HEALTHCARE
FACILITIES LAW

HEALTHCARE FACILITIES LAW

Critical Issues for Hospitals, HMOs, and Extended Care Facilities

ANNE M. DELLINGER
General Editor

Professor of Public Law and Government, Institute of Government, The University of North Carolina at Chapel Hill Member, North Carolina Bar

LITTLE, BROWN AND COMPANY
Boston   Toronto   London

Library of Congress Catalog Card No. 90-63881

ISBN 0-316-18040-8

This publication is designed to provide accurate and authoritative information in regard to the subject matter covered. It is sold with the understanding that the publisher is not engaged in rendering legal, accounting or other professional services. If legal advice or other expert assistance is required, the services of a competent professional person should be sought.

> —*From a Declaration of Principles jointly adopted by a Committee of the American Bar Association and a Committee of Publishers.*

MV-NY

PUBLISHED SIMULTANEOUSLY IN CANADA BY
LITTLE, BROWN & COMPANY (CANADA) LIMITED

PRINTED IN THE UNITED STATES OF AMERICA

Summary of Contents

Contents

2   The Healthcare Facility as Employer   65

Contents

Contents

4 Tort Liability, Immunities, and Defenses 257

Contents

Contents

7 Consent to Treatment 455

8   Medical Records   531

9   Patients' Rights: An Overview   607

Contents

Contents

12 Organ Procurement and Transplantation   771

13 Acquired Immunodeficiency Syndrome 841

Contents

Contents

15   Legal Characteristics of the Extended Care Facility   993

Contents

16 Legal Characteristics of the Health Maintenance Organization   1051

Contents

Preface

This book is a collective effort by attorneys with varied experiences in health law to assist both their colleagues who represent healthcare facilities and the men and women who administer them. Among the authors are teachers and writers on health topics as well as lawyers who have served as staff and retained counsel for facilities. Although the text emphasizes the legal problems of hospitals, the distinctive features of care rendered by health maintenance organizations and extended care facilities also receive attention. Supplementing chapters on the legal characteristics of those entities, Timothy Jost and Barbara Shickich have reviewed other chapters from the viewpoint of extended care facilities and health maintenance organizations, respectively.

No book substitutes for advice of counsel on a particular matter. As a general discussion of the legal issues related to operating healthcare facilities, however, this volume is a beginning point for research on specific questions and should be a useful reference for attorneys and administrators. While law changes rapidly, and health precedents faster than many other areas, frequent supplements should keep the reader current.

The book describes the legal structure of facilities, common aspects of their management, conditions under which services are delivered, and the most difficult and significant new problems for facilities. The last include terminal care decision-making, recently addressed by the Supreme Court; manipulation of previously unknown reproductive mechanisms; the complex organ procurement and transplantation system; and the peculiar legal issues involving people with AIDS.

I acknowledge with great appreciation the considerable effort of each author as well as the encouragement and support of John L. Sanders, director of the Institute of Government, The University of North Carolina at Chapel Hill. My thanks too, for editorial assistance, to Anna Jean Mayhew; and, for research assistance, to Celia Jones and Anne Harper, students at the Duke Law School.

Anne M. Dellinger

November, 1990

About the General Editor and Contributors

Anne M. Dellinger is a health attorney on the faculty of the Institute of Government, The University of North Carolina at Chapel Hill. She is a graduate of Duke Law School, a member of the North Carolina bar, former president of the North Carolina Society of Health Care Attorneys, and a member of the American Law Institute.

Stephen Allred is an associate professor of public law and government at the Institute of Government, The University of North Carolina at Chapel Hill, where he specializes in labor law. Before joining the Institute faculty, he practiced with a labor law firm in Washington, D.C. Professor Allred received his B.A. and MPA from the University of North Carolina at Chapel Hill and his J.D. from Catholic University of America, where he was associate editor of the law review.

Joan Brannon is a professor of public law and government at the Institute of Government, The University of North Carolina at Chapel Hill. She holds an A.B. from Smith College and a J.D. with high honors from The University of North Carolina at Chapel Hill, where she was editor-in-chief of the law review. Professor Brannon has taught numerous classes in the field of mental health legal issues and has authored and co-authored several publications on mental health legal issues, including *Law of Health Records in North Carolina*. She has served as counsel to the Mental Patients Commitments Committee of the North Carolina Legislative Research Commission and provided legal assistance to the North Carolina Mental Health Study Commission.

William A. Campbell is professor of public law and government and associate director of the Institute of Government, The

University of North Carolina at Chapel Hill. He received a B.A. from Rhodes College and an LL.B. from Vanderbilt University, where he served as case editor of the Vanderbilt Law Review and was elected to membership in the Order of the Coif. He recently served as a member of the National Academy of Science's Committee on Contraceptive Development.

Jean Gordon Carter is an associate in the law firm of Hunton & Williams in its Raleigh office, where she practices primarily in the taxation area with an emphasis on tax-exempt entities, including hospitals. She holds a B.S. magna cum laude with honors in accountancy from Wake Forest University and a J.D. with high honors from Duke University School of Law, where she served on the editorial board of the Duke Law Journal and was a member of the Order of the Coif. Ms. Carter is a member of the taxation and health law sections of the North Carolina Bar Association and is on the council for the estates section. She is an initial director and officer of the North Carolina Planned Giving Council and an officer of the Wake County Estates Council. Ms. Carter is a certified public accountant and a board-certified specialist in estate planning and probate law.

Elena N. Cohen is an associate of the law firm of Kalkines, Arky, Zall & Bernstein in Manhattan, which primarily represents healthcare institutions. Before assuming her current position, she was a staff attorney at the Society for the Right to Die. She has authored several publications concerning the death and dying field. Ms. Cohen holds a B.A. from Harvard University and a J.D. from New York University. She is a member of the New York and Washington, D.C. bars, the American Bar Association, the National Lawyers Guild, the National Health Lawyer's Association, and the American Society of Law and Medicine.

Douglas Colton is a partner in the Washington, D.C. law firm of Verner, Liipfert, Bernhard, McPherson and Hand, where he practices antitrust law and complex litigation on behalf of, among others, healthcare industry participants, largely hospitals.

Mr. Colton attended Yale University and the University of Texas School of Law, and in addition to his private practice has served as special assistant to the assistant attorney general in charge of the Antitrust Division of the United States Department of Justice. Mr. Colton frequently writes and speaks on topics relating to economic competition in the healthcare field and healthcare economics.

Arlene J. Diosegy is the general counsel for the North Carolina Medical Society. Ms. Diosegy holds a B.A. from Allegheny College and a J.D. from Temple University School of Law. She is a member of the board of governors of the North Carolina Bar Association and served as chairman of its health law section for two years. She has authored a number of continuing legal education manuscripts for the Bar Association, including *AIDS in the Workplace: A Legal Conundrum* and *The Durable Power of Attorney for Healthcare Decision Making*, and is the editor of *Body Medical, Body Legal: A Look at Health Law in North Carolina*. She is a member of the Pennsylvania, Colorado, and North Carolina bars.

Sara Jones is an associate of the law firm of Crowell & Moring in Washington, D.C., where she practices primarily in health and science litigation matters. She received her J.D. from Duke University Law School, where she was a legal writing and advocacy teaching assistant and a member of the Alaska Law Review. Ms. Jones is a member of the pro bono committee of the young lawyer's section of the District of Columbia Bar Association and is a member of the litigation section of the ABA. She is a member of the bars of the District of Columbia and Kentucky.

Timothy Stoltzfus Jost, professor of law and of hospital and health services, Ohio State University, holds a B.A. from Adlai Stevenson College, the University of California at Santa Cruz and a J.D. from the University of Chicago. He is a co-author of Health Law: Cases, Materials and Problems. He is the author of the American Bar Association's Model Recommendations: Intermediate Sanctions for Enforcement of Quality of Care in Nursing Homes and of numerous articles on health law. He has served as a consultant to the Institute of Medicine and the Administrative Conference of the United States.

Kathryn Kelly is a partner with the Washington, D.C. law firm of Crowell & Moring, where she practices principally in the areas of product liability and healthcare. She is an arbitrator for Maryland's Health Claims Arbitration Office. She received her J.D. from the University of Notre Dame, where she was the articles editor of the law review.

Ms. Kelly has been a vicechair of the committee on uniform state laws of the tort and insurance practice section and is a member of the litigation and TIPS sections of the ABA. She has lectured and written various articles in the areas of product liability, healthcare, and trial tactics, and she co-authored the *Guide to Multistate Litigation, Product Liability: Cases & Trends,* and *Product Liability: A Practice Guide.* She contributed two chapters to *AIDS and the Law.* She is a member of the bars of the District of Columbia and Maryland.

Nancy M. P. King received her law degree from the University of North Carolina at Chapel Hill in 1980 and has worked in health law, policy, and ethics in many capacities since that time. She is assistant professor in the Department of Social Medicine at the School of Medicine, The University of North Carolina at Chapel Hill, where she teaches legal and moral issues in healthcare and is especially interested in informed consent, refusal of treatment, and the physician-patient relationship. With Ruth Faden and Tom Beauchamp, she wrote *A History and Theory of Informed Consent;* she is also senior editor of *The Physician as Captain of the Ship: A Critical Reappraisal* and author of the forthcoming *Making Sense of Advance Directives.*

Jeffrey S. Koeze is assistant professor of public law and Government at the Institute of Government, The University of North Carolina at Chapel Hill, where he specializes in health law. He is a graduate of the University of North Carolina at Chapel Hill and the University of Virginia School of Law and is a member of the North Carolina bar.

S. Wade Malone is an attorney with the law firm of King & Spalding in Atlanta, Georgia. He received his bachelor's degree from Georgetown University and his law degree from the George Washington National Law Center. After law school, he clerked for the Honorable John L. Coffey of the United States Court of Appeals for the Seventh Circuit.

Glen A. Reed is a partner in the law firm of King & Spalding in Atlanta, Georgia. He is a graduate of the University of Tennessee and the Yale Law School. He is a member of the board of the American Academy of Hospital Attorneys and is the President-Elect of the Georgia Academy of Hospital Attorneys. He is the chairman of the annual *Fundamentals of Healthcare Law Program* of the American Hospital Association. Mr. Reed lectures frequently on health law.

Lois L. Shepherd is an attorney with the firm of Robinson, Bradshaw & Hinson, P.A., in Charlotte, North Carolina. She graduated with highest honors from The University of North Carolina at Chapel Hill and received her J.D. from the Yale Law School. Ms. Shepherd is a member of the North Carolina bar.

Barbara Allan Shickich is a solo practitioner in Seattle, Washington. She is the former vice-president and general counsel of Group Health Cooperative of Puget Sound. She has been a member of the National Health Lawyers Association, served on the board of directors of the Washington State Society of Hospital Attorneys, and lectured for both organizations on issues pertaining to HMOs. She holds a B.A. from Washington State University and a J.D. from New York University School of Law, where she was a Root-Tilden scholar.

Caroline T. Wilson is a member of the law firm of Robinson, Bradshaw, and Hinson, P.A. in Charlotte, North Carolina. She holds a B.A. and a J.D. from The University of North Carolina at Chapel Hill and an M.S. from Vanderbilt University in Nashville, Tennessee. Ms. Wilson is a member of the North Carolina bar.

HEALTHCARE
FACILITIES LAW

I   LEGAL ISSUES IN THE MANAGEMENT OF HEALTHCARE FACILITIES

1   Staff Membership and Clinical Privileges

Caroline T. Wilson
Anne M. Dellinger

§1.0 Introduction

Responsible allocation of the right to practice in the hospital is among the hospital governing body's most serious legal duties—

and there are many possibilities for error in performing it. The hospital's first obligation is to its patients, and therefore the hospital must regulate staff membership and clinical privileges so as to ensure competent patient care. The second consideration that influences the hospital's staffing decisions is its own interest in the efficient administration and operation of the hospital. For administrative reasons, a hospital may prefer to limit the physicians or other health professionals on its staff, and it may want to reserve privileges exclusively for those who are not only competent but also efficient users of the facility.

As a legal matter, the hospital may not consult its own interests entirely. Because the ability to gain and keep clinical privileges often determines a medical practitioner's success, the courts and other bodies that control hospitals require them to act carefully in extending these privileges. At a minimum, medical practitioners are entitled to rely on the protection provided by the hospital and medical staff bylaws, and practitioners enjoy even greater protection when dealing with public or governmental hospitals. Courts and legislators do not treat as equals, however, all who would like to practice in the hospital. While the law now easily acknowledges certain rights of physicians, it is only beginning to concede some of the same rights to other healthcare practitioners.

The hospital must balance the medical practitioner's right to practice against the patient's right to competent medical care and its own interest in efficiency. To encourage the hospital to undertake its duty to regulate staff membership and clinical privileges, federal and state legislators have enacted laws to protect the hospital from liability in certain circumstances. Even though the hospital must recognize practitioners' rights, the hospital, its staff, and its employees may be protected from liability for wrong decisions about extending staff membership and clinical privileges.

A. Organization of the Hospital Medical Staff

§1.1 Staff Membership

Both the Conditions of Participation for Medicare and Medicaid (the Conditions of Participation) and the standards of the Joint Commission on Accreditation of Healthcare Organizations (JCAHO)[1] require the hospital to have an organized medical staff.[2] The medical staff must include licensed physicians and may also include other healthcare practitioners who are permitted by state law to provide patient care services independently.[3] The medical staff is generally an unincorporated association that functions independently from but is accountable to the hospital's governing board.[4] There may be several categories of staff

---

§1.1 [1]The Joint Commission on Accreditation of Healthcare Organizations is a nonprofit corporation that sets standards for and accredits hospitals. Its policymaking body, the board of commissioners, consists of representatives of the American Medical Association (which selects about one-third of the commissioners), the American Hospital Association, the American College of Surgeons, the American College of Physicians, and the American Dental Association. JCAHO accreditation is voluntary; however, hospitals that have this accreditation are thereby exempt from much state and federal regulation.

[2]42 C.F.R. §482.22 (1988); Joint Commission on Accreditation of Healthcare Organizations, Accreditation Manual for Hospitals 1991, MS .1, at 99 (1990) (hereinafter JCAHO Accreditation Manual). Some state statutes also specifically address the organization of the medical staff. (See, e.g., Ind. Code Ann. §16-10-1-6.5 (Burns Cum. Supp. 1989)).

[3]See 42 C.F.R. §482.22(a) (1988); JCAHO Accreditation Manual, MS .1.1.1, at 99. The JCAHO Accreditation Manual specifically defines individuals permitted to provide patient care services independently as "[a]ny individual who is permitted by law and who is also permitted by the hospital to provide patient care services without direction or supervision, within the scope of his license and in accordance with individually granted clinical privileges." Id. at footnote.

[4]42 C.F.R. §482.22(b) (1988); JCAHO Accreditation Manual, MS .1, at 99. If the medical staff is totally independent from the governing board and the hospital, the medical staff may be sued independently as an unincorporated association. (See, e.g., Corleto v. Shore Memorial Hosp., 138 N.J. Super. 302, 350 A.2d 534 (1975)).

membership, including categories reserved specifically for temporary or probationary members. Although it is ultimately responsible for granting medical staff membership, the governing board generally acts on the recommendations of the medical staff.[5] The standards for selection of medical staff and the distinctions between the categories of medical staff membership must be set out specifically in the staff bylaws.[6]

The primary function of the medical staff is to ensure the quality of the professional services rendered in the hospital. The medical staff accomplishes this goal by establishing and supervising the delineation of clinical privileges among the individuals who practice in the hospital.[7]

§1.2 Clinical Privileges

The JCAHO standards define clinical privileges as "[p]ermission to provide medical or other patient care services in the granting institution, within well defined limits, based on the individual's professional license and his experience, competence, ability and judgment."[1] Any individual who practices independently in the hospital must have clinical privileges whether or not he or she is a member of the medical staff.[2] Included in the privileges granted to the individual may be the privilege of independently admitting patients to the hospital.[3] Although the medical staff may recommend individuals for specific privileges, the governing board of the hospital is ultimately responsible for the delineation

---

[5]42 C.F.R. §482.22(a) (1988); JCAHO Accreditation Manual, MS .1.2.3.1.1, at 100.

[6]42 C.F.R. §482.22(c) (1988); JCAHO Accreditation Manual, MS .1.2.2 at 100 and MS .2.4.4, at 103.

[7]42 C.F.R. §482.22 (1988); JCAHO Accreditation Manual, MS .1, at 99-102.

§1.2 [1]JCAHO Accreditation Manual, MS .1, at 99 at footnote.

[2]Id. at MS .4.1, at 108.

[3]Id. at MS .4.3, at 111 (all individuals who have the privilege of independently admitting patients to the hospital must be active members of the medical staff).

of clinical privileges.[4] The process and criteria for the delineation of clinical privileges must be set out in the medical staff bylaws.[5]

§1.3 Staff Bylaws

The Conditions of Participation and JCAHO standards both require that the medical staff enact bylaws that contain criteria for staff membership and the granting of clinical privileges.[1] Similarly, some states have enacted statutes specifically requiring hospital medical staffs to adopt bylaws or rules governing staff membership and clinical privileges.[2] These bylaws are adopted by the medical staff and approved by the governing body before becoming effective.[3] The medical staff bylaws are separate from the bylaws of the hospital and specifically relate to procedures affecting the hospital medical staff. Once these bylaws have been

---

[4]Id. at MS .4.2.1, at 108; see infra §1.4, nn.25 and 26 and accompanying text.

[5]42 C.F.R. §482.22(c)(6) (1988); JCAHO Accreditation Manual, MS .4 at 107 and MS .4.2.2, at 108.

§1.3 [1]42 C.F.R. §482.22(c)(6) (1988); JCAHO Accreditation Manual, MS .2, at 102, MS .1.2.3.1.2, at 100, and MS .4.2.2, at 108.

[2]An example of this is Cal. Bus. & Prof. Code §2282 (West Cum. Supp. 1990):

2282. Practice in hospital with staff of five or more physicians and surgeons without adoption of certain rules

The regular practice of medicine in a licensed general or specified hospital having five or more physicians and surgeons on the medical staff, which does not have rules established by the board of directors thereof to govern the operation of the hospital, which rules include, among other provisions, all the following, constitutes unprofessional conduct:

(a) Provision for the organization of physicians and surgeons licensed to practice in this state who are permitted to practice in the hospital into a formal medical staff with appropriate officers and bylaws and with staff appointments on an annual or biennial basis. . . .

See also, e.g., Fla. Stat. Ann. §395.011(6) (West 1986 & Cum. Supp. 1989); Wash. Rev. Code Ann. §70.43.010 (Cum. Supp. 1989).

[3]42 C.F.R. §482.22(c) (1988); JCAHO Accreditation Manual, MS .2.1, at 102.

adopted, JCAHO standards provide that neither the governing body nor the medical staff may unilaterally amend them.[4]

B. Regulation of Staff Membership and Clinical Privileges

§1.4 The Hospital's Duty to Regulate Staff Membership and Clinical Privileges

The hospital is expected to make reasonable efforts to improve a patient's condition; if that proves impossible, at least it must try to do no harm. The hospital's efforts to ensure competent patient care must include the regulation of staff membership and clinical privileges. This duty is fairly new in the history of health law, and it has several sources.

§1.4.1 Sources of the Duty

The duty to regulate staff membership and clinical privileges is defined by federal statutes and regulations, and JCAHO standards, state statutes, and case law.

Federal Statutes and Regulations. The federal government imposes a patient care obligation on hospitals that seek Medicare or Medicaid reimbursement and are not accredited by the JCAHO or the American Osteopathic Association. The Conditions of Participation require in general that the governing body of the hospital "[e]nsure that the medical staff is accountable to the governing body for the quality of care provided to patients."[1]

---

[4]JCAHO Accreditation Manual, MS .2.1, at 102.
§1.4 [1]42 C.F.R. §482.12(a)(5) (1988).

The federal Health Care Quality Improvement Act,[2] which provides some immunity for hospitals that comply with its provisions, imposes an additional statutory duty on hospitals that want to come within the protection of the Act. Before extending privileges to a physician or other healthcare practitioner, the hospital must request information regarding the physician or healthcare practitioner from the National Practitioner Data Bank, which is established by the Act.[3] Every two years the hospital also must request information from the National Practitioner Data Bank on all members of the hospital's medical staff and any physician or healthcare practitioner who has been granted privileges at the hospital.[4] Whether or not the hospital actually requests the information, for the purposes of any medical malpractice action the hospital will be presumed to have knowledge of any information that has been reported to the National Practitioner Data Bank.[5]

JCAHO Standards. The JCAHO also requires hospitals to regulate staff membership and clinical privileges. JCAHO accreditation, which the federal government accepts as a substitute for

---

[2]42 U.S.C.A. §11101 et seq. (1989).

[3]Although the other provisions of the Act (discussed infra, §1.11, nn.1-9 and accompanying text) apply to all healthcare entities, the duty to obtain information regarding each physician from the National Practitioner Data Bank, as discussed in this section, applies only to hospitals. For a more complete discussion of the National Practitioner Data Bank see infra §1.10, nn. 2-3 and accompanying text. See also 54 Fed. Reg. 42,722 (1989) (to be codified at 45 C.F.R. §60) as corrected by 54 Fed. Reg. 43890 (1989) for regulations governing the National Practitioner Data Bank.

[4]The hospital is not expected to request information at the two-year anniversary of each physician on staff, but rather the hospital can obtain information on the entire staff every two years. H.R. Rep. 903, 99th Cong., 2d Sess. 18, reprinted in U.S. Code Cong. & Ad. News 6401.

[5]This presumption is not a presumption of malpractice, but rather a presumption that holds the hospital to the standard of care of a person in possession of this information. Id. Recognizing the trend toward imposing liability on hospitals for the negligent acts of staff physicians (discussed infra, §1.4, nn.13-39 and accompanying text), this presumption could be quite significant.

its Conditions of Participation, depends on hospital compliance with a requirement that the medical staff have "overall responsibility for the quality of the professional services provided by individuals with clinical privileges, as well as the responsibility of accounting therefor to the governing body."[6] Other standards require that the criteria for granting staff membership and clinical privileges be "designed to assure the medical staff and governing body that patients will receive quality care."[7]

State Statutes. Some states have enacted statutes that impose an obligation on hospitals to regulate staff admissions and performance on behalf of patients.[8] These statutes are often part

---

[6]JCAHO Accreditation Manual, MS .1, at 99.

[7]Id. at MS .1.2.3.1.2.1, at 100 and MS .4.2.2.1, at 108.

[8]Some states have also enacted statutes related to the regulation of medical staff with the apparent purpose of protecting the medical staff rather than the patients. Such statutes may state that staff membership and clinical privileges cannot be denied without good cause, that the denial or termination of staff membership or clinical privileges must be reported to the medical governing body of that state, that the doctor who is denied staff membership or clinical privileges must receive a written report stating the reasons for the denial, or that any staff member who participates on peer review committees is immune from liability for decisions of the committee. For a discussion of these statutes see infra §1.11, nn.10-26 and accompanying text.

Some states have also adopted risk management statutes. Although these statutes are not aimed directly at regulating staff membership and clinical privileges, they provide additional protection for patients. A good example is Alaska Stat. §18.20.075 (1986 & Cum. Supp. 1989):

Sec. 18.20.075 Risk management. (a) To be eligible for a license each hospital shall have in operation an internal risk management program which shall

(1) investigate the frequency and causes of incidents in hospitals that cause injury to patients;

(2) develop and implement measures to minimize the risk of injury to patients; in developing these measures each hospital shall take into account recommendations of its medical staff, the Medical Indemnity Corporation of Alaska, private underwriters, industry standards, experience of other hospi-

of the state's hospital licensure legislation,[9] but the statutes themselves vary considerably in their specificity and scope. Some statutes impose a duty on the hospitals to review the qualifications and performance of their medical staff,[10] while others give

---

tals, and recommendations of licensing boards of other health care providers; and

(3) analyze patient grievances and relate to patient care.

(b) the department shall adopt by regulation standards for the risk management programs in hospitals in the state which may vary according to the size of the hospital, the type of care provided by the hospital, and other factors found relevant by the department. Regulations adopted under this subsection are subject to the Administrative Procedure Act (AS 44.62) (§39 ch. 102 SLA 1976).

[9]Statutes addressing the regulation of staff membership and clinical privileges also may be located with general statutes on public health and safety, medical professions, or tort liability. A few states' codes contain peer or organizational review sections. Because the statutes are not always readily identifiable by title, it is necessary to carefully check the statutes of each state to determine whether there is any statutory duty or authority to regulate staff membership and clinical privileges.

[10]An example of this is N.Y. Pub. Health Law §2805-K (McKinney Cum. Supp. 1990):

§2805-K. Investigations prior to granting or renewing privileges.

(1) Prior to granting or renewing professionalized privileges or association of any physician, dentist or podiatrist or hiring of physician, dentist or podiatrist, a hospital or a facility approved pursuant to this article shall request from the physician, dentist or podiatrist and the physician, dentist or podiatrist shall be required to provide the following information:

(a) The name of any hospital or facility with or at which the physician, dentist or podiatrist had or has any association, employment, privileges or practice;

(b) Where such association, employment, privilege or practice was discontinued, the reasons for its discontinuation;

(c) Any pending professional medical, dental or podiatric misconduct proceedings or any pending medical malpractice actions in this state or another state, the substance of the allegations in such proceedings or actions, and any additional information concerning such proceedings or actions as such physician, dentist or podiatrist may deem appropriate;

(d) The substance of the findings in such actions or proceedings and

hospitals the power to regulate staff without specifically requiring them to do so.[11] States that do not impose a statutory duty on hospitals to regulate staff membership and clinical privileges or states that impose a general statutory duty may impose such a duty or elaborate on that duty through the promulgation of regulations.[12]

Case Law.   Acknowledging the hospital's patient care obligation, courts have increasingly recognized the hospital's duty to regulate clinical privileges and have held the hospital liable if

---

any additional information concerning such actions or proceedings as the physician, dentist or podiatrist may deem appropriate;

(e) A waiver by the physician, dentist or podiatrist of any confidentiality provisions concerning the information required to be provided to hospitals pursuant to this subdivision; and

(f) A verification by the physician, dentist or podiatrist that the information provided by [him or her] is true and accurate.

(2) Prior to granting privileges or association to any physician, dentist or podiatrist, or hiring a physician, dentist or podiatrist, any hospital or facility approved pursuant to this article shall request from any hospital with or at which such physician, dentist or podiatrist had or has privileges, was associated, or was employed, the following information concerning such physician, dentist or podiatrist:

(a) Any pending professional medical conduct proceedings or any pending medical malpractice actions, in this state or another state;

(b) Any judgment or settlement of a medical malpractice action and any finding of professional misconduct in this state or another; and

(c) Any information required to be reported by hospitals pursuant to section twenty-eight hundred three-e of this article. . . .

[11]An example is R.I. Gen. Laws §23-17-23 (1985 & Cum. Supp. 1988):

23-17-23. Hospital disciplinary powers.—(a) The board of trustees of a hospital or other appropriate authority licensed pursuant to the laws of the state is authorized to suspend, deny, revoke or curtail the staff privileges of any staff member for good cause which shall include the grounds specified in §5-37-5.1 for unprofessional conduct. Provided, however, that the procedures for such actions shall comply with the procedures, if any, that may from time to time be outlined by the joint commission for accreditation of hospitals. . . .

Even if the state statute is permissive, the courts may impose a duty on the hospital. See, e.g., Johnson v. Misericordia Community Hosp., 99 Wis. 2d 708, 301 N.W.2d 156 (1981).

[12]See, e.g., S.C. Code Ann. §R61-16-301 et seq. (Law. Co-op. Cum. Supp. 1989).

a patient is harmed as a result of lack of supervision. Some jurisdictions, in a trend that disturbs hospitals, recognize hospitals' independent nondelegable duty of care for the medical treatment of patients. This duty may give rise to liability under the theory of "corporate negligence."

Corporate negligence was first set out in an Illinois case, Darling v. Charleston Community Memorial Hospital.[13] In *Darling* a hospital's emergency room physician treated a boy for a broken leg. The boy was admitted to the hospital and placed in a cast that caused gangrene. Eventually, the leg had to be amputated. The Illinois court criticized the inaction of the hospital's employees, who probably should have intervened at several points.

> At that point [when nurses identified a circulation problem] it became the nurses' duty to inform the attending physician, and if he failed to act, to advise the hospital authorities so that appropriate action might be taken. As to consultation, there is no dispute that the hospital failed to review Dr. Alexander's work or require a consultation; the only issue is whether its failure to do so was negligence. On the evidence before it the jury could reasonably have found that it was.[14]

Courts of several jurisdictions have cited *Darling* for the proposition that the hospital owes a duty to its patients to monitor the quality of medical care.[15] As stated by the California Court of Appeals in Elam v. College Park Hospital, the "hospital is in the best position to evaluate the competence of physicians it, in its discretion, allows to perform surgery and to practice within its premises. . . ."[16]

---

[13]33 Ill. 2d 326, 211 N.E.2d 253 (1965), cert. denied, 383 U.S. 946 (1966).

[14]211 N.E.2d at 258.

[15]See, e.g., Johnson v. Misericordia Community Hosp., 99 Wis. 2d 708, 301 N.W.2d 156 (1981).

[16]132 Cal. App. 3d 332, 183 Cal. Reptr. 156, 164 (1982).

§1.4.2 Elements of the Duty

There are at minimum two elements of the hospital's duty to regulate staff membership and clinical privileges: (1) the duty to use care in the selection of the medical staff and (2) the duty to supervise and review the medical staff's performance, as seen in *Darling.*[17]

Duty to Select. The Health Care Quality Improvement Act and the Conditions of Participation require hospitals to examine the credentials of candidates for medical staff membership.[18] The JCAHO standards demand that the hospital establish specific criteria as a basis for granting staff membership.[19] The criteria should pertain to "evidence of current licensure, relevant training and/or experience, current competence, and health status."[20] Some states also have enacted specific legislation requiring the hospital to examine the credentials of all applicants for staff membership.[21]

Some jurisdictions recognize a hospital's legal duty to

---

[17]The hospital also has a duty to maintain the grounds and to furnish supplies free of defects. See Comment, The Hospital-Physician Relationship: Hospital Responsibility for Malpractice of Physicians, 50 Wash. L. Rev. 385, 412 (1975). See also Cal. Health and Safety Code §1276 (West 1979 & Cum. Supp. 1990):

> ### §1276 Standards for physical plant, staff and services; exceptions; program flexibility; applications; approval or denial
>
> (a) . . . the regulations adopted by the state department shall, as applicable, prescribe standards of adequacy, safety, and sanitation of the physical plant, of staffing with duly qualified licensed personnel, and of services, based on the type of health facility and the needs of the persons served thereby . . .

[18]42 U.S.C.A. §11135 (1989); 42 C.F.R. §482.22(a)(2) (1988).
[19]JCAHO Accreditation Manual, MS .1.2.3.1.2, at 100.
[20]Id. at MS .1.2.3.1.2.2, at 100.
[21]See, e.g., Ind. Code Ann. §16-10-1-6.5 (Burns Cum. Supp. 1989).

exercise reasonable care when selecting medical staff.[22] Holding that the hospital has a duty to exercise due care in the selection of its medical staff, the Supreme Court of Wisconsin, in Johnson v. Misericordia Community Hospital,[23] affirmed the lower court's decision holding the hospital liable for negligently appointing an unqualified physician to its medical staff. The court stated:

> [t]he failure of a hospital to scrutinize the credentials of its medical staff applicants could forseeably result in the appointment of unqualified physicians and surgeons to its staff. Thus the granting of staff privileges to these doctors would undoubtedly create an unreasonable risk of harm or injury to their patients. Therefore the failure to investigate a medical staff applicant's qualification for the privileges requested gives rise to a foreseeable risk of unreasonable harm.[24]

In most hospitals, the medical staff is responsible for supervising the delineation of clinical privileges. Stating that the hospital must act in good faith and use reasonable care in selecting physicians, the Georgia Court of Appeals, in Joiner v. Mitchell County Hospital Authority,[25] concluded that members of the staff are agents of the hospital and therefore the hospital authority "is responsible for any default or negligence on its part in properly selecting new members of the staff." Therefore, even if a physician is recommended by other physicians on the medical staff, the hospital may not be able to escape liability for negligently granting privileges to an unqualified physician.[26]

---

[22]Although it is generally accepted that employers can be held liable for negligently selecting independent contractors, most jurisdictions have not yet directly addressed the issue in the context of hospitals' selection of staff physicians. See generally Annot., 51 A.L.R.3d 981 (1973 & Cum. Supp. 1989).

[23]99 Wis. 2d 708, 301 N.W.2d 156 (1981).

[24]301 N.W.2d at 164.

[25]125 Ga. App. 1, 186 S.E.2d 307, 308 (1971), affd., 229 Ga. 140, 189 S.E.2d 412 (1972).

[26]But the hospital will not be held liable unless the plaintiff can show that if the hospital had followed proper procedures it would have denied privileges to the physician. See, e.g., Rule v. Lutheran Hosp. & Homes Socy. of Am., 835 F.2d 1250 (8th Cir. 1987); Ferguson v. Gonyaw, 64 Mich. App. 685, 236 N.W.2d 543, 550 (1975).

Duty to Supervise. In Purcell v. Zimbelman,[27] the Arizona Court of Appeals recognized that hospitals have an independent duty to supervise the competence of their staff physicians. The standard of care articulated by the majority of courts that have recognized this duty is "reasonable care based on the hospital's actual or constructive knowledge."[28] Liability for failure to supervise or review the performance of the physician is more likely to arise when the staff member has a history of negligent medical practice.[29] The *Purcell* court affirmed the trial court's judgment holding the hospital liable for failing to take action against an incompetent staff physician. The hospital knew that the physician had been sued for malpractice four times before he treated Mr. Purcell.

Federal and state legislatures and regulatory bodies also have recognized the hospital's duty to evaluate and supervise the quality of medical treatment rendered on its premises. The Conditions of Participation state that the medical staff must periodically conduct appraisals of its members.[30] Similarly, the Health Care Quality Improvement Act requires hospitals to request updated information from the National Practitioner Data Bank on each of its staff physicians every two years.[31] The JCAHO standards demand that the medical staff provide effective mechanisms for monitoring and evaluating "the quality and appropriateness of patient care and the clinical performance of all individuals with delineated clinical privileges."[32] In addition, some states have enacted legislation that requires the hospital to monitor the performance of each member of its medical staff.[33]

When asking whether a hospital exercised reasonable care in selecting and supervising staff physicians, a court may consider whether the hospital followed licensing regulations, federal

---

[27]18 Ariz. App. 75, 500 P.2d 335 (1972).
[28]See, e.g., Fridena v. Evans, 127 Ariz. 516, 622 P.2d 463 (1980).
[29]See generally Annot., 12 A.L.R.4th 46 (1982 & Cum. Supp. 1989).
[30]42 C.F.R. §482.22(a)(1) (1988).
[31]42 U.S.C.A. §11135 (1989).
[32]JCAHO Accreditation Manual, MS .6.1, at 114.
[33]See, e.g., Fla. Stat. Ann. §395.011 (West Cum. Supp. 1989).

accreditation standards, and its own bylaws.[34] Courts have been willing to hold hospitals liable for not devising adequate rules and regulations,[35] but compliance with bylaws alone is probably not sufficient to protect the hospital from liability.[36] Although not all jurisdictions have recognized corporate negligence, with the abrogation of the immunity doctrines[37] and the expansion of the doctrine of respondeat superior[38] it is advisable for

---

[34]See, e.g., Sheffield v. Zilis, 170 Ga. App. 62, 316 S.E.2d 493 (1984) (concerning negligent selection); Johnson v. St. Bernard Hosp., 79 Ill. App. 3d 709, 399 N.E.2d 198 (1979), 35 Ill. Dec. 364 (concerning negligent supervision).

[35]See, e.g., Bilonoha v. Zurbitzky, 233 Pa. Super. 136, 336 A.2d 351 (1975).

[36]W. Isele, The Hospital Medical Staff 66 (1984).

[37]See Chapter 4, infra, for an in-depth discussion of the immunity doctrines.

[38]Respondeat superior is a legal doctrine holding employers liable for the actions of their employees. Although under traditional analysis respondeat superior would not apply to nonemployee staff physicians, several jurisdictions reject this type of analysis and apply the doctrine of respondeat superior to hold the hospital liable for the negligence of staff physicians on the basis of ostensible or apparent agency. These courts look to the patient's reasonable expectations. See, e.g., Smith v. St. Francis Hosp., 676 P.2d 279, 283 (Okla. App. 1983); Arthur v. St. Peter's Hosp., 169 N.J. Super. 575, 583, 405 A.2d 443, 447 (1979). Whether the patient understands that the doctor is not an employee of the hospital and the degree of the patient's involvement in the selection of the physician also may affect whether the doctrine applies. See, e.g., Grewe v. Mt. Clemens Gen. Hosp., 404 Mich. 240, 273 N.W.2d 429, 433 (1978); Adamski v. Tacoma Gen. Hosp., 20 Wash. App. 98, 579 P.2d 970 (1978). The court is more likely to find hospital liability for acts of physicians, such as emergency room physicians, with specialties that the hospital has an obligation to offer. See, e.g., Paintsville Hosp. Co. v. Rose, 683 S.W.2d 255 (Ky. 1985); Mduba v. Benedictine, 52 A.D.2d 450, 384 N.Y.S.2d 527 (1976). More recently, several courts have rejected the application of principles of ostensible agency and have applied the principles of agency by estoppel to conclude that public policy requires that the hospital be held liable for the malpractice of its emergency room physicians. Martell v. St. Charles Hosp., 137 Misc. 2d 980, 523 N.Y.S. 2d 342 (1987). Even if no liability attaches for the negligent medical acts of nonemployee physicians, the hospital still may be liable under the older case law that imposed liability for negligent administrative decisions of nonemployee physicians. See, e.g., Keene v. Methodist Hosp., 324 F. Supp. 233, 234-235 (N.D. Ind. 1971). For a discussion

hospitals to follow the guidelines set out by the JCAHO in the selection of staff physicians.[39] For the same reasons, it is important for the hospital to have and to follow standard procedures for the supervision of, and consultation among, the medical staff.

§1.5 Efficient Operation of the Hospital

Another of the hospital's interests in regulating staff membership and clinical privileges is in preserving efficiency. The hospital may protect this interest in a variety of ways, including enforcement of bylaws and internal regulations, execution of exclusive contracts for services, and "closing" of privileges to any additional staff. The hospital's interest in efficiency has been specifically recognized by the JCAHO standards. The standards include "reasonable qualifications" such as "the ability of the hospital to provide adequate facilities and supportive services for the applicant and his patients; [and] patient care needs for additional staff members with the applicant's skill and training" among the criteria that hospitals may consider in granting or continuing staff privileges.[1] The JCAHO standards also support the hospital's right to enforce its interest by requiring that each staff member agree in writing that his or her activities as a member of the

---

of the development of the application of the doctrine of respondeat superior to the acts of physicians see Adamski v. Tacoma Gen. Hosp., 20 Wash. App. 98, 579 P.2d 970 (1978). See also Comment, The Hospital-Physician Relationship: Hospital Responsibility for Malpractice of Physicians, 50 Wash. L. Rev. 385 (1975). See generally Annot., 51 A.L.R.4th 235 (1987 & Cum. Supp. 1989).

[39]Several commentators cite a California trial court opinion, Gonzales v. Nork, for the proposition that compliance with JCAHO standards may not be sufficient to protect a hospital from liability. However, the issue was not before the court when the case went up on appeal (20 Cal. 3d 500, 143 Cal. Rptr. 240, 573 P.2d 458 (1978)), and the few courts that have considered this issue do not appear to have followed the California trial court's lead.

§1.5   [1]JCAHO Accreditation Manual, MS .1.2.3.1.2.3.1, at 100.

medical staff will be bound by the bylaws, rules, and policies of the medical staff and the hospital.[2]

Several states have enacted statutes that recognize the hospital's interest in efficiency.[3] Some statutes directly acknowledge the hospital's interest in "the efficient and effective utilization of hospital resources,"[4] while others simply state that clinical privileges can be restricted if the physician fails to abide by hospital rules, and procedures.[5]

Case law suggests that hospitals may grant, deny, or modify clinical privileges on the basis of institutional convenience (efficiency). Courts have upheld the hospital's right to terminate clinical privileges of physicians who refuse to comply with the bylaws and regulations that the hospital enacted in the interest of efficient and effective administration. In Yeargin v. Hamilton Memorial Hospital,[6] a 54-year-old staff physician who had performed occasional required emergency room duty for 20 years alleged that he was now physically unable to do so in addition to treating his own patients. The assignment, required of all staff doctors under 60, consisted of four days per month of backup for the full-time emergency room physicians. After finding Dr. Yeargin physically fit to fulfill the obligation, the court ruled that the facilities of the public hospital were available to him "only upon his accepting the corresponding burden of reasonable public service for emergency duty." A Pennsylvania court reached a similar conclusion concerning a state hospital's requirement that a staff obstetrician-gynecologist accept every third indigent ob-gyn patient.[7] The requirement, imposed by the state's health commissioners to ensure compliance with Hill-

---

[2]Id. at MS .1.2.3.1.1.1, at 100.

[3]Some statutes may indirectly recognize the hospital's interest in efficiency by incorporating the JCAHO standards or suggesting that state agencies take the standards into account when promulgating the rules that govern hospitals.

[4]Ind. Code Ann. §16-10-1-6.5 (Burns Cum. Supp. 1989). See also, e.g., N.C. Gen. Stat. §131E-85 (1988 & Cum. Supp. 1989).

[5]See, e.g., Colo. Rev. Stat. §25-3-103.5 (Cum. Supp. 1988).

[6]229 Ga. 870, 195 S.E.2d 8 (1972).

[7]Clair v. Centre Community Hosp., 317 Pa. Super. 25, 463 A.2d 1065 (1983).

Burton regulations, was found to be burdensome but neither unreasonable nor arbitrary.

In other cases the courts have supported the hospital's decisions regarding the internal administration of the hospital. The Montana Supreme Court upheld a hospital administrator's decision not to permit the husbands of women in labor in the delivery room.[8] A doctor who wished to admit an expectant father saw the rule as an unlawful infringement of his clinical privileges, but the court adopted the view that "licensed hospitals have the authority, acting on the advice of their medical staffs, to adopt rules of self-regulation governing the hospital's physicians. Licensed physicians must live according to the rules adopted by their colleagues. . . ." While the court noted that the decision was not necessarily wise, it deferred to the judgment of the administrator; she in turn had deferred to the staff's recommendation on grounds that the issue was primarily medical and deference was necessary in most instances in order to preserve staff harmony.

Similarly, the Eighth Circuit Court of Appeals upheld the hospital's decision to terminate a staff member who was director of pathology because he could no longer work effectively with the hospital administration "due to conflicting ideas about the way the department should operate."[9] Finding that the loss of the position in question was not a revocation of clinical privileges that invoked certain of the physician's constitutional rights, the court concluded that "[t]he hospital administrator's discretion in [choosing a department head] is generally regarded as essential to the proper and efficient operation of the hospital."

A hospital may attempt to protect its interest in efficiency by executing an exclusive contract for service with a particular physician or group of physicians.[10] The Ohio Court of Appeals supported the hospital's right to terminate the clinical privileges of a radiologist who had been excluded from the group that by exclusive contract was to provide all of the hospital's radiology

[8]Hulit v. St. Vincent's Hosp., 164 Mont. 168, 520 P.2d 99, 100 (1974).
[9]Engelstad v. Virginia Mun. Hosp., 718 F.2d 262, 269 (8th Cir. 1983).
[10]See generally Annot., 74 A.L.R.3d 1268 (1976 & Cum. Supp. 1989).

services. The court stated that "[e]xclusive contracts have been generally upheld as a reasonable exercise of the hospital's power to provide for the proper management of the hospital."[11] In Adler v. Montefiore Hospital Association of Western Pennsylvania,[12] a staff physician who also served as head of the cardiology laboratory was replaced in that position (a lucrative one, since only the occupant of that post was allowed to perform cardiac catheterizations) by a full-time director of the laboratory who was retained through an exclusive contract. The court upheld the contract arrangement as a reasonable decision by the hospital intended to improve patient care, teaching, and administrative efficiency.

Because the efficient operation of the hospital also can be affected by the size of the medical staff, hospitals sometimes withhold privileges from new applicants in one or more areas of practice. New Jersey's supreme court reversed trial and appellate courts to uphold a hospital board's decision that its surgical staff must be limited in size.[13] The board feared that its new hospital, already operating above expected occupancy levels with a 3:1 ratio of nonsurgical patients to surgical patients, could not meet the requirements of additional surgical staff without turning away nonsurgical patients. Although the court warned that excluding newcomer physicians merely to benefit present staff was impermissible, it accepted the hospital's decision as a reasonable exercise of discretion on behalf of the community.

A decade later, the New Jersey Supreme Court invalidated one element of a hospital's closed staff policy. The institution excluded new physicians unless they were joining the private practice of a physician already on the medical staff of the hospital.[14] The court found that although the hospital's closed staff policy was reasonable, the exception was invalid since it

---

[11]Williams v. Hobbs, 9 Ohio App. 3d 331, 460 N.E.2d 287, 292 (1983).

[12]453 Pa. 60, 311 A.2d 634 (Pa. 1973), cert. denied, 414 U.S. 1131 (1974).

[13]Guerrero v. Burlington County Memorial Hosp., 70 N.J. 344, 360 A.2d 334 (1976).

[14]Desai v. St. Barnabas Med. Center, 103 N.J. 79, 510 A.2d 662, 668 (1986).

did not serve a public health objective and arbitrarily discriminated against qualified applicants. The court concluded that "[i]f a hospital policy decision reasonably serves an evident public-health purpose, it will be sustained, even though it may have a discriminating effect," but if it cannot be shown that the policy furthers a legitimate healthcare objective it is invalid. This opinion, together with other case law, indicates that hospitals must be prepared to prove the need for exclusive contracts and closed staff policies.

Efficiency-based denials of clinical privileges are sometimes attacked through state and federal antitrust claims. In 1984 the United States Supreme Court ruled in a case that raised these issues in the context of an exclusive contract with a single group of physicians.[15] The question before the Court was whether a hospital's contract to extend privileges to only one anesthesiology group constituted an illegal restraint of trade.[16] The plaintiff sought a judgment invalidating the exclusive contract and appointing him to the hospital staff. Under the existing arrangement, the hospital staffed each of its 13 operating rooms with a nurse anesthetist, and physicians from the anesthesiology group with which it had the contract circulated among the rooms to provide supervision. According to the hospital, the system assured 24-hour-a-day coverage and close monitoring of professional standards and also fixed legal and medical responsibility on one party, the group.

The Supreme Court found no evidence of adverse effects on competition from the exclusive contract and held that it did not constitute an illegal restraint of trade. This decision relieved concerns over the legality of exclusive contracts,[17] but strengthened awareness of the Supreme Court's determination to subject healthcare to antitrust regulation.[18] Although the Health Care

---

[15]Jefferson Parish Hosp. Dist. No. 2 v. Hyde, 466 U.S. 2 (1984).

[16]15 U.S.C.A. §1 (1973 & Cum. Supp. 1989).

[17]In subsequent cases, lower courts have relied on the Supreme Court's antitrust analysis to uphold exclusive contracts. See, e.g., Ezpeleta v. Sisters of Mercy Health Corp., 621 F. Supp. 1262 (N.D. Ind. 1985), affd., 800 F.2d 119 (7th Cir. 1986).

[18]More recently, in Patrick v. Burget, 486 U.S. 94, rehg. denied, 487 U.S.

Quality Improvement Act may protect hospitals from some antitrust suits, the Act does not apply to efficiency-based denials of staff membership.[19]

C. Staff Membership and Allocation of Clinical Privileges

§1.6 Procedures

Physicians must complete an application for staff membership and clinical privileges in which the physician consents to the inspection of records and documents pertaining to his or her license, specific training, experience, current competence, and health status; agrees to be bound by the bylaws and rules of the medical staff and the hospital; and releases the hospital and medical staff from any civil liability in acting on his or her application.[1] These procedures, together with the procedures for granting or renewing staff membership and delineating clinical privileges, are generally set out in the medical staff bylaws. The bylaws also must include due process procedures for physicians who are denied privileges or membership on the medical staff.

The JCAHO standards require that an appointment to the medical staff or for clinical privileges cannot be for a period longer than two years.[2] Therefore, the staff bylaws also must include procedures for reappointment to the medical staff and reapplication for clinical privileges. According to the JCAHO

1243 (1988), the Supreme Court held that medical staff peer review activities are not immune from antitrust scrutiny.

[19]42 U.S.C.A. §11151(9) (1989).

§1.6 [1]JCAHO Accreditation Manual, MS .1.2.3.1.4, at 100; MS .1.2.3.1.1.1, at 100; and MS .1.2.3.1.7, at 101. For a more detailed discussion of the release from liability, see infra §1.13, nn.1-4 and accompanying text.

[2]JCAHO Accreditation Manual, MS .1.2.3.1.11, at 101 and MS .4.2.10.1, at 110.

standards, the basis of the reappointment must be a reappraisal at the time of the renewal and may include peer recommendations and departmental recommendations.[3]

§1.7 Criteria for Staff Membership and Clinical Privileges

Both the Conditions of Participation and the JCAHO standards specify that there must be in the staff bylaws criteria for determining admittance to the medical staff and criteria for delineating clinical privileges.[1] The courts of various states also have considered what bases are appropriate for granting staff membership and clinical privileges. While reported decisions cannot always safely predict future decisions, it is useful to know what reasons for denying or limiting staff membership or clinical privileges have been accepted or rejected by courts of various jurisdictions.

§1.7.1 Valid Criteria

Some courts have found that the following to be valid criteria for refusing to grant staff membership or clinical privileges:

References.　　Failure to provide satisfactory references regarding the physician's competence in the area of practice for which the physician has applied for privileges is generally a valid reason for denial of privileges.[2] However, failure to obtain

---

[3]Id. at MS .5.5, at 114.

§1.7　[1]42 C.F.R. §482.22(c) (1988); JCAHO Accreditation Manual, MS .1.2.3.1.2, at 100 and MS .4.2.2, at 108.

[2]See, e.g., Rao v. Board of County Comm., 80 Wash. 2d 695, 497 P.2d 591, cert. denied, 409 U.S. 1017 (1972) (private hospital but dicta as to public hospitals). Denial of privileges based on the receipt of negative or ambiguous recommendations has also been upheld. See, e.g., Theissen v. Watonga Mun. Hosp. Bd., 550 P.2d 938 (Okla. 1976); Sosa v. Board of Mgrs. of Val Verde Memorial Hosp., 437 F.2d 173 (5th Cir. 1971).

references from existing staff members of the hospital is generally not a justified basis for exclusion.[3]

Malpractice Insurance. Courts have generally found that requirements that staff members carry insurance are reasonable.[4] The JCAHO also has recognized that the hospital is justified in establishing this criterion.[5]

Availability. Denials based on concern about the physician's other commitments (as evidenced by clinical privileges at other hospitals, for example) have been upheld.[6] Courts also have found that hospitals were justified in excluding physicians who were unavailable or unwilling to provide emergency care.[7] Although the JCAHO allows hospitals to impose geographic restrictions,[8] the courts are split on whether the hospital can reasonably restrict the location of the doctor's office or home.[9]

---

[3]See, e.g., Foster v. Mobile County Hosp. Bd., 398 F.2d 227 (5th Cir. 1968). But see La. Rev. Stat. Ann. §37:1301 (West 1988 & Cum. Supp. 1989).

[4]See, e.g., Wilkinson v. Madera Community Hosp., 144 Cal. App. 3d 436, 192 Cal. Rptr. 593 (1983) (upholds state regulation requiring malpractice insurance, thereby overruling Rosner v. Peninsula Hosp. Dist., 224 Cal. App. 2d 115, 36 Cal. Rptr. 332 (1964), which struck down a hospital's insurance requirement). However, some courts have indicated that the hospital must be flexible in applying this requirement, because if the physician had good reason for not carrying insurance (i.e., no insurance was available) the enforcement of the regulation by the hospital would not be reasonable. See, e.g., Holmes v. Hoemako Hosp., 117 Ariz. 403, 573 P.2d 477 (1977) (en banc). See generally Annot., 7 A.L.R.4th 1240 (1981 & Cum. Supp. 1989).

[5]JCAHO Accreditation Manual, MS .1.2.3.1.2.3.3, at 100.

[6]See, e.g., Stone v. William Beaumont Hosp., 782 F.2d 609 (6th Cir. 1986); Robinson v. Magovern, 521 F. Supp. 842, 917-918 (W.D. Pa. 1981), affd., 688 F.2d 824 (3d Cir. 1982), cert. denied, 459 U.S. 971 (1982) (private hospital).

[7]See, e.g., Yeargin v. Hamilton Memorial Hosp., 229 Ga. 870, 195 S.E.2d 8 (1972).

[8]JCAHO Accreditation Manual, MS .1.2.3.1.2.3.4, at 100.

[9]Compare Sams v. Ohio Valley Gen. Hosp. Assn., 413 F.2d 826 (4th Cir. 1969) (striking down a requirement that staff members maintain an office within the county) with Kennedy v. St. Joseph Memorial Hosp. of Kokomo, Ind., 482 N.E.2d 268 (Ind. App. 1985) (the rule that staff members must live "[close] enough to the hospital to provide continuous care to their patients" was reasonable).

Limitations on Size of Staff.   Courts in at least one jurisdiction (New Jersey) have generally upheld the hospital's right to "close" staff privileges as long as the restriction is reasonably related to the hospital's duty of patient care[10] and is not a long-term moratorium.[11]

Exclusive Contracts.   Challenges to exclusive arrangements, either on antitrust grounds or as unreasonable exercises of authority by the board, have generally failed.[12]

Loss of Tied Appointment.   Requirements that staff members retain medical school faculty status or affiliation with a group with which the hospital has an exclusive contract have been upheld.[13]

Higher Standards.   Requirements that staff members meet newly imposed standards for additional knowledge or expertise have been upheld.[14]

Refusal to Comply with Hospital Rules.   Courts have generally upheld hospitals' enforcement of reasonable rules[15] through denial or removal of privileges.[16]

---

[10]See supra §1.5, nn.13 and 14 and accompanying text.

[11]See, e.g., Walsky v. Pascack Valley Hosp., 145 N.J. Super. 393, 367 A.2d 1204 (1976), affd., 156 N.J. Super. 13, 383 A.2d 154 (1978).

[12]See, e.g., Jefferson Parish Hosp. Dist. No. 2 v. Hyde, 466 U.S. 2 (1984); Capili v. Shott, 620 F.2d 438 (4th Cir. 1980); Dattilo v. Tucson Gen. Hosp., 23 Ariz. App. 392, 533 P.2d 700 (1975) (antitrust grounds only); Rush v. City of St. Petersburg, 205 So. 2d 11 (Fla. App. 1967); Blank v. Palo Alto-Stanford Hosp. Center, 234 Cal. App. 2d 377, 44 Cal. Rptr. 572 (1965); Benell v. City of Virginia, 258 Minn. 559, 104 N.W.2d 633 (1960). See also supra §1.5, nn.10, 11, 12, 15, and 16.

[13]See, e.g., Dillard v. Rowland, 520 S.W.2d 81 (Mo. App. 1974). See also supra §1.5, nn.10 and 11 and accompanying text.

[14]See, e.g., Khan v. Suburban Community Hosp., 45 Ohio St. 2d 39, 340 N.E.2d 398 (1976).

[15]As an example of the latitude permitted hospitals, see the Supreme Court's decision upholding a public hospital's rules prohibiting abortions. Poelker v. Doe, 432 U.S. 519 (1977).

[16]See, e.g., Clair v. Centre Community Hosp., 317 Pa. Super. 25, 463

Difficulty in Working with Others.   The courts are split on whether negative actions based on the applicant's or staff member's difficulty in getting along with others are reasonable. Some courts have allowed hospitals to rely on this criterion when denying or revoking staff privileges,[17] particularly when the physician's actions constituted a disruptive force at the hospital.[18]

Incompetence.   Many cases support negative decisions based on incompetence; apparently, in every reported case on the subject incompetence has been a sufficient basis for denying or limiting staff membership or clinical privileges.[19]

Misconduct.   Courts have generally supported hospital actions based on physicians' misconduct.[20]

A.2d 1065 (1983) (physician required to treat every third indigent ob/gyn patient); Cobb County-Kennestone Hosp. Auth. v. Prince, 242 Ga. 139, 249 S.E.2d 581 (1978) (physicians required to use hospital's CAT scan machine); Yeargin v. Hamilton Memorial Hosp., 229 Ga. 870, 195 S.E.2d 8 (1972) (physician required to take share of emergency room duty).

[17]See, e.g., Robbins v. Ong, 452 F. Supp. 110 (S.D. Ga. 1978).

[18]See, e.g., Pick v. Santa Ana-Tustin Community Hosp., 130 Cal. App. 3d 970, 182 Cal. Rptr. 85 (1982).

[19]See, e.g., Storrs v. Lutheran Hosp. and Homes Socy. of Am., 661 P.2d 632 (Alaska 1983) (but remanded because the hospital's bylaws promised no diminution of privileges except in instances of "proven gross negligence," and the hospital had not even alleged gross negligence); Pontius v. Children's Hosp., 552 F. Supp. 1352 (W.D. Pa. 1982); Scappatura v. Baptist Hosp. of Phoenix, 120 Ariz. 204, 584 P.2d 1195 (1978) (private hospital); Paine v. Brunswick County Hosp. Auth., 470 F. Supp. 28 (E.D.N.C. 1978); Peterson v. Tucson General Hosp., 114 Ariz. 66, 559 P.2d 186 (1976); Klinge v. Lutheran Charities Assn. of St. Louis, 523 F.2d 56 (8th Cir. 1975); Duffield v. Memorial Hosp. Assn. of Charleston, 361 F. Supp. 398 (1973), affd. on other grounds, 503 F.2d 512 (4th Cir. 1974); Moore v. Board of Trustees of Carson-Tahoe Hosp., 88 Nev. 207, 495 P.2d 605, cert. denied, 409 U.S. 879 (1972); Sosa v. Board of Mgrs. of Val Verde Memorial Hosp., 437 F.2d 173 (5th Cir. 1971) (but remanded for additional procedural protection for plaintiff); Citta v. Delaware Valley Hosp., 313 F. Supp. 301 (E.D. Pa. 1970); Dayan v. Wood River Township Hosp., 18 Ill. App. 2d 263, 152 N.E.2d 205 (1958).

[20]See, e.g., Leonard v. Board of Directors, Prowers County Hosp. Dist.,

§1.7.2 Invalid Criteria

The courts have usually found that the following are invalid criteria for refusing to grant staff membership or clinical privileges:

Race.   Privileges may not be denied on the basis of race.[21]

Sex.   At least one court has stated that denial of privileges on the basis of sex is impermissible.[22]

Medical Society Affiliation or Board Certification.   Requirements that applicants be members of or approved by local medical societies have uniformly been struck down on the basis that such a requirement is an invalid delegation of power to an

---

673 P.2d 1019 (Colo. App. 1983) (refusal to meet with board, insulting letter); Unterthiner v. Desert Hosp. Dist. of Palm Springs, 33 Cal. 3d 285, 188 Cal. Rptr. 590, 656 P.2d 554 (1983), cert. denied, 464 U.S. 1068 (1984) (falsification of qualifications); Miller v. National Medical Hosp., 124 Cal. App. 3d 81, 177 Cal. Rptr. 119 (1981) (conviction of conspiracy to murder wife); Battle v. Jefferson Davis Memorial Hosp., 451 F. Supp. 1015 (S.D. Miss. 1976), affd., 575 F.2d 298 (5th Cir. 1978) (falsification of qualifications); Sosa v. Board of Mgrs. of Val Verde Memorial Hosp., 437 F.2d 173 (5th Cir. 1971) (felony convictions; abandoning patients); Anderson v. Board of Trustees of Caro Community Hosp., 10 Mich. App. 348, 159 N.W.2d (1968) (screaming and profanity in hospital; slander of staff; unauthorized inspection of patient records); Koelling v. Board of Trustees of Mary Frances Skiff Memorial Hosp., 259 Iowa 1185, 146 N.W.2d 284 (1966) (deceptive entries on patient charts to conceal incompetence). But see Wyatt v. Tahoe Forest Hosp. Dist., 174 Cal. App. 2d 709, 345 P.2d 93 (1959) (where there was no evidence of current misconduct and the denial was based on past misconduct alone, the court held that the exclusion of the physician was arbitrary).

[21]See, e.g., Chowdhury v. Reading Hosp. and Medical Center, 677 F.2d 317 (3d Cir. 1982), cert. denied, 463 U.S. 1229 (1983); Cypress v. Newport News Gen. and Nonsectarian Hosp. Assn. 375 F.2d 648 (4th Cir. 1967). Even if courts did not find that it was arbitrary, capricious, or unreasonable to deny privileges on the basis of race, this criterion for staff membership or clinical privileges is constitutionally impermissible.

[22]Dorsten v. Lapeer County Gen. Hosp., 521 F. Supp. 944 (E.D. Mich. 1981). Like distinctions based on race, denial of staff membership or clinical privileges based on sex is also unconstitutional.

independent agency.[23] Similarly, a requirement that applicants be board-certified or board-eligible has been rejected.[24] The Conditions of Participation also forbid withholding privileges for lack of "certification, fellowship, or membership in a specialty body or society."[25]

Refusal to Perform Abortions. No hospital may take any adverse action against a staff physician who refuses to take part in abortions. Federal law offers specific protection for physicians in an act covering any hospital that receives funds under the Public Health Services Act, the Community Mental Health Centers Act, or the Developmental Disabilities Assistance and Bill of Rights Act.[26] Some states have similar statutes.[27]

Difficulty in Working with Others. As discussed in §1.7.1, supra, the courts are split on whether staff membership can be denied because an applicant or staff member has difficulty getting along with others. Some courts have held that exclusion based on the physician's difficulty in working with others is unreasonable.[28]

---

[23]See, e.g., Foster v. Mobile County Hosp. Bd., 398 F.2d 227 (5th Cir. 1968); Ware v. Benedikt, 225 Ark. 185, 280 S.W.2d 234 (1955); Hamilton County Hosp. v. Andrews, 227 Ind. 217, 84 N.E.2d 469, rehg. denied, 227 Ind. 217, 85 N.E.2d 365, cert. denied, 338 U.S. 831 (1949).

[24]See, e.g., Armstrong v. Board of Directors of Fayette County Gen. Hosp., 553 S.W.2d 77 (Tenn. App. 1976).

[25]42 C.F.R. §482.12(a)(7) (1988).

[26]42 U.S.C.A. §300a-7(e) (Cum. Supp. 1989).

[27]See, e.g., N.C. Gen. Stat. §14-45.1(e) (1986 & Cum. Supp. 1989).

[28]See, e.g., Rosner v. Eden Township Hosp. Dist., 58 Cal. 2d 592, 25 Cal. Rptr. 551, 375 P.2d 431 (1962). *Rosner* seems to present good reasons for general judicial skepticism of this ground for negative actions. The court noted that the plaintiff appeared more in the right than those with whom he was not able to get along, citing an incident in which the plaintiff warned another physician (his superior) of a nurse's incompetence, without effect. Two days later, when the nurse's negligence resulted in a baby's death, the plaintiff expressed the opinion that his superior too was guilty of obvious malpractice for failure to heed the warning. Thereafter, his superior found the plaintiff hard to work with.

School of Practice. Although there are a variety of views, courts may require that hospitals have a reason other than preference for allopathy for excluding osteopathic physicians from the staff.[29] The courts have not held, however, that osteopaths have a right to staff privileges.[30] Although podiatrists and chiropractors have not been as successful in gaining support from the courts,[31] the courts at least require that these physicians be given adequate due process.[32] Some states have enacted statutes to address this issue.[33]

D. Denial or Revocation of Staff Membership or Clinical Privileges

§1.8 Physicians' Rights

In trying to fulfill their duty to regulate staff membership or clinical privileges, hospitals sometimes take the following nega-

---

[29]See, e.g., Greisman v. Newcomb Hosp., 40 N.J. 389, 192 A.2d 817 (1963).

[30]See, e.g., Hayman v. City of Galveston, 273 U.S. 414 (1927); Silverstein v. Gwinnett Hosp. Auth., 861 F.2d 1560 (11th Cir. 1988); Taylor v. Horn, 189 So. 2d 198 (Fla. App. 1966), appeal dismissed, 201 So. 2d 228 (1967).

[31]See, e.g., Samuel v. Curry County, 55 Or. App. 653, 639 P.2d 687, review denied, 292 Or. 863, 648 P.2d 850 (1982).

[32]See, e.g., Shaw v. Hospital Auth. of Cobb County, 507 F.2d 625 (5th Cir. 1975).

[33]Mo. Ann. Stat §205.300 (Vernon 1983 & Cum. Supp. 1987) states:

205.300. Equal privileges to practitioners—rights of patient

1. In the management of such public hospital no discrimination shall be made against practitioners of any school of medicine recognized by the laws of Missouri, and all such legal practitioners shall have equal privileges in treating patients in said hospital . . .

See also, e.g., La. Rev. Stat. Ann. §37:1301 (West 1988 & Cum. Supp. 1989) (prohibits discrimination against podiatrists); Tex. Civ. St. §4551k (Vernon Cum. Supp. 1987) (prohibits discrimination against dentists).

tive actions: failure to act on or rejection of an application; suspension, revocation, or limitation of clinical privileges; or failure to reappoint to the staff. Although hospitals enjoy some legal protections in so acting, their staff members also have legal rights. Because of the difficulty of balancing the institution's rights against those of the individual, each kind of adverse decision by the hospital has produced litigation.

The legal rights extended to the staff may apply to both physicians and other healthcare practitioners. The rights of physicians, however, are more clearly defined and of longer standing than the rights of other practitioners. To summarize the physicians' rights that are reasonably well established: doctors are at least entitled to rely on the protection provided by the hospital bylaws, and they generally can expect basic fairness from any hospital where they seek privileges. From a public hospital, they are entitled to the due process and equal protection guaranteed by the Fifth and Fourteenth Amendments to the United States Constitution. A hospital also must comply with applicable federal and state antidiscrimination statutes. Finally, there is a growing recognition that hospitals must take care that their actions do not violate state and federal antitrust laws.

§1.8.1 Constitutional Rights: Due Process and Equal Protection

The extent of a physician's rights largely depends on whether the hospital where he or she practices or seeks privileges is a public or a private hospital. Although this would appear to be a simple distinction, it is often difficult to determine whether a hospital is acting in a public or a private capacity. A hospital that is privately owned may act with a public character for certain purposes. Moreover, with today's heavy reliance on federal funding and the increase in federal regulations, there are few hospitals that do not have some public characteristics.[1]

---

§1.8 [1]Cary, Due Process Considerations in Hospital Staff Privileges Cases,

A hospital is treated as public if it is "an instrumentality of the state"[2] or engages in "state action."[3] The courts have articulated diverse views on what action is considered sufficient to constitute state action.[4] In most cases, neither a hospital's involvement with state and federal reimbursement programs for patient care nor even its acceptance of direct aid will change its character from private to public;[5] but this finding in conjunction with other factors may be sufficient to do so. Factors the court may consider[6] include: public control of the governing board,[7] leases or conveyances from the government,[8] or a monopoly by the hospital.[9]

Before classifying a hospital as public, most courts, in addition to weighing and balancing these factors, require that

---

3 Specialty Law Dig.: Health Care 5 (Dec. 1981). Private hospitals with public characteristics are referred to by some courts as "quasi-public" hospitals.

[2]See, e.g., Edson v. Griffin Hosp., 21 Conn. Supp. 55, 57, 144 A.2d 341, 343 (1958).

[3]See, e.g., Manning v. Greensville Memorial Hosp., 470 F. Supp. 662 (E.D. Va. 1979).

[4]For a summary of court decisions on action sufficient to constitute state action see Annot., 42 A.L.R. Fed. 463 (1979 & Supp. 1989).

[5]See, e.g., Barrett v. United Hosp., 376 F. Supp. 791 (S.D.N.Y. 1974), affd., 506 F.2d 1395 (2d Cir. 1974). Prior to 1982, the Fourth Circuit took the position that an otherwise private hospital's participation in state and federal regulatory and financial assistance programs could render the hospital "public" for certain purposes, including the regulation of staff membership and clinical privileges. The court reversed itself in Modaber v. Culpepper Memorial Hosp., 674 F.2d 1023, 1027 (4th Cir. 1982), holding that "[t]he staff privileges decisions of a hospital which receives Hill-Burton Act funds, accepts Medicare and Medicaid patients and reports privileges revocations to state medical licensing authorities do not constitute 'state action.' "

[6]In addition to the factors listed, some physicians have argued variously that licensing by the state, regulation by the state, and the hospital's tax exempt status are sufficient to constitute state action, but courts have rarely accepted these arguments.

[7]See, e.g., Chiaffitelli v. Dettmer Hosp., 437 F.2d 429 (6th Cir. 1971) (per curiam).

[8]See, e.g., O'Neill v. Grayson County War Memorial Hosp., 472 F.2d 1140 (6th Cir. 1973).

[9]See, e.g., Meredith v. Allen County War Memorial Hosp. Comm., 397 F.2d 33 (6th Cir. 1968).

there be a nexus between the government involvement and the action of the hospital.[10] In determining whether the necessary nexus exists, courts often follow the test articulated by the Supreme Court in Jackson v. Metropolitan Edison Co.,[11] which required that: (1) there be "a sufficiently close nexus between the state and the challenged action of the regulated entity so that the action of the latter may be fairly treated as that of the State itself" and (2) the initiative for the action come from the state. Even where there is no nexus, however, the First Circuit Court of Appeals has suggested that "the relationship between the state and private institution may be so intertwined that the state will be held responsible for conduct of the institution with which it had no direct connection."[12]

Private Hospitals.   Traditionally, the actions of private hospitals have not been subject to any significant judicial review. Both courts and state legislatures, however, are increasingly requiring certain protection for staff members of private hospitals. Even where courts cannot find sufficient "state action" to invoke the protection of the Fifth and Fourteenth Amendments, they have found other ways of extending protection to physicians practicing in private hospitals.

On the theory that a hospital's purpose is to serve the public welfare, the courts of some jurisdictions have determined that there is a fiduciary relationship between the hospital and the staff and the public.[13] The New Jersey Court, in Greisman v. Newcomb Hospital, stated that "while the managing officials [of the hospital] may have discretionary powers in the selection of the medical staff, those powers are deeply embedded in public aspects, and are rightly viewed as fiduciary powers to be exercised reasonably and for the public good."[14] Due to this fiduciary

---

[10]See, e.g., Briscoe v. Bock, 540 F.2d 392 (8th Cir. 1976).

[11]419 U.S. 345, 351 (1974).

[12]Downs v. Sawtelle, 574 F.2d 1, 9 (1st Cir. 1978), cert. denied, 439 U.S. 910 (1978).

[13]See, e.g., Silver v. Castle Memorial Hosp., 53 Haw. 475, 497 P.2d 564, cert. denied, 409 U.S. 1048 (1972).

[14]40 N.J. 389, 192 A.2d 817, 824 (1963).

relationship, the allocation of clinical privileges becomes an activity subject to judicial scrutiny. Therefore, "[i]f the exclusion of a person from [the hospital's] medical or surgical staff is based on the sound and reasonable exercise of discretionary judgment, courts will not intervene, but if the exclusion stems from unreasonable, arbitrary, capricious or discriminatory considerations, equitable relief is available."[15] Although courts relying on this theory find legal rights outside of the United States Constitution, a determination that the hospital is acting in a fiduciary capacity depends on the same factors that the courts consider when finding "state action" sufficient to give rise to constitutional protection.

Some jurisdictions have relied on principles of fairness to apply common-law due process requirements to private hospitals. In Ascherman v. St. Francis Memorial Hospital, California's Court of Appeals struck down a private hospital's action that was based on a bylaw that the court concluded was not "substantially rational and procedurally fair."[16] The court imposed the common-law due process requirement bringing the private hospital to a level of procedural fairness similar to that required of public hospitals. Two years later, citing *Ascherman,* the California Superior Court refused to allow a private hospital to dismiss a surgical resident without explanation or review, thus stretching the review standard even further.[17] The court's opinion directs California hospitals to examine JCAHO standards on medical staff hearings for an indication of what procedures will be considered sufficiently fair when they dismiss either staff or physician employees, such as residents. The existence of the standards, the court claimed, proves that all hospitals are accustomed to granting due process in connection with staff decisions; thus, the California rule would not impose "insuper-

---

[15]Davidson v. Youngstown Hosp. Assn., 19 Ohio App. 2d 246, 250 N.E.2d 892, 896 (1969).

[16]45 Cal. App. 3d 507, 119 Cal. Rptr. 507 (1975). The bylaw permitted rejection of applications that were not accompanied by three references from active staff members.

[17]Ezekial v. Winkley, 20 Cal. 3d 267, 142 Cal. Rptr. 418, 572 P.2d 32, 40 (1977).

able administrative burdens." In a third case the California Supreme Court directed trial courts to exercise their own independent judgment on the merits of hospitals' staffing decisions rather than determining merely whether the hospital acted on the basis of substantial evidence.[18]

Other jurisdictions have not subjected the decisions of private hospitals to the scrutiny imposed by the California courts but, like the court in *Greisman*, have stated that the hospital's clinical privileges decisions will be subject to judicial review if they are arbitrary, capricious, or unreasonable.[19] In Gianetti v. Norwalk Hospital,[20] the Supreme Court of Connecticut subjected the decision of the hospital administration to judicial review based on a different theory. At the outset, the court acknowledged that issues of contractual rights and duties are subject to judicial review. The court then concluded that the medical staff bylaws were an integral part of the contractual relationship between the physician and the hospital. The rights and duties arising out of the contractual relationship between the physician and the hospital, as in any contractual relationship, were subject to judicial review, and therefore actions by the hospital under the bylaws were subject to review.[21] The court concluded that the public-private distinction is inappropriate where there is a contractual relationship between the parties.

Most jurisdictions still allow private hospitals to afford fewer legal rights to staff members than public hospitals are obliged to, but there is a trend toward imposing more requirements on private hospitals than previously.[22] This trend, together

---

[18]Anton v. San Antonio Community Hosp., 19 Cal. 3d 802, 140 Cal. Rptr. 442, 567 P.2d 1162 (1977).

[19]See, e.g., Bricker v. Sceva Speare Memorial Hosp., 111 N.H. 276, 281 A.2d 589 (1971), cert. denied, 404 U.S. 995 (1971).

[20]211 Conn. 51, 557 A.2d 1249 (1989).

[21]It should be noted that the *Gianetti* court was careful to frame the question on which it was ruling, limiting it to the specific physician, bylaws, and hospital at issue in this case.

[22]In spite of this trend, the courts in some jurisdictions continue to hold that private hospitals' hiring decisions should not be subjected to substantive judicial review. See, e.g., Rosenberg v. Holy Redeemer Hosp., 351 Pa. Super.

with the possibility that a hospital that thinks itself private could be adjudged public, makes it advisable for all hospitals to accord their medical staff the elements of due process. In addition, if the hospital wants to qualify for the immunity provided by the Health Care Quality Improvement Act, the hospital must make certain that the physician is afforded adequate notice and hearing procedures.[23]

Public Hospitals. Applicants or members of the medical staff of public hospitals are entitled to the due process and equal protection guaranteed by the Fifth and Fourteenth Amendments to the United States Constitution.[24] The consideration that a hospital owes a practitioner varies, however, according to the seriousness of the hospital's action. All decisions affecting privileges are not accorded identical weight. A reason or a process deemed fair enough for denying an application for privileges, for example, might not be sufficient if the issue were instead revocation of privileges.[25] Judged by their impact on the

---

399, 506 A.2d 408, appeal denied, 514 Pa. 643, 523 A.2d 1132 (1986); Barrows v. Northwestern Memorial Hosp., 121 Ill. Dec. 244, 123 Ill. 2d 49, 525 N.E.2d 50 (1988).

[23]For discussion see infra nn.65-69 and accompanying text. The JCAHO standards also require the hospital to have fair hearing procedures when the action is adverse to the applicant for staff membership or clinical privileges. JCAHO Accreditation Manual, MS .1.2.3.1.9, at 101 and MS .4.2.11, at 111.

[24]Courts have found that clinical privileges are a property interest within the Fourteenth Amendment. See, e.g., Poe v. Charlotte Memorial Hosp., 374 F. Supp. 1302, 1312 (W.D.N.C. 1974). Courts also have held that the actions of the hospital in revoking clinical privileges may affect the physician's liberty interest. See, e.g., Hoberman v. Lock Haven Hosp., 377 F. Supp. 1178, 1185 (M.D. Pa. 1974). A court might not find a protectable property interest if the physician is an applicant for privileges or the employment contract is terminable at will. See, e.g., Engelstad v. Virginia Mun. Hosp., 718 F.2d 262 (8th Cir. 1983). For discussion see Cary, Due Process Considerations in Hospital Staff Privileges Cases, 3 Specialty Law Dig.: Health Care 5 (Dec. 1981).

[25]The California Supreme Court stated the principle in the context of a residency program. When the plaintiff was dismissed without explanation after he had completed three of four years, the court noted that his stake was greater than if he had never been accepted. Ezekial v. Winkley, 20 Cal. 3d 267, 142 Cal. Rptr. 418, 572 P.2d 32 (1977).

staff member's reputation or income, the following actions are likely to be of increasing gravity: (1) failure to respond to or rejection of an application; (2) limitation of privileges; (3) probation of the staff member; (4) suspension of privileges; (5) failure to reappoint to the staff; (6) revocation of privileges. Reflected in this hierarchy is the tendency of courts to grant greater protection to members of the staff than to applicants.

The facts of each case also are crucial to an assessment of how grave the action by the hospital might be in its effect. Take category (2), for example. "Limitation of privileges" could mean a decision to keep a physician on staff but forbid her to perform a particular procedure because she is thought to perform it incompetently. Or it might refer to a nonjudgmental decision, such as allowing a hospital-employed physician to perform all procedures of a certain type, which were formerly performed by the staff member. Hospital attorneys and administrators must be sensitive to these differences so that the hospital's policies and actions in contested situations assure staff members of the greatest protection when their interests are most severely threatened. When in doubt, as a matter of both fairness and prudence, the choice should be to provide fuller due process than may be necessary. Any action impugning a physician's competence should be viewed as serious, even though the direct economic loss from it may be slight.

As a matter of what is sometimes called "substantive due process," the action of the hospital cannot be arbitrary, capricious, or unreasonable.[26] For a summary of reported decisions, see the discussion of criteria for staff membership and clinical privileges in §1.7 of this chapter.[27]

---

[26]See, e.g., Ritter v. Board of Commrs. of Adams County Public Hosp. Dist. No. 1, 96 Wash. 2d 503, 637 P.2d 940 (1981) (en banc).

[27]Because traditionally the decisions of private hospitals have not been subject to judicial review, the majority of appellate decisions that consider substantive due process requirements deal with public hospitals. It can generally be assumed, however, that the courts will not require more of a private hospital than of a public hospital. Therefore, although there are some exceptions, where courts have found a public hospital justified in denying or limiting staff membership or clinical privileges, a private hospital would also

Courts have frequently considered what procedures must, in the interest of minimal fairness, be extended to a person being denied privileges. The physician may be entitled to sufficient notice of the charges against him or her (if any), a timely hearing before an unbiased jury, a right to defend against charges or present a case for privileges, a right to confront adverse witnesses, a written decision stating reasons, and a record of the proceedings. Some jurisdictions grant the physician a right to an attorney,[28] while others say that the physician has no such right.[29] The physician may be entitled to some or all of these procedures.[30] The timing and the extent of the procedures depend on the seriousness of the accusations against the physician and the potential consequences.[31] For example, although summary suspension has been upheld in emergency situations,[32] it is improbable that summary revocation would be upheld.[33]

Where the physician is entitled to a hearing, it must be held before an unbiased jury. In In re Zaman,[34] the South Carolina Supreme Court stated that having three of the physician's "original accusers sit also as his jury is a direct violation of [his] right to a fair and meaningful hearing under the due

---

be justified. Similarly, if the court finds that a restriction imposed by a private hospital is unreasonable, the court is not likely to uphold the same restriction when imposed by a public hospital. For a summary of case law in this area see Annot., 37 A.L.R.3d 645 (1971 & Cum. Supp. 1987).

[28]See, e.g., Garrow v. Elizabeth Gen. Hosp. and Dispensary, 79 N.J. 549, 401 A.2d 533 (1979) (private hospital).

[29]See, e.g., Anton v. San Antonio Community Hosp., 19 Cal. 3d 802, 140 Cal. Rptr. 442, 567 P.2d 1162 (1977) (private treated as public).

[30]Although the procedural standards set out in the Health Care Quality Improvement Act (discussed infra nn.65-69 and accompanying text) are more extensive than the law of many states, the due process requirement imposed by the Act can apparently be met by compliance with existing state law.

[31]See supra n.25 and accompanying text.

[32]See, e.g., Duby v. Baron, 369 Mass. 614, 341 N.E.2d 870 (1976). The JCAHO Accreditation Manual, MS .2.4.3, at 103 also provides support for summary suspensions in emergency situations.

[33]See, e.g., Park Hosp. Dist. v. District Court of the Eighth Judicial Dist., 192 Colo. 69, 555 P.2d 984 (1976) (en banc).

[34]285 S.C. 345, 329 S.E.2d 436, 437 (1985).

process clause." However, where the juror did not initiate the proceedings, but merely assisted in preparing the charges against the physician, the Illinois Court of Appeals, in Landenheim v. Union County Hospital District,[35] held that the physician's due process rights had not been violated. Stating that "due process does not require that every member of an administrative tribunal be completely unfamiliar with the factual issues presented at the hearing," the court concluded that the bias and familiarity necessary to disqualify a member of the jury must come from an extrajudicial source and thus incline toward a decision based on something other than the information learned from participation in the case.

In addition to substantive and procedural due process rights, staff members are entitled to equal protection. Generally, the court will not find a violation of the equal protection clause if the hospital has a rational basis for its decision to exclude an individual or a class of individuals.[36] On some issues, however, like exclusion based on race, the court will look at the hospital's action with strict scrutiny.[37]

Before seeking judicial review of the hospital's decision, the staff member must exhaust the internal grievance procedures provided by the hospital.[38] On review, the court will generally uphold the hospital's action if there is substantial evidence supporting the hospital's decision.[39] Only in California have courts adopted an independent judgment test giving little or no deference to the hospital's decision, at least where the action of the hospital substantially affects fundamental vested rights of the physician, such as terminating existing clinical privileges.[40]

---

[35]31 Ill. Dec. 568, 76 Ill. App. 3d 90, 394 N.E.2d 770, 774 (1979).

[36]See, e.g., Sosa v. Board of Mgrs. of Val Verde Memorial Hosp., 437 F.2d 173 (5th Cir. 1971).

[37]See, e.g., Cypress v. Newport News Gen. and Nonsectarian Hosp. Assn., 375 F.2d 648 (4th Cir. 1967) (private hospital).

[38]See, e.g., Sanchez v. Hosp. Auth. of Walker, Dade & Catoosa Counties, 146 Ga. App. 734, 247 S.E.2d 534 (1978).

[39]See, e.g., Kaplan v. Carney, 404 F. Supp. 161 (E.D. Mo. 1975).

[40]Anton v. San Antonio Community Hosp., 19 Cal. 3d 802, 140 Cal. Rptr. 442, 567 P.2d 1162 (1977) (private hospital treated as public hospital).

§1.8.2 Compliance with Bylaws

Although the courts and legislatures of various jurisdictions differ in the rights afforded to staff members, all jurisdictions agree on one point: hospitals must follow their own bylaws. Some courts reach this conclusion by construing bylaws as a contract between hospital and staff. In a South Dakota case,[41] the medical staff won a declaratory judgment that bylaws adopted in 1947 were a binding contract and could be amended only as provided therein—that is, by a two-thirds vote of the staff. Consequently, bylaws adopted by the hospital administration in 1972 were null.[42] Other courts simply assert that bylaws, once properly adopted,[43] must be adhered to.[44] The Illinois Court of Appeals's pronouncement is typical: "[W]here a physician's existing staff privileges are revoked or reduced, a private hospital must follow its own bylaws in doing so or be subject to limited judicial review."[45]

This widely accepted legal principle is a major protection for practitioners at private hospitals because the Conditions of Participation, the JCAHO standards, and, in some instances, state law all require that hospitals and their medical staffs have

---

[41]St. John's Hosp. Medical Staff v. St. John Regional Medical Center, 90 S.D. 674, 245 N.W.2d 472 (1976).

[42]The result seems somewhat extreme. One can imagine circumstances—adding a right to suspend privileges summarily in the interest of patient care, for example—in which a bylaw change might be highly advisable from the hospital's point of view and yet unacceptable to one-third of the medical staff.

[43]Staff members cannot rely on improperly adopted bylaws. See, e.g., Greenspan v. National Medical Care, 485 F. Supp. 311 (E.D. Va. 1980) (the plaintiff wrote and adopted the bylaws himself while serving as acting director of the medical center, without submitting them to the corporation's owners).

[44]See, e.g., Shulman v. Washington Hosp. Center, 319 F. Supp. 252 (D.D.C. 1970); Scappatura v. Baptist Hosp. of Phoenix, 120 Ariz. 204, 584 P.2d 1195 (1978); Spencer v. Community Hosp. of Evanston, 42 Ill. Dec. 272, 87 Ill. App. 3d 214, 408 N.E.2d 981 (1980); Knapp v. Palos Community Hosp., 80 Ill. Dec. 442, 125 Ill. App. 3d 244, 465 N.E.2d 554 (1984).

[45]Spencer v. Community Hosp. of Evanston, 42 Ill. Dec. 272, 87 Ill. App. 3d 214, 408 N.E.2d 981, 984 (1980), quoting Jain v. Northwest Community Hosp., 24 Ill. Dec. 341, 67 Ill. App. 3d 420, 385 N.E.2d 108, leave to appeal denied, 75 Ill. 2d 591 (1978).

bylaws. Thus, it is not possible for a hospital to avoid obligations to its staff by simply not enacting bylaws.

Although the bylaws may grant significant protection to staff members, some jurisdictions do not extend the protection to applicants for staff membership. In Bello v. South Shore Hospital,[46] four physicians brought an action for a declaratory judgment regarding the propriety of the denial of their applications for staff membership, claiming that the hospital's action was inconsistent with its own bylaws. The court stated that rights under the bylaws "do not arise upon application for membership but only when such application is accepted" and, therefore, "the physicians have no standing to challenge the hospital's compliance with its bylaws." JCAHO standards also allow this differential treatment between applicants and members of the medical staff.[47] In jurisdictions where judicial review of private hospitals is limited to a determination of whether the hospital followed its bylaws, and those bylaws, either by their terms or as applied, do not cover those seeking staff membership or privileges, applicants must look to state and federal statutes and regulations for legal protection.

§1.8.3 Statutory and Regulatory Protection

A physician who has been denied staff membership or clinical privileges may be able to invoke the protection of state and federal law[48] as well as the standards of the accrediting agency.

State Statutes. Many state statutes apply equally to public and private hospitals. For example, Colorado's statute provides

---

[46]384 Mass. 770, 429 N.E.2d 1011, 1016 (1981).

[47]JCAHO Accreditation Manual, MS .2.4.2, at 103.

[48]The Health Care Quality Improvement Act (discussed infra nn.65-69 and accompanying text) states that the peer review procedure must provide adequate due process. Although the statute does not provide direct protection for the physician, it may be an incentive for hospitals, because the due process requirement must be met before they can invoke the immunity provided by the Act.

that a physician threatened with hospital discipline has a right to notice of the hearing, a right to be present, a right to be represented by counsel, and a right to offer evidence.[49] New York has adopted a grievance process whereby any person dissatisfied with the hospital's decision has an opportunity to be heard by the Public Health Council.[50] Many states also have enacted statutes that prevent the hospital from discriminating against physicians based on their school of practice.[51]

Federal Statutes. Federal acts protect individuals from discrimination[52] that is based on sex,[53] religion,[54] race,[55] national origin,[56] handicap,[57] or age;[58] but there is considerable doubt as to whether the antidiscrimination statutes apply to the medical staff member. Among the questions not yet determined are: (1) whether the statutes apply to every hospital that receives any form of federal financial assistance (nearly all hospitals) or only

---

[49]Colo. Rev. Stat. §12-43.5-102(3)(b)(II) (1985 & Cum. Supp. 1988).

[50]N.Y. Pub. Health Law §2801-b (McKinney 1985 & Cum. Supp. 1990).

[51]See supra §1.7, n.33.

[52]Section 1983 of the Civil Rights Act of 1971, 42 U.S.C.A. §1983 (1981 & Cum. Supp. 1989) forbids deprivation of anyone's federal constitutional or statutory rights by a person acting "under color of state law." If a person is deprived of his or her rights, the individual acting "under color of state law" shall be liable to the injured party. Section 1983 applies to public, not private, hospitals.

[53]Title VII of the 1964 Civil Rights Act, 42 U.S.C.A. §§2000e to 2000e-17 (1981 & Cum. Supp. 1989) (it can be argued that this statute does not apply to the majority of medical staff members, who are not employees for most purposes).

[54]Id.

[55]Id.; Title VI of the 1964 Civil Rights Act, 42 U.S.C.A. §2000d (1981 & Cum. Supp. 1989) (forbids discrimination in all federally funded activities).

[56]Title VII of the 1964 Civil Rights Act, 42 U.S.C.A. §§2000e to 2000e-17 (1981 & Cum. Supp. 1989); Title VI of the 1964 Civil Rights Act, 42 U.S.C.A. §2000d (1981 & Cum. Supp. 1989).

[57]The Rehabilitation Act of 1973, 29 U.S.C.A. §794 (1985 & Cum. Supp. 1989) (forbids discrimination in any federally funded activity).

[58]The Age Discrimination Act, 29 U.S.C.A. §§621 to 634 (1985 & Cum. Supp. 1989) (forbids discrimination in employment and therefore may not extend to most staff members, who are not usually considered employees).

to those that are publicly owned or supported or receive direct federal grants; (2) whether all operations of a covered hospital are subject to the statutes or only those functions that directly benefit from federal assistance (not a simple distinction, in any case); and (3) assuming that the statutes do cover either the entire hospital or the area in which the staff member works, whether the staff member himself or herself is protected by them. Some courts accept the argument that hospital employees and staff members are not the intended beneficiaries of federal assistance, and hence are not covered by the civil rights statutes.[59] Finally, there is a question whether the acts that regulate employment practices cover staff members, who are not considered employees by the hospital. (These issues are treated at greater length in Chapter 2, infra.)

Medical staff members or applicants who have been denied privileges often invoke the protection of state and federal antitrust laws.[60] Until the 1980s it was usually assumed that hospitals were exempt from antitrust law. Now, however, each defense that has been relied on by healthcare agencies against federal antitrust prohibitions—that the practice of a profession like medicine is not "trade or commerce,"[61] that in any case it is not interstate commerce,[62] and that hospital policies (because hospitals are regulated by the state) are exempt as "state

---

[59]For a holding to this effect, see Vuciecevic v. MacNeal Memorial Hosp., 572 F. Supp. 1424 (N.D. Ill. 1983).

[60]A survey of health attorneys indicated that more than half of the antitrust actions in which their clients were involved were medical staff decisions. 12, no. 3 Health Lawyer's News Report 8 (March 1984). The federal statutes are principally the Sherman Act, 15 U.S.C.A. §§1, 2 (1973 & Cum. Supp. 1989); the Clayton Act, 15 U.S.C.A. §§13, 14 (1973 & Cum. Supp. 1989); and the Federal Trade Commission Act, 15 U.S.C.A. §45 (1973 & Cum. Supp. 1989).

[61]Holdings to the contrary are found in Goldfarb v. Virginia State Bar, 421 U.S. 773 (1975); National Socy. of Professional Engineers v. United States, 435 U.S. 679 (1978); and Arizona v. Maricopa County Medical Socy., 457 U.S. 332 (1982).

[62]The Supreme Court held that hospitals may be engaged in interstate commerce in United States v. Oregon State Medical Socy., 343 U.S. 326 (1952), and again more recently in Hospital Building Co. v. Trustees of Rex Hosp., 425 U.S. 738 (1976).

action"[63]—has been undermined by Supreme Court decisions.[64] (For a complete discussion of the antitrust liability of healthcare facilities, see Chapter 3, infra.)

The Health Care Quality Improvement Act sets out notice and hearing standards.[65] The standards require that the physician receive notice of the proposed action; notice of the hearing; a hearing before a mutually acceptable arbitrator, an appointed hearing officer, or a panel of individuals who are not in direct economic competition with the physician;[66] a right to representation; the opportunity to call, examine, and cross-examine witnesses; the opportunity to present evidence; the right to submit a written statement at the close of the evidence; the right to a record of the proceedings; and the right to the written recommendation and written final decision of the healthcare entity.

These standards are fairly extensive, and provide much more procedural protection than the law of many states,[67] but a failure to meet these standards does not necessarily constitute inadequate due process in violation of the statutory requirements. The legislative history suggests that the "adequacy" requirement may also be met by compliance with applicable law even if the plaintiff physician is afforded fewer due process rights.[68] Procedural protection is only necessary if negative action is actually taken by the healthcare entity. The Act recognizes that the healthcare entity reasonably may take immediate action (without

---

[63]Unless the state exercises ultimate control over the conduct in question, this premise is now questionable. See, e.g., Patrick v. Burget, 486 U.S. 94, rehg. denied, 487 U.S. 1243 (1988).

[64]For discussion of the denial of staff membership and clinical privileges as a violation of the Sherman Act, see generally Annot., 89 A.L.R. Fed. 452 (1988 & Cum. Supp. 1989).

[65]42 U.S.C.A. §11112 (1989).

[66]The requirement that the panel or officer not be in direct economic competition with the physician is intended to ensure that the panel or officer is impartial and fair.

[67]See supra §1.8, nn. 49-51 and accompanying text. This is particularly true for private hospitals. See supra nn.13-23 and accompanying text.

[68]H.R. Rep. No. 903, 99th Cong., 2d Sess. 10, reprinted in 1987 U.S. Code Cong. & Ad. News 6384, 6393.

a hearing and notice) in emergency situations. The healthcare entity also may suspend the physician's privileges for 14 days or less for the purpose of investigation without having to comply with the statutory due process requirements.[69]

Regulations. Both the federal Conditions of Participation and JCAHO standards also refer to procedures for decision-making about staff. The JCAHO requires a fair hearing when recommendations regarding clinical privileges are adverse to the applicant; "appellate review mechanisms" that may differ for applicants and those already holding staff membership or clinical privileges; reappointment intervals of not more than two years; staff recommendations on appointments, reappointments, and terminations; and final decision by the governing body.[70] The Conditions of Participation simply state that a hospital's bylaws must include criteria for determining the privileges to be granted and a procedure for applying the criteria to individuals requesting privileges.[71]

§1.9 Rights of Nonphysician Practitioners[1]

For the last half-century American medical practice has been hospital-centered. Patients have become accustomed to having all but minor procedures performed in hospitals, and hospital affiliation confers prestige on practitioners. Not surprisingly, a variety of individuals and classes of nonphysician healthcare practitioners are seeking hospital privileges. To date, their efforts have not been widely successful, but momentum may be building toward an expanded concept of staff. Groups that have sought

---

[69]Congress did not intend for this to be a back door for harassment of physicians through repeated suspensions or investigations. Id.

[70]JCAHO Accreditation Manual, MS .1.2.3.1-2.4.2 at 100-103.

[71]42 C.F.R. §482.22(c)(6) (1988).

§1.9 [1]The term, used here for convenience to designate all health professionals other than doctors of medicine, is inaccurate as applied to osteopathic physicians. Vis-a-vis osteopaths, the correct but little-used term for an M.D. is "allopath."

admission to staff include osteopaths, podiatrists, chiropractors, psychologists, physician's assistants, physical therapists, nurse anesthetists and midwives, family nurse practitioners, and dentists. Most of those groups have initiated litigation to that end.

In 1927 the United States Supreme Court found no denial of due process or equal protection in a municipal hospital's exclusion of the entire class of osteopaths.[2] Regarding due process, the Court decided that "it cannot, we think, be said that all licensed physicians have a constitutional right to practice their profession in a hospital maintained by a state or a political subdivision. . . ." As for equal protection, the Court found it permissible for the hospital's trustees to select only one among "the numerous systems or methods of treatment authorized to practice in Texas." The Texas statute forbidding preference by law for any school of medicine was said to mean merely preference in licensure, not in who may practice or teach in state institutions. By 1940 (osteopathy was founded in 1874), osteopaths were licensed to practice in every state but were still nearly universally denied staff membership and clinical privileges at (allopathic) hospitals.[3]

Despite the fact that osteopaths have no constitutional right to practice in a public hospital,[4] there are an increasing number of state statutes that prohibit discrimination against osteopaths who apply for staff membership and clinical privileges.[5] These statutes do not guarantee osteopaths a position on the hospital staff, but rather they generally require the hospital to consider

---

[2]Hayman v. City of Galveston, 273 U.S. 414 (1927).

[3]Helminski, "That Peculiar Science:" Osteopathic Medicine and the Law, 12 Law, Medicine and Health Care 32-36 (February 1984). As a result, osteopaths developed their own institutions—about 200 hospitals by 1977. Id. at 36, n.41.

[4]For more recent cases following the holding in Hayman v. City of Galveston, 273 U.S. 414 (1927) (discussed supra, text accompanying nn.2 and 3), see Silverstein v. Gwinnett Hosp. Auth., 861 F.2d 1560 (11th Cir. 1988) and Stern v. Tarrant County Hosp. Dist., 778 F.2d 1052 (5th Cir. 1985), cert. denied, 476 U.S. 1108, rehg. denied, 477 U.S. 909 (1986).

[5]See, e.g., Fla. Stat. Ann. §395.011(1) (West 1986 & Cum. Supp. 1989); Colo. Rev. Stat. §25-3-103.5 (Burns Cum. Supp. 1989).

the osteopath for staff membership and clinical privileges based on his or her individual credentials and skills.[6] The medical establishment also has become more favorably inclined toward osteopathy. The American Medical Association, for instance, supports the merger of state medical and osteopathic societies[7] and use of the same criteria to evaluate osteopathic and allopathic applicants for hospital privileges.[8]

Other types of health professionals also are pressing claims against hospitals that deny them staff membership and clinical privileges. Members of the National Health Lawyers' Association report a substantial number of legal actions brought against hospitals by groups heretofore excluded from staff.[9] Though decisions in these cases do not consistently favor the previously excluded practitioners,[10] and courts do appear to recognize a need for general supervision of nonphysicians by physicians, it is increasingly likely that hospitals will be found to have a legal duty not to limit access to their facilities arbitrarily.

Legislation adopted by the District of Columbia provides that qualified certified registered nurse anesthetists, certified

---

[6]See, e.g., D.C. Code Ann. §32-1307(a) (1988 & Cum. Supp. 1989); Fla. Stat. Ann. §395.011(5) (West 1986 & Cum. Supp. 1989). However, the court may not find discrimination where the osteopath does not allege that the hospital's requirements discriminate against all osteopaths. See, e.g., Berman v. Florida Med. Center, 600 F.2d 466 (5th Cir. 1979).

[7]Helminski, supra n.3, at 36, n.59.

[8]W. Isele, The Hospital Medical Staff: Its Legal Rights and Responsibilities 91 (1984).

[9]Antitrust Survey 12, no. 3 Health Lawyers News Report 8 (March 1984).

[10]For example, see Grodjesk v. Jersey City Medical Center, 135 N.J. Super. 393, 343 A.2d 489 (1975) (oral surgeons may not be excluded without a rational basis; basis found to be sufficient); Davidson v. Youngstown Hosp. Assn., 19 Ohio App. 2d 246, 250 N.E.2d 892 (1969); Shaw v. Hospital Auth. of Cobb County, 614 F.2d 946 (5th Cir.), rehg. denied, 620 F.2d 300, cert. denied, 449 U.S. 955 (1980) (limited practice rights of podiatrists reasonable basis for exclusion); Todd v. Physicians and Surgeons Community Hosp., 165 Ga. App. 656, 302 S.E.2d 378 (1983) (private hospital may exclude podiatrists without violating equal protection rights); Herbert v. Women's Hosp. Found., 377 So. 2d 1340 (1979), writ denied, 379 So. 2d 254 (La. 1980) (damages awarded to staff nurse anesthetists who were fired when exclusive contract given to anesthesiologist).

nurse midwives, certified nurse practitioners, podiatrists, and psychologists shall not be prohibited from "being accorded clinical privileges and appointed to all categories of staff membership at those facilities and agencies that offer the kind of services that can be performed by either members of these health professions or physicians."[11] The statutory standards for clinical privileges and staff membership that require that clinical privileges be determined based on the individual's qualifications also apply to these nonphysician health professionals. In addition, the statute requires hospitals to provide specific procedural protection for any health professional whose staff membership or clinical privileges are being denied, reduced, or revoked.

Although the Maryland Supreme Court has held that a statute requiring hospitals that offer foot care to admit podiatrists is constitutional,[12] courts appear to construe such statutes strictly. Applying a state statute that prohibits hospitals from discriminating against medical and osteopathic physicians, podiatrists, and dentists, the Ohio Supreme Court held that a hospital's unreasonable requirement that podiatrists have a two-year residency in addition to board certification was illegally discriminatory.[13] In another case, however, the Supreme Court refused to extend the protection of the statute beyond its express provisions and held that a hospital's exclusion of chiropractors was not arbitrary and capricious.[14]

The Fifth Circuit Court of Appeals has held that podiatrists who apply for staff membership are entitled to the protection of a due process hearing.[15] Again, however, the actual protection extended to podiatrists appears to be minimal. On remand, the podiatrist was given a due process hearing and then excluded from the staff based on a hospital bylaw that allowed only

---

[11]D.C. Code Ann. §32-1307 (1988 & Cum. Supp. 1989).

[12]State of Md. v. Good Samaritan Hosp. of Md., 299 Md. 310, 473 A.2d 892, appeal dismissed, 469 U.S. 802 (1984).

[13]Dooley v. Barberton Citizens Hosp., 11 Ohio St. 3d 216, 465 N.E.2d 58 (1984).

[14]Fort Hamilton-Hughes Memorial Hosp. Center v. Southard, 12 Ohio St. 3d 263, 466 N.E.2d 903 (1984).

[15]Shaw v. Hospital Auth. of Cobb County, 507 F.2d 625 (5th Cir. 1975).

physicians with unrestricted licenses and dentists to be members of the hospital staff. The court of appeals upheld the hospital's decision, stating that a state-created right to practice podiatry does not confer an absolute constitutional right to practice at a particular public hospital.[16]

Some nonphysician practitioners have brought suit against hospitals and physicians claiming antitrust violations. The United States Supreme Court in 1984[17] declined to review such a complaint, brought by chiropractors against the AMA, the JCAHO, the American Hospital Association, and others concerning (among other issues) hospital access. The Seventh Circuit Court of Appeals decision that was thus left standing would first require chiropractors to show that the exclusion of chiropractors by the physicians and the hospital reduces competition.[18] If the chiropractors succeed in this showing, the court will then allow the medical groups to defend themselves by proving that the opposition to chiropractors rests on a reasonable concern for their own patients (not the general public) that cannot be dealt with in a manner less restrictive of competition.

The Federal Trade Commission has for some time encouraged the expansion of staff membership and clinical privileges. Commenting favorably on the District of Columbia statute before it was passed, a commissioner observed that "denials of hospital privileges to groups such as those listed in the bill can violate the antitrust laws when they constitute boycotts of one professional group by another professional group of horizontal competitors."[19] The commissioner then said that it was a "fundamental premise of the Commission's work . . . that appropriate access to hospitals by enumerated health care providers who meet the necessary standards would substantially benefit competition and

---

[16]Shaw, supra n.10. The bylaw was found to be reasonably related to the operation of the hospital.

[17]Wilk v. American Medical Assn., 719 F.2d 207 (7th Cir. 1983), cert. denied, 467 U.S. 1210 (1984).

[18]Id.

[19]Letter to Polly Shackleton, Council of the District of Columbia, from Patricia P. Bailey, Federal Trade Commission (June 22, 1983), p.2.

consumers. . . ."[20] The entire commission has criticized the American Medical Association's preference for barring podiatrists and clinical psychologists and, in what may have been a pointed reference to the possibility of antitrust violation, noted that JCAHO standards have reflected the AMA position.[21]

The JCAHO has since altered its standards to allow hospitals greater latitude in granting privileges. Formerly limited to physicians and dentists, medical staffs may now include other practitioners licensed to provide care independently, and clinical privileges may be offered to still others.[22] Nevertheless, only medical staff may admit patients under the standards. A physician (doctor of medicine or osteopathy) or an oral surgeon must examine each patient on admission, and a physician must take responsibility for the patient's general condition.[23]

The Conditions of Participation for Medicare and Medicaid go further than the JCAHO standards. The hospital staff must be "composed of doctors of medicine or osteopathy and, in accordance with State law, may also be composed of other practitioners appointed by the governing body."[24] Patients may be admitted to the hospital by a doctor of medicine or osteopathy, a dentist, a podiatrist, an optometrist, or a chiropractor. However, a doctor of medicine or osteopathy is responsible for problems that are outside of the scope of practice of the nonphysician practitioners. In addition, on admission, the patient must be examined by a doctor of medicine or osteopathy, or, if the patient is being admitted for oromaxillofacial surgery, an oral surgeon who has been granted privileges under state law may complete the examination.

As nonphysician practitioners increasingly ask for staff membership and clinical privileges and seek legal remedies for

---

[20]Id. at 5.

[21]American Medical Assn. v. Federal Trade Comm., 94 F.T.C. 701 (1978), affd., 638 F.2d 443 (2d Cir. 1980), affd. by an equally divided court, 455 U.S. 676, rehg. denied, 456 U.S. 966 (1982). The AMA is a founder of the JCAHO and appoints 7 of its 20 commissioners.

[22]JCAHO Accreditation Manual, MS .1.1, at 99.

[23]JCAHO Accreditation Manual, MS .4.3, at 111.

[24]42 C.F.R. §§482.12, 482.22 (1988).

denial, hospitals should develop procedures for dealing with potential applicants. The AMA has advised its members that "[t]he central issue to be confronted is the development of membership provisions in the medical staff bylaws on how to establish objective criteria that will assure the provisions of quality care without appearing to prohibit arbitrarily any category of health care practitioner from joining the staff."[25] The hospital should be able to defend its decision to exclude an entire category of healthcare professionals on the basis of objective criteria related to quality of care and efficiency.[26]

§1.10 The Hospital's Duty to Report

Both federal and state laws require hospitals to report incompetent physicians.

§1.10.1 State Law Requirements

In order to monitor the competence of practicing physicians, some states have enacted statutes requiring hospitals and other healthcare agencies to report any disciplinary procedure to the state licensing authority.[1]

§1.10.2 The National Practitioner Data Bank

So that healthcare entities can make informed decisions about whether to grant privileges to a physician, the Health Care Quality Improvement Act establishes a National Practitioner Data Bank and imposes reporting requirements on insurance

---

[25]American Medical Association, Bylaws: A Guide for Hospital Medical Staff (1985).

[26]Alex M. Clarke and G. Lane Earnest, Chiropractors and Other Allied Health Practitioners, paper presented at the annual meeting of the American Academy of Hospital Attorneys (1989).

§1.10 [1]See, e.g., Ohio Rev. Code Ann. §4731.224 (1987).

companies, boards of medical examiners, and healthcare entities.[2] Monthly reports regarding any malpractice payments made
in settlement or satisfaction of a judgment, negative actions
affecting a physician's license, negative actions by professional
review committees, and any surrender of a physician's clinical
privileges[3] must be made to the National Practitioner Data Bank.
The statute imposes various sanctions for failing to comply with
the reporting requirements. An insurance committee that fails
to report will be fined. If a board of medical examiners neglects
its duty to report, its responsibility for gathering information
from healthcare providers will be assigned to another entity. A
healthcare entity that fails to report will lose the immunity
provided by the Act for three years.

E. Legal Protection for Those Who Allocate Privileges

A physician whose staff membership or clinical privileges have
been terminated or denied may bring an action against the
hospital or its administrators, staff, or employees claiming
antitrust violations, interference with contract, discrimination,
denial of due process, negligence, or (most commonly) defamation. The law recognizes, however, that important public

---

[2]42 U.S.C.A. §11133 (1989). Although the Act requires insurance companies to report malpractice insurance payments made for the benefit of
physicians as well as other healthcare practitioners, the Act allows but does
not require healthcare entities to report adverse professional review actions
taken with respect to nonphysician practitioners. It should be noted, however,
that the Medicare and Medicaid Patient and Program Protection Act of 1987
requires the state to report to the National Practitioner Data Bank any adverse
action of any state licensing authority against *any* healthcare practitioner. See
42 U.S.C.A. §§1396a(a)(49), 1396r-2.

[3]This reporting requirement is intended to prevent hospitals from making
a deal with the physician that the hospital will not report the physician if the
physician will voluntarily surrender his or her privileges.

interests will be served if the hospital and its staff are not afraid to exercise their best judgment in denying, suspending, limiting, or revoking privileges or reporting disciplinary actions to others with a legitimate interest. For this reason, both the common law and the statutory law offer some protection against these legal actions. Provisions in the application for staff membership or the hospital bylaws may give additional protection.

§1.11 Statutory Immunity

There are both federal and state laws that provide some immunity for individuals who participate in the allocation of clinical privileges.

§1.11.1 The Health Care Quality Improvement Act

To encourage medical peer review activities, Congress enacted the Health Care Quality Improvement Act of 1986.[1] The Act partially protects healthcare entities[2] or individuals who take part in the professional peer review process[3] from actions for damages brought under federal and state laws by physicians (doctors of medicine, osteopathy, or dentistry) who were negatively affected by the peer review process.[4] The statute protects only those decisions that are based on the competence of the

---

§1.11 [1] 42 U.S.C.A. §11101 et seq. (1989).

[2] "Health care entities" includes hospitals, entities that provide healthcare services (including health maintenance organizations and group medical practices), and some professional societies.

[3] The Act also provides an immunity for any person who provides information to a professional review body as long as the person does not knowingly provide false information. The Act discourages frivolous litigation by awarding reasonable attorneys' fees and the costs of litigation to the defendant physician or hospital if the defendant prevails and the plaintiff physician's action was frivolous, unreasonable, without foundation, or in bad faith.

[4] The Act does not apply to actions brought by other healthcare providers.

physician. The Act does not apply to decisions based on the hospital's efficiency interest,[5] actions for declaratory or injunctive relief, civil rights actions, or actions brought by the United States or the state attorney general.

The provision for immunity from federal claims (for example, claims based on federal antitrust law) became effective on November 14, 1986, the date the statute was enacted. The section providing immunity from state claims (for example, claims based on state antitrust law) became effective October 14, 1989, unless the state legislature approved an earlier effective date.[6] The immunity provided does not supplant any existing state or federal immunity that does not conflict with the Act. Instead, the Act offers additional protection, particularly in antitrust actions.[7]

To gain immunity through the Act, a peer review committee's action must be taken:

1. in the reasonable belief[8] that it furthers quality health-care;

---

[5]The hospital's attempt to close staff privileges, execute an exclusive contract, or require certain training may be challenged by the affected physicians. Although physicians often challenge these acts with antitrust suits, the hospital will have to continue to rely on other federal and state immunity provisions. See infra nn.10-26 and accompanying text.

[6]The Act originally provided that states could opt out of the state law immunity, but this option was eliminated by the 1989 amendments to the Act.

[7]Some states were initially concerned that the Act would preempt state immunity statutes. In 1989, Congress amended the Act to address those fears. For a further discussion of the 1989 amendments to the Act, see Peer Review Immunity Task Group, American Academy of Hospital Attorneys, American Hospital Association, Immunity for Peer Review Participants in Hospitals: What Is It? Where Does It Come From? How Do You Protect It? (December 1989). Although some courts have found that federal antitrust law does not apply if the restraint is based on state action, in the absence of a specific immunity, state antitrust law may continue to apply.

[8]The committee originally considered using a "good faith" standard, but changed the standard to one of "reasonableness" due to concerns that "good faith" may be misinterpreted as requiring only a test of the subjective state of mind of the individuals conducting the professional review action. H.R. Rep.

2. after a reasonable effort to obtain the facts;
3. after adequate due process (notice and hearing standards that fulfill this requirement are set out in the Act);
4. in the reasonable belief that the action was warranted by the known facts.

The hospital is presumed to have met these standards unless the plaintiff physician rebuts this presumption by a preponderance of the evidence.[9]

In summary, although the Act may offer some protection that is not provided by other federal and state legislation or common law, the immunity extended by the Act may not apply if:

1. the hospital did not meet the due process requirements imposed by the Act;
2. the hospital's immunity has been suspended due to its failure to follow the reporting requirements set out in the Act;
3. the professional review action was not based on the competency of the physician;
4. the state opted out of the state law immunity provisions (so that the Act does not apply to any claims based on state law);
5. the action is brought by a healthcare practitioner other than a medical doctor, an osteopath, or a dentist;
6. the action is brought by the United States or the State Attorney General;
7. the action is for declaratory or injunctive relief;
8. the action is a civil rights action.

Because of these exceptions, it is important to consider other sources of protection for physicians and hospitals that participate in the peer review process.

No. 903, 99th Cong., 2d Sess. 10, reprinted in 1987 U.S. Code Cong. & Ad. News 6384, 6392-6393.

[9]The legislative history suggests that this presumption only applies to the first standard. Id. However, the Act as finally enacted does not reflect that intent.

§1.11.2 State Statutes

All states have now enacted immunity statutes that try to protect individuals who participate in the peer review process. The immunity granted in most statutes applies to all civil liability and damages.[10] Some states, however, extend the immunity granted to include all criminal actions.[11] The scope of these statutes varies considerably in terms of who receives immunity and for what behavior it is granted. The statutes also impose a variety of qualifications that must be met before immunity attaches.

A few state statutes extend immunity to the members of the committee, the hospital, and anyone who provides information or participates in the peer review process.[12] Most statutes, however, exclude the hospital, and many also exclude the hospital's administrators, its employees, or both.[13] These omissions may present legal difficulties for hospitals, since employees can be a common source of information about incompetence and the hospital bears the final legal responsibility for deciding who will have privileges.

Each statute must be read carefully to determine what behavior is protected. Some states grant statutory immunity only to those who report practitioners to the state licensing authority,[14] while other states protect those who participate in either the peer review or licensing proceedings.[15] The statute also may limit the grant of immunity to actions of a particular hospital committee, which may or may not be the committee responsible for the peer review process.[16]

---

[10]See, e.g., Wis. Stat. Ann. §146.37 (1) (West 1989 & Cum. Supp. 1989).

[11]See, e.g., Del. Code Ann. tit. 24 §1768 (1981 & Cum. Supp. 1988).

[12]See, e.g., R.I. Gen. Laws §5-37.3-7 (1987 & Cum. Supp. 1988); La. Rev. Stat. §44:78 (West 1982 & Cum. Supp. 1989).

[13]See, e.g., Vt. Stat. Ann. tit. 26 §1442(a) (Cum. Supp. 1988).

[14]See, e.g., S.C. Code Ann. §40.47.212 (1986 & Cum. Supp. 1989).

[15]See, e.g., Utah Code Ann. §§58-12-25, 58-12-43 (6) (1986 & Cum. Supp. 1989).

[16]See, e.g., Idaho Code §§39-1392a(b), 39-1392c (1977 & Cum. Supp. 1989).

Although a few states grant an absolute statutory immunity,[17] the majority provide for a qualified immunity requiring that the individual must have acted within the scope of his or her responsibilities and without malice.[18] "Malice" has been defined by the courts in a variety of ways, including (1) a primary purpose other than the safeguarding of patients,[19] (2) personal spite or ill will,[20] and (3) making statements not believing they are true or with no grounds to believe they are true.[21] Many states also require that the behavior of the individual be reasonable,[22] which leaves the door open for suits in negligence.

Because there is considerable variation among state statutes, it is important to look at the statutes of the applicable jurisdiction to determine accurately what amount of statutory protection is granted. It is also important to consult the relevant case law for proper definitions of the statutory terms and judicial interpretation of ambiguities.

Another effective method of precluding physicians from bringing legal actions based on the denial or termination of their privileges is to limit their access to the records of medical staff committees. Some states have enacted statutes that provide that these records are privileged and are not subject to discovery except in certain circumstances.[23] Some of the "nondiscovery" statutes are only intended to prevent patients bringing malprac-

---

[17]See, e.g., Ind. Code Ann. §16-10-1-6.5(d) (Burns Cum. Supp. 1989). Some states may apply the absolute statutory immunity granted in judicial proceedings to the peer review process. See, e.g., Ascherman v. Natanson, 23 Cal. App. 3d 861, 100 Cal. Rptr. 656 (1972) (applying Cal. Civil Code §47).

[18]See, e.g., La. Rev. Stat. §44:7D (West 1982 & Cum. Supp. 1989); Duby v. Baron, 369 Mass. 614, 341 N.E.2d 870 (1976) (analyzing whether the committee's actions were within the scope of its responsibilities).

[19]Scappatura v. Baptist Hosp. of Phoenix, 120 Ariz. 204, 584 P.2d 1195, 1201 (1978).

[20]Greenfield v. Kanwit, 546 F. Supp. 220 (S.D.N.Y. 1982), affd., 714 F.2d 113 (2d Cir. 1982).

[21]Spencer v. Community Hosp. of Evanston, 87 Ill. App. 3d 214, 408 N.E.2d 981, 42 Ill. Dec. 272 (1980).

[22]See, e.g., Mont. Code Ann. §37-2-201 (1989).

[23]See, e.g., Tenn. Code Ann. §63-6-219(c) (1986 & Cum. Supp. 1989).

tice actions from gaining access to medical committee records and specifically state that they do not apply to physicians' discovery of records related to the consideration or review of their staff membership or clinical privileges.[24] In the absence of a specific exception, some courts have relied on these statutes to deny discovery to physicians who were the subject of medical committee investigation,[25] while other courts have refused to extend the application of the statutes beyond medical malpractice actions.[26]

§1.12 Common-Law Protection

The case law in the area of defamation (the area of greatest hazard) provides additional protection for physicians and hospitals involved in the peer review process. When a person denied staff membership or clinical privileges brings a lawsuit that is based on a charge of defamation, the hospital or whoever is charged may be able to use either the fact that the statement was true[1] or some type of "privilege" as a defense.

Privilege, the right to make a statement that may be construed as defamatory, may be either absolute or qualified. If the plaintiff has consented to the utterance, the defendant's privilege is absolute. In Schechet v. Kesten,[2] Dr. Schechet requested that Dr. Kesten send a letter to the credentials committee specifying the charges that caused Dr. Kesten to require that Dr. Schechet be supervised during surgery. The Michigan Court of Appeals concluded that Dr. Schechet had consented to Dr. Kesten's written statements and therefore Dr. Kesten was entitled to an absolute privilege.

The privilege also may be absolute if the law requires the

---

[24]See, e.g., Alaska Stat. §18-23.030 (1986 & Cum. Supp. 1989).

[25]See, e.g., Franco v. Dist. Ct., 641 P.2d 922 (Colo. 1982) (en banc).

[26]See, e.g., Good Samaritan Hosp. Assn. v. Simon, 370 So. 2d 174 (Fla. App. 1979).

§1.12 [1]See, e.g., Franklin v. Blank, 86 N.M. 585, 525 P.2d 945 (1974).

[2]3 Mich. App. 126, 141 N.W.2d 641 (1966).

statement (as in judicial proceedings). In Franklin v. Blank,[3] the New Mexico Court of Appeals stated that a letter that initiated peer review of a doctor's professional misconduct was part of "quasi-judicial" proceedings and therefore was entitled to an absolute privilege. Other courts, however, have held that the peer review process is not judicial in nature and therefore not entitled to absolute protection.[4]

More often, the privilege available to the hospital will be the qualified one reserved for people considered to be making the statement in the course of doing their duty or otherwise acting reasonably. The broad categories of statements to which a qualified privilege applies[5] are:

- Statements made in the speaker's own defense, to protect his or her reputation;[6]
- Statements made to protect the safety of a member of the speaker's family;[7]
- Statements made to protect a person to whom the speaker has a legal or moral duty;[8]
- Statements made to one with whom the speaker has a common (often, business) interest;[9]

---

[3]86 N.M. 585, 525 P.2d 945 (1974).

[4]DiMiceli v. Klieger, 58 Wis. 2d 359, 206 N.W.2d 184 (1973).

[5]This list combines the areas of qualified privilege identified by Prosser and Keeton, The Law of Torts 824-832, 836-838 (5th ed. 1984) and the American Law Institute, Restatement (Second) of Torts §§594-598, 611 (1977). Some of the common-law privileges have been codified in various states.

[6]See, e.g., McBride v. Sears, Roebuck & Co., 306 Minn. 93, 235 N.W.2d 371 (1975) (action for slander and wrongful termination of employment—business had legitimate interest in protecting itself and therefore a qualified privilege was properly invoked.)

[7]See, e.g., MacConnell v. Mitten, 131 Ariz. 22, 638 P.2d 689 (1981) (defendant was protected by a qualified privilege when discussing with his son possible acts of his former employee (plaintiff) that he believed were adversely affecting his wife).

[8]See, e.g., Greenfield v. Kanwit, 546 F. Supp. 220 (S.D.N.Y.), affd., 714 F.2d 113 (2d Cir. 1982) (physician, chairman of medical society, was privileged in communicating to the secretary of the society matters concerning another member's professional misconduct).

[9]See, e.g., Seidenstein v. National Medical Enter., 769 F.2d 1100 (5th Cir.

- Statements made to one who has authority to act in the public interest;[10]
- Fair comment on matters in the public domain;[11]
- Statements that merely report the content of public proceedings.[12]

While a hospital may be able to claim privilege on the basis of one or more of these kinds of statements in a given case, only an attorney reviewing the specific circumstances can estimate whether a privilege is available. Moreover, it should be noted that a privilege will be lost if the speaker was motivated by malice[13] or disclosed information to people other than those with a legal right to know.[14]

A typical decision recognizing a hospital's privilege in the staffing area is Spencer v. Community Hospital of Evanston.[15] In that case the court rejected a libel claim by a suspended staff physician against peers who reported negatively to the hospital's board of trustees. The report was judged to be conditionally privileged because (1) it was made for the purpose of satisfying the hospital's strong interest in learning the quality of the health

---

1985) (physician who was head of governing board was privileged when he made a statement regarding the defendant to a group of physicians because they had a common and legitimate interest in the suspension of plaintiff's clinical privileges).

[10]See, e.g., Segall v. Piazza, 46 Misc. 2d 700, 260 N.Y.S.2d 543 (1965) (correspondence from student's parent to school principal regarding the practices of a certain teacher was privileged).

[11]See, e.g., Brinkley v. Fishbein, 110 F.2d 62, cert. denied, 311 U.S. 672 (1940) (publication in AMA magazine stating that plaintiff was a "quack" was privileged since it involved a matter of public concern).

[12]See, e.g., Morton v. Stewart, 153 Ga. App. 636, 266 S.E.2d 230 (1980) (report of medical licensing board activities was privileged).

[13]See, e.g., Spencer v. Community Hosp. of Evanston, 42 Ill. Dec. 272, 87 Ill. App. 3d 214, 408 N.E.2d 981 (1980).

[14]See, e.g., Berry v. Moench, 8 Utah 2d 191, 331 P.2d 814 (1958).

[15]42 Ill. Dec. 272, 87 Ill. App. 3d 214, 408 N.E.2d 981 (1980). See also Kinney v. Daniels, 574 F. Supp. 542 (S.D.W. Va. 1983) (summary judgment for chief of staff in defamation action over letter to plaintiff-physician).

care it provided; (2) the report was specific and did not go beyond its purpose; (3) it was submitted to the board in a proper manner; and (4) it was not otherwise released. These points should be emphasized to hospital personnel who participate in medical staffing decisions.

§1.13 Release from Liability

As an additional source of protection, some hospitals may require that any applicant for admission to the staff sign a release from liability (absolute immunity) for the hospital and its staff for acts connected to the peer review procedure. Concluding that the immunity granted was "intended to be a justifiable means of providing a complete, candid and up-to-date professional history of the candidates," the Indiana Court of Appeals upheld the hospital's right to require employees to sign such a release.[1] In DeLeon v. St. Joseph Hospital,[2] the Fourth Circuit Court of Appeals upheld the district court's finding that a release executed by a physician in connection with his application for privileges barred his defamation claim absent a showing of extreme or wanton conduct.

The Kentucky legislature has reached the same result by enacting a statute that states that "[a]ny person who applies for or is granted staff privileges . . . shall be deemed to have waived as a condition of such application or grant, any claim for damages for any good faith action taken by any person who is a member, participant in or employee of or who furnishes professional counsel or services to any committee, board, commission or other entity. . . ."[3] Although hospitals may act prudently by including such provisions in their bylaws, at least one court held that an immunity provision in a hospital's bylaws was void as against public policy.[4]

---

§1.13 [1]King v. Bartholomew County Hosp., 476 N.E.2d 877 (Ind. App. 1985).

[2]871 F.2d 1229 (4th Cir.), cert. denied, 105 S. Ct. 87 (1989).

[3]Ky. Rev. Stat. §311.377(1) (1983 & Cum. Supp. 1988).

[4]Westlake Community Hosp. v. Superior Ct. of L.A. County, 17 Cal. 3d 465, 131 Cal. Rptr. 90, 551 P.2d 410 (1976).

F. Extended Care Facilities

§1.14 Rights and Obligations of Nursing Homes and Other Extended Care Facilities

Nursing homes and other extended care facilities also have an interest in regulating staff membership and clinical privileges, both because of their patient care obligation and their interest in the efficient operation of the facility. There is little case law, however, dealing with the rights and obligations of nursing homes and other extended care facilities with respect to such regulation.

As a general guide to determining the rights and obligations of the extended care facility with respect to staff membership and clinical privileges, it is important to look at the statutory law in the state where the facility is located. The state may have specific statutes governing extended care facilities, or it may cover extended care facilities in the statutory law governing hospitals. If the state statutes define "hospital" to include extended care facilities, extended care facilities in that state probably have the same rights and obligations as hospitals with respect to staff membership and clinical privileges.[1] It is important to recognize, however, that in some states, extended care facilities may be governed by some but not all of the statutes that govern hospitals. For example, under Georgia law, only hospitals must comply with the statutory provisions on the revocation of clinical privileges,[2] but all institutions, including hospitals and extended care facilities, must report to the Composite State Board of Medical Examiners the names of physicians whose privileges are denied, revoked, or restricted.[3]

Without specific statutory law, it is difficult to identify with certainty the rights and obligations of extended care facilities

---

§1.14 [1]See, e.g., Hauptman v. Grand Manor Health Related Facilities, 121 A.D.2d 151, 502 N.Y.S.2d 1012 (1986).

[2]Ga. Code Ann. §31-7-7 (1985 & Cum. Supp. 1989).

[3]Ga. Code Ann. §31-7-8 (1985 & Cum. Supp. 1989).

with respect to staff membership and clinical privileges. The Kansas Court of Appeals is among the few to rule on the subject. Acknowledging that nursing homes are specifically excluded from the Kansas medical care facility licensure statutes, the court in State ex rel. Walker v. Bergman[4] concluded that the patients' right to choose their own physicians overrode the nursing home's interest in the efficient operation of the facility. The court recognized that, although the nursing home was obligated to exercise reasonable care to avoid injuring the patients, the physicians, not the nursing home, were ultimately responsible for the healthcare of the patients. Comparing nursing homes with hospitals, the court stated that "[t]he hospital's authority to select its staff reflects the liability it assumes for patient care." The court concluded that the nursing home could fulfill its limited patient care obligation without impinging on the patients' rights to choose their own physicians. The court affirmed the lower court's decision enjoining the nursing home from revoking the clinical privileges of certain physicians.

G. Conclusion

Because they are responsible for patients, hospitals must scrutinize the qualifications and performance of applicants and current practitioners and may deny staff membership or clinical privileges on the basis of deficiencies. Efficiency and convenience are other justifiable grounds for denying privileges. Even so, the hospital should expect legal challenges to its procedures, its reasons for exclusion, and their effects on competition.

For their protection, hospitals should check the credentials and disciplinary records of applicants for privileges as far as is practicable. Once applicants are admitted, the hospital must review their and other staff members' competence on a contin-

---

[4]State ex rel. Walker v. Bergman, 12 Kan. App. 2d 695, 755 P.2d 557 (1988).

uing basis. The hospital should also periodically examine its bylaws on staff membership and clinical privileges. Ideally, bylaws should comply with current law on practitioners' rights without making the institution's duties more onerous than necessary.

2 The Healthcare Facility as Employer

Stephen Allred

A. Overview

§2.0 General Attributes of the Healthcare Facility as Employer

The healthcare industry in the United States has become a major employer. According to the Census Bureau, healthcare occupations are among the fastest-growing in the country.[1] As healthcare facilities increase in number and size, the opportunity for employment problems to arise increases as well.

Healthcare facilities are also faced with the prospect of a workforce that is increasingly composed of minority employees. As more persons of diverse cultures and backgrounds gain access to employment opportunities, conflicts among co-workers and allegations that personnel decisions were improperly motivated by discriminatory intent become more common.

At the same time, employees are increasingly demanding more meaningful work. Unlike their parents, new employees may not have a strong sense of loyalty to a particular employer or, indeed, to a given career field. The willingness of many employees to change jobs and even career directions creates an unending need for the healthcare facility to deal with a constantly changing workforce.

There has also been a substantial increase in the number of two-career couples, among both healthcare facilities and other employers. The problems inherent in juggling work demands, child care, and family responsibilities may sometimes affect performance in the workplace.[2]

Like any other employer, the healthcare facility is more and

---

§2.0   [1]U.S. Census Bureau, Earnings by Occupation and Education 29-36 (U.S. Govt. Printing Office) (1984); see also Statistical Abstract of the United States 375 (U.S. Govt. Printing Office) (1988).

[2]An example is found in Lesley J. Levin, Managing the Two Career Marriage, Public Management 9-10 (May-June 1983), describing how a manager of a hospital social services department manages her career and family. See generally BNA Special Report, Work & Family: A Changing Dynamic (Bureau of National Affairs, Washington, D.C.) (1986).

more concerned with the prospect of an applicant's or employee's bringing a legal challenge to a personnel decision. As discussed below, there is a wide range of statutes and common-law bases by which individuals may challenge the healthcare facility's decision to reject an applicant, deny a promotion, reassign and reorganize employees, turn down a training request, or dismiss an employee. For better or worse, in recent years there has been a marked increase in the incidence of employee challenges to employer personnel decisions. The possibility that a particular decision will be met with a legal challenge is not confined to employers in the healthcare industry. And yet, there are certain aspects of the healthcare facility as employer that make the employment relationship unique.

§2.1 Special Attributes of the Healthcare Facility as Employer

One special attribute of the healthcare facility as employer is that it employs individuals who may face moral questions of whether to use technological advances in ways that are repugnant to their ethical or religious beliefs. For example, a nurse's refusal, on religious grounds, to follow a procedure requiring families to be asked for organ donations may present the healthcare facility with the dilemma of whether to dismiss her for insubordination (and possibly risk a wrongful discharge action, as discussed below) or to attempt to work around her refusal by using another employee. In such instances a solution to an employee's moral dilemma may be hard to come by; and the legal principles that govern the situation are unclear.[1]

Another special attribute of the healthcare facility as employer is that its workforce is sharply divided, comprising both professionals and nonprofessionals. It is difficult, under the best of circumstances, to provide a harmonious employment envi-

------

§2.1   [1]For a full discussion of this issue, see Davis, Defining the Employment Rights of Medical Personnel Within the Parameters of Personal Conscience, 1986 Det. C.L. Rev. 847-878.

ronment in which both technicians and professional specialists can work well together. In a medical setting, in which cooperation is not only desirable but essential to ensure adequate patient care, the ability of professional and nonprofessional staff to work together becomes critical. The healthcare facility, as employer, must anticipate possible sources of conflict among staff with divergent backgrounds and expectations and take steps to ensure that conflict is held to a minimum.

Related to this sharp division along professional versus nonprofessional status lines is the fact that professions in the healthcare field tend to be sex-concentrated. That is, certain occupations are dominated by women (e.g., nursing, speech pathology, and nutrition) and others by men (e.g., surgery and hospital administration). The fact that occupational groupings can be characterized as predominantly male or female can lead to allegations of sex discrimination, most recently in the form of "comparable worth" claims.

The fourth special attribute of the healthcare facility as employer is that it is not always clear whether it is a "public" or "private" employer. Also, various federal and state labor statutes define employers in different ways; whether a healthcare facility meets the definition of "employer" under those statutes is a critical jurisdictional prerequisite. Although the public-versus-private question is treated briefly in various parts of this chapter, the reader is cautioned that the answer to the question is not always clear and that additional research into the matter may be required.

The final special attribute of the healthcare facility as employer to be discussed here is that it is frequently in the public eye; as a result, public expectations about its employees are higher than, for example, expectations about the assembly workers at the local factory. The healthcare industry has cultivated an image of professionalism and competence. When healthcare facility employees, by their conduct, act in a manner inconsistent with that image, the public perception of the facility as professional and competent may suffer.

This chapter summarizes the various legal bases by which employment decisions may be challenged, including the recent development of exceptions to the employment-at-will doctrine; describes various federal statutes governing the full range of personnel decisions an employer in the healthcare industry may make; discusses the constitutional issues that may arise when the facility is a public employer; and explores some critical issues faced by the healthcare provider as it attempts to deal effectively with its employees.

B. The Employment-at-Will Doctrine

§2.2 In General

When an employer hires an applicant, the legal presumption that governs their working relationship is that the employment is "at will"—that is, employment is at the will of either party, and the employer is free to dismiss the employee at any time without explanation or legal penalty.[1] Reduced to its harshest terms, the employment-at-will doctrine has been described as granting employers the right to dismiss an employee "for good cause, for no cause, or even for cause morally wrong."[2]

Perhaps because the doctrine in its purest form is so harsh, however, a substantial number of exceptions have recently been recognized by the courts to the presumption of employment at will. These may be grouped into two broad categories: statutory and common-law exceptions. The first group, statutory exceptions, includes federal and state legislative modifications of an employer's ability to dismiss employees. For example, as discussed in §2.6, the Civil Rights Act of 1964 prohibits dismissal

---

§2.2 [1]This is referred to as the "American Rule," as originally stated (arguably, without support) by Horace G. Wood in his 1877 treatise Law of Master and Servant. For a full discussion of the development of the American Rule, see L. K. Larson and P. Borowsky, Unjust Dismissal §2.04 (1986).

[2]Payne v. Watkins & A.R.R., 81 Tenn. 507, 519-520 (1884), overruled on other grounds; Hutten v. Waters, 132 Tenn. 527 (1915).

for discriminatory reasons. Similarly, numerous state statutes prohibit dismissal for employee activities such as serving on a jury or filing a workers' compensation claim. The second group, common-law exceptions, are judicially created exceptions based on a finding of breach of contract or the tort of wrongful discharge (as opposed to the legislature's or Congress's having created a statutory exception). In other words, in this second group of exceptions the court finds either that the parties themselves, through their actions, have created a contractual exception to the employment-at-will rule or that the employer's motive in dismissing an employee violates some tenet of public policy.

The statutory exceptions to the doctrine of employment at will are discussed in the sections on federal labor statutes and employment discrimination. The judicially created exceptions to the employment-at-will doctrine are the major focus of this section and are discussed below.

§2.3 Application of the Employment-at-Will Doctrine to Healthcare Facilities

§2.3.1 Exceptions Based on Implied Contracts of Employment

Obviously, one way in which an employer and employee may avoid an at-will employment relationship is to execute a written contract setting forth the terms and conditions of employment for a specified length of time. Indeed, in many employment settings such as public schools and professional sports franchises the use of employment contracts is commonplace.

In many workplace settings, however, including health-care facilities, employment contracts are not routinely used. Nonetheless, a court may find that an employment contract has been created by implication, by representations made at the time of hiring,[1] by statements contained in personnel hand-

---

§2.3 [1]See, e.g., Filcek v. Norris-Schmid, 156 Mich. App. 80, 401 N.W.2d

books,[2] or even by an implied covenant of good faith and fair dealing.[3] Examples of each of these bases for finding an employment contract follow.

The court found that representations made at the time of hiring created an exception to the employment-at-will doctrine in Sides v. Duke Hospital.[4] The plaintiff, Marie Sides, worked as a nurse anesthetist at Duke Hospital in Durham, North Carolina. She brought a wrongful discharge action after being discharged after 11 years' service. Sides was held entitled to maintain her claim of wrongful discharge, based on representations made to her that if she were to leave Michigan and come to work in North Carolina she would only be discharged for incompetence. The court held that her move from Michigan constituted

---

318 (1986); Unker v. Joseph Markovits, 643 F. Supp. 1043 (S.D.N.Y. 1986); Janda v. Iowa Indus. Hydraulics, 326 N.W.2d 339 (Iowa 1982); Cleary v. American Airlines, 111 Cal. App. 3d 443, 168 Cal. Rptr. 722 (1980).

[2] See, e.g., Pine River State Bank v. Metille, 333 N.W.2d 622 (Minn. 1983); Weiner v. McGraw-Hill, 57 N.Y.2d 458, 443 N.E.2d 441, 457 N.Y.S.2d 193 (1982); Toussaint v. Blue Cross and Blue Shield of Mich., 408 Mich. 579, 292 N.W.2d 880 (1980).

[3] Only three states—California, Montana, and Massachusetts—have recognized this exception to the employment-at-will doctrine. See, e.g., Flanigan v. Prudential Fed. Sav. and Loan Assn., 221 Mont. 419, 720 P.2d 257 (1986); Gram v. Liberty Mut. Life Ins. Co., 384 Mass. 659, 429 N.E.2d 21 (1981); Pugh v. See's Candies, 116 Cal. App. 3d 311, 171 Cal. Rptr. 917, modified, 117 Cal. App. 3d 520 (1981). Many state courts have considered and rejected the implied covenant of good faith and fair dealing as an exception to the employment-at-will doctrine. See, e.g., Murphy v. American Home Prod. Corp., 58 N.Y.2d 293, 448 N.E.2d 86, 461 N.Y.S.2d 232 (1983); Grunn v. Hawaiian Airlines, 162 Ga. App. 474, 291 S.E.2d 779 (1982); Daniel v. Magma Copper Co., 127 Ariz. 320, 620 P.2d 699 (Ct. App. 1980). For a full discussion of this issue, see Diamond, The Tort of Bad Faith Breach of Contract: When, if at All, Should It Be Extended Beyond Insurance Transactions?, 64 Marq. L. Rev. 425 (1981).

[4] 74 N.C. App. 331, 328 S.E.2d 818, review denied, 314 N.C. 331, 333 S.E.2d 490 (1985). Sides is also discussed infra as an exception to employment at will on public policy grounds. A contrary decision is Murphine v. Hospital Auth., 151 Ga. App. 722, 261 S.E.2d 457 (1979), in which a promise to promote on the basis of seniority was held unenforceable where the employee's entire employment contract was terminable at will.

sufficient consideration to protect her employment contract from the terminable-at-will rule.

The court found statements contained in a personnel handbook sufficient to create an employment contract in Renny v. Port Huron Hospital.[5] The plaintiff, Karen Renny, was employed by Port Huron Hospital as a registered nurse. She was discharged for "deliberate restriction of work" (essentially, insubordination), and she appealed her discharge through the grievance procedure set forth in the hospital's employee handbook. Following unsuccessful pursuit of her grievance through this procedure, Renny filed suit for wrongful discharge, claiming that the handbook established a contractual requirement that hospital employees only be discharged for good cause and that the grievance procedure denied her due process.

The hospital argued that the handbook was not a contract, but merely provided guidance on employer policies. The hospital conceded that the handbook was issued to all employees and that they were required to read it as part of their orientation. However, the hospital argued that, even if the handbook were to be construed as a contract, Renny had not signed it in a manner that indicated her intent to be bound, since she had drawn a line through the words "I agree to abide by the rules and regulations it [the handbook] outlines" and substituted the words "I don't agree, but will abide."

The court found that the handbook constituted a just-cause employment contract, irrespective of the signature of the employee, or, indeed, of the employee's knowledge of the hospital's policies before being hired. Stated the court:

> A provision in the employment contract providing that an employee shall not be discharged except for cause is legally enforceable whether by express agreement, oral or written, or as a result of an employee's legitimate expectations grounded in an employer's policy statements. These legitimate expectations may

---

[5]427 Mich. 415, 398 N.W.2d 327 (1986). Cf. Berry v. Doctor's Health Facilities, 715 S.W.2d 60 (Tex. App. 1986) (personnel handbook with signed disclaimer that employee understood handbook held not an employment contract or a guarantee of continued employment, but merely a policy guide).

be grounded in an employer's written policy statements as set forth in the manual of personnel policies.[6]

The court noted that an employer could still enter into terminable-at-will employment arrangements by requiring prospective employees to acknowledge that they serve at the will or pleasure of the company. Moreover, noted the court, there is no requirement that an employer establish any personnel policies or practices. In the Port Huron Hospital case, however, the employer had done so, with the result that its policies were held to constitute an enforceable contract.

Finally, the court found an implied covenant of good faith and fair dealing in Crenshaw v. Bozeman Deaconess Hospital.[7] The plaintiff in this case was Shirley Crenshaw, a respiratory therapist. Crenshaw was discharged by the hospital while still a "probationary" employee (defined by the hospital's policy manual as an employee with less than 500 hours of employment) for a variety of alleged offenses, including insubordination and unsatisfactory work performance (which were later found to be false). Crenshaw filed a wrongful discharge suit against the hospital, alleging that her employer breached an implied covenant of good faith and fair dealing with her.

The Montana courts had previously recognized the theory that there is an implied covenant of good faith and fair dealing in employment contracts.[8] One court described the covenant exception to employment at will this way:

> Whether a covenant of good faith and fair dealing is implied in a particular case depends upon objective manifestations by the employer giving rise to the employee's reasonable belief that he or she has job security and will be treated fairly. . . . [T]he implied covenant protects the investment of the employee who in good faith accepts and maintains employment reasonably

---

[6]427 Mich. at 428, 398 N.W.2d at 334.

[7]213 Mont. 488, 693 P.2d 487 (1984).

[8]Gates v. Life of Mont., 196 Mont. 178, 638 P.2d 1063 (1982) (*Gates I*); Gates v. Life of Mont., 668 P.2d 213, 40 St. Rep. 1287 (Mont. 1983) (*Gates II*).

believing their job is secure so long as they perform their duties satisfactorily, [and] such an employee is protected from bad faith or unfair treatment by the employer.[9]

The court found that Crenshaw was led to believe that her job was secure and that as an employee she was entitled to the protection of good faith and fair dealing by the hospital, irrespective of her probationary status. The court further found that the charges and allegations in her discharge notice were false and resulted not only in her losing her job but in jeopardizing her career. Crenshaw's discharge, held the court, was motivated by bad faith and thus breached the implied covenant of good faith and fair dealing under Montana law.

These cases, while not controlling beyond the states in which they were decided, show the trend of many courts in recognizing exceptions to the employment-at-will doctrine based on contract theory. A healthcare facility wishing to avoid the results of these cases should review its recruitment and interviewing policies and practices, determine whether its employee personnel manual, if any, arguably confers a contract of employment so as to make the employment relationship other than at will, and evaluate each proposed dismissal to determine whether it is likely to be challenged as in violation of an implied covenant of good faith and fair dealing.

§2.3.2 Exceptions Based on the Tort of Wrongful Discharge

Courts in a number of jurisdictions have recognized an exception to the employment-at-will rule based on the tort of wrongful or abusive discharge. This theory, in its narrowest form, holds that an employer may not dismiss an employee in violation of a

---

[9]Dare v. Montana Petroleum Marketing Co., 687 P.2d 1015, 41 St. Rep. 1735 (Mont. 1984).

public policy set forth in a statute.[10] In its broader form, the theory holds that an employer may not dismiss an employee for reasons of malice, bad faith, or retaliation, since to do so contravenes public policy.[11]

The question of whether the dismissal of an employee violates public policy is obviously one subject to differing interpretations. The Arizona Supreme Court attempted to define the scope of the tort of wrongful discharge for violation of public policy in this way:

> There is no precise definition of the term. In general, it can be said that the public policy concerns what is right and just and what effects the citizens of the state have collectively. It is to be found in the state's constitution and statutes and, when they are silent, in its judicial decisions. Although there is no precise line of demarcation dividing matters that are the subject of public policies from matters purely personal, a survey of cases in other states involving retaliatory discharge shows that a matter must strike at the heart of a citizen's social rights, duties, and responsibilities before the tort will be allowed.[12]

---

[10]Hansrote v. American Indus. Technologies, 586 F. Supp. 113 (W.D. Pa. 1984), affd., 770 F.2d 1070 (3d Cir. 1985); Brockmeyer v. Dun & Bradstreet, 113 Wis. 2d 561, 335 N.W.2d 834 (1983); Wiskotoni v. Michigan Nat. Bank-West, 716 F.2d 378 (6th Cir. 1983); Murphy v. City of Topeka-Shawnee County, 6 Kan. App. 2d 488, 630 P.2d 186 (1981); Lally v. Copygraphics, 85 N.J. 668, 428 A.2d 1317 (1981); Kelsay v. Motorola, 74 Ill. 2d 172, 384 N.E.2d 353 (1978); Frampton v. Central Ind. Gas Co., 260 Ind. 249, 297 N.E.2d 425 (1973). The California Court of Appeals is credited with first recognizing the public policy exception to the doctrine of employment at will in Petermann v. International Bhd. of Teamsters, 174 Cal. App. 2d 184, 344 P.2d 25 (1959).

[11]Howard v. Dorr Woolen Co., 120 N.H. 295, 414 A.2d 1273 (1980); Geary v. United States Steel Corp., 456 Pa. 171, 319 A.2d 174 (1974); Sheets v. Teddy's Frosted Foods, 179 Conn. 471, 427 A.2d 385 (1980); Parnar v. Americana Hotels, 65 Haw. 370, 652 P.2d 625 (1982); Palmateer v. International Harvester Co., 85 Ill. 2d 124, 421 N.E.2d 876 (1981); Trombetta v. Detroit, Toledo & Ironton R.R. Co., 81 Mich. App. 489, 265 N.W.2d 385 (1978); Nees v. Hocks, 272 Or. 210, 536 P.2d 512 (1975); Reuther v. Fowler & Williams, 255 Pa. Super. 28, 386 A.2d 119 (1978); Harless v. First Nat. Bank, 246 S.E.2d 270 (W. Va. 1978).

[12]Wagenseller v. Scottsdale Memorial Hosp., 147 Ariz. 370, 710 P.2d 1025 (1985).

Two recent cases involving healthcare facilities illustrate the narrow and broad approaches of the courts in dealing with the tort of wrongful discharge.

The narrow approach is typified by Sides v. Duke Hospital[13] (discussed supra §2.3.1). The plaintiff, a nurse anesthetist, brought a wrongful discharge action against the hospital, alleging that she had been dismissed in retaliation for her refusal to commit perjury in a medical malpractice trial. The court agreed that such a dismissal was a wrongful discharge, stating:

> [W]hile there may be a right to terminate a contract at will for no reason, or for an arbitrary or irrational reason, there can be no right to terminate such a contract for an unlawful reason or purpose that contravenes public policy. . . . We hold, therefore, that no employer in this State, notwithstanding that an employment is at will, has the right to discharge an employee and deprive him of his livelihood without civil liability because he refuses to testify untruthfully or incompletely in a court case, as plaintiff alleges happened here.[14]

Subsequent decisions of the North Carolina courts have made it clear that this public policy exception requires the showing of a violation of a specific statutory mandate, and further that the statute itself evinces important public policy concerns.[15] Read narrowly, the *Sides* case stands merely for the proposition that one cannot be dismissed for refusal to commit an illegal act—in this case, perjury.

A broader view of the wrongful discharge tort holds that an employer may not terminate an employee for refusal to commit unlawful acts, for performing important public obliga-

---

[13]74 N.C. App. 331, 328 S.E.2d 818, review denied, 314 N.C. 331, 333 S.E.2d 490 (1985).

[14]74 N.C. App. at 342, 328 S.E.2d at 826.

[15]In Trought v. Richardson, 78 N.C. App. 758, 338 S.E.2d 617 (1986), the court refused to recognize an abusive discharge claim where a nurse alleged she was discharged in retaliation for transferring licensed practical nurses out of the emergency room because they were performing procedures in violation of hospital policy and state law.

tions, or for exercising certain legal rights or privileges.[16] A case typifying the broader view is Wagenseller v. Scottsdale Memorial Hospital.[17] In that case, Catherine Sue Wagenseller, a paramedic coordinator, was dismissed by the hospital following her refusal to engage in activities she found morally objectionable during a rafting trip with other hospital employees. The court held that her refusal to join her co-workers in displays of nudity was an impermissible basis for her subsequent dismissal, finding that such motives by the employer contravened important public policy interests embodied in the state's indecent exposure statutes. Further, stated the court, "the interests of society as a whole will be promoted if employers are forbidden to fire for cause which is 'morally wrong.' "[18] The court remanded the case for a determination of whether Wagenseller's termination was caused by her refusal to perform some act contrary to public policy.

Even the broad view of the public policy exception has its limits, however. In Staggie v. Idaho Falls Consolidated Hospital,[19] the Court of Appeals of Idaho refused to extend the public policy exception to cover "bad faith" firings of employees whose activities are not otherwise worthy of judicial protection. Thus, a hospital maintenance engineer was not entitled to the public policy exception where he had engaged in an unauthorized shift-scheduling swap and the hospital had discharged him; there was no requirement that the hospital demonstrate "good faith" in dismissing him for his misconduct.[20]

---

[16]A discussion of these cases is found in Note, Protecting Employees at Will Against Wrongful Discharge: The Public Policy Exception, 96 Harv. L. Rev. 1931 (1983).

[17]147 Ariz. 370, 710 P.2d 1025 (1985).

[18]710 P.2d at 1033.

[19]110 Idaho 349, 715 P.2d 1019 (Ct. App. 1986).

[20]See also Lampe v. Presbyterian Medical Center, 41 Colo. App. 465, 590 P.2d 513 (1979) (no public policy violation for dismissal of nurse who refused to reduce nurse overtime for fear that to do so would jeopardize patient care); Rozier v. St. Mary's Hosp., 88 Ill. App. 3d 994, 411 N.E.2d 50 (1980) (no public policy violation for dismissal of employee who made allegations to press that hospital was abusing patients; employee had lied to newspaper); MacNeil v. Minidoka Memorial Hosp., 108 Idaho 588, 701 P.2d 208 (1985) (no public

As these cases make clear, the healthcare facility may find its decision to terminate an employee challenged under a variety of wrongful discharge tort theories. Employers are advised to become familiar with the exceptions to the employment-at-will rule doctrine, if any, in their state (particularly the public policy exceptions), since there is substantial variation from one jurisdiction to the next in the type of claim that will be recognized. By monitoring the development of the law in this area, healthcare employers can reduce the risk of a successful challenge to a dismissal action.

C. Federal Labor Statutes

§2.4 The Fair Labor Standards Act

The Fair Labor Standards Act (FLSA),[1] originally enacted during the Great Depression, is designed to ensure that employers meet federally mandated minimum wage and overtime standards. In addition, the Act requires equal pay for equal work (thus prohibiting wage differentiation solely on the basis of sex)[2] and requires employers to maintain specified wage and hour records.[3] Further, the FLSA places certain restrictions on child labor.[4] The FLSA is administered and enforced by the U.S. Department of Labor.

The FLSA originally applied only to private employers engaged in commerce. In 1966, the Act was amended to cover school, hospital, nursing home, and local transit employees. In 1974, the Act was again amended to extend its coverage to

---

policy violation where hospital substantially complied with personnel manual in dismissing cleaning person).

§2.4   [1] 29 U.S.C. §201 et seq., 52 Stat. 1060 (June 25, 1938), as amended.
[2] 29 U.S.C. §206(d), The Equal Pay Act of 1963.
[3] 29 C.F.R. pt. 516.
[4] 29 C.F.R. pt. 570.

include state and local governments. Although the 1974 amendments were initially held unconstitutional,[5] since 1985, with the Supreme Court's decision in Garcia v. San Antonio Metropolitan Transit Authority,[6] the FLSA has also governed the wage and overtime practices of all public employers.

§2.4.1 Covered Employees; Exempt and Nonexempt Employees

Most, but not all, employees are covered by the FLSA.[7] This is not to say, however, that most employees are subject to all the requirements of the Act. The critical inquiry under the FLSA is whether a given individual is *exempt* or *nonexempt*. Exempt employees are subject to the FLSA's equal pay provisions and recordkeeping requirements; they are not, however, subject to the Act's minimum wage and overtime provisions.

Who, then, is exempt from the FLSA?

The Act provides that executive, administrative, and professional employees are exempt from its minimum wage and overtime provisions.[8] Two tests, the "long test" and the "short test," have been adopted by the Department of Labor to

---

[5]National League of Cities v. Usery, 426 U.S. 833 (1976) (holding that the "traditional" functions of state and local governments, including the power to determine wage rates to be paid to their employees, could not, under the Tenth Amendment, be interfered with by the federal government).

[6]469 U.S. 528 (1985) (holding that the federal minimum wage and overtime laws can constitutionally be applied to state and local governments and that the attempt to define certain governmental activities as "traditional" had proven unworkable in the period since Usery, supra n.5, was decided).

[7]Those excluded from coverage are, for example, persons who serve on the personal staff of public elective office holders, 29 U.S.C. §203(e)(2)(C)(ii)(II), members of the immediate family of an employer engaged in agriculture, 29 U.S.C. §203(e)(3), or an employee who works in a foreign country, see, e.g., Hornstein v. Negev Air Base Const., 110 A.D.2d 884 (N.Y. App. Div. 1985). Other than the very few exceptions found in the Act, however, all other employees are covered.

[8]29 U.S.C. §213.

determine whether an employee meets one or more of these exemptions.

The long test for executives[9] requires a showing that the individual (1) has a primary duty (i.e., 50 percent or more of the time) of managing an enterprise or department; (2) customarily and regularly directs the work of two or more employees; (3) has the authority to hire and fire employees or effectively recommend such actions; (4) customarily and regularly exercises discretionary powers; (5) devotes no more than 20 percent of his or her time to nonmanagerial duties; and (6) is paid on a salary basis at least $155 per week. The short test for executives requires a showing that the individual (1) is paid on a salary basis at least $250 per week; (2) regularly directs the work of at least two employees; and (3) has a primary duty of managing an enterprise or department.

In the healthcare arena, hospital administrators would typically be held to meet the executive exemption.

The long test for administrative personnel[10] requires a showing that the individual (1) has a primary duty of office or nonmanual work directly related to management policies or general business operations of the employer, or responsible work directly related to academic instruction or training in an educational institution; (2) customarily and regularly exercises discretion and independent judgment; (3) regularly assists an executive or administrator, works under only generalized supervision along specialized or technical lines that require special training, experience, or knowledge, or executes special assignments under general supervision; (4) devotes no more than 20 percent of his or her time to other duties; and (5) is paid on a salary basis at least $155 per week. The short test for administrative personnel requires a showing that the individual (1) is paid on a salary basis at least $250 per week; (2) has a primary duty of office or nonmanual work directly related to management policies or general business operations of the employer, or responsible work

---

[9] 29 C.F.R. §§541.1, 541.101.
[10] 29 C.F.R. §§541.2, 541.201.

directly related to academic instruction or training in an educational institution; and (3) performs work requiring the exercise of discretion and independent judgment.

Healthcare facility employees who typically would meet the administrative exemption include personnel directors, administrative assistants, special assistants to facility directors, executive secretaries, purchasing agents, and safety directors.

The long test for professional[11] employees requires a showing that the individual (1) performs work requiring advanced knowledge in a field of science or learning customarily obtained by a prolonged course of specialized study;[12] (2) consistently exercises discretion and judgment; (3) does work that is predominantly intellectual and varied in character; (4) devotes no more than 20 percent of his or her time to other duties; and, except for physicians, who qualify if they meet the preceding four conditions irrespective of salary, (5) is paid on a salary or fee basis at least $170 per week. The short test for professional personnel requires a showing that the individual (1) is paid at least $250 a week; and (2) performs work requiring advanced knowledge in a field of science or learning.

Employees in the healthcare industry who generally fit within the professional exemption include physicians, registered nurses,[13] physician assistants, registered or certified medical technologists, speech pathologists, and physical therapists.

Employees who meet none of these exemptions, and are thus subject to the Act's minimum wage and overtime provisions, include licensed practical nurses, nurse's aides, laboratory assistants, laboratory technicians, orderlies, cafeteria workers, and clerical employees.

---

[11]29 C.F.R. §§541.3, 541.301.

[12]This first criterion may also be met by two other means, neither of which is applicable in the healthcare field: being an artist or being a certified educator. 29 C.F.R. §§541.3, 541.301.

[13]Although not all registered nurses study a traditional four-year college curriculum, the DOL provides at 29 C.F.R. §541.302(e)(1) that nurses registered by a state examining board are professionals for purposes of the FLSA.

§2.4.2 Calculating Overtime Entitlement

The typical nonexempt employee is entitled to overtime compensation at the rate of 1½ hours' pay for every hour worked over 40 hours in a 7-day workweek. The FLSA contains an alternative method of calculating overtime compensation, however, for nonexempt employees who work in healthcare facilities.[14] Under this method, overtime is calculated on a 14-day period and requires premium payment for all hours worked over 8 per day *or* over 80 in a 14-day cycle. This differs from the standard FLSA requirement that an employee work a certain number of hours in a cycle before any entitlement to overtime payment accrues.

To illustrate, suppose a nurse's aide works 11 hours in one day, but only a total of 72 hours in a 14-day period. The aide would nonetheless be entitled to 3 hours of overtime pay, since she worked over 8 hours one day, although her net total of hours is still under 80. Or, if another aide worked 8 hours per day over a 13-day span, and on the 14th day worked another 4 hours, she would likewise be entitled to 4 hours of overtime payment, even though she never worked more than 8 hours on any one day.

The healthcare employer who desires to use the 14-day period to calculate overtime entitlement may only do so after reaching an agreement with its employees or their representatives.[15] The Act does not require that such agreement be reduced to writing, but it is advisable to do so.

---

[14]"Healthcare facilities" are defined as 29 U.S.C. §207(j) as hospitals or establishments "primarily engaged in the care of the sick, the aged, or the mentally ill or defective who reside on the premises." Healthcare facilities designated as eligible to use the 14-day period for calculating overtime entitlement include a home for emotionally disturbed children (W.H. Admin. Op. Ltr., June 7, 1967); a nursing home (W.H. Admin. Op. Ltr., Aug. 27, 1974); a home for the aged (W.H. Admin. Op. Ltr., July 18, 1967); and a home for the blind (W.H. Admin. Op. Ltr., June 16, 1967). Public hospitals, nursing homes, or mental institutions would qualify as employers eligible to use the 14-day alternative as well.

[15]29 U.S.C. §207(j). Failure to prove the existence of an agreement may

§2.4.3 The Equal Pay Act

All employees, whether exempt or nonexempt, are covered by a 1963 amendment to the FLSA known as the Equal Pay Act.[16] The Act, which is administered and enforced by the U.S. Equal Employment Opportunity Commission (EEOC), provides that an employer may not pay an employee of one sex less than an employee of the opposite sex for work performed under similar working conditions that requires equal skill, effort, and responsibility. The Act thus mandates equal pay for equal work.

The act contains four exceptions to the requirement of equal pay for equal work.[17] An employer may maintain a wage differential where the difference in pay is attributable to (1) a bona fide seniority system; (2) a merit system; (3) a system that bases pay on quality or quantity of work produced; or (4) some factor other than sex. An employer is barred from complying with the equal pay requirement by reducing the wage rate of any employee.

To be considered "equal work" under the Act, jobs need not be identical, but only substantially equal.[18] The EEOC regulations note that the question of "what constitutes equal skill, equal effort, or equal responsibility cannot be precisely defined."[19] Each term constitutes a separate requirement, each of which must be met in order for the equal pay standard to apply. Substantial differences, not minor differences, are required to be shown by an employer to justify pay differences.

The equal skill requirement is measured in terms of job performance, taking into consideration experience, training, education, and ability. The critical focus is on the position, not the incumbent. Thus, even if an incumbent has particular skills

---

result in back pay liability. See, e.g., Beebe v. United States, 640 F.2d 1283 (Ct. Cl. 1981) (lack of agreement over adoption of alternative schedule for firefighters entitled employees to overtime payment).

[16]29 U.S.C. §206(d).

[17]29 U.S.C. §206(d).

[18]Corning Glass Works v. Brennan, 417 U.S. 188 (1974); 29 C.F.R. §1620.13(a).

[19]29 C.F.R. §1620.14(a).

exceeding those needed for adequate job performance, those additional skills cannot be taken into consideration in determining equal skill requirements between two jobs.[20]

The equal effort requirement examines the amount of physical or mental exertion needed to perform a job. It is the degree of effort, not the type of effort (i.e., physical versus mental) that is measured to determine equality.[21]

The equal responsibility standard focuses on the degree of accountability required for adequate job performance, with emphasis placed on the importance of the job's obligation.[22]

§2.4.4 The Equal Pay Act and Comparable Worth

It should be noted that the Equal Pay Act only requires equal pay for equal work; it does not require equal pay for work of comparable worth. Comparable worth refers to the movement to raise the ratio of wages in traditionally women's jobs to wages in traditionally men's jobs. Proponents argue that society is dominated by men and thus has steered women into certain jobs and kept the wages in those jobs below what the jobs were actually worth to the employer, because most of the incumbents were women. The solution, they contend, is to apply job analysis techniques to determine the relative worth of jobs.

In its purest form, comparable worth involves a comparison between workers of one sex in one job category with workers of the other sex in a totally different job category. Proponents argue that although the work is not the same, it is of comparable worth to the employer.[23]

---

[20]29 C.F.R. §1620.15(a).

[21]29 C.F.R. §1620.16(a).

[22]29 C.F.R. §1620.17(a).

[23]See, e.g., Lemons v. City and County of Denver, 620 F.2d (10th Cir.), cert. denied, 449 U.S. 888 (1980) (comparing the worth of nurses to that of tree trimmers). There is a rich literature on the comparable worth debate. See, e.g., Booker and Nuckolls, Legal and Economic Aspects of Comparable Worth, 15 Pub. Personnel Mgmt. 189-206 (Summer 1986); Chi, Comparable Worth, 57 State Government 34-45 (1985); Bunzel, To each according to her

The less rarefied comparable worth concept involves a comparison between workers of one sex in one job category with workers of the other sex in a similar job category. Proponents argue that although the two groups are not performing work that meets the Equal Pay Act standard (meaning the jobs require equal skill, effort, and responsibility, performed under similar working conditions), the work is nonetheless of comparable worth to the employer.

To fully understand the scope of the Equal Pay Act regarding comparable worth claims, it is necessary to also consider part of Title VII of the Civil Rights Act of 1964. (Title VII is discussed fully in Part D of this chapter, infra.) Title VII, which prohibits discrimination on the basis of sex (among other grounds), contains a reference to the Equal Pay Act, stating:

> It shall not be an unlawful employment practice under this subchapter for any employer to differentiate upon the basis of sex in determining the amount of wages or compensation paid or to be paid to employees of such employer if such differentiation is authorized by the provisions of Section 206(d) of Title 29 [the Equal Pay Act].[24]

Initially, the courts interpreted this provision, which allows employers in Title VII cases to invoke the four affirmative defenses to equal pay under the Equal Pay Act (discussed above), as restricting Title VII's scope to only those actions that could also be brought under the Equal Pay Act. The courts thus read the equal pay for equal work standard into Title VII, with the result that comparable worth claims were precluded.[25]

---

worth?, 67 The Public Interest 77-93 (Spring 1982); Lois Friss, Equal Pay for Comparable Worth, 2 Rev. of Pub. Per. Adm. 37-48 (Summer 1982); Reynolds, Comparable Worth: Bad Policy and Bad Law, 9 Harv. J.L. & Pub. Pol. 89-94 (Winter 1986); England, A Dissenting View in Favor of Pay Equity, 9 Harv. J.L. & Pub. Pol. 99-106 (Winter 1986).

[24]42 U.S.C. §2003-2(h). This section is known as the Bennett Amendment, after its congressional sponsor.

[25]See, e.g., Lemons v. City and County of Denver, supra n.23; Molthan v. Temple Univ., 442 F. Supp. 448 (E.D. Pa. 1977).

This narrow view of the relationship of the Equal Pay Act of Title VII sex discrimination claims ended, however, with the Supreme Court's decision in County of Washington v. Gunther.[26] In this case, the County of Washington, Oregon paid substantially lower wages to female guards than to male guards in the county jail. The female guards sued under Title VII, claiming that the county intentionally set the pay scale for female guards at a lower level than that warranted by its own survey of outside markets and the worth of the jobs.

The Court declined the opportunity to endorse the comparable worth theory. It did rule, however, that Title VII reaches claims of sex discrimination not covered by the Equal Pay Act (that is, where female plaintiffs cannot show that they were doing equal work requiring skill, effort, and responsibility, but were being paid less than men). Although the Court in *Gunther* found that the jobs of the female prison guards were not substantially equal to those of the male guards, the Court recognized the claim that the female guards were the victims of intentional sex discrimination, and the case was remanded for further evidence of discriminatory intent.

While *Gunther* opened the door for comparable worth claims under Title VII, subsequent plaintiffs have fared poorly in pursuing such claims in the courts. Typical is the result in American Nurses Association v. State of Illinois.[27] In that case, the Illinois Commission on the Status of Women commissioned a study of state employee jobs using a method of job classification called "point factor analysis." In a nutshell, point factor analysis compares jobs on a numerical scale of difficulty, using several predetermined job worth factors. The study found, based on principles of comparable worth, that the 12 predominantly female job classifications were underpaid by between 29 and 56 percent. For example, an electrician whose job was "pointed" at 274 had an average monthly salary of $2,286.00, while a nurse with 480 points was paid, on average, only $2,104 a month. The union representing the nurses filed suit, alleging

[26]452 U.S. 161 (1981).
[27]783 F.2d 716 (7th Cir. 1986).

86

that the failure of the state of Illinois to correct this imbalance by reconfiguring its wage system in accordance with the findings of the study violated Title VII.

The court rejected the claim that the failure to accept the recommendations of a comparable worth study was actionable. Mere knowledge of a wage disparity, held the court, is not the same thing as an intent to cause or maintain it. If the state's intention was to pay market rates, its knowledge that the consequences would be that men got higher wages on average than women, and that the difference might exceed any premium attributable to a difference in relative worth, would not make it guilty of intentionally discriminating against women.

As in *Gunther,* the case was remanded for a determination of intentional discrimination—that is, proof that the state of Illinois overpaid workers in predominantly male jobs because they were male. The court characterized this burden of proof as "a tough row to hoe."[28]

§2.5 The National Labor Relations Act

The National Labor Relations Act (the Wagner Act),[1] like the Fair Labor Standards Act, was a product of the Great Depression.

---

[28]783 F.2d at 730. The only other circuit courts to consider the matter have reached the same conclusion. See AFSCME v. State of Washington, 770 F.2d 1401 (9th Cir. 1985) (basing wages on a complex set of market forces does not constitute a clearly delineated employment policy that suffices to support a claim of sex discrimination); United Auto Workers v. Michigan, 886 F.2d 766 (6th Cir. 1989) (failure of state to implement results of state-commissioned study finding workers in female-dominated positions paid less than workers in male-dominated positions not a violation of Title VII absent showing of intent to discriminate).

§2.5 [1]49 Stat. 449 (1935), 29 U.S.C. §§151-168, as amended by Pub. L. No. 101, 80th Cong., 1st Sess., 1947, and Pub. L. No. 257, 86th Cong., 1st Sess., 1959. This section provides only a brief overview of the NLRA as applied to healthcare facilities. For a full discussion of the Act and the myriad issues that arise in its application, see C. J. Morris, ed., The Developing Labor Law (2d ed. BNA 1983); F. Bartosic and R. C. Hartley, Labor Relations Law in the Private Sector (2d ed. ALI/ABA 1986).

Enacted in 1935, the Act declared the national labor policy to be one of encouraging collective bargaining and employee representation by labor organizations as a means of eliminating substantial obstructions to the free flow of interstate commerce.[2] The Act gave employees the right to form, join, or assist labor organizations, to engage in collective bargaining, and to engage in concerted activities for collective bargaining or mutual aid or protection.[3] The Act also proscribed certain aspects of employer conduct as unfair labor practices,[4] and created the National Labor Relations Board (NLRB) to interpret and administer the Act.[5] As originally enacted, the Act only placed restraints on employers.

In 1947, Congress made substantial amendments to the Act with the passage of the Taft-Hartley Act. Largely due to the wave of strikes following the end of World War II and the growing perception that labor unions were becoming too powerful, the Act added certain unfair labor practices for labor organizations,[6] amended the existing unfair labor practices section to permit noncoercive employer "free speech" on the question of union representation,[7] outlawed the closed-shop union security arrangement (whereby an individual could only be hired if already a union member),[8] outlawed secondary boycotts,[9] and increased the NLRB from three to five members.

Finally, in 1959, as part of the Landrum-Griffin Act (which established separate requirements for labor organization financial reporting and disclosure), the Act was amended to permit states

---

[2]§1, 29 U.S.C. §151. The constitutionality of the Wagner Act was upheld in NLRB v. Jones & Laughlin Steel Co., 301 U.S. 1 (1937).

[3]§7, 29 U.S.C. §157.

[4]§8(a), 29 U.S.C. §158(a).

[5]§3, 29 U.S.C. §153.

[6]§8(b), 29 U.S.C. §158(b).

[7]§8(c), 29 U.S.C. §158(c), provides that "[t]he expression of any views, argument, or opinion or the dissemination thereof, whether in written, printed, graphic, or visual form, shall not constitute or be evidence of an unfair labor practice under any of the provisions of this Act, if such expression contains no threat of reprisal or force or promise of benefit."

[8]§7, 29 U.S.C. §157.

[9]§§8(b)(4)(A), (B), U.S.C. §158(b).

to handle cases over which the NLRB lacked jurisdiction,[10] to further restrict secondary boycott practices,[11] and to outlaw hot cargo clauses (which permitted an employer to agree with a union to refuse to handle another employer's goods).[12]

As originally enacted, the Act covered both for-profit and nonprofit healthcare institutions. In 1947, however, the Taft-Hartley amendments exempted nonprofit healthcare facilities, largely because they were experiencing financial difficulties. The question of healthcare facility coverage was reexamined by Congress in the 1970s, with the result that in 1974 the Act was amended to again govern labor relations at nonprofit healthcare institutions, but with special provisions in recognition of the unique nature of those institutions. Specifically, the Act was amended to curtail the employee right to strike and engage in picketing and to make special provisions regarding contract termination and mediation.[13]

Note that public healthcare facilities are excluded from NLRA coverage by §2(2) of the Act, which provides that the term "employer" shall not include the United States or any of its political subdivisions.[14] Private healthcare institutions subject to the Act, whether operated for profit or as nonprofit organizations, are defined as "any hospital, convalescent hospital, health maintenance organization, health clinic, nursing home, extended care facility, or other institution devoted to the care of the sick, infirm, or aged person."[15]

The National Labor Relations Board has discretion to

---

[10]§14(c)(1), 29 U.S.C. §164(c).

[11]§8(b)(4)(A), 29 U.S.C. §158(b). See generally NLRB v. Servette, Inc., 377 U.S. 46 (1964).

[12]§8(e), 29 U.S.C. §158(e). See generally Connell Constr. Co. v. Plumbers Local 100, 421 U.S. 616 (1975).

[13]§8(d), 8(g), 29 U.S.C. §§158(d), and (g).

[14]In applying this exemption, the NLRB has distinguished between actual administrative control by a governmental entity and mere financial support of the healthcare facility by the government. Facilities in the latter category have been held to be subject to the Act's jurisdiction, as long as the operation of the facility is privately controlled. See, e.g., Mental Health Management, 237 N.L.R.B. 12 (1978).

[15]Sec. 2(14), 29 U.S.C. §152(14).

exercise its power over all enterprises affecting commerce; it has enacted jurisdictional standards to exclude employers in various types of enterprises whose annual dollar volume of business falls below certain levels. For a private healthcare facility to come under the NLRB's jurisdiction, its total annual volume of business must be at least $250,000 if a hospital, at least $100,000 if a nursing home, visiting nurse's association or related facility, and at least $250,000 if any other private healthcare facilities as defined above.[16]

§2.5.1 Bargaining Units in Healthcare Facilities

Under §9 of the National Labor Relations Act, the NLRB is responsible for certifying proposed groupings of employees as appropriate for the purpose of collective bargaining. These certified groupings are called "bargaining units." It has long been the case that the Board, in exercising this responsibility, has relied primarily on the finding of a "community of interest" among the employees whom the union proposes to represent,[17] and that the courts have given broad deference to the Board's expertise in determining the appropriateness of bargaining units.[18]

In enacting the healthcare amendments to the National Labor Relations Act in 1974, Congress expressed the view (albeit in a committee report and not by amending §9 of the Act) that the NLRB should avoid undue proliferation of bargaining units.[19] Although the Board initially appeared to pay little attention to

---

[16]East Oakland Community Health Alliance, 218 N.L.R.B. 1270 (1975).

[17]This standard began with the decision in In re Chrysler Corp., 1 N.L.R.B. 164, 169-170, (1936) and has continued to the present time.

[18]See, e.g., Allied Chem. & Alkali Workers, Local No. 1 v. Pittsburgh Plate Glass Co., 404 U.S. 157, 171-172 (1971); NLRB v. Hearst Publications, 322 U.S. 111, 134 (1944); Local No. 627, Intl. Union of Operating Engineers v. NLRB, 595 F.2d 844, 848 (D.C. Cir. 1979).

[19]S. Rep. 766, 93d Cong., 2d Sess. 5 (1974), reprinted in 1974 U.S. Code Cong. & Admin. News 3946.

congressional preference and judicial admonition[20] for fewer, larger units in the healthcare industry, in 1984 the Board adopted, with its decision in *St. Francis Hospital (St. Francis II)*,[21] a standard favoring broad professional and nonprofessional units.

In *St. Francis II* the Board adopted a "disparity-of-interest" standard, which implicitly began with a presumption that the broadest bargaining units possible—one for all professional employees and one for all nonprofessional employees of the employer—were the most appropriate units. The Board held that, although it would continue to apply the traditional criterion of community of interest to determine appropriate bargaining units for all employers, only where "sharper than usual differences (or 'disparities') between the wages, hours, and working conditions, etc., of the requested employees and those in an overall professional or nonprofessional unit"[22] existed would a separate unit for those employees be found. In other words, where a union sought to represent in a separate unit, for example, a group of skilled maintenance employees, it could only do so where the NLRB found "sharp differences" between the working conditions of those employees and other nonprofessional employees.

The *St. Francis II* decision was not to be the last word on healthcare facility bargaining units, however. The NLRB decision was appealed by the union in the case to the U.S. Court of Appeals for the District of Columbia, and that court held that there was nothing in the Act to mandate the Board's conclusion that it was to presume that only two appropriate bargaining units exist in the healthcare industry.[23] Stated the court:

---

[20]See, e.g., Southwest Community Health Serv. v. NLRB, 726 F.2d 611 (10th Cir. 1984); NLRB v. Frederick Memorial Hosp., 691 F.2d 191 (4th Cir. 1982); NLRB v. HMO Intl., 678 F.2d 806 (9th Cir. 1982); Mary Thompson Hosp. v. NLRB, 621 F.2d 858 (7th Cir. 1980); Allegheny Gen. Hosp. v. NLRB, 608 F.2d 965 (3d Cir. 1979); NLRB v. Mercy Hosp. Assn., 606 F.2d 22 (2d Cir. 1979), cert. denied, 445 U.S. 971 (1980).

[21]271 N.L.R.B. 948 (1984).

[22]Id. at 953.

[23]International Bhd. of Electrical Workers, Local Union 474 v. NLRB, 814 F.2d 697, 708 (D.C. Cir. 1987). In so holding, the court rejected the numerous holdings to the contrary by other circuit courts of appeals noted supra, n. 20.

When we consider the Committee Reports' admonition and the statements of individual legislators against the backdrop of this policy favoring collective labor organization in the health-care industry, we think it plain that Congress did not intend to mandate a standard that burdens hospital employees with a presumption in favor of wall-to-wall units. Rather, Congress was satisfied that the Board would continue to exercise its discretion under the Act in striking the "appropriate balance between the interests of hospital employees, patients, and employers."[24]

The court remanded the case to the NLRB for reconsideration. The Board, on remand, decided to resolve the issue by a method common in administrative law but only exercised once previously by the Board in its 53-year history: instituting rulemaking proceedings to establish rules for determining appropriate bargaining units in the healthcare industry.[25]

In 1989, the NLRB published final rules on the criteria to be used in determining appropriate bargaining units in the healthcare industry.[26] The Board has fashioned eight bargaining units for all nonpsychiatric hospitals, as follows:

1. all registered nurses
2. all physicians
3. all professional employees except registered nurses and physicians
4. all technical employees

---

[24]814 F.2d at 714.

[25]The Board's previous rulemaking involved the promulgation of standards for the exercise of jurisdiction over private colleges and universities. The Board's reluctance to use rulemaking was upheld in NLRB v. Bell Aerospace Co., 416 U.S. 267 (1974). The proposed rules for healthcare facility bargaining units are found in the Federal Register of June 14, 1988. Interestingly, Board Member Dennis, in her concurring opinion in *St. Francis II*, suggested that precisely this approach was needed, reasoning that "[u]nder the 'disparity-of-interests' standard we adopt today, it is not possible to give as much guidance to health care employers and unions as I would like, for each case must be judged on its own particular facts." 271 N.L.R.B. at 955 (Dennis, concurring).

[26]These rules were upheld in American Hosp. Assn. v. NLRB, 899 F.2d 651 (7th Cir. 1990).

5. business office clerical employees
6. skilled maintenance employees
7. all service and other clerical employees
8. all guards

The effect of moving from only two to eight units will be to make it easier for labor organizations to obtain recognition, since they will no longer be required to seek broad-based support from employees with differing interests.

§2.5.2 Strikes and Picketing in the Healthcare Industry

The 1974 amendments to the Labor Management Relations Act further recognized the unique nature of healthcare facilities as employers by establishing limits on strikes and picketing.[27] Specifically, §8(g) of the Act requires that a union representing employees at a healthcare institution must give a minimum of ten days' written notice to the institution and to the Federal Mediation and Conciliation Service (FMCS) of its intention to engage in a strike, a picket, or any other concerted refusal to work. The notice is to inform the employer and FMCS of the date and time the action will commence.[28] Once given, the notice may be extended by the written agreement of the employer and the union. Additional notice requirements, arising where a contract is to be terminated, are discussed in §2.5.3, infra.

In no other employment setting is this type of advance notice of labor protest required. Clearly, Congress's intent in requiring this notice was to minimize the risk to critically ill patients by ensuring adequate time for the healthcare provider

---

[27]The effect of §8(g) is to preempt all state statutes that prohibit strikes by healthcare facility employees. In re State of Minnesota, 219 N.L.R.B. 1095 (1975).

[28]Note that the notice must be in writing. In Retail Clerks Union Local 727 (Devon Gable Health Care Center, Inc.), 244 N.L.R.B. 586 (1979), the NLRB held that mere oral notice of a strike or picketing, even if timely given, does not satisfy the requirements of §8(g).

to make alternative care arrangements. Failure of a union to comply with the notice requirements may permit the healthcare facility to dismiss the striking employees.

Note, however, that the notice requirement only pertains to unions. Employees who are not represented by a union but who wish to picket or strike their employer may do so irrespective of §8(g)'s notice requirements.[29] Illustrative of the limits of §8(g) is Montefiore Hospital and Medical Center v. NLRB.[30] In that case, two physicians, not themselves union members or part of a bargaining unit, walked out without notice to the hospital in sympathy with an ongoing strike by the employer's unionized employees. The physicians were dismissed for failure to comply with the Act's notice requirements, but the court overturned their dismissal, holding that §8(g) applies only to labor organizations, not to individual employees. Although the employees' actions were not in violation of the Act, the court noted that "[w]hen, as in this case, a union has given notice of its intention to strike, the hospital would be well-advised to inquire of the rest of its employees whether they plan to stay out in sympathy."[31]

This is not to suggest, however, that in absolutely every instance an employee is free to engage in disruptive concerted activity. When, by its timing or unexpectedness, a strike creates great danger or is likely to damage the employer's business excessively, prior notice may be required irrespective of §8(g)'s applicability.[32] But in the *Montefiore* case, as the court noted,

> although prior notice by [the physicians] would have been more considerate and in keeping with their ethical duties to the Hospital and their patients, we cannot say that their failure to give it created such a danger or risk of harm to patients as to justify

---

[29]*Walker Methodist Residence and Health Care Center,* 227 N.L.R.B. 1630 (1977); NLRB v. Long Beach Youth Center, 591 F.2d 1276 (9th Cir. 1979); NLRB v. Rock Hill Convalescent Center, 585 F.2d 700 (4th Cir. 1978).

[30]621 F.2d 510 (2d Cir. 1980).

[31]Id. at 515.

[32]See, e.g., Southern Steamship Co. v. NLRB, 316 U.S. 31 (1942); Dobbs Houses, Inc. v. NLRB, 325 F.2d 531 (5th Cir. 1963).

depriving them of the Act's protection. This was not a case in which patients were left lying on the operating table, emergency room personnel walked off, or people in need of immediate treatment were left to fend for themselves.[33]

Obviously, where a healthcare facility encounters situations more like those described by the court that would endanger patients, the decision to dismiss those responsible may well be upheld.

§2.5.3 Contract Termination and Mediation in Healthcare Facilities

The NLRA provides for all employers, at §8(d),[34] a means of ensuring that a "cooling off" period occurs between the decision of one party to a collective bargaining agreement to terminate the agreement and resort to the use of economic weapons such as strikes or concerted activities. Specifically, §8(d) requires: (1) 60 days' notice of proposed termination or modification of the agreement; (2) 30 days' notice to the FMCS of the existence of a bargaining dispute; and (3) continuation of the agreement for the 60-day period. For employers and employees in healthcare facilities, however, these rules are more stringent. As is the case with strikes and picketing, the NLRA has been modified to alleviate the disruptive impact of labor unrest on patient care by increasing the notice requirements and making special provisions for the resolution of bargaining disputes.

Section 8(d) was amended in 1974 to increase the notice period from 60 to 90 days for parties to collective bargaining agreements in the healthcare industry. FMCS notice must be given within 60 days, as opposed to the 30-day requirement for other employers. Finally, the parties are prohibited from resorting to strikes, lockouts, or other disruptive activities for a period of 90 days, not 60 days as is the case elsewhere.

---

[33]*Montefiore*, 621 F.2d at 516.
[34]29 U.S.C. §158(d).

FMCS use is mandated for dispute resolution in the health-care industry. While the FMCS is heavily used in other industries as well, the decision to invoke its assistance in resolving a bargaining dispute is discretionary in those industries.

Further, a special procedure has been established by the FMCS to assist in resolving bargaining disputes in the healthcare area: the use of a special board of inquiry to conduct fact-finding. A board of inquiry may be created at the discretion of the director of the FMCS in those situations where a threatened strike or lockout would severely impair healthcare delivery and patient care. The board may consist of a multi-member panel, but is often a single arbitrator appointed from the list of qualified individuals maintained by the FMCS.

There is some indication that the increased notice require-ments and the use of special FMCS boards of inquiry may have lessened the frequency of strikes and lockouts in the healthcare industry.[35] In any event, the healthcare employer must be aware of the special rules governing the resolution of bargaining impasses in the industry.

D. Employment Discrimination

§2.6 Title VII of the Civil Rights Act of 1964

No single piece of legislation has had greater impact on the employment relationship than Title VII of the Civil Rights Act of 1964.[1] Originally applicable only to private employers of 15 or more employees, the Act was amended in 1972 to extend to public employers as well.

The Act bars discrimination by employers on the basis of

---

[35]Comment, Labor Relations in the Health Care Industry—The Impact of the 1974 Health Care Amendments to the National Labor Relations Act, 54 Tulane L. Rev. 416, 451 (1980).

§2.6 [1]42 U.S.C. §2000e et seq.

race, color, religion, sex, or national origin.[2] Specifically, Title VII makes it unlawful for an employer to refuse to hire or discharge any individual or otherwise to discriminate against any individual with respect to compensation or terms and conditions of employment.[3] An exception is made and discrimination is permitted where religion, sex, or national origin is a bona fide occupational qualification (bfoq) reasonably necessary to the operation of the business.[4]

Since the passage of Title VII of the Civil Rights Act of 1964, the courts have recognized two theories by which discrimination may be proved: disparate treatment and disparate impact.

§2.6.1 The Disparate Treatment Theory of Discrimination

Disparate treatment analysis is a means of proving intentional discrimination. An employer will be found to have violated Title VII if it is shown that the employer treats some employees or applicants less favorably because of their race, sex, creed, color, or national origin. This different (or disparate) treatment may be shown either by direct evidence or, as is usually the case, by indirect evidence.

The Supreme Court has recognized a means by which disparate treatment may be inferred, sufficient to require the employer to rebut the inference of discrimination. Under the model set forth in McDonnell Douglas Corp. v. Green,[5] an

---

[2]42 U.S.C. §2000e-2(a)e.

[3]42 U.S.C. §2000e(k).

[4]42 U.S.C. §2000e-2(e)(1). Although the Act provides the bfoq exception, in practice employers have found this exception extremely difficult to meet. See B. Schlei and B. Grossman, Employment Discrimination Law 340-360 (BNA 1983).

[5]411 U.S. 792, 802 (1973). Elaboration on the *McDonnell Douglas* standard is found in Teamsters v. United States, 431 U.S. 324, 335 n.15 (1977); Furnco Const. Corp. v. Waters, 438 U.S. 567, 577 (1978); Texas Dept. of Community Affairs v. Burdine, 450 U.S. 248, 253-255 (1981); United States Postal Serv. Bd. of Governors v. Aikens, 460 U.S. 711, 715 (1983).

applicant can create a prima facie case of discrimination in hiring by showing that:

1. he or she belongs to a protected class;
2. he or she applied and was qualified for a job for which the employer was seeking applicants;
3. he or she was rejected, despite the fact that he or she met the qualifications for the job; and
4. after his or her rejection, the employer continued to seek applicants from persons with the same qualifications as the applicant.

The employer then has the burden of presenting evidence to the court that the applicant was rejected not on a basis prohibited by Title VII, but because of a legitimate, nondiscriminatory reason. Such reasons might include the fact that another applicant possessed superior qualifications or that the applicant did poorly in the employment interview. Finally, once the employer has advanced its legitimate reason for the applicant's rejection, the applicant has an opportunity to show that the employer's proffered reason for rejection is a pretext and that the real reason is discrimination. It is always the case in disparate treatment analysis that the plaintiff has the ultimate burden of proof and that this burden remains with the plaintiff at all times.[6]

The plaintiff failed to make a prima facie case of race discrimination under the disparate treatment theory in Williams v. HMO of Florida.[7] In this case, the plaintiff, Lavonne Williams, claimed that her employer, HMO of Florida, discriminated against her by refusing to hire her for a marketing representative's position and failing to provide her with adequate training in her position as a marketing assistant because she was black.

On the first issue, refusal to hire, the court found that the marketing representative's position required a bachelor's degree

---

[6]See, e.g., Board of Trustees of Keene State College v. Sweeney, 439 U.S. 24, 25 (1978).

[7]46 FEP Cases 539 (M.D. Fla. 1986).

and required the incumbent to make presentations to groups of 20 or more people. Williams had a degree and several years' experience in the healthcare and insurance fields, but no previous sales experience and no experience speaking before large groups.

Williams was not able to make out a prima facie case on her first claim. Although she was a member of a class protected by Title VII and applied for a position with HMO of Florida, the court held that she did not meet the qualifications for the position. Specifically, she lacked the sales and speaking experience required of all candidates for the position. The court added that she failed to present evidence showing who, if anyone, was hired in place of her, or whether that person was outside the protected class; further, she failed to present evidence that she was equally or more qualified than the other persons hired as marketing representatives.

On the second issue, failure to train, Williams was similarly unable to make out a prima facie case. Although the company did not offer her a marketing representative's position, she was given a job as a marketing assistant, conditioned on her passing a typing test. She did not pass the test, but claimed that the reason was those responsible for training her were hostile and unfriendly. As the court noted, however, personal animosity, even if proven, is not the equivalent of the racial discrimination proscribed by Title VII.

Even if Williams had made out a prima facie case of failure to train, stated the court, the employer articulated nondiscriminatory reasons sufficient to rebut the inference of discrimination. Specifically, the court found that the plaintiff was given adequate opportunity to become proficient in typing and that she lacked the skills necessary to participate in the training offered.

The plaintiff was able to establish a prima facie case of race discrimination in Wrenn v. New York City Health & Hospitals Corp.[8] In this case, Curtis Wrenn, a black, applied for 15 different executive-level positions at the defendant employer's facilities and was rejected for all 15. He challenged the employer's failure to hire him for the first position for which he had applied,

---

[8] 664 F. Supp. 773 (S.D.N.Y. 1987).

executive director at Metropolitan Hospital, as one based on race, and alleged that the remaining 14 rejections were in retaliation for his filing an EEOC complaint concerning his Metropolitan Hospital rejection.

The court agreed that Wrenn had established a prima facie case of discrimination, but credited the employer's explanation of its selection of another candidate, a Hispanic male, over the plaintiff. The applicant chosen to be executive director was proficient in both English and Spanish, which was important since Metropolitan Hospital, located in East Harlem, served a large Spanish-speaking community. Further, the selected candidate had previously served as acting executive director of the hospital. In the court's view, these factors made the selected candidate "uniquely qualified" for the job. In rejecting the contention of the plaintiff that the selection decision was racially motivated, the court stated that "it is well-established that an employer need not prove that the person selected 'had superior objective qualifications, or that it made the wisest choice, but only that the reasons for the decision were nondiscriminatory.' "[9]

As demonstrated by the above cases, the disparate treatment model is often used to challenge subjective employment practices such as selection for promotion by the use of interviews.[10] In

---

[9]Id. at 777 (citing Davis v. State Univ. of N.Y., 802 F.2d 638, 641 (2d Cir. 1986).

[10]See also Price Waterhouse v. Hopkins, 109 S. Ct. 1775, 104 L. Ed. 2d 268 (1989), in which the Supreme Court held that if a Title VII plaintiff can prove that her gender played a motivating part in an employment decision, the burden of proof shifts to the employer to show that the same decision would have been made in any event, based on other legitimate considerations. This burden shift only occurs in cases in which the plaintiff can show that an unlawful motive was a substantial factor actually relied on by the employer in deciding to act. Elaborating on the burden of the employer in a mixed motive case, the Court said:

> [I]n most cases, the employer should be able to present some objective evidence as to its probable decision in the absence of an impermissible motive. . . . An employer may not . . . prevail in a mixed-motive case by offering a legitimate and sufficient reason for its decision if that reason did not motivate it at the time of the decision. Finally, an employer may not meet its burden in such a case by merely showing that at the time of the decision it was motivated only in part by

contrast, where objective means of screening or selecting candidates (such as scored tests or credential requirements) are used, plaintiffs alleging discrimination have relied on a second theory of discrimination: disparate impact analysis.

§2.6.2 The Disparate Impact Theory of Discrimination

The seminal disparate impact analysis case is Griggs v. Duke Power Company.[11] In that case the employer required employees to possess a high school diploma and to obtain a passing score on a personnel test in order to be eligible for promotion from laborer positions to any other jobs in the company. A group of black employees sued the company under Title VII, claiming the requirements for promotion out of the laborer jobs were racially discriminatory. Duke Power's response was that the job requirements applied to all applicants alike, black or white, and that it did not intend to discriminate.

The Supreme Court held that even if an employer does not intend to discriminate, it may nonetheless be in violation of Title VII if the employer's practices have a disparate impact on a protected group and are insufficiently job-related. Unlike the disparate treatment theory, in a disparate impact case the plaintiff is not required to prove a discriminatory motive on the part of the employer as part of the prima facie case. Rather, a plaintiff may establish a prima facie case by showing that an employment practice that is facially neutral (such as a requirement that all applicants pass a scored test or possess certain educational credentials) has the effect of disproportionately excluding members of a protected class. In challenging the use of a scored test, for example, a black plaintiff may use statistics to show that a significantly greater number of blacks than whites fail the test.

---

a legitimate reason. The very premise of mixed-motive cases is that a legitimate reason was present. . . . The employer instead must show that its legitimate reason, standing alone, would have induced it to make the same decision.

[11] 401 U.S. 424 (1971).

Where statistically significant difference in scores is shown, it is determined that there is "substantial adverse impact." The inference is drawn that this difference constitutes a pattern or practice of discrimination.

The magnitude of disparity needed and the amount of statistical proof required to establish substantial adverse impact sufficient to constitute a prima facie case varies from case to case; there is no one method that has been universally accepted by the courts. In Griggs the plaintiffs showed that 34 percent of the white males in North Carolina had a high school diploma while only 12 percent of the black males possessed this credential. The Court held that this statistical showing was sufficient to constitute a prima facie case.

Once the prima facie case is established, the employer may rebut the inference of discrimination by: (1) submitting countervailing statistical proof;[12] (2) showing that the statistics offered by the plaintiff are not sufficiently probative;[13] or (3) demonstrating that the practice, although having substantial adverse impact, is directly related to job performance and may be fairly characterized as a "business necessity" (discussed in §2.6.3, infra).[14] In Griggs, the company was unable to demonstrate that its high school diploma and testing requirements, which the plaintiffs' statistical evidence clearly showed had adverse impact on blacks, were job-related.

After Griggs, the lower courts were faced with numerous challenges to employment practices used to differentiate among applicants. The question arose whether disparate impact analysis was only to be applied to specific, objective job requirements or was also appropriate for subjective employment practices. The circuit courts reached different answers.[15] To resolve the split in

---

[12]Hazelwood School Dist. v. United States, 433 U.S. 299 (1977).

[13]Castaneda v. Partida, 430 U.S. 482 (1977).

[14]Griggs, 401 U.S. at 431.

[15]Cases limiting the application of disparate impact analysis to objective, identifiable employment criteria include Lewis v. NLRB, 750 F.2d 1266, 1271 (5th Cir. 1985) and Zahorik v. Cornell Univ., 729 F.2d 85, 95-96 (2d Cir. 1984). Cases allowing the application of disparate impact analysis to subjective employment decisions include Regner v. City of Chicago, 789 F.2d 534, 538-

the circuits, the Supreme Court in 1988 agreed to hear Watson v. Ft. Worth Bank and Trust.[16]

Clara Watson, a black, was hired as a proof operator by Fort Worth Bank and Trust in 1973. She was promoted to teller's positions of increasing responsibility from 1975 until 1980. Between February 1980 and January 1981, Watson applied and was turned down for four separate promotion opportunities with the bank. In each instance either a white male or a white female (all of whom were also current bank employees) was selected for the position. The method used to evaluate the employees for promotion was to allow a single managerial bank official to select the employee he or she thought was the best for the position, relying on each candidate's performance evaluation and previous experience. In August 1981, following her four rejections for promotion, Watson filed a Title VII suit claiming that the bank discriminated against her and other similarly situated persons on the basis of race in making promotion decisions.

The district court analyzed Watson's case under the disparate treatment theory and held that, although Watson demonstrated a prima facie case of discrimination, she failed to demonstrate that the bank's articulated reasons for not promoting her were a pretext. On appeal, the Fifth Circuit Court of Appeals similarly held for the bank on the merits.[17] In so doing, the court rejected Watson's argument that the district court should have applied disparate impact analysis to her claims of discrimination in promotion. The Fifth Circuit instead held that "a Title VII challenge to an allegedly discretionary promotion system is properly analyzed under the disparate treatment model rather than the disparate impact model."[18] It was this failure to allow

---

539 (7th Cir. 1986); Segar v. Smith, 738 F.2d 1249, 1270 (D.C. Cir. 1984), cert. denied, 471 U.S. 1115 (1985); Griffin v. Carlin, 755 F.2d 1516, 1522-1525 (11th Cir. 1985); and Atonio v. Wards Cove Packing Co., 810 F.2d 1477 (9th Cir. 1987) (en banc).

[16]108 S. Ct. 2777, 101 L. Ed. 2d 827 (1988).

[17]798 F.2d 791, 798 (5th Cir. 1986).

[18]798 F.2d at 797.

Watson to present her case under a disparate impact theory that the Supreme Court addressed.

The Court held that disparate impact analysis may be applied to cases in which subjective criteria are used to make employment decisions.

Justice O'Connor, who wrote the plurality opinion, conceded that in each of the Court's opinions following *Griggs* the Court had applied disparate *impact* analysis to situations involving standardized employment tests or criteria. In Albemarle Paper Co. v. Moody,[19] the challenged employment practice was the use of written aptitude tests; in Washington v. Davis,[20] a written test of verbal skills; and in Connecticut v. Teal,[21] a written examination. In contrast, stated Justice O'Connor, the Court had always used disparate *treatment* analysis in reviewing hiring and promotion decisions that were based on the exercise of personal judgment or the application of subjective criteria.[22]

But the fact that the Court had not previously applied disparate impact analysis to subjective means of selection did not mean that such analysis was not appropriate. Rather, stated Justice O'Connor, "disparate impact analysis is in principle no less applicable to subjective employment criteria than to objective or standardized tests."[23]

Recall that under disparate impact analysis, once a statistical showing of disparate impact is made, the employer must justify the use of the offending selection device as a business necessity. Turning to the evidentiary standards that should apply to such cases, the Court acknowledged the difficulty in validating subjective methods of selection:

> Standardized tests and criteria, like those at issue in our previous disparate impact cases, can often be justified through formal "validation studies," which seek to determine whether discrete selection criteria predict actual on-the-job performance. Respon-

---

[19]422 U.S. 405 (1975).
[20]426 U.S. 229 (1976).
[21]457 U.S. 440 (1982).
[22]See cases listed in n.5.
[23]108 S. Ct. at 2786, 101 L. Ed. 2d at 842.

dent warns, however, that "validating" subjective selection criteria in this way is impracticable. Some qualities—for example, common sense, good judgment, originality, ambition, loyalty, and tact—cannot be measured accurately through standardized testing techniques. . . . Because of these difficulties, we are told, employers will find it impossible to eliminate subjective selection criteria and impossibly expensive to defend such practices in litigation. [Their] only alternative will be to adopt surreptitious quota systems in order to ensure that no plaintiff can establish a statistical prima facie case.[24]

While acknowledging that the threat of proof of disparate impact by statistics could indeed pressure employers into adopting quota systems, Justice O'Connor warned that such a result would "be contrary to Congress' clearly expressed intent, and it should not be the effect of our decision."[25] The Court then offered further explanation as to why employers should not be forced to adopt such systems to prevent a prima facie case from being made.

First, the Court emphasized that the plaintiff in a disparate impact case must do more than merely present statistics showing that there are different hiring rates for blacks and whites. Rather, the individual claiming that an employer's hiring practices are discriminatory has the burden of isolating and identifying the specific practice (e.g., use of word-of-mouth referral) that has produced the disparity. This task may be difficult where subjective selection criteria are used.

Second, even if the specific employment practice is identified, stated the Court, the plaintiff must prove causation; that is, "the plaintiff must offer statistical evidence of a kind and degree sufficient to show that the practice in question has caused the exclusion of applicants for jobs or promotions because of their membership in a protected group."[26] The Court declined to specify what level of statistical proof will establish causation. Noting that no consensus has developed around any mathemat-

---

[24]108 S. Ct. at 2787, 101 L. Ed. 2d at 843.

[25]108 S. Ct. at 2788, 101 L. Ed. 2d at 844.

[26]108 S. Ct. at 2788-2789, 101 L. Ed. 2d at 845.

ical standard, the Court held that "at this stage in the law's development, we believe . . . a case-by-case approach"[27] is appropriate.

Third, the Court stated clearly that, even if an employer is required to demonstrate that the employment practice in question is job-related, "the ultimate burden of proving that discrimination against a protected group has been caused by a specific employment practice remains with the plaintiff at all times."[28]

In 1989, the Supreme Court substantially altered the law regarding disparate impact claims with the issuance of its decision in Wards Cove Packing Company v. Atonio.[29] This case was brought by a class of Asian and Alaskan salmon cannery workers who alleged that the Wards Cove Packing Company violated Title VII by hiring minorities for low-paying unskilled jobs while filling skilled and supervisory jobs with white applicants. The result was racial stratification of the workforce.

Specifically, the workers claimed that the employer's hiring and promotion practices of nepotism, having a rehire preference, using word-of-mouth referrals from white employees, and not using objective hiring criteria, among others, had a substantial disparate impact on the minority employees.

In a 5-4 opinion, Justice White, writing for the majority, first addressed the question of the proper basis for comparison in a statistical showing of disparate impact. The lower court had ruled that the plaintiffs had established a prima facie statistical

---

[27]108 S. Ct. at 2789 n.3, 101 L. Ed. 2d at 846 n.3. The Court thus declined to endorse the EEOC's 80-percent rule as set forth in the Uniform Guidelines on Employee Selection Procedures. That rule holds that, where an employer's selection rate for one group of applicants is less than 80 percent of the selection rate of another group of applicants, the first group has a statistically established prima facie case of discrimination. The Court also declined to endorse the "standard deviation" analysis sometimes used in jury selection cases. See, e.g., Rivera v. Wichita Falls, 665 F.2d 531, 536 n.7 (5th Cir. 1982).

[28]108 S. Ct. at 2790, 101 L. Ed. 2d at 847. It was this characterization of the burden of proof that prompted the opinion by Justice Blackmun, who stated that the correct formulation of the burden of proof was to shift it to the employer once a prima facie statistical showing had been made.

[29]109 S. Ct. 2115, 104 L. Ed. 2d 733 (1989).

showing by comparing two groups of Wards Cove Company employees: the high percentage of nonwhite workers holding unskilled jobs versus the low percentage of nonwhite workers holding skilled jobs. Such a comparison, stated the Court, is irrelevant. Rather, the proper comparison is between the racial composition of the qualified persons in the labor market and the persons holding those jobs in the employer's workforce. Stated Justice White: "If the absence of minorities holding [those jobs] is due to a dearth of qualified nonwhite applicants (for reasons that are not [the employer's] fault), [the employer's] selection methods or employment practices cannot be said to have had a 'disparate impact' on nonwhites."[30] If the Court were to hold otherwise, he reasoned, then an employer with any segment of its workforce that was racially imbalanced when compared to any other segment of its workforce would be required to engage in the expensive and time-consuming task of defending the business necessity of the methods used to select the other segment and would be forced to adopt strict quotas to comply with the Act, a result Congress rejected in drafting Title VII. The opinion continued: "As long as there are no barriers or practices deterring nonwhites from applying for [the skilled] positions, if the percentage of *selected* applicants who are nonwhite is not significantly less than the percentage of *qualified* applicants who are nonwhite, the employer's selection mechanism probably does not operate with a disparate impact on minorities."[31]

The second question addressed by the Court was whether the plaintiffs could establish a disparate impact claim merely by showing there were statistical disparities in the company's workforce. The Court held that such a showing was insufficient. Rather, the plaintiffs in a disparate impact case "also have to demonstrate that the disparity they complain of is the result of one or more of the employment practices they are attacking here, specifically showing that each challenged practice has a significant disparate impact on employment opportunities for

---

[30]104 L. Ed. 2d at 748.
[31]Id. at 749.

whites and nonwhites."[32] In other words, the plaintiff's burden is now to isolate the specific employment practice that causes the different rates of hiring among applicant groups.

As noted above, the Court's prior disparate impact opinions required a demonstration of "business necessity" by the employer to defeat the prima facie case. In *Wards Cove*, however, the Court reexamined the business necessity defense and lowered the burden on employers of justifying the use of particular employment practices by recasting "business necessity" as "business legitimacy." Stated the Court:

> the dispositive issue is whether a challenged practice serves, in a significant way, the legitimate employment goals of the employer. The touchstone of this inquiry is a reasoned review of the employer's justification for his use of the challenged practice. A mere insubstantial justification in this regard will not suffice, because such a low standard of review would permit discrimination to be practiced through the use of spurious, seemingly neutral employment practices. At the same time, though, there is no requirement that the challenged business practice be 'essential' or 'indispensable' to the employer's business for it to pass muster: this degree of scrutiny would be almost impossible for most employers to meet, and would result in a host of evils we have identified above.[33]

Finally, the Court addressed the question of the burden of proof in a disparate impact case. As the plurality had held in Watson v. Ft. Worth Savings and Loan, the majority in *Wards Cove* held that the burden of proof remains with the disparate impact plaintiff at all times. In explaining this holding, the opinion acknowledged that the Court's earlier opinions could be read otherwise, "but to the extent that those cases speak of an employer's 'burden of proof' with respect to a legitimate business justification defense, they should have been understood to mean an employer's production—but not persuasion—burden."[34]

---

[32]Id. at 751.
[33]Id. at 752.
[34]Id. at 753.

The majority opinion thus changed the elements of disparate impact analysis in three ways: first, by barring the use of internal workforce statistical comparisons to establish a prima facie case; second, by requiring plaintiffs to identify the specific employment practice that caused the disparity to exist, and, where such a showing is made, to lower the standard an employer must meet to justify that practice; and third, by placing the burden of proof in a disparate impact case on the plaintiff.

In sum, discrimination claims may be brought under two distinct theories to challenge objective and subjective employment decisions, both of which require the plaintiff to carry the ultimate burden of proof. Whether the employer can rebut the plaintiff's claims is the subject of the next section.

§2.6.3 Employer Defenses

The most frequently used employer defense against a Title VII claim is a rebuttal of the inference that discrimination occurred— in other words, the employer's articulation of a legitimate, nondiscriminatory reason for the personnel action taken. This defense prevailed in the *Wrenn* case discussed in the preceding section. Two other recent cases involving healthcare facilities illustrate the successful use of this defense.

In Logan v. St. Luke's-Roosevelt Hospital,[35] a black former supervisory food service worker established a prima facie case of race discrimination by demonstrating that she was discharged though she had satisfied the normal requirements for her work. The hospital, however, demonstrated that she was fired not because of her race, but because of dissatisfaction with her performance and her poor interpersonal relationships with her subordinates. The plaintiff failed to offer evidence that the hospital's dissatisfaction with her was a pretext for race discrimination. The court noted that such evidence might have included a showing that white employees with similarly poor work records were retained, that a statistical pattern of discrimination

---

[35]636 F. Supp. 226 (S.D.N.Y. 1986).

existed, or that direct expressions of bias had been made; in this case, no such evidence was presented.

In another case, Carlton v. Interfaith Medical Center,[36] a black woman employed by a hospital as a registrar in the outpatient clinic was laid off. She claimed the reason was race discrimination. The employer successfully defended its action by articulating a legitimate nondiscriminatory reason for its action, in this case that the state of New York had mandated massive layoffs as a condition of certifying the hospital's operation; in other words, the layoff decision was motivated not by race but by economics. The court noted that, while this state mandate did not remove the employer's actions from scrutiny, it did place a greater emphasis on the requirement that the plaintiff prove discriminatory intent.

A second defense is one noted in the preceding section, the business necessity defense. Where a plaintiff demonstrates (usually through statistical evidence) that an employer's employment practice has a substantial adverse impact on a protected group, the burden then shifts to the employer to show that the practice has a manifest relationship to the employment in question and is justified by business necessity. Even if the employer successfully demonstrates that the practice is justified by business necessity, the plaintiff may still prevail by showing that other practices would accomplish the employer's objectives without the attendant discriminatory effects.[37]

A "business necessity" has been explained by one court as a discriminatory employment practice that is "necessary to safe and efficient job performance. . . . For a practice to be a 'necessity,' however, it need not be the sine qua non of job performance; indispensability is not the touchstone. Rather, the practice must substantially promote the proficient operation of the business."[38] Another court described the term this way:

---

[36]12 F. Supp. 118 (C.D.N.Y. 1985).

[37]See, e.g., Connecticut v. Teal, 457 U.S. 440, 445-446 (1982); Dothard v. Rawlinson, 433 U.S. 321, 328-329; International Bhd. of Teamsters v. United States, 431 U.S. 324, 335 n.15 (1977); Albemarle Paper Co. v. Moody, 422 U.S. 405, 425 (1975); *Griggs,* 401 U.S. at 430-432 (1971).

[38]Chrisner v. Complete Auto Transit, 645 F.2d 1251, 1262 (6th Cir. 1981).

110

"[T]he practice must be essential, the purpose compelling."[39] Obviously, the business necessity defense is a difficult one to sustain, in that it has been narrowly construed by reviewing courts. Clearly, the challenged employment practice must be more than merely desirable for the employer; it must be essential to the safe and efficient operation of the business.[40]

A third defense, also noted briefly above, is the express provision in Title VII than an employer does not unlawfully discriminate where it can show that a challenged employment practice is a bona fide occupational qualification. Title VII states:

> Notwithstanding any other provision of this subchapter, (1) it shall not be an unlawful employment practice for an employer to hire and employ employees . . . on the basis of . . . religion, sex, or national origin in those certain instances where religion, sex, or national origin is a bona fide occupational qualification reasonably necessary to the normal operation of that particular business or enterprise.[41]

Like the business necessity defense, however, the bfoq exception has been narrowly construed.[42] One case in which the bfoq defense prevailed was Dothard v. Rawlinson,[43] in which

---

[39]Williams v. Colorado Springs School Dist., 641 F.2d 335, 342 (10th Cir. 1981).

[40]Robinson v. Lorillard Corp., 444 F.2d 791 (4th Cir.), cert. denied, 404 U.S. 1006 (1971). One of the few instances in which the business necessity defense prevailed is described in United States v. South Carolina, 445 F. Supp. 1094 (D.S.C. 1977), affd., 434 U.S. 1026 (1978), in which the use of a minimum score requirement on the National Teachers' Examination to make certification and salary decisions was upheld, notwithstanding a disproportionate failure rate among blacks. See also Newman v. Crews, 651 F.2d 222 (4th Cir. 1981). A more recent (but still rare) case in which the business necessity defense prevailed is Chambers v. Omaha Girls Club, 834 F.2d 697 (8th Cir. 1987), in which a girl's club rule requiring employees to act as role models for teenage members justified the termination of a pregnant single woman as a club counselor.

[41]42 U.S.C. §2000e-2(e).

[42]See, e.g., Gunther v. Iowa State Men's Reformatory, 612 F.2d 1079, 1085 (8th Cir.), cert. denied, 446 U.S. 966 (1980).

[43]433 U.S. 321 (1977).

the Supreme Court found that a rule banning women as prison guards at an all-male prison rife with violence was a bfoq. By contrast, the courts have held that sex is not a bfoq allowing airlines to employ only women as flight attendants,[44] and have rejected "customer preference" as a basis to show a discriminatory job requirement is a bfoq.[45]

Another defense also expressly found in the text of Title VII[46] is an exception for employers following the requirements of a bona fide seniority system. In International Brotherhood of Teamsters v. United States,[47] the Supreme Court held that an otherwise neutral seniority system may be maintained under Title VII even though it may perpetuate pre-Title VII discrimination.

In determining whether a seniority system is bona fide, the courts consider a number of factors, including (1) whether the system adversely affects both minority and majority workers; (2) whether the system serves a legitimate business purpose and follows industry practice; (3) whether the system was intentionally created to discriminate; and (4) whether the system is maintained and negotiated free of any illegal purpose.[48]

Finally, depending on the employment status of the plaintiff, a jurisdictional defense may be made by a hospital employer: namely, that a physician with staff privileges is not an "employee" as defined by the Act and thus has no standing to bring a Title VII complaint. The case law indicates that a physician is probably not an employee, but the hospital's conduct in suspending or denying staff privileges may still be a violation of Title VII as an interference with the physician's employment opportunities with other employers, specifically, prospective patients.

The general test to determine whether a physician is an employee for purposes of Title VII is the same one that is used

---

[44]Wilson v. Southwest Airlines Co., 517 F. Supp. 292 (N.D. Tex. 1981).
[45]Fernandez v. Wynn Oil Co., 653 F.2d 1273 (9th Cir. 1981).
[46]42 U.S.C. §2000e-3(h).
[47]431 U.S. 324 (1977).
[48]Pullman-Standard v. Swint, 456 U.S. 273, 279-281 (1982).

with respect to any other individual.[49] The test involves analyzing the "economic realities" of the working relationship in light of "common law principles of agency and the right of the employer to control the employee."[50] The economic reality is the extent to which the worker is economically dependent on the employer, and agency analysis focuses mostly on the employer's control over the individual's work activities. In applying this test to physicians and considering a number of factors, the court in Beverly v. Douglas held that a physician with voluntary staff privileges was not an employee of the hospital, citing the fact that the doctor's practice and office, from which she was compensated directly by the patients, were outside of the hospital.[51]

Knowing whether a physician is an employee of the hospital does not end the inquiry of whether that physician has standing to sue the hospital under Title VII. Assuming that the hospital is an "employer" as defined in Title VII, it is prohibited from discriminating against "any individual" with respect to "employment privileges."[52] The statutory reference is to "individual," and, as some courts explain, nothing in the statute restricts that reference to employees of the employer.[53]

An often-cited case in which an individual was held to have standing to sue a hospital under Title VII is Sibley Memorial Hospital v. Wilson.[54] *Sibley* involved a male nurse who sued a hospital for discriminating against him by refusing to refer him to female patients for private duty nursing. Although the nurse was not employed by the hospital, he participated in a referral service that the hospital offered its patients. The court held that the nurse had standing to sue the hospital under Title VII because by discriminatorily refusing to refer him to female patients the

---

[49]Beverly v. Douglas, 591 F. Supp. 1321 (S.D.N.Y. 1984).

[50]*Beverly,* 591 F. Supp. at 1326; Mares v. Marsh, 777 F.2d 1066 (5th Cir. 1985).

[51]*Beverly,* 591 F. Supp. at 1328 (S.D.N.Y. 1984).

[52]41 U.S.C. §2000e(2)(a)(1).

[53]See, e.g., Doe on behalf of Doe v. St. Joseph's Hosp., 788 F.2d 411 (7th Cir. 1986).

[54]488 F.2d 1338 (D.C. Cir. 1973).

hospital interfered with his prospective employment by those patients. The court explained that to permit the hospital to interfere with an individual's employment by another employer in a manner that it could not with regard to employment in its own service would be to "condone continued use of the very criteria for employment that Congress has prohibited."[55]

By contrast, in Beverly v. Douglas, discussed above, the court held that denial or suspension of staff privileges does not interfere with the physician's employment opportunities because the relationship of physician to patient is not one of employment.[56] Rather, the court concluded, the doctor-patient relationship is one of independent contract. The physician, therefore, lacked standing under Title VII because the link between the hospital's conduct and an employment relationship was missing.

§2.6.4 The Procedure for Resolution of Discrimination Complaints

Discrimination charges are filed with the EEOC. The time limits for filing charges vary depending on whether there exists a state fair employment practices law. States with such laws, under which a state or local agency is designated to receive discrimination charges, are called "deferral" states, so called because the

---

[55]Id. at 1341. Some courts follow the Sibley reasoning and hold that a physician does have standing under Title VII. See, e.g., Mitchell v. Frank R. Howard Memorial Hosp., 47 FEP Cases 954 (9th Cir. 1988); Diggs v. Harris Hospital-Methodist, 847 F.2d 270 (5th Cir. 1988); Doe on behalf of Doe v. St. Joseph's Hosp. 788 F.2d 411 (7th Cir. 1986); Gomez v. Alexian Bros. Hosp., 698 F.2d 1019 (9th Cir. 1983); Pao v. Holy Redeemer Hosp., 547 F. Supp. 484 (E.D. Pa. 1982). These courts reason that by engaging in discriminatory conduct affecting a physician's staff privileges a hospital deprives the physician of prospective patients desiring the resources of that hospital. These prospective patients are the physician's "ultimate employers," Pao, 547 F. Supp. at 494, and the hospital's conduct interferes with the physician's employment opportunities in violation of Title VII. See, e.g., Gomez v. Alexian Bros. Hosp., 698 F.2d 1019 (9th Cir. 1983).

[56]Beverly, 591 F. Supp. at 1328. See also Diggs v. Harris Hospital-Methodist, 847 F.2d 270 (5th Cir. 1988).

EEOC must defer processing of the charge until the state entity has had an opportunity to resolve the matter. In states without such a law, a plaintiff must file a charge with the EEOC within 180 days of the alleged violation. In deferral agency states, a plaintiff ostensibly has 300 days to file with the EEOC; however, because the EEOC will not process a charge or consider it filed until the deferral agency has had 60 days to act on the matter, the plaintiff must in fact file the charge with the EEOC within 240 days of the alleged violation to ensure it is considered timely filed.[57]

The requirement that charges be timely filed is not a jurisdictional prerequisite to federal court suits; thus, it may be tolled or waived in appropriate circumstances, such as reliance by a plaintiff on false information from EEOC officials as to applicable time periods.[58]

Within 10 days of receipt of a charge, the EEOC sends written notification to the facility alleged to have discriminated (termed the respondent) and begins its investigation. The EEOC official handling the charge will typically meet with the charging party and representatives of the employer to examine any relevant documents and to take written statements of each side's position. In investigating the charge, the EEOC has broad authority to examine an employer's personnel practices, limited only by the requirement that the information be relevant to the charge.

At the conclusion of the investigation, the EEOC determines whether there is reasonable cause to believe that discrimination has occurred. The parties to the charge (the complainant employee, or applicant, and the respondent employer) are given an opportunity to resolve the matter and to execute a conciliation agreement. The agreement may simply require the reversal of an earlier employer personnel decision, such as a disciplinary

[57] 42 U.S.C. §2000(e)(5)(e) sets forth the time limits for filing charges. The 240-day limitation is explained in Mohasco Corp. v. Silver, 447 U.S. 807, 815-817 (1980).
[58] Zipes v. Trans World Airlines, 455 U.S. 385, 393 (1982); Delaware State College v. Ricks, 449 U.S. 250 (1980).

action, or may go further and prescribe affirmative action to be taken by the employer.

If efforts at conciliation fail, the EEOC provides notice to the charging party of his or her right to bring suit in federal or state court within 90 days of receipt of the notice.[59] Failure of a charging party to timely bring suit will result in dismissal of the case.

§2.6.5 Sex Discrimination

A healthcare facility may encounter Title VII sex discrimination claims of three general types: (1) disparate treatment or disparate impact claims (see §§2.6.1 and 2.6.2); (2) pregnancy discrimination claims (see §2.6.6); and (3) sexual harassment claims (see §2.6.7).

The same two theories of discrimination (disparate treatment and disparate impact) described in §§2.6.1 and 2.6.2 may be used to prove sex discrimination. Like race discrimination claims, a plaintiff claiming sex discrimination must establish a prima facie case; likewise, an employer may rebut the inference of sex discrimination by articulating a legitimate, nondiscriminatory reason for its personnel action. If the plaintiff cannot undercut that reason by showing it to be a pretext, the employer's decision will stand. Two recent cases illustrate the application of Title VII disparate treatment theory to sex discrimination claims.

In Ross v. William Beaumont Hospital,[60] the plaintiff, a female surgeon, alleged that her staff privileges were terminated on the basis of sex. Her prima facie case showed that in the history of the hospital, only two doctors had ever been placed on probation because of their behavior, and that both were women. She alleged that her discipline was attributable to a sexist attitude on the part of the hospital director. The employer rebutted by showing that the decision to terminate her staff privileges was not based on her sex, but rather on demonstrated

---

[59]42 U.S.C. §§2000e-5(f)(1), (3).
[60]678 F. Supp. (E.D. Mich. 1988).

instances of disruptive behavior by the female surgeon toward patients, nurses, and other physicians. The court found the employer credible and the infractions well-documented, and noted that it was not its role to intrude on the sound managerial judgment of the hospital, even if that judgment was subjective in nature.

Similarly, in Mousavi v. Beebe Hospital of Sussex County[61] a female neurologist claimed that her failure to be hired was attributable to sex discrimination. The employer rebutted her prima facie case by showing that it had hired the male applicant over the plaintiff not because of her sex, but because it sought a full-time neurologist, located in the area, willing to make a "primary commitment" to the hospital—which qualities the male applicant exhibited. By contrast, the plaintiff did not express a willingness to relocate and to make a full-time commitment. The court credited the employer's explanation as a legitimate, nondiscriminatory reason for its hiring decision.

§2.6.6 Pregnancy Discrimination

A second type of sex discrimination charge involves an allegation that a healthcare facility violated the Pregnancy Discrimination Act, a 1978 amendment to Title VII. With the passage of this Act, Congress overruled a 1976 ruling by the Supreme Court[62] that Title VII did not extend its prohibitions to discrimination on the basis of pregnancy; under the Act, discrimination on the basis of pregnancy is discrimination on the basis of sex. Two cases illustrating the application of the pregnancy discrimination amendment follow.

The first case, Hayes v. Shelby Memorial Hospital,[63] concerned a hospital x-ray technician who was fired after she informed her supervisor that she was pregnant. The court held the hospital violated the Pregnancy Discrimination Act, since

---

[61]674 F. Supp. 145 (D. Del. 1987).
[62]General Electric Co. v. Gilbert, 429 U.S. 125 (1976).
[63]726 F.2d 1543 (11th Cir. 1984).

firing a woman because she is pregnant is discriminatory on its face. The hospital argued the bfoq defense, asserting that the risk of harm to the fetus justified its discriminatory action. The court rejected the employer's argument, holding that when a policy designed to protect employee offspring from workplace hazards proves facially discriminatory, there is no bfoq defense unless the employer shows a direct relationship between the policy and the actual ability of a pregnant or fertile female to perform her job.[64]

A second case, Maddox v. Grandview Care Center,[65] held that a healthcare facility's maternity leave policy was facially discriminatory in that it limited maternity leave to a maximum of three months, while leave for all other illnesses as well as temporary disabilities was allowed for up to six months. Thus, the forced resignation of a nurse's aide who requested, at her doctor's advice, a six month's leave of absence was a violation of the Act.[66]

Healthcare employers should analyze their policies concerning maternity leave and employee assignment to determine whether they are risking a possible violation of the Pregnancy Discrimination Act. The key is to analyze the case using the same sex discrimination theories discussed in §2.6.5 and to consider whether any affirmative defense is likely to prevail.

§2.6.7 Sexual Harassment

In addition to disparate treatment or disparate impact sex discrimination and pregnancy discrimination, employees may allege a third type of sex discrimination: sexual harassment.

Recall that Title VII prohibits discrimination "against any

---

[64]But cf. UAW v. Johnson Controls, 886 F.2d 871 (7th Cir. 1989), cert. granted, 110 S. Ct. 1522, 108 L. Ed. 2d 762 (1990); Wright v. Olin Corp., 697 F.2d 1172 (4th Cir. 1982).

[65]780 F.2d 987 (11th Cir. 1986).

[66]A similar result is found in Zuniga v. Kleberg County Hosp., 692 F.2d 986 (5th Cir. 1982).

individual with respect to . . . compensation, terms, conditions, or privileges of employment because of such individual's . . . sex."[67] Like the pregnancy discrimination question, it was not initially clear that claims of sexual harassment could be brought under Title VII. Beginning with the case of Barnes v. Costle,[68] however, many federal courts ruled that Title VII's prohibition of sex discrimination included discrimination in the form of sexual harassment.[69] Following these initial court rulings, the Equal Employment Opportunity Commission issued guidelines to employers in 1980 defining sexual harassment as one type of sex discrimination prohibited by Title VII.[70] According to the EEOC:

> Unwelcome sexual advances, requests for sexual favors, and other verbal or physical conduct of a sexual nature constitute sexual harassment when (1) submission to such conduct is made either explicitly or implicitly a term or condition of an individual's employment, (2) submission to or rejection of such conduct by an individual is used as the basis for employment decisions affecting such individual, or (3) such conduct has the purpose or effect of unreasonably interfering with an individual's work performance or creating an intimidating, hostile, or offensive working environment.

It is now well-settled that sexual harassment, although not specifically prohibited as an unlawful employment practice in Title VII, may be challenged as a violation of that Act. There are two types of sexual harassment cases that may be brought under Title VII: "quid pro quo" claims and "hostile environment" claims. These are discussed in turn below.

The courts refer to cases in which an employee claims she

---

[67]42 U.S.C. §2000e-3(a)(1).

[68]561 F.2d 983 (D.C. Cir. 1977).

[69]Id. at 995. See also Miller v. Bank of Am., 600 F.2d 211 (9th Cir. 1979); Garber v. Saxon Business Prod., 552 F.2d 1032 (4th Cir. 1977) (per curiam); Tompkins v. Public Serv. Electric & Gas Co., 568 F.2d 1044 (3d Cir. 1977).

[70]EEOC Regs., 29 C.F.R. §1604.11(a).

was denied a tangible economic benefit, such as a promotion or salary increase, because of her refusal to succumb to an unwanted sexual relationship as "quid pro quo" cases. A quid pro quo is a trade of one valuable thing for another. In this instance, the employee is either rewarded for her cooperation or punished for her refusal to trade sexual favors for job benefits. These are the most common types of sexual harassment cases. The case of Henson v. City of Dundee[71] is illustrative.

Barbara Henson was a dispatcher in a city police department. She alleged in her Title VII claim that, among other violations, she was denied permission to attend a police academy because of her refusal to have a sexual relationship with her supervisor. In evaluating her claim, the court described four elements necessary to prove a quid pro quo case.[72]

First, the employee must belong to a protected group. Because Title VII prohibits discrimination against either sex, this requirement is automatically satisfied.

Second, the employee must show that she was subjected to unwelcome sexual harassment. In defining unwelcome sexual harassment, the court noted with approval the EEOC guidelines, adding that the conduct in question must be "unwelcome in the sense that the employee did not solicit or incite it, and in the sense that the employee regarded the conduct as undesirable or offensive."[73]

Third, the harassment complained of must have been based on sex. That is, the employee must show that but for her sex, she would not have been subjected to the harassment. Of course, the easiest means of proof of this element is to show that the offending supervisor, if male, treated only females in the offending manner.

Fourth, the employee's reaction to the harassment must have affected some tangible aspect of the employee's terms of employment. The employee must show that she was deprived of a job benefit (here, opportunity for training at the police

---

[71]682 F.2d 897 (11th Cir. 1982).
[72]Id. at 909.
[73]Id. at 903.

academy) to which she was otherwise entitled because of her refusal to tolerate the harassment or to succumb to unwanted advances.

If an employee proves all four elements of a quid pro quo case, the healthcare facility may be held liable for the acts of the offending supervisor.

Further, an employee may be able to recover damages for sexual harassment even without showing the loss of a tangible job benefit. In the Supreme Court's only decision concerning sexual harassment, Meritor Savings Bank v. Vinson,[74] the Court addressed the question of the circumstances under which an employer could be found liable for the existence of a "hostile environment."

Mechelle Vinson was an employee of a Washington, D.C. bank who alleged that she was required to submit to the sexual demands of her supervisor or risk losing her job. Her supervisor denied the existence of any sexual relationship, and the lower court found in favor of the bank. On appeal, the Court of Appeals for the District of Columbia reversed the lower court, finding that Vinson's allegation that she was required to participate in an involuntary sexual relationship constituted a hostile environment claim under Title VII. The Supreme Court agreed, and ruled that an employee states a claim of sexual harassment by proving the existence of a hostile or abusive work environment. The Court remanded the case to the district court so that further evidence on the question of the existence of a hostile environment could be heard.

The Court cited with approval the EEOC definition of a hostile environment noted above. The court also relied in part on the language of the court in *Henson:*

> Sexual harassment which creates a hostile or offensive environment for members of one sex is every bit the arbitrary barrier to sexual equality at the workplace that racial harassment is to racial equality. Surely, a requirement that a man or woman run a gauntlet of sexual abuse in return for the privilege of being

---

[74]477 U.S. 57 (1986).

allowed to work and make a living can be as demeaning and disconcerting as the harshest of racial epithets.[75]

The Court recognized, however, that not all inappropriate conduct that may occur in the workplace constitutes harassment. Rather, the Court ruled, the sexual harassment must be sufficiently severe or pervasive as to alter the conditions of the victim's employment, thus creating an abusive workplace environment. In Mechelle Vinson's case, sufficient allegations of the existence of an abusive workplace environment were shown. Significantly, Ms. Vinson did not have to quit or be fired or show any other economic effect on her employment to state a claim of sexual harassment; the Court held that the adverse psychological effects of the workplace environment were actionable.

Unlike the court of appeals, however, the Court rejected the view that an employer should be held automatically liable for the acts of its supervisors in creating a hostile environment. Although the Court declined the opportunity to declare a definitive rule on employer liability, it did rule that the lower courts should look to principles from the law of agency for guidance—that is, ask whether the circumstances of the case suggest that the individual supervisor was acting on behalf of the employer, or acting purely as an individual whose conduct cannot be fairly attributed to his employer. The Court determined that Title VII should be construed to place some limits on the acts of employees for which employers are to be held responsible, but noted that absence of notice to an employer that harassment is taking place does not necessarily protect that employer from liability. In other words, a defense asserted by an employer that it simply did not know the harassment was taking place would not insulate it when the harassment occurred in the open and co-workers and supervisors knew of it, yet no one in management moved to stop it. By contrast, an employer might avoid liability when the harassment took place in such a manner that no one but the two parties involved would be aware of it (for

---

[75]Id. at 67, citing Henson v. Dundee, 682 F.2d 897, 902 (11th Cir. 1982).

example, where a supervisor made suggestive remarks to an employee in the privacy of his office) and, on discovery by another manager that the harassment was occurring, the employer disciplined the offending supervisor immediately.

In sum, Title VII enables an employee to bring two different types of claims of sexual harassment: the quid pro quo claim, in which actual economic loss is demonstrated, and the hostile environment claim, in which the purely psychological aspects of the workplace may be challenged.[76] How, then, may a healthcare facility reduce its liability for sexual harassment claims?

Obviously, no employer can guarantee that its employees will not engage in sexual harassment. But a healthcare facility *can* take steps to show that such harassment is not consistent with its policies or practices and thus reduce the chances that a court attributes the harassment to the employer.

First, the facility should develop and publicize a strong policy statement on sexual harassment, indicating that harassment in any form will not be tolerated and may lead to dismissal of the offenders. Given the acceptance by the courts of the EEOC's definition of sexual harassment and the difficulty of formulating a clear definition of what constitutes such conduct, it is suggested that an employer simply incorporate the EEOC definition noted above. The policy should be posted on all official bulletin boards and reviewed in orientation sessions for new employees. In this way, the facility is officially on record as opposing sexual harassment.

Second, training should be provided. The existence of a policy and adherence to it are sometimes two different things. The facility should train all supervisors and employees on sexual harassment to help them understand what conduct is prohibited

---

[76]But note that Title VII's ban on sex discrimination does not include sexual liaisons; rather, it is limited to membership in a class delineated by gender. Thus, Title VII was not violated when a male administrator of a hospital respiratory therapy department created certain requirements for a supervisory position that excluded male staff therapists from the position so as to favor a woman with whom the official was engaged in a romantic relationship. DeCintio v. Westchester County Medical Center, 821 F.2d 111 (2d Cir. 1986), cert. denied, 44 FEP 1672 (1987).

and to increase their understanding of the possible legal conse-quences of harassment.

Third, the healthcare facility should review its grievance procedure and, where necessary, revise it to include complaints of sexual harassment. It is important that the grievance procedure allow an employee alleging sexual harassment to bypass the immediate supervisor if that individual is the alleged offender. In *Vinson,* the employer argued that Ms. Vinson's claim of harassment should be dismissed because she failed to file a grievance under the bank's grievance procedure. But as the Supreme Court noted, since the grievance procedure required Ms. Vinson to file her complaint with her supervisor—the alleged perpetrator of the harassment—this failure was not surprising. The Court stated that such an argument would be "substantially stronger if [the employer's] procedures were better calculated to encourage victims of harassment to come for-ward."[77] Thus, it is in the employer's interest to revise its grievance procedure (or perhaps establish a completely separate procedure) to encourage those who suffer harassment to come forward.

§2.7 The Civil Rights Acts of 1866 and 1871

After the Civil War, Congress passed two civil rights enforcement statutes to give effect to the Thirteenth, Fourteenth, and Fifteenth Amendments. These acts, codified at §1981 and §1983 of Title 42 of the U.S. Code, have been used by plaintiffs to bring claims of discrimination in employment separate and apart from the Title VII claims discussed in §2.6. A brief review of the scope of these Acts is set forth below.

§2.7.1 The Civil Rights Act of 1866

The Civil Rights Act of 1866 is found at 42 U.S.C. §1981.[1] It provides that "all persons . . . shall have the same right . . .

---

[77]*Meritor,* 477 U.S. at 73.

§2.7 [1]The primary purpose of the Civil Rights Act of 1866 was to provide

to make and enforce contracts . . . as is enjoyed by white citizens." The effect of this language is to allow a plaintiff to seek redress against a governmental or private employer for discrimination in employment on the basis of race or national origin.[2] How, then, do these claims differ from Title VII actions?

One critical distinction between §1981 claims and Title VII claims is that §1981 claims must prove intent to discriminate. In General Building Contractors Association v. Pennsylvania,[3] the Supreme Court held that an employer could not be held liable for discrimination merely because the construction industry unions through whom hiring referrals were made did not refer black applicants. Rather, stated the Court, proof of discriminatory intent by the employer is required to establish liability. Thus, the disparate impact theory discussed in §2.6.2 has no applicability to a §1981 claim.

A second critical distinction between §1981 claims and Title VII suits is that a plaintiff has a much longer period of time in which to bring a claim under §1981. In Johnson v. Railway Express Agency,[4] the Supreme Court held that suits filed under §1981 are not governed by the same procedural requirements of Title VII claims, but are governed instead by state statutes of limitation governing similar actions. In Goodman v. Lukens

---

an enforcement mechanism for the Thirteenth Amendment generally as well as to outlaw the "Black Codes" enacted by the southern states after the war. See B. Schwartz, From Confederation to Nation: The American Constitution 1835-1877 191 (1973). The Supreme Court held in Runyon v. McCrary, 427 U.S. 160 (1976), that the Civil Rights Act of 1866 applied to private businesses as well as government employers. In Patterson v. McLean Credit Union, 109 S. Ct. 2363, 105 L. Ed. 2d 132 (1989), the Court held that, although §1981 applied to private employers, it did not provide a cause of action for racial harassment or breach of contract.

[2]In St. Francis College v. Al-Khazraji, 481 U.S. 604 (1987), and Shaare Tefila Congregation v. Cobb, 481 U.S. 615 (1987), the Supreme Court held that §1981 claims were not limited to race discrimination. Rather, the statute protects those who are subjected to intentional discrimination solely because of their ancestry or ethnic characteristics, such as Arabs or Jews.

[3]458 U.S. 375 (1982).

[4]421 U.S. 454 (1975).

Steel Co.,[5] the Court clarified its ruling in *Johnson* to specify that the appropriate state statute of limitations for timely filing of §1981 claims is the one governing personal injury actions (one to three years).

A third critical distinction between the two statutes is that a plaintiff who prevails under a §1981 claim may be awarded punitive damages and payment for pain and suffering. Such damages are unavailable under Title VII.

Finally, it should be noted that §1981 has no applicability to claims of discrimination based on sex or religion.[6] Although the courts have taken a broad view of what constitutes an allowable claim for discrimination based on race or national origin, to allow sex or religion discrimination claims under §1981 would be contrary to the intent of Congress at the time the statute was enacted.[7]

Of course, where an employee has filed and lost a Title VII claim, the employee may not relitigate the claim as a §1981 action.[8]

§2.7.2 The Civil Rights Act of 1871

The Civil Rights Act of 1871 is found at 42 U.S.C. §1983. The Act provides:

> Every person who, under color of any statute, ordinance, regulation, custom or usage, of any State or Territory, subjects, or causes to be subjected, any citizen of the United States or other person within the jurisdiction thereof to the deprivation of any rights, privileges or immunities secured by the Constitution and

---

[5]482 U.S. 656 (1987).

[6]Runyon v. McCrary, 427 U.S. 160, 167 (1976).

[7]See e.g., Bobo v. ITT, Continental Baking Co., 27 FEP Cases 502 (5th Cir. 1981).

[8]See, e.g., Nanavati v. Tomlin Memorial Hosp., 47 FEP Cases 1126, 1136 (3d Cir. 1988) (discharged physician's discrimination claim under §1981 barred as res judicata where previous discrimination complaint failed).

laws, shall be liable to the party injured in an action at law, suit in equity, or other proper proceeding for redress.

Note one key difference between this Act and the Civil Rights Act of 1866: §1983 only applies to persons acting "under color of" state law. In other words, purely private conduct is not actionable under this statute; only actions taken by government entities, such as a county hospital, are covered.

The Supreme Court described §1983 as intended "to interpose the federal courts between the States and the people, as guardians of the people's federal rights."[9] Section 1983 does not provide an independent source of rights, however; it is a vehicle by which one can challenge an action taken by a local government entity[10] for the alleged violation of a right protected under the U.S. Constitution or a federal statute.

Local government entities may be sued under §1983 for deprivation of constitutional or federal rights. In order to bring suit, however, the plaintiff must show that the deprivations were caused by an established government custom or by a "policy statement, ordinance, regulation, or decision officially adopted and promulgated by the body's officers."[11] Thus, where a municipal or county healthcare facility acts in such a way as to cause the plaintiff to be subjected to a deprivation of constitutional or federal rights, either by formal governing board action or by the policy decisions or upper-level administrators, then §1983 liability may be found.

The same procedural and substantive distinctions between Title VII and §1981 discussed in §2.7.1 can be drawn between Title VII and §1983 as well. Thus, §1983 claims involving Fourteenth Amendment issues require proof of intent to discriminate, may be brought under the applicable state statute of limitations, and may entitle the successful plaintiff to both

---

[9]Mitchum v. Foster, 405 U.S. 225, 242 (1972).

[10]The Supreme Court held in Will v. Michigan Dept. of State Police, 105 L. Ed. 2d 45 (1989), that state governments are immune from liability under §1983 because the Eleventh Amendment bars suits against states for damages and equitable relief.

[11]Monell v. New York Dept. of Social Serv., 436 U.S. 658, 694 (1978).

equitable and legal relief. Unlike §1981, however, §1983 claims may encompass allegations of sex discrimination. For example, §1983 may be used to redress claims of sexual harassment.

Section 1983 claims alleging sexual harassment are a recent phenomenon. It is important to remember that a claim of sexual harassment brought under Title VII, as discussed in §2.6.7, may result in liability for the employer even when the employer did not know of the harassment. A key difference between the Title VII and §1983 cases is that, in the latter, the offending acts are presumed to be the individual acts of the supervisor. In other words, a plaintiff in a §1983 action has the burden of proving not only that the harassment occurred, but also that the employer maintained a policy of sexual harassment or, at least, maintained a policy of tolerating sexual harassment.

An illustration of a sexual harassment claim brought under §1983 is Bohen v. City of East Chicago.[12] In that case, an employee named Hortentia Bohen was subjected to repeated attempts at sexual fondling by her supervisor and was forced to leave the office bathroom door open when she occupied it. Repeated complaints by the employee to higher management about her supervisor's behavior met with no response. Bohen alleged that her employer maintained a policy of "deliberate indifference" to claims of sexual harassment, thus depriving her of her constitutional guarantees of equal protection. In other words, she argued, because her supervisors knew of the ongoing sexual harassment and failed to take steps to stop it, the supervisors' indifference was fairly attributable to the city as official policy. Finally, claimed Bohen, because the actions of the supervisors constituted not only the deliberate acts of individuals, but also the policy of the employer, the city itself was liable for damages.

The court agreed with Bohen, ruling that the city did in fact know of and tolerate the sexual harassment. The court noted the failure of Bohen's supervisors to take corrective action:

> In sum, sexual harassment was the general, on-going, and accepted practice at the East Chicago Fire Department, and high-

---

[12]799 F.2d 1180 (7th Cir. 1986).

ranking, supervisory, and management officials responsible for working conditions at the department knew of, tolerated, and participated in the harassment. This satisfies §1983's requirement that the actions complained of be the policy or custom of the state entity.[13]

Thus, a local government healthcare facility may be liable for sexual harassment under §1983 when the practice of sexual harassment can be shown to be the accepted policy or custom of the employer.

§2.8 The Age Discrimination in Employment Act

The Age Discrimination in Employment Act (ADEA)[1] prohibits discrimination on the basis of age for all persons age 40 and over. The ADEA covers all private employers engaged in an industry affecting commerce who have 20 or more employees for each working day in each of 20 or more weeks per year.[2] The Act also covers a state and local government employers[3] and the federal government.[4]

The ADEA is similar to Title VII of the Civil Rights Act of 1964 in that it prohibits discrimination in employment and is enforced by the EEOC. The ADEA differs from Title VII in that

---

[13]Id. at 1189.

§2.8 [1]Pub. L. No. 90-202, 81 Stat. 602, effective June 12, 1968, as amended, 29 U.S.C. §621 et seq. The 1986 amendments to the ADEA redefined the protected class to include all persons aged 40 and above; previously, the protected class was defined as all persons aged 40 to 70. However, persons employed in a "bona fide executive or a high policymaking position" may be required to retire after age 70 if they have held their position for at least two years and are entitled to a pension of at least $44,000 a year. 29 U.S.C. 631(c)(1).

[2]29 U.S.C. §630(a).

[3]29 U.S.C. §630(b)(2); EEOC v. Wyoming, 460 U.S. 226 (1983) (upholding application of the ADEA to state and local governments as constitutional under the Tenth Amendment).

[4]29 U.S.C. §633(a).

plaintiffs under the ADEA have the right to a trial by jury.[5] Like Title VII, ADEA claims may be brought using disparate treatment or disparate impact theories of discrimination.

§2.8.1 Prohibited Practices Under the ADEA

Specifically, the ADEA makes it unlawful for an employer:

> (1) to fail to refuse to hire or to discharge any individual or otherwise to discriminate against any individual with respect to his compensation, terms, conditions, or privileges of employment, because of such individual's age;
>
> (2) to limit, segregate, or classify his employees in any way which would deprive or tend to deprive any individual of employment opportunities or otherwise adversely affect his status as an employee, because of such individual's age; or
>
> (3) to reduce the wage rate of any employee in order to comply with this Act.[6]

§2.8.2 Employer Defenses

The ADEA provides four employer defenses to an age discrimination claim. They are summarized below.

First, the ADEA permits discrimination on the basis of age where age is a "bona fide occupational qualification reasonably necessary to the normal operation of the particular business."[7] As is the case with respect to Title VII cases, however, the bfoq defense has been construed very narrowly by the courts.[8] An employer asserting the bfoq defense must show that the age limitation is reasonably necessary to the essential aspects of the

---

[5] 29 U.S.C. §626(c)(2); Lorillard v. Pons, 434 U.S. 575 (1978).

[6] 29 U.S.C. §623(a).

[7] 29 U.S.C. §623(f)(1).

[8] See, e.g., Marshall v. Westinghouse Elec. Corp., 576 F.2d 588 (5th Cir. 1978); Western Airlines v. Criswell, 472 U.S. 400 (1985).

business, and that it is not feasible to make a case-by-case determination of individual ability to perform the job.[9]

Second, discrimination is permitted where the action is in observance of the terms of a "bona fide seniority system or any bona fide employee benefit plan which is not a subterfuge to avoid the purposes of the Act."[10]

Third, the ADEA permits an employer to take a personnel action based on "reasonable factors other than age."[11] This defense, sometimes referred to as the "rfoa defense," permits the employer to show that a legitimate, nondiscriminatory reason motivated the decision in question (e.g., that the employee was not performing the job properly).

Fourth, the Act allows an employer to discharge or discipline an employee for good cause.[12]

§2.8.3 Proving the ADEA Case

What must a plaintiff show to prevail in an ADEA action? Lovelace v. Sherwin-Williams Co.[13] illustrates an unsuccessful attempt by an employee to prove age discrimination. In 1978, plaintiff Wilbur Lovelace, then 55, was demoted from the position of store manager to salesman for a Sherwin-Williams paint store in Asheville, N.C. The employer had rated his overall performance as "high standard" in 1977. Although the store's profits increased from 1970 to 1974, its profit trend declined for the following four years. Following repeated visits by the district manager and instructions to make operational changes that Lovelace ignored, he was demoted, and a new manager, aged 49, was appointed. Lovelace claimed the demotion was based on age.

To establish a prima facie case, the court required the

[9]*Criswell,* 472 U.S. at 422-423.
[10]29 U.S.C. §623(f)(2).
[11]29 U.S.C. §623(f)(1).
[12]29 U.S.C. §623(f)(3).
[13]681 F.2d 230 (4th Cir. 1982).

plaintiff to show that an employee covered by the Act has suffered an unfavorable employment action by an employer covered by the Act under circumstances in which the employee's age was a determining factor in the sense that, but for his employer's motive to discriminate against him because of his age, he would not have suffered the action.[14] The court explained that a plaintiff may establish the third element of the prima facie case by producing evidence (1) that he was at the time of demotion performing his job at a level that met his employer's legitimate expectations, and (2) following his demotion his employer sought someone else to perform the same work.[15]

In rebutting the prima facie case, the burden of producing evidence on the issue shifts to the defendant, who must "rebut the presumption by producing evidence that the plaintiff was [disfavored] for a legitimate, nondiscriminatory reason."[16] Failure of the defendant to carry this burden of production requires submission of the issue to the jury. On the other hand, where the defendant produces evidence to "destroy the legally mandatory inference,"[17] the effect is to recast the dispositive motivational issue at "a new level of specificity."[18] As a result, the plaintiff once again has the burden of production, and must be given the opportunity to counter the defendant's evidence of the specific reason for the action with evidence that the reason given is "pretextual" or "not the true reason."[19] This new evidence may be designed to directly attack the credibility of the defendant's specific explanation or simply to prove that, as against that specific reason, age is the "more likely" explanation.

In *Lovelace,* the plaintiff established a prima facie case that he was performing his job at a level that met his employer's

----

[14]*Lovelace,* 681 F.2d at 238; Spagnuolo v. Whirlpool Corp., 641 F.2d 1109, 1112 (4th Cir. 1981); Loeb v. Textron, 600 F.2d 1003 (1st Cir. 1979).

[15]*Lovelace,* 681 F.2d at 238; *Loeb,* 600 F.2d at 1014; Smith v. University of N.C., 632 F.2d 316, 332 (4th Cir. 1980).

[16]Texas Dept. of Community Affairs v. Burdine, 450 U.S. 248, 255 (1980).

[17]*Burdine,* 450 U.S. at 255 n.10.

[18]Id.

[19]Id. at 256.

expectations. This presumption is supportable only to the extent that the inference was created by the two-year-old satisfactory performance appraisal. However, the employer successfully rebutted this inference by showing more recent specific instances of failure in performance by the employee, and further showed that the employee had ignored suggested corrective measures. Thus, the court found no ADEA violation.

In this case and in many others,[20] the courts have made it clear that for a plaintiff to prevail in an ADEA case age need not be shown to be *the* determining factor. It is legally sufficient if the plaintiff can prove that age is *a* determining factor.

Numerous age discrimination cases involving healthcare facilities have been litigated applying the burden of proof discussed above, with varying results. In Buckley v. Hospital Corporation of America,[21] a dismissed 62-year-old nurse supervisor prevailed against her employer by introducing evidence that the hospital administrator had voiced a need to recruit younger employees and had referred to the plaintiff as being of "advanced age." By contrast, in Corrigan v. New York University Medical Center,[22] two plaintiffs, aged 51 and 53, who were rejected for orderly positions were unable to show that the employer's decision to hire another applicant was based on age; rather, the employer rebutted the prima facie case by showing these applicants had done poorly in their employment interviews. Similarly, in Snyder v. Washington Hospital Center,[23] a discharged 57-year-old director of public affairs failed to prove her termination was motivated by age when the employer presented evidence to show that a number of complaints about the employee's rudeness and "attitude problems" made her an unsatisfactory employee.

---

[20]See, e.g., Krodel v. Young, 748 F.2d 701 (D.C. Cir. 1984); Monroe v. United Airlines, 736 F.2d 394 (7th Cir. 1984); Fink v. Western Elec. Co., 708 F.2d 909 (4th Cir. 1983).

[21]758 F.2d 1525 (11th Cir. 1985).

[22]606 F. Supp. 345 (S.D.N.Y. 1985).

[23]36 FEP Cases 445 (D.D.C. 1984).

§2.9 Handicap Discrimination

Since the early 1970s, the federal government and 47 of the 50 states[1] have enacted laws prohibiting employment discrimination on the basis of handicapping conditions. The state statutes vary considerably; a description of them is beyond the scope of this chapter. Suffice it to say that most state statutes are modeled on the federal handicap discrimination statute, the Rehabilitation Act of 1973.[2] Because the federal statute is the most common basis for handicap discrimination claims and because similar claims may be brought under most state statutes, this section focuses on the Rehabilitation Act; an employer should, however, also review the applicable state statute to be fully aware of its responsibilities in this area.

§2.9.1 The Rehabilitation Act of 1973

The Rehabilitation Act of 1973 prohibits discrimination in employment against handicapped persons. The Act defines "handicapped person" very broadly to include any person who "(i) has a physical or mental handicap which substantially limits one or more major life activities, (ii) has a record of such an impairment, or (iii) is regarded as having such an impairment."[3] The Act excludes "any individual who is an alcoholic or drug abuser whose current use of alcohol or drugs prevents such individual from performing" her or his job or who constitutes a direct threat to the property or safety of others.[4]

---

§2.9 [1]Fair Employment Practices Manual, 451:102-104 (Bureau of National Affairs, 1988).

[2]Pub. L. No. 93-112, 87 Stat. 394, 29 U.S.C. §§701 et seq.

[3]29 U.S.C. §706. Major life activities are defined by the Department of Labor's Office of Federal Contract Compliance (OFCCP) as "communication, ambulation, selfcare, socialization, education, vocational training, employment, transportation, adapting to housing, etc." 41 C.F.R. §60.741, Appendix A (1981).

[4]29 U.S.C. §706. Cases interpreting this provision include Walker v. Weinberger, 600 F. Supp. 757 (D.D.C. 1985) (dismissal for absences due to

The Act covers recipients of federal contract funds. Specifically, §503 of the Act provides that any person who enters into a contract for more than $2,500 with the federal government for the procurement of personal property and nonpersonal services "shall take affirmative action to employ and advance in employment qualified individuals with handicaps." Section 504 of the Act provides that "no otherwise qualified individual with handicaps . . . shall, solely by reason of his handicap, be excluded from the participation in, be denied the benefits of, or be subjected to discrimination under any program or activity receiving Federal financial assistance."

In 1984, the Supreme Court held that §504 only applies to the specific program of an employer receiving federal funds.[5] With congressional passage of the Civil Rights Restoration Act[6] in 1988, however, the effect of the 1984 ruling was overturned, affirming that the entire corporation or other covered employer is subject to the requirements of the Act, not just the particular subunit of the employer receiving the federal funds.[7] At least one court has held that the Civil Rights Restoration Act should

---

treatment for alcoholism overturned); Davis v. Bucher, 451 F. Supp. 791 (E.D. Pa. 1978) (per se rule requiring rejection of all applicants with drug use history, including those who no longer use drugs, violation of Act); New York City Transit Auth. v. Beazer, 440 U.S. 568 (1978) (refusal to hire methadone users upheld as business necessity in Title VII challenge).

[5]Consolidated Rail Co. v. Darrone, 465 U.S. 624, 636 (1984). The Court similarly held that Title IX of the Education Amendments of 1972 only applied to the particular program or activity receiving federal funds, not the entire educational institution. Grove City College v. Bell, 465 U.S. 555 (1984).

[6]Pub. L. No. 100-259, 102 Stat. 28, 29 U.S.C. §794.

[7]A hospital receiving Medicare and Medicaid payments is a recipient of federal funds and thus covered by the Act. United States v. Baylor Univ. Medical Center, 736 F.2d 1039, 1040-1041 (5th Cir. 1984), cert. denied, 464 U.S. 1040 (1985); Scanlon v. Atascadero State Hosp., 735 F.2d 359 (9th Cir. 1984). A private contractor of services "integral to the operation of a recipient hospital" may also be considered a recipient for purposes of the Act. Frazier v. Northwest Miss. Regional Medical Center Bd. of Trustees, 765 F.2d 1278 (5th Cir. 1985); contra, United States v. Cabrini Medical Center, 639 F.2d 908 (2d Cir. 1981); Eivins v. Adventist Health System/Eastern Inc., 651 F. Supp. 340 (D. Kan. 1987).

be applied retroactively, in that instance to allow a discharged hospital employee to bring his handicap discrimination suit.[8]

The Rehabilitation Act protects "otherwise qualified" persons from discrimination based on handicap. In 1979, the Supreme Court defined an "otherwise qualified" person as "one who is able to meet all of a program's requirements in spite of his handicap."[9] That is, an otherwise qualified person is one who can perform the essential functions of a particular job.[10] The Act requires employers to reasonably accommodate otherwise qualified individuals, as discussed in §2.9.2.

Whether a given individual is an otherwise qualified handicapped person is often a difficult question to answer. Each case is unique and is therefore of limited precedential value. Nonetheless, it is useful to note the wide range of conditions found to constitute handicaps in recent years in order to get a sense of the breadth of the Act's protections. Conditions found to be handicaps include chronic contagious diseases,[11] mental disorders,[12] dyslexia,[13] legal blindness,[14] ankylosing spondylitis (stiffening of the joints),[15] nervous conditions,[16] hypersensitivity to tobacco smoke,[17] former drug addiction,[18] and epilepsy.[19]

---

[8]Leake v. Long Island Jewish Medical Center, 47 FEP 783 (E.D.N.Y. 1988). Section 504 of the Act is enforceable by a private right of action in federal court. For a discussion of the damages available to a successful plaintiff in a §504 action, see Note, Safeguarding Equality for the Handicapped: Compensatory Relief Under Section 504 of the Rehabilitation Act, 1986 Duke L.J. 197 (1986).

[9]Southeastern Community College v. Davis, 442 U.S. 397, 406 (1979).

[10]45 C.F.R. §84.3(k).

[11]School Board of Nassau County v. Arline, 480 U.S. 273 (1987).

[12]Schmidt v. Bell, 33 FEP Cases 839 (E.D. Pa. 1983).

[13]Stutts v. Freeman, 30 FEP Cases 1121 (11th Cir. 1983).

[14]Norcross v. Sneed, 755 F.2d 113 (8th Cir. 1985).

[15]Sisson v. Helms, 751 F.2d 991 (9th Cir.), cert. denied, 106 S. Ct. 137 (1985).

[16]Treadwell v. Alexander, 707 F.2d 474 (11th Cir. 1983).

[17]Vickers v. Veterans Admin., 549 F. Supp. 85 (W.D. Wash. 1982).

[18]Davis v. Bucher, 451 F. Supp. 791 (E.D. Pa. 1978).

[19]Smith v. Administrator of Veterans Affairs, 32 FEP Cases 986 (C.D. Cal. 1983).

§2.9.2 The Americans with Disabilities Act of 1990

The Americans with Disabilities Act of 1990 (42 U.S.C. §§12111 to 12213) was signed into law by the president on July 25, 1990. The act essentially extends the prohibition against handicap discrimination in the Rehabilitation Act of 1973 to private and public employers, including healthcare facilities, that do not receive federal funding.

Title I of the Act, which bars handicap discrimination in employment, is effective for all employers with at least 25 employees as of July 25, 1992; the Act is effective for employers with at 15 employees as of July 25, 1994. The Act prohibits employment discrimination against qualified individuals with disabilities and defines "disabilities" as is now done under the Rehabilitation Act, to include "(A) a physical or mental impairment that substantially limits one or more of the major life activities of such individual; (B) a record of such impairment; or (C) being regarded as having such an impairment."

Employers are required to make reasonable accommodation for otherwise qualified individuals. "Reasonable accommodation" is defined to include making existing facilities used by employees readily accessible to and usable by individuals with disabilities; job restructuring; modifying work schedules; reassigning employees; acquisition or modification of equipment or devices; appropriate adjustment or modification of examinations and training materials; adoption or modification of procedures or protocols; and provision of qualified readers or interpreters.

The Act bars the use of pre-employment physicals unless they are shown to be job-related. Further, physicals may only be required after an offer of employment has been made. However, a job offer may be conditioned on the results of the physical if all employees are required to undergo them and the information obtained is maintained in a confidential manner.

The Act neither requires nor prohibits drug testing. Employers may prohibit the use of drugs and alcohol at the workplace. Most important, the Act excludes from the definition of "handicapped individuals," current illegal drug users and alcoholics who cannot safely perform their jobs. However, a recovered individual, or one who is participating in a rehabilitation program and is not using drugs, is covered by the Act.

The Act is to be enforced by the EEOC under regulations to be promulgated in the next year. Remedies are to be the same as those allowed under Title VII of the Civil Rights Act of 1964.

§2.9.3 The Employer's Duty to Accommodate

As noted above, both the Rehabilitation Act and the Americans with Disabilities Act require employers to make reasonable efforts to accommodate handicapped individuals. If a handicapped person is unable to perform the essential functions of a particular job, then the employer must consider whether reasonable accommodation would enable the person to perform those functions. For example, a healthcare facility could probably make a reasonable accommodation for an otherwise qualified secretary who uses a wheelchair. Accommodation is not reasonable, however, if it requires "a fundamental alteration" of the job or imposes "undue financial and administrative burdens" on the employer.[20] "Where reasonable accommodation does not overcome the effects of a person's handicap, or where reasonable accommodation causes undue hardship to the employer, failure to hire or promote the handicapped person will not be considered discrimination."[21]

A number of cases illustrate the employer's duty to accommodate individuals with handicaps. In Smith v. Administrator of Veterans Affairs,[22] an epileptic nursing assistant was dismissed from his job following two instances in which he blacked out. He sued the Long Beach Veterans Hospital under the Act, claiming that the employer had failed to reasonably accommodate his handicap. The court held that the employee, who was under medication to control his epilepsy, was fully capable of

---

[20]*Southeastern,* 442 U.S. at 410-412.
[21]Id. at 413.
[22]32 FEP Cases 986 (C.D. Cal. 1983).

performing his nursing assistant duties with reasonable accommodation by the hospital, and that the employer had not made such accommodation. The court suggested that such actions as providing additional supervision, administering a blood test to determine whether the employee was taking his medication, or reassigning the employee to a clerical position were reasonable means of accommodating the employee's epilepsy. Similarly, in Carter v. Casa Central,[23] the court found that a reasonable accommodation of a director of nursing with multiple sclerosis would be to allow her to perform her duties without requiring her to stand or walk for prolonged periods.

§2.9.4 Handicap Discrimination and the Employee with AIDS

A complete discussion of handicap discrimination and the employee with AIDS will be found in Chapter 13 of this book, "AIDS and the Healthcare Facility." Thus far, the greatest source of protection for employees with AIDS who suffer adverse employment decisions has been the Rehabilitation Act of 1973. The Americans with Disabilities Act of 1990 will offer additional protection for these employees.

E. Affirmative Action

§2.10 In General

Affirmative action is the deliberate use of race and sex preferences in selection or promotion. Affirmative action may result from an employer's decision to voluntarily adopt an affirmative action plan or from a consent decree or court order requiring its use. Affirmative action plans have been challenged under both Title

---

[23]47 FEP Cases 257 (7th Cir. 1988).

VII of the Civil Rights Act of 1964 and the Constitution; by and large, however, affirmative action as a legal remedy to past discrimination has survived both types of challenge.[1] A brief review of the major affirmative action decisions rendered by the Supreme Court is set forth below.

The first Supreme Court case to examine the affirmative action issue was not decided until 1978, and it did not involve affirmative action in employment. Nonetheless, that case, Regents of the University of California v. Bakke,[2] upheld the principle of affirmative action and stands for the proposition that government may take race into account to remedy past racial injustice, at least where appropriate findings of past discrimination have been made by a court, an administrative agency, or a legislative body. In *Bakke,* the affirmative action taken was to set aside 16 of 100 places in the entering class at the University of California medical school for minority applicants. The Court upheld this practice as not violative of the Constitution's equal protection clause.[3]

In 1979, the Court decided its first affirmative action-in-employment case, United Steelworkers of America v. Weber,[4] in which a white employee sued his employer and his union, challenging a voluntarily adopted job training program that mandated a one-for-one quota for minority employees. The

---

§2.10   [1] The view that affirmative action is alive and well is reflected in a series of recent law review articles on the subject. See, e.g., Schwartz, The 1986 and 1987 Affirmative Action Cases: It's All Over but the Shouting, 86 Mich. L. Rev. 524 (1987); Rutherglen and Ortiz, Affirmative Action Under the Constitution and Title VII: From Confusion to Convergence, 35 UCLA L. Rev. 467 (1988); Selig, Affirmative Action in Employment: The Legacy of a Supreme Court Majority, 63 Indiana L.J. 301 (1988).

[2] 438 U.S. 265 (1978).

[3] As is the case with many of the Supreme Court's opinions on affirmative action, there was no clear majority in *Bakke.* Five justices upheld taking race into account in admissions, but disagreed on the level of scrutiny to be applied to affirmative action and on the constitutionality of the particular practice at issue in the case. See 438 U.S. at 291, 305, 319-320 (Powell, J.); id. at 359, 379 (Brennan, White, Marshall, and Blackmun, JJ., concurring in the judgment in part and dissenting in part); id. at 387, n.7 (White, J.).

[4] 443 U.S. 193 (1979).

Court upheld the program, ruling that Title VII's ban on racial discrimination does not prohibit voluntary affirmative action plans.[5] The Court set forth four criteria to guide employers in adopting affirmative action plans: (1) a showing of prior discrimination should be made; (2) the plan should be reasonably related to remedying the prior discrimination; (3) the plan should not trammel the rights of the majority race workers or serve as a complete bar to their advancement; and (4) the plan should be a temporary measure to eliminate an existing racial imbalance.[6]

The Court next upheld, in Fullilove v. Klutznick,[7] the constitutionality of a federal requirement that recipients of federal funds for public works projects set aside 10 percent of those funds for minority contractors.

In 1984, the Court seemed to retreat from its earlier approval of affirmative action with the issuance of Firefighters Local Union No. 1784 v. Stotts.[8] That decision struck down a lower court's order requiring layoffs of white employees so that a specified level of black employment could be maintained. The Court held that Title VII protects bona fide seniority systems and that it is inappropriate to deny an innocent (white) employee the benefit of his or her seniority in order to provide a class remedy for others.[9] Most significantly, the Court stated that Title VII relief was available "only to those who have been actual victims of illegal discrimination."[10] The U.S. Justice Department reacted by moving to modify over 50 court-approved affirmative action plans by eliminating goals or quotas if persons who were not actual victims of discrimination were marked for preferential treatment. These efforts met with meager success, however, and were abandoned when the Court retreated from the broad implications of *Stotts* just two years later.

In 1986, the Supreme Court decided three affirmative action

---

[5]Id. at 200-208.
[6]Id. at 208.
[7]448 U.S. 448 (1980).
[8]467 U.S. 561 (1984).
[9]Id. at 566-567.
[10]Id. at 580.

cases: Wygant v. Jackson Board of Education,[11] Local 28, Sheet Metal Workers International Association v. EEOC,[12] and Local 93, International Association of Firefighters v. City of Cleveland.[13] In *Wygant,* the Court held that, for a public employer, a voluntary affirmative action plan must comply with the equal protection clause of the Constitution and that an affirmative action plan's requirement that white employees with greater seniority be laid off while black employees with less seniority retain their jobs was unconstitutional. The justification offered for the plan, that black students needed black teachers as role models, was found insufficient to justify layoffs of more senior white teachers. In *Sheet Metal Workers,* the Court held that affirmative race-conscious relief may be ordered by a court under Title VII to remedy past discrimination even if it benefits individuals who were not themselves identified victims of past discrimination. Similarly, in *Firefighters,* the Court held that Title VII does not prohibit parties from entering into consent decrees that benefit individuals who are not actual victims of discrimination. The effect of *Sheet Metal Workers* and *Firefighters,* then, was to undercut the apparent limitation of the 1984 *Stotts* case: that only actual victims of discrimination are entitled to relief.

In 1987, the Court rendered two far-reaching affirmative action decisions. In U.S. v. Paradise,[14] the Court held that a one-black-for-one-white promotion requirement is permissible under the equal protection clause where justified because of pervasive, systematic, and obstinate discriminatory practices on the part of the employer (in this case, the Alabama Department of Public Safety). Thus, in appropriate circumstances, the use of quotas is permissible. And in Johnson v. Transportation Agency, Santa Clara County,[15] the Court held that a public employer's voluntary affirmative action plan that did not establish quotas but did allow consideration of sex as one factor when evaluating

---

[11]476 U.S. 267 (1986).
[12]478 U.S. 421 (1986).
[13]478 U.S. 501 (1986).
[14]480 U.S. 149 (1987).
[15]480 U.S. 616 (1987).

qualified job applicants for positions in which women were underrepresented was lawful under Title VII. The sex-conscious relief was found justified by the existence of a manifest imbalance reflected in sex-segregated job categories and by the fact that the rights of innocent third parties were not unnecessarily trammeled, nor were they barred from further advancement. Significantly, the Court in *Johnson* added that it is not necessary that a public employer using an affirmative action plan in which race or sex is one factor in the decision to promote or hire prove or admit that it has illegally discriminated in past employment decisions.

In 1989, the Supreme Court decided two cases that undercut the previous vitality of affirmative action in employment. In J. A. Croson Company v. City of Richmond,[16] the Court struck down a minority contractor set-aside program of the city of Richmond as violative of the equal protection clause. The Court held that a public entity is subject to strict scrutiny under the Constitution in taking race-based action and that the action taken must be narrowly tailored to achieve a compelling government interest. The city had failed to demonstrate either that discrimination in building contracting was present or that the minority set-aside was necessary to achieve any compelling interest in overcoming past discrimination. And, in Martin v. Wilks,[17] the Court held that a collateral attack by white employees could be allowed against a consent degree establishing an affirmative action plan where those employees chose not to intervene in the original litigation.

In sum, then, these are the "rules" for voluntary affirmative action plans:

1. Plans with race or sex preferences are lawful under Title VII if they are designed to correct manifest imbalances reflecting underrepresentation of minority groups in traditionally segregated job categories.

2. It is not necessary that a public employer admit past discrimination in order to adopt an affirmative action plan.

---

[16]109 S. Ct. 706 (1989).
[17]109 S. Ct. 2180 (1989).

However, mere "societal discrimination" or the "role model" theory will not support race-conscious plans.

3. Race or sex may be considered as one factor in a decision to promote or hire; however, all candidates, irrespective of race or sex, must be qualified.

4. The plan may not unnecessarily trammel the rights of white or male employees or applicants; nor may it create an absolute bar to their advancement.

5. Such plans are temporary, and are aimed only at attaining a balanced workforce, not maintaining a permanent race or sex balance.

Similarly, the "rules" for court-ordered affirmative action plans are:

1. Court-ordered plans may benefit individuals who prove they are victims of discrimination.

2. Courts may order plans that benefit individuals who were not victims of past discrimination. Remedies are prospective only, and must be necessary to remedy the employer's past discrimination.

3. Title VII does not prohibit entry of consent decrees that may benefit individuals who were not actual victims of discrimination. However, the consent decrees may later be challenged by those affected by their administration, even though they knew of the possible ramifications of the consent decree but chose not to be parties to the original litigation.

§2.11 Affirmative Action Requirements of Federal Contracts

Title VII, as interpreted by the courts, sets forth certain rules for affirmative action, noted above. A hospital or other healthcare facility that enters into contracts with the federal government may be required to follow other affirmative action rules as well. These rules, as promulgated by the U.S. Department of Labor's Office of Federal Contract Compliance (OFCCP), set forth certain affirmative action requirements, described below.

Executive Order 11,246, signed by President Lyndon Johnson in 1965, establishes a requirement that government contractors and subcontractors "take affirmative action to ensure that applicants are employed, and that employees are treated during employment, without regard to their race, color, religion, sex, or national origin."[1] Unlike Title VII, which merely prohibits employers from discrimination and allows voluntary adoption of affirmative action plans, E.O. 11,246 requires employers to take affirmative action to enhance the employment opportunities of minorities and women.

Under OFCCP regulations,[2] a prime nonconstruction contractor or subcontractor with 50 or more employees and a contract of at least $50,000 must file a written affirmative action plan, which must include goals and timetables. Under the plan, the contractor agrees to make a good-faith effort to correct any underrepresentation of protected groups in its workforce, including special outreach efforts as part of its recruitment and selection practices.

The current OFCCP regulations have been in effect since 1980. Substantial changes were proposed by the Reagan administration in April 1981 to increase the threshold dollar limit triggering the affirmative action requirements, but the effective date of those changes was postponed indefinitely in August 1981. A full discussion of the OFCCP regulations is beyond the scope of this chapter, but healthcare facilities are advised to check the current regulatory requirements if contemplating execution of a federal contract.

F. Constitutional Protection of Employees of Public Hospitals

§2.12 The Dual Role of Government as Employer

Public healthcare facilities are like their private sector counterparts in many respects. Both provide patient care, both are

---

§2.11 [1]E.O. 11246 §202, as amended.
[2]41 C.F.R. pt. 60.

subject to federal and state nondiscrimination statutes, and both have their share of personnel problems. But the public healthcare facility, as a governmental entity, has additional responsibilities: it deals with its individuals in the capacity of employer (to its employees) *and* in the capacity of "the government" (to citizens). In other words, because a public healthcare facility is both an employer and a governmental entity, it must ensure that certain constitutional rights enjoyed by its employees as citizens are respected. In a nutshell, the meaning of the dual role of the government as employer is simply this: the employer is still the government; and employees may not be required to leave their constitutional rights at the workplace door merely because they work for a public employer. The scope of these rights is summarized in this section.

§2.13 First Amendment Free Speech Rights

For the public healthcare employer seeking to determine the exact scope of the free speech rights of its employees, no bright line emerges from the Supreme Court's rulings either to define speech on a matter of public concern or to predict how the balancing test will be struck in a particular circumstance. A brief review of the Court's rulings in this area follows; the public healthcare facility is advised, however, to proceed carefully when determining whether an employee's speech should be the basis for disciplinary action.

It was not until 1968, in Pickering v. Board of Education,[1]

---

§2.13 [1]391 U.S. 563 (1968). *Pickering* evolved from a series of cases involving the freedom of association under the First Amendment. Many states in the 1950s and 1960s had requirements that public school teachers take loyalty oaths. These oaths were challenged as unconstitutional, beginning with Weiman v. Updegraff, 344 U.S. 183 (1952). In *Weiman,* a loyalty oath that excluded from public employment persons who had innocent, as opposed to knowing, association with certain subversive associations was held to constitute "an assertion of arbitrary power" by the state. 344 U.S. at 191. In Shelton v. Tucker, 363 U.S. 479 (1960), a school teacher refused to sign an affidavit listing organizations to which he belonged. The *Shelton* Court held that a

that the Supreme Court squarely recognized the free speech right of public employees. In *Pickering*, a public school teacher was dismissed for writing a letter to the local newspaper criticizing the school board and the superintendent of schools for funding athletic programs at the expense of academic excellence.[2] The Court held that firing the school teacher was an impermissible infringement of his free speech right, rejecting the notion that "teachers may constitutionally be compelled to relinquish the First Amendment rights they would otherwise enjoy as citizens to comment on matters of public interest."[3] Instead, the Court framed the proper inquiry as follows: "The problem in any case is to arrive at a balance between the interests of the teacher, as a citizen, in commenting upon matters of public concern and the interest of the State, as an employer,

---

state's indiscriminate requirement that membership be disclosed in any and all organizations was an abuse of due process. 364 U.S. at 490. In Cramp v. Board of Public Instruction, 368 U.S. 278 (1961), the Court invalidated a requirement that school teachers sign a statement that they had never aided or supported the communist party as too vague to constitutionally warrant termination for refusal to sign. Finally, in Keyishian v. Board of Regents, 385 U.S. 589 (1967), faculty members of the State University of New York successfully argued that the New York statute requiring them to sign a loyalty oath was an unconstitutional infringement on their First Amendment right of association.

[2]*Pickering*, 391 U.S. at 566.

[3]Id. at 568. Note that the First Amendment right recognized by *Pickering* is the citizen's right to comment on matters of public interest; private speech— that is, speech that does not implicate the relationship of the government to the citizen—does not rise to the level of protected speech recognized in *Pickering*. The subsequent decisions of the Supreme Court proceed from this premise. Thus, there are three categories of speech: first, protected speech, implicating important First Amendment interests; second, routine speech, which, although perfectly permissible, constitutes no more than common conversations among persons on subjects of private interest having no First Amendment implications (see, e.g., Yoggerst v. Hedges, 739 F.2d 293 (7th Cir. 1984) (public employee's comment to a co-worker concerning rumor that agency director had been fired, "Did you hear the good news?," not protected speech); and, third, outlawed speech, such as obscenity (see, e.g., Paris Adult Theatre I v. Slaton, 413 U.S. 49 (1973)) or recklessly false statements (see, e.g., New York Times Co. v. Sullivan, 376 U.S. 254, 279-280 (1964)).

in promoting the efficiency of the public services it performs through its employees."[4]

The balancing test established in *Pickering* was, of necessity, stated in general terms. The Court noted the impossibility of anticipating the variety of circumstances in which a public employee's speech might need to be balanced against the employer's exercise of managerial efficiency, and held instead that in this type of case three factors are to be considered in striking the balance.[5] These factors are: (1) the parties' working relationship; (2) the detrimental effect, if any, of the speech on the employer; and (3) the nature of the issue on which the employee spoke and the relationship of the employee to that issue.[6]

Three cases decided after *Pickering* provided opportunities for the Court to clarify the balancing test. First, in Perry v. Sindermann,[7] the Court provided further elaboration of factor (3), the relationship of the employee to the issue. Sindermann, a college professor, was denied renewal of his employment contract with Odessa State College after he testified before the Texas legislature in favor of a proposal to elevate all junior colleges to four-year institutions. The proposal was opposed by the Board of Regents of Odessa State. In evaluating his free speech claim, the Court noted that Sindermann was both a teacher in the system to be changed and a spokesman for the local teachers' association. As such, he was a member of the

---

[4]*Pickering*, 391 U.S. at 568. Note that while the *Pickering* balancing test only applied to speech on matters of public concern and not to speech of purely private interest, the Court provided no further guidance on distinguishing the two.

[5]*Pickering*, 391 U.S. at 569. Justice Marshall, writing for the Court, indicated "some of the general lines along which an analysis of the controlling interest should run" in evaluating public employee free speech cases, but left open the possibility that factors other than those in *Pickering* might be controlling, given the "enormous variety of fact situations in which critical statements by teachers and other public employees may be thought by their superiors, against whom the statements are directed, to furnish grounds for dismissal." Id. at 569-573.

[6]391 U.S. at 570-572.

[7]408 U.S. 593 (1972).

public who, by virtue of his position, was likely to have special insight on this matter of public concern.[8] Second, in Mount Healthy City School District Board of Education v. Doyle,[9] the Court set forth the burden of proof an employer must meet in dismissing an employee for exercising free speech rights. In *Mount Healthy*, a school teacher was dismissed both for his reporting to a local radio station on the establishment of a teacher dress code and for unprofessional conduct in dealing with staff and students. The Court held that the burden is initially on the employee to show that he was engaged in constitutionally protected conduct and that this conduct was a motivating factor in the decision to dismiss. Once this prima facie showing is made, the burden then shifts to the employer to show that the termination would have occurred irrespective of the protected activity.[10] Third, in Givhan v. Western Line Consolidated School District,[11] the Court held that the *Pickering* test applied to speech even in a private setting. In *Givhan*, a school teacher expressed her opposition to certain school board policies as racially discriminatory in one-on-one meetings with her supervisor. She claimed that her subsequent termination was in retaliation for her expressing her concerns.[12] The Court held that *Pickering* applied to private discussions between employer and employee and that, in determining the proper balance between free speech and the efficiency of the service, the time, place, and manner of the speech could be considered.[13]

In 1983, with the decision in Connick v. Myers,[14] the Supreme Court reexamined the scope of the free speech rights of public employees and held that a threshold examination of the speech involved must be made to determine whether the *Pickering* balancing test was to be applied. The Court constructed a continuum along which speech by a public employee could

---

[8]Id. at 594-595.
[9]429 U.S. 274 (1977).
[10]Id. at 287.
[11]439 U.S. 410 (1979).
[12]Id. at 412-413.
[13]Id. at 415 n.4.
[14]461 U.S. 138 (1983).

fall—from speech that has so little value that the state could prohibit it to speech of vital interest to the public.[15] The Court held that, for a public employee's speech to be protected, it could not simply by characterized as falling generally within the realm of matters of public concern; instead, a threshold determination must be made by examining "the content, form and context of a given statement, as revealed by the whole record."[16] Thus, a two-pronged test was framed: (1) is the speech on a matter of public concern? and (2) if so, does the employee's First Amendment interest outweigh the employer's interest in efficient public service? If the answer to both prongs of the *Connick* test is "yes," then the rule in *Mt. Healthy* requires a showing by the employee that her speech was a substantial or motivating factor in the decision to discipline her, which the employer can only rebut by proving that the discipline would have been imposed irrespective of the protected conduct of the employee.[17]

Finally, in 1987, the Court made a slight adjustment in the law governing free speech of public employees in Rankin v. McPherson.[18] The Court held that greater latitude must be given to lower-level workers than to higher-ranking employees in weighing the competing interests of the parties. Stated the Court: "The burden of caution employees bear with respect to the words they speak will vary with the extent of authority and public accountability the employee's role entails."[19]

The Supreme Court has interpreted the First Amendment's guarantee of free speech in the context of public employment to recognize legitimate interests on both sides of the scales.[20] The

---

[15]Id. at 147. Justice White gave as an example of the former, obscenity, and as an example of the latter, Pickering's letter concerning allocation of school funds.

[16]Id. at 147-148.

[17]Id. at 147-154.

[18]483 U.S. 378 (1987).

[19]Id. at 390.

[20]A case in which speech by a public employee was held outside the realm of matters of public concern is Davis v. West Community Hosp., 755 F.2d 455, 461-462 (5th Cir. 1985) (surgeon with staff privileges at community

Court's rulings, while instructive, do not provide a clear set of rules to govern the limits of free speech.

§2.13.1 Strike Prohibitions

Unlike their private sector counterparts covered under the National Labor Relations Act (See §2.5.2), public healthcare facility employees are frequently prohibited by state statute from engaging in strikes or work slowdowns. Although ten states permit at least some public employees to strike, a survey conducted in 1981[21] found that one-half of all states not only prohibit public employees from striking, but also provide for economic or disciplinary penalties against those employees who do so. Twelve states have legislation requiring discontinuation of pay for striking employees; 16 states authorize disciplinary action against employees for striking; still other states provide for imprisonment of employees or their union officers for engaging in strikes.[22]

In 1985, the California Supreme Court reexamined the question of whether a state common law barred public employees from striking. That case, County Sanitation District No. 2 v. Los Angeles County Employees Assn. Local 660,[23] held that there was no common-law bar on the right of California public employees to strike. The court held that the right to strike

---

hospital criticized hospital personnel and claimed ineffective treatment of patients; speech held to involve only personal grievances against various co-workers and administrators). By contrast, a case in which the speech in question was held to constitute speech on a matter of public concern is Rookard v. Health and Hosps. Corp., 710 F.2d 41, 46 (2d Cir. 1983) (exposing corruption and waste in government is "obviously" a matter of public concern).

[21]H. S. Tanimoto and J. M. Najita, Guide to Statutory Provisions in Public Sector Collective Bargaining, Industrial Relations Center, University of Hawaii (1981). The study is summarized in J. Straussman, S. Bretschneider, and R. Rodgers, Public Unions and Penalties for Striking Across the States, 6 Review of Public Personnel Administration, 19-36 (Summer 1986).

[22]Straussman et al., supra, n.21, at 20.

[23]214 Cal. Rptr. 424, 699 P.2d 835, cert. denied, 474 U.S. 995 (1985).

"represents a basic civil liberty"[24] that could not be abridged "unless or until it is clearly demonstrated that such a strike creates a substantial and imminent threat to the health or safety of the public."[25] The court declined to reach the constitutional question of strike prohibitions, but intimated that the issue, if presented, would be resolved in favor of the right to strike.

California is the only state thus far to hold that strikes by public employees are permitted absent clear legislative authorization. Whether any other state will follow California's lead remains to be seen.[26]

§2.14 Fourteenth Amendment Property and Liberty Rights

Since 1972 the Supreme Court has held that the Fourteenth Amendment's guarantee that no state shall "deprive any person of life, liberty, or property, without due process of law"[1] extends, in two distinct circumstances, to a public employee's job security.[2] First, a public employee's liberty interest is impaired where a public employer dismisses an employee for reasons "that might seriously damage his standing and associations in his community"[3] or that might stigmatize the employee and impair "his freedom to take advantage of other employment opportunities."[4] Where such stigmatizing charges are made public by the employer, the employee is entitled to notice and an opportunity

---

[24]699 P.2d at 848.

[25]Id. at 850.

[26]For a full discussion of the *County Sanitation* case, see Hogler, The Common Law of Public Employee Strikes: A New Rule in California, 37 Labor L.J. 94-103 (Feb. 1986).

§2.14 [1]U.S. Const. amend. XIV, §1.

[2]Board of Regents v. Roth, 408 U.S. 564, 577 (1972); Perry v. Sindermann, 408 U.S. 593, 597 (1972); Arnett v. Kennedy, 416 U.S. 134, 157 (1974); Bishop v. Wood, 426 U.S. 341, 343 (1976); Cleveland Bd. of Educ. v. Loudermill, 470 U.S. 532, 541 (1985).

[3]Board of Regents v. Roth, 408 U.S. at 573.

[4]Id.

for a hearing to clear his or her name.[5] Second, where a public employee demonstrates a vested property interest in the job—that is, a status conferred by the public employer other than "at-will" employment—the employee may only be removed for cause after notice and an opportunity to respond to the proposed dismissal.[6]

§2.14.1 Substantive Due Process

The public employee's substantive due process property right in employment is conferred by statute, ordinance, or express or implied contract under state law.[7] In other words, this right arises not from the Constitution itself, but from specific state action, such as enactment of a statute providing that no state employee may be dismissed except for just cause. The effect of this statutory provision is to create a property interest for due process purposes: the employee may no longer be terminated at will, but has a sufficient "claim of entitlement" to continued employment to constitute a protected Fourteenth Amendment interest.[8] The Supreme Court held in Board of Regents v. Roth[9] that, in order to demonstrate a property right in employment, the public employee "clearly must have more than an abstract need or desire for it. He must have more than a unilateral expectation of it. He must, instead, have a legitimate claim of entitlement to it." The question of what process is due—that is, the procedural requirements necessary to satisfy the Fourteenth Amendment—are determined by reference to the Constitution. Those requirements are discussed in the next section.

---

[5]Board of Regents v. Roth, 408 U.S. at 573; see *Bishop*, 426 U.S. at 348-349; Boston v. Webb, 783 F.2d 1163, 1166 (4th Cir. 1986); McGhee v. Draper, 564 F.2d 902 (10th Cir. 1977).

[6]*Loudermill*, 470 U.S. at 541-542 and cases cited therein.

[7]*Bishop*, 426 U.S. 341, 344 (1976).

[8]Perry v. Sindermann, 408 U.S. 593, 601 (1972).

[9]408 U.S. 564, 577 (1972).

§2.14.2 Procedural Due Process

When a public healthcare facility decides to dismiss an employee, what steps are necessary to ensure that procedural due process requirements are met? The steps to be taken must be adequate to protect the Fourteenth Amendment property rights created by an expectation of continued indefinite employment. There are at least three components of procedural due process:

1. *Adequate notice.* Notice of the proposed dismissal must be "reasonably calculated, under all circumstances, to appraise [the employees] of the pendency of the action and afford them an opportunity to present their objections."[10] The basic standard for notice and an opportunity to be heard is set forth in the Supreme Court's opinion in Greene v. McElroy:[11] "Where governmental action seriously injures an individual, and the reasonableness of the action depends on fact findings, the evidence used to prove the Government's case must be disclosed to the individual so that he has an opportunity to show that it is untrue."

2. *A neutral decisionmaker.* The person reviewing the decision to dismiss should be a "neutral factfinder."[12] It is not necessary, however, that the "neutral factfinder" be an independent third party; indeed, it will usually be a management official of the healthcare facility. It is necessary, however, that the neutral factfinder not enter the hearing with an irrevocably closed mind, and that the factfinder be truthful about any pre-hearing involvement in the matter.[13]

3. *An opportunity to be heard, to present evidence, and to contest the evidence against the employee.* Under the Supreme Court's

---

[10]Mullane v. Central Hanover Trust Co., 339 U.S. 306, 314 (1950).

[11]360 U.S. 474 (1959).

[12]Parham v. J.R., 442 U.S. 584, 607 (1979).

[13]Compare Boston v. Webb, 783 F.2d 1163 (4th Cir. 1986) (fact that the ultimate decisionmaker in a dismissal action was involved in an earlier stage of the decision did not mean dismissed employee was denied due process) with Crump v. Board of Ed., 326 N.C. 603 (1990) (failure of school board members to disclose prior involvement in case constitutes disqualifying bias in violation of due process requirements).

holding in Cleveland Board of Education v. Loudermill,[14] a public employee with a vested property interest is entitled, as a matter of due process, to a pretermination hearing. The procedure requires that an employee dismissed for performance or conduct be afforded a predismissal conference between the supervisor and/or the department head and the employee. It further requires the supervisor or department head to specify the reasons for the proposed dismissal during this conference and to afford the employee an opportunity to respond.

Similarly, protection of a public employee's liberty interest requires that procedural safeguards be observed. In McGhee v. Draper,[15] the court listed these as: (1) reasonable notice of the substance of the charges against the employee; (2) the opportunity for cross-examination of the employee's accusers; and (3) a statement of the reasons for the dismissal of the employee.

§2.15 Fourth Amendment Freedom from Unreasonable Searches

The Fourth Amendment to the United States Constitution states:

> The right of the people to be secure in their persons, houses, papers, and effects, against unreasonable searches and seizures, shall not be violated, and no Warrants shall issue, but upon probable cause, supported by Oath or affirmation, and particularly describing the place to be searched and the persons or things to be seized.

It should be noted that the Constitution does not prohibit *all* searches; it prohibits only *unreasonable* searches.[1] As the Supreme Court has stated, the question of what constitutes an unreasonable search

---

[14]470 U.S. 532 (1985).

[15]564 F.2d 902 (10th Cir. 1977).

§2.15 [1]Carroll v. United States, 267 U.S. 132 (1925).

is not capable of precise definition or mechanical application. In each case it requires a balancing of the need for the particular search against the invasion of personal rights that the search entails. Courts must consider the scope of the particular intrusion, the manner in which it is conducted, the justification for initiating it, and the place in which it is conducted.[2]

In other words, the Fourth Amendment protects against intrusions in circumstances in which the individual has a legitimate expectation of privacy.[3] That expectation in turn depends on two requirements: "first, that [the] person have . . . an actual (subjective) expectation of privacy, and second, that the expectation be one that society is prepared to recognize as 'reasonable.' "[4]

Public employees have challenged the use of drug tests and the conduct of workplace searches as violations of their constitutional right to be free of unreasonable searches. The results of those challenges are summarized below.

§2.15.1 Drug Testing

Whether a public employer's decision to implement drug testing will be deemed "reasonable" appears to be a function of the nature of the work performed by the employees to be tested. Simply stated, some employees have less of a privacy right than others. Although the cases are not uniform, some courts have ruled that employees whose work does not involve high risk to themselves or to the public may be tested only if an employer has "probable cause"—reasonable grounds for believing that a particular employee is probably using drugs. When, on the other hand, questions of public safety are paramount, some courts

---

[2]Bell v. Wolfish, 441 U.S. 520, 559 (1979).

[3]Terry v. Ohio, 392 U.S. 1 (1968); Schmerber v. Calif., 384 U.S. at 767. ("The overriding function of the Fourth Amendment is to protect personal privacy and dignity against unwarranted intrusion by the State.")

[4]Katz v. United States, 389 U.S. 347, 361 (1967) (Harlan, J., concurring); see also Smith v. Maryland, 442 U.S. 735, 740 (1979).

have applied a less stringent standard: that an employer have a "reasonable suspicion" that an employee is using drugs. Although this standard requires only that the employer have reasonable grounds to suspect the drug use, there still must be evidence to support a suspicion that a particular employee is using drugs. A third standard, that the nature of the work is such that a "special need" exception to the Fourth Amendment requirement of "at least reasonable suspicion" may be made, was recently announced by the Supreme Court, and is discussed below.

Under any standard, employee privacy interests are balanced with employer safety and performance interests. The weighing of these interests by various courts has led to mixed results.

The Supreme Court rendered two decisions on public employee drug testing in 1989, Skinner v. Railway Labor Executives Association[5] and National Treasury Employees Union v. Von Rabb.[6]

The *Skinner* case involved a challenge by a union representing railroad employees to regulations of the Federal Railroad Administration (FRA). The regulations mandated blood and urine tests of employees following a major train accident and authorized testing of employees who violated certain safety rules. The regulations were promulgated in response to uncontroverted evidence that there is significant intoxication and drug use on the job in the railroad industry.

The Court held the FRA program constitutional. Even where a warrant or probable cause is not required, noted the Court, Fourth Amendment searches traditionally have been justified only where there is "some quantum of individualized suspicion" to conclude that a search is reasonable. In this case, however, not only was there no warrant required to conduct a drug test (and thus no determination of probable cause to believe the person to be tested had violated the law), but no individualized suspicion was required. The Court found that the privacy interest of the employees was limited since the testing only momentarily

---

[5]109 S. Ct. 1402, 103 L. Ed. 2d 639 (1989).
[6]109 S. Ct. 1384, 103 L. Ed. 2d 685 (1989).

interfered with the employees' freedom of movement, a blood test is typical of procedures that are commonplace in physical examinations, with virtually no risk, trauma, or pain, the urine collection procedure was done in such a manner as to minimize its intrusiveness, and the employees work in a highly regulated industry in which drug and alcohol abuse has been documented.

Against this minimal privacy interest, the Court found a compelling government interest in testing without individualized suspicion, since the risk to the public of damage caused by impaired employees was great, the requirement of particularized suspicion would make it more difficult for the railroad to obtain the needed information, and the drug testing requirements would have a deterrent effect on employees because they'd be less likely to use drugs if they knew they'd be tested in the event of an accident.

The *Von Rabb* case arose when the National Treasury Employees Union challenged the drug testing program of the United States Customs Service, in which drug tests were made a condition of employment for persons seeking positions directly involved in drug interdiction, positions in which the incumbent carries a firearm, or positions in which the incumbent handles classified material. In the period between May 1986, when the program was begun, and November 1988, when the case was argued before the Supreme Court, 3,600 employees were tested; of these, only five employees had positive test results.

Notwithstanding the few employees found with positive test results, the Court held the Customs Service program constitutional. As in *Skinner,* stated the Court, where a search under the Fourth Amendment serves "special governmental needs, beyond the normal need for law enforcement," it is necessary to balance individual privacy interests against governmental interests in order to decide whether a warrant or individualized suspicion is constitutionally required. Government offices could not function if warrants were mandated, since to do so "would only divert valuable agency resources from the Service's primary mission." Nor would a warrant provide additional protection of personal privacy, since the Customs Service employees seeking to transfer to the listed positions know that a drug test is required and that there is no discretionary determination to search.

The Court determined that compelling governmental interests outweighed the privacy interest of the employees in drug interdiction and firearms-carrying positions. Employees in these positions had a greatly diminished expectation of privacy, in the Court's view. The Court remanded the question of the drug tests as applied to employees in so-called sensitive positions. The lower court was directed to reexamine the criteria used by the Customs Service to determine what constitutes classified material and which employees are to be tested.

Since the Supreme Court rulings, a number of lower courts have addressed the constitutionality of public employee drug testing, with mixed results.[7]

A number of rules emerge from these recent cases to guide public healthcare facilities.

First, if a public healthcare facility has probable cause to believe that an employee is using drugs, drug testing is constitutionally permitted. However, as noted above, a court may hold a public employer to the less stringent reasonable-suspicion standard in circumstances in which public safety concerns are high. Note that in each case discussed above, in balancing these interests the Court considered the nature of the employee's duties and responsibilities.

---

[7]See, e.g., Guiney v. Roache, 873 F.2d 1557 (1st Cir. 1989) (program mandating drug testing of all sworn and civilian personnel of Boston police department is constitutional as to police officers who carry firearms or participate in drug interdiction, since court finds no relevant distinction between them and customs officers in *Von Rabb*); Bangert v. Hodel, 705 F. Supp. 643 (D.D.C. 1989) (random testing of Department of Interior employees in sensitive positions constitutes unreasonable search and seizure under Fourth Amendment, since there are no reasonable grounds for suspecting that search would turn up evidence of work-related drug use); Fraternal Order of Police, Lodge No. 5 v. Tucker, 868 F.2d 74 (3d Cir. 1989) (police department had reasonable suspicion of drug use by off-duty officers, justifying dismissal for refusing to submit to testing); AFGE Local 1616 v. Thornburg, 4 IER Cases 516 (N.D. Cal. 1989) (INS random testing plan held unconstitutional where no showing that drug use is potential or current problem by INS employees).

Second, whether a court holds an employer to the higher or lower standard it still appears that blanket testing (that is, testing without any evidence of drug use) is not permissible, absent a showing of a special needs exception to the Fourth Amendment.

Third, although the courts closely scrutinize across-the-board drug testing of employees, they seem prepared to give job applicants less protection. It would appear that a public healthcare facility may require drug testing as part of its applicant screening process; but when the person to be tested is already an employee, the balancing test noted above is to be applied.

Fourth, the mere fact that blanket drug testing nets some employees who test positive does not seem that the testing itself will be upheld. The positive results do not justify the constitutionally impermissible means.

Fifth, the employer should use reasonable procedures to ensure the validity of the test results.

§2.15.2 Workplace Searches

Interestingly, the only case in which the Supreme Court has considered the question of whether the Fourth Amendment protects public employees from unreasonable searches of their workplace arose in a healthcare facility.[8] In O'Connor v. Ortega,[9] a hospital physician was suspected of various acts of misconduct, including theft of hospital property and sexual harassment. The executive director of the hospital suspended the physician pending completion of an investigation into the alleged misconduct. As part of that investigation, the executive director and

---

[8]Indeed, the Court noted the paucity of case law on the appropriate standard for public workplace searches in O'Connor v. Ortega, 480 U.S. 709, 723 (1987).

[9]480 U.S. 709 (1987).

other management officials entered the physician's office and conducted a search of his file cabinets and desk. Certain materials found in that search were used in the subsequent administrative proceeding to remove the physician.

The physician maintained that the search of his office by hospital officials violated the Fourth Amendment's prohibition against unreasonable searches. The Court, in a 5-4 ruling, held that searches and seizures of government offices by government employers are subject to Fourth Amendment restraints, but held that the search of the physician's office in this case was, on balance, reasonable.

The Court held that the physician had a reasonable expectation of privacy in his office, including his desk and file cabinets. Finding whether a search of his office was reasonable, then, required a balance of "the invasion of the employee's legitimate expectations of privacy against the government's need for supervision, control and the efficient operation of the workplace."[10] The Court held that the reasonableness of a search is essentially to be determined on a case-by-case basis, "judged by the standard of reasonableness under all the circumstances."[11] In *O'Connor*, the Court declined to rule whether the search of the physician's office was reasonable, because there were unresolved issues of fact properly to be considered by the lower court; it therefore remanded the matter to the district court.

The significance of this case for the healthcare facility is obvious: before conducting a workplace search of employee lockers, offices, files, or other areas in which it may fairly be said the employee has a "legitimate expectation of privacy," the employer should consider whether the need for supervision, control, and efficient operation of the facility outweighs the employee's privacy interest. Healthcare facilities are advised to proceed with caution in this area, and to consult legal counsel as needed.

---

[10]Id. at 725.
[11]Id.

G. ERISA and Healthcare Facilities

§2.16 The Scope of ERISA

The Employee Retirement Income Security Act of 1974 (ERISA)[1] is designed to protect employees and their beneficiaries under employee pension benefit plans and employee welfare benefit plans. ERISA actually consists of two sets of laws: those found in Titles I, III, and IV of the Act (which provide certain employee protections, enforcement procedures, and a system of benefits insurance) and those found in the Internal Revenue Code (which govern the tax treatment of employer-sponsored benefit plans). These provisions will be referred to as "Act" provisions and "Code" provisions, respectively.

ERISA covers private-sector employers, including for-profit hospitals, private nonprofit healthcare facilities, and other private healthcare facilities. ERISA does not cover public employees,[2] employees under tax-exempt church plans,[3] and certain other employee plans.[4]

The Act establishes strict fiduciary standards for those involved with the management of employee benefit funds, requiring that administrators act "with the care, skill, prudence and diligence under the circumstances that a prudent man acting in like capacity and familiar with such matters would use . . ."[5] The Act also prohibits fiduciaries from engaging in certain "prohibited transactions," essentially of the type that would inure to the personal benefit of the fiduciary.[6] Further, the Act bars discrimination against plan participants or their beneficiaries because they have exercised or may exercise their rights under the Act or because they participate in administrative or judicial proceedings to determine their rights under the Act. For example,

---

§2.16 [1] 29 U.S.C. §1001 et seq.
[2] 29 U.S.C. §1003(b)(1).
[3] 29 U.S.C. §1002(b)(2).
[4] 29 U.S.C. §§1003(b)(3), 1003(b)(5).
[5] §404(a)(1)(B).
[6] §§406 to 408.

an employee may not be dismissed in order to prevent her eligibility for benefits.[7]

In 1980 Congress amended ERISA by enacting the Multi-Employer Pension Plan Amendments Act, which provides that if multiple-employer pension plans are terminated, the participating employers are liable for certain levels of guaranteed benefits to employees. Congress further amended ERISA in 1984, as part of the Retirement Equity Act, to ensure that benefit plan administrators would comply with court-ordered child support, alimony, or property right divisions.

A complete discussion of ERISA is beyond the scope of this chapter. Healthcare employers should consult an attorney who specializes in ERISA to ensure compliance with the Act and its complex provisions.

H. Conclusion

State and federal statutes, the United States Constitution, and the common law comprise the sources of employment law for healthcare facilities. As made evident by this chapter, it is important to consider all these sources in determining the proper course of action to take in establishing a personnel policy or making a personnel decision. The healthcare facility must stay current in employment law, which is subject to significant shifts over time; what is an acceptable employment practice today may well be struck down by a court tomorrow.

Still, it is usually the case that what makes good practical sense also makes good legal sense. The healthcare facility that takes the time to evaluate its personnel actions is likely to discover that those actions can withstand legal challenge.

---

[7]See, e.g., Gavalik v. Continental Can Co., 812 F.2d 834 (3d Cir. 1987).

3   Antitrust Law

Douglas J. Colton

§3.0 Introduction

§3.0.1 The Nature of Antitrust Law

Antitrust law governs economic competition. The basic model according to which our economy operates assumes independent self-interested decisions made by millions of individuals and enterprises. We call this the free enterprise system, in which the desire to make a profit through competition leads businesses to expand production, improve quality, reduce costs, and sell more. There are many exceptions to the free enterprise model, but in general American society still organizes its business and economic affairs on the competitive model rather than through the centralized governmental control used in many other societies.

Raw economic competition has only one measure of success for a business: profit. However, unbridled competition can have side effects that as a society we do not want, and it can be conducted in ways of which we do not approve. For a hundred years or more our society has recognized that some restraint on the competitive economic process is probably necessary. Even more important, although we approve of competition, individual businesses sometimes may find it more comfortable, or profitable, not to compete. They may decide to divide up the available business among themselves and their competitors or may attempt to destroy their competitors, leaving purchasers with only one seller from whom to buy. Consumers, as a result, will likely be forced to pay higher prices for the goods and services they desire. The origins of antitrust law are found in the dual desire to (a) avoid the harsher consequences of unrestricted competition and (b) ensure that those who are supposed to compete do so instead of rigging the game.

Like most models that try to describe human behavior, the competitive model is oversimplified and often hard to reconcile with reality. Even so, our society prefers this model to any other. Sometimes we must accommodate the model to actual behavior, but just as often we try to modify our behavior to make it follow the model more closely. Antitrust law permits us, on a regular basis, to redefine what we expect our economy to look like and to create rules so that participants in the competitive economic process will know what they may and may not do.

Antitrust law should not be regarded as a foreign or undesired imposition on American life. This body of law was adopted as a means to preserve the economic identity we have chosen for ourselves. The following pages will discuss particular applications of antitrust concepts to the field of healthcare—and especially to the hospital industry. These concepts have been applied to healthcare only relatively recently; as a result, there is still much uncertainty about how existing rules will be applied in this area. It's not that antitrust law is encroaching on healthcare; rather, the economics of healthcare have changed. Healthcare is moving into the mainstream of the American economy, and it must learn to accommodate itself to the rules of competition.

§3.0.2 The Source of Antitrust Law

Antitrust law, unlike much of the law that affects hospitals and other healthcare providers, is not regulatory in the sense of involving a lot of specific statutes and rules. The applicable rules for such subjects as Medicare and Medicaid reimbursement, licensure of hospitals and physicians, certificates of need, and the like are set forth in page after page of fine print. In contrast, antitrust law is very briefly stated. The fundamental laws are two brief paragraphs enacted in 1890, §§1 and 2 of the federal Sherman Act.[1] Section 1 declares illegal every "contract, combination or conspiracy . . . in restraint of trade." Section 2 declares illegal every act of "monopolization . . . or attempt to monopolize."

Nothing in the Sherman Act—which has remained essentially unchanged for a century—specifically says what is legal and what is not. Instead, the courts have defined those categories in case decisions over the decades. Illegal combinations are those that the courts find to be in unreasonable restraint of trade.[2] Monopolization has been defined as certain kinds of conduct committed by enterprises with a certain amount of strength ("market power") in the marketplace that has the potential effect of unjustifiably limiting the quantity of goods or services available to consumers, thereby raising the prices that consumers will have to pay for those goods and services.[3] The courts have intended that these concepts of impermissible restraints of trade be applied to virtually all industries, not just the industry at question in a particular case.[4] As a result, probably no two cases

---

§3.0   [1]Sherman Antitrust Act of 1890, 15 U.S.C. §§1, 2 (1982).

[2]In a classic statement, Chief Justice White launched what has become the touchstone of the antitrust laws: "If the criterion by which it is to be determined in all cases whether every contract, combination, etc., is a restraint of trade within the intendment of the law, is the direct or indirect effect of the acts involved, then of course the rule of reason becomes the guide. . . . [I]n every case where it has been claimed that an act or acts are in violation of the [Sherman Act] the rule of reason, in light of the principles of law and the public policy which the act embodies, must be applied." Standard Oil Co. v. United States, 221 U.S. 1, 66 (1911).

[3]United States v. Aluminum Co. of Am., 148 F.2d 416, 429-430 (2d Cir. 1945). See also Aspen Skiing Co. v. Aspen Highlands Skiing Corp., 472 U.S. 585 (1985).

[4]See Arizona v. Maricopa County Medical Socy., 457 U.S. 332, 349 (1982) ("Whatever may be its peculiar problems and characteristics, the Sherman Act, so far as price-fixing agreements are concerned, establishes one

will ever have the same fact situations, and in an economy of billions of transactions, some conduct will inevitably not fit within recognized antitrust rules and principles.

Moreover, because antitrust law is essentially judge-made law, it reflects changes in society's values over time. The Supreme Court has sometimes reversed an earlier position and announced new rules to be applied thereafter to business conduct. Also, as new areas of the economy—such as healthcare—develop, new kinds of problems arise for which no solution in antitrust law has previously been needed.

This means that the rules of competition are not carved in stone, especially in the healthcare field. Some kinds of conduct clearly are and will be illegal as long as we have antitrust law. Others equally clearly are legal and proper. In the middle lie many novel and complex transactions for which antitrust law has not yet found a definitive rule. Healthcare poses increasingly difficult antitrust questions, which is one reason why hospital administrators find that they must seek antitrust advice more frequently than in the past.

Because the Sherman Act is federal law, it is applied in federal court.[5] Other federal sources of antitrust law include legislation that deals with mergers,[6] tie-ins,[7] price discrimination,[8] and other matters that usually are of little concern to hospital officials.[9] The Federal Trade Commission Act,[10] which

---

uniform rule applicable to all industries alike.") (quoting United States v. Socony-Vacuum Oil Co., 310 U.S. 150, 222 (1940)).

[5]Unlike most other types of suits brought under federal law, the jurisdiction of the federal courts under the antitrust laws is exclusive. See Blumenstock Bros. Advertising Agy. v. Curtis Publishing Co., 252 U.S. 436, 440-441 (1920). If a federal antitrust claim is initiated in state court, the defendant may remove the action to federal court, 28 U.S.C. §1441(b), whereupon the case may be dismissed because the removal jurisdiction of the federal courts is derivative and the state court lacked jurisdiction. State of Washington v. American League of Professional Baseball Clubs, 460 F.2d 654, 658 (9th Cir. 1982).

[6]Clayton Act, §7, 15 U.S.C. §18 (1982).

[7]Clayton Act, §3, 15 U.S.C. §14 (1982).

[8]Robinson-Patman Act of 1936, 15 U.S.C. §13 (1982).

[9]See, e.g., Clayton Act §8, 15 U.S.C. §19 (1982) (forbidding interlocking corporate directorates).

[10]15 U.S.C. §§41-58 (1982).

proscribes "unfair and deceptive" trade practices, is enforced *only* by the Federal Trade Commission (FTC) in Washington, D.C. and in various branch offices. The FTC historically has not brought action against not-for-profit entities unless those entities arguably were acting for the financial benefit—the profit—of others (for example, the FTC has prosecuted the not-for-profit American Medical Association when that group was found to be acting for the economic benefit of member physicians).[11] The FTC is now evidently reconsidering whether or not it may have jurisdiction to challenge at least some hospital activities, such as mergers. Although FTC cases generate publicity, they are somewhat less likely than private civil actions to constitute a threat of antitrust liability; FTC actions may be prosecuted only by the Commission itself, not by private parties, and these administrative proceedings generally do not involve damage awards. That private individuals and corporations may not sue for violations reduces the impact of the FTC Act, although more kinds of conduct (such as advertising) are subject to FTC scrutiny than to litigation under the Sherman Act.

Virtually every state also has its own antitrust law, and sometimes state laws will contain analogues both to the Sherman Act and to parts of other federal antitrust laws.[12] Generally, state courts have interpreted state antitrust laws remarkably rarely, even though the laws have been on the books for many years. The antitrust laws of most states embody the same basic principles as do the federal laws, although with a few twists, such as those state laws prohibiting enterprises from making sales at "below cost" with the motive to harm competitors.[13] The unusual aspects of these state laws have rarely been invoked, but it cannot be assumed that there are *no* differences between state and federal antitrust laws.

State courts have overwhelmingly interpreted their own

---

[11]American Medical Assn., 94 F.T.C. 701 (1979), affd., 638 F.2d 443 (2d Cir. 1980), affd. by an equally divided Court, 455 U.S. 676 (1982).

[12]See, e.g., N.C. Gen. Stat. §§75-1 et seq.; N.Y. Gen. Bus. Law §§340 et seq. (Donnelly Act); Colo. Rev. Stat. §§6-4-101 et seq.; Cal. Bus. & Prof. Code §§16700-16760, 17000-17101; Ohio Rev. Code §§1331.01 et seq.

[13]See, e.g., Colo. Rev. Stat. §6-2-105; Idaho Code §48-404.

state antitrust statutes in a fashion that is largely consistent with federal antitrust laws.[14] It is rare that conduct found illegal under state antitrust law would not also be illegal under federal antitrust law, and because of federal treble damages and attorneys' fees for victorious plaintiffs (provisions not found in all state antitrust laws), by far the majority of all antitrust cases decided to date have been brought in federal court under federal law. Since the federal courts have been largely inhospitable to health industry antitrust claims—especially those brought by physicians—there may well be an impending increase in such cases brought under state antitrust laws in state courts. Even now, alleged violation of state antitrust law is frequently joined in the same case with a claim of violation of federal law. Such claims, since they invoke federal antitrust law, must be brought in federal court. Unless otherwise noted, the principles discussed below are those of federal law.

§3.0.3 The Enforcement of Antitrust Law

Federal and state antitrust laws can be enforced either by government authorities or by private individuals and businesses. The Federal Trade Commission Act can be enforced only by the FTC.[15] Most antitrust lawsuits are filed by private parties complaining about the conduct of another business enterprise. Only about ten percent of all federal antitrust cases are brought

---

[14]But see, for example, New York's Donnelly Act, N.Y. Gen. Bus. Law §§340 et seq., which has been interpreted by New York courts not to cover the activities of doctors, People v. Roth, 419 N.Y.S.2d 851, affd., 425 N.Y.S.2d 904, affd., 438 N.Y.S.2d 737 (1981); or the Texas antitrust law, Tex. Bus. & Com. Code §§15.01 et seq., which has a provision specifically exempting professionals such as doctors from treatment under "per se" analysis except for stated categories of conduct.

[15]See Hester v. Martindale-Hubbell, 493 F. Supp. 335 (E.D.N.C. 1980), affd., 659 F.2d 433 (4th Cir. 1981), cert. denied, 455 U.S. 981 (1982); Cameron v. New Hanover Memorial Hosp., 58 N.C. App. 414, 293 S.E.2d 901, cert. denied & app. dismissed, 307 N.C. 127, 297 S.E.2d 399 (1982); Rose v. Vulcan Materials Co., 282 N.C. 643, 194 S.E.2d 521 (1973).

by the federal government. In recent years most of these have been criminal enforcement activities directed against the most serious violations. Many of the rest of the government cases are civil suits, usually intended to establish a precedent for an industry or for a kind of conduct not previously challenged.

Federal law intentionally encourages private parties to bring antitrust cases. When the antitrust laws were drafted late in the nineteenth century, it was already clear that policing a large and dynamic economy for violations of the rules of competition would be impossible. That remains true today. Enforcement of antitrust law simply cannot depend on the availability of government prosecutors. Instead, the law provides that the successful plaintiff in most antitrust cases shall receive *treble damages*—three times the actual, proven loss during the four years before the suit was filed, and prospectively for perhaps an extended period.[16] The successful plaintiff is also entitled to attorneys' fees, which can be an enormous sum in protracted cases. Those fees can be awarded even when the court grants no damages but does issue an injunction.

A successful antitrust plaintiff is deemed to have served the goals of society by uncovering and prosecuting anticompetitive practices. The windfall treble-damages provision is meant to encourage such suits. In addition, the awarding of attorneys' fees prompts attorneys to take on cases that otherwise might not be filed, because they know that they will be paid if the suit succeeds. These provisions have been much criticized, but they serve a purpose. While injustices occasionally may occur (the provisions could, for example, compel a defendant who cannot afford the risk of an adverse judgment plus attorneys' fees to settle an antitrust claim even though the defendant is right), legislators have not been persuaded sufficiently by that fact to change the rules.

Criticism of the treble damages provision has, however, had some effect. In recent years awards of treble damages against cities, counties, and other local government units have prompted complaints that the purpose of antitrust law is not served when

---

[16]Clayton Act, §4, 15 U.S.C. §15 (1982).

a taxing entity is forced to raise taxes in order to satisfy antitrust judgments.[17] In late 1984 the United States Congress enacted and the president signed legislation that made local government entities immune from antitrust damage claims.[18] This new law certainly will protect cities and counties, but it may also protect county hospitals and state-connected hospitals that are not themselves units of government, such as hospitals created by "hospital authorities" or "public trusts."

Many hospitals exist through special corporations created to own and operate them, with some involvement of local government units. Most of these hospitals do not receive tax revenues, have no tax-levying or tax-collecting authority, and are operated by officials who are neither elected nor directly accountable to elected officials. Yet these hospitals may enjoy the benefit of tax-exempt municipal bond financing; their boards of trustees may be approved, if not appointed, by a unit of local government; and they are viewed as serving public functions in their communities. The question of whether the actions of such hospitals constitute local government actions—and therefore are immune from the treble-damages provision—has arisen only recently.[19] For purposes of antitrust law, the issue will soon be reviewed by appellate courts. There is some reason to believe that these quasi-governmental entities—and their officers, directors, and other "agents"—will be immunized from antitrust damages and attorneys' fees awards, although not necessarily

---

[17]See H. Rep. No. 965, 98th Cong., 2d Sess. 10-11, reprinted in U.S. Code Cong. & Admin. News 4602, 4611-4612 (1982).

[18]Local Government Antitrust Act, Pub. L. No. 98-544, 98 Stat. 2750 (1984) (codified at 15 U.S.C.A. §§34-36 (West Supp. 1987)).

[19]One federal district court has held that California hospital districts are absolutely immune from damages under the Local Government Antitrust Act. Palm Springs Medical Clinic v. Desert Hosp., 628 F. Supp. 454 (C.D. Cal. 1986). Similarly, in Sandcrest Outpatient Serv., P.A. v. Cumberland County Hosp. Sys., 853 F.2d 1139 (4th Cir. 1988), the court affirmed the district court's holding that a county hospital system, created pursuant to state law, was protected by the Act, as were various individuals associated with the hospital system. State laws creating hospital "districts" and "authorities" vary, so the issue remains open elsewhere.

from federal injunctions or damage awards under state law.[20]
The federal immunity statute does not require that state laws
provide the same protection to these entities.

The chief enforcement mechanism for antitrust law is the
private lawsuit, usually for damages but often for an injunction
either in addition to or instead of an award of damages. Such a
suit can be filed under federal law by any person "injured in
his business or property"[21]—either a consumer injured by

---

[20]Indeed, a major unanswered question is the extent to which doctors
who participate in peer review activities can be found guilty of conspiring
with their hospital or with each other. Courts of appeal have split on this
issue, in part by dividing it into almost metaphysical distinctions as to who
competes with whom and who acts on behalf of whom. See, e.g., Weiss v.
York Hosp., 745 F.2d 786 (3d Cir. 1984), cert. denied, 470 U.S. 1060 (1985),
ruling that doctors can conspire with each other but not with the hospital;
Potters Medical Center v. City Hosp. Assn., 800 F.2d 568 (6th Cir. 1986),
ruling that doctors cannot conspire with the hospital; Bolt v. Halifax Hosp.
Medical Center, 891 F.2d 810 (11th Cir. 1990), suggesting that doctors can
conspire with the hospital as well as with each other. Federal legislation
exempting healthcare facilities and doctors from antitrust claims arising from
peer review was passed several years ago, Health Care Quality Improvement
Act of 1986, 42 U.S.C. §§11101-11152 (Supp. 1987), see Austin v. McNamara,
1990 U.S. LEXIS 3550 (C.D. Cal. 1990). In any event, that law denies
exemption for peer review undertaken with economic motives—an allegation
that can easily be made and is at the heart of all antitrust cases anyway. 42
U.S.C. §112(a) (protection exists only if peer review was taken "in the
reasonable belief that the action was in furtherance of quality health care").

[21]Clayton Act, §4, 15 U.S.C. §15 (1982). The requirement of "antitrust
injury," or standing, can be a significant obstacle for antitrust plaintiffs. The
injury of which the plaintiff complains must be more than simply causally
related to the defendant's conduct. "Plaintiffs must prove *antitrust* injury,
which is to say injury of the type that the antitrust laws were intended to
prevent and that flows from that which makes the defendants' acts unlawful."
Brunswick Corp. v. Pueblo Bowl-O-Mat, 429 U.S. 477 (1977). This requirement
barred a physician's claim that his termination by the defendant hospital after
the expiration of a four-year contract violated the antitrust laws. The physician
alleged that his termination was the result of pressure put on the hospital by
its competitors in response to the plaintiff's support of a new hospital to be
built in the area. The court held that the plaintiff lacked standing to assert an
antitrust violation because the defendant's anticompetitive conduct, if any,
was directed not at the plaintiff but at the hospital about to be constructed.
The plaintiff's injury was not the result of any "price-fixing, elimination of

improper competitive conduct or a business that claims to have been put at an unfair disadvantage or otherwise injured by its competitors.

Most private cases are of the latter sort: one person or business asserting that it has been unfairly kept from competitive opportunities by the conduct of its (usually larger and more powerful) competitors. Certainly this is true in the healthcare industry. The cases involve physicians against other physicians or against hospitals, hospitals against hospitals, nurses and allied practitioners against doctors or hospitals, hospitals and doctors against insurance companies, and a wide variety of other groupings of professional competitors. Virtually no important healthcare antitrust cases have been initiated by patients as consumers of healthcare services. Such cases are not impossible, but the complex economics of healthcare are such that patients will rarely have both a large economic motive and a tenable antitrust claim to assert.

Private antitrust enforcement is usually a long and expensive process. An ordinary case in the federal courts in most jurisdictions will go to trial about 18 to 24 months after it is filed. In some places, the wait for a trial date is twice that long. Filing itself occurs long after the conduct that it challenges. Because antitrust law involves complex economic dealings, these cases usually take longer at trial that cases that depend on relatively simple facts. Because antitrust law is a specialized area of law— only a comparative handful of cases are filed every year in the entire country—these cases are usually handled by attorneys who specialize in this area. Federal and state investigations in the healthcare industry are becoming more common, but are still statistically rare, and government prosecutions against healthcare providers are even rarer. However, at both the federal and state levels, antitrust enforcement authorities have commented on the enormous role that healthcare plays in our lives and our economy, and these authorities have indicated intentions to step up the pace of government enforcement activities. As the

---

competition or a monopoly. . . ." Trepel v. Pontiac Osteopathic Hosp., 599 F. Supp. 1484, 1492-1493 (E.D. Mich. 1984).

application of antitrust law to healthcare becomes more visible, the volume of private litigation will inevitably rise as well.

§3.1 The Impact of Antitrust Law on the Healthcare Industry

There are several reasons for the expanding use of antitrust law in healthcare, especially with regard to hospitals but also for physicians and other practitioners as well as for third-party payors such as insurance companies and health maintenance organizations. Ultimately these factors all derive from the growing recognition that economic competition plays a vital role in the provision of healthcare.

§3.1.1 The Application of Antitrust Law to the "Learned Professions"

Only since the mid-1970s has antitrust law been applied by federal courts to the healthcare sector of the economy.[1] Today the commercial nature and sheer economic size of the healthcare sector are almost universally acknowledged, but this has not always been true. Until well into the twentieth century, hospitals were not places that the sick or infirm could have much faith in, and medicine was not a high-income or high-status profession.[2] Medical knowledge and technology have advanced rapidly and dramatically. More and more of our national resources have been devoted to procuring high-quality healthcare for a larger proportion of the population. Within the last 30 years the economic consequences of these changes have become clear: healthcare has entered commerce.

---

§3.1 [1]Virtually all antitrust activity involving the healthcare industry to date has centered on hospitals. The concepts are equally applicable to other healthcare facilities.

[2]See generally P. Starr, The Social Transformation of American Medicine (1982).

Antitrust law is the law of trade or commerce. It generally is considered to be less appropriate for application to supposedly nonmarket activities such as education, religion, and family life—a list that until recently was deemed to include the "learned professions," especially law and medicine. Until fairly recently antitrust cases in the healthcare sector were quite rare.[3] In 1975 the United States Supreme Court decided Goldfarb v. Virginia State Bar, a case involving accusations of antitrust violations made against the Virginia Bar Association.[4] The Court declared that the practice of law was part of commerce and thus subject to antitrust law. The case determined that professionals can no longer assert "worthy purpose" defenses to justify plainly anticompetitive conduct and obtain automatic antitrust immunity. This was made even clearer in National Society of Professional Engineers v. United States,[5] in which the Court stated:

> [T]he purpose of [antitrust] analysis is to form a judgment about the competitive significance of the [challenged] restraint; it is not to decide whether a policy favoring competition is in the public interest, or in the interest of the members of an industry. . . . [P]etitioner's attempt to [justify the challenged conduct] on the basis of the potential threat that competition poses to the public safety and the ethics of its profession is nothing less than a frontal assault on the basic policy of the Sherman Act.[6]

In subsequent cases the Court has held not only that hospitals, and the healthcare industry in general, are engaged in commerce[7] but also that generally recognized antitrust principles should be

---

[3]In part this is explained by the courts' past reluctance to regard the practice of medicine as commerce and thus within the reach of the antitrust laws. See United States v. Oregon Medical Socy., 243 U.S. 326, 338-339 (1952); FTC v. Raladam Co., 283 U.S. 643, 653 (1931) ("medical practitioners . . . follow a profession and not a trade"); Wolf v. Jane Phillips Episcopal Memorial Hosp. Center, 513 F.2d 684, 686 (10th Cir. 1975) (discussing the "learned professions" exception to antitrust scrutiny).

[4]Goldfarb v. Virginia State Bar, 421 U.S. 773 (1975).

[5]435 U.S. 679 (1978).

[6]Id. at 692, 695.

[7]Hospital Bldg. Co. v. Trustees of Rex Hosp., 425 U.S. 738 (1976).

applied in determining the legality of healthcare practices,[8] albeit perhaps with some recognition of the behavior and economic conduct peculiar to the healthcare industry.[9]

Now that the healthcare sector is no longer assumed to be exempt from antitrust law, the economic complexity that developed there during the protected period has been made manifest. The division of the industry into patients who consume but often do not "choose" for themselves the healthcare they receive; into doctors who "choose" and provide care but do not themselves consume it or pay for it; into hospitals that provide care but do not "choose" it or pay for it; and into insurers and other third-party payors who pay for healthcare services, but neither choose nor consume them, created anomalous economic motivations and conduct never before addressed by antitrust law. Once the courthouse door was opened to healthcare antitrust cases, lawyers and participants in the healthcare industry quickly found that antitrust law is a powerful tool to promote change and to attack traditional practices.

Healthcare has turned out to be rife with arrangements and behavior unlike those found elsewhere in the economy— arrangements that may appear suspect, if not clearly illegal, when viewed through the prism of antitrust law. Much of the shock for hospitals in complying with antitrust rules comes simply from adjusting to rules developed for other industries under other circumstances. Right or wrong, they must adjust. Failure to do so risks legal challenges sanctioned by courts and antitrust enforcement authorities, who now view the healthcare industry as prime territory. In fact, the 1980s were characterized by economic turmoil and upheaval in the healthcare industry, attributable in part to the discovery by healthcare providers that they must play by the same economic rules as the rest of American commerce and in part to the determination by third-

---

[8] Arizona v. Maricopa County Medical Socy. 457 U.S. 332 (1982).

[9] See, e.g., Jefferson Parish Hosp. Dist. No. 2 v. Hyde, 466 U.S. 2, 27-28 (1984) (noting the "market imperfections" inherent in the healthcare industry, such as the prevalence of third-party payment and consumers' lack of adequate information).

party payors—including the federal government—that health-care costs might best be contained by making the industry adhere to the competitive model on which antitrust law rests.

§3.1.2 Hospitals as the Center of Healthcare's Economic Activity

The development of modern healthcare is in many ways the development of the modern hospital.[10] The complexity and cost of diagnostic and therapeutic procedures and modalities often require centralized sources of capital and expertise. As the causes of disease and injury have been discovered and methods to treat them have been found, medical specialties have proliferated. As a result, modern healthcare requires contributions from and coordination of a variety of technological components and healthcare specialists. It is at hospitals that all these resources come together for treatment of patients.

Hospitals themselves have expanded their roles by dealing with patients both earlier and later in the course of treatment. From "wellness" services and outpatient clinics through nursing facilities, home health agencies, and equipment companies, hospitals have extended the scope of their dealings with patients; indeed, even the line separating the responsibility of hospitals to arrange for healthcare services from the province of other entities who devise programs for paying for those services, has become blurred.[11] Accordingly, hospitals have grown in economic importance as well as sheer size. Physicians, nurses, technicians, therapists, equipment suppliers—all these and others—increasingly have viewed hospitals as the focal point of their own economic activity. For the growing number of healthcare practitioners and enterprises that seek to ply their

---

[10]See generally C. Rosenberg, The Care of Strangers: The Rise of America's Hospital System (1987).

[11]See Reazin v. Blue Cross & Blue Shield, 635 F. Supp. 1287 (D.C. Kan. 1986), supplemented, 663 F. Supp. 1360 (D.C. Kan. 1987), affd. in part and remanded in part, 1990 U.S. App. LEXIS 4565 (10th Cir. 1990).

services (their business), access to the hospital is essential to economic success. Accordingly, outsiders tend to fight to get in, and insiders tend to fight to keep others out.

As hospitals grow, their economic impact on their communities and on other businesses around them increases. In addition to individual providers and competing hospitals, laboratories, freestanding diagnostic or treatment clinics, laundries, nursing facilities, equipment suppliers, and other enterprises gain or lose by what goes on in each hospital. As hospitals take more aggressive steps to keep beds full, develop outpatient care centers, and expand revenue through expansion into "downstream" or even nonhealthcare ventures, they affect or even threaten an increasing number of other economic players. As a result, these players have strong incentives either to fight to gain rights to participate in the economic activity generated by hospitals or to oppose hospitals' expansion into such areas.

§3.1.3 Economic Pressure on the Healthcare Industry

The final, and perhaps most important, factor promoting the surge in healthcare antitrust litigation is economic pressure within the industry.[12] The national consensus is that the quality of care should be maintained while the cost of care is lowered (or at least, while the rate of increase is abated). Government programs, employers, insurance companies, and individuals are trying to contain the rapid inflation of healthcare costs that occurred in the 1960s and 1970s and slowed only briefly in the 1980s. The Medicare program alone suddenly changed its system of reimbursement to hospitals, forcing new economies in treatment of the over-65 population.[13] Even with the change to a

---

[12]See generally Alpert and McCarthy, Beyond *Goldfarb:* Applying Traditional Antitrust Analysis to Changing Health Markets, 29 Antitrust Bull. 165, 171-178 (1984).

[13]See Social Security Amendments of 1983, Pub. L. No. 21, 97 Stat. 65, 98th Cong., 1st Sess. (1983) (codified in scattered sections of 42 U.S.C.).

"prospective payment system" for the Medicare population, that group continues to grow in size and average age, so that expenses for necessary medical services to this major group are still increasing for demographic reasons even before the direct costs for life-extending advances in medical knowledge are calculated.

While patients and third-party payors have tried to minimize the growth in the number of dollars per capita devoted to healthcare, the number of providers seeking to participate has grown. There are many more hospital beds, physicians, nurses, and allied health professionals today than there were 10 or 15 years ago.[14] At current price levels, most communities have more than enough sellers of virtually every healthcare service to meet existing and projected demand. Traditional economics argues that prices will therefore come down.[15] Hospitals are discounting prices, and individual providers' incomes are falling. Those who are selling healthcare services have no choice but to compete for the business available.

Changes in the law, in the growth and importance of hospitals, and in the degree of economic turmoil in healthcare are all related. Courts and regulatory agencies seem to have concluded that applying competitive principles to the industry is more likely to hold down costs than is regulation. The changes that have led to the recent resolve to apply antitrust concepts to healthcare are deep-seated and probably permanent. So long as these factors are still at work—that is, for the forseeable future—

---

[14]Indeed, the oversupply of beds in some communities, coupled with the pressures of reimbursement—especially from Medicare, but from private payors as well—has set off an imposition of the hospital industry. Many rural hospitals are closing, and many inner-city hospitals with high charity and bad-debt loads are finding it necessary to cut back services, merge with other hospitals, or close. For these hospitals, the current "marketplace" solution to the cost of healthcare is not working.

[15]In the author's experience, almost all hospitals and physicians are under substantial pressure from insurers, employers, and others to lower either prices or the total cost per case, and most providers feel compelled to accommodate some of these pressures. At the very least the rate of increase in healthcare costs declined in the 1980s, although it shows signs of picking up again.

antitrust disputes over a static or insufficiently growing economic "pie" will be common. Because each community is virtually a separate marketplace for the sale of these services, and because there are thousands of independent hospitals and tens of thousands of different individual economic participants in this industry, issues are unlikely to be resolved on a national scale in one or a few antitrust cases. Litigants will offer slightly variant facts to distinguish their cases from those already decided, and the same kinds of issues will be (have been) litigated over and over again as competition takes its toll on less successful competitors.

§3.2 Basic Antitrust Concepts for Hospitals

Like other technical areas of the law, antitrust law has its own vocabulary and set of fundamental concepts.

§3.2.1 Horizontal, Vertical, and Other Arrangements

Antitrust law usually tries to place economic dealings into familiar descriptive models. Analysis often proceeds from the use of labels that identify the relationships between business enterprises. The most common of these labels are "horizontal" and "vertical."

"Horizontal" relationships are those between competitors. A hospital competes with another hospital in the same fairly small city; any agreement between them would be a horizontal agreement. A hospital in Chicago or Springfield, Illinois probably does not compete much with a hospital in Los Angeles or Tustin, California, so agreements between them are not horizontal, even though the Illinois hospitals are both in the same business as the California hospitals. The Chicago and Springfield hospitals may not compete even though they are in the same state. In large cities such as Chicago or Los Angeles, it is probable that the hospitals really do not compete for the same patients, because travel time between the facilities is too great, or patient and physician preferences are too well-established, for the hospitals effectively to seek the same business. If, however, the only two medical devices of a certain kind in the United States were in the hospital in Chicago and the hospital in Los Angeles, then, at least with regard to that service, those two hospitals would be competitors. An agreement between them dealing with that service would be horizontal, because they both seek to draw business for that service from the same national pool of patients. Whether an agreement is horizontal or not effectively depends on whether the sellers of the service at issue are both trying (or realistically could try) to attract the same purchasers.

Antitrust enforcers tend to suspect horizontal agreements. Competitors are supposed to act independently, bidding against each other for business, not agree on how business will be conducted between them. Nearby hospitals, however, frequently need to work together more than competing grocery stores, gas stations, or steel mills do. Cooperation on a regional emergency medical system, for instance, should not be and generally is not presumed illegal under antitrust law. Hospitals also provide more than a single service; they are really bundles of services,[1] some of which compete with others in the community and some of which have little or no competition. Whether a particular agreement is horizontal in violation of antitrust law depends on whether it is between competitors regarding a service in which they do or should compete. If the answer is yes, antitrust enforcers learning of such agreements may carefully examine the conduct.[2]

---

§3.2 [1]See, e.g., In re Am. Medical Intl., F.T.C. Dkt. 9158 (July 2, 1984) (relevant product market in hospital merger case consisted of the "cluster" of general acute care hospital services).

[2]For example, in the spring of 1990, an investigation was launched by the Antitrust Division of the U.S. Department of Justice regarding an agreement by hospitals in Des Moines, Iowa to limit the amount they spent on advertising. The hospitals had reached their agreement in response to tremendous public pressure to hold down costs, and the state legislature had nearly enacted a draconian statute intended to limit such "non-productive" hospital costs. The agreement was publicly and proudly announced by the hospitals, but was

"Vertical" conduct occurs between buyers and sellers. Vertical arrangements lie at the heart of most transactions in our economy, and most are *not* suspect under antitrust law. Every buyer and every seller is deemed to act to protect its own economic best interest. The bargaining for economic self-interest between buyers and sellers defines a competitive marketplace. Antitrust law approves of "hard bargains," in which a purchaser manages to drive down the price of what it buys.[3] Sellers are assumed to know their own best interest and the lowest price at which they are willing to make a sale (or can without losing money). If there are enough buyers and enough sellers in the marketplace, and reasonably accurate information regarding the market is available to the buyers and sellers, then prices should be driven down to a level sufficient to provide reasonable profit to an efficient producer.

This is the ideal. In practice, markets rarely contain enough buyers and sellers for perfect competition; moreover, the healthcare marketplace has certainly been distorted by the presence of extremely large purchasers (such as the Medicare program and some private insurance payors) as well as by a lack of good information on the part of many of the market's participants. Nonetheless, the healthcare business in the United States does consist of buyers and sellers seeking economic self-interest. In this broad respect it resembles other sectors of the economy.

In other respects healthcare is very different. The relationship between physicians and the hospitals in which they have staff privileges is neither horizontal nor vertical as comprehended in the standard definitions. Hospitals generally do not purchase the

---

investigated when the enforcement authorities learned of it from various publications. As of this writing, the investigation is still under way.

[3] See, e.g., Kartell v. Blue Shield, 749 F.2d 922, 924-925 (1st Cir. 1984), cert. denied, 471 U.S. 1029 (1985); Ball Memorial Hosp. v. Mutual Hosp. Ins., 784 F.2d 1325, 1340 (7th Cir. 1986). At least in theory, however, a dominant purchaser can be found to have abused its large purchasing power as a means of suppressing competition. See Reazin v. Blue Cross & Blue Shield, 635 F. Supp. 1287, at 1328-1333 (D.C. Kan. 1986), supplemented, 663 F. Supp. 1360 (D.C. Kan. 1987), affd. in part and remanded in part, 1990 U.S. App. LEXIS 4565 (10th Cir. 1990).

services of their staff physicians, but they must obtain those services in order to obtain patients and revenues. Furthermore, hospitals may have several relationships at the same time with a single physician. The hospital may sell a service (through salaried physicians or otherwise) that competes directly with services offered by physicians who have staff privileges. The hospital can thus be in a horizontal relationship with physicians even as it depends on them for the patient admissions that generate revenue. To take a rather common example, a hospital may receive substantial revenues from its CAT scanner. A physicians' group that has staff privileges at the hospital may also own a CAT scanner. The hospital competes with the physicians for CAT scan revenues at the same time that it obtains patient admissions from those physicians. The relationship between the hospital and these physicians is complex—economically, politically, and legally. If the owners of the outpatient CAT scanner are radiologists who practice at the hospital, then the hospital finds itself competing with the very doctors it may need to provide its own competitive service.

Antitrust law must learn to deal with such complex relationships. Some courts have ignored that fact and have used the convenient pigeonhole labels of horizontal and vertical analysis, with questionable results.[4] Until courts learn more about health-

---

[4]Compare Dos Santos v. Columbus-Cuneo-Cabrini Med. Center, 684 F.2d 1346, 1352 (7th Cir. 1982) (treating exclusive contract as a "vertical combination"), with Jefferson Parish Hosp. Dist. No. 2 v. Hyde, 466 U.S. 2 (1984) (treating exclusive contract as a tying arrangement under the hospital's control). Most striking in these cases is the courts' differing opinions on who is to be considered the "purchaser" and on the nature of the market to which the alleged illegal restraint on competition applies. In *Dos Santos* the United States Court of Appeals for the Seventh Circuit suggested that the relevant purchaser was the hospital because "[t]he patient . . . receives the service but does so without making any significant economic decision." *Dos Santos,* 684 F.2d at 1354. In contrast, the Supreme Court clearly considered the patients as the relevant purchasers, concluding that "[o]nly if patients are forced to purchase . . . services as a result of the hospital's market power would the [exclusive contract] have anticompetitive consequences." *Hyde,* 466 U.S. at 25. The distinction may be critical in determining whether the defendant hospital has sufficient market power to raise antitrust concerns. In *Dos Santos,* for example,

care, some of the traditional concepts of antitrust law will be simplistically and wrongly applied to it.

§3.2.2 Monopoly

In economic terms a firm is a monopoly if, by its decisions alone, the total quantity of a particular product or service available to customers can be reduced and (or) the price of the product can be increased. In antitrust law a monopoly usually will be found when the seller has about two-thirds or more of the sales of a given product in a defined geographic area, plus an (ill-defined) ability to "control prices or exclude competition."[5] This definition fails to provide solid guidance to many firms (especially in the healthcare industry) because it is extremely difficult to determine how much power a seller has in a highly regulated environment and because tests of the ability to set prices without regard to others, or to drive would-be competitors from the marketplace, are rarely found. Nonetheless,

---

the court explained its analysis as follows:

> Because the patient generally takes no part in the selection of a particular anesthesiologist . . . and because the expense of anesthesia services to the patient is ordinarily at least partially insured or otherwise payable by a third party, it might be somewhat anomalous to treat the patient as a buyer. . . . It may thus be more appropriate for antitrust purposes to treat the *hospital* as the purchaser, in view of the hospital's responsibility for assuring the availability of anesthesia services for its patients, its incentives to maximize the use of its surgical facilities and its potential liability for negligent rendition of anesthesia services in its operating rooms. . . . Such a recharacterization could therefore alter dramatically the definition of the relevant market and with it the lawfulness of the exclusive contract.

684 F.2d at 1354. For a general discussion of the characterization problems that arise in relations between hospitals and physicians, see Kissam, Webber, Bigus, and Holzgraefe, Antitrust & Hospital Privileges: Testing the Conventional Wisdom, 70 Calif. L. Rev. 595, 603-613 (1982); Havighurst, Doctors and Hospitals: An Antitrust Perspective on Traditional Relationships, 1984 Duke L.J. 1071.

[5]United States v. Grinnell Corp., 384 U.S. 563, 570-571 (1966); United States v. E. I. du Pont de Nemours & Co., 351 U.S. 377, 391 (1956). See also Smith v. Burns Clinic Medical Center, 779 F.2d 1173, 1175 (6th Cir. 1985).

monopolies are frequently found in healthcare. Any sole provider in a community is probably a monopoly—for example, a hospital to which residents must turn because there is no other within a convenient distance. The only anesthesiologist or pathology lab in a community separated from any other by 20, 30, or 40 miles may have a practical monopoly on that service.[6] Hospital monopolies are probably more common than those in any other major line of commerce outside of regulated utilities, and monopolies by individual providers or facilities over specialty areas are even more common (e.g., the only orthopedic surgeon or the only CAT scanner in a community.) These monopolies frequently result from (and are protected by) certificate-of-need laws (CONs).

It is *not* illegal to be or to have a monopoly. However, it is illegal to *try* to become a monopoly (other than through use of licenses such as CONs)[7] or, having legally obtained a monopoly,

---

[6]See Coastal Neuro-Psychiatric Assoc. v. Onslow County Hosp. Auth., 607 F. Supp. 49 (E.D.N.C. 1985), revd. on other grounds, 795 F.2d 340 (4th Cir. 1986).

[7]Competitors of hospitals seeking a certificate of need (CON) for specific equipment or licensing may oppose the granting of the CON through state administrative processes without fear of incurring antitrust liability as long as the opposition is not a sham enacted solely for anticompetitive reasons; good-faith use of administrative proceedings to block competition is legal even if the motive for doing so is anticompetitive. See Garst v. Stoco, 604 F. Supp. 326 (W.D. Ark. 1985). The protection afforded hospitals in this respect derives from the Noerr-Pennington doctrine developed by the Supreme Court to protect the rights of individuals and entities to collectively seek to influence governmental action, including action that limits competition. This doctrine is premised on the First Amendment, which provides rights to petition the government. See United Mine Workers v. Pennington, 381 U.S. 657 (1965); Eastern R.R. Presidents Conf. v. Noerr Motor Freight, 365 U.S. 127 (1961). The "sham" exception to this protection was first articulated by the Court in California Motor Transp. Co. v. Trucking Unltd. 404 U.S. 508 (1972). If, for example, competing hospitals seek to influence state administrative processes by deliberately falsifying information given to a state agency, that conduct will not receive Noerr-Pennington protection. See St. Joseph's Hosp. v. Hospital Corp. of Am., 795 F.2d 948, 956 (11th Cir. 1986); 404 U.S. at 512-513 ("Misrepresentations, condoned in the political arena, are not immunized when used in the adjudicatory process.").

to take steps to exclude competition. Antitrust law frowns on monopolies, tolerating them only if they abide by rules not imposed on non-monopolies. Those rules can be very hard to describe; it can be even harder to determine how to apply them in the special-service oriented monopolies of limited geographic scope that are often found at hospitals. The traditional monopoly rules demand that the monopolist compete only in ways that are "honestly industrial."[8] That is, the monopolist may do things intended to increase business or reduce costs but may not take steps intended primarily to crush a competitor. The difference between permissible competition by a monopoly and prohibited acts of monopolization can be extremely difficult to determine, and often seems almost metaphysical; no antitrust lawyer or judge can comfortably claim to understand clearly what is or is not legal for a particular monopolist.[9]

Although numerous healthcare antitrust cases have involved accusations of monopoly against hospitals or providers, the responsibilities of the sole or dominant hospital in the community (or specialty practice group) have not yet been clearly set forth. It is clear, however, that such entities may be held to account for conduct that puts would-be competitors at a considerable economic disadvantage.[10]

---

[8]United States v. Aluminum Co. of Am., 148 F.2d 416, 431 (2d Cir. 1945); United States v. United Shoe Mach. Corp., 110 F. Supp. 295, 341 (D. Mass. 1953), affd. per curiam, 347 U.S. 521 (1954).

[9]For example, in *Aspen Skiing* the Supreme Court upheld a finding of illegal conduct based on the refusal of the monopolist to continue historic joint marketing with its only—and much smaller—competitor. Had the losing defendant not been a monopolist, joint marketing with its competitor may have been an illegal horizontal agreement. Aspen Skiing Co. v. Aspen Highlands Skiing Corp., 472 U.S. 585 (1985).

[10]Potters Medical Center v. City Hosp., 800 F.2d 568, 575-577, 580 (6th Cir. 1986) (allegations of monopolization through restrictions on physician hospital-staff membership sufficient to preclude summary judgment for defendant hospital); Reazin v. Blue Cross & Blue Shield, 635 F. Supp. 1287 (D.C. Kan. 1986), supplemented, 663 F. Supp. 1360 (D.C. Kan. 1987), affd. in part and remanded in part, 1990 U.S. App. LEXIS 4565 (10th Cir. 1990).

§3.2.3 Per Se and Rule-of-Reason Analysis

Alleged antitrust violations are analyzed and judged under either of two very different legal standards, "per se" rules and the "rule of reason."

Per Se Analysis.   Per se cases involve conduct that the courts have decided cannot be defended under antitrust law. The only question for a court to answer is whether the conduct occurred, not why it occurred or with what impact. Per se cases involve the only antitrust violations for which criminal penalties have historically been invoked, and they represent conduct with the most serious anticompetitive effects. Most of them involve horizontal agreements: price fixing,[11] bid rigging,[12] agreements to divide up customers or territories,[13] and so forth. Most of this conduct on its face reflects agreements between competitors not to compete with each other. Customers are almost certain to be the losers in such arrangements, because their freedom of choice will be limited or they will be forced to pay higher prices for desired goods and services.

Per se litigations are easy to assert but not so easy to prove, especially in the healthcare industry. The limits of permissible cooperation between providers such as hospitals and physicians have not yet been drawn. Among the most serious of alleged violations are group boycotts, which involve decisions by one group of competitors to place one or more other competitors at an economic disadvantage.[14] But in some matters, such as staff-privilege and peer-review proceedings at hospitals, cooperation between competing hospitals and healthcare professionals—with the attendant economic consequences—is not only common but probably inevitable. This is not true in other areas of the

---

[11]See Arizona v. Maricopa County Medical Socy., 457 U.S. 332, 343-348 (1982).

[12]See Las Vegas Merchant Plumbers Assn. v. United States, 210 F.2d 732 (9th Cir.), cert. denied, 348 U.S. 817 (1954).

[13]See United States v. Topco Assocs., 405 U.S. 596 (1972).

[14]See Klor's v. Broadway-Hale Stores, 359 U.S. 207 (1959); Fashion Originators' Guild of Am. v. FTC, 312 U.S. 457 (1941).

economy, and thus unreflective application of per se doctrine as traditionally applied to those other industries often breaks down in the healthcare field. Fortunately, courts usually have not applied per se notions simplistically to conduct involving complex economic relationships.[15] For instance, even though per se violations generally preclude any investigation into the motives for the challenged conduct, motive continues to matter in healthcare, particularly with respect to credentialing and peer review.[16]

---

[15]There has been a general trend away from simplistic application of per se analysis to collective refusals to deal, or boycotts. See, e.g., Northwest Wholesale Stationers v. Pacific Stationery and Printing Co., 472 U.S. 284 (1985). In the healthcare field, and especially in peer review cases, courts have tended to dodge the rigidity of per se boycott analysis either through a determination that refusals to deal really have not been a result of agreements between competitors. See, e.g., Cooper v. Forsyth County Hosp. Auth., 1986 Trade Cas. (CCH) ¶67,065, at 62,493 (4th Cir. 1986); Smith v. Northern Michigan Hosp., 703 F.2d 942, 950-951 (6th Cir. 1983); Harron v. United Hosp. Center, 522 F.2d 1133 (4th Cir. 1975), cert. denied, 424 U.S. 916 (1976); Robinson v. Magovern, 521 F. Supp. 842, 907-913 (W.D. Pa. 1981), affd., 688 F.2d 824 (3d Cir.), cert. denied, 459 U.S. 971 (1982); or that, even if a horizontal agreement has been shown, the conduct is protected under supervening doctrines. See, e.g., Marrese v. Interqual, 748 F.2d 373 (7th Cir. 1984), cert. denied, 472 U.S. 1027 (1985) (activities of peer review committee immunized from antitrust attack under state action doctrine); Coastal Neuro-Psychiatric Assoc. v. Onslow Memorial Hosp., 795 F.2d 340, 342 (4th Cir. 1986) (state statute immunizes privilege decisions from antitrust attack under state action doctrine). In Bolt v. Halifax Hosp. Medical Center, 891 F.2d 810 (11th Cir. 1990), the court rejected the hospital's claim to state action immunity, holding that the hospital was not acting as a sovereign in imposing the alleged restraint, and that the alleged conspiracy was not a foreseeable result of the hospital's enabling legislation.

[16]See, e.g., Wilk v. American Medical Assn., 719 F.2d 207, 225-229 (7th Cir. 1983), later proceedings, 735 F.2d 217 (7th Cir. 1983), cert. denied, 467 U.S. 1210 (1984); Smith v. Northern Mich. Hosp., 703 F.2d 942, 953 (6th Cir. 1982); Chiropractic Co-op Assn. v. American Medical Assn., 617 F. Supp. 264, 269-270 (E.D. Mich. 1985); Rockland Physicians Assocs. v. Grodin, 616 F. Supp. 945-955 (D.C.N.Y. 1985); Pontius v. Children's Hosp., 552 F. Supp. 1352, 1369-1370, 1372 (W.D. Pa. 1982); Williams v. Kleaveland, 534 F. Supp. 912, 919 (W.D. Mich. 1981). Courts seem willing to examine conduct under the per se label, but carry out what is essentially a rule-of-reason analysis. See, e.g., Robinson v. Magovern, infra n.32; Bolt v. Halifax Hosp.

Rule-of-Reason Analysis. If the per se label does not fit, courts use the rule of reason in analyzing alleged antitrust violations. This standard requires that a court consider both the motive and the impact on competition of the challenged conduct. Defendants may defend themselves on grounds that (a) their conduct was necessary for noneconomic reasons[17] or (b) whatever the reason for their conduct, it did not unreasonably restrain competition.[18] Rule-of-reason analysis permits nearly any relevant factor or argument offered in justification of challenged conduct to be considered.

Trial courts seem less comfortable with the use of per se rules in healthcare antitrust controversies than are courts of appeals, which are removed from the communities in which the conduct occurs and from the courtroom in which that conduct is explained by live witnesses. Often, the battle in healthcare antitrust cases involves the defendant's efforts to persuade the court to use rule-of-reason analysis. Those efforts are worthwhile: healthcare defendants rarely lose rule-of-reason cases, and trial courts have rarely applied per se analysis.

§3.2.4 Mergers and Joint Ventures

A "merger" is the consolidation of two previously independent enterprises. "Joint ventures" occur when two or more independent enterprises cooperate in establishing a new business. Both mergers and joint ventures can have antitrust significance; they may lead to monopolization, facilitate collusion among compet-

---

Medical Center, 891 F.2d 810 (11th Cir. 1990). Thus, although labels are often outcome-determinative for other kinds of antitrust cases, they may be much less so in the healthcare arena.

[17]See Wilk, 719 F.2d at 225-229. The Supreme Court has made it clear, however, that "the Rule of Reason does not support a defense on the assumption that competition itself is unreasonable." National Socy. of Professional Engrs. v. United States, 435 U.S. 679, 696 (1978).

[18]See Jefferson Parish Hosp. Dist. No. 2 v. Hyde, 466 U.S. 2, 29-31 (1984); Chicago Bd. of Trade v. United States, 246 U.S. 231, 238 (1918).

itors, decrease the possibility of greater competition by making it virtually impossible for aspiring competitors to enter the market, or deprive the market of needed competition by joining two or more actual or potential competitors. As more and more healthcare providers consolidate to obtain efficiency or seek new markets and new businesses through cooperation with others, these areas of antitrust law are increasing in importance.

Traditionally, mergers occur through the purchase and sale of stock or through the purchase and sale of physical assets. Not-for-profit institutions such as hospitals rarely transfer ownership through a sale of stock, but they sometimes sell or assign their assets or enter a "statutory merger" that transfers control to a different entity.[19] Frequently, though, change of control over hospitals occurs through execution of management contracts that give essentially all operating authority to a professional management company. Although there is little law on the topic, a transfer of operating control over physical assets of a hospital probably will be viewed as a merger for purposes of antitrust law.[20]

Joint ventures have become a major force in the hospital industry. Whether they are undertaken as economic ventures to pool the resources of various entities or as "political" gestures by a hospital to win even greater allegiance from its medical staff or others, joint ventures are seen as an advantageous way of doing business. What little law there is regarding joint ventures suggests that they will be viewed as mergers between the parent organizations.[21]

---

[19]See Clayton Act, §7, 15 U.S.C. §18 (1982).

[20]The FTC has held that acquisition of management contracts will be regarded as acquisition of an asset for purposes of antitrust analysis. The Commission found that "management arrangements enhance the ability to coordinate behavior between [commonly] owned and managed hospitals so that any collusion in the market is . . . more likely." Hospital Corp. of America, 3 Trade Reg. Rep. (CCH) ¶22,301 (FTC Oct. 25, 1985), affd., 807 F.2d 1381 (7th Cir. 1986).

[21]United States v. Penn-Olin Chem. Co., 378 U.S. 158, 170 (1964).

§3.2.5 Exclusive Contracts and Tie-Ins

Two kinds of hospital conduct have recently raised substantial antitrust questions: exclusive contracts and tie-ins.

An exclusive contract grants one party the sole right to provide a good or service to another. If both a purchaser *and* a seller agree not to deal with anyone else regarding a particular good or service, the contract is a "bilateral" exclusive. If the purchaser agrees to buy only from the contracting seller but that seller can also sell to others, the contract is a "conventional" exclusive.

In a typical exclusive contract a health maintenance organization (HMO) might agree to purchase all of its hospitalization needs in a given community from a single hospital or a small group of hospitals. Or, a hospital might agree to buy all of its baked goods for a certain period from a single baker. Or, most commonly, a hospital will grant an exclusive right to perform a particular kind of service—usually radiology, pathology, anesthesiology, or emergency room medicine—to a specific individual or group of physicians. The contract can be tailored in many ways to meet particular needs.

Exclusive contracts do not inherently violate antitrust law.[22] In the hospital context, however, they have evoked much litigation, usually arising out of exclusive agreements between hospitals and physicians. These generally are not traditional exclusive contracts regarding which there is at least a handful of decided antitrust cases, because the hospital may not actually purchase anything from the contracting physicians. Frequently, the hospital instead grants an exclusive "franchise" to one or more physicians to provide a particular service at the facility. The effect of such agreements will be to prevent competitors of the contracting doctors from providing the service at the facility.

---

[22]See, e.g., Tampa Electric Co. v. Nashville Coal Co., 365 U.S. 320, 327 (1961) ("[E]ven though a contract is found to be an exclusive-dealing arrangement, it does not violate [the antitrust laws] unless the court believes it probable that performance of the contract will foreclose competition in a substantial share of the line of commerce affected.").

Courts faced with the issue generally accepted exclusive hospital-physician contracts without much antitrust concern, and analyzed them as a kind of vertical arrangement, until the Supreme Court decided Jefferson Parish Hosp. Dist. No. 2 v. Hyde.[23] *Hyde* involved an exclusive contract for anesthesia services at a New Orleans hospital. The Court found no antitrust violation in that case, but noted that in effect the exclusive contract might, on somewhat different facts, constitute a "tying arrangement," something that is rarely found but, when found, is considered illegal under per se analysis. A tie-in occurs when the seller of a product for which there is little competition (the "tying product") makes the sale of that product conditioned on the buyer's purchase of some other product (usually, but not necessarily, one offered by the seller) for which there is more competition (the "tied product"). In other words, a tie-in occurs when a seller with market power over some good or service uses that market power to force the sale of some other product.[24]

Hospitals provide bundles of services, many of which are actually sold by physicians in the role of independent entrepreneurs. Hospitals are now under pressure to unbundle these services so that some can be sold by entities other than the hospital itself. Yet many hospitals fear that this process, carried too far, can destroy the great value a hospital derives from bringing together many different disciplines and services. The process also threatens the traditional budgetary and fiscal practices of most hospitals whereby basic room-and-board ("hotel") services are offered at a price that may not include fully allocated costs of the facility, while other services, such as ancillaries (x-ray, lab services) or use of the surgical suite are offered at higher prices that effectively cross-subsidize other parts of the hospital. Those more profitable areas of the hospital are frequently the ones that offer the most profit opportunity for physicians or

---

[23]466 U.S. 2 (1984).

[24]See generally P. Areeda, Antitrust Analysis: Problems, Text, Cases 732-739 (3d ed. 1981). A critical question in the area of tie-in law is whether there are actually two *separate* products involved or a combined "package" that is really only one product: can or should, for example, reading x-rays be a different product from taking x-rays?

others who want to "unbundle" them from other hospital operations and offer them at a lower but still profitable price. Much of this battle may be fought out under the label of tie-in law, because the hospital grants an exclusive franchise to one group of doctors as a means of blocking competition regarding that service, and outsiders claim that the exclusive contract illicitly "ties" use of, for instance, the hospital's hotel services or surgical suite to use of particular radiologists, anesthesiologists, or pathologists. Thus far, there are no definitive court decisions regarding the legality of exclusive contracts that are alleged to constitute tie-ins, although this theory has been raised unsuccessfully in a number of cases. Pertinent appellate decisions should start to appear over the next several years.

§3.2.6 Group Boycotts and Exclusionary Behavior

Another violation frequently alleged in the healthcare field is the group boycott. Courts struggle with defining a boycott in *any* context,[25] but some hospital situations appear to fit the most logical and consistent definitions. A classic boycott occurs when some competitors agree among themselves to deprive another competitor of an economic benefit.[26] For example, if a board of realtors decided to deny access to a multiple-listing service to someone who did not keep its minimum commission schedule, the participating realtors would be guilty of a group boycott against the excluded competitor. This violation would almost certainly constitute a per se offense.[27] Or suppose that a group of obstetricians, hoping to suppress competition from nurse midwives, pressured a malpractice insurance carrier to deny coverage to the nurses or even to obstetricians who cooperated with them.[28] This action would appear to be a boycott accom-

---

[25]See generally Heidt, Industry Self-Regulation and the Useless Concept "Group Boycott," 39 Vand. L. Rev. 1507 (1986).

[26]See, e.g., Klor's v. Broadway-Hale Stores, 359 U.S. 207 (1959).

[27]United States v. Realty Multi-List, 629 F.2d 1351 (5th Cir. 1980).

[28]Nurse Midwifery Assocs. v. Hibbett, 549 F. Supp. 1185 (M.D. Tenn. 1982).

plished through pressure on someone other than a competitor but aimed at suppressing competition.[29]

In the hospital setting the most frequent allegations of boycott are heard from (1) physicians against hospitals and other physicians; and (2) alternative financing entities (such as health maintenance organizations) against physicians. Any decision to exclude a particular physician or group of practitioners of a particular classification (e.g., nurse midwives, podiatrists, osteopathic doctors), if done by competing practitioners (obstetricians, orthopedic surgeons, allopathic doctors) in order to suppress competition, could be a per se illegal group boycott.[30] Similarly, an agreement among physicians that none of them will contract with a health maintenance organization, perhaps in addition to pressure from them to prevent their hospital from doing so, would probably constitute a boycott of the HMO, making the physicians and perhaps even the hospital, if it agreed not to contract with the HMO, guilty of an antitrust violation.[31]

Because hospitals and their medical staffs often cooperate closely in deciding about staff privileges and related hospital

---

[29]See Reazin v. Blue Cross & Blue Shield, 635 F. Supp. 1287 (D.C. Kan. 1986) supplemented, 663 F. Supp. 1360 (D.C. Kan. 1987), affd. in part and remanded in part, 1990 U.S. App. LEXIS 4565 (10th Cir. 1990).

[30]See Virginia Academy of Clinical Psychologists v. Blue Shield, 624 F.2d 476 (4th Cir. 1980), cert. denied, 450 U.S. 916 (1981), in which the United States Court of Appeals for the Fourth Circuit held that Blue Shield's policy of reimbursing psychologists for services only when provided in connection with and billed through a physician constituted a violation of the Sherman Act. The court found that Blue Shield acted as an "agent[s] of the member physicians" who dominated Blue Shield, resulting in an unjustifiable attempt to limit competition between psychologists and physicians. See also Bolt v. Halifax Hosp. Medical Center, 891 F.2d 810 (11th Cir. 1990) (each staff physician is a separate economic entity potentially in competition with other physicians); Weiss v. York Hosp., 745 F.2d 786, 818 (3d Cir. 1984) (medical staff constitutes a conspiracy, combination, etc., for purposes of §1 of the Sherman Act).

[31]See American Medical Assn. v. United States, 317 U.S. 519 (1943); Ohio v. Mahoning County Medical Socy., 1982-1 Trade Cas. (CCH) ¶64,556 (N.D. Ohio 1982); United States v. Halifax Hosp. Medical Center, 1981-1 Trade Cas. (CCH) ¶64,151 (M.D. Fla. 1981); Forbes Health System Medical Staff, 94 F.T.C. 1042 (1979).

policy, and because those decisions frequently result in a practitioner's losing privileges having considerable economic value, allegations of group boycotts by physicians are probably the most common of all healthcare antitrust claims. In addition, because someone who knowingly assists a group boycott may himself or herself be guilty of the violation, a hospital that facilitates a "boycott" orchestrated by others could also commit an antitrust violation.[32]

Hospitals must therefore be conscious of the legal liabilities that may be created for them by members of their own medical staff or others. A critical determination is whether doctors who act as part of a credentialing or peer review process are acting as a *part* of the hospital, and thus are incapable of conspiring with the hospital, or whether those doctors remain independent economic actors who may be found guilty of conspiring with each other, and with the hospital, to orchestrate a "boycott" or other restraint of trade by denying a competitor some privileges at that hospital. Since boycotts and other antitrust conspiracies can only exist if two or more *independent* economic entities consciously agree to a common cause, this issue of the "identity" of doctors in peer review contexts is critically important. Thus far, federal courts of appeal have split on this issue, and it will probably require a Supreme Court decision to resolve it.[33]

---

[32]See Robinson v. Magovern, 521 F. Supp. 842, 907 (W.D. Pa. 1981) ("A court will find the necessary collaboration even where the first entity does not receive any benefit from the concerted activity and acts only in response to coercion."), affd. mem., 688 F.2d 824 (3d Cir.), cert. denied, 459 U.S. 971 (1982); St. Paul Fire & Marine Ins. Co. v. Barry, 438 U.S. 531, 544-545 (1978) ("The enlistment of third parties in an agreement not to trade, as a means of compelling capitulation by the boycotted group, long has been viewed as conduct supporting a finding of unlawful boycott.").

[33]See, e.g., Bolt v. Halifax Hosp. Medical Center, 891 F.2d 810 (11th Cir. 1990) (hospital can conspire with its medical staff); Oltz v. St. Peter's Community Hosp., 861 F.2d 1440 (9th Cir. 1988) (following *Bolt*); Potters Medical Center v. City Hosp. Assn., 800 F.2d 568 (6th Cir. 1986) (staff physician lacked capacity to conspire with hospital); Weiss v. York Hosp., 745 F.2d 786 (3d Cir. 1984), cert. denied, 470 U.S. 1060 (1985) (hospital cannot conspire with staff).

§3.2.7 Price Discrimination

Many who work in the healthcare industry are vaguely aware of and concerned about legal restrictions on discrimination in price between customers. The federal Robinson-Patman Act[34] forbids some such discrimination, but that Act will rarely apply to not-for-profit hospitals. Although the law limits to some degree the ability of the sellers of physical goods or commodities to charge similar customers different prices for similar products, it explicitly excludes from its coverage the sale of services, which is what most hospitals and physicians sell.[35] Thus, preferred-provider arrangements, differential contracting between different third-party payors, and similar agreements should not face antitrust liability as *price discrimination.* The only notable risk in this area occurs if not-for-profit hospitals purchase goods—such as pharmaceuticals or parenteral solutions—at a discount offered to them by the manufacturers on the basis that the hospitals are charitable institutions[36] and then sell those goods outside the hospital (whether to patients or to a third party for resale) in competition with sellers who do not have the benefit of the charitable discount.[37] Hospitals should not sell such discount-priced merchandise to their own downstream subsidiaries, whether or not those subsidiaries are for-profit, without consulting counsel.

The antitrust concepts defined above are those most often encountered in court decisions and opinions of counsel, though many other terms and concepts may arise in litigation. Understanding these concepts will help the hospital administrator

---

[34]15 U.S.C. §13 et seq. (1982).

[35]Issues of liability under the Robinson-Patman Act may arise, for example, when an institution purchases pharmaceuticals at discount prices for not-for-profit uses but then resells those pharmaceuticals to "downstream" buyers— not the hospital's patients—in competition with pharmacies, home health agencies, or others. See Abbott Laboratories v. Portland Retail Druggists Assn., 425 U.S. 1 (1976).

[36]Not-for-Profit Institutions Act, 15 U.S.C. §13c (Supp. 1987).

[37]425 U.S. 1 (1976).

recognize the kinds of situations that can lead to antitrust problems.

§3.3 *Identifying Potential Antitrust Problems*

Some conduct so clearly violates antitrust law that it can be spotted easily and avoided: agreeing with one's competitors on what price everyone will charge for services constitutes price fixing no matter what explanations or justifications are offered.[1] It is unlikely that a court hearing such a case would even permit the explanations or justifications to be presented. Most violations alleged in the healthcare field are not so clear-cut. Nonetheless, hospital administrators and healthcare providers should not feel hemmed in by antitrust law. A little common sense will head off most problems. The violations most likely to result in civil liability or government prosecution usually can be identified by asking a few questions about a proposed course of conduct.

Most antitrust violations arise from some type of transaction—a contrast entered, a new policy implemented, a joint venture created. Yet even conduct that has long been accepted may be attacked in the new economic environment, and it might be hard to identify potential problems arising from long-standing practices without an "antitrust audit" by experienced counsel. Most such audits will probably disclose no major problems, and it would not be imprudent for a hospital administrator to forego such an expense until some complaints are heard by the hospital involving competition or antitrust concepts. Still, such a review can serve as prophylaxis and can sensitize Administration to future potential problems. If even one relatively minor antitrust problem can be headed off, the audit will pay for itself many times over.

In considering possible antitrust liability from proposed hospital transactions, a few mental questions should be posed.

---

§3.3 [1]Arizona v. Maricopa County Medical Socy., 457 U.S. 332 (1982); National Socy. of Professional Engrs. v. United States, 435 U.S. 679 (1978).

§3.3.1 Who Will Be Hurt, and How Much?

The antitrust violations most likely to create problems for a hospital arise from transactions that cost someone money. Many technical antitrust violations no doubt occur all the time but do not result in economic loss to any identifiable party, and therefore escape notice and governmental inquiry unless publicized.

Nearly all antitrust claims are asserted by those who have lost, or stand to lose, from the practice at issue and want to recover their losses, three times over, in court. The probability that conduct will be attacked under the antitrust laws increases with the amount that a competitor stands to lose by virtue of being excluded from a market it intends to enter. Most likely to draw antitrust suits are decisions that take away an *existing* opportunity for profit or that threaten an *existing* investment. Those whose economic position is threatened by a new decision or new policy often have substantial vested interests to protect.

Thus, the question to be asked is, "Whose ox is gored?" Identify the party or parties who may lose as a consequence of the decision at hand and try to estimate the size of the loss. If you cannot find someone who might be angered by an economic decision, there probably is no antitrust problem (except, perhaps, in the area of mergers and joint ventures, but even there the risks of committing a violation are small, and the hospital almost certainly already has legal advice regarding the transaction, including at least a brief antitrust analysis if the transaction is of more than minimal size).

So whose ox *is* gored? In a decision to exclude a particular physician from the medical staff, the complainant would be the excluded physician. In a decision to deny staff privileges to an entire class of practitioners, *any* local member of the excluded class (for example, podiatrists, nurse midwives, or osteopaths) might initiate action if the exclusion denies the practitioner significant income. In an exclusive contract between the hospital and specialists, all practitioners of the specialty who are not granted contract rights could attack the contract, especially if it removes them from privileges and economic opportunities they previously enjoyed. In a requirement that hospital inpatients use equipment or services offered by the hospital (as opposed to those offered by others), outside sellers of the goods or services that the patients must buy from the hospital could initiate antitrust action. In an exclusive contract between the hospital and an HMO, any other hospital in the community that will lose business it had been obtaining from the HMO might challenge the transaction. In a decision by a hospital and its staff not to cooperate with an HMO, the HMO might sue, threaten suit, or complain to enforcement authorities if participation by that hospital and those doctors is important to the HMO's participation in that market. In a decision by a group of hospitals and a pathology group practice to build a consolidated lab that will obtain all hospital business, the pathologists and clinical labs that would lose business are likely complainants or plaintiffs. And so on.

Many decisions being made by hospitals today are economically attractive to the hospital precisely because they will take business away from someone. That someone need not sit still for the loss of revenue that the decision will cause. The disadvantaged entity can fight back by making business arrangements of its own to regain lost advantage or, as is occurring more and more frequently in the healthcare sector, by commencing antitrust litigation to stop the harmful conduct, or at least by trying to interest an enforcement agency in challenging the conduct. Of course, not all, nor most, nor even many forms of conduct that hurt someone are antitrust violations; most "good deals" are *not* illegal just because they obtain revenues that someone else would otherwise obtain. If one hospital in a two-hospital community simply underbids its competitor for a large volume of business and the competitor cannot afford to meet the lower price, there should be little antitrust risk in the conduct. The loss suffered by the competitor in this situation is the result of competition, the very process that the antitrust laws seek to foster. Sometimes, however, the advantage derived from a business transaction arises from something other than pure price competition. Any activity that forecloses another business entity's opportunities to obtain customers (patients) by competing on the basis of price or quality is likely to lead the losing competitor at least to check to see whether antitrust laws have been broken—or if a plausible claim can be made that they have.

§3.3.2 Who Is Making the Decision?

If a decision that hurts a business entity is made by or at the insistence of a group of its competitors, it should be examined for its antitrust risks. For example, if the decision not to admit another surgeon to the staff of a hospital is made either by staff surgeons or by the hospital at the request of those surgeons, a group boycott could easily be alleged.[2] If all of the hospitals in a community agree that they will not accept referrals from, or perform laboratory services for, a competing independent surgi-care center, the hospitals may well be engaged in a boycott.[3]

The risks are much lower when only one competitor of the business (or businesses) that stands to lose is involved in the decision. Such an action is not likely to constitute a group boycott. If a single hospital obtains an exclusive contract with a local HMO, antitrust violations can still be alleged, but they probably would not involve per se claims and should be less likely to succeed than joint decisions made by two or more hospitals.[4] If the business transaction involves no competitor of

---

[2]See, e.g., Patrick v. Burget, 800 F.2d 1498 (9th Cir. 1986), revd., 486 U.S. 94 (1988); Weiss v. York Hosp., 745 F.2d 786 (3d Cir. 1986).

[3]See Feminist Women's Health Center v. Mohammad, 586 F.2d 530, 546-547 (5th Cir. 1978), cert. denied, 444 U.S. 924 (1979). But see McDonald v. Saint Joseph's Hosp., 524 F. Supp. 122 (N.D. Ga. 1981).

[4]For purposes of antitrust law, businesses that share or are controlled by common owners are almost certainly a single entity incapable of entering into a conspiracy or agreement. See Copperweld Corp. v. Independence Tube Corp., 467 U.S. 752 (1984). Similarly, an employer and its own executives, employees, or board members do not constitute the multiple independent entities necessary to enter into a conspiracy or agreement. See Nelson Radio & Supply Co. v. Motorola, 200 F.2d 911, 914 (5th Cir. 1952). As the court stated in Potters Medical Center v. City Hosp. Assocs., 800 F.2d 568, 573 (6th Cir. 1986), "The rationale [of these cases] is that officers or agents of a single firm share a unity of economic purpose with the firm, so that agreements,

the party that stands to lose, then the risk of an antitrust violation should be quite small.

§3.3.3 May Monopoly Power Be a Factor?

If there is no cooperation between competitors in the conduct, there is probably no antitrust violation—except when monopoly power is involved, which is relatively rare, although more common in healthcare than in other industries. Monopoly power exists when a particular seller is dominant in its marketplace— that is, when it generally accounts for two-thirds or more of sales in its line of business (a common situation in a one-hospital town).[5]

---

combinations or concerted actions among them do not impermissibly coalesce economic power that was previously directed toward divergent goals."

The relationship between a hospital and its own medical staff can be murkier. The possibility of a hospital-staff conspiracy remains, although some courts appear reluctant to adopt such a view. See Potters Medical Center v. City Hosp. Assn., 800 F.2d 568, 573 (6th Cir. 1986); Weiss v. York Hosp., 745 F.2d 786, 817 (3d Cir. 1984), cert. denied, 470 U.S. 1060 (1985); Moles v. Morton F. Plant Hosp., 1980-1 Trade Cas. (CCH) ¶63,600 (M.D. Fla. 1978), affd. mem., 617 F.2d 293 (5th Cir.), cert. denied, 449 U.S. 919 (1980); Quinn v. Kent Gen. Hosp., 617 F. Supp. 1226 (D. Del. 1985); Seglin v. Esau, 1984-2 Trade Cas. (CCH) ¶65,835 (N.D. Ill. 1984), affd. on other grounds, 769 F.2d 1274 (7th Cir. 1985); McMorris v. Williamsport Hosp., 597 F. Supp. 899 (M.D. Pa. 1984). But see Robinson v. Magovern, 521 F. Supp. 842, 906-907 (W.D. Pa. 1981), affd. mem., 688 F.2d 824 (3d Cir.), cert. denied, 459 U.S. 971 (1982); Bolt v. Halifax Hosp. Medical Center, 891 F.2d 810 (11th Cir. 1990); Williams v. Kleaveland, 534 F. Supp. 912, 920 (W.D. Mich. 1981). Moreover, hospitals managed by independent management companies that may have economic motives distinct from those of the hospital might be found capable of conspiring with management. See St. Joseph's Hosp. v. Hospital Corp. of Am., 795 F.2d 948, 956 (11th Cir. 1986). This so-called independent stake exception has been recognized by the Supreme Court, but it was neither explicitly approved nor disapproved. See Copperweld, 467 U.S. at 769 n.15.

[5]See United States v. Paramount Pictures, 334 U.S. 131 (1948) (market share of 70 percent deemed sufficient to establish monopoly power). Although market *share* is often a reliable indicator of market *power*, some courts have not viewed the correlation as dispositive. In Reazin v. Blue Cross & Blue Shield, for example, the court noted: "[W]hile market share is indicative of

The monopoly seller has obligations to its small competitors that do not exist in a more competitive marketplace. It must be careful not to use its power in such a way as to crush competition: failed businesses that have tried to compete with a monopoly have many advantages in antitrust cases. A monopoly need not go out of its way to help its competitor, but it should be wary of conduct that is reasonably calculated to destroy that competitor.[6] Similarly, a monopoly *may* (antitrust law is not clear on this point) have an obligation even to those who do not compete with it to refrain from excluding them unfairly from an opportunity to compete in their own line of business.[7] For example, it may be argued that in a one-hospital town the hospital may not exclude from access to its facilities, and patients, those practitioners who are economically dependent on it. The hospital might be regarded as an "essential facility," exclusion from which hinders competition among practicing healthcare professionals.[8] This doctrine is not now widely accepted, but the

---

market power, it is not the sole matter to be considered in assessing a defendant's market strength. Evaluating a firm's ability to achieve a monopoly by controlling prices and eliminating competition is a complex assessment based on as much information as is available to provide one with a broad understanding and appreciation of the market and competition in general." 635 F. Supp. 1287, 1330 (D. Kan. 1986) (quoting Shoppin' Bag of Pueblo v. Dillon Co., 783 F.2d 159 (10th Cir. 1986)), supplemented, 663 F. Supp. 1360 (D.C. Kan. 1987), affd. in part and remanded in part, 1990 U.S. App. LEXIS 4565 (10th Cir. 1990); see also Ball Memorial Hosp. v. Mutual Hosp. Ins., 784 F.2d 1325, 1335-1337 (7th Cir. 1986).

[6]See Aspen Skiing Co. v. Aspen Highlands Skiing Corp., 472 U.S. 585 (1985).

[7]See Reazin v. Blue Cross & Blue Shield, 635 F. Supp. 1287 (D.C. Kan. 1986); supplemented, 633 F. Supp. 1360 (D.C. Kan. 1987), affd. in part and remanded in part, 1990 U.S. App. LEXIS 4565 (10th Cir. 1990).

[8]The Supreme Court has recently suggested that if a competitor is excluded from "unique access to a business element necessary for effective competition" by a group possessing market power, the exclusion may constitute a boycott amounting to a per se violation of the antitrust laws (at least, if the exclusion is based on a demonstrable intent to affect competition). Northwest Wholesale Stationers v. Pacific Stationery & Printing Co., 472 U.S. 284 (1985). This is stated by some courts as the "essential facilities" doctrine. In M.C.I. Communications Corp. v. AT&T, 708 F.2d 1081, 1132-1133 (7th Cir.), cert. denied,

emerging oversupply of practitioners who need access to a hospital may force courts to consider whether a monopoly hospital *must* open its doors to all who want to use it for profit.[9]

§3.3.4 Is Anyone Actually Complaining?

Whether or not a particular course of conduct is likely to be challenged on antitrust grounds often becomes clear only after

---

464 U.S. 891 (1983), the court of appeals set forth the following elements of the essential facilities doctrine: "(1) control of the essential facility by a monopolist; (2) a competitor's inability practically or reasonably to duplicate the essential facility; (3) the denial of the use of the facility to a competitor; and (4) the feasibility of providing the facility." See also Twin Laboratories v. Weider Health & Fitness, 900 F.2d 566, 569 (2d Cir. 1990); City of Malden v. Union Electric Co., 887 F.2d 147 (8th Cir. 1989). In Hecht v. Pro-Football, 570 F.2d 982, 992 (D.C. Cir. 1977), cert. denied, 436 U.S. 956 (1978), the court explained the doctrine in simple terms: "The essential facilities doctrine, also called the 'bottleneck principle,' states that 'where facilities cannot practicably be duplicated by would-be competitors, those in possession of them must allow them to be shared on fair terms. It is illegal restraint of trade to foreclose the scarce facility.' " See also Otter Tail Power Co. v. United States, 410 U.S. 366, 377-378 (1973); United States v. Terminal R.R. Assn., 224 U.S. 383 (1912). See generally Note, Unclogging the Bottleneck: A New Essential Facilities Doctrine, 63 Colum. L. Rev. 441 (1983).

In Robinson v. Magovern, 521 F. Supp. 842, 913 (W.D. Pa. 1981), affd. mem., 688 F.2d 824 (3d Cir.), cert. denied, 459 U.S. 971 (1982), the court rejected the plaintiff's contention that the defendant hospital was an essential facility because the plaintiff had staff privileges at three competing facilities. This, held the court, negated the conclusion that denial of privileges "impose[d] a severe handicap on [plaintiff's] competitive position." See also Pontius v. Children's Hosp., 571 F. Supp. 1352 (E.D. Pa. 1982) (essential facilities doctrine not applicable to hospital staff privileges decisions).

[9]Some federal courts appear to be willing to grant hospitals wide latitude in deciding what kind of practitioners may have access to hospital facilities. For example, categorical exclusion of podiatrists has been found acceptable. See Cooper v. Forsyth County Hosp. Auth., 604 F. Supp. 685, 687-688 (M.D.N.C. 1985), affd., 789 F.2d 278 (4th Cir. 1986), cert. denied, 476 U.S. 972 (1987); Shaw v. Hosp. Auth., 614 F.2d 946 (5th Cir. 1980); Levin v. Joint Comm. on Accreditation of Hosps., 354 F.2d 515 (D.C. Cir. 1965); Kaczanowski v. Medical Center Hosp., 612 F. Supp. 688 (D. Vt. 1985); Feldman v. Jackson Memorial Hosp., 571 F. Supp. 1000 (S.D. Fla. 1983). Even when a hospital competes with those it excludes, federal courts have upheld such practices.

204

the conduct has started or the transaction has been completed. It is at that point, when the economic consequences of the conduct become known, that potential plaintiffs begin to be heard.

Usually there is some warning before an antitrust suit is filed. Those who view themselves as victims of a new policy or practice make their views known and often threaten litigation. If the conduct being contested has been going on for a long time, the plaintiff may file suit to recover for past loss. If the conduct is new, the loss is unlikely to be significant for some time after the conduct begins. During that period, it may not be economically worthwhile for a plaintiff to file suit if it can convince the prospective defendant to abandon its conduct.

Typically, the "victim" will accuse the "defendant," either orally or in writing, of unfair competitive conduct. If the conduct does not cease, a threatening letter—often from a local attorney who invokes antitrust law—may follow without much explanation. The final step before litigation may involve presentation to the defendant of a "draft" antitrust complaint, ready to be filed in federal court, or may involve contact from an antitrust expert retained by the putative plaintiff. Although this scenario is not invariable, some version of it is found in many cases. Thus, hospitals may have notice before they are actually sued. At this point experienced antitrust counsel could tell you how likely it is that you will be sued and, if sued, what the prospects are. Still, unless the conduct at issue had an obvious victim, or unless two or more competitors coordinated it, or unless a monopoly put a competitor at a disadvantage, the risk of an antitrust suit is probably not high enough to warrant calling on antitrust experts when the transaction is being arranged, or even before a complaint is received. If obvious danger signs are absent, vague complaints or threats do not mean that an actual suit is imminent.

Occasionally, of course, antitrust lawsuits are filed without prior warning or complaint. *Some* antitrust violations would not be spotted even if all of the questions above were faithfully asked and answered. These occasions, however, should be rare. Understanding these rules of thumb should provide a sufficient guide for conducting day-to-day transactions. However, if one of the following risk factors is noted, a stronger possibility of antitrust litigation arises: (1) Will the conduct clearly cause significant economic harm to someone? (2) Does it involve agreement between competitors? (3) Does it involve acts by a monopolist that will put one of its competitors in jeopardy?

§3.4 Common Antitrust Problems

The diversity and rapid evolution of hospital practices plus economic pressures on the healthcare industry create an almost infinite variety of potential antitrust problems. Many of these problems will be more theoretical than real (such as the decision by an HMO or a preferred provider organization not to contract with a doctor known to be an excessive utilizer of hospital resources). Most past and present healthcare antitrust cases fall into relatively well-defined categories. The antitrust principles discussed below should be applied to decisions in various areas of substantial concern to hospitals in which there has been litigation.

§3.4.1 Access Restrictions in General

The prime producer of healthcare antitrust litigation has been restriction of access to hospitals, either through denial (or restriction) of staff privileges or through use of exclusive contracts. Denials of privileges to physicians have always been a concern and an economic threat to them, because most doctors depend on the ability to admit and treat patients in a hospital for a substantial portion of their income. Malpractice litigation has forced hospitals to investigate the history of applicants; denials of privileges based on documented records of practice problems probably will not provoke antitrust lawsuits that are likely to succeed.[1]

---

§3.4 [1]The Health Care Quality Improvement Act of 1986, 42 U.S.C.A. §§11101-11152 (Supp. 1987), a federal law, protects credentialing and peer

Changing hospital economics now require many institutions to withhold privileges, or the practical right to *use* privileges even if they are not modified or revoked, on grounds *other than* the applicant's technical competence. A hospital may deny privileges because it cannot handle any additional physician and patient load in certain areas (e.g., cardiac catheterization labs); because it has determined that it should close its staff generally; or because it concludes that the applicant simply consumes too many resources (is not cost-effective) in his or her hospital practice. The hospital may conclude that it needs or wants to give a physician or group an exclusive franchise (e.g., in radiology) without affecting the clinical "privileges" of doctors already on staff; those doctors would retain their privileges but not the economic benefit of them. These matters are all harder to document than is the malpractice experience of a particular physician. These reasons for denying privileges (or granting exclusive contracts) are also potentially susceptible to manipulation by staff physicians who wish to exclude a competitor from their field.

§3.4.2 Staff Privileges Issues

Perhaps the best extant discussion of the antitrust principles that govern a challenge to a hospital's decision to deny privileges to a particular physician is that by the trial court in Robinson v. Magovern,[2] an early antitrust staff privileges case. This decision, often cited by courts hearing challenges to decisions on privileges, is a fairly comprehensive statement of emergent governing law, although there has been considerable elaboration on the topic since the case was decided.[3]

---

review conduct of hospitals and doctors serving on their committees *provided that* "due process" is given and that only "quality-of-care" factors are considered. See, e.g., Patrick v. Burget, 486 U.S. 94 (1988); Austin v. McNamara, 1990 U.S. LEXIS 3550 (C.D. Cal. 1990).

[2]521 F. Supp. 842 (W.D. Pa. 1981), affd. mem., 688 F.2d 824 (3d Cir.), cert. denied, 459 U.S. 971 (1984).

[3]Oltz v. St. Peter's Community Hosp., 861 F.2d 1440 (9th Cir. 1988);

Dr. Robinson was a highly regarded cardiovascular surgeon who had privileges for heart surgery at a number of hospitals in the Pittsburgh area. When he was denied privileges at Allegheny General Hospital, he sued. Allegheny General had been a hospital of declining reputation until it consciously changed its image. Its trustees determined that it should build a reputation as a high-quality research, teaching, and tertiary-care institution with highly respected physicians on its staff. Toward that end the hospital recruited and supported Dr. Magovern, who eventually became chief of surgery, chief of staff, and head of a very successful cardiac surgery unit that worked primarily at the hospital. As part of his staff role at the hospital, Dr. Magovern supervised the credentialing process that ultimately resulted in denial of privileges to Dr. Robinson.

Dr. Robinson claimed that Dr. Magovern and his group were conspiring to keep him off the staff at Allegheny General in order to preserve their alleged monopoly of heart surgery at that hospital. The case took several years to prepare and six weeks to try. It reputedly cost each side hundreds of thousands of dollars. It ended in a complete defeat for Dr. Robinson. That is, no antitrust violations were found.

The case was tried without jury before a judge who explained his reasoning at length. First, the judge denied that there could be such a thing as monopolization of the heart surgery practice at Allegheny General because the "relevant geographic market" for heart surgery extended over a number of counties in which many other facilities, with which Allegheny General had to compete, were located. Patients from the Pittsburgh area and beyond could choose from among several hospitals in deciding where they would have heart surgery performed. Thus, even if Magovern's group *was* dominant at

McKenzie v. Mercy Hosp. of Independence, Kan., 854 F.2d 365 (10th Cir. 1988); Tarabishi v. McAlester Regional Hosp., 827 F.2d 648 (10th Cir. 1987); Castelli v. Meadville Medical Center, 702 F. Supp. 1201 (W.D. Pa. 1988); Jiricko v. Coffeyville Memorial Hosp. Medical Center, 700 F. Supp. 1559 (D. Kan. 1988); Drs. Steur and Latham v. National Medical Enter., 672 F. Supp. 1489 (D.S.C. 1987).

Allegheny General, it did not have a monopoly in heart surgery in the geographic market in which Allegheny General competed.

More important, the court found that Dr. Robinson had not established that his exclusion from the staff resulted from of any conspiracy on the part of Dr. Magovern or his group. Instead, it found that Dr. Robinson's exclusion was supported by excellent motives not involving the kind of anticompetitive features that are the essence of an antitrust violation. Those reasons revolved around the hospital's self-definition and the means by which the hospital chose to compete.

Allegheny General changed from a declining facility to a premier referral hospital, especially in cardiac care, by cultivating an image of high quality. This market position was established by promoting teaching and research activities. Staff physicians were expected to engage in one or both of these activities. Dr. Magovern was the chief overseer of this new identity for the hospital, and the plan succeeded very well in enhancing the reputation of the hospital and creating for it a solid business foundation.

The main objection to Dr. Robinson was not that he was incompetent but that he showed no interest in promoting the hospital's chosen identity. In all his years of practice he had not engaged in research. Moreover, it was his stated intention to maintain privileges at a number of other area hospitals; thus, he was likely to impose a work burden on the residents at Allegheny General without a demonstrated willingness to help train them.

In sum, the evidence indicated that staff privileges for Dr. Robinson at Allegheny General would further *his* professional and economic goals but not necessarily the hospital's interests. Because the choice of whether to grant staff privileges was ultimately for the hospital and its board to make, the court found that denying privileges was justifiable as being in the best interests of the *institution*. The court was not persuaded that the cardiac surgeons already working at the hospital had somehow orchestrated Dr. Robinson's rejection.

The lesson of *Robinson* is simple but extremely important. A denial of staff privileges will generally not be condemned as a per se violation; the hospital's conduct will be examined for its reasonableness and competitive effects, at least unless the plaintiff makes a strong showing that the decision was actually instigated by competitors of the rejected doctor. The peer review process will nominally be exempt from antitrust attack under the Health Care Quality Improvement Act,[4] but that immunity is currently uncertain, and may require a virtual antitrust trial to establish. The court in *Robinson* provides workable guidance to hospitals. Under this standard a denial of staff privileges should survive an antitrust challenge if it is shown to be a decision made by the hospital to further its own, independent business goals. Conversely, a decision by the hospital unsupported by such reasons and that appears to be instigated by staff physicians to favor their economic interests may well be suspect.[5] In fact, as of early 1990, physicians had succeeded in only a small handful of antitrust cases revolving around their denial of access to facilities, and nearly all of those cases involved claims that groups of competing practitioners had caused the exclusion. It cannot be determined how many such cases have been filed and settled without a reported court decision.

More difficult questions are created when the hospital's motive in denying privileges is to protect itself from competition from the physician. For example, if the physician seeking privileges operates an independent business that competes directly with the hospital, then the decision to deny privileges *may* be viewed as monopolistic and an antitrust violation.[6] A sham use of the peer review process as a means for the hospital to destroy a doctor's nearby surgicenter, for example, might well be a violation (assuming that the impact on competition, as well as the sham, could be proved). For most decisions, however, the *Robinson* lesson will suffice: if the decision is made by and

---

[4]42 U.S.C.A. §§11101-11152 (Supp. 1987).

[5]See Weiss v. York Hosp., 745 F.2d 786, 814-816 (3d Cir. 1984), cert. denied, 470 U.S. 1060 (1985).

[6]Coastal Neuro-Psychiatric Assocs. v. Onslow County Hosp. Auth., 607 F. Supp. 49, 53-54 (E.D.N.C. 1985), revd. on other grounds, 795 F.2d 340 (4th Cir. 1986).

for the hospital and not for its physicians or other practitioners, the risk of antitrust violation should be small.

Many lawsuits have been filed by physicians claiming antitrust violations when hospital privileges have been denied or limited—nearly always without success. In the early years some of them were dismissed by obviously unsympathetic trial courts for failure to prove that the challenged conduct affected or was part of "interstate commerce" (an essential element of an antitrust claim),[7] or on grounds that the credentialing process for staff privileges was immune from antitrust challenge because it is conduct sanctioned and supervised by state government,[8]

---

[7]The Supreme Court has held that allegations by the plaintiff that the defendant's conduct would lessen (1) purchases and sales of supplies from out-of-state sources, (2) revenues obtained from third-party payors, (3) management fees, and (4) out-of-state financing to build or add new facilities were sufficient to satisfy the jurisdiction prerequisite that interstate commerce be implicated. Hospital Bldg. Co. v. Trustees of Rex Hosp., 425 U.S. 738, 742 (1976). Some lower courts have applied these criteria strictly and have not hesitated to dismiss physicians' complaints on the ground that an insufficient nexus with interstate commerce has been alleged. The courts of appeals are split on the proper standard to be applied, some requiring that the conduct at issue itself result in interstate commerce effects, see Furlong v. Long Island Hosp., 710 F.2d 922, 926 (2d Cir. 1983); Stone v. William Beaumont Hosp., 782 F.2d 609 (6th Cir. 1986); Seglin v. Esau, 769 F.2d 1274, 1279-1284 (7th Cir. 1985); Crane v. Intermountain Health Care, 637 F.2d 715, 723-724 (10th Cir. 1981) (en banc), while others hold that as long as the defendant's general business activities involve or affect interstate commerce, Sherman Act jurisdiction is proper. See Hahn v. Oregon Physicians Serv., 689 F.2d 840, 844 (9th Cir. 1982), cert. denied, 462 U.S. 1133 (1983); McElhinney v. Medical Protective Co., 549 F. Supp. 121, 127-128 (E.D. Ky. 1982), remanded without opinion, 738 F.2d 439 (6th Cir. 1984). Generally, it should not be difficult for a plaintiff sufficiently to *plead* interstate commerce to remain in court at least through the discovery phase.

[8]The state action doctrine is generally associated with the Supreme Court's decision in Parker v. Brown, 317 U.S. 341 (1943), and exempts anticompetitive actions taken by state governments from antitrust scrutiny. The Court has further refined the test, holding that state action will be present if: "First, the challenged restraint [is] 'one clearly articulated and affirmatively expressed as state policy'; second, the policy [is] 'actively supervised' by the state itself." California Retail Liquor Dealers' Assn. v. Midcal Aluminum, 445 U.S. 97 (1980) (quoting City of Lafayette v. Louisiana Power & Light Co., 435 U.S.

or for a general and perhaps not well-explained failure to establish a violation.[9] The "interstate commerce" and "state action" defenses no longer have much credibility in this kind of case.[10] Denial of staff privileges is not inherently an antitrust violation, and it is likely to become a violation only when it occurs at least in part to limit competition. When there are reasonable explanations for the exclusion that do not involve suppression of competition between the applicant and someone else, the denial will probably be upheld in antitrust litigation under the rule of reason.[11]

389, 410 (1978)); see 324 Liquor Corp. v. Duffy, 479 U.S. 335 (1987); Town of Hallie v. City of Eau Claire, 471 U.S. 34 (1985). Some trial or intermediate appellate courts have found that this standard was satisfied by state statutes immunizing the activities of peer review committees, see Patrick v. Burget, 800 F.2d 1498 (9th Cir. 1986), revd., 486 U.S. 94 (1988) (state involvement in hospital peer review process insufficient to confer state action immunity); Marrese v. Interqual, 748 F.2d 373 (7th Cir. 1984), cert. denied, 472 U.S. 1027 (1985), or statutes conferring immunity on hospitals for decisions regarding staff privileges. See Coastal Neuro-Psychiatric Assocs. v. Onslow County Hosp. Auth., 795 F.2d 340 (4th Cir. 1986). Other courts have been more reluctant to apply the doctrine, finding that whatever policy may have been articulated by the state, the activity challenged is insufficiently supervised by the state to constitute state action. Quinn v. Kent Gen. Hosp., 617 F. Supp. 1226, 1236-1240 (D. Del. 1985); Bolt v. Halifax Hosp. Center, 891 F.2d 810 (11th Cir. 1990) (availability of judicial review for hospital peer review decisions insufficient state involvement to invoke state action doctrine).

[9]See, e.g., Trepel v. Pontiac Osteopathic Hosp., 599 F. Supp. 1484 (E.D. Mich. 1984) (lack of standing); Capili v. Shott, 620 F.2d 438 (4th Cir. 1980) (per curiam); Harron v. United Hosp. Center, 522 F.2d 1133 (4th Cir. 1975), cert. denied, 424 U.S. 916 (1976) (describing claim as "frivolous").

[10]Courts increasingly accept a plaintiff's showing of "interstate commerce." See Cardio-Medical Assocs. v. Crozer-Chester Medical Center, 721 F.2d 68 (3d Cir. 1983); Shahawy v. Harrison, 778 F.2d 636 (11th Cir. 1985); Sweeney v. Athens Regional Medical Center, 709 F. Supp. 1563 (M.D. Ga. 1989); Quinn v. Kent Gen. Hosp., 617 F. Supp. 1226 (D. Del. 1985). The Supreme Court decision in Patrick, discussed infra, casts doubt on state action defenses. Patrick v. Burget, 486 U.S. 94 (1988); Bolt v. Halifax Hosp. Center, 891 F.2d 810 (11th Cir. 1990); Shahawy v. Harrison, 875 F.2d 1529 (11th Cir. 1989); Jiricko v. Coffeyville Memorial Hosp. Medical Center, 700 F. Supp. 1559 (D. Kan. 1988).

[11]See, e.g., Robinson v. Magovern, 521 F. Supp. 842 (W.D. Pa. 1981), affd. mem., 688 F.2d 824 (3d Cir.), cert. denied, 459 U.S. 971 (1984).

One of the very few antitrust cases won by a plaintiff physician alleging a conspiracy to deprive him of his staff privileges was Patrick v. Burget, decided by the United States Supreme Court in 1988.[12] The plaintiff surgeon had lost a bitter struggle with his former partners resulting in his eventual ouster from the hospital where he had practiced. After he succeeded in convincing the jury at trial that his ouster was the result of a conspiracy in restraint of trade rather than deficiencies in his ability to practice medicine, the U.S. Court of Appeals for the Ninth Circuit reversed the verdict in his favor on the ground that the hospital peer review activities at issue constituted "state action" sufficiently to provide antitrust exemption for the physicians involved.[13] The Supreme Court found that the state of Oregon had neither mandated nor supervised the peer review activities at issue. Thus, there being no immunity based on state action, the trial court verdict was reinstated.

In part because of physician lawsuits like *Patrick,* Congress in 1987 enacted the Health Care Quality Improvement Act.[14] The Act supposedly provides antitrust immunity to the participants (both institutions and individuals) in peer review activities. This immunity is linked to establishment of a nationwide reporting system intended to enable hospitals and others to learn whether applicants for privileges have previously been disciplined at another hospital or have suffered malpractice judgments or settlements arising out of their activities. The immunity requires both that the national reporting system be checked and that the peer review process be uncontaminated by "economic interests" of the reviewers. The reporting system was not operational as this book went to press, so the immunity has not yet often been invoked. In any event, it appears that the immunity may be avoided if a plaintiff *alleges* that the peer review process was tainted by economic interests of the reviewers. Once alleged, the issue of economic motive presumably will

---

[12]Patrick v. Burget, 486 U.S. 94 (1988), reversing 800 F.2d 1498 (9th Cir. 1986).

[13]800 F.2d 1498 (9th Cir. 1986).

[14]42 U.S.C.A. §§11101-11152 (Supp. 1987).

be subject to proof. Proving this point is tantamount to proving an antitrust case on the merits. Thus, invoking the statutory immunity may require virtually as much time and expense as defense of the antitrust claim itself. Presumably, as well, defendants who lack an economic motive for their actions during the peer review process will be able to prove that and invoke the defense—but, even without the statutory immunity, doctors lacking financial motives have not been found liable for antitrust violations arising from peer review (although many of them have had to go through the ordeal of litigating a case to be exonerated).

The federal statutory immunity thus may have little impact, although it is too early to tell. It remains clear that access to hospitals is critical to practitioners in many disciplines. So long as that access is in whole or in part under the control of other healthcare practitioners, denial of access will spawn antitrust complaints and suits.

§3.4.3 Exclusions Based on the Class of Practitioner

Besides making case-by-case determinations regarding physician applicants, hospitals must also decide whether to exclude or limit the granting of privileges to entire classes of practitioners. Usually those practitioners are in the "allied health professions," including such disciplines as podiatry, dentistry, chiropractic, psychology, respiratory therapy, midwifery, and nurse anesthesia. These practitioners are not medically licensed, but they are licensed to provide particular healthcare services that may substantially overlap with those provided by medical licensees. In fact, it may be argued that nonphysician practitioners in some fields may have more training and expertise in their specialty than do most physicians who are not specialists in that field but whose privileges may nonetheless entitle them to provide the service.

The question then arises whether a hospital can justify denying such a class of practitioners access to its facilities—and thereby deny them the opportunity to treat patients for profit on hospital premises. The model staff bylaws and accreditation guidelines of the Joint Commission on Accreditation of Healthcare Organizations (JCAHO) really do not answer the question.[15] Not only are hospitals generally free to resolve these questions themselves without risking their accreditation by the JCAHO, but the JCAHO itself has been trying to sidestep these issues (if only to avoid antitrust litigation of its own).

Very few antitrust court decisions have involved challenges to such exclusions by a member of an excluded class of practitioners. One such case arose in North Carolina. In Cooper v. Forsyth County Hospital Authority,[16] the United States Court of Appeals for the Fourth Circuit affirmed the right of a hospital to decide what classes of practitioners it would permit on its premises. A podiatrist sought privileges at a hospital that did not grant them to podiatrists. The court found that the hospital's trustees had the power to decide what was in the best interest of patients. If the podiatrists alleged conspiracy (perhaps by orthopedic surgeons) against them, the allegations were not a problem for the court. In a brief decision, the court found it appropriate for the hospital board to set its own standard of patient care in terms of the kinds of practitioners who would be permitted access to patients.

This decision should be helpful to hospital boards in defining their own institutional character. But it is still possible that an excluded class of practitioners will claim that they were excluded because of pressure from and a conspiracy by their competitors. In such instances antitrust liability can arise. Moreover, courts may be more willing to permit limitation or exclusion of practitioners who clearly have less training or education than their medical counterparts (e.g., nurse anesthetists versus M.D. anesthesiologists) than they will be to allow economic discrim-

---

[15]See Joint Commission on Accreditation of Hospitals, Accreditation Manual for Hospitals 95-98 (1990). The standards state: "[The medical staff] includes fully licensed physicians and may include other licensed individuals permitted by law and by the hospital to provide patient care services independently in the hospital." Id. at 95, *Medical Staff,* Required Characteristic 1.1.1.

[16]789 F.2d 278 (4th Cir. 1986).

ination between similarly trained but differently licensed practitioners (e.g., osteopathic versus allopathic physicians).

In Weiss v. York Hospital,[17] for example, an osteopathic
physician asserted that the denial of privileges he sought was
part of a pattern of exclusion by the hospital and its allopathic
physicians. The court held that the hospital was legally incapable
of conspiring with its medical staff but found that the staff itself
was "a combination of individual doctors and therefore . . .
any action taken by the medical staff satisfies the 'contract,
combination, or conspiracy' requirement of section 1 [of the
Sherman Act]."[18] Given this finding, the court concluded that a
"group of firms at one level of distribution, i.e., the doctors'
level, have used their existing relationship with a supplier [the
hospital] to exclude their competitors from dealing with the supplier."[19] It is important that the court also noted that the
defendant hospital possessed market power in the geographic
market for inpatient healthcare services. Because the staff offered
no "public service or ethical norm" that justified their exclusionary conduct, the court found that the staff's actions were
illegal per se.[20] This decision has frequently been criticized, but
it does demonstrate the force of a conspiracy allegation: if
conspiracy by the hospital with competitors of the excluded class
can be established to the judge's or jury's satisfaction, antitrust
liability might arise even if the board believed that it had its
own independent reasons for denying privileges. In *Weiss,* the
hospital was obliged to treat osteopaths and allopaths the same—
and to pay the plaintiff's very high legal fees.[21]

---

[17]745 F.2d 786 (3d Cir. 1984).

[18]Id. at 814.

[19]Id. at 819; see also id. at 822 n.61 ("[T]he purpose and effect of the
defendants' discriminatory conduct was 'to foreclose so much of the market
from penetration by [the M.D.s'] competitors [i.e., the D.O.s] as to unreasonably
restrain competition in the affected market for [inpatient medical care]"
(quoting Jefferson Parish Hosp. Dist. No. 2 v. Hyde, 466 U.S. 2, 30 n.51
(1984)) (interpolations the court's).

[20]*Weiss,* 745 F.2d at 821.

[21]The osteopath-allopath struggle has produced legislation and court
decisions on non-antitrust grounds in many states and state courts. There is

All across the country allied health professionals are seeking to obtain new or expanded access to hospitals and the patients who use them. Legislators occasionally mandate such access under pressure from the allied professional groups, as well as from insurers and employers who see these groups as potentially less expensive alternatives to traditional forms of practice.[22] Even some hospitals are recognizing that it may be to their advantage to permit at least some allied professionals on staff. To the extent that this prospect threatens practitioners who now have access (usually physicians), resistance arises and the hospital is caught in the middle. If courts come to view hospitals—especially those with no relatively close competing hospital—as public institutions with special obligations not only to patients but also to those who make their living at hospitals, it may be increasingly hard to deny access to licensed and trained professionals who want to practice in a hospital setting.

In general, the following guidelines should be observed: If a practitioner or a group of allied professionals seeks access and privileges in a hospital beyond those (if any) currently permitted by staff bylaws, the decision on that request should *not* be turned over to the medical staff. Instead, the board of trustees may ask the applicant group to provide information about the services it wishes to provide and about its members' training and competence to perform those services in a hospital setting. If the applicant group's approach is serious, potentially backed with a threat of litigation, then some kind of informal hearings may be advisable.[23] Certainly, the medical staff members' views should be solicited as to whether it would be appropriate for services to be provided in the hospital by the allied professionals. In soliciting such views, however, the board must be aware that the interests of physicians who wish to preserve their prerogatives

---

no uniform or consistent rule as to whether hospital trustees may or may not exclude osteopathic physicians or, if so, under what circumstances.

[22]See, e.g., D.C. Code Ann. §32-1307(c) (1986 Cum. Supp.).

[23]See Silver v. New York Stock Exch., 373 U.S. 341 (1963). But see Northwest Wholesale Stationers v. Pacific Stationery & Printing Co., 472 U.S. 284 (1985) (no hearing required when participant in joint venture is expelled if venture possessed no market power).

and stature (as well as their finances) and the interests of the allied group may conflict. The medical staff's advice should be accepted with the awareness that it may contain inherent professional bias, sometimes philosophic or care-oriented, but also sometimes economically driven. Such bias may exist even if the physicians would not themselves be competitors of the allied professionals. Many physicians presume that certain services will always be rendered more appropriately by physicians than by anyone else. While this may or may not be true, the board must exercise independent judgment on the matter.[24]

If the hospital decides to exclude a class of practitioners at the request of or even under pressure from staff physicians, then a boycott may have been committed, not only by the physicians but also by the hospital itself. Acquiescence under pressure to a request to boycott may be no less an antitrust violation than active support of the boycott.[25] Judges and juries are human and may tend to excuse hospitals' behavior as due to coercion, but the letter of the law demands that a hospital that supports its physicians in an improper exclusionary decision be found as liable as the physicians.

Some solution to this dilemma might be obtained through state legislative action with regard to the specific rights and duties of allied health professionals. Of course, legislation is subject to political pressures perhaps beyond the control of hospitals, and it often may do as much harm as good by removing the flexibility to adapt to individual circumstances. Whether or not legislative solutions are proposed, the issues surrounding when and how allied professionals can practice in hospitals will no doubt generate considerable controversy (and

---

[24]See Monsanto Co. v. Spray-Rite Serv. Corp., 465 U.S. 752, 761 (1984) (an entity typically "has a right to deal, or refuse to deal, with whomever it likes, as long as it does so independently"); United States v. Colgate & Co., 250 U.S. 300, 307 (1919) ("In the absence of any purpose to create or maintain a monopoly, the [Sherman Act] does not restrict the long recognized right of a trader or manufacturer . . . freely to exercise his own independent discretion as to parties with whom he will deal.").

[25]See §3.2, n.32, supra.

probably litigation) over the next decade, a matter that a hospital may not take lightly.

§3.4.4 Exclusive Contracting

Another prominent source of healthcare antitrust litigation involves exclusive contracts between hospitals and physicians or physician groups. In some disciplines, especially (but not solely) the hospital-based specialties of anesthesiology, radiology, pathology, and emergency room medicine, exclusive contracts are common, and they provoked little legal attention for many years. Sometimes those contracts were prompted by vagaries of reimbursement law or by particular institutional needs. In other instances exclusive contracts, effectively granting a franchise over a particular area of practice in a hospital, arose from the political need to placate and maintain the support of certain physicians whom the hospital viewed as important to the institution's financial success. Under such contracts, a practitioner who wanted access to the hospital in one of the contracted fields had to seek a position with the exclusive contracting group or forego the opportunity to practice in that hospital absent special circumstances.

As the supply of physicians has grown, exclusive contracting has emerged as a substantial barrier to economic success for some physicians. No longer can a physician who has been rejected because of an exclusive arrangement be confident of finding another nearby hospital either willing to accept her or him on staff or able to do so in light of its own contract commitments. If the only hospital in a community has an exclusive contract, then a physician who is not a party to that contract must either commute or move to some other community to sustain her or his practice. Even in large cities, as exclusive contracts have become more prevalent, physicians who lose or are denied privileges at one hospital cannot always move easily to some other convenient facility. To those practitioners for whom hospital access is a virtual economic necessity—surgeons, radiologists, and so on—breaking through exclusive contracts may become essential to economic survival. Accordingly, a substantial number of antitrust suits have challenged the legal validity of such arrangements, and the issue is still not definitively resolved.

At first these cases met with little, if any, success. The arrangement between a hospital and its contracting physicians was viewed as vertical, subject to rule-of-reason, rather than per se, analysis.[26] Hospitals justified the use of exclusive contracting on grounds of administrative convenience, provision of constant coverage, and ability to control quality of care, among others.[27] Courts that heard challenges to such contracts were not sympathetic to plaintiffs.[28]

The rationale offered by the courts in upholding exclusive contracts was that the hospital was "buying" the services of the contracting physicians and had the right to do so on an exclusive or nonexclusive basis, as it deemed appropriate.[29] Exclusive contracts were (and are) generally deemed acceptable in non-health contexts unless they tie up a sizable proportion of the available business for a long time.[30] Even then, they are by no means presumptively illegal.

When challenges to hospital exclusive contracts predicated on "vertical" antitrust analysis failed, the challengers rummaged around for another antitrust theory on which the attack could be based. They characterized exclusive contracts as tie-ins between the hospital or some department in it and the services of a contracting physician. Under this theory, a patient who used the operating room at a particular hospital was "deprived"

---

[26]See, e.g., Dos Santos v. Columbus-Cuneo-Cabrini Medical Center, 684 F.2d 1346, 1352 (7th Cir. 1982); McMorris v. Williamsport Hosp., 597 F. Supp. 899, 916 (M.D. Pa. 1984).

[27]See, e.g., Smith v. Northern Michigan Hosps., 518 F. Supp. 664, 668 (W.D. Mich. 1981) ("An exclusive contract permits more control over standards, personnel and procedures.").

[28]See, e.g., Capili v. Shott, 620 F.2d 438 (4th Cir. 1980) (per curiam); Harron v. United Hosp. Center, 522 F.2d 1133 (4th Cir. 1975) (characterizing physician's claims as "frivolous"), cert. denied, 424 U.S. 916 (1976).

[29]Harron v. United Hosp. Center, 522 F.2d 1133 (4th Cir. 1975).

[30]See Burnham Hosp., 101 F.T.C. 991 (1983) (advisory opinion).

of the opportunity to choose his or her own anesthesiologist if anesthesia services were covered by an exclusive contract.

Precisely this argument was made by a New Orleans anesthesiologist in Jefferson Parish Hospital District No. 2 v. Hyde.[31] To the surprise of many observers, although the plaintiff lost before the trial court he prevailed in the United States Court of Appeals for the Fifth Circuit.[32] That court characterized the conduct as a clear tie-in—that is, a per se violation. The court obviously was influenced by the fact that the hospital itself, under the unusual arrangement involved, made a profit from the provision of anesthesia services by the contracting group. The court of appeals asserted, in effect, that once a patient had chosen the defendant hospital, it was not fair to confine the patient's choice to any particular group of anesthesiologists. By extension, *any* exclusively contracted services of the hospital might be viewed as a tie-in, because patients could not choose their own providers once they had chosen the hospital.

The Supreme Court reversed the Fifth Circuit's decision, but in doing so it left open many important questions regarding such exclusive contracting. The Court found no liability, but it did not expressly reject the tie-in theory. Instead, it noted that there are numerous hospitals in the city of New Orleans from which patients can choose. A patient who did not wish to use the anesthesia group with which a particular hospital—including the hospital involved in the case—had an exclusive contract could choose a different hospital in order to obtain the anesthesiologist of his or her choice (or at least not to have to use a disfavored anesthesiologist). Because the patient could avoid the so-called tie-in altogether and not be compelled to purchase services from an undesired provider, the exclusive contract agreement in *Hyde* was not an antitrust violation.

The basic determinant in the Supreme Court's decision was that New Orleans had a number of competing hospitals. Patients, as a result, were not in any real sense forced to purchase either of the services offered by the defendant hospital. In communities

---

[31]Jefferson Parish Hosp. Dist. No. 2 v. Hyde, 466 U.S. 2 (1984).
[32]Id. at 8.

in which there are only a few hospitals, or only one, any exclusive contract will more likely take on the appearance of a tie-in. If patients have little or no choice about where they will be hospitalized, any exclusive contract that ties the patient to some provider of medical services might be construed as a tie-in.

The Court itself left a potential loophole by noting that some kinds of medical practitioners have traditionally been "hospital based" and *might* be exempt from tie-in analysis.[33] In other cases courts have somehow decided that no exclusive contract exists,[34] or, as in the Supreme Court's decision in *Hyde,* they have concluded that somehow the elements of compulsion essential for a tie-in have not been shown.[35] It is clear that hospitals throughout the country are continuing to enter exclusive contracts. The wisdom, or legality, of such conduct cannot be definitively determined, although if the hospital involved has numerous competitors and no "market power" in the inpatient service that is alleged to be the "tying product," a tie-in analysis is unlikely to succeed for a plaintiff. Big city hospitals probably remain free to enter exclusive arrangements without significant antitrust risk (in antitrust law, one can virtually never say that a transaction has *no* risk, unless it presents facts identical to those in a recent favorable Supreme Court decision!), but hospitals in smaller communities, or hospitals offering some unique service to which the exclusive product is somehow related, should probably obtain antitrust advice before entering such contracts—at least if there is an identifiable economic "loser."

When we consider whose ox is really gored, we realize that not all exclusive contracts create immediate risk. If the exclusive contract is used in a service area in which the only potential

---

[33]Id. at 23 n.36.

[34]See, e.g., Konik v. Champlain Valley Physicians Medical Center, 733 F.2d 1007, 1017-1018 (2d Cir. 1984).

[35]See, e.g., Ezpeleta v. Sisters of Mercy Health Corp., 800 F.2d 119 (7th Cir. 1986); Kuck v. Bensen, 647 F. Supp. 743, 746 (D. Me. 1986); White v. Rockingham Radiologists, 1986-1 Trade Cas. (CCH) ¶67,142, at 62,889 (W.D. Va. 1986); Mays v. Hospital Auth. of Henry County, 596 F. Supp. 899 (M.D. Pa. 1984).

service providers are those who become parties to the contract, then no immediate risk of antitrust liability is created by the contract. Even if there are, for example, radiologists located in a community that has several hospitals one of which enters into a contract that excludes some of the radiologists in town from access to that hospital, the excluded doctors may already be concentrating their practices at other hospitals so that they all have an opportunity to earn a living somewhere despite the exclusive contract. This state of affairs appears unlikely to last as the use of exclusive contracts in some disciplines becomes the norm in many communities. Physicians completing their training and attempting to establish a practice, or even established doctors changing communities or perhaps even staying in the same place, may encounter exclusive contracts that create a barrier to providing service to *any* hospital in the community where the doctor would like to practice.

Most young physicians will probably not have the resources to commence antitrust litigation (an important item in evaluating antitrust risks stemming from any particular conduct), and in any event they may view doing so as politically unwise. But whether challenges come from new physicians or from more mature practitioners whose economic opportunities are being limited, litigation over this issue will certainly continue in places where there is a limited number of hospitals in which the physician may seek to practice—and in many communities where established practitioners are ousted from a lucrative niche by a new exclusive contract.[36] There are no hard and fast rules, but it is likely that exclusive contracts in any community with four or fewer hospitals should be examined for their impact on potential plaintiffs and for justification.

The concept of justification means simply that the reasons why the *hospital* wishes to enter an exclusive contract are relevant. If the services involved are already available and of satisfactory quality, coverage, and continuity, the hospital may

---

[36]Indeed, it is not unknown for physicians who have themselves benefited from an exclusive contract to turn around and challenge the validity of the contract when it is awarded to a competitor.

gain nothing through entering an exclusive contract. Concerns about on-call availability, maintenance of quality, and so on can often be addressed through staff bylaws and regulations, conditioning staff privileges on the provision of certain services, and assurances to the hospital. In other words, the hospital may be able to obtain these services and assurances without excluding by contract any practitioners willing to abide by such conditions.[37] From the hospital's perspective there may well be few good quality-of-care justifications for granting an exclusive franchise. Doctors who are excluded by contract from working in a hospital certainly cannot admit patients to that hospital, and that may be contrary to the institution's own interests. Most of the stated clinical goals traditionally used to justify exclusive contracts are subject to at least reasonable dispute. That does not mean that the use of such contracts will become a substantial risk, but that justifications should not be after-the-fact clinical "needs" that close analysis will demonstrate do not really exist.

The exclusive contract may be used by a hospital as a means, for example, of reacting to physicians who both use the hospital's capital investment to make a very nice living and at the same time set up a competing facility (such as a surgicenter or outpatient radiology clinic) across the street. In these circumstances, an exclusive contract that excludes the "disloyal" physicians *may* be an appropriate response. In any event, it is far wiser to consult competent healthcare antitrust counsel about the risks of proceeding with an exclusive that is frankly intended to remove offending doctors from the facility than to create

---

[37]In Stone v. William Beaumont Hosp., 782 F.2d 609 (6th Cir. 1986), the defendant hospital claimed that it denied staff privileges to the plaintiff precisely because the plaintiff refused to comply with conditions the hospital deemed essential to its interests. Specifically, the hospital denied privileges because of the plaintiff's heavy commitments to other hospitals, the plaintiff's lack of ability to provide the necessary backup services, and the inconsistency between granting privileges to the plaintiff and the hospital's objectives of maintaining a specialized staff of full-time "geographic" cardiologists. The court, however, did not assess the reasonableness of these justifications; instead, it dismissed the plaintiff's claim for failure to plead that the hospital's conduct had a significant effect on interstate commerce.

make-weight arguments that the exclusive is necessary for quality-of-care reasons. Such arguments may fool some courts or juries some of the time, but are as prone as any other untrue justification to dissolve in the heat of a legal battle.

If a hospital's board and administration are being asked to enter an exclusive contract that the hospital did not propose, then pointing out the Court's decision in *Hyde* and the potential for litigation may be a useful means of resisting pressure. But often the hospital has decided on its own to grant an exclusive contract in some area, perhaps specifically to provide economic protection to a specialty practitioner who otherwise would not make his or her services available at the hospital. For example, a neurosurgeon might agree to move to a community and establish a practice *only* if exclusive privileges are granted, at least for some agreed-upon period of time.[38] If the hospital board believes that a neurosurgeon is necessary for the well-being of its patient community, granting the exclusive contract may be the only available means of obtaining a necessary service. This would be a clinical, or quality-of-care, justification that would stand up to close scrutiny and should survive antitrust challenge.

Once again, if the exclusive contract is based on a *real* need of the institution, and if the institution is not simply foreclosing competition with itself[39] through use of an exclusive contract,

---

[38]For an example of such an arrangement, see McMorris v. Williamsport Hosp., 597 F. Supp. 899 (M.D. Pa. 1984). The court, however, refused to grant summary judgment for the defendant hospital. The plaintiff alleged that an exclusive contract with a salaried nuclear medicine physician was a tying arrangement. In refusing summary judgment the court noted that the hospital, unlike the one in *Hyde,* had some measure of market power.

[39]The "need" may be economic, not clinical, as when physicians who benefit from use of the hospital's plant and equipment also seek to divert some of the hospital's revenue stream to their own competing facility. The hospital may see this conduct as disloyal or creating a conflict of interest and may seek to deprive the offending doctors of access to its capital plant through grant of an exclusive contract to someone else (e.g., granting an anesthesia exclusive that shuts out the anesthesiologist who financed and works at the outpatient surgery center across the street from the hospital's own surgicenter). Note that the exclusive does not actually attack competition: the anesthesiologist can continue to work at his surgicenter regardless of whether or not he also is

the contract should survive attack even under a tie-in theory.[40] Such a case has evidently not yet come up in a reported federal antitrust decision, and the facts on which it would be based may be rare. There may be little justification for most exclusive contracts from the hospital's perspective. That being so, the trend of the law suggests that exclusive contracts should be used with some caution in communities with only one or a few hospitals unless there is a compelling reason to use them, such as the need to attract an otherwise-unavailable specialist.

§3.4.5 Requiring Patients to Use Hospital Facilities or Personnel

A little-explored problem that could become a major hospital antitrust issue is the practice of requiring inpatients to obtain certain services only from facilities or personnel provided by the hospital. Because such policies may block access to markets and revenue for willing sellers, they are likely to stir up litigation. This problem resembles the exclusive contract and tie-in concerns discussed above, with the difference that in this situation the

---

able to work in the hospital. However, in some instances actions of this sort by the hospital may tend to create a monopoly, especially if the loss of access to the hospital renders the competing physician or his facility unable to survive economically. Moreover, the anesthesiologist's loss of access to the hospital may send a warning to other doctors not to try to compete with the facility, thereby having a chilling effect on possible future competition. This scenario is just starting to appear, and the rules regarding permissible hospital responses to physician competition are not yet clear. The concept of removing a doctor's privileges (or access to the hospital plant and equipment) for nonclinical reasons has been accepted in some jurisdictions; the hearing process invoked for clinical privilege reductions is not required. See, e.g., Sternberg v. Hospital Corp. of Am., Case No. 87-35327 (23), Circuit Court of the 17th Judicial District in and for Broward County, Fla., Summary Final Judgment for Defendants, entered Feb. 27, 1990.

[40]This set of facts occurred in Coastal Neuro-Psychiatric Assocs. v. Onslow County Hosp. Auth., 795 F.2d 340 (4th Cir. 1986), but the court of appeals held that the hospital's conduct was immune from antitrust attack under the state action doctrine. See also nn.121 and 122 below and accompanying text.

hospital is itself the seller of the required service rather than an outside doctor with an exclusive contract.

Hospitals have always assumed the right to compel patients to purchase various goods and services from them rather than from any other supplier. For example, inpatients are not told that pharmaceutical goods or intravenous solutions might be purchased from a competing vendor across the street. Patients are not told that they have a choice of using the hospital's x-ray machines or someone else's. For that matter, patient meals are included in the daily charges, while patients are kept ignorant of the fact that they may get their food from another source. Traditionally, when an inpatient has bought hospital services, she has bought the entire bundle: whatever her healthcare needs, the patient has usually relied exclusively on the hospital. Even as physicians are protesting exclusive contracts (while others are trying to obtain them), other parts of the traditional hospital bundle of services represent areas of economic opportunity potentially worth fighting over.

An example is a CAT scanner owned and installed by the hospital on its premises. Quite naturally, the hospital might require that all of its inpatients in need of CAT scans receive them from its own scanner. If there are no other scanners in town, no problem is likely to arise. But suppose another scanner, used by hospital physicians and patients before the hospital installed its own, is located in physicians' offices near the hospital. Now that the hospital has its own equipment, it might illegally tell people that they may not use the scanner down the street while they are inpatients at the hospital.

The economic stakes in such a scenario can be high, at least from the perspective of the individuals involved. The physicians who purchased the outside scanner may well have depended greatly on hospital-generated revenues to pay for their machine and return a profit to them. Suddenly, that source of revenue may be cut off as the hospital installs both its own scanner and a policy that inpatients cannot use the scanner in the physicians' clinic (at least, not without being discharged from the hospital). To the physician-owners, it appears that the hospital is simply suppressing competition by creating a captive market for its own machine. They may argue that patients are deprived of choice and are tied to the hospital's CAT scanner purely because they are inpatients at the facility. The doctors may also claim that they are themselves deprived of business and that patients are deprived of free choice and of the benefits of competition in the sale of these services.

The hospital will certainly see things differently. Hospital administrators assert that it is not good practice to ship patients from the hospital to an outside machine—a practice presumably followed previously only because no other machine was available. The hospital's own concerns about tort liability and about providing the best quality of care are thus invoked as strong reasons for not permitting patients to use the outside machine. Moreover, the hospital can point out that *it* does not compel any patient to use its machine. Doctors on staff decide when a diagnostic or therapeutic modality is required, so patients are not really tied in the sense of having to purchase the service. Only if a physician prescribes a service will the service be provided. In fact, hospitals can often point to greater, undisclosed self-interest on the part of physicians who tell patients that they need diagnostic work of the sort their (the doctors') machine provides. Indeed, if the physicians restrict the use of their scanner to patients who also contract with them for physicians' services and the scanner is one of only a few available, the physicians' conduct itself conceivably could constitute a tie-in: patients would be told they could only get the services of, say, the only orthopedic surgeon in town if they also agreed to use the scanner in which she held an ownership interest. The services of the surgeon could be the tying product, and use of the scanner the tied product, to the detriment of the machine owned by the hospital (for which charges might be lower than those charged by the orthopedist).

The debate over mandatory use of hospital-provided services is likely to focus on the medical need and justification for the hospital policy, the economic impact of the policy, and whether the hospital has an implicit right to prohibit competition with itself. Such a situation arose in Coastal Neuro-Psychiatric Associates v. Onslow County Hospital Authority.[41] The plaintiff

---

[41]607 F. Supp. 49 (E.D.N.C. 1985), revd. on other grounds, 795 F.2d 340 (4th Cir. 1986).

physicians, who owned a CAT scanner, challenged two of the defendant's practices: (1) patients who used the hospital's services were forced to use the hospital's own CAT scanner if such a procedure was needed, and (2) patients who used the hospital's CAT scanner were forced to use a certain group of radiologists chosen by the hospital to interpret the scans. The court held that the practice of barring inpatients' use of CAT scanners other than the one owned by the hospital did *not* constitute a tying arrangement because not all patients who used the hospital's services were required to submit to CAT scan diagnosis. The complexities of this situation make the court's conclusions questionable, because it is unlikely that many patients who require the use of a CAT scanner will seek such a method of diagnosis without the need for other services offered exclusively by hospitals: these patients really do not have a choice about using the only hospital in the area, and the hospital uses that need to compel use of its scanner instead of one outside the hospital. In effect, the hospital's policy could foreclose any possibility of competition from independent owners of CAT scanners that cannot simultaneously provide complementary inpatient hospital services. In fact, the plaintiffs in *Onslow* owned their own CAT scanner, and the hospital's practices clearly limited the occasions on which the plaintiffs could effectively compete with the hospital.

On the other hand, the court did find that a tying arrangement had been sufficiently *alleged* by the plaintiffs with respect to the hospital rules concerning the physicians patients were required to employ to read the films generated by the CAT scanner. This claim mirrored the allegations in *Hyde*. Unlike *Hyde*, however, the district court concluded that Onslow Memorial Hospital enjoyed a virtual monopoly, clearing the way for plaintiffs to prove their allegations at trial. On appeal, however, the United States Court of Appeals for the Fourth Circuit reversed this decision,[42] holding that the defendant's conduct was autho-

---

[42]Coastal Neuro-Psychiatric Associates v. Onslow County Hosp. Auth., 795 F.2d 340, 342 (4th Cir. 1986). For a discussion of the state action doctrine, see n.89.

rized by state statute and thus immune under the "state action" doctrine first articulated by the Supreme Court in Parker v. Brown.

A lot of the goods and services offered at hospitals can in fact be sold to inpatients by outsiders, at least theoretically— quite probably without jeopardizing patient care.[43] For example, regular x-ray services can also be provided in physicians' offices. Many pathology services are already being performed off hospital premises by independent laboratories. There is no inherent reason why pharmaceutical goods *must* come only from the hospital pharmacy, and there is no intuitively obvious reason why services provided by hospital employees cannot be provided by outsiders brought into the hospital for specific cases. For example, at many hospitals anesthesiologists bring into the hospital, and supervise and bill patients for, their own nurse anesthetist employees or contractors. Some hospitals have nurse anesthetists as their own employees and do not permit physicians to bring their employees in to compete with the hospital's. The same may be true with regard to respiratory therapy, physical therapy, or other services up to and including regular nursing service.

Many parts of a hospital's bundle of services offer attractive economic opportunities that, in theory, outsiders might wish to exploit in the name of "vigorous competition." Frequently, issues of quality and liability may be resolved without precluding the outsider from competing with the hospital. Yet permitting outsiders to strip from the hospital one after another of its profitable services may leave the hospital as nothing more than a hotel with linoleum floors, offering minimal services at high prices while the clinical activities are performed by others. This,

---

[43]Cf. Jefferson Parish Hosp. Dist. No. 2 v. Hyde, 466 U.S. 2, 22 (1984) ("Unquestionably, the anesthesiological component of the package offered by the hospital could be provided separately and could be selected by the individual patient or by one of the patient's doctors if the hospital did not insist on including anesthesiological services in the package it offers to its customers.")

at least, is the hospital's justification, resting both on economic and quality-of-care premises: if courts do not permit hospitals to "bundle" services and protect the more profitable of them from outside encroachment, then hospitals *as* unique bundles of services may cease to exist. Unbridled competition may destroy the institutions so that the purity of the antitrust economic model can be preserved.

Such a development can harm not only the hospital but also the community it serves. Not-for-profit hospitals in particular consider themselves obligated by their very nature to provide a broad array of services, especially when they are the only hospital in town. The pricing of services at hospitals is something of an art form at even the most sophisticated institutions, and the desire to keep basic rates for room and board as low as possible causes many ancillary services to be priced well over direct cost and even well over fully allocated cost. This situation creates an opportunity for a competitor to claim to provide the same service more cheaply—without resolving the question of the hospital's need for revenue to maintain its services.

The *Onslow* decision is scarcely the end of litigation on this topic. Hospital boards must be aware that requiring inpatients to buy from the hospital a service that an outsider has been selling to inpatients, or is claiming it should be permitted to sell to inpatients, may lead to litigation. Such a decision may be the right one, and challenges to these practices may not succeed; apparently none have to date. But the well-established prerogative of a hospital to dictate what the patient will buy, and where, is now being questioned, with (perhaps) enormous and unforeseen consequences. If an outside vendor protests being denied access to inpatients, antitrust counsel should be consulted.

§3.4.6 Closing or Limiting Staff Size

In recent years there has been much discussion as to whether the size of an entire medical staff, or departments within the staff, should or can be limited. In a few instances size has been restricted without antitrust challenge. But any wholesale move to restrict staff size could potentially deprive a lot of physicians of economic opportunities and quite possibly would prompt litigation. Again, the motives behind such conduct should be examined.

Why might a hospital limit its staff or department size? The most often-mentioned justification is lack of capacity: the facility as a whole, or certain parts of it, simply cannot take any more patients. While this argument has an immediate appeal, and is almost invariably invoked as the justification for closing all or part of a staff, in many instances it probably is not valid.

First, in the early 1990s, relatively few hospitals are seriously or persistently overloaded. Usually, more admissions would be welcome. Moreover, new members of the medical staff do not necessarily generate new admissions; they may merely redistribute existing admissions across a different physician grouping. Perhaps in communities with several hospitals a physician may switch his own loyalties, and admissions, from one facility to another, prompting overcrowding at the new recipient. But to a considerable degree the number of admissions in a given department may ultimately rest on the size and demographics of the population from which the hospital draws (and, perhaps, on the hospital's marketing efforts). Cynics might say that more doctors will generate more admissions because physicians will do whatever is necessary to support their own incomes. There is little evidence on this assertion, but conventional wisdom suggests that it is usually good to add doctors to the staff in the hope that they will generate more admissions.[44]

Absent a hospital's actually being overloaded and having good reason to believe that having more doctors on staff will unacceptably increase the burdens on the institution, what justifications exist for closing or limiting staff size? Perhaps scheduling is a problem, especially in operating rooms. Also, adding physicians can mean a greater administrative burden. But again, unless the hospital's beds are full, it is difficult to

---

[44]See Potters Medical Center v. City Hosp. Assn., 800 F.2d 568, 575-576 (6th Cir. 1986).

imagine that this burden is so great as to warrant keeping physicians off staff or limiting departmental size.

Most often, freezes or limitations on staff size will be proposed by existing medical staff. Consciously or otherwise, practitioners may view the pool of available business as static, and they may not be eager to invite competition into the market. Limitations on staff help preserve the business of those already there. A hospital that closes its staff (or certain departments) at the prompting of its physicians may well commit an antitrust violation. This action would be a classic group boycott, orchestrated by physicians against their competitors, with the hospital as the mechanism to carry it out. Both the physicians and the hospital could be liable at law if this were found by a court to be the basis for the staff exclusion policy.

A much more difficult question is created by staff limitations that the hospital actually does initiate for its *own* interests— including protecting its staff physicians from competition without their requesting or reaching an agreement that such protection should be accorded them. That is, a hospital may conclude that in order to maintain the good will, or even the presence, of some physicians whose services are essential to its financial and institutional well-being, *it* must shelter those physicians from too much competition. For example, an outstanding neurosurgeon may be willing to remain on staff at a hospital in a relatively small community only as long as he knows that he has the entire market to himself. If another neurosurgeon is accepted on staff, the first one may leave. Under these circumstances the hospital *may* be acting in its own best interest in unilaterally deciding to limit the size of the neurosurgical staff, precisely to protect the economic interests of the person who is already there. Similarly, a hospital wishing to institute a sophisticated program may need to have a sophisticated team of doctors to control that program, which might only be achieved by giving exclusive access to a certain department to the specialists; a heart transplant program might require closing the cardiac surgery or cardiology departments or substantially turning control of them over to the physicians who will manage the transplant program.

This may appear to be very much like the kind of conduct potentially viewed as a group boycott, discussed above. The difference, though, is in the self-interest of the institution and in the furthering of efficiency-creating practices. If the hospital *ought* to have an interest in (or at least little reason to fear) obtaining additional staff members, then a decision to limit staff size that occurs after consulting with present staff members may be risky, especially if the hospital is a high-profile, successful institution at which new doctors in the community would like to establish their practices. A threat by an entire staff or large department to leave town if it does not get a closed unit is not credible in most communities, since doctors cannot necessarily switch to another community or even another hospital in the same community without a lot of inconvenience to themselves; thus, such a threat is probably not justification for closing all or part of the staff. But a department with one or two practitioners who are of particular value to the institution may be worth protecting, and "protection" may mean a unilateral choice by the hospital to close the department, in effect granting an exclusive franchise to the doctors but without an "agreement" to that effect with them. These are difficult decisions, and should not be undertaken without some reflection and perhaps some legal counsel—especially if the closure will cause economic harm to one or more identifiable excluded physicians.

The line between proper and improper closures will not be easy to draw, but the problem is not likely to come up often. In the face of pressure from incumbent practitioners to turn down new applicants for privileges, the hospital should consult counsel and try to find out the real motivations for the proposal. If the proposal really is in the best interest of the hospital, that should not be difficult to discern, and the plan probably can be implemented without legal risk. As admissions decline but the number of physicians increases, there may be more and more pressure to restrict hospital staffs but less and less justification for it. Hospitals may well be able to deflect such pressures by pointing out to the current staff the antitrust risks that can go along with proposals to limit additional staff.

§3.4.7 Joint Ventures

The term "joint venture" is often used to describe new business activities in the healthcare industry.[45] Generically, joint ventures are new business enterprises created by two or more unrelated parent entities. The antitrust significance of a joint venture will depend on such factors as who the parents are, the line of business in which the new enterprise will engage, the relationship between the parents and the new enterprise, and the likelihood that the enterprise will limit or preclude competition.[46]

What antitrust law[47] there is on joint ventures suggests that these arrangements generally should be viewed as a kind of merger between the parent enterprises.[48] The Supreme Court has expressed concern that when two or more enterprises, each wishing to start a new business, combine their efforts, then competition is reduced. That is, instead of two or more new businesses being started by two or more parents, only one is started.[49]

---

[45]Professor Brodley has defined a joint venture as "an integration of operations between two or more separate firms, in which the following conditions are present: (1) the enterprise is under the joint control of the parent firms, which are not under related control; (2) each parent makes a substantial contribution to the joint enterprise; (3) the enterprise exists as a business entity separate from its parents; and (4) the joint venture creates significant new enterprise capacity, new technology, a new product, or entry into a new market." Brodley, Joint Ventures and Antitrust Policy, 95 Harv. L. Rev. 1523, 1526 (1982).

[46]United States v. Penn-Olin Chem. Co., 378 U.S. 158 (1964).

[47]Joint ventures may raise questions under other areas of law, such as Medicare or Medicaid "fraud and abuse." Those considerations are not addressed in this chapter.

[48]*Penn-Olin*, 378 U.S. at 170.

[49]In United States v. Penn-Olin Chemical Co. the Supreme Court expressed this concern: "If the parent companies are in competition, or might compete absent the joint venture, it may be assumed that neither will compete with the progeny in its line of commerce. Inevitably, the operations of the joint venture will be frozen to those lines of commerce which will not bring it into competition with the parents, and the latter, by the same token, will be foreclosed from the joint venture's market." 378 U.S. at 169. See also FTC v.

Of course, the prospect that a joint venture will keep one or more of the parents out of a particular new line of business matters only if competition in that area is sparse. If General Motors and IBM decided to create a joint venture to market hot dogs in downtown Manhattan, that enterprise might reduce the prospect that either parent company would start such a business alone in competition with all other hot dog stands. That scarcely matters, though, because there are already so many hot dog stands in downtown Manhattan—and, even more important, there are many other companies that are able to enter that business if competitive opportunity in it is attractive.[50]

In contrast, if two of the largest outboard motor manufacturers in the world agree to start a joint venture to manufacture and sell outboard motors in the United States, that may substantially restrict competition, because each company could have started the new venture on its own and there are very few other companies with the knowledge or experience to do so. The latter joint venture was found illegal,[51] but the hot dog stand venture certainly would not be.

For a hospital-sponsored joint venture, the first question is whether the enterprise is likely to suppress competition in some form. If the answer is yes, other questions arise, such as whether such competition would probably have arisen if the joint venture had not occurred.

Procter & Gamble Co., 386 U.S. 568 (1967); United States v. Marine Bancorporation, 418 U.S. 602 (1974); Yamaha Motor Co. v. FTC, 6757 F.2d 971, 981 (8th Cir. 1981), cert. denied, 456 U.S. 915 (1982); Engine Specialties v. Bombardier, 605 F.2d 1, 9-11 (1st Cir. 1979), cert. denied, 446 U.S. 983 (1980); Tenneco v. FTC, 689 F.2d 346 (2d Cir. 1982); United States v. Siemens Corp., 621 F.2d 499 (2d Cir. 1980); BOC Intl. v. FTC, 557 F.2d 24 (2d Cir. 1977); Union Carbide Corp. v. Nisley, 300 F.2d 561 (10th Cir. 1961), cert. dismissed, 371 U.S. 801 (1962). See generally Brodley, Potential Competition Under the Merger Guidelines, 71 Calif. L. Rev. 377 (1983).

[50]If potential competitors of the joint venture can enter the product market easily—that is, if there are no significant barriers to entry, such as high capital requirements—then the anticompetitive effects of the joint venture will be minimal and probably not suspect under the antitrust laws. Cf. FTC v. Rhinechem Corp., 459 F. Supp. 785, 789-790 (N.D. Ill. 1978).

[51]Yamaha Motor Co. v. FTC, 657 F.2d 971 (8th Cir. 1981).

For example, suppose that two hospitals in the same community decide to create a pathology laboratory. If they are the only two hospitals in town, such a joint venture almost certainly will make it impossible for a competing laboratory that is at all dependent on hospital-derived work to survive. If each parent hospital is assumed to make all of its own laboratory purchases from the joint venture, the joint venture will suppress competition through three mechanisms. First, the largest customers in town for lab services will already have been foreclosed to any other potential seller of such lab services; second, the jointly owned facility will probably operate at such a high volume (giving it great economy of scale) that no new, low-volume laboratory could compete with it on price; and third, by combining, the hospitals will have removed themselves as independent potential or actual competitors in the market for furnishing lab services. Under such circumstances the joint-venture laboratory will almost certainly capture not only the hospital work generated by its parents but a lot of outpatient work as well as work from hospitals in outlying communities. Thus, the joint venture is likely either to forestall creation of any new competition or at least to keep a new competitor from succeeding.

The results of this analysis would differ if there were many more available purchasers of pathology lab services than the two hospitals sponsoring the joint venture if a well-financed competitor were willing to sell to other hospitals on the basis of superior quality or cost, or if for other reasons competition in the laboratory business could survive even in the face of the joint venture. Moreover, even if the joint venture suppressed potential competition between the participants in the venture, it might not be an antitrust violation if it could be shown that neither parent was likely to start a pathology lab on its own.[52] Unless both hospitals were able and willing to enter the business

---

[52]If the capital requirements of an enterprise are such that either parent would be unable to enter the market independently, it is likely that no antitrust violation will be found. See United States v. FCC, 652 F.2d 72 (D.C. Cir. 1980) (en banc).

alone, the joint venture would not be inherently responsible for suppressing competition—*unless*, as in this example, the parents and the joint venture were in a buyer-seller relationship in which use of a joint venture would probably deprive any competitors of the laboratory of the customers it needs to survive. This joint venture might be an "agreement in restraint of trade" or it might be viewed as an effort at monopolization of the pathology laboratory business in the community.

Hospitals buy services from pathology laboratories; they may also create a joint-venture cement company, which would not depend on hospitals for its business. In that instance, the fact that the parent enterprises are hospitals would not ensure the success of the joint venture against its competition. In this respect joint ventures in the hospital industry are different from those in most other industries, because hospital joint ventures tend to be in some kind of vertical relationship with the hospital parents and can draw on the strength of the hospitals or their purchases to compete more effectively.

Some hospital-sponsored joint ventures (such as pathology laboratories) may create public benefit because their economies of scale permit lower prices. The strength of this argument may depend on the actual operation of the joint venture. If the savings created by economies of scale actually are passed on as lower prices to consumers rather than returned to the parents in the form of profits, the transaction is much more likely to survive antitrust attack.

Of course, many joint ventures now being structured involve not hospital with hospital, but rather hospital with physician, hospital with home health agency, and so on. Sometimes several hospitals are involved, sometimes several physician groups, and sometimes three or more distinct groups of players. For the most part, the joint ventures created by hospitals—pathology laboratories, health maintenance organizations, or imaging centers, for example—are not big enough to require reporting to federal antitrust authorities.[53] These authorities are unlikely to be aware

---

[53]Federal law requires substantial mergers and acquisitions to be reported to the Department of Justice and the FTC. See Hart-Scott-Rodino Antitrust

of these ventures, much less to investigate or attack them. Nevertheless, the risk of antitrust violations in joint ventures is real, because most enterprises proposed by joint ventures pose distinct economic threats to existing players in the community. Joint ventures intended to bring a new service to the community may present minimal antitrust risk, but ventures intended to capture business in the community currently conducted by others are quite likely to evoke at least the threat of antitrust action. In the whose-ox-is-gored analysis, usually distinct businesses or individuals can be identified whose economic interest might be harmed by the joint venture. If they are identifiable, the impact of the joint venture on them should be considered, and the joint venturers should be prepared to have to defend their conduct against claims made by a sinking competitor.

For example, consider a venture between a hospital, some members of its medical staff, and a local home health equipment company. The parties are to share in the benefits of a newly created company formed to market services and merchandise likely to be needed by many hospital patients when they are discharged. To such a business, the hospital can bring capital and access to patients just when they need to make a purchasing decision. Physicians can bring capital and some ability to influence patient choice (although they may be included more for political reasons than for what they bring to the enterprise). The home health company brings its expertise in the line of business. The net effects of such a combination may well be a home health equipment company with enormous competitive advantages over anyone else in that business in the community. Competing enterprises may not be able to survive. If greatly threatened, experience indicates they may sue, and antitrust grounds are the most likely to be invoked.

To the extent that the business advantage of such a joint venture rests in the hospital's ability to generate customers for

---

Improvement Act of 1976, 15 U.S.C. §18A(d) (1982). Pre-acquisition notice is generally required only if the firm to be acquired has assets of at least $15 million and the acquiring firm has sales and assets of at least $100 million, or vice versa. 16 C.F.R. §§801.40(b)(2)(ii), 801.40(b)(2)(iii) (1989).

it, the joint-venture form may be irrelevant to the reasons for success. Even if the hospital simply started its own home health agency, that company might have enormous advantages that could drive its competitors out of business. Such a development might well be viewed as monopolization, discussed above. But the joint-venture mechanism makes the enterprise even more vulnerable to attack, because the enterprise involves an agreement between two or more independent enterprises. Thus, the aggrieved competitor could assert a "combination in restraint of trade" instead of the much-harder-to-prove monopolization claim that would apply if the hospital had acted alone.

If two or more of the joint-venture parents are competitors of one another, an antitrust attack by a losing competitor of the joint venture is likely to be even stronger. Such cases are now being litigated; joint ventures of this nature are themselves relatively new in the industry. Perhaps most such joint ventures provide economic advantage to the parents without greatly harming any existing competitor. But sometimes competitors are threatened, and some of them have sued.[54]

Accordingly, no categorical statements can be made about the legality of joint ventures. As a rule of thumb, the more attractive they seem to be as business opportunities, the more likely it is that they will gore someone's ox and that precautions should be taken to assure that any harm to competitors results from appropriate competition, not from illegal combination or use of market dominance. More and more, hospitals and physicians find it worthwhile to cooperate in dealing with the rapidly changing economics of healthcare. They may find partic-

---

[54]For example, in *Key Enterprises* the sole hospital in a Florida community joint-ventured a home health service with a company already in that business. A small home health company found itself in economic peril and sued. A jury returned a multi-million dollar verdict for the plaintiff, but the trial judge reversed the verdict and dismissed the case on the basis that the plaintiff had not shown an antitrust violation. Both the adverse jury verdict and the reversal when the facts were analyzed by a jurist more conversant than are juries with antitrust concepts are suggestive of the fate of a lot of healthcare antitrust cases to date and to be anticipated. Key Enterprises of Delaware v. Venice Hospital, 703 F. Supp. 1513 (M.D. Fla. 1989).

ipating in joint ventures to be a good and workable idea. But the risks of antitrust violation are high enough to warrant an antitrust analysis of any enterprise larger than all but the smallest and most informal, at least if the venture is to offer a service already being sold by someone else in the community.

§3.4.8 Special Issues for Health Maintenance Organizations and Preferred Provider Organizations

In many respects, the most visible manifestation of the new competitive environment in healthcare has been the spectacular growth of health maintenance organizations (HMOs) and pre-ferred-provider organizations (PPOs),[55] along with the entire notion of reducing healthcare costs through implementation of "managed care" in those and other contexts. HMOs or PPOs are being either implemented or at least discussed in almost every community and almost every hospital in the country.

HMOs and PPOs constitute both a different form of organization for the payment and delivery of healthcare services and a means by which hospitals and physicians now compete for patients. HMOs and PPOs make the price of healthcare services a consideration for both patients and their employers when a healthcare "system" is chosen. In turn, that system dictates, or at least limits, the choice of providers available to the patients. By choosing one of these systems as an insurer or payor for healthcare costs, the patient may be choosing a limited panel of available physicians to provide primary and specialty care, and she almost certainly will be confining herself to one or a few of the hospitals in her community.

This is a sharp break with the pattern of the last several generations, during which the notion of "freedom of choice" was embedded in state insurance codes to keep insurance

---

[55]See Alpert and McCarthy, Beyond *Goldfarb:* Applying Traditional Anti-trust Analysis to Changing Health Markets, 29 Antitrust Bull. 165, 176-176 (1984).

companies from attempting to influence patients' health provider choices. After about 1983 freedom of choice as a right all but vanished in most jurisdictions, through either specific legislation or regulatory "benign neglect," leading to direct contractual relations between payors on the one hand and healthcare providers on the other. In nearly every state insurers can pay reduced benefits for an insured patient who does not use the "preferred providers" with which the insurer has contracted. Because these contracts can substantially affect the flow of patients in a community, they are a prime means by which healthcare providers compete with each other for a static or diminishing pool of available non-Medicare or Medicaid, "charge-paying" business.

HMOs are creatures of explicit statutes at either the federal[56] or state levels.[57] Essentially, they are insurance companies that provide the services for which insurance premiums are paid. That is, the subscriber (or his employer) pays a fixed premium in advance every month, in return for which he is to be provided all the basic healthcare services he needs—whether from a physician, a hospital, or possibly other providers. The HMO's risk lies in the unpredictable rate at which its subscribers will use health services under the plan. Generally, the more subscribers use the plan, in the form of physician encounters or hospital visits, the higher the insurer's costs (except for the still relatively rare plans in which both doctors and hospitals are "capitated"). HMOs attempt to control that use through various incentive mechanisms applied to the physicians and hospitals that sell services to the HMO. The various means of utilization review and control ("managed care") can, in the aggregate, reduce the amount of services necessary to take care of a given population by a considerable amount. At the same time, the prospect that the HMO can channel a significant number of patients to a limited number of doctors and hospitals, can enable the HMO to bargain for better prices from providers with which it contracts than are charged to traditional third-party insurance companies.

---

[56]42 U.S.C. §300e et seq. (1982).
[57]E.g., Mo. Rev. Stat. §354.400 et seq.

HMOs have grown rapidly in the last several years, and according to the Group Health Association, at the end of 1989 enrollment in approximately 600 plans totaled nearly 35 million lives.

PPOs are similar to HMOs in that they contract with physicians and hospitals to provide services to enrolled subscribers. However, a PPO may not involve the insurance component of premium prepayment. Many PPOs still provide traditional, if perhaps discounted, fee-for-service payments to providers every time service is rendered. The payment may be lower than the provider's posted charges, and virtually every PPO attempts to reduce the total amount of healthcare service required for its patient population, much as HMOs do. However, in a PPO the actuarial risk *may* remain with either the patient or her employer rather than being shifted to an insurance company. But even this is changing. Many insurance companies are now developing hybrid products that are very similar to HMOs in that subscribers incur a fixed premium payment for their coverage and the insurer signs up a panel of providers that may be fewer than all providers in the community to meet the healthcare needs of the PPO's enrollees.

The whole area of alternative delivery systems is so complex and changes so rapidly that it cannot adequately be described here. But these systems do raise antitrust issues, because they are becoming primary tools of competition between providers. Hospitals and physicians should be aware of some issues that can arise in the context of such systems.

Inclusion, Exclusion, and Exclusivity. Virtually by definition, HMOs and PPOs will not want to sign up all physicians in a community, and if the town has more than one hospital, these systems almost certainly will want to contract with fewer than all hospitals. (It is difficult to envision a "Preferred Provider Organization" in a one-hospital town.) When these alternative delivery systems began to attract attention in the 1980s, it was only by promising to deliver new patients to physicians and hospitals that they could gain price concessions and other contractual benefits from providers. Now, the systems can threaten to move existing patients away from providers who do not grant concessions. Such quid pro quo arrangements are not antitrust violations. No physician or hospital has any inherent right to be included in an alternative delivery system. It would be hard to prosecute an antitrust case against an organizer of a HMO or PPO who decides not to include a particular practitioner or facility for good business reasons (such as the need to be able to commit all available patients to a single hospital in order to get a good price from that hospital). If a physician or hospital were excluded because of a collaborative decision by a group of that provider's competitors, perhaps an action could be brought; but even then the plaintiff would have to show that the exclusion was motivated by a desire to hurt competition rather than a desire to create a viable competitive enterprise by reasonable means.[58]

In fact, it appears that including too many of a community's providers may itself create antitrust problems. If a high proportion of the providers in a given place participate in a particular system, then rival systems may find it hard to get started. That is, those who have a stake, whether or not it involves equity, in a particular system may be less willing to sign up with and provide necessary services to a competing system. Thus, the theoretical possibility of overinclusion has been referred to by the head (at that time) of the Antitrust Division of the United States Department of Justice.[59] The risks incurred by an over-

---

[58]See Reazin v. Blue Cross & Blue Shield, 635 F. Supp. 1287 (D.C. Kan. 1986); supplemented, 633 F. Supp. 1360 (D.C. Kan. 1987), affd. in part and remanded in part, 1990 U.S. App. LEXIS 4565 (10th Cir. 1990).

[59]P. McGrath, Asst. Atty. Genl., Antitrust Div., Remarks before the Thirty-Third American Bar Association Antitrust Spring Meeting 7-10 (Mar. 22, 1985). In a business review letter to Hospital Corporation of America, the Department of Justice expressly addressed the anticompetitive implications of overinclusiveness: "[I]f a large percentage of hospitals . . . or if a large percentage of doctors in any geographic market should become affiliated only with [HCA's proposed PPO], the Antitrust Division would be likely to give further consideration to the question of whether [the PPO] operation in Southern Florida has the purpose or effect of impeding the development of other PPOs, facilitating collusion, or otherwise reducing competition among providers or hospitals." Department of Justice, Business Review Letter to HCA (Sept. 21, 1983). Subsequent pronouncements from the Antitrust Division

inclusive system are probably quite small unless it is established that overinclusion has indeed kept a rival system from getting started or succeeding. Such a suit would be difficult to prosecute and probably could not be brought without strong evidence of anticompetitive effect. The government enforcement authorities may be the most likely plaintiffs in that kind of suit, and they have shown no inclination actually to bring such suits.[60]

The possibility of antitrust violation may be substantially higher if the contract between a provider and an alternative delivery system prohibits the provider from selling services to a competing system (a kind of "exclusivity" provision).[61] There is little procompetitive justification for this conduct. Simply put, this arrangement appears to deprive competing systems of access to necessary practitioners or facilities. Exclusivity provisions that prevent a significant number of providers from selling services to a competing buyer, when these providers actually have the capacity to service the other system, almost certainly are not enforceable and therefore should be resisted when suggested by a PPO or HMO. That does not, however, mean that the provider

---

have reconfirmed that there are potential problems inherent in "overinclusiveness," and a "35 percent rule" has developed: the Antitrust Division has indicated that overinclusiveness concerns will generally not be present unless the HMO or PPO in question has a 35 percent share in the relevant market. See, e.g., Charles F. Rule, Antitrust in the Health Care Field: Distinguishing Resistance from Adaptation, remarks at the Antitrust and Health Care Seminar of the Antitrust Section of the Connecticut Bar Assn. and the Connecticut Health Lawyers Assn. (March 11, 1988). It is unclear, however, whether the percentage applies to the proportion of current business being conducted, the proportion of capacity, or the proportion of providers in the market. This ambiguity has reflected antitrust authorities' lack of familiarity with healthcare markets, and also has probably reflected a perceived lack of need to focus on these definitions in the absence of "close" cases for investigation or prosecution.

[60]But see *Medical Group to Close in Face of Opposition By Justice Department*, Wall St. J., Oct. 15, 1984, at 16. For useful guidance, see FTC, Enforcement Policy with Respect to Physician Agreements to Control Medical Prepayment Plans, 46 Fed. Reg. 48,982 (1981). See generally Miles and Philp, Hospitals Caught in the Antitrust Net: An Overview, 24 Duq. L. Rev. 489, 555-584 (1985).

[61]See Blue Cross v. Kitsap Physicians Serv., 1982-1 Trade Cas. (CCH) ¶64,588 (W.D. Wash. 1981); FTC, supra n.60, at 48,991.

must sell to all systems at equal prices: hospitals and doctors have no legal compulsion *not* to price discriminate, and may by *individual* decision choose to favor one system over another. So long as the impetus for such favoritism arises from the seller of services, and is not an effort by one purchaser of services— HMO or PPO—to block others from the market, the favoritism by itself should not occasion any antitrust liability.

In most communities, unless an alternative delivery system controls a very large proportion of the available patients, a hospital can legally obligate the PPO or HMO to send all of *its* patients to that facility. The total number of patients obtained by a hospital through such a provision may be relatively small compared to the overall business available in the community, but the patients thus obtained by the hospital that are new, or "incremental," can be highly profitable. These patients in effect will be taken directly from competing institutions to which they might otherwise have been admitted, and exclusivity of this sort is likely to be protested even if it is legal. Such contracts can be highly beneficial both to the alternative delivery system and to the hospital that contracts with it on an exclusive basis, and should withstand antitrust challenge—even though a small body of law suggests that exclusive contracts may under certain limited circumstances be antitrust violations.[62]

Pricing Considerations. The other area of antitrust concern with regard to alternative major delivery systems is price setting. In Arizona v. Maricopa County Medical Socy.,[63] the Supreme Court disapproved the method by which a PPO-like entity representing approximately 70 percent of the physicians in a community set its prices (through a poll of its members). Because of that decision, it was feared that PPOs and even perhaps HMOs that were sponsored by providers or that involved a considerable

---

[62]See Standard Oil Co. of California (Standard Stations) v. United States, 337 U.S. 293 (1949); FTC v. Motion Picture Advertising Serv. Co., 334 U.S. 392 (1953). But see Tampa Elec. Co. v. Nashville Coal Co., 365 U.S. 320 (1961).
[63]457 U.S. 332 (1982).

number of them would have trouble establishing prices. In other words, it was feared that only insurer-sponsored systems would be feasible because the amount of cooperation necessary for physicians, hospitals, or both to get together to establish their own systems would invoke application of antitrust laws.

Not true. Despite the Court's holding in *Maricopa,* there are provider-sponsored systems throughout the country that appear to be approved, or at least accepted, by antitrust enforcement authorities. Enforcement authorities have recognized that alternative delivery systems are a procompetitive alternative to traditional fee-for-service arrangements and should be encouraged rather than discouraged by antitrust law.[64] The result has been a *laissez faire* environment in which enforcement authorities will not challenge an arrangement unless it clearly is likely to suppress competition.

The circumstances under which any healthcare provider enters into an alternative delivery system contract, or even itself forms such a system, will vary from community to community. In general, the risk that such an action will constitute an antitrust violation is now very low. If and when these systems emerge as a dominant force in determining who will succeed and who will fail as a healthcare provider, then the antitrust issues that they raise will become more urgent.

§3.4.9 Mergers

As mergers and acquisitions of hospitals have become commonplace, they have become subject to antitrust law.[65] During the 1980s the standards used to evaluate mergers were relaxed

---

[64]For a discussion of the practices of the FTC and the Department of Justice in this area, see Miles and Philp, supra n.60, at 561-568, 580-584.

[65]North Carolina ex rel. Edmisten v. P.I.A. Asheville, 740 F.2d 274 (4th Cir. 1984), cert. denied, 471 U.S. 1003 (1985); American Medicorp v. Humana, 445 F. Supp. 589 (E.D. Pa. 1977); United States v. Hosp. Affiliates Intl., 1980-1 Trade Cas. (CCH) ¶63,721 (E.D. La. 1980); American Medical Intl., 3 Trade Reg. Rep. (CCH) ¶22,170 (FTC July 2, 1984); Hospital Corp. of Am., 3 Trade Reg. Rep. (CCH) ¶22,301 (FTC Oct. 25, 1985).

somewhat, both by federal enforcement authorities at the Department of Justice and the Federal Trade Commission and by many federal courts.[66] Preliminary indications are that in the 1990s, as the pace of hospital mergers increases, more of them will be challenged as economic pressures compel consolidation of facilities.

If the hospitals involved in a merger or acquisition transaction are not in the same community and do not compete with each other, then antitrust risk will be minimal. A "large" transaction may have to be reported to federal authorities,[67] but in the absence of real competition between the facilities, an antitrust challenge is remote. If the facilities compete or are in the same community, then antitrust concerns will arise, whether or not the transaction is big enough to be reported. Antitrust enforcement authorities now regularly read the healthcare trade publications, and mergers that are not formally reportable may become known to the FTC or the Department of Justice through routine news articles—if they have not first become known through objections voiced by other hospitals, service purchasers, or distressed physicians in the community.

In all but the largest cities, merger of two hospitals will probably raise the concentration of business at the surviving facility to a level that would be troublesome under traditional antitrust analysis. But mergers are always evaluated in context, and that context today includes the financial plight of many institutions. A showing that one of the facilities would certainly fail unless they merged may allow invocation of a recognized defense to an antitrust challenge, the "failing company" doctrine.[68] This doctrine, or more properly this administrative and

---

[66]Compare United States Department of Justice, Merger Guidelines (June 14, 1984), reprinted in 2 Trade Reg. Rep. (CCH) ¶4,490, with United States Department of Justice, Merger Guidelines (1968), reprinted in 2 Trade Reg. Rep. (CCH) ¶4,510.

[67]See n.53, supra.

[68]See Citizens Publishing Co. v. United States, 394 U.S. 131 (1969); United States Department of Justice, Merger Guidelines §5.1 (June 14, 1984), reprinted in 2 Trade Reg. Rep. (CCH) ¶4,490.

judicial policy, may increasingly be appropriate for hospitals. In fact, a showing that one of the proposed merger partners will eventually be forced to curtail quality of care due to economic pressures, even if its "failure" as a competitor is not imminent, may permit a more relaxed application of the doctrine, especially if the surviving (acquiring) hospital has not shown a predilection for profit-maximizing conduct. If the acquirer is a not-for-profit hospital, the transaction may be acceptable even though a comparable merger in another industry, or involving a for-profit acquirer, would face harsher scrutiny. The "quasi-failing-company" defense has been invoked successfully to permit several mergers that otherwise would have been challenged by the government, such as a merger of the only two hospitals in Danville, Illinois in 1988.[69]

Unless there is proof that one of the institutions that are planning to merge is failing, a court that is considering a challenge to a hospital merger will try to determine whether the transaction will be likely "substantially to lessen competition" in the hospital field.[70] It was thought for a while that approval of a transfer of ownership through certificate-of-need (CON) laws might confer some antitrust immunity on a transaction, and this position was accepted by a federal district court. But after first affirming this decision, the United States Court of Appeals for the Fourth Circuit determined that CON approval in North Carolina did not confer antitrust immunity on a merger and found a particular transaction involving psychiatric facilities

---

[69]The author of this chapter represented a party in the Danville merger. Although the transaction ultimately was not challenged, that decision was made by the Department of Justice only after exhaustive inquiry into the facts surrounding the transaction. The local Antitrust Division field office recommended that suit be filed to challenge the transactions, but was overruled by officials in Washington. This was not a large transaction compared with those reported daily in the financial press, but a great deal of effort was expended by the parties and the government in the investigations: even small-town deals are subject to antitrust scrutiny.

[70]Clayton Act, §7, 15 U.S.C. §18 (1982). See also United States v. Philadelphia Natl. Bank, 374 U.S. 321 (1963); United States v. Bethlehem Steel Corp., 168 F. Supp. 576 (S.D.N.Y. 1958).

to be unacceptable.[71] In states where CON or state licensure mechanisms require close scrutiny of proposed mergers, or in states where rate regulation mitigates or removes the possibility of price gouging by a hospital obtaining market power through a merger or acquisition, challenge of the transaction is unlikely, and may well be unsuccessful if attempted.[72] These cases may be heard before a local federal district court judge, whose sympathies may well be with the hospitals, not the government.

Two recent cases demonstrate the wide range of outcomes possible in antitrust challenges to hospital mergers. More or less at the same time, the Department of Justice sued to stop mergers in Roanoke, Virginia and in Rockford, Illinois. The underlying facts of these cases were fairly similar, but not identical. Each involved an apparent accretion of market power beyond that usually permitted in mergers. The government won the Rockford case and lost the Roanoke case.[73] Both decisions were affirmed on appeal.[74] Interestingly, even while the Rockford decision was being affirmed on appeal, denying permission for the merger, Judge Posner of the U.S. Court of Appeals for the Seventh Circuit noted that the focus of inquiry in hospital merger cases should be on probable price impact, not statistical indices of "concentration" or market share.[75]

---

[71]North Carolina ex rel. Edmisten v. P.I.A. Asheville, 740 F.2d 274 (4th Cir. 1984) (en banc), cert. denied, 471 U.S. 1003 (1985).

[72]For example, New Jersey currently exercises such pervasive control over hospital prices, not to mention mergers or other transactions that may affect the quantity or quality of services available, that a merger between two New Jersey hospitals is unlikely to be challenged by federal antitrust authorities no matter what the post-merger market structure looks like. In general, the more a state regulates the hospital industry, the easier it should be for a merger to survive antitrust scrutiny.

[73]United States v. Rockford Mem. Corp., 717 F. Supp. 1251 (N.D. Ill. 1989); United States v. Carilion Health Sys., 707 F. Supp. 840 (W.D. Va. 1989).

[74]United States v. Rockford Memorial Corp., 717 F. Supp. 1251 (N.D. Ill. 1989), affd., 1990 U.S. App. LEXIS 4805 (7th Cir. 1990); United States v. Carilion Health Sys., 707 F. Supp. 840 (W.D. Va. 1989), affd. without opinion, 892 F.2d 1042 (4th Cir. 1989), reported in full, 1989-2 CCH Trade Cases ¶68859 (4th Cir. 1989).

[75]"It is regrettable that antitrust cases are decided on the basis of theoretical

The wisdom gained from these cases is that each case is different. The government does not win all of its attacks on mergers, and the Roanoke case suggests the importance of a "home town sentiment" that is favorable to the hospitals. Theoretical economic models introduced by economists from the Justice Department or FTC in Washington may not fare well next to the testimony of community leaders that the merger is a good idea; if there is considerable local support for the transaction, the government may face a difficult case. Of course, if the case is not heard in the community at issue, or involves a for-profit acquirer, or is opposed by large-scale purchasers such as HMOs, PPOs, or employers, then the slight leniency evident regarding some transactions in the late 1980s may not be available in other transactions.

In any matter as substantial as a merger of hospitals or a large-scale sale of one hospital's assets to another hospital owner in the same community, attorneys obviously will be involved. If the transaction involves arguably competing facilities, then the attorneys will work with the antitrust issues virtually from the inception of the deal. Hospitals come in for such pervasive regulation, in addition to their quasi-public identity, that a hospital merger must anticipate scrutiny. If the discussions of possible consolidation or merger lead to agreement, with regard either to actual consolidation or perhaps just cooperation on competitive matters, the hospitals must seek advice on the antitrust considerations before proceeding. If the transaction does involve competing facilities, that does not mean it is automatically illegal or will be attacked. Some deals may not be doable under antitrust law, but few are unthinkable. Moreover, negotiation of a merger that is problematic under antitrust law is not itself illegal: so long as the negotiations do not lead to any side-bar agreements restraining competition between the facilities, the talks are legal even if the deal itself is not.

---

guesses as to what particular market-structure characteristics portend for competition. . . . We would like to see more effort put into studying the actual effect of concentration on price in the hospital industry as in other industries." Judge Richard Posner, in United States v. Rockford Memorial Corp., 1990 U.S. App. LEXIS at 4828-4829.

Sometimes, counsel can help craft a way of structuring the transaction to make it more defensible under antitrust law. Some mergers just cannot be sustained under reasonable interpretations of the law,[76] but many obviously will be legal, and many more will reside in a grey area in which the only answer as to legality will have to come from the courts (if the parties are willing to take it that far).

§3.4.10 Control over the Hospital's Revenue-Generating Departments

Earlier we said that hospitals may be characterized as bundles of complementary services centered in a common facility. Physicians and others have learned that some of those services might be unbundled from the hospital and sold at a profit in competition with the hospital. Thus, radiology, CAT scanning, pathology, anesthesia services, and so on, all of which have historically been provided by a hospital, could be, and in fact *are* being, sold by physicians or other entrepreneurs either in direct competition with the hospital or in the place of the hospital.

Voluntary Unbundling. If the hospital willingly surrenders control of a revenue-generating department to outsiders and gives them an exclusive franchise that precludes others from providing the same service, illegal tie-ins or monopolization might be charged as discussed above, depending on the number and strength of other competitors for the service at issue. It could be argued, for example, that if a hospital permits outside physicians to provide CAT scans to hospital patients using the

---

[76]For example, if a town had three hospitals of roughly equivalent size, and all were doing well financially while competing vigorously with each other, it is difficult to imagine how any two of them could legally merge— *unless* the degree of state regulation made it possible to invoke the "state action" defense or state rate regulation undercut antitrust concerns about pricing in a duopoly situation. Deals that are apparently hopeless can sometimes but not always, be done.

physicians' off-site machine, then this right should not be given exclusively to one group without compelling justification. To compel patients who use the hospital also to use a contracted-for service that might otherwise be purchased in a competitive marketplace arguably constitutes a tie-in of the hospital facility to the other service. In fact, that was the circumstance at issue in Jefferson Parish Hospital District No. 2 v. Hyde,[77] except that the service involved in that case was anesthesiology, regarding which the defendant hospital had an exclusive contract arrangement with the defendant anesthesia group.

In *Hyde* the Supreme Court found for the defendant, but not because such exclusive arrangements are inherently legal. Instead, it held that because the community had many other hospitals, patients could choose another hospital if they did not want to use the anesthesia group designated by the defendant hospital. Therefore the critical component of "forcing" was absent, and as a result there was no antitrust violation. Under the same circumstances in a one- or two-hospital town, arguments of restraint of trade based on exclusive contracts might appear more reasonable.

Involuntary Unbundling. The foregoing discussion assumes that a hospital has voluntarily surrendered control over one of its revenue departments to physicians or others. Different problems may arise when staff physicians attempt to wrest control of a department and its revenues from the hospital against its will.

That was the situation, for example, in a case involving a typical small community hospital in North Carolina.[78] In the late 1970s the hospital concluded that it needed to obtain the services of a full-time anesthesiologist to supervise the hospital-employed nurse anesthetists who, until then, had provided all anesthesia services at the institution. An anesthesiologist was recruited to establish a fee-for-service practice with certain

---

[77]466 U.S. 2 (1984).

[78]Watauga Anesthesia Assocs. v. Watauga Hosp., (W.D.N.C.—directed verdict for defendant Jan. 28, 1986) (No. St-C-84-76).

contractual responsibilities for supervision and direction of the nurse anesthetists. The physician recruited was authorized to assign cases to himself but was explicitly forbidden either to charge patients for supervision provided to nurse anesthetists employed by the hospital or to bring his own nurse anesthetists into the hospital.

Gradually, the anesthesiologist gained more and more of the anesthesia business at the hospital. His proportion rose to over 50 percent when he brought in another doctor as an associate. The original anesthesiologist repeatedly requested the right to bring his own nurses into the hospital (who would then be in direct competition with the nurses in the hospital's employ). Finally, the anesthesiologist hired two nurse anesthetists away from the hospital and proclaimed his intention to bring them back into the hospital as his employees. The hospital's board rejected this demand and arranged for the hospital to contract directly with yet another anesthesiologist to provide medical supervision to the hospital's remaining nurse anesthetists. Even without being able to use his own nurse anesthetists, the original anesthesiologist quickly gained, and maintained, approximately 70 percent of the anesthesia business generated at the hospital.

The original anesthesiologist filed a federal antitrust suit against the hospital and its administrator and trustees. The case alleged that the hospital's refusal to permit him to compete with the hospital in providing doctor-supervised nurse anesthetist services constituted an illegal tie-in, monopolization, or other restraint of trade. The case was tried in January 1986. At the close of plaintiffs' case, a directed verdict was granted in favor of the hospital on all counts. Although the court issued no written opinion in this case, the trial judge made clear that the conduct involved did not appear to be an antitrust violation. The conduct did not constitute a tie-in because no patient was compelled to use the hospital's anesthesia service. The anesthesiologist was still able to sell his own services in the hospital even if he could not sell the services of a nurse anesthetist. Furthermore, the hospital's conduct in recruiting the anesthesiologist and generally supporting his activities seemed to refute the charge of an intention to monopolize anesthesia practice by the hospital, as did the overwhelming fact that the anesthesiologist was able to obtain and maintain more than twice as much anesthesia business hospital-generated as the hospital itself could maintain.

The facts of this case do not support the proposition that a hospital may *always* restrain the manner in which a staff physician can compete with it. But it was brought out at the trial that a hospital has responsibilities and costs that physicians who have the privilege of practicing at the institution do not bear. The court seemed to recognize that under these circumstances abstract notions about the desirability of competition should not be applied mechanically to what goes on at a hospital. Because there is no reported decision in this litigation, the case cannot be used as a precedent. Still, the attitude of this court when confronted with a clash between the needs of a not-for-profit community hospital and the demands of a physician may suggest a continued willingness of federal courts, when dealing with such matters, to find that the hospital acted in good faith with little effect on competition. As more and more economic opportunities are available to be carved out of hospitals, these issues are almost certain to recur. Thus far, the courts have indulged hospitals in such cases. Inevitably, however, a case with bad facts will appear and a decision will be rendered in favor of a physician or other competitor who tries to unbundle a profitable piece of the hospital's services. Then, precedent will be established and litigation will be used even more as a tool to carve out the profitable pieces of hospital operation over the strenuous objections of hospitals.

Conclusion

Antitrust suits involving hospitals remain relatively rare, although the threat of them is commonplace at a large number of institutions. The proportion of those cases that involve simple refusals to grant or renew staff privileges appears to be increasing again, after a slight downturn of several years. Quite possibly, the Health Care Quality Improvement Act, with its (limited) antitrust immunity, will cut down on the number of pure staff privilege cases. The other kinds of cases now being filed in increasing numbers are raising questions about the fundamental nature of hospitals, an issue that has only briefly been explored in the past: are hospitals, especially not-for-profits, "businesses" in a conventional sense, or are they public institutions, public utilities, or something else? The Supreme Court has decided that hospitals are in commerce and capable of committing antitrust violations and that no special antitrust rules should apply to the healthcare professions. Yet the economics of healthcare and of hospitals remain substantially different from the economics of other sectors, and the not-for-profit nature of most hospitals in the United States blunts many of the traditional arguments made in support of conventional antitrust law as it has evolved over the past 100 years.

This is not to say that not-for-profit hospitals cannot and do not engage in anticompetitive conduct that should, and will, be subject to antitrust law. Still, hospital boards and administrators are probably more worried about antitrust law than the actual decided cases warrant. Involvement in such litigation is unpleasant and expensive for all defendants, and it must be assumed that some plaintiffs are right and some defendants will have to pay substantial damages even in the hospital context. But in the final analysis, if economic decisionmakers remember to ask who stands to lose and why, and if they apply plain common sense, most antitrust problems can be avoided. Application of antitrust law will not be permitted to destroy the necessary operation of healthcare facilities or the necessary practices of healthcare providers. The challenge will be determining what economic aspects of our healthcare system are in fact "necessary" in a competitive marketplace. The rules under which health industry players operate are changing, primarily as a result of economic pressures. Those economic pressures will bring with them some new responsibilities under antitrust law. This result arises from—but does not cause—the changes now being felt in the healthcare delivery system.

256

4   Tort Liability, Immunities, and Defenses

Kathryn Kelly and Sara Jones

§4.0 Tort Liability: General Negligence Principles

Under the legal system in the United States, people can be held liable for injury they cause to others through their negligence under principles of tort law. In order to prove an action in tort, whether under medical malpractice or another theory, claimants must establish each of four elements:

1. the existence of a *duty* owed to them;
2. the *breach* of that duty;
3. that the breach of the duty owed *caused* an injury; and
4. the extent of that injury and its monetary value or *damages*.[1]

§4.0.1 Duty

Historically, courts imposed liability on people for harm caused by their unreasonable and imprudent actions, but were reluctant to impose such liability for inaction. Today, courts routinely hold people liable for both acts *and* omissions that present an unreasonable risk of harm to others. Those who do not act as reasonable and prudent persons would under the same or similar circumstances are liable for the consequences of their actions. Courts do not hold persons liable for occurrences that could not be foreseen or prevented by reasonable precautions. Such occurrences are considered "unavoidable accidents."

"Reasonable and prudent" behavior is judged by an objective, rather than a subjective, standard. Thus, the standard of reasonableness may be altered by the actor's physical attributes (for example, blindness), but is not generally adjusted for mental capabilities or temperament except in the case of children.[2]

Through the gradual development of case law based in part on societal expectations, certain types of actors have been found to owe a specialized duty of care to others. This special duty

---

§4.0 [1]See generally W. Prosser and W. P. Keeton, The Law of Torts, §30, at 164-168 (5th ed. 1984).

[2]Severely mentally handicapped plaintiffs may be held to a different standard when contributory negligence is an issue. See Prosser and Keeton, supra n.1, §32, at 178.

exceeds the ordinary person's level of required care.[3] For example, an ordinary person would have no reason to know of a neighbor's dangerous propensities—and if she did know, would have no obligation to take steps to protect third persons from harm caused by the neighbor. The tort law recognizes no duty under these circumstances. A psychiatrist who has undertaken to treat the neighbor, however, has by virtue of that fact and of his special skill and training, assumed the duty to take steps to protect third parties from the dangerous propensities of a patient.[4]

§4.0.2 Breach

Breach of the duty of reasonable care is an issue of fact to be determined by the jury. In most instances, that determination is based on the jury's own experience and knowledge of reasonable and prudent behavior as ordinary men and women. In order to determine what is reasonable and prudent in specialized circumstances, however, "expert testimony" is necessary. Testimony by expert witnesses on the prevailing standard of treatment is required to assist lay people in determining whether or not a healthcare provider has met the appropriate standard of care.[5] For example, suppose someone who has fallen and injured an ankle is treated by an emergency room physician who examines the injured ankle but does not x-ray it. The patient is sent home with a diagnosis of "sprain" and told to keep the ankle elevated and apply ice. It's later learned that the ankle was in fact broken. In order to evaluate the emergency room physician's conduct, the jury would have to know whether the prevailing standard of care required an x-ray (because broken bones cannot always

---

[3]See generally Prosser and Keeton, supra n.1, §§31-32, at 169-193 and §§53-56, at 356-385.

[4]See, e.g., Tarasoff v. Regents of Univ. of Cal., 17 Cal. 3d 425, 551 P.2d 334 (1976) (psychiatrist had duty to warn third person that patient had threatened her).

[5]See generally Prosser and Keeton, supra n.1, §§37-40, at 235-262.

be detected by physical examination) or whether it did not
(because physical examination usually is sufficient to detect a
broken bone).

§4.0.3 Causation

Once the existence of a duty and the breach of that duty have
been shown, a claimant must prove that the negligent acts "proximately caused" the harm. "Proximate cause" simply means
that the breaching actions of one who owed a duty are sufficiently connected to the harmful event to warrant imposing
liability on the actor. In some cases, even though an act may
have been the "cause in fact" of some harm, the particular result
may be so unforeseeable and so extraordinary that it is not seen
as being sufficiently connected to the breach to warrant the
imposition of liability.[6]

If the harm would have occurred whether or not the
"unreasonable" action or omission took place, such "breach" is
not considered to be sufficiently connected to impose liability.
If, however, the jury finds the negligent conduct was a "substantial factor" contributing to bringing about the harm, then it
may be found sufficiently connected to satisfy "proximate" cause
requirements.[7]

To return to the example above, suppose that the patient
visited another physician the next day and was correctly diagnosed and treated. Treatment consisted of wearing a cast for six
weeks and physical therapy for another four weeks. Assuming
that there was expert testimony that the standard of care required
that an x-ray should have been taken at the emergency room,
the patient could demonstrate breach. A medical malpractice
case against the first doctor could proceed only if the patient
also could show that the negligent failure to diagnose caused
injury. If, on the other hand, the six weeks in the cast and four
weeks of physical therapy would have been necessary even if

---

[6]See Prosser and Keeton, supra n.1, §43, at 280-300.
[7]See generally Prosser and Keeton, supra n.1, §§41-45, at 263-321.

the break had been diagnosed at the first visit, there would be no causal link between the negligent act and the injuries.

§4.0.4 Damages

Finally, it is necessary for a claimant to show actual loss flowing from the negligent conduct in order to recover any damages. Even if a person owes a duty to another and breaches it, there is no tort liability if no harm results.[8] For example, even if a physician's late diagnosis of a disease is found to be negligent, there may be no cause of action if the claimant is unable to show that such failure to diagnose actually diminished the patient's chances of recovery.[9]

A. Negligence Elements and Defenses in the Medical Setting: Medical Malpractice

Claimants are required to prove each of the four elements of a negligence action in order to support a claim for medical malpractice. The following sections discuss special applications of each of these requirements in the medical setting. It should be emphasized that failure to establish *any* of the four elements means that the claimant's case fails. In addition, failure to comply with the appropriate statute of limitations and, in some circumstances, application of some form of governmental immunity may defeat a claimant's cause of action in the medical setting. These defenses are also addressed below.

---

[8]See Prosser and Keeton, supra n.1, §30, at 165.

[9]See §4.7 for a discussion of the damage elements of "loss of a chance" cases.

§4.1 Duties, Defenses, and Standards of Care in the Medical Malpractice Setting

§4.1.1 The Requirement of Special Relationship: The Physician-Patient Relationship

The delivery of healthcare by a physician, in the healthcare facility or otherwise, is one of the areas in which the actor is held to a higher standard of care than the ordinary reasonably prudent man or woman. Although a physician generally is not obligated to accept a patient for treatment, once such acceptance is made the physician enters the physician-patient relationship and all the duties it imposes. Because no duty arises until a physician-patient relationship is formed, the claimant must prove the existence of the relationship.[1] Although this is usually not an issue because both sides agree that the relationship exists, it may be disputed in some cases whether a relationship exists or when it was established. A single visit may be enough to establish a relationship.[2] A telephone consultation may not be, particularly when the physician simply recommends that the patient continue treatment already prescribed by another physician and come in for examination in the morning.[3] A physician-patient relationship generally does not exist where examination is made for a purpose other than treatment, as, for example, a

---

§4.1 [1] See generally Annot., What Constitutes Physician-Patient Relationship for Malpractice Purposes, 17 A.L.R.4th 132 (1982) (acceptance of patient—especially when the patient directly contacted the physician without referral—begins physician-patient relationship).

[2] See, e.g., Baird v. National Health Found., 235 Mo. App. 594, 144 S.W.2d 850 (1940) (visit to patient in hospital at request of other physician enough to show physician-patient relationship).

[3] See, e.g., Clanton v. Von Haam, 177 Ga. App. 694, 340 S.E.2d 627 (1986) (patient-physician relationship not established when patient called doctor late at night, he recommended she continue the treatment prescribed by her other physician and call him in the morning; no independent treatment had begun; he only listened to her symptoms); Doran v. Priddy, 534 F. Supp. 30 (D. Kan. 1981) (applying Kansas law) (no doctor-patient relationship when obstetrician declined to see a hospitalized patient after receiving a phone call from a nurse concerning the case).

physical for employment purposes or to obtain insurance.[4] As a matter of public policy, physicians who render aid in emergency situations (other than in the emergency room) are often exempt from ordinary liability for such assistance.[5]

Once a physician-patient relationship is established, the physician is then required to conform to the standard of care in diagnosis, obtaining informed consent for any procedures, and giving continuing attention or referring to another qualified physician.[6]

§4.1.2 The Requirement of Special Relationship: The Healthcare Facility-Nonphysician Provider Relationship

A claim against a healthcare facility also begins with the establishing of a relationship from which a special duty arises. The claimant may not be able to meet that burden if, for example, the facility can show that the patient was never

---

[4]See, e.g., Keene v. Wiggins, 69 Cal. App. 3d 308, 138 Cal. Rptr. 3 (1977) (employee's reliance on copy of worker's compensation report that insurance company physician prepared for employer rating injury of employee does not establish relationship absent any evidence of treatment or intent to treat); Thomas v. Kenton, 425 So. 2d 396 (La. Ct. App. 1982) (no physician-patient relationship with employer's staff physician when physician was hired by the employer to annually check overall health of employees and did not respond to, or treat, individual complaints of employees). Compare Lodico v. Cohn, 132 Misc. 2d 866, 505 N.Y.S.2d 818 (1986) (physician-patient relationship existed between worker compensation claimant and state insurance fund's physician, who was asked not only to render opinion on the cause of the disability but also to determine necessity of further treatment).

[5]See, e.g., Matts v. Homsi, 106 Mich. App. 563, 308 N.W.2d 284 (1981) (applying Missouri "Good Samaritan" statute to physician who responded to an emergency request although he was not on call that evening and had no obligation to do so). See 61 Am. Jur. 2d 306 (1981) (discussion of public policy behind "Good Samaritan" statutes). See also N.C. Gen. Stat. §90-21.14 (1959) (exempting volunteers from liability for care rendered in emergency situations absent gross negligence).

[6]See generally Dooley, Modern Tort Law, §§34.13-34.15 (Medical Malpractice) (1983).

admitted for treatment. In Weldon v. Seminole Municipal Hospital, the Supreme Court of Oklahoma affirmed the trial court's dismissal of the claims against facility-defendant because the claimant was never admitted to the hospital after being seen in the emergency room by her private physician, who recommended she see a specialist in another hospital: "There should not be a duty on a hospital to supervise treatment given by doctor acting within his own discretion as to care of his patient where patient is not subsequently admitted and subject to hospital's care."[7] This defense may not apply if the healthcare facility had refused to admit a patient in need of emergency care.[8]

Once a patient has been admitted, the healthcare facility owes a duty to exercise the degree of care and attention that is reasonable given the physical and mental capacities of the patient.[9] The facility is generally not, however, an insurer of the patient's safety required to anticipate all contingencies.[10] In a case involving a disoriented patient with a medical illness who had no known suicidal tendencies, the hospital was not liable when the patient managed to unlock his window and jump. The hospital's decision to place the patient in a secure ward, but not a psychiatric unit, complied with the standard of care because not all suicide attempts can be predicted.[11] Finally, there

---

[7]See Weldon v. Seminole Mun. Hosp. 709 P.2d 1058, 1061 (Okla. 1985).

[8]See, e.g., Gonzalez v. United States, 600 F. Supp. 1390 (W.D. Tex. 1985) (applying Texas law) (liability imposed for failure to admit patient suffering from peritonitis in emergency room). See also §4.10.

[9]See, e.g., Rogers v. Baptist Gen. Convention, 651 P.2d 672, 674 at n.1 (Okla. 1982) (hospitals are held to standard of ordinary care commensurate with patient's physical and mental condition); Mellies v. National Heritage, Inc., 636 P.2d 215 (Kan. Ct. App. 1981) (hospital bound to exercise such care as patient's known physical and mental ailments required).

[10]See, e.g., Nichols v. Green Acres Rest Home, 245 So. 2d 544, 545 (La. App. 1971) (appellate court affirmed lower court ruling that nursing home was not liable for the death of a patient who had a heart attack while walking unattended on the grounds, stating that a "nursing home is not the insurer of the safety of its patients").

[11]See Caldwell v. United States, 548 F. Supp. 91 (E.D. La. 1982) (applying Louisiana law) (although standard adjusts to condition of patient, hospital was

are some statutory exemptions from liability for the healthcare facility under certain circumstances.[12]

§4.1.3 Standard of Care: Physicians

The standard of care required of physicians varies slightly from state to state, depending on developments in case law or statutorily set standards.[13] Historically, physicians were required to exercise that degree of care exercised by physicians in the same community. This traditional standard was known as the "strict locality" rule.[14] This rule was based on the rationale that physicians in rural areas did not have the same opportunities for professional development and access to modern technology as their urban counterparts.[15] The strict locality rule fell into disfavor because, as its critics charged, it reinforced the status quo of care in any given community, served as a disincentive for elevation of standards, and sometimes made it difficult for

---

not negligent in placing mentally disoriented patient in secured medical ward rather than psychiatric ward). Compare Cowan v. Doering, 111 N.J. 451, 545 A.2d 159 (1988) (court upheld jury verdict finding healthcare facility liable for injuries incurred when patient jumped from window in intensive care unit where patient was being treated for drug overdose).

[12]See, e.g., La. Rev. Stat. Ann. 9:2797.1 (1989) (statute exempting nonprofit poison centers from liability for good-faith provision of information).

[13]Many states have statutorily set standards of care. See, e.g., Vt. Stat. Ann. tit. 12, §1908 (West Supp. 1989) and N.C. Gen. Stat. §90-21.11 (1985) (setting the degree of care and skill of reasonable provider in a similar practice in similar circumstances). See also Va. Code §8.01-581.20 (1984) (setting standard as a reasonable provider within the state). Compare Okla. Stat. Ann. tit. 76, §20.1 (West 1987) (setting standards at nationwide level).

[14]See Annotation, Malpractice Testimony: Competency of Physician or Surgeon from One Locality to Testify, in Malpractice Case as to Standard of Care Required of Defendant Practicing in Another Locality, 37 A.L.R.3d 426 (1971).

[15]See Small v. Howard, 128 Mass. 131 (1980) (establishing standard as that which physicians and surgeons of ordinary capability and practicing in similar localities with similar opportunities ordinarily possess), overruled in Brune v. Belinkoff, 354 Mass. 102, 235 N.E.2d 793 (1968) (abandoning geographic standard).

the claimant to find expert testimony because physicians within the same community were reluctant to testify against each other.[16]

Most jurisdictions now have adopted the "similar community in similar or like circumstances" standard, holding physicians to the standard of care of physicians of the same type in a similar type of community with similar equipment and comparable access to continuing education opportunities.[17] The similar community rule balances the need to avoid evaluating a general practitioner in a rural area by the same standard as a specialist at an urban teaching hospital with the need of the claimant for access to expert testimony.

In some jurisdictions, courts and legislatures have gone one step beyond the similar community rule to a national standard because they perceive the community standard to be inconsistent with the realities of medical practice.[18] Particularly within fields of specialty, physicians are increasingly held to a national standard because they are seen as having relatively equal opportunities for professional development[19] and because they must meet national board standards within their specialty areas.[20]

---

[16]See, e.g., McGulpin v. Bessmer, 241 Iowa 1119, 43 N.W.2d 121, 127 (1950) (court criticized requirement of expert testimony of physician from same community).

[17]See, e.g., Wiggins v. Piver, 276 N.C. 134, 171 S.E.2d 393 (1970) (adopting similar community rule).

[18]Brune v. Belinkoff, 354 Mass. 102, 235 N.E.2d 793 (1968) (general practitioners and specialists held to national standard, although availability of resources can be taken into account as one factor).

[19]See Shilkret v. Annapolis Emergency Hosp. Assn., 276 Md. 187, 198, 349 A.2d 245, 252 (1975) (in rejecting traditional locality rules as "ignoring the realities of medical life," court noted superior training, communication, and transportation technologies, proliferation of literature and seminars as indicative of equalization of opportunity for physicians). See generally Annot., Standard of Care Owed to Patient by Medical Specialist as Determined by Local, "Like Community," State, National or Other Standards, 18 A.L.R.4th 603 (1982). But see Dewitt v. Brown, 669 F.2d 516 (8th Cir. 1982) (applying Arkansas law) ("like community" rather than national standard applied to orthopedic surgeon).

[20]See, e.g., Shilkret v. Annapolis Emergency Hosp. Assn., 276 Md. 187, 198, 349 A.2d 245, 251 (1975) (because "medical profession itself recognizes

Despite the trend to a national standard for physicians who specialize, many jurisdictions still adhere to a similar locality rule for general practitioners[21] or at least consider it to be one factor to be taken into account in establishing the appropriate standard of care.[22]

§4.1.4 Standard of Care: Nonphysician Healthcare Providers

The strict locality rule presents the same disincentives for elevating community standards of care and the same difficulty in obtaining expert testimony for nurses and other providers as it does for physicians. Thus, the strict locality rule generally has been abandoned for nurses and nonphysician providers as well. There is much less movement, however, toward national standards of care for nonphysician providers than for physicians. Most jurisdictions still hold nurses and other nonphysician healthcare providers to the standard of care of the same type of providers in similar communities under like circumstances.[23]

---

national standards for specialists that are not determined by geography, the law should follow suit"). See also Aasheim v. Humberger, 695 P.2d 824 (Mont. 1985) (rejecting same or similar locality rule in favor of national standards with respect to board-certified specialists); Shamburger v. Behrens, 418 N.W.2d 299 (S.D. 1988) (specialists held to the "national standards of profession").

[21]See N.C. Gen. Stat. §90-21.11 (1985) (requiring subjective standard of similar community with similar knowledge and experience). See also Vt. Stat. Ann. tit. 12, §1908 (West Supp. 1989) (requiring skill of similar type of professional in same or similar circumstances).

[22]See Blair v. Eblen, 461 S.W.2d 370, 373, (Ky. Ct. App. 1970) (evidence of a reasonably competent practitioner in the same or similar community should be considered along with availability of facilities and proximity of specialists and special facilities and whether physician is a general practitioner or specialist).

[23]See, e.g., Holbrooks v. Duke Univ., 63 N.C. App. 504, 305 S.E.2d 69 (1983) (nurse "expert" testimony required as to nursing standard of care); Page v. Wilson Memorial Hosp., 49 N.C. App. 533, 272 S.E.2d 8 (1980) (nurse with knowledge of nursing standards in nearby communities allowed to testify to standard in similar community). See also Biggs v. Cumberland

§4.1.5 Standard of Care: The Healthcare Facility

The precise standard to be applied with respect to the healthcare facility varies somewhat from jurisdiction to jurisdiction. The strict locality rule was abandoned in many jurisdictions because in many communities there is only one hospital.[24] The prevailing standard applied to the healthcare facility, as with general practitioners and nonphysician healthcare providers, remains that of the similar or like community under similar circumstances.[25] There has been some movement toward applying a national standard to the healthcare facility, particularly when the procedure involved is nationally recognized[26] or is regulated by hospital accreditation standards promulgated by the Joint Commission on Accreditation of Healthcare Organizations (JCAHO).[27]

County Hosp. Sys., 69 N.C. App. 547, 317 S.E.2d 421 (1984) (nurse's aide allowed to testify as to nursing community standard of care in action against hospital for negligence of nurse in failing to assist a patient after showering). Compare Wade v. John D. Archbold Memorial Hosp., 252 Ga. 118, 311 S.E.2d 836 (1984) (physical therapists are not limited by location and resources and therefore are subject to national standard) and Haney v. Alexander, 323 S.E.2d 430 (N.C. Ct. App. 1984), cert. denied, 313 N.C. 329, 327 S.E.2d 889 (1985) (nurse from different community allowed to testify about common nursing test when test is purportedly the "same throughout country").

[24]See generally Annot., Locality Rule as Governing Hospital's Standard of Care to Patient and Expert's Competency to Testify Thereto, 36 A.L.R.3d 440-457 (1971).

[25]See, e.g., Lamont v. Brookwood Health Serv. 446 So. 2d 1018 (Ala. 1983) (hospital owes degree of care exercised by hospitals engaged in the same type of operation in similar conditions). See also Clites v. State, 322 N.W.2d 917 (Iowa Ct. App. 1982) (applying standard of hospitals "generally" under similar circumstances); Tripp v. Pate, 49 N.C. App. 329, 271 S.E.2d 407 (1980); Sawyer v. United States, 465 F. Supp. 282 (E.D. Va. 1978) (applying Virginia law); Smith v. John C. Lincoln Hosp., 118 Ariz. App. 549, 578 P.2d 630 (1978) (hospital's duty to patient is to exercise skill and knowledge possessed by like institutions in similar communities).

[26]Haney v. Alexander, 323 S.E.2d 430 (N.C. Ct. App. 1984) cert. denied, 313 N.C. 329, 327 S.E.2d 889 (1985) (nurse from different community allowed to testify where test was same throughout country). See also Rodgers v. Baptist Gen. Convention, 651 P.2d 672 (Okla. 1982) (dictum) (hospital duty does not vary from community to community).

[27]See, e.g., Shilkret v. Annapolis Emergency Hosp. Assn., 276 Md. 187,

§4.2 *Proof of Breach*

§4.2.1 The Requirement of Expert Testimony

Proof that a healthcare provider did not meet the applicable standard of care must usually be established by expert testimony.[1] There are several exceptions, however. If the question of negligence is so obvious as to be within the common knowledge and experience of lay jurors, expert testimony may not be required.[2] Statutory standards regarding nursing homes may, in some circumstances, be used as evidence of the requisite standard of care in place of expert testimony.[3] In some cases, contractual

---

349 A.2d 245 (1975) (evidence of national JCAHO standards for pregnancy, child delivery, and infant care were sufficient to take issue to jury).

§4.2 [1] See, e.g., Folger v. Corbett, 118 N.H. 737, 394 A.2d 63 (1978) (expert testimony required to show breach of duty to obtain informed consent); Christianson v. Downs, 90 Wis. 2d 332, 279 N.W.2d 918 (1979) (expert testimony required to show breach of duty to diagnose). See generally Annot., Necessity of Expert Evidence to Support Action Against Hospital for Injury to or Death of Patient, 40 A.L.R.3d 515-552 (1971). See also Rosemont, Inc. v. Marshall, 481 So. 2d 1126 (Ala. 1985) (expert testimony required to determine standard of care for nursing home in caring for depressed patient); Thomas v. McPherson Community Health Center, 155 Mich. App. 700, 400 N.W.2d 629 (1986) (failure to produce expert testimony to show health center breached standard of care properly resulted in directed verdict for hospital); Mielke v. Condell Memorial Hosp., 124 Ill. App. 3d 42, 463 N.E.2d 216 (2d Dist. 1984) (expert testimony required because standard for drug dispensing not within knowledge of jury).

[2] See, e.g., Robbins v. Jewish Hosp., 663 S.W.2d 341 (Mo. Ct. App. 1983) (failure to raise bed rails falls within ordinary comprehension of jury); Veesart v. Community Hosp. Assn., 211 Kan. 896, 508 P.2d 506 (1973) (expert testimony not required to establish hospital negligence in relation to a fall); Winters v. City of Jersey City, 120 N.J. Super. 129, 293 A.2d 431 (1972) (expert testimony not required where issue of negligence on failing to raise bed rails of elderly man resulted in fall because the matter is within the common knowledge of the jury). See also Kujawski v. Arbor View Health Care Ctr., 407 N.W.2d 249 (Wis. 1987) (Supreme Court of Wisconsin remanded nursing home malpractice case that was dismissed for insufficiency of evidence holding that expert testimony was not required to establish standard of care with respect to use of safety belt on wheelchair).

[3] See, e.g., Dusine v. Golden Shores Convalescent Center, 249 So. 2d 40,

provisions between patient and facility may serve to establish the standard of care in the absence of expert testimony.[4]

If expert testimony is required, both claimant and defendant must be able to satisfy the court that their experts are qualified to testify about the applicable standard, whether it be the locality, similar community, national, or specialist standard.[5] Cross-examination of experts as to prior testimony and fees is considered to be necessary and appropriate to show bias.[6] It should also be noted that cross-examination of a defendant may be used by a claimant to prove the standard of care to which his or her conduct may be held.[7] A testifying expert may be

---

41-42 (Fla. App. 1971) (appellate court remanded malpractice action against nursing home for failure to monitor a restrained patient based on lower court's error in not allowing state regulations as evidence of the applicable standard of care for nursing homes administering restraint of patient; no expert testimony given as to standard of care in nursing home); Nichols v. Green Acres Rest Home, 245 So. 2d 544, 545 (La. App. 1971) (appellate court affirmed judgment in favor of nursing home defendant, citing compliance with all state requirements as one factor relevant to the issue of compliance with the requisite nursing home standard of care); cf. Stogsdill v. Manor Convalescent Home, 35 Ill. App. 3d 634, 343 N.E.2d 589, 611-612 (1976) (court remanded nursing home malpractice case for trial, holding that statutory standards submitted were "too vague to be sufficient indicators of the standard of due care required of nursing homes" and that "[s]ince the regulations do not clearly set forth the standard of care required, expert testimony was still required in this case").

[4]See, e.g., Free v. Franklin Guest Home, 397 So. 2d 47 (La. App. 1981) (court remanded lower court's dismissal of plaintiff's action against nursing home for breach of contract based on standard of care provisions of nursing home contract that provided "patient was to be free from mental and physical abuse and was to be treated with consideration, respect, and full recognition of his dignity and individuality").

[5]See Siirila v. Barrios, 398 Mich. 576, 248 N.W.2d 171 (1976) (although trial court should not have excluded expert testimony of specialist as to general practitioner standard of care, specialist could not testify anyway because not familiar with practice in community).

[6]See Trower v. Jones, 121 Ill. 2d 211, 520 N.E.2d 297 (1988) (testimony relevant to whether experts were also "expert" in the art of persuasion).

[7]See e.g., Rice v. Jaskolski, 412 Mich. 206, 313 N.W.2d 893 (1981) (dentist defendant's own testimony as to standard of care for warning patients of possibility of facial numbness sufficient to put issue of his violation of standard to jury).

270

cross-examined with learned treatises, if it is established that they are authoritative.[8]

§4.2.2 The Doctrine of Res Ipsa Loquitur

In meeting its burden of proof as to a defendant's alleged breach, a plaintiff may make use of the doctrine of res ipsa loquitur to establish an inference that the damage occurred through the negligence of a healthcare provider if the claimant can show each of three elements:

- that the injury is of a type that would not normally occur in the absence of negligence;
- that the claimant's well-being was totally subject to the control of the defendant healthcare provider; and
- that the claimant did not assume the risk or act in a way that was contributorily negligent.[9]

This doctrine was adopted to allow for certain situations in which the defendant is in such control of the information necessary to make out a case of malpractice that it is almost impossible for the claimant to meet the burden of coming forward with sufficient evidence to go to the jury. Res ipsa loquitur most commonly arises in the operating room after injury to portions of the body not operated on[10] or failure to remove surgical tools and sponges from patient prior to closing the wound.[11] The effect of the inference of negligence through res ipsa loquitur is not uniform throughout jurisdictions. The ma-

---

[8]See Fed. R. Evid. 803(18).

[9]See generally W. Prosser and W. P. Keeton, The Law of Torts, §39, at 242 (5th ed. 1984). See also §4.3.3, infra, for a discussion of contributory negligence and causation.

[10]See, e.g., Ybarra v. Spangard, 25 Cal. 2d 486, 154 P.2d 687 (1944) (applying elements and policies of res ipsa loquitur to healthcare providers present in operating room).

[11]Rudeck v. Wright, 709 P.2d 621 (Mont. 1985) (leaving a foreign object in a patient's body is negligence per se).

jority of states use the doctrine to allow the issue to be put to the jury and protect the claimant against nonsuit.[12] The minority view is that the application of the res ipsa loquitur doctrine actually shifts the burden of proof to the defendant.[13] Finally, although the doctrine has been used to impose an inference of negligence against multiple defendants,[14] most states do not allow the claimant to make out a case against several defendants by showing that an injury would not have occurred without the negligence of one or another of them[15]

Ultimately, whether through the use of res ipsa loquitur or direct evidence, the claimant must show that it is more likely than not that the physician breached the applicable standard in order for the issue of negligence to be properly submitted to the jury.[16]

§4.3 Causation

The claimant in a malpractice case also must prove through expert testimony that the negligent conduct of the physician or healthcare facility was the proximate cause of the injury complained of.[1] It is not necessary to show the breach was the sole

---

[12]See Gilbert v. Korvette's, Inc., 457 Pa. 602, 327 A.2d 94 (1974) (rejecting burden shifting interpretation previously applied, noting it was error for trial court to apply rebuttable presumption). See also Louiselle and Williams, Res Ipsa Loquitur—Its Future in Medical Malpractice Cases, 48 Calif. L. Rev. 252, 263 (1960); Prosser and Keeton, supra n.9, §40, at 257-259.

[13]See, e.g., Toussant v. Guice, 414 So. 2d 850 (La. Ct. App. 1982).

[14]See Ybarra v. Spangard, 25 Cal. 2d 486, 154 P.2d 687 (1944) (doctrine invoked against all healthcare providers present in operating room).

[15]See Prosser and Keeton, supra n.9, §39, at 251-253. See also McCafferty and Meyer, Medical Malpractice Bases of Liability §2.38, at 42 (1985).

[16]See Rauschelbach v. Benincasa, 372 S.W.2d 120 (Mo. 1963) (requiring reasonable probability—if negligence matter of conjecture, issue not for jury). See also Ericksen v. Wilson, 266 Minn. 401, 123 N.W.2d 687 (1963) (poor result of treatment alone not sufficient to put issue to jury).

§4.3 [1]See, e.g., Raitt v. Johns Hopkins Hosp., 22 Md. App. 196, 322 A.2d 548 (1974) (plaintiff showed breach by proffer of rejected expert testimony but not causation because proffer did not encompass issue of causation), revd. on other grounds, 274 Md. 489, 336 A.2d 90 (1975).

cause, but only that it was a substantial cause in bringing about the harm.[2] In the medical setting, proving causation is often complicated by the fact that the patient seeking medical attention is already ill or suffering from some type of harm, rendering it difficult to show that a negligent act separately contributed toward any injury.[3]

§4.3.1 Causation and Intervening Acts

If the physician's negligent act is found to have substantially contributed toward a separate harm or to have aggravated the existing illness or injury, then the physician is liable for all foreseeable consequences of the negligence. Thus, in the medical malpractice context, the defendant not only will be liable for the injury caused by his or her own negligence, but also may be liable for any injury caused by a second physician if the treatment by the second physician was made necessary by the original negligence.[4] Because the intervention of the second physician was necessary to restore the plaintiff to the position he or she was in before the original negligence, the intervention of the second physician generally does not supersede the

---

[2]See Bender v. Dingwerth, 425 F.2d 378 (5th Cir. 1970) (applying Texas law) (trial court's charge that there could be more than one proximate cause did not sufficiently correct error in another instruction that it must be sole cause).

[3]See Monahan v. Weichert, 82 A.D.2d 102, 442 N.Y.S.2d 295, 299 (1981) (issue whether arthritic patient's loss of mobility in knees after surgery was caused by physician's negligence or was inevitable outcome of disease was one for the jury). See also Monahan v. Weichert, 93 A.D.2d 984, 461 N.Y.S.2d 633 (1983) (quoting previous case and reinstating jury verdict on issue of causation). See §4.7 re loss of a chance.

[4]See Lindquist v. Dengel, 92 Wash. 2d 257, 595 P.2d 934 (1979) (stating no special exception to the rule of liability for foreseeable harm, court held proper jury instruction must clarify physician cannot avoid liability for harm caused by treatment from other physicians if his own negligence was the cause of the injury that necessitated that treatment), citing Restatement (Second) of Torts §457 (1965).

negligence of the original physician.[5] To put it another way, someone injured in an automobile accident due to the driver's negligence or someone injured by a doctor's incorrect diagnosis may be further injured by medical malpractice. Thus, both the negligent driver and the negligent healthcare provider would be liable for the harm caused by the second provider's negligence.

For example, in Carter v. Shirley, an obstetrician's negligence during follow-up care to a complicated delivery resulted in severe infection. The infection had to be treated by a surgeon, who performed colorectal surgery. That allegedly negligent surgery resulted in permanent impairments of the claimant. The court held the obstetrician would be liable for all of the injuries, even those caused by the second physician's negligent diagnosis and surgery.[6]

If, on the other hand, the physician's initial treatment of an existing ill is not successful but does not necessitate the patient's seeking additional treatment, that physician will not be liable for the cost of the second physician's treatment and any damages flowing from it. For example, when a surgeon unsuccessfully attempted to correct the spinal deformities of a claimant, but did not make the condition more severe, he was not held liable for the injuries caused by a subsequent back operation performed by another physician.[7] In such a case, the general rule of liability

---

[5]According to the Restatement:

If the negligent actor is liable for another's bodily injury, he is also subject to liability for any additional bodily harm resulting from normal efforts of third persons in rendering aid which the other's injury reasonably requires, irrespective of whether such acts are done in a proper or a negligent manner.

Restatement (Second) of Torts §457 (1986).

[6]See Carter v. Shirley, 21 Mass. App. 503, 488 N.E.2d 16, 20 (1986) ("[T]he law is well settled that, in an action of tort for negligence causing bodily injury, the negligence of a physician, properly chosen, in treating that injury does not destroy the causal connection between that injury and the consequent suffering, even so much of the suffering as arises from the negligent treatment and would not have arisen if the injury had been properly treated."), citing Sacchetti v. Springer, 303 Mass. 480, 81, 22 N.E.2d 42 (1939) and W. Prosser and W. P. Keeton, The Law of Torts, §44, at 309-310 (5th ed. 1984).

[7]See Harrington v. Cohen, 374 N.E.2d 344 (Mass. Ct. App. 1978) (court

for foreseeable consequences does not apply, because no injury was inflicted by the initial operation. This logic reflects the standard "but for" principle of causation in that the harm from the second operation might have occurred whether or not the first physician had performed the operation that left the patient in the same condition. Although the second operation may not have occurred if a cure had been effected, the initial physician is not liable for subsequent treatment in the absence of an express contract to cure.[8]

A physician generally will not be liable for subsequent injuries *intentionally* (as opposed to negligently) inflicted on the claimant or for injuries arising from treatment of a different injury from the one caused by defendant.[9]

§4.3.2 The Standard of Proof of Causation

The traditional standard of proof required of the claimant to establish the causation element of malpractice is "reasonable probability" that the breach was "a substantial factor" in bringing about the harm.[10] The standard of proof can also be expressed as a requirement that a preponderance of the evidence show the defendant's breach was a cause of the claimant's injury.[11] If

---

affirmed denial of motion for new trial against physician whose negligence did not leave plaintiff in worse condition than before), citing Restatement (Second) of Torts §457 (1965).

[8]374 N.E.2d at 346.

[9]See Prosser and Keeton, supra n.6, §44, at 309. See also Restatement (Second) of Torts §457 (1965).

[10]See, e.g., Laws v. Harter, 534 S.W.2d 449, 451 (Ky. Ct. App. 1976) (applying reasonable "probability" as opposed to "possibility," court concluded not enough evidence to support connection between doctor leaving sponge in patient and patient's chronic abscess in chest cavity); Cooper v. Sisters of Charity of Cincinnati, 27 Ohio St. 2d 242, 272 N.E.2d 97 (1971) (court applied reasonable probability standard, rejecting the substantial possibility standard).

[11]See, e.g., Borowski v. Von Solbrig, 14 Ill. App. 3d 672, 303 N.E.2d 146, 152 (1973) (noting great weight of authority "holds a fair preponderance of evidence" is required).

sufficient evidence of reasonable probability is not offered, a directed verdict can be entered for the defendant.

For example, in a case involving the alleged negligence of a doctor who failed to diagnose a skull fracture of a boy complaining of a headache after being hit by a car, the court held that the issue of proximate cause could not be submitted to the jury without sufficient evidence showing that with the proper diagnosis and treatment the patient probably would have survived.[12] Similarly, a summary judgment for the defendant physician has been affirmed when expert testimony has been given that despite the negligence of the initial treating physician in failing to take skull x-rays of patient who struck his head falling from a truck, the injury was of a type "which would lead to death and is irreversible or irretrievable."[13]

Another standard of causation used in a few jurisdictions is the "substantial possibility" requirement. The Restatement (Second) of Torts §323(a), which imposes liability for a breach that merely "increases the risk of harm," has been used in some medical malpractice cases to require that a claimant need only show the breach increased the risk of harm, not that it necessarily caused the harm.[14] This has been interpreted by some to require only a showing that there is a "substantial possibility" the defendant's conduct contributed toward the harm.

In Jones v. Montefiore Hospital, the Supreme Court of

---

[12]See Cooper v. Sisters of Charity of Cincinnati, 272 N.E.2d 97 (Ohio 1971) (court affirmed entry of directed verdict for defendant). See also §4.7 re loss-of-a-chance cases.

[13]Neal v. Welker, 426 S.W.2d 476, 477 (Ky. Ct. App. 1968) (defendant's summary judgment proper when claimant gave no expert testimony to rebut defendant's expert evidence of lack of causation).

[14]See Jones v. Montefiore Hosp., 494 Pa. 410, 431 A.2d 920 (1981) (court remanded case for retrial based on new standard) (citing the Restatement (Second) of Torts §323(a)). See also Hamil v. Bashline, 224 Pa. Super. 407, 307 A.2d 57 (1973) (reversed trial court opinion based on reasonable medical certainty standard of causation; relying on the Restatement (Second) of Torts §323, court ruled that only an increased risk of harm must be shown). But see Hamil v. Bashline, 481 Pa. 256, 392 A.2d 1280 (1978) (on appeal of remand, court held the jury and not the expert was to balance probabilities showing likelihood that defendant's conduct resulted in harm to plaintiff).

Pennsylvania vacated and remanded a lower court decision that required the claimant show that the defendant's conduct was a direct cause "without which it [the injury] would not occur."[15] The court rejected this instruction in favor of one that allowed the jury to impose liability "if it decided that appellees' negligent conduct increased the risk of harm, and that such increased risk was a substantial factor in bringing about the harm actually inflicted."[16] The court in Thomas v. Corso applied this standard somewhat differently in holding that a jury could base its finding on a showing that "substantial possibility of survival" was effectively precluded by the breach of the defendant.[17]

Most jurisdictions, however, continue to apply the "reasonable probability" standard that the breach was a substantial factor in bringing about harm and that mere possibility of decreased chance of survival or increased risk of harm is not enough to support a finding of causation.[18] For example, in Walden v. Jones, claimant's expert testified that if defendant physician had performed surgery to correct a herniated disc immediately after the patient experienced some paralysis the claimant *might* not have been permanently paralyzed and would have had a *chance* to recover lower limb mobility. In light of testimony that there would only have been a possibility of recovery, the Court of Appeals of Kentucky held that sufficient evidence was not produced to preclude a directed verdict for defendant.[19]

---

[15]431 A.2d at 923.

[16]Id. at 924.

[17]Thomas v. Corso, 288 A.2d 379, 390 (Md. Ct. App. 1972) (verdict upheld when jury could reasonably conclude defendant's failure deprived plaintiff of substantial possibility of survival). See also Hicks v. United States, 368 F.2d 626, 632 (4th Cir. 1966) (applying Virginia law) ("If there was any substantial possibility of survival and the defendant has destroyed it, he is answerable.") See §4.7 re loss-of-a-chance cases.

[18]See, e.g., Laws v. Harter, 534 S.W.2d 449, 451 (Ky. Ct. App. 1976) (applying reasonable "probability" as opposed to possibility); Short v. Downs, 537 P.2d 754 (Colo. Ct. App. 1975) (court acknowledged mere possibility not enough); Gibson v. Avery 463 S.W.2d 277 (Tex. Civ. App. 1970) (plaintiff's evidence showing conduct was only a "possible cause" did not meet reasonable probability standard).

[19]Walden v. Jones, 439 S.W.2d 571 (Ky. Ct. App. 1968).

§4.3.3 Contributory Negligence and Causation

At common law, a claimant was precluded from recovery of any damages for injury caused primarily by the negligence of others *if* that claimant's own deviation from ordinary and prudent behavior contributed in any way to the harm.[20] Although there have been many reasons offered for this defense, the primary one is that the claimant's behavior in such cases negates proximate cause because the claimant's conduct is an intervening cause.[21] Examples of actions or omissions of patients that have reduced their recovery include concealing important medical facts from the physician,[22] failing to take medication as prescribed, and otherwise failing to follow a doctor's orders.[23] It is generally not considered negligent for patients to follow the instructions of, or to otherwise rely on, their physicians.[24]

---

[20]See generally W. Prosser and W. P. Keeton, The Law of Torts, §65, at 451 (5th ed. 1984).

[21]See generally id. §65, at 452 (citing cases, but disagreeing with premise).

[22]See, e.g., Moodie v. Santoni, 292 Md. 582, 441 A.2d 323 (1982) (plaintiff contributorily negligent when evidence showed plaintiff failed to disclose important symptoms); Skar v. City of Lincoln, 599 F.2d 253 (8th Cir. 1979) (applying Nebraska law) (patient refused to give accurate information about medical history). See also Annotation, Patient's Failure to Reveal Medical History to Physician as Contributory Negligence or Assumption of Risk in Defense of Malpractice Action, 33 A.L.R.4th 790 (1984).

[23]See, e.g., Fall v. White, 449 N.E.2d 628 (Ind. Ct. App. 1983) (failure to follow doctor's instructions for further care or further diagnostic tests); Brazil v. United States, 484 F. Supp. 986 (N.D. Ala. 1979) (applying Alabama law) (failure to follow doctor's orders not to move). See also Annot., Medical Malpractice: Patient's Failure to Return, as Directed, for Examination or Treatment as Contributory Negligence, 100 A.L.R.3d 723 (1980). Compare Stager v. Schneider, 494 A.2d 1307 (D.C. Ct. App. 1985) (although plaintiff has duty to cooperate with doctor in proper diagnosis and treatment, plaintiff had no affirmative duty to call and inquire as to test results of a secondary procedure and as such was not contributorily negligent).

[24]Johnson v. United States, 271 F. Supp. 205 (W.D. Ark. 1967) (not contributorily negligent for failing to consult another doctor when patient had no reason to believe that the doctor's negligence caused injury); O'Neil v. State, 323 N.Y.S.2d 56 (N.Y. Ct. Cl. 1971) (not contributorily negligent for failure to diagnose own illness); Fairchild v. Brian, 354 So. 2d 675 (La. Ct. App. 1977) (may rely on assurances of doctor and need not seek opinion of

Today, contributory negligence of the claimant operates as a complete bar to recovery in only a handful of states.[25] The general rule now is that damages will be apportioned between the parties based in some fashion on their "comparative negligence," or degree of fault.[26] The major premise on which the imposition of comparative liability is based is that although the claimant's "contributory" negligence "proximately causes" his own injury, at least in part, it should not operate to absolve entirely the defendant for her role in bringing about the claimant's harm.[27]

The consequences of a finding that the claimant contributed to his own injury vary by state. In a few remaining jurisdictions, the claimant's contributory negligence operates as a complete bar to any recovery.[28] In a majority of states, there is some form of comparative negligence: pure comparative negligence, modified or "equal division" comparative negligence, the "slight gross" system of comparative negligence,[29] or the 50-percent system.[30]

About a dozen states have adopted a pure comparative negligence system, under which the claimant's award is reduced by the percentage of fault attributable to him.[31] In these states, a claimant can recover 5 percent of his proven damages even if

---

others). Compare Santoni v. Moodie, 53 Md. App. 129, 452 A.2d 1223 (1982) (hearsay evidence as to the decedent's state of mind in continuing to take a prescribed drug long after serious side effects arose and failing to report those symptoms to clinic physicians was relevant to issue of contributory negligence).

[25]See V. Schwartz, Comparative Negligence §1.1, at 3 (2d ed. 1986). Some form of comparative negligence has been adopted in all but six jurisdictions.

[26]Id. §2.1, at 29.

[27]See generally Prosser and Keeton, supra n.20, §67, at 468-479.

[28]The jurisdictions are Alabama, the District of Columbia, Maryland, North Carolina, South Carolina, and Virginia.

[29]See Notes, Comparative Negligence, 81 Colum. L. Rev. 1668 (1981).

[30]See V. Schwartz, Comparative Negligence (2d ed. 1986).

[31]States using a pure comparative negligence system include Mississippi, Rhode Island, Washington, New York, Michigan and Louisiana by statute, and Florida, California, Alaska, New Mexico, Illinois, Missouri and Kentucky. See V. Schwartz, supra n.30, §3.2, at 47-49.

he was 95 percent at fault. Some states that initially adopted pure comparative negligence later enacted statutes that call for some form of modified comparative negligence.[32]

Modified comparative negligence can take several forms. The most straightforward, the old "equal division" system, simply cut the award to the claimant in half when both the defendant and claimant were found to be at fault, regardless of the degree of contribution of each in bringing about the harm.[33] The equal division system was seen as vastly unfair and was eventually overruled by the Supreme Court in United States v. Reliable Transfer Co.[34]

Under the fairly archaic slight-gross system, the claimant is allowed to recover completely, even if contributorily negligent, if the claimant's negligence was comparatively "slight" and the defendant's negligence was comparatively "gross."[35] Under this system the only "apportionment" is in determining whether the claimant's negligence is "remote" in comparison with that of the defendant—there is no relative apportionment of damages.[36]

The 50-percent system is the most pervasive comparative negligence scheme, used in 28 states.[37] Under the 50-percent

---

[32]See, e.g., Ark. Stat. Ann. §27-1765 and Iowa Code Ann. §668 (West 1987).

[33]See V. Schwartz, supra n.30, §3.3, at 54.

[34]421 U.S. 397 (1975), (Court ruled the ease of administering the equal division was outweighed by the unjust results of its application).

[35]See V. Schwartz, supra n.30, §3.4, at 59-60.

[36]Id., noting Tennessee is the only state that continues to apply the slight-gross rule.

[37]Id. at 67 (listing Ark. Stat. Ann. §27-1764; Colo. Rev. Stat. §13-21-111; Conn. Gen. Stat. Ann. §52-572h; Del. Code Ann. tit. 10, §8132; Ga. Code Ann. §§46-8-291, 51-11-1; Haw. Rev. Stat. §663-31(a); Idaho Code §6-801; Ind. Code §34-4-33-4; Iowa Code Ann. ch. 668; Kan. Stat. Ann. §60-258a; Me. Rev. Stat. Ann. tit. 14, §156; Mass. Gen. Laws Ann. ch. 231, §85; Minn. Stat. Ann. §604.01, subd. 1; Mont. Code Ann. §27-1-702; Nev. Rev. Stat. §41.141; N.H. Rev. Stat. Ann. §507:7-a; N.J. Stat. Ann. §2A:15-5.1; N.D. Cent. Code §9-10-07; Ohio Rev. Code Ann. §2315.19; Okla. Stat. Ann. tit. 23, §11; Or. Rev. Stat. §18.470; Pa. Stat. Ann. tit. 42, §7102; Tex. Rev. Civ. Stat. Ann. art. 2212a, §1 (Vernon); Utah Code Ann. §78-27-37; Vt. Stat. Ann. tit. 12, §1036; Bradley v. Appalachian Power Co., 163 W. Va. 332, 256 S.E.2d 879 (1979); Wis. Stat. Ann., §895.045; Wyo. Stat. §1-1-109).

system, claimants are generally not entitled to recover if they are more than 50 percent at fault. Some 50-percent states, however, bar recovery if the claimant is equally, or exactly 50 percent, at fault.[38] Thus, only a claimant who is *less than* 50 percent at fault can recover the remaining proportion of his or her damages from the defendant. In several states, the defendants' liability is expressly joint and several (i.e., the comparative fault only operates as between claimant and defendants—not among defendants). Thus, a defendant hospital 10 percent at fault could pay 80 percent of the damages if one of its doctors was 70 percent at fault and the claimant was only 20 percent at fault.[39]

§4.4 Damages

In addition to establishing a duty, its breach, and its causal connection to an injury, the claimant must prove the scope and extent of injuries and their monetary value in order to recover damages. The problem of calculating the monetary value of a claimant's injuries is compounded in the medical malpractice setting by the fact that a portion of the damage may be due to the original illness or injury.[1] In malpractice actions that involve elderly patients, the actual losses may be low because the claimant is experiencing high medical expenses and has a short life expectancy even before the allegedly negligent or intentional conduct caused harm.[2]

---

[38]Id. at 68.

[39]Id. at 74.

§4.4 [1]See generally 61 Am. Jur. 2d §367 (1981) citing Borowski v. Von Solbrig, 14 Ill. App. 3d 672, 303 N.E.2d 146 (1973), affd., 60 Ill. 2d 418, 328 N.E.2d 301 (1975) (doctor whose negligence aggravated injury liable only for portion of injury he caused).

[2]Some statutes governing actions against nursing homes permit multiple damages and attorneys' fees to address this concern. See, e.g., N.Y. Pub. Health Law §§2801d(2), 2801d(6) (providing for punitive damages and award of attorneys' fees to prevailing party). See also Mo. Ann. Stat. §198.093.3 (Vernon 1988); Ohio Rev. Code Ann. §3721.17(I) (Page 1989); Ill. Ann. Stat. ch. 111½ §4153-602 (West 1989).

§4.4.1 Compensatory Damages

In medical malpractice cases, the claimant is entitled to recover compensation for the monetary value of the difference between the position he or she would have been in had it not been for the defendant's negligence and the position he or she is in because of that negligence.[3] Both economic and noneconomic losses generally are considered recoverable in putting the claimant back to his or her prior position. Economic damages include compensation for lost wages, reduced earning capacity, medical expenses, and the cost of special equipment.[4] Computation of such awards is complicated by the need to consider such issues as adjustments for future projected productivity and inflation and, in some states, adjustments for the effect of income taxes.[5]

Noneconomic losses include damages for pain and suffering, disfigurement, loss of consortium, and emotional distress. Such damages are among the most difficult to quantify because there is no monetary reference point.[6] Some commentators have suggested that juries, contrary to their instructions, include in their noneconomic damages awards compensation for attorneys' fees that they may be aware will ultimately lessen the award to the plaintiff.[7] Some states have imposed caps on total awards for noneconomic damages.[8]

---

[3]See, e.g., Gleitman v. Cosgrove, 49 N.J. 22, 227 A.2d 689 (1967) (court cited measure of damages as that required to put claimant in position he or she would have been in had it not been for defendant's negligence) (overruled on other grounds).

[4]See V. Schwartz, et al., Product Liability: A Practical Guide, ¶75.201 (1988).

[5]See Kaczkowski v. Bolubasz, 421 A.2d 1027 (Pa. 1980) (court held increases in productivity and inflation should be considered).

[6]See Annot. Excessiveness or Adequacy of Damages Awarded to Injured Person for Injuries to Arms, Legs, Feet and Hands, 11 A.L.R.3d 9 (1967) (discussing spread of awards for disfiguring loss of various appendages).

[7]See M. G. MacDonald and K. C. Meyer, Health Care Law: A Practical Guide, §11.05[1], at 11-54 (1988).

[8]See, e.g., Alaska Stat. §09.17.010 (Supp. 1986); Colo. Rev. Stat. §13-21-102.5 (Supp. 1986); Fla. Stat. §768.80 (Supp. 1986); Haw. Rev. Stat. §663.xx (Supp. 1986); Idaho Code §6-1603 (Supp. 1986); Kan. H.B. 2472

Historically, damages for mental anguish or emotional distress have been recoverable if such distress causes bodily pain and suffering or is caused by it. Mental or emotional distress as a separate cause of action, without any showing of accompanying physical or monetary injury, generally was not compensable without some physical manifestation of its severity or extreme and outrageous conduct by the defendant.[9] More recently, however, the California Supreme Court awarded such damages without a showing of actual physical injury when a doctor erroneously diagnosed the claimant's wife as having syphilis. The incorrect diagnosis resulted in the claimant's suffering of emotional distress and serious marital difficulties.[10] The court rules that the "universally accepted gravity of a false imputation of syphilis" is sufficient proof that the distress was significant enough to verify the genuineness of the claim.[11] Less proof of actual distress is typically required if the defendant's conduct is particularly outrageous.[12]

§4.4.2 Wrongful Death and Survival Actions

At common law, an injured claimant's cause of action for tortious injury died with her. Now, virtually every state allows

---

(approved May 15, 1987); Md. Cts. & Jud. Proc. §11-108 (1989); Minn. Stat. §549.23 (Supp. 1986); N.H. Rev. Stat. Ann. §508:4-d (Supp. 1986); Wash. Rev. Code §4.56xxx (Supp. 1986).

[9]See W. Prosser and W. P. Keeton, The Law of Torts, §12, at 55 (5th ed. 1984) quoting Lynch v. Knight, Eng. Rep. 854 (1861) ("mental pain or anxiety, the law cannot value and does not pretend to redress, when the unlawful act causes that alone").

[10]Molien v. Kaiser Found. Hosp., 27 Cal. 3d 916, 167 Cal. Rptr. 831, 616 P.2d 813 (1980) (claim for damages for emotional distress upheld because the potential for emotional suffering for such a negligent diagnosis was foreseeable).

[11]Id. at 821. (Court also noted couple had to undergo expense of marital counseling).

[12]See Annot., Recovery for Emotional Distress Resulting from Statement of Medical Practitioner or Official, Allegedly Constituting Outrageous Conduct, 34 A.L.R.4th 688 (1984). See, e.g., Seitz v. Humana of Kentucky, No. 87-CA-2511-S (Ky. Ct. App. Nov. 4, 1988) (available on LEXIS).

a cause of action for wrongful death and perhaps also allows the survival of the estate's cause of action. Under early wrongful death statutes, damages were limited to the actual economic loss to the qualifying relative. Pain and suffering, loss of consortium, and emotional distress damages were not recoverable.[13] Although the primary basis for recovery in wrongful death actions is still economic loss to the claimant, many wrongful death statutes now allow recovery of both economic and noneconomic compensatory damages, and some even allow punitive damages.[14] Survival statutes generally allow compensation for all losses—economic and noneconomic—to which the decedent would have been entitled had she survived, subject to any defenses that would have been valid against the decedent.[15] Generally, wrongful death and survival actions both may be brought as a result of a patient's death allegedly due to malpractice.

§4.4.3 Punitive Damages

Since punishment is not the main thrust of tort law, punitive damages are awarded only in egregious cases of negligence bordering on intentional conduct.[16] Intentional conduct typically requires an element of either malicious or recklessly indifferent

---

[13]See V. Schwartz, supra n.4, ¶¶75,501 to 75,801.

[14]Id. at ¶75,631. Note that some statutes governing the rights of nursing home residents create a cause of action that allows recovery for pain and suffering of decedent nursing home residents regardless of the existence of wrongful death statutes limiting such damages. See, e.g., Stiffelman v. Abrams, 655 S.W.2d 522, 532 (Mo. banc 1983), citing Mo. Ann. Stat. §198.0931 et seq. (Vernon 1988). In *Stiffelman,* the decedent's estate was allowed to proceed with a cause of action based on the pain and suffering of the decedent as a result of the intentionally tortious acts of the defendant nursing home rather than be limited to the statutory wrongful death damages of loss of support and other pecuniary damages. The court further noted punitive damages were available provided the plaintiff (the estate) was able to prove intentional conduct by the nursing home that brought about the injuries.

[15]V. Schwartz, supra n.4, at ¶75,641.

[16]See Prosser and Keeton, supra n.9, §2, at 9.

behavior that warrants an award of punitive damages designed to punish the defendant and discourage such behavior.[17] Because of the peculiarly vulnerable status of nursing home residents, several states have adopted special statutes that expressly authorize punitive damages for intentional, and in some cases even negligent, acts that result in injury to the resident.[18]

Punitive damages generally are not insurable for public policy reasons.[19] There is an increasing trend, however, toward upholding coverage for punitive damages awarded in gross negligence cases.[20] Thus, a healthcare facility may be able to insure against vicarious liability for reckless behavior of employees provided that it does not have actual or constructive notice of these propensities.[21] Insurance coverage for punitive damages

---

[17]See e.g., Wargelin v. Sisters of Mercy Health Corp., 149 Mich. App. 75, 385 N.W.2d 732 (1986) (parents allowed to take issue of punitive damages to jury where obstetrician, after negligent delivery, presented dead fetus to mother as if it were alive). See also Short v. Downs, 537 P.2d 754 (Colo. Ct. App. 1975) (punitive damages awardable where doctor used silicone labeled "not for human use" for injecting into patient's breast without attempting to discover what the effects might be).

[18]See, e.g., Ill. Ann. Stat. ch. 111½ §§4153-601, 2 (West 1989) (statute permits recovery of treble damages for both intentional and negligent acts that result in injury to nursing home residents), upheld in Harris v. Manor Healthcare Corp., 489 N.E.2d 1374 (Ill. 1986) (Supreme Court of Illinois upheld treble damage statute against state constitutional challenge as prohibited "special legislation," stating, "the potential for long-term abuse and neglect is far greater for nursing home residents than it is for hospital patients"; therefore, the rational basis test for distinguishing between hospitals and "long-term care" facilities was met). See also Ohio Rev. Code Ann. §3721.17(I) (Page 1989) (intentional conduct not specified as a requirement for punitive damages); Mo. Ann. Stat. §198.093(3) (Vernon 1988) (court may award punitive damages limited to five times the amount of special damages unless the injury is the result of an intentional act or omission); N.Y. Pub. Health Law §2801d(2) (provides for punitive damages where the act is "willful or in reckless disregard for the lawful rights of the patient").

[19]See W. Prosser and W. P. Keeton, The Law of Torts, §2, at 13 (5th ed. 1984) ("[I]f punitive damages are supported by any sound policy, that policy would appear to demand that they shall not be covered by liability insurance.").

[20]See, e.g., Mazza v. Medical Mutual Ins. Co., 311 N.C. 621, 319 S.E.2d 217 (1984) (public policy does not prohibit insurance coverage for punitive damages awarded in an action for physician's gross negligence).

[21]See §§4.12.2.2 and 4.13.1.2, infra.

resulting from an insured's intentional conduct is still not allowed in most jurisdictions.[22]

Legislatures in at least ten states have enacted statutory schemes to limit punitive damage awards.[23]

§4.4.4 Payment of Damages

Traditionally, payments of damages for medical malpractice-related injuries have been made in a lump sum. In order to make an award, the jury must calculate the present value of the losses they have predicted will occur over a number of years.[24] Once it is determined, for example, that the claimant would have earned an additional $300,000 over his lifetime but for the injury, the jury must determine what lesser sum should be awarded that, together with the interest earned on it, would be sufficient to provide $300,000 over the claimant's working life. Several legislatures have enacted statutes that allow for periodic payment of these damages because such payments help reduce liability insurance costs.[25] Although many of these statutes have been subjected to constitutional challenges on the basis of denial of "due process," "equal protection," and "trial by jury," most have survived.[26]

---

[22]See, e.g., Continental Ins. Co. v. Hancock, 507 S.W. 146 (Ky. Ct. App. 1974) (punitive damages may be covered if they are due to gross negligence as opposed to intentional conduct).

[23]See Ala. Code §6-11-21 (1987); Colo. Rev. Stat. §13.21.102(1) (1986); Conn. Gen. Stat. §52-240b (1979); Fla. Stat. §768.73(1)(a) (1986); Ga. Code Ann. §51-12-5.1(g) (1987); Kan. Stat. Ann. §60-3701(e) (1988); Nevada Acts 1989, ch. 218; Okla. Stat. tit. 23, §9 (1986); Tex. Civ. Prac. & Rem. Code Ann. §41.007 (1987); Va. Code Ann. §8.01-38.1 (1987).

[24]See 22 Am. Jur. 2d, Damages, §§676, 678 (1988).

[25]See, e.g., Ariz. Rev. Stat. Ann. §12-567 (1980).

[26]See, e.g., Annot., Validity of State Statute Providing for Periodic Payment of Future Damages in Medical Malpractice Action, 41 A.L.R.4th 275 (1985), citing American Bank & Trust Co. v. Community Hosp., 36 Cal. 3d 359, Cal. Rptr. 671, 683 P.2d 670 (1984).

For a discussion of structured settlements, see V. Schwartz et al., Guide to Multistate Litigation §13.03, at 269-271 (1985).

Periodic payment of damages can be beneficial to both claimant and defendant. It provides a steady income to the claimant while ensuring that the award is not dissipated.[27] Defendants are not subjected to the total weight of the projected injury at once, and some of the funds may be earned through other investments during the payout period.[28]

§4.5 The Statute-of-Limitations Defense

One defense available to a healthcare provider is that the cause of action is barred by the statute of limitations. The statute of limitations, which does not depend on the merits of the case, is a complete defense to an action that is not commenced within the statutory period of time. The purpose of the statute is to protect the defendant healthcare facility from having to defend itself from a stale claim for which witnesses and evidence may have disappeared.

§4.5.1 Limitation of Actions

Although every state has a statute of limitations, the period during which a cause of action must be brought varies from state to state. Within a state, the time period may vary depending on whether the action is brought in tort, contract, malpractice, or wrongful death. The periods generally range from one to three years for a malpractice action, one to six years for a negligence action, three to fifteen years for a contract action, and one to three years for a wrongful death action.

In a medical malpractice action, there may be an issue as to whether the contract or tort statutory limitation applies. Many

---

[27]According to the Journal of Commerce (Mar. 1978), cited in Schwartz, supra n.26, §13.03, at 270, n.29, studies show that 90 percent of those that received substantial sums through prizes, lotteries, or settlements dissipated the entire amount within five years.

[28]See Schwartz, supra n.26, §13.03 at 269-271 for a discussion of structural settlements.

claimants have attempted to bring their medical malpractice actions as contract actions because the statute of limitations for breach of contract is generally longer than it is for tort. The courts typically have held that the tort statute of limitations applies, regardless of the form of the action.[1] There is case law to the contrary, however, when there is a written contract or an express contract warranting a cure.[2] If the claimant brings a contract action, the court may limit the damages to those available in contract and refuse any award for pain and suffering.[3] Many states have settled the issue by adopting specific medical malpractice statutes of limitations. The majority of these states provide for one uniform statute of limitations whether the malpractice action is brought in tort or in contract.[4] Other malpractice statutes apply only to actions brought in tort and specifically exclude contract actions.[5]

§4.5.2 Accrual of the Cause of Action

Another question that often arises is, when does the statute of limitations begin to run? There are several events that could commence the running of the statute, depending upon the wording of the statute and the case law interpreting it.

---

§4.5 [1]See, e.g., Kozan v. Comstock, 270 F.2d 839 (5th Cir. 1959) (applying Louisiana law) (court affirmed trial court dismissal based on application of one-year tort statute of limitations although the action was brought in contract).

[2]See Kozan, 270 F.2d 839 (court acknowledged cause of action in contract could exist if there were an express contract); Zostautas v. St. Anthony de Padua Hosp., 178 N.E.2d 303 (Ill. 1961) (court recognized contract cause of action in some instances but dismissed contract cause of action when it was alleged at common law rather than under wrongful death statute).

[3]See, e.g., Robbins v. Finestone, 308 N.Y. 543, 127 N.E.2d 330 (1955).

[4]See Ala. Code §6-5-482 (1977 & Supp. 1988); Colo. Rev. Stat. §13-80-102 (1974 & Supp. 1988); and Mass. Gen. Laws Ann. ch. 260, §4 (West 1959 & Supp. 1989) (providing a uniform statute of limitations for actions arising against medical professionals regardless of legal theory on which based).

[5]See Kan. Stat. Ann. §60-513 (1983 & Supp. 1987); Miss. Code Ann. §15-1-36 (Supp. 1987) (setting out statutory period for claims against medical professionals *not* based on contract).

The Traditional Rule. Under the general tort statutes of limitations, which are based on common law, the cause of action accrues when the wrongful act or omission occurs. Ordinarily, the negligent act and the injury occur simultaneously and the injury is apparent. In the medical malpractice context, however, this rule may produce harsh results, because many injuries are not, and could not be, discovered until many years after the negligent act took place. Many courts and state legislatures have created exceptions to the traditional rule to avoid these harsh results.[6]

The Discovery Rule. One of the earliest exceptions, later known as the "discovery rule," originally stated that the statute of limitations did not begin to run until the presence of a foreign object negligently left in a patient's body had been discovered.[7] This rule has been expanded in most states to include the discovery of injury in all forms of medical malpractice, although a few states continue to apply the rule only to the discovery of foreign objects.[8] Under one variation of the rule, a cause of action accrues when the claimant discovers, or through the use of reasonable diligence should have discovered, *the injury.*[9] The rule adopted by a majority of jurisdictions, however, states that the statute of limitations does not begin to run until the plaintiff discovers, or through the use of reasonable diligence should

---

[6]Reeves and Hirsh, For Whom the Bell Tolls: The Statute of Limitations and Medical Malpractice, 1986 Med. Trial Tech. Q. 414.

[7]Fernandi v. Strully, 35 N.J. 434, 173 A.2d 277 (1961) (period of limitation began to run when patient had reason to know about the foreign object, a wing nut, left in body after an operation).

[8]See, e.g., Ark. Code Ann. §16-114-203 (1987); Idaho Code §5-219 (1979 & Supp. 1988). See also Myrick v. James, 444 A.2d 987 (Me. 1982) (court extended discovery rule to surgical malpractice only); Ivey v. Scoggins, 163 Ga. App. 741, 295 S.E.2d 164 (1982) (discovery rule application to foreign objects); N.Y. Civ. Prac. L. & R. §214(a) (McKinney Supp. 1989) (extends discovery rules to continuous treatment and foreign object situations but limits "foreign" objects to exclude "compounds, fixation devices or prosthetic aids").

[9]See Conn. Gen. Stat. Ann. §52-584 (West 1960 & Supp. 1988); Haw. Rev. Stat. §657-7.3 (1976 & Supp. 1987).

have discovered, that she has a *cause of action*.[10] This not only requires that the plaintiff be aware of the injury, but also that the plaintiff be aware that it was the defendant's negligence that caused the injury.[11]

For example, in Wallish v. Fosnaugh,[12] a high-protein dietary treatment prescribed by a physician for an infant's rash resulted in severe mental retardation. The parents of the child knew that he was retarded for over 20 years before they learned that a high-protein diet can produce phenylketonuria, which in turn produces severe mental retardation if untreated. The court ruled that the statute of limitation began to run when the parents learned of the causal connection with the defendant's improper treatment rather than the "discovery" of the injury, the mental retardation.

The Continuous-Treatment Rule. Several jurisdictions have adopted the continuous-treatment rule, either by statute or case law, as another exception to the traditional rule for the accrual of the cause of action. Under it, physicians are regarded as negligent not only in the original act, but also in continuing the negligent treatment or in the continuous failure to remedy the situation. The statute of limitations in these jurisdictions does not commence until the treatment for the medical problem in question is terminated.[13] In determining whether continuous

---

[10]See Ala. Code §6-5-482 (1977 & Supp. 1988); Fla. Stat. Ann. §95.11 (West 1982 & Supp. 1988).

[11]Bayless v. Philadelphia Natl. League Club, 579 F.2d 37, 41 (3d Cir. 1978) (applying Pennsylvania law) (court remanded issue of running of statute of limitations based on Pennsylvania rule that statute does not run until claimant knows "who or what" caused the harm).

[12]126 Mich. App. 418, 336 N.W.2d 923 (1983). See also Call v. Kezirian, 185 Cal. Rptr. 103, 135 Cal. App. 3d 189 (2d Dist. 1982) (court held statute of limitations for parents of 7-year-old born with Down's Syndrome did not run until the parents knew or should have known, as intelligent people without specialized knowledge, that the defect could have been discovered with amniocentesis).

[13]See, e.g., N.Y. Civ. Prac. L. & R. 214-a (McKinney Supp. 1989); Ishler v. Miller, 384 N.E.2d 296 (Ohio 1978) (statutory period does not commence until termination of patient-physician relationship). See also Collins v. Wil-

treatment is involved, the courts consider the continuity of treatment, the date of the last contact, and whether the continued treatment was for the particular medical problem in question.[14]

Two situations may arise that fall outside the scope of the rule. First, a claimant may "discover" the injury but continue treatment. In a majority of states, the statute of limitations will commence running on the claimant's discovery of the cause of action, whether or not treatment continues.[15] A few jurisdictions, however, follow the continuous-treatment rule regardless of when the claim is discovered because to do otherwise would force claimants to discontinue treatment by physicians against whom they may have a claim without giving them a chance to correct their mistake.[16] Second, a claimant may communicate with a physician solely for the purpose of extending the statute of limitations. In the second situation, courts will refuse to toll (delay) the running of the statute when it appears that claimant's last contact with the physician was made merely to delay commencing the running of the statute.[17]

---

mington Medical Center, 311 A.2d 885 (Del. Super. 1973) (cause of action began to accrue at least as early as date doctor told patient he "could do no more" and terminated physician-patient relationship).

[14]*Ishler*, 384 N.E.2d at 298. See also Eagleston v. Mount Sinai Medical Center, 144 A.D.2d 427, 533 N.Y.S.2d 992 (N.Y. App. Div. 1988) (court found continuous-treatment rule did not apply when claimant failed to show post-surgery visits were a continuation of the initial surgery).

[15]See Lane v. Lane, 752 S.W.2d 25 (Ark. 1988) (statutory period did not begin to accrue until patient discovered cause of her drug addiction regardless of length of time of treatment or of existing injury). See also Hundley v. St. Francis Hosp., 161 Cal. App. 2d 800, 327 P.2d 131 (1958).

[16]See Ishler v. Miller, 56 Ohio St. 2d 447, 384 N.E.2d 296 (Ohio 1978) (court affirmed that discovery rule is not applicable during the physician-patient relationship). See also Saultz v. Funk, 64 Ohio App. 2d 29, 410 N.E.2d 1275 (1979) (discovery rule can extend continuous-treatment rule in cases of foreign objects).

[17]Compare Shane v. Mouw, 116 Mich. App. 737, 323 N.W.2d 537 (1982) (when no evidence that telephone call to physician was solely for purpose of extending the statute of limitations, telephone conversation may extend period under continuous-treatment rule); DeGrazia v. Johnson, 105 Mich. App. 356, 306 N.W.2d 512 (1981) (court allowed telephone conversation to extend

Wrongful Death Statutes. The statute of limitations for wrongful death begins to run on the date of death of the decedent. As with contract actions, some claimants have attempted to bring a malpractice action as a wrongful death action to take advantage of different time limits or different damages available. In some circumstances, this is an advantage to the claimant because the statute runs from the date of death and not from the date of the injury or negligent act. The courts are split on the issue whether the wrongful death or medical malpractice statute would control. Several courts have applied the wrongful death statute,[18] while others have applied the malpractice statute.[19]

Exceptions to the Accrual Rules. There are two major exceptions to the accrual rules, one that extends the period during which suit may be brought and one that limits it. The first is the fraudulent concealment doctrine, which has been adopted legislatively or judicially in most states. Under this doctrine, if the plaintiff has not discovered the cause of action because the physician fraudulently concealed the negligence, then the statute will be tolled until the plaintiff discovers, or should have discovered, the fraud.[20] Fraudulent concealment is hard to prove,

---

period under continuous-treatment rule only when no evidence of fraudulent purpose).

[18]Brown v. St. Paul Mercury Ins. Co., 732 S.W.2d 130 (Ark. 1987) (wrongful death statute applies when patient dies before two-year malpractice period has run); Baxter v. Zeller, 601 P.2d 902 (Or. Ct. App. 1979) (three-year wrongful death statute applied when cause of action based on death as a result of physician's negligence).

[19]See, e.g., DeRogatis v. Mayo Clinic, 390 N.W.2d 773 (Minn. 1986) (malpractice statutory period applied to wrongful death actions; period began to run when underlying medical malpractice claim would); Camp. v. Martin, 256 S.E.2d 657 (Ga. Ct. App. 1979) (court affirmed dismissal of wrongful death action because medical malpractice period had run).

[20]See, e.g., Fla. Stat. Ann. §95.11 (West 1982 & Supp. 1988) (if fraud, concealment, or intentional misrepresentation of fact prevented the discovery of the injury, then period of limitations is extended); Mont. Code Ann. §27-2-205 (1986) (tolled if there has been a failure to disclose any act, error, or omission on which such action is based). See also Van Bronckhorst v. Taube,

since it requires proof that the physician had actual or constructive knowledge and either deliberately concealed the negligence or failed to inform the claimant of the cause of an injury.[21]

The second important exception is the maximum time limit for bringing an action. Several states that have adopted the discovery rule also have provided for maximum periods of time during which a cause of action must be brought, regardless of when the injury, cause of action, or foreign object is discovered.[22] Occasionally, there will be a maximum time limit for bringing an action with an exception for either the discovery of a foreign object or the discovery of fraudulent concealment. These exceptions may provide for longer maximum periods[23] or no maximum periods for the discovery of a foreign object or fraudulent concealment.[24]

§4.6 Governmental Immunity and the Healthcare Facility

§4.6.1 Overview

Although largely inapplicable in the medical malpractice setting, in certain circumstances some form of governmental immunity

---

168 Ind. App. 132, 341 N.E.2d 791 (2d Dist. 1976) (court held physician's fraud in concealing true nature of patient's condition equitably estopped his assertion of statute of limitations).

[21]See, e.g., Ray v. Scheibert, 484 S.W.2d 63 (Tenn. Ct. App. 1972). (Court dismissed claimant's continuous-treatment claim because no evidence of fraudulent concealment despite claimant's testimony that he pointed out redness and inflammation to defendant and they indicated it was not a problem).

[22]See Ill. Ann. Stat. ch. 110, ¶13-212 (Smith-Hurd Supp. 1988); N.C. Gen. Stat. §1-15(c) (1983).

[23]See Fla. Stat. Ann. §95.11 (West 1982) (longer maximum limit for fraud); N.C. Gen. Stat. §1-15(c) (1983) (longer maximum limit for discovery of foreign objects).

[24]Ga. Code Ann. §9-3-71 (1982 & Supp. 1987) (no maximum limit for fraud); Mont. Code Ann. §27-2-205 (1987) (no maximum limit for discovery of foreign object).

may block an action against a governmental healthcare facility. Governmental immunity is rooted in the doctrine of sovereign immunity that originated in English common law derived from the fiction "the King can do no wrong." Without much further justification, the doctrine was then used by early American judges to bar suits against the United States absent its consent.[1] Thus, the immunity of the United States is based on common law. The immunity of the states themselves is additionally based on the Eleventh Amendment to the Constitution.[2]

Whether based on the Eleventh Amendment or on the common law, governmental immunity is generally referred to as "sovereign immunity."[3] Initially, it applied broadly to the federal government, federal agencies, and state agencies (as well as states), but not to political subdivisions. Later, some form of sovereign immunity was judicially extended to municipal corporations in many states, but the doctrine as it applied to municipalities was much narrower, even from its inception.[4] A distinction was drawn between governmental[5] and proprietary activities.[6] Municipalities traditionally have been immune for injury caused by activities of theirs that are classified as governmental functions, but liable for those caused by their proprietary activities.[7]

---

§4.6 [1]W. Prosser and W. P. Keeton, The Law of Torts, §131, at 1032, 1033 (5th ed. 1984).

[2]The Eleventh Amendment was proposed after a state was held liable to a citizen of another state in Chisholm v. Georgia, 2 U.S. (2 Dall.) 419 (1793).

[3]Prosser and Keeton, supra n.1.

[4]See Owen v. City of Independence, Mo., 445 U.S. 622, 638-650 (1980) (§1983 case discussing history and narrow development of municipal immunity as compared to federal and state immunity).

[5]Black's Law Dictionary (5th ed. 1979) defines the governmental functions of a municipality as those which are essential to its existence, in the sense of serving public at large. One example of a governmental function is the operation of a police department.

[6]Black's Law Dictionary defines proprietary functions as those exercised for the "peculiar benefit and advantage" of citizens of municipality. One example of a proprietary function is the operation of the public utilities.

[7]Lee and Lindahl, Modern Tort Law: Liability and Litigation §16.09, at 574 (rev. ed. 1988).

Over time, the cloak of sovereign immunity became riddled with a myriad of statutory and case law exceptions. In an effort to reduce the level of confusion surrounding the uneven application of sovereign immunity, the federal government and most states enacted broad "immunity statutes" that serve to lift governmental immunity and impose liability for all but a few retained exceptions.

§4.6.2 The Present Scope of Sovereign Immunity: Federal Immunity

Congress first consented to liability on a broad scale by enacting the Tucker Act, which dealt with contract claims,[8] in 1887. It was not until 1946, however, that the federal government consented, with several exceptions, to tort liability by enacting the Federal Tort Claims Act (FTCA).[9] The FTCA provides that, absent specified exceptions, the United States is liable

> for injury or loss of property, or personal injury or death caused by the negligent or wrongful act or omission of any employee of the government while acting within the scope of his office or employment, under circumstances where the United States, if a private person, would be liable to the claimant in accordance with the law of the place where the act or omission occurred.[10]

The government did not waive immunity for certain types of claims. For example, the federal government is not liable for claims based on the exercise or performance or the failure to exercise or perform what are considered "discretionary" (or "policy" judgment) functions.[11] To further complicate applica-

---

[8] 28 U.S.C. §§507, 1346, 1402, 1491, 1496, 1501, 1503, 2071, 2411, 2501, and 2512.

[9] Act of Aug. 2, 1946, ch. 753, tit. IV, 60 Stat. 842. See also 28 U.S.C. §§1346, 1402, 1504, 2110, 2401, 2402, 2411, 2412, 2671 et seq.

[10] 28 U.S.C. §1346(b).

[11] 28 U.S.C. §2680(a). See Dalehite v. United States, 346 U.S. 15 (1953) (government not liable for policy judgment to adopt fertilizer export program to increase food supply in militarily occupied areas when explosive fertilizer manufactured by government erupted in ship).

tion of the FTCA, distinctions have been drawn between discretion at the planning level and discretion at the operational level. The former function retains immunity, while the latter does not.[12] Courts generally have considered only medical decisions relating to the admitting process of government hospitals to be discretionary.[13] Most other medical decisions are not considered discretionary and are therefore subject to liability.[14]

For example, in Denny v. United States, the Court of Appeals for the Fifth Circuit considered the army's decision whether to promptly dispatch an ambulance to an officer's wife in labor a discretionary one, because the army was only obligated to attend to the families of officers and soldiers free of charge "whenever practicable."[15] Although the *Denny* case actually involved the timing of the dispatch of an ambulance, it was distinguished as a case based on the "discretionary" decision to admit in Costley v. United States.[16] In *Costley*, an officer's wife, already admitted to the hospital for childbirth, was paralyzed by a negligently administered injection. The government was held liable for the negligent medical *treatment* rendered, which, once the patient was admitted, was considered nondiscretionary. Several courts have similarly held the government liable for various negligent medical treatment decisions, noting that once the decision to admit or to give treatment has been made,

---

[12] W. Prosser and W. P. Keeton, The Law of Torts, §131, at 1040 (5th ed. 1984).

[13] See Denny v. United States, 171 F.2d 365 (5th Cir. 1948), cert. denied, 337 U.S. 919 (1949) (army's failure to promptly dispatch ambulance to officer's wife was considered discretionary; therefore, tort claim barred).

[14] Beins v. United States, 695 F.2d 591, 614 at n.31 (D.C. Cir. 1982) (citing cases in support of proposition that "medical decisions by government personnel are beyond its [discretionary function's] pale" and are therefore subject to liability); Surratt v. United States, 582 F. Supp. 692 (N.D. Ill. 1984) (medical decisions of government physicians are not within discretionary function and are therefore subject to liability). See also Thomas v. United States, 660 F. Supp. 216, 219 (D.D.C. 1987) (plaintiff required to establish usual elements of medical malpractice claim in such claims against United States).

[15] Denny v. United States, 171 F.2d 365, 366 (5th Cir. 1948).

[16] 181 F.2d 723 (5th Cir. 1950).

administering the treatment is nondiscretionary.[17] Although some courts have occasionally referred to the implementation of actual medical treatment as being "discretionary at the operational level," this essentially means it is nondiscretionary and thus subjects the government to liability.[18]

Several cases also have deemed the decision whether to commit or detain a mental patient for treatment "discretionary," holding the government immune from liability for any negligence in such decisions.[19] In contrast, decisions to release mental patients are generally not considered discretionary and can subject a governmental healthcare facility to liability—although there is at least one case to the contrary.[20]

In Fair v. United States, the government was held liable for the release of a patient who had previously threatened the life of a student nurse. The previous threats had been so extreme

---

[17]See, e.g., Grigalauskas v. United States, 103 F. Supp. 543 (D. Mass. 1951) (government liable for negligent injection of infant by doctor because once discretion to admit has been exercised, government employees under duty to exercise due care); Hunter v. United States, 236 F. Supp. 411 (M.D. Tenn. 1964).

[18]See, e.g., Fair v. United States, 234 F.2d 288 (5th Cir. 1956) (government liable for decision to release mental patient when it was at the operational level).

[19]See, e.g., Fahey v. United States, 153 F. Supp. 878 (S.D.N.Y. 1957) (government not liable for death allegedly resulting from its failure to commit an allegedly mentally disturbed veteran). See also Blitz v. Boog, 328 F.2d 596 (2d Cir. 1964) (government not liable for its decision to retain patient for examination for psychotic problems rather than for the medical treatment sought); Teasley v. United States, 662 F.2d 787 (D.C. Cir. 1980) (government hospital was not liable for injuries to woman by nondetained patient when it had initiated involuntary commitment proceedings, disclosing patient's serious sexual offense, mental condition, and dangerousness to women, and such petition was denied).

[20]See, e.g., *Fair,* 234 F.2d 288 (5th Cir. 1956) (government liable for release of dangerous patient and failure to warn victims); Merchants Nat. Bank & Trust Co. of Fargo v. United States, 272 F. Supp. 409 (D.N.D. 1967) (government liable for failing to warn employer of mental patient's homicidal tendencies). Compare Smart v. United States, 207 F.2d 841 (10th Cir. 1953) (government not liable when released mental patient struck and injured claimant with stolen automobile because release was "discretionary").

that a detective agency had been hired for her protection. The hospital had promised to contact the detective agency if a decision was made to release. The hospital, however, not only failed to contact the agency, but also was found to have conducted only a cursory psychiatric examination prior to release of the patient. The released patient almost immediately killed the nurse and two bodyguards before killing himself. The court held that the government was liable for this release.[21]

Similarly, the government was held liable for the work release of a patient who was committed as a "chronic schizophrenic" in Merchants National Bank & Trust Co. v. United States. The patient's wife was a former psychiatric nurse with a documented fear of her husband. The government hospital and its agents did not warn the work release employer of the extent of the patient's mental disturbances, nor did it warn the employer to monitor the patient's nonwork-related activities in any way. Further, the hospital did not notify the patient's wife of her husband's work release. The husband killed his wife on his second weekend off.[22]

In contrast, the government was not held liable in Smart v. United States for the release of a veteran whose mental condition improved through treatment and who was released for a 90-day trial visit to his home. While on the journey home, he stole a car and injured the claimant while driving recklessly. The decision to release in that case was seen as falling within the discretionary function and was therefore immune from liability.[23] Thus, those cases that hold the government liable for release seem to suggest foreseeability of the harm, whereas the instrument of injury and the patient's history in *Smart*, the exception to the rule, do not appear to imply a foreseeable harm.

Decisions involving "something more" than whether to admit or treat, even if arguably in relation to the admitting process, can be considered outside the "discretionary" exception to liability in some circumstances. In Santa v. United States, the

---

[21]*Fair*, 234 F.2d 288.
[22]*Merchants Nat. Bank & Trust*, 272 F. Supp. 409.
[23]*Smart*, 207 F.2d 841.

government was held liable when a patient transfer and a decision not to admit involved a series of negligent acts.[24] One Mrs. Santa was told that her husband, who was suffering from a heart attack, was being hospitalized and that she could go home. After she went home, the hospital discharged her husband. Mr. Santa was then removed to a government mental hospital, which decided not to admit him because he appeared to be suffering from a medical, rather than a mental, condition. The patient was then left unattended at the mental hospital for several hours prior to any government personnel contacting his family. The patient died in the passenger car of relatives en route to a third state hospital.[25]

In addition to the discretionary exception, the FTCA also retains immunity for claims arising out of assault, battery, false imprisonment, libel, slander, misrepresentation, or deceit.[26] State law in some jurisdictions considers failure to obtain informed consent a battery.[27] Several courts, however, interpret the FTCA exclusions under federal rather than state law.[28] Although actions based on failure to obtain informed consent may be considered a battery under applicable state law, courts in some jurisdictions, applying federal law, consider them as negligence actions and therefore subject the government to liability.[29]

---

[24]252 F. Supp. 615 (D.P.R. 1966).

[25] Id.

[26]28 U.S.C. §2680(a).

[27]See, e.g., Moos v. United States, 118 F. Supp. 275 (D. Minn. 1954), affd. 225 F.2d 705 (8th Cir. 1955) (under Minnesota law, operation without consent constitutes an "assault and battery" that falls within exception to Federal Tort Claims Act and therefore precludes suit against federal hospital); Lojuk v. Quandt, 706 F.2d 1456 (7th Cir. 1983), cert. denied, 474 U.S. 1067 (1986) (under Illinois law, claims alleging total lack of consent to medical procedures are treated as batteries that fall within exception to Federal Tort Claims Act).

[28]Ramirez v. United States, 567 F.2d 854, 856 (9th Cir. 1977) (relying on United States v. Neustadt, 366 U.S. 696, 705-706 (1961) (failure to warn of risk not "misrepresentation" under meaning of FTCA exclusion; exclusions to be interpreted under federal law).

[29]Lane v. United States, 225 F. Supp. 850 (E.D. Va. 1964) (operation on wrong knee not an assault and battery within the FTCA exemption because it

Similarly, the communication of an improper diagnosis could be considered a misrepresentation within the meaning of 28 U.S.C. §2680(h). Courts in several cases, however, have held that the exclusion does not apply if the gravamen of the complaint implies that the government had an additional duty to render proper care and was negligent in its performance of that duty.[30] The exclusion may apply if the gravamen of the complaint is misrepresentation, even though negligence is asserted.[31]

The Supreme Court has interpreted the FTCA to exclude an additional area from liability. Under the *Feres* doctrine, the government is not liable in tort for injuries to members of the armed services that arise out of or are in the course of activity incident to service.[32] This doctrine operates to preclude suit by members of the services for injuries sustained through negligent treatment in a military or government hospital if the member is still on active duty or continues to receive orders and assignments from superiors.[33] Claims of spouses for loss of consortium and even infant genetic damage resulting from a military parent's chromosomal injury caused by the government's negligence also

---

was not an *intentional* act but merely a negligent one). See also Fontenelle v. United States, 327 F. Supp. 801 (S.D.N.Y. 1971) (issue of informed consent was one for trial and was not subject to dismissal under FTCA exemption).

[30]See, e.g., Beech v. United States, 345 F.2d 872 (5th Cir. 1965) (court remanded issue of negligence to jury when physician failed to diagnose broken hip after fall, stating that although a claim for breach of duty to communicate proper diagnosis may be barred by FTCA, duty to render proper care for treatment was not).

[31]See, e.g., Wright v. Doe, 347 F. Supp. 833 (M.D. Fla. 1972) (even if claimant couched complaint solely on misrepresentation so as to be beyond purview of the Federal Tort Claims Act, court will not bar it if claimant might have made negligence claim as well).

[32]Feres v. United States, 340 U.S. 135 (1950).

[33]See, e.g., Rayner v. United States, 760 F.2d 1217 (11th Cir. 1985), cert. denied, 474 U.S. 851 (*Feres* doctrine barred suit by serviceman for negligent treatment in military hospital because medical treatment was considered a benefit and as such it was "incident" to military service); Lampitt v. United States, 753 F.2d 702 (8th Cir. 1985) (soldier's action for negligent injury while on convalescent leave was barred nonetheless because he continued receiving orders and assignments from superiors at that time).

may not be recoverable.[34] Military spouses and family members, however, usually may sue for negligence in the treatment of their own injuries because they are not considered "incident to service."[35]

§4.6.3 The Present Scope of Sovereign Immunity: State Immunity

States began abrogating sovereign immunity beginning in 1961 with the California case Muskopf v. Corning Hospital District.[36] Thereafter, several other states abandoned sovereign immunity by broad judicial decree.[37] Some of these blanket repeals were modified by subsequent legislation.[38] By now, virtually all states have followed the federal government's lead in limiting sovereign immunity, at least to some extent. Some 30 states have modified the doctrine in a very substantial way by case law or statute.[39] Several of these state statutes specifically limit the types of claims that may be brought, along the lines of the exceptions listed in

---

[34]Heath v. United States, 663 F. Supp. 1340 (E.D. Cal. 1986) (patient's claim for severe birth defects of child due to prescription of drug administered to mother during pregnancy while on active duty was barred by *Feres* doctrine).

[35]Grigalauskas v. United States, 103 F. Supp. 543 (D. Mass. 1951), affd., 195 F.2d 494 (1st Cir. 1952). (*Feres* doesn't bar claims of dependent for negligent injection at military hospital).

[36]359 P.2d 457 (Cal. 1961) (doctrine of state governmental immunity was "mistaken and unjust").

[37]See, e.g., Holytz v. City of Milwaukee, 17 Wis. 2d 260, 115 N.W.2d 618 (1962) (since the doctrine was created judicially it could be abandoned judicially); Ryan v. State, 134 Ariz. 308, 656 P.2d 597 (1982) (overruling previous judicial establishment of sovereign immunity in Arizona).

[38]Molitor v. Kaneland Community Unit Dist. No. 302, 18 Ill. 2d 11, 163 N.E.2d 89 (1959) (superseded by statute as stated in Oppe v. Missouri, 525 N.E.2d 1189 (Ill. Ct. App. 4th Dist. 1988)); Muskopf v. Corning Hosp. Dist. 55 Cal. 2d 21, 359 P.2d 457 (1961) (superseded by statute as stated in Ramirez v. City of Redondo Beach, 229 Cal. Rptr. 917 (Cal. App. 1986)).

[39]Lee and Lindhal, Modern Tort Law: Liability and Litigation 570 (rev. ed. 1988), citing Jones v. State Highway Commn., 557 S.W.2d 225, 227 (Mo. 1977) (listing the 29 other jurisdictions) (superseded by statute as stated in Bartley v. Special School Dist. of St. Louis County, 649 S.W.2d 864 (1983)).

the FTCA,[40] while others pattern their entire act after the FTCA.[41] Some of these states also limit the amount[42] and nature[43] of damages recoverable for any claimant or for any accident.

In addition, a number of states have enacted statutes that provide administrative forums in which most claims against a state can be heard.[44] These acts typically define the amount of liability and the procedures to be followed in order to impose liability in the alternative forum. In some states, these procedures may require submission of a written claim to an agency for a period of time before commencing suit in state courts.[45]

Some states have waived immunity in a limited class of cases. One example is the waiver of immunity to the extent that the state,[46] or its agency,[47] has procured liability insurance. Finally, some states have followed the traditional distinction of municipal immunity and have waived immunity for proprietary activities while retaining it for governmental activities.[48]

§4.6.4 The Present Scope of Sovereign Immunity: Municipal Immunity

The trend abrogating the immunity of local governments began in 1957.[49] Soon thereafter, many jurisdictions enacted state

---

[40]See, e.g., Alaska Stat. §09.50.250 (1983).

[41]See Iowa Code Ann. §25A.1 et seq. (1978).

[42]See, e.g., Minn. Stat. Ann. §3.736 (West 1977 & Supp. 1989).

[43]See, e.g., Ind. Code Ann. §34-4-16.5-4 (Burns 1983) (no punitive damages). Compare Md. State Govt. Code Ann. §12-104 (Supp. 1988) (immunity not waived for punitive damages and interest before judgment).

[44]See W. Prosser and W. P. Keeton, The Law of Torts §131, at 1044-1046 (5th ed. 1984) (listing Ala., Ark., Ga., Ky., N.C., Tenn., W. Va., and Wisc.).

[45]See, e.g., Cal. Govt. Code §945.4 (West 1980 & Supp. 1989); Iowa Code Ann. §25A.5 (1978 & Supp. 1988); Colo. Rev. Stat. §24-10-109 (1988); Idaho Code §6-901 et seq. (1979).

[46]See S.D. Codified Laws Ann. §21-32-16 (1987).

[47]See, e.g., Minn. Stat. Ann. §3.736 (West 1977 & Supp. 1989) (any state agency); Kan. Stat. Ann. §§74-4707, 74-4708 (1980).

[48]See, e.g., Mich. Comp. Laws Ann. §3.996(107), cited in Prosser and Keeton, supra n.44, §131, at 1045.

[49]Hargrove v. Town of Cocoa Beach, 96 So. 2d 130 (Fla. 1957) (court

legislation that restored at least a part of the immunity.[50] Typically, these municipal tort claims acts impose liability but retain exceptions for legislative, judicial, and certain policy decisions.[51] Many municipal immunity acts also prescribe the procedures that must be followed before suit may be brought.[52]

Today, about half of the states have abolished municipal immunity, and it has been recognized as the majority position by the Restatement (Second) of Torts that local government entities are not immune from liability.[53] In the states that retain some form of municipal immunity, entities are generally liable for proprietary, but not governmental, functions. Cases are split as to whether community hospitals perform governmental (and therefore immune) or proprietary (and therefore liable) functions.[54] Although a number of factors are noted by courts considering the issue (e.g., whether or not a fee is charged), there is no uniform standard for this determination.[55] Whether or not a particular municipal hospital is considered to be carrying out governmental or proprietary functions depends solely on the case law in the jurisdiction.

---

broadly held that city may be liable for torts of public officers in case re prisoner's death from smoke inhalation in unattended jail).

[50]See, e.g., Ind. Code Ann. §34-4-16.5-3 (Burns 1986); N.J. Stat. Ann. §59:2-1 et seq.

[51]See, e.g., Cal. Govt. Code §810 et seq. (West 1980 & Supp. 1989).

[52]Prosser and Keeton, supra n.44, §131, at 1055.

[53]Restatement (Second) of Torts §895C comment f (1982).

[54]See Annot., Immunity from Liability for Damages in Tort of State or Governmental Unit or Agency in Operating Hospital, 25 A.L.R.2d 203 (1952). See also Later Case Service, 25 A.L.R.2d 203-249 (1981).

[55]See Sides v. Cabarrus Memorial Hosp., 287 N.C. 14, 213 S.E.2d 297, 302-303 (1975) (hospital activities proprietary because they involve a monetary charge and are not historically performed by the government). Compare Harrison v. City of Pontiac, Mich., 285 F.2d 305, 306 (6th Cir. 1961) (hospital acting in governmental capacity may remain immune even if it charges fees greater than actual costs, provided the income is only incidental to its main purpose).

B. Negligence Principles Applied in Particular Causes of Action in the Medical Setting

§4.7 Liability for Loss of a Chance or Diminished Chance to Survive or Recover

§4.7.1 Overview

The failure of a healthcare provider to timely and properly diagnose a patient can result in the wrong treatment, no treatment, or a delay in treatment. If the failure to diagnose is a result of behavior below the standard of care, it can constitute medical malpractice just as a failure to give proper treatment does.[1] In order to recover, the claimant must prove that this missed diagnosis was a result of a failure to meet the standard of care and that the negligence was the proximate cause of the harm.

Under some circumstances, a failure to diagnose does not actually cause a separate harm, but rather diminishes or destroys the claimant's chances for recovery by allowing the underlying condition to progress. For example, in Rewis v. United States,[2] a child was brought to an emergency room after ingesting a large quantity of adult aspirin. The emergency room physicians diagnosed her as having a virus and sent her home. The next day, she was brought back to the hospital, where the correct diagnosis was made and heroic, although futile, efforts were made to save her. In the malpractice action brought by her parents, the healthcare providers argued that even if the correct diagnosis had been made at the time of the first emergency room examination, she probably would have died anyway and that their actions thus did not "cause" her death.

In another case, Herskovits v. Group Health Cooperative of

---

§4.7　[1] Wilkinson v. Vesey, 295 A.2d 676, 682 (R.I. 1972).
[2] 503 F.2d 1202 (5th Cir. 1974) (applying New Mexico law).

Puget Sound,[3] the claimant argued that his lung cancer was diagnosed six months later than it should have been, reducing his chance of surviving from 39 percent to 25 percent. The providers who missed the diagnosis argued that it was more likely than not (i.e., there was a 61 percent chance) that the cancer rather than the malpractice was the proximate cause of his death.

These cases are examples of the two types of cases that raise the issue of compensation for a diminished chance of recovery: cases of acute danger in which proper diagnosis and treatment may have saved the patient and cases of chronic illness in which earlier diagnosis and treatment may have extended the patient's life or increased the patient's chance of survival. The cases usually involve chances of survival but sometimes involve chances of more complete recovery.[4]

§4.7.2 The Traditional Rule

Under common-law causation requirements, the claimant had to show that the injury would not have occurred ''but for''[5] the defendant's conduct. Traditionally, damages could be recovered in cases like those discussed above only if an expert witness could testify that it was more likely than not (i.e., at least a 51 percent chance existed) that the claimant would have survived but for the tortious conduct.[6] This means that if the chance of

---

[3]99 Wash. 2d 609, 664 P.2d (1983).

[4]See, e.g., Cooper v. Hartman, 533 A.2d 1294 (Md. 1987) (plaintiff alleged that earlier diagnosis and treatment of osteomyelitis (bone infection) would have resulted in better result than the one obtained, life saved at cost of permanent shortening of leg).

[5]W. Prosser and W. P. Keeton, The Law of Torts, §41, at 266 (5th ed. 1984).

[6]Restatement (Second) of Torts §433B comment a (1986); *Rewis,* 503 F.2d 1202, 1211 (in action for failure to diagnose aspirin poisoning in a young child, plaintiff must show that it was more likely than not that the child's life would have been saved if proper diagnosis had been made when the child was first presented to emergency room).

survival for the underlying condition (e.g., the aspirin poisoning or lung cancer) was 50 percent or less, the preexisting condition—and not the tortious conduct—was the probable (more likely than not) cause of death. Thus, the claimant could not recover for the malpractice. The traditional approach has been criticized for producing results that are unfair and contrary to public policy.[7]

An oft-quoted passage from Hicks v. United States sums up the criticism: "When a defendant's negligent action or inaction has effectively terminated a person's chance of survival, it does not lie in the defendant's mouth to raise conjectures as to the measure of the chances that he has put beyond the possibility of realization."[8] Under the traditional theory, if the provider's negligence caused the claimant's chance of recovery to fall from 45 percent to 5 percent, the provider would not be liable for any damages, but if the provider caused a decrease in the chance of survival from 90 percent to 75 percent, the provider could be liable for at least some damages. Some courts find the rule unacceptable because it is a "blanket release from liability for doctors and hospitals any time there was less than a 50% chance of survival, regardless of how flagrant the negligence."[9]

§4.7.3 The Recent Trend

Although some courts have retained the traditional approach in the face of this criticism,[10] the recent trend allows recovery even

---

[7]See generally King, Causation, Valuation, and Chance in Personal Injury Torts Involving Preexisting Conditions and Future Consequences, 90 Yale L.J. 1353, 1376 (1981); Comment, Proving Causation in "Loss of a Chance" Cases: A Proportional Approach, 34 Cath. U.L. Rev. 747 (1985).

[8]Hicks v. United States, 368 F.2d 626, 632 (4th Cir. 1966) (applying Virginia law) (in case in which patient "would have survived" abdominal obstruction with proper diagnosis and surgery).

[9]Herskovits v. Group Health Coop. of Puget Sound, 99 Wash. 2d 609, 664 P.2d 474, 476 (1983).

[10]*Rewis*, 503 F.2d 1202, Morgenroth v. Pacific Medical Center, 126 Cal. Rptr. 681, 54 Cal. App. 3d 521 (1976); Gooding v. University Hosp. Bldg.,

if the original chance of survival was 50 percent or less. The courts that have moved away from the traditional "all or nothing" approach have done so by different methods. Some have simply relaxed the standards regarding causation to allow recovery in cases involving less than an even chance,[11] while others have left the traditional rules of causation intact but have recognized the reduction of the chance of survival as a way to measure damages.[12]

§4.7.4 The Causation Approach

The courts that have approached the problem by defining the injury as death but altering the proof requirements have done so in a variety of ways. For example, some jurisdictions alter the standard for proof of causation by requiring that the negligence only be a "substantial factor" in causing the injury.[13] Other courts have required the plaintiff to show that there was a "substantial possibility" of survival absent the negligence. This line of cases allows the jury to find that the reduction of a "substantial possibility" of survival actually caused the patient's death.[14] Finally, several courts follow the two-step analysis of

---

Inc., 445 So. 2d 1015 (Fla. 1984); Cornfeldt v. Tongen, 295 N.W.2d 638 (Minn. 1980); Clayton v. Thompson, 475 So. 2d 439 (Miss. 1985); Cooper v. Sisters of Charity, 27 Ohio St. 2d 242, 272 N.E.2d 97 (1971); Hanselmann v. McCardle, 275 S.C. 46, 267 S.E.2d 531 (1980).

[11]See, e.g., Thompson v. Sun City Community Hosp., 141 Ariz. 597, 606, 688 P.2d 605, 615 (1984); Sharp v. Kaiser Found. Health Plan, 710 P.2d 1153, 1155 (Colo. Ct. App. 1985); Roberson v. Counselman, 235 Kan. 1006, 1013, 686 P.2d 149, 158 (1984); Evers v. Dollinger, 95 N.J. 399, 413, 471 A.2d 405, 412 (1984); Hamil v. Bashline, 481 Pa. 256, 269, 392 A.2d 1280, 1288 (1978).

[12]DeBurkarte v. Louvar, 393 N.W.2d 131, 137 (Iowa 1986); McKellips v. St. Francis Hosp., 741 P.2d 467, 476-477 (Okla. 1987); *Herskovits,* 99 Wash. 2d 609.

[13]Daniels v. Hadley Memorial Hosp., 566 F.2d 749 (D.C. Cir. 1977); *Roberson,* 235 Kan. 1006; Jones v. Montefiore Hosp., 494 Pa. 410, 431 A.2d 920 (1981); *Hamil,* 481 Pa. 256.

[14]Brown v. Koulizakis, 229 Va. 524, 331 S.E.2d 440 (1985); Jeanes v.

the Restatement[15] and allow the jury to determine the causation issue once the court finds that the provider in some way increased the risk of harm:

> Once a plaintiff has introduced evidence that a defendant's negligent act or omission increased the risk of harm to a person in plaintiff's position, and that the harm was in fact sustained, it becomes a question for the jury as to whether or not that increased risk was a substantial factor in producing the harm.[16]

This allows the jury, rather than the medical experts, to determine the issue of causation based on its evaluation of the increased risk. One court has limited the jury by requiring a finding that the increased risk "probably" caused the death,[17] while another requires only that it be a "substantial factor" in causing the death.[18]

§4.7.5 The Damages Approach

The second methodology for allowing recovery is to define the reduction in chance, rather than the death, as the injury and to consider it in assessing damages.[19] The causation question then becomes one of whether it is more likely than not that the

---

Milner, 428 F.2d 598 (8th Cir. 1970) (applying Arkansas law) (jury may conclude that the loss of an 11-percent chance of survival caused the patient's death).

[15]Restatement (Second) of Torts §323(a) (1965).

[16]*Hamil*, 481 Pa. 256. See also Thompson v. Sun City Community Hosp., 141 Ariz. 597 (jury should decide if the loss of a five-to-ten percent chance probably caused the harm); Aasheim v. Humberger, 695 P.2d 824 (Mont. 1985); *Herskovits*, 99 Wash. 2d 609 (jury could find the reduction in the chance of survival from 39 percent to 25 percent caused the patient's death).

[17]See *Thompson*, 141 Ariz. 597.

[18]See *Hamil*, 481 Pa. 256.

[19]See, e.g., *DeBurkarte*, 393 N.W.2d 131 (Iowa 1986); O'Brien v. Stover, 443 F.2d 1013, 1019 (8th Cir. 1971) (applying Arkansas law); *Jeanes*, 428 F.2d 598 (8th Cir. 1970) (applying Iowa law); James v. United States, 483 F. Supp. 581 (N.D. Cal. 1980).

provider caused the reduction in the patient's chance for survival, rather than whether it is more likely than not that the provider caused the patient's death.[20]

In loss-of-a-chance cases, it is important to distinguish between theories of causation and damages. Even in those jurisdictions whose altering of the causation standard allows the jury to determine that the provider's negligence "caused" the patient's death by diminishing the chances for survival, many hold the provider liable only to the extent the negligence allowed the preexisting condition to progress. Compensation is awarded to the plaintiff for those damages directly caused by the negligence, such as lost earnings and additional medical expenses.[21]

Several methods have been used to calculate damages for a reduction in the chances of survival.[22] Some courts allow the jury to value the lost chance without any guidelines,[23] while others have spelled out the method by which the determination is to be made.[24] Oklahoma, for example, has the jury determine the total wrongful death damages (e.g., $500,000), the original chance of survival (e.g., 40 percent), and the reduced chance due to the negligence (e.g., 25 percent), and then award as compensation the difference between the two (e.g., 15 percent of $500,000).[25]

---

[20]See, e.g., Waffen v. United States Dept. of Health & Human Servs., 799 F.2d 911, 918 (4th Cir. 1986) (applying Maryland law) (burden of proving causation by a preponderance of the evidence is not lessened, but plaintiff now may recover damages for causation of a new kind of harm—loss of a substantial possibility of survival).

[21]See, e.g., *Herskovits*, 99 Wash. 2d 609 ("decedent's shortened life expectancy is not recoverable as a separate item of damages, but will be considered as it affects loss of value of future earning capacity").

[22]See Comment, Proving Causation in "Loss of a Chance" Cases: A Proportional Approach, 34 Cath. U.L. Rev. 747, 782 (1985); King, Causation, Valuation, and Chance in Personal Injury Torts Involving Preexisting Conditions and Future Consequences, 90 Yale L.J. 1353, 1381.

[23]See, e.g., DeBurkarte v. Louvar, 393 N.W.2d 131 (Iowa 1986).

[24]See Jordan v. Bero, 210 S.E.2d 618, 640-1 (W. Va. 1974) (Neely, J., concurring); Mays v. United States, 608 F. Supp. 1476, 1483 (D. Colo. 1985), revd. on other grounds, 806 F.2d 976 (10th Cir. 1986), cert. denied, 55 U.S.L.W. 3820 (1987).

[25]McKellips v. Saint Francis Hosp., 741 P.2d 467, 476 (Okla. 1987).

§4.7.6 Procedural Issues

The choice of approach (causation or damage) made by the jurisdiction can have an important impact on the procedural posture of the case (i.e., whether a wrongful death action can be maintained against the provider). Historically, wrongful death actions[26] and survival actions[27] were separate causes of action. They have different statutes of limitations (e.g., one year from the date of death versus three years from the date of injury), different plaintiffs (e..g., the statutory beneficiaries versus the heirs of the estate), and different types of damages recoverable (e.g., loss of support, loss of consortium, and pain and suffering of beneficiaries versus medical expenses, funeral expenses, lost earnings, pain and suffering of decedent). Although the causes of action have been merged in some states, they remain distinct in others.[28] In those states where the causes of action remain distinct and the loss of a chance is defined as the injury, it cannot be recovered through a wrongful death action.[29]

---

[26]A wrongful death statute creates a new cause of action at the time of death for the benefit of certain statutory categories of people who were economically or emotionally dependent on the decedent.

[27]A survival statute allows the decedent's cause of action for injury to him to survive his death. Whatever damages the decedent would have been entitled to thus inure to the benefit of his estate.

[28]See V. Schwartz et al., Product Liability: A Practical Guide, ¶75,501 (1988) (discussing the wrongful death and survival schemes of various states).

[29]Weimer v. Hetrick, 309 Md. 536, 525 A.2d 643, 652 (1987) (because no damages for injuries or losses sustained by decedent prior to death are recoverable under the wrongful death statute, cannot recover for loss of a chance). See also Herskovits v. Group Health Coop. of Puget Sound, 99 Wash. 2d 609, 664 P.2d 474 481 (1983) (Pearson, J., concurring) (raised question whether action for reduction of chance of survival can be brought under wrongful death statute).

§4.8 *Informed Consent and Liability for Failure to Act in Its Absence*

§4.8.1 Overview

The doctrine of informed consent[1] evolved out of the tort of battery.[2] Mr. Justice Cardozo was one of the first to articulate the doctrine, in the case of Schloendorff v. Society of New York Hospital:

> Every human being of adult years and sound mind has the right to determine what should be done with his own body; and a surgeon who performs an operation without the patient's consent commits an assault for which he is liable in damages.[3]

This doctrine requires generally that the physician disclose "any facts which are necessary to form the basis of an intelligent consent by the patient to the proposed treatment."[4] Because of perceived inadequacies in recovery under a battery theory, most states now allow recovery for failure to adequately inform under negligence theory as well.[5] Some of these states distinguish between lack of informed consent and total lack of consent, with only the latter treated as a battery.[6] This distinction is important because the statutes of limitations, the types of damages recoverable, and the elements of proof differ for the

---

§4.8 [1]See Chapter 7, infra, for a more detailed discussion of consent to treatment.

[2]Battery is the intentional touching of another without permission.

[3]105 N.E. 92, 93 (N.Y. 1914) (overruled on other grounds).

[4]Salgo v. Leland Stanford Jr. Univ. Bd. of Trustees, 317 P.2d 170, 181 (Cal. Ct. App. 1957).

[5]Natanson v. Kline, 186 Kan. 393, 350 P.2d 1093, clarified, 187 Kan. 186, 354 P.2d 670 (1960).

[6]Lojuk v. Quandt, 706 F.2d 1456 (7th Cir. 1983), cert. denied, 474 U.S. 1067 (1986) (applying Illinois law); Moore v. Eli Lilly and Co., 626 F. Supp. 365, 368 (D. Mass. 1986) (rejecting allegation of battery where patient did not allege total lack of consent); Scott v. Bradford, 606 P.2d 554 (Okla. 1979) (discussing distinction between lack of informed consent and total lack of consent).

two theories.[7] The statute of limitations for battery is usually much shorter than for negligence. The plaintiff may recover under a battery theory for any unpermitted touching, whether or not the plaintiff was injured. Conversely, the plaintiff under a negligence theory must have been injured by the lack of informed consent. The negligence action is more difficult to prove because it requires expert testimony as to what must be disclosed to establish deviation from the standard of care while battery requires no more than proof that no consent was given.

§4.8.2 What Must Be Disclosed

The types of information that must be disclosed are fairly uniform among the states.[8] The patient should be informed of the diagnosis, the nature and purpose of the proposed treatment, all of the relevant risks and benefits of the proposed treatment, and reasonable alternatives to the proposed treatment. The most common allegation in a malpractice action based on lack of informed consent is failure to disclose all relevant risks. This allegation typically arises in cases in which the plaintiff is unable to prove that the healthcare provider did anything wrong in the course of the treatment. The patient then argues that he never would have consented to the treatment if he had known about the risks associated with it.

---

[7]See, e.g., McKinley v. Stripling, 763 S.W.2d 407 (Tex. 1989) (Supreme Court of Texas ruled that legislative enactment that limited claims based on lack of informed consent to actions in negligence, as opposed to battery, implicitly included the common-law negligence requirement of proof of proximate cause).

[8]See, e.g., Cross v. Trapp, 294 S.E.2d 446 (W. Va. 1982) (must disclose risks involved, alternative methods of treatment, risks of alternatives, and likely results without treatment); McPherson v. Ellis, 305 N.C. 266, 287 S.E.2d 892 (1982) (patient must be apprised of risks of proposed treatment); Sard v. Hardy, 281 Md. 432, 379 A.2d 1014 (1977) (duty to disclose nature of ailment, nature of proposed treatment, probability of success of contemplated therapy, alternative to therapy, and risk of unfortunate consequence); Wilkinson v. Vesey, 110 R.I. 606, 295 A.2d 676 (1972) (duty to disclose all material risks).

§4.8.3 Who Has the Duty to Disclose

Traditionally, the duty to disclose information and obtain an informed consent is solely that of the physician and does not extend to the healthcare facility.[9] The leading case on the subject of hospital liability for informed consent states that

> So long as it cannot be said that a spinal-jack operation is per se an act of malpractice, the hospital does not share and should not share in the responsibility to advise patients of the novelty and risks attendant on the procedures. . . .
>
> Assuming whatever degree of reprehensibility in the surgeon's conduct and however drastic or radical the operation, liability does not attach to the hospital unless it knew or should have known that there was lacking an informed consent or that the operation was not permissible under existing standards.[10]

A hospital may be vicariously liable, under a respondeat superior theory, if the doctor who failed to obtain the informed consent is an employee of the hospital.[11]

§4.8.4 Determining the Standard: Reasonable Physician Versus Reasonable Patient

The standard against which the disclosure is evaluated varies among the states. The majority view follows the reasonable physician standard, which requires the physician to disclose all information a reasonable and prudent physician would under

---

[9]See, e.g., Cooper v. Curry, 92 N.M. 417, 589 P.2d 201 (Ct. App. 1978) (hospital could not be liable for admission clerk's failure to fill out consent form because clerk was only performing administrative function for doctor who was not employee of hospital).

[10]Fiorentino v. Wenger, 19 N.Y.2d 407, 227 N.E.2d 296, 301 (1967).

[11]See, e.g., Seneris v. Haas, 45 Cal. 2d 291, 291 P.2d 915 (1955); Ohio Rev. Code Ann. §2317.54 (Page 1981 & Supp. 1987) (hospital not liable unless physician is an employee). See also §4.12, infra, on vicarious liability.

like circumstances.[12] This is premised on the view that the extent of disclosure is a medical question. Expert testimony is required to establish the standard. Allowing doctors to determine what the patient should be told has been criticized as paternalistic.

The minority view follows the reasonable patient standard, under which a physician must disclose all information that a reasonable person would find material in deciding whether or not to undergo the treatment.[13] Supporters of this view argue that the patient has a right to determine for himself or herself what risks should be taken. It has gained acceptance with the growth of the patient-as-consumer movement.

§4.8.5 Exceptions

There are several exceptions to the duty to obtain consent. The most common example is for medical emergencies. No consent is required as long as the patient is *incapacitated* and delay in treatment would result in significant harm. "Significant harm" is usually defined as a life- or health-threatening injury or disease.[14] It is not enough for the situation to be life-threatening; the harm must be *imminent* (i.e., there is clearly no time to obtain consent).[15]

---

[12]See, e.g., Neb. Rev. Stat. §44-2816 (1984); N.Y. Pub. Health Law §2805-d (McKinney 1985 & Supp. 1989); Natanson v. Kline, 186 Kan. 393, 350 P.2d 1093, clarified, 187 Kan. 186, 354 P.2d 670 (1960).

[13]Approximately one-third of the jurisdictions have adopted this standard. See Scott v. Bradford, 606 P.2d 554 (Okla. 1979); *Wilkinson*, 110 R.I. 606; Cobbs v. Grant, 8 Cal. 3d 229, 502 P.2d 1 (1972); Canterbury v. Spence, 464 F.2d 772 (D.C. Cir.), cert. denied, 409 U.S. 1064 (1972); Utah Code Ann. §78-14-5 (1987).

[14]See Ga. Code Ann. §31-9-3 (1985) (harm significant if it would jeopardize life or health or result in disfigurement or impaired faculties); *Canterbury*, 464 F.2d 772, 778 (D.C. Cir.) (harm from failure to treat is imminent and outweighs any harm threatened by the proposed treatment).

[15]Kozup v. Georgetown Univ. Hosp., 851 F.2d 437 (D.C. Cir. 1988) (on battery count, healthcare facility's argument that it was not required to obtain parental consent for life-saving transfusion of newborn rejected because no showing that danger was so imminent that there was no time to obtain consent).

Another common example is the therapeutic privilege, under which a physician may withhold information if the physician reasonably believes that disclosure of the information would adversely and substantially affect the patient's mental or physical well-being.[16]

Third, there are a number of legally required procedures for which it is not necessary to obtain the patient's consent. These vary by jurisdiction, but include treatment for venereal disease,[17] drug addiction,[18] alcoholism,[19] and infectious diseases,[20] as well as diagnostic testing prior to marriage[21] and of neonatal infants (e.g., for hypothyroidism or metabolic disorders)[22] and vaccinations of school-aged children.[23]

§4.8.6 Consent for Incompetent Patients

State statutes and case law ordinarily determine who can consent for an incompetent patient.[24] If the patient is declared incompetent, a court will appoint a legal guardian who has final say

---

[16]See N.Y. Pub. Health Law §2805-d (McKinney 1985 & Supp. 1989); Alaska Stat. §09.55.556 (1983); Utah Code Ann. §78-14-5 (1987); *Canterbury*, 464 F.2d at 789 (risk of disclosure poses such a threat of detriment to the patient as to become unfeasible or contraindicated from a medical point of view).

[17]See, e.g., N.J. Stat. Ann. §26:4-49.7 (West 1987).

[18]Minn. Stat. Ann. §254.09 (West 1982 & Supp. 1987).

[19]Colo. Rev. Stat. §25-1-301 (1982).

[20]Va. Code Ann. §54-325.2(D)(1) (1982 & Supp. 1987).

[21]See, e.g., Fla. Stat. Ann. §741.051 (West 1986 & Supp. 1988) (venereal disease); N.J. Stat. Ann. §37:1-20 (West 1968) (same); Idaho Code §32-412 (1983 & Supp. 1988) (rubella immunity); R.I. Gen. Laws §15-2-3 (1981) (same).

[22]See, e.g., D.C. Code §6-311 et seq. (1981).

[23]See, e.g., Conn. Gen. Stat. Ann. §10-204a (West 1986); Vt. Stat. Ann. tit. 18, §1121 (1982).

[24]See, e.g., Ill. Ann. Stat. ch. 111½ §4152-202 (West 1989) (statute outlining who may contract for nursing home care in case of incapacity of patient).

in medical decisions.[25] If there is no legal guardian, it is common practice to rely on the consent of close relatives even though there is little legal authority for this.[26] A custodial institution, such as a nursing home, may be subject to liability for false imprisonment in the absence of any formal proceeding to confine or commit if the patient is competent. The consent of close relatives is not enough.[27]

Ordinarily, minors are legally incompetent to consent to treatment. A minor is typically one who is less than 18 years old. The parents or other legal guardians generally have been given the right to give consent, but there are some exceptions. Some states allow "mature" minors to consent to treatment,[28] and many states allow emancipated minors to consent. Although the states vary, a minor is usually considered emancipated if he or she is married,[29] is a parent,[30] or is self-supporting and not living at home.[31] Finally, several states have statutes and case law that carve out specific exceptions for types of medical procedures or treatment, such as venereal disease or abortion,

---

[25]See, e.g., In re Quinlan, 70 N.J. 10, 355 A.2d 647 (N.J. 1976), cert. denied, 429 U.S. 922 (1976).

[26]But see Ark. Code Ann. §20-9-602 (1987) (close relative may consent for someone of "unsound mind"); Miss. Code Ann. §41-41-3 (1972 & Supp. 1988); Farber v. Olkon, 40 Cal. 2d 503, 254 P.2d 520 (1953).

[27]See, e.g., Big Town Nursing Home v. Newman, 461 S.W.2d 195 (Tex. Ct. App. 1970) (nursing home subject to exemplary damages for confining competent elderly patient against his will when no formal proceeding to confine plaintiff had occurred despite nephew's signature on admission papers).

[28]Younts v. St. Francis Hosp. and School of Nursing, 205 Kan. 292, 469 P.2d 330 (1970) (17-year-old could appreciate nature of procedure and consent to skin graft); Lacey v. Laird, 166 Ohio St. 12 139 N.E.2d 25 (Ohio 1956) (18-year-old consented to plastic surgery); Bonner v. Moran, 126 F.2d 121 (D.C. Cir. 1941) (child close to maturity can consent to therapeutic treatment).

[29]Franco v. Davis, 51 N.J. 237, 239 A.2d 1 (1968) (overruled on other grounds); Ditmar v. Ditmar, 48 Wash. 2d 373, 293 P.2d 759 (Wash. 1956); Md. Health-Gen. Code Ann. §20-102 (1987); Va. Code Ann. §54-325.2(E) (1982 & Supp. 1987).

[30]See Md. Health-Gen. Code Ann. §20-102 (1987).

[31]Smith v. Seibly, 72 Wash. 2d 16, 431 P.2d 719 (1967); Buxton v. Bishop, 185 Va. 1, 37 S.E.2d 755 (Va. 1946); Alaska Stat. §09.65.100 (1983).

that can be administered without the consent of parents in some circumstances.[32]

Sometimes the parent is also a minor. Several state statutes allow minors who are parents to consent to treatment for their children.[33] Even in the absence of any statute, obtaining consent from the minor parent is preferable to obtaining it from another relative. If the minor parent is not capable of understanding the situation, a court order should be obtained appointing a legal guardian.

§4.8.7 The Right to Refuse Treatment

If the patient cannot consent because of unconsciousness or legal incompetence, a physician usually may rely on a relative's consent for treatment[34] but may not rely on a relative's refusal to consent because there are no state statutes authorizing substituted refusal to consent.[35] In this situation, a physician may be liable for failure to treat unless some type of affirmative action is taken, such as obtaining a court order directing treatment or one appointing a legal guardian to make the decision to refuse treatment.[36]

Some states allow parents to refuse medical treatment for minor children for religious reasons.[37] Parents refusing life-saving treatment, however, may have their refusal overridden by

---

[32]See N.Y. Pub. Health Law §2305(2) (McKinney 1985) (venereal disease); Md. Health-Gen. Code Ann. §20-102 (1987) (venereal disease, alcoholism, drug abuse, pregnancy, and contraception); Me. Rev. Stat. Ann. tit 32 §3292 (1979). See also Bellotti v. Baird, 443 U.S. 622 (1979) (state statute must give minor opportunity to show maturity to consent to abortion).

[33]See, e.g., Fla. Stat. Ann. §743.065 (West 1986); Mass. Gen. Laws Ann. ch. 112, §12F (West 1983 & Supp. 1989); N.Y. Pub. Health Law §2504 (McKinney 1985).

[34]See, e.g., Steele v. Woods, 327 S.W.2d 187, 198 (Mo. 1959); Ark. Stat. Ann. §82-363 (1981).

[35]See Collins v. Davis, 254 N.Y.S.2d 666 (1964) (wife would not authorize surgery for husband in coma).

[36]See Va. Code §54-325.2 (1982 & Supp. 1987).

[37]See, e.g., N.J. Stat. Ann. §26:1A-66 (West 1987 & Supp. 1988).

court order[38] or may be found guilty of violation of child neglect statutes or other statutes that allow a child to be temporarily removed from the custody of the parents.[39] The courts may then intervene and compel life-saving treatment, if it is determined to be in the child's best interest. Courts are reluctant to intervene if the condition is not life-threatening.[40] A few states allow treatment over parental objection, if there is an emergency and no time to obtain a court order.[41]

§4.9 *Abandonment or Failure to Monitor*

§4.9.1 Provider Liability

Physicians generally have broad discretion in determining whether or not to accept a particular patient.[1] Once a relationship is formed, however, the law assumes that both parties intend it to continue for the duration of the treatment. This means that a physician must monitor, observe, and diligently attend to a

---

[38]See, e.g., Me. Rev. Stat. Ann. tit. 22, §4071 (West Supp. 1988). See also State v. Pericone, 37 N.J. 463, 181 A.2d 751, cert. denied, 371 U.S. 890 (1962) (statute providing for temporary custody in case of neglect and trial court's action pursuant to it was not unconstitutional given parental refusal of necessary blood transfusion for child); People ex rel. Wallace v. Labrenz, 411 Ill. 618, 104 N.E.2d 769, cert. denied, 344 U.S. 824 (1952) (child whose parents refused to consent to life-saving blood transfusion was "neglected child" within statute authorizing appointment of temporary guardian).

[39]See, e.g., Mitchell v. Davis, 205 S.W.2d 812 (Tex. Civ. App. 1947) (12-year-old boy declared neglected and placed in state custody because mother believed in healing through prayer and refused to consent to treatment for degenerative arthritis).

[40]See, e.g., In re Green, 448 Pa. 338, 292 A.2d 387 (1972), revg. 220 Pa. Super. 191, 286 A.2d 681 (Pa. 1971) (mother's refusal to consent to surgery to correct damage to spine from polio upheld because life not in imminent danger); In re Seiferth, 309 N.Y. 80, 127 N.E.2d 820 (1955) (father's refusal to consent to surgery to correct cleft palate and harelip upheld because life not endangered).

[41]See N.C. Gen. Stat. §90-21.1 (1985 & Supp. 1987).

§4.9 [1]See Chapter 6 for a detailed discussion of access to treatment and the duty to treat.

patient until the illness or injury is abated, the physician is discharged, or the physician properly withdraws.[2] Absent proper withdrawal, a physician may be liable for both malpractice and breach of contract, commonly called "abandonment."

Abandonment has been defined as the unilateral severance or termination of the professional relationship between physician and patient at an unreasonable time or without giving the patient an opportunity to safely obtain medical treatment elsewhere.[3] When a physician wishes to terminate the relationship, notice to the patient is required. Such notice must give the patient sufficient opportunity to arrange for other medical attendance.[4] As in other malpractice cases, the claimant must show that the abandonment was the proximate cause of the injury. If no harm resulted from the abandonment, no damages may be recovered.[5]

These instances of intentional termination of care by the physician should be distinguished from those situations in which the physician fails to properly monitor or diligently attend to the patient. Such a failure is allegedly malpractice, but an abandonment instruction is not appropriate.[6]

---

[2]See, e.g., Thomas v. Corso, 265 Md. 84, 288 A.2d 379, 388 (1972) ("A physician cannot properly withdraw from a case under diagnosis or treatment without giving reasonable notice.").

[3]See, e.g., Miller v. Greater Southeast Community Hosp., 508 A.2d 927 (D.C. 1986); Capps v. Valk, 187 Kan. 287, 369 P.2d 238 (1962); Vann v. Harden, 187 Va. 555, 47 S.E.2d 314 (1948).

[4]See, e.g., Groce v. Myers, 224 N.C. 165, 29 S.E.2d 553 (1944) (once relationship established, cannot be terminated merely by will of physician); Stohlman v. Davis, 117 Neb. 178, 220 N.W. 247 (1928) (physician must secure patient's permission to have physician's son cover for him or give patient sufficient notice to secure another physician of his choice).

[5]Skodje v. Hardy, 47 Wash. 2d 557, 288 P.2d 471 (1955) (asserted abandonment not actionable because led to no delay in obtaining treatment where spouse of patient immediately telephoned another physician and patient's appendix was removed later that night by new physician).

[6]Johnson v. Bernard, 388 A.2d 490 (D.C. 1978) (failure of oral surgeon to properly monitor patient in recovery room may be malpractice but not abandonment); Dicke v. Graves, 668 P.2d 189 (Kan. Ct. App. 1983) (failure of dentist to respond quickly and to treat diligently is negligence claim not abandonment claim).

Failure to monitor or diligently attend, whether it be abandonment or negligence, arises from the duty to provide continued care throughout the professional relationship. The physician need not be physically present, but must have provided adequate coverage.[7] How often the physician must monitor and attend to the patient is dependent on the particular circumstances. A physician will only be liable if the failure to monitor or diligently attend deviates from the standard of care required in the circumstances. There may be situations, however, in which expert testimony is not necessary to establish the violation.[8]

Many of the constructive abandonment cases are against surgeons, for failure to perform appropriate post-surgical procedures and monitoring.[9] As in other malpractice cases, there must be proximate cause between the failure to monitor or attend and the injury. If proximate cause is demonstrated, the plaintiff may only recover for the additional injury caused by the failure.[10]

§4.9.2 Healthcare Facility Liability for Abandonment

Although most of the case law in this area involves physician liability, the healthcare facility also may be liable for abandonment, for not ensuring that decisions made by physicians are

---

[7]Capps v. Valk, 189 Kan. 287, 369 P.2d 238 (1962) (surgeon may rely on hospital resident to monitor patient post-operatively and to remove patient's drainage tube, but surgeon responsible if resident fails to do so).

[8]Thomas v. Corso, 265 Md. 84, 288 A.2d 379, 389 (Md. Ct. App. 1972) (expert testimony not necessary if physician on call at emergency room failed to attend patient at all).

[9]See, e.g., Baulsir v. Sugar, 266 Md. 390, 293 A.2d 253 (1972); Dashiell v. Griffth, 84 Md. 363, 35 A. 1094 (1896).

[10]See, e.g., Lee v. Dewbre, 362 S.W.2d 900 (Tex. Crim. App. 1962) (Obstetrician left town day after patient's difficult delivery of baby. No causal connection between patient's subsequent hysterectomy and doctor's abandonment because patient had been transferred to another hospital and was under new doctor's care when her condition worsened).

appropriate and consistent with accepted medical standards[11] or for not providing the reasonable care or attention that conditions require.[12]

Because the healthcare facility is not liable until a professional relationship has been established, a threshold question that may arise in abandonment cases is whether a relationship was formed between the facility and the patient. The courts have considered the following factors in making that determination: whether the facility is obligated to provide emergency services; what steps the facility has taken to admit the patient; and what treatment, if any, has been rendered to the patient. In one case, a Florida appellate court found that a hospital had admitted a patient simply by examining him, even though no steps had been taken in the admitting process.[13] In another case, the Alabama Supreme Court found that no relationship was established when the patient had been examined and given pain medication but not formally admitted.[14]

§4.10 Refusal to Treat

§4.10.1 Overview

At common law, *private* healthcare facilities were free to admit or refuse patients based on whatever criteria they chose.[1] A private hospital owed no duty to accept a patient it did not desire, and thus was not required to give any reason for its refusal to accept a patient.[2] *Public* healthcare facilities, on the

---

[11]Meiselman v. Crown Heights Hosp., 285 N.Y. 389, 34 N.E.2d 367 (1941).

[12]Miller v. Greater Southeast Community Hosp., 508 A.2d 927 (D.C. 1986) (allegation that hospital did not provide adequate medical care while patient waiting for own physician).

[13]Le Juene Road Hosp. v. Watson, 171 So. 2d 202 (Fla. Ct. App. 1965).

[14]Harper v. Baptist Medical Center-Princeton, 341 So. 2d 133 (Ala. 1976).

§4.10 [1]Hill v. Ohio County, 468 S.W.2d 306 (Ky. Ct. App. 1970), cert. denied, 404 U.S. 1041 (1972).

[2]See Wilmington Gen. Hosp. v. Manlove, 54 Del. 15, 174 A.2d 135, 138 (1961) (quoting with approval 41 C.J.S. Hospitals §8, p. 345).

other hand, were treated differently, because the charters under which they were created often set forth requirements as to the number and types of patients that they would treat. Although the common-law rule allowing private hospitals to refuse to admit some patients still exists, most states, through either court decisions or statutes, have created restrictions on the freedom of both public and private healthcare facilities to choose their patients.[3]

§4.10.2 The Healthcare Facility's Duty to Treat Emergency Patients

One of the first limitations on the right to choose patients was imposed in the Wilmington General Hospital v. Manlove.[4] In that case, an infant was brought to the emergency room of a hospital with a high fever and diarrhea. The baby had been seen by his own doctor the day before and was taking prescribed medication. The intake nurse refused to examine the infant and sent him home because his private physician could not be reached. He died a few hours later of bronchial pneumonia. The Delaware Supreme Court acknowledged that a hospital has no legal obligation to provide an emergency ward, but went on to state that a hospital that *does* have an emergency ward could not refuse service to a patient in an emergency in which the patient (or, in this case, his parent) is relying on the custom of the hospital to render emergency aid.[5]

Other jurisdictions have followed the lead of the Delaware court and imposed a duty to treat in emergency situations.[6]

---

[3]See, e.g., *Wilmington Gen. Hosp.*, 54 Del. 15; Cal. Health & Safety Code §1317 (West 1979 & Supp. 1989); Ill. Ann. Stat. ch. 111½, ¶86 (Smith-Hurd 1977 & Supp. 1988).

[4]54 Del. 15, 174 A.2d 135 (1961).

[5]Id. at 140.

[6]See, e.g., Thompson v. Sun City Community Hosp., 142 Ariz. App. 1, 688 P.2d 647 (1983) (hospital that maintains emergency room has duty to provide immediate and necessary emergency care); Carr v. St. Paul Fire and Marine Ins. Co., 384 F. Supp. 821 (W.D. Ark. 1974) (same).

Arizona has extended this duty to treat in emergencies to severely burned children who had come across the border from Mexico to seek medical attention at a private hospital.[7] The court based its decision on the patients' reliance on the well-established custom of the hospital to provide emergency care and on the Arizona licensing statutes, which require hospitals to provide emergency service. The court refused to read an exception for nonresident aliens into the statutory requirement.[8]

Many states also have enacted statutes that require hospitals to provide emergency services to all patients requiring immediate attention.[9]

New federal requirements in the area of emergency admissions were enacted as part of the Consolidated Omnibus Budget Reconciliation Act of 1985 (COBRA).[10] The requirements in COBRA apply to all hospitals that participate in the Medicare program, whether public or private. Under COBRA, hospitals that have emergency departments are required to provide medical screening to any person who comes to the hospital and requests examination or treatment for a medical condition. If the patient does have an emergency condition or if the patient is in labor, the hospital must either treat the patient or transfer

---

[7]Guerrero v. Copper Queen Hosp., 112 Ariz. 104, 537 P.2d 1329 (1975).

[8]Id., at 1332 ("The proximity of the . . . [facility] to the international border presents special problems to it and other hospitals similarly situated. The lack of modern medical facilities in the Mexican border cities is the primary factor. Despite this obvious condition, we decline to find an exception in the statutes; this condition was equally obvious to the legislators, and they chose not to make an exception . . .").

[9]See, e.g., Cal. Health & Safety Code §1317 (West 1979 & Supp. 1989) (requiring that emergency services be provided by any licensed health facility that has an emergency room to any person requesting and in need of such services); Ill. Ann. Stat. ch. 111½, ¶86 (Smith-Hurd 1977 & Supp. 1988) (requiring hospitals to provide emergency services to anyone seriously hurt or ill).

[10]Consolidated Omnibus Budget Reconciliation Act of 1985, Pub. L. No. 99-272 §9121, 1986 U.S. Code Cong. & Admin. News (100 Stat.) 82, 164-167 (codified as amended at 42 U.S.C.A. §1395dd) (West Supp. 1988) (section setting out standards for "[e]xamination and treatment for emergency medical conditions and women in active labor").

the patient to another facility. The transferor hospital, however, is liable to the transferee hospital for its expenses in treating the patient.[11] A hospital may not transfer a patient until the patient's condition is stabilized, unless the patient requests transfer or a physician certifies that the benefits of transfer to another facility outweigh the risks. As a result of COBRA, virtually every hospital that maintains an emergency room must now admit or appropriately transfer emergency patients.

Hospitals that willfully or negligently fail to comply with COBRA may be suspended or terminated from the Medicare program, and knowing violations may result in a fine against a hospital or physician of up to $25,000 per violation. Also, COBRA authorizes any individual who is injured as a result of a hospital's violation of COBRA to bring a civil suit against the hospital.[12]

The JCAHO requires every hospital to have a well-defined plan for emergency care that includes a procedure whereby the ill or injured who come to the hospital for emergency care are assessed and either treated or referred to an appropriate facility.[13] Violation of the JCAHO standard would jeopardize accreditation and could be used by the patient as evidence of negligence (failure to act reasonably).

§4.10.3 The Healthcare Facility's Duty to Treat Indigent Patients

A common reason for denying a patient admission, when the hospital has the capability to treat the patient, is that the patient

---

[11]See 42 U.S.C.A. §1395dd(d)(3)(B) (West Supp. 1988).

[12]See, e.g., Reid v. Indianapolis Osteopathic Medical Hosp., 709 F. Supp. 853 (S.A. Ind. 1989) (patient whose individual action against the "dumping" healthcare facility was authorized under COBRA was not required to first submit claim under state review panel process).

[13]JCAHO, Accreditation Manual for Hospitals (1990). See also Jackson v. Power, 743 P.2d 1376 (Alaska 1987) (court referred to JCAH standards in holding that the providing of emergency room services is a nondelegable healthcare facility duty).

is uninsured and unable to pay for treatment. Under the common law, private hospitals have no affirmative duty to treat members of the general public. They may select for admission whomever they choose on whatever criteria they choose.[14] Absent emergency situations as discussed above, private hospitals can refuse to admit a patient for financial reasons. Public hospitals, on the other hand, are often required by state law or their charter to accept all patients. Because treating uninsured patients is expensive, hospitals have an incentive to transfer patients that are unable to pay or to simply turn them away. This is known as "patient dumping." The federal government[15] and many states[16] have tried to provide access to healthcare for indigents and to equalize the burden of indigent healthcare among hospitals.

Congress' first attempt to deal with this problem was in 1946, through the Hill-Burton Act.[17] In return for the receipt of federal funds for construction, hospitals were required to make their services available to all persons residing in the territorial area of the facility and provide, for a 20-year period, a reasonable volume of free or below-cost care to any person unable to pay. The Hill-Burton regulations applied to all facilities for either 20 years after completion of construction or for the period of the loan.[18] Hill-Burton was criticized because it did not contain an

---

[14]See, e.g., Birmingham Baptist Hosp. v. Crews, 229 Ala. 398, 399, 157 So. 224, 225 (1934) (a private hospital has no duty to treat a patient that it deems unacceptable).

[15]See, e.g., Hospital Survey & Construction (Hill-Burton) Act, Pub. L. No. 79-725, 60 Stat. 1040 (1946) (codified as amended at 42 U.S.C.A. §§291 to 291o-1 (West 1982 & Supp. 1988)). The Hill-Burton Act provides federal funds for the construction and modernization of hospitals on the condition that the hospital provide care to indigent patients.

[16]See, e.g., Cal. Health & Safety Code §1317 (West 1979 & Supp. 1989) (providing for emergency services regardless of sex, race, age, handicap, or ability to pay).

[17]42 U.S.C.A. §291 et seq. (West 1982 & Supp. 1988).

[18]Although the 20-year commitments of the original grantees have run, the requirements of the Hill-Burton Act continue to have some relevance. In 1975, a new federal assistance program for hospital construction and modernization, Title XVI of the Public Health Service Act, was established with essentially the same requirements for a reasonable volume of free or below-

express cause of action under which an individual could enforce its provisions, did not provide for punitive damages, and did not respond to the immediate needs of the uninsured.[19] Because of Hill-Burton's failure to fully address the problem of "patient dumping," Congress recently passed federal antidumping legislation as part of COBRA.[20]

§4.10.4 The Healthcare Facility's Duty to Treat Patients with AIDS

Although under the common law a private healthcare facility may refuse to admit any patient, a refusal by a hospital to admit or treat a patient suffering from Acquired Immune Deficiency Syndrome (AIDS) may be a violation of federal or state antidiscrimination laws if the facility has appropriate facilities for treatment. Hospitals that receive federal funds are bound by §504 of the Federal Rehabilitation Act of 1973.[21] Section 504 provides that handicapped individuals that are otherwise qualified may not be excluded from or denied the benefits of any program receiving federal financial assistance. Persons with AIDS have been found to be "handicapped" within the meaning of the statute.[22] Thus, hospitals, private or public, receiving federal funds are prohibited from discriminating against AIDS patients unless the restrictions on care are rational, as, for example, if the hospital is not medically equipped to handle such patients. Most states also have statutes prohibiting discrimination against the disabled or handicapped. Although the definition of protected

---

cost care. 42 U.S.C. §300q et seq. (West 1982 & Supp. 1988). In 1979, Congress provided for additional capitalization of the fund through September 30, 1982. See 42 U.S.C. §300q-2(e)(2) (West 1982 & Supp. 1988).

[19]Cf. Cook v. Ochsner Found. Hosp. 319 F. Supp. 603, 606 (E.D. La. 1970) (finding an *implied* private cause of action).

[20]42 U.S.C.A. §1395dd (West Supp. 1988) (discussed in the previous section).

[21]29 U.S.C.A. §794 (West Supp. 1988).

[22]Thomas v. Atascadero Unified School Dist. 662 F. Supp. 376 (C.D. Cal. 1986).

person varies from state to state, some states already have indicated that persons with AIDS will be afforded protection under state law.[23]

In addition, if an AIDS patient is suffering from a medical emergency, the facility may have a duty to provide emergency services under Hill-Burton, COBRA, or state law.[24]

The American Medical Association Council on Ethical and Judicial Affairs recently published a report that condemned the refusal to care as unethical and stated that those who are HIV-seropositive should not be the subject of any form of discrimination.[25]

C. Bases for Liability of the Healthcare Facility

§4.11 Overview

The liability of the healthcare facility for patient welfare has evolved along a circuitous route. Traditionally, the healthcare facility was not liable for the acts of healthcare providers in the treatment of patients, under the now-defunct doctrine of charitable immunity.[1] As charitable immunity eroded, the courts

---

[23]See, e.g., Lewis, Acquired Immunodeficiency Syndrome: State Legislative Activity, 258 J.A.M.A. 2410, 2412 (Nov. 6, 1987) (listing Connecticut, Florida, Illinois, Maine, Massachusetts, Michigan, Minnesota, Missouri, New Jersey, New Mexico, New York, Oregon, Washington, and Wisconsin). But see Elstein v. State Div. of Human Rights, N.Y.L.J. (Onondaga County Aug. 18, 1988) (antidiscrimination law covering public accommodation does *not* prohibit discrimination by private physician who allegedly refused to treat AIDS patient).

[24]See, e.g., American Hosp. Assn. v. Schweiker, 721 F.2d 170, 172 (7th Cir. 1983) (regulations under Hill-Burton prohibit discrimination on basis of race, sex, national origin, or any other ground unrelated to need for care).

[25]See Wash. Post, Nov. 13, 1987, at A3, col. 4.

§4.11 [1]See Schloendorff v. Society of N.Y. Hosp., 211 N.Y. 125, 128-129, 105 N.E. 92, 93 (1914); §4.11.1 on charitable immunity.

began to impose liability on the healthcare facility using several approaches. First, traditional employer liability principles were used to impose vicarious liability on the facility for the acts of its employees (usually nurses, orderlies, physical therapists, and so on, but sometimes physicians).[2] Second, courts sometimes found the facility vicariously liable for the negligent acts of independent physicians through use of estoppel or apparent agency theories.[3] Third, the facility was found to have its own direct duty to provide for the safety of its patients in accordance with their needs.[4]

Although vicarious liability and direct liability are conceptually distinct, the courts frequently discuss them interchangeably. Thus, courts that hold a healthcare facility liable while discussing the presence or absence of some form of "agency" (i.e., vicarious liability) may do so in a case that appears to involve a breach of what could be characterized as a direct healthcare facility duty.[5] Conversely, courts have characterized what appears to be respondeat superior or agency liability as direct "corporate" negligence.[6] Findings of agency as a basis for vicarious liability often appear most attenuated when a strong, though perhaps unarticulated, independent healthcare facility duty exists.[7]

---

[2]See, e.g., Keyser v. St. Mary's Hosp., 662 F. Supp. 191 (D. Idaho 1987) (hospital liable for physician's negligence if acted as employee).

[3]See, e.g., Paintsville Hosp. Co. v. Rose, 683 S.W.2d 255 (Ky. 1985) (hospital held liable for nonemployee emergency room physician's negligence on principles of "ostensible agency"). See §4.12.4.

[4]Jackson v. Power, 743 P.2d 1376 (Alaska 1987) (negligent emergency room doctor not employee but hospital breached its own nondelegable duty to provide emergency services).

[5]See, e.g., Mduba v. Benedictine Hosp., 52 A.D.2d 450, 384 N.Y.S.2d 527 (1976) (hospital liable for independent contractor emergency room physician's actions under agency theory although arguably negligent in own duty to establish emergency room procedure, availability of blood supply, and organization of emergency room).

[6]See, e.g., Fridena v. Evans, 127 Ariz. 516, 622 P.2d 463 (Ariz. 1980) (court affirmed jury verdict finding "corporate" negligence in failing to oversee treatment of negligent doctor who, as chief surgeon, chairman of the board of trustees, the medical director, and controlling stockholder, was clearly an agent of the hospital).

[7]This independent duty is often thrown into the judicial analysis as a

The body of direct duties owed by the healthcare facility to its patients is ever-expanding. Even as the facility finds itself charged with additional direct duties, vicarious liability remains an issue for the torts of both physician and nonphysician employees.[8] The sections that follow cover trends in both vicarious liability for negligent acts of others (as employees or agents) and direct liability for breach of evolving direct and independent duties of healthcare facilities.

§4.11.1 Background: The Demise of the Charitable Immunity Doctrine

Hospitals were once protected from liability for negligence by the doctrine of charitable immunity. The doctrine, developed in England and first adopted in the United States in McDonald v. Massachusetts General Hospital, was based on the rationale that it was improper to divert trust funds to pay hospital damage awards and that the actions of physicians and nurses, who were considered independent contractors, could not be controlled and supervised by hospitals.[9]

Various unwieldy exceptions and limitations to this doctrine developed as the courts struggled to avoid the harsh results in individual cases. First, courts attempted to distinguish between administrative (nonmedical) and medical (treatment) acts. Using

---

"public policy" consideration. See, e.g., Hannola v. City of Lakewood, 68 Ohio App. 2d 61, 426 N.E.2d 1187 (1980) (holding hospital vicariously liable for independent emergency room doctor's negligence, stressing "the public assumes, correctly or not, that the hospital exerts some measure of control over the medical activities taking place there"). See also Southwick, Hospital Liability: The Theories Have Been Merged, 4 No. 1 J. Legal Med. (1983). Compare Jackson v. Power, 743 P.2d 1376 (Alaska 1987) (Supreme Court of Alaska distinguished operation and applicability of apparent agency and estoppel vicarious liability theories from independent nondelegable duties of hospital). See also §4.12.4.

[8]See §4.12.

[9]120 Mass. 432 (1876) (overruled by Colby v. Carney, 356 Mass. 527, 254 N.E.2d 407 (1969)).

this characterization, courts limited hospital immunity to medical acts and held facilities liable for administrative acts, because such acts were seen as being within the hospital's control. Predictably, a number of inconsistent characterizations for whether an act was administrative or medical developed.[10] Other courts limited immunity to the beneficiaries of charity (i.e., the patients themselves and not third parties on the premises, such as spouses),[11] and to specific assets that the doctrine was designed to protect.[12] Another related exception was the extension of liability if the patient had paid for services and therefore was not the "beneficiary" of any charitable trust.[13]

The District of Columbia was one of the first jurisdictions to abolish charitable immunity, in the case of President and Directors of Georgetown College v. Hughes.[14] The D.C. Court of Appeals abolished hospital charitable immunity because of the increasing control over professional employees and the advent of liability insurance (which solved the problem of diversion of trust funds). Soon thereafter, a New York court, in the oft-cited case of Bing

---

[10]See Bing v. Thunig, 2 N.Y.2d 656, at 660-661, 163 N.Y.S.2d 3, 6, 143 N.E.2d 3, 4-5 (N.Y. 1957) (citing with disfavor cases for the propositions that "[p]lacing an improperly capped hot water bottle on a patient's body is administrative, while keeping a hot water bottle too long on a patient's body is medical [and a]dministering blood, by means of a transfusion, to the wrong patient is administrative, while administering the wrong blood to the right patient is medical") (citations omitted).

[11]See, e.g., Alabama Baptist Hosp. Bd. v. Carter, 145 So. 443 (Ala. 1932) later app., 151 So. 62 (1933) (although court stated charitable immunity would not operate to bar liability of hospital for negligence to third persons, hospital not liable when patient's wife fell in poorly lighted stairway, due to her own negligence).

[12]See, e.g., YMCA v. Bailey, 146 S.E.2d 234 (Ga. Ct. App. 1965), cert. denied, 385 U.S. 868 (1966) (court held charitable immunity inapplicable when hospital had insurance policy that was seen as a noncharitable asset).

[13]See, e.g., Sheehan v. North Country Community Hosp., 273 N.Y. 163, 7 N.E.2d (1937) (charitable hospital corporation held not exempt from liability to paying patient injured in ambulance accident); Nicholson v. Good Samaritan Hosp., 199 So. 344, 348-349 (Fla. 1940) (court held charitable immunity inapplicable to paying patient whether or not funds used to supply care to charity patients).

[14]130 F.2d 810 (D.C. Ct. App. 1942) (making new law).

v. Thunig, abandoned the healthcare facility exemption from respondeat superior liability for employees' actions, stating that

> [t]here is no reason to continue their exemption from the universal rules of respondeat superior. The test should be, for these institutions, whether charitable or profit-making, as it is for every other employer, was the person who committed the negligent injury-producing act one of its employees, and, if he was, was he acting within the scope of his employment.[15]

Today, only a few jurisdictions continue to provide some protection from liability for charitable institutions.[16]

Even with the virtual elimination of charitable immunity and the growing application of traditional respondeat superior liability to healthcare facilities, some courts remain reluctant to impose liability premised on healthcare facility control on the medical judgments of healthcare professionals.[17] This reluctance, however, never extended to the administrative actions of healthcare providers. Thus, artifacts of the traditional distinction of "medical" versus "administrative" acts remain. Although many courts have abandoned the distinction,[18] these characterizations serve as a useful basis for predicting which duties will be seen

---

[15]2 N.Y.2d 656, 667, 163 N.Y.S.2d 3, 11, 143 N.E.2d 3, 8 (1957) (case also noted for abandoning the distinction between medical and administrative acts necessitated by charitable immunity).

[16]See W. Prosser and W. P. Keeton, The Law of Torts, §133, at 1070 (5th ed. 1984) (even in those states that continue to provide charitable immunity, e.g., Arkansas and Maine, the charity waives immunity if it carries liability insurance).

[17]See, e.g., Kitto v. Gilbert, 570 P.2d 544, 550 (Colo. Ct. App. 1977) (both hospital and physician could not be liable for employee physician's negligence in performing medical services; due to physician's control, his liability supersedes hospital's). Compare Darling v. Charleston Community Memorial Hosp., 33 Ill. 2d 326, 211 N.E.2d 253 (1965), cert. denied, 383 U.S. 946 (1966), discussed infra, §4.11.2.

[18]See Bing v. Thunig, 2 N.Y.2d 656, 163 N.Y.S.2d 3, 11, 143 N.E.2d 3, 8 (N.Y. 1957) (*Bing* court attempted to eliminate artificial administrative-versus-medical acts distinction and relied instead on traditional test of respondeat superior: whether act was committed by employee within the scope of employment). See, infra §4.12.2.1, nn.5-8 and accompanying text.

as direct (formerly "administrative") duties and which are viewed as medical (within the control of the professional).[19]

§4.11.2 *Darling* and Its Progeny

Courts often confuse direct duties and vicarious liabilities in the hospital or HCF setting.[20] For example, in the per curiam opinion rendered by the Louisiana Supreme Court in the case of Sibley Board of Supervisors v. Louisiana State University, the majority remanded the issue of the "independent negligence" of the LSU Board of Supervisors "in permitting psychiatric treatment and administration of drugs by teams without independent patient care review."[21] Justice Calogero, however, as one of four separate dissenters, wrote that the claimant had not sufficiently alleged negligence against the LSU board, stating that the claimant's argument for liability for "permitting treatment" was actually "a thinly disguised espousal of the state's vicarious liability for the suspect treatment instituted by State medical professionals."[22]

Similarly, in Fridena v. Evans, a doctor who was the chief surgeon of the hospital, the chairman of its board of trustees, the medical director, and the controlling stockholder negligently performed surgery on the claimant, causing her leg to be shortened by three inches. The trial court found the hospital vicariously liable based on the physician's agency. Although the appellate court affirmed a finding against the hospital, it did so

---

[19]See §4.13 on direct liability.

[20]See, e.g., Sibley v. Board of Supervisors of La. State Univ., 477 So. 2d 1094 (La. 1985), on remand, 490 So. 2d 307 (La. Ct. App. 1986) (per curiam decision running the gamut of bases for hospital liability for physician's acts). See also Mduba v. Benedictine Hosp., 52 A.D.2d 450, 384 N.Y.S.2d 527 (1976) and Fridena v. Evans, 127 Ariz. 516, 622 P.2d 463 (Ariz. 1980), summarized supra at nn. 5 and 6.

[21]*Sibley*, 477 So. 2d at 1098 (primary issue was whether the Louisiana statutory cap on recovery for healthcare providers also applied to a healthcare facility and whether it was constitutional as applied to either physician or facility).

[22]Id. at 1111 (dissenting in part, concurring in part) (no recovery above caps for facility vicariously liable for actions of healthcare professionals).

based on the hospital's breach of an "independent" duty to supervise treatment—which was not specifically pleaded by the claimant—in lieu of the finding of vicarious liability through agency theory espoused by the lower court.[23]

Conversely, in Mduba v. Benedictine Hospital, the administrator of an estate filed an action against the hospital for wrongful death based on the negligence of the hospital in failing to promptly administer blood to the decedent, who had been injured in an automobile accident. The healthcare facility in question did not keep blood on its premises for use during emergencies, but instead relied on a laboratory located two blocks away for its blood supply. The trial court dismissed the complaint, based on the fact that the doctor operating the emergency room was not a hospital "employee." The appellate court reversed and remanded the issue of whether the physician was an "agent" of the facility to the jury. Although the appellate court noted that the hospital held itself out as being equipped to furnish emergency treatment and was under a duty to perform such services, it did not consider whether the facility breached any independent direct duty to furnish such an essential emergency medical supply as blood. Instead, the court based its reversal solely on the appearance of the employment relationship and vicarious liability theories.[24]

The confusion demonstrated by the *Sibley*, *Fridena*, and *Mduba* courts is understandable given the lack of clarity of the primary case cited for establishing the "corporate" or direct liability doctrine, Darling v. Charleston Community Memorial Hospital.[25] In *Darling*, the Supreme Court of Illinois upheld a jury's verdict finding a hospital liable for the breach of its own duty to supervise the quality of care rendered by a staff physician. Darling was a college athlete who came to the hospital's emergency room with a broken leg. The physician on call, an employee of the hospital, set the leg. After three days of

---

[23]*Fridena*, 622 P.2d at 466-467.

[24]*Mduba*, 384 N.Y.S.2d at 529-530.

[25]33 Ill. 2d 326, 211 N.E.2d 253 (1965), cert. denied, 383 U.S. 946 (1966).

complications, including swelling and darkening of the toes, the cast was removed. The leg eventually had to be amputated because the swelling had interfered with circulation.[26]

Although *Darling* often has been cited as support for holding a hospital liable for negligent medical acts of nonemployee physicians,[27] the doctor rendering care in *Darling* was in fact an employee.[28] In *Darling,* the Illinois Supreme Court found the jury's verdict "supportable" on the basis that: the hospital's *employed* nurses did not perform their duties of monitoring patient symptoms and reporting them to the attending physician and the hospital failed to require consultation by physicians skilled in surgical treatment "or to review the treatment rendered."[29] Thus, the *Darling* holding arguably contains elements of both vicarious liability for the negligence of the employed nurses and physicians and direct hospital liability for the failure to require certain review procedures and systems.

Since the *Darling* decision, Illinois appellate courts in the first and fourth districts, citing *Darling*, have stated that

> a hospital may be liable for injuries suffered by a patient in its care under two distinct theories. The hospital may be liable for a physician's misconduct on a respondeat superior theory when an employer-employee or principal-agent relationship is present *or* for the violation of an independent duty owed by the hospital to review and supervise medical care administered by the patient. . . . [30]

---

[26]Id.

[27]See, e.g., Thompson v. Nason Hosp., 535 A.2d 1177, 1181 (Pa. Super. Ct. 1988) (court remanded issue of hospital's liability for negligent supervision of patient care by nonemployee physician, citing *Darling*), appeal granted, 518 Pa. 641, 542 A.2d 1370 (1988); Bost v. Riley, 262 S.E.2d 391, 396 (N.C. Ct. App. 1980) (court noted hospital could be liable for failing to monitor and oversee treatment rendered by independent physician, citing *Darling*).

[28]The employment relationship is not explicitly set out in the court's opinion, but a subsequent Illinois decision distinguished the *Darling* case on the basis that in *Darling* the "treating physician was an employee." See Lundahl v. Rockford Medical Hosp. Assn., 93 Ill. App. 2d 461, 235 N.E.2d 671, 674 (1968).

[29]*Darling*, 211 N.E.2d at 258.

[30]See Alford v. Phipps, 523 N.E.2d 563, 571 (Ill. Ct. App. 4th Dist. 1988)

A hospital is not an insurer of a patient's safety, but it owes him a duty of protection and it must exercise a degree of reasonable care toward him as his known condition requires . . .[31]

There is no duty on the part of the hospital, however, to insure that each of its staff physicians will always perform his duty of due care to his patient.[32]

The Fourth District Court of Appeals of Illinois in Alford v. Phipps affirmed the trial court's dismissal of two negligence counts against the hospital for failure to state a cause of action despite an allegation that the hospital, through its nurses and agents (independent physicians with staff privileges), failed to consult with other physicians for the purpose of improving the quality of care as the patient's condition deteriorated.[33] Similar situations have been interpreted by courts in other states to constitute a breach of a direct "corporate" healthcare facility duty based on *Darling*.[34]

The First District Court of Appeals of Illinois dismissed counts against a hospital based on a vicarious liability theory of "joint enterprise" for doctor's negligence where the plaintiff had not shown breach of any independent duty to the patient, nor had it shown that the staff physician was an employee: "[M]erely supplying the doctor with equipment and personnel does not

---

(plaintiff's pleading stating failure of physician to consult with other physicians regarding patient's care insufficient to state cause of action for breach of direct duty) and Barton v. Evanston Hosp., 513 N.E.2d 65, 67 (Ill. Ct. App. 1st Dist. 1987) (surgeon was independent contractor and therefore respondeat superior not applicable).

[31]*Alford*, 523 N.E.2d at 571 and *Barton*, 513 N.E.2d at 66.

[32]*Alford*, 523 N.E.2d at 571 and *Barton*, 513 N.E.2d at 67.

[33]*Alford*, 523 N.E.2d at 570-571 (court, however, remanded because the dismissal should not have been with prejudice).

[34]See, e.g., Bost v. Riley, 262 S.E.2d 391 (N.C. Ct. App. 1980) (Hospital seen as breaching its direct duty to "monitor and oversee treatment" of nonemployee physicians by failing to take action against surgeons who failed to make progress notes as required. Hospital not liable, however, because causation not established).

evidence a right to govern his conduct."[35] Thus, courts of the state that purportedly gave birth to the "corporate duty" to monitor and oversee professional conduct have placed limits on the scope of this independent duty.

§4.12 Vicarious Liability of the Healthcare Facility

§4.12.1 The Decline of the "Captain of the Ship" and "Borrowed Servant" Doctrines

The "captain of the ship" and the "borrowed servant" doctrines traditionally operated to hold private physicians, rather than the employing facility, liable for the negligence of nonphysician facility employees on the theory that the staff members were under the professional control of the "borrowing" physician.[1] These doctrines were created so that some "deep pocket" could be held liable for the acts of nurses and other nonphysician employees at a time when their actual employer, the healthcare facility, was immune from suit under principles of charitable immunity. Today, these theories of respondeat superior liability are rarely applied to healthcare facility employees who assist physicians.[2] In fact, now that the facility itself can be liable for its employees' negligent acts, facility employees are generally

---

[35] *Barton*, 513 N.E.2d at 66-68.

§4.12 [1] See McConnell v. Williams, 361 Pa. 355, 65 A.2d 243 (1949) (if employee acted as servant of physician, physician rather than hospital would be liable). See also Ybarra v. Spangard, 25 Cal. 2d 486, 154 P.2d 687 (1944).

[2] See Annot. Liability of Hospital for Negligence of Nurse Assisting Operating Surgeon, 29 A.L.R.3d 1065, 1068-1069 (1970) (hospitals generally liable for employed nurse's administrative acts even when assisting surgeon, unless clearly a "medical act" under the surgeon's supervision. But see Austin v. Litvak, 682 P.2d 41 (Colo. 1984) (the hospital and its employees subserve the physician, who has sole control over diagnosis, treatment, and surgery); Krane v. St. Anthony Hosp. Sys., 738 P.2d 75 (Colo. Ct. App. 1987) (endorsed borrowed servant doctrine in operating room by implication); Kitto v. Gilbert, 570 P.2d 544, 549-550 (Colo. Ct. App. 1977) (surgeon who assumed control of operating room was liable for acts of hospital employees assisting).

not considered "borrowed servants" under the control of private physicians, even when they are acting on that physician's orders.[3]

§4.12.2 Liability for the Acts of Staff Members

Negligent Acts. In applying traditional tort law to the healthcare facility setting, a court first must determine whether the allegedly negligent individual is an employee or agent of the facility. This usually is not a difficult issue with respect to acts of the nonphysician staff, because their relationship most closely resembles the traditional employer-employee relationship.[4] Even with respect to nonphysician staff, courts sometimes found that the facility was not liable for the "medical," or professional, acts of its staff, but rather was liable only for the "administrative" acts.[5]

The artificial and unpredictable nature of the distinction between medical and administrative acts was pointed out by the court in *Bing*:

---

[3]See, e.g., Variety Children's Hosp. v. Perkins, 382 So. 2d 331 (Fla. Ct. App. 3d Dist. 1980) (nurses carrying out surgeon's orders in intensive care unit were not borrowed servants); Simpson v. Sisters of Charity of Providence in Or., 284 Or. 547, 588 P.2d 4 (1978) (x-ray technicians acting under orders not "employees" of physician). See also Dessauer v. Memorial Gen. Hosp., 628 P.2d 337 (N.M. Ct. App. 1981) (trial court properly refused instruction that doctor was responsible for negligence of assistants).

[4]See, e.g., Porter v. Patterson, 107 Ga. App. 64, 129 S.E.2d 70 (1962) (hospital liable for negligence of employees even if performing treatment-related tasks). See also Daniel v. St. Francis Cabrini Hosp. of Alexandria, 415 So. 2d 586, 589 (La. Ct. App. 3d Cir. 1982) ("[I]t is the settled jurisprudence of this State that a hospital is responsible for the negligence of its employees including, inter alia, nurses and attendants, under the doctrine of respondeat superior.") (citing general Louisiana statute on liability of "Master" for acts of "servants" in footnote).

[5]See, e.g., Annot. Liability of Hospital for Negligence of Nurse Assisting Operating Surgeon, 29 A.L.R.3d 1065, 1068-1069 (1970) (citing cases that use "administrative" versus "medical" acts distinction in determining liability of hospital for nurse's acts).

[P]lacing an improperly capped hot water bottle on a patient's body is administrative, while keeping a hot water bottle too long on a patient's body is medical. Administering blood, by means of a transfusion, to the wrong patient is administrative, while administering the wrong blood to the right patient is medical.[6]

The *Bing* court dismissed these distinctions as unworkable and substituted the more practical test that liability would result if the employee was acting within the scope of his or her employment.[7] The rationale for applying this form of respondeat superior to healthcare facilities is based primarily on patient expectations:

Certainly, the person who avails himself of "hospital facilities" expects that the hospital will attempt to cure him, not that its nurses or other employees will act on their own responsibility.[8]

This generally imposes respondeat superior liability on the healthcare facility for all negligent acts of its employees committed within the scope of employment, even if the acts involved the exercise of professional judgment.

Not all courts, however, impose liability on the facility for all negligent acts of employees. At least one commentator has suggested that the theories of respondeat superior and corporate

---

[6]Bing v. Thunig, 2 N.Y.2d 656 at 660-661, 163 N.Y.S.2d 3, 6, 143 N.E.2d 3, 4-5 (N.Y. 1957), citing Berg v. New York Socy. for Relief of the Ruptured and Crippled, 1 N.Y.2d 499, 136 N.E.2d 523 (1956) (administering wrong blood to right patient is medical) and Necolayff v. Genesee Hosp., 296 N.Y. 936, 73 N.E.2d 117 (1947) (administering blood to wrong patient is administrative). See also Johnson v. Sears, Roebuck & Co., 355 F. Supp. 1065 (E.D. Wisc. 1973) (applying Wisconsin law) (court held distinction between "professional" and "administrative" services for purposes of imposing strict liability on hospital is vague and the decision should be made on an ad hoc basis). See generally Mobilia, Hospital Corporate Liability: Toward a Stricter Standard for Administrative Services, 35 Def. L.J. 157 at 181-184 (1986) (discussing *Johnson*).

[7]*Bing*, 2 N.Y.2d 656, 143 N.E.2d 3 (N.Y. 1957). See also 53 Am. Jur. 2D Master Servant §404 (1970).

[8]*Bing*, 2 N.Y.2d at 666. See also Rabon v. Rowan Memorial Hosp., 269 N.C. 1, 152 S.E.2d 485 (1967).

negligence have merged so that courts tend to require breach of an independent healthcare facility duty in imposing vicarious liability for employee acts.[9] For example, in Starnes v. Charlotte-Mecklenberg Hospital Authority, the hospital was not liable when an infant was burned by a hot water bottle used by a nurse anesthetist during surgery. The court based this finding on the fact that there was no showing of any facility duty to train the employee anesthetist on how to properly use hot water bottles, nor was it shown the facility breached its duty to provide safe equipment or to exercise care in selection and retention of employees. This would be true even if the employee herself were negligent.[10]

On the other hand, when a patient's wound became infected because it was exposed to unsterile bathwater and towels through a nonphysician employee's mishandling, or when an infant was infected through handling by infectious hospital personnel, courts have held the healthcare facility liable.[11] These findings were based in part on the direct duty to provide a sterile environment that does not aggravate infections or illness.[12] Similarly, hospital can be held liable for failure of staff members to properly attend a patient,[13] failure to raise the bed rails of

---

[9]See generally Southwick, Hospital Liability: Two Theories Have Been Merged, 4 J. Legal Med. No. 1 (1983) (arguing that liability under the theories of respondeat superior and corporate or independent negligence have "become one," implying that liability for employees' acts requires breach of an independent hospital duty as well), citing Fridena v. Evans, 127 Ariz. 516, 622 P.2d 463 (1980).

[10]Starnes v. Charlotte-Mecklenburg Hosp. Auth., 28 N.C. App. 418, 221 S.E.2d 733, 736-737 (1976) (court affirmed hospital's motion for directed verdict and remanded issue of anesthetist's negligence to jury).

[11]See, e.g., St. Paul Fire & Marine Ins. Co. v. Prothro, 266 Ark. App. 1020, 590 S.W.2d 35 (1979) (hospital liable for negligence when fall during physical therapy reopened wound, which was bathed in unsterile bath water and patient developed staph infection). See also Kapuschinsky v. United States, 248 F. Supp. 732 (D.S.C. 1966) (hospital liable for failure to protect premature infant from infection by nurse who had worked in infected wards prior to her handling of infant).

[12]See also §4.13.2.

[13]See, e.g., Daniel v. St. Francis Cabrini Hosp. of Alexandria, 415 So. 2d

weak patients,[14] failure of the staff to report obvious symptoms to physicians and to administer basic diagnostic tests,[15] and even for the unprofessional behavior of a staff member,[16] because a hospital has an independent duty to provide competent and diligent staff.[17]

Although there are cases in which nurses, and therefore their employing healthcare facility, have been exonerated for following physicians' orders,[18] some of these same cases imply that the facility may be liable in some circumstances when its staff fails to question a doctor's order.[19] It is generally held that nonphysician staff members are "not responsible for the diagnosis and treatment of patients" and that absent a "showing of how the handling of [the] case was so obviously negligent that [the] [staff member] was obliged to intervene and order a different treatment," there is no staff negligence, and hence no healthcare

---

586 (La. Ct. App. 1982) (hospital liable for injuries due to nurse's negligence in failing to attend patient after administering enema).

[14]See, e.g., Winters v. Jersey City, 120 N.J. Super. 129, 293 A.2d 431 (1972) (hospital liable for injuries due to negligence of hospital employees in failing to raise bed rails of elderly patient who fell from the bed).

[15]Darling v. Charleston Community Memorial Hospital, 33 Ill. 2d 326, 211 N.E.2d 253 (1965), cert. denied, 383 U.S. 946 (1966). See also Goff v. Doctors Gen. Hosp. of San Jose, 166 Cal. App. 2d 314, 333 P.2d 29 (1958) (despite profuse bleeding, hospital nurses failed to procure medical attention for plaintiff); Utter v. United Hosp. Center, 236 S.E.2d 213 (W. Va. 1977) (nurse failed to report complications and worsening condition to physicians).

[16]See, e.g., Hall v. Bio-Medical Application, Inc., 671 F.2d 300 (8th Cir. 1982) (applying Arkansas law) (facility held liable to patient for nurse's unacceptable and unprofessional behavior in leaving dialysis needles in patient's arm, notwithstanding "extreme provocation" by plaintiff).

[17]See §§4.13.1 and 4.13.2.

[18]See, e.g., Paris v. Kreitz, 75 N.C. App. 365, 331 S.E.2d 234, review denied, 315 N.C. 185, 337 S.E.2d 858 (1985) (nurse not responsible for diagnosis and treatment of patient); Byrd v. Marion Gen. Hosp., 202 N.C. 337, 162 S.E. 738, 740 (1932) (nurse not liable for following doctor's orders because she had duty to "obey and diligently execute" them). See also Jackson v. Joyner, 236 N.C. 259, 262, 72 S.E.2d 589, 592 (1952).

[19]See, e.g., Byrd, 202 N.C. 337 (in dicta, court suggested nurse should disobey an order any reasonable person would anticipate might cause harm).

facility liability, for failure to question physicians' orders.[20] Although nurses may disobey doctors' instructions that are patently wrong, a *duty* to disobey does not arise when there is a mere difference in medical opinion.[21] Courts are reluctant to impose liability on the facility for the acts of nurses and other nonphysicians who fail to interfere with a physician's orders in all but the most egregious circumstances.[22] The standard to be used in determining whether the nurse breached a "duty to disobey" must generally be established by expert testimony of similar providers in similar communities under similar circumstances.[23]

Intentional Acts. The healthcare facility may be liable for the intentional acts of its employee or agent if the employee is acting

---

[20]*Paris,* 75 N.C. App. 365, citing *Byrd,* 202 N.C. 337. Compare Poor Sisters of St. Francis v. Catron, 435 N.E.2d 305, 307 (Ind. Ct. App. 2d Dist. 1982) (court affirmed finding against hospital based on its nurses' substantial departure from accepted standards of care in failing to question physician's orders regarding length of use of endotracheal tube).

[21]Id.

[22]See *Byrd,* 202 N.C. 337, 341 ("Certainly, if a physician or surgeon should order a nurse to stick fire to a patient, no nurse would be protected from liability."). See also Walker v. United States, 549 F. Supp. 973 (W.D. Okla. 1982) (applying Oklahoma law) (hospital personnel not liable for failure to object to use of surgical tool where they did not know, or have reason to know, that instrument used by surgeon may cause kidney stones); Killeen v. Reinhardt, 71 A.D.2d 851, 419 N.Y.S.2d 175, 177 (1979) (hospital staff not liable when following doctor's orders unless staff knows the doctor's orders are "so clearly contra indicated by normal practice that ordinary prudence requires inquiry").

[23]See, e.g., §4.1.4. See also N.C. Gen. Stat. §90-21.12 (1985), which sets forth a subjective standard of care: "the same health care profession with similar training and experience situated in the same or similar communities at the time of the alleged act . . ."; Conn. Gen. Stat. Ann. §52-184c (West. Supp. 1988): "prevailing professional standard of care for a given health care provider shall be that level of care, skill and treatment which, in light of all relevant surrounding circumstances, is recognized as acceptable and appropriate by reasonably prudent similar health care providers." See also Note, When Doctrines Collide: Corporate Negligence and Respondeat Superior When Hospital Employees Fail to Speak Up," 61 Tul. L. Rev. 85 (1986).

within the scope of employment.[24] Whether an employee is acting within the scope of employment, however, is not always clear. One relevant factor to be considered is whether the employee is acting in furtherance of her own self-interest or with intent to benefit the employer. An employee acting in her own self-interest is seen as acting outside the scope of employment.[25]

A second factor to be considered is whether the intentional tort of the employee was "foreseeable" to the facility. This factor arises out of the facility's duty to exercise reasonable care in selecting and retaining its employees. The facility may be liable for the intentional acts of an employee, even if the employee was not acting within the scope of employment, if the facility knew or should have known of propensities of the employee that would place patients at risk.[26] Several courts have held that a facility must verify references supplied by an applicant and check for a criminal record in order to avoid liability for intentional acts based on constructive knowledge of a propensity (e.g., to violence).[27]

---

[24]W. Prosser and W. P. Keeton, The Law of Torts §70 at 501 (5th ed. 1984). See, e.g., Hall v. Bio-Medical Application, Inc., 671 F.2d 300 (8th Cir. 1982) (applying Arkansas law) (facility liable when nurse left needles in patient's arm after disconnecting him from dialysis, calling him a "black son of a bitch").

[25]See, e.g., Focke v. United States, 597 F. Supp. 1325 (D. Kan. 1982) (applying Kansas law) (hospital not liable because social worker's sexual encounters with wife and daughter of patient-client were for his own sexual gratification).

[26]See §4.13.1.2 on negligent selection and retention of staff members.

[27]See, e.g., Wilson N. Jones Memorial Hosp. v. Davis, 553 S.W.2d 180 (Tex. Ct. App. 1977) (hospital liable for acts of orderly because it failed to investigate background prior to employment). See also Hipp v. Hospital Auth. of City of Marietta, 104 Ga. App. 174, 121 S.E.2d 273 (1961) (hospital failed to discover orderly had criminal record as a "peeping tom" and was therefore liable for molestation of 11-year-old patient); Focke v. United States, 597 F. Supp. 1325 (D. Kan. 1982) (applying Kansas law) (where social worker associate interviewed for two hours and civil service check performed, hospital not liable); Taylor v. Doctors Hosp. (West), 21 Ohio App. 3d 154, 486 N.E.2d 1249 (1985) (hospital not liable where employee's sexual acts were considered beyond scope of employment and there were no allegations of negligence in selecting employee).

§4.12.3 Liability for Physicians as Employees

Negligent Acts. The vicarious liability of hospitals for negligent acts of physicians turns primarily on two issues: whether the physician is an "employee" of the hospital and whether the physician-employee is free from (or subject to) any control by the employer of the time, method, or manner of performance of the work.[28]

The answers to both questions require an in-depth review of the surrounding factual circumstances and do not turn on the mere facial appearance of contractual relationships.

In determining whether an employment relationship exists for purposes of imposing respondeat superior liability on the healthcare facility, courts look at a variety of factors:

The Financial Arrangement

- whether the physician receives a salary from the hospital;[29]
- whether the patient receives only one bill for the services of both the hospital and the physician;[30]
- the extent to which the doctor's fees are included in the facility's combined bill;[31] and
- in the case of an HMO, whether the member physician

---

[28]See Murphy v. Clayton County Hosp., 333 S.E.2d 15, 16 (Ga. Ct. App. 1985) (physicians considered independent contractors where hospital does not control "time, method or manner of performing medical services by the physicians").

[29]See Beeck v. Tucson Gen. Hosp., 18 Ariz. App. 165, 500 P.2d 1153 (1972) (radiologist received full compensation from hospital for five years). See also Kober v. Stewart, 417 P.2d 476 (Mont. 1966); Niles v. City of Rafael, 116 Cal. Rptr. 733, 42 Cal. App. 3d 320 (1974) (institution liable for negligence of part-time salaried director of pediatrics department).

[30]Adamski v. Tacoma Gen. Hosp., 20 Wash. App. 98, 579 P.2d 970, 972 (1978) (in reversing summary judgment in favor of hospital on issue of employment, court noted that hospital billed for physician's fees and remanded issue to jury).

[31]*Beeck*, 18 Ariz. App. 165 (1972) (if hospital bills for physicians, it can be seen as evidence of a contractual relationship by jury).

is on a lump-sum, "capitation" system of compensation or the more traditional "fee-for-services" system.[32]

Physical Setup

- whether the doctor is prohibited from having his or her own private office located outside of the facility;[33]
- whether the physician has an office inside the facility;[34]
- whether the hospital provides the equipment, staff, room, or radiology services used in the physician's practice;[35]
- the explicit terms of the contract regarding facilities and services between the facility and its physicians;[36]
- whether the physician is a "resident" physician technically considered to be employed by the university that also operates the hospital;[37] and
- whether a "resident" physician on rotation at a non-university hospital is still within the control of the university hospital.[38]

---

[32]See Oakley and Kelly, HMO Liability for Malpractice of Member Physicians: The Case of IPA Model HMOs (hereinafter HMO Liability), XXIV Tort & Ins. L.J. (Spring 1988), 624 at 628. The authors suggest the lump-sum system is more indicative of an integrated, employment-type relationship although as yet there is no case law on the issue.

[33]Adamski, 579 P.2d at 973 (court noted contractual prohibition of private practice in remanding issue of employment).

[34]See, e.g., Gamble v. United States, 648 F. Supp. 438 (N.D. Ohio 1986).

[35]See Beeck, 18 Ariz. App. 165.

[36]See HMO Liability, supra n.32. Courts give more weight to actual control and operation than to contractual terms purporting to absolve hospital of liability (citing Bing v. Thunig, 2 N.Y.2d 656, 666 (N.Y. 1957)).

[37]Cornell v. Ohio State Univ. Hosp., 36 Ohio Misc. 2d 25, 28 521 N.E.2d 857, 860 (Ohio Ct. Cl. 1987) (residents held to be hospital employees).

[38]Kelley v. Rossi, 48 N.E.2d 1340 (resident generally employee except when on rotation to private hospital) (Mass. 1985). See also Smock v. Brantley, 76 N.C. App. 73, 331 S.E.2d 714 (1985), rev. denied, 315 N.C. 590, 341 S.E.2d 30 (1986) (outlying hospital not liable because had no control over resident activities).

Patient Choice

- whether the patient has any choice in selecting the physician or whether the hospital arbitrarily assigns;[39] and
- whether there is a preexisting patient-physician relationship outside of facility's treatment plan.[40]

In addition to the legal and contractual factors that characterize the relationship, courts look to the degree of actual control exercised by the healthcare facility, that is, the power of the facility to define "the time, method or manner of performing medical services by the physician defendants."[41] Because the facility strives to comply with the extensive standards and guidelines promulgated by the JCAHO, they are sometimes seen as satisfying the "time, method or manner" requirement in areas that fall within JCAHO standards. For example, JCAHO and JCAH (the predecessor to JCAHO) standards have long required hospitals to implement a "well-defined plan" for community emergency services.[42] The Supreme Court of Alaska, in Jackson v. Powers, used the JCAH standard as evidence that the provision of emergency service is a nondelegable duty. Thus, the hospital was liable for service rendered by physicians performing emergency room services, even though they were under an independent contract.[43]

---

[39]See *Adamski*, 579 P.2d at 977.

[40]Weldon v. Seminole Mun. Hosp., 709 P.2d 1058 (Okla. 1985) (mother called doctor with whom family had preexisting doctor-patient relationship); Thompson v. Nason Hosp., 535 A.2d 1177, 1180 (Pa. Super. 1988) (court reversed summary judgment on issue of employment and noted that the physician had treated the patient as family physician within the last five years), appeal granted, 542 A.2d 1370 (1988).

[41]Murphy v. Clayton County Hosp., 333 S.E.2d 15, 16 (Ga. Ct. App. 1985).

[42]See JCAHO, Accreditation Manual for Hospitals, Standard I (1990).

[43]See Jackson v. Power, 743 P.2d 1376 (Alaska 1987) (JCAH-accredited hospital had to implement "well defined plan" for community emergency room to maintain accreditation) (nondelegable nature of duty). See also Mduba v. Benedictine Hosp., 52 A.D.2d 450, 384 N.Y.S.2d 527 (1976).

Other indicia of control that may impose a corresponding liability include hospital bylaws (setting out an express or implied facility duty to supervise and aid the physician staff members)[44] and quality assurance mechanisms (which might impute knowledge of the negligent procedures used by the physician).[45] Healthcare facilities may be exempt from liability, however, for medical decisions over which the physician, rather than the hospital, has primary control (such as obtaining informed consent), regardless of the characterization of the employment relationship.[46] Even when it can be shown that some indicia of control exist, the plaintiff must demonstrate control over the specific act for which the hospital is allegedly vicariously liable. Finally, in some states certain types of healthcare facilities are statutorily exempt from vicarious liability for physicians.[47]

---

[44]See JCAHO, Accreditation Manual for Hospitals, §4.1, at 41 (1990) (requiring the governing body of healthcare facilities to set up bylaws requiring peer review and quality assurance of physician staff members).

[45]See JCAHO, Accreditation Manual for Hospitals §17, at 205-208 (1985) (quality assurance standards).

[46]See, e.g., Pauscher v. Iowa Methodist Medical Center, 408 N.W.2d 355 (Iowa 1987) (hospital not responsible for seeing that physician adequately inform patient about treatment); Keyser v. St. Mary's Hosp., 662 F. Supp. 191 (D. Idaho 1987) (Idaho statutorily places duty to obtain informed consent on the physician); Krane v. St. Anthony Hosp. Sys., 738 P.2d 75 (Colo. Ct. App. 1987) (duty to obtain informed consent lay with physician, not hospital). See also Cooper v. Curry, 92 N.M. 417, 589 P.2d 201 (1978) (hospital not liable for nonemployed physician's failure to obtain informed consent); Fiorentino v. Wenger, 19 N.Y.2d 407, 280 N.Y.S.2d 373, 227 N.E.2d 296 (1967) (duty to obtain informed consent is doctor's, not hospital's). Compare Valcin v. Public Health Trust of Dade County, 473 So. 2d 1297 (Fla. Ct. App. 3d Dist. 1984) (though duty of physician to obtain informed consent, hospital may be liable if relationship between physician and hospital is such that hospital is vicariously liable for doctor's acts).

[47]See, e.g., Ill. Rev. Stat. ch. 32, ¶595 (1983) et seq. (providing that HMO shall not be held liable for negligent acts of member physicians) (cited in HMO Liability, supra n.32, at 635); Ark. Stat. Ann. §23-75-116 (1959 & Supp. 1987) (establishing nonliability of certain "hospital service corporations" and "medical service corporations" to subscribers for negligence of hospitals). See also Brown v. Michael Reese Health Plan, 150 Ill. App. 3d 959, 502 N.E.2d 433 (1986) (upholding constitutionality of HMO exemption); Utah Code Ann. §58-12-28(4)(a) (Supp. 1988) (unlawful for anyone other than a licensed

Intentional Acts.   The intentionally tortious acts of doctors are rarely considered to be within the scope of employment and thus do not generally subject the healthcare facility to vicarious liability.[48] A facility can nevertheless be liable for its own negligence in selecting, retaining, or extending privileges to a doctor who has a record indicative of intentionally tortious or otherwise harmful conduct.[49]

Under certain circumstances, an HMO might be liable for the intentionally tortious acts of doctors on its staff who refuse to authorize necessary services or procedures, since the very premise of an HMO is to encourage economically efficient healthcare delivery. This liability might rest primarily on the HMO's own contribution of producing an incentive for not providing necessary services. For example, some HMO plans pay an annual bonus to enrolled physicians whose referral of patients for specialized care is below a certain dollar amount. Such limitations on care may not always be in the best interests of the patient member, and arguably limitation of services might be seen as "within the scope of employment" in those HMOs with such a policy. It has been suggested that an HMO might be subject to punitive damages for encouraging financial motives for the conduct of providers against the best interests of patient members, depending on applicable state law.[50] Any HMO with

---

physician to "diagnose, treat, correct, advise or prescribe"). This statute has been interpreted by the federal district court of Utah to mean hospitals cannot be held liable for a physician's misdiagnosis. See Tolman v. IHC Hospitals, 637 F. Supp. 682 (D. Utah 1986) (hospital not liable under agency theory for radiologist's misdiagnosis).

[48]See Annot., Liability of Hospital or Clinic for Sexual Relationships with Patients by Staff Physicians, Psychologists, and Other Healers, 45 A.L.R.4th 289 (1986); See also Smith v. St. Paul Fire & Marine Ins. Co., 353 N.W.2d 130 (Minn. 1984) (doctor's sexual contact with minor patients not considered "professional services" and therefore not covered by professional liability insurance policy).

[49]See Annot., supra n.48. See, e.g., Simmons v. United States, 805 F.2d 1363 (9th Cir. 1986) (applying Washington law) (healthcare facility liable when informed of sexual relationship between counselor and patient and did nothing to prevent further harm to client). See also §4.13.1 on negligent selection and retention.

[50]See HMO Liability at 637.

a bonus policy for limiting referral or access to services should take great care in drafting and administering this policy to ensure that it is only unnecessary care that is limited and that necessary care is provided.

§4.12.4 Liability for the Acts of "Independent" Physicians

Overview.　Although some jurisdictions still refuse to hold healthcare facilities liable for the negligent acts of "independent contractor" physicians, many have over the years developed special applications of agency and estoppel theories in order to hold the facility liable for the malpractice of nonemployee physicians.[51] Despite early popularity, the concept of "apparent agency"[52] may now be giving way to the somewhat higher

---

[51]See, e.g., Alford v. Phipps, 523 N.E.2d 563 (Ill. Ct. App. 4th Dist. 1988) (hospital may be liable for a physician's misconduct on a respondeat superior theory when an employer-employee or principal-agent relationship exists or for the violation of an independent duty); Jackson v. Power, 743 P.2d 1376 (Alaska 1987) ("[W]e have applied the theory of respondeat superior only in an employer/employee context."). See also Weldon v. Seminole Mun. Hosp., 709 P.2d 1058 (Okla. 1985) ("[T]he majority of courts, including Oklahoma, do not extend the theory of respondeat superior to a hospital where the doctor . . . is an independent contractor."); Murphy v. Clayton County Hosp., 175 Ga. App. 152, 333 S.E.2d 15 (1985) (doctors are independent contractors if not subject to hospital's control as to "time, method or manner of performing medical services"); Jeffcoat v. Phillips, 534 S.W.2d 168 (Tex. Civ. App. 1976) (no respondeat superior where doctor is independent contractor), distinguished in Park North Gen. Hosp. v. Hickman, 703 S.W.2d 262 (Tex. Ct. App. 4th Dist. 1985) (court noted hospital in *Jeffcoat* not liable when doctor was patient's independent physician prior to hospital admission; in *Park North* hospital only liable for breach of its independent duty to exercise care in selection of medical staff and authorization of specialized privileges).

[52]See Seneris v. Haas, 45 Cal. 2d 811, 291 P.2d 915, 927 (1955) (lead case in establishing facility liability for conduct of a nonemployee where "record reveals [facility] did nothing to put [patient] on notice that the X-ray laboratory was not an integral part of [the] institution, and it cannot seriously be contended that [patient] . . . should have inquired whether the individual

standard of proof embodied in the doctrine of "agency by estoppel," which generally requires more facility conduct to justify the patient's asserted reliance.[53]

The Supreme Court of Alaska, in Jackson v. Power, articulated the difference between the doctrines of apparent agency and agency by estoppel (although it did not apply either.)[54] The *Jackson* court noted that "[c]ases from other jurisdictions show a strong trend toward liability against hospitals that permit or encourage patients to believe that independent contractor/physicians are, in fact, authorized agents of the hospitals."[55] According to the court, the "apparent" or "ostensible" agency theory is grounded in the Restatement (Second) of Torts §429 (1966) and the "agency by estoppel" theory is based on the Restatement (Second) of Agency §267 (1958).

The Restatement (Second) of Torts §429 describes "ostensible" or "apparent" agency as applicable in the following circumstance:

> One who employs an independent contractor to perform services for another which are accepted in the reasonable belief that the services are being rendered by the employer or by his

doctors who examined him were employees"). Compare Tolman v. IHC Hospitals, 637 F. Supp. 682 (D. Utah 1986) (applying Utah law) (hospital not liable under agency theory for radiologist's misdiagnosis).

[53]See, e.g., Stratso v. Song, 17 Ohio App. 3d 39, 477 N.E.2d 1176 (1984) (appellate court stated agency by estoppel could be used against healthcare facility for acts of independent contractor where plaintiff testified he would otherwise have "checked out" the doctor's reputation but instead reasonably relied on the hospital's reputation).

[54]743 P.2d 1376 (Alaska 1987) (Supreme Court of Alaska affirmed lower court's denial of claimant's motion for summary judgment, holding that genuine issue of fact as to apparent agency existed but holding general acute care hospital's duty to provide emergency room care nondelegable and therefore facility liable for emergency room physician's acts as a matter of law).

[55]Id. at 1380 (citing Paintsville Hosp. Co. v. Rose, 683 S.W.2d 255, 257 (Ky. 1985). See also Hannola v. City of Lakewood, 68 Ohio App. 2d 61, 426 N.E.2d 1187, 1192 (1980); Grewe v. Mt. Clemens Gen. Hosp., 404 Mich. 240, 273 N.W.2d 429, 432-433 (1978); Mehlmen v. Powell, 281 Md. 269 378 A.2d 1121 (Md. 1977).

servants, is subject to liability for physical harm caused by the negligence of the contractor in supplying such services, to the same extent as though the employer were supplying them himself or by his servants.[56]

On the other hand, the Restatement (Second) of Agency §267, most often used in describing requirements of agency by estoppel, provides:

> One who represents that another is his servant or agent and thereby causes a third person justifiably to rely upon the care or skill of such apparent agent is subject to liability to the third person for harm caused by the lack of care or skill of the one appearing to be a servant or other agent as if he were such.[57]

This distinction is important because, under the latter (the agency-by-estoppel theory), there must be a showing of *actual* reliance by the claimant before the hospital is estopped from denying agency. Under the former (the apparent agency theory), no showing of reliance is necessary. Unfortunately, however, courts often confuse the elements required by the two separate theories.

For example, in Paintsville Hospital Co. v. Rose, the Kentucky Supreme Court applied some version of the doctrine of apparent agency to the emergency room setting while purporting to rely on the Restatement (Second) of Agency §267, the passage generally cited as setting out the more stringent requirements of agency by estoppel.[58] Nevertheless, under the Kentucky court's reading of apparent agency, it is not necessary for the claimant to show an express representation by the facility

---

[56]Cited in Jackson v. Power, 743 P.2d at 1380.

[57]Id.

[58]Paintsville Hosp. Co. v. Rose, 683 S.W.2d 255, 257 (Ky. 1985) (invoking the Restatement (Second) of Agency §267 (1958), which requires justifiable reliance). Most courts interpret this standard's "justifiable reliance" more stringently than the Supreme Court of Kentucky and use it as a standard for "agency by estoppel." See, e.g., *Jackson*, 743 P.2d at 1380 (cites this section as setting forth requirements of agency by estoppel). See also §4.12.4.3 on agency by estoppel, citing primarily the Restatement (Second) of Agency §267.

or to provide testimony as to reliance on any representation. Absent opposing testimony that the patient knew or should have known the doctor was independent, the facility will be liable for independent emergency room physicians' negligent acts.[59]

On the other hand, the Eighth Circuit, in Porter v. Sisters of St. Mary, did require proof of justifiable reliance of the patient. Despite its use of "apparent agency" language, the court appears to have applied the doctrine of agency by estoppel.[60] Although it cited Missouri case law framed in terms of apparent agency, the Eighth Circuit in *Porter* also cited, and applied the Restatement (Second) of Agency §267 (agency by estoppel) standard, finding no "justifiable reliance" despite testimony that a doctor in the emergency room had stated that the independent physician in question was "our best person for the job" and had called him into the area.[61] The court found no agency because there was no showing that the third party "justifiably relied" on the employment status of the physician or his appropriateness for follow-up care subsequent to the emergency procedures.[62]

The Standard for "Apparent Agency." The Restatement (Second) of Torts §429 (apparent agency) standard is generally considered easier to meet for plaintiffs.[63] It may actually be more

---

[59]*Paintsville*, 683 S.W.2d at 256.

[60]756 F.2d 669, 673-674 (8th Cir. 1985) (applying Missouri law) (court applies §267 rather than §429, but cites Missouri case law utilizing "apparent" authority language), citing Jeff-Cole Quarries v. Bell, 454 S.W.2d 5, 13 (Mo. 1970). See also Richmond County Hosp. Auth. v. Brown, 257 Ga. 507, 361 S.E.2d 164 (1987).

[61]See *Porter*, 756 F.2d 669 (doctor was, however, dressed casually and plaintiff's injury resulted from services rendered upon further retention beyond emergency room service).

[62]Id. at 673. See also *Richmond Co. Hosp. Auth.*, 257 Ga. 507 (Georgia Supreme Court characterized issue as one of apparent agency but required justifiable reliance standard or agency by estoppel).

[63]See generally Reed, Expanding Theories of Hospital Liability: A Review, 21 J. Health & Hosp. L. No. 9, at 217, 224-226 (1988). See also Ferraro and Camarra, Hospital Liability: Apparent Agency or Agency by Estoppel? 76 Ill. B.J. 364 (1988).

stringent than the Restatement (Second) of Agency §267, however, as that standard was applied by the court in *Paintsville*, discussed above.[64] Most courts adopting apparent agency, whether using the requirements of the Restatement (Second) of Torts as described in Jackson v. Power[65] or the Restatement (Second) Agency §267 (the "estoppel standard," set forth in the next section), require the claimant to prove some requisite level of representation of the employment status of the physician.[66]

If the treating physician was not requested by the patient but merely appeared, even when that physician had a prior relationship with the patient, apparent agency may be established. For example, in Thompson v. Nason Hospital, the healthcare facility moved for summary judgment, arguing that the claimant should have known the independent contractor status of a physician with whom she had a prior patient-physician relationship. The claimant had testified that the defendant physician had been her family doctor. The court rejected this argument, however, because the claimant did not request treatment by that physician and the record was unclear as to when the patient was last treated by the physician.[67] When a claimant directly requests a family physician to treat in the emergency room, however, generally no apparent agency is

---

[64]*Paintsville*, 683 S.W.2d at 256 (hospital required to set forth "evidence that the patient knew or should have known that the treating physician was not a hospital employee") (plaintiff not required to give testimony as to reliance).

[65]*Jackson*, 743 P.2d at 1380 (doctrine of apparent agency requires showing that plaintiff looked to hospital rather than doctor for treatment and hospital "held out" doctor as employee).

[66]See, e.g., Adamski v. Tacoma Gen. Hosp., 20 Wash. App. 98, 579 P.2d 970, 979 (1978) (claimant's evidence sufficient to show agency under Restatement (Second) of Agency §267 when claimant not advised of lack of employment status of emergency room physician, hospital gave claimant a form indicating patient could call emergency room to remove stitches if personal doctor not available, and claimant believed he was treated by the hospital's agent).

[67]Thompson v. Nason Hosp., 535 A.2d 1177, 1180 (Pa. Super. 1988) (no request for physician in question made by patient and prior treatment record was unclear.)

found.[68] Generally, in "apparent agency" jurisdictions, liability continues to rest on appearances and public expectations (subjective issues) rather than on actual proof of justifiable reliance (an objective issue).[69]

The Standard for Agency by Estoppel. The emerging theory of healthcare facility liability for independent contractors is agency by estoppel. Agency-by-estoppel liability typically is based on §267 of the Restatement (Second) of Agency.[70] In Illinois, the founding state of corporate liability, the recent case law that allows any finding of agency for independent contractors appears to require the higher standard of proof of justifiable reliance that is embodied in the agency-by-estoppel theories.[71]

According to one commentator, agency by estoppel is a "conservative and well-grounded alternative to the more radical theories of apparent agency" because it also requires "good faith reliance and action upon the representation of the principal by a third party to his or her detriment."[72] Under agency-by-estoppel theory, the claimants must "plead and prove that if they had known the purported agents were not employees of

---

[68]Weldon v. Seminole Mun. Hosp., 709 P.2d 1058, 1060 (Okla. 1985) (patient who sought treatment directly from family physician by calling and asking him to meet in the emergency room could not claim "apparent agency").

[69]See Gamble v. United States, 648 F. Supp. 438, 441-442 (N.D. Ohio 1986) (applying Ohio law); Hannola v. City of Lakewood, 68 Ohio App. 2d 61, 426 N.E.2d 1187 (1980).

[70]See Jackson v. Power, 743 P.2d 1376 (Alaska 1987) (citing §267 of the Restatement (Second) of Agency as the standard for agency by estoppel). But see Smith v. St. Francis Hosp., 676 P.2d 279 (Okla. App. 1983) (citing §429 of the Restatement (Second) of Torts in holding healthcare facility "estopped" from denying physician's employment).

[71]See, e.g., Johnson v. Sumner, 160 Ill. App. 3d 173, 175, 513 N.E.2d 149, 151 (3d Dist. 1987) (court rejected apparent agency because it was not persuaded the doctrine recognized realities of hospital-physician relationships); Gasbarra v. St. James Hosp., 85 Ill. App. 3d 32, 45, 406 N.E.2d 544, 555 (1st Dist. 1980) and Crittendon v. State Oil Co., 78 Ill. App. 2d 112, 116, 222 N.E.2d 561, 564 (1966).

[72]See Reed, supra n.63, at 225, citing Ferraro and Camarra, Hospital Liability: Apparent Agency or Agency by Estoppel? 76 Ill. B.J. 364 (1988).

the hospital then they would have refused to be treated by them or would have taken a different course of action."[73] If the plaintiff meets agency by estoppel's higher requirement of proof of inducing acts and actual reliance, the hospital is "estopped" from denying agency.[74]

   Public Policy.   Some courts have held the healthcare facility liable for the acts of independent physicians regardless of both the actual contractual relationship between the facility and its emergency room physicians and any reason the claimant may have to know that the physicians are independent contractors because

> [i]t is the hospital's location and reputation which draw patients to its emergency room, as well as the exigencies of the moment, and, in this regard, the contractual relationship between the hospital and the emergency room physicians is irrelevant as a practical matter.[75]

The public policy principle has been articulated in this way by an Ohio court:

> [P]ublic outrage, and possibly even an effect on admissions at a typical hospital, would surely follow a public announcement by the hospital that it regards all staff doctors as completely independent professionals, conducts no supervision of their performance and takes no interest in their competence. The public assumes, correctly or not, that the hospital exerts some measure of control over the medical activities taking place there.[76]

---

[73]Ferraro and Camarra, supra n.72, at 365.

[74]See Jackson v. Power, 743 P.2d 1367 (Alaska 1987) citing *Mehlman*, 378 A.2d at 1123.

[75]Martell v. St. Charles Hosp., 523 N.Y.S.2d 342, 253 (Sup. 1987) (court dismissed hospital's motion for summary judgment, holding hospital liable for malpractice of emergency room physician based on public policy reasons "without regard for whether the patient has reason not to rely upon the appearance that the physician is a hospital employee").

[76]Hannola v. City of Lakewood, 68 Ohio App. 2d 61, 426 N.E.2d 1187, 1191 (1980).

In Jackson v. Power, the Supreme Court of Alaska declined to apply agency theory, but rather found that the duty of an acute care hospital to provide emergency services was nondelegable due to "public policy" considerations.[77] Thus, public policy required that the facility be liable for the acts of independent emergency room physicians whether or not they were deemed to be the agents of the hospital.

§4.13 Direct Liability

§4.13.1 Negligent Selection and Retention

Physicians. It is almost universally accepted that the healthcare facility has a direct duty to its patients to exercise reasonable care in the selection and retention of its medical staff. Liability for breach of this duty is separate and apart from any vicarious liability that the facility may incur for negligent acts of employed medical staff or for actions of independent, but "apparent," agents or agents engaged in nondelegable duties. The facility will be liable regardless of the employment status of physicians to whom the privilege of performing medical services at the hospital is negligently extended.[1]

In the leading case establishing healthcare facility liability for negligent selection and retention, Joiner v. Mitchell County Hospital Authority, the Georgia Court of Appeals rejected the defendant's argument that the duty to screen candidates was a function of the medical staff, not of the hospital administration.[2] The court noted that the Georgia Health Code authorized the delegation of this duty from the facility to the staff. Medical

---

[77] 743 P.2d 1367 (Alaska 1987).

§4.13 [1] But see Schenck v. Government of Guam, 609 F.2d 387 (9th Cir. 1979) (no liability for failing to review treatment given by a private physician because no duty to review). Note, however, that the duty to review treatment is related to, but not the same as, the duty to hire carefully.

[2] 186 S.E.2d 307 (Ga. Ct. App. 1971) (required hospital to demonstrate more than mere fact physician was licensed to practice medicine and was recommended by staff).

staff, however, are agents of the facility. Thus, the court held the facility liable for the medical staff's negligence in the selection of new member agents.[3] Similarly, in Corleto v. Shore Memorial Hospital,[4] the Superior Court of New Jersey cited general principles of tort and agency in concluding that although (at that time) the independent contract of a physician was a good defense against respondeat superior liability, a hospital is directly liable for its own negligent engagement of an incompetent contractor.

Although *Darling* did not itself deal with the issue of negligent selection and retention of staff, the court in *Darling* used what has become the major tool for demonstrating the duty to reasonably select and retain staff by favorably citing "regulations, standards, and bylaws" as evidence of the standard of care to be exercised by hospitals.[5] By implication, such standards also could be considered as evidence of facility duties in selection and retention of medical staff.

Courts have noted that, in some instances, the governing body of the healthcare facility is actually required to set up regulations for peer review and to refuse privileges to those who do not meet the required standards.[6] Any facility that has such

---

[3]*Joiner*, 186 S.E.2d at 308 (hospital "must act in good faith and with reasonable care in the selection of a physician").

[4]Corleto v. Shore Memorial Hosp., 138 N.J. Super. 302, 350 A.2d 534, 537 (1975), citing Majestic Realty Assocs. v. Toti Contracting Co., 30 N.J. 425, 431, 153 A.2d 321 (1959) and Fiorentino v. Wenger, 19 N.Y.2d 407, 280 N.Y.S.2d 373, 227 N.E.2d 296 (1967). New Jersey Hospital Association's amicus brief filed in *Corleto* at 538 cited JCAHO standards and hospital bylaws in support of leaving such determinations and duties to professionals. Accord *Joiner*, 186 S.E.2d at 308.

[5]*Darling*, 211 N.E.2d at 257 (the court held the jury was properly instructed that such evidence was to be considered but was not conclusive of the standard of care to be exercised).

[6]See Moore v. Board of Trustees of Carson-Tahoe Hosp., 88 Nev. 207, 495 P.2d 605, cert. denied, 409 U.S. 879 (1972) (Supreme Court of Nevada affirmed district court's denial of writ of mandate to restore doctor's privileges and upheld the hospital's actions based on its obligation to set up a system under bylaws to guarantee that the staff continually reviews and evaluates the quality of care being rendered within the institution by regular peer review.)

bylaws is required to follow them.[7] JCAHO standards require that the facility establish a procedure for appointing staff physicians in the bylaws of the governing body.[8] Although not every facility may have such a requirement embodied in its bylaws, JCAHO standards generally are admissible as proof of the standard of care required of both the hospital's board or governing body and its medical staff.[9]

A number of courts in various jurisdictions have enumerated specific procedures that should be performed by the facility in the selection and retention of staff. It is now considered prudent for hospitals to ascertain the qualifications of physicians *prior* to extending privileges by thoroughly checking all representations made on any physician's application for privileges.[10] Failure to investigate such representations constitutes "constructive knowledge" of any erroneous assertions and as such it can render the facility liable if a reasonable hospital armed with such knowledge would not have extended privileges.[11] The facility also is required

---

[7]See, e.g., Purcell v. Zimbelman, 500 P.2d 335 (Ariz. Ct. App. 1972) (citing the Basic Accreditation Requirements of the American Osteopathic Association and the By-Laws of the Professional Staff of Tucson General Hospital in support of the hospital's duty to review competence of staff doctors).

[8]JCAHO, Accreditation Manual for Hospitals §4.1.13, at 43 (1990).

[9]JCAHO standards are not conclusive proof of the standard but may be given presumptive weight. See *Darling*, 211 N.E.2d at 257. Compare Livingston v. Gribetz, 549 F. Supp. 238, 239 (S.D.N.Y. 1982) ("suggested guideline promulgated by health organizations . . . is not to be equated with negligence or considered to have implicated as negligence any omission from any such recommended procedures").

[10]Rule v. Lutheran Hosp. & Homes Socy. of Am., 835 F.2d 1250 (8th Cir. 1987) (applying Nebraska law) (hospital required to check physician qualifications with respect to specific operation for which privileges extended); see also Johnson v. Misericordia Community Hosp., 99 Wis. 2d 708, 301 N.W.2d 156 (1981) (no investigation by hospital of representations in physician's application). Accord Robinson v. Duszynski, 36 N.C. App. 103, 243 S.E.2d 148 (1978) (hospital not liable for punitive damages where reputable agency retained to investigate qualifications of physician). See generally Oakley and Kelly, HMO Liability for Malpractice of Member Physicians: The Case of IPA Model HMOs, XXIV Tort & Ins. L.J. 633 (Spring 1988).

[11]See Purcell v. Zimbelman, 500 P.2d 335 (Ariz. Ct. App. 1972) (evidence of prior malpractice suit against physicians based on similar treatment was

to check a physician's credentials with respect to the particular procedures for which privileges are requested to be extended.[12]

Effective October 14, 1989, in those states that have not legislatively opted out, the Health Care Quality Improvement Act requires the healthcare facility, among other entities, to report all professional review actions that adversely affect the clinical privileges of a physician for longer than 30 days to a federal data bank and provides immunity from liability to the complying facility for such professional review actions under "any law of the United States or of any State."[13] In addition, the Act requires the facility to check with the federal data bank at the time a physician is credentialed and every two years thereafter. In a medical malpractice claim against a healthcare facility, any facility that fails to request such information as required "is presumed to have constructive knowledge" of any information it would have learned had it consulted the registry.[14] An attorney or claimant who has filed a medical malpractice action against a healthcare facility may obtain information regarding a specific healthcare provider only on submitting evidence that the facility failed to request the information as required, and the claimant may only use that information in a

---

sufficient to impute constructive knowledge of surgeon's lack of skill for that treatment). But cf. Hull v. North Valley Hosp., 498 P.2d 136 (Mont. 1972) (hospital not liable when it had no actual knowledge of professional reputation until after negligence of staff member) (representing the minority view).

[12]See *Rule*, 835 F.2d 1250 (court affirmed trial court's finding against hospital for granting special obstetrical privileges without investigating whether doctor was qualified to perform the procedures in question at any of the three hospitals where the doctor previously had privileges. Evidence at trial indicated that investigation would have revealed he was qualified to perform such procedures only under supervision).

[13]42 U.S.C. §11111 et seq. See, e.g., Vankirk v. Board of Trustees of White County Memorial Hosp., No. 91C01-8809-CP-128 (Ind. Cir. Ct.) (filed Nov. 9, 1988) (Indiana legislatively opted in to several provisions under the Health Care Quality Improvement Act; in suit by physician against hospital the court ruled in favor of the hospital, which complied with the Act as an alternative to its existing bylaws).

[14]See 42 U.S.C. §11135.

claim against the facility, not against the healthcare provider.[15]

The fact that a physician performs a high volume of a specific type of operation, absent a showing of negligence in the physician's recommendation or performance of those operations, will not alone create "constructive" knowledge of a problem sufficient to impose liability on the facility for negligent retention of that doctor.[16] A facility that is aware of a physician's performance of an unusually high volume of a certain type of operation and that has reason to believe these operations are unnecessary, however, can be exposed to liability for failing to ensure that the operations are necessary. For example, a hospital whose executive committee became aware that an "inordinate number of craniotomies were being performed on patients whose brain tissue samples indicated no need for such procedures" was found to have breached an independent duty to supervise and review the operating physician despite its oral and written instruction requiring consultation on all craniotomies.[17]

Some courts and commentators have confused the clear duty to periodically review staff credentials and performance to determine whether to continue extending privileges with the highly controversial "duty" to monitor and oversee current treatment rendered by a staff physician.[18] The origination of the

---

[15]See National Practitioner Data Bank for Adverse Information on Physicians and Other Health Care Providers, 54 Fed. Reg. 42722 (1989) (to be codified at 45 C.F.R. pt. 60, §60.11(a)(5)).

[16]See Braden v. Saint Francis Hosp., 714 P.2d 505, 507 (Colo. Ct. App. 1985) (hospital not liable when physician who performed a large number of amputations was not shown to have a record of either negligent or unnecessary performance of them).

[17]See Western Ins. Co. v. Brochner, 682 P.2d 1213, 1217 (Colo. Ct. App. 1983) (hospital liable for breach of an independent duty to supervise and review; court held, however, hospital entitled to complete indemnification by physician), reversed on other grounds, Brochner v. Western Ins. Co., 724 P.2d 1293 (Colo. 1986) (Supreme Court of Colorado reversed on indemnity grounds, abolishing doctrine of indemnity requiring total reimbursement of one joint tortfeasor by another).

[18]See, e.g., Southwick, Hospital Liability: Two Theories Have Been Merged, 4 J. Leg. Med. (1983) (discussing Schenck v. Government of Guam as rejecting duty to exercise care in staff selection when the case itself appears merely to reject a requirement of staff review *simultaneous* with performance of procedure.

so-called duty to monitor and oversee treatment by independent staff physicians is often erroneously attributed to *Darling*, a case in which the physician and nurses involved were employees.[19] Although a North Carolina court seemed to imply a duty to monitor and oversee treatment in an independent contractor setting in 1980, subsequent case law in North Carolina has not supported a duty to monitor treatment.[20]

The view that the facility has a direct duty to monitor and review current treatment is most persistent in the arena of the facility's own recordkeeping procedures. Hospitals occasionally have been found liable for deviation from hospital procedures with respect to recordkeeping and follow-up requirements when such deviation results in a failure to catch a healthcare provider's negligence prior to its causing patient harm.[21] Any claim of facility liability based solely on breach of a duty to oversee *current* medical decisions should be vigorously contested. It is not the majority view.[22]

On the other hand, a healthcare facility does have a

There was no mention of any prior negligence of the physician who enjoyed staff privileges).

[19]See §4.11.2.

[20]See Bost v. Riley, 44 N.C. App. 638, 262 S.E.2d 391, 392 (1980) (though hospital must make "reasonable effort to monitor and oversee treatment," no causation established from hospital's failure to take action against surgeon for failure to make periodic postoperative progress notes). Compare Burns v. Forsyth County Hosp. Auth., 344 S.E.2d 839 (N.C. App. 1986) (stating "it is overly burdensome to impose a legal duty on [a healthcare facility] to read through entire medical records" in affirming dismissal of action against hospital).

[21]See, e.g., Thomas v. United States, 660 F. Supp. 216 (D.D.C. 1987) (hospital liable for failure to keep proper notes of patient's condition). See also Mays v. United States, 608 F. Supp. 1476, (D. Colo. 1985) (army medical center liable for failure to properly maintain records and ensure appropriate followup), reversed on other grounds, 806 F.2d 976 (1986), cert. denied, 107 S. Ct. 3184 (1987); Valcin v. Public Health Trust of Dade County, 473 So. 2d 1297 (Fla. Ct. App. 3d Dist. 1984) (although it is duty of doctor to make operative note, hospital has separate duty to see that records contain surgical notes).

[22]See Illinois case law subsequent to *Darling* discussed supra §4.11.2, nn. 30-33 and accompanying text.

continuing obligation to monitor, review, and oversee trends in the quality of treatment given by a staff physician over time (both within and outside of its facility) in determining whether or not it is appropriate to renew or continue to extend privileges.[23] Although every "incident" may not warrant suspension of privileges, it does warrant close review. In Elam v. College Park Hospital, the facility was denied summary judgment by the court, which noted that the facility had notice of at least one malpractice claim against the physician. The issue of whether or not the requisite standard of peer review was met in light of this fact was remanded for the trier of fact.[24] In Edmonds v. Chamberlain Memorial Hospital, the facility was found not liable for negligent selection or retention of a physician when it initially verified credentials and performance in the physician's residency program and subsequently the physician performed one negligent act. Four months later, after determining the doctor was suffering from mental illness, the facility suspended the physician's privileges. Reviewing physicians indicated by affidavit that there was no indication of incompetency until some time after the negligent act and just prior to suspension.[25]

Once it has suspended privileges, the facility should take great care before reinstating them. One hospital that had initially required and received proof of a physician's qualifications suspended his privileges for medical reasons. The hospital allowed reinstatement only on formal application; it also required an updating of application letters attesting to physical and mental

---

[23]See Elam v. College Park Hosp., 183 Cal. Rptr. 156, 132 Cal. App. 3d 332 (4th Dist. 1982) (court reversed summary judgment in favor of hospital and remanded issue of negligent peer review to jury despite regular committee review of doctor's charts when facility admitted knowledge of at least one malpractice claim against the physician in question). See also JCAHO, Accreditation Manuals for Hospitals §§13.7, 14.6, 18.6, and 22.6 (1990) (setting out requirements of various peer review committees).

[24]Elam, 183 Cal. Rptr. 156.

[25]See Edmonds v. Chamberlain Memorial Hosp., 629 S.W.2d 28 (Tenn. Ct. App. 1981) (court of appeals affirmed summary judgment in favor of hospital on negligent retention grounds but remanded issue of vicarious liability based on physician's agency).

condition to return to work and required a staff physician to sponsor him. These procedures were found to be reasonable, and the hospital was not held liable for the physician's subsequent malpractice.[26]

Nonphysician Employees. In addition to the vicarious liability that the facility may incur for negligent acts of its nonphysician employees, the facility is directly liable for its own negligence in failing to exercise reasonable care when selecting and retaining employees.[27] This responsibility is similar to the duty of care in selecting staff physicians. One of the earliest cases discussing negligent employee selection predates the corporate liability doctrine.[28]

The healthcare facility is required to both have and *follow* regular procedures for investigating the suitability and fitness of employees for the position for which they are retained.[29] This includes some degree of investigation of both personal references and prior employment references[30] as well as some effort to determine whether or not the applicant has any sort of criminal

---

[26]Sheffield v. Zilis, 170 Ga. App. 62, 316 S.E.2d 493 (1984).

[27]See §4.13.1. Employers may escape vicarious liability for intentional acts beyond the scope of employment.

[28]See Hipp v. Hospital Auth. of City of Marietta, 104 Ga. App. 174, 121 S.E.2d 273 (1961) (hospital held liable for negligent employment of orderly when it failed to investigate his record and "moral character") (citing several earlier hospital cases in Georgia).

[29]See Wilson N. Jones Memorial Hosp. v. Davis, 553 S.W.2d 180 (Tex. Ct. App. 1977) (court found disregard of stated hiring practices basis of liability). See also *Hipp,* 121 S.E.2d at 274, citing 29 Am. Jur., Innkeepers, at 49, §60:

> The obligation of the proprietor to protect his patrons from injury or mistreatment includes the duty to select and retain only such employees as are fit and suitable to look after the safety and comfort of his guests and who will not commit acts of violence against them . . ."

[30]See generally Wilson N. Jones Memorial Hosp. v. Davis, 553 S.W.2d 180 (hospital liable for failure to check prior employment and personal references). Compare Focke v. United States, 597 F. Supp. 1325 (D. Kan. 1982) (applying Kansas law) (hospital not liable if hires outside agency to perform reference check and conducts own personal interview).

record that would put the employer on notice of potential harm to patients.[31]

Even though there was no written application or psychological testing, a hospital's personal interview and reliance on a "civil service check" in the hiring of a "social work associate" was sufficient to satisfy its duty to investigate where no evidence of the facility's customary procedures to the contrary was submitted.[32] On the other hand, a hospital that required four employment references and three personal references and whose customary policy was to verify at least one of each was found "recklessly" negligent in hiring an orderly without investigating references until after hiring and without contacting his training institution, despite its justification of a "critical need" for employees and lack of cooperation of certain institutions. The facility was held liable in that case for punitive damages.[33]

In addition to care in selecting, the healthcare facility has a duty to exercise reasonable care in retaining employees. While the facility should be aware of exposure to liability for wrongful discharge,[34] any notice of negligent, reckless, or intentional behavior of employees that could be potentially harmful to a patient should be investigated at once. In Focke v. United States, a social work associate's supervisor testified that "there were two occasions in which he felt [the associate] exhibited poor judgment." In holding the hospital not liable for retention of the employee, the court seemed persuaded by the fact that these incidents were not considered "significant" by the supervisor, that they were subsequently discussed fully with the employee,

---

[31]See *Wilson*, 553 S.W.2d at 182 (hospital liable for failure to investigate criminal record and training of employee where such investigation would have revealed drug problem and lack of skill to perform as an orderly). See also *Hipp*, 104 Ga. App. 174 (hospital liable for failing to investigate criminal record and moral character of orderly where investigation would have revealed conviction of "cursing in public" and history of being a "peeping tom").

[32]See, e.g., *Focke*, 597 F. Supp. 1325 (hospital not negligent in selection or retention of social worker associate who engaged in sexual conduct with family members of client).

[33]*Wilson*, 553 S.W.2d at 183.

[34]See Chapter 2.

and that all evidence of his sexual contact with the patient's family had been carefully concealed from the hospital by the employee.[35] In a case alleging vicarious liability of a healthcare facility for the sexual acts of an orderly, the court noted favorably the discharge of the employee after timely investigation and verification of the conduct by a third-party witness.[36]

§4.13.2 Selection of Equipment, Supplies, and Devices

"The duty of provide safe and proper equipment is analogous to and equally compelling as the long standing requirement that a charitable institution exercise due care in the selection and retention of its employees."[37] This direct duty is nondelegable and its breach also constitutes direct "corporate negligence."[38]

The traditional standard for reasonable care in the selection and supply of equipment is one of usual and customary practice. Under this standard, hospitals have been found negligent for failure to supply "properly working oxygen supply,"[39] failure to have a cardiac stimulator available,[40] failure to separate sterile and unsterile items in an equipment cabinet,[41] failure to have

---

[35]See *Focke*, 597 F. Supp. at 1347 (facility not liable for negligent retention of the employee).

[36]Taylor v. Doctors Hosp. (West), 486 N.E.2d 1249 1250 (Ohio Ct. App. 1985) (respondeat superior, not negligent retention, was the issue expressly addressed by the court).

[37]Starnes v. Charlotte-Mecklenburg Hosp. Auth., 28 N.C. App. 418, 421, 221 S.E.2d 733, 736 (1976). See also Milner v. Huntsville Memorial Hosp., 398 S.W.2d 647, 648 (Tex. Civ. App. 1966).

[38]See Davidson v. Methodist Hosp. of Dallas, 348 S.W.2d 400 (Tex. Ct. App. 1961).

[39]Bellaire Gen. Hosp. v. Campbell, 510 S.W.2d 94 (Tex. Ct. App. 1974).

[40]Id.

[41]Suburban Hosp. Assn. v. Hadary, 22 Md. App. 186, 322 A.2d 258 (Md. Ct. Spec. App. 1974) (as a result of a facility practice, patient had to undergo painful treatment to protect against infection because not known whether sterile or unsterile item was used). See also Peck v. Charles B. Towns Hosp., 275 A.D. 302, 89 N.Y.S.2d 190 (1949) (hospital liable for failure to sterilize hypodermic needles by steam under pressure).

access to an endotracheal tube in the emergency room,[42] and failure to repair equipment.[43] Conversely, the facility was not liable for the selection of a hot water bottle heating device that burned a baby during surgery, despite the fact that safer heating devices (such as heating blankets) could have been used.[44] Similarly, there was no breach of the facility's duty to provide safe equipment when a baby was burned in a nondefective incubator that used an unshielded bulb not controlled by a thermostat.[45]

It has been argued that the facility may become subject to "reasonable prudence" standards that impose a duty to protect from foreseeable harm presented by equipment under the Supreme Court of Washington's analysis in Helling v. Carey.[46] Under the "reasonable prudence" standard, a healthcare facility would be subject to liability for using equipment that causes a foreseeable harm whether or not the equipment is the standard, customary model used by similar facilities in similar communities.[47] The increased use of JCAHO standards, bylaws, regulations, and rules as evidence of the standard of reasonable care

---

[42]Garcia v. Memorial Hosp., 557 S.W.2d 859 (Tex. Ct. App. 1977) (access to the equipment might have saved child's life).

[43]Berg v. United States, 806 F.2d 978 (10th Cir. 1986) (applying Colorado law) (healthcare facility liable for failure of previously failing cerebral angiogram equipment absent evidence of repair).

[44]Starnes, 28 N.C. App. 418, (no showing equipment was defective nor showing heating blankets customarily used by other hospitals).

[45]Emory Univ. v. Porter, 103 Ga. App. 752, 120 S.E.2d 668 (1961) (action dismissed because no allegation that the incubator was defective for purposes intended despite fact that thermostatically controlled incubators existed).

[46]See Southwick, Hospital Liability: Two Theories Have Been Merged, 4 J. Legal Med. (1983) citing Helling v. Carey, 83 Wash. 2d 514, 519 P.2d 981 (1974) (an often-cited medical malpractice case requiring duty to protect from foreseeable harm as opposed to the status quo (customary standard of care) in glaucoma testing).

[47]See, e.g., Vuono v. New York Blood Center, 696 F. Supp. 743 (D. Mass. 1988) (in denying the summary judgment motion of a healthcare facility that argued compliance with federal and industry standards, the court noted industry custom is inconclusive on the issue of negligence because a whole industry may be lagging in responsible standards and a "reasonable prudence" standard should be imposed).

may further operate to require hospitals to supply equipment that exceeds "customary" equipment in some areas.[48]

Finally, although the majority of jurisdictions are still reluctant to extend strict liability for defective products and services to healthcare facilities on the grounds that they are not sellers of products,[49] there is a growing number of cases that have imposed strict liability under certain circumstances in the healthcare facility setting.[50] There are also cases that suggest the facility may be strictly liable for "administrative" (as opposed to "medical") services,[51] thereby reviving the relevance of the traditional distinctions "abolished" in Bing v. Thunig.[52]

---

[48]See Perdue, Direct Corporate Liability of Hospitals: A Modern Day Legal Concept of Liability for Injury Occurring in the Modern Day Hospital, 24 S. Tex. L.J. 773, at 790 (1983).

[49]See, e.g., Hector v. Cedars-Sinai Medical Center, 225 Cal. Rptr. 595, 180 Cal. App. 3d 493 (2d Dist. 1986) (facility not liable for allegedly defective pacemaker because not a seller of product, but a provider of medical services); Dubin v. Michael Reese Hosp. & Medical Center, 83 Ill. 2d 277, 415 N.E.2d 350 (1980) (reversing lower court holding that strict liability was applicable to supplying of blood); Silverhart v. Mount Zion Hosp., 98 Cal. Rptr. 187, 20 Cal. App. 3d 1022 (1st Dist. 1971).

[50]See, e.g., Kirk v. Michael Reese Hosp. & Medical Center, 483 N.E.2d 906, 913 (Ill. Ct. App. 1st Dist. 1985) (court held hospital strictly liable for unreasonably dangerous conditions of drugs as opposed to medical decision to administer them); Skelton v. Druid City Hosp. Bd., 459 So. 2d 818 (Ala. 1984) (hospital liable for "breach of warranty" when suture needle broke); Thomas v. St. Joseph Hosp., 618 S.W.2d 791 (Tex. Civ. App. 1st Dist. 1981) (hospital construed as being seller of inflammable gown in which patient burned to death); Providence Hosp. v. Truly, 611 S.W.2d 127 (Tex. Civ. App. 1980) (facility strictly liable for contaminated fluid used by staff physician that came from hospital pharmacy).

[51]See Hoven v. Kelble, 79 Wis. 2d 444, 256 N.W.2d 379 (1977) (Supreme Court of Wisconsin implied that strict liability may be permitted only for mechanical or administrative services and not professional ones), citing Johnson v. Sears, Roebuck & Co., 355 F. Supp. 1065 (E.D. Wis. 1973). See also Grubb v. Albert Einstein Medical Center, 255 Pa. Super. 381, 387 A.2d 480 (1978) (court held facility strictly liable for the "administrative service" of supplying a defective surgical tool).

[52]2 N.Y.2d 656, 163 N.Y.S.2d 3, 143 N.E.2d 3 (N.Y. 1957). See also §4.12.2.1, supra, text and accompanying nn. 5-8.

§4.13.3 Design, Maintenance, and Security of the Physical Plant

The liability of the healthcare facility for negligence in facility upkeep is based on the fundamental tort principle that property owners are obligated to keep their premises in a "reasonably safe condition for the expected use" of invitees.[53] Some states prescribe statutory standards of care for the facility in the area of maintenance of the physical plant.[54]

As part of the duty to safely maintain the premises, the healthcare facility is obligated to warn patients and other invitees of all hidden dangers of which it has actual or constructive knowledge. Although the facility generally is not liable for failure to warn patients of *obvious* dangers,[55] it is required to exercise care to protect patients from *reasonably foreseeable* hidden dangers.[56]

Serious risk of harm to a patient has been considered reasonably foreseeable when a hospital allowed another patient to keep scissors near her bed, despite the fact that that patient

---

[53]See, e.g., Methodist Hosp. of Ind. v. Rioux, 438 N.E.2d 315 (Ind. Ct. App. 4th Dist. 1982) (hospital liable for failure to keep premises in good condition); Hill v. Walker Memorial Hosp., 407 F.2d 1036 (4th Cir. 1969) (applying N.C. law) (hospital has duty to exercise reasonable care for safety of patients). See also Perdue, supra n.48, at 789-790, citing Charrin v. Methodist Hosp., 432 S.W.2d 572, 574 (Tex. Civ. App. 1968). See generally W. Prosser and W. P. Keeton, The Law of Torts, §61, at 419-432 (5th ed. 1984).

[54]See, e.g., Tex. Rev. Civ. Stat. Ann. at 4442c, §7(a)(1), (3), (5), and (6) (Vernon Supp. 1989) (authorizing licensing agency to set standards for construction, maintenance, and equipment in nursing homes).

[55]See, e.g., Durrance v. Bacon County Hosp. Auth., 321 S.E.2d 767, 172 Ga. App. 1 (1984) (hospital not liable for failing to warn of uneven sidewalk equally obvious to plaintiff); Prevette v. Wilkes Gen. Hosp. 37 N.C. App. 425, 246 S.E.2d 91 (1978) (where defects in ramp should have been apparent to anyone, jury could find contributory negligence); Charrin v. Methodist Hosp., 432 S.W.2d 572 (Tex. Civ. App. 1968) (hospital not liable for failure to warn patient of unconcealed television cord).

[56]See, e.g., Clinton v. City of New York, 528 N.Y.S.2d 108, 109 (N.Y. App. Div. 1988).

had no history of mental disturbance.[57] On the other hand, injury was not considered to be reasonably foreseeable when a potentially disturbed patient who was transferred to a hospital "for the sake of his nerves" threw a chair at another patient.[58] The most logical explanation for this discrepancy in the interpretation of foreseeability is in its focus on the ordinary use of the instrument of injury rather than on the dangerous propensity of the third party.

Finally, as to the adequacy of the facilities themselves, healthcare facilities appear to have a duty to exercise reasonable care in providing emergency backup facilities in the event that their customary facilities prove inadequate.[59] A healthcare facility has been held liable for failing to warn a pregnant patient of its inability to perform caesarean sections and its failure to have in place backup arrangements at alternative facilities in the event a patient should require them.[60]

§4.13.4 Innovative (Nonstandard) Therapies

Although medical science would not advance without the use of innovative modes of therapy,[61] the traditional standard for malpractice is based on *customary*, rather than nonstandard, practice. Thus, the healthcare facility must deal with the tension between encouraging development in medical science and prudence in the treatment of patients. Courts are reluctant to impose an absolute duty on the facility to provide nonstandard therapy, but they do generally require that they not block access to it.[62]

---

[57]Id.

[58]Burns v. Forsyth County Hosp. Auth. 344 S.E.2d 839 (N.C. App. 1986) (court did not require facility to read all records of transferee and seemed to focus on the ordinary nature of the instrument of injury).

[59]Wade v. John D. Archbold Memorial Hosp., 166 Ga. App. 487, 304 S.E.2d 417 (1983), reversed. 252 Ga. 118, 311 S.E.2d 836, on remand, 318 S.E.2d 839 (1984) (hospital has duty to provide facilities reasonably suited to general use in similar circumstances).

[60]See, e.g., Hernandez v. Smith, 552 F.2d 142 (5th Cir. 1977).

[61]See generally, Fried, Medical Experimentation 4 (1974).

[62]See Chapter 6.

Direct and vicarious liability for negligence relating to utilization of nonstandard and experimental treatment, however, is a threat to the facility that can take various forms.[63]

The most obvious type of liability can arise from adopting a mode of treatment whose effect is so uncertain that its application constitutes an "experiment." Although all medical treatment is to some extent uncertain, the National Commission for the Protection of Human Subjects of Biomedical and Behavioral Research (Commission on Biomedical Research) distinguishes experimentation from therapeutic "practice" by its purpose to test a hypothesis.[64] Experimentation is separately defined as using "the human as the subject, not as a patient" for purposes of structured research (as opposed to therapy).[65] Although formal distinctions between therapeutic innovation and experimentation suggest the existence of a structured experimental design, in reality such distinctions are not so easy to make.

According to the Commission on Biomedical Research, healthcare facilities could be liable for drastically innovative therapies even if they are not the subject of a formal design:

> Radically new procedures . . . should . . . be made the object of formal research at an early stage in order to determine whether they are safe and effective. Thus it is the responsibility of medical practice committees for example to insist that a major innovation be incorporated into a formal research project.[66]

If an innovative therapy is the subject of formal research, the facility clearly has a duty to regulate the parameters of that

---

[63]See generally Cowan and Bertsch, Innovative Therapy: The Responsibility of Hospitals, 33 Def. L.J. 623-653 (1984).

[64]Id., citing The Belmont Report: Ethical Principles and Guidelines for the Protection of Human Subjects of Research (hereinafter Belmont Report) (DHEW Pub. No. (OS) 78-0012) (1978).

[65]Ladimer, Ethical and Legal Aspects of Medical Research on Human Beings, 3 J. Pub. L. 467, 472 (1954).

[66]See Belmont Report, at 3-4, quoted in Cowan and Bertsch, supra n.63, at 628. See also Fortner v. Koch, 272 Mich. 273, 261 N.W. 762 (1935) (therapeutic experimentation must not vary too radically from accepted method).

experimentation through institutional review boards (IRBs).[67] IRBs are required to approve and review all experiments involving human subjects.[68] The facility is obligated to review innovative therapy that is not part of a formal research project to ensure that any systematic variation from accepted therapy is detected by its practice area peer review committees.[69] Healthcare facilities are thus directly liable for establishing IRBs to review experimentation and to be sure that ongoing "therapeutic" experimentation is incorporated into formal projects.

Aside from this ongoing monitoring function, healthcare facilities generally are not liable for an independent physician's own negligent choice to adopt a nonstandard therapy in a given situation unless such choices become a pattern.[70] The facility is not liable for a physician's failure to obtain properly informed consent for an innovative therapy.[71] The rationale for not imposing such liability is found in Fiorentino v. Wenger:

> [T]he hospital does not share . . . in the responsibility to advise patients of the novelty and risks attendant on the procedure. . . . Nor is it desirable, as a matter of public policy, that more and more hospitals (and the better ones are more likely to do so than the inferior ones) should either close their doors to, or by interventions discourage, less conventional or even experimental operations.[72]

Thus, the healthcare facility should not discourage physicians from conducting innovative procedures within it, but

---

[67]The amount of federal support and the ultimate use of the results of the research may invoke certain federal statutes. The federal Food, Drug and Cosmetic Act (FDCA) (21 U.S.C. §301 eq seq.) regulatory provisions for protection of human subjects can be found at 46 Fed. Reg. 8950 et seq. (1981) and IRBs at 46 Fed. Reg. 8975 et seq. (1981).

[68]Id.

[69]See Cowan and Bertsch, supra n.63, at 651-654.

[70]See Fiorentino v. Wenger, 19 N.Y.S.2d 407, 280 N.Y.S.2d 373 (1967) (hospital not liable for physician's failure to advise patient of risks incumbent in spinal-jack operation).

[71]See Chapter 7 generally.

[72]*Fiorentino*, 280 N.Y.S.2d at 380.

should set up appropriate monitoring and review boards to ensure that nonstandard treatment that borders on experimentation is incorporated into a controlled and approved design.

§4.13.5 Liability of Trustees or Directors

Overview. Most healthcare facilities, whether for-profit or non-for-profit, are separate corporate entities. Directors of a for-profit facility are elected by, and are accountable to, the shareholders of the corporation.[73] The not-for-profit facility does not generally have shareholders, but some state statutes authorize the election of the facility's directors by shareholder equivalents, or "members" of the corporation, who do not receive dividends.[74] If there are no "members," directors may be appointed initially by the incorporators of the facility and thereafter through a method set forth in its bylaws.[75] Directors of both incorporated and unincorporated not-for-profit organizations are sometimes referred to as "trustees."[76] There is no legal distinction between a trustee and a director of an *incorporated* not-for-profit organization. Moreover, there is a trend toward fewer distinctions between directors and true trustees of traditional charitable trusts for the *unincorporated* healthcare facility as well.

The scope of the facility's board's duties and responsibilities generally is defined in its charter and bylaws in combination with state statutes and accreditation requirements. Less commonly, the deed of trust for a charitable trust defines those duties. Whether composed of trustees or directors, healthcare

---

[73]See Chapter 14 for a discussion of the healthcare facility and corporate governance.

[74]See, e.g., Pa. Stat. Ann. tit. 15 §7752 (Purdon Supp. 1988); N.Y. Not-For-Profit Corp. Law §601 (McKinney 1970 and Supp. 1984-1985), cited in MacDonald, Meyer, and Essig, Health Care Law: A Practical Guide §2.04[1] (1988) (authorizing certain nondividend receiving "members" to perform some shareholder functions).

[75]See H. Oleck, Nonprofit Corporations, Organizations and Associations §7, at 32 (4th ed. 1980).

[76]Id. §213, at 590.

facility boards are required to set out long-range fiscal and operational goals including goals for raising capital and maintaining the facility. They have the additional responsibilities of setting up bylaws to govern the medical staff and quality assurance or peer review boards and approving or terminating of members of the medical staff.[77]

The directors of a not-for-profit healthcare facility are required to perform the same fiduciary duties of loyalty and care in administering their responsibilities as board members of any other corporation.[78] The lead case in establishing not-for-profit facility director liability for breach of those duties is Beard v. Achenbach Memorial Hospital Association.[79] In applying corporate standards to the performance of fiduciary duties at a not-for-profit hospital, the Court of Appeals for the Tenth Circuit held that

> [t]he directors of a corporation are charged with the duty of managing its affairs honestly and in good faith, and they must *exercise ordinary and reasonable care* in the performance of their duties. They must *act with fidelity to the interests of the corporation*, and they are jointly and severally liable for losses of the corporation proximately resulting from bad faith, fraudulent breaches of trust, or gross or willful negligence in the discharge of their duties.[80]

At one time, "trustees" of charitable public hospitals also were obligated to preserve the trust and to refrain from engaging in potentially "interested" transactions absent approval of the beneficiaries. Because there is no one beneficiary legally possessed of an enforceable entitlement, it was often impossible to

---

[77]JCAHO, Accreditation Manual for Hospitals §4.1, at 41-44 (1990). See also case law cited in §4.13 on liability for negligent selection and retention of staff.

[78]See H. Oleck, supra n.75, §213, at 591-592. See also D. Kurtz, Board Liability: Guide for Nonprofit Directors 23 (1988).

[79]170 F.2d 859 (10th Cir. 1948) (applying Kansas law) (not-for-profit corporation had been set up to manage, operate, and control public hospital per testamentary trust).

[80]Id. at 862 (emphasis supplied).

obtain "approval" of the beneficiaries of a public charitable hospital.[81] Today, it has been argued that "trustees" of not-for-profit charitable corporations and trusts should be bound by the same standard in performing their duties as for-profit corporate directors[82] and should not be subject to the full obligations of trustees.

The Duty of Care. The standard for both for-profit and not-for-profit healthcare facility directors in exercising the "duty of care" is established in a majority of states by statute. Statutory duties of care usually require that the director or trustee act in good faith and act with the care that an ordinarily prudent person in a similar position would use under similar circumstances.[83] Courts usually apply similar standards in the absence of state statutes.[84]

---

[81]See Moody, State Statutes Governing Directors of Charitable Organizations, 18 U.S.F.L. Rev. 749, 795-756 (1984), citing Hone, Position Paper Prepared for Committee on Nonprofit Corporation Law, ABA Section of Corporations, Business, and Banking Law (1980).

[82]See H. Oleck, supra n.75, at 612, n.26a and Moody, supra n.81, at 755-756, both citing Stern v. Lucy Webb Hayes Natl. Training School for Deaconesses and Missionaries, 381 F. Supp. 1003 (D.D.C. 1974) (applying D.C. law) (discussed in the following section). See also D. Kurtz, supra n.78, at 22-23 (1988) (all statutes that provide standard for not-for-profit directors and nearly all cases dealing with the subject apply corporate, as opposed to trust standards, to not-for-profit directors). Compare Note, A Call to Reform the Duties of Directors Under State Not-For-Profit Corporation Statutes, 72 Iowa L. Rev. 725 (1987) (suggesting higher standard should be required of public benefit nonprofit corporation directors, as opposed to mutual benefit corporations, because of lack of body of enforcing "members"); Lynch v. Redfield, 88 Cal. Rptr. 86, 9 Cal. App. 3d 293 (2d Dist. 1970) (the only case that imposes liability on not-for-profit directors by applying trust standard).

[83]See, e.g., Cal. Corp. Code §309(a) (West 1977 & Supp. 1989); Wash. Rev. Code Ann. §4.24.264 (1988); W. Va. Code §55-7C-3 (Supp. 1988) (not-for-profit standards).

[84]See, e.g., *Stern*, 381 F. Supp. 1003 (lead case establishing standard for liability at not-for-profit private charitable hospital). See also Beard v. Achenbach Memorial Hosp. Assn., 170 F.2d 859 (10th Cir. 1948) (applying Kansas law) (court held not-for-profit public hospital directors to ordinary and reasonable standard of care and good faith in carrying out interests of facility).

The duty of care imposes an affirmative duty to manage the facility and to exercise due care in making judgments. At a minimum, this requires that the director or trustee attend enough board meetings to keep abreast of the general affairs of the facility in order to oppose any actions that are not in its best interests and to supervise any activities or committees for which he or she is directly responsible.[85] Total abdication of these duties may subject a director to liability for nonmanagement.[86]

Directors and trustees may delegate certain of their responsibilities to others.[87] In addition, directors may rely on competent expert advice and generally will not be held personally liable for such good-faith reliance.[88] Directors and trustees are, however, charged with knowledge of all information that would have been obtained had the director discharged his or her duties diligently.[89] Though special functions of board members may be taken into account in judging diligence (e.g., being a fund-raising director as opposed to an attorney director), no special consideration is given to "nominal" directors who hold positions primarily based on contributions or position in the community.[90]

The healthcare facility's directors and trustees are subject

---

[85]See Kurtz, supra n.78, at 26 (1988) (although this duty of attendance is not explicitly set out by statute, it is noted in case law).

[86]See, e.g., *Stern*, 381 F. Supp. at 1014. See also N.Y. Not-For-Profit Corp. Law §719(b) (McKinney 1970) (imposing liability on directors for unlawful actions of board with which they do not formally dissent).

[87]See, e.g., N.Y. Not-For-Profit Corp. Law §717 (McKinney 1970 & Supp. 1989) (authorizing reliance and delegation for certain investment functions). But see N.Y. Not-For-Profit Corp. Law §712(a) (McKinney 1970) (setting out fundamental corporate changes, bylaw amendments, and modification of member rights as nondelegable functions).

[88]See, e.g., Ohio Rev. Code Ann. §1702 et seq. (Anderson 1985); N.Y. Not-For-Profit Corp. Law §717(b) (McKinney 1970). See also Revised Model Nonprofit Corporation Act (RMNCA) §8.30(b) (Exposure Draft 1986).

[89]See, e.g., *Stern*, 381 F. Supp. at 1014.

[90]See, e.g., Ray v. Homewood Hosp., 27 N.W.2d 409, 411 (Minn. 1947) (court affirmed invalidity of incorporators' agreement for two nominal director spots, stating no director can be merely nominal. Incorporator's bargain was found invalid for self-dealing as well). See also Kurtz, supra n.78, at 26 (suggesting board membership not be offered as a mechanism for recognition of benefactors).

to the standard fiduciary obligations of all corporate directors. They are to exercise the care of an ordinarily prudent person in similar circumstances.[91] Under the "business judgment" rule, courts scrutinize the decisionmaking process of directors and trustees to see that they act in good faith and on an informed basis. The merits of the decision, however, usually will not be reviewed.[92] Directors can be held personally liable for the extreme conduct involved in acts of fraud, improper motive, or personal interest.[93]

The leading case dealing with a trustee's breach of a fiduciary duty at a not-for-profit private charitable hospital is Stern v. Lucy Webb Hayes National Training School for Deaconesses and Missionaries.[94] In *Stern*, the entire board was charged with mismanagement, nonmanagement, and self-dealing for failing to scrutinize the investment of a substantial amount of hospital funds in low- and non-interest-bearing accounts at financial institutions with which certain trustees had affiliations. The *Stern* court adopted what it called the "modern" trend to apply corporate rather than trust principles in determining the liability of directors of charitable corporations because their functions were virtually indistinguishable from those of their "pure" corporate counterparts.[95] Applying a modified standard based on the hospital's own recently adopted bylaws, the court held that a director must perform his or her duties "honestly,

---

[91]See, e.g., Ga. Code Ann. §14-3-13 (1982); La. Rev. Stat. Ann. §12:226 (West 1969); Minn. Stat. Ann. §317.20(6) (West 1969).

[92]See, e.g., Beard v. Achenbach Memorial Hosp. Assn., 170 F.2d 859, 862-863 (10th Cir. 1948) (no liability for good-faith decision, even if poor one, absent "gross or willful negligence" or "reckless" "extravagant" expenditure). See generally Block, Barton, and Radin, The Business Judgment Rule: Fiduciary Duties of Corporate Directors and Officers 1-20 (2d ed. 1988).

[93]See, e.g., Stern v. Lucy Webb Hayes Natl. Training School for Deaconesses and Missionaries, 381 F. Supp. 1003, 1014-1015 (D.D.C. 1974) (although directors and trustees can be personally liable for self-dealing, court ordered monitoring sanctions on self-dealing directors in this case). See also Ohio Rev. Code Ann. §1702 et seq. (Anderson 1985) (imposing fine for false statements or reports of directors).

[94]*Stern*, 381 F. Supp. 1003 (D.D.C. 1974).

[95]Id. at 1013.

in good faith, and with a reasonable amount of diligence and care"[96]—the same standard to which any corporate director is held.[97]

The Duty of Loyalty.   In addition to exercising due care and diligence, directors and trustees must act in the best interests of the healthcare facility rather than in their own. This duty most commonly arises when there is a transaction between the hospital and a director or trustee or a company in which the director or trustee has an interest.[98] At common law, these transactions were automatically void. Today, corporate statutes in the majority of states permit some of these transactions in special circumstances.[99] The typical statute dealing with interested transactions allows those transactions that: (1) are approved by some number of disinterested directors on the board or (2) on the merits are fair and reasonable to the hospital.[100]

Courts have adopted similar approaches to the problem of transactions between the healthcare facility and a director.[101] In

---

[96]Id. at 1015.

[97]See Block, et al., supra n.92, at 1-20.

[98]See, e.g., *Stern*, 381 F. Supp. 1003 (D.D.C. 1974) (applying D.C. law) (directors alleged to have breached duty of loyalty by placing large amounts of hospital funds in low- or non-interest bearing accounts at banks with which they were affiliated).

[99]See E. Brodsky and M. Adamski, Law of Corporate Officers and Directors §3.01 (1984). See, e.g., Fla. Stat. Ann. §617.641 (West 1977); Nev. Rev. Stat. §81.630 (1986); N.J. Stat. Ann. §15A:6-8 (West 1984); N.Y. Not-For-Profit Corp. Law §715 (McKinney 1977). See also Block, et al., supra n.92, Appendix E (listing the 45 states that have enacted interested director statutes—all but Alaska, Massachusetts, Mississippi, South Dakota, and Utah, as well as the District of Columbia).

[100]See, e.g., Del. Code Ann. tit. 8, §144. According to Block, et al., supra n.92, Appendix E, at 587, some 31 states have statutes based on the Delaware interested transaction statute.

[101]See, e.g., Virginia Mason Hosp. Assn. v. Larson, 9 Wash. 2d 284, 114 P.2d 976, 983 (1941) (court noted favorably the substantial number of debts forgiven by potentially interested physician-directors in approving transaction transferring title of formerly for-profit facility (which owed funds to directors) to not-for-profit corporation. As a whole, court found transaction was fair and reasonable to not-for-profit corporation).

Stern, the court stated that in order to be upheld the interested transaction must be fair, the conflict of interest must be disclosed to the board, and the transaction must be approved by the disinterested directors.[102]

D. Alternative Dispute Resolution (ADR)

§4.14 Overview

Several states have enacted various statutory schemes involving alternative dispute resolution in the medical malpractice setting in response to the rising costs of healthcare delivery attributable to insuring against medical malpractice litigation costs. Although ADR has many critics, it continues to be advocated as a weapon against the high cost of malpractice claims.[1] These ADR statutory schemes take various forms, but they can be divided into two general categories: (1) standards for agreement by the parties to submit disputes to some form of binding arbitration and (2) requirements for preliminary review of malpractice claims by boards or screening panels with the panel's decision usually not binding (although it may be admissible at a subsequent trial).

§4.15 Arbitration

Potential parties to medical malpractice litigation may agree to settle any disputes that arise between them through arbitration

---

[102]*Stern*, 381 F. Supp. at 1015-1016 (holding that the trustees breached their fiduciary duties by failing to disclose self-dealing and failing to monitor the growth of investments made in accounts at banks with which they were affiliated).

§4.14 [1]See Alternative Dispute Resolution Report, vol. 1, at 9 (BNA) (April 30, 1987) (ADR limited weapon against the high cost of malpractice claims). See also Margolick, Mediation Isn't Cure for Patients' Claims, 1980 Natl. L.J. 1.

rather than litigation. There are two general categories of arbitration agreements. One is between the facility and the patient and may cover physician providers on the facility's staff as well. The other is negotiated by a third-party healthcare plan insurer to cover any disputes that may arise between the subscribers and the providers.

In order to enforce an arbitration clause, the healthcare facility must show that the patient knew and understood the rights she was waiving in signing the agreement to arbitrate. Without such a showing, the agreement between patient and facility may be voided as a contract of adhesion.[1] Arbitration agreements embodied in healthcare plans usually are upheld because they were freely negotiated and entered into by knowledgeable employers on behalf of their employees.[2]

In Wheeler v. St. Joseph Hospital, the court held that there is no public policy against arbitration agreements between a patient and a hospital. The particular agreement was voided, however, because it was buried in a hospital admission form and was to be "effective" unless the patient initialed the form to indicate nonagreement or sent written communication of nonagreement to hospital within 30 days. Thus, the court found

---

§4.15 [1]See, e.g., Wheeler v. St. Joseph Hosp., 133 Cal. Rptr. 775, 63 Cal. App. 3d 345 (1976) (court held arbitration agreement placed inconspicuously in hospital admission form was unenforceable because lack of clarity of purpose and lack of explanation rendered it a contract of adhesion); Obstetrics and Gynecologists v. Pepper, 101 Nev. 105, 693 P.2d 1259 (Nev. 1985) (arbitration agreement unenforceable when terms of contract not explained to patient); Sanchez v. Sirmons, 121 Misc. 2d 249, 467 N.Y.S.2d 757 (Super. Ct. 1983) (arbitration agreement inconspicuously placed in form entitled "consent to abortion" was voidable).

[2]See, e.g., Madden v. Kaiser Found. Hosp., 17 Cal. 3d 699, 131 Cal. Rptr. 882, 552 P.2d 1178 (1976) (court upheld group insurance contract negotiated by state agency and hospital on behalf of state employees); Wilson v. Kaiser Found. Hosps., 190 Cal. Rptr. 649, 141 Cal. App. 3d 891 (1983) (newborn infant's claims subject to arbitration agreement embodied in group health plan of mother, which provided that all newborn infants of group members become group members at birth). Compare Benyon v. Garden Grove Medical Group, 161 Cal. Rptr. 146, 100 Cal. App. 3d 698 (4th Dist. 1980) (certain provisions of group arbitration agreement that were never called to subscribers' attention were unenforceable).

it to be an unenforceable contract of adhesion. The court reasoned that, in order to be binding, the clause must be called to the attention of the patient and explained.[3]

In an effort to establish standards for binding arbitration, several states have enacted "arbitration acts."[4] The schemes set forth in these arbitration statutes vary in their provisions. Most schemes provide for voluntary arbitration.[5] A few schemes provide for some form of "arbitration" as a mandatory prerequisite to traditional litigation. These schemes actually more closely resemble preliminary review boards, discussed in the next section.[6] The results of the arbitration may be binding[7] or merely advisory.[8] As a general rule, schemes that provide for

---

[3]*Wheeler,* 133 Cal. Rptr. 775.

[4]See, e.g., Ala. Code §6-5-485 (1988) (providing for voluntary, binding agreements to settle disputes by arbitration in medical liability actions); Alaska Stat. §09.55.535 et seq. (1988) (providing for voluntary arbitration by agreements revocable up to 30 days and then binding); Cal. [Civ. Proc.] Code §1295 (West 1989) (setting out valid contract provisions for binding arbitration of medical malpractice); Ill. Rev. Stat. ch. 10, ¶201 et seq. (Smith-Hurd Supp. 1989) (detailed Health Care Arbitration Act provides requirements for binding arbitration agreements); Mich Comp. Laws §27A.5040 et seq. (1975) (sets out extensive procedures for binding arbitration clauses and agreements); N.Y. Civ. Prac. L. & R. 7550 (Consol. 1989) (Health Care Arbitration Act provides for voluntary arbitration of claims, binding if by agreement); Ohio Rev. Code Ann. §2711.21 et seq. (1987 Supp.) (as amended) (arbitration board to hear medical claims by agreement—nonbinding); S.D. Codified Laws Ann. §21-25B-1 (1987) (providing for binding arbitration agreements relating to medical services, revocable to future services); Vt. Stat. Ann. tit. 12, §7001, et seq. (Supp. 1989) (voluntary arbitration).

[5]See, e.g., Alaska Stat. §09.55.535 et seq. (1988); N.Y. Civ. Prac. L. & R. 7550 (Consol. 1989); and Ohio Rev. Code Ann. §2711.21 et seq. (1987 Supp.) (as amended).

[6]See, e.g., Fla. Stat. Ann. §768.575 (West Supp. 1988) (mandatory notice of claim, period of negotiation and court-ordered "arbitration" at the request of either party); Haw. Rev. Stat. §671-11 et seq. (1976) (provides for nonbinding mandatory medical claim conciliation panels); Md. Cts. & Jud. Proc. Code Ann. §3-2A-01 et seq. (1987) (Maryland Uniform Arbitration Act provides for "arbitration" via preliminary review panel minitrials).

[7]See, e.g., Cal. [Civ. Proc.] Code §1295 (1975); Ill. Rev. Stat., ch. 10, ¶201 et seq. (1976); Mich. Comp. Laws §27A.5040 et seq. (1975).

[8]See, e.g., Ohio Rev. Code Ann. §2711.21 et seq. (Page 1975 and 1987 Supp.) (as amended).

voluntary binding arbitration have been upheld,[9] but mandatory arbitration-preliminary review schemes, even when nonbinding, may not survive judicial scrutiny.[10]

Courts have enforced binding arbitration schemes that contain the following elements:

- agreements must either be set forth in a document separate from the hospital admission form or, if in the admission form, in a conspicuous typeface;
- the matters at stake must be explained to the patient, or the patient must be given adequate time to read the agreement prior to signing; and
- there must be an adequate period after discharge to revoke the agreement.[11]

Parents and other agents, such as employers, may negotiate binding arbitration agreements on behalf of third parties, provided that they have met with all other statutory requirements.[12]

---

[9]See, e.g., Mich. Comp. Laws §27A.5040 et seq. (1975), referred to favorably by court in Stefani v. Bhagat, 149 Mich. App. 431, 386 N.W.2d 203 (1986); Cal. [Civ. Proc] Code §1295 (1975), cited favorably by court in Wheeler v. St. Joseph Hosp., 133 Cal. Rptr. 775, 63 Cal. App. 3d 345 (1976) (enacted after action arose). See also Annotation, Arbitration of Medical Malpractice Claims, 84 A.L.R.3d 375 (1978) (such statutes are generally upheld if they require sufficient evidence of voluntary agreement in order to be binding). See also Annot., Medical Malpractice Reform Statutes, 80 A.L.R.3d 583 (1977).

[10]See, e.g., Simon v. St. Elizabeth Medical Center, 3 Ohio Op. 3d 164, 355 N.E.2d 903 (Ct. C.P. 1976) (holding Ohio compulsory nonbinding mediation was a violation of the right to jury trial, which the Ohio Constitution provided "shall be inviolate"). The Ohio statute was later amended to provide for voluntary, rather than compulsory, arbitration. See also the discussion of constitutionality of preliminary review board provisions in §4.16 infra.

[11]See, e.g., Stefani, 149 Mich. App. 431 (upholding agreement that complied with Michigan's requirement to set out agreement separately and provide brochure explaining terms) and Morris v. Metriyakool, 418 Mich. 423, 344 N.W.2d 736 (1984) (upholding agreements that included Michigan's statutory 60-day revocation period). See also Wheeler, 133 Cal. Rptr. 775, (noting with approval new California requirement that arbitration clauses be in 10-point type in red ink and placed near the signature line).

[12]See, e.g., Madden v. Kaiser Found. Hosp., 17 Cal. 3d 699, 131 Cal.

§4.16 Preliminary Review Boards

A number of states have enacted statutes that provide for either voluntary or mandatory screening of medical malpractice claims by a panel composed of "experts" prior to traditional litigation.[1] The main difference between a preliminary review board and an arbitration board is that preliminary review is designed to screen out nonmeritorious claims before they reach the court system and arbitration is generally designed as an alternative, and potentially cost-effective, forum for final resolution of claims.

Rptr. 882, 552 P.2d 1178 (1976) (state agency's negotiation of arbitration agreement with hospital on behalf of state employees for purposes of group medical plan); Doyle v. Giuliucci, 62 Cal. 2d 606, 43 Cal. Rptr. 697, 401 P.2d 1 (1965) (father's consent to arbitration enforced against minor).

§4.16 [1]See, e.g., Conn. Gen. Stat. Ann. §38-19b et seq. (West 1977) (voluntary participation, unanimous finding admissible in evidence); Del. Code Ann. tit. 18, §6801 et seq. (Supp. 1986) (combination voluntary-mandatory screening with findings admissible at subsequent proceeding); Haw. Rev. Stat. §671-11 (1976) (mandatory screening, confidentiality of findings); Ill. Rev. Stat. ch. 110, ¶2-1013 et seq. (1985) (mandatory scheme with election to opt out becomes binding by default if findings unanimous and no written rejection by either party within 28 days); Ind. Code §16-9.5-9-1 et seq. (1977) (mandatory screening, findings admissible); La. Rev. Stat. Ann. §40:1299.47 et seq. (West 1977 & Supp. 1989) (mandatory review, opinion admissible); Md. Cts. & Jud. Proc. Code Ann. §3-2A-01 et seq. (1989) (mandatory preliminary review panel's findings admissible unless vacated); Me. Rev. Stat. Ann. tit. 24, §2851 et seq. (1987) (mandatory screening, limited admissibility); Mass. Gen. Laws Ann. ch. 231, §60B (West 1985) (mandatory screening, requirement of bond for unsuccessful plaintiff to proceed); Mont. Code Ann. §27-6-101 et seq. (1983) (mandatory review, findings not admissible); Neb. Rev. Stat. §44-2840 et seq. (1988) (mandatory review, report admissible); Nev. Rev. Stat. §41A.003 (1986) (mandatory review, subsequent bond required for unsuccessful claimant); N.H. Rev. Stat. Ann. §519-A:1 et seq. (1974) (mandatory review, findings not admissible); N.M. Stat. Ann. §41-5-14 (1978) (mandatory review, findings not admissible); Tenn. Code Ann. §29-26-113 (1980) (mandatory hearing, findings not admissible); Utah Code Ann. §78-14-12 et seq. (1987) (mandatory review, not admissible into evidence); Va. Code Ann. §8.01-581.1 (1984) (mandatory review, finding admissible); Wis. Stat. §655.02 et seq. (voluntary scheme, adverse findings against healthcare providers are referred to examining boards); Wyo. Stat. §9-2-1501 et seq. (voluntary screening, not admissible).

There are important distinctions between the various sorts of review panel schemes. The major distinctions include

- whether screening is mandatory prior to commencement of court action;
- whether the determination of the preliminary review board is to be binding; and
- whether the board's findings may be admitted into evidence at a subsequent proceeding.

§4.16.1 Binding Versus Nonbinding Decisions

In most states, the decisions of preliminary review boards, whether voluntary or mandatory, are generally not binding unless accepted by the parties.[2] The rare preliminary review board whose findings are binding or can be binding through inaction by the claimant may not survive constitutional challenge because of their denial of claimants' access to courts.[3] Some mandatory screening statutes have been held unconstitutional,

---

[2]See, e.g., Connecticut, Delaware, Hawaii, Indiana, Louisiana, Maryland, Maine, Massachusetts, Montana, Nebraska, Nevada, New Hampshire, Utah, Virginia, and Wyoming statutes cited supra n.1. See also Lacy v. Green, 428 A.2d 1171 (Del. Super. Ct. 1981); Cha v. Warnick, 455 N.E.2d 1165 (Ind. Ct. App. 3d Dist. 1983); Attorney Gen. v. Johnson, 282 Md. 274, 385 A.2d 57 (Md. 1978); and Linder v. Smith, 629 P.2d 1187 (Mont. 1981), all upholding preliminary review statutes against claims that provisions constitute an unconstitutional denial of right of access to courts.

[3]See, e.g., Ill. Rev. Stat. ch. 110, ¶2-1009 et seq. (mandatory review in which unanimous decisions are binding in the absence of written rejection by a party within 28 days). See also Bernier v. Burris, 113 Ill. 2d 219, 497 N.E.2d 763 (1986) (Illinois panel scheme considered unconstitutional delegation of judicial power by court noting the binding nature of decision absent revocation by claimant). But see Md. Cts. & Jud. Proc. Code Ann. §3-2A-01 et seq. (1989) (Maryland scheme of binding decision if not rejected within 30 days survived constitutional challenge based on denial of access to courts in Wyndham v. Haines, 305 Md. 269, 503 A.2d 719 (1986)).

even though they are not technically binding, because they create extreme delays in access to courts.[4]

§4.16.2 Admissible Versus Inadmissible Findings

Just over half of the statutes governing preliminary review panels provide that the findings of the panels are admissible in subsequent judicial proceedings.[5] In addition, some states admit decisions of preliminary review panels if they are unanimous.[6] Statutes that allow admission of findings into evidence, but do not require the jury to be bound by them, are generally upheld.[7]

---

[4]Gallagher v. Caliguiri, 287 Pa. Super. 250, 429 A.2d 1195 (1981) (Pennsylvania Health Care Services Malpractice Act unconstitutional because gives exclusive original jurisdiction that results in oppressive delay.) See also Aldana v. Holub, 381 So. 2d 231 (Fla. 1980) (Florida's Medical Mediation Act deemed unconstitutional, though it was nonbinding, because its arbitrary and capricious time limitations were violative of due process); Jiron v. Mahlab, 99 N.M. 425, 659 P.2d 311 (1983) (although New Mexico statute not per se unconstitutional, when it demands preliminary review by medical commission while defendant escapes personal jurisdiction for purposes of subsequent court proceeding, it unconstitutionally deprives patient of access to courts). Compare Jones v. State Bd. of Medicine, 97 Idaho 859, 555 P.2d 399 (1976) (court noted that due process does not require that the statutory substitute for common-law rights be exactly coextensive as to speediness of justice).

[5]See statutes regarding admissibility of panel findings in Connecticut, Delaware, Louisiana, Maine, Maryland, Nebraska, Virginia, and Wisconsin, supra n.1. See also Everett v. Nejad, 493 A.2d 969 (Del. Sup. 1985) (plaintiff waived right to object to admissibility of findings when failed to file timely motion for review under Del. Code Ann. tit. 18, §6811(d)) (combination system).

[6]See, e.g., Treyball v. Clark, 65 N.Y.2d 589, 493 N.Y.S.2d 1004, 483 N.E.2d 1136 (1985) (statute authorizing unanimous recommendation of panel to be admitted into evidence upheld); Lipsius v. White, 91 A.D.2d 271, 458 N.Y.S.2d 928 (2d Dept. 1983) (unanimous recommendation of medical malpractice panel to be considered with all other evidence); Dubler v. Stetser, 179 N.J. Super. 139, 430 A.2d 962 (1981) (unanimous decision admissible). See also Ill. Rev. Stat. ch. 110, ¶2-1009 et seq.

[7]See, e.g., Halpern v. Gozan, 85 Misc. 2d 753, 381 N.Y.S.2d 744 (Super. Ct. 1976) (court upheld admissibility of medical review panel decision provision against constitutional challenge of impingement on right to jury trial because

In a few states, legislatures have created prescreening panels whose findings are not admissible in any subsequent trial of the issues.[8] The Massachusetts scheme requires the claimant to post a bond in bringing an unsuccessfully reviewed claim to the court system,[9] but does not provide for admissibility of *findings*. As interpreted by the Supreme Court of Massachusetts, however, the *fact* that the panel exercises its option to request additional information via a "tribunal-appointed" expert, in addition to the testimony of that expert, is admissible under the statute as evidence at subsequent proceedings.[10] Courts have enforced prohibitions against admission of findings at subsequent proceedings.[11]

Some preliminary review board statutes have been challenged because the composition of the panels is allegedly prejudicial to one or both parties. Courts are split on the issue of whether a review panel consisting of one judge and some combination of lay persons (usually one physician and one attorney) is an unconstitutional delegation of judicial power. In Bernier v. Burris, the Supreme Court of Illinois ruled that the

---

either party may call and cross-examine panel members at subsequent proceedings). See also Speet v. Bacaj, 237 Va. 290, 377 S.E.2d 397 (1989); Lacy v. Green, 428 A.2d 1171 (Del. Super. Ct. 1981), Seoane v. Ortho Pharmaceuticals, 660 F.2d 146 (5th Cir. 1981) (applying Louisiana law); and Johnson v. St. Vincent Hosp., 404 N.E.2d 585 (Ind. 1980), all upholding schemes that allow admission of findings against claim of denial of right to trial by jury.

[8]See Haw. Rev. Stat. §671-11; Mont. Code Ann. §27-6-01 et seq.; N.H. Rev. Stat. Ann §519-A:1 et seq. (1974); N.M. Stat. Ann. §41-5-14 (1978); Utah Code Ann. §78-14-12 et seq. (1987); Wyo. Stat. §9-2-1501 et seq.

[9]Mass. Gen. Laws Ann. ch. 231, §60B (West 1985) (statute requires mandatory screening and posting of bond by unsuccessful claimant).

[10]See Beeler v. Downey, 387 Mass. 609, 442 N.E.2d 19 (1982) (Supreme Court of Massachusetts interpreted provisions to not allow admissibility of *findings*, as opposed to admissibility of the tribunal's decision to summon an expert and that expert's testimony).

[11]See, e.g., Linder v. Smith, 629 P.2d 1187 (Mont. 1981) (upholding Montana provision as to inadmissibility of findings as direct evidence but striking provisions prohibiting use of any prior inconsistent statements of experts for impeachment purposes). See also statutes in Hawaii, New Hampshire, New Mexico, Utah, and Wyoming, supra n.8.

Illinois preliminary review scheme unconstitutionally delegated judicial power to a three-member review panel consisting of one circuit judge, one practicing attorney, and one healthcare professional.[12] On the other hand, the Massachusetts scheme providing for panels with precisely the same composition has been upheld.[13] One factor that may be decisive on the constitutionality of a mixed panel is whether the findings of the panel are binding. The court in *Bernier* noted that judgment could be entered based on a unanimous finding of the panel if the finding was not rejected within 28 days, prior to stating its holding that the Illinois statute unconstitutionally delegated judicial power.[14] Findings under the Massachusetts scheme, however, are neither binding nor admissible.[15]

Similarly, the inclusion of a healthcare provider on a review panel may be subject to constitutional challenge based on denial of due process in some situations, because of the potential bias it presents in favor of the defendant. The Supreme Court of Michigan, however, reversed a lower court ruling that the Michigan scheme, which required that at least one member of the "arbitration board" be from the same medical specialty as the defendant, was unconstitutional.[16] The higher court stated that such a panel would be valid absent a showing of "actual bias on the part of a particular arbitration panel."[17] The Louisiana scheme, which *requires* all three medical members of the panel to be of the "same class and specialty of practice" as the

---

[12]Bernier v. Burris, 113 Ill. 2d 219, 497 N.E.2d 763, 100 Ill. Dec. 585 (1986).

[13]*Beeler*, 387 Mass. 609.

[14]Bernier v. Burris, 497 N.E.2d at 769, and Wright v. Central Du Page Hospital Assn., 63 Ill. 2d 313, 347 N.E.2d 736 (1976).

[15]*Beeler*, 387 Mass. 609. See also Eastin v. Broomfield, 116 Ariz. 576, 570 P.2d 744 (1977) (not unconstitutional delegation of power to nonjurists if not binding).

[16]Morris v. Metriyakool, 418 Mich. 423, 344 N.W.2d 736, 739 (Mich. 1984) (statute requiring at least one member of arbitration board to be from same medical speciality as defendant survived constitutional challenge based on denial of due process, reversing lower court).

[17]Id.

defendant, also has been enforced.[18] This requirement can be enforced even when the physicians happen to practice at the same hospital,[19] but physicians who are partners with the defendant generally may not sit as review panelists.[20] Further, ex parte communication between the defendant doctor and the trier of fact as to the issues prior to decision may be grounds for vacating the findings of even a "constitutionally composed" board. In Santola v. Eisenberg, the panel's decision was vacated when it was discovered that the physician panel member had attended a departmental staff meeting in which the provider defendant had led a discussion of the case at issue prior to the panel's recommendation.[21]

E. Conclusion

The application of tort law principles to the healthcare facility has drastically expanded over the past 40 years. WIth charitable immunity definitively discarded, those defending the healthcare facility in tort suits should attempt to narrow the issue to whether there is a direct and independent facility duty. If the scope of the facility duty is successfully narrowed, it is likely to be more difficult for the claimant to establish the requisite

---

[18]See, e.g., Re Calongne, 447 So. 2d 1217 (La. Ct. App. 1984) (physician specializing in internal medicine not qualified to be panel member reviewing claims against general practitioner in process of becoming board-certified in emergency medicine), citing La. Rev. Ann. §40:1299.47 et seq. (West 1977 & Supp. 1989). See also Mass. Gen. Laws. Ann. ch. 231, §60B (West 1985) (providing medical member be within field of medicine and reside outside county of defendant), upheld in Beeler v. Downey, 387 Mass. 609, 442 N.E.2d 19.

[19]See, e.g., Derouen v. Kolb, 397 So. 2d 791 (La. 1981) (fact that physician member on panel was staff member of same hospital as defendant did not violate constitutional due process).

[20]See, e.g., Landry v. Martinez, 415 So. 2d 965 (La. Ct. App. 1982).

[21]96 A.D.2d 716, 465 N.Y.S.2d 91 (4th Dept. 1983).

breach, causation, and damages flowing from that breach.[1] For example, suppose an otherwise competent physician who is an independent contractor in a hospital emergency room injures a patient through negligence. If the hospital's duty is only the direct duty to exercise care in extending staff privileges, the claimant must show both that the duty to investigate was breached and that had the investigation been made, the privileges would not have reasonably been extended.[2] On the other hand, if the claimant successfully argues that the hospital is vicariously liable for all of the physician's actions because he or she is apparently the agent of the hospital, then the claimant only needs to show the underlying negligence of the physician to prove its case against the hospital.[3]

---

[1]See §§4.1 to 4.4 on the elements and standards required in medical malpractice cause of action against the healthcare facility.

[2]See §4.13.1.

[3]See §4.12.4.

5   Risk Management

Arlene J. Diosegy

§5.0 Introduction

This chapter introduces the reader to the concept of risk management and its goals, describes the contemporary risk management techniques most often employed by healthcare facilities, and outlines the major considerations and procedures involved in creating a risk management system for the facility.

A. The Concept of Risk Management

§5.1 Definitions and Origins

"Risk management," a term apparently coined by two professors of insurance in 1963, is the process of reducing the costs of

389

predictable business losses. For healthcare facilities, risk management means identifying areas of potential liability exposure, avoiding or at least reducing exposure whenever possible, and thus minimizing loss from malpractice litigation and other civil claims.[1] "Quality assurance" is a related term, often used interchangeably with risk management. Risk management, however, focuses on the patient's interests, not the facility's. "[R]isk management is concerned with an *acceptable* level of care from the legal perspective. Quality assurance, on the other hand, is concerned with an *optimal* level of care. . . ."[2] Risk management is the broader term; it encompasses the identification, assessment, and financing of all risk, of which inadequate provision of medical services is but one kind.

Seen merely as an aspect of good business practice, risk management techniques—insurance, for example—are certainly not new. However, these techniques have become increasingly relevant to healthcare in the United States in the past quarter-century. With the advent of Medicare and Medicaid in the mid-1960s, the federal government, as the largest purchaser of care, began to require increased accountability from facilities seeking reimbursement. The insurance industry responded to sharp increases in malpractice litigation in the mid-1970s and mid-1980s by emphasizing to facilities the need to prevent malpractice claims and other forms of loss.[3] At the same time, health institutions sought to identify their most costly risks and to handle them prudently.

At least ten states require risk management programs as a

---

§5.1   [1]J. Orlikoff, W. Fifer, and H. Greeley, Malpractice Prevention and Liability Control for Hospitals 28-29 (1981).

[2]Orlikoff and Lanham, Why Risk Management and Quality Assurance Should Be Integrated, 1981 Hospitals 54 (June 1, 1981).

[3]The experience of St. Paul Marine and Fire Insurance Co., one of the nation's major health facility underwriters, is an example. Beginning in the mid-1970s, St. Paul made a significant financial commitment to encouraging risk management within facilities by hiring registered nurses to visit hospitals to review operations. Telephone conversation with Robert Coderre, St. Paul Marine and Fire Insurance Company, St. Paul, Minnesota (June 14, 1989).

condition of licensure for hospitals.[4] The Joint Commission on Accreditation of Healthcare Organizations (JCAHO) requires both a quality assurance and a risk management program[5] and requires that they be linked.[6]

§5.2 The Goals of Risk Management

The goals of risk management are to protect the financial assets of the facility and, if possible, to increase profitability. Despite sharp and sustained growth over a 15-year period in the size and number of damage claims paid by healthcare facilities, there is some evidence that risk management is effective in meeting these goals and also in improving care. When malpractice claims decreased in 1988, spokespersons for both insurance and medicine gave first credit to health facilities' efforts to prevent negligence. An official of the American Medical Association specifically pointed to the success of "new routines intended to avert actions or omissions that could lead to lawsuits."[1] These routines are a major component of an institution's risk management program.

---

[4]Alaska Stat. §18.20.075 (1986); Florida Stat. §395.041 (1986), as amended, Florida Stat. §395.041 (Supp. 1988); regulations at Fla. Admin. Code Ann. 10D-75.001 (1987); Kan. Stat. Ann. §§65-4921 to 65-4930 (1985); Md. Health-Gen. Code Ann. §19-319 (1987); Mass. Ann. Laws ch. 111, §203 (Law. Co-op. Supp. 1988); N.Y. Comp. Codes R. & Regs. tit. 10, §405.41 (1986); N.C. Gen. Stat. §131E-96 (1988), regulations at 10 N.C.A.C. 3C§.0307; R.I. Gen. Laws §23-17-24 (1985); S.C. Code Ann. §38-33-40 (Law. Co-op. Supp. 1987); Wash. Rev. Code Ann. §§43.19.1936 to 43.19.200 (Supp. 1988).
[5]JCAHO, 1989 Accreditation Manual for Hospitals §GB .1.18, at 52.
[6]JCAHO, supra n.5, at 219-223.
§5.2 [1]James S. Todd, Vice-President of the American Medical Association. Dr. Todd observed more colloquially in the same interview that "Happy patients don't sue. We're trying to figure out how to keep them happy." Milt Freudenheim, *Costs of Medical Malpractice Drop After an 11-Year Climb*, N.Y. Times, June 11, 1989, at 1, cols. 1-2.

B. Identifying, Controlling, and Financing Risk

§5.3 Identifying and Assessing Risk

Since a facility's risk exposure is at least as large as its total assets, risk management begins with knowledge of corporate assets. A careful listing of both tangible (real estate, buildings, and furnishings) and intangible (e.g., current revenue, investments, good will) property is a logical beginning point for risk management. Budget analysis is next. Precise knowledge of how the facility generates revenue is essential, because tolerance for risk potential in an activity will be tied to the activity's profitability.

A risk manager must know how the facility functions as well as what it owns. Thorough understanding of operations should be supplemented frequently by personal inspections, called "safety rounds" in risk management literature. One source recommends following the same routes that patients follow through the facility as a reminder of potential hazards.[1]

To assess risk, the manager must have a working knowledge of legal theories of liability, though most managers are not lawyers. The manager should also be familiar with licensing and accreditation standards for facilities and with state and federal law pertaining to the health and safety of patients and the public.

When the manager has identified as many forms of risk as practicable, an assessment should be made of the probable frequency and gravity of each event should it occur.[2] This assessment is the most important and most difficult task of risk management. Besides personal knowledge of current operations and the risks they entail, the manager will rely on several kinds of historical data such as the particular facility's loss experience and state-wide or industry-wide trends. Information on such

---

§5.3 [1]Schmitt, Risk Management—It's More than Just Insurance, 37 Healthcare Fin. Mgmt. 16 (March 1983).

[2]Id.

trends is often available from the insurance department of the state government. In addition, professional liability carriers in each state are often obligated to keep accessible records of claims and payments.

The identification of new types of risk is especially challenging. Technological advances in treatment and administration improve care but at the same time create opportunities for grave liability. Computerization is the best example. Computer-aided diagnosis and patient recordkeeping, automated calculation and delivery of drug and radiation dosage—these are valuable tools for medicine. But when they fail, as all systems do, the harm to a patient may be vast.[3]

James E. Orlikoff and Audrone Vanagunas of the American Hospital Association have compiled a list of situations in which particular attention to liability potential may be warranted. Though developed for hospitals, the guide should be equally useful for other facilities. Orlikoff and Vanagunas advise facilities to be alert for legal danger whenever:

1. Changing demographics are significantly increasing the potential patient population for the area, service, or treatment.
2. The health care financing and delivery system is changing or has changed in such a way as to dramatically increase the need for the service, area, or treatment.
3. The program, area, service, technology, or treatment is growing at an accelerating rate.
4. The service, program, or treatment has become recently available or practical in a new setting because of technological advances.
5. Standards and protocols to ensure quality of care are not yet developed or are just emerging in the area.

---

[3]See Metzger, Legal Implications of Computer-Aided Medical Diagnosis, 9 J. Legal Medicine 313-328 (1988); Lawrence, Strict Liability, Computer Software and Medicine: Public Policy at the Crossroads, 22 Tort and Ins. L.J. 1-18 (Fall 1987); Hyman, Risks Associated with Diagnostic Devices, 11 J. Clinical Engineering 273-278 (July-August 1986).

6. There are currently no or minimal risk management programs or protocols in the area, treatment, or technology.
7. There is no current, significant malpractice litigation in the area, nor has there ever been such litigation. Hence, there is no case law defining the boundaries of liability in the area.
8. There is the potential for severe patient injury, missed diagnosis or misdiagnosis, or other liability in the area.
9. There is no malpractice liability insurance coverage yet developed and available in the area. Or, if insurance coverage is available, the boundaries of it are vague.
10. Malpractice or other insurance coverage was available in the past for the area but has recently become unavailable, unaffordable, or offered with severe restrictions and exclusions in coverage.
11. The area represents a new business activity for the hospital.
12. The area represents a new disease of epidemic proportions.
13. There are existing shortages in allied health care professionals or changing demographics that portend future shortages.
14. Programs, systems, and protocols [are] implemented in the area to reduce the risk of patient injury and improve the quality of care.[4]

§5.4 Deciding How to Handle Risk

Once the probable nature and extent of the facility's risk is known insofar as possible, plans can be made for coping with it. Adam P. Sielecki, Jr.'s related articles in Topics in Health

---

[4]J. Orlikoff with A. Vanagunas, Malpractice Prevention and Liability Control for Hospitals 139-140 (2d ed. 1988). Reprinted with permission. It is striking how many of their criteria apply to the treatment of AIDS and to other services, preeminently transfusions, in light of AIDS.

Care Financing suggest a framework for planning. He characterizes a facility's choices as risk avoidance, loss control, separation of exposures, and transfer of risk to others.[1] Sielecki's first proposal, risk avoidance, entails dropping an activity entirely—a decision he believes facilities should always consider.[2] Loss control involves both preventing events—relocating psychiatric patients to the ground floor to forestall suicide, for example—and reducing the cost of those that do occur—for example, planning for quick recovery of confused patients who may wander from a nursing home. Separation of exposure means duplicating service capacity in order to insure against system failures—an alternative power supply for the operating room, for instance. Transfer of risk refers to an entity's ability to use contracts and leases to divest itself of legal and financial responsibility for certain aspects of its operations.[3] A major hospital, for instance, might have sufficient economic power to require indemnification from equipment, computer software, or drug manufacturers if their products fail. Teaching centers could require medical or nursing schools to insure against their students' malpractice as a condition of the training.

§5.5 Financing Unavoidable Risk

Since an enterprise cannot escape most risk generated by its activities, the question becomes how to pay if loss occurs. The facility may choose to bear the cost itself ("risk retention"), but Sielecki advises doing so only in one of these cases:

---

§5.4 [1]Sielecki, Current Philosophy of Risk Management, 9 Topics in Health Care Financing 4 (Spring 1983).

[2]Discouraging certain behavior by raising its cost is a time-honored practice with continued viability. For example, in North Carolina in 1987, Medical Mutual's insurance rates for family practitioners who delivered babies increased from approximately $4,800 to $27,000. The new premium was necessitated, according to many if not all insurers, by litigation costs from such births. Subsequently, the majority of family practitioners in the state ended their practice of obstetrics.

[3]Sielecki, supra n.1, at 4-5.

1. when losses are reasonably predictable and the cost of paying for them will be less than that of transferring the risk;
2. when the probability of loss is sufficiently remote;
3. when the projected cost of the loss could easily be borne; or
4. when it is not possible to transfer the risk.[1]

If risks are retained for these or other reasons, all but the most affluent facilities will need to set aside funds for future losses and, most likely, purchase supplemental insurance for catastrophic losses.

Though self-insurance is becoming more frequent,[2] most facilities continue to rely heavily on traditional insurance. Under an insurance contract or policy, the responsibility to pay for loss is, in specified circumstances, transferred to another entity. Note, though, that a policy is merely a private contract transferring financial responsibility; it cannot transfer legal responsibility. If the insurer fails to pay, the insured retains its responsibility to the claimant.

With assistance from counsel, the risk manager should play a major role in the process of insuring the facility. Probably both should carefully review policies before purchase to determine the extent of coverage and the principal exclusions. For instance, if a policy will not cover antitrust violations or pay punitive damages (both common exclusions), alternatives must be found for handling these risks. When insurance is obtained, the risk manager should oversee reviewing policies annually, seeing that the facility's responsibilities under each are fulfilled, and searching the insurance market for better alternatives to the current coverage.

---

§5.5 [1]Sielecki, Risk Management Philosophy and Techniques—An Overview, 9 Topics in Health Care Financing 3 (Summer 1983). Sielecki also observes that risk retention can be intentional or not, depending on whether the facility is aware of it.

[2]"Today the objective of every risk manager is to buy as little insurance as they need," an insurance executive observes. Collins, 20 Years of Growth: Professional Risk Management Emerges, 1987 Bus. Ins. 6 (Oct. 26, 1987).

C. Establishing a Risk Management Program

§5.6 The Form of the Program

A successful program must be tailored to the particular facility. The system should reflect the institution's corporate goals— above all, its own standards for patient care—and should have the support of the governing board, employees, and staff.[1] Beyond that, no form of risk management is more inherently desirable than another; organizational structure in a risk management department should be as simple as it can be and still achieve the goals outlined in Part B above.

Several matters deserve consideration at the outset. First is the establishment of good communication within the system. Efforts to promote communication should probably include (a) locating the manager's position near the top of the corporate hierarchy[2] and deciding who reports to the manager and through what processes (see §5.8 on Incident Reporting); and (b) automating risk management's information-gathering process insofar as possible.[3] A manual available to all personnel could

---

§5.6 [1]Risk managers tend to consider the success of a program to be closely tied to the extent of physician participation. James E. Orlikoff with Androne M. Vanagunas, Malpractice Prevention and Liability Control for Hospitals 34, 36 (2d ed. 1988). For their part, physicians seem proud of their historical leadership in quality assurance (Purcell, Quality Assurance/Utilization Management and Risk Management: Deterrents to Professional Liability, 31 Clinical Obstetrics and Gynecology 163-164 (March 1988) but threatened by perceived disciplinary and personal liability implications of quality assurance or risk management schemes (Berwick, Continuous Improvement as an Ideal in Health Care, 320 New Eng. J. Med. 53-55 (January 5, 1989)). On physicians' ambivalence, see also Confronting Professional Liability: A Roundtable Discussion of Medical Risk Management, 70 Minnesota Med. 142-148 (March 1987).

[2]Risk managers naturally prefer to be highly placed in the administration, and a few studies show that the position works better at that level. Risk Managers Need Clout, Backup to Cut Losses, 1989 Hospitals 72 (Feb. 20, 1989).

[3]A 1986 survey by the JCAHO found that a slight majority of hospitals

also be a useful communication tool. Adam Sielecki strongly recommends providing a manual that describes risk management policies, departmental safety rules, disaster plans, incident reporting procedures, and insurance programs.[4]

The second issue in establishing a risk management program is the necessity for staff training and regular retraining. Healthcare workers cannot be expected to understand fully the legal implications of medical situations, but with instruction can easily master basic legal principles and risk management procedures. Training should emphasize the legal significance of medical recordkeeping, careful documentation of actions taken, and reporting of potentially troublesome events.

A third issue, the proper relationship between risk management and quality assurance systems in the facility, receives much attention in the literature of hospital administration. The ultimate purposes of the two functions differ, though there is a large area of congruence. Much of the same information is essential to both operations, however, and close cooperation can eliminate duplication of effort and increase the efficiency of each. As noted earlier, JCAHO guidelines now require some integration of the two functions in hospitals.[5]

A final consideration is what part the risk manager will play in the facility's legal defense. The manager's role may vary from inactive (approval of attorneys' fees) to moderately active (reviewing monthly or quarterly reports from counsel) to active (developing case strategy, attending depositions, assisting in preparation of documents). The scope of the role is less important than that it be well understood by counsel and the manager.

(and no doubt a larger percentage of other healthcare facilities) had not computerized risk management and quality assurance information. The JCAHO recommends automation and has developed specifications for a software system. Shanahan, Confronting the Software Dilemma: Specifications for a QA/RM Information Management System, 1988 QRB 345-347 (Nov. 1988).

[4]Sielecki, Current Philosophy of Risk Management, 9 Topics in Health Care Financing 3 (Spring 1983).

[5]"There are operational linkages between the risk management functions related to the clinical aspects of patient care and safety and quality assurance functions." JCAHO, 1989 Accreditation Manual for Hospitals QA.1.4.

398

§5.7 Designing and Filling the Position of Risk Manager

The basic tasks of a risk manager can be extrapolated from the preceding descriptions of the nature and goals of risk management. In addition, the list below of principal duties may be helpful to administrators creating or redesigning one or more positions for their facility. The list was compiled by the participants in the 25th annual meeting of the Risk & Insurance Management Society.[1] This group of experienced risk managers considered the following their most important responsibilities:

1. Reminding all employees and staff of the importance of doing their jobs well and of documenting what they do.
2. Following the facility's activities for the purpose of identifying risk. This may mean reviewing minutes of staff and governing body meetings, contacting departments regularly to determine whether they are developing new loss exposures, and talking frequently to the facility's attorney.
3. Reviewing the facility's business activity (as opposed to service functions as in items 1 and 2). The risk manager should communicate at frequent intervals with the facility's comptroller and its insurers.
4. Closely monitoring the financial strength and management skills of the facility. If the facility is not insuring or is underinsuring a potential liability, the risk manager should be the person to identify the problem and bring it to the attention of management.
5. Exploring alternatives to the current risk management program. This requires attendance at continuing education programs for risk managers as well as efforts to keep abreast of the latest insurance mechanisms.

---

§5.7   [1]Las Vegas, Nevada, 1987. This session is described in Taravella, Risk Managers Could Be Liable for Errors, 1987 Bus. Ins. 3, 14 (April 13, 1987).

6. Analyzing available insurance offerings and recommending the best product and vendors to the facility's executives and governing body.[2]

Although the Insurance Institute of America confers an "Associate in Risk Management" degree and a few schools offer majors,[3] risk managers for health facilities present a variety of credentials. In the days when a risk manager's leading or exclusive function was to purchase insurance, the task could be given to any executive. Most often, an accountant, or perhaps the institution's treasurer, was chosen.[4] Today, a healthcare facility selecting among candidates for a risk manager's position would probably consider business management degrees and experience, knowledge of the insurance industry, and experience in healthcare, either as a medical professional or an administrator.

D. Operating the Program

§5.8 Incident Reporting

The essence of risk management is the identification of particular events, past or future, that may ultimately result in loss. For risk management to work, each such incident or occurrence must be recognized by those involved and must be brought to the attention of risk managers. In healthcare facilities today, the most commonly used method for achieving these ends is an incident reporting system.

The American Hospital Association defines "incident" as

---

[2]The principal speaker, George L. Head, reminded the participants of the possibility of risk managers themselves incurring liability if their negligence, such as failing to secure or maintain insurance coverage, costs the facility. Id. 3, 14.

[3]Collins, 20 Years of Growth: Professional Risk Management Emerges, 1987 Bus. Ins. 4 (Oct. 26, 1987).

[4]Id.

"any happening . . . not consistent with the routine operation of the hospital or the routine care of a particular patient,"[1] a description that encompasses events as diverse as a fatal drug reaction, a nursing home resident's fall in the shower, an automobile accident in the parking deck, or a family member's threat of suit. Many facilities use incident reporting because their insurers require it as a condition of coverage, particularly under "claims made" policies. Policies often contain a "reservation of rights" clause that exempts losses from an event for which an incident report was completed late or not at all.

There are good reasons besides insurance requirements for making incident reporting the basis of a risk management program. The American College of Surgeons has identified several, including these:

1. Reports allow early identification of a problem or potentially compensable event, permitting the risk manager to try to avoid further damage and perhaps litigation through efforts to remedy the situation. At a minimum, early warning enables the manager to gather evidence for defense of a lawsuit.

2. An incident reporting system is a database that can facilitate the detection and analysis of problems over a period of time. Data on trends help control losses and indicate areas of possible liability that are good candidates for insurance coverage.

3. The system enhances and is enhanced by cross-reference with any other risk detection system the facility employs. Incident reporting data, for example, can be combined with information from the quality assurance system for their mutual benefit.[2]

The first step in establishing incident reporting, and one that would profit from the risk manager's continuous efforts, is

---

§5.8 [1]American College of Surgeons, Patient's Safety Manual 71 (2d ed. 1985).
[2]Id.

to persuade staff members that reporting is in their own interest. The manager should consult widely, particularly among physicians and department heads, in developing guidelines on what kinds of occurrences are to be reported. Following the lead of the AHA definition above, the manager should encourage formulation of a broad definition of reportable events. Reporting should be made as simple as possible, and standardizing the process is advisable. While information needs vary with the type of incident, it should be possible to group events within categories that use a single format for reporting; accidents, for instance, whether to patients, visitors, or business invitees, might use the same form. Injuries to employees are often handled through a separate workers' compensation process.

It may be unwise for the manager to insist on a written format, at least as the initial step in reporting. Perhaps telephone reports, which can be transcribed and supplemented later, would work better. In any case, the manager will want to canvas staff and employees from time to time to solicit their support and suggestions on the most satisfactory procedures.

Though widely used and acknowledged as among the most effective tools of risk management, incident reporting sometimes fails to fulfill its purposes. Orlikoff, Fifer, and Greeley note the characteristics that tend to weaken a system's effectiveness:

1. It is not clear who is responsible for reporting—nurses or physicians involved in an untoward medical situation, for example. (Probably a physician should report, if one was present).
2. Reporting is viewed as a routine task and given low priority.
3. Many incidents, especially those involving physicians, are not reported.
4. No criteria exist for deciding which incidents are serious enough to merit investigation.
5. There is no process for detecting patterns of potential liability among large numbers of reports.
6. Reports are incomplete or improperly done.

7. Staff and employees view reporting as threatening and potentially punitive.[3]

Managers should be alert to these situations.

Even an efficient incident reporting system has one serious risk that the risk manager must try to minimize: the incidents reports, which the facility created for its own use, may eventually be available to ("discoverable" by) parties suing the facility. The legal status of incident reports is not settled. Most states have not ruled on the matter, and those that have do not seem to have disposed of the question entirely. Some states use the attorney-client privilege to protect reports from discovery;[4] other states use the attorney work product doctrine.[5] The trend, however, seems to be toward allowing plaintiffs access.[6] Thus, it is essential for the risk manager to know current state law on the point and to seek advice from the facility's attorneys and insurers on lessening both the probability of discovery and the damage to the facility if release is ordered. To these ends, one legal treatise suggests that facilities:

1. Treat incident reports as confidential documents, clearly marked as such.
2. Strictly limit the number of copies made and the distribution of the reports in the institution.

---

[3]J. Orlikoff, W. Fifer, and H. Greeley, Malpractice Prevention and Liability Control for Hospitals 37 (1981).

[4]Enke v. Anderson, 783 S.W.2d 462 (Mo. App. 1987).

[5]Johnson v. United States, 780 F.2d 902 (11th Cir. 1986).

[6]John C. Lincoln Hosp. and Health Center v. Superior Ct. of the State of Ariz., in and for the County of Maricopa, 768 P.2d 188 (Ariz. App. 1989); Mole v. Millard, 762 S.W.2d 251 (Tex. App. 1988); Shotwell v. Winthrop Community Hosp., 531 N.E.2d 270 (Mass. App. 1988); Sakosko v. Memorial Hosp., 522 N.E.2d 273 (Ill. App. 1988), allowing discovery of letters written by a risk management consultant to the risk management committee reviewing the defendant's liability claims; Sims v. Knollwood Park Hosp., 511 So. 2d 154 (Ala. 1987); Monah v. Western Pa. Hosp., No. G.D. 86-8881, Allegheny County (Pa.) Ct. C.P., Feb. 23, 1987; Bernardi v. Community Hosp. Assn., 443 P.2d 708 (Colo. 1982).

3. Do not place a copy of the report in the patient's medical record or in the unit file.
4. Limit the content of the report to facts, not conclusions or assignment of blame.
5. Address the report to the . . . attorney or claims manager by name.
6. Train . . . personnel to complete incident reports with the same care used in completing a medical record.[7]

§5.9 Other Screening Methods

Incident reporting is not the only method risk management systems employ for locating areas of potential loss. Other procedures might be used instead of or in conjunction with the reporting of unusual events by those involved in them. Some facilities are finding that more nearly automatic identification of incidents is helpful. American Healthcare Systems, for instance, has developed a computerized checklist for its approximately 1,100 hospitals. The program identifies any aberrational event, including an unusual test result, that occurs in the course of treatment—an unplanned second surgery, for example, or readmission to the facility shortly after discharge.[1] Another computer program used in a few hospitals monitors respiratory therapy, blood transfusions, and medication effectiveness; the program also identifies patients receiving potentially dangerous combinations of diets or drugs.[2]

A facility may choose to screen patient records at regular intervals during and after treatment. Orlikoff and Vanagunas describe one such system:

> Using a list of screening criteria . . . all patient records are reviewed within 48 to 72 hours of admission and every 3 or 4

---

[7]Aspen Hospital Law Manual, Medical Records, §§4-5, at 78 (December 1986).

§5.9 [1]Richman, Hospitals Explore Innovative Techniques to Prevent Litigation and Hold Down Costs, 1987 Modern Healthcare 8 (May 8, 1987).

[2]Id. at 62.

days thereafter until the patient is discharged in an attempt to identify any adverse patient occurrences. The chart is also reviewed approximately two weeks after discharge to insure that compliance with all criteria has been assessed.[3]

§5.10 Analyzing the Information

The risk manager must develop a process for screening raw data from the various reports the facility creates, looking for events in certain categories: those that occur frequently; those that are likely to produce claims against the institution; those that are especially likely to result in settlements or losing judgments; and those that, if lost, will be expensive. Only by quantifying these and similarly relevant factors can the manager address risks appropriately. The manager should therefore allocate a considerable portion of her or his time to data analysis.

A risk manager might wish to assign a numerical value to each of the criteria above—for example, to the probability that a particular kind of incident will result in a lawsuit. (The facility's attorney should be a valuable resource in making predictions of this kind.) Some incidents might be ignored; others with a higher number could be marked for further inquiry, while those with the highest score would be investigated immediately.

The information sought to be derived from risk management data will vary from one facility to another and should depend in part on past loss experience and present concerns. A leading text recommends collecting at least the following items: the date of the incident—information that over time will indicate trends in frequency; the type of incident; the severity of the injury, if any; and where in the facility the injury occurred. This information will help concentrate training-for-prevention efforts on the departments, will determine categories of employees and patients, and will identify the activities most likely to involve risk.[1]

---

[3] J. Orlikoff with A. Vanagunas, Malpractice Prevention and Liability Control for Hospitals 60 (2d ed. 1988).

§5.10 [1] J. Orlikoff with A. Vanagunas, Malpractice Prevention and Liability Control for Hospitals 68 (2d ed. 1988).

It should be noted that data analysis of the sort described is not a mechanical task. When incident reporting is the basis of a facility's system, judgment is required to determine from the written narratives how to categorize events (often in more than one way) and when further information is needed before final assessment. The risk manager's entire staff must be carefully trained in the principles of the system in order to advise staff on the filing of incident reports and in order to screen the reports filed.

E. Conclusion

At least since the charitable immunity doctrine disappeared from American law, the activities of healthcare facilities have contained the potential for extremely serious risk. It is in facilities' interests to deal with that fact systematically, to plan for losses, and to reduce their effect by all available means. Certainly, chief among the ways of preventing civil claims is the rendering of the best possible care to patients.

The process of managing risk begins with canvassing assets and potential liabilities. If, as is usually the case, the latter is much greater, the facility will probably try to transfer some portion of its loss exposure through insurance. A variety of insurance mechanisms exist today and should be considered. Whatever the arrangements for handling loss, one or more employees should be assigned to monitor the facility's operations from the perspective of minimizing risk. No healthcare facility can afford to ignore risk management.

II

DELIVERY OF SERVICES

6 Access to Treatment

Jeffrey S. Koeze

§6.0 Introduction

Until the beginning of the twentieth century, sick individuals would seek healthcare in a hospital or other institution only as a last resort. Before then healthcare facilities were often hellish places, with the sick, the insane, and the dying indiscriminately herded together in crowded wards. The pressing question for the ill of one hundred years ago was not how to get enough money to get into a hospital, but how to get enough money to stay out of one.

After 1870 the growing abilities of medical science contributed to a revolution in healthcare facilities by creating demand for services, especially surgery, that were difficult to provide in the home.[1] Although in recent years technology formerly avail-

---

§6.0 [1]See generally C. Rosenberg, The Care of Strangers: The Rise of the American Hospital System (1987).

able only in healthcare facilities has moved into healthcare providers' offices and even into the home, healthcare facilities, and hospitals in particular, remain the center of our healthcare system. So long as that is true, the facility door will remain the key to access to healthcare. This chapter focuses on some of the legal issues that arise as individuals pass through that doorway. It addresses how the law may (1) require or encourage healthcare facilities to provide care to those who cannot pay for it; (2) grant persons rights to healthcare that they may exercise in healthcare facilities; (3) limit facilities' ability to discriminate among patients based on characteristics such as race; and (4) limit facilities' regulatory power over therapies and medical practice.

A. Access and Ability to Pay

§6.1 Indigent Care

Healthcare providers are in general free to refuse to care for those who cannot pay for it. As a result, the primary barrier to adequate healthcare in the United States, in spite of large public expenditures, is lack of the money needed to buy it. While the controversy continues over comprehensive plans to provide medical care to all, those seeking to prevent discrimination based on ability to pay have won limited victories in the courts and legislatures. These victories have put pressure on both public and private healthcare facilities to provide care to persons regardless of their ability to pay.[1]

---

§6.1 [1]Facilities have been accused of inflating the amount of uncompensated care they provide by including all bad debts, regardless of whether or not the patient could in fact have paid, and by using the amount of their charge, rather than the cost of the service, as a basis for calculating their charitable contribution. We need not determine the "right" way to calculate uncompensated care here; I will use the term although its definition is disputed.

§6.1.1 The Hill-Burton Mandates

Congress addressed a post-Depression, postwar shortage of medical facilities with the 1946 federal Hospital Survey and Construction Act, known as Hill-Burton.[2] Hill-Burton provided states with loans and grants for the construction of healthcare facilities. Between 1947 and 1974 the federal government provided over $4.4 billion in grants and $2 billion in loans and loan guarantees to almost 7,000 healthcare facilities.[3] To qualify for federal assistance, states were required to prepare a plan that provided adequate healthcare facilities for every state resident and necessary services to persons unable to pay.[4] Before a facility could receive Hill-Burton funds, the facility had to provide "assurances" that it would be available to all those living in its territorial area (the "community service" assurance) and that it would provide a reasonable amount of care to those unable to pay (the "reasonable volume" or "uncompensated care" assurance).[5]

Despite giving assurances, healthcare facilities provided little uncompensated care.[6] Compounding the problem was the fact that until 1973 the regulations governing these assurances neither required facilities to report uncompensated care nor set a minimum amount of care for each facility.[7]

In 1975 Congress replaced Hill-Burton with Title XVI of the Public Health Service Act.[8] Like Hill-Burton, Title XVI requires facilities receiving aid to make community service and uncom-

---

[2]Pub. L. No. 79-725, 60 Stat. 1040 (1946).

[3]American Hosp. Assn. v. Schweiker, 721 F.2d 170, 173 (7th Cir. 1983), cert. denied, 466 U.S. 958 (1984); Dowell and Parks, Defending Against Suits by Medical Providers: Medicaid, Hill-Burton, and Beyond, 20 Clearinghouse Rev. 454, 460 (1986).

[4]42 U.S.C. §291c(e) (1982).

[5]See *American Hosp. Assn.*, 721 F.2d at 172–173.

[6]S. Rep. No. 1285, 93d Cong., 2d Sess. 61, reprinted in 1974 U.S. Code Cong. & Ad. News 7842, 7900.

[7]See 42 C.F.R. §§53.61-53.63 (Supp. 1947) and 42 C.F.R. §53.111(b)(1972); see also Newsom v. Vanderbilt Univ., 653 F.2d 1100, 1108-1109 (6th Cir. 1981).

[8]Pub. L. No. 93-641, §4, 88 Stat. 2257, 2264 (1975).

pensated care assurances.[9] In addition, Congress required the Secretary of Health and Human Services to issue rules to enforce compliance with assurances given by recipients of money under both Hill-Burton and Title XVI.[10]

Those regulations, in effect since 1979, limit Hill-Burton uncompensated care assurances to 20 years after the completion of construction or until any direct or federally guaranteed loans are repaid.[11] Title XVI uncompensated care assurances have no time limit.[12] Each year uncompensated care under Hill-Burton and Title XVI must total the lesser of three percent of a facility's operating costs for the last fiscal year or ten percent of all federal assistance provided to the facility as adjusted for inflation.[13]

If a facility fails to provide that level of care, it must make up the deficit in the next year or its obligation period will be extended until the deficit is made up.[14] However, this rule does not apply if the deficit results from a lack of eligible patients[15] or from a financial inability to provide care. A Hill-Burton facility may make up deficits incurred for those reasons at any time during or immediately following its period of obligation.[16] A Title XVI facility need never make up such a deficit.[17]

The 1979 rules also contain provisions that help define and

---

[9] 42 U.S.C. §300s-1(b)(1)(K) (1988).

[10] Id. §300s(3).

[11] 42 C.F.R. §124.501(b)(1) (1989). These regulations are not meant to have retroactive effect. *American Hosp. Assn.*, 721 F.2d at 174. The pre-1979 regulations appear at 42 C.F.R. §§53.111 ˜3.113 (1989).

[12] 42 C.F.R. §124.501(b)(2) (1989).

[13] Id. §124.503(a). For definitions of "uncompensated services," "operating costs," and "federal financial assistance" see id. §124.502. Not all uncompensated services must be uncompensated; facilities may count services for which they receive reimbursement under state indigent care programs against Hill-Burton obligations. Lile v. Univ. of Iowa Hosp. and Clinics, 886 F.2d 157 (8th Cir. 1989).

[14] 42 C.F.R. §124.503(b) (1989). Provision of uncompensated services above the mandated amounts may be carried forward to reduce the obligation in subsequent years. Id. §124.503(c)(1).

[15] Whether a person is eligible for uncompensated services is determined under 42 C.F.R. §124.505 (1989).

[16] Id. §124.503(b)(2)(A).

[17] Id. §124.503(b)(2)(B).

enforce the community service mandate under Hill-Burton and Title XVI. These obligations have no time limit and they require facilities assisted by either program to provide medical services to all those living within a defined geographic area.[18]

Unlike the uncompensated care obligation, the community service obligation does not require a facility to treat patients who cannot pay for services unless they require emergency care[19] or are eligible for services, under the uncompensated care obligation.[20] However, the community service obligation does prohibit discrimination against patients because payment will be sought from the Medicare or Medicaid programs,[21] in which the facilities are required to participate.[22]

The community service regulations also forbid admission requirements or facility practices that have the effect of limiting the services available to eligible individuals.[23] For example, if few staff physicians will accept Medicare or Medicaid patients, the facility must find ways to make services available to those individuals.[24] Similarly, policies requiring preadmission deposits or requiring that patients be admitted by physicians with staff privileges are improper if they have the effect of excluding eligible persons from the facility.[25] Also invalid are rules that

---

[18]Id. §§124.603(a).

[19]"Emergency services" is not defined. Ritter v. Wayne County Gen. Hosp., 174 Mich. App. 490, 436 N.W.2d 673 (1988) (per curiam). For additional discussion of the obligation to provide emergency care, see §6.2.

[20]42 C.F.R. §124.603(a) (1989).

[21]Id. §124.603(c).

[22]Id. See also McNulty v. Marin Gen. Hosp., administrative complaint (Heath and Human Services Region IX filed Oct. 16, 1989) (arguing that California hospitals must also participate in that state's indigent care program); but see Natl. Rural Health Assn. v. Bowen, No. 88-3248 (D.D.C. filed Nov. 8, 1988) (claiming that rural hospitals need not participate in Medicaid and Medicare because reimbursement under those programs does not meet actual costs).

[23]42 C.F.R. §124.603(d) (1989).

[24]For an unsuccessful challenge to a hospital bylaw requiring staff physicians to treat certain patients so that the facility could comply with Hill-Burton obligations, see Clair v. Centre Community Hosp., 317 Pa. Super. 25, 463 A.2d 1065 (1983).

[25]42 C.F.R. §124.603(d) (1989).

restrict services to the eligible population, such as rules against providing labor and delivery services to women who received little or no prenatal care.[26]

The regulations contain a number of provisions that aid enforcement of the uncompensated care and community service mandates.[27] Facilities must give public notice of the availability of services,[28] file reports documenting compliance,[29] and maintain public records necessary to support compliance claims.[30] Any person who believes that a facility is out of compliance with the uncompensated care obligation must file a complaint with the Secretary of Health and Human Resources before pursuing action in court.[31]

§6.1.2 State Statutory Mandates to Provide Care

State laws requiring facilities to provide uncompensated care (other than emergency care) are uncommon, but they do exist. North Carolina law contains several such mandates and will serve to illustrate the variety of ways in which facilities may acquire mandates to provide care.

Healthcare facilities in North Carolina must get a certificate of need before expanding services. Applicants for certificates of

---

[26]See A. Freifield, The Right to Health Care: An Advocate's Guide to the Hill-Burton Uncompensated Care and Community Service Requirements, 43-44, 81 n.59 (1986).

[27]Certain public facilities, facilities with small annual obligations (generally less than $10,000 per year), community health centers, migrant health centers, and certain National Health Service Corps sites may claim exemptions from this compliance scheme. 42 C.F.R. §§124.513-124.515 (1988).

[28]42 C.F.R. §§124.504, 124.604 (1989).

[29]Id. §§124.509, 124.605.

[30]Id. §§124.510, 124.605.

[31]Id. §§124.511(a), 124.606. Facility failure to comply with uncompensated care regulations may be a defense to a suit for collection of patient charges. See, e.g., Creditors Protective Assn. v. Flack, 93 Ore. App. 719, 763 P.2d 756 (1988); see also Dowell and Parks, Defending Against Suits by Medical Providers: Medicaid, Hill-Burton, and Beyond, 20 Clearinghouse Rev. 454, 460 (1986).

need must demonstrate the impact of the proposed facility on "the health-related needs of the elderly and of members of medically underserved groups, such as the medically indigent or low income persons, Medicaid and Medicare recipients, racial and ethnic minorities, women, and handicapped persons. . . ."[32] In addition, state regulators must require facilities to demonstrate compliance with their promises to serve those populations made in certificate-of-need applications.[33] Failure to comply with promises may result in sanctions, including withdrawal of the certificate.[34]

Mandates to provide indigent care may also arise when a public hospital is sold or leased to a private nonprofit or for-profit corporation. In either case the local government making the conveyance may specify in the agreement that the new operators of the facility will provide a specified amount of care to the indigent.[35]

Finally, the statutes that create certain public facilities may contain mandates to provide certain types of care or care to certain groups of people.[36] In North Carolina, services provided by state-established regional mental health, mental retardation, and substance abuse authorities must be provided without regard to ability to pay.[37] Such statutory mandates to provide care may form the basis for lawsuits by individuals who don't get it.[38]

---

[32]N.C. Gen. Stat. §131E-183(a)(13) (1988). See also id. §§131E-183(a)(3), (3a).

[33]N.C. Gen. Stat. §131E-181 (Supp. 1989).

[34]N.C. Gen. Stat. §§131E-189(b), 131E-190 (1988).

[35]Id. §§131E-8, 131E-13.

[36]Facilities may have similar obligations to provide care under trust documents, bylaws, or facility policies. See, e.g., Chandler v. Hospital Auth., 548 So. 2d 1384 (Ala. 1989).

[37]N.C. Gen. Stat. §122C-146 (1989).

[38]Cf. Klassette v. Mecklenberg County Area Mental Health, Mental Retardation, and Substance Abuse Auth., 88 N.C. App. 495, 364 S.E.2d 179 (1988). State courts may be more willing than federal courts to permit individuals to sue alleging violations of statutes in which the legislature has not provided explicitly for private causes of action. McClurg, Your Money or Your Life: Interpreting the Federal Act Against Patient Dumping, 24 Wake Forest L. Rev. 173, 194-196 (1989); see, e.g., Guerrero v. Copper Queen Hosp., 112 Ariz. 104, 537 P.2d 1329 (1975) (en banc).

§6.1.3 Federal Statutory Entitlements to Care

Beginning in the 1960s, attorneys argued that the U.S. Constitution required the government to provide at public expense the facilities to care for those who could not obtain care elsewhere. The argument failed.[39] However, in Title XIX of the Social Security Act, commonly known as the Medicaid program, Congress created a statutory entitlement to healthcare, including care in healthcare facilities.[40] Medicaid patients have become an important source of revenue for many healthcare facilities, and litigation brought by facilities has helped protect eligible patients' rights to treatment.

Medicaid is a cooperative state-federal program to provide medical assistance to indigent persons. As a condition of receiving federal financial assistance in providing healthcare, states participating in Medicaid must prepare a medical assistance plan consistent with federal statutes and regulations.[41] At a minimum, these plans must provide eligible poor persons with a broad range of medical services, including inpatient hospital services, outpatient hospital services, other laboratory and x-ray services, physician's services, skilled nursing facility services, early and periodic screening and diagnosis and treatment, family planning services, home health services, and, as permitted by state licensing laws, nurse-midwife services.[42]

States' obligation to provide care is not unlimited. They need only provide "medically necessary"[43] services "sufficient in amount, duration, and scope to reasonably achieve [their] purpose."[44] States may not, however, limit services to an eligible person "solely because of the diagnosis, type of illness, or

---

[39]See, e.g., Maher v. Roe, 432 U.S. 464, 469 (1977). Persons in state custody are constitutionally entitled to some care. See, e.g., Youngblood v. Romero, 457 U.S. 307 (1982).

[40]Pub. L. No. 89-97, §121, 79 Stat. 291, 343 (1965).

[41]42 U.S.C. §1396(a) (1988).

[42]42 C.F.R. §440.210 (1988). These services are defined in id. §§440.10 to 440.50, 440.70, 440.165.

[43]Beal v. Doe, 432 U.S. 438, 444 (1977).

[44]42 C.F.R. §440.230(b) (1988); 42 U.S.C. §1396a(a)(17) (1988).

condition."[45] Nor may they set reimbursement rates below a level "reasonable and adequate to meet the costs which must be incurred by efficiently and economically operated facilities. . . ."[46]

States' compliance with these standards has been the subject of much litigation.[47] Rapidly rising healthcare costs placed great pressure on state Medicaid budgets, and in 1981 Congress amended Title XIX, giving states flexibility in designing reimbursement schemes to control costs. Many states took advantage of the opportunity and developed new reimbursement methods that lowered the amounts paid to providers of medical care.

A number of these new reimbursement methods were challenged in court as being inconsistent with Title XIX.[48] These challenges have had mixed success; courts only overturn states' determinations that a reimbursement method resulted in "adequate and reasonable" payments if the determination was "arbitrary and capricious."[49] Nevertheless, courts have invalidated methods of reimbursement that resulted in payments so low that they did not meet the costs of any of the facilities in a state, threatened to drive facilities out of the program, or endangered the financial stability of those remaining in it.[50]

Lowering reimbursement payments is one way to reduce Medicaid budgets; reducing services is another. In general, states have been successful in defending limits on services. For example, courts have approved provisions in state plans limiting coverage for visits to physician's offices to three per month,[51] reducing

---

[45]42 C.F.R. §440.230(c) (1988).

[46]42 U.S.C. §1396a(a)(13)(A) (1988).

[47]For a more detailed discussion of the issues raised in this section see Perkins, Increasing Provider Participation in the Medicaid Program: Is There a Doctor in the House?, 26 Hous. L. Rev. 77 (1989).

[48]These suits are brought against state officials under 42 U.S.C. §1983. See Wilder v. Virginia Hosp. Assn., 58 U.S.L.W. 4975 (June 12, 1990).

[49]E.g., Mississippi Hosp. Assn. v. Heckler, 701 F.2d 511 (5th Cir. 1983).

[50]See, e.g., AMISUB (PSL), Inc. v. Colorado Dept. of Social Serv., 879 F.2d 789, 797-801 (10th Cir. 1989). Illinois Hosp. Assn. v. Illinois Dept. of Public Aid, 576 F. Supp. 360 (N.D. Ill. 1983).

[51]Curtis v. Taylor, 625 F.2d 645 (5th Cir.), modified on other grounds, 648 F.2d 946 (5th Cir. 1980).

covered days of inpatient hospital care from 40 to 12 and outpatient visits from an unlimited number to 18,[52] requiring prior authorization for certain services,[53] and prohibiting reimbursement for all experimental treatments.[54]

Despite judicial approval of these broad limits on Medicaid coverage, attempts to eliminate coverage for particular treatments, or to limit the treatments to certain persons, often fail. For example, Pennsylvania's attempt to restrict Medicaid coverage for eyeglasses to vision problems resulting from eye disease was unsuccessful.[55] Similarly, courts have invalidated state refusals to provide patients with electronic speech devices,[56] sex change operations,[57] and certain drugs.[58]

Two specific therapies, abortion and transplants, receive special treatment under Title XIX. Since 1986, transplants have been subject to special rules that permit states to choose whether or not they will provide transplant coverage.[59] However, if transplants are part of the state plan, they must be reasonably funded and be offered under standards ensuring that similarly situated persons are treated alike.[60]

The United States Congress began tight controls on the expenditure of federal funds for abortions in 1976. The terms of the restriction have varied from year to year. The most restrictive provision, in place in fiscal 1976, provided for Medicaid abortion funding only when "the life of the mother would be endangered if the fetus were carried to term."[61]

---

[52]Charleston Memorial Hosp. v. Conrad, 693 F.2d 324 (4th Cir. 1982).

[53]Cowan v. Myers, 187 Cal. App. 3d 968, 232 Cal. Rptr. 299 (1986), cert. denied, 484 U.S. 846 (1987).

[54]Rush v. Parham, 625 F.2d 1150 (5th Cir. 1980).

[55]White v. Beal, 555 F.2d 1146 (3d Cir. 1977).

[56]Myers v. Reagan, 776 F.2d 241 (8th Cir. 1985).

[57]Pinneke v. Preisser, 623 F.2d 546 (8th Cir. 1980).

[58]Weaver v. Reagan, 886 F.2d 194 (8th Cir. 1989). Note that coverage limitations in Medicaid state plans are also subject to challenge under state law. See, e.g., Montana Low Income Coalition v. Gray, No. CDV-87-629 (Mont. Super. Ct., Feb. 5, 1988) (elimination of certain state Medicaid benefits invalid under state constitution).

[59]42 U.S.C. 1396b(i) (1988).

[60]Ellis v. Patterson, 859 F.2d 52, 55-56 (8th Cir. 1988).

[61]Harris v. McRae, 448 U.S. 297, 325 n.27 (1980).

In Harris v. McRae the United States Supreme Court held that the statute did not offend the Fifth Amendment to the Constitution.[62] In addition, it rejected the argument that Title XIX required states to provide abortions even though federal funding was unavailable.[63]

Although *McRae* made it clear that as a matter of federal law states need not provide Medicaid-funded abortions for which federal support is barred, some state courts, relying on state constitutions, have struck down state legislative attempts to restrict Medicaid funding for medically indicated abortions. For example, in Moe v. Secretary of Administration and Finance, the Massachusetts Supreme Court held that the state could not provide funding for childbirth, one form of the treatment of pregnancy, while restricting funding for abortion, another way of treating pregnancy.[64]

§6.1.4 State Statutory Entitlements to Care

Recognizing that the Medicaid program does not provide care for all who need it, states have set up their own programs to increase access to care for the poor. The plans vary considerably in method of financing, care provided, eligibility requirements, and obligations placed on providers. All these plans cannot be described in detail here,[65] but healthcare facility administrators

---

[62]Id. at 315-318.

[63]Id. at 308-310.

[64]382 Mass. 629, 655, 417 N.E.2d 387, 402 (1981). See also Doe v. Maher, 40 Conn. Supp. 394, 515 A.2d 134 (1986); Right to Choose v. Byrne, 91 N.J. 287, 450 A.2d 925 (1982); Committee to Defend Reproductive Rights v. Myers, 29 Cal. 3d 252, 172 Cal. Rptr. 866, 625 P.2d 779 (1981); but see Fischer v. Dept. of Public Welfare, 509 Pa. 293, 502 A.2d 114 (1985). The Court approved elimination of federal funding for nontherapeutic abortions in Maher v. Roe, 423 U.S. 464 (1977). The Oregon Supreme Court struck down state administrative restrictions on elective abortions on statutory grounds in Planned Parenthood Assn. v. Department of Human Resources, 297 Or. 563, 687 P.2d 785 (1984) (en banc).

[65]For a description of some of the programs, see Dowell, State and Local Government Responsibilities to Provide Medical Care for Indigents, 3 J. Law & Health 1 (1988-89).

should realize that state indigent care programs have been the basis for suits by providers seeking payment for services provided to nonpaying patients. For example, in Sandegren v. State of Florida ex rel. Sarasota County Public Hospital Board, a hospital successfully sued Sarasota County for over $150,000 in funds that the county was obligated by state law to appropriate for community mental health services.[66]

§6.1.5 Tax Incentives for Indigent Care

Additional pressure to supply uncompensated care has come from the tax system. Many healthcare facilities are exempt from state and local property taxes,[67] other state and local taxes, and federal income tax. These tax exemptions first applied to hospitals—institutions that began as charities serving the sick poor. But healthcare facilities have changed dramatically, and competition between profit and not-for-profit facilities, governments' need for additional tax revenues, and the perception that some facilities inadequately serve the poor have brought numerous recent challenges to these tax exemptions, especially in the state courts.

Under the federal income tax laws, a facility need not provide uncompensated care to enjoy tax-exempt status. That was not always the case. In Revenue Ruling 56-185, the Internal Revenue Service (IRS) stated that a hospital could qualify for tax-exempt status under §501(c)(3) of the Internal Revenue Code only if it provided care to those unable to pay to the extent of its financial ability.[68]

The IRS abandoned that position in 1969, reasoning that the delivery of healthcare services is a charitable purpose whether or not patients pay for the care.[69] However, whether or not a

---

[66]397 So. 2d 657 (Fla. 1981); see also Madera Community Hosp. v. Madera County, 155 Cal. App. 3d 136, 201 Cal. Rptr. 768 (1984).

[67]Also known as ad valorem taxes.

[68]Rev. Rul. 56-185, 1956-1 C.B. 202.

[69]Rev. Rul. 69-545, 1969-2 C.B. 117; see also Eastern Kentucky Welfare Rights Org. v. Simon, 506 F.2d 1278 (D.C. Cir. 1974), revd. on other grounds, 426 U.S. 26 (1976).

facility provides emergency care without regard to ability to pay remains a factor in the IRS decisions to grant tax-exempt status.[70] In addition, a failure to provide uncompensated care is a factor that the IRS may take into account in deciding whether an ostensibly nonprofit facility is in fact operated for private purposes and therefore ineligible for federal tax exemption.[71]

The situation at the state level is more complex. In many states, property dedicated to charitable purposes is exempt from ad valorem taxes (and occasionally other taxes) under broad statutory or constitutional provisions.[72] Other states exempt hospitals and other healthcare facilities under more specific state statutes,[73] including some that tie exemptions directly to the facilities' status under §501(c)(3).[74]

The outcomes of cases addressing tax-exempt status of necessity depend on the specific language of the tax exemption in question, but it is fair to say that the provision of uncompensated care can be an important factor in deciding whether a facility is tax-exempt. In Utah County v. Intermountain Health Care, the Utah Supreme Court set out a six-factor test to measure qualifications for tax exemptions under Utah law. The provision of free care, it held, was "[o]ne of the most significant of the factors," and the fact that the value of the free care provided by the hospitals in that case was less than 1 percent of their gross revenues helped doom their tax-exempt status.[75]

In an Illinois case,[76] an outpatient walk-in clinic argued that it was entitled to tax-exempt status because it provided uncompensated care equal to 6 percent of its total revenue,

---

[70]Rev. Rul. 69-545, 1969-2 C.B. 117; see also Internal Revenue Service, Exempt Organizations Handbook §349.2 (1988).

[71]See Harding Hosp. v. United States, 505 F.2d 1068 (6th Cir. 1974); Sonora Community Hosp. v. Commissioner, 46 T.C. 519 (1966).

[72]See, e.g., Pa. Const. art. VIII, §2; 72 Pa. Stat. Ann. tit. 72, §5020-204(a)(3) (Purdon Supp. 1989).

[73]See, e.g., Wis. Stat. Ann. §70.11(4m) (West 1989).

[74]See, e.g., Fla. Stat. Ann. §196.197(1) (West 1988).

[75]709 P.2d 265, 269-270, 274 (Utah 1985).

[76]Highland Park Hosp. v. State, 155 Ill. App. 3d 272, 507 N.E.2d 1331 (1987).

relying on an earlier case from the same state that granted an exemption to a hospital at which 5 percent of the total patient load consisted of charity patients.[77] The court disagreed, pointing out that the clinic did not, as the hospital in the earlier case did, provide charity care to all who sought it, but instead billed every patient, tried diligently to collect on those bills, and did not publicly admit that it treated charity patients.[78] In other jurisdictions, however, limits on access to free care, such as requiring preadmission deposits and transferring nonpaying patients to public facilities, have not resulted in the loss of tax-exempt status.[79]

Other jurisdictions place little or no weight on the provision of uncompensated care in the decision to grant tax exemptions. In some, it is not the amount of indigent care, but the fact that it is available to some patients (even if only in small amounts) that makes a facility eligible for tax-exempt status.[80] Others ignore charity care altogether, arguing, much like the Internal Revenue Service, that the provision of healthcare is by nature a charitable purpose.[81]

§6.2 Access to Emergency Care

The public has long expected hospital emergency departments to provide care to all who arrive at the door. Many hospitals, however, have resisted that expectation, most commonly by

---

[77]Sisters of Third Order of St. Francis v. Board of Review, 231 Ill. 317, 83 N.E. 272 (1907).

[78]*Highland Park*, 155 Ill. App. 3d at 281, 507 N.E.2d at 1336-1337.

[79]See, e.g., Callaway Community Hosp. Assn. v. Craighead, 759 S.W.2d 253 (Mo. Ct. App. 1988).

[80]See, e.g., Lamb County Appraisal Dist. v. South Plains Hospital-Clinic, 688 S.W.2d 896, 905-908 (Tex. Ct. App. 1985).

[81]See, e.g., Medical Center Hosp. of Vermont v. City of Burlington, 566 A.2d 1352 (Ver. 1989); Harvard Community Health Plan v. Board of Assessors, 384 Mass. 536, 427 N.E.2d 1159 (1981) (granting tax-exempt status to prepaid health plan); but see Supervisor of Assessments v. Group Health Assn., 308 Md. 151, 517 A.2d 1076 (Md. 1986) (denying status to health maintenance organization).

transferring uninsured or underinsured poor patients to other facilities, a practice known as "dumping." Under current state and federal law, refusing to provide emergency services involves significant legal risks.[1]

§6.2.1 Common Law

State common law has played a significant (though narrow) role in increasing access to the emergency department by penalizing facilities for inappropriate refusals to treat, whether the refusal is based on a patient's ability to pay or is caused by the incompetence or indifference of emergency department personnel.[2] In examining these cases, it is helpful to keep two issues separate. The first is, may a facility with an emergency department refuse to provide basic emergency care to a patient in need? The second is, if it does offer emergency care to a patient, under what circumstances may the patient be transferred to another facility for further care?[3]

Despite some courts' claim of adherence to the rule that a hospital "owes the public no duty to accept any patient not desired by it,"[4] no case has held that a facility may turn away or transfer an emergency patient before providing an examina-

---

§6.2 [1]The existence of this practice has been demonstrated in several studies. See, e.g., Kellerman and Hackman, Emergency Department Patient "Dumping": An Analysis of Interhospital Transfers to the Regional Medical Center at Memphis, Tennessee, 78 Am. J. Pub. Health 1287 (1988); Schiff, Ansell, Schlosser, Ahamed, Adris, Morrison, and Whitman, Transfer to a Public Hospital: A Prospective Study of 467 Patients, 314 New Eng. J. Med. 552 (1986).

[2]For purposes of this discussion, it is assumed that the hospital is liable for the conduct of emergency department personnel in treating, refusing to treat, or transferring patients. That will not always be the case. See §4.12.

[3]These issues have been the subject of much commentary. See, e.g., Annas, Your Money or Your Life: "Dumping" Uninsured Patients from Hospital Emergency Wards, 76 Amer. J. Pub. Health 74 (1986).

[4]Crews v. Birmingham Baptist Hosp., 229 Ala. 398, 399, 157 So. 224, 225 (1934); see also Le Jeune Road Hosp. v. Watson, 171 So. 2d 202, 203 (Fla. Dist. Ct. App. 1965).

tion and basic emergency care.[5] Today, the emergency department's duty to provide care to all who seek it is "essentially universal and noncontroversial."[6]

Courts have arrived at this position by two different routes.[7] The first seeks to avoid the traditional "no duty" rule by finding that the patient is admitted and the provider-patient relationship established while the patient receives, or, more typically, waits for, treatment in the emergency department. For example, in Methodist Hospital v. Ball, an intern briefly examined an auto accident victim, left him largely unattended for 45 minutes, and then transferred him to another facility, where he died of internal bleeding. In the resulting lawsuit the court held that while waiting in the emergency room the victim had become a "patient" to whom the hospital owed a duty of care, "even though he was never given a room in the hospital and stayed in emergency room only forty-five minutes."[8] Once the patient-

---

[5]But cf. Hill v. Ohio County, 468 S.W.2d 306 (Ky. 1971), cert. denied, 404 U.S. 1041 (1972) (holding hospital may turn away woman in labor based on dubious conclusion that active labor is not an emergency); Campbell v. Mincey, 413 F. Supp. 16 (N.D. Miss. 1975), affd., 542 F.2d 573 (5th Cir. 1976) (same). Notwithstanding those cases, a duty to treat in an emergency probably exists in Kentucky and Mississippi. See Richard v. Adair Hosp. Foundation Corp., 566 S.W.2d 791, 793 (Ky. Ct. App. 1978); New Biloxi Hosp. v. Frazier, 245 Miss. 185, 146 So. 2d 882 (1962).

[6]See Annas, Legal Risks and Responsibilities of Physicians in the AIDS Epidemic, 18 Hastings Center Report 26, 27 (April/May 1988).

[7]A third route, one that has received more attention from commentators than from courts, would hold hospitals, whether public or private, to be the equivalent of public utilities, with a corresponding "fiduciary" relationship to the public. See, e.g., Doe v. Bridgeton Hosp. Assn., 71 N.J. 478, 485-489, 366 A.2d 641, 644-646 (1976), cert. denied, 433 U.S. 914 (1977); Fine, Opening the Closed Doors: The Duty of Hospitals to Treat Emergency Patients, 24 Wash. U.J. Urb. & Contemp. L. 123 (1983).

[8]Methodist Hosp. v. Ball, 50 Tenn. App. 460, 469, 362 S.W.2d 475, 479 (1961); see also O'Neill v. Montefiore Hosp., 11 A.D.2d 132, 202 N.Y.S.2d 436 (N.Y. App. Div. 1960) (nurse assisting possible heart attack victim may by calling a doctor create provider-patient relationship with facility); Bourgeois v. Dade County, 99 So. 2d 575 (Fla. 1957); cf. Klassette v. Mecklenburg County Area Mental Health, Mental Retardation, and Substance Abuse Auth., 88 N.C. App. 495, 364 S.E.2d 179 (1988) (action by facility may be gratuitous undertaking resulting in duty to provide care).

provider relationship is established, the facility may not unilaterally terminate it by discharging or transferring the patient.[9]

Wilmington General Hospital v. Manlove illustrates the second approach. In *Manlove* the court held that a duty to treat all emergency patients who sought care at an emergency room arose from the public's reliance on the "established custom" that the facility would render it.[10] This rule has been applied to public[11] and private[12] facilities alike.

The approach a court picks to establish a duty to provide emergency care may have practical consequences. Courts tempted to find informal admissions based on the conduct of emergency department personnel create a difficulty for emergency departments, because the duty owed to an admitted patient may be greater than that owed to an emergency patient. A comparison of two cases illustrates the problem.

In Joyner v. Alton Oschner Medical Foundation, the Oschner Clinic emergency department received an auto accident victim and after four hours of treatment transferred him, in stable condition, to a Veterans' Administration hospital for further care. The transfer was made because the patient did not have the money for the clinic's preadmission deposit. The patient sued, but the court found the clinic's action appropriate and denied the victim recovery for alleged pain and suffering caused by the delay in his being admitted to a hospital.[13]

In Le Jeune Road Hospital, Inc. v. Watson, the facility treated an 11-year-old boy with appendicitis for about two hours and then asked him and his mother to leave when they were unable to put down a deposit for the required appendectomy. The child was successfully treated several hours later at

---

[9]See §6.4.

[10]54 Del. 15, 23, 174 A.2d 135, 139 (1961); see also Valdez v. Lyman-Roberts Hosp., 638 S.W.2d 111, 114 n.1 (Tex. Ct. App. 1982).

[11]See, e.g., Williams v. Hospital Auth., 119 Ga. App. 626, 627, 168 S.E.2d 336, 337 (1969).

[12]See, e.g., Mercy Medical Center v. Winnebago County, 58 Wis. 2d 260, 268, 206 N.W.2d 198, 201 (1973).

[13]Joyner v. Alton Ochsner Medical Found., 230 So. 2d 913, 915-916 (La. Ct. App. 1970).

another hospital. In this case the court held that the boy had been admitted to the facility and that requiring him to leave was abandonment. On that court's interpretation of abandonment doctrine,[14] the child was entitled to recover for the pain and suffering caused by the delay in obtaining treatment.[15]

Jurisdictions that follow *Manlove* create other problems. First, *Manlove* contains no definition of an emergency. In practice, this has proved to be a difficulty for patients who would sue a hospital: the plaintiff in Campbell v. Mincey[16] must have been surprised to learn that active labor is no emergency.

Second, *Manlove* says nothing about how to assess the expectations of potential emergency patients. One consequence of this ambiguity is that prudent facilities exercise caution in the way they publicize services to avoid creating inaccurate perceptions in the community. For example, some freestanding outpatient treatment facilities have dropped the word "emergency" from their names, lest patients begin arriving expecting care for heart attacks and gunshot wounds.

Furthermore, while *Manlove* establishes a duty to provide emergency care, it does not provide guidance to facilities attempting to decide precisely what sorts of care it must provide as part of that duty. National accreditation standards permit a wide variety in levels of emergency care, ranging from basic emergency care to highly sophisticated care for victims of severe trauma.[17] Would a facility in a community with five Level III emergency departments be able to operate one at Level I, or would that be inconsistent with the "established custom" in the community? What would the custom be in a community served by a single emergency department? Whatever services that

---

[14]See §6.3.

[15]Le Jeune Road Hosp. v. Watson, 171 So. 2d 202, 203-204 (Fla. Dist. Ct. App. 1965).

[16]413 F. Supp. 16 (N.D. Miss. 1975).

[17]The Joint Commission on Accreditation of Healthcare Organizations classifies emergency departments on a scale of I to IV based on the level of service they provide. See Joint Commission on Accreditation of Healthcare Organizations, 1990 Accreditation Manual for Hospitals 31-46 (1991).

facility routinely provided, or perhaps what facilities in similar communities customarily provide?[18]

Manlove does not answer this question. However, phrasing the duty owed under *Manlove* in terms of the practice in the same or a similar community makes it easy to transform the *Manlove* duty into the ordinary tort law duty to conform to the standard of care. In some jurisdictions this transformation has in fact taken place, and arguments about special or limited duties to emergency patients are not taken seriously.[19]

Once a court creates a duty to treat emergency patients, the issue becomes whether, and at what point, emergency patients requiring further care may be released or transferred to another facility. This issue has been litigated for almost 70 years.

On a cold, rainy day in the early 1930s a man took his 2½-year-old daughter to Birmingham Baptist Hospital. She was near death from diphtheria. Doctors in the emergency room administered oxygen, took a throat culture, and gave her an antitoxin. Her condition improved and, applying a hospital rule against admitting patients with communicable diseases, the doctors sent her home, where she promptly died. In Crews v. Birmingham Baptist Hospital, the father sued and lost, the Alabama Supreme Court determining that the hospital had no duty to admit the girl for further treatment.[20]

Relying on *Crews*, healthcare facilities have argued that once a facility gives basic emergency care it has no duty to admit a patient requiring further care.[21] In response to this argument

---

[18]Cf. Baxter v. Alexin Bros. Hosp., 214 Cal. App. 3d 722, 262 Cal. Rptr. 867 (1989).

[19]See, e.g., Carr v. St. Paul Fire and Marine Ins. Co., 384 F. Supp. 821 (W.D. Ark. 1974).

[20]The case suggests, but need not be read to hold, that the hospital might have turned the girl away without offering any treatment. A better reading of this case is that the hospital's rule against admitting patients with communicable diseases was acceptable given the limited ability to control infections in 1934. See Rothenburg, Who Cares?: The Evolution of the Legal Duty to Provide Emergency Care, 26 Houston L. Rev. 21, 30-31 (1989).

[21]See, e.g., Harper v. Baptist Medical Center-Princeton, 341 So. 2d 133, 134 (Ala. 1976) (per curiam).

most courts ignore facilities' claim to be absolutely free to refuse admission and instead analyze refusals of admission using negligence principles, asking whether the facility's conduct in transferring or releasing a patient was consistent with good medical practice or was reasonable under the circumstances. Thus, in most jurisdictions today, a facility must decide on a case-by-case basis which patients may safely be transferred and which must be admitted for further treatment.[22]

As this discussion suggests, the development of special, limited common-law duties to emergency patients from *Crews* in 1934 through *Manlove* in 1961 and on to the present has led to unfortunate confusion. Although attorneys and courts continue to make carefully drawn distinctions among duties owed to emergency patients at various points between the facility door and a bed, these distinctions may be expected to collapse under their own weight. Today, prudent healthcare facilities with emergency rooms will assume, regardless of case law to the contrary, that their duty to emergency patients is at all times to provide reasonable care under the circumstances.

§6.2.2 State Statutes

The practical significance of the common-law duty to provide emergency care has been reduced by state and federal legislation establishing duties to treat and limiting facility discretion in making transfers. Over 20 states have statutes or regulations that prohibit facilities from denying emergency care based on ability to pay[23] (although few of them have effective enforcement provisions).

---

[22]See, e.g., Reeves v. North Broward Hosp. Dist., 191 So. 2d 307 (Fla. Dist. Ct. App. 1966), cert. denied, 201 So. 2d 232 (Fla. 1967); New Biloxi Hosp. v. Frazier, 245 Miss. 185, 197, 146 So. 2d 882, 887 (1962). Negligence principles are discussed more fully in Chapter 4.

[23]See, e.g., Ill. Ann. Stat. ch. 111½, para. 86 (Smith-Hurd 1988); Mass. Gen. Laws Ann. ch. 111, §70E(m)(e) (1985). See generally, Dowell, Indigent Access to Hospital Emergency Room Services, 18 Clearinghouse Rev. 483 (1984).

Courts, however, have been willing to permit lawsuits based on such statutes against facilities by patients refused emergency treatment, even when the statutes themselves do not explicitly establish private causes of action. For example, reasoning from state regulations requiring certain hospitals to maintain an emergency department, the court in Guererro v. Copper Queen Hospital held that a patient who was denied emergency care could sue the facility for damages.[24]

§6.2.3 Emergency Care Under Federal Law

The United States Congress supplemented state statutory and common-law duties to provide emergency care with the "anti-dumping" provisions of the Consolidated Omnibus Budget Reconciliation Act of 1985 (COBRA).[25] COBRA requires hospitals that have emergency departments and that participate in the Medicare program[26] to provide basic emergency treatment to all patients and forbids inappropriate patient transfers to other facilities.[27]

Under COBRA, hospitals must screen all emergency department patients, within the staff and facilities available, to determine whether they have an emergency medical condition.[28] "Emergency medical condition" means a "condition manifesting

---

[24]Guerrero v. Copper Queen Hosp., 112 Ariz. 104, 537 P.2d 1329 (1975); cf. Klassette v. Mecklenburg County Area Mental Health, Mental Retardation, and Substance Abuse Auth., 88 N.C. App. 495, 364 S.E.2d 179 (1988).

[25]Pub. L. No. 99-272, §9121, 1986 U.S. Code Cong. & Admin. News (100 Stat.) 82, 164-167 (codified as amended at 42 U.S.C. §1395dd) (hereinafter COBRA).

[26]42 U.S.C.A. 1395cc(a)(1)(I) (West Supp. 1990).

[27]COBRA does not address the steering of emergency patients to particular facilities by emergency transportation systems. In Hosp. Auth. v. Jones, 386 S.E.2d 120 (Ga. 1989), the parents of a burn victim sent for financial reasons to a hospital without proper treatment facilities recovered $1,310,000, including $1,300,000 in punitive damages. For a case finding no liability under federal law for such steering see Wideman v. Shallowford Community Hosp., 826 F.2d 1030 (11th Cir. 1987).

[28]42 U.S.C.S. §1395dd(a) (Law. Co-op. Supp. 1990).

itself by acute symptoms" that in the absence of immediate treatment is expected to place the patient's health (or the health of a fetus) in serious jeopardy, impair seriously the patient's bodily functions, or cause serious dysfunction of an organ or body part. When applied to a woman having contractions the term means that there is not enough time to make a transfer before delivery or that transfer would pose a threat to the mother or fetus.[29]

If the facility determines that a patient has an emergency medical condition, it must provide the treatment necessary to stabilize him "within the staff and facilities available at the hospital" or transfer him in accordance with COBRA's provisions.[30] "Stabilized" means that no material deterioration is likely to result from or occur during a transfer to another facility, or, with respect to a woman in labor, that she has delivered.[31]

COBRA places strict limits on a facility's power to transfer unstable patients. Such a patient may be transferred if the patient (or the patient's legally responsible representative) requests the transfer in writing after having been informed of the facility's obligations under COBRA and of the risks of the transfer. Otherwise, transfer of an unstable patient requires a physician to certify in writing that the benefits of the transfer are expected to outweigh the risks associated with it. If a physician is not present in the emergency department, another qualified provider may sign such a form in consultation with a physician, provided that the physician later counter-signs the form.[32]

In addition to completing the paperwork, the facility must ensure that the transfer is "appropriate."[33] An appropriate transfer is one in which the transferring facility does everything in its capacity to limit medical risks and in which (1) the receiving facility has the space and personnel to provide treatment and consents to the transfer, (2) the transferring facility

----

[29]Id. §1395dd(e)(1).
[30]Id. §1395dd(b)(1).
[31]Id. §1395dd(e)(3).
[32]Id. §1395dd(c)(1).
[33]Id.

provides copies of all records relating to treatment, including lab results and, (3) the transfer is made using proper equipment and personnel.[34] Facilities on the receiving end of a transfer, whether proper under COBRA or not, should remember that the COBRA rules governing evaluation, stabilizing treatment, and transfer apply with equal force to them on receipt of the transferred patient.[35]

Violations of COBRA may result in termination or suspension of the offending healthcare facility's Medicare provider agreement, and each knowing violation subjects a facility to civil monetary penalties of up to $50,000. In addition, any person harmed by a violation may bring a civil suit directly against the facility and collect such damages as are permitted under the law of the state in which the facility is located. Finally, a facility that suffers financial loss because of an improper transfer may recover those losses from the offending hospital. Suits by patients and other facilities are subject to a two-year limitations period.[36]

The reach of COBRA will not be known for several years. Regulations interpreting the statute have been proposed but at this writing are not final.[37] The first lawsuits brought under the statute are just beginning to work their way through the courts,[38] and many questions about the statute remain unanswered.[39] Among the most important is whether in civil suits by patients facilities will be strictly liable for making transfers that violate

---

[34]Id. §1395dd(c)(2).

[35]See Thompson v. St. Anne Hosp., 716 F. Supp. 8, 9-10 (N.D. Ill. 1989).

[36]42 U.S.C.S. §1395dd(e) (Law. Co-op. Supp. 1990). In addition, COBRA does not preempt state law except in the case of a direct conflict between COBRA and state law. Thus, an individual harmed by an inappropriate transfer may bring actions under COBRA as well as for negligence or the violation of state statutes. Id. §1395dd(f).

[37]53 Fed. Reg. 22513 (1988) (proposed June 16, 1988).

[38]See Taylor, *Cracking Down on Patient Dumping*, Natl. L.J., June 6, 1988, at 1, col. 1.

[39]Two articles discussing COBRA are McClurg, Your Money or Your Life: Interpreting the Federal Act Against Patient Dumping, 24 Wake Forest L. Rev. 173 (1989) and Enfield and Sklar, Patient Dumping in the Hospital Emergency Department: Renewed Interest in an Old Problem, 8 Am. J.L. & Med. 561 (1988).

the Act, or whether patients will have to prove facilities negligent (for example, in assessing a patient's condition) in making an improper transfer or refusing care.[40]

Another issue, the relationship between COBRA and state malpractice reform schemes, has been the subject of one case thus far and will be the subject of more. In Reid v. Indianapolis Osteopathic Medical Hospital, the court held that a suit under COBRA need not be submitted to a state malpractice review panel, but that COBRA did incorporate the state's cap on damages in malpractice cases.[41]

The last significant subject of litigation has been whether or not a plaintiff seeking damages under COBRA must prove that the transfer or refusal to care complained of was motivated by financial concerns. Surprisingly, since the text of the statute itself gives no basis for such a conclusion, two of the first courts to consider this question held that such proof is required in a COBRA action.[42] In DeBerry v. Sherman Hospital Association the court reached the opposite, and probably correct, conclusion that proof of financial motivation for COBRA violations is not required.[43]

Controversies will arise over many other issues as well, including the meaning of terms and phrases such as "stabilize" and "emergency medical condition"; the role of peer review in investigating complaints; the extent of the screening a hospital must do to determine if an emergency exists; and the interaction of COBRA and state immunity rules.[44]

---

[40]See Reid v. Indianapolis Osteopathic Medical Hosp., 709 F. Supp. 853, 855 (S.D. Ind. 1989) (stating that COBRA sets "strict liability standard").

[41]Id. at 854-856; but see Wilson v. Atlanicare Medical Center, 868 F.2d 34 (1st Cir. 1989) (suggesting in dicta that state procedural requirements in malpractice cases may apply in COBRA cases).

[42]See Evitt v. University Heights Hosp., 727 F. Supp. 495 (S.D. Ind. 1989); Stewart v. Myrick, 731 F. Supp. 433 (D. Kan. 1990).

[43]No. 90-C-1173 (N.D. Ill., June 15, 1990) (LEXIS, Genfed library, Dist file).

[44]Estate of Banks v. Chambers Memorial Hosp. Auxiliary, 865 F.2d 696 (5th Cir. 1989), held that sovereign immunity barred suit against a county hospital arising from its refusal to treat an uninsured 1-year-old girl who later died from choking on a bean. Whether suit would be permitted under COBRA in these circumstances is open to question.

§6.3 Common-Law Constraints on Discharges

Whether a patient gets in the door as an emergency or ordinary admission, facilities often face the question of whether to continue to provide care if the patient, the patient's insurers, or other third parties cannot or will not pay for it. The primary common-law constraint on the decision to discharge[1] for financial or other nonmedical reasons is the possibility of a lawsuit alleging abandonment.[2]

The relationship between a healthcare provider and a patient continues, and the provider is required to provide care, until (1) both parties agree to end it; (2) the patient ends it; (3) the provider's services are no longer needed; or (4) the provider withdraws after reasonable notice to the patient and the patient is able to obtain alternative care without suffering damage in the process.[3] If the provider terminates care inappropriately, it can be liable for any resulting damage.

Meiselman v. Crown Heights Hospital is one of the few cases applying this rule in a suit against a healthcare facility.[4] In *Meiselman*, a hospital's chief of staff admitted a boy for treatment of osteomyelitis. After 18 weeks of care, the bill came to about $1,000, of which the child's father had paid $349. The physician discharged the boy, who continued to have severe problems.[5] In the resulting lawsuit, the highest court of New York reversed a summary judgment in favor of the doctor and the hospital, stating that the "jury might have found that the defendants had

---

§6.3 [1]The attending physician makes the decision to order discharge. When and under what circumstances the facility will be held accountable for the physician's acts will vary depending on the jurisdiction and the circumstances. See §4.12. This discussion assumes that the facility has some legal responsibility for the discharge decision. See, e.g., Morrison v. Washington County, 700 F.2d 678 (11th Cir. 1983).

[2]See §4.9.2.

[3]Annas, Legal Risks and Responsibilities of Physicians in the AIDS Epidemic, 18 Hastings Center Report 26, 27 (April/May 1988).

[4]285 N.Y. 389, 34 N.E.2d 367 (1941); see also Le Jeune Road Hosp. v. Watson, 171 So. 2d 202, 204 (Fla. Dist. Ct. App. 1965).

[5]*Meiselman*, 285 N.Y. at 393-394, 34 N.E.2d at 369.

prematurely and willfully discharged themselves from attention to the case while the patient was desperately ill . . ." and that this act was responsible for damage to the child from the continuing infection.[6]

The patient in *Meiselman* required continual inpatient care. However, the discharge of an individual who needs some further healthcare but does not need the facility's inpatient services could also create a risk of liability. Those lacking a home, family or friends who can help, or the means to obtain needed follow-up care should not be discharged if harm could result.[7]

Although it is sensible to assume that there is a limit to a healthcare facility's duty to provide free care to patients who can neither pay nor be safely discharged, that limit has not been spelled out by the courts.[8] Facilities approach difficult discharge decisions paying careful attention to ethical, legal, financial, and public relations concerns. In some instances, no good solution is found. Thus, many children infected with the human immunodeficiency virus and abandoned by their parents spend long periods of time in hospitals at great expense, because there is no place for them to go.

B. Discrimination and Access

§6.4 Overview

Local, state, and federal laws prohibit healthcare facilities from discriminating in the availability of or in the manner of providing

---

[6]Id. at 370, 285 N.Y. at 385-396.

[7]Report of the Task Force on Legal Issues in Discharge Planning, Office of the General Counsel, American Hospital Association, Discharging Hospital Patients: Legal Implications for Institutional Providers and Health Care Professionals, Legal Memorandum No. 9, at 41-44 (June 1987).

[8]Cf. Payton v. Weaver, 131 Cal. App. 3d 38, 182 Cal. Rptr. 225 (1982) (approving refusal to continue treating noncompliant patient in end-stage renal disease program).

services.[1] Discrimination based race, color, gender, sexual preference, national origin, religion, age, or handicap, or a combination of these, may, depending on the circumstances and the jurisdiction, cause legal problems and result in lawsuits, loss of funding, loss of tax-exempt status, and loss of licensure. Because of its general applicability, the following discussion will focus on federal law, but facilities should remember that state and local laws may provide protections that are as strong or stronger against discrimination.

§6.5 Constitutional Protections Against Discrimination

The Fifth and Fourteenth Amendments to the United States Constitution[1] limit the power of public and quasi-public facilities to discriminate in admissions, programs, or services. However, current constitutional doctrine does not treat all discrimination alike. To oversimplify the matter,[2] the Constitution bars discrimination based on race, national origin, or the exercise of a right expressly granted by Constitution (such as the right to freely practice one's religion), unless a compelling reason for the discrimination exists. Discrimination based on gender "must

---

§6.4 [1]Discrimination in employment and on medical staffs is discussed in Chapters 1 and 2.

§6.5 [1]U.S. Const. amend. V, amend. XIV, §1. The Fourteenth Amendment provides in part: "No state shall make or enforce any law which shall abridge the privileges or immunities of citizens of the United States; nor shall any state deprive any person of life, liberty, or property, without due process of law; nor deny to any person within its jurisdiction the equal protection of the laws." U.S. Const. amend. XIV, §1. The Fifth Amendment, applicable to the federal government, does not contain an equal protection clause, but the Supreme Court has held that the concepts of equal protection apply to the federal government because they are inherent in the Fifth Amendment's due process guarantee. See, e.g., Davis v. Passman, 442 U.S. 228, 234 (1979).

[2]For a thorough introduction to equal protection doctrine see R. Rotunda, J. Nowak, and N. Young, 2 Treatise on Constitutional Law: Substance and Procedure 314-362 (1986).

serve important governmental objectives and must be substantially related to the achievement of those objectives."[3]

In suits under the Fifth and Fourteenth Amendments the plaintiff must prove (1) intentional discrimination[4] by (2) the government or by a person or entity so closely identified with the government that its actions constitute "state action."[5] Both of these elements of the plaintiff's case can be difficult to establish.

Proof of intentional discrimination requires the plaintiff to demonstrate that the defendant "selected or reaffirmed a particular course of action at least in part 'because of,' not merely 'in spite of,' its adverse effects upon an identifiable group."[6] Changing the facts of Personnel Administrator v. Feeney[7] yields an example to illustrate this rule. Imagine that in response to a shortage of nursing home beds, the board of a public extended care facility decided to give preference in admission to veterans in an effort to reward them for their service to the nation. This preference would place a substantial burden on women, who would lose admission opportunities to veterans, almost all of whom are men. Nevertheless, because the board did not act with the intent to discriminate against women, the preference would not be unconstitutional.

The "state action" requirement presents another difficult hurdle for plaintiffs asserting constitutional claims against health-care facilities.[8] By their terms, the Fifth and Fourteenth Amend-

---

[3]Craig v. Boren, 429 U.S. 190, 197 (1976).

[4]Washington v. Davis, 426 U.S. 229, 238-244 (1976).

[5]Suits against local governmental entities and state officials for violations of constitutional rights may be brought under 42 U.S.C. §1983. See S. Nahmod, Civil Rights and Civil Liberties Litigation: The Law of Section 1983, at 13-15 (2d ed. 1986). Suits against the federal government may be brought directly under the Constitution. See Davis v. Passman, 442 U.S. 228, 236-244 (1979). There are important differences between suits under §1983 and under the Constitution, differences that are beyond the scope of this chapter.

[6]442 U.S. 256, 279 (1979) (holding that Massachusetts law giving preference for civil service jobs to veterans does not violate equal protection clause).

[7]Id.

[8]In the equal protection context, conduct by a defendant that is "state

ments apply only to the government; private facilities are not subject to the Constitution's ban on discrimination. However, extensive state and federal involvement in the healthcare system often makes it difficult to determine where government action leaves off and private action begins.

Government financial and regulatory involvement with private facilities can make those facilities subject to suit under the Constitution. In 1963, the United States Court of Appeals for the Fourth Circuit required Moses H. Cone Memorial Hospital and Wesley Long Community Hospital in Greensboro, North Carolina to stop discriminating based on race in patient admissions and medical staff appointments. The court held that the hospitals' participation in the construction funding program of the Hill-Burton Act made them state actors subject to the Fifth and Fourteenth Amendments.[9]

Today, receipt of funds under Hill-Burton or government participation in a facility's planning process would not suffice to make a facility's acts state action.[10] A private facility may become a state actor if it (1) exercises powers traditionally reserved for the state,[11] (2) acts for the state's benefit or shares the rewards and responsibilities of a private venture with the state,[12] or (3) acts pursuant to the state's direction or encouragement.[13]

---

action" under the Constitution satisfies the requirement in a §1983 action that the defendant act "under color of law." Rendell-Baker v. Kohn, 457 U.S. 830, 838 (1982).

[9]Simkins v. Moses H. Cone Memorial Hosp., 323 F.2d 959 (4th Cir.) (en banc), cert. denied, 376 U.S. 938 (1963).

[10]See Modaber v. Culpepper Memorial Hosp., 674 F.2d 1023 (4th Cir. 1982), applying Jackson v. Metropolitan Edison Co., 419 U.S. 345 (1974); Lubin v. Crittenden Hosp. Assn., 713 F.2d 414 (8th Cir. 1983), cert. denied, 465 U.S. 1025 (1984); see generally Action of Private Hospital as State Action under 42 U.S.C.S. §1983 or Fourteenth Amendment, 42 A.L.R. Fed. 463 (1979).

[11]See, e.g., Finch v. Mississippi State Medical Assn., 585 F.2d 765, 778 (5th Cir. 1978) (medical society performs public function when it appoints members of the Mississippi State Board of Health).

[12]See, e.g., Burton v. Wilmington Parking Auth., 365 U.S. 715, 725 (1961); Modaber, 674 F.2d at 1025.

[13]Modaber, 674 F.2d at 1025; Clair v. Centre Community Hosp., 317 Pa. Super. 25, 436 A.2d 1065 (1983).

Unfortunately, no firm rule exists for determining when a facility is sufficiently tied to the state to become a state actor. The issue is determined by "sifting facts and weighing circumstances"[14] in an effort to determine "whether there is a sufficiently close nexus" between the state and the private actor "that the action of the latter may fairly be treated as that of the State itself."[15]

The strongest case for a determination of state action is when a public entity has direct control over a facility's governing board. For example, in 1973 the chief of staff of the Milo Community Hospital in Milo, Maine sterilized Georgia Downs, a deaf-mute, four days after the birth of her second out-of-wedlock child. She sued the hospital and several other defendants, claiming that the sterilization violated her constitutional rights. On appeal, the court held that the Milo Community Hospital was a state actor, emphasizing that the Board of Selectmen of the town of Milo appointed the entire board of directors of the hospital.[16]

Short of direct control through the power to appoint the governing board, a public body may make a state actor of a private facility through control conferred by financing arrangements and by retaining an interest in the facility's revenues.[17] On the other hand, a slightly more distant relationship between the state and the private facility is enough to insulate the facility from the claim that it is a state actor. For example, a physician sued the Orange Memorial Hospital Corporation in an attempt to invalidate a rule prohibiting abortions in Orange Memorial Hospital.[18] The hospital was built on land donated to Orange

---

[14]*Burton*, 365 U.S. at 722.

[15]Jackson v. Metropolitan Edison Co., 419 U.S. 345, 351 (1974).

[16]Downs v. Sawtelle, 574 F.2d 1, 6-9 (1st Cir. 1978), cert. denied, 439 U.S. 910 (1978).

[17]Jatoi v. Hurst-Euless-Bedford Hosp. Auth., 807 F.2d 1214, 1220-1222 (5th Cir. 1987), modified on other grounds, 819 F.2d 545 (1987), cert. denied, 484 U.S. 1010 (1988).

[18]Greco v. Orange Memorial Hosp. Corp., 513 F.2d 873 (5th Cir. 1975), cert. denied, 423 U.S. 1000 (1975). For a discussion of the validity of such rules, see §6.10.

County, Texas using a combination of Hill-Burton funds and bonds issued by the county. The bonds were repaid out of the county's tax proceeds; they were not self-liquidating revenue bonds. The county leased the facility to the nonprofit, tax-exempt Orange Memorial Hospital Corporation for $1 per year. The corporation was run by an independent board of directors. The county retained only the right to obtain financial and other information about the facility and to approve the disposal of equipment. The United States Court of Appeals for the Fifth Circuit held that the relationship between the county and the hospital was not close enough to make the hospital a state actor.[19]

§6.6 Federal Antidiscrimination Statutes

Congress supplemented constitutional protections against discrimination with Title VI of the Civil Rights Act of 1964,[1] §504 of the Rehabilitation Act of 1973,[2] and Title III of the Older Americans Amendments of 1975.[3] Title VI prohibits discrimination based on race, color, or national origin, §504 prohibits discrimination based on handicap, and Title III prohibits discrimination based on age in any program or activity, whether public or private, receiving federal financial assistance.[4]

"Federal financial assistance" is broadly defined in regulations to cover direct funding, grants, loans, and use of federal personnel and property.[5] Most healthcare facilities are subject to

---

[19]Id. at 882.

§6.6 [1]Pub. L. No. 88-352, §§601-04, 78 Stat. 241, 252.

[2]Pub. L. No. 93-112, §504, 87 Stat. 355, 394.

[3]Pub. L. No. 94-135, §206, 89 Stat. 713, 728.

[4]For a case in which all three statutes were used to challenge a major hospital consolidation plan see National Assn. for the Advancement of Colored People v. Medical Center, Inc., 453 F. Supp. 280 (D. Del. 1978), revd., 599 F.2d 1247 (3d Cir. 1979), on remand, 491 F. Supp. 290 (D. Del. 1980), affd., 657 F.2d 1981 (3d Cir. 1981) (en banc).

[5]45 C.F.R. §§80.2 (Title VI), 84.3(h) (Section 504), 90.4 (Title III) (1988).

these statutes through receipt of Medicaid and Medicare funds[6] or other federal support for their operations.[7]

If any one program or activity of a healthcare facility receives federal financial assistance, the Civil Rights Restoration Act of 1988[8] applies Title VI, §504, and Title III to the entire facility. Furthermore, if any single facility of a multi-facility healthcare organization receives federal financial assistance, the entire organization is subject to the Acts.[9] For example, if a hospital corporation receives federal aid for its emergency room, then the antidiscrimination laws apply to all other activities of the hospital. Similarly, if a single nursing home in a five-home chain receives federal funds, the entire chain is subject to antidiscrimination provisions.[10]

Title VI provides: "No person in the United States shall, on the ground of race, color, or national origin, be excluded from participation in, be denied the benefits of, or be subjected to discrimination under any program or activity receiving federal financial assistance."[11] The conduct prohibited under Title VI is more completely described in regulations[12] that prohibit obvious forms of discrimination (such as denial of services to or physical segregation of particular classes of patients) as well as practices that are not as directly discriminatory (such as a decision to

---

[6]See 45 C.F.R. pt. 80, app. A, pt. 1, No. 121 and pt. 2, No. 30 (1989); United States v. Baylor Univ. Medical Center, 736 F.2d 1039 (5th Cir. 1984), cert. denied, 469 U.S. 1189 (1985).

[7]45 C.F.R. pt. 80, app. A (1989) provides an extensive list of sources of federal financial assistance for purposes of Title VI. Receipt of assistance under any of those programs should also subject a facility to §504 and Title III. See *Baylor Univ. Medical Center*, 736 F.2d at 1047.

[8]Pub. L. No. 100-259, 1988 U.S. Code Cong. & Admin. News (102 Stat.) 28.

[9]42 U.S.C.A. §2000d-4a(3)(A)(ii) (West Supp. 1989); 42 U.S.C.A. §6107(4)(c)(i)(II) (West Supp. 1989); 29 U.S.C.A. §794(3)(A)(ii) (West Supp. 1989).

[10]These examples are contained in S. Rep. No. 100-64, 100th Cong., 2d Sess. 18, reprinted in 1988 U.S. Code Cong. & Admin. News 3, 20.

[11]42 U.S.C. §2000d (1982).

[12]45 C.F.R. §80.3 (1989).

close a facility[13] or to deny staff privileges to a physician whose patients are largely of one race or nationality).[14]

Section 504 provides: "No otherwise qualified individual with handicaps in the United States . . . shall, solely by reason of his handicap, be excluded from the participation in, be denied the benefits of, or be subjected to discrimination under any program of activity receiving federal financial assistance."[15] "Handicapped individual" is defined as any person who has a physical or mental impairment that substantially limits one or more of such person's major life activities, who has a record of such impairment, or who is regarded as having such an impairment.[16] "Physical or mental impairment" is broadly defined in regulations[17] and includes virtually any physical limitation or disorder, mental impairment, or mental illness, as well as infection with chronic diseases and conditions such as tuberculosis and the human immunodeficiency virus.[18]

Regulations describe a number of specific discriminatory practices that §504 forbids.[19] In general, under §504 persons who have handicaps are entitled to "meaningful access" to healthcare facilities and healthcare programs.[20] Section 504 requires healthcare facilities to strike "a balance between the statutory rights of the handicapped to be integrated into society and the legitimate interests of federal grantees in preserving the integrity of their programs." Thus, the statute requires facilities to take "reasonable" steps to accommodate the needs of persons with handicaps, but not to make "fundamental" or "substantial" changes in the way they do business.[21]

---

[13]See, e.g., Bryan v. Koch, 627 F.2d 612 (2d Cir. 1980); Harper v. Wolf, No. 89-C-427-B (N.D. Ill. July 12, 1989) (LEXIS, Genfed library, Dist file).

[14]The possibility of such an action is discussed in Doe on Behalf of Doe v. St. Joseph's Hosp. of Fort Wayne, 788 F.2d 411, 421 (7th Cir. 1986).

[15]29 U.S.C. §794 (1988).

[16]Id. §706(8)(B) (1988).

[17]45 C.F.R. §84.3(j)(2)(i) (1989).

[18]School Bd. v. Arline, 480 U.S. 273 (1987).

[19]45 C.F.R. §84.52(a) (1989).

[20]Alexander v. Choate, 469 U.S. 287, 301 (1985).

[21]Id. at 300.

Title III prohibits discrimination based on age in programs or activities receiving federal financial assistance,[22] but statutory exceptions substantially narrow its scope when compared with Title VI or §504. Many public and publicly supported programs explicitly discriminate based on age. Title III permits such discrimination if the action "reasonably takes into account age as a factor necessary to the normal operation or the achievement of any statutory objective of the program or activity involved" or if the "differentiation made by such action is based upon reasonable factors other than age." In addition, programs "established under the authority of any law" that provide benefits or assistance, establish criteria for participation, or describe intended beneficiaries in age-related terms are exempt from the Title III prohibition of discrimination.[23]

Both individuals and the government may enforce Title VI, §504, and Title III. Government enforcement of these statutes with regard to healthcare facilities is handled by the Office of Civil Rights (OCR) in the Department of Health and Human Services[24] in accordance with federal regulations.[25]

The OCR enforcement procedures are essentially identical for both Title VI and §504.[26] These regulations require facilities to cooperate with investigations and provide information necessary to audit compliance;[27] they also provide for periodic compliance reviews as well as investigation of complaints by persons who believe they have been unlawfully discriminated against.[28] A primary weapon of the OCR is the power to terminate federal financial assistance,[29] but it may also take

[22]42 U.S.C. §6102 (1982).

[23]Id. §6103(b).

[24]For a general description of the operation and authority of the Office of Civil Rights see Congressional Quarterly, Inc., Federal Regulatory Directory 641 (5th ed. 1985).

[25]45 C.F.R. §§80.1 to 80.13 (Title VI), 84.1 to 84.55, 84.61 (Section 504), 90.1 to 90.62 (Title III) (1989).

[26]See 45 C.F.R. §§80.6 to 80.10, 84.61 (1989).

[27]42 C.F.R. §80.6 (1989). See United States v. Baylor Univ. Medical Center, 736 F.2d 1039 (5th Cir. 1984), cert. denied, 469 U.S. 1189 (1985).

[28]45 C.F.R. §80.7 (1989).

[29]Id. §§80.8 to 80.10.

advantage of any other remedies available under state or federal law.[30] The Title III enforcement provisions are quite similar in structure and substance, but are less detailed.[31]

Enforcement by private individuals is slightly more complex. Title III[32] and §504[33] contain provisions authorizing persons who are victims of discrimination to seek relief in court. Title VI does not, but courts have held that individuals may sue to enforce it by finding an implied private right of action.[34]

Under Title III, "any interested person" may bring an action in federal court seeking an injunction to prevent or cure violations of Title III.[35] However, before such an action may be brought, the plaintiff must seek administrative remedies by filing a complaint with the ORC.[36] Damages are not available for violations of Title III, but a prevailing plaintiff may recover costs and attorneys' fees.[37]

Title VI does not generally require persons to file an administrative complaint before bringing suit.[38] If successful in proving a Title VI violation, individuals may obtain injunctions against future discrimination, declaratory judgments finding discriminatory practices unlawful, and compensatory damages. While proof of intentional discrimination is not necessary in a Title VI action, it is a prerequisite to recovery of compensatory damages.[39]

Private enforcement of §504 is essentially the same as that

---

[30]Id. §80.8.

[31]Id. §§90.41 to 90.50.

[32]42 U.S.C. §6104(e) (1982).

[33]29 U.S.C. §794a(a)(2) (1988). Pushkin v. Regents of Univ. of Colo. 658 F.2d 1372, 1376-1380 (10th Cir. 1981) is one of many cases holding that this provision grants a private right of action.

[34]See Adams v. Bell, 711 F.2d 161, 167 n.35 (D.C. Cir. 1983) (en banc), cert. denied, 465 U.S. 1021 (1984); Cheyney State College Faculty v. Hufstedler, 703 F.2d 732 (3d Cir. 1983).

[35]42 U.S.C. §6104(e) (1982).

[36]Id.

[37]Id.

[38]*Cheyney State College Faculty*, 703 F.2d at 737.

[39]Guardians Assn. v. Civil Service Commn., 463 U.S. 582 (1983) (plurality decision); see also Alexander v. Choate, 469 U.S. 287, 292-299 (1985).

under Title VI,[40] and courts have applied the same rules regarding procedural matters such as exhaustion.[41] However, whether §504 requires proof of intentional discrimination is determined not with reference to Title VI but in accordance with the terms of §504 itself.[42] Nevertheless, and despite some analytic difficulties, courts have tended to interpret the statutes similarly and have held that proof of intentional discrimination is required when the plaintiff seeks compensatory damages.[43]

Persons with disabilities obtained additional sweeping protections from discrimination in the 1990 Americans with Disabilities Act (ADA).[44] Section 302 of that Act provides: "No individual shall be discriminated against on the basis of disability in the full and equal enjoyments of the goods, services, facilities, privileges, advantages, or accommodations of any place of public accommodation by any person who owns, leases, leases to, or operates a place of public accommodation."[45] Most, if not all, healthcare facilities are "places of public accommodation" as the Act defines the term.[46]

Under the ADA, healthcare facilities may not deny services to individuals based on their disabilities, provide services that are unequal to those provided to persons without disabilities, or offer different or segregated services based on a person's disability. The ADA requires facilities to take the following steps to avoid discrimination: (1) changing eligibility criteria that screen

---

[40]29 U.S.C. §794a(2) (1988).

[41]See, e.g., Camenisch v. University of Texas, 616 F.2d 127, 135-136 (5th Cir. 1980), vacated on other grounds, 451 U.S. 390 (1981).

[42]Pushkin v. Regents of Univ. of Colo., 658 F.2d 1372, 1383-1387 (10th Cir. 1981); but see Carter v. Orleans Parish Pub. Schools, 725 F.2d 261, 264 (5th Cir. 1984) (per curiam).

[43]See, e.g., Georgia State Conf. of Branches of NAACP v. Georgia, 775 F.2d 1403, 1427-1428 (11th Cir. 1985). This issue has not been settled by the Supreme Court, see Alexander v. Choate, 469 U.S. 287, 292-299 (1985), and courts have come to different conclusions. See generally Note, Safeguarding Equality for the Handicapped: Compensatory Relief Under Section 504 of the Rehabilitation Act, 1986 Duke L.J. 197 (1986).

[44]Pub. L. No. 101-336, 104 Stat. 327 (1990).

[45]42 U.S.C.S. §12182(a) (Law. Co-op. Supp. Oct. 1990).

[46]Id. §12181(7).

out or tend to reduce access to services or quality of services to individuals with disabilities (regardless of the purpose of the criteria) unless the criteria are "necessary"; (2) making "reasonable modifications" in policies, practices, and procedures when required to ensure access to services, unless the modifications would "fundamentally alter" the nature of the services provided; (3) making available auxiliary aids and services, unless doing so would fundamentally alter the nature of services provided or entail an "undue burden"; and (4) removing architectural barriers when removal is "readily achievable."[47]

The ADA definition of "disability is the same as the definition of "handicap" in the Rehabilitation Act of 1973.[48] However, compulsive gambling, kleptomania, and pyromania, as well as homosexuality, bisexuality, transvestism, transsexualism, pedophilia, exhibitionism, voyeurism, gender identity disorders not resulting from physical impairment, and other sexual behavior disorders, are all excluded from that definition.[49]

In addition, psychoactive substance use disorders resulting from current illegal use of drugs are not disabilities, but facilities may not deny a person health services or drug rehabilitation if the individual is otherwise entitled to those services.[50] A facility may refuse to provide other services to persons because they are currently using drugs; they may not discriminate against former drug users.[51]

The ADA protects two other classes of persons. A facility violates the ADA if it discriminates against a person who has a "relationship or association" with a person with a known disability.[52] The ADA also prohibits retaliation against a person who opposes an act prohibited by the ADA or who participates in ADA enforcement, and it forbids coercion or intimidation of those who exercise or who encourage others to exercise their rights under the Act.[53]

---

[47]Id. §12182(b).

[48]Id. §12102(2); see supra n.16 and accompanying text.

[49]42 U.S.C.S. §12211 (Law. Co-op. Supp. Oct. 1990).

[50]Id. §§12210, 12211.

[51]Id. §§12114, 12210.

[52]Id. §12182(b)(1)(E).

[53]Id. §12203.

The construction and alteration of healthcare facilities are subject to the ADA as well. The Act requires new construction to be "readily accessible" and "usable" by individuals with disabilities unless this is "structurally impracticable." Alterations must make the facility readily accessible and usable to "the maximum extent feasible," including making alterations to bathrooms, telephones, and drinking fountains, unless alterations to those things are "disproportionate" in cost or scope to the entire project.[54]

The ADA's rules for new facility construction apply to facilities scheduled for occupancy 30 months or more after the ADA's enactment.[55] The other provisions described above take effect 18 months after enactment, but facilities with 25 or fewer employees and gross receipts of $1 million or less are exempt for an additional six months, and those with 10 or fewer employees and gross receipts of $500,000 or less are exempt from civil suits for an additional year.[56]

Both the government and private individuals may enforce the ADA. Private enforcement is limited to actions for injunctive relief under the public accommodations provisions of the Civil Rights Act of 1964.[57] Damages are not available in such lawsuits, but a prevailing plaintiff is entitled to attorneys' fees.[58] The U.S. Department of Justice may also enforce the ADA in federal court. A court hearing such a lawsuit may grant injunctions to prevent or remedy discrimination, award damages to individuals harmed by the discrimination, and assess civil penalties of up to $50,000 for a first violation and $100,000 for subsequent violations of the Act.[59]

Finally, healthcare facilities should be aware that the ADA

---

[54]Id. §12183.

[55]ADA, Pub. L. No. 101-336, §§303, 310. The ADA was signed by President Bush on July 25, 1990.

[56]Id. §310. These extensions of time do not apply to suits concerning construction projects.

[57]42 U.S.C.S. §12188 (Law. Co-op. Supp. Oct. 1990); 42 U.S.C. §2000a-3(a).

[58]42 U.S.C. §2000a-3(b) (1982).

[59]42 U.S.C.S. §12188 (Law. Co-op. Supp. Oct. 1990).

did not repeal the Rehabilitation Act, nor did it repeal or preempt other federal, state, or local laws that provide equal or greater protections to persons with disabilities.[60]

§6.7 State and Local Antidiscrimination Laws

State and local laws often parallel federal antidiscrimination statutes. Others expand on federal laws by covering additional forms of discrimination, including gender and sexual preference, and by covering all facilities within the jurisdiction, not just those that receive federal funds.

The District of Columbia's human rights law provides an example of how comprehensive a local civil rights statute can be. Healthcare facilities in the District may not discriminate[1] in providing services based on race, color, religion, national origin, sex (including pregnancy, childbirth, or related conditions), age, marital status, personal appearance, sexual orientation, family responsibilities, physical handicap, matriculation, political affiliation, source of income, or place of residence or business."[2] The District of Columbia Commission on Human Rights and the District of Columbia Office on Human Rights enforce this statute.[3] Individuals may file complaints with the Office, which may investigate, seek a conciliation agreement, seek injunctions against discrimination, and refer violations to licensing agencies.[4] In addition, the Commission has the power to order compliance with the human rights law and award compensatory damages to victims of discrimination.[5] Alternatively, individuals claiming discrimination may file a lawsuit seeking damages and other "appropriate" remedies.[6]

---

[60]Id. §12201.

§6.7 [1]D.C. Code Ann. §§1-2502, 1-2519 (1987).

[2]Id. §1-2519.

[3]Id. §1-2541.

[4]Id. §§1-2544, 1-2545, 1-2547, 1-2557.

[5]Id. §1-2553.

[6]Id. §1-2556.

C. Access to Specific Therapies

§6.8 Overview

For some individuals, getting through the facility door is only the first step in obtaining the healthcare they want. Healthcare facilities bear legal responsibility for regulating both who may provide healthcare and the way in which it is provided. This authority is limited by law in a number of important ways, including antitrust statutes and statutes that regulate staff privileges.[1] Those topics are discussed fully in other chapters; the following discussion focuses on common-law and constitutional limits on facilities' power to control the delivery of patient care by barring the use of particular therapies or otherwise limiting their availability.

§6.9 Private Facilities

The power of private facilities to regulate patient care by limiting services is not subject to constitutional limits and is rarely interfered with by the common law. For example, courts have often upheld the power of private facilities to bar abortions on their premises.[1]

The general rule, however, is subject to a number of exceptions. In some jurisdictions the courts have required private facilities to justify the reasonableness of their rules.[2] Thus, in

---

§6.8 [1] See Chapters 1 and 3.

§6.9 [1] See, e.g., Greco v. Orange Memorial Hosp. Corp., 513 F.2d 873 (5th Cir. 1975), cert. denied, 423 U.S. 1000 (1975); cf. Walker v. Pierce, 560 F.2d 609 (4th Cir. 1977), cert. denied, 434 U.S. 1075 (1978) (private physician may refuse to deliver children of Medicaid patient unless patient agrees to have tubal ligation).

[2] See, e.g., Greisman v. Newcomb Hosp., 40 N.J. 389, 192 A.2d 817 (1963) (hospital rules must be "reasonable" and must take the public interest into account); cf. Hulit v. St. Vincent's Hosp., 164 Mont. 168, 520 P.2d 99 (1974) (holding that hospital prohibition on practice of Lamaze method of

Doe v. Bridgeton Hospital Association, the court struck down a private nonprofit hospital's rule that prohibited the performance of elective abortions[3] in the facility.[4] In addition, limits on treatments may interfere with licensure, accreditation for residency programs,[5] and contracts with medical staff[6] or expose the facility to liability for malpractice.[7]

§6.10 Public Facilities

A public healthcare facility's power to regulate patient care is limited by the federal Constitution and by the constitution of the state under whose power it is established. In this respect, public healthcare facilities are no different from legislatures or other public agencies, and their rules are equally subject to judicial review for constitutional validity.

The most successful federal constitutional attacks on government's regulatory power over healthcare involve matters of human procreation. In Griswold v. Connecticut[1] the United States Supreme Court declared unconstitutional a law prohibiting married couples from using contraceptives. Subsequent cases invalidated state laws prohibiting the distribution of contracep-

---

childbirth is not arbitrary and capricious). Most cases discussing judicial oversight of private hospital rulemaking involve the denial and granting of staff privileges. See §1.8.1.

[3]Many states have statutes that permit facilities to decline to provide abortion services. See, e.g., N.C. Gen. Stat. §14-45.1 (1986).

[4]71 N.J. 478, 366 A.2d 641 (1976), cert. denied, 433 U.S. 914 (1977); see also Suenram v. Society of the Valley Hosp., 155 N.J. 593, 383 A.2d 143 (1977). *Suenram* is odd because the court appears to have applied the provisions of the U.S. and New Jersey constitutions to the decisions of a private facility without a finding of state action.

[5]See St. Agnes Hosp. of the City of Baltimore v. Riddick, 668 F. Supp. 478 (D. Md. 1987).

[6]See St. Francis Memorial Hosp. v. Superior Ct., 205 Cal. App. 3d 438, 252 Cal. Rptr. 380 (1988).

[7]See Brownfield v. Daniel Freeman Marina Hosp., 208 Cal. App. 3d 405, 256 Cal. Rptr. 240 (1989).

§6.10 [1]381 U.S. 479 (1965).

tives to single persons,[2] prohibiting persons other than licensed pharmacists from distributing nonprescription contraceptives,[3] and prohibiting the distribution of contraceptives to persons under sixteen.[4]

From state regulation of contraception the Supreme Court proceeded to state regulation of abortion, striking down in Roe v. Wade[5] a Texas law that made it a criminal offense to perform an abortion except to save the life of the mother. Under *Roe*, the state's ability to regulate abortion depended on the duration of the pregnancy. As summarized by Justice Blackmun:

> (a) For the stage prior to approximately the end of the first trimester, the abortion decision and its effectuation must be left to the medical judgment of the pregnant woman's attending physician.
> (b) For the stage subsequent to approximately the end of the first trimester, the State, in promoting its interest in the health of the mother, may, if it chooses, regulate the abortion procedure in ways that are reasonably related to maternal health.
> (c) For the stage subsequent to viability, the State in promoting its interest in the potentiality of human life, may, if it chooses, regulate, and even proscribe, abortion except where it is necessary, in appropriate medical judgment, for the preservation of the life or health of the mother.[6]

In response to *Roe* the U.S. Congress, state legislatures, and municipalities began to search for constitutional ways to limit the availability of abortion. These cases have produced a steady stream of litigation, including more than a dozen cases decided by the Supreme Court. These cases have upheld provisions requiring, for example, that women give informed consent to abortion,[7] that physicians perform abortions,[8] that physicians

---

[2] Eisenstadt v. Baird, 405 U.S. 438 (1972).
[3] Carey v. Population Services Intl., 431 U.S. 678 (1977).
[4] Id.
[5] 410 U.S. 113 (1973).
[6] Id. at 164-165.
[7] Planned Parenthood v. Danforth, 428 U.S. 52, 65-67 (1976).
[8] *Roe*, 410 U.S. at 165; Connecticut v. Menillo, 423 U.S. 9 (1975) (per curiam).

report abortions for statistical purposes,[9] that abortions after the first trimester be performed in licensed in- or outpatient clinics,[10] and that a second physician be present during the abortion of viable fetuses, except in emergency situations.[11]

However, the Court has also struck down a number of restrictions on abortion. These include provisions that, for example, required detailed information tending to discourage abortion to be provided to women considering abortions,[12] forbade anyone save the attending physician from conducting the discussion in which informed consent was obtained,[13] imposed a 24-hour waiting period between obtaining informed consent and the performance of the abortion,[14] forced physicians to do detailed reporting on each abortion,[15] mandated abortions performed after the first trimester be done in a full-service hospital,[16] and compelled physicians aborting viable fetuses to balance the health risks to the mother with the health risks of the fetus in selecting the method of abortion.[17]

In addition to its implications for procreative freedom, *Roe* has been a model and a starting point for injecting constitutional arguments into other legal controversies in healthcare. Both courts and commentators debate whether *Roe* created a broad fundamental constitutional right that might be (quite ambiguously) called a right to medical privacy or a narrower right to procreative freedom.[18] Among the rights that creative lawyers

---

[9]*Danforth*, 428 U.S. at 80-81.

[10]Simopoulos v. Virginia, 462 U.S. 506, 508-519 (1983).

[11]Planned Parenthood v. Ashcroft, 462 U.S. 476, 482-486 (1983).

[12]City of Akron v. Akron Center for Reproductive Health, 462 U.S. 416, 442-445 (1983); Thornburgh v. American College of Obstetricians and Gynecologists, 476 U.S. 747, 759-764 (1986).

[13]*City of Akron*, 462 U.S. at 446-449.

[14]Id. at 449-451.

[15]*Thornburgh*, 476 U.S. at 765-767.

[16]*City of Akron*, 462 U.S. at 431-439.

[17]*Thornburgh*, 476 U.S. at 768-769.

[18]Compare People v. Privitera, 23 Cal. 3d 697, 701-705, 153 Cal. Rptr. 431, 433-435, 591 P.2d 919, 921-923 (en banc), cert. denied, 444 U.S. 949 (1979) and Capron, So Quick Bright Things Come to Confusion, 8 Am J.L. & Med. 169, 174 (1987) with Andrews v. Ballard, 498 F. Supp. 1038, 1044-

have tried, with little success, to derive from *Roe* are a doctor's right to practice medicine,[19] a patient's right to be treated by the physician of his choice,[20] a physician's right to select her patients,[21] a right to die,[22] and a right to have access to unapproved or banned drugs and therapies.[23]

The Supreme Court, in Webster v. Reproductive Health Services,[24] significantly reduced the prospects for rights to medical privacy, gave new hope to those who seek limits on abortion, and removed any doubt that public healthcare facilities have broad freedom under the Constitution to limit abortion and other services.

The most direct effect of *Webster* is on abortion rights. The Court plurality abandoned the *Roe* trimester framework quoted above;[25] under *Webster*, the state's "compelling interest" in protecting fetal life and the health of the mother, restricted under

---

1052 (S.D. Tex. 1980) and Robertson, Gestational Burdens and Fetal Status: Justifying Roe v. Wade, 8 Am..J.L. & Med. 189, 191-192 n.17 (1987).

[19]See generally Koh, Rebalancing the Medical Triad: Justice Blackmun's Contributions to Law and Medicine, 8 Am. J.L. & Med. 315, 320-321 (1987).

[20]See, e.g., Fitzgerald v. Porter Memorial Hosp., 523 F.2d 716 (7th Cir. 1975), cert. denied, 425 U.S. 916 (1976); Adler v. Montefiore Hosp. Assn., 453 Pa. 60, 311 A.2d 634 (1973), cert. denied, 414 U.S. 1131 (1974).

[21]See, e.g., Clair v. Centre Community Hosp., 317 Pa. Super. 25, 463 A.2d 1065 (1983).

[22]See, e.g., Superintendent of Belchertown State School v. Saikewicz, 373 Mass. 728, 370 N.E.2d 417 (1977); In re Quinlan, 70 N.J. 10, 355 A.2d 647, cert. denied, 429 U.S. 922 (1976).

[23]See, e.g., Rutherford v. United States, 616 F.2d 455, 457 (10th Cir.), cert. denied, 449 U.S. 937 (1980); People v. Privitera, 23 Cal. 3d 697, 701-705, 153 Cal. Rptr. 431, 433-435, 591 P.2d 919, 921-923 (en banc), cert. denied, 444 U.S. 949 (1979). The spread of human immunodeficiency virus infection has created an intense debate on this subject. See, e.g., Freedman and McGill Boston Research Group, Nonvalidated Therapies and HIV Disease, 19 Hastings Center Report 14 (May/June 1989).

[24]109 S. Ct. 3040 (1989).

[25]In *Webster*, Justices Rehnquist, White, and Kennedy voted to abandon the trimester framework. Justice Scalia voted to overrule *Roe* entirely. Justice O'Connor thought it unnecessary to address the issue, but she has previously advocated the end of distinctions based on trimesters. See, e.g., *Thornburgh*, 476 U.S. at 828.

Roe to the time after fetal viability,[26] now extends throughout pregnancy.[27] This opens the door to broader state, and hence public facility, regulation of abortion, and may signal the end of *Roe* altogether.[28] In addition, although the *Webster* plurality did not address the broad issue of the status of a fundamental right to privacy in procreative, medical, or other personal matters, a reversal of *Roe* would cast a shadow extending perhaps all the way back to *Griswold*.[29]

Most significant for healthcare facilities, under *Webster* public facility restrictions on therapies are largely immune from challenge under the Constitution.[30] Prior to *Webster*, several courts had struck down facility rules restricting access to procedures such as abortion and sterilization.[31] *Webster* upheld Missouri's law that prohibited public employees from performing or assisting in the performance of abortions not necessary to save the life of the mother and placed the same restriction on the use of public facilities.[32] Under the *Webster* plurality's analysis, there are no special constitutional limits on public facilities' freedom to control patient care, even when procreation is involved.[33] On

---

[26]City of Akron v. Akron Center for Reproductive Health, 462 U.S. 416, 428-429 (1983).

[27]*Webster*, 109 S. Ct. at 3057. Justice Rehnquist, writing for the plurality, did not indicate in his opinion whether pregnancy begins at the time of fertilization or at implantation of the fertilized ovum in the uterine wall. Since several contraceptives work during the interval between fertilization and implantation, a determination that the state's interest extends to the time of fertilization might permit limits on the sale or use of those products. See id. at 3080-3084 (Stevens, J., concurring in part and dissenting in part).

[28]Id. at 3067 (Blackmun, J., concurring in part and dissenting in part).

[29]See id. at 3072.

[30]Cf. State of New York v. Sullivan, 889 F.2d 401 (2d Cir. 1989), cert. granted, 58 U.S.L.W. 3749 (May 29, 1990) (upholding restrictions on abortion counseling in federally funded family planning clinics).

[31]See, e.g., Hathaway v. Worcester City Hosp., 475 F.2d 701, 705 (1st Cir. 1973); but see Poelker v. Doe, 432 U.S. 519 (1977).

[32]*Webster*, 109 S. Ct. at 3052-3053.

[33]Id. at 3052 (plurality opinion), 3059 (O'Connor, J., concurring). The restriction, however, must be put into place by an authority with the power to do so. State legislatures have the power to promote moral and social values such as the protection of potential human life. By contrast, the rulemaking

the other hand, courts relying on state constitutions are not be bound by *Webster*, and some may be expected, as some already have,[34] to continue to protect and expand privacy rights.

To summarize, after *Webster*, facility rules restricting health-care services are valid if "it is conceivable that the [restriction] bears a rational relationship to an end of government which is not prohibited by the Constitution."[35] Few restrictions are invalid under this standard,[36] and in most cases a facility should expect the courts to respect its judgment in regulating patient care. For example, the court in Fitzgerald v. Porter Memorial Hospital, citing conflicting opinions in the medical literature about the wisdom of having fathers in the delivery room, rejected an expectant father's challenge to a rule that prohibited him from being present at the birth of his child.[37] Although that case might be decided differently today, the important thing is that the court did not attempt to assess the merits of the policy; the existence of a scrap of support in the medical literature was enough to justify deference to the judgment of facility administrators.

---

power of public facility governing boards may extend only to subjects over which the legislature has given them authority. Therefore, while public facilities may make rules based on the dictates of medical practice, they may not have the power to regulate morals or set social policy. Cf. Doe v. Bridgeton Hosp. Assn., 71 N.J. 478, 489, 366 A.2d 641, 647 (1976), cert. denied, 433 U.S. 914 (1977) ("Moral concepts cannot be the basis of a non-sectarian eleemosynary hospital's regulations. . . ."); Rogers v. State Bd. of Medical Examiners, 371 So. 2d 1037 (Fla. Dist. Ct. App. 1979), affd., 387 So. 2d 937 (Fla. 1980).

[34]See cases supra §6.1.3 n.64.

[35]R. Rotunda, J. Nowak, and J. Young, 2 Treatise on Constitutional Law: Substance and Procedure 324 (1986).

[36]Cf. Hathaway v. Worcester City Hosp., 475 F.2d 701, 705 (1st Cir. 1973) (suggesting that a rule prohibiting sterilizations might not survive review under a rationality standard); McCabe v. Nassau County Medical Center, 453 F.2d 698 (2d Cir. 1971) (same).

[37]523 F.2d 716, 721 (7th Cir. 1975), cert. denied, 425 U.S. 916 (1976).

7   Consent to Treatment

Nancy M. King

§7.0 Introduction

This chapter addresses the law of informed consent to healthcare treatment and research: a concept that is straightforward in its philosophy, uncertain and complex in practice, and still controversial after decades of debate. A single chapter cannot attempt to address in detail all of the variations in state law that are important to the informed consent practices of healthcare facilities. Instead, this chapter's goals are, first, to provide a strong general understanding of the doctrine; second, to convey knowledge of the issues that are likely to be addressed by the law of particular jurisdictions; and third, to give guidance to individuals and institutions faced with filling in the many remaining gaps in order to develop a sensible and consistent informed consent practice.[1]

There are two distinct, fundamental, and longstanding rationales for imposing on healthcare providers the obligation to obtain the informed consent of patients before performing procedures or giving treatments. The first is simply the patient's rights of bodily control and self-determination, often expressed by quoting Mr. Justice Cardozo's language in the 1914 *Schloendorff* decision: "Every human being of adult years and sound mind has a right to determine what shall be done with his own body."[2]

This rationale is absolute, exceptionless, and more readily accepted by nonphysicians than by physicians. The second rationale focuses, in contrast, on the consequences of consent, holding that "it is reasonable that a patient should be told what is about to be done to him, that he may take courage and put himself in such a situation as to enable him to undergo the operation."[3] By this reasoning, obtaining informed consent is generally, but not necessarily, good for patients, and should be a matter of the physician's best judgment, like the rest of the provision of healthcare.

---

§7.0 [1]For more extensive reading on informed consent, the following sources are excellent: P. S. Appelbaum, C. W. Lidz, and A. Meizel, Informed Consent: Legal Theory and Clinical Practice (1987); R. Faden and T. Beauchamp with N. M. P. King, A History and Theory of Informed Consent (1986); F. Rozovsky, Consent to Treatment: A Practical Guide (2d ed. 1990).

[2]Schloendorff v. Society of N.Y. Hosps., 211 N.Y. 125, 126, 105 N.E. 92, 93 (1914), overruled on other grounds; Bing v. Thunig, 2 N.Y.2d 656, 143 N.E.2d 3, 163 N.Y.S.2d 3 (1957).

[3]Slater v. Baker & Stapleton, 95 Eng. Rep. 860, 861, 2 Wils. K.B. 359, 360 (1767).

The modern legal doctrine of informed consent represents a combination of these viewpoints—an attempt to serve simultaneously the potentially incompatible goals of promoting both the autonomy of patients and their best interests, medically defined. It is this difficult blending that makes the doctrine appear, to many healthcare providers, like a patchwork of generalities and exceptions.

This can be corrected easily by recognizing that informed consent is a process, rather than a product, with its own natural place in the provider-patient relationship. The sharing of information between caregiver and patient is necessary so that treatment goals can be articulated and achieved; for providers, the informed consent process can help guide good practice and good recordkeeping as well. Accordingly, this chapter is intended as a practice guide rather than a discussion of the courtroom management of informed consent claims.

A. The Doctrine of Informed Consent

§7.1 The Duty to Obtain Informed Consent

Although the informed consent doctrine has its historical and philosophical origins in the intentional tort of battery for unauthorized bodily invasion,[1] in most jurisdictions the failure to obtain informed consent is now treated almost exclusively as a matter of negligence law.[2] This means that, conceptually, obtaining informed consent is part of good patient care and that the failure to do so must be proved in court as malpractice is proved, by a showing that the provider's duty to obtain informed

---

§7.1 [1]See, e.g., early cases such as Mohr v. Williams, 95 Minn. 261, 104 N.W. 12 (1905); Pratt v. Davis, 224 Ill. 300, 79 N.E. 562 (1906); Rolater v. Strain, 39 Okla. 572, 137 P. 96 (1913).

[2]Meisel and Kabnick, Informed Consent to Medical Treatment: An Analysis of Recent Legislation, 41 U. Pitt. L. Rev. 407 (1980).

consent was breached, causing financially measurable injury to the patient that could have been avoided with due care.

Informed consent differs from most malpractice matters in that the basic dual duty to disclose information and to obtain consent is both measured by expert testimony[3] and stated as a matter of law.[4] According to battery law, any failures of disclosure that caused the particular plaintiff to lack adequate knowledge of the proposed bodily invasion will give rise to liability.[5] In contrast, under negligence standards, duties are measured by reasonable conduct, so that in malpractice, professional custom generally dictates the standard of care.[6] However, informed consent makes little sense when viewed solely as a creature of professional custom, since it is the patient's own self-determination that forms the basis of the duty to begin with. Therefore, customary professional disclosure is generally expected to bear some relationship to the information wanted or needed by reasonable patients so that they may make decisions about whether to consent to the procedures and treatments offered.[7] It is important for institutions to know the law of their own jurisdictions, but the differences that exist have much more effect on whether a patient's claim succeeds in court than they do as guides to good informed consent practice.

The traditional case law litany of informed consent disclosure includes the nature, consequences, risks, and alternatives of a proposed procedure, including no treatment as an alternative.[8] This litany is largely the same whether it is the product of

---

[3]E.g., Troy v. Long Island Jewish-Hillside Med. Center, 86 A.D.2d 631, 446 N.Y.S.2d 347 (1982).

[4]Canterbury v. Spence, 464 F.2d 772 (D.C. Cir.), cert. denied, 409 U.S. 1064 (1972).

[5]E.g., Gray v. Grunnagle, 423 Pa. 144, 223 A.2d 663 (1966).

[6]*Canterbury*, 464 F.2d at 789. Thus, even in jurisdictions not requiring expert testimony to establish the standard of disclosure, experts are often used to provide medical evidence about the existence of risks to be disclosed. Wilkinson v. Vesey, 110 R.I. 606, 295 A.2d 676 (1972).

[7]See the extensive discussion in *Canterbury*, 464 F.2d at 782-787. See also Natanson v. Kline, 186 Kan. 393, 350 P.2d 1093 (1960).

[8]See, e.g., McPherson v. Ellis, 305 N.C. 266, 287 S.E.2d 892 (1982); Sard v. Hardy, 281 Md. 432, 379 A.2d 1014 (1977); Wilkinson v. Vesey, 110 R.I. 606, 295 A.2d 676 (1972).

a professional standard of disclosure, that is, what doctors usually tell patients,[9] or a reasonable person standard, measured by the information that is viewed by reasonable patients as material to the decision at hand.[10] Most case law embraces the professional standard; though the better-reasoned cases use the reasonable person standard, they are in the minority.[11] Nonetheless, their impact and their logic have been significant enough to influence physicians' informed consent practice in many jurisdictions not officially employing that standard, through scholarly writing and teaching.[12]

§7.1.1 Who Gets Consent

The duty to obtain the patient's informed consent before the administration of proposed procedures and treatments is a

---

[9]E.g., Bloskas v. Murray, 646 P.2d 907 (Colo. 1982); Bly v. Rhoads, 222 S.E.2d 783 (Va. 1976); Natanson v. Kline, 186 Kan. 393, 350 P.2d 1093 (Kan. 1960).

[10]E.g., Largey v. Rothman, 110 N.J. 204, 540 A.2d 504 (1988); Cobbs v. Grant, 8 Cal. 3d 229, 104 Cal. Rptr. 505, 502 P.2d 1 (1972); Wilkinson v. Vesey, 110 R.I. 606 (1972); Cooper v. Roberts, 220 Pa. Super. 260, 286 A.2d 647 (1971).

[11]President's Commission for the Study of Ethical Problems in Medicine and Biomedical and Behavioral Research, Making Health Care Decisions: The Ethical and Legal Implications of Informed Consent in the Patient-Practitioner Relationship, vol. 3, Appendix L (U.S. Govt. Printing Office) (1982); Annot., 52 A.L.R.3d 1084 (1977); Annot., 88 A.L.R.3d 1008 (1978).

[12]Many, if not most, articles, commentaries, and treatises discuss the three major patient-centered, reasonable person standard cases—Canterbury v. Spence, Cobbs v. Grant, and Wilkinson v. Vesey—extensively and with approval. See sources cited in §7.0, n.1. As a result, much of the formal and informal teaching and modeling about informed consent to which physicians are exposed during their training years begins with the reasoning of these cases and a generally patient-focused disclosure duty. Further, it has not been shown that what physicians generally disclose is affected by the law of their jurisdiction. Faden et al., Disclosure of Information to Patients in Medical Care, 19 Med. Care 718 (1981). Presumably, the eventual result of physician practice that looks to patient preferences as a guide to disclosure will be a change in professional practice and therefore in the professional standard of disclosure.

nondelegable duty owed by the provider of the proffered services to the patient or the patient's representative.[13] Physicians who delegate the task of getting the patient's signature on consent forms to nurses or other personnel thus remain responsible for securing informed consent, and therefore responsible for what those others do or fail to do to obtain consent.

§7.1.2 When Consent Is Needed

One of the first questions that looms for healthcare providers and facilities is, simply, What, of all we do, do we need to get consent for? Perhaps surprisingly, the available law doesn't address the question precisely in those terms, since case law, statutes, and commentary all usually begin by applying the general disclosure duty to particular interventions. However, it is often broadly stated that informed consent is necessary for all surgery or for all medical "interventions," "procedures" or "treatments."[14]

Even having said this much, it is still necessary to determine what those terms mean for informed consent practice. Many treatment plans consist of numerous potentially discrete elements; others may entail preliminary diagnostic testing, periodic monitoring for and management of side effects, or necessary followup care. How to decide what to get consent for—The whole thing at once? Just parts? Which parts? In what order?— has not been well considered. Some general rules can be deduced, however.

---

[13]Miller v. Kennedy, 11 Wash. App. 272, 522 P.2d 852 (1974), affd. per curiam, 85 Wash. 2d 151, 530 P.2d 334 (1975).

[14]"The context in which the duty . . . arises is . . . the . . . decision as to whether a particular treatment procedure is to be undertaken." Canterbury v. Spence, 464 F.2d at 781. "It is well established that the physician must seek and secure his patient's consent before commencing an operation or other course of treatment." Id. at 782 (footnote omitted). The author of an authoritative treatise suggests that consent is required for "a proposed diagnostic, medical, or surgical intervention," but does not address the question further or define those terms. F. Rozovsky, Consent to Treatment: A Practical Guide 51 (1984).

Most fundamentally, because the purpose of informed consent is to prepare the patient (or the patient's representative) to make healthcare decisions, the duty to obtain informed consent arises whenever there is a healthcare decision to be made and the issues that go into that decision are significant for the patient.[15] The duty to obtain informed consent arises when a proposed intervention is invasive—when it has an ascertainable impact on the patient—and when it entails more than minimal risk.

Thus, *any risk-bearing intervention*—including diagnostic testing that poses risks to the patient, whether those risks are physical, psychic, or sociopolitical (as in HIV testing)—requires the patient's informed consent. Within these broad boundaries, specific and particular consent policy decisions should be made by reference to customary clinical practice and the perceptions of patients. Information disclosure should be specific, but should also help the patient to see the relationship between a whole procedure or course of treatment and its component parts. When consent to a course of treatment includes consent to a collection of elements of the treatment, the disclosure process should include discussion of all the elements, but should not preclude further discussion at the time each element comes up. Similarly, general consents should be supplemented by particular disclosures and consents regarding elements of the treatment. Consents once given must be amended whenever the risks change for particular patients. When routine or non-risky procedures are combined with procedures carrying risks, as is common, medical judgment must be able to present a picture of the treatment plan that places the risky pieces in perspective but does not slight the informed consent requirement for those portions.[16]

------

[15]*Canterbury*, 464 F.2d at 781.

[16]An illustrative example of a common but surprisingly complex treatment regimen is a total abdominal hysterectomy and oophorectomy for the removal of benign recurrent uterine tumors. The surgery itself carries certain risks; there are different types of incisions and incision closures involved; the choice of anesthesia may be significant; and disclosure of anesthesia risks is necessary. Moreover, there should be consent to preoperative testing, disclosure regarding preparation for surgery (e.g., diet, enema, and medications), information about

Overall, informed consent is best served by the cooperative attempt of physicians and patients to provide patients with a useful understanding of what is being proposed and an ongoing understanding of what is being accomplished. All risk-bearing interventions appear within the context of tests, treatments, or treatment plans, and should be discussed with patients within that context as well as in terms of the elements of disclosure for particular interventions. Informed consent is not an isolated issue. The amount and nature of informed consent discussion and documentation should be dictated by clinical common sense, so that information-sharing is a question of thoroughness, timing, and the understanding patients need to be well-informed, rather than merely a question of whether consent is required for a whole or for its parts.[17]

"What to get consent for" may be a question that is best answered indirectly, by institutional sensitivity to the problem and by development of informed consent policies that help providers to think usefully about it. For example, policies that require clinical departments to determine for themselves which procedures should be accompanied by written documentation of informed consent, and whether that documentation should be in the medical record or by means of a form, encourages the view that consent policy reflects an integrated model of the physician-patient relationship including discussion, decision-

---

the postoperative course (e.g., intravenous fluids and medication, catheterization, diet, resumption of mobility, length of hospitalization, wound care, and activity limitation), and discussion of complications, if any, and of necessary aftercare—in this case, the desirability of hormone replacement therapy. In order to give the patient a complete picture of her surgery, a commonsense plan of information disclosure is likely to blend classic informed consent components such as the surgery and anesthesia with discussion of routine procedures such as postsurgical catheterization and diet restriction, as well as more general information and advice designed to preview the experience for the patient. Disclosure is likely to be made by various parties (the physician, the surgeon, the anesthesiologist, and the nursing staff), and to be further developed over time as appropriate (before admission, upon admission, if problems arise, upon discharge, and at post-discharge checkup).

[17]R. Faden and T. Beauchamp with N. King, A History and Theory of Informed Consent (1986).

making, and documentation—rather than just a list of mandatory forms outside of which informed consent has no existence.[18]

§7.1.3 Disclosing Information

The "elements" of informed consent—the nature, consequences, risks, and alternatives of a proposed intervention—form the core of the disclosure requirement of informed consent.[19] Once it has been determined that informed consent is necessary for a particular intervention, the specific information to be given about that intervention is determined by reference to that list of elements. The questions that arise here are about how much to tell and how to tell it.

Generalizations about an appropriate body of information to be disclosed can never be secure, because they are based on examination of scattered state court decisions attempting to clarify things for juries rather than on careful description of disclosure standards to guide physicians' practice. Healthcare facilities should develop policy with an eye to the law of their own states; however, good policy will need to be based on an understanding that goes beyond state law if it is to succeed in promoting informed consent.

In addition, the form and manner of information disclosure are important. Caregivers are not required to be insurers of the understanding of their patients; yet, informed consent disclosure is meaningless if it is not reasonably understandable. The language used should be accurate but not overly technical. Information should be "translated," supplemented, and made concrete with examples and analogies. Caregivers should not hesitate to give patients their advice and their reasons for the advice; this helps to place disclosure in a comprehensible perspective. And caregivers should take ample time for disclosure, in a setting that does not interfere with communication

---

[18]F. Rozovsky, Consent to Treatment: A Practical Guide (2d ed. 1990).

[19]See cases cited supra n.8; see also P. Appelbaum, C. W. Lidz, and A. Meisel, Informed Consent: Legal Theory and Clinical Practice 49 (1987).

and comprehension and under unpressured circumstances. This requires a certain amount of planning. These are issues addressed only extremely rarely, if at all, in case law and in statutes. Nonetheless, attention to them in policy and practice is highly likely to reduce litigation risks by increasing patients' understanding of and involvement in decisions about their care.

The Nature and Consequences of the Procedure.   Many courts and legislatures specifically require caregivers to disclose the nature of the procedure offered. This means more than just the procedure's name; it includes the reason why it is being contemplated and its expected outcome or consequences, including anticipated benefits and expected adverse effects and even later decisions or interventions that will necessarily follow.[20] For example, consent to a diagnostic test may necessitate a discussion of the need for further testing, of the treatment decision to be faced if the definitive test result is positive, and of later procedures that will or may be needed once a course of treatment is begun—all by way of explaining the significance of the first test. Patients should be told whether the procedure is diagnostic or therapeutic, or if it is for research rather than treatment.[21] A description of what is involved in performing the procedure is also part of disclosing its nature, including attention to such information as the following: Is it physically invasive, or a drug, or an x-ray? What instruments are used? How long does it take? Will anesthesia be used? What will it feel like? What will recovery be like and how long will it take? And who will do it?[22]

Part and parcel of the description of the nature of a proposed intervention is a description of its *consequences*—of what will happen if everything goes as planned. It may seem simpleminded to emphasize the need for discussion of the expected

---

[20]E.g., Gray v. Grunnagle, 423 Pa. 144, 223 A.2d 663, 674 (1966); Wash. Rev. Code Ann. §7.70.050(3)(a) (Supp. 1985); Ohio Rev. Code. Ann. §2317.54(A) (Page, 1981).

[21]E.g., Estrada v. Jacques, 70 N.C. App. 627, 321 S.E.2d 240 (1984).

[22]Appelbaum, supra n.19, at 50.

outcome, since that is presumably why the procedure is being suggested in the first place; but without specific attention to this disclosure, patient and physician may have very different expectations of the intervention. In addition, there can be adverse but inevitable consequences or side effects associated with the procedure that must be disclosed—as when prostate surgery necessarily results in infertility.[23]

Risks. Adverse consequences that are not inevitable but yet do not result from negligence are risks. Risk disclosure is what informed consent is often perceived to be about; thus, the informed consent doctrine has been described as a mere duty to warn.[24] Much judicial and scholarly ink has been spilled on the problem of deciding which risks must be disclosed. Risk disclosure is also of greatest concern to practitioners, owing to their concern that overdisclosure may be counterproductive. However, the guidance that is offered by cases and statutes is less than complete, leaving much to the clinical discretion of individual practitioners and their knowledge of their patients.

The professional standard of disclosure refers only to customary practice. Although in theory the patient-centered disclosure standard is likely to result in more risk disclosure than the professional standard, in practice both are likely to draw on the same sources: expert professional judgments about what risks in fact exist and some sense of what patients need to know or reasonably ought to be told. Courts applying the patient-centered standard have focused, using a variety of terms, on the importance of the risks involved. Most commonly, the courts have said that risks that are "material"—significant to patients' decision-making, though not necessarily dispositive of the actual decision—must be disclosed,[25] and they have further said that materiality should be measured by considering a combination of the likelihood that the risk will materialize and

---

[23]Bang v. Charles T. Miller Hosp., 251 Minn. 427, 88 N.W.2d 186 (1958).

[24]Katz, Informed Consent—A Fairy Tale? Law's Vision, 39 U. Pitt L. Rev. 137 (1977).

[25]E.g., *Canterbury*, 464 F.2d at 786-787.

the severity of the harm if it does.[26] Thus, a remote risk of death or serious harm should be disclosed; more significant risks of major but not extreme harm should also be disclosed; and, generally, less serious harms should probably be disclosed as well, if they are highly likely to occur.

Naturally, it is the gray area between what should clearly be disclosed and what clearly need not be that is largest, most commonly at issue, and most troubling. Few useful cutoff percentages are available to give content to the determination of materiality. Though some cases mandate disclosure of 1 percent or smaller risks of serious harm,[27] it seems misdirected to seek absolute numbers and far more fruitful simply to examine the likelihood and severity of anticipated risks to determine what disclosure would be dictated by medical practice, what disclosure seems necessary to give the patient an adequate understanding, and what disclosure patients might reasonably want. The cases give even less help on the question of how to measure the risk to begin with: A national percentage? The experience with this intervention in the state? In the region? In the hospital? The attending physician's experience only? Experience with all patients? Or with a group of patients similar in age, demographics, or severity of illness?

It is prudent, in light of the entirety of the informed consent doctrine, to err on the side of disclosure and to base disclosure on the individual as much as possible. The provider who makes decisions about how to assess the risks of a proposed intervention by looking at (1) how his or her colleagues measure risks for this intervention, (2) what meaningful data are available to use as the basis for this measurement, and (3) commonsense consideration of what medically relevant characteristics of the patient might reasonably affect the risk assessment is unlikely to run legal risk in any jurisdiction. It also makes sense to be

---

[26]*Canterbury*, 464 F.2d at 788.

[27]E.g., *Canterbury*, 464 F.2d 772 (1 percent risk of paralysis from exploratory surgery); Scott v. Wilson, 396 S.W.2d 532 (Tex. Ct. App. 1965), affd., 412 S.W.2d 299 (Tex. 1967) (1 percent chance of loss of hearing); McPherson v. Ellis, 305 N.C. 266, 287 S.E.2d 892 (1982) (1 in 500 chance of paralysis, when all expert testimony held disclosure customary).

frank with patients about the range of possibilities inherent in risk percentages, so that they may receive risk information as attempted prediction rather than as gospel.

There are also some commonly cited instances of permissible nondisclosure of risks in both case law and statutes. When risks are common knowledge;[28] too remote, even if serious;[29] or too minor, even if highly likely, they need not be disclosed. Risks that are already known to the patient, or should be because everybody knows them, need not be disclosed because patients may be expected to have and to exercise ordinary reasonable awareness; risks that are too small to disclose are arguably not material to a reasonable patient's decisional process. Some states even provide exhaustive lists of risks that must be disclosed (see §7.3).

Alternatives. Disclosure of alternatives to the proposed intervention is central to the idea of informed consent.[30] Since informed consent is about choice, if there were no choice, there would be no need for informed consent. But, in fact, there is always a choice: "no treatment" is an alternative the consequences of which must always be disclosed.[31] See the further discussion of this issue in §7E, Refusal of Treatment.

In addition to no treatment, the physician must disclose medically acceptable alternatives. Disclosure must be as thorough as for the recommended intervention, so that patients may weigh the differences (in, e.g., invasiveness, effectiveness, burdensomeness, or cost) according to their own preferences. There is no obligation to disclose medically unacceptable alternatives (except to the extent that "no treatment" is viewed as unacceptable);

---

[28]*Canterbury,* 464 F.2d at 788 ("[T]here is no obligation to communicate those [risks] of which persons of average sophistication are aware.") (footnote omitted).

[29]E.g., Stottlemire v. Cawood, 213 F. Supp. 897 (D.D.C. 1963) (1 in 800,000 chance of aplastic anemia); Starnes v. Taylor, 272 N.C. 386, 158 S.E.2d 339 (1968) (1 in 250 to 1 in 500 chance of perforation of esophagus).

[30]Logan v. Greenwich Hosp. Assn., 191 Conn. 282, 465 A.2d 294 (1983).

[31]Cobbs v. Grant, 8 Cal. 3d 229, 243, 104 Cal. Rptr. 505, 514, 502 P.2d 1, 10 (1972).

however, physicians may not withhold information about options they do not favor, or do not offer, if those options nonetheless constitute acceptable care.[32]

Additional Disclosure. Establishing the duty to disclose the elements of informed consent generally exhausts what the courts and legislatures have to say about giving information but does not answer all that physicians and other caregivers in healthcare facilities are likely to face. Additional disclosures not falling within these categories will frequently be necessary. Patients have the right to know the identities of all their caregivers and to refuse any unwanted interventions by them.[33] In addition, healthcare settings typically contain fiduciary patient-provider relationships where circumstances may arise in which withholding information is deceptive, becoming the equivalent of misrepresentation by caregivers.[34] As a general principle, whenever caregivers are, or should be, aware that patients' lack of information is leading to preventable misunderstanding, disclosure is necessary.

§7.1.4 Obtaining Consent

Although nearly all the judicial attention given to informed consent has gone to the content of the disclosure, the caregiver who offers to perform an intervention on the patient is also responsible for obtaining the patient's consent *after* that disclo-

---

[32]E.g., Smith v. Karen S. Reisig, M.D., Inc. 686 P.2d 285 (Okla. 1984); *Logan*, 191 Conn. 282; Keogan v. Holy Family Hosp., 95 Wash. 2d 306, 622 P.2d 1246 (1980); Sard v. Hardy, 281 Md. 432, 379 A.2d 1014 (1977).

[33]This very basic expression of the battery principle is one of the rights enshrined in the Joint Commission on Accreditation of Healthcare Organizations' Patients' Bill of Rights. See Chapter 9.

[34]Berkey v. Anderson, 1 Cal. App. 3d 790, 805, 82 Cal. Rptr. 67, 77 (1969) ("If appellant was simply told a myelogram was nothing to worry about and that the most uncomfortable thing about it was being tilted about on a cold table, the jury could have concluded that under the facts the statement was actually deceptive.")

sure. The informed consent doctrine holds that valid consents must be not only informed but also voluntary and made with understanding.[35] Because the caregiver has the duty to inform, it is important to ask whether the caregiver has any similar duty to ensure or at least to promote understanding and voluntariness in patients' consents as well.

The short answer is no. The few court decisions that address the issues of patients' voluntariness and understanding are equivocal and confused about whether and to what extent physicians are responsible for creating those states.[36] Though it is very clear that consents are invalid without these qualities regardless of how much disclosure has preceded them, they are both problematic to measure and difficult to ensure. However, there are some things that caregivers and healthcare facilities can readily do to promote understanding and voluntariness, and these are worth discussing, if only because they flow naturally from the previous discussion of information disclosure.

Understanding means two things: it means the patient's understanding that he or she is making a decision, not merely being informed of or acquiescing to someone else's decision; and his or her understanding what the decision entails. That is, patients must know what an informed consent *is*, in addition to being informed about the particular decision faced.[37] The first part is easily accomplished by prefacing information disclosure with a brief explanation of the reasons for giving patients information, the patient's decisionmaking responsibility, and the caregiver's role in supporting the patient's choices through information and advice. The second part is enhanced, as discussed above, by using accessible language, example, and analogy, and choosing a time and setting for disclosure that

[35]E.g., Gray v. Grunnagle, 423 Pa. 144, 223 A.2d 663, 674 (1966) (consent must be based on "true understanding"); Relf v. Weinberger, 372 F. Supp. 1196 (D.D.C. 1974) (coercion by caregiver would invalidate patient's consent).

[36]E.g., Cooper v. Roberts, 220 Pa. Super. 260, 286 A.2d 647 (1971); Dunham v. Wright, 423 F.2d 940 (3d Cir. 1970).

[37]R. Faden and T. Beauchamp with N. King, A History and Theory of Informed Consent 300-304 (1986).

promote reflection by the patient and dialogue between patient and caregiver.

In addition, there are a number of barriers to understanding that are at least partially within the control of caregivers and healthcare facilities. To the extent that these barriers can be eliminated, caregivers bear some responsibility for doing so in order to enhance the patient's capacity to understand.[38] This does not represent a heavy burden so much as a commonsense recognition of factors affecting understanding. For example, both excessive sedation and inadequate analgesia may make concentration difficult; both are often easy to adjust temporarily to permit the consent process to operate with maximal effectiveness.

Soliciting exchanges with the patient during and after disclosure—from questions as simple as, Do you understand the procedure? Do you have any questions about it? to asking patients to explain in their own words what they have just been told—is a standard means of checking whether the disclosure is adequate and whether patients are satisfied and understand it (or think they do). Some feedback like this should be sought, and it is often required in formal consent procedures and consent forms.[39]

The adult patient's general capacity to understand is presumed in law.[40] This is why there is some obligation to attempt to remove barriers to understanding: the barriers are presumed to be removable. It is appropriate, however, for caregivers to remain alert at all times to the possibility of permanent barriers to understanding, which render the patient incapable of making

---

[38]Id. at 316-329.

[39]For example, a North Carolina hospital's recently revised model consent form contains a witness certification statement that the patient has answered the following questions: "Did your doctor explain the procedure/treatment to you? Do you have any questions about the treatment that have not been answered? Is this your signature on the consent form? Have you given your consent to the proposed treatment?" The University of North Carolina Hospitals, University of North Carolina Hospitals Policy Manual, Request and Authorization for Operation or Other Procedure, Policy Number I-04, Informed Consent (Sept. 18, 1988).

[40]See §7.6 infra.

informed decisions. These checks of understanding are good ways to discover signs of possible "incompetence," which is discussed in §§7.2.2 and 7.8 below. A patient who is incapable of making healthcare decisions can give neither a valid refusal of nor a valid consent to treatment.

"Voluntariness" refers to the patient's perception that he or she is choosing freely, without undue pressure from the caregiver. Patients who believe they have no other choice but to decide as they do are not consenting voluntarily. However, only certain external pressures are within the control or influence of the caregiver. If patients feel that the severity of their illness gives them no choice but to try dangerous therapies, for example, they may not be making a fully voluntary choice, yet they are not really being coerced—that is, the influence constraining them is not within anyone's control. If they are being pressured by their families to make certain choices, we may decide that they are being coerced without being able to require their physicians to try to relieve the pressure. But if patients feel that their physicians are pressuring them to make certain choices— for example, to choose an experimental treatment—we can require that the perceived threat be eliminated. Some patients fear, for example, that if they refuse the physician's advice they may lose his or her approval and concern; or that if they refuse certain heroic treatments their basic care may suffer. Patients should always be assured that they may disagree with their caregivers and refuse treatments or participation in research without detriment to the rest of their care. Further discussion of this issue as regards consent to research is considered in §7.13 below.

§7.1.5 Documenting Consent

Although signed consent forms are often required by healthcare facilities for at least some interventions, and many state laws provide limited liability protection to physicians who obtain patients' signatures on approved forms, there is no general requirement that consent must be obtained in writing to be valid.[41] Simple verbal consents should be regarded as minimally adequate for patient care where no policy exists requiring a writing.

Documentation of the patient's informed consent is the last step in the informed consent process; it cannot take the place of the entire process of information disclosure and exchange between caregivers and patients. However, written documentation of the patient's consent is desirable for practical reasons. A writing has evidentiary value in case of later legal action; it facilitates good recordkeeping and continuity of care; and it aids the memory of both physician and patient.

Except in the rare instances in which a signed consent form is required by statute (as for certain procedures such as sterilization), consent forms are only one of the ways in which informed consent to treatment may be documented. Besides consent forms, documentation may be by means of a detailed note in the medical record, dated and signed by the caregiver who sought the consent and indicating the content of the disclosure that was made. Use of a well-designed consent form can have the same effects as placing notes in the medical record, provided that the form indicates what was disclosed and a copy of the form is retained by the facility. In addition, if the patient retains a copy the patient's memory and understanding will be supported. Finally, it is sometimes argued that requiring the patient's signature reinforces the seriousness of the patient's decision and thus helps ensure that it is carefully considered. This effect is probably more significant for elective procedures and refusals of treatment than for other choices.

For consent forms to have evidentiary value they must have some specificity. The frequently encountered blanket admission consent form and the standard operative permit are too broad and vague to be useful unless they are substantially modified to

---

[41]Hernandez v. United States, 465 F. Supp. 1971 (D. Kan. 1979). Even when informed consent statutes provide that signed consent forms create a presumption of valid consent, no signature requirement is thereby created. Doss v. Hartford Fire Ins. Co., 448 So. 2d 813 (La. App. 1984). See also the discussion in §7.1.3 supra. Written consent is usually required, however, for participation in federally funded research; see Part D infra.

provide appropriate information about the specific procedure or procedures performed. Most hospitals are by now experienced in drafting good surgical consent forms. Many model forms are available as well in treatises, handbooks, statutes, and educational materials, as well as from many other sources.[42]

The process of identifying interventions for which consent must be obtained and drafting consent forms to fit them is one that should be undertaken by a healthcare facility's caregivers, using legal advice but starting from professional expertise. It must be remembered that forms are not usually required, so even when they are in use, they do not excuse caregivers from the performance of the rest of the informed consent duty.[43] Many cases are likely to have special circumstances that call for disclosure different from or in addition to that prescribed by a form. Moreover, there will often be additional interventions for which no form exists but for which informed consent is nonetheless required.[44]

It seems always to be the healthcare facility's hope that a well-drafted consent form can protect it and its caregivers from legal difficulties. No consent form, however "airtight," can be entirely immune from challenge on grounds of fraud, deception, misrepresentation, incapacity of the patient, or other imperfections.[45] The best way to use consent forms is as evidence that an adequate informed consent process took place. This means that healthcare facilities are best advised to put their energies into making the consent process a meaningful one.

§7.2 Exceptions to the Duty

There are, of course, certain circumstances that excuse the caregiver from the duty to obtain informed consent, for generally commonsense reasons.

---

[42]E.g., F. Rozovsky, Consent to Treatment: A Practical Guide §12.1 (2d ed. 1990).

[43]See the discussion in §7.1 supra of the informed consent process.

[44]See §7.1.2 supra.

[45]Many informed consent statutes and cases specifically acknowledge these challenges to the presumption that a signed consent form is valid.

§7.2.1 Emergencies

The emergency exception permits caregivers to treat patients without consent when they are in need of immediate treatment and under the circumstances are incapable of making an informed choice. To excuse the failure to obtain consent, the delay that would be required to obtain a legally valid consent must be dangerous to the patient and there must be no reason to believe the patient would not consent if able to do so.[1] An emergency need not be life-threatening, but must be a serious threat to health. It can encompass any situation in which fast action is needed to prevent a significant harm or increase in harm.[2] The patient need not be unconscious or completely incapable of expressing preferences; it need only be true that obtaining informed consent from either the patient or an authorized representative would take too much time under the circumstances.[3]

The basis for this exception is that patients generally wish to be made well, and therefore it is reasonable, in an emergency, to presume consent to necessary treatment unless something appears to challenge the presumption. Such a challenge might be the discovery that the patient has religious beliefs incompatible with accepting certain treatments. The presumption may not be applied to experimental or otherwise unusual or nonstandard treatments.[4]

As soon as is reasonably possible, retrospective consent should be obtained from the patient or the patient's representative. This will often be after the emergency, but it may be

---

§7.2 [1] E.g., Luka v. Lowrie, 136 N.W. 1106 (Mich. 1912).

[2] Compare Cunningham v. Yankton Clinic, 262 N.W.2d 508 (S.D. 1978) with Sullivan v. Montgomery, 279 N.Y.S. 575 (City Ct. 1935). Many courts do not even attempt to define an emergency when they find one to exist. See, e.g., Kennedy v. Parrott, 243 N.C. 355, 90 S.E.2d 754 (1956); Franklyn v. Peabody, 249 Mich. 363, 228 N.W. 681 (1930).

[3] See Crouch v. Most, 78 N.M. 406, 410, 432 P.2d 250, 254 (1967); Dunham v. Wright, 423 F.2d 940, 941 (3d Cir. 1970).

[4] W. P. Keeton, D. B. Dobbs, R.E. Keeton and D. G. Owen, Prosser and Keeton on the Law of Torts §18 (5th ed. 1984).

while the treatment is still taking place. Thus, the way in which information disclosure proceeds and the kind of prior agreement obtained from the patient, if any, depends on the nature of the emergency and the patient's capacity to choose, with complete abrogation of all disclosure and consent requirements obtaining at one end of the spectrum only. Note that with the expansive definition of emergency that can be employed in this exception, some emergencies may be anticipatable. It is generally better practice to anticipate and discuss possible future interventions with patients and their representatives than to await the emergency. Informed consent may thus be previewed, making it possible to obtain a valid consent quickly at the time of the intervention.[5]

A number of state statutes address the emergency exception, especially as regards treatment of minors. They usually provide procedures to follow and sometimes offer definitions, and should be consulted where they exist.

§7.2.2 Incompetence, or Decisional Incapacity

Whether or not there is an emergency, if the patient is not capable of making an informed, understanding, and voluntary choice it is futile, and therefore unnecessary, to seek informed consent from the patient. Moreover, the caregiver may not rely on any consent given while the patient lacks capacity to consent. As an exceptive case, incompetence often overlaps with emergency. If the patient's incapacity is temporary but competence cannot be restored without taking more time than is safe for the patient, the exceptions are coextensive. When the incompetence exception arises, consent must be obtained from the patient's representative, if possible. Issues surrounding the patient's lack of capacity are discussed more fully in §§7.7 and 7.8 below.

---

[5]The courts must "develop a delicate balance between the right of the patient to choose the treatment he wishes to undergo and the freedom of the physician to practice responsible and progressive medicine without fear of frequent litigation." *Dunham*, 423 F.2d at 942.

§7.2.3 Waiver

If the patient is an adult, is currently capable of decisionmaking, and elects not to receive information disclosure, not to make the treatment choice, or both, the patient is waiving exercise of the right to information, the right to decide, or both. Informed consent is intended to promote the patient's right to make his or her own decisions. One consequence of this is that deciding irrationally or stupidly or ignorantly is the patient's right so long as the patient is capable of reasonable decisions. Thus, the patient may refuse information and even has the right to surrender the decision itself.[6] When the patient says, Please don't tell me, it will upset me, or I can't decide, Doctor, I'll do whatever you say, these are waivers.

Very little has been said about the waiver exception. However, waiver is a familiar legal concept outside of the consent setting,[7] and by analogy to that body of law it is reasonable to require that caregivers make some effort to ensure that waivers of informed consent are knowing and voluntary before acting on them.[8] Because patients may be passive, timid, and hesitant to assert themselves in the unfamiliar circumstances of illness, physicians and other caregivers must not mistake passivity for waiver. Patients must know that they hold the right to make their own healthcare decisions and that they will be supported in their decisionmaking efforts if they feel over-whelmed by them. If they give up the exercise of this right they must do so voluntarily; as with the voluntariness of the decision itself, they should not be made to feel that they have no other choice if they wish to receive the care they need. The result is

---

[6]Kaimowitz v. Michigan Dept. of Mental Health, 1 Ment. Dis. Law. Rptr. 147 (Cir. Cit. Wayne County Mich. 1976); Holt v. Nelson, 523 P.2d 211, 219 (Wash. App. 1974); Cobbs v. Grant, 8 Cal. 3d 229, 104 Cal. Rptr. 505, 502 P.2d 1 (1972); Putensen v. Clay Adams, Inc., 12 Cal. App. 3d 1062, 1083-1084 (1970).

[7]28 Am. Jur. 2d, Estoppel and Waiver, §154, at 836 (1966).

[8]Miranda v. Arizona, 384 U.S. 436, 475-476 (1966); Johnson v. Zerbst, 304 U.S. 458, 464 (1938) (defining waiver as voluntary and intentional relinquishment of the exercise of a known right).

that patients should make an explicit declaration of waiver and their reasons before the caregiver should rely on it.[9]

Finally, the caregiver should ask the patient to identify a chosen decisionmaker if decision is waived. Patients may wish the caregiver to decide. However, many patients may want a relative or friend to decide. If a friend or relative is identified, this person needs to receive full informed consent disclosure in order to prepare for deciding on the patient's behalf. (The patient should be reminded of this, since it means a voluntary breach of confidentiality.) As a safeguard, the caregiver should also offer to make disclosure to a person designated by the patient any time the patient waives disclosure or names the caregiver as decisionmaker. This affords the caregiver the opportunity to discuss the patient's needs and interests with someone who is not a healthcare provider and who knows the patient, even though the patient is not willing to engage in this discussion.

§7.2.4 Therapeutic Privilege

Bad news can be upsetting. It is in part for this reason that the waiver exception to the informed consent requirement exists for patients whose feeling is, Don't tell me, Doctor, I can't take it. But sometimes a family member, rather than the patient, may ask the physician not to inform the patient, or the physician may determine that certain information would be harmful for the patient to hear. The justification for the physician's therapeutic privilege to withhold information from the patient is avoidance of this harm.[10]

---

[9]Functionally, this means that when a patient says, Don't tell me anything, or You decide, the caregiver should make sure, through discussion with the patient, that the patient knows he or she is giving up the exercise of a right and has some notion of what it means to do so. See Meisel, The "Exceptions" to the Informed Consent Doctrine: Striking a Balance Between Competing Values in Medical Decisionmaking, 1979 Wisc. L. Rev. 413, 457 (1979).

[10]Roberts v. Wood, 206 F. Supp. 579 (S.D. Ala. 1962); Watson v. Clutts, 262 N.C. 153, 136 S.E.2d 617 (1964). See also Waltz and Scheuneman, Informed Consent to Therapy, 64 Nw. U.L. Rev. 628, 641-643 (1970).

The privilege permits physicians to make a selective disclosure to a patient, leaving out important information about risks but not telling the patient it is being left out, and then to accept as valid a consent based on this incomplete disclosure.[11] Little has been said about the therapeutic privilege in the courts, but it has been much discussed in commentary. Plainly, the privilege must be very narrowly construed, or it has the potential to swallow up the entire informed consent doctrine by permitting physicians to withhold information simply because it may distress patients. When formulated narrowly, the privilege may not be invoked simply to avoid frightening patients away from interventions the physician considers necessary. Only when the physician has reason to believe that certain disclosures would render the patient so upset as to make rational choice impossible, or otherwise would result in significant harm to the patient, is this narrow exception justified.[12] However, though commentators generally agree that a narrow view of the privilege is preferable, a few courts have construed it more broadly.[13]

If the privilege is invoked, the withheld disclosure should be made to a family member or other representative for the patient.[14] The better course, however, is to proceed with full disclosure to vulnerable patients and to provide extensive support for them in the informed consent process.[15]

---

[11]Nishi v. Hartwell, 52 Haw. 188, 198, 473 P.2d 116, 122 (1970).

[12]Canterbury v. Spence, 464 F.2d 772, 789 (D.C. Cir. 1972), cert. denied, 409 U.S. 1064 (1972).

[13]*Nishi*, 52 Haw. 188, citing Salgo v. Leland Stanford Jr. Univ. Bd. of Trustees, 154 Cal. App. 2d 560, 317 P.2d 170 (1957). See also Barclay v. Campbell, 683 S.W.2d 498, 501 (Tex. Civ. App. 1984).

[14]*Canterbury*, 464 F.2d at 789. As with the waiver exception, disclosure to a family member may help the physician to make better choices on the patient's behalf when, as here, the patient's decision is based on incomplete disclosure.

[15]Alan Meisel, who has in the past recommended abolition of the privilege, suggests beginning disclosure by telling vulnerable patients that some information may upset them, offering support, and then allowing them to choose whether to hear all of the details—that is, allowing them to decide whether to waive full disclosure. P. Appelbaum, C. Lidz, and A. Meisel, Informed Consent: Legal Theory And Clinical Practice 77 (1987).

§7.2.5 Public Health Emergencies

The last category of potential exceptions to the informed consent requirement may arise when the public health or the public safety is so severely threatened as to justify imposing tests or treatments on individuals because of the risks they pose to others. This is not so much an informed consent issue as it is one of bare consent; the effect of such an exception is to force a patient to undergo an unwanted intervention. Mandatory vaccination is a commonly cited example of this exception;[16] so is mandatory blood testing for marriage license applicants. Enforced treatment of contagious diseases has been justified under this exception, especially in confined populations. Current controversies about mandatory HIV testing raise the issue of this exception in the way it is most likely to be pertinent for healthcare facilities. In the absence of legislation permitting or requiring HIV testing without the patient's informed consent for public health reasons, HIV testing of hospitalized patients should not be performed nonconsensually, because of the risks associated with breach of confidentiality about the patients' HIV status. Similarly, when the concerns of public safety and the criminal justice system call for the gathering of evidence in healthcare settings (e.g., blood samples for blood alcohol levels, taken by emergency room personnel), caregivers should not proceed without disclosure or consent or over patients' objections unless state legislation authorizes them to do so or a court order is sought and obtained.[17]

---

[16]Jacobson v. Massachusetts, 197 U.S. 11, 24 S. Ct. 358, 49 L. Ed 643 (1905).

[17]The features common to this exception are that the enforced interventions bear risks for the patient or detainee that are not outweighed by benefits to the patient or detainee. Thus, the state is obliged to show—by law, state penal regulations, or court order—that the public health need outweighs the risk to the individual. Healthcare facilities should have access to legal advisors knowledgeable about their state's law in these areas. See generally chapter 4 of F. Rozovsky, Consent to Treatment: A Practical Guide (2d ed. 1990).

§7.3 *Informed Consent Statutes*

Many states have passed legislation dealing with informed consent, usually as part of the malpractice reform efforts undertaken by state legislatures in the 1970s.[1] The effect of such statutes is to supersede the common law, taking the privilege of deciding what the informed consent doctrine should be like away from the courts. This effect was sought because of a widespread but largely unfounded fear that informed consent was contributing substantially to the increase in malpractice litigation and awards.[2]

It is not possible to summarize these statutes effectively. Providers should be familiar with their own state's laws and should seek interpretation of them from the health law bar in the state.[3] Generally, these statutes specify the standard of disclosure, in broad terms, and the causation standard, which dictates when a patient may recover for a provider's failure to disclose. Perhaps a "typical" statute could be described as one that specifies a professional standard of disclosure and a reasonable person causation standard, meaning that (1) the required disclosure is what physicians in similar communities would disclose under the circumstances and that (2) patients can recover if they can show that a reasonable person in the patient's position would have refused the procedure had they been given the requisite information.[4] Often, these statutes list exceptions

---

§7.3 [1]Meisel and Kabnick, Informed Consent to Medical Treatment: An Analysis of Recent Legislation, 41 U. Pitt. L. Rev. 407 (1980).

[2]Informed consent was the most significant issue in only 2.4 percent of all appellate malpractice decisions nationwide up to 1971. Report of the Secretary's Commission on Medical Malpractice (DHEW) (U.S. Govt. Printing Office) (1973). Moreover, in a survey of all the malpractice claims resolved between 1975 and 1976, informed consent was raised as an issue in only 3 percent of the cases. S. Law and S. Polan, Pain and Profit: The Politics of Malpractice 113 (1978).

[3]In addition to the survey of state laws in Meisel and Kabnick, supra n.1, a slightly more recent comprehensive analysis of state law appears in President's Commission for the Study of Ethical Problems in Medicare and Biomedical and Behavioral Research, Making Health Care Decisions, vol. 3, Appendix L, 205-245 (1982).

[4]See, e.g., N.C. Gen. Stat. §90-21.13 (1975).

to the duty to inform and defenses for failure to inform.[5] Many of them also provide that a consent in writing, in a form prescribed by the statute, will be presumed valid.[6] A few states provide, in their statutes or by regulation, a list of required disclosures.[7]

"Living will" statutes, a special form of consent statute, also exist in most states. They are considered in Chapter 15, and compilations of them for all the states are readily available.

Finally, there are several kinds of special consent statutes that healthcare facilities in many states must know about. These are special disease-specific or procedure-specific disclosure statutes passed for patients' rights reasons, intended to address the problems of vulnerable groups of patients. Many of these special statutes mandate disclosure directly, rather than merely prescribing the cause of action for failure to disclose. Statutes in a few states require the disclosure of treatment options to breast cancer patients.[8] A number of states have passed statutes regulating the provision of electroconvulsive therapy, including requirements for obtaining the consent of the patient or a representative and, in many instances, listing required disclosure.[9] Many states also have statutory schemes governing sterilizations, both for men and women generally[10] and for mentally disabled adults[11] and

---

[5]E.g., Ga. Code §§88-2901 to 88-2907 (1971); Idaho Code §§39-4301 to 39-4306 (1975); Alaska Stat. §09.55.556 (1976); N.Y. Pub. Health Law §2805-d (McKinney 1975).

[6]E.g., N.C. Gen. Stat. §90-21.13 (1975); Fla. Stat. Ann. §786.46 (West 1975); Ohio Rev. Code Ann. §2317.54 (Baldwin 1977).

[7]E.g., Iowa Code Ann. §147.137 (West 1975) (statutory risk list); Hawaii Rev. Stat. §671-3 (1976); Tex. Stat. Ann. art. 4590i (Vernon 1976) (administrative boards given authority to set disclosure standards).

[8]Cal. Health & Safety Code §1704.5 (West 1980); Mass. Gen. Laws Ann. ch. 111, §70E (West 1979).

[9]E.g., Cal. Welf. & Inst. Code §5326.85 (West 1981); Fla. Stat. §458.325 (West 1979); Mass. Gen. Laws Ann. ch. 123 (West 1981); Mo. Ann. Stat. §630.130 (Vernon 1980); N.M. Stat. Ann. §43-1-15 (1970).

[10]E.g., Calif. Welf. & Inst. Code §14191 (West 1975); Ga. Code Ann. §24-4536 (Harrison 1981).

[11]E.g., Ohio Rev. Code Ann. §5122.271 (Baldwin 1981); Va. Code §§54-325.9 to 325.12 (1981).

minors.[12] There are also federal regulations mandating informed consent for sterilizations performed with federal funds.[13] Other state statutes prescribe informed consent for mentally ill and disabled institutionalized persons receiving psychotropic medication,[14] psychosurgery,[15] and other interventions.[16]

§7.4 Healthcare Facility Liability for Failure to Obtain Informed Consent

Although the task of obtaining the patient's written consent is often delegated by the patient's physician to nurses or other healthcare personnel, the duty to obtain informed consent still remains the physician's, because the duty belongs to the health-care provider who offers to perform the service.[1] (Usually this is a physician, but other caregivers may also provide services independently from physicians and therefore will also have

---

[12]E.g., Mont. Code Ann. §53-23-104 (1974); N.C. Gen. Stat. §§35-36, 35-37 (1981).

[13]42 C.F.R. §§441.253, 441.257-258 (1981) (Medicaid funding; includes detailed consent requirements and forms).

[14]Many such provisions are found in statutory institution codes (e.g., Ill. Ann. Stat. ch. 91½, §2-107 (Smith-Hurd 1979)), mental health legislation (e.g., Wis. Stat. Ann. §51.61 (West 1978)), and patients' bills of rights (e.g., Fla. Stat. Ann. §394.459 (West 1980)).

[15]E.g., N.J. Stat. Ann. §30:4-24.2 (West 1975); N.D. Cent. Code §25-03.1-40 (1977).

[16]E.g., Mont. Code Ann. §53-20-146 (1979) (behavioral modification with aversive stimuli). Many states also legislatively permit but regulate use of isolation or restraints. Where this is so, consent concerns focus on the content of disclosure to patients entering the institution, who should be told that their treatment may by law include these measures.

§7.4 [1]This means that consulting physicians who propose treatments to patients take on informed consent duties as regards those treatments—duties not shared by the referring physician. Gray v. Grunnagle, 423 Pa. 144, 233 A.2d 663 (1966).

informed consent duties.)[2] Anyone who, acting as the physician's agent, fails to obtain informed consent has rendered the physician responsible for that failure.[3]

The healthcare facility that presides over informed consent practice is likely to find itself with informed consent duties only in unusual circumstances. Physicians and others who are employees of a healthcare facility and have informed consent duties can potentially make the facility liable through the vicarious liability doctrine of respondeat superior, or "let the master answer" for the negligence of the servant.[4] This employment relationship, though still uncommon for caregivers with independent informed consent responsibilities, is certainly not unheard of, especially since HMOs and other alternative delivery systems have been developing employment relationships with physicians.[5]

Note that the employment relationship does not give the facility its own informed consent duty. It may, however, have a supervisory duty: if the facility's employees (e.g., nurses) regularly obtain patients' signatures on consent forms, and therefore have the opportunity to observe whether the patients have been adequately informed or not, it is reasonable to expect that the facility is thereby put on notice about defects in the consent process and in patients' understanding. Therefore, if an employee of the facility such as a nurse or a clerk obtains a patient's signature but the patient claims that the consent process was suspect, the facility could be held vicariously responsible for the employee's negligent failure to check the validity of the consent before obtaining the signature. This is particularly true where the facility's policy requires, as many do, that, as part of the process of witnessing the patient's signature, the nurse must ask

---

[2]Dentists, nurses, physical therapists, psychologists, respiratory therapists, and some diagnostic technicians are among the many healthcare providers who could have independent informed consent responsibilities.

[3]This is the standard agency law principle that was once denominated the "captain of the ship" doctrine when applied in medical (and especially surgical) contexts, e.g., Sparger v. Worley Hosp., 547 S.W.2d 582 (Tex. 1977).

[4]Fruit v. Schreiner, 502 P.2d 133 (Alaska 1972).

[5]See Chapter 16.

the patient whether she understands the procedure or has questions.[6]

There is a possibility, based on some scholarly discussion, that a facility could be held to have a direct and independent informed consent duty to patients as part of its own duty to provide patients with safe facilities and to honor their basic rights. Argument in support of such an independent duty could be based on the facility's conformance with JCAHO accreditation standards, which contain a Patient's Bill of Rights. This basis for liability has yet to find its way into case law, but the time may be near.[7]

§7.5 Consent to Special Conditions of Healthcare Facilities

Although informed consent law has been directed exclusively toward procedure-specific information conveyed to patients by the person offering to perform the procedures, healthcare facilities are increasingly facing consent questions in new contexts that reflect both changes in service delivery and emerging societal concerns. A discussion of these emerging issues cannot be exhaustive, but all healthcare facilities should be sensitive to the potential need to discuss certain policies and practices with patients. The general rationale for requiring such discussion is as follows: When important aspects of any facility's service delivery run counter to what patients are likely to assume

---

[6]See the discussion of hospital consent policy in §7.1.4 supra, n.39. See also Fiorentino v. Wenger, 19 N.Y.2d 407, 280 N.Y.S.2d 373, 227 N.E.2d 296 (1967). Cf. Darling v. Charleston Community Mem. Hosp., 50 Ill. App. 2d 253, 200 N.E.2d 149 (1964), affd., 33 Ill. 2d 326, 211 N.E.2d 253 (1965) (nurses' duties included checking patient's leg cast; proper checks would have timely discovered negligent cast application).

[7]This line of argument was pursued, but neither well-addressed nor ruled on, in Campbell v. Pitt County Mem. Hosp., 321 N.C. 261 (1987) (nursing staff secured father's signature on labor-and-delivery consent form after delivery; timely seeking consent could have revealed parents' lack of knowledge about method of delivery chosen by obstetrician).

without discussion, the faculty may risk liability based on the patient's reasonable expectations rather than on the facility's actual practices.

§7.5.1 HMO Coverage Limitations

The questions of what care will be provided and what care will be paid for by an HMO are a matter of contract, and the details of such agreements are outside the scope of the current discussion. It is clear, however, that many HMO contracts contain ample room for confusion and dispute about the conditions of coverage. Most common is the familiar confusion about coverage and reimbursement for the services of consultants and other referrals and for procedures performed outside the HMO or in facilities not on the HMO's approved list. It is plainly in the HMO's best interest to ensure that enrollees are well-informed about coverage limitations, precertification requirements, the circumstances under which emergency exceptions apply, and so forth, so as to minimize later confusion and reduce the likelihood that patients can successfully claim coverage for noncovered services on the ground that they reasonably assumed it would be forthcoming.

Even more difficult questions may arise if the HMO seeks to eliminate coverage for certain services altogether. A plan might choose to contain costs by eliminating certain arguably marginal services—for example, routine internal fetal monitoring during labor. Such a limitation, though controversial, could conceivably survive a malpractice challenge; if so, a pregnant woman enrolled in the HMO would be unable to obtain routine monitoring, even at extra cost, when delivering her baby in the HMO's facility. If such efforts at curbing expenditures are to survive legal challenge, they must surely be discussed fully with enrollees, first at the time of enrollment and, later, as part of the informed consent process surrounding pregnancy. Otherwise, such restrictions are very likely to be found to constrain the free choice of patients unreasonably and without their knowledge.[1] Well-informed enrollees, on the other hand, might be viewed as making a supportable choice to enroll in a less costly program that eliminated some marginal services.[2]

§7.5.2 Extended Care Facility Policies

Many extended care and special service facilities maintain policies or practices concerning resuscitation, use of ventilatory support, and artificial nutrition and hydration that are of direct concern to elderly, chronically ill, and terminally ill patients.[3] These policies and practices have two general sources.

First, extended care facilities may find it difficult to establish and maintain Do Not Resuscitate (DNR) status for patients when they do not have medical staff available around the clock. Nurses and paramedical personnel are not permitted to exercise discretion in resuscitation decisions. Therefore, neither the nursing staff nor rescue squads will be able to respond to patients' wishes to forgo resuscitation in the absence of a physician's orders. Physicians attending in the facility must maintain a sound DNR policy—consulting with patients and their families, giving a clear indication of the patient's DNR status, and regularly reviewing and updating orders—so that nurses and paramedics can respond appropriately.

Second, some facilities may choose to establish morally based institutional policies prohibiting the withholding or withdrawal of ventilators, artificial nutrition and hydration, and possibly other "extraordinary" care from patients in the facility. Sometimes such policies are well-established, but often are not made known to patients until an attempt is made to refuse treatment.

For facilities subscribing to practices or policies that, like

---

§7.5 [1]See discussion in C. Havighurst, Health Care Law and Policy 816-817 (1988).

[2]See Chapter 16.

[3]Policies on the use of drugs, seclusion, and restraint may have even more significance for many patients (see §7.3 supra) and should be viewed similarly.

the above, purport to limit patients' power to refuse treatments, the issues are two. First, does the facility have a duty to disclose such policies and practices to potential patients on or before admission, so that they will have knowledge of them? Second, can the facility maintain adherence to such policies and practices over the objection of patients on the ground that they knew of them on admission and therefore agreed to them?

The second question lies within the scope of Chapter 15. The first and necessarily prior question must be answered in the affirmative if the facility hopes to escape liability for policies and practices running counter to the reasonable expectations of patients. If patients may reasonably expect that their treatment refusals will be honored, then policies and practices precluding refusal of certain treatments may subject the facility to liability when there is no prior discussion of them.

In the only reported decision thus far to address these issues squarely, In re Requena,[4] the patient, who was suffering from amyotrophic lateral sclerosis, had been hospitalized for 15 months. She decided that when she became unable to eat normally, she would not accept feeding through a nasogastric tube. When the hospital was told of her decision it informed her of an institutional policy against withdrawing or withholding artificial nutrition and hydration and asked her to leave because it could not comply with her wishes. The court ordered the hospital to honor Mrs. Requena's decision because she had been there for so long before learning of the policy and had formed many strong attachments to staff members there. In the court's view, under the circumstances it was fairer to expect the hospital to suffer a violation of its policy than to ask Mrs. Requena to give up either her chosen caregivers or her preferred course of treatment. Having left open the question of how it would rule had Mrs. Requena been informed of the hospital's policy on her admission, this court has opened the possibility that such policies might, under some circumstances, be ruled valid, but only if

---

[4]In re Requena, 213 N.J. Super. 443, 517 A.2d 869 (App. Div. 1986), affirming 213 N.J. Super. 475, 517 A.2d 886 (Ch. Div. 1986).

patients receive adequate notice of them, understand their consequences, and freely choose to enter the facility nonetheless.

When a facility's reasons for failing to have policies are practical rather than ideological, it is becoming clear that under some circumstances the lack of a DNR policy could give rise to liability for treatment without the patient's consent. Facilities that do not make some effort to establish policies for instituting and honoring DNR orders, within the limits made necessary by the availability of attending physicians, may someday face liability on that account.[5]

A separate but related issue for residents of extended care facilities is the matter of consent to the placement itself. When residents who have decisional capacity are placed without their consent or held against their will (as, for example, when a resident withdraws consent to the placement on learning of policies and restrictions he or she deems unacceptable), they are being falsely imprisoned.[6] Because nursing home admissions often come at the behest of the patient's relatives, hospital social workers, and other third parties, the facility that does not independently assess a new resident's decisional capacity and confirm his or her consent to placement could be liable for false imprisonment. Facilities should also make it a policy to inform residents promptly of its policies and restrictions and develop mechanisms to investigate and deal with residents' decisions to leave the facility, in order to preclude false imprisonment liability.

B. Capacity to Consent

§7.6 The Presumption of Capacity

The patient's "competence"—or, more precisely, the patient's capacity to make healthcare decisions—is not always an issue,

---

[5]See the discussion in §7.17.3 and accompanying notes 19 and 20 of the *Strachan* and *Leach* cases.

[6]Big Town Nursing Home v. Newman, 461 S.W.2d 195 (Tex. Civ. App. 1970).

but when it is, it is a particularly difficult and confusing one. Consents must be intentional, made with understanding, and free from control by others in order to be valid, but there is no requirement that a consent also be competent per se. Rather, decisional capacity is an attribute of the patient, not the choice, an ability that forms the basis for producing a valid decision.[1]

All adults are presumed by law to have decisional capacity.[2] The presumption of capacity can be overcome by reliable evidence of the patient's incapacity. Confinement in a mental institution—even involuntary commitment—does not necessarily overcome the presumption of decisional capacity, nor does any particular diagnosis.[3] If the patient has been legally determined to be incompetent, or a guardian or conservator of the patient's person has been legally appointed, the presumption is overcome, and the appointed decisionmaker holds authority to choose for the patient in all decisions to which the determination of incapacity extends.[4] In all other cases, a particular examination of the patient's capacity must be made in order to overcome the presumption.

---

§7.6 [1]Thus, the consent of a patient who currently lacks decisional capacity is not valid. Demers v. Gerety, 85 N.M. 641, 515 P.2d 645 (Ct. App. 1973).

[2]E.g., Grannum v. Berard, 70 Wash. 2d 304, 422 P.2d 812 (1967). Minors, by contrast, are presumed to lack capacity; however, in many instances they may demonstrate that they are able to make certain choices, and they will be permitted to consent to some treatments even without demonstrating their capacity; for further discussion see Part C infra.

[3]See Wilson v. Lehman, 379 S.W.2d 478 (Ky. 1964) (patient undergoing electroconvulsive therapy still presumed competent until shown otherwise).

[4]Statutory schemes for the determination of incapacity and appointment of guardians generally require specific and detailed findings and often provide for limited guardianships for persons who lack capacity in some areas (e.g., financial management) but not others (e.g., independent living). Formal guardianship proceedings may be triggered by the onset of illness or disability; or, the incompetency of a mentally disabled young adult might be judicially determined at the time he or she attains majority.

§7.7 The Assessment of Capacity

Because capacity is presumed for all adults not legally determined to be incompetent, it is not necessary to assess each patient's capacity to make every healthcare decision. However, caregivers and facilities must have at least some guidelines regarding what should prompt an assessment. Perhaps advanced age, certain diagnoses, and residence in an extended care facility are together sufficient to create a suspicion that would justify assessing the patient's capacity. Caution must then be used in the assessment, so that triggering the assessment does not itself overcome the presumption.

The questions of who should be testing patients' decisional capacity and what should give rise to the need for testing are not settled, and should be determined pragmatically. First, caregivers should be alert to the existence of appointed guardians for patients and should request proof of the person's guardianship or durable power of attorney, as required by state law, from anyone purporting to have decisional authority for a patient. Second, caregivers should derive any suspicion of a patient's lack of capacity from the patient's behavior, not from the patient's status, diagnosis, or age, or from the family's assertions about the patient.

Of necessity, many determinations about a patient's capacity are made at the bedside by physicians—sometimes, but not always, with the assistance of psychiatric, neurological, or psychological expertise. Because decisional capacity is task-specific, a global determination of lack of capacity, such as that provided by a mental status examination, cannot necessarily show that the patient cannot make a given decision—especially if the determination of incapacity is made before the need for the decision arises. Therefore, global determinations of incapacity should be considered preliminary, and either should be reexamined when a decision is needed or should provide evidence in a judicial proceeding to determine the patient's capacity (except where the emergency exception applies). Though some commentators have argued that the courts should always be consulted for determinations about patients' decisional capacities, except where statutes permit otherwise, by custom many such determinations are made by attending physicians without judicial review. Because the machinery of justice is cumbersome and costly, in the great majority of cases, where no controversies appear to exist, customary practice seems appropriate. It is of course always advisable to document the reasons and evidence for each determination of incapacity, to indicate who acted as substitute decisionmaker, and to seek judicial review when not doing so would create a serious risk of unfaithfulness or injury to the patient.

The capacity to make a healthcare decision is in essence no different from the capacity to make any life decision of comparable significance. And although we rarely scrutinize people's capacity to engage in ordinary transactions, from major purchases to marriage, career, and childbearing, we often scrutinize healthcare decision-making very closely. The risk naturally arises that standards of capacity may rise too high in healthcare by comparison with other sorts of decisions. When the standards rise, caregivers are placed at greater risk when they honor patients' informed choices. Thus, it is in the best interest of caregivers and healthcare facilities to assess patients' capacities fairly and consistently and to keep written records of the reasons prompting assessment and the reasons supporting the conclusion reached.

It is always risky not to honor a patient's choice, or even to fail to involve the patient in the decision, because the patient lacks capacity. In many cases the risk is somewhat reduced by the clear necessity for the procedure, the existence of an emergency, or the establishment of a good understanding between the physician and the patient's family. However, whenever decisions involve more than minimal risk or uncertainty, whenever they are highly consequential or implicate personal values, and whenever there is time to anticipate a future lack of capacity, it is wise to discuss the decisions at hand and to line up alternative decisionmakers. In such cases, the physician's decision to foreclose the patient's involvement in the choice without consulting a court for permission is very risky. Facilities are best advised to develop a policy that can help physicians to decide when to seek judicial sanction for their determinations that patients lack capacity. Extended care facilities in particular need such policies, because so much of their population suffers from diminishing or intermittent decisional capacity.

§7.7.1 Standards of Decisional Capacity

In essence, decisional capacity (or "competence") in the context of healthcare decision-making means the ability to give an informed consent (that is, the ability to give a consent that is intentional, based on understanding, and free from control by others). Setting the standards for understanding, voluntariness, and intention means determining how much of each of those attributes is necessary. Legally, decisional capacity is a minimal threshold standard, below which it is not reasonable to honor the patient's choices because the patient is not sufficiently capable of making them. Moreover, decisional capacity is specific; that is, patients may be competent in some ways and not in others, and therefore capable of making healthcare choices but not financial decisions, or capable of making minor or familiar decisions but not of grasping complex technical information necessary for other decisions. Finally, decisional capacity is not fixed, but may wax and wane with the patient's condition. Decisions made during a "window of capacity" should be honored during incapacity. Thus, standards of capacity must establish minimum threshold levels of decisional ability and must be specific, both temporally and to the ability being measured.

§7.7.2 Tests of Decisional Capacity

Many tests of decisional capacity have been suggested.[1] Logically, the best test for the ability to perform a task is a <u>trial performance</u>

_____

§7.7 [1]The most complete general discussion of the tests most commonly employed is still Roth, Meisel, and Lidz, Tests of Competency to Consent to Treatment, 134 Am. J. Psychiatry 279 (1977).

of the task. Thus, at first glance it would appear that the best test for decisional capacity is the informed consent process. However, this is not necessarily so. For persons who are unconscious, comatose, or otherwise unresponsive, it is futile and foolish to proceed with the consent process only to obtain a lack of response. Similarly, when patients are able to interact but, as a result of their conditions, are unable to "sit through" the consent process, it should be possible to judge them incapable without taking the process to the bitter end. On the other hand, because the doctrine of informed consent cannot preclude patients from making foolish or unreasonable choices, and because patients may refuse information or decide against medical advice, requiring patients to have the *ability* to make a fully informed, well-reasoned choice is different from requiring them to actually make such a choice every time. Thus, simply putting the patient through the informed consent process could result in the application of too high a standard unless careful attention is given to how the test purports to reflect ability to decide.

The presence of a decision is sometimes offered as a test of decisional capacity. This test requires only the expression of assent or dissent.[2] Such a test is insufficient because it does not necessarily reflect the patient's ability to understand and to decide freely. It may mask any number of cognitive or psychological disorders and is likely to result in many false positive determinations of capacity. It can even give rise to false negative determinations, where anything from language barriers to massive motor-neural disorders could prevent the communication of a decision.

The patient's understanding of the decision faced is sometimes tested as a way of gauging capacity as well as a way of determining whether the duty to obtain informed consent has

---

[2]Thus, only a patient who does not express a decision would be incompetent. An example of a conscious patient unable to express a decision might be a profoundly retarded adult like Joseph Saikewicz, see Superintendent of Belchertown State School v. Saikewicz, 373 Mass. 728, 370 N.E.2d 417 (1977), though Mr. Saikewicz did display aversion to the therapy at issue.

been met. Such a test examines whether the patient has grasped the basic issues disclosed by the caregiver and has some sense of why they, and the decision faced, are important.[3] The most common means of testing understanding is to ask the patient to repeat information back to the caregiver in his or her own words. Sometimes more standardized written multiple-choice questionnaires are used.[4]

The risk of false negatives in this test derives from its unavoidable bias in favor of the caregiver's definition of "understanding." Moreover, it must be carefully administered to ensure that it does not become a test of the patient's recall. Since this test deals only with understanding and not with the patient's reasoning process, however, its principal risk is that caregivers may overestimate the degree of understanding that is sufficient for patients to make informed choices. This is probably the best test, and it has the advantage of already being built into the informed consent process. Asking patients whether they understand and if they have questions, and even soliciting patients' own versions of disclosed information, are standard features of many facilities' informed consent policies.

Another test, frequently used, is examination of the patient's decisionmaking process[5]—that is, asking patients to explain the basis for their choices and evaluating their reasons and their reasoning. If a patient has not considered a decision fully enough or taken all of the important considerations into account in

---

[3]E.g., In re Quackenbush, 156 N.J. Super. 282, 287, 383 A.2d 785, 788 (1978).

[4]Meisel and Roth, Toward an Informed Discussion of Informed Consent, 25 Ariz. L. Rev. 288-289, 292-295 (1983); Stuart, Protection of the Right to Informed Consent to Participate in Research, 9 Behavioral Therapy 73 (1978).

[5]Courts appearing to apply this test have differed in their conclusions. Compare In re B., 156 N.J. Super. 231, 234, 383 A.2d 760, 762 (1977) (patient's refusal to take psychotropic medication "not based entirely on rational considerations, but reflects delusional thinking") and In re Quackenbush, 156 N.J. Super. 282, 287, 383 A.2d 785, 788 (1978) with Lane v. Candura, 6 Mass. App. 377, 376 N.E.2d 1232 (1978) (patient's irrational refusal of treatment does not amount to incompetence) and In re Yetter, 62 Pa. D. & C. 2d 619 (Northampton County 1973) (patient not incompetent, though refusal of treatment partly based on delusional reasoning).

making it, the patient will be judged lacking in decisional capacity. This test runs a high risk of false negatives, since it clearly favors decisionmaking processes that resemble those of whoever is evaluating the process in question and thus may be biased against cultural, social, and religious differences in decisional priorities.

Finally, the decision itself has been known to serve as a test of decisional capacity. This test is also substantially biased. Whether the patient makes the "right" choice may be as much a matter of legitimate differences in viewpoint as of defects in decisional capacity; thus, false negatives may be caused by value conflicts. Like the test for the presence of a decision, this test could also give rise to false positives, since a patient with no capacity to understand the situation could still by chance announce the "right" choice.

§7.8 Deciding for Decisionally Incapable Adults

In general, there is no clearly authoritative decisionmaker for adults who lack capacity to make their own healthcare decisions and no clearly evident decisionmaking standard to be used by substitute decisionmakers. Statutes and sometimes case law have addressed this problem when dealing with particular circumstances. For example, the emergency doctrine authorizes physicians to treat patients after using their best medical judgment to make choices in the best interests of the patient; see §7.2.1 above. Much discussion about deciding for patients who lack capacity has focused on death and dying and whether and when lifesaving treatment may be refused on a patient's behalf. The reader should consult Chapter 10 for an in-depth analysis of cases and statutes in this area. Despite these developments, however, for most ordinary, nonemergency treatments and interventions for adult patients not terminally ill but not capable of decisionmaking, there is no approved procedure.

Healthcare facilities should establish a policy requiring caregivers to record in writing, in the medical record or other appropriate place, not only the physician's determination of the patient's decisional incapacity but also what happens next: who assumes decisional authority in each instance and on what basis. Such a record will help to demonstrate, should it become necessary, that the caregivers acted in good faith when proceeding in the absence of the patient's consent. Extended care facilities in particular should have policies regarding the use of substitute decisionmakers—family members, guardians, ombudsmen, patient advocates, or courts—for all risk-bearing decisions made on behalf of residents permanently or temporarily lacking decisional capacity.

§7.8.1 Who Has Authority

The list of potential decisionmakers for an adult lacking decisional capacity includes physicians and other caregivers; family members (e.g., the spouse, adult children, parents, or siblings); close friends; the court; and anyone named by the patient or appointed by the court. In practical terms, decisions for patients are probably most often made by the caregivers and family (or friends) together, and not infrequently by the caregivers alone when the friends and family are nonexistent, unavailable, or uninvolved. Unless the case law or a statute in a particular state prescribes a hierarchy of approved decisionmakers for certain kinds of decisions for incompetent patients,[1] or requires that courts,[2] committees,[3] or ombudsmen[4] make them, this ad hoc approach is appropriate. However, if there is disagreement— among family members, between family and friends, among

§7.8 [1]E.g., N.C. Gen. Stat. §90-322 (1983) (lifesaving treatment may be withheld or withdrawn from terminally ill incapacitated adult patients by decision of the attending physician with the patient's spouse, guardian, or a majority of the patient's relatives in the first degree (i.e., parents and adult children), in that order.

[2]Superintendent of Belchertown State School v. Saikewicz, 373 Mass. 728, 370 N.E.2d 417 (1977).

[3]In re Quinlan, 70 N.J. 10, 355 A.2d 647, cert. denied, 429 U.S. 922 (1976).

[4]In re Conroy, 98 N.J. 321, 486 A.2d 1209 (1985).

caregivers, or between caregivers and others—or if there is reason to suspect any conflict of interest on the part of anyone involved in the decision, it becomes especially important to consider the appropriate basis for the decision when deciding who is the right decisionmaker.

§7.8.2 Standards of Decision

There is a clear complementarity between choice of the appropriate decisionmaker and choice of the applicable standard of decision. As discussed in more detail in Chapter 10, decision-making on behalf of another who lacks capacity should generally be made according to one of two possible standards: either by determining what the patient would want if he or she did not lack capacity, or by acting in the patient's best interests. The first standard, substituted judgment, requires decisionmakers to assemble evidence of the patient's personality, values, previous choices, and expressions of preference in order to best determine what the patient would have wanted.[5] Decisionmakers who lack access to this kind of information about a patient or who disagree with or misassess the patient's likely choice because of their own emotions and values should be disqualified from making decisions according to this standard.

Very often there is insufficient evidence to make a choice for the patient according to this standard, especially when the decision faced is less monumental than the life-and-death issues about which people are most likely to reflect in advance or when the patient never had the capacity to reflect that makes the standard meaningful. Use of the alternative "best interests" standard requires cooperation between caregivers, who make

---

[5]When patients have left instructions, while decisionally capable, about decisions to be made if they lose decisional capacity, honoring their wishes does not require the substituted judgment process. However, their instructions may not be specific or clear enough to apply to the decision at hand, in which case they form part of the evidence of what the patient would have wanted. See Chapter 10.

medical assessments and recommendations, and family or friends, who can contribute evidence of the patient's preferences and values—evidence that falls short of a substituted judgment but helps those involved to focus on the best interests, medical *and otherwise*, of *this particular patient*. The best interests standard does not center on the physician's medical advice, but may rest there when other information about the patient's interests is unavailable or insufficient.

C. Consent and Minors

§7.9 Parental Consent

Only adults are presumed capable of giving informed consent to their own treatment. The general age of majority is now 18 in all states. When minor children are in need of treatment, the consent of a parent or legal guardian is generally sought. Children, especially older children, may in fact have decisional capacity; nonetheless, initiating treatments when parents are unavailable or over parental objection is not without risks for providers, even though in most cases the risks of liability are quite small. A commonsense case-by-case approach to decision-making and recordkeeping in the treatment of minors will help to ensure that informed consent is obtained from the appropriate party so that children receive needed treatments without risk to the provider.[1]

The purpose of informed consent is not simply to ensure that medical advice is followed but to allow patients to make their own healthcare choices (or to allow their representatives to make choices on their behalf). Parents are their minor children's legal representatives, and as such may make decisions for their children based not only on medical advice but also on the child's nonmedical interests and on family values. Although

---

§7.9 [1]The bible for consent questions in the treatment of minors is still A. Holder, Legal Issues in Pediatrics and Adolescent Medicine (2d ed. 1985).

a high degree of concern exists that parents not injure their children through medical neglect, parents are presumed to be acting in their child's best interests; the final determination of whether this is so belongs not with the provider but with the courts.

Parental consents, as well as refusals, can raise questions about the child's best interests. There are some treatment authorizations made by parents on behalf of their children that have been recognized as deserving special scrutiny because of the need to make sure that the child's best interests are being served. For example, any decision to sterilize mentally retarded minors must conform to statutory requirements designed to ensure that the power to reproduce is not being withdrawn merely for parental convenience.[2] Similarly, the courts have mandated special scrutiny of procedures not primarily for the medical benefit of the child—for example, donation of a kidney by the child to a sibling.[3] Any time a parental decision, whether consent or refusal, does not seem clearly to be in the child's best interests, some measure of further scrutiny should be initiated by the healthcare providers.[4] Of course, a child's refusal of treatments to which parents have consented raises concerns as well. Minors' refusals may be valid when their consents would be valid; see §7.12 and especially Chapter 10.

§7.10 Parental Unavailability and Refusal

The consent of only one parent is required in order to authorize treatment for a child; therefore, if only one parent is available,

---

[2]See the discussion in §7.3 supra.

[3]E.g., Hart v. Brown, 29 Conn. Supp. 368, 289 A.2d 386 (1972); Little v. Little, 576 S.W.2d 493 (Tex. Civ. App. 1979). Many decisions conclude by authorizing such "nontherapeutic" treatments; the significant fact for present purposes is that whatever conclusion is reached comes after very careful consideration of all the evidence and reasoning.

[4]Providers should have a general knowledge of the avenues of scrutiny open to them in their states, including social services involvement, ethics committees, statutes governing organ donation, mental health treatment, and other kinds of care for minors, and judicial precedent.

one consent is sufficient, and disagreements between parents may safely be left to them to resolve. It is when neither parent is available or both refuse to authorize treatment that significant legal questions arise.[1]

§7.10.1 Emergencies

The emergency exception to the duty to obtain informed consent applies to minors as well as to adults. "Emergency" is often broadly construed whatever the age of the patient. Thus, if the parents of minors cannot be reached in time, necessary treatments may be given without their consent.[2] Many state statutory schemes provide procedures for certifying the existence of an emergency, sometimes requiring the signatures of two physicians, before treating a minor in the absence of parental consent.[3] In the absence of such statutes or institutional policies, the provider should attest in the record to the need to treat immediately, the attempts made to contact the parents, and any other reasons for proceeding without parental consent.

If the parents are available but refuse to consent to emergency treatment for their minor child, their objections should be investigated. It is at least possible that a parent has reasons that should be honored. Unless the child's life will be endangered by the delay needed to inquire into the parent's choice, the caregiver should so inquire. When the parent continues to refuse, the

---

§7.10 [1]In Hodgson v. Minnesota, 58 U.S.L.W. 4957 (U.S., June 26, 1990), the Supreme Court upheld a statute providing that when a minor seeks an abortion, both her parents must be *notified* unless she obtains a judicial bypass of that notification for reasons of emancipation, judicial determination of maturity, or one of several other exceptions. In previous cases, the Supreme Court has struck down statutes that required the *consent* of one or both parents without providing for judicial bypass. See A. Holder, Legal Issues in Pediatrics and Adolescent Medicine 286-288 (2d ed. 1985).

[2]E.g., Tabor v. Scobee, 254 S.W.2d 474 (Ky. 1952); Wells v. McGehee, 39 So. 2d 196 (La. 1949); Jackovach v. Yocum, 212 Iowa 914, 237 N.W. 444 (1931).

[3]E.g., Fla. Stat. Ann. §743.064 (West 1979); Ill. Ann. Stat. ch. 111, §4503 (Smith-Hurd 1972); N.C. Gen. Stat. §90-21.1 (1977).

facility should proceed with emergency treatment. Sometimes statutes authorizing emergency treatment also give physicians authority to act in emergencies despite parental refusal. In the absence of such authority, healthcare facilities should have procedures in place for seeking emergency court orders granting temporary custody of the child to the physician or to the social services department for the purpose of administering treatment.

§7.10.2 Necessary Treatment

When both parents refuse to consent to treatments considered necessary by providers, if there is no emergency, the provider may not proceed to treat unless (1) the minor is capable of giving valid consent (see §7.12) and is willing to do so, or (2) a court order authorizing treatment is obtained.

If the parents cannot be found and a child is in need of treatment, but there is no emergency, it is prudent but not always necessary to seek court authorization for treatment. Older children may often possess actual decisional capacity and, where necessary care is at issue, physicians are very unlikely to be found liable for relying on the consent of a child aged 15 or older (see §7.12 below).

§7.10.3 Religious Objections to Treatment

The most difficult instance of parent-provider disagreement to resolve is when a parent has religious objections to treatment of a child. Religiously motivated treatment refusals by adults for themselves should be honored, even when death will result;[4] however, it is less clear whether the treatment of children should be governed by the beliefs of their parents.

If the child is truly able to make the decision, it is the

---

[4]E.g., In re Melideo, 88 Misc. 2d 974, 390 N.Y.S.2d 523 (1976); In re Osborne, 294 A.2d 372 (D.C. App. 1972).

child's decision that providers should seek to honor.[5] Minors' decisions to refuse lifesaving treatment for any reason are very problematic and should be examined with great care; for a child near the age of majority, however, some religiously motivated refusals should certainly be honored, depending on the circumstances. When the child is not mature enough to decide, the parents' religious refusals of treatment may be overridden by court order if the treatment is lifesaving or will prevent serious damage to the child.[6] The most familiar religious objections to treatment are Jehovah's Witnesses' refusal of blood and blood products for themselves and their children. When forgoing transfusions is not safe for the child, most courts will routinely override parental refusals on a proper showing by providers.[7]

§7.11 The Baby Doe Regulations

When parents refuse treatment for an "infant," a child less than one year old, that refusal will also be examined according to

---

[5]When the child's condition is not life-threatening, it may be feasible to postpone a final decision until the child can act as an independent decision-maker and either affirms or disaffirms the parental choice. E.g., In re Green, 448 Pa. 338, 292 A.2d 387 (1972), revg. 220 Pa. Super. 191, 286 A.2d 681 (1971); In re Seiferth, 309 N.Y. 80, 127 N.E.2d 820 (1955). See also the discussion of mature minors in §7.12.3 infra and the discussion of minors in Chapter 10.

[6]E.g., Gates v. Jensen, 20 Wash. App. 81, 579 P.2d 374 (1978). One difficulty with religiously motivated treatment refusals is that the parents' religious reasons for refusal may draw attention away from real risks in the proposed treatment and real uncertainties about its benefits. In every case, regardless of the reasons parents give for refusing treatment, providers must be certain that the treatment they recommend is in their view genuinely necessary, not just a long shot or a last resort.

[7]E.g., Morrison v. State, 252 S.W.2d 97 (Mo. Ct. App. 1952). Many providers agree to perform bloodless surgery when possible or to substitute the transfusion of artificial volume expanders for that of whole blood. When such measures are not possible, courts have compelled transfusions for competent adult pregnant women, despite religious objections, in order to preserve the life of the fetus. E.g., Raleigh Fitkin-Paul Morgan Mem. Hosp. v. Anderson, 42 N.J. 421, 201 A.2d 537, cert. denied, 377 U.S. 985 (1964).

the standards set forth in the federal government's "Baby Doe" child abuse regulations.[1] These regulations have been adopted by all of the states in exchange for federal matching funds for state programs for the prevention of child abuse and neglect.[2] They purport to spell out with specificity when parents may refuse lifesaving medical treatment for their infant children and when such refusal constitutes "medical neglect," to be treated according to the state's social services mechanism for handling child abuse and neglect.[3] The only times treatments may be refused for infants are: (1) when they are permanently comatose; (2) when treatment would merely prolong dying and thus be futile; or (3) when treatment would be "virtually futile" in terms of the infant's survival and thus would be "inhumane."[4]

Facilities that treat infants with serious illnesses and injuries must be conversant with the Baby Doe regulations; even if the facility's only capacity to treat infants is in the emergency room, the emergency room staff and transport teams must at least be aware of the treatment exceptions and should know whether the facilities to which children are likely to be transferred have infant care review committees.[5]

§7.11.1 Infant Care Review Committees

These committees are suggested, but not mandated, by the federal regulations in order to advise parents and physicians about treatment decisions for severely ill infants.[6] Many children's hospitals and hospitals with neonatal and pediatric

---

§7.11 [1]Child Abuse and Neglect Prevention and Treatment, 45 C.F.R. pt. 1345 (1985).

[2]Child Abuse Amendments of 1984, Pub. L. No. 98-457, 98 Stat. 1749 (1984).

[3]45 C.F.R. §1340.15(b)(1).

[4]45 C.F.R. §1340.15(b)(2).

[5]For further discussion of treatment refusal on behalf of children and the Baby Doe regulations, see Chapter 10.

[6]Model Guidelines for Health Care Providers to Establish Infant Care Review Committees, 50 Fed. Reg. 14893 (1985).

intensive care units have such committees, much of whose function is educational and policymaking.[7]

Where such committees exist, parents of severely ill infants should be informed of the availability of the committee to give advice on different treatment decisions and must be informed when the committee is to be consulted about their child. Committees do not replace parents as the decisionmakers for their children, however. When a committee disagrees with the parents' treatment decision, its only power is to refer the disagreement to the local social services department or to the courts.[8]

§7.11.2 Healthcare Facility Liability and the Baby Doe Regulations

No healthcare facility has the automatic authority to treat patients over their objections, or minor patients over their parents' objections, even if the parents refuse clearly necessary treatment; therefore, facilities and providers offering treatment to infants will incur no federal penalties for failure to perform it over parental objections.[9] If, however, facilities believe an infant should be treated under the regulations, and they fail to contact the social services department or the courts to decide whether treatment should be ordered, the ultimate sanction provided by the federal regulations is the state's loss of federal matching funds for its child abuse programs. Once the facility engages the state's social services mechanisms in these cases, parents may be convicted of child neglect for refusing treatments not falling within the regulatory exceptions, and the state, as custodian of neglected children, may take the regulations as guidance for difficult treatment decisions.[10] Thus, the regulations have the

---

[7]Id. at 14894-14895.

[8]Id. at 14896.

[9]See Bowen v. American Hosp. Assn., 476 U.S. 610 (1986).

[10]The "Baby Lance" case was apparently the first treatment decision case decided under the new regulations to gain national attention. In 1986, when

potential to affect infant care significantly, regardless of parental wishes, in at least some cases. Since their introduction in 1984, these regulations have apparently had considerably less impact on treatment than originally expected.[11] They have, however, focused much-needed attention on the role of parents and caregivers in informed consent and on moral dilemmas in the intensive care nursery.

§7.12 Valid Consent by Minors

It has long been recognized that many children, especially older children, may possess decisional capacity comparable to that considered sufficient in adults. That decisional capacity is being more and more widely acknowledged, so that, as Angela Holder points out, in the past 25 years there have been no reported successful challenges to a provider's reliance on the consent of anyone age 15 or over to healthcare treatment.[1] A provider relying on the consent of a child must satisfy all the ordinary

---

he was five weeks old, Lance Steinhaus was abused by his father and received serious and irreversible brain damage, rendering him permanently unconscious. Five months later, Lance's mother, in consultation with his physicians, placed a Do Not Resuscitate order in his medical record as well as a direction not to administer antibiotics. On learning of this, the Redwood County, Minnesota Welfare Department, which had had custody of Lance since the beating, challenged the mother's right to make treatment decisions and argued that the Baby Doe regulations required treatment because Lance's "persistent vegetative state" was not the chronic and irreversible coma that the regulations specified as an exceptive case. On October 13, 1986, after hearing expert testimony that Lance's condition fit the regulatory language, the Redwood County court ordered that, in the language of the regulations, only "appropriate nutrition, hydration, warmth, and medication" were *required*. Left undecided was whether the child's family or the Welfare Department had decisional authority over treatment not required by the regulations. Gianelli, *Minnesota Judge: Baby Lance Can Die*, Am. Med. News, October 24-31, 1986, at 1, col. 1.

[11]50 Fed. Reg. 14885-14887 (1985) (regulatory impact analysis claiming that only a fraction of a very small fraction of births will involve "even a potential allegation of medical neglect" under the regulations).

§7.12 [1]A. Holder, Legal Issues in Pediatrics and Adolescent Medicine 133 (2d ed. 1985).

requirements of informed consent and should give special attention to making the determination, in the medical record, that the child understands the decision and its implications. In addition to this general rule, there are several more specific statutory and judicial doctrines that help both to protect providers from liability risks and to focus attention on the capacities and needs of the child.

§7.12.1 Statutes Regarding Treatment of Minors

Virtually all states have enacted statutes permitting minors (often of any age, sometimes of a specified age and up) to consent to certain types of treatment—usually treatment for venereal diseases and communicable diseases, often for drug or alcohol abuse, psychiatric and emotional problems, and prenatal care, and sometimes for birth control.[2] The exact terms of these statutes vary greatly from state to state. In general, such statutes do not so much presume that minors are capable of giving consent to these treatments as they reason that requiring parental consent would increase the likelihood that children would not seek needed care because of the breach of confidentiality entailed in contacting parents about stigmatizing conditions. Thus, these statutes are more a codified exception to the informed consent requirement than an acknowledgment that children always have sufficient decisional capacity to consent to these treatments.

Many states have also directly addressed the question of the child's capacity by codifying the general proposition that children who demonstrate capacity may give consent without parental notification.[3] Such statutes overlap substantially with common-

---

[2]See, e.g., N.C. Gen. Stat. §90-21.5 (1983) (any minor may consent to prevention, diagnosis, and treatment of venereal and reportable communicable diseases, pregnancy, substance abuse, and emotional disturbance, not including abortion, sterilization, or psychiatric commitment). The best compilation of such statutes is found in Ewald, Medical Decisionmaking for Children: An Analysis of Competing Interests, 25 St. Louis L.J. 689 (1982).

[3]E.g., N.C. Gen. Stat. §90-21.5(b): "Any minor who is emancipated may consent to any medical treatment, dental and health services for himself and his child."

law formulations of the "emancipated" and "mature minor" doctrines.

§7.12.2 Emancipation

Emancipation describes the condition of a minor no longer under the protection and control of his or her parents. This legal status has long been recognized. It varies in its precise definition from one jurisdiction to another, but minors who are married, in the armed services, or simply living away from home and self-supporting are usually considered emancipated.[4] Emancipation is a general status, applying to most legal capacities (such as entering into contracts, including contracting for health services). The premises behind it are, first, that parents of emancipated minors may be hard to reach or uninvolved in their children's decisions, and, second, that their lives demonstrate that emancipated minors have decisional capacity.

In addition, in many states some categories of minors may be considered emancipated for medical care purposes though not necessarily for all purposes.[5] College students living away from home but financially dependent on their parents fall into this category; although parental notification regarding major risk-bearing decisions is always prudent, in many instances it is not necessary. Unmarried minor mothers living with their parents may also be permitted to make their own healthcare decisions, because they already have the power to decide on behalf of their children. A few states, however, may not recognize the minor mother's right to make her own healthcare decisions unless she demonstrates the decisional capacity of a "mature minor."

Finally, there are children who have left home without

---

[4]E.g., Bach v. Long Island Jewish Hosp., 267 N.Y.S.2d 289 (1966) (marriage); Swenson v. Swenson, 227 S.W.2d 103 (Mo. 1950) (military service); Blue v. Blue, 152 Nev. 82, 40 N.W.2d 268 (1949) (financial self-sufficiency).

[5]A. Holder, supra n.1, at 128.

parental consent whose parents do not consider themselves to have surrendered decisional authority. It is difficult to determine whether runaways are emancipated according to the above definitions. However, if runaways seeking treatment refuse to help providers contact their parents, the issue is moot. They may receive emergency care or care authorized by minor treatment statutes without concern about consent; they may receive necessary care under the presumption that they are emancipated so long as their refusal of parental notification is well-documented, including the child's signature; and they may well fall under the mature minor doctrine anyway.

§7.12.3 The Mature Minor Doctrine

The "mature minor doctrine" is the term used for judicial recognition that children who have the capacity to give consent should be permitted to do so without the need for parental notification. It is probably best known as a result of the many Supreme Court decisions delineating abortion rights. As the law now stands, in most states, minors seeking abortions may generally obtain them without parental consent if they appear before a judge and demonstrate their understanding of the abortion decision and its implications.[6] However, states may require notification of one[7] or both[8] parents, as long as a judicial bypass is available as an alternative. For most other medical decisions, the physician may make a determination of the child's maturity, even if all the accoutrements of emancipation are not present, and treat with the child's consent alone, without seeking judicial approval.[9]

---

[6]Matter of Mary Moe, 12 Mass. App. 727, 446 N.E.2d 740 (Mass. 1983); Orr v. Knowles, 215 Neb. 49, 337 N.W.2d 699 (Neb. 1983).

[7]Ohio v. Akron Center for Reproductive Health, 58 U.S.L.W. 4979 (U.S., June 26, 1990).

[8]Hodgson v. Minnesota, 58 U.S.L.W. 4957 (U.S., June 26, 1990).

[9]E.g., Carter v. Cangello, 164 Cal. Rptr. 361 (1980) (17-year-old girl, living independently but supported by parents, consented to surgery); Younts v. St. Francis Hosp. and School of Nursing, 205 Kan. 292, 469 P.2d 330

The mature minor doctrine is decision-specific, functioning in general the same way a determination of decisional capacity does for an adult whose capacity is in question. The provider who would rely on it must make, justify, and document the finding that this child has the capacity to make this decision. Then the child must give an informed consent (or an informed refusal; see Part E), exactly as an adult would. Common sense would indicate that the younger the child and the more serious the decision, the more difficult it will be to show maturity sufficient to satisfy a court. Children younger than 14 or 15, facing major procedures and life-threatening situations, should ordinarily not be determined mature by the physician alone without judicial guidance. However, providers should never hesitate to explore the possibility that any child may have the capacity to make or take part in healthcare decisions, regardless of age.[10]

D. Consent to Participation in Research

§7.13 Informed Consent: Research Versus Treatment

Treatment and research have differing goals. Though research may be described as "therapeutic," that is, capable of benefitting individual research subjects, modern medical research, unlike

---

(1970) (17-year-old girl consented to simple surgery on broken finger; parents not immediately available).

[10]The question of the child's capacity to consent is distinct from that of the parents' financial responsibility. Fully emancipated minors are usually deemed fully financially responsible for their contracts by the courts, but could be held to pay only the fair value of the services in some cases. Their parents have no financial responsibility for them. Parents of mature minors (or any other children) remain responsible for *necessary* services received by their children, even if they were not consulted or when treatment was provided by court order over their objections.

treatment, does not focus exclusively on the needs of individual patients. Instead, in order to assess the future therapeutic value of the protocol being tested, researchers must ensure that the information they gather about the protocol's effects is generalizable, reproducible, isolatable, and objective. Tailoring new protocols to the needs of individuals is not compatible with these research goals. Thus, though it may seem cruel to individual patients, the use of double-blind placebo studies of potentially lifesaving protocols and the long testing periods that postpone the availability of new protocols are seen as necessary by researchers for the general welfare. Essentially, the balance between advocacy for individual patients and society-wide responsibility is very different for clinicians and researchers.

This difference in focus raises informed consent issues. Most fundamentally, patients are patients and research subjects are research subjects, and the difference must be made clear to everyone who is asked to participate in research.[1] The disclosure requirements for informed consent begin from the central assumption of the patient-provider relationship: the reason the caregiver is proposing an intervention is to help the patient. But that is never the only reason for requesting research participation, and it may not be a reason at all in many research projects. Therefore, at the top of the list of basic disclosure for research is disclosing that the proposed intervention is research and what that means for the patient.

In nontherapeutic research, the reasons for participation are different enough to cause subjects to evaluate the risks very differently from the way they might if benefit to them were possible. In therapeutic research, the constraints of research design and the lack of knowledge about the protocol being tested make the risks greater and the benefits less likely than for common and well-proven treatment. Thus, knowing that research, not treatment, is contemplated deeply affects the patient's decision-making. Patients may be less willing to consent to

---

§7.13 [1]Cf. Estrada v. Jacques, 70 N.C. App. 627, 321 S.E.2d 240 (1984) (holding that healthcare providers have duty to inform patients if proposed procedure is experimental).

participation in research, even "therapeutic" research, than to treatment. If they do consent, their principal reasons may be different: altruism, perhaps, or, in the case of therapeutic research, the sense of having no other hope.

The chances that patients may mistake research for treatment are high, because of the ever-present hope of benefit and the association of physicians with caregiving. The risk that patients' misunderstandings will not be corrected by researchers—or even that patients might be inadvertently deceived into thinking they are receiving treatment—is also high, possibly resulting in harm both to patients' decisional autonomy and to their well-being. Thus, research deserves both special scrutiny and special regulation as regards informed consent.

One issue deserving particular consideration is who obtains consent when the prospective subjects are already patients. Informed consent to treatment is the responsibility of the treatment provider. However, if the researcher is also the patient-subject's primary provider, there is a high risk of confusion or the appearance of coercion when the researcher seeks consent. Patients may find it very difficult to distinguish research from treatment when both are provided by their own physician. Even if they can manage the distinction, patients approached by their physicians to participate in research may find it difficult to say no, out of feelings of gratitude, debt, or concern that refusal will compromise their continuing care. For these reasons researchers should try to separate their patient populations and their subject populations; if that is not possible, they should delegate the task of obtaining consent to a research colleague not associated, in the minds of the patient-subjects, with their doctor.

There is almost no modern case law on consent to research.[2]

---

[2]Karp v. Cooley, 493 F.2d 408, rehearing denied, 496 F.2d 878, cert. denied, 419 U.S. 845 (1979), perhaps the best-known case, concerns consent to innovative treatment but finds no liability for claimed imperfection in the consent process. Halushka v. University of Sask., 53 D.L.R.2d 436 (Saskatchewan Ct. App. 1965), a well-known Canadian case, establishes the requirement of informed consent for nontherapeutic research, using American case law precedents regarding informed consent to treatment. The research at issue in Hyman v. Jewish Chronic Disease Hosp., 251 N.Y.S.2d 818 (1964), 206 N.E.2d

Only a few states have statutory schemes regulating research in state-supported institutions.[3] The federal government regulates research extensively, however—all testing of new drugs[4] and all research conducted at institutions receiving federal funding[5] is regulated. These regulatory schemes, as well as research policies sometimes adopted by professional societies or certifying bodies whose members engage in research, and, occasionally, policies of private industry, for all intents and purposes establish standards of care for consent in research.[6]

Readers seeking more detail about the entire scheme of research regulation than is possible to include here should consult some of the many excellent discussions of federal research regulation in other works[7] or read the regulations themselves. At least a brief acquaintance with the federal regulations pertaining to consent to research is advisable, both because they pertain to research at many institutions and because they also provide good policy guidance for institutional oversight of otherwise unregulated research.

---

338 (1965), was arguably harmless, but was undertaken without the subjects' consent or knowledge and without the knowledge or approval of the hospital's research review committee.

[3]New York and California have such laws. See Note, Ensuring Informed Consent to Human Experimentation, 58 N.C.L. Rev. 137 (1979). So do several other states. See F. Rozovsky, Consent to Treatment: A Practical Guide §8.4 (2d ed. 1990).

[4]Food and Drug Administration regulations regarding consent to research appear at 21 C.F.R. pt. 50 (1985).

[5]DHHS regulations appear at 45 C.F.R. pt. 46 (1985).

[6]It does not necessarily follow from the existence of such regulations and policies that the failure to conform to them constitutes failure to obtain informed consent for the purpose of damages liability, but it is reasonable to assume that a court would probably so find. E.g., Whitlock v. Duke Univ., 637 F. Supp. 1463, 1466 (M.D.N.C. 1986) ("The Court concludes that North Carolina would analyze informed consent in the nontherapeutic content consistent with 45 C.F.R. §46.116(a)(2) (1985).").

[7]P. Appelbaum, C. Lidz, and A. Meisel, Informed Consent: Legal Theory and Clinical Practice Part IV (1987); R. Faden and T. Beauchamp with N. M. P. King, A History and Theory of Informed Consent, chapters 5 and 6 (1986); J. Katz, Experimentation with Human Beings (1972); F. Rozovsky, Consent to Treatment: A Practical Guide (2 ed. 1990).

§7.14 Federal Regulations

The Department of Health and Human Services (DHHS) regulations on biomedical research,[1] which differ from the FDA regulations[2] only in some of their details, take a comprehensive, laundry list approach to informed consent disclosure. There are eight basic elements of informed consent and six optional elements set forth in the regulations. The basic elements are:

1. A statement that the study constitutes research, an explanation of its purposes and the expected duration of subject involvement, and a description of the procedures involved, with experimental procedures identified as such.
2. A description of risks and discomforts that are "reasonably foreseeable."
3. A description of possible benefits to subjects and others.
4. Disclosure of appropriate alternative treatments, if any.
5. A statement describing the extent of confidentiality of records generated.
6. An explanation of whether compensation or treatment will be available if injuries occur.
7. A note as to who can be contacted with questions or reports of injuries.
8. A statement as to the voluntary nature of participation and the subject's right of withdrawal at any time.[3]

The optional elements are:

1. A statement that unforeseen risks may arise.
2. A description of circumstances in which subjects' participation may be terminated without their consent.
3. A note as to any additional costs to the subject as a result of participation.

---

§7.14 [1] 45 C.F.R. pt. 46 (1985).
[2] 21 C.F.R. §§50.1-50.27, 56.100-56.124 (1985).
[3] 45 C.F.R. §46.116(a) (1985).

4. A description of the consequences of premature withdrawal.
5. A statement that subjects will be informed of any findings that may affect their willingness to continue.
6. The number of subjects to be involved.[4]

Written consent and consent forms are usually required, and the regulations provide for both verbal and written disclosure.[5] They also require that consent be sought only under circumstances that give potential subjects enough time to decide and that minimize the risks of coercion and undue influence to participate; they further require that information be provided in language that prospective subjects are likely to understand.[6]

Under the federal regulations, certain kinds of minimally risk-bearing research may be exempt from review for regulatory compliance[7] or eligible for expedited review.[8] Exempt research, mostly data collection from existing specimens and records, surveys, and observation of public behavior, does not carry informed consent requirements and is unlikely, in any case, to be misleading to patients. "Expedited review" research, though also minimally risk-bearing, involves new collection of data and specimens, and informed consent is therefore required.

§7.15 IRB Review

Prospective review of proposed research is the central feature of the federal regulations. It is done by institutional review boards (IRBs), created by each institution housing federally funded research. These IRBs are extensively described in the regulations.[1]

---

[4] 45 C.F.R. §46.116(b) (1985).

[5] 45 C.F.R. §46.117 (1985).

[6] 45 C.F.R. pt. 46 (1985).

[7] 45 C.F.R. §46.101(b) (1985).

[8] Activities Which May Be Reviewed Through Expedited Review Procedures Set Forth in HHS Regulations for Protection of Human Research Subjects, 46 Fed. Reg. 8392 (1981).

§7.15   [1] 45 C.F.R. pt. 46 (1985).

Their size, composition, and functions are given by regulation, as well as the substantive criteria on which their review is to be based, the procedures for review, requirements for protection and monitoring of subjects, and the scope of their discretionary decisionmaking authority.

The essence of what IRBs do is to balance the potential value and potential risks of proposed research in order to decide whether the research should take place at all.[2] Thus, it is given that there is no preeminent right of autonomy either to conduct research or to participate in it: some research is just too risky, or promises too little societal benefit, even for the best-informed altruist's consent to participation to be valid. Informed consent may seem a small issue next to the determination of whether research should even take place, but the bulk of the regulatory guidance given to IRBs lies in how to get informed consent for participation in research, once approved. Even so, little guidance is given to the IRB about how to ensure that subjects have decisional capacity and give consent voluntarily and with understanding. Much of the consent practice of researchers, and the oversight given by IRBs, is likely to be guided by the general informed consent principles already discussed.

§7.16 Special Populations

As with informed consent to treatment, children and others lacking decisional capacity merit special attention in the research setting. The central problem is whether substitute decisionmakers may ever consent to the research participation of persons lacking decisional capacity. Because the best interest of the incompetent subject is not the principal goal of research participation, the proposed enrollment of incompetents in research almost automatically raises the same kinds of concerns about their best interests that controversial treatment decisions would. However, some degree of altruism may be ascribable to vulnerable populations. Moreover, the chance of benefit, especially when there

---

[2]Id.

are no effective alternative treatments and when enrollment provides the only access to a drug or protocol, may conceivably also be a valid motivation for enrolling minors and incompetents in research. A set of special regulations applying to children codifies this, permitting children to be enrolled in certain low-risk research with the consent of their parents.[1] IRBs are also able to require the "assent" of children old enough to have some grasp of the proposed research and the consequences of a decision to participate or not.[2]

Research involving fetuses, products of human in vitro fertilization, and pregnant women is also subject to special regulations.[3] These regulations limit a pregnant woman's ability to participate in research in order to protect her fetus. If she is permitted to participate, the regulations require both her consent and that of the father of the fetus. IRBs must see that researchers monitor the informed consent process to ensure that it is full and fair.

Special regulations also apply to research on prisoners.[4] Prisoners are extremely limited in their power to consent to participate in research, despite their own argument that they should be permitted to make their own risk-benefit determinations. Other populations especially vulnerable to coercion and undue influence may be afforded additional protections, at the discretion of the IRB.[5] The other populations usually considered most at risk are other institutionalized populations, the elderly, and the mentally impaired. Though possible protections are not specified, they could include the use of patient advocates or ombudsmen to oversee the consent process; expanded use of "living will" documents so that competent patients may express their views on research participation in the anticipation of incompetence; or IRB development of special policies similar to those applied to minors, prisoners, and fetal research. All of

---

§7.16 [1] 45 C.F.R. pt. 46, subpt. D (1985).
[2] 45 C.F.R. §46.408 (1985).
[3] 45 C.F.R. pt. 46, subpt. B (1985).
[4] 45 C.F.R. pt. 46, subpt. C (1985).
[5] 45 C.F.R. §46.111(b) (1985).

these vulnerable groups are of course covered by the existing consent-to-research provisions in the regulations, which include protections for incompetent subjects.

Another vulnerable population not specifically contemplated by the regulations is terminally ill patients for whom an experimental protocol or innovative treatment is the last hope. The "situational coercion" of terminal illness can affect patients, their substitute decisionmakers, and researchers alike, making them feel as though participation in research, or risky unproven treatment, is the only available choice.

Although the federal regulations' balancing of risks and benefits helps to curb the temptation to offer anything and everything to patients as a last resort, there are still major unresolved questions about innovative treatments and informed consent when life is at stake. For example, should parents be permitted to consent to multiple successive liver transplants for their infant child? Should the artificial heart be made available to anyone, given its risks? These questions plumb the depths of the intersection of the patient's right to informed consent and choice of treatment, the medical profession's mandate to preserve life, and the setting of standards of safe and acceptable practice in untried fields. Caregivers and institutions are advised to proceed with great caution whenever proposed clinical trials or innovative treatments raise concerns that cannot be addressed, at least in part or by implication, by the general plan of the DHHS regulations and the law of consent to treatment.

E. Refusal of Treatment

§7.17 The Legal Issues in Treatment Refusal

"Informed consent" is fundamentally a misnomer in that the term appears to presume that patients always consent. By now it is well understood, however, that what is really at issue in informed consent law is the process of informing the patient (or his or her representative) for decision—and that decision could as easily be refusal as consent.

The reader is referred to Chapter 10, Terminal Care Decisionmaking, for a much more detailed discussion of the law of treatment refusal as developed in case law and statutes pertaining to serious and terminal illness. A brief discussion of treatment refusal in its most general terms is appropriate here, however, because refusal of treatment is common in many circumstances besides death and dying and also because understanding refusal is necessary to an adequate understanding of consent.

The basic modern informed consent claim is fundamentally a claim that the patient would have refused treatment if properly informed. It hinges on demonstration of an injury that would have been avoided if the patient had indeed refused.[1] Added to this, however, is a very different, purely dignitary component dating back to informed consent's common-law battery origins: acknowledgment of the underlying right to make an informed choice.[2] In ordinary modern informed consent cases, the negligence law form of the doctrine and its essentially philosophical dignitary component are fairly well merged. "Treatment refusal" cases, however, have tended to surface in two quite different forms, which highlight the two components separately.

§7.17.1 The Common Law of "Informed Refusal"

The essence of the informed refusal cause of action is that the duty to give information and to encourage the patient to make a free, informed, and reasonable choice applies both when the patient accepts the physician's proposed treatment *and* when the

---

§7.17 [1]Canterbury v. Spence, 464 F.2d 772 (D.C. Cir.), cert. denied, 409 U.S. 1064 (1972); Natanson v. Kline, 186 Kan. 393, 350 P.2d 1093 (1960). An exhaustive historical or theoretical account of the development of informed consent law or the elements of a successful consent lawsuit is beyond the scope of this volume; readers who would like more background are advised to consult the texts cited in §7.0.

[2]Schloendorff v. Society of N.Y. Hosps., 211 N.Y. 125, 126, 105 N.E. 92, 93 (1914); Mohr v. Williams, 95 Minn. 261, 104 N.W. 12 (1905).

patient refuses the treatment. This may seem obvious; yet before the first decisions in this area appeared it was not inherently implausible to claim that the duty to give information should be triggered only by the patient's willingness to undergo a physical intrusion. The defendant doctor in Truman v. Thomas[3] reasoned this way when his deceased patient's children sued him for failing to warn their mother of the risk she took in refusing a Pap smear test. After Mrs. Truman's death from cervical cancer that was detected only in its late stages, her children were permitted to argue that, had her physician informed her of the magnitude of the risk that she might have undetected cancer, she would have decided to have the test and would have pursued earlier, successful treatment. The court's reasoning was that the duty to inform cannot depend on the choice made by the patient because the information is meant to assist in that choice.[4] Therefore, anytime the patient faces a choice, all the medically reasonable alternatives *and* the possibility of no treatment must be discussed.

The fact that *Truman* concerned a diagnostic test does not give rise to new duties regarding tests and screening, because it does not require substantial new disclosure about tests. If a test is risky, disclosure is already required.[5] This disclosure will necessarily include the physician's reason for wanting to perform a test or diagnostic procedure in the first place, which presumably is to detect treatable abnormalities. However, since the risks of not doing a test or procedure are not fully implicated until the test or procedure is refused, a complete discussion of those risks may reasonably be put off unless and until the patient refuses.

---

[3]27 Cal. 3d 285, 165 Cal. Rptr. 308, 611 P.2d 902 (Cal. 1980).

[4]*Truman*, 611 P.2d at 906.

[5]Id. In fact, many informed consent cases are about diagnostic or exploratory procedures, as opposed to treatments. E.g., Berkey v. Anderson, 1 Cal. App. 3d 790, 82 Cal. Rptr. 67 (1970) (intravenous myelogram); Terry v. Albany Med. Ctr. Hosp., 78 Misc. 2d 1035, 359 N.Y.S.2d 235 (1974) (coronary arteriography); *Canterbury*, 464 F.2d 772 (D.C. Cir. 1972) (exploratory laminectomy); Salgo v. Leland Stanford Jr. Univ. Bd. of Trustees, 154 Cal. App. 2d 560, 317 P.2d 170 (1957) (translumbar aortography); Cooper v. Roberts, 220 Pa. Super. 260, 286 A.2d 647 (1971) (fiberoptic gastroscopy).

Such discussion seems a natural part of the physician's duties
(1) to explore the patient's refusal thoroughly in order to
ascertain that it is a free and informed choice and (2) to use
education and reasonable persuasion to change the patient's
mind about the intervention.

The "informed refusal" cases, though there are few of them
to date,[6] serve powerfully to reinforce the view of consent as a
process that is both part of the physician-patient relationship
and directed toward the patient's control of healthcare decision-
making. Cost-conscious healthcare providers have grown accustomed to asking themselves and their colleagues whether another
test, x-ray, or diagnostic study in warranted for a given patient's
care by inquiring, How likely is this procedure to show us
something that will cause us to change our current care plan?
If the answer is, not at all (because, for example, it will reveal
an untreatable condition, or distinguish between two conditions
whose treatment is the same, or merely duplicate a clinically
based assessment), the procedure is not done. The converse
proposition is true by implication: tests are done in the hope of
obtaining information that could change the care plan.

Similarly, in order to take appropriate legal account of both
informed consent and informed refusal, providers need only
consider whether there is any information *the patient* does not
yet have that is likely to change *the patient's* course of action.
All such information must be disclosed, even though some or
most of the choices facing the patient may not be purely medical.
For example, genetic counseling and information about incurable
conditions are given to patients so that they will have the
opportunity to make decisions—not necessarily all medical
ones—that take the health issues involved into consideration.
Decisions about childbearing, financial preparation for the burdens of illness, and many other kinds of decisions reflect the
myriad ways in which medical information affects patients' life
choices. From this perspective, "what to seek informed consent

---

[6]Moore v. Preventive Medicine Medical Group, 178 Cal. App. 3d 728,
223 Cal. Rptr. 859 (1986); Crisher v. Spak, 471 N.Y.S.2d 741 (Sup. Ct. 1983).

for" becomes "what to inform patients about to prepare them for decisions."

§7.17.2 The Prospective Cause of Action: Common-law and Constitutional Claims

The better-known variety of treatment refusal case is very different from "informed refusal" cases. It does not even reach the issue of information disclosure, but turns solely on establishing the patient's right to refuse treatment under the circumstances.

Mrs. Truman had simply said no, repeatedly, to a proffered test, and left the doctor's office. At trial, her children were not permitted to argue simply that a physician who fails to perform a Pap smear on a female patient over the age of 23 is negligent. The appeals court explained: "The suggestion that a physician *must* perform a test on a patient, who is capable of deciding whether to undergo the proposed procedure, is directly contrary to the principle that it is the *patient* who must ultimately decide which medical procedures to undergo."[7] Thus, in *Truman* the physician's duty was limited to informing the patient for decision. It remained to be determined whether she would have refused if informed; if so, she was not injured by the failure to inform.[8]

Most treatment refusal cases, however, are brought prospectively, by patients (or their representatives) whose caregivers or healthcare facilities do not wish to honor treatment refusals— as if Dr. Thomas had warned Mrs. Truman that he must test her and she was seeking the court's permission to say no. Naturally, these cases arise when the patient is unable to use Mrs. Truman's means of avoiding unwanted interventions (e.g., not seeking care at all or leaving the premises) or when the controversial refusal is being made *for* the patient by someone else whose authority to do so is challenged. Thus, most of these treatment refusal cases deal with death and dying; however, the

---

[7]*Truman*, 611 P.2d at 908.
[8]Id. at 907.

common-law and constitutional bases for the right to refuse treatment are the same for less apocalyptic decisions as well.

Failing to honor a refusal to be treated means treating a patient without his or her consent; therefore, the common-law right to refuse treatment and the basis for the battery cause of action for failure to obtain consent are essentially the same.[9] So well-established has the common-law right of decision seemed that the early refusal cases scarcely saw the need to discuss the nature of the common-law claim, but concentrated on the more powerful constitutional claim.

The constitutional right of treatment refusal has been held by many courts to be based on the right of privacy,[10] which encompasses personal decision-making and bodily integrity[11] and may be invoked only against governmental actions.[12] When the courts began to hear treatment refusal cases involving the refusal of artificial nutrition and hydration, some legislatures amended their state "living will" statutes to exclude this category of treatment refusals from statutory recognition.[13] As a result, in some states patients' claims of the right to refuse certain treatments rest entirely on the constitutional cause of action. At the end of its 1990 term, the United States Supreme Court at last tackled the question of the constitutional claim and acknowledged that patients have a Fourteenth Amendment liberty interest in refusing unwanted medical care, including artificial

---

[9]Tort claims such as informed consent are usually claims for damages after the injury occurs. However, in treatment refusal cases patients often can be viewed as suffering or risking continuous or repeated injury when caregivers refuse to withhold or withdraw continuous or repeated treatments such as respirators, feeding tubes, chemotherapy, or dialysis. Rather than requiring the patient to suffer and claim damages periodically, courts can declare the parties' rights and permanently enjoin continuous or repeated injury.

[10]Gray v. Romeo, 709 F. Supp. 325 (D.R.I. 1988).

[11]Superintendent of Belchertown State School v. Saikewicz, 373 Mass. 728, 370 N.E.2d 417 (1977); In re Quinlan, 70 N.J. 10, 355 A.2d 647, cert. denied, 429 U.S. 922 (1976).

[12]Thus, the conduct of a private physician or facility cannot violate this constitutional right, but the actions of a state-supported facility, a district attorney, or the courts themselves could do so.

[13]See Chapter 10.

nutrition and hydration. States may institute appropriate procedural safeguards to ensure an accurate determination of the patient's wishes when the patient is not decisionally capable.[14]

§7.17.3 Healthcare Facility Liability and Refusal of Treatment

Like the question of healthcare facility liability for failure to obtain informed consent, a facility's liability for failure to honor treatment refusal depends on (1) whether the facility can be held accountable for the actions of its staff and (2) whether it may be seen to have any independent responsibility. As discussed in §7.4 above, healthcare facilities are liable through respondeat superior for the acts of their employees; this would certainly include liability for discrete instances of intervention over the patient's objections by anyone, from a technician or nurse's aide up to a physician employee acting in the course of employment. Normally, routine patient care contacts are considered to be consensual by implication; that is, a patient's acquiescence to institutional routine constitutes implied consent to the manipulations necessary to that routine.[15] However, if a patient refuses anything, from a bath to a blood drawing to a catheterization, any employee who performs such interventions over the patient's objections without a showing of their necessity to prevent injury to the patient and the patient's decisional incapacity (or, in rare circumstances, the need to prevent immediate harm to others) can be found liable for common-law battery[16]—and so can the employing institution, so long as the battery occurred as part of the employee's fulfillment of assigned duties. According to the

---

[14]Cruzan v. Director, Mo. Dept. of Health, 58 U.S.L.W. 4916 (U.S., June 26, 1990).

[15]Cf. O'Brien v. Cunard Steamship Co., 154 Mass. 272, 28 N.E. 266 (1891) (passenger gave implied consent to vaccination by joining line of people receiving injections on ship).

[16]The earliest reported American decisions upholding the patient's right to give consent before treatment were battery cases. See especially Rolater v. Strain, 39 Okla. 572, 137 P. 96 (1913).

principles of common-law battery, the defendant may be held accountable in damages for all of the consequences of the nonconsensual contact, including the cost of even beneficial treatments.

Extended care facilities are at particular risk of liability for battery, because matters of daily routine and activities may be a source of ongoing decisional conflict between the needs of the institution and the lifestyle preferences of residents, for whom the institution is home. Nursing home residents represent a vulnerable population who may need protection of their decisionmaking role. Federal[17] and state[18] laws provide such protection, but in addition facilities are well-advised to establish policies encouraging discussion and negotiation of decisions on such matters as daily care, institutional schedules, social and recreational activities, and other amenities, that do not carry risks but that significantly affect the quality of residents' lives.

Related to the simple battery cause of action is the recent development of a third type of treatment refusal suit that combines some of the attributes of both the prospective and retrospective claims already discussed. The important new element in these suits is a battery claim for damages for delay in honoring the patient's treatment refusal.

Suits claiming damages for delay and failure to honor treatments refusals and decisions to withdraw treatment are new because, until recently, it could not be denied that the sometimes lengthy intervals between patients' decisions and their eventual implementation were good-faith delays by healthcare providers genuinely uncertain of their legal responsibilities and liabilities. The delays caused by obtaining legal advice and then court approval were unfortunate and difficult but undeniably necessary. However, there certainly may be circumstances in which

---

[17]42 U.S.C. §§1395i-3(c), 1396r-3(c) (1987).

[18]E.g., New Jersey's Ombudsman for the Institutionalized Elderly, N.J. Stat. Ann. §52:27G (1986) (The ombudsman's function in cases in which treatment is to be withheld or withdrawn has been quite controversial. See Price and Armstrong, New Jersey's "Granny Doe" Squad: Arguments About Mechanisms for Protection of Vulnerable Patients, 17 L., Med., & Health Care 255 (1989).

the rights of the patient are clear, the courts of the state in question have provided guidance, and the institution still drags its feet. In such cases the institution that fails to respond promptly and appropriately when patients or their families assert a desire to refuse treatment or to have it withdrawn could face liability for damages, in at least the amount of the hospital and physicians' bills from the point at which a court determines treatment should reasonably have been stopped[19] and possibly also for emotional distress for either the patient or the patient's family.[20] Institutional providers can effectively reduce or eliminate this liability risk by developing, and educating staff and patients about, procedures for the determination and declaration of brain death, mechanisms and guidelines for discussion and implementation of treatment withdrawal under appropriate circumstances and with reasonable dispatch, and provisions for judicial review and intervention when necessary. The risk of liability in this area is small, but the benefits of developing and implementing policies to address these concerns may be considerable.

§7.18 Decisionally Capable Adults

The right of a decisionally capable adult to refuse treatment of any kind for any reason is generally well-established.[1] With the proviso that some choices—especially those likely to result in death—and some reasons may provide reason to inquire further into the patient's decisional capacity,[2] treatment refusals should be honored. It is worth mentioning, however, that treatment refusals may be difficult to accommodate in some institutional settings; that honoring them may sometimes be ethically trou-

---

[19]Cf. Estate of Leach v. Shapiro, 13 Ohio App. 3d 393, 469 N.E.2d 1047 (1984).

[20]Cf. Strachan v. John F. Kennedy Mem. Hosp., 109 N.J. 523, 538 A.2d 346 (1988).

§7.18 [1]See Chapter 10.

[2]See the discussion of decisional capacity in Part B supra.

bling for caregivers; that they can sometimes cause patients to be viewed as troublemakers; and that they may be based on fear, misinformation, or the desire to regain control of life rather than on the genuine desire to forgo a treatment. For these reasons, facilities are advised to discourage staff from negatively labeling refusing patients; to attempt to reconcile patients' lifestyle preferences with institutional needs; and to encourage extensive discussion of refusals with patients and staff.

§7.19 Adults Lacking Decisional Capacity

Patients without decisional capacity need substitute decision-makers to exercise the right of healthcare decision-making on their behalf. Once it has been determined that, either generally or for a particular decision, a patient lacks capacity, a substitute decisionmaker must be identified and the basis on which the decision should be made must also be identified. Substitute decisionmakers are empowered to refuse treatment on behalf of patients, provided there is sufficient evidence to show that refusal *was* the patient's choice,[1] that refusal *would be* the patient's choice if choice were possible now,[2] or that refusal would be in the patient's *best interests*.[3]

§7.19.1 Statutes

For life-and-death decision-making, many states have passed legislation to assist patients in expressing their treatment choices. These statutes enable patients to express their wishes while competent so that they may be honored later, after the patient

---

§7.19 [1]For example, that before becoming incapacitated the patient had made statements refusing the exact intervention at issue.

[2]This is the principle of substituted judgment. See Superintendent of Belchertown State School v. Saikewicz, 373 Mass. 728, 370 N.E.2d 417 (1977).

[3]E.g., In re Conroy, 98 N.J. 321, 486 A.2d 1209 (1985).

has lost decisional capacity. See Chapter 10 for detailed discussion of these "natural death acts."

§7.19.2 Healthcare Facility Policies

Whatever form is taken by such a statute in a given state, however, healthcare facilities need to recognize that such statutes do not capture the full scope of treatment refusal—that patients are still empowered to make choices not encompassed by such statutes, as well as to express their choices in ways not enumerated in a given statute. Thus, not only must facilities not assume that patients without "living wills" have chosen not to refuse treatment, but they should also be prepared to recognize and deal appropriately with treatment refusals well outside the scope of natural death acts. Such recognition ought to include a mechanism for examining and evaluating any documents, directives, or other expressions of will offered by patients or their family or friends as a refusal of treatment or in support of a refusal; the availability of legal advice from the institution's counsel or the courts; and a plan for negotiation with patients' representatives about the course of treatment during the time needed to reach a final decision about the treatment refusal in question.

§7.19.3 Ethics Committees

In addition to polices like those described above, facilities likely to face many treatment refusal situations—extended care facilities, for example—may benefit substantially from the formation of an institutional ethics committee as an advisory body and forum for discussion of treatment refusals and other care controversies. Like the Infant Care Review Committees discussed above, ethics committees may not take decisional authority away from patients and physicians, either by fiat or by coercion. If conscientiously assembled, however, they can help to ensure that all necessary facts and issues are identified and to assure patients and their representatives of the institution's commitment to upholding the patient's decisional authority—both of which are important concerns for institutionalized patients.

F. Conclusion

Generally speaking, patients (when they have decisional capacity) or their authorized representatives (when they do not) hold the ultimate power to authorize or to refuse healthcare interventions on their own behalf—except in those few instances in which the risk of harm to others is found to outweigh the patient's free choice. So that this power may be implemented effectively, patients or their representatives have a right of access to all information material to a decision about whether to authorize any intervention. Material information includes the nature and consequences of the intervention; its significant risks; and the nature, risks, and consequences of all medically reasonable alternative interventions as well as those of not intervening at all. Although some jurisdictions measure this required disclosure according to professional custom and some according to the reasonable information needs of patients, there are likely to be few differences in core disclosure requirements under these different standards. Caregivers and institutions in all jurisdictions would be well-advised to base their informed consent practice on professional standards, careful discussion with patients, and common sense, supplemented by clear documentation and by advice from legal counsel as regards specific relevant statutory and case law.

The primary responsibility for obtaining informed consent rests with the caregiver proposing the intervention. However, healthcare facilities may also bear responsibility for the acts of employees who intervene without consent or in the face of a patient's refusal of an intervention. Moreover, facilities that involve themselves in any way in the consent process—by requiring signed consent forms before permitting certain procedures to take place, by delegating nurses or other employees to obtain consent signatures or act as consent witnesses, or even by responding poorly to a patient's or a family's treatment refusal decision—may incur independent liability if they should have been able to ameliorate or correct a defect in the consent process.

In the very great majority of situations, the patient's best interests and the patient's interest in making medical decisions go hand in hand. Exceptions to this convenient fit occur (1) when patients declare them, as by refusing treatment, and (2) when the patient's decisional interest cannot be effectuated, as during emergencies or when the patient is incapacitated. The best way that caregivers and healthcare facilities can promote both interests, recognize exceptions, and limit their own liability on consent issues is by developing policies and practices that (1) encourage disclosure and discussion, (2) anticipate problems and emergencies, (3) facilitate thorough documentation of the decisional process between caregivers and patients, and (4) build on existing statutory and case law in their jurisdiction.

8 Medical Records

Anne M. Dellinger
*with Joan G. Brannon**

§8.0 Introduction

Handling medical records is among the most important and complex functions of healthcare facilities. Few areas generate as many questions for attorneys. Defining the record, and certainly agreeing on what constitutes its confidential portions, can occasionally be problematic. Uncertainty about these areas will

---

*Joan G. Brannon is the author of Part E of this chapter.

increase as technology changes the forms of records. While most facilities still use paper records, a commentator predicts that "the computer's capacity for image processing, graphic display, and analog input, in addition to data and word processing, makes a completely computerized medical record inevitable in the near future."[1]

This chapter describes the multiple legal interests involved in records: interested parties include the facility, its staff and employees, patients and their representatives, civil litigants, law enforcement authorities, accrediting agencies, the press and public, employers, and third party payors. The chapter treats confidentiality issues at some length and discusses general requirements for creating, maintaining, and releasing records. It concludes with a brief listing of liability concerns associated with recordkeeping. (Theories of liability are dealt with at length in Chapter 4 and the management of liability risks is discussed in Chapter 5.) These risks include the potential legal consequences of failing to document care or to transfer information needed in treatment and the possible penalities for disclosing information without authorization or withholding it from parties with a legal right to it.

A. Background

§8.1 Purposes of Recordkeeping

The benefit, indeed the necessity, to providers of keeping good treatment records is obvious. Oddly, the value of good record-keeping was not always apparent. A 1918 study by the American College of Surgeons reported that 89 of the 5,323 AMA-

---

§8.0 [1]Fulton, Legal Problems Arising in the Automation of Medical Records, Topics in Health Record Mgmt. 73 (December 1987). According to Fulton, computerized records are explicitly or implicitly accepted under the licensing regulations of about half of the states. Id. at 74.

registered hospitals kept "accurate and complete case records
. . . written for all patients and filed in an accessible manner."[1]
Today, all reputable providers keep records, primarily to trace
the course of illness and to assist treatment. Secondary objectives
include:

- to satisfy legal and regulatory agencies' requirements;
- to coordinate and evaluate the care given by the facility
  and individual staff members and employees;
- to keep in touch with patients after discharge and
  preserve information of possible future use to them;
- to increase economic efficiency and justify billing;
- to provide research data;
- to defend against legal claims.

§8.1.1 The Legal Duty

State law (statutory and decisional) usually recognizes the
individual provider's and the facility's duties to keep records and
use them in treatment. The requirements may appear in statute[2]
and often appear in a state's administrative code, particularly
the sections of the code dealing with facility licensure.[3] Case
law recognizes an institutional obligation to see that records are
maintained and that the information therein is disseminated
properly.[4] The professional's duty is illustrated by decisions
holding that failure to keep records is failure to adhere to

---

§8.1 [1]Privacy Protection Study Commission, Personal Privacy in an
Information Society 277-278 (1977) (hereinafter Privacy Commission Report).

[2]E.g., Fla. Stat. Ann. §458.331(1)(m) (West Supp. 1990) (provider's duty);
Fla. Stat. Ann. §395.016 (West 1986) (facility's duty).

[3]A.A.C. R9-10-221 (1982).

[4]Public Health Trust of Dade County v. Valcin, 507 So. 2d 596 (Fla. 1987)
(hospital required to see that records of employee physicians contain notes on
surgery); Washington Healthcare Corp. v. Barrow, 531 A.2d 226 (D.C. 1987)
(recovery for delay in cancer diagnosis with evidence tending to show hospital
did not forward radiology report to private physician).

accepted standards of medical practice.[5] The consequences of omission for the practitioner may include loss of staff privileges[6] or a threat to licensure itself.[7] Besides the direct admonitions in state law, compliance with state-imposed obligations such as the reporting of communicable diseases or suspicious injuries would be impossible without recordkeeping.

§8.1.2 As a Medical Tool

The record is crucial in treatment and the evaluation of treatment. As has been noted, "Today's physician . . . must learn more and remember more about his patients than his predecessors. To aid memory and to meet the demands for precise documentation, he incorporates more and more of what he learns about patients in their medical records."[8] For better and worse,[9] the record of a modern patient is the principal outline of and justification of her medical care. In fact, keeping accurate records and consulting them before beginning or continuing with

---

[5]Failure to keep adequate records was one ground, though not the most serious, for a license revocation upheld in Keigan v. Board of Registration in Medicine, 399 Mass. 719, 506 N.E.2d 866 (1987).

[6]Jones v. Yonkers Gen. Hosp., 143 A.D.2d 885, 533 N.Y.S.2d 522 (1988).

[7]Nadell v. Ambach, 136 A.D.2d 804, 523 N.Y.S.2d 637 (1988); Kieffer v. Department of Licensing and Regulation, 169 Mich. App. 312, 425 N.W.2d 539 (1988).

[8]Privacy Commission Report, at 283.

[9]Patients probably lose as well as gain from increased reliance on records. A study of house officers on the night shift concluded that "while on call, house officers spend relatively little time in direct patient contact, but they spend considerable time charting." Lurie, et al., How Do House Officers Spend Their Nights?, 320 New Eng. J. Med. 1673 (1989). Another observer of house staff has noted that "[a]ction ceased when there was no chart" and that "[t]he chart actually seemed to replace the patient at times, as when the staff talked about a patient while pointing to and looking at the chart—in the patient's presence as well as absence." T. Mizrahi, Getting Rid of Patients: Contradictions in the Socialization of Physicians 88-89 (1986). A practicing physician also complains, "Physicians may spend as much time with records as with patients." Burnum, The Misinformation Era: The Fall of the Medical Record, 110 Annals of Internal Med. 482, 484 (March 15, 1989).

treatment is so integral to good practice that failure to do so rather readily suggests malpractice.[10]

To ensure acceptable care, the facility has two general responsibilities with respect to recordkeeping: to insist that each practitioner keep records[11] and to establish procedures for disseminating the recorded information to proper parties. The latter is a central function of the administration of a healthcare facility and, as has been noted for the corresponding duty of practitioners, its neglect may well result in liability.[12]

§8.1.3 For the Future Needs of Patients

Very few Americans possess a full set of their medical records. Since records are passed from one provider to the next throughout a lifetime, patients depend on facilities to retain records of the care given and to provide copies on request. Moreover, developments in medicine may necessitate a facility's recalling former patients or at least notifying them of previously unknown aspects of their condition or the treatment they received (see §8.8). In these situations records are essential and may save lives.

§8.1.4 For Business Purposes

Good records are central to the efficient management of a facility. Individuals, private insurers, and the state and federal health-funding programs require extensive records as justification for billing.[13] The Diagnostic Related Group (DRG) reimbursement

---

[10]See Haley v. United States, 739 F.2d 1502 (10th Cir. 1984); In re Jascelevich License Revocation, 182 N.J. Super. 455, 442 A.2d 635 (1982).

[11]Brown v. Sims, 538 So. 2d 901 (Fla. App. 1989).

[12]Washington Healthcare Corp. v. Barrow, 531 A.2d 226 (D.C. 1987). Byerly v. Madsen, 41 Wash. App. 495, 704 P.2d 1236 (1985).

[13]For example, to participate in Medicaid the federal government requires nursing facilities to maintain clinical records on all residents and specifies in general terms the contents of the records. 42 U.S.C.A. §1396r(b)(6) (1989).

system places far greater emphasis than previously on accuracy and timeliness.[14] Diagnoses must be precise and correct from the beginning, and delay in completing discharge summaries will delay payment. In order to operate a facility profitably, its administrators must be able to allocate costs to particular patterns of practice and services.

§8.1.5 For Research

Patient records are highly valuable research tools. Indeed, many studies, especially those in epidemiology, consist entirely of analyses of records. In addition to the use of records themselves as the subject of research, research on live subjects must be carefully documented, thus generating more records. (See, for example, the consent requirements for participation in federally funded research, §7.14). A facility's ability to conduct research improves the quality of care for future patients as well as the institution's ability to attract staff and employees.

§8.1.6 For Protection from Liability

The 1977 Privacy Protection Study Commission called records "the physician's only real defense against malpractice."[15] They are even more important for a healthcare facility, since the facility cannot testify from memory about disputed events. In most instances, records are the facility's memory.

The importance of records in risk management and in preventing or defending against unjustified claims cannot be overestimated. When records suggest that the provider's actions may be difficult to defend, the facility has the opportunity to avoid litigation through early settlement of claims.

---

[14]For a contrary view, that billing and recordkeeping requirements in general and DRGs in particular have seriously distorted the truthfulness of medical records, see Burnum, supra n.9.

[15]Privacy Commission Report, at 283.

§8.2 Definitions of the Record

Because various legal consequences follow from designating an item of information a medical record, it is important to apply the label carefully. The facility's definition should try to avoid under- or over-inclusiveness since items so defined must be treated with care.

§8.2.1 Health Organization Definitions

Several national healthcare organizations define medical records. The American Hospital Association (AHA) terminology guide speaks of "the record of a patient maintained by a hospital or a physician for the purpose of documenting clinical data on diagnosis, treatment, and outcome,"[1] while the American Medical Association (AMA) describes the record simply as "notes made in treating a patient."[2] According to the American Medical Record Association, "The medical record is a compilation of a patient's life and health history including past and present illnesses and treatment written by the health professionals contributing to that patient's care."[3] The Joint Commission on the Accreditation of Healthcare Organizations (JCAHO) requires that, in an accredited hospital, "[t]he medical record contain[s] sufficient information to identify the patient, support the diagnosis, justify the treatment, and document the course and results accurately."[4] The JCAHO further specifies the contents of hospital medical records as follows:

---

§8.2   [1]American Hospital Association, Hospital Administration Terminology 35 (2d ed. 1986).

[2]American Medical Association, Reference Guide to Policy and Official Statements 60 (1988) (hereinafter AMA Reference Guide).

[3]Huffman, Medical Record Management 45 (8th ed. 1985).

[4]Joint Commission on Accreditation of Healthcare Organizations, Accreditation Manual for Hospitals 85 (1991) (hereinafter JCAHO Accreditation Manual). For a decision recognizing the manual as an industry-wide standard, see Brown v. Sims, 538 So. 2d 901 (Fla. App. 1989).

1. identification data
2. the patient's medical history
3. a summary of patient's psychosocial needs
4. reports of physical examinations
5. diagnostic and therapeutic orders
6. evidence of informed consent
7. clinical observations
8. reports of and results from tests and procedures
9. conclusions at end of hospitalization, evaluation, or treatment.[5]

All items but 1 and 6 are described as key factors in the accrediting process. Perhaps these two are not because, as the Manual notes, they are occasionally unobtainable.[6]

§8.2.2 State Statutory and Regulatory Definitions

Some states define "medical record" by statute. Florida, for example, which requires both providers and facilities to keep records, defines it as a "problem-oriented" system that must include "basic client data collection; a listing of the patient's problems; the initial plan with diagnostic and therapeutic orders as appropriate for each problem identified; and progress notes including a discharge summary."[7] It is more common to find "medical record" defined—and indeed its exact contents specified—in an administrative code[8] than in statute. A facility's attorney must be aware of definitions in state law when questions arise about records.

---

[5]JCAHO Accreditation Manual, at 85.

[6]This cannot be the full explanation for the rather puzzling omission of item 6, however. The absence of clear evidence of the patient's consent would seem to make it more important than usual for the record to note the alternative theory of consent on which the patient is being treated.

[7]Fla. Stat. Ann. §395.016 (West 1986).

[8]See, e.g., Wis. Admin. Code §HSS 124.14(3)(a) (1988).

§8.2.3 Problems in Definition

The traditional notion of the medical record has expanded. Records now take many forms besides words on paper: the definition might encompass x-rays, photographs, videotapes, and microfilm as well as computer systems using optical storage disks or other technology. When disputes arise, a court must decide whether particular information held by a facility, whatever its physical form, is a medical record.[9] To answer the question, one may ask, Does the information refer to a person who is a patient? Is it the kind of patient information that a provider must keep confidential? Does it serve a purpose for which medical records are intended? In examining these issues it is useful to consider the following: the reason for recording the information, the understandings of the parties when it was recorded, the use to which it will be put, the relationship between the provider and the person to whom it refers, and the probable effect of disclosure.

The Formation of the Medical Relationship. When a person has discussed his medical condition with another, the question may arise whether a doctor-patient relationship exists between them. The matter may be raised in order to determine whether information revealed during the relationship is part of the medical record and governed by confidentiality. Such an inquiry may take several paths: is one of the parties a physician or her agent? Is the other party a patient? Did the two meet in the context of medical care? On the first point, one unreported decision has held that when a hospitalized patient talked to the facility's security guard, the patient did not do so within a protected medical relationship.[10] The court refused to consider the guard a delegate of the physician—an understandable conclusion, though not necessarily a distinction a mental patient

---

[9]In Laubach v. Franklin Square Hosp., 79 Md. App. 203, 556 A.2d 682 (1989), plaintiff successfully maintained that fetal monitoring tracings were medical records and as such should have been released.

[10]Kincaid v. Harper-Grace Hosp., No. 92598 (Mich. App. 1988).

would draw before deciding in whom to confide. A similar question arose when a news reporter who was present in a hospital's waiting room and examining room photographed an AIDS patient.[11] Though the patient knew he was dealing with a reporter, he still alleged that the interview and picture-taking occurred within a medical relationship, that public disclosure was improper, and that the facility bore some responsibility.

The dispute may revolve around whether the person who confided information qualified as a "patient." Not everyone undergoing a medical examination so qualifies. For example, though the matter is still litigated, it is the traditional view that someone subjected to a medical examination required by, paid for, and conducted for the benefit of another party does not become a patient of the examiner. This category of 'nonpatients' may include job applicants and employees, as well as people for whom a court orders examinations.[12]

Courts divide on whether other categories of people enjoy the privacy accorded to patients. In cases involving AIDS transmitted by transfusion, facilities have sought with mixed success to guard the identity of blood donors;[13] one facility has succeeded in guarding the identity of potential transplant donors.[14] One court denied a request for in camera inspection of records the purpose of which was to learn whether a patient's parents knew of her dangerous propensities. (The parents and patient were defendants in a personal injury suit arising

---

[11]Anderson v. Strong Memorial Hosp., 5 A.D.2d 1033, 542 N.Y.S.2d 96 (1989); for lower court decision, see 140 Misc. 2d 770, 531 N.Y.S.2d 735 (1988).

[12]Baker v. Alexander, 745 S.W.2d 112 (Tex. App. 1988).

[13]The Colorado Supreme Court and the Court of Appeals of Texas both refused to characterize blood donors as patients. Though acknowledging that donors have a privacy interest, the courts allowed malpractice plaintiffs to discover the donors' identities. Belle Bonfils Memorial Blood Center v. Denver District Court, 763 P.2d 1003 (Colo. 1988); Tarrant County Hosp. Dist. v. Hughes, 734 S.W.2d 675 (Tex. App. 1987). Florida's Supreme Court protected blood donors' identities in similar circumstances, though suggesting that plaintiff might be entitled to know their HIV status. South Florida Blood Serv. v. Rasmussen, 500 So. 2d 533 (Fla. 1987).

[14]Head v. Colloton, 331 N.W.2d 870 (Iowa 1983).

from the patient's actions.) The court ruled that the patient-psychotherapist privilege covered communications of the third parties as well as of the patient.[15] Whether the dead are still 'patients' for purposes of record confidentiality is unsettled. A New York newspaper was able to obtain a death certificate because a court concluded that the dead have no privacy rights.[16] On the other hand, a Massachusetts paper lost its fight to see autopsy records because the court held that a privacy interest of the dead person was at issue.[17] A person has been held not to have entered a doctor-patient relationship because he communicated falsely with his physician.[18]

What Constitutes the Medical Record. Though conceding that a bona fide medical relationship has existed, parties can still differ over whether certain information is part of the medical record. Practitioners sometimes claim a right to memorialize encounters with patients outside of and in addition to the official record. The AMA's statement that "notes made in treating a patient are primarily for the physician's own use and constitute his personal property" seems supportive of that right.[19] Occasionally a patient litigates the matter. While most reported cases concern photographs or videotapes, the same principles would apply to records in any form.[20] One patient sought his surgeon's videotape of an operation to determine whether malpractice had

---

[15]Grosslight v. Superior Court, 72 Cal. App. 3d 502, 140 Cal. Rptr. 278 (1977).

[16]Tri-State Publishing Co. v. City of Port Jervis, 138 Misc. 2d 147, 523 N.Y.S.2d 954 (1988).

[17]Globe Newspaper Co. v. Chief Medical Examiner, 404 Mass. 132, 533 N.E.2d 1356 (1989).

[18]State of Ohio ex rel. Buchman v. Stokes, 36 Ohio App. 3d 109, 521 N.E.2d 515 (1987).

[19]AMA Reference Guide, at 60.

[20]Patients may be especially sensitive about pictorial records of treatment. If so, obtaining consent for the use of pictures would be extremely important, but an article in the New England Journal of Medicine implies that it is often overlooked. Slue, Occasional Notes: Unmasking the Lone Ranger, 321 New Eng. J. Med. 550, 551 (Aug. 24, 1989).

occurred,[21] but more often the patient's concern is privacy. He may object to the fact that the record is made at all[22] or to its use in embarrassing circumstances that he has not authorized.[23] The frequency with which patients prevail in these (admittedly rare) cases suggests caution is advisable when information is gathered or used for purposes other than the patient's benefit.

Healthcare facilities, like practitioners, assert that some information they compile should not be viewed as a medical record—for instance, descriptions of staff performance (peer review records) or of unusual events in treatment (incident reports). Thus far the facilities have been moderately successful. A number of states designate "peer review" or "medical review" records generated by hospitals as belonging solely to the hospital, not subject to access by patients, investigative agencies, or others. For a sampling of decisions on the discoverability of incident reports and suggestions on how to lessen its probability, see §5.8.

Another definitional issue is whether—and, if so, when— summary can substitute for the whole. Again, the AMA presumably expresses the physician's preference when it speaks of her providing "a copy *or a summary* of the record" to the patient or other inquirer.[24] The JCAHO does not directly address the question of whether summaries may substitute for the medical record but seems to suggest that they may. The JCAHO 1991 Accreditation Manual for Hospitals recognizes the patient's right to "complete and current information concerning his diagnosis

---

[21]Hill v. Springer, 132 Misc. 2d 1012, 506 N.Y.S.2d 255 (1986) (patient failed to gain access to the tape). See also Laubach v. Franklin Square Hosp., 79 Md. App. 203, 556 A.2d 682 (1989).

[22]Estate of Berthiaume v. Pratt, 365 A.2d 792 (Me. 1976); for one of several early cases, see Clayman v. Bernstein, 38 Pa. D.&C. 543 (1940).

[23]For recent examples of such litigation, see Vassiliades v. Garfinckel's, Brooks Bros., 492 A.2d 580 (D.C. 1985) (plastic surgeon promoted his work through showing plaintiff's photographs publicly) and Anderson v. Strong Mem. Hosp., 5 A.D.2d 1033, 542 N.Y.S.2d 96 (1989) (patient's photo taken by reporter and published in newspaper story on AIDS). For a ruling of the British Health Commissioner on point, see §8.5, note 33, infra.

[24]AMA Reference Guide, supra n.2 (emphasis supplied).

(to the degree known), treatment, and any known prognosis."[25] On the other hand, the guidelines on medical record services speak of a "clinical résumé" that is to be made available to those who may treat the patient subsequently. That résumé, as described, is clearly a summary.[26]

The practice of providing only summaries has been criticized by some physicians,[27] as well as by patients and their lawyers.[28] A facility's decision not to provide entire records might be challenged, though the use of summaries might be upheld in certain circumstances.[29] If a patient seeks to discover records in the course of litigation, it is especially likely that he will be entitled to the whole.

B. Access and Confidentiality

§8.3 Ownership and Control

Traditional concepts of ownership are not easily applied to medical records. While it is generally agreed that records, as physical entities, belong to a healthcare facility, it is almost equally well accepted that health professionals and patients have rights in them. As a practical matter, none of these groups usually claims exclusive jurisdiction. The JCAHO states, "The

---

[25]Id. at xii.

[26]"The clinical résumé concisely recapitulates the reason for hospitalization, the significant findings, the procedures performed and treatment rendered, the condition of the patient on discharge, and any specific instructions given to the patient and/or family, as pertinent." Id. at 89.

[27]Kaufman, Barriers Between Patients and Their Medical Records, 319 New Eng. J. Med. 1672 (1988).

[28]Essen, Medical Records and Treating Physicians: Access, Privilege and Confidentiality, Trial Briefs 8 (3d Quarter 1989). See Lipsman v. New York City B. of Ed., 133 A.D.2d 812, 520 N.Y.S.2d 396 (1987) (teacher entitled to actual medical records and fitness report rather than summary).

[29]Mitchell v. Subramanya, 27 Mass. App. 365, 538 N.E.2d 319 (1989).

medical record is the property of the hospital and is maintained for the benefit of the patient, the medical staff, and the hospital."[1] The AHA position is similar: "Although the medical record is kept for the benefit of the patient, the physician, and the health-care institution, it is the property of the health-care institution with other interests recognized by law."[2] Even though the AMA insists that "[n]otes made in treating a patient are primarily for the physician's own use and constitute his personal property," it recognizes patients' entitlement to the information.[3]

Naturally, concessions that parties have rights in records do not ensure agreement on the scope of the rights, nor do they guarantee that rights are accorded to all parties in practice.[4] Changes in professionals' and facilities' relative control over records parallel the change in their relationship during this century. In 1900, physicians, usually practicing alone, rendered almost all professional healthcare and controlled most medical records. Today, when no more than one-third of the typical hospital record is created by the attending physician, ultimate control over it is usually exercised by the facility.[5] The president of a state medical society regretfully noted the change more than a decade ago: "Those records that the physician makes in the hospital we feel are also his own, but because of the necessity of having organized medical staffs, this private, privileged communication has been turned over to the hospital for safe-

---

§8.3 [1] Joint Commission on Accreditation of Healthcare Organizations, Accreditation Manual for Hospitals 90 (1991).

[2] American Hospital Association, Technical Advisory Bulletin: Preservation of Medical Records in Health Care Institutions 1 (1975).

[3] American Medical Association, Reference Guide to Policy and Official Statements 60 (1988).

[4] An older source cites two surveys of Massachusetts hospitals in which a majority denied patients' requests for information (25 of 28 in one study, 9 of 10 in the other), despite a state statute assuring patient access to records. A. Westin, Computers, Health Records and Citizen Rights 28 (1976) (United States Bureau of Standards Doc. No. 157). While enforcement of the right to access seems more likely at present, most states still lack an access statute.

[5] Testimony of an AHA representative, in Privacy Protection Study Commission, Personal Privacy in an Information Society 278 (1977).

keeping.''[6] The older relationship may have lingered longer in extended care facilities. A representative of that industry told a congressional subcommittee in 1979 that the facilities saw themselves merely as intermediaries in the doctor-patient relationship. Thus, records belonged primarily to the physician, who was usually notified and asked to consent if a patient sought access.[7]

Four cases illustrate the shift from physician to facility control of records. In the earliest, an employer refused to pay for care when the doctor refused to send the employer copies of x-rays. The state supreme court held that the physician's offer to let other doctors examine the x-rays in his office was sufficient to justify the fee.[8] This decision contrasts sharply with several from the 1980s.

In one, a physician being investigated for misconduct was barred, like any other member of the public, from using the state freedom of information law to obtain copies of his patients' medical records from the board of medical examiners.[9] In another, a state's highest court eventually upheld a physician's right to review the records of his patients, but there were three dissenters.[10] In the fourth case, a medical school operating a clinical program was allowed to repossess patient records that a former faculty member (the treating physician) had taken with him, subject to the physician's right to obtain copies.[11]

---

[6]Statement of Arvine G. Popplewell, President, Indiana Medical Association, in Privacy of Medical Records: Hearings on H.R. No. 2979 and H.R. No. 3444 Before the Govt. Information and Individual Rights Subcomm. of the House Comm. on Govt. Operations, 96th Cong., 1st Sess. 860 (1979).

[7]Id. at 854-855.

[8]McGarry v. J. A. Mercier Co., 272 Mich. 501, 262 N.W. 296 (1935).

[9]John P. v. Whalen, 54 N.Y.2d 89, 429 N.E.2d 117 (1981).

[10]Beth Israel Hosp. v. District Court, 683 P.2d 343 (Colo. 1984). The issue was whether the records had become ''records of a review committee'' and thus protected from discovery by the physician in his suit against the hospital. The dissenters would have denied the doctor access; they saw ''no significance in the fact that the hospital records may have been those of [his] patients or that these records may have been available to him when he was previously attending them as their doctor.'' Id. at 348.

[11]Albany Med. College v. McShane, 66 N.Y.2d 982, 489 N.E.2d 1278 (1985).

For its legal protection, a facility should assert ownership of the records of treatment administered there. At the same time, the facility should permit the staff members and employees who create the record, that is, who are responsible for the treatment, to consult or copy it in appropriate circumstances. One such circumstance would be when the treatment may become the subject of a malpractice claim.

§8.4 Patient Access

Attitudes toward patient access to records have also changed. Before mid-century the nearly universal practice was not to allow it. While vestiges of that pattern remain and certain circumstances increase providers' reluctance to allow access, the common view today is that the patient does have a right to review the entire record.

§8.4.1 Attitudinal Changes

The older view appears in a treatise on hospital records the first edition of which was published in 1947:

> It is undesirable to allow a patient or his family to inspect his chart. He or they may find comments by nurses, interns, or other members of the professional staff which may be considered uncomplimentary or incorrect. The patient may then attempt to have the record changed, or cause annoyance to the administration or the professional staff. He may even bring a lawsuit for libel or some other fancied grievance. It is, therefore, advisable to have the abstract of the record omit characterizations or other remarks which may offend the patient.[1]

---

§8.4 [1]E. Hayt, Medicolegal Aspects of Hospital Records 114 (1977). Nearly identical language appeared in E. Hayt and L. Hayt, Law of Hospital, Physician and Patient 516 (1947).

Another reason, no longer considered necessary, for keeping records from patients was fear that they would discover serious diagnoses. A survey of physicians in 1961 found 90 percent unwilling to tell a patient of a cancer diagnosis; a 1978 study determined that almost all would tell.[2] Advocates of access have suggested numerous benefits: relieving patients' anxiety; making them participants in their treatment and ultimately responsible for their own health; permitting them to make meaningful waivers of confidentiality; putting them on a par with others who have access to their records; protecting them from inaccurate or obsolete record data; avoiding unnecessary duplication of treatment; allowing patients to take medical information with them as they move; and reducing litigation through better understanding of what has occurred. They tend to discount the most often-voiced objections, administrative inconvenience and cost.[3]

In 1972 the American Hospital Association issued a "Patient's Bill of Rights," guaranteeing a right to know the diagnosis, major treatment risks, and prognosis. This guarantee certainly implies a right of access to one's records. Since at least 1979 the AHA has explicitly recommended access unless "medically contraindicated."[4] Federal study commissions in 1976, 1977, and 1979 found widespread support for patient access, both

---

[2]Cited in Leblang and King, Tort Liability for Nondisclosure: The Physician's Legal Obligations to Disclose Patient Illness and Injury, 89 Dick. L. Rev. 1, 22 (1984).

[3]Testimony before a congressional subcommittee suggested that requests would not prove burdensome: The Thomas Jefferson University Hospital, Philadelphia, reported 15 requests annually (out of 21,000 patients discharged each year). Privacy of Medical Records: Hearings on H.R. No. 2979 and H.R. No. 3444 Before the Govt. Information and Individual Rights Subcomm. of the House Comm. on Govt. Operations, 96th Cong., 1st Sess. 315. The U.S. Indian Health Service reported a high of 700 requests per year from 2.2 million patients and former patients, id. St. Elizabeth's Hospital, Washington, D.C., reported 1 request among 600 patients, id. at 623. The Public Health Service reported only 26 requests ever received for amendment or correction, all but one of them settled locally, id. at 608.

[4]American Hospital Association, Institutional Policies for Disclosure of Medical Record Information 6 (1979) (hereinafter AHA Guidelines).

among the general public and the medical community, and
recommended it.

§8.4.2 Statutory and Case Law Support

The federal Privacy Act of 1974 ensures access to one's records
for any person about whom a federal agency, including a
hospital, keeps records.[5] While Medicaid regulations do not
directly state that residents of extended care facilities may see
their records, the right might be inferred from the right "to
participate in planning care or treatment or changes in care and
treatment."[6] A large minority of states ensure access by statute,[7]
and even those without a general statute on access may grant it
to particular categories of patients.[8]

Courts seem increasingly supportive of the right.[9] The
Supreme Court of Florida has required compliance with the
state's patient access statute even though the patient thereby
learned the names of his natural parents, presumably against
their wishes.[10] Since a facility's unjustified refusal to grant access

---

[5] 5 U.S.C.A. §552a(d)(1977). The Act also affords people the right to
request correction or deletion of errors in the record. See R. R. v. United States
Dept. of the Army, 482 F. Supp. 770 (D.D.C. 1980).

[6] 42 U.S.C.A. §1396r(c)(1)(A)(i) (1989).

[7] As early as 1979 several estimates, of from 10 to 15 states, were given
to a congressional subcommittee. Privacy of Medical Records, supra n.3, at
214, 237, 307.

[8] The access of mental patients to their records is frequently protected by
statute; see, e.g., N.C. Gen. Stat. §122C-53(c) (1986). Georgia does have a
broad access statute, applicable to HMOs and hospitals as well as to other
providers, Ga. Code Ann. §31-33-2 (1985). A separate statutory provision
guarantees access for residents of extended care facilities, Ga. Code Ann. §31-
8-108(b)(6) (1985).

[9] E.g., Ruffin v. Strange, 434 So. 2d 1200 (La. App. 1983); Cynthia B. v.
New Rochelle Hosp. Med. Center, 60 N.Y.2d 452, 458 N.E.2d 363, 470
N.Y.S.2d 122 (1983); Oliver v. Harborview Med. Center, 94 Wash. 2d 559,
618 P.2d 76 (1980).

[10] Atwell v. Sacred Heart Hosp. of Pensacola, 520 So. 2d 30 (Fla. 1988).

may toll a malpractice statute of limitations[11] or even result in a damage award,[12] and since denying access is rarely justifiable, the presumption and operating practice in a facility should be to grant patients access.

§8.4.3 Considerations in Granting Access

Arrangements for patient access involve a number of considerations intended to ensure the security of the record and the facility's convenience. Though procedures will vary, they should include efforts to verify that the person viewing or receiving a record is the patient or someone legally authorized to act for her. The facility must also decide when, how, and to what information access will be given.

Identifying the Requester. When a request is received for a record, the facility should take reasonable precautions to verify the validity of the request, that is, whether it comes from a patient or her authorized representative. Facility procedures on this point have twice been upheld, though they inconvenienced the patient. In one case, the hospital required that requests be signed by the patient and dated no earlier than 90 days before presentation. Plaintiff, the patient's attorney, had been refused access when he presented a form signed by the patient but perhaps not signed within the preceding 90 days.[13] In another, a hospital was found not to have breached any duty by ignoring a form letter requesting a patient's records.[14]

---

[11]Emmett v. Eastern Dispensary & Casualty Hosp., 396 F.2d 931 (D.C. Cir. 1967); Cassidy v. County of Nassau, 84 A.D.2d 742, 443 N.Y.S.2d 742 (1981).

[12]In Pierce v. Penman, 357 Pa. Super. 225, 515 A.2d 948 (1986), the appeals court awarded the patient $2,500 compensatory demages and $10,000 punitive damages for emotional distress occasioned by repeated refusals to give her copies of her record.

[13]Thurman v. Crawford, 652 S.W.2d 240 (Mo. App. 1983).

[14]Young v. Madison Gen. Hosp., 337 So. 2d 931 (Miss. 1976).

Access for the Patient, the Patient's Representative, or Both.   A
facility must decide to whom it will grant access in the patient's
name—to the patient as well as to any representative designated
by the patient such as a health professional, attorney, or other
person, or to a representative only. (Presumably, it would be
unreasonable to limit access to the patient only, that is, to refuse
to allow him to designate a representative for the purpose.)
Some facilities are reluctant to release records to patients. The
earlier custom, echoed in current statements of the AMA Council
on Ethical and Judicial Affairs,[15] was to transfer records from
provider to provider. In most circumstances insistence on a
representative seems unnecessary today and might even be
successfully challenged by the patient.[16]

*Access when the Patient Is a Minor or Otherwise Incompe-
tent.*   The records of minor patients occasionally raise special
issues for facilities. (See §8.9.5 infra.) These can include whether
to grant the minor access, whether to honor the patient's request
not to grant access to parents, and which parent in divorced
families controls access to the record. Some answers may depend
on who controlled the treatment. If the minor patient consented
to her own treatment, presumably she should control access to
the records of it as an adult patient would. In dealing with
divorced families the facility might ask for a copy of the custody
agreement, which may describe the parties' respective rights
concerning the children's medical care. In addition, the facility's
attorney must determine whether parental rights in healthcare
are addressed by statute in the jurisdiction.

Historically, facilities have been more reluctant to grant
access to their records to mental patients than to others. The
stated reason, usually, is fear of harm to the patient. Again, this
is a question that has been settled by statute or regulation in a

---

[15]See "Availability of Information to Other Physicians" and "Information
and Patients" in American Medical Association, Reference Guide to Policy and
Official Statements (1988) (hereinafter AMA Reference Guide).

[16]Lipsman v. New York City Bd. of Ed., 133 A.D.2d 812, 520 N.Y.S.2d
396 (1987).

number of states. If not, the attorney will wish to consult the case law of other jurisdictions, much of which supports the patient's right of access.[17]

Access to the Entire Record. This point has been discussed earlier (see §8.2.3) as an aspect of defining the medical record. There is no consensus on whether a provider may provide less than the whole record to a patient. Though very few state statutes address the point,[18] in some instances the distinction between a summary and the entire record may be important to the patient.[19] Certainly an attorney wants access to the whole in preparing a case, and the patient may have other uses for it as well. The AMA[20] and the JCAHO[21] seem to approve a physician's decision to release summaries only, but individual providers have claimed that subsequent care suffers.[22] Two reported decisions on the practice reach opposite results.[23]

Conditions for Access. The facility may impose reasonable conditions on the requester. These might include a refusal, absent special need, to allow the record to be reviewed before it is complete. Some facilities do resist allowing a patient access who is still being treated—a hospitalized acute care patient, for

---

[17]See *Cynthia B.*, 60 N.Y.2d 452 (supra n.9); Doe v. Commr. of Mental Health, 372 Mass. 534, 362 N.E.2d 920 (1977).

[18]For a statute approving the use of summaries, see Cal. [Health & Safety] Code §1795.20(a) (West Supp. 1990).

[19]A related question, with medical and legal consequences, is what the facility itself will denominate as the record and keep. As diagnosis and treatment become more technically complex and the records of care are automated, it becomes harder to say whether data are preliminary—and hence perhaps disposable—or of some ultimate significance.

[20]AMA Reference Guide, at 60.

[21]Joint Commission on the Accreditation of Healthcare Organizations, Accreditation Manual for Hospitals 89 (1991).

[22]Kaufman, "Barriers Between Patients and Their Medical Records," 319 New Eng. J. of Med. 1672 (1988).

[23]Lipsman v. New York City Board of Education, 133 A.D.2d 812, 520 N.Y.S.2d 396 (1987) (summary insufficient); Mitchell v. Subramanya, 27 Mass. App. 365, 538 N.E.2d 319 (1989) (summary sufficient).

instance. Though requiring the patient to wait for discharge or later would be less reasonable for a long-term care facility, it might insist on some degree of completion or on regular intervals for access. Most facilities have an employee present when others are viewing a record, both to ensure its safety and to explain it if necessary.[24] A facility never releases the original of its records. (Even courts usually accept copies.) Instead, it arranges for the requester to be provided with copies, for which a reasonable charge may be made.[25] One condition that is not reasonable is that payment for the care be received before access is granted.[26]

§8.5 Medical Confidentiality

Many people have a need or desire for information about the health status of others. Representatives of these interests often approach healthcare facilities seeking access to medical records. Responding properly to such requests is a major challenge, since it is a well-established ethical and, to some extent, legal principle that the medical relationship should remain confidential. This section examines society's ambivalence about medical confidentiality as well as its sources and boundaries.

§8.5.1 Confidentiality's Uncertain Legal Status

United States jurisprudence clearly reveals a lack of consensus as to how much privacy should be afforded to medical care relationships. Medical ethics, from the Hippocratic Oath to

---

[24]For an example of how confused a patient can become, see Fitzgerald v. Caplan, 184 Ga. App. 567, 362 S.E.2d 103 (1987).

[25]How high the fee may be has been litigated several times in New York. See, for example, Hayes v. County of Nassau, 127 A.D.2d 742, 512 N.Y.S.2d 134 (1987).

[26]The self-help remedy of withholding access is not an appropriate means for collection of a civil debt and could create serious liability for the facility if harm to the patient resulted. The AMA disapproves of the practice. AMA Reference Guide, at 60.

current formulations of the AMA,[1] place confidentiality high among medical values. Physicians take the matter seriously and in doing so reflect their patients' preferences, as two examples from the Privacy Commission's hearings suggest: First, the National Center for Health Statistics acknowledged that its data on the incidence of venereal disease are unreliable because physicians will not report these diseases for fear of stigmatizing patients.[2] Second, in one group of nearly 1,000 patients, only 20 percent agreed to have information about them sent to a state registry (once they were assured there would be no penalty for refusing).[3]

While doctors and patients agree on the desirability of confidentiality, American law is frankly ambiguous. The majority of states have no general statutory right to confidentiality of medical records, and the group of cases upholding a cause of action against providers for improper disclosure is quite small. (However, certain kinds of records—mental health records, for example—are well-protected by statute.) Nearly all states recognize a doctor-patient testimonial privilege, but it is usually weaker than the attorney-client privilege. Under the federal rules of evidence the doctor-patient testimonial privilege is strongly disfavored.[4]

---

§8.5 [1]American Medical Association, Reference Guide to Policy and Official Statements 14 (1988) (hereinafter AMA Reference Guide).

[2]Privacy Protection Study Commission, Personal Privacy in an Information Society 287 (1977).

[3]The experiment took place at four mental health clinics in Georgia. When read both formally and informally worded statements allowing information to be sent to the state department of mental health, 100 percent of the patients signed waivers. But when read the informal statement and then told that they truly had an option—that is, that they would receive the same service in either case—the majority declined (59 percent when told by a clerk, 80 percent when told by a physician). A. Westin, Computers, Health Records and Citizen Rights 243-245 (1976) (United States Bureau of Standards Doc. No. 157).

[4]Federal rules of evidence do not recognize the privilege. However, federal judges may protect what information they think best. Holder, The Biomedical Researcher and Subpoenas: Judicial Protection of Confidential Medical Data, 12 Am. J. Law and Med. 405, 412, citing Deitchman v. E. R. Squibb and Sons, 740 F.2d 556 (7th Cir. 1984).

The United States Supreme Court once discussed extensively, but did not rule on, the confidentiality question. In Whalen v. Roe,[5] the Court unanimously upheld a state law requiring limited disclosure, but the opinions (a majority opinion and two concurrences) revealed disagreement within the Court on central points. At issue in *Whalen* was the constitutionality of a New York requirement that pharmacists report every prescription for a Schedule II drug (those with high potential for abuse) to the state health department. The trial court invalidated the statute as an infringement on a constitutionally protected zone of privacy, the doctor-patient relationship.[6] The Supreme Court majority explicitly refused to decide whether the Constitution protects the confidentiality of medical information, holding instead that the New York statute did not breach confidentiality. Only 17 health department employees and 24 investigators had access to the registry; they could be criminally penalized for unlawful disclosures; and records were destroyed after five years. Referring to "the cases sometimes characterized as protecting 'privacy,'" the Court found they protect two interests: (1) avoiding disclosure of personal matters and (2) personal choice in making certain important decisions. Neither interest, it said, was seriously threatened in this instance. The Court did observe that when government gathers private data, it must keep them safe, and noted cautiously, "[I]n some circumstances that duty arguably has its roots in the Constitution."[7]

Justice Brennan wrote a separate opinion to emphasize the point: "[B]road dissemination by state officials of such information [as that collected by the health department] would clearly implicate constitutionally protected privacy rights and presumably be justified only by compelling state interests."

[5]429 U.S. 589 (1977). See Planned Parenthood v. Danforth, 428 U.S. 52, 80 (1976) for an earlier reference to medical confidentiality as an aspect of privacy, cited in Carter v. Broadlawns Medical Center, 667 F. Supp. 1269 (S.D. Iowa 1987).

[6]Roe v. Ingraham, 403 F. Supp. 931 (S.D.N.Y. 1975).

[7]429 U.S. 589, 605 (1977).

Justice Stewart, on the contrary, denied the existence of a general constitutional right to privacy. Thus *Whalen* left unanswered the question of whether the federal constitution protects a patient's confidentiality in his dealings with health providers.[8] Changes on the Supreme Court since *Whalen* probably make it less likely that the Court would recognize such a protection today.

§8.5.2 Sources of the Right

Besides medical ethics,[9] what accounts for the widespread perception that disclosures to health providers are confidential? As noted above, there is some support within the Supreme Court for the premise that health care is a basic aspect of privacy, and a majority of the Court has not as yet stated the contrary. The privacy rights of those using federal healthcare facilities are guaranteed by statute.[10] In the states, besides nearly unanimous recognition of a doctor-patient testimonial privilege, statutes[11] or case law[12] may provide a broader assurance of privacy. Finally, the doctor-patient agreement can be viewed as a contract, one (implied) term of which is preservation of confidentiality.[13]

---

[8]For circuit court interpretations of *Whalen*, see General Motors Corp. v. Director of NIOSH, 636 F.2d 163 (6th Cir. 1980) and United States v. Westinghouse Elec. Corp. 638 F.2d 570 (3d Cir. 1980). In Carter v. Broadlawns Medical Center, a federal district court held patients have a Fourteenth Amendment right not to have unauthorized people view their medical records, 667 F. Supp. 1269 at 1282.

[9]AMA Reference Guide, at 14.

[10]5 U.S.C.A. §552(b)(6); 5 U.S.C.A. §552a(b) (1977).

[11]E.g., Fla. Stat. Ann. §395.017(3) (West Supp. 1990) and §455.241(2) (West 1981 & Supp. 1990). New York guarantees confidentiality to HMO patients, N.Y. Pub. Health Law art. 44, §4410(2) (1985).

[12]Alberts v. Devine, 395 Mass. 59, 479 N.E.2d 113 (1985), cert. denied, 474 U.S. 1013 (1985).

[13]Id.

§8.5.3 The Extent of the Right

If medical privacy is a right, what material does it protect? The attorney researching the answer in her jurisdiction will want to review the state's testimonial privilege statute and its judicial interpretations. Though the law of doctor-patient privilege is not coextensive with medical privacy law, knowledge of the former is a good beginning in understanding a jurisdiction's present and perhaps its future positions on the issue.

One privilege statute, for example, reads in pertinent part, "No person . . . shall be required to disclose any information which he may have acquired in attending a patient in a professional character, and which information was necessary to enable him to prescribe for such patient as a physician, or to do any act for him as a surgeon. . . ."[14] The state's courts have interpreted the statute to mean that it covers any information necessary for treatment—more than oral communications, but not information irrelevant to the medical relationship. Information gathered either by an individual provider or by a facility is covered. Ordinarily, only the patient can waive or assert his right to confidentiality, but he may waive by means of certain acts as well as words. The privilege extends to communications to a nurse or other person working under a physician but not to nonphysician health professionals practicing independently (an optometrist, for instance). The privilege does not come into being unless a proper doctor-patient relationship is formed and it does not survive the patient's death. The privilege does not apply in involuntary commitment proceedings or (under another statute) when the evidence sought to be excluded concerns child abuse or neglect.[15] Most important, the privilege may be set aside by a judge who finds that the protected evidence is "necessary to a proper administration of justice."

None of these holdings can be assumed true for other jurisdictions. Each point noted above and others must be

---

[14]N.C. Gen. Stat. §8-53 (1986).

[15]Dellinger, Medical Records in Joan G. Brannon and A. Dellinger, The Law of Health Records in North Carolina 27-28 (1987).

researched for the state within which the facility is located. Holdings from other jurisdictions may, however, interest an attorney whose jurisdiction has not decided what is protected from disclosure. A small body of cases can be consulted on such commonly unsettled questions as: Is it necessary to conceal the patient's identity, that is, the mere fact that he or she is a patient? Does concealing identification completely eliminate other privacy concerns? Is information obtained about third parties entitled to protection?

Patient Identification.   Whether identification of a person as a patient is confidential has been an issue for a hundred years, especially in New York. While the answer has more often than not been no, several newer cases and legislative enactments are to the contrary. Federal legislation, for instance, strongly protects the identities of patients in federally funded alcohol and drug treatment programs.[16] (See Part E of this chapter.) When the state of North Carolina revised its mental health code it overwhelmingly disapproved public access to the names of involuntarily committed patients.[17]

Decisions that protect identity often arise from situations in which releasing a patient's name, address, or other seemingly neutral data actually discloses more than that she or he has seen a doctor. In Alaska, a doctor elected to local office challenged a conflict of interest statute requiring elected officials to publish lists of their clients, in his case, patients. The Alaska Supreme Court held that the resulting violation of patients' privacy rights rendered the statute unconstitutional. The court concluded that patients' names must be private, at least when a physician deals with a particular kind of stigmatizing condition such as mental illness, venereal disease, abortions, or contraception. It also recognized privacy concerns when minors seek treatment without their parents' knowledge or spouses without each other's.[18]

---

[16]42 U.S.C.A. §290ee-3 (Supp. 1989); 42 U.S.C.A. §290dd-3 (Supp. 1989).

[17]General Assembly Roundup, News and Observer (Raleigh, N.C.), June 20, 1985.

[18]Falcon v. Alaska Pub. Affairs Commn., 570 P.2d 469 (Alaska 1977).

Other courts have disapproved of disclosure when (1) malpractice plaintiffs wanted the names of those who received similar operations;[19] (2) a prosecutor trailing a murderer asked for the identity of anyone treated for stab wounds within a three-day period;[20] (3) a person who contracted AIDS from a blood transfusion sought the names of donors;[21] (4) an adopted child obtained her birth mother's name and address from the obstetrician;[22] and (5) a local medical society sought names and addresses of all Medicare beneficiaries in the area.[23] In each instance, revealing the patient's identity did or would have also revealed facts about diagnosis, treatment, or other highly private matters.[24]

The older and perhaps still dominant view is expressed in an 1892 opinion of New York's highest court. It held that a doctor could testify that a patient visited him for care, on what dates, where, and so on without breaching confidentiality.[25] New York courts continue to affirm the point,[26] as do courts of several other jurisdictions.[27] Federal appeals courts have declined

---

[19]Mack v. Beacon Light Clinic, 461 So. 2d 799 (Ala. App. 1984) (abortions); Leikensohn v. Cornwell, 434 So. 2d 1030 (Fla. App. 1983); Ziegler v. Superior Court, 640 P.2d 181 (Ariz. App. 1982).

[20]Grand Jury Investigation of Onandaga County No. 235, 59 N.Y.2d 130, 450 N.E.2d 678, 463 N.Y.S.2d 758 (1983).

[21]South Florida Blood Serv. v. Rasmussen, 467 So. 2d 798 (Fla. App. 1985).

[22]Humphers v. First Interstate Bank of Or., 68 Or. App. 573, 684 P.2d 581 (1984).

[23]Multnomah County Medical Soc. v. Scott, 825 F.2d 1410 (9th Cir. 1987).

[24]The protection of identification might not, however, extend to a person seen entering a facility. Chico Feminist Women's Health Center v. Scully, 256 Cal. Rptr. 194, 208 Cal. App. 3d 230 (1989).

[25]Patten v. United Life & Accident Ins. Assn., 133 N.Y. 450, 31 N.E. 342 (1892).

[26]Henry v. Lewis, 102 A.D.2d 430, 478 N.Y.S.2d 263 (1984).

[27]In re Warrant for 2045 Franklin, 709 P.2d 597 (Colo. App. 1985); People v. Florendo, 95 Ill. 2d 155, 447 N.E.2d 282 (1983); Chidester v. Needles, 353 N.W.2d 849 (Iowa 1984); Koudsi v. Hennepin County Med. Center, 317 N.W.2d 705 (Minn. 1982).

to protect the identities of psychiatric patients[28] and of veterans exposed to atomic testing.[29]

Nonidentifiable Medical Information. If courts are satisfied that information to be released from medical records does not identify patients, they are likely to approve the disclosure.[30] For example, Justice Brennan first stayed an order of the Texas Supreme Court requiring production of records of abortion patients, then dissolved the stay, then reinstituted it. The decisive issue, in his view, was whether the order removed patient identifiers.[31] A few courts, however, recognize the existence of a greater privacy interest for the patient, one that attaches even though his identity will be concealed.[32] Still other courts are dubious about the *ability* to conceal identity even though a good-faith effort is made; they fear for the patient's privacy once *any* information is released. If publishing a name sometimes reveals medical facts, here the concern is the obverse: releasing medical histories may help identify individuals.

Concerns about identification are particularly acute with respect to photographs that illustrate the effects of disease and treatment. The existence of several cases based on photos suggests that this is a particularly painful form of disclosure for patients.[33]

---

[28]In re Zuniga, 714 F.2d 632 (6th Cir. 1983); In re Doe, 711 F.2d 1187 (2d Cir. 1983); In re Pebsworth, 705 F.2d 261 (7th Cir. 1983).

[29]National Assn. of Atomic Veterans v. Director, Defense Nuclear Agency, 583 F. Supp. 1483 (D.D.C. 1984).

[30]N. O. v. Callahan, 110 F.R.D. 637 (D. Mass. 1986); C. L. v. Edson, 409 N.W.2d 417 (Wis. App. 1987); State ex rel. Cox Med. Center v. Keet, 678 S.W.2d 813 (Mo. 1984); Ziegler v. Superior Court, 656 P.2d 1251 (Ariz. App. 1982).

[31]Reproductive Servs. v. Walker, 439 U.S. 1307 (1978); 439 U.S. 1354 (1978).

[32]Lora v. Board of Ed. 74 F.R.D. 565 (E.D.N.Y. 1977); Leikensohn v. Cornwell, 434 So. 2d 1030 (Fla. App. 1983); Argonaut Ins. Co. v. Peralta, 358 So. 2d 232 (Fla. App. 1978) (unidentifiable records released because other interests judged stronger than remaining privacy interest; court observed, however, that many people resist giving information to researchers through anonymous instruments).

[33]Anderson v. Strong Memorial Hosp. 5 A.D.2d 1033, 542 N.Y.S.2d 96

Certain traditional methods used to conceal identity in photographs are sometimes ineffective.[34] Facilities should secure informed consent from patients before publicly displaying their images and should strictly limit secondary users' access to photographs.[35]

Nonpatient Information.   Medical records frequently contain material about people other than the patient. One of the JCAHO standards for social work services in hospitals illustrates this fact.

SO.4.2 As appropriate, pertinent information relating to the following is included in the medical record:

SO.4.2.1 Observations and social assessment of the patient and as relevant, of the patient's family;

SO4.2.2 The proposed plan for providing any required social work services;

SO4.2.3 Any social therapy/rehabilitation provided to the patient and the patient's family;

SO4.2.4 Social work summaries, including any recommendations for follow-up; and

SO.4.2.5 As appropriate, other pertinent information also is included in the medical record, such as home environment

---

(1989); Estate of Berthiaume v. Pratt, 365 A.2d 792 (Me. 1976). In two other cases, photographs that were probably taken for the record were later used for unauthorized purposes and the patient was held aggrieved thereby. In Vassiliades v. Garfinckel's, Brooks Bros., 492 A.2d 580 (D.C. 1985), a plastic surgeon promoted his work by showing plaintiff's photographs. In England, a patient discovered full-length nude photos of himself in a textbook written by his physician. The British Health Commissioner allocated responsibility for this invasion of privacy to the hospital where treatment occurred as well as to the physician and publisher. Report of the British Health Commissioner, Use of Medical Records 39-44 (1985) (on file with the author). An important early case is Bazemore v. Savannah Hospital, 155 S.E. 194 (Ga. 1930). California protects residents of extended care facilities from use of their photos for any but identification or health care purposes. Cal. Health & Safety Code §1599.80 (West Supp. 1990).

[34]Slue, Occasional Notes: Unmasking the Lone Ranger, 321 New Eng. J. Med. 550-551 (1989).

[35]Binder v. Superior Court, 242 Cal. Rptr. 231 (Cal. App. 1987). Malpractice plaintiff sought to discover photos of other patients.

evaluations for the attending practitioner, cooperative activities with community agencies, and follow-up reports.[36]
The records of extended care facilities or psychiatric units are particularly likely to involve the privacy of many people besides the patient. The records may note the patient's interactions with other named patients and family members and also may include statements solicited from relatives, friends, and acquaintances.

Before releasing records, a facility would do well to consider what rights of confidentiality belong to third parties mentioned in the records. There are surprisingly few precedents to inform the consideration. However, at least one case has held that when family members participate in counseling sessions for the sake of a patient, the contents of records concerning them cannot be divulged without the family members' consent.[37] Likewise, the Seventh Circuit Court of Appeals rejected a Freedom of Information Act request for the records of the Indiana "Baby Doe" case, stating that removing identification of the infant would not suffice to protect the privacy of his parents.[38]

Uncertainty about balancing the multiple privacy interests implicated in their records leads some facilities to keep more than one set for a single case. Two authors writing on nonpatient information in records recommend keeping separate files (for example, one for each person in family therapy).[39] In the 1979 congressional hearings on medical record privacy, a psychiatrist described "double recordkeeping" as a growing phenomenon—one set for disclosure, one not.[40] At the same hearing, the president of the American Academy of Pediatrics, while conced-

---

[36]Joint Commission on Accreditation of Healthcare Organizations, Accreditation Manual for Hospitals 247 (1991).

[37]Grosslight v. Superior Court, 72 Cal. App. 3d 502, 140 Cal. Rptr. 278 (1977).

[38]Marzen v. Department of Health and Human Serv., 825 F.2d 1148 (7th Cir. 1987).

[39]Huber and Roth, Preserving the Confidentiality of Medical Record Information Regarding Nonpatients, 66 Va. L. Rev. 583, 592-595 (1980).

[40]Privacy of Medical Records: Hearings on H.R. No. 2979 and H.R. No. 3444 Before the Govt. Information and Individual Rights Subcomm. of the House Comm. on Govt. Operations, 96th Cong., 1st Sess. 892-893.

ing the occasional desirability of segregating information, predicted that an orderly division of material into "confidential"
and "not confidential" would prove impossible.[41] An alternative
to separating material about nonpatients from the patient's
record is to secure consent from each person mentioned in a
record before releasing it.

§8.6 Exceptions to Confidentiality

Law and custom have always recognized exceptions to medical
confidentiality, and the trend is accelerating. An early commentator on medical records and privacy divided potential users of
records into three categories: (1) direct-service providers (that
is, healthcare and other institutions—schools, for example—
that are performing a service for the patient); (2) providers of
support services (primarily, third-party payors and reviewers of
the quality of care); and (3) secondary users (that is, those who
want health data to serve some social need apart from the
patient's need). Secondary uses might include: credential and
evaluative decisions (for such purposes as insurance, employment, or licensing); judicial process, in both civil litigation and
criminal prosecution or defense; medical and social research;
public health protection; or public information needs, as judged
by news media.[1] In addition, patients' families and employers,
or people dealing with emergencies, may want information, and
the healthcare provider may sometimes need to warn others
that the patient threatens them or himself. The legitimacy of
each of these claims as an exception to confidentiality is
considered below.

§8.6.1 Direct Service

It is inaccurate to say that direct service providers enjoy an
exception to medical confidentiality. Rather, it is *their* interchange

---

[41]Testimony of Dr. Adele Hofman, id. at 975-976.

§8.6 [1]A. Westin, Computers, Health Records and Citizen Rights 9-10
(1976) (United States Bureau of Standards Doc. No. 157).

with a patient that is confidential. The Supreme Court has pointed out the "host of . . . unpleasant invasions of privacy that are associated with many facets of health care," adding that "disclosures of private medical information to doctors, to hospital personnel, to insurance companies, and to public health agencies are often an essential part of modern medical practice even when the disclosure may reflect unfavorably on the character of the patient."[2] Given the complexity of medical treatment today, patients can be assumed to understand that many people other than their personal physicians must be privy to information about them in the course of treatment. If the provider's internal access policy is reasonable, such sharing does not breach confidentiality.[3] (All staff and employees, of course, must keep the data confidential.) As patients move from one facility to another, however, the decision of whether to make records of their past treatment available to new providers is theirs. The provider would breach confidentiality by doing so without patient consent.[4]

§8.6.2 Support Services

Certain functions provide such vital support to the medical care relationship that they are allowed to intrude on its privacy.

---

[2]Whalen v. Roe, 429 U.S. 589, 602 (1977).

[3]But see Carter v. Broadlawns Medical Center, 667 F. Supp. 1269 (S.D. Iowa 1987), a successful challenge to a facility's practice of allowing chaplains access to records, and Cassingham v. Lutheran Sunburst Health Serv., 748 S.W.2d 589 (Tex. App. 1988), denying summary judgment for a facility that opened a record to a counselor recommended by their physician.

[4]For an extreme example of provider access demands, see Privacy of Medical Records: Hearings on H.R. No. 2979 and H.R. No. 3444 Before the Govt. Information and Indiv. Rights Subcomm. of the House Comm. on Govt. Operations, 96th Cong., 1st Sess. 275-276 (hereinafter Privacy of Medical Records), describing a pharmacy that allegedly refused to fill prescriptions unless prospective customers consented to disclosure of their medical records. Perhaps a more common, and therefore better, example would be a provider's sharing information with a school without patient consent. Iverson v. Frandsen, 237 F.2d 898 (10th Cir. 1956) raises but does not settle the question of whether this may be an actionable breach of confidentiality.

Foremost among these are insurance and quality assurance. Some measure of privacy may still be appropriate, however, even within these categories.

Third-Party Payment. The majority of healthcare is paid for by private insurance. In addition, government insurance programs for the elderly and some of the indigent require vast public outlays. Thus, it is unsurprising that insurers' access to medical information is the best-established exception to confidentiality.[5] The propriety of a facility's disclosing to a patient's insurer has apparently rarely been questioned and is usually upheld.[6] Still, there is a body of opinion—probably stronger among mental health providers than others—that insurers' requests are on occasion overbroad and potentially harmful.[7]

----

[5]From another point of view, this is not an exception to confidentiality but an instance of release with patient's consent. Under that theory, the patient chooses to execute a written waiver of confidentiality in favor of the insurer, and the provider then supplies the information requested as a favor to the patient.

[6]Hague v. Williams, 37 N.J. 328, 181 A.2d 345 (1962); Patten v. United Life & Accident Ins. Assn., 133 N.Y. 450, 31 N.E. 342 (1892). But see Prince v. St. Francis-St. George Hosp., 484 N.E.2d 265 (Ohio App. 1985), in which doctors' bungled attempt to secure insurance reimbursement for their care resulted in disclosure of patient's alcoholism to co-workers of the patient's husband.

[7]The Preyer Subcommittee on Privacy of Medical Records recorded these protests:

> I see continuing hardship on almost a daily basis concerning patients who are being asked for information which I, as a psychiatrist and as a person who has worked as a medical advisor for H.E.W. for over 16 years, know is not necessary to make an adjudication of the validity of the claim.

Letter from John Reckless, M.D., Durham, North Carolina, in Privacy of Medical Records, at 1198-1199.

> I realize the necessity of the review of records to determine liability under the FEP [Federal Employees Program]. However, I seriously question whether or not all of these records are needed. . . . [W]hy is it necessary to submit an entire medical record, which increases our costs and breaches confidentiality, and then have that chart reviewed by a non-physician clerk?

Letter of John D. Olofson, psychiatric hospital administrator, Asheville, North

A 1983 decision of the Seventh Circuit Court of Appeals acknowledged the incursion health insurance has made on privacy. In connection with the prosecution of a psychotherapist for criminal fraud, the court approved a subpoena to require Blue Cross to surrender the doctor's records, including patients' names, listings of their visits, and diagnoses. In a decision that is itself a milestone in the trend it describes, the court asserted that confidentiality is compromised "to a large degree already . . . in the system of third party medical reimbursement. . . . [P]atients were aware that substantial intrusion upon their privacy was entailed in their consent to the processing and verification of the information at issue by numerous employees in a large, anonymous corporation." Furthermore, the court alleged, the possibility that the insurer might have to reveal confidential data as part of a criminal investigation is one the insured probably did consider, or should have considered, when he waived confidentiality on behalf of his insurer.[8]

Quality Assurance. Patients' confidentiality rights are regularly set aside, often by statute, to allow review of providers' care. The extensive subpoena powers associated with fraud investigations will be discussed below; but even when fraud is

---

Carolina, id. at 247-248.

The chairman of the National Commission on Confidentiality of Health Records complained to Representative Preyer of an insurance form that asked psychiatrists: "Was a transference effected with your patient? Describe some of the patient's fantasy life." Statement of Dr. Alfred M. Freedman, id. at 239.

A spokesman for the American Psychological Association suggested that insurers' imperfect grasp of psychiatric problems (all rooted to some degree in childhood, he asserted) may force psychiatrists to dissemble. He recalled an incident from his own career in which his full case report to the insurer resulted in rejection of the patient's claim as a "pre-existing condition." Statement of Dr. Beigler, id. at 456.

Alan Westin states that some providers let insurers handle the record themselves or send an entire page rather than excerpting the item needed. "The costs of locating the relevant data, masking out parts not pertinent, and explaining such procedures to the requesting parties are often more than overworked records departments can expend." A. Westin, supra n.1, at 117.

[8]In re Pebsworth, 705 F.2d 261 (7th Cir. 1983).

not an issue, quality control reviewers require access to records. The extent of the access needed—whether it must include identifiable patient records, for instance—is debatable.

State agencies licensing healthcare facilities may have statutory or regulatory authority to review patient records as part of their duty to inspect licensees. The facility's attorney should consult state law on the point. As a condition of participation in Medicaid, states must require providers to supply the state or the secretary of Health and Human Services (HHS) with requested information,[9] presumably including patient records. Both federal statute[10] and regulation[11] require that Medicare providers release patient data to peer review organizations with which HHS contracts for utilization and quality control. Survey teams from the JCAHO inspect selected groups of patient records in the course of their inspections.

§8.6.3 Secondary Uses

Medical information is useful to many people besides those categorized above as primary users (those treating a patient, paying for treatment, or charged with ensuring that care is adequate). Even if the facility sympathizes with the motives behind other requests, careful consideration should be given to whether there is a legal basis for granting access to confidential material. All requesting units, including governmental agencies and law enforcement personnel, should be asked to prove their entitlements, while the facility should be prepared to assert those of patients.

Professional Licensing.   Boards that license and discipline medical professionals need to examine the professionals' performance through medical records. State statutes often permit such

---

[9]42 U.S.C. §1396a(a)(27) (1983 & Supp. 1989).
[10]42 U.S.C. §1395cc(a)(1)(e) (Supp. 1989).
[11]42 C.F.R. §476.111 (1988).

boards to inspect records without patient consent, though a showing of probable cause to suspect misconduct may be required,[12] or the inspection right may be otherwise limited.[13] The right of a board is occasionally challenged. California's courts require the board to show "good cause" for the subpoena of records;[14] New York too has on occasion denied a professional board's request.[15] One of the latter decisions illustrates the degree to which investigations of physicians' conduct can threaten the privacy of patients. The examining board sought records of a psychiatrist's former patient—but not the records of his treatment. Instead, the board, presumably looking for more evidence against the psychiatrist, wished to examine the records of the patient's subsequent treatment by two other therapists. The court rejected the board's request for a subpoena of "the entire files of two separate health care professionals, neither of whom are under investigation, for records of a patient who has filed no charges, and who objects to the disclosure of her files."[16] If a facility receiving such a request considers it an unjustified infringement of patient privacy, the facility's attorney should seek modification of the subpoena or advise the facility to refuse to comply without a court order. He might also advise the facility to inform the affected patients.

---

[12]Fla. Stat. Ann. §455.421(2) (West 1989), applied in Nach v. Department of Professional Regulation, Bd. of Med. Examiners, 528 So. 2d 908 (Fla. App. 1988).

[13]Manthey v. Ohio State Med. Bd., 36 Ohio App. 3d 181, 521 N.E.2d 1121 (Ohio App. 1987).

[14]Division of Medical Quality Assurance v. Gherardini, 93 Cal. App. 3d 669, 156 Cal. Rptr. 55 (1979).

[15]Shankman v. Axelrod, 137 A.D.2d 255, 528 N.Y.S.2d 937 (1988) (rather than sending a subpoena, the Board's representative entered the physician's office pursuant to an inspection warrant and removed records); In re A-85-04-38, 138 Misc. 2d 786, 525 N.Y.S.2d 479 (1988).

[16]In re A-85-04-38, id. at 480. An opinion of the Florida Attorney-General is a further reminder that patients have serious interests at stake when their doctors are investigated. The opinion states that the Department of Professional Regulation may not release patient records or information identifying a patient by name to law enforcement or regulatory agencies. Op. Atty-Gen. 89-12 (March 1, 1989).

Employment. Employers are concerned with health data because employee health affects both job performance and the cost of job-related health insurance. Conversely, patients have reasons (including fear of discrimination) to guard health data from employers. The American Cancer Society has concluded that a minority of cancer patients returning to work and a larger number seeking new work encounter prejudice.[17] Each of the three major national studies of medical confidentiality identified employers' interest in records as a problem.[18] The 1977 report warned,

> [S]o long as there are no absolute barriers to an employer's use of its employee medical and insurance claims records, and as long as employers are in some cases *required* to use such records, a privacy problem of potentially major proportions exists. For example, Department of Defense Industrial Security regulations require employers to report any information that would reflect on the reliability of employees who work on classified projects. Information on employees and their dependents in medical treatment or insurance claim files is not excluded from this requirement.[19]

Under current rules, Department of Defense contractors must report any adverse information about employees with access to classified information. As examples, the Department manual lists "bizarre . . . conduct; treatment for mental or emotional disorders; excessive use of intoxicants; use of illegal, controlled substances. . . ."[20]

---

[17]The American Cancer Society and the Legal Aid Society of San Francisco fund a National Cancer Employment Law Project that promotes antidiscrimination legislation. See also Mellette, The Problem of Employability After Cancer Treatment, Proceedings of the American Cancer Society Fourth National Conference on Human Values & Cancer, New York City (March 15-17, 1984).

[18]A. Westin, supra n.1, at 64-67. Privacy of Medical Records, at 256-257. According to the Privacy Protection Study Commission, "employers have begun to rival insurance companies as major keepers and users of medical record information." Privacy Protection Study Commission, Personal Privacy in an Information Society 297 (1977).

[19]Id. at 229.

[20]The Industrial Security Manual for Safeguarding Classified Information (DoD 5220.22-M) (1989) at 40, n.13.

No clear trend emerges from the cases in which patients challenge a provider's decision to release data to an employer. Some courts have been persuaded of the employer's right to know.[21] Others have found a clear duty on the part of providers not to disclose.[22] Given the probability of adverse consequences for the patient from disclosure, the American Hospital Association's recommendation to its members not to disclose to employers without specific statutory authority[23] seems prudent.

Law Enforcement. State, federal, and local law enforcement officials may seek information from healthcare facilities to pursue criminal or civil violations of law. The FBI, for instance, believes that lives have been saved because it has sometimes had access to the medical records of people involved in hostage situations. From time to time police ask healthcare facilities to watch for fugitives needing certain kinds of treatment.[24] The Secret Service attempts to identify potentially dangerous people through inquiries to mental institutions and psychiatrists.[25] The Department of Health and Human Services sought access (unsuccessfully) to the records of handicapped infants to determine whether §504 of the Rehabilitation Act of 1973 had been violated,[26] and NIOSH, the federal agency charged with protecting industrial health, has won access to employee health records.[27]

Medical records can be valuable evidence of various kinds of fraud against the government, a use to which courts have

---

[21]Bratt v. IBM Corp., 785 F.2d 352 (1st Cir. 1986); Davis v. Monsanto, 627 F. Supp. 418 (D.W. Va. 1986).

[22]Crippen v. Charter Southland Hosp., 534 So. 2d 286 (Ala. 1988); Alberts v. Devine, 395 Mass. 59, 479 N.E.2d 113 (1985).

[23]American Hospital Association, Institutional Policies for Disclosure of Medical Records Information 6 (1979) (hereinafter AHA Guidelines).

[24]In Bryson v. Tillinghast, 749 P.2d 110 (Okla. 1988), the state supreme court refused to impose liability for breach of confidentiality on a physician who informed police he had treated a man being sought for rape.

[25]Statement of H. Stuart Knight, Secret Service Director, in 38 Cong. Q. Weekly Rep. 1347 (1980).

[26]Bowen v. American Hosp. Assn., 476 U.S. 610 (1986).

[27]United States v. Westinghouse Elec. Corp., 638 F.2d 570 (3d Cir. 1980); General Motors Corp. v. Director of NIOSH, 636 F.2d 163 (6th Cir. 1980).

generally proved sympathetic.[28] The Internal Revenue Service discovers tax violations through examination of taxpayers' (including health providers') records.[29] In policing Medicare and Medicaid, federal and state government personnel extensively review the patient records of providers.[30]

Prosecutors, usually through grand juries, may seek records to identify suspects; prove intoxication, drug abuse, rape, or child abuse; or attack legal defenses such as insanity. (Their record of success in such efforts is mixed.)[31] Medical examiners investigating suspicious deaths need to inspect the decedent's records and typically may do so under state statute. Criminal defendants sometimes request records as well.[32]

Facilities should release confidential information sought by law enforcement authorities only in response to a valid subpoena or court order. Unless a court specifically directs otherwise, sealed copies of the records should be submitted to the court

---

[28]The following exemplify numerous state and federal decisions upholding government access to medical records for purposes of investigating fraud. In re Search Warrant (Sealed), 810 F.2d 67 (3d Cir. 1987); United States v. Fishman, 726 F.2d 125 (4th Cir. 1983); In re Pebsworth, 705 F.2d 261 (7th Cir. 1983). Among the smaller group of contrary holdings are Doe v. Stephens, 851 F.2d 1457 (D.C. Cir. 1988) and Hawaii Psychiatric Socy. v. Ariyoshi, 481 F. Supp. 1028 (D. Haw. 1979).

[29]United States v. Texas Heart Inst. 755 F.2d 469 (5th Cir. 1985). But see Wisconsin Psychiatric Serv. v. Commissioner, 76 T.C. 839 (1981) (denying IRS access).

[30]A physician "may have hundreds of patients whose records contain the information which we need to make the case against one provider." Statement of Richard Lowe, Inspector-General, Department of Health, Education and Welfare, in Privacy of Medical Records, supra n.4, at 805. See In re Search Warrant (Sealed), 810 F.2d 67 (3d Cir. 1987).

[31]People v. Hawkrigg, 138 Misc. 2d 764, 525 N.Y.S.2d 752 (1988) (suspect judged to have waived right to prevent grand jury access to records); Scull v. Superior Court of the State of Cal., 206 Cal. App. 3d 784, 254 Cal. Rptr. 24 (1988) (district attorney not entitled to names of suspect's former patients).

[32]People v. Boyette, 201 Cal. App. 3d 1527, 247 Cal. Rptr. 795 (1988) (burglary defendant entitled to have court examine medical records of witness to alleged act. Court will determine relevance and weigh defendant's need for disclosure against witness-patient's privacy interest.)

itself, rather than to the party requesting the subpoena. In some circumstances a facility may be legally obligated to protect the patient by moving to quash a subpoena that appears too broad, by notifying the patient so that he may contest it[33] or by refusing to comply without a court order.[34] Service with a search warrant for patient records is far less common but presents similar issues.[35]

Litigation. A person's entitlement to her medical records for litigation purposes is fully recognized by law,[36] even in states without a general right of access for patients. At the same time, by initiating legal action against a health provider, the patient is considered to have waived her right of privacy so that the provider may defend itself.[37] Since, however, it is debatable when and to what extent the waiver occurs, a facility should proceed cautiously in sharing records or information on the assumption of waiver.[38]

A more difficult issue is raised when parties need others' medical records to defend or prosecute a case. Courts are divided on the point. A few permit disclosure because the people concerned (blood donors) are not "patients";[39] others approve

---

[33]California requires a party issuing a subpoena for a physician's medical records to inform the patient before requiring production of the record. Cal. Civ. Proc. Code §1985.3 (West Supp. 1990).

[34]Allen v. Smith, 368 S.E.2d 924 (W. Va. 1988) (physicians may be liable for releasing records on basis of "bare, untested subpoena" rather than court order). See §8.14.5 for a discussion of a covered facility's obligation under federal law to resist subpoenas for records of patients in alcohol and drug abuse treatment programs.

[35]Samaritan Health Serv. v. City of Glendale, 184 Ariz. 394, 714 P.2d 887 (1986) approved the facility's compliance with search warrants.

[36]Emmett v. Eastern Dispensary & Casualty Co., 396 F.2d 931 (D.C. Cir. 1967); Cassidy v. County of Nassau, 84 A.D.2d 742, 443 N.Y.S.2d 742 (1981).

[37]Caesar v. Mountanos, 542 F.2d 1064 (9th Cir. 1976). Rea v. Pardo, 132 A.D.2d 442, 522 N.Y.S.2d 393 (1987).

[38]Nelson v. Lewis, 130 N.H. 106, 534 A.2d 720 (1987); Dalley v. LaGuardia Hosp., 130 A.D.2d 543, 515 N.Y.S.2d 276 (1987).

[39]Belle Bonfils Memorial Blood Center v. Denver Dist. Court, 763 P.2d 1003 (Colo. 1988).

it because another social need—protection of children, for instance—outweighs the medical privacy interest.[40] A number of decisions, including an in-chambers opinion of Justice Brennan,[41] compromise by disclosing the information sought but not the patient's identity.[42] Some courts, though, simply protect the nonlitigant patient's privacy interest.[43]

Research.   The medical community generally recognizes the needs of scientific research as legitimate reasons for breaching confidentiality. The JCAHO states that one purpose of medical records is to "provide data for use in continuing education and in research,"[44] that consent of the patient or the patient's representative is unnecessary when releasing information for "educational purposes and research programs,"[45] and that records should be kept long enough to accommodate research needs.[46] The AHA offers guidance to chief executive officers in approving research requests.[47] Two circuit courts of appeals have authorized release of records to federal agencies for research purposes without the consent of individuals or their employers.[48] To suggestions that they should obtain consent or remove

---

[40]Richard v. Tarzetti, 510 So. 2d 1361 (La. App. 1987).

[41]Reproductive Services, Inc., v. Walker, 439 U.S. 1307 (1978); 439 U.S. 1354 (1978); 439 U.S. 1133 (1979).

[42]Farnsworth v. Proctor & Gamble, 101 F.R.D. 355 (N.D. Ga. 1984), affd. 758 F.2d 1545 (11th Cir. 1985); Deitchman v. E. R. Squibb & Sons, 740 F.2d 556 (7th Cir. 1984).

[43]*Dalley*, 130 A.D.2d 543.

[44]Joint Commission on Accreditation of Healthcare Organizations, Accreditation Manual for Hospitals, MR .1.2.5 (1991) (hereinafter JCAHO Accreditation Manual), at 83.

[45]MR .3.3.1.5, id. at 91. This position seems inconsistent with the Joint Commission's assurance to the patient that his medical record will be "read only by individuals directly involved in his treatment or in the monitoring of its quality." Id. at xii.

[46]MR .4.6, id. at 94.

[47]AHA Guidelines, at 5.

[48]General Motors Corp. v. Director of NIOSH, 636 F.2d 163 (6th Cir. 1980); United States v. Westinghouse Elec. Corp., 638 F.2d 570 (3d Cir. 1980).

identification from records, some researchers reply (1) that personally identifiable information is essential to the research; (2) that patient consent would be impossible to secure in broad, retrospective studies; and (3) that vital medical information has and will continue to emerge from such studies.[49]

There are few sources of legal advice for facilities considering research requests. A facility's attorney will be familiar with the federal regulations applicable to grantees or contractors, which require that research with humans be approved by an institutional review board operating under federal guidelines.[50] In addition, the attorney should consider the confidentiality problem created by the federal Freedom of Information Act (FOIA), under which research may become available to the public. The Supreme Court held that data on 1,000 diabetes patients was not an "agency record" under FOIA and thus need not be released to a requester.[51] Despite the decision, one commentator cautions that, often, promises of confidentiality from federal researchers cannot be kept due to FOIA.[52] In fact, a district court ordered release, under FOIA, of the names and addresses of 30,000 veterans;[53] but the Ninth Circuit Court of Appeals refused

---

[49]Statement of Leon Gordis for the Association of American Medical Colleges and the Society for Epidemiologic Research, in Privacy of Medical Records, at 469, 478-479, 495. Dr. Gordis named as triumphs of nonconsensual research with records studies of the cause of preventable blindness in premature newborns, the benefits of anticoagulants for heart attack patients, the connection between DES and vaginal cancer, the connection between smoking and fetal defects, the harmful effects of oral contraceptives, and the improved survival of leukemic children.

[50]45 C.F.R. §§46.101 through 46.409 (1988).

[51]Forsham v. Harris, 445 U.S. 169 (1980). The decision's premise is that the researchers—university faculty and clinicians—merely reported to rather than were controlled by a federal agency.

[52]O'Reilly, Medical Privacy and Medical Research: Is Government the Problem or the Solution?, 12 U. Dayton L. Rev. 243, 260-265 (1986).

[53]They had identified themselves, after promises of confidentiality, as having suffered atomic exposure. Finding the privacy interest weaker than the public interest, the court did not directly address the problems attendant on the fact that the release would publicly identify each veteran as being at higher risk of a number of serious diseases. National Assn. of Atomic Veterans v. Director, Defense Nuclear Agency, 583 F. Supp. 1483 (D.D.C. 1984).

a request for the names and addresses of all Medicare beneficiaries in a geographic area.[54]

Nor is the problem of compelled disclosure of research data
confined to FOIA; courts sometimes allow parties in litigation
to subpoena researchers and the records that underlie their
published works.[55] Receipt of a subpoena in these circumstances
creates a serious dilemma. Angela R. Holder warns that

> If a researcher violates a subject's confidentiality, even under
> subpoena, the employing institution under whose aegis the
> research was conducted may be vicariously liable to the subject
> [citation omitted]. . . . Because of its own responsibilities, the
> institution itself may wish to intervene on its own behalf if a
> subpoena is served.[56]

In deciding whether to grant a researcher's request for access
to records, a facility must weigh the potential gain from a project
against the possibility of embarrassment or harm to patients and
the legal consequences of such harm for the facility. If a request
is granted, the researcher should certainly be required to give
assurances that the information will remain confidential and
that published results will not identify individuals.[57] At the same
time, facility administrators must recognize that researchers may
not be able to honor such commitments.

Protection of Public Health. The principle that public health
needs preempt individual rights, including that to privacy, is
well-established in American law. A typical formulation appears
in dicta from the Alabama Supreme Court to the effect that a

---

[54]Multnomah County Med. Socy. v. Scott, 825 F.2d 1410 (9th Cir. 1987).

[55]Farnsworth v. Proctor & Gamble, 101 F.R.D. 355 (N.D. Ga. 1984), affd.
758 F.2d 1545 (11th Cir. 1985); Deitchman v. E. R. Squibb & Sons, 740 F.2d
556 (7th Cir. 1984).

[56]Holder, The Biomedical Researcher and Subpoenas: Judicial Protection
of Confidential Medical Data, XII Am. J. Law and Med., 405, 419.

[57]As noted in §8.5.3, concealment of identity is difficult. A subject who
claims her condition was revealed to co-workers by published research findings
filed a $10 million action against the researchers. L. Goodstein, *Doctor Tells
AIDS Trial of "Distress,"* The Washington Post, Jan. 23, 1990, at cols. 4-6.

patient's privacy interest (which the court in this case upheld) could without doubt be "superseded when, for instance, the deleterious or contagious effects of a patient's condition require disclosure to the public health authorities to protect the greater societal interests."[58] The Supreme Court acknowledged in Whalen v. Roe that "disclosures of private medical information to . . . public health agencies are often an essential part of modern medical practice. . . . Requiring such disclosures to representatives of the State having responsibility for the health of the community does not automatically amount to an impermissible invasion of privacy."[59] State statutes often require facilities to report communicable disease to state authorities,[60] who may also be permitted to inspect records and release the information if necessary.[61] Occasionally, federal agencies exercise similar authority.[62] The AMA's position is that "[t]he confidentiality of the doctor-patient relationship is vitally important but not absolute. There must be a judicious balance between the well being of the patient and the protection of the public health."[63]

Protection of Individuals. A related legal principle asserts that in certain circumstances the health or welfare of specific people (including the patient) preempts the patient's privacy interest. This tenet formed the basis of several early decisions[64] but takes its current vitality from the California Supreme Court

---

[58]Mull v. String, 448 So. 2d 952, 955 n.3 (Ala. 1984).

[59]429 U.S. 589, 602 (1977).

[60]Cal [Health & Safety] Code §3125; applied in Derrick v. Ontario Community Hosp., 47 Cal. App. 3d 145, 120 Cal. Rptr. 566 (1975).

[61]N.C. Gen. Stat. §130A-144(b) (1989); N.C. Gen. Stat. §130A-143(8) (1989).

[62]The Food and Drug Administration (FDA) requires that records be kept of all complaints about adverse reactions to receipt of blood or blood products. If the product is considered responsible for the reaction, the record must be sent to the manufacturer or collecting agency. If death follows any complication of blood transfusion, a report must be submitted to the FDA. 21 C.F.R. §606.170 (1989).

[63]American Medical Association, Reference Guide to Policy and Official Statements 5-6 (1988).

[64]E.g., Simonsen v. Swenson, 104 Neb. 224, 177 N.W. 831 (1920).

decision in Tarasoff v. Regents of the University of California.[65] The *Tarasoff* case held that

> a psychiatrist or therapist may have a duty to take whatever steps are reasonably necessary to protect an intended or potential victim of his patient when he determines, or should determine, in the appropriate factual setting and in accordance with the standards of his profession established at trial, that the patient is or may present a probability of danger to that person.[66]

A number of courts have extended *Tarasoff*, suggesting that medical professionals not only may, but must, reveal patients' secrets when necessary to prevent harm to the patient or others; AIDS has kept the issue in the forefront of public, legal, and medical awareness in recent years. The AMA addresses the general subject of warnings in the context of AIDS. Its conclusion is that if others (preferably the patient) do not warn a third party, the HIV-infected person's physician should do so. The AMA correctly notes, however, that that may be forbidden under state law.[67] Before allowing staff to breach confidentiality to protect third parties, facilities must have the advice of counsel familiar with state law on required and permissible procedures.

News Releases. How much, if any, patient information to release publicly is a continuing problem for facilities. The media, representing the public, have a strong interest in prominent individuals and in certain types of patients. Opinion is divided on whether healthcare facilities should indulge this interest. The AHA recommends that disclosure be "limited to name, date of admission, and general condition" and would not release even this if the patient or her representative asked for complete nondisclosure.[68]

Most hospitals (and presumably other facilities that receive numerous requests) do seem to accommodate the news media

---

[65]17 Cal. 3d 425, 551 P.2d 334 (1976).
[66]Id. at 345.
[67]American Medical Association, supra n.63, at 6.
[68]AHA Guidelines, at 4.

to some extent. That facilities choose to do so is somewhat surprising, since the Aspen Hospital Law Manual states that releases to news media are "[p]erhaps the hospital practice most likely to give rise to questions of the invasion of privacy."[69] The manual also correctly notes that there is "no obligation whatsoever" to release information to news media.[70] While some courts have upheld media access when the privacy interest is judged minimal,[71] more decisions seem to deny it.[72]

The common practice of cooperating with the media has its critics. The 1977 Privacy Protection Study Commission concluded that each "patient's desire not to have his admission and general condition known should be respected."[73] The Uniform Health-Care Information Act would at least allow a patient to ask not to have these facts revealed.[74] Broader disclosure, even when unquestionably newsworthy, is still more problematic.[75] The better policy for facilities may be to take the view of the Missouri Supreme Court half a century ago. The court said, "[c]ertainly if there is any right of privacy at all, it should include the right to obtain medical treatment . . . (at least if it is not contagious or dangerous to others) without personal publicity."[76]

Family Access.   Probably the most frequent, but least considered, exception to confidentiality is that made for members

---

[69]Aspen Systems Corporation, Hospital Law Manual 63 (1986).

[70]Id.

[71]Tri-State Publishing Company v. City of Port Jervis, 523 N.Y.S.2d 954 (N.Y. Sup. Ct. 1988); C. L. v. Edson, 409 N.W.2d 417 (Wis. App. 1987).

[72]Globe Newspaper Company v. Chief Medical Examiner, 404 Mass. 132, 533 N.E.2d 1356 (1989); News-Press Publishing Co. v. Kaune, 511 So. 2d 1023 (Fla. App. 1987).

[73]Privacy Protection Study Commission, Personal Privacy in an Information Society 311 (1977).

[74]Uniform Health-Care Information Act §2-104(b)(1), recommended by the National Conference of Commissioners on Uniform State Laws (Chicago 1985). Montana has adopted the act.

[75]A Hastings Center staff member deplored the release by Jackson Pollock's analyst of drawings done as part of therapy. Bermel, The Therapist's Duty—To Patients, Art, or History? 16 Hastings Center Report 2 (Feb. 1986).

[76]Barber v. Time, Inc., 348 Mo. 1199, 1207, 159 S.W.2d 291, 295 (1942).

of the patient's family (or close friends). Because family and friends are often present at the facility, express a desire to be informed and to help, and may be functioning better than the patient, medical personnel usually assume that otherwise confidential information may be shared with them—perhaps on an "implied consent" theory.

In most instances the assumption is reasonable. Still, health professionals in a facility should recognize that sharing information with families represents a judgment and, according to one writer, "the judgment should always be based on the general principle 'Is breaking confidentiality, even with the family, for the patient's interest or destructive to the patient's interest?' "[77] While it may usually be safe to assume family harmony, any evidence that a patient does not want information divulged to his family or other visitors should receive attention, and his instructions should be followed.

C. Healthcare Facility Record-Handling Procedures

§8.7 Creating and Maintaining Records

Each healthcare facility has its own procedures for creating and maintaining records. The arrangements incorporate the administration's formal and informal decisions on contents, who has authority to record data, storage and security measures, internal access, and the process for amendment.

---

[77]Grossman, Confidentiality in Medical Practice, 28 Ann. Rev. of Med. 43, 48 (1977). Disclosures to a patient's spouse that become evidence in divorce or child custody proceedings have been litigated, with mixed results. See, e.g., Allen v. Smith, 368 S.E.2d 924 (W. Va. 1988) and Werner v. Kliewer, 710 P.2d 1250 (Kan. 1985). See also Matter of Wollan (390 N.W.2d 839 (Minn. App. 1986)), where a mental patient's sister inspected his records and used the information to protest his being granted leave. The appellate court upheld the trial court's decision to allow inspection.

What goes into the patient's record and how it is kept are in large part a matter of law, regulation, or accrediting requirements. "Conditions of Participation" for Medicare and Medicaid, state licensing statutes and regulations, and the standards of such organizations as the JCAHO specify what must be included and in what manner. Instructions from these sources are similar, though not identical. Each must be consulted for its details, but in general their criteria address the following aspects of record-keeping:

- identifying the patient;
- obtaining essential information;
- ensuring that qualified people form the conclusions in the record and that the individual responsible for each item is identified;
- separating fact from opinion in the record;
- gathering scattered data in one location;
- recording events soon after their occurrence;
- ensuring that information is recorded accurately and legibly;
- ensuring that the record is handled by competent, authorized staff;
- indexing to maximize the record's utility;
- keeping the record safe but available for quick retrieval;
- releasing the record only with patient consent or other legal authorization.

§8.7.1 Record Entries

The record must contain at minimum all information necessary to comply with state or federal law; for most facilities the contents must also satisfy accrediting bodies. (See §8.2.1 for JCAHO requirements on the contents of hospital records.) In addition, the facility will probably collect information for its own purposes (see §8.1). Attention must also be paid to the possible effects of omissions from records; on occasion these can be as legally significant as entries.[1]

The facility must decide and specify which staff members and employees will enter information in records. The matter deserves careful consideration, and a facility's requirements should be incorporated in formal policy.[2] In general, diagnoses, orders, treatment descriptions, and other significant information should be recorded by the person legally and actually responsible for them. If an action is performed by a person who practices under supervision, her record entries should be signed by her and her supervisor. If an action is recorded by someone other than the person who performed it, both should sign the entry. Timeliness, legibility, and accuracy of entries are crucial—to keep the record useful in treatment, to meet accrediting and reimbursement agencies'[3] requirements, and to ensure that the record is an authoritative defense of malpractice claims.

§8.7.2 Storage

The primary goal in developing a storage plan is security, with accessibility for authorized people next in importance.[4] An

---

§8.7 [1]In Collins v. Westlake Community Hosp., 57 Ill.2d 388, 312 N.E.2d 614 (1974) liability depended on whether nurses had observed a patient during a period for which no entries appeared in the record. There was testimony that the nurses' practice was to record only abnormal findings and the trial court directed a verdict for the hospital despite a jury verdict for the plaintiff. On appeal, the court reversed, finding that the jury might have appropriately concluded that the patient had not been checked.

[2]JCAHO hospital standards require this. Joint Commission on Accreditation of Healthcare Organizations, Accreditation Manual for Hospitals MR 3.5.1, at 91 (1991).

[3]For example, the Medicare Conditions of Participation for hospitals require that records be completed no later than 30 days after discharge. 42 C.F.R. §482.24(c)(2)(viii) (1988).

[4]The Medicare Condition of Participation on medical recordkeeping in skilled nursing facilities is standard. It states, "The facility safeguards medical record information against loss, destruction, or unauthorized use." 42 C.F.R. §405.1132(b) (1988).

original record should not leave the facility's premises unless subpoenaed by a court that will not accept copies. If possible, a facility employee should be present when a record is read or copied by someone not affiliated with the facility. Security procedures differ but are no less important in a computerized record system. Passwords for computer access should be required and changed frequently. Under any system, the facility will want to arrange for training and periodically retraining employees and staff in the importance of treating records carefully and preserving confidentiality. For storage, as for all aspects of medical record-keeping, a facility must satisfy the specific requirements of federal programs, state licensure, and accrediting agencies.[5]

§8.7.3 Internal Access

A facility's policy on internal access to records has a significant effect on their physical security and confidentiality. Since there is little regulation of this area, the facility may designate which individuals and categories of people affiliated with the institution have access. Rarely, questions about the appropriateness of access reach the courts; when they do, the right of employees or other affiliated groups to inspect records is usually vindicated.[6] A state supreme court, in one of the few decisions on this point, described the standard thus:

> While a patient may legitimately expect that confidential information will not be disclosed . . . to hospital personnel unconcerned with his treatment, his expectation of privacy does not

---

[5]For example, under the Conditions of Participation for Medicare hospitals must be able to retrieve records both by diagnosis and medical procedure performed, 42 C.F.R. §482.24(b)(2) (1988); skilled nursing facilities need only index by diagnosis, 42 C.F.R. §405.1132(g) (1988).

[6]Hyman v. Jewish Chronic Disease Hosp., 15 N.Y.2d 317, 206 N.E.2d 338 (1965) (hospital board of directors entitled to review charts (perhaps with names deleted)); Knecht v. Vandalia Medical Center, 14 Ohio App. 3d 129, 470 N.E.2d 230 (1984); Group Health Plan v. Lopez, 341 N.W.2d 294 (Minn. 1983).

extend to hospital administrators or employees who need the information in order to facilitate the patient's treatment or properly administer the hospital in accordance with approved standards.[7]

In establishing guidelines, the facility may wish to consider such issues as whether a staff physician may consult any record for guidance in treating his own patients or show his patients' records to other doctors for their advice.[8] AHA guidelines specifically recognize the access right of the governing board and chief executive officer and recommend that others' access depend on the person's authority and responsibility, reason for request, and the kind of information at issue.[9]

§8.7.4 Amendment

The basic principle in amending records is simple and universally agreed to: never amend a record so that the original entry is obliterated. As applied to paper records, this usually means striking a single line through the erroneous entry and inserting or attaching the new information along with the date and the name or initials of the person making the correction. To accomplish the same purpose, a computerized record system must allow transfer of records at frequent intervals to files that are no longer accessible to any but the few individuals authorized to amend. The program for amendment should be designed to record all alterations along with the date made, the code of the person amending the record, and the original entry.

An obvious corollary of the principle is that no amendment should occur after the facility has notice that litigation is planned

---

[7]State v. Smith, 298 N.C. 115, 132, 257 S.E.2d 399, 408 (1979).

[8]Privacy of Medical Records: Hearings on H.R. No. 2979 and H.R. No. 3444 Before the Govt. Information and Individual Rights Subcomm. of the House Comm. on Govt. Operations, 96th Cong., 1st Sess. 43. The House Subcommittee answered these questions in the affirmative.

[9]American Hospital Association, Institutional Policies for Disclosure of Medical Records Information 6-7 (1979).

or that the record or underlying event is in any way disputed. To do so can create a perception of bad faith on the part of the facility.[10]

Occasionally, a patient objects to information in her record and asks that it be modified or eliminated. The 1979 House subcommittee investigating medical records heard several accounts of patients threatened by inaccuracies.[11] At least one court has granted a patient the right to have false factual assertions deleted.[12] In that case the Veterans Administration had added the patient's corrective statements to his record at his request but had refused to delete even information that had been proved false. Before establishing its procedure for considering requests to amend records, a facility might consult the AHA guidelines. They recommend notifying the responsible physician of the request, notifying the patient of the action taken, and establishing a body to review denials of such requests.[13]

§8.8 Retention Periods

It is not possible to give a definitive answer to the question of how long medical records should be kept. The JCAHO does not attempt it, saying simply, "[t]he length of time medical records are to be retained is dependent on the need for their use in continuing patient care and for legal, research, or educational purposes."[1] The "Conditions of Participation" for hospitals require that records be kept for at least five years,[2] and Medicare

---

[10]For allowable inferences from a facility's delay in producing or failure to produce records in contemplation of litigation, see Thor v. Boska, 38 Cal. App. 3d 558, 113 Cal. Rptr. 296 (1974) and Wickliffe v. Sunrise Hosp., 766 P.2d 1322 (Nev. 1988).

[11]Privacy of Medical Records, supra n.8, at 625, 644, 964.

[12]R. R. v. United States Dept. of the Army, 482 F. Supp. 770 (D.D.C. 1980).

[13]AHA Guidelines, supra n.9, at 6-7.

§8.8 [1]Joint Commission on Accreditation of Healthcare Organizations, Accreditation Manual for Hospitals 94 (1991).

[2]42 C.F.R. §482.24(b)(1) (1988).

guidelines require that discharge summaries, clinical records, and other medical records relating to health insurance claims be kept "for a period of five years after the month the cost report to which the materials apply is filed with the intermediary."[3]

A 1975 bulletin jointly issued by the AHA and the American Medical Record Association (AMRA) states that most purposes for which records are kept can be satisfied by ten years' retention of the whole record. The associations suggest, though, that "basic information" be kept permanently. Basic information includes dates of admission and discharge, names of physicians, diagnoses, records of operations and surgical procedures, pathology reports, and discharge summaries. Records of legally incompetent patients (minors and the mentally disabled) should be kept until the end of the disability period (for minors, age 18 plus the statute of limitations). Finally, the bulletin recommends keeping records longer if requested by the patient, the physician, or anyone with a legal interest in the record.[4]

A facility's attorney should determine whether state law requires that records be kept for a specific period. Alaska, for example, requires retention for seven years after discharge or two years after the patient turns 19, whichever is later.[5] Texas cites 10 years from the date of last treatment (or until a minor's 20th birthday if later) and adds an admonition not to destroy records pertaining to any unresolved matter in litigation.[6] Wisconsin's administrative code specifies "at least 5 years."[7] In addition, the attorney must consider the statutes of limitations in the state for malpractice, corporate negligence, and other causes of action possibly relevant to the facility's operation.

No recommendation, however, can remove all uncertainty. One source speaks of balancing "the foreseeable need for information versus the potential harm that can result from

---

[3] 2 Medicare & Medicaid Guide (CCH) §2304 6420.85 (1988).

[4] American Hospital Association, Technical Advisory Bulletin: Preservation of Medical Records in Health Care Institutions (1975).

[5] Alaska Stat. §18.20.085 (1987).

[6] Tex. Health & Safety Code Ann. §241.103 (Vernon 1990).

[7] Wis. Admin. Code HHS §124.14(2)(c) (1988).

disseminating obsolete data."[8] And, of course, medical needs are not always foreseeable. The discovery that asbestos is a carcinogen, for example, led to a request that the Occupational Safety and Health Administration (OSHA) order employers to keep medical records for the duration of a person's employment plus 40 years.[9] Thyroid irradiation and the effects of diethylstilbestrol on the fetus are other examples of records' being needed for therapeutic reasons many years after their normal usefulness. Nor can legal needs always be foreseen. A facility may comply with its state's statutes of limitation but find itself sued in another state and subjected to a more generous statute of limitations there.[10] Records could then be needed for a considerably longer period.

While several cases serve as reminders that loss of records

---

[8]J. Bruce, Privacy and Confidentiality of Health Care Information 12 (1984).

[9]Spokesman for Public Citizens' Health Research Group, testifying before OSHA Board, March 30, 1979, in Privacy of Medical Records: Hearings on H.R. No. 2979 and H.R. No. 3444 Before the Govt. Information and Individual Rights Subcomm. of the House Comm. on Govt. Operations, 96th Cong., 1st Sess. 883-885.

[10]It would be imprudent for facilities to assume they are answerable only under the laws of their jurisdictions. Many facilities treat nonresidents. Those that do incur at least a slight risk of being sued in the patient's home state with the court applying the law of the state. In Rosenthal v. Warren (475 F.2d 438, cert. denied, 414 U.S. 856 (1973)), the Second Circuit allowed New York to apply its law in a malpractice action brought by a New York resident against a Massachusetts hospital and physician. That was justified, the court said, because the hospital was a national institution in terms of patients, staff, reputation, and efforts to obtain out-of-state contributions. 475 F.2d at 446. The hospital could therefore be held accountable for its actions in any state with a significant interest in its activities. A Louisiana resident has been allowed to file suit there against his Texas physicians and hospital. Gurvich v. Tyree, 694 S.W.2d 39 (Tex. App. 1985). In the 1980s the United States Supreme Court alternately expanded and contracted its requirement of the "minimum contacts" required between defendants and the state in which they are sued before suit will be allowed. Worldwide Volkswagen Corp. v. Woodson, 444 U.S. 286 (1980); Burger King Corp. v. Rudzewicz, 471 U.S. 462 (1985); Asahi Metal Industry Co. v. Superior Court of California, Solano County, 480 U.S. 102 (1987).

will seriously hurt the defense in malpractice litigation,[11] there is no indication that scheduled destruction after a reasonable period of time would be prejudicial. To the contrary, limiting the growth of archives by an orderly process would seem to be competent management. The difficulty will be in defining "reasonable" and "orderly."

§8.9 Releasing Records with Consent

Before releasing records at a patient's request, a healthcare facility must settle several issues concerning the patient's waiver of confidentiality. These include the validity, voluntariness, scope, and time limits of the consent to release information. Minors' records raise additional problems.

§8.9.1 Ascertaining the Authenticity of the Request

Facilities must be concerned with whether a purported request for release of information is authentic. To that end, nearly all would refuse to honor a request that was not in writing and signed by the patient. The JCAHO requires a patient's written consent,[1] and in one case a court severely rebuked psychotherapists for relying on oral consent. The court refused to recognize

---

[11]Carr v. St. Paul Fire & Marine Ins. Co., 384 F. Supp. 821 (W.D. Ark. 1974) (jury may infer that destroyed record would show hospital acted improperly); Thor v. Baska, 38 Cal. App. 3d 558, 113 Cal. Rptr. 296 (1974) (plaintiff entitled to instruction that doctor's loss of original records supports her claim); Public Health Trust of Dade County v. Valcin, 507 So. 2d 596 (Fla. 1987) (hospital negligent not to create and preserve records); Fox v. Cohen, 84 Ill. App. 3d 744, 406 N.E.2d 178 (1980) (cause of action stated, though premature, by allegation that hospital lost, misplaced, or destroyed EKG); but in Hyrniak v. Nathan Littauer Hosp. Assn., 86 A.D.2d 699, 446 N.Y.S.2d 558 (1982), the court dismissed plaintiff's claim against a hospital that could not locate her three-year-old x-rays. The court found no duty to preserve the x-rays and no evidence that she was damaged by the loss.

§8.9 [1]Joint Commission on Accreditation of Healthcare Organizations, Accreditation Manual for Hospitals 90 (1991).

such consent as a defense to breach of confidentiality.[2] Facilities' refusals to release information when they doubt the authenticity of the requests have been upheld.[3]

§8.9.2 The Scope of the Request

Exactly what the patient wants released and to whom can be difficult to communicate, and misunderstandings are occasionally litigated.[4] Commentators disagree on whether it is appropriate to allow—much less to ask—patients to sign "blanket" releases. Behind that issue is the question of whether patients are likely to realize what is (or may later appear) in their records. The AMRA advises against honoring requests to release "any and all information."[5] The 1977 Privacy Protection Study Commission urged that "disclosure . . . be strictly limited to the particular information needed for the user's particular stated purposes" and that the entire record never be sent; rather, a completed claim form or abstract should be returned to the requester.[6] Yet despite similar arguments from the American Civil Liberties Union[7]

---

[2]Doe v. Roe, 93 Misc. 2d 201, 400 N.Y.S.2d 668 (1977). The fact that the consent was extracted from a psychoanalytic patient by the therapist was probably as important as the fact that it was oral. Moreover, the patient had tried to withdraw the consent.

[3]Young v. Madison Gen. Hosp., 337 So. 2d 931 (Miss. 1976); Thurman v. Crawford, 652 S.W.2d 240 (Mo. Ct. App. 1983).

[4]A woman who authorized filming of her Caesarean "for medical societies and in the interests of science" sued over its exhibition in theaters. Feeney v. Young, 191 A.D. 501, 181 N.Y.S. 481 (1920); another who agreed to display of her photographs to others considering plastic surgery sued when the pictures appeared on television and in department stores. Vassiliades v. Garfinckel's, Brooks Bros., 492 A.2d 580 (D.C. 1985).

[5]Privacy of Medical Records: Hearing on H.R. No. 2979 and H.R. No. 3444 Before the Govt. Information and Individual Rights Subcomm. of the House Comm. on Govt. Operations, 96th Cong., 1st Sess. 309.

[6]Privacy Protection Study Commission, Personal Privacy in an Information Society 312-313 (1977).

[7]John Shattuck, of the New York Civil Liberties Union, attributed many

and the American Psychiatric Association[8] during hearings, the 1979 Subcommittee on Records did not, in the end, propose eliminating blanket consents. The Subcommittee concluded that some patients indeed want all information released—when changing providers, for instance.

Consent forms should specify to what person or entity information is to be given. A facility employee should help patients comprehend the scope of their consent if there is reason to believe they do not. For example, some employers contract with firms that audit employees' use of medical insurance benefits. The firms, acting as agents of the employer or its insurer, request information from facilities not only after but during the patient's stay, to determine the patient's condition and whether charges will be reimbursed. It is debatable whether the patient-employee's customary waiver in favor of his insurer is sufficient to cover this relatively new type of release. Such questions are best resolved by the facility's informing patients of the kinds of requests they may not anticipate.

§8.9.3 Time Limitations

A frequent question is how long a consent to release of records is valid. There is almost no law on this point in the United States, and recommendations vary widely. The Privacy Protection Study Commission suggested a "reasonable time not to exceed one year,"[9] while the 1979 Subcommittee decided not to propose legislation on the issue. The statute proposed by the National Conference of Commissioners on Uniform State Laws[10] has

---

problems with breach of confidentiality to the pro forma nature of releases. "Such 'consent' is not informed, because patients do not know what is in their own records or what the insurer will do with the records, and it is not freely given, because there is no effective choice." Privacy of Medical Records, supra n.5, at 585-586.

[8]Id. at 397-398, 407.

[9]Privacy Protection Study Commission, supra n.6, at 315.

[10]See Uniform Health-Care Information Act, recommended by the National Conference of Commissioners on Uniform State Laws (Chicago 1985).

consent expire after six months if no time is specified. Under the proposed act it is permissible for releases to specify expiration dates of up to 30 months after execution. The uniform law also allows prospective consent; that is, the patient could authorize release of records of care received six months after the date consent was given, and longer for a waiver in favor of third-party payors. The AMRA, on the other hand, has expressed disapproval of prospective consent.[11] Each facility in its own discretion establishes policy on time limitations for honoring consent to release records.

§8.9.4 Voluntariness

It is sometimes debated whether voluntariness is a meaningful concept in the context of release of medical information. Both the American Civil Liberties Union and the Privacy Protection Study Commission think not. Even a textbook on medical records accepts the premise that patient waiver is frequently not voluntary.[12] If that observation is accurate, it still does not follow that consent need not be sought. As the Study Commission noted, "This is not to say that authorization procedures are useless; to the contrary, they are essential instruments of control over the content and subsequent use of what is disclosed."[13] Although recognizing that patients' choices about waiver of confidentiality are increasingly limited, a facility should continue its efforts to inform them of the scope of the waiver and its possible significance, so that they may exercise whatever choice is still available.

---

[11]Statement of Jane Rogers for the AMRA, in Privacy of Medical Records, supra n.5, at 308.

[12]J. Bruce, Privacy and Confidentiality of Health Care Information, American Hospital Association 63-64 (1984). Bruce concludes that pursuing the issue of voluntariness with individual patients would be "inadvisable" and "unrealistic."

[13]Privacy Protection Study Commission, supra n.6, at 291.

§8.9.5 Minors' Records

It is usually assumed that whoever consents to treatment has authority to waive confidentiality regarding the treatment. Thus, a minor would control access to records of treatment to which she alone consented. The parent, guardian, or other consenting party would control records of treatment to which they consented on the minor's behalf. In the absence of specific law on the subject, these assumptions are reasonable.

Nevertheless, certain situations present special problems. When one parent disputes the other's rights of access to records, for instance, the healthcare facility should consider requiring presentation of a custody order and, unless it clarifies the respective rights, might be well advised to await a court order before complying with a request for access.[14] If consent to treatment was obtained from both parent and child, as is usually recommended in the treatment of older minors, consent to disclosure should also be secured from both (if possible). The American Academy of Pediatrics has recommended that both parents and children be offered opportunities to review and expunge records, pointing out that children's records could trouble them for a lifetime by conveying information that is both detrimental and no longer medically relevant.[15]

D. Liability Concerns

§8.10 Defense of Negligence Claims

As stated above, complete, contemporaneous documentation of adequate care is the best defense available to a healthcare facility

---

[14]State law may settle the point. E.g., N.C. Gen. Stat. §50-13.2(b) (1987) reads in part, "Absent an order of the court to the contrary, each parent shall have equal access to the records of the minor child involving the health, education, and welfare of the child."

[15]Statement of Adele Hofmann, in Privacy of Medical Records, supra n.5, at 964-970.

facing a negligence claim from a former patient. Records are even more valuable for an institutional than for an individual provider, because the institution has no personal memory of events from which to testify. If a patient has access to his records, their condition can influence his decision to sue and may also incline parties to settle, which would prevent or at least shorten litigation. The 1973 Secretary's Commission on Medical Malpractice found that "the unavailability of medical records without resort to litigation creates needless expense and increases the incidence of malpractice litigation."[1]

While a facility usually benefits from keeping good records of care and sharing them with the patient at his request, its position in litigation can be adversely affected by patient access to peer review records (see §8.2.3 above) or incident reports (see §5.8). The facility should seek legal advice on how to prevent required disclosure of these records.

§8.11 Failing to Keep or Mishandling Records

Practitioners' duty to keep records, the violation of which can result in such severe sanctions as termination of staff privileges or license to practice, was discussed in §8.1.1. Healthcare facilities may have a separate duty of the same kind. Several, though not all, courts asked to consider the facility's failure to maintain records have found a breach of duty.[1]

Healthcare facilities are clearly responsible for establishing procedures adequate to process the information that staff physicians and employees produce. Delays in conveying diagnoses or medical orders constitute obvious examples of malpractice. In one instance, a hospital was found liable for failure to notify

---

§8.10 [1]Department of Health, Education, and Welfare, Report of the Secretary's Commission on Medical Malpractice 75 (DHEW Pub. No.(OS) 73-88) (1973).

§8.11 [1]Thomas v. United States, 660 F. Supp. 216 (D.D.C. 1987); Mays v. United States, 608 F. Supp. 1476 (D. Colo. 1985), reversed on other grounds, 806 F.2d 976 (1986), cert. denied, 482 U.S. 913 (1987); but see Bost v. Riley, 44 N.C. App. 638, 262 S.E.2d 391 (1980).

the patient for almost a year that her x-ray indicated a malignancy. The evidence tended to show that the facility did not forward its radiologist's report to the patient's doctor. The patient was awarded a large sum.[2]

§8.12 Refusal to Disclose or Improper Disclosure

The extent of patients' right of access to their records is still unsettled in most jurisdictions. If a patient's request for access fails, she will usually succeed by means of the discovery process of civil litigation. What is less certain, however, is whether denial of access by the facility could be considered a compensable wrong. At least two decisions find that it may be.[1]

More than a dozen reported decisions hold that a healthcare provider is or may be liable for improper disclosure of medical information, that is, disclosure to which the patient objects. Most successful claims rest on one or more of these grounds: invasion of privacy,[2] breach of a professional duty to maintain confidentiality,[3] defamation,[4] or breach of contract.[5] Breach of a statutory duty might also be claimed, as in one early New York case.[6] In one instance, recovery was held to be possible on the basis of

---

[2]Washington Healthcare Corp. v. Barrow, 531 A.2d 226 (D.C. App. 1987); see also Byerly v. Madsen, 704 P.2d 1236 (Wash. App. 1985) and Keene v. Methodist Hosp., 324 F. Supp. 233 (N.D. Ind. 1971).

§8.12 [1]Laubach v. Franklin Square Hosp., 556 A.2d 682 (Md. App. 1989); Pierce v. Penman, 357 Pa. Super. 225, 515 A.2d 948 (1986) (defendants were physicians, not a facility).

[2]E.g., Horne v. Patton, 291 Ala. 701, 287 So. 2d 824 (1974) and Bazemore v. Savannah Hosp., 171 Ga. 257, 155 S.E. 194 (1930).

[3]Alberts v. Devine, 395 Mass. 59, 479 N.E.2d 113 (1985), cert. denied, 474 U.S. 1013 (1985).

[4]Berry v. Moench, 8 Utah 2d 191, 331 P.2d 814 (1958).

[5]Breach of contract is cited in several cases but apparently has not been the sole ground for recovery in any decision. It usually appears in tandem with breach of confidentiality, as in Alberts v. Devine, supra n.3.

[6]Griffin v. Medical Socy. of N.Y., 7 Misc. 2d 549, 11 N.Y.S.2d 109 (1939).

intentional infliction of emotional distress.[7] Finally, it is occasionally asserted that unjustified disclosure constitutes malpractice,[8] a claim closely related to that of breach of a professional duty to maintain confidentiality.

E. Federal Law Governing Alcohol and Drug Abuse Records*

§8.13 Application of the Law

In 1974 Congress enacted two laws governing records of persons receiving treatment for alcohol or drug abuse.[1] These statutes and the implementing regulations[2] seek to encourage people to seek treatment for drug and alcohol abuse by assuring them that neither the fact that they are in treatment nor any information they reveal to healthcare providers will be disclosed except in extraordinary circumstances. This federal law controls over state laws or regulations dealing with records created and maintained during treatment for alcohol or substance abuse to the extent the state laws would allow disclosure prohibited by the federal law.[3]

§8.13.1 Coverage of a Facility's Program

The federal law applies to records of the identity, diagnosis, or treatment of a patient maintained by a federally assisted drug or

---

[7]Chuy v. Philadelphia Eagles Football Club, 595 F.2d 1265 (3d Cir. 1979).

[8]See the concurring opinion in MacDonald v. Clinger, 84 A.D.2d 482, 446 N.Y.S.2d 801 (1982).

§8.13 *Part E of this chapter was written by Joan G. Brannon.

[1]Drug Abuse Prevention, Treatment, and Rehabilitation Act, 42 U.S.C.A. §290ee-3 (1985); Comprehensive Alcohol Abuse and Alcoholism Prevention, Treatment, and Rehabilitation Act, id. §290dd-3 (1985).

[2]42 C.F.R. §2.1 et seq. (1987).

[3]Id. §2.20.

alcohol program. A program is federally assisted if it is carried out under a license or other authorization granted by the United States, (e.g., certification of provider status under the Medicare program); is supported either directly or indirectly by federal funds; or has tax-exempt status. Although "program" is broadly defined as a person who provides alcohol or drug abuse diagnosis, treatment, or referral for treatment, the regulations are limited in their application to general care facilities. A general care facility is *not* a program unless it has an identified unit that provides alcohol or drug abuse diagnosis, treatment, or referral for treatment or it has staff whose primary function is to provide substance abuse services and who are identified as substance abuse providers. Thus, a general hospital that has no separate ward for or special staff identified as treating substance abusers is not covered by the federal law, even though it might diagnose and treat substance abusers (along with others) in its emergency room or on its medical floor.[4] On the other hand, if a provider is operating a drug clinic or is a hospital with a ward for substance abusers *and* it is exempt from federal taxation, receives federal grant money for its substance abuse program, or is licensed by the federal government, then the records of all patients being treated for alcohol or drug abuse are covered. The regulations cover programs, not patients. If a program is covered, then records on all its patients are covered. If a program is not covered, then records of its patients, even if they indicate alcohol or drug abuse diagnosis or treatment, are not covered.[5]

---

[4]See 52 F.R. 21797 (June 9, 1987). But see United States v. Eide, 875 F.2d 1429 (9th Cir. 1989).

[5]The first set of regulations, issued in 1975, were broader and covered patients who received federal assistance even if the program did not receive assistance. See 40 F.R. 27806; 42 C.F.R. §2.12-1 and Opinion 77-28 (Nov. 22, 1977) to Ms. Crisp, East Tennessee Baptist Hospital, in Legal Opinions on the Confidentiality of Alcohol and Drug Abuse Patients' Records 1975-1978, at 187 (United States Dept. of Health and Human Services) (hereinafter Legal Opinions).

§8.13.2 The Effects of Coverage

If the program is covered, then all records that would identify a patient as an alcohol or drug abuser are covered by the federal law. "Records" are defined as any information relating to a patient, whether recorded or not, received or acquired by a federally assisted alcohol or drug program. In State v. Magnuson,[6] the court said that one critical criterion is whether the information contained in the record was acquired in connection with the performance of an alcohol or drug abuse treatment function.[7]

In *Magnuson*, a defendant in a criminal trial for driving while under the influence of liquor was trying to have his conviction stricken on the ground that the information leading to his arrest was gained by the improper release of alcohol abuse treatment records.[8] The facts were as follows: The defendant's friend called the Alcoholics Anonymous 24-hour telephone number and told the person who answered that the defendant was drunk and was driving a blue Ford Bronco. The person who answered the AA telephone was the director of a treatment program for alcohol abuse, and the defendant was a patient in the program (a fact the friend who called did not know). The program director immediately called the sheriff, informing him that the defendant was seen driving while impaired and telling

---

[6] 210 Mont. 401, 682 P.2d 1365.

[7] The definition of "records" was slightly different in the original regulations.

[8] Most courts have held that, even though evidence for a criminal trial may have been obtained in violation of the confidentiality statutes, the remedy under those statutes is not suppression of the evidence, particularly when "records" are not released. United States v. Johnson, 810 F.2d 841 (8th Cir. 1987); Armenta v. Superior Court of Santa Barbara County, 61 Cal. App. 3d 584, 132 Cal. Rptr. 586 (1976); State v. Brown, 376 N.W.2d 451 (Minn. App. 1985); State v. Magnuson, 210 Mont. 401, 682 P.2d 1365 (1984); State v. Bethea, 35 N.C. App. 512, 241 S.E.2d 869 (1978). But see State v. Eide, 875 F.2d 1429 (9th Cir. 1989). Although the commentary to the 1987 rules makes no mention of any change regarding admissibility of evidence, the regulations themselves seem to provide that any information obtained in violation of the law must be suppressed at a criminal trial. 42 C.F.R. §2.12(d).

him where the defendant could probably be found. The court held that the information given to the sheriff was not a record under the confidentiality laws and regulations since the program director was not acting as a provider of treatment to the defendant when he took the telephone call from the friend. And in State v. Brown,[9] the court held that a counselor's direct personal observations are not a record, even if reduced to writing.

Under the federal law, no information may be released unless a specific provision authorizes the release. The law prohibits *any* disclosure about patients, including whether they are attending treatment programs, their physical location, and their status as patients. Any request for disclosure that may not legally be honored must be met with a noncommittal response. The Department of Health and Human Services attorneys' opinions suggest the following possible responses: "Federal regulations prohibit this treatment program from disclosing any information about a patient unless a court order authorizes such disclosure"; "Our program may not disclose information in violation of federal statutes, under 42 U.S.C. 290ee-3 or 42 U.S.C. 290dd-3 and regulations, 42 C.F.R. §2.1 et seq";[10] or "Federal law prohibits this hospital from informing you whether a particular person is or is not a patient." Nevertheless, the regulations allow a program to state that a particular individual is not and has never been a patient.[11]

The federal law's specificity about nondisclosure raises two often-asked questions. First, What must the program do if relatives or friends of the patient telephone or come to see him? Without the patient's consent, a noncommittal response must be given. (However, programs may ask the patient on admission to consent to disclosure of his presence to specific family members and friends.) Second, How should a facility respond if a law

---

[9] 376 N.W.2d 451 (Minn. App. 1985). See also State v. White, 169 Conn. 223, 363 A.2d 143 (1975).

[10] Opinion 77-22 (Oct. 3, 1977) and Opinion 77-29 (Dec. 8, 1977) to Mr. Bybee, Office of the Attorney General, Columbia, S.C., in Legal Opinions, supra n.5, at 165, 190.

[11] 42 C.F.R. §2.13(b)(2).

enforcement officer comes to the premises of a covered facility with an arrest warrant for a person the officer believes is a patient? In the Department of Health and Human Services' view, an arrest warrant does not constitute an authorizing court order for purposes of release of information under the regulations.[12] Thus, a program staff member must give a noncommittal response to a police officer's request for assistance in making an arrest unless the officer has, in addition to the warrant, a court order issued after a hearing.[13]

§8.13.3 Penalties

Violation of the federal laws or regulations is a crime punishable by a fine of not more than $500 for the first offense and not more than $5,000 for each subsequent offense.[14] It appears unlikely, however, that the Department of Justice will prosecute a violation of the statute, since no reported cases of prosecution can be found. Two civil actions have been filed against treatment programs on the ground that they violated the confidentiality

---

[12]Opinion of Department of Health and Human Services to Duncan M. Shrout (Dec. 1, 1982); Opinion 78-2(A) (Jan. 26, 1978) to Mr. Westergren, Legal Opinions, supra n.5, at 7.

[13]See the discussion on access by court order in §8.14.5. Although a program staff member would be prohibited from disclosing patient information, the regulations do not require the staff member to resist forcibly execution of an arrest warrant. The law enforcement officer may enter the facility and search for the person. As long as the law enforcement officer removes no patient records, he is not in violation of the regulations. Opinion of Department of Health and Human Services to Duncan M. Shrout, id.

[14]In Town of Huntington v. New York State Drug Abuse Control Commn., 84 Misc. 2d 138, 373 N.Y.S.2d 728 (Sup. Ct. 1975), the court held that the town of Huntington had standing to assert the rights of drug abuse program participants to anonymity when it sought an injunction to challenge the propriety of certain forms that the town refused to compile on individuals participating in the city's drug abuse program. Though town officials were being threatened with a cut-off of state and local funds if they refused to file the forms, they objected on the grounds that filing would subject them to criminal prosecution for disclosure of confidential records.

statutes and regulations. In both of those cases, the court held that there is no private right of action under the federal laws; the sole remedy under federal law is punishment for a crime.[15]

§8.14 Access to Records in Covered Programs

If the federal laws and regulations apply to a facility's program, they will determine most, though not all, of the confidentiality issues involving records of people enrolled in the program. Under the law, certain specified disclosures may be made without violating confidentiality. Some matters, such as patient access to records, are referred to state law. Among the issues the federal law addresses are: what information may be released with and without a patient's consent; how to handle records of minor and incompetent patients; the proper response to court orders seeking information; and the reporting of patients as suspected perpetrators or victims of child abuse and neglect.

§8.14.1 The Patient's Access

The federal regulations do not require that the patient be given access to her records; they merely provide that the regulations may not prohibit a program from giving a patient access.[1] Because the federal law does not answer the question, healthcare providers should look to state law to determine whether the patient has a right of access to her records. If state law does not speak to the issue, providers are free to determine their own access policy.[2]

§8.14.2 Disclosure Without the Patient's Consent

The regulations list three instances in which a covered program may release records without the patient's consent. First, it may

---

[15]Logan v. District of Columbia, 447 F. Supp. 1328 (D.D.C. 1978); Dixon v. United States, No. 79 Civ. 5467 (S.D.N.Y. 1981).
   §8.14 [1]42 C.F.R. §2.23.
   [2]See the discussion on patient's access to his or her records in §8.4.

release information to medical personnel to the extent necessary to meet bona fide medical emergencies.[3] For example, if a known diabetic being treated for alcohol abuse suffers a seizure and is taken to a hospital emergency room, the program that is treating him may tell the emergency room physician that the patient is a diabetic and an alcohol abuser, since that information would be important in treating him for the seizure. Second, the provider may release information to persons who are conducting research.[4] And, third, it may release information to persons conducting an evaluation or audit of the treatment program.[5]

§8.14.3 Release with the Patient's Consent

If a patient gives written consent, the provider may disclose records in accordance with the consent.[6] There are some special rules about release to the patient's probation or parole officer. The program may release information to these parties or to a court official when participation in treatment is made a condition of probation, parole, pretrial release, or sentence. Note that the patient must give written consent to release of this information, but that the consent could be given when the patient is placed on probation or parole or is sentenced.[7]

---

[3] 42 C.F.R. §2.51.

[4] Id. §2.52.

[5] Id. §2.53.

[6] Under the regulations issued in 1975, the law did not allow unlimited release when the patient consented. Those regulations listed certain circumstances under which the provider could release records if the patient had given written consent, such as releasing only information that would be reasonably necessary for evaluation and payment of the claim to third party payors or disclosing information to employers only if the information would be used to help the patient and not deny him or her employment. 42 C.F.R. §§2.37, 2.38 (1985); 40 F.R. 27813, §§2.37, 2.38. The regulations that took effect in 1987 removed all restrictions on release when the patient gives proper written consent.

[7] In United States v. Hopper, 440 F. Supp. 1208 (N.D. Ill. 1977), the federal court in a probation violation proceeding emphasized the court's continuing jurisdiction over a probationer and said the failure expressly to

§8.14.4 Records of Minors and Incompetent Persons

If state law requires parental consent for a minor's substance abuse treatment, the federal regulations provide that the minor and her parent both must consent to release of the minor's records. In those states, if a minor seeks treatment but will not give consent to notify her parents, the program may notify the parents of the application only if the minor lacks capacity to decide on consent *and* the minor's condition poses a serious threat to her own health or to any other person.[8]

If, under the particular state's law, the minor may consent to her own treatment, then only she need consent to disclosure. And if state law authorizes the minor to consent to treatment, a provider of drug or alcohol abuse services to the minor may not inquire about the parents' financial responsibility or bill the parents without the minor's express written consent. However, unless a provider is required to furnish services irrespective of the patient's ability to pay, it may refuse to treat the minor unless she will consent to the billing of her parents.

A person who has been adjudicated incompetent may not consent to disclosure of his records; consent must be given by his guardian.[9]

The confidentiality of substance abuse records survives the patient. Except for information relating to the cause of death that is needed under state law for vital statistics, disclosures that would have required patient consent before death require consent of the patient's personal representative after death. If there is no personal representative, the patient's spouse may consent to disclosure. And if there is no spouse, any responsible member of the patient's family may consent.

---

order that probationer release his records as a condition of probation did not preclude court access to the records when the probationer refused to consent to release. The judge held a hearing and issued a court order requiring the release of the records. See also People v. Silkworth, 142 Misc. 2d 752, 538 N.Y.S.2d 692 (1989).

[8]42 C.F.R. §2.14.
[9]Id. §2.15.

§8.14.5 Access by Court Order

A provider must release alcohol and drug abuse treatment records if it receives a court order listing the specific records to be released. Before issuing such an order, however, the judge must hold a hearing to determine whether there is good reason to require disclosure of the records.[10] A subpoena alone is not sufficient to compel the disclosure of the records. Both a subpoena and a specific court order issued after a hearing are necessary before the program may release the records. The program may respond to notice of a hearing by filing a written response or by appearing at the hearing. At the hearing, the judge must weigh the public interest and the need for disclosure against possible injury to the patient, the physician-patient privilege, or the treatment service. Evidence that the disclosure would impair either the patient's or the program's effectiveness should be very carefully considered. The program should be prepared to offer evidence at the hearing as to any probable damaging effects to the patient or program if the records are released.[11]

Courts frequently seek records of a patient treated for drug or alcohol abuse in proceedings to protect abused or neglected children. (See §8.14.6.) In several cases in which a conflict arose between the confidentiality of treatment records and a child's interests, the child's interests prevailed, and the courts ordered

---

[10]Id. §§2.61-2.67.

[11]If the program received a subpoena to produce substance abuse records, federal law would prohibit release of records. But state law generally requires the program to comply with the subpoena for alcohol or drug abuse treatment records by taking the records to the place ordered or to seek an order to quash the subpoena. When a program gets a subpoena, it cannot ignore it. If the program does not seek to have the subpoena quashed, the person subpoenaed should appear at the place and time set for producing the records. At that time the person subpoenaed should inform the judge that federal law prohibits release without a special hearing. The person subpoenaed might want to take a copy of the federal regulations that deal with the court hearing—42 C.F.R. §2.61-2.67 (1985)—to give to the judge, since many state court judges are not familiar with the federal regulations.

disclosure of the treatment records.[12] Courts have been less likely to allow access to substance abuse records in criminal trials where defendants seek records of witnesses testifying for the government.[13]

The regulations are even more stringent regarding release of records for criminal investigation or prosecution of a present or former patient in the program. In such a case, the court may authorize disclosure of the records only if the crime was extremely serious or was believed to have been committed on program premises or against program personnel.

The regulations provide that a court order may not allow disclosure of confidential communications made by a patient to a program staff member in the course of diagnosis or treatment unless the disclosure is necessary to protect against a threat to life or of serious bodily injury or it is necessary in connection with an investigation or prosecution of an extremely serious crime.[14]

---

[12]In re Baby X, 97 Mich. App. 111, 293 N.W.2d 736 (1980); State v. Andring, 342 N.W.2d 128 (Minn. 1984); In re Dwayne G., 97 Misc. 2d 333, 411 N.Y.S.2d 180 (1978); In re Doe Children, 93 Misc. 2d 479, 402 N.Y.S.2d 958 (1978). Although no cases have been found, the same reasoning might apply to child custody cases in which the court needs to determine what is in the best interest of the child. But see Matter of Stephen F., 118 Misc. 2d 655, 460 N.Y.S.2d 856 (1982), in which the court denied access to drug treatment records of a parent in a child neglect proceeding when the fact of drug dependency had already been disclosed.

[13]In United States v. Graham, 548 F.2d 1302 (8th Cir. 1977), the court found that the patient's right to privacy and the interest in preserving the drug prevention program outweighed any benefit to the party seeking to have the records disclosed, and therefore it refused to order the disclosure of records. The facts of the case were as follows. A state's witness in a criminal drug conspiracy trial had been treated for drug abuse. At the trial, the witness testified that she had been addicted to drugs. The defendant had issued a subpoena for the drug treatment program records; the judge examined the records and denied access to them. See also United States v. Cresta, 825 F.2d 538 (1st Cir. 1987); United States v. Smith, 789 F.2d 196 (3d Cir. 1986). For refusal to disclose in another fact situation, see In re Matter of Commr. of Social Services, 55 N.Y.2d 588, 436 N.E.2d 451, 451 N.Y.S.2d 1 (1982) (the court in a civil paternity suit denied defendant access to plaintiff's drug treatment records; the defendant hoped the records would show that the plaintiff was promiscuous and had previously had an abortion).

[14]See United States v. Corona, 849 F.2d 562 (11th Cir. 1988) (violation

§8.14.6 Reporting Child Abuse and Neglect

Originally, the federal law had no exception for reporting suspected child abuse or neglect. Drug and alcohol treatment programs were told that if the report of suspected child abuse could be made without identifying a person as receiving treatment for alcohol or drug abuse, it would not conflict with the federal regulations.[15] If, however, it were necessary in the report to so identify a person, the report—with its identifying information—could not be released without a specific court order or a written hospital-agency agreement that made the agency to whom abuse must be reported a qualified service provider.[16]

But in 1986, the United States Congress, as part of the Children's Justice Act, amended both federal confidentiality laws to provide that they do *not* apply to the reporting under state law of incidents of suspected child abuse and neglect to the appropriate state or local authorities.[17] Thus, it is now clear that people providing drug or alcohol abuse treatment must comply fully with the state's mandatory child abuse and neglect reporting laws. When making such reports, the reporter must give his name, address, and telephone number as required by state laws, even though that information could identify a client as receiving treatment for alcohol or drug abuse. However, the amended law does not authorize release of substance abuse records *after* a

---

of federal Drug Control Act by purchasing firearms while addicted to cocaine is an extremely serious crime). In *Corona*, the court upheld trial judge's disclosure of substance abuse records even though judge had not made specific findings conforming to 42 U.S.C. §2.65. The appellate court found on a de novo review that all the criteria were met.

[15]Opinion of Department of Health and Human Services to John T. Brennan, Jr. (Dec. 7, 1981) (loose-leaf folder of opinions on file with the author).

[16]Joint Policy Statement of Confidentiality of Alcohol and Drug Abuse Patient Records and Child Abuse and Neglect Reporting, in Legal Opinions on the Confidentiality of Alcohol and Drug Abuse Patients' Records 1975-1978, at 313 (United States Dept. of Health and Human Services).

[17]42 U.S.C.A. §§290dd-3(3), 290ee-3(e) (West Supp. Dec. 1986) as amended Aug. 27, 1986, Pub. L. No. 99-401, 100 Stat. 907.

report of suspected child abuse or neglect has been made. Thus, if an agency seeks access to substance abuse records for proceedings relating to child abuse or neglect, the patient must consent in writing or a court must issue an order compelling disclosure.

§8.14.7 Exempt Disclosures

Federal law provides that certain disclosures are not protected and can be made without the patient's consent and without consideration for the effect of the disclosure. One is information exchanged within a program among those who need it in connection with their duties or between a program and an entity that has direct administrative control over the program. For example, any staff member of a drug treatment center where the person is a patient may have access to the patient's record if she needs the record in connection with her duties.[18]

Another exempted disclosure is information transmitted from a program to a qualified service organization that the organization needs to perform its services to the program.[19] ("Service organization" is an entity that provides such services to the treatment program as data processing; dosage preparation; laboratory analyses; legal, medical, accounting, or other professional services, or services to prevent or treat child abuse or neglect, including training on nutrition and child care and individual and group therapy.) The qualified service organization must enter into a written agreement with the treatment program that it will be bound by the federal confidentiality regulations. Before the regulations were amended to specifically include services to prevent child abuse, some of the official opinions issued by the Department of Health and Human Services indicated that it might be possible for programs to enter into qualified service organization contracts with any human services

---

[18]42 C.F.R. §2.12(c)(3).
[19]42 C.F.R. §2.12(c)(4).

agency.[20] If those opinions were followed, healthcare providers could disclose information to any human services agency with which it had a written agreement. However, such a broad use of the term "qualified service organization" would undermine the underlying reasoning of the statutes and regulations. Programs should probably limit qualified service organization agreements to the kinds of service organizations specifically mentioned in the definition above.

Finally, information is exempted that will not identify individual patients. Covered providers are free to release statistical information on recipients of treatment or other information in a way that does not identify individuals.

---

[20]Opinion 76-52 (1976), to Mr. Dempsey, in Legal Opinions, supra n.16, at 305.

9

Patients' Rights:
An Overview

Anne M. Dellinger

§9.0 Introduction

Patients' rights are considered separately in this chapter although they—above all, the right to competent care—are the basis of numerous other chapters. Separate discussion seems merited for three reasons: First, a patient's subjective reaction to his or her total experience with a healthcare facility probably influences most decisions to litigate; not every patient who suspects lack of professional skill in his or her care seeks legal redress. Second, at present there is a noticeable amount of criticism of the behavior of healthcare providers toward patients. Patients, a small but expressive minority of providers, and neutral parties (national commissions, state legislatures, and Congress) have registered dissatisfaction or acted in ways that imply it. Third, important aspects of the relationship between providers and patients appear to be changing. In the last three decades, American society has been altered by consumerism and by movements for women's and civil rights; these factors have affected healthcare as well. The growing power of the elderly is an additional factor militating in favor of change. Many in this age group both fear and value medicine's life-prolonging capability and seek a greater role in decisions about its use.

A note about terminology. "Patients' rights" suggests assumptions about the appropriate relationship between patients and providers that some in both categories reject. The term has a consumerist coloration, implying that patients have lacked power in the medical relationship and seek more. Because the word "rights" implies the potential for enforcement against others, it has adversarial connotations as well. The term "patients' rights" is used here, however, primarily for lack of an alternative, the author having tried and failed to identify a phrase reflecting patients' hopes for compassion as well as justice.

A. The Framework of Provider-Patient Relations

§9.1 The Historic Legacy

In many societies healers have reduced their ideals to writing and have used the formulations to instruct aspirants in the behavior proper to the profession. These documents form a kind of abbreviated history of the practitioner's view of the medical contract. A brief examination of historic terms may illuminate contemporary behavior.

The medical codes of past eras are a problematic legacy for

today's physician. The codes do explain the frequent veneration of medicine: most codes exhort practitioners to show industry and compassion, to keep patients' confidences, and to avoid the temptations of ambition, wealth, and sexual opportunity. But historic codes also limn an authoritarian world in which doctors obeyed their elders in medicine while exacting obedience from patients. Loyalty to the profession—one of the highest medical values—was used to discourage internal disputes and thus the acknowledgment of uncertainty; doctors, for both selfish and altruistic reasons, kept their own counsel.[1] An observer notes that the forms of the codes reveal these underlying attitudes. The earliest were personal affirmations by the practitioner; then came codes written in third-person "should" terms. Rights language appears only in modern codes.[2]

§9.1.1 Paternalism, Professional Loyalty, and Silence

Paternalism was implicit in most historic codes. A physician who took the Hippocratic oath promised to take "measures for the benefit of the sick according to my ability and judgment; I will keep them from harm and injustice."[3] A later Hebrew code praised God for "implant[ing] in the hearts of sages skill to heal . . . and to declare marvels to the multitudes," while warning the sages lest "haughtiness cause you to lift up your eyes and hearts in pride."[4] In another document influential in the West, the "Prayer of Moses Maimonides," the physician asked the

---

§9.1 [1]For a comprehensive collection of medical codes, see W. T. Reich and L. Walters, eds., Encyclopedia of Bioethics 1731-1757 (1978), (Appendix, §I) (hereinafter Encyclopedia of Bioethics).

[2]Veatch, Codes of Medical Ethics: Ethical Analysis, in Encyclopedia of Bioethics 172 (vol. 1) (1978), (hereinafter Codes of Medical Ethics).

[3]Veatch notes that the pledge to benefit the patient according to the physician's judgment presumably takes precedence over other possible needs, such as a patient's need for personal freedom or truth. Id. at 173-174.

[4]Oath of Asaph, probably written between the third and seventh centuries. Appendix, Encyclopedia of Bioethics, at 1733.

Deity to "[G]rant that my patients have confidence in me and my art and follow my directions and my counsel."[5]

The American Medical Association's first code, adopted in 1847 and not replaced until 1957, advised the physician to "unite tenderness with firmness, and condescension with authority,"[6] and said of the patient that "obedience . . . to the prescriptions of his physician should be prompt and implicit. He should never permit his own crude opinions as to their fitness, to influence his attention to them."[7]

The codes revealed the existence—indeed what sometimes seemed the primacy for physicians—of a fraternity of healers. Most codes required the physician to commit himself to teachers in medicine and to fellow practitioners as fully as to patients. Those who passed on the art (and presumably wrote codes) claimed the same fealty as parents, even as masters in one formulation.[8] Fully one-quarter of the lengthy 1847 AMA code was devoted to the duties of physicians to one another and to the profession, described in exacting detail.

The codes also reveal the antiquity and persistence over centuries of what has been called "the silent world of doctor and patient."[9] Indian medical aspirants of the first century learned to conceal a fatal diagnosis: "Even knowing that the patient's span of life has come to its close, it shall not be mentioned by thee there [in the home], where if so done, it would cause shock to the patient or to others."[10] So, apparently, did nineteenth-century American practitioners, whose code advised that a physician

---

[5]Id. at 1737-1738. The encyclopedia tentatively attributes the prayer to late eighteenth-century Germany, where it was first printed, though it purports to date from the twelfth century.

[6]Code of Ethics, American Medical Association 1847, ch. I, art. I, at 1, in id. at 1739.

[7]Code of Ethics, American Medical Association 1847, ch. I, art II, at 6, in id. at 1740.

[8]Oath of Initiation from a first-century Indian medical text, the *Caraka Samhita*, id. at 1732.

[9]J. Katz, The Silent World of Doctor and Patient 1981.

[10]Appendix, Encyclopedia of Bioethics, at 1732.

not be forward to make gloomy prognostications . . . [though] not fail, on proper occasions, to give to the friends of the patient timely notice of danger . . . and even to the patient himself, if absolutely necessary. This office, however, . . . ought to be declined whenever it can be assigned to any other . . . [f]or the physician should be the minister of hope . . . smooth the bed of death . . . and avoid all things which have a tendency to discourage the patient and to depress his spirits.

That document's prescription of silence extended further than protecting a patient from knowledge of imminent death; patients were also to be shielded from the fact that physicians disagreed. Elaborate rules tried to prevent more than one physician's involvement in a case—one rule said patients ought to "if possible, avoid even the *friendly visits of a physician* who is not attending him—and when he does receive them, he should never converse on the subject of his disease. . . ."[11] While patients were strongly discouraged from seeking consultations, the code recognized that some were inevitable and attempted to minimize the harm by establishing protocol: the original attendant would preside in the presence of the patient and family; debate among consultants would be private; in case of disagreement ("a circumstance much to be deplored") a majority vote won; and the patient, if at all possible, was to learn only the result.[12]

§9.1.2 Issues of Discrimination

Some patients are more attractive than others. Medical encounters presumably incorporate an era's prevailing social views of

---

[11]Code of Ethics, American Medical Association 1847, ch. I, art. II, at 7, in id. at 1741. The code's effort to regulate speech was remarkable. Another provision admonished that the patient should "never weary his physician with a tedious detail of events or matters not appertaining to his disease. . . . Neither should he obtrude the details of his business nor the history of his family concerns." Code of Ethics, American Medical Association 1847, ch. I, art. II, at 5, in id. at 1740.

[12]Code of Ethics, American Medical Association, 1847, ch. II, art. IV, at 2-10, in id. at 1743-1744.

equality and discrimination, though perhaps softened by medicine's ethos of care. Most medical codes distinguished among patients by class, sex, and various personal characteristics and also reflected the struggle to reconcile medical ethics with the desire for compensation. Though more than one code urged resolving the last point in favor of care,[13] most seem to assume that payment for service is a condition of the relationship. (The 1847 American code tried to extract more than money from patients; it asked that the patient "entertain a just and enduring sense of the value of the services rendered him . . . for these are of such character, that no mere pecuniary acknowledgment can repay or cancel them.")[14] Care of women presents difficulties in many societies because the proximity to the male healer threatens either to violate patriarchal rights or to sway the healer from his task. Other characteristics that render a patient unattractive, now and under the historic codes, are immorality, unpopularity, political radicalism, and failure to comply with medical regimens. Codes varied as to whether undesirable patients should be served.[15]

Throughout United States history, the social status of the ill has strongly influenced their treatment. Until the twentieth century, people preferred home care if at all possible. Eighteenth- and nineteenth-century hospitals were avoided by anyone who could do so, making them the preserve of the lowest classes. Medical staff positions, on the contrary, were usually sought-after posts awarded to well-educated and -connected physicians. Thus, the social gulf between hospital patient and doctor was enormous; it surely affected patients' treatment. Common attri-

---

[13]E.g., the tenth-century Persian "Advice to a Physician," id. at 1734-1735 and a seventeenth-century Chinese text, id. at 1735-1736.

[14]Code of Ethics, American Medical Association 1847, ch. I, art. II, at 10, in id. at 1741.

[15]Compare the first-century Indian oath with the seventeenth-century Chinese: "No persons, who are hated by the king or who are haters of the king or who are hated by the public or who are haters of the public, shall receive treatment." Id. at 1732; "Prostitutes should be treated just like patients from a good family and gratuitous services should be given to the poor ones." Id. at 1735.

butes of ward life included impersonality; lack of comfort, sanitation, and privacy; and a substantial restriction of freedom. In this context the notion of "patients' rights" had little meaning.[16]

In addition to class distinctions, through most of U.S. history hospital inmates were further stratified by gender, race, religion, diagnosis, or a combination of these. Because respectable women were so likely to be cared for at home, the few women patients were disproportionately alcoholic, infected with venereal disease as a result of prostitution, or unmarried maternity cases—any of which conditions consigned them to a low position in the patient hierarchy. The chronically ill and the contagious were also disfavored as patients.[17] Discrimination on the basis of ethnic origin and religion was sufficiently common to lead to the creation of separate hospitals by Catholic and Jewish communities.[18] The harshest discrimination, however, was reserved for blacks. As hospital patients they encountered rigid segregation and extreme overcrowding—and yet knew themselves to be among the fortunate members of their race because they had gained admittance.[19]

While the most obvious discrimination against patients had faded by mid-twentieth century in the United States, vestiges remain. The class barrier between physicians and patients is narrower, for instance, but still exists. Racial discrimination is not history but present or remembered personal experience for large numbers of providers and patients. Non-English speakers

---

[16]See C. E. Rosenberg, The Care of Strangers: The Rise of America's Hospital System (1987) and P. Starr, The Social Transformation of American Medicine (1985), especially ch. four, "The Reconstitution of the Hospital." See also H. F. Dowling, City Hospitals: The Undercare of the Underprivileged 51 (1982).

[17]Charles Rosenberg notes that "[a]s late as 1909 none of New York City's general hospitals would accept cancer patients." Rosenberg, supra n.16, at 306.

[18]Starr, supra n.16, at 173-176.

[19]Rosenberg, supra n.16, at 301-303. See also E. H. Beardsley, A History of Neglect: Health Care for Blacks and Millworkers in the Twentieth Century South 36-39 (1987) and M. Seham, Blacks and American Medical Care (1973).

continue to encounter difficulties in obtaining care in the average facility, and the indigent perhaps still more (see §15.9 and §15.10 on Medicaid discrimination). Contagion is feared, as ever, though most health professionals are meeting the challenge with honor. These and similar issues have affected care in America from the beginning.

§9.2 The Contemporary Relationship

It is hazardous to attempt to characterize any broad social phenomenon, and above all a contemporary one. Recognizing that fact, the following description of provider-patient relations is confined to these few observations: Neither patients nor providers in the second half of the twentieth century have been fully satisfied with the medical contract. Conflict between the parties is multi-determined, complex, and, to some extent, unavoidable. Patients as a group seem to seek a more egalitarian form of medical interaction and their preferences appear to be altering traditional patterns of practice.

§9.2.1 Criticism and Desire for Change

If, as has been claimed,[1] medicine's old authoritarianism is being replaced by negotiation between doctor and patient, the pace of change is slow and the formation of a new bond still incomplete. Late-nineteenth-century patients were addressed by their bed numbers even unto death,[2] and today's patient may still meet a provider who patronizes by first name use.[3] In narrow time frames progress can be hard to see. Two reports written 30 years apart identified the same deficiency in United States medical

---

§9.2 [1]M. Haug and B. Lavin, Consumerism in Medicine: Challenging Physician Authority 37-39 (1983).

[2]C. Rosenberg, The Care of Strangers: The Rise of America's Hospital System 292, 308 (1987).

[3]J. Katz, The Silent World of Doctor and Patient 211 (1981) (hereinafter Silent World).

training: it does not sufficiently attend to patients' emotional needs or the importance of communication, with the result that patients (and not infrequently doctors) are fearful and isolated.[4]

Still, there is some evidence that change has occurred. Writing in 1961 about patients' views of medical practice, Eliot Friedson asserted, citing Hippocrates and Benvenuto Cellini, that doctor-patient conflict is ageless.[5] But Friedson also assumed that any doctor who tells the truth will demoralize patients—an assumption questioned far more often now than in 1961.[6] It is difficult, of course, to organize people around the experience of their own illness. Yet patients as a group do seem to be expressing their dissatisfaction and desire for change. The forms of this expression include the more than sixfold increase in the rate of malpractice filings over the past 15 years, the acceptance in this country of hospice care for the dying, the emergence of bioethics as a branch of philosophy and of law-and-medicine as a distinct field of legal studies, the formation of patient advocacy groups,[7] and the popularity of the concept of personal control over health.[8]

---

[4]Brant and Kutner, Physician-Patient Relations in a Teaching Hospital, 32 J. Med. Educ. 703-706 (October 1957); the second report is described in J. Berger, New Medical School Challenge: Human Values, N.Y. Times, Nov. 16, 1988, at 23, cols. 5-8.

[5]E. Friedson, Patients' Views of Medical Practice 172-173 (1961) (hereinafter Patients' Views).

[6]Id. at 55.

[7]Such as the Public Citizen Health Research Group, National Citizens' Coalition for Nursing Home Reform, National Women's Health Collective, People's Medical Society, United Seniors' Health Cooperative, Children's Defense Fund, and the National Council on Patient Information and Education.

[8]This is evidenced in, for example, "The People's Pharmacy" radio show and syndicated column, the "People's Advocate" column of The Washington Post's Health section, and the Columbia University public television series on law and ethics in medicine, as well as the stream of first-person accounts of illnesses and medical confrontations (including Betty Rollin's *Last Wish*, Norman Cousins's *Anatomy of an Illness*, Martha Lear's *Heartsounds*, and many others). Public and private agencies operate national "hotlines" offering information on various diseases—Alzheimer's Disease, eating disorders, cancer, AIDS, and others. Ann Landers's advice column repeatedly addresses medical issues and regularly recommends self-help texts, e.g., *Your Good Health* from Harvard University Press.

Certain groups of patients—those that were frequently discriminated against in the past—have been especially active in their own behalf and have in part succeeded. Although marked differentials in the health status of blacks and whites persist, healthcare facilities have been racially integrated for a quarter-century.[9] The agenda of the women's movement in America includes greater power over reproductive health.[10] As a result, since the 1970s more than a dozen states have required disclosure to breast cancer patients of all acceptable treatment alternatives. At least one state (Massachusetts) also requires preadmission disclosure of a facility's statistics on caesarean deliveries and breastfeeding.[11] California forbids facilities to limit sterilizations on the basis of age, marital status, or number of natural children.[12] The mid-1960s Medicare and Medicaid enactments substantially improved the health status of the elderly and the indigent, though the latters' gains have since been eroded. In Massachusetts, the elderly won additional concessions guaranteeing treatment—and at Medicare rates.[13]

The appearance of acquired immune deficiency syndrome (AIDS) challenged the assumption that nondiscriminatory care was available for patients with serious contagious disease and for those from social categories considered undesirable. In large measure, American society—above all, American medicine—

[9]Integration was required for healthcare facilities receiving federal funds by Simkins v. Moses Cone Hosp., 323 F.2d 959 (4th Cir. 1963), cert. denied, 376 U.S. 938 (1964).

[10]Haug and Lavin, supra n.1, at 18, noting especially the 1973 publication of *Our Bodies, Ourselves* by the Boston Women's Health Collective. George G. Annas's influential 1975 formulation of patients' rights stated that "[w]hile the legal rights of women in the hospital are not essentially different from other patients, women are at greater risk of certain violations of their rights, especially in the area of reproduction." American Civil Liberties Union, The Rights of Hospital Patients (1975).

[11]Mass. Ann. Laws ch. 111, §70E (Law. Co-op. 1985 & Supp. 1989).

[12]Cal. Health & Safety Code §1232 (West 1979).

[13]Mass. Ann. Laws ch. 111, §51D (Law. Co-op. 1985 & Supp. 1989); Medical Socy. v. Dukakis, 815 F.2d 790 (1st Cir. 1987), cert. denied, 484 U.S. 896 (1987).

responded well. Despite many injustices to individuals, AIDS patients as a group have not been denied healthcare.[14]

Patients' own efforts to establish their rights have been supplemented by the efforts of health professionals. Sensitive providers are in an excellent position to observe and comment on patients' rights. Their testimony is among the best evidence available that the modern sensibility rebels against an authoritarian healthcare system. Contemporary accounts by physicians,[15] medical students, and interns[16] as well as nurses[17] have frequently noted the human costs of "the world's best healthcare." These intimate witnesses note the usual (though perhaps avoidable) indignities of confinement in any large institution, the arrogance of some colleagues, the tendency of medical training and practice to blunt sympathy, and the strong pressure to conserve time and money at the expense of other values. Thomas Szasz spoke for a number of his medical colleagues when he warned the rest: "[W]e must keep in mind that people want and need not only health but also dignity, that often they can obtain health only at the cost of dignity, and that sometimes

---

[14]The AMA has struggled with physicians' ethical duties to treat, whether testing should be mandatory or voluntary, and the appropriate degree of confidentiality of the results. Health providers' courage in dealing with AIDS is not diminished by their fear or the fact that some (25 percent in one study) would avoid the duty if possible. Link and Feingold, et al., Concerns of Medical and Pediatric House Officers about Acquiring AIDS from Their Patients, 78 Am. J. Pub. Health 455 (April 1988). For essays rating our society in dealing humanely with victims of fearful disease, see Special Supplement, "AIDS: The Responsibilities of Health Professionals," Hastings Center Report 1-32 (April-May 1988).

[15]D. Hilfiker, Healing the Wounds (1985) (hereinafter Healing the Wounds); T. Preston, The Clay Pedestal (1981) (hereinafter The Clay Pedestal). These physicians write from their experience as patients: Vital Signs: A Young Doctor's Struggle with Cancer (1975) and E. E. Rosenbaum, A Taste of My Own Medicine (1988).

[16]C. LeBaron, Gentle Vengeance (1982) (hereinafter Gentle Vengeance); M. Konner, Becoming a Doctor (1987) (hereinafter Becoming a Doctor); R. E. Peschel and E. Rhodes Peschel, When a Doctor Hates a Patient (1986).

[17]B. Huttmann, The Patient's Advocate (1981); J. Storch, Patients' Rights (1982); S. Tisdale, Harvest Moon: Portrait of a Nursing Home (1987).

they prefer not to pay this price."[18] Providers who are not direct caregivers will sometimes take up patients' causes. As a means of reducing costs, administrators may align themselves with patients' desire for less aggressive treatment.[19] Many institutions support a patient advocate and some a bioethicist or an ethics committee to advise on difficult issues.

National commissions and federal legislation and regulation have sought directly or implicitly to change patients' status. The Commission on Medical Malpractice, reporting to the Secretary of Health, Education, and Welfare in 1973, identified the slighting of "the rights of patients as human beings" as a factor in the increase of malpractice litigation.[20] Two presidential commissions of the 1980s advocated increasing patients' roles in decision-making about treatment[21] and urged facilities to make stronger efforts to reduce patients' sense of alienation and loss of control.[22] In setting eligibility standards for Medicare and Medicaid reimbursement, the federal government has required recognition of certain rights by hospitals, mental health facilities, and, more recently, nursing homes and home health agencies. Following exposés of dangerous laxity in some clinical laboratories, Congress established standards for those facilities. The Health Care Financing Administration's publication of facilities' mortality rates (actual compared to expected rates) is potentially a powerful tool for patients. Efforts to improve patients' status, however (and even the partial success of such efforts), simply bring the remaining barriers into sharper focus.

---

[18]Szasz, Illness and Indignity, 227 J.A.M.A. 543 (No. 5, Feb. 4, 1974).

[19]Summers, Take Patients' Rights Seriously to Improve Patient Care and to Lower Costs, 10 Health Care Mgmt. Rev. 55-62 (Fall 1985).

[20]Report of the Secretary's Commission on Medical Malpractice 67-81 (U.S. Govt. Printing Office, DHEW Pub. No. (OS) 73-88) (1973).

[21]President's Commission for the Study of Ethical Problems in Medicine, Making Health Care Decisions. (U. S. Govt. Printing Office, 1982).

[22]President's Commission for the Study of Ethical Problems in Medical and Biomedical and Behavioral Research, Deciding to Forego Life-Sustaining Treatment. (U.S. Govt. Printing Office, 1983). For a powerful fictional account of a patient's reaction to helplessness and pain, see J. Stafford, "The Interior Castle," in C. Fadiman, ed., The World of the Short Story (1986).

§9.2.2 Reasons for Conflict

Since providers and patients both seek to return the patient to health, why does their relationship generate conflict? One answer is that "[t]he professional expects patients to accept what he recommends on his terms; patients seek services on their own terms. In that each seeks to gain his own terms, there is conflict."[23] In short, the parties have divergent interests as well as a common interest. The conflict between them is not simple, and is caused by, among other reasons, (1) a reluctance to acknowledge medical uncertainty that is supported by the weight of medical tradition; (2) providers' loyalty to the healthcare professions; (3) the stress of medical training and practice; (4) the imbalance of power between patients and providers; (5) patients' personal failings of intellect or character; and, finally, (6) the barriers to communication that inhere in the relationship. Each issue is examined further below.

Despite the scientific advances of this century, vast areas of medical uncertainty remain. To Lewis Thomas the recognition of this ignorance is "the major discovery of the past 100 years of biology . . . the most significant contribution of twentieth-century science to the human intellect."[24] Not everyone, however, shares Thomas's enthusiasm. According to Jay Katz and others,[25] confessing ignorance frightens physicians for both altruistic and selfish reasons. For one, sharing uncertainty may eventually require sharing authority.[26] Patients may lose the therapeutic benefits of hope and of belief in the physician's

---

[23]Patients' Views, at 171. Jay Katz agrees that conflict arises from doctors' and patients' differing preferences for modes of treatment—a situation not improved by the fact that the difference is usually covered by silence. Silent World, at 99-100. Katz advocates exploration of preferences because "no single right decision exists for how the life of health and illness should be lived." Id. at 102.

[24]The Medusa and the Snail: More Notes of a Biology Watcher 73-74 (1979) cited in Silent World, at 181.

[25]Preeminently, E. Cassell, Talking with Patients (2 vols.) (1985).

[26]Shultz, From Informed Consent to Patient Choice: A New Protected Interest, 95 Yale L.J. 219, 270 (1985).

powers.[27] The time required for explanation and deliberation may reduce efficiency,[28] raising costs. Both providers and patients may have to restrain what has been observed to be their mutual preference for action.[29] The costs of nondisclosure, though, are high. Besides the psychological burden pretense imposes on the professional, the failure to disclose uncertainty diminishes the patient's trust and opportunities for choice. Viewed in that light, the provider's concealment of ignorance is among the principal sources of conflict in the provider-patient relationship.

Providers disinclined to communicate for any reason can turn to authority to bolster their position. Considerable opinion exists that medical tradition does devalue truthful conversation with patients. As a leading proponent of the view asserts, "The humane care that physicians have extended to patients throughout the ages rarely has been based on the humaneness of consensual understanding; rather it has been based on the humaneness of service silently rendered."[30] This concept has also been stated more starkly: "Patient self-determination is an idea alien to medicine."[31] Robert Burt, writing on the way medicine was practiced before 1900, observes that "the proposition that patients should give 'informed consent' for their treatment was not seriously entertained; it was simply not plausible, because both physician and patient assumed that they approached one another without distinct psychological boundaries. . . ."[32] Thomas Preston finds the custom still strong, although past its social usefulness:

---

[27]Silent World, at xvii; The Clay Pedestal, at 82-89; and recall the position of the 1847 AMA code described above.

[28]Healing the Wounds, at 58-71.

[29]"Both patient and physician hope for beneficial action, but both prefer action with little chance of benefit to no action at all." The Clay Pedestal, at 147.

[30]Silent World, at xvi-xvii.

[31]Id at 104.

[32]Taking Care of Strangers 101 (1979). A 1957 study concluded that physicians did not think of communication as part of the essential work of medicine. Brant and Kutner, Physician-Patient Relations in a Teaching Hospital, 32 J. Med. Educ. 703-706 (October 1957).

[D]eception in clinical medicine is not random and individual; it is part of accepted professional practice. Medical students learn subtle deceptions by example, by observing their teachers and senior colleagues. From using evasive or incomprehensible language to exclude the patient from communication among professionals at the bedside, to conscious lying about the purpose or result of a test, deception of the patient is systematically if unconsciously taught to the medical student from the beginning of his clinical experience, all in support of the notion of the healer.[33]

The problem with nondisclosure is that, as noted earlier, a provider's commitment to a patient's welfare does not necessarily produce unanimity between them—and unanimity is the only condition under which patient compliance and provider authoritarianism are acceptable. Frequently, provider and patient will define "welfare" somewhat differently. A physician, for example, in keeping with medical norms, may value longevity more than the patient does. To complicate the matter further, providers are often mistaken in believing they can intuit patients' preferences.[34]

A second source of conflict or distancing between provider and patient is the provider's loyalty to her own and the other health professions. Despite their competition, members of any profession share economic interests. In addition, since provision of healthcare is frequently a group effort, the training of its professionals includes deliberate attention to team building. While professional socialization is necessary and useful, it can be criticized for reducing providers' identification and sympathetic interaction with patients. Studies show, for example, that physicians and interns on hospital wards each spend more time talking within their own group than to patients.[35]

---

[33]The Clay Pedestal, at 167-168. Eric Cassell suggests another reason patients are usually excluded from the diagnostic process: they are thought to be unreliable witnesses. Talking with Patients 123 (vol. 2) (1985).

[34]Wolf, Conflict Between Doctor and Patient, 16 Law, Medicine and Health Care 198 (Fall-Winter 1988).

[35]J. D. Stoeckle, "Introduction," in J. D. Stoeckle, ed., Encounters between Patients and Doctors 53-54 (1987) (hereinafter Encounters).

Eliot Friedson cited numerous other studies for his conclusion that "the medical practitioner is typically a colleague in a structure of institutions and organizations, the patient being an essentially minor contingency."[36] Thomas Preston, author of *The Clay Pedestal*, and Melvin Konner, a chronicler of his own internship, reserve their harshest criticism for this point. Preston recounts a formative experience in which a colleague humiliated a patient. "If any of us other physicians in that corridor felt indignation at the shameful behavior of our colleague, we didn't betray it, even in the expressions on our faces. For on this point, the code was clear: one physician does not interfere with another physician's professional relationships. . . . Somehow, in the process of becoming a physician, loyalty is focused on the profession that nurtures and sustains, and everything else becomes subordinated to that end—including the patient."[37]

Konner suggests that the process of professional socialization occurs during internship. He claims to have identified with patients through most of the year and then finally capitulated, joining the team whose job, as he saw it, was "to deal with patients, but patients are outside it." Konner interpreted the message to interns thus: "Relations with [patients] should be smooth, cordial, and efficient, but . . . certainly not personal." Moreover, "[d]isloyalty to the team is always dangerous, and it can be remarkably subtle. Too great an involvement with patients can in itself be sufficient to suggest it . . . through an implied accusation leveled against the other team members: I care more than you do for patients, therefore you do not care enough. Avoiding this implication helps to suppress at least some nurturing impulses toward patients."[38]

A third reason for stress between patient and provider is the stress of medical training and practice. For patients, who are

---

[36]E. Friedson, "Client Control and Medical Practice," in Encounters, at 180-191.

[37]The Clay Pedestal, at xiv-xv. Ruth Macklin, staff bioethicist for the Albert Einstein College of Medicine, primarily blames practitioners' reluctance to challenge one another for the rare instances of harm and injustice to patients she has witnessed. Mortal Choices 201-216 (1987).

[38]Becoming a Doctor, at 365.

by definition people with problems, behavior allowances are made. Caregivers' difficulties, on the other hand, are less frequently recognized and tolerated. Still, few doubt that the medical professions are stressful to learn and to practice, and providers' stress is sometimes cited as an origin of dysfunctional behavior toward patients.[39] Working hours, salaries, and conditions in most facilities discourage providers from focusing full attention on patient rights. Harry F. Dowling refers to "the hardening effect" of dealing with more sick patients than there are means or time to help.[40] In addition, stress may reinforce a practitioner's reliance on tradition, including its less beneficial aspects. Katz, for instance, surmises that doctors cling to silence (nondisclosure of pertinent medical information to patients) because it is entrenched custom and therefore comforting.[41] Konner notes the feeling of safety from practicing according to traditional norms, "the spiritual comfort the practitioner derives from keeping to ritualistic routines, held firmly in common with other practitioners."[42]

A fourth factor in patient-provider conflict is that the power of those involved in medical relationships is unequal; the patient, as the weaker party, may not express dissatisfaction on this score but is quite likely to feel it. Providers' authority is far-reaching, extending beyond the individual contract. It has been alleged of physicians, for instance, that as a group they "determine what services are available and when, who is eligible for them, where doctors' offices and hospitals are located, how many specialists and generalists practice medicine, the quality of health services (which practices are acceptable and which are not), and the cost of health care."[43] Certainly providers are

---

[39]Physicians are considered the most privileged providers, but see David Hilfiker, Healing the Wounds, generally for an eloquent analysis of physicians' frustrations.

[40]H. F. Dowling, City Hospitals: The Undercare of the Underprivileged 134 (1982).

[41]Silent World, generally.

[42]Becoming a Doctor, at 375.

[43]The Clay Pedestal, at 171.

better-informed than patients about diagnosis,[44] treatment alternatives, and prognosis. The difference in the parties' comprehension of science and medical technology insures inequality,[45] and a typical patient labors under additional disadvantages. He needs the provider's help, initiates and conducts the relationship while ill, must function in a complex, unfamiliar environment,[46] and has an ambiguous but clearly lower status than the provider. Individual characteristics may reduce a patient's power still more: 60 percent of patients in the United States are female (70 percent, if mothers of pediatric patients are included) and 92 percent of physicians male;[47] in one study women and blacks waited longer to obtain appointments and to be seen than white males;[48] some observers allege that students are allowed to intrude more often on nonpaying than on paying patients;[49] working-class patients receive less information than middle-class

---

[44]Two observers hypothesize that doctors and patients actually negotiate a diagnosis acceptable to both, but especially to the doctor. T. J. Scheff, "Negotiating Reality: Notes on Power in the Assessment of Responsibility," in Encounters, at 193-213, and Aaron Lazare et al., "Studies on a Negotiated Approach to Patienthood," in Encounters, at 413-432.

[45]Haug and Lavin analogize the physician's monopoly of information to capitalists' control of the means of production. Consumerism in Medicine, at 15. Howard Waitzkin agrees that with doctors (as well as other professionals) "information control is used, at least in part, to maintain patterns of dominance and subordination." H. Waitzkin, "Information Control and Micropolitics," in Encounters, at 348.

[46]According to Ruth Ravich, "[T]he modern teaching hospital may have as many as 250 different job classifications in 50 different occupational groups. This division of labor puts patients and their families into brief contact with, and under the care of, many different people at a time when they are least able to form new interpersonal relationships." R. Ravich, "Patient Advocacy," in J. H. Marks, ed., Advocacy in Health Care 53 (1985). Evidence on medical technicians, a group with which hospital patients have numerous contacts, suggests the technicians make little effort to personalize the relationship. Stoeckle, in Encounters, at 66.

[47]According to 1980 census data, Stoeckle, in Encounters, at 38-39.

[48]Stoeckle, in Encounters, at 43-44.

[49]Becoming a Doctor, at 220.

patients,[50] and members of some ethnic groups are diagnosed differently than those whose culture is familiar to providers.[51]

Patients' failings of intelligence and character are another barrier to good relations between patient and provider. Patients' unreasonable expectations and inappropriate dependence have been noted.[52] Two other charges are harder to assess: that patients make diagnosis difficult by concealing information and that they refuse to follow orders. Based on his study of physician-patient interviews, Eric Cassell defends patients from the accusation that they often lie. He offers other explanations: first, that the logic of their comments, though it always exists, is not always readily apparent; second, that each patient—and to some extent each American subculture as well—has a "palette of language" whose unfamiliar terms can mislead the listener;[53] and third, that patients' utterances may honestly—and understandably—be at war with one another.[54]

---

[50]Waitzkin, in Encounters, at 351.

[51]I. Zola, "Problems of Communication, Diagnosis, and Patient Care: The Interplay of Patient, Physician, and Clinic Organization," in Encounters, at 323.

[52]Freidson, in Encounters, at 186; L. V. Pratt, "Reshaping the Consumer's Posture in Health Care," in E. B. Gallagher, ed., The Doctor-Patient Relationship in the Changing Health Scene 204 (U.S. DHEW Conference Proceedings, April 26-28, 1976), Hilfiker, Healing the Wounds, especially ch. 3: The Limits of Help and ch. 4: The Boundaries of Knowledge. "Even the routine health consumer today expects the physician not only to provide accurate diagnosis and treatment of organic illness, but also to alleviate symptoms, provide sympathy and support, and relieve the fear associated with illness." Hilfiker at 52.

[53]E. Cassell, Talking with Patients 53-55 (vol. 1) (1985).

[54]"Even a very sick person might be of two minds about going to the doctor. Some do not like physicians, others are afraid of illness, still others do not like tests or needles, many have severe demands on their time; perhaps a hundred additional good reasons could be found for not wanting to be sick. Unfortunately, however, the patient's body is not well and demands attention, so the person reluctantly takes his or her body off to the doctor. Since the body does not have its own voice, the person is forced to report the symptoms and answer questions. It is little wonder that the part of the patient that did not want to come occasionally says things to counter the impression of illness—ergo contradictions that sound like deliberate evasions." Id. at 101.

Failure to follow orders—noncompliance—is extremely common patient behavior. (Research suggests that one-third of patients disregard a material component of the advice they receive.) Yet despite the frequency, there is no consensus on whether noncompliance is, on balance, obstructive or constructive behavior. In the consumer model of health care " . . . the physician is a part-time consultant with specialized expertise but limited knowledge of or interest in the consumer's total health needs. The consumer is responsible for choosing his consultants wisely and monitoring their services carefully. He then complies selectively, not automatically, with advice given."[55] Katz cautions, "it may turn out that what a physician first perceived to be an expression of a patient's 'irrational' behavior was based on different value preferences about the importance of longevity, quality of life, bodily invasions, or the risks a patient is willing to take for purposes of greater well-being."[56] Most providers can probably accept noncompliance in theory, but may find it a legal and management concern, particularly with respect to in-patients.

Finally, in examining the potential for conflict between providers and patients, one must acknowledge certain inherent barriers to their mutual understanding. First, illness is inescapably subjective, an experience for which one's descriptive powers are usually insufficient. Moreover, as Eric Cassell warns his fellow physicians, each illness, even each symptom, may have peculiar significance to a patient that arises from his own history.[57] Take for example a middle-aged man whose father died from stroke at 40. Such a patient probably notes in himself the symptom of numbness and mentions it to his doctor differently than other men would—but his communication may be less rather than more direct. Patients have emotional needs that few health professionals are trained to deal with. Jay Katz, a psychiatrist, discounts the likelihood that most will cope well enough: "It is dangerous nonsense to assert that in the practice of their art and

---

[55]Pratt, supra n.52, at 197-214, quotation at 209.
[56]Silent World, at 118.
[57]Cassell, Talking with Patients 135-141 (vol. 2).

science physicians can rely on their benevolent intentions, their abilities to judge what is the right thing to do, or their capacities for conducting their rounds with humanity, patience, prudence and wisdom—all supposedly acquired through on-the-job training."[58]

Certain aspects of training raise additional barriers to empathy with patients. Medicine, like other sciences, encourages objectivity. The practitioner is to focus on the problem, disease, and to preserve an attitude of scientific inquiry about the disease process. These requirements inevitably create an emotional distance from patients that can prove difficult to modulate. A physician complains, "what begins as a necessary tool in certain areas of medicine easily becomes a generalized defensive response."[59] The patient is objectified and the physician may find himself increasingly dependent on the safety of distancing.[60]

Even the formal language of medicine, with its Latinate and technical vocabulary, separates provider and patient.[61] Informal medical language reveals still more powerfully the provider's need for and achievement of separation. The habit of referring to patients by their chief complaint objectifies them—"the gunshot wound in the ER"—and certain terms commonly used among professionals subtly suggest that patients are to blame

---

[58]Silent World, at xxi. See also Healing the Wounds, at 53-54. Hilfiker (Healing the Wounds, at 28) and Konner (Becoming a Doctor, at 32) describe nearly identical personal experiences to illustrate that training also slights doctors' emotional needs. Each felt he had severely embarrassed his clinical instructor by asking how to deal with feelings of sexual arousal from examining a patient; neither received any guidance on the matter.

[59]Healing the Wounds, at 127.

[60]Id. at 125-127.

[61]While medicine, like other learned professions, defends its vocabulary as essential, some are skeptical. A study of physicians treating lower-income Scottish patients found doctors sometimes deliberately choosing terms they believed patients did not understand (in fact, the patients grasped more than they were expected to) and concluded that "limited communication may, in various ways, serve the professional interests and needs of physicians." McKinlay, Who Is Really Ignorant—Physician or Patient? 16 J. Health and Social Behavior 3-11 (1975).

for their condition—"she coded," "she blew her IV."[62] A few physicians who criticize the profession's socialization process recall incidents of callousness and mockery of patients.[63] It is their view that medical training actively promotes emotional distancing. Whether it does, or whether it simply fails to help providers deal with their own and patients' fears, the result is a measure of loneliness and frustration for both.

Despite their common focus on the patient's health, then, providers and patients are seldom of one mind. They clash in defining health and in the course of advancing goals not shared by the other. While conflict cannot be eliminated, it might be reduced by acknowledging medical uncertainty, rendering training less stressful, focusing on patients' psychological as well as physical needs, reexamining medical tradition, affirming the caregiver's primary loyalty to the patient, and above all structuring the patient-provider relationship so as to bolster patient autonomy.

§9.2.3 Restructuring the Relationship

Even if they do not receive deliberate attention, provider-patient interactions naturally change as patterns of care change. For example, increased hospitalization (a long trend now reversing), the growth of group practice, the advent of health maintenance

---

[62]Becoming a Doctor, at 289-290, 373. George J. Annas makes the point as well in The Emerging Stowaway: Patients' Rights in the 1980s, 10 Law, Medicine and Health Care 34 (Feb. 1982) (hereinafter The Emerging Stowaway). New interest in mind-body interaction, though it has many benefits, may exacerbate the tendency to blame. S. Sontag, Illness As Metaphor (1977). For an example of the genre promising great physical rewards for positive thinking, see B. S. Siegel, Love, Medicine and Miracles (1986).

[63]Healing the Wounds, at 28-29; R. E. Peschel and E. Rhodes Peschel, When a Doctor Hates a Patient 102-115 (1986). Melvin Konner, especially, was deeply troubled by his observations on this point. Becoming a Doctor, at 18, 47-48, 53, 60, 125, 152-153, 266, 269-270 (mocking a doctor who cried for his patient), and 287. Konner and others are discomfited too by colleagues' attitudes toward cadavers, 245-246; Peschel and Peschel, at 31-47; Gentle Vengeance, at 243-248. LeBaron is also disturbed by indifference to the suffering of laboratory animals, id. at 73-78.

organizations, and institutionalization of the elderly all encourage patients to form their primary relationship with a facility and its changing staff rather than with a single practitioner. Thus, facilities themselves become actors in provider-patient relationships and, if they choose, enforcers of patient rights.

Most facilities have chosen to do so, for several reasons. A facility's concern for its patients is one. As early as 1927 a physician complained of the tendency of modern hospitals "to deteriorate into dehumanized machines" in which a patient "loses his personal identity."[64] This tendency has grown along with the size, distance from the patient's home, and technical sophistication of modern facilities. A second reason is the loss in every state of the protection of "charitable immunity," the legal doctrine formerly preventing recovery from charitable institutions for their negligence. A further legal development in a number of jurisdictions encourages facilities' intervention in the relations between patients and employees or staff; that is the "corporate negligence" concept, which under some circumstances creates facility responsibility for staff derelictions.

In 1973 a federal commission urged facilities to adopt patient grievance mechanisms (then present in only 27 percent of the largest hospitals),[65] and the American Hospital Association submitted to its member institutions the first patients' bill of rights. Today half of American hospitals have a patient representative (though questions of status and authority for the position remain); many also have ethics committees to help staff, patients, and families define choices. At least one institution (Sarah Lawrence College) offers a master's degree in health advocacy, to train patient mediators. The American Civil Liberties Union

---

[64]F. W. Peabody, "The Care of the Patient," in Encounters, at 389-390.

[65]The commission's researchers were unimpressed with existing programs, noting that, in most cases, the single person charged with the duty lacked training and authority. One respondent described its eight-woman Patient Relations staff as "airline stewardess types." F. Thompson et al., Patient Grievance Mechanisms in Health Care Institutions, Appendix: Report of the Secretary's Commission on Medical Malpractice 758-759, quotation at 769, DHEW Pub. No. (OS) 73-89 (1973).

published a Hospital Patient's Bill of Rights in 1975,[66] and the People's Medical Society issued another in 1983. A growing minority of states protects some aspects of patients' rights. A few states, preeminently Massachusetts, have legislated extensively in the area. The federal government protects beneficiaries of Medicare and Medicaid, and indirectly all patients, through Conditions of Participation for its programs that require facilities (and recently home health agencies) to acknowledge certain rights. In 1987 Congress enacted legislation on nursing home rights described as "the culmination of ten years of effort by consumer groups." The written standards of the Joint Commission on Accreditation of Healthcare Organizations begin with "Rights and Responsibilities of Patients." Numerous official statements of the American Medical Association adopted in the 1970s and 1980s affirm patient entitlements.

These changes have certainly not transformed the provider-patient relationship; at most they are a beginning. A major impediment to restructuring the relationship is that in the United States the elemental patient right—to basic care regardless of ability to pay—is not guaranteed and is available to a shrinking majority of the population.[67] Other barriers are patients' and providers' opposition to change (or at least ambivalence about it),[68] the fact that few people identify themselves as members of the interest group *patients*,[69] and the widely shared perception

---

[66]The document's premises were that (1) the medical consumer has some rights he should not have to forfeit when hospitalized and (2) most hospitals do not recognize them. G. Annas, The Rights of Hospital Patients 1 (1975).

[67]By contrast, the basic Canadian document in the field, "Consumers' Rights to Health Care," from the Consumers' Association of Canada, can assert a right to equal access to care as one of its four points because of governmental guarantees.

[68]For example, a study showed 80 percent of patients but only 20 percent of physicians support patients' right to read their records. At the same time, 43 percent of doctors accepted patients' right to make the final treatment decision but only 40 percent of patients wished to do so. As the researchers noted, each group's views seem self-contradictory. Haug and Lavin, Consumerism in Medicine, at 68-69.

[69]Stoeckle observes that ". . . doctors, . . . unlike patients, have the position, time, capacity, and responsibility to enhance their relationships. For

that health costs must be curbed. The last raises the question of what further efforts to humanize medical interactions are desirable or possible. After all, American healthcare is very good indeed for those who can afford it. The current state of patients' rights, described below, represents an intermediate point between medicine's tradition of paternalism and an ideal of provider-patient equality that may never be attained.

B. The Kinds of Rights at Issue

§9.3 Generally Acknowledged Basic Rights

Patients are widely understood to enjoy certain entitlements in their relationship with providers. These include

1. the right to know what the provider knows about the patient's illness and treatment;
2. the right to make significant medical decisions, including that of terminating treatment;
3. the right to competent care;
4. the right to have medical information kept confidential;
5. the right to be treated courteously;
6. the right not to be exploited; and
7. the right to continued care until the relationship is properly ended.

In extended care facilities there is additional emphasis, as there must be, on rights. (See §15.12 through §15.18.) When patients remain in a facility for long periods, such rights as protection of property or funds and the right not to be summarily discharged assume importance.

---

this task, professional leadership and commitment are needed alongside a more educated patient in a more humane and equitable society." Encounters, at 386.

Consensus on basic rights exists only at a rather high level of generality. Each premise above leads to practical questions that are resolved differently by various providers. In addition, some matters that seem basic—the criteria for selecting among those who wish to be patients—command no consensus.[1]

Opinions and practices differ, for example, on such aspects of the relationship as these: Does the patient herself have the right to read records? In what form? During the course of treatment or only at its conclusion? What *are* the significant medical decisions, and what information does the patient need in order to make them? How much information concerning risk and uncertainty is helpful? What deference is due to a patient's known or possible idiosyncratic preferences? What constitutes competent care and appropriate consequences for its absence? (Because they are the subject of the law of medical malpractice, these issues are among the best-defined.) Are lengthy waiting periods, lack of privacy, or hurried consultations discourteous, and, if so, are they avoidable? At what point does lack of continuity in the medical relationship (assignment of HMO enrollees, for instance, to a succession of physicians) become unacceptable? Which business decisions of providers—joint venturing, ownership of facilities to which patients are referred, cost shifting to the insured, bonuses from insurers for not referring to specialists—could be fairly thought to exploit patients as financial resources? What necessities of teaching and research is it just to expect patients and their families to bear? What patient behavior justifies refusing to continue care?

---

§9.3   [1]For one selection from the extensive literature on this subject, see Arras, The Fragile Web of Responsibility: AIDS and the Duty to Treat, Hastings Center Report 10-20 (April/May 1988).

632

§9.4 Derivative Specific Rights

At least the following jurisdictions[1] incorporate some aspects of patients' rights in statute: California,[2] Colorado,[3] the District of Columbia,[4] Illinois,[5] Indiana,[6] Maryland,[7] Massachusetts,[8] Michigan,[9] Minnesota,[10] New Hampshire,[11] North Dakota,[12] Rhode Island,[13] South Dakota,[14] Texas,[15] and Vermont.[16] A few statutes address a single issue—the right to records,[17] for instance, or, more significantly, refusal of diagnosis or emergency services for any discriminatory reason including inability to pay.[18] Others are

---

§9.4 [1]Every state has enactments affecting patients' rights, if only by setting time limits for filing malpractice claims or ratifying the existence of a bond of confidentiality between physician and patient in some circumstances (the "doctor-patient privilege.") For example, concern about malpractice litigation in the early 1970s led many states to shorten statutes of limitations on the claims; similar fears in the late 1980s prompted several (such as California and Virginia) to attempt to limit the amount of recovery. The states named in the text have additional legislation that deliberately promotes rights.

[2]Cal. Civ. Code §§56 to 56.37 (West 1982 & Supp. 1990); Cal. Welf. & Inst. Code §§5510 to 5550, §§9700 to 9741 (West 1984 & Supp. 1989).

[3]Colo. Rev. Stat. §§25-1-120 to 25-1-121 (1989).

[4]D.C. Code Ann. §§32-1301 to 32-1309 (1988 & Supp. 1989).

[5]Ill. Ann. Stat. ch. 111½, ¶¶4152-101 to 4153-215 (extended care facilities); id. ch. 111½, ¶5403 (medical patients) (Smith-Hurd 1988).

[6]Ind. Code §§16-14-1.6-1 to 16-14-1.6-11 (1983 & Supp. 1988).

[7]Md. Health-Gen. Code Ann. §§19-301 (1990), 19-342 to 19-350, 19-370 to 19-374 (1990). See also Md. Regs. Code tit. 10, §10.07.10.13 (Supp. 1988).

[8]Mass. Ann. Laws ch. 111, §§70E to 70F (Law. Co-op. 1985 & Supp. 1989).

[9]Mich. Comp. Laws Ann. §§333.20201 to 333.20203 (West 1980 and Supp. 1989).

[10]Minn. Stat. Ann. §§144.651 to 144.652 (West 1989).

[11]N.H. Rev. Stat. Ann. §§151:19 to 151:29 (1989).

[12]N.D. Cent. Code §§50-10.2-01 to 50-10.2-04 (Supp. 1989).

[13]R.I. Gen. Laws §§23-17-19.1 to 23-17.5-24 (1985 & Supp. 1988).

[14]S.D. Codified Laws Ann. §36-2-16 (1986).

[15]Tex. Health & Safety Code Ann. §311.022 (Vernon 1990).

[16]Vt. Stat. Ann. tit. 18, §§1851, 1852 (Supp. 1989) (hospital patients); §§2101-06 (Supp. 1989) (nursing home patients).

[17]S.D. Codified Laws Ann. §36-2-16 (1986).

[18]Tex. Health & Safety Code Ann. §311.022. (Vernon 1990).

broader. The language of the Massachusetts statute, reproduced in part below, has been copied by several other states; it exemplifies the most comprehensive enactments.

Besides guaranteeing written notice of rights, an itemized bill and explanation of charges on request, and freedom in choice of facility if the facility can accommodate the patient, the Massachusetts statute provides as follows:

Every patient or resident of a facility shall have the right:

(a) upon request, to obtain from the facility in charge of his care the name and specialty, if any, of the physician or other person responsible for his care or the coordination of his care;

(b) to confidentiality of all records and communications to the extent provided by law;

(c) to have all reasonable requests responded to promptly and adequately within the capacity of the facility;

(d) upon request, to obtain an explanation as to the relationship, if any, of the facility to any other health care facility or educational institution insofar as said relationship relates to his care or treatment;

(e) to obtain from a person designated by the facility a copy of any rules or regulations of the facility which apply to his conduct as a patient or resident;

(f) upon request, to receive from a person designated by the facility any information which the facility has available relative to financial assistance and free health care;

(g) upon request, to inspect his medical records and to receive a copy thereof in accordance with section seventy, and the fee for said copy shall be determined by the rate of copying expenses;

(h) to refuse to be examined, observed, or treated by students or any other facility staff without jeopardizing access to psychiatric, psychological, or other medical care and attention;

(i) to refuse to serve as a research subject and to refuse any care or examination when the primary purpose is educational rather than therapeutic;

(j) to privacy during medical treatment or other rendering of care within the capacity of the facility;

(k) to prompt life saving treatment in an emergency without discrimination on account of economic status or source of payment and without delaying treatment for purposes of prior discussion of the source of payment unless such delay can be imposed without material risk to his health, and this right shall also extend to those persons not already patients or residents of a facility if said facility has a certified emergency care unit;

(l) to informed consent to the extent provided by law;

(m) upon request to receive a copy of an itemized bill or other statement of charges submitted to any third party by the facility for care of the patient or resident and to have a copy of said itemized bill or statement sent to the attending physician of the patient or resident;

(n) if refused treatment because of economic status or the lack of a source of payment, to prompt and safe transfer to a facility which agrees to receive and treat such patient. Said facility refusing to treat such patient shall be responsible for: ascertaining that the patient may be safely transferred; contacting a facility willing to treat such patient; arranging the transportation; accompanying the patient with necessary and appropriate professional staff to assist in the safety and comfort of the transfer, assure that the receiving facility assumes the necessary care promptly, and provide pertinent medical information about the patient's condition; and maintaining records of the foregoing.[19]

The attending physicians as well as the facilities must confer the above rights. In addition, physicians are obliged, if asked, to explain their relationship to any other facility or educational institution, including any ownership or financial interest, "insofar as said relationship relates to . . . care or treatment." Physicians must also explain "all alternative treatments which are medically viable" for breast cancer. Before admitting a maternity patient, the facility must inform her of its rates of caesarean delivery and breastfeeding among patients and usage rates of various anesthetics. Finally, both facilities and physicians are forbidden to test for the HTLV-III antibody without the patient's written consent or to disclose the result or identify the subject of the test.[20]

---

[19]Mass. Ann. Laws ch. 111, §70E (Law. Co-op. 1985 & Supp. 1989).
[20]Mass. Ann. Laws ch. 111, §70F (Law. Co-op. 1985 & Supp. 1989).

Though the Massachusetts statute is as comprehensive as any single formulation, it omits certain guarantees made by other states, the federal government, or the health facility accrediting agency, the JCAHO. These include such privacy or autonomy rights as wearing one's own clothes whenever possible,[21] declining to see staff not involved in care,[22] not being housed with smokers,[23] keeping the source of payment for care confidential,[24] and having a same-sex staff member present during examinations.[25] Vermont's statute allows constant family presence for patients who are children or who are terminally ill.[26] JCAHO standards and the laws of several states address particular communication problems, sometimes ensuring access to an interpreter[27] or the right to speak one's own language.[28] Connection to the outside world is assured by enactments on

---

[21]Joint Commission on Accreditation of Healthcare Organizations (JCAHO), Accreditation Manual for Hospitals 1991 (Chicago 1990), xii (hereinafter Accreditation Manual); Vt. Stat. Ann. tit. 18, §1852(6) (1989 Supp.); Md. Health-Gen. Code Ann. §19-344(1) (1990); Minn. Stat. Ann. §144.651(22) (West 1990). It is interesting, though, that the current Minnesota statute is less permissive than its predecessor, which allowed use of personal clothing and possessions "unless medically contraindicated and documented by [the] physician in the medical record."

[22]Accreditation Manual, at xi; Ill. Ann. Stat. ch. 111½, ¶4152-110 (Smith-Hurd 1988) (nursing homes); Cal. Health & Safety Code §5530 (West 1984 and Supp. 1989).

[23]Accreditation Manual, at xii; Vt. Stat. Ann. tit. 18, §1852 (Supp. 1989).

[24]Accreditation Manual, at xii.

[25]Accreditation Manual, at xii; Vt. Stat. Ann. tit. 18, §1852 (Supp. 1989).

[26]Vt. Stat. Ann. tit. 18, §1852 (Supp. 1989); George Annas argues that parents' right to consent for a child necessarily includes the right to be with the child unless this interferes with the facility's treatment of other patients. He rejects the argument that parents' presence may interfere with treatment of their own child since they must be present in order to consent to it. Annas, The Rights of Hospital Patients, at 142.

[27]Accreditation Manual, at xiii; Vt. Stat. Ann. tit. 18, §1852 (Supp. 1989); Minn. Stat. Ann. §144.651 (West 1989) (promising "reasonable accommodations"); Md. Health-Gen. Code Ann. §19-344(e) (1990) requires that treatment information be "in language that the resident reasonably can be expected to understand."

[28]Tex. Health & Safety Code Ann. §242.011 (Vernon 1990).

visitors,[29] mail,[30] and the exercise of civil rights such as voting.[31] Some protection is afforded for the desire to stay in a facility[32] and more for the right to leave.[33] Finally, patients are entitled to specific information on cost.[34]

The National Association of Insurance Commissioners's

---

[29]Cal. Health & Safety Code §9722 (West 1984 & Supp. 1989) (long-term care facilities); Colo. Rev. Stat. §25-1-120 (1989) (nursing and intermediate care facilities).

[30]Mich. Comp. Laws Ann. §333.20201(k) (West 1980 & Supp. 1989).

[31]Vt. Stat. Ann. tit. 17, §2122 (Supp. 1989) provides that no one shall gain or lose residency in a hospital, nursing home or other healthcare facility as a result of voting. See also Ga. Code Ann. §31-8-111(1) (1985 & Supp. 1989).

[32]The Supreme Court denied patients' claim against the government to prevent closing a facility for violations, but speculated that patients might have a damage claim against the facility. O'Bannon v. Town Court Nursing Center, 447 U.S. 773, 787 (1980). California's State Department of Health Services or the facility must help patients relocate before a facility stops serving them. West's Ann. Cal. Health & Safety Code §§1336 to 1336.2 (Supp. 1990). As for exclusion of a single patient, the Medicare and Medicaid Conditions of Participation require facilities to explain and honor an array of discharge rights. See, e.g., 42 C.F.R. §405.1121(k)(4) (1988). When a provider is suspended from the programs, his patients must be told that no further bills for his services will be paid, 42 C.F.R. §§1001.125(d) and (e) (1988). No patient may be discharged whose condition is not stable (see Chapter 6, Access to Care). Several states have also enacted transfer rights. Md. Health-Gen. Code Ann. §19-345 (1990); Mass. Ann. Laws ch. 111, §70E(n) (Law. Co-op. 1985 & Supp. 1989); N.H. Rev. Stat. Ann. §151:21 (IV), §151:26 (Supp. 1989); Minn. Stat. Ann. §144.651, Subd. 29 (West 1989).

[33]Unless a patient has been committed to a facility she is free to leave in nearly every circumstance including 'against medical advice' and without arranging for payment. Mildred I. Freel states that some patients are given the contrary impression or flatly told otherwise. M. Freel, "Consumer Rights and the Health Care Industry," in J. C. McCloskey and H. K. Grace, eds., Current Issues in Nursing 589 (2d ed. 1985). Though the right to leave need not be set out, some states do so. Minn. Stat. Ann. §144.651 (West 1989); Ga. Code Ann. §31-8-112(d) (1985); West's Ann. Cal. Health & Safety Code §1285 (Supp. 1990).

[34]Medicare patients are entitled to information about charges, coverage, and their rights to appeal denials of payment. For hospital patients the right is codified at 42 U.S.C.A. §1395cc(a)(1)(M); for home health patients at 42 U.S.C.A. §1395bbb(a)(1)(E). State law may assure the same right; e.g., Colo. Rev. Stat. §25-1-120(1)(e) (1989); Ga. Code Ann. §31-8-106 (1985); Md. Health-Gen. Code Ann. §19-344 (1990).

model act governing health maintenance organizations guarantees a role for patients. Under the act, every HMO must allow some patient participation in governance and establish a mechanism for soliciting and resolving complaints. (See §16.9.6.) Utah's statute is illustrative.

§31A-8-401. Enrollee participation

Every organization shall provide a reasonable procedure for allowing enrollees to participate in matters of policy of the organization and for resolving complaints and grievances initiated by enrollees or providers.[35]

§9.5 Rights Patients Seek

Despite the entitlements noted above and a generally high quality of care, Americans are dissatisfied with significant aspects of the health system.[1] The most troubling issue, as noted above, is the absence of basic services for all. The size of the uninsured and inadequately insured population is often estimated at 25 percent of the total population. In one large poll, 7 percent reported forgoing needed medical care in the preceding year because of cost.[2] Congress regularly considers expansion of Medicaid, the program that once met most of the needs of the medically indigent, and serious proposals have emerged for restructuring by other methods.[3] Meanwhile, lack of care for

---

[35]Utah Code Ann. (1986).

§9.5 [1]Eighty-nine percent of Americans in one poll want "fundamental change," compared to 42 percent of Canadians and 69 percent of Britons. D. Hevesi, "Polls Show Discontent With Health Care," N.Y. Times, Feb. 15, 1989, at 8, cols. 1-3.

[2]Id. Fewer than 1 percent in Britain and Canada reported the same.

[3]Enthoven and Kronick, A Consumer-Choice Health Plan for the 1990's: Universal Health Insurance in a System Designed to Promote Quality and Economy, 320 New Eng. J. Med. 94-101 (Jan. 12, 1989). Himmelstein, Woolhandler, et al., A National Health Program for the United States, 320 New Eng. J. Med. 102-108 (1989). On January 30, 1989, the National Leadership Commission on Health Care published its proposal. Congressional Quarterly Weekly Report 221 (February 4, 1989).

some creates negative perceptions of the healthcare system even among the majority for whom care is affordable.

A closely related issue is the limitations on access to inexpensive providers that characterize medicine in the United States.[4] Whether the patient-plaintiffs are nursing home residents suing to remain in a substandard facility[5] or pregnant women seeking hospital privileges for their doctors,[6] efforts to force recognition of their preference in providers usually fail.[7] Licensure is the initial hurdle eliminating many unorthodox healers.[8] Even for licensed nonphysician practitioners, staff privileges in healthcare facilities have been[9] and remain[10] an elusive goal. Though there may be little support for a truly free market in health services,[11] nonphysician practitioners are doubtless correct

---

[4]For a historical account of the transition in the United States from an open to a limited market in medical services, see P. Starr, The Social Transformation of American Medicine, Book I: A Sovereign Profession: The Rise of Medical Authority and the Shaping of the Medical System (1985).

[5]O'Bannon v. Town Court Nursing Center, 447 U.S. 773 (1980).

[6]Bello v. South Shore Hosp., 384 Mass. 770, 429 N.E.2d 1011 (1981).

[7]But see Virginia Academy of Clinical Psychologists v. Blue Shield, 469 F.2d 476 (4th Cir. 1980), in which patients won the right to reimbursement for psychologists' services not billed through a physician.

[8]N.C. Gen. Stat. §90-18 (1985), a typical "practicing without license" statute, reads in part, "No person shall practice medicine or surgery, or any of the branches thereof, nor in any case prescribe for the cure of diseases unless he shall have been first licensed and registered so to do. . . . Any person shall be regarded as practicing medicine or surgery . . . who shall diagnose or attempt to diagnose, treat or attempt to treat, operate or attempt to operate on, or prescribe for or administer to, or profess to treat any human ailment, physical or mental, or any physical injury to or deformity of another person. . . ." Upheld in State v. Nelson, 69 N.C. App. 633, 640-641, 317 S.E.2d 711, 713 (1984).

[9]In 1927 the Supreme Court found no denial of due process or equal protection in a municipal hospital's denial of privileges to osteopaths. Hayman v. City of Galveston, 273 U.S. 414 (1927).

[10]Stern v. Tarrant County Hosp. Dist., 755 F.2d 430 (5th Cir. 1985), reversing 565 F. Supp. 1440 (N.D. Texas 1983), 778 F.2d 1052 (5th Cir. 1985), cert. denied, 476 U.S. 1108 (1986); Cooper v. Forsyth County Hosp. Auth., 604 F. Supp. 685 (M.D.N.C. 1985).

[11]The proposal has been well argued, however, by Milton Friedman in Capitalism and Freedom (1982).

in asserting that patients would like a wider spectrum of choice.

It is also likely that many patients want better information on the nature, quality, and cost of available services—information without which economists agree a market cannot function efficiently. Although the American Medical Association urges its members to volunteer fee information, few do so; patients also find it difficult to determine which practitioners use particular techniques and treatments. The Long-Term Care Ombudsman program (described in §15.3) has been of some help in identifying problems for residents of extended care facilities, but more assistance is needed. Judging the quality of care is the patient's hardest task, and the few assessment tools available are controversial. The Health Care Financing Administration publishes facilities' deviations from expected mortality rates and other standards and has proposed releasing data for individual practitioners; in December 1988 it published survey standards for extended care facilities. The JCAHO proposes to identify publicly facilities that have failed inspection and are scheduled to lose accreditation. These steps and similar efforts by governmental and private agencies are welcomed by consumer groups but often criticized as misleading and damaging by provider organizations, thus increasing patients' uncertainties.

Several sources recommend that facilities provide an advocate for patients or allow the patient to designate someone to assist in understanding the information needed for decision-making, for overseeing care, or for challenging costs.[12] As noted earlier, many facilities do provide an advocate. Some states appoint, and then require certain facilities to receive, visitors who represent patients.[13] The federal Conditions of Participation

---

[12]George J. Annas, like the Secretary's Commission on Medical Malpractice, favors a professional advocate provided by the facility. Annas, The Emerging Stowaway: Patients' Rights in the 1980s, 10 Law, Medicine and Health Care 35 (1982). Others recommend the patient's selecting her own advocate. Huttmann, The Patient's Advocate (1981); E. E. Rosenbaum, A Taste of My Own Medicine 37 (1988); People's Medical Society, Code of Practice, in C. B. Inlander, L. S. Levin, and E. Weiner, Medicine on Trial 221 (1988).

[13]Cal. Welf. & Inst. Code §5521 (West 1984); N.C. Gen. Stat. §131E-128

usually include a complaint mechanism.[14] Still, a competent patient's need for and right to help in coping with a healthcare facility is not uniformly acknowledged.

C. The Sources of Rights

§9.6 The Provider-Patient Contract

"The creation of the physician-patient relationship is contractual in nature. Generally, both the physician and the patient are free to enter into or decline to enter the relationship."[1] This statement of the American Medical Association reflects our societal understanding, based on the model of patient and physician coming together as independent contractors. In the context of private outpatient care and in hospitals the contract is largely unwritten and, more important, unspoken. Though the execution of consent-to-treatment forms is commonplace, no attempt is made to reduce to writing the totality, or even the essential elements of, the healthcare relationship. Presumably, its most basic terms are, from a patient's viewpoint, competently rendered care to which he assents and, for the provider, payment and, if the relationship is to continue, an acceptable level of cooperation. But even these major terms are implicit, to be inferred from the parties' behavior. The same is true of subsidiary conditions such as preservation of confidentiality, termination of the contract at

---

(1988) (nursing home advisory committees). These appointees are heirs to the responsibilities exercised until the twentieth century by the trustees of hospitals and similar institutions. C. Rosenberg, The Care of Strangers 263-267 (1987).

[14]Pub. L. No. 100-203, §4025, amending 42 U.S.C. §1395aa(a) to require a "hotline" for complaints about home health agencies.

§9.6 [1]American Medical Association, Reference Guide to Policy and Official Statements 19 (1987). The 1988 Guide makes similar statements: "A physician may choose those persons whom he will accept as patients" (63) and "free choice of physicians is the right of every individual" (12).

will by the patient, and a provider's duty to notify the patient
before terminating.

Fortunately, unspoken agreements work well enough for
countless contracts to be performed with no need to examine
their content. When one party is disappointed, relatively little
effort is expended on reconstructing the actual expectations of
the individuals. The law, most often using tort or contract
principles, looks instead to the assumptions and behavior of a
"reasonable patient" and compares the practitioner to similarly
situated practitioners of the same profession. Thus, the contract's
outlines vary over space and time. A change in expectations on
either side, such as patients' growing assumption of autonomy
in decision-making, will eventually alter the contract—and can
do so in spite of the other side's preferences.[2] As a result,
although the legal concept of a provider-patient contract is
among the most important sources of hospital patients' rights, it
is an indefinite and evolving standard.

The patient-provider contract is far more explicit with
respect to extended care facilities and health maintenance
organizations. Most extended care facilities enter into written
contracts with residents. Some states, in fact, require that each
patient be admitted pursuant to contract.[3] The contracts, which
usually list specific rights, have occasionally been held enforceable. In one instance, a plaintiff whose husband was severely
abused was able to take advantage of the ten-year period for
filing contract claims; her suit would have been barred under
the statute of limitations for tort actions.[4] The relationship
between HMOs and their enrollees is also explicitly contractual.
A statute such as Illinois's, for example, regulates HMOs as
"administrators" of insurance contracts; patients are described

---

[2]"Even if doctors' expectations about authority differ, they have reason to
know, and under contract principles therefore to be bound by, the intent of
patients." Shultz, From Informed Consent to Patient Choice: A New Protected
Interest, 95 Yale L.J. 219, 282, citing Restatement (Second) of Contracts §201
(1979).

[3]Ill. Ann. Stat. ch. 111½, ¶4152-202 (1988).

[4]Free v. Franklin Guest Home, 397 So. 2d 47 (La. App. 1981).

as contract beneficiaries.[5] The statute lists in some detail what matters must be addressed in the contract.[6]

§9.7 Legislation

Legislation is a more definite guide and an important source of rights. State laws will usually set out in general terms a performance standard for professionals, deviation from which will be adjudged medical malpractice. A large number of states legislate the confidentiality of and access to records, and consent-to-treatment statutes are common. State legislatures have addressed even the most difficult issues in medical ethics. The majority allow competent adults to arrange to have treatment terminated at some future point by means of "living wills" or designation of a decisionmaker through transfer of a durable power of attorney. To further these processes (and other goals, such as organ transplantation), states have enacted determination-of-death statutes based on cessation of certain brain functions. If a pattern of preference for particular categories of patients can be discerned in legislation, it is a higher level of protection for the handicapped, the mentally ill, and residents of nursing homes.

Federal statutes and regulations, usually tied to funding, play major roles in the creation and enforcement of rights. For

---

[5] Ill. Ann. Stat. ch. 73, ¶982m (1989 Supp.).

[6] Id. According to Illinois law,

Each administrator shall provide to any beneficiary of any program subject to this Article a document which (1) sets forth those providers with which agreements or arrangements have been made to provide health care services to such beneficiaries, a source for the beneficiary to contact regarding changes in such providers and a clear description of any incentives for the beneficiary to utilize such providers, (2) discloses the extent of coverage as well as any limitations or exclusions of health care services under the program, (3) clearly sets out the circumstances under which reimbursement will be made to a beneficiary unable to use the services of a provider with which an arrangement or agreement has been made, (4) a description of the process for addressing a beneficiary complaint under the program, and (5) discloses deductible and coinsurance amounts charged to any person receiving health care services from such a provider.

example, institutions receiving federal funds for research involving human subjects must scrutinize and vouch for the projects'
adherence to ethical standards. The Food and Drug Administration requires that patients be warned of the effects of drugs and
regulates the process of obtaining consent for participation in
investigative drug research. The Conditions of Participation in
the Medicare and Medicaid programs strongly influence facilities'
functioning, as when hospital emergency rooms are required to
stabilize patients without regard to ability to pay and must
accept any woman in active labor. The Department of Health
and Human Services (HHS) tried to regulate hospitals' care of
handicapped newborns under the federal handicapped persons
protection act. (The regulations were withdrawn after rejection
by the Supreme Court.)[1] Using its power to regulate funds for
family planning programs, HHS has forbidden (and, at another
point in time, required)[2] providers to insist that minor patients
have parental consent to participate in the programs. In 1986,
Congress funded organizations created to advocate for the
mentally ill and investigate patient abuse or neglect. Thus, the
federal government's impact on treatment of patients is substantial and tends to produce a national uniformity that would not
otherwise exist.

§9.8 Litigation

Litigation defines rights as well as enforces them; it gives content
to the provider-patient contract and fixes the intent and effect
of legislation. For example, decisions of the Supreme Court
spanning half a century protect reproductive freedom by forbidding state-ordered sterilization[1] and governmental bans on

---

§9.7 [1]Bowen v. American Hosp. Assn., 476 U.S. 610, 647 (1986).

[2]The regulations were withdrawn after federal courts in New York and
the District of Columbia found they exceeded HHS authority. New York v.
Schweiker, 557 F. Supp. 354 (S.D.N.Y. 1983); Planned Parenthood Federation
v. Schweiker, 559 F. Supp. 658 (D.D.C. 1983), affd. sub nom. Planned
Parenthood Federation v. Heckler, 712 F.2d 650 (D.C. Cir. 1983).

§9.8 [1]Skinner v. Oklahoma, 316 U.S. 535 (1942).

contraception[2] and abortion.[3] Adjudication of legal rights follows advances in medical technology. Surrogate parenting[4] and the development of cell lines from diseased organs[5] are examples of new arenas in which rights must be assigned. The Supreme Court, presumably acting on behalf of the public, has recently rescinded healthcare facilities' longstanding exemption from antitrust laws.[6]

On the other hand, the Court declined to protect patients in another significant medical decision, its "most comprehensive attempt thus far to define the constitutional right of privacy."[7] In Whalen v. Roe, the Court unanimously upheld New York's recordkeeping on narcotic drug prescriptions, a program that required pharmacies to report patients by name to a state registry. The Court considered, but the majority did not decide, whether the Constitution protects the confidentiality of medical information; the majority held instead that the New York statute did not violate confidentiality. The opinion does posit that when government gathers private data it must keep them safe, and it observes cautiously, "[I]n some circumstances that duty arguably has its roots in the Constitution."[8] State courts and the lower federal courts rule frequently in the area, particularly if malpractice litigation and decisions concerning physician-patient privilege are considered adjudications of patients' rights.

Several courts have upheld state statutes protecting the rights of patients in extended care facilities. The Supreme Court of Missouri held that its statute does create enforceable rights

---

[2]Griswold v. Connecticut, 381 U.S. 479 (1965).

[3]Roe v. Wade, 410 U.S. 113 (1973).

[4]In re Baby M, 109 N.J. 396, 537 A.2d 1227 (1988).

[5]Moore v. Regents of the Univ. of Cal., 249 Cal. Rptr. 494 (1988); rev. granted, 252 Cal. Rptr. 896, 763 P.2d 479.

[6]"[W]hatever may be its peculiar problems and characteristics, the Sherman Act, so far as price-fixing agreements are concerned, establishes one uniform rule applicable to all industries alike." Arizona v. Maricopa County Med. Socy., 457 U.S. 332, 349 (1982), quoting United States v. Socony-Vacuum Oil Co., 310 U.S. 150, 222 (1940).

[7]L. Tribe, American Constitutional Law 886 (1978).

[8]Whalen v. Roe, 429 U.S. 589, 605 (1977).

separate from those available under the wrongful death statute[9] and that the statute is clear enough to justify criminal penalties for violation.[10] The Supreme Courts of Iowa[11] and Louisiana,[12] as well as a New York trial court,[13] found the nursing home statutes of the respective states placed facility employees on notice that physical abuse of patients violated the law. In each case the question was whether the statute's criminal penalties could be imposed. The federal district court decision construing North Carolina's "Nursing Home Patients' Bill of Rights"[14] is a minority view. That court, though highly sympathetic, dismissed plaintiff's claim because the statute appeared "so general and nebulous that a trier of fact could not determine whether the standard had been violated. . . ."[15]

§9.9 Statements of Providers' and Patients' Organizations

Though almost entirely without legal effect, the codes of ethics and official statements of providers and the few patients' manifestos do affect expectations. Perhaps the best-known patient document is the 23-point "A Model Patient's Bill of Rights," written by George J. Annas for the American Civil Liberties Union (ACLU) in 1975.[1] The ACLU statement is meant to be adopted by facilities and, except for calling for "access to the highest degree of care without regard to the source of payment for that treatment and care," its provisions represent goals that

---

[9] Stiffelman v. Abrams, 655 S.W.2d 522 (Mo. banc 1983).

[10] State v. Dale, 775 S.W.2d 126 (Mo. banc 1989).

[11] State v. McKee, 392 N.W.2d 493 (Iowa 1986).

[12] State v. Brenner, 486 So. 2d 101 (La. 1986).

[13] People v. Coe, 131 Misc. 2d 807, 501 N.Y.S.2d 997 (Sup. 1986, affd., 510 N.Y.S.2d 470 (A.D. 1 Dept. 1987).

[14] Makas v. Hillhaven, 589 F. Supp. 736 (M.D.N.C. 1984).

[15] Id. at 742.

§9.9 [1] George Annas, Rights of Hospital Patients 233-235 (1975).

most facilities acknowledge, though few guarantee.[2] In 1983, a newly formed group called the People's Medical Society[3] proposed legislation, a "Model Hospital Disclosure Act," drafted by Lori B. Andrews.[4] This document asks far more of facilities; for example, it requires annual publication of "number and types of malpractice claims *filed*, decided, or *settled* against the institution . . . listing the names of physicians or hospital staff named in the suit [and] . . . descriptions of clinical trials and clinical experiments *proposed* or conducted in the institution" (emphasis supplied). The following excerpt indicates the scope of facilities' duties under the proposal:

> Health care practitioners or institutions shall not proceed with a [therapy] . . . before disclosing the nature of the procedure, its risks and benefits, its success rate generally and in the institution, cost range, number and type of hospital personnel likely to be involved, the type of equipment likely to be involved, the type of diagnostic procedures and monitoring procedures used in conjunction with the procedure, a summary of the literature justifying and opposing such procedures, a list of specific references in the literature on the procedure, and whether such materials are available in the hospital library.

The complete formulation is unduly burdensome to administrators and therefore is unlikely to be adopted voluntarily. No state

---

[2]Many facilities would find several other specified rights difficult or inconvenient to honor, such as "9. We recognize the right of any patient who does not speak English to have access to an interpreter," "10. The patient has a legal right to all the information contained in his medical record while in the health-care facility and to examine the record upon request," and "22. At the termination of his stay at the health care facility we recognize the right of a patient to a complete copy of the information contained in his medical record."

[3]The Society, based in Allentown, Pennsylvania, is a nonprofit consumer advocacy organization claiming 80,000 members. Author telephone conversation with Society representative (April 10, 1989).

[4]C. B. Inlander, L. V. Levin, and E. Weiner, Medicine on Trial 214-220 (1988). The Society also sponsors a Code of Practice that it urges physicians to adopt and display. Id. at 221.

has enacted it as legislation to date. It is, however, a reminder of patients' fears about illness[5] and the strength of the desire to maintain control.

Providers' organizations are sensitive to patients' fears, particularly as healthcare becomes a more competitive industry. In 1973, the American Hospital Association (AHA) sent to member institutions a 12-point Patient's Bill of Rights and suggested its adoption as hospital policy. The document encourages providers and patients to demonstrate consideration and respect for one another and advocates privacy for patients, information sharing, and providers' avoidance of undisclosed conflicts of interest. Though the code has been criticized for vagueness, for lacking an enforcement mechanism, and for depending on providers to define and grant rights,[6] it is probably the most influential formulation in current use. At least half of AHA member facilities have formally adopted it.[7] A second influential institution, the Joint Commission on Accreditation of Healthcare Organizations, begins its *Accreditation Manual for Hospitals* with a section entitled "Rights and Responsibilities of Patients." This document incorporates and amplifies the major points of the AHA bill, adding specific guarantees.[8] As to its

---

[5]As one patient put it, "[W]hen we enter a hospital, we often feel like the guests of some giant in a fairy story—we are not quite sure whether we have been invited for dinner or whether we *are* the dinner." M. Siegler and H. Osmond, Patienthood 89 (1979).

[6]Annas and Healey, The Patient Rights Advocate: Redefining the Doctor-Patient Relationship in the Hospital Context, 27 Vand. L. Rev. 243, 256 (1974).

[7]Telephone conversation with Alexandra Geikas, American Hospital Association, Chicago, Illinois (April 10, 1989). The Association has not surveyed members on adoption since the late 1970s.

[8]For example, the first point of the AHA bill is "The patient has the right to considerate and respectful care." The JCAHO states, "The patient has the right to considerate, respectful care at all times and under all circumstances, with recognition of his personal dignity." The AHA guarantees privacy, advising that "[c]ase discussion, consultation, examination and treatment are confidential and should be conducted discreetly. Those not directly involved in his care must have the permission of the patient to be present" (point 5). The JCAHO enumerates eight specific aspects of privacy, including the rights to have a person of one's own sex present during examination, not to remain disrobed longer than necessary, and to have the source of payment kept confidential.

effect on accreditation decisions, the manual says merely, "The following basic rights and responsibilities of patients are considered reasonably applicable to all hospitals."

The final body of materials that can be considered a source of patients' rights is the codes of ethics of the various healthcare professions. Though some object to the codes as inadequate in this regard,[9] each of them does suggest the profession's ideals. Serving both as an appeal to conscience and a yardstick for professional performance, the codes doubtless influence the treatment of patients (though their effect cannot be measured). A code's basic principles are usually expressed in quite general terms ("service to humanity with full respect for the dignity of man" is the physician's first principle), but these are supplemented by official interpretations that are more specific. For example, Point 1 of the American Nurses' Association code provides in part, "The nurse provides services with respect for human dignity and the uniqueness of the client. . . ." Portions of the Commentary on Point 1 are more explicit, as the following passage demonstrates:

1.3 Personal Attributes of Clients

Age, sex, race, color, personality, or other personal attributes, as well as individual differences in background, customs, attitudes, and beliefs, influence nursing practice only insofar as they represent factors the nurse must understand, consider, and respect in tailoring care to personal needs and in maintaining the individual's self-respect and dignity. Consideration of individual value systems and life-styles should be included in the planning of health care for each client.[10]

---

[9]Thomas Preston differentiates between physicians' personal and professional ethics. The former "generally favors the patient" but is often overwhelmed by the latter. The Clay Pedestal 167 (1981). According to Robert Veatch, "[t]he most important event in medical ethics in the past fifteen years has probably been the challenging of the assumption that the codes of organized medical professionals are the definitive summary of ethical norms governing medicine." "Challenging the Power of Codes," Hastings Center Report 16:5 (October 1986, 14).

[10]W. T. Reich and L. Walters, eds., Encyclopedia of Bioethics, Appendix, §IV, Codes of Specialty Health-Care Associations, at 1789-1790 (1978).

While the codes must be further interpreted by each member of the profession, they contain some guidance for the conscientious practitioner. Together with legislation, litigation, the formal statements of advocacy groups, and the expectations embedded in the implied contract between patient and provider, they contribute to the process of reaching agreement on patients' genuine needs and acceptable preferences.

D. Suggestions for Improving Provider-Patient Relations

§9.10 Improving the Quality and Conditions of Medical Training

Analyzing patients' attitudes three decades ago, Eliot Friedson predicted that the patient of the future would "continue to get along but will present the evasive, resentful but desperately demanding face to the medical world that all people present when confronted by forces they cannot control, which they know are sometimes indifferent to them, but which they cannot do without."[1] That disturbing description, though harsher than today's reality, is too close to the mark to ignore. Numerous observers of healthcare suggest changes in the behavior of both providers and patients that deserve consideration. With one exception, the changes are within the power of individual facilities to influence; the exception is modification of the selection and training of healthcare professionals.

On that subject, in 1989 a shift of emphasis in the Medical College Admissions Test was announced. The schools training physicians apparently agreed that science "can be taught much more easily—and to people of more widely varying aptitude to begin with—than the far more subtle abilities to grasp what is

---

§9.10   [1] E. Friedson, Patients' Views of Medical Practice 230 (1961).

650

bothering a patient and to give advice in the context of the patient's own concerns"[2] and that selecting for and developing the latter abilities would help the profession. In commenting favorably on the proposal, the Washington Post sought further changes, particularly in what it called "the boot-camp ambience" of medical school.[3] To further that goal, one state, New York, has established maximum on-duty hours for interns and residents.

§9.11 Improving the Ambience of Healthcare Facilities

Healthcare facilities themselves control the ambience for licensed practitioners (as opposed to students). If it chose, an institution might structure a reward system that recognized physicians, nurses, and others for sensitivity to patients' emotional as well as their physical needs. Administrators could reject the "Theory of Bad Apples," assuming instead that workers "are trying hard, acting in good faith, and not willfully failing to do what they know to be correct." The alternative "Theory of Continuous Improvement" might improve care by constantly testing processes and results and acting on the information.[1]

Facilities have the power to add significantly to patients' well-being through attention to their preferences. They could adopt the suggestions of a national commission that patients be allowed to decorate their rooms and wear their own clothes, to go and come from the facility more freely, to return home to rest, and to decide on treatment.[2] They might, one advocate

---

[2]*The Well-Rounded Doctor*, The Washington Post, March 22, 1989, at A18, cols. 1-2.

[3]Id.

§9.11 [1]Berwick, Continuous Improvement as an Ideal in Health Care, 320 New Eng. J. Med. 53-56 (Jan. 5, 1989).

[2]President's Commission for the Study of Ethical Problems in Medical and Biomedical and Behavioral Research, Deciding to Forego Life-Sustaining Treatment 108 (U.S. Govt. Printing Office, 1983). Admittedly, admission and discharge possibilities are controlled by third-party payors as much as by facility and physician preferences.

insists, truly individualize care, abandoning such demeaning routines as sleeping pills for everyone, mandatory wheelchair transportation, and a standard battery of admissions tests.[3] Greater concessions to privacy could be made.[4] Above all, facilities could use their authority to open up conversation between provider and patient. A wider dialogue, which Jay Katz persuasively argues must begin with providers' conceding uncertainty, promises inestimable benefit. It would lift the provider's burden of omnipotence; supply data for improving care; increase the patient's comforting and healing sense of control; and help the parties identify misunderstandings and distinguish between them and genuine disagreement.[5] Though they can expect resistance, facilities could try to persuade healthcare workers to accept conflict rather than suppress it.[6] (A harder task, perhaps, will be persuading patients that conflict does not jeopardize care.)[7] To encourage dialogue, facilities must freely

---

[3]Annas, The Emerging Stowaway, 10 Law, Medicine and Health Care 35 (Feb. 1982).

[4]John H. Seyle, a nursing home administrator, calls attention to the particular privacy needs of long-term patients, including sexual privacy for spouses. Seyle, Privacy Rights and Rights Related to Physical Security, 11 Am. Health Care Assn. J. 21-22 (May 1985).

[5]In these cases facilities bear considerable responsibility—Susan M. Wolf points out that if the patient and the provider cannot resolve a difference, an individual provider is relatively free to withdraw services, but a facility should be less so. Wolf, Conflict Between Doctor and Patient, 16 Law, Medicine and Health Care 200 (Fall/Winter 1988).

[6]Id. at 202.

[7]An intriguing study suggests that most patients are highly compliant until reassured on this point. One hundred percent of patients at mental health clinics who were read a formally worded waiver allowing their records to be sent to the state mental health agency signed the waivers. All patients who were read an informal statement to the same effect also signed. But in a group who were read the informal statement and then assured verbally that they truly had a choice—that is, their decision would not affect service—most declined to sign (59 percent when told by a clerk, 80 percent when told by a physician). The researcher surmised that the physician's reassurance was more credible. A. Westin, Computers, Health Records and Citizen Rights 243-245 (1976) (United States Bureau of Standards Doc. No. 157).

offer patients information, especially access to their own records.[8]
These measures require commitment to a broader definition of
patient needs than has been customary. Many will argue that
efficiency would suffer. On the other hand, such changes are
possible, merciful—and may even be prudent.

---

[8]George Annas joins the many who advocate greater patient access to
records but adds a more controversial proposal. It is that before consenting to
treatment patients learn the full facts about the experience of the person
performing a procedure, including how many times she has performed it and
her complication rate. Annas, The Emerging Stowaway, 10 Law, Medicine
and Health Care 35 (Feb. 1982).

III EMERGING ISSUES IN HEALTHCARE FACILITIES LAW

10

Terminal Care Decision-making

Elena N. Cohen

657

§10.0 Introduction

The duty of healthcare facilities and professionals to prolong life is not absolute. A patient is entitled to decide when the limits of useful intervention in illness have been reached and should be able to rely on health providers for help in understanding and effectuating his or her choices. This chapter reviews the legal principles involved in terminal care decision-making; suggests methods by which facilities can assist in the making and carrying out of decisions; describes commonly used dispute resolution procedures; and points out certain liability potentials associated with these areas.

A. The Legal Framework

§10.1 History of Terminal Care Decision-making

Treatment decisions have traditionally been made in the context of physicians consulting with patients and their families. Until recently, doctors would recommend a course of treatment, with varying degrees of explanation, and patients usually accepted the recommendation. (See §9.1.) If the physician thought the patient could not understand the recommendation, he would deal with the patient's family members as patient surrogates. The entire process usually occurred without institutional or judicial involvement.

In the last several decades, the physician-directed approach to treatment has evolved in the direction of a physician-patient partnership. (See §9.2.) Increasingly, the law has been called on to structure the partners' understandings. Following the acceptance in the 1960s of the "informed consent doctrine" (treated in Chapter 7), the concept of "advance medical directives" became popular. These directives, discussed below, may take a variety of forms. Some are authorized by statute (see Appendix 10-1); others, by courts. Most request that certain treatment possibilities be forgone in the event of serious irreversible illness, but they may also be used to request treatment. Sample statutory documents are included in Appendices 10-2, 10-3, and 10-4.

In 1976, the New Jersey Supreme Court ruled in the Quinlan case[1]—thereby acknowledging, however reluctantly, a role for the legal system in resolving the conflicts associated in the modern era with dying. California enacted the first "natural death" statute, granting immunity to healthcare providers who honor documents in which individuals try to express in advance a preference for rejecting life-sustaining treatment should certain medical events occur.[2] By the end of the 1980s, courts in over half the states had ruled on rejection of life-sustaining treatment (sometimes referred to as "right-to-die" cases), and more than 40 state legislatures had enacted "natural death" or medical proxy laws.[3]

For the foreseeable future, healthcare facilities must continue to focus on terminal care decision-making. A number of factors suggest that this aspect of facilities' operations may become increasingly important and problematic in coming years. These elements include the aging of the United States population; the high incidence of debilitating illnesses, such as AIDS and Alzheimer's disease; the growing technological capacity for extended life support; and patients' growing sense that they should and can control healthcare decisions.

---

§10.1 [1] In re Quinlan, 70 N.J. 10, 355 A.2d 647, cert. denied sub nom. Garger v. New Jersey, 429 U.S. 922 (1976), diverged from in part, In re Conroy, 98 N.J. 321, 486 A.2d 1209 (1985).

[2] Cal. Health & Safety Code §§7185 to 7195 (West Supp. 1990).

[3] For statutory citations, see Appendix 10-1. For the most up-to-date citations on right-to-die cases, living will laws, and healthcare proxies, as well as copies of unreported cases, statutory forms, and a statutory checklist chart (summarizing basic living will provisions in each state), write to: Legal Department, The Society for the Right to Die, 250 W. 57th St., NY, NY 10107.

Although many commentators claim that the phrase "right to die" inaccurately describes cases because there is no recognized right to die (only a right to refuse treatment), this chapter uses the phrase for convenience.

§10.2 Sources of Law

With a few exceptions, the controlling law on "death and dying" emanates not from federal authorities but from state courts, legislatures, and regulatory agencies. This section describes (1) the kinds of statutes most often encountered, (2) the bases for a number of the judicial decisions construing such statutes or constitutional or common-law rights, and (3) the categories of authority (including accreditation standards) to be consulted in the absence of statutory or decisional law.

§10.2.1 State Statutory and Regulatory Authority

The most significant statutes in the majority of states are those that deal directly with the extent to which individual preferences concerning terminal care will be honored and the approved means for indicating those preferences. Such legislation is known by a variety of names; among them natural death, living will, and right-to-die laws. Other statutes, too, may affect terminal care. A listing of the most relevant categories is included to assist the facility's attorney in researching the law of her jurisdiction.

A living will (also called "directive" or "declaration") is one form of advance directive. As noted above, it is a document intended to memorialize the treatment preferences of the maker ("declarant" or "patient") for later use should he be unable to state his preference at that time. Living wills may be expressly authorized by statute (see Appendix 10-1) or, if not, may be created by individuals and authorized by judicial precedents. Most such statutes authorize "competent adults" to indicate in writing their future wish to reject "life-sustaining treatment" if they are in a "terminal" condition and can no longer express themselves.

The statutes offer legal immunity to healthcare professionals and facilities that honor living wills meeting the statutory requirements. Many enactments also attempt to require that the provider honor the documents or make a "reasonable attempt" to transfer care of the patient to another professional or facility that will comply.

Sample statutory living wills appear in Appendices 10-2 and 10-3.

In determining the laws of her jurisdiction on terminal decision-making, the attorney should consult available statutes and regulations in the following areas:

1. Determination of death. Most states recognize death as occurring when there is irreversible cessation of either the functioning of the cardiopulmonary system or the entire brain, including the brain stem.[1]

2. Patient-appointed medical or healthcare proxies. Such statutes, often referred to as creating "durable powers of attorney for healthcare," authorize a patient to appoint another person to make healthcare decisions on her behalf should she become incapable of decision-making. See §10.6.4.

3. Patient's rights. See Chapter 7, Consent to Treatment; Chapter 9, Patients' Rights; and Chapter 15, Extended Care Facilities

4. Anatomical gifts. See Chapter 12, Organ Procurement and Transplantation.

5. Child abuse and neglect. See §10.3.

6. Adult abuse and neglect.[2] (Federal and state ombuds-

---

§10.2 [1]For a list of most states adopting the brain death standard by statute, see Uniform Brain Death Act, 12 U.L.A. 16 (Supp. 1990); Uniform Determination of Death Act, 12 U.L.A. 320 (Supp. 1990). Some states have also adopted the brain death standard by case law or regulation. For a discussion of these authorities, see citations in §10.3 n.11. For discussion of clinical criteria for determination of brain death, see 261 J.A.M.A. 2205-2210, 2222-2228, 2246 (April 21, 1989) (collection of articles); Korein, The Diagnosis of Brain Death, 4 Seminars in Neurology 52 (March 1984).

[2]See, e.g., 42 U.S.C.A. §3027(a)(12) (Supp. 1989); Del. Code Ann. tit. 16, §§1130-1140 (Michie Supp. 1988); Iowa Code Ann. §235.B (West Supp. 1990); In re Peter, 108 N.J. 365, 529 A.2d 419 (1987); In re Estate of Greenspan, 137 Ill. 2d 1, 558 N.E.2d 1194 No. 69703, slip op. at 15-17, 1990 Ill. LEXIS 82. (Ill. July 9, 1990) (not providing adequate nutrition when nonprovision is based on patient's knowing refusal is not neglect); New York

men programs create a mechanism whereby a governmental official, an ombudsman, is appointed to investigate complaints of potential abuse and neglect of the institutionalized elderly.)
7. Hospice care.[3]
8. Medical decisionmakers for incapacitated patients without directives. See §10.6.4.

§10.2.2 Federal Statutory and Regulatory Authority

Federal statutes and regulations should be consulted in the following circumstances: when the facility is a federal facility or receives Medicare or Medicaid funds;[4] if the facility is an extended care facility[5] (see Chapter 15 on residents' rights and extended care facilities' reimbursement); or if the facility treats severely impaired newborns in a state that receives federal funds for child abuse and neglect programs[6] (see §7.11). In addition,

---

State Department of Health Memorandum, Series 89-84 (Oct. 20, 1989) (same); Price and Armstrong, New Jersey's "Granny Doe" Squad: Arguments About Mechanisms for Protection of Vulnerable Patients, 17 L. Medicine & Health Care 255 (Fall 1989).

[3]For general information on hospices, contact the National Hospice Association, 1901 North Moore St., Suite 901, Arlington, VA 22209. See also Crowley, The Hospice Movement: A Renewed View of the Death Process, 4 J. Contemp. Health L. & Poly. 295 (1988), reprinted in Specialty Law Digest: Health Care 7 (Dec. 1988). For a discussion of cardiopulmonary resuscitation and hospices, see New York State Department of Health Memorandum, Series 89-56 (July 13, 1989).

[4]In re Application of Deel, 729 F. Supp. 231 (N.D.N.Y. 1990); Tune v. Walter Reed Army Medical Hosp., 602 F. Supp. 1452 (D.D.C. 1985). The Patient Self-Determination Act (H. 4449 and S. 1766), Pub. L. No. 101-508, §§4206, 4751 (effective December 1, 1991), requires providers receiving Medicare and Medicaid funds to inform patients about their right to execute advance directives.

[5]See, e.g., 42 C.F.R. §§442.311, 442.312, 483.10 (Oct. 1, 1989 edition); 54 Fed. Reg. 5316-73 (Feb. 2, 1989) (including discussion of regulations in relation to terminal care decision-making).

[6]42 U.S.C.A. §§5101-5117d (1983 & Supp. 1989); 45 C.F.R. §84.55, pt. 1340 (Oct. 1, 1989). For information on the history of these federal authorities,

the standards for institutional accreditation set forth by the JCAHO should be consulted.[7]

§10.2.3 Judicial Authority

Before the United States Supreme Court's decision in Cruzan v. Director, Missouri Department of Health,[8] legal issues of terminal care decision-making had been adjudicated almost entirely in state courts. In *Cruzan*, the Court held that competent adults have a liberty interest in rejecting medical treatment (including artificially administered nutrition and hydration) that is protected by the due process clause of the federal Constitution. The Court also held that the Constitution does not prohibit states from requiring that there be "clear and convincing" evidence that a currently incompetent patient would want treatment rejected before treatment is forgone. It did not, however, *require* that such a test be used.

Most cases in state courts arose in one of two circumstances: either a state's natural death statute failed to resolve the controversy (perhaps because it did not cover the medical condition or treatment at issue or the patient did not have a living will) or the statute was challenged as a restriction of a constitutional or common-law right.

Most courts have acknowledged that the right to refuse life-sustaining treatment may be an aspect of privacy, a liberty

---

see U.S. Commission on Civil Rights, Medical Discrimination Against Children with Disabilities (Washington, D.C.) (Sept. 1989). See also §7.11 and §10.3 n.3. There are also state child abuse and neglect laws and cases interpreting them.

For helpful secondary authorities on treatment of severely impaired newborns, see Imperiled Newborns, Hastings Center Report 5-32 (Dec. 1987); Fleischman, Bioethical Review Committees in Perinatology, 14 Clinics in Perinatology 379 (June 1987); 17 Law, Medicine & Health Care 295-347 (Winter 1989) (collection of articles on the Linares case).

[7]Joint Commission on Accreditation of Healthcare Organizations, Accreditation Manual for Hospitals §§MA .1.4.12 (1991).

[8]Cruzan v. Director, Mo. Dept. of Health, 110 S. Ct. 2841, 111 L. Ed. 2d 224 (1990); Cruzan v. Mouton, No. CV384-9P (Mo. Cir., Jasper Co., Dec. 14, 1990).

interest,[9] or an issue of self-determination.[10] Until *Cruzan*, most courts that decided that the right to reject treatment was constitutionally protected concluded that the protection was derived from the federal constitutional right of privacy. The Court in *Cruzan*, however, refused to find protection based on privacy, holding instead that the right was protected by the due process clause of the Fourteenth Amendment.[11] It is unclear, however, whether state courts will continue to recognize the right as being protected under the *state* constitutional right of privacy. The right of self-determination is recognized by the common law. The right to refuse treatment, whether based on constitutional or common law, is not absolute. After recognizing its existence, a court will weigh it against competing state interests, discussed in §10.3.

If a statute is being construed, the court must judge its effect on constitutional rights, previously enacted statutes, and common-law rights. Many statutes make the task easier by stating that they do not impair currently existing rights.

Facility attorneys must familiarize themselves with decisions from their state's courts on the rights of the dying.

§10.2.4 Persuasive Authority

Terminal care decision-making is a relatively new legal concern for healthcare facilities, and it touches on issues of medicine,

---

[9]See, e.g., Rasmussen v. Fleming, 154 Ariz. 207, 214-215, 741 P.2d 674, 681-682 (1987) (citing authorities in other jurisdictions); In re Application of Deel, 729 F. Supp. 231 (N.D.N.Y. 1990); Gray v. Romeo, 697 F. Supp. 580, 584-586 (D.R.I. 1988) (rights of self-determination and privacy grounded in the liberties protected by the federal constitutional due process clause).

[10]In re Estate of Longeway, 133 Ill. 2d 33, 549 N.E.2d 292, 297-298 (Ill. 1989); In re Gardner, 534 A.2d 947, 950-952 (Me. 1987) (and authorities cited therein); In re Storar (Eichner), 52 N.Y.2d 363, 376-383, 420 N.E.2d 64, 70, 438 N.Y.S.2d 266, 272-276, cert. denied, 454 U.S. 858 (1981).

[11]Cruzan v. Director, Mo. Dept. of Health, 110 S. Ct. 2841, 111 L. Ed. 2d 224, 241-243 (1990). In In re Guardianship of Browning, No. 74,174, slip op. at 7, 1990 Fla. LEXIS 1154 (Fla. 1990), decided shortly after *Cruzan*, the Florida Supreme Court recognized the right as being protected under the state constitutional right of privacy.

philosophy, religion, and public policy as well as issues of law. For those reasons, legislators, judges, and health professionals working in the area have consulted not only legally binding authority but also persuasive nonbinding authorities. State appellate courts, for example, have relied on such nonbinding authorities as trial court decisions, opinions from courts in other states, governmental reports, and medical and ethical writings.[12]

In reaching its own positions or in offering legal arguments to support them, a facility may also wish to include references to sources outside the law. Within the law, the facility's attorney

---

[12]See, e.g., In re Jobes, 108 N.J. 394, 529 A.2d 434 (1987), stay denied sub nom. Lincoln Park Nursing & Convalescent Home v. Kahn, 483 U.S. 1036 (1987) (citing nonbinding authorities). State attorneys general have also addressed these issues. See, e.g., 73 Op. Atty. Gen. No. 88-046 (Md. Oct. 17, 1988); N.Y. Op. Atty. Gen. 84-F16 (Dec. 1984). State health departments have also issued clarifications. See, e.g., California Department of Health Services, Revisions to the Guidelines Regarding Withdrawal or Withholding of Life-Sustaining Procedure(s) in Long-Term Care Facilities, OHLP 88-79 (Dec. 14, 1988); New York State Department of Health Memoranda Series 89-84 (Oct. 20, 1989). Among the most often-cited persuasive authorities in the medicolegal literature are: President's Commission for the Study of Ethical Problems in Medicine and Biomedical and Behavioral Research, Deciding to Forego Life-Sustaining Treatment (1983); American Medical Association Council on Ethical and Judicial Affairs, Withholding or Withdrawing Life-Prolonging Medical Treatment §§2.20, 2.21, Current Opinions of the Council on Ethical and Judicial Affairs of the American Medical Association (1989); American Academy of Neurology, Position Paper of the American Academy of Neurology on Certain Aspects of the Care and Management of the Persistent Vegetative State Patient, 39 Neurology 123-126 (Jan. 1989); U.S. Congress Office of Technology, Life-Sustaining Technologies and the Elderly (July 1987); Wanzer et al., The Physician's Responsibility Toward Hopelessly Ill Patients, 310 New Eng. J. Medicine 955 (April 12, 1984). Other statements on professional ethics include American College of Physicians, Ethics Manual, 111 Annals of Internal Medicine 245 (Aug. 1, 1989), 327 (Aug. 15, 1989).

For helpful overviews of the death and dying field, see A. Meisel, The Right to Die (1989 & Supp. 1990); Living Wills and Health-Care Proxies, Murphy's Wills Clauses (Dec. 1988 and Supp. 1989); N. Cantor, Legal Frontiers of Death and Dying (1987); Death and Dying (Chapter 12), BioLaw (1986, July 1989 and supplements); D. Humphry and A. Wickett, The Right to Die (1986); Rhoden, Litigating Life and Death, 102 Harv. L. Rev. 375 (Dec. 1988). A subscription service with updated medicolegal developments is available from The Society for the Right to Die, 250 W. 57th St., NY, NY 10107.

665

is most likely to find analogies for medical directives in the law of property. Precedents involving wills and powers of attorney for financial matters may be helpful, for example, in determining whether a document was voluntarily executed.

§10.3 Frequently Accepted Principles

The following principles concerning terminal care are established in the statutory or case law of a number of jurisdictions. The list may serve as a beginning point for developing facility policy and for the research of the facility's attorney. Each principle must be checked against binding precedents in the state where the facility is located.

1. Decisionally capable adults may refuse any medical treatment, including life-sustaining treatment, regardless of age, medical condition, or prognosis[1] (the definition of decisional incapacity is discussed in §10.6.1).
2. The right to refuse treatment is not necessarily lost when a person becomes decisionally incapable.[2]
3. Parents usually cannot refuse life-sustaining treatment for their minor children when the treatment is expected to be clearly beneficial. In some jurisdictions, however, they may reject life support on the child's behalf if doing so is generally consistent with accepted medical standards or the child is irreversibly ill (permanently unconscious, for example) and the parents conclude that refusal is in the child's best interest. Minors

---

§10.3   [1]Cruzan v. Director, Mo. Dept. of Health, 110 S. Ct. 2841, 111 L. Ed. 2d 224, 241, (1990); Fosmire v. Nicoleau, 75 N.Y.2d 218, 228-229, 551 N.E.2d 77, 551 N.Y.S.2d 876, (1990); Delio v. Westchester County Medical Center, 129 A.D.2d 1, 21-22, 516 N.Y.S.2d 677, 690-691 (2d Dept. 1987); In re Conroy, 98 N.J. 321, 355, 486 A.2d 1209, 1226 (1985) (and authorities cited therein).
[2]John F. Kennedy Memorial Hosp. v. Bludworth, 452 So. 2d 921, 924-926 (Fla. 1984); In re L.H.R., 253 Ga. 439, 446, 321 S.E.2d 716, 722 (1984).

usually cannot refuse life-sustaining treatment for themselves, although there have been recent holdings to the contrary involving "mature minors."[3]

4. The right to refuse treatment must be balanced against competing state interests. The most often articulated interests are (a) the preservation of life (while this is usually considered the strongest state interest, it alone is insufficient to outweigh the right to refuse treatment);[4] (b) the prevention of suicide; (c) the protection of innocent third parties; and (d) the ethical integrity of the medical professions.[5]

5. In the balancing test of Principle 4 above, "innocent third parties" does not include healthcare workers who are disturbed by patient preferences. The category is usually limited to (a) those who could develop a

---

[3]Bowen v. American Hosp. Assn., 476 U.S. 610 (1986); In re Guardianship of Barry, 445 So. 2d 365 (Fla. Dist. Ct. App. 1984); Custody of a Minor, 375 Mass. 733, 379 N.E.2d 1053 (1978); Custody of a Minor, 378 Mass. 732, 393 N.E.2d 836 (1979); In re Rosebush, No. 88 349180 AZ (Mich. Cir. Ct. Oakland County July 29, 1988) (Kuhn, J.); In re Hofbauer, 47 N.Y.2d 648, 393 N.E.2d 1009, 419 N.Y.S.2d 936 (1979); Scheb, Termination of Life Support Systems for Minor Children: Evolving Legal Responses, 54 Tenn. L. Rev. 1 (1986). Cf. Franson v. Radich, 84 Or. App. 715, 720-722, 735 P.2d 632, 635-636 (Ct. App. 1987) (right-to-life organization that caused neglect proceedings against parents of severely impaired newborns for failing to provide life support could be sued for custodial interference); D. Margolick, In Child Deaths, a Test for Christian Science, The N.Y. Times (New York late edition), Aug. 6, 1990, at A1 (overview of Twitchell case in Massachusetts and other cases involving criminal prosecution of parents who refuse treatment for their children for religious reasons). But see In re E.G., 133 Ill. 2d 98, 549 N.E.2d 292 (Ill. 1989) (mature minor may refuse medical treatment); In re Swan, 569 A.2d 1202 (Me. 1990) (artificial feeding could be refused on behalf of adolescent in persistent vegetative who had expressed wishes before he fell into that state). See also §10.2 n.6.

[4]State v. McAfee, 259 Ga. 579, 385 S.E.2d 651, 652 (1989); In re Conroy, 98 N.J. 321, 353, 486 A.2d 1209, 1225 (1985); Fosmire v. Nicoleau, 75 N.Y.2d 218, 227-231, 551 N.E.2d 77, 81-84, 551 N.Y.S.2d 876, 880-883 (1990).

[5]Rasmussen v. Fleming, 154 Ariz. 207, 216-218, 741 P.2d 674, 683-685 (1987); Superintendent of Belchertown State School v. Saikewicz, 373 Mass. 728, 740-745, 370 N.E.2d 417, 425-727 (1977).

contagious disease because of patient refusal or (b) a patient's minor children if they would not otherwise be adequately cared for and the patient has the prospect of full recovery following treatment.[6]

6. In the balancing test of Principle 4 above, medical ethics is adjudged to be enhanced by honoring patient preference, even if it results in the patient's death.[7]

7. In the event of conflict, the patient's wishes, expressed when decisionally capable, override those of family members or healthcare professionals (see §§10.6.1, 10.10).

8. Forgoing life-sustaining treatment is sometimes referred to as "passive euthanasia." It does not constitute suicide, assisted suicide, or murder so long as it is consistent with the patient's wishes, if known, or, if not, with the patient's best interest (in some jurisdictions) (see §10.6.4). The cause of death is not the act of forgoing treatment, but the underlying condition that prevents natural functioning. In contrast, deliberately shortening a person's life—by lethal injection, for example—is called "active euthanasia." It is a crime.[8]

---

[6]Jacobson v. Massachusetts, 197 U.S. 11 (1905) (compulsory smallpox vaccine); Public Health Trust v. Wons, 541 So. 2d 96 (Fla. 1989) (children otherwise adequately cared for); In re Requena, 213 N.J. Super. 475, 487-488, 517 A.2d 886, 893 (Super. Ct. Ch. Div.), affd., 213 N.J. Super. 443, 517 A.2d 869, 893 (Super. Ct. App. Div. 1986) (per curiam) (healthcare workers upset by patient decision are not innocent third parties); In re Farrell, 108 N.J. 335, 352-353, 529 A.2d 404, 412-413 (1987) (mother would not be able to care for minor children even with treatment). But see Fosmire v. Nicoleau, 75 N.Y.2d 218, 229-331, 551 N.E.2d 77, 82-84, 551 N.Y.S.2d 876, 881-883 (1990) (state interest in preserving even sole parent does not outweigh right to refuse treatment).

[7]Elbaum v. Grace Plaza of Great Neck, 148 A.D.2d 244, 255-257, 544 N.Y.S.2d 840, 847-848 (2d Dept. 1989) (and authorities cited therein); In re Application of Deel, 729 F. Supp. 231, 234 (N.D.N.Y. 1990) (and authorities cited therein). See also §10.2 n.12.

[8]Bouvia v. Superior Court (Glenchur), 179 Cal. App. 3d 1127, 1145, 225 Cal. Rptr. 297, 306 (Ct. App. 1986), review denied (Cal. June 5, 1986) (motive

9. There is no legal distinction between withholding and withdrawing treatment.[9]

10. Health professionals may be liable if they provide treatment against a person's known wishes, or if they negligently fail to provide treatment. (See §§10.9 and 10.10, as well as Chapter 6 on the latter point.)

11. By statute, healthcare providers are immune from civil and criminal liability if they honor statutorily authorized advance directives.

12. Providers are likewise protected in honoring nonstatutory directives or oral statements that meet constitutional or common-law standards, that is, if the directives and statements are adequate evidence of an incapacitated person's decision to reject life support, made when he was capable.[10]

---

not relevant); McConnell v. Beverly Enter., 209 Conn. 692, 710-711, 553 A.2d 596, 605-606 (1989) (and authorities cited therein); In re Application of Deel, 729 F. Supp. 231, 234 (N.D.N.Y. 1990); In re Conroy, 98 N.J. 321, 355, 486 A.2d 1209, 1226 (1985). See also Gilbert v. State, 487 So. 2d 1185 (Fla. Dist. Ct. App.), review denied, 494 So. 2d 1150 (Fla. 1986) (appellate court upheld murder conviction of husband who shot wife and claimed it was a mercy killing since euthanasia is not a defense to murder); Barber v. Superior Court, 147 Cal. App. 3d 1006, 196 Cal. Rptr. 484 (Ct. App. 1983) (criminal charges were thrown out against physicians who withdrew life-sustaining treatment from a permanently unconscious patient based on family preferences and patient's best interest); L. Belkin, Doctor Tells of First Death Using His Suicidal Device, The N.Y. Times, June 6, 1990, at A1 (describing Jack Kevorkian's device, used in the death of Janet Adkins in Michigan). For a discussion of comfort care and shortening life, see §10.6 nn.45-54.

[9]Rasmussen v. Fleming, 154 Ariz. 207, 222 n.24, 741 P.2d 674, 689 n.24 (1987) (and authorities cited therein); In re Guardianship of Grant, 109 Wash. 2d 545, 747 P.2d 445 (1987), modified on other grounds, 757 P.2d 534 (1988); President's Commission for the Study of Ethical Problems in Medicine and Biomedical and Behavioral Research, Deciding to Forego Life-Sustaining Treatment 61-77 (1983).

[10]For discussions of nonstatutory documents, see John F. Kennedy Memorial Hosp. v. Bludworth, 452 So. 2d 921 (Fla. 1984) (discussed document executed before Florida enacted living will act); In re Peter, 108 N.J. 365, 378, 529 A.2d 419, 426 (1987); In re Westchester County Med. Center (O'Connor), 72 N.Y.2d 517, 531, 531 N.E.2d 607, 613-614, 534 N.Y.S.2d 886, 892-893 (1988) (dicta); Saunders v. State, 129 Misc. 2d 45, 492 N.Y.S.2d 510 (Sup.

13. There is no legal obligation to provide futile treat-
     ment (including treatment of any kind to brain-dead
     persons).[11]

B. Making and Implementing Terminal Care Decisions

§10.4 The Facility's Obligations

The healthcare facility itself, in addition to individual professionals, is responsible for ascertaining patient wishes about terminal
care, explaining the facility's policies, and seeing that both are
accommodated to the extent possible. The facility should take

---

Ct. Nassau County 1985); In re Guardianship of Browning, No. 74,174, 1990
Fla. LEXIS 1154 (Sept. 13, 1990). For drafting suggestions for nonstatutory
provisions in advance directives, see Living Wills and Health-Care Proxies,
Murphy's Wills Clauses (Dec. 1988 & Supp. 1989). For the propositions that
the statutory rights are not exclusive and that other rights to reject life-
sustaining treatment exist, see Camp. v. White, 510 So. 2d 166, 169-170 (Ala.
1987); Bartling v. Superior Court, 163 Cal. App. 3d 186, 194, 209 Cal. Rptr.
220, 224 (Ct. App. 1984); Corbett v. D'Alessandro, 487 So. 2d 368, 370-371
(Fla. Dist. Ct. App.), review denied, 492 So. 2d 1331 (Fla. 1986); State v.
McAfee, 259 Ga. 579, 385 S.E.2d 651, 652-653 (Ga. 1989); In re Gardner,
534 A.2d 947, 952 (Me. 1987). See also §10.6 n.49.

[11]For recent cases on brain death, see Gallups v. Cotter, 534 So. 2d 585
(Ala. 1988); White v. St. Joseph Health Center, No. CV88-14759 (Mo. Cir.
Ct. Jackson County July 7, 1988) (Clark, J.); Strachan v. John F. Kennedy
Memorial Hosp., 109 N.J. 523, 538 A.2d 346 (1988). For a discussion of
futility, see Hastings Center, Guidelines on the Termination of Life-Sustaining
Treatment and the Care of the Dying 32 (1987); Blackhall, Sounding Board:
Must We Always Use CPR?, 317 New Eng. J. Med. 1281 (Nov. 12, 1987);
Youngner, Who Defines Futility?, 260 J.A.M.A. 2094 (Oct. 14, 1988); N.Y.
Pub. Health Law §§2961(9) (McKinney Supp. 1990); 10 N.Y. Admin. Code
tit. 10, §405.43(b)(9) (definition of medical futility in DNR context). But see
N.Y. Pub. Health Law §§2965(7), 2966(3) (McKinney Supp. 1990) (if patient
or appropriate surrogate objects to entry of DNR order, such an order shall
not be entered).

the initiative in establishing policy, educating staff and patients, and ensuring that decisions are carried out and carefully documented. The alternatives open to staff members and employees who may disagree with patients' decisions or facility policy should also be explored and explained.

§10.4.1 Creating Facility Policy

A facility should establish policy on terminal care decision-making as a service to patients and their families and to give guidance to the institution's employees and staff. (Policy is legally required in some circumstances, and, in all instances, should reduce the possibility of liability.)[1] The following steps may be useful in formulating policy.

Identify the legal constraints. When does the law of the jurisdiction require, prohibit, or allow health professionals to take certain steps? For example, in New York, they are required to inform patients about "do not resuscitate" options;[2] they are prohibited from shutting off the respirator of a patient in a persistent vegetative state when there is not clear evidence of the patient's wishes, even if physicians and family agree that it would be in the patient's best interests;[3] they are allowed, but not required, to go to court seeking judicial immunity before they honor patient preferences.[4]

---

§10.4 [1]See Patient Self-Determination Act (supra p. 662 n.4) (advance directive policies); Joint Commission on Accreditation of Healthcare Organizations, Accreditation Manual for Hospitals §MA .1.4.12 (1991) (do-not-resuscitate policies); 42 C.F.R. §§442.311, 442.312 (Oct. 1, 1989); Ill. Ann. Stat. ch. 111½, ¶4152-210 (Smith-Hurd 1988) (nursing home resident rights).

[2]N.Y. Pub. Health Law §2978 (McKinney Supp. 1990); 10 N.Y. Admin. Code tit. 10, §405.7(c)(10); W. Va. Code §16-30A-19 (Supp. 1990) (healthcare proxy).

[3]See In re Westchester County Med. Center (O'Connor), 72 N.Y.2d 517, 531 N.E.2d 607, 534 N.Y.S.2d 886 (1988); In re Storar, 52 N.Y.2d 363, 420 N.E.2d 64, 438 N.Y.S.2d 266, cert. denied, 454 U.S. 858 (1981).

[4]In re Guardianship of Browning, No. 17,174, 1990 Fla. LEXIS 1154 (Sept. 13, 1990); In re Jobes, 108 N.J. 394, 529 A.2d 434 (1987), stay denied sub nom. Lincoln Park Nursing & Convalescent Home v. Kahn, 483 U.S. 1036

Thorough understanding of the law of the jurisdiction shortens the process of developing policy and helps later in evaluating specific cases that arise in the facility. In addition, problems in the law may be identified that the facility or its professionals can help change through proposing legislation.

In drafting and in reviewing drafts of a policy, involve members of each of the health professions represented in the facility. Each group faces different problems in dealing with life-sustaining treatment, and its representatives may be better able than other people to identify the problems and possible solutions. Social workers or patient advocates, for example, may know the questions that patients or their families most often ask. Physicians and nurses will want to know who must implement a decision to stop treatment and whether they can refuse to participate. Emergency personnel may want to know what resuscitation efforts to undertake on a patient whose living will rejects treatment in certain circumstances.

Assemble a collection of terminal care protocols from similar facilities. Borrowing from these can save time and can also identify important issues that may have been overlooked.[5]

Establish an interdisciplinary committee to review the work-

(1987); In re Application of Deel, 729 F. Supp. 231, 234 (N.D.N.Y. 1990); In re Storar, 52 N.Y.2d 363, 382, 420 N.E.2d 64, 73-74, 438 N.Y.S.2d 266, 276, cert. denied, 454 U.S. 858 (1981); In re Guardianship of Hamlin, 102 Wash. 2d 810, 689 P.2d 1372 (1984). Cf. Cruzan v. Director, Mo. Dept. of Health, 110 S. Ct. 2841, 111 L. Ed. 224 (1990) (discussing procedural safeguards that states may impose before life-sustaining treatment may be forgone). See also §10.6 n.63.

[5]For sample policies, see U.S. Congress Office of Technology Assessment, Institutional Protocols for Decisions About Life-Sustaining Treatments (July 1988); Hastings Center, Guidelines on the Termination of Life-Sustaining Treatment and the Care of the Dying (1987); Ruark et al., Initiating and Withdrawing Life Support: Principles and Practice in Adult Medicine, 318 New Eng. J. Med. 25 (Jan. 7, 1988); Meisel et al., Hospital Guidelines for Deciding About Life-Sustaining Treatment: Dealing with Health "Limbo," 14 Critical Care Medicine 239 (March 1986); Carlson et al., Development of a Comprehensive Supportive Care Team For the Hopelessly Ill on a University Hospital Medical Service, 259 J.A.M.A. 378 (Jan. 15, 1988). For other sample policies, write to The Society for the Right to Die, 250 W. 57th St., NY, NY 10107, and the Hastings Center, 755 Elm Rd., Briarcliff Manor, NY 10510.

ing of the policy at regular intervals and research new developments in the area.

§10.4.2 Educating Staff and Patients

Once the policy is formulated, it must be explained to the facility's entire healthcare team.[6] A well-trained staff can then participate in the efforts to educate patients about the policy. The affected staff groups include, but are not limited to, physicians, nurses, admissions employees, ethics committee members (see §10.6), emergency personnel, attorneys, administrators, chaplains and other counselors, and patient advocates. Each person should receive a copy of the policy as well as a copy of the information given to the potential patient or patient representative. The policy should name a person within the facility to whom questions or comments may be addressed. When the policy is introduced, sessions should be scheduled to explain it to facility personnel. Thereafter, an annual training session would be beneficial.

Patients, too, must be educated about the policy. Informing them and their families may avoid both legal complications and those unfortunate circumstances in which family members, acting out of uncertainty and frustration, take matters into their own hands.[7] In this regard, explanations of the dispute resolution procedures and the time frame for decision-making are especially helpful. Patients and families should be reminded that they are

---

[6]For statutory requirements on staff education, see Patient Self-Determination Act, supra p. 662 n.4; Del. Code Ann. tit. 16, §1124 (Repl. 1983); Ill. Ann. Stat. ch. 111½, ¶4152-212 (Smith-Hurd Supp. 1988).

[7]For discussion of the controversial *Linares* case (in which a father disconnected his vegetative son's respirator in a hospital) and the importance of family-institution discussion, see 17 Law, Medicine & Health Care 295-346 (Winter 1989) (collection of articles); Medical Ethics Advisor 101-111 (Aug. 1989), 69-73 (June 1989), 138-140 (Oct. 1989); Chambers, Sua Sponte: Did Lawyers for Hospital Act Properly?, Natl. L.J. (June 19, 1989). See also Hudson, A Case Study: How to Alienate a Family (part of executive report on right to die), 1989 Hospitals 40 (Nov. 20, 1989).

free to seek judicial involvement, which might result in quicker resolution than that offered by the facility's policy.

Since a major factor in determining appropriate care is patient preference, the facility's procedure should encourage patients to express their wishes. Ideally, the means chosen will not be intrusive, threatening, or unduly time-consuming for either the patient or facility personnel. On admission, patients (or family members or other appropriate representatives, if the patient cannot speak for herself) are routinely asked for basic information about insurance, religious preference, people to contact in case of emergency, and consent to treatment in general. Certain questions could easily be added to the admissions form, such as "Do you have a living will or have you appointed in writing someone to make healthcare decisions?" "If yes, please provide a copy. If not, and you would like information about these legal options, contact [named individual] in this facility." "If you cannot make decisions about your care, who would you like to make medical decisions on your behalf? (List name, address and telephone number.)" "Are there any decisions you do NOT want this person to make?"

Such questions may help avoid decisionmaking crises should the patient become decisionally incapacitated; may well relieve rather than burden patients and their families; and are unlikely to make the admissions process significantly more inconvenient.[8]

---

[8]For the importance of discussion with patients and their families, see In re Jobes, 108 N.J. 394, 418 n.11, 529 A.2d 434, 446 n.11 (1987), stay denied sub nom. Lincoln Park Nursing & Convalescent Home v. Kahn, 483 U.S. 1036 (1987); Lo et al., Patient Attitudes to Discussing Life-Sustaining Treatment, 146 Arch. Internal Med. 1613 (Aug. 1986); Wanzer et al., The Physician's Responsibility Toward Hopelessly Ill Patients: A Second Look, 320 New Eng. J. Med. 844, 845 (March 30, 1989); Ruark et al., Initiating and Withdrawing Life Support: Principles and Practice in Adult Medicine, 318 New Eng. J. Med. 25, 26 (Jan. 7, 1988); Finucane et al., Planning with Elderly Outpatients for Contingencies of Severe Illness: A Survey and Clinical Trial, 3 J. Gen'l Internal Med. 322 (July/Aug. 1988); Stolman, Evaluation of the Do Not Resuscitate Orders at a Community Hospital, 149 Arch. Internal Med. 1851 (Aug. 1989); McCrary and Botkin, Hospital Policy on Advance Directives: Do Institutions Ask Patients About Living Wills?, 262 J.A.M.A. 2411 (Nov. 3, 1989); Davidson et al., Physicians' Attitudes on Advance Directives, 262 J.A.M.A. 2415 (Nov.

If a facility imposes restrictions on honoring patient preferences, those limitations should be clearly set out in the admissions material. Patients might be asked to sign a statement indicating awareness and acceptance of the restrictions. Some facilities, for example, may wish to insist on artificial feeding for anyone who cannot take adequate nutrition orally. Although it is not certain that such restrictions are enforceable, they are more likely to be if the facility makes them known to patients on admission (as discussed in §10.5).

Both staff and patients should be informed that advance directives may be easily revoked. Most statutes specifically list the methods of revocation; some allow it even when the patient is considered decisionally incapacitated. Although the latter contradicts, in theory, the idea of informed consent—since a person is allowed to make a decision she may not understand— it probably represents a policy choice to encourage healthcare providers to give rather than withhold care.

A brief informational brochure, distributed at or soon after admission, can be an effective educational tool. It should outline facility policy as well as the rights and responsibilities of patients admitted to the facility, some of which may be required by law.[9] The brochure should describe the dispute resolution procedures, the location in the facility where further information is available, and outside informational resources.[10]

3, 1989); Ridley, Accommodating Jehovah's Witness' Choice of Nonblood Management, 10 Perspectives in Healthcare Risk Mgmt. 17 (Winter 1990). But see Ga. Code Ann. §31-32-9(d) (Michie 1985 & Supp. 1990) (no healthcare facility may provide living wills except at patient's specific request).

[9]See §10.4 n.1.

[10]Some helpful resource organizations include: American Bar Association, Commission on Legal Problems of the Elderly, 1800 M St. N.W., Washington, D.C. 20036; New Jersey Commission on Legal & Ethical Problems in the Delivery of Health Care, 321 W. State St., CN, Trenton, NJ 08625 (state governmental commission); New York State Task Force on Life and Law, 5 Penn Plaza, 3d Floor, NY, NY 10001-1803; (state governmental task force); Oregon Health Decisions (grassroots organization); Vermont Ethics Network, 102 South Main St., Waterbury, VT 05676 (grassroots organization); Society for the Right to Die, 250 W. 57th Street, NY, NY 10107 (patient advocacy organization and national resource center). See also §10.7 n.4.

§10.4.3 Documenting and Communicating the Decision

Until recently, many healthcare professionals feared that documenting decisions about life-sustaining treatment could subject them to liability. Even if that was the case in the past, today the opposite is true. Documentation of terminal care decisions is good practice, both of law and of medicine. Facilities should encourage physicians to document the patient's consent to all life-sustaining measures—nasogastric tubes, respirators, suctioning, tracheotomies, and transfusions—to reduce claims that the treatment was provided without consent.[11]

Whenever a decision is made to seek or forgo life-sustaining treatment, the attending physician should enter the fact in the medical record. The entry should consist, at a minimum, of the date, the treatment at issue, a summary of its risks and benefits, who participated in making the decision, a summary of their discussion, and the outcome. The record should also contain copies of any written documents associated with the decision (e.g., living will, proxy appointment, or release of liability). (Living will statutes usually require that a copy of the document be inserted in the medical record.)

The facility should institute procedures to ensure that, when a patient changes physicians, either within the facility or as a result of discharge or transfer, any directions about terminal care follow the patient.[12] Both patient and physician should be reminded that anyone who received a copy of an advance directive as originally executed should be given another copy if it is revised and should be informed if it is revoked.

---

[11]Some patients' rights statutes provide immunity for documented refusals. Ga. Code Ann. §31-8-108(b)(3) (1985); Ill. Ann. Stat. ch. 111½, ¶4152-104(b) (Smith-Hurd 1990); see generally Cohen, Patient's Rights Laws and the Right to Refuse Life-Sustaining Treatment in Nursing Homes: A Hidden Weapon for Patient Advocacy, 2 BioLaw S:231 n.37 (Aug. 1989). Documentation of advance directives is required for providers receiving Medicare and Medicaid funds. See Patient Self-Determination Act, supra p. 662 n.4.

[12]N.Y. Pub. Health Law §2971 (McKinney Supp. 1990) (transfer requirements for do-not-resuscitate orders); Miles, Advance Directives to Limit Treatment: The Need for Portability, 35 Amer. Geriatrics Socy. 74 (Jan. 1987).

At the time terminal care decisions are reduced to writing, it is important for patients to discuss the directives with providers, family, and any decisionmaking representative. This process can identify ambiguities or other factors that deserve consideration, including whether particular professionals now caring for the patient would have difficulty honoring the directive should the time for implementation arrive (see §10.5). The patient can then consider substituting doctors at a time when she is still in a position to do so.

§10.4.4 Reducing Concerns About Validity

Healthcare professionals often express concern about the legality of advance directives. The facility's attorney can perform a valuable function by anticipating the most troublesome issues and offering the professionals specific information, guidance, and reassurance. A sampling of frequently voiced questions follows.

1. Was the declarant (patient) capable of executing a legal document when she did so, and did she do so voluntarily and without coercion? If, as is true in many jurisdictions, the state's living will statute establishes a presumption of capability and voluntary execution, health professionals should be told this. Such statutory provisions give legal protection to those who rely on the documents without specific confirmation. Healthcare professionals should also be instructed to investigate if evidence that might rebut the presumption comes to their attention. If necessary, judicial clarification can be sought.

2. What is a healthcare professional's obligation to confirm that a patient's directive is authentic? This concern includes the question of whether the procedural requirements for executing the document were fulfilled and whether the patient understood the substance of her action. The former is addressed in this section and the latter in paragraph 3 below. Usually, the professional may presume that the directive was validly executed, unless she knew or should have known otherwise. While all

living will and healthcare proxy statutes have execution requirements, these vary from state to state. The most important are
that declarants be "competent" and that they sign the document
voluntarily and without coercion in the presence of two qualified
witnesses. (Requirements for qualifying as a witness also vary.)

3. What standards are helpful in gauging the authenticity
of a nonstatutory directive? The law is not clear on this question,
and a nonstatutory directive should not be ignored solely because
it differs from the statutory prescription. If the state has a living
will statute, it is best that the nonstatutory document satisfy its
execution requirements. If not, execution requirements for wills
of property provide the closest analogy. Video- or audiotaped
discussions with patients may also be helpful evidence of their
preferences. If there is no durable power of attorney statute
directly relating to healthcare decisions, healthcare language
could be inserted in a general durable power of attorney form,
in which case the general durable power execution requirements
are preferable. (See §10.6.4.)

A directive should be signed by the declarant and dated.
Some statutes permit another to sign at the declarant's direction
and in her presence if she is physically incapable of signing.
Most statutes require that witnesses be competent adults and
impose additional restrictions on family members or healthcare
providers. Very few statutes provide that a directive lapses unless
re-executed; therefore, it remains valid unless revoked. Still, it
is wise to ask patients to update the document periodically. The
facility's policy might ask patients, on admission, to do one of
the following: initial and date their directive in the presence of
admissions personnel; add a paragraph, signed and dated, stating
that the directive still represents their wishes; or execute a new
directive, particularly if the desired changes are significant. (It
should be noted, however, that some living will statutes impose
additional execution requirements if the declarant signs the will
when she is in a healthcare facility.)

4. Do patients really understand the substance of what they
have requested? For instance, does a patient truly wish to reject
"artificial feeding" when she rejects "life-sustaining treatments"
or comprehend such phrases as "terminal condition"? Though
statutory living wills are presumed to be valid, the facility should

encourage its staff to discuss a patient's directive with him for clarification.

5. Is a directive that varies the statutory form still valid? Most statutes set out language that must be "substantially followed" in order for the act to apply to the document; some statutes also expressly allow declarants to add personal instructions. Courts have not defined "substantial compliance" in this context, though, so the enforceability of variant documents will depend on the nature of the variations and cannot safely be predicted. Directives that are adjudged to "substantially comply" provide the declarant and healthcare provider with full statutory protection. Those that do not comply—for example, a document that rejects a form of treatment explicitly excluded from statutory coverage—may still be enforceable under a common-law or constitutional right to control treatment (discussed in §10.6.3). In that case, the right could still be exercised. Even if portions of the document are invalid, the remaining portions are usually enforceable, under either statutory provisions or common-law precedents about construing documents.

§10.5 Healthcare Professionals' Obligations

Healthcare professionals, and above all physicians, have a duty in this area that differs somewhat from the facility's. The latter must develop and implement policy on terminal care decision-making, but physicians ultimately are responsible for obtaining informed consent to (or refusal of) treatment. In addition, it is arguable that physicians bear a responsibility to initiate conversations with terminally ill patients to elicit their preferences; and it is certain that it is physicians who should honor those preferences or arrange (with administrative assistance) for them to be honored by others.

Though physicians have no legal obligation to discuss with patients any future refusal of or consent to treatment, such discussions would seem to be a part of humane care (not to mention orderly administration).[1] One consequence of conver-

---

§10.5 [1]See §10.4 nn.7, 8 and §10.5 nn.5, 6.

sation on the subject might be the patient's decision to execute an advance directive. If so, physicians can offer extremely useful advice. Patients should be encouraged to make a directive as specific as possible, both in terms of the treatments at issue and the circumstances in which the document is meant to apply. Potentially ambiguous terms should be defined, with any interpretive guidelines also articulated. (Certain adjectives commonly found in early right-to-die literature, such as "heroic," "extraordinary," "invasive," and "imminent," were discovered through experience to be too ambiguous to be helpful.)[2]

Health professionals, like the facility administration, should also be prepared to direct patients to attorneys or advocacy groups for assistance in drafting a directive. (No health professional should offer assistance of this sort. His expertise is most valuable in identifying medical possibilities for the patient to consider.)[3]

Whether a patient has a living will before admission or decides to execute one thereafter, health professionals can improve the document by asking questions of the patient that identify and clarify the choices. The professional could then make record entries on these points or the patient could amend his advance directive to explain them.

Finally, professionals should be encouraged to explore their doubts or convictions about whether they find a patient's choices ethically and professionally acceptable. By voicing concerns in a timely manner to patients, families, and the administration, an attending physician helps preserve his and the patient's options. First, after further communication on the subject, the physician may come to accept the patient's choice. If not, there may be time to transfer the patient to another physician within the facility who is willing to comply and is acceptable to the patient or his representative. Third, if no willing physician can be identified within the facility, it may be possible to find a suitable person at another facility or one who will supervise care of the patient at home.

---

[2]See, e.g., President's Commission for the Study of Ethical Problems in Medicine and Biomedical and Behavioral Research, Deciding to Forego Life-Sustaining Treatment 82-90 (1983). See also §10.6 n.13.

[3]See §10.4 n.8.

If none of the above occurs, the facility and physician together must consider the possibility of liability. Whether providers can refuse to honor the patient's preference without engaging in "abandonment" of the patient (or violating medical ethics) is still an open question. Most living will statutes include a "conscience" clause, requiring only that the objecting physician, and sometimes the facility, make a "reasonable effort" to transfer the patient to a physician willing to comply with the patient's wishes.[4]

Courts have split on the scope of the obligation of health professionals to honor patient preferences to reject life support. Some courts have declined to compel doctors to participate in terminating unwanted treatment; others have implied they would permit refusals only when the physician let the patient know in advance and the patient could easily seek care elsewhere.[5] Still others have forced physicians to participate if a willing physician could not be found in time.[6]

---

[4]See, e.g., Iowa Code Ann. §144A.8 (West 1989) (physician must take reasonable steps to effect transfer); Alaska Rev. Stat. §18.12.050(a) (1986) (physician must actually transfer, not just make reasonable effort); Minn. Stat. Ann. §§145B.06, 145B.07 (West Supp. 1990) (physicians' options are greater if physician communicates hesitation).

[5]Conservatorship of Morrison, 206 Cal. App. 3d 304, 253 Cal. Rptr. 530 (Cal. Ct. App. 1988); Brophy v. New Eng. Sinai Hosp. 398 Mass. 417, 440 n.39, 497 N.E.2d 626, 639 n.39 (1986); In re Estate of Longeway, 133 Ill. 2d 33, 549 N.E.2d 292, 299 (1989); Delio v. Westchester County Med. Center, 129 A.D.2d 1, 26, 516 N.Y.S.2d 677, 693 (2d Dept. 1987); In re Guardianship of Grant, 109 Wash. 2d 545, 567 n.6, 747 P.2d 445, 456 n.6 (1987), modified on other grounds, 757 P.2d 534 (1988). See also Miles et al., Conflicts Between Patients' Wishes to Forgo Treatment and the Policies of Health Care Facilities, 321 New Eng. J. Med. 48 (July 6, 1989); American Academy of Neurology, Position Paper of the American Academy of Neurology on Certain Aspects of the Care and Management of the Persistent Vegetative State Patient, 39 Neurology 124 (Jan. 1989); Hastings Center, Guidelines on the Termination of Life-Sustaining Treatment and the Care of the Dying 32-33 (1987); Uniform Rights of the Terminally Ill Act §8, 9B U.L.A. 78 (Supp. 1990); Ridley, Accommodating Jehovah's Witness' Choice of Nonblood Management, 10 Perspectives in Healthcare Risk Mgmt. 17 (Winter 1990).

[6]Bouvia v. Superior Court (Glenchur), 179 Cal. App. 3d 1127, 1145-

§10.6 Assessing the Patient's Circumstances

A variety of factors affect the facility's handling of termination-of-care decisions. In each case, judgments must be made about the patient's ability to make life-or-death decisions and about her physical condition and prospects. Another consideration is the kinds of treatment being refused. What arrangements exist for this patient's healthcare decision-making? Is she currently able to decide for herself? If not, has she previously appointed a proxy or executed a living will? Or, in the absence of written directives, are there other automatic surrogate decisionmakers, or has a court appointed or become the decisionmaker? If no arrangements have been made, how should the facility proceed?

§10.6.1 The Patient's Capacity to Decide

Although treatment may be refused or terminated for both "competent" and "incompetent" adults,[1] the procedures will differ for the two groups. As a general rule, the law presumes that adults are competent. Competence to make treatment decisions, however, may differ from competence for other purposes—managing personal or financial affairs, for example. Thus, the medicolegal literature often uses another term (for example, "decisionally incapable" or "decisionally incapaci-

---

1146, 225 Cal. Rptr. 297, 306-307 (Ct. App. 1986), review denied (Cal. June 5, 1986); Bartling v. Superior Court, 163 Cal. App. 3d 186, 197 n.8, 209 Cal. Rptr. 220, 226 n.8 (Ct. App. 1984); In re Rodas, No. 86PR139, slip op. at 31-34 (Colo. Dist. Ct. Mesa County Jan. 22, 1987), as modified (April 3, 1987) (Buss, J.); 73 Op. Atty. Gen., No. 88-046, slip op. at 41-45 (Md. Oct. 17, 1988); In re Jobes, 108 N.J. 394, 424-426, 529 A.2d 434, 450 (1987); In re Requena, 213 N.J. Super. 475, 517 A.2d 886 (Super. Ct. Ch. Div.), affd., 213 N.J. Super. 443, 517 A.2d 869 (Super. Ct. App. Div. 1986) (per curiam); Elbaum v. Grace Plaza of Great Neck, 148 A.D.2d 244, 255-257, 544 N.Y.S.2d 840, 846-848 (2d Dept. 1989); Gray v. Romeo, 697 F. Supp. 580, 590-591 (D.R.I. 1988); Annas, Transferring the Ethical Hot Potato, Hastings Center Report 20 (Feb. 1987).
    §10.6 [1]See §10.3 n.2.

tated") to describe those who are not able to make medical decisions.[2] (See Chapter 7 for a discussion of competence in the medical care context.)

To consent to or refuse treatment, a patient need only be able to understand the consequences of accepting or rejecting it and be able to communicate the decision. If these conditions are met, the patient is decisionally capable.[3] Depending on the jurisdiction, the relevant conditions may exist even if the patient has been judicially declared "incompetent," is a "mature minor," has unrelated psychiatric problems, has vacillating treatment preferences, or has so-called idiosyncratic preferences (and perhaps is considered foolish or unwise by family members or physicians).[4]

A physician attending someone he believes to be decisionally capable may still be properly concerned about whether the patient fully appreciates the consequences of the decision. The physician should take the initiative in clarifying the specific consequences and should summarize his discussions with the patient in the medical record. An entry might read:

> I asked Ms. Blank if she wanted to reject the use of antibiotics in her treatment for AIDS, explaining that the antibiotic treatment

---

[2]D.C. Code Ann. §§21-2202(5) (1989); N.Y. Pub. Health Law §2961(3) (McKinney Supp. 1990); Tenn. Code Ann. §32-11-103(1) (Supp. 1989); Vt. Stat. tit. 14, §3452(3) (Supp. 1988).

[3]Id. and §10.6 n.4.

[4]Bartling v. Superior Court, 163 Cal. App. 3d 186, 193, 209 Cal. Rptr. 220, 223-224 (Ct. App. 1984); In re Rodas, No. 86PR139, slip op. at 13-23 (Colo. Dist. Ct. Mesa County Jan. 22, 1987), as modified (April 3, 1987) (Buss, J.); Lane v. Candura, 6 Mass. App. 377, 376 N.E.2d 1232 (Ct. App. 1978); In re Quackenbush, 156 N.J. Super. 282, 383 A.2d 785 (Morris County Ct. 1978); In re Milton, 29 Ohio St. 3d 20, 25, 505 N.E.2d 255, 259, cert. denied sub nom. Ohio Dept. Mental Health v. Milton, 484 U.S. 820 (1987); State Dept. of Human Serv. v. Northern, 563 S.W.2d 197 (Tenn. App. 1978). For mature minors, see In re E.G., 133 Ill. 2d 98, 549 N.E.2d 322 (1989); In re Swan, 569 A.2d 1202 (Me. 1990). For a discussion of capacity, see also Chapter 7; U.S. Congress Office of Technology Assessment, Life-Sustaining Technologies and the Elderly 102-108 (July 1987); A. Meisel, The Right to Die, chs. 7-8 (1989 & Supp. 1990).

was painless, inexpensive, and had an 80% probability of restoring her to an asymptomatic state for at least several weeks (though it would not cure the AIDS). Told her that without the treatment she would almost certainly die in a matter of weeks or months. She said she understood and still wanted to reject the treatment.

On the other hand, if there is reason to doubt whether a patient is decisionally capable, that question must be resolved before any variations in standard treatment are undertaken. Some courts have established guidelines for making the determination.[5] One effect of such a determination may be to trigger the implementation of a living will. The typical statute provides that a living will maker must be determined to be incapable of making medical decisions before the living will becomes effective. Some statutes leave the determination to the treating physician; others have more stringent requirements for determining incapacity.[6] Accordingly, before consulting an advance directive or patient surrogate, health professionals must be sure they have taken the prescribed steps to ascertain that the patient cannot express her preferences.

If the patient cannot decide, then advance directives should be followed. When advance directives first appeared, some questioned whether they could ever embody "informed" consent since they were executed when the declarant was not suffering from a particular illness or considering a particular treatment.[7] The living will acts have largely satisfied the legal aspects of that

---

[5]In re Farrell, 108 N.J. 335, 353-359, 529 A.2d 404, 413-416 (1987), criticized in Annas, In Thunder, Lightning or in Rain: What Three Doctors Can Do, Hastings Center Report 28 (Oct./Nov. 1987); In re Estate of Dorone, 517 Pa. 3, 534 A.2d 452 (Pa. 1987); University of Cincinnati Hosp. v. Edmund, 30 Ohio Misc. 2d 1, 4, 506 N.E.2d 299, 302 (Ct. Comm. Pleas 1986).

[6]Haw. Rev. Stat. §327D-10(c) (Supp 1989); Wyo. Stat. §35-22-102(c)(1988). See also Kirby v. Spivey, 167 Ga. App. 751, 754, 307 S.E.2d 538, 541 (Ct. App. 1983).

[7]In re Westchester County Med. Center (O'Connor), 72 N.Y.2d 517, 530-535, 531 N.E.2d 607, 613-616, 534 N.Y.S.2d 886, 892-894 (1988); Dresser, Life, Death and Incompetent Patients: Conceptual Infirmities and Hidden Values in the Law, 28 Ariz. L. Rev. 373 (1986).

concern: by definition, a state legislature that has adopted a sample form has determined that the statutory form meets the requirements of informed consent. Nonstatutory living wills have been evaluated on a case-by-case basis. As a general rule, the more specific they are, the greater their chance of being upheld.[8]

§10.6.2 The Patient's Physical Condition

Reasonably accurate determination of a patient's physical condition is essential to complying with various legal responsibilities in terminal care decision-making. It can be extremely difficult, however, to describe the condition of a seriously ill person. In the decades since the *Quinlan* case, the medical and legal communities have searched for a common vocabulary with which to discuss particular patients' situations.

The Legal Significance of Determining the Patient's Condition. Some members of the medicolegal community argue that a patient's physical condition and prognosis should affect her ability to reject life support.[9] The theory is that the state's interest in preserving life is stronger than the individual's right to reject treatment except when the patient's prognosis, even with treatment, is dim.[10] Increasingly, however, it is agreed that a

---

[8]73 Op. Atty. Gen.—, No. 88-046, slip op. at 19-25 (Md. Oct. 17, 1988); In re Peter, 108 N.J. 365, 379-380, 529 A.2d 419, 426-427 (1987); In re Westchester County Med. Center (O'Connor), 72 N.Y.2d 517, 530-535, 531 N.E.2d 607, 613-616, 534 N.Y.S.2d 886, 892-894 (1988). See also §10.6 n.30.

[9]In re Quinlan, 70 N.J. 10, 40-41, 355 A.2d 647, 664, cert. denied sub nom. Garger v. New Jersey, 429 U.S. 922 (1976), diverged from in part, In re Conroy, 98 N.J. 321, 486 A.2d 1209 (1985); Fosmire v. Nicoleau, 75 N.Y.2d 218, 228-229, 551 N.E.2d 77, 82-83, 551 N.Y.S.2d 876, 881-82 (1990) (discussed and rejected argument). For the role of prognosis in making terminal care decisions, see also Smedira et al., Withholding and Withdrawal of Life Support from the Critically Ill, 322 New Eng. J. Med. 309 (Feb. 1, 1990).

[10]Id.

decisionally capable adult, regardless of age, medical condition or prognosis, can refuse treatment.[11]

Still, the patient's physical condition is significant in several contexts in terminal care decision-making. It is highly relevant, for instance, to (1) the question of when a living will becomes effective; (2) whether it is a statutory or nonstatutory document; and (3) interpreting the provisions of the document so that it can be carried out.[12]

Most living will statutes require that the patient be "qualified" before the statute goes into effect. The term is usually interpreted as describing a person currently incapable of expressing preferences and suffering from a "terminal" condition, illness, or disability that is, based on reasonable medical judgment, without hope of improvement. Readers will recognize the interpretive problems raised by such language. Courts, physicians, and patients have disagreed on terms such as "terminal" and "imminent death." Some people apply the phrases to life expectancy, likelihood of improvement, or recovery *with* treatment; others think the language is meant to apply to the same states *without* treatment.[13] Other frequently used terms are even more vague. Health professionals who receive from patients living wills that say the declarant rejects life support if she will not "improve," "recover," "regain" a "meaningful quality of life," or die a "dignified death" should ask the patient to define those terms if at all possible, preferably in writing. (See §10.5.)

---

[11]See §10.3 n.1.

[12]Fosmire v. Nicoleau, 75 N.Y.2d 218, 228-229, 551 N.E.2d 77, 82-83, 551 N.Y.S.2d 876, 881-882 (1990); In re Guardianship of Browning, No. 74,174, 1990 Fla. LEXIS 1154 (Sept. 13, 1990).

[13]See, e.g., *Browning*, supra n.12; In re Estate of Greenspan, 137 Ill. 2d 1, 558 N.E.2d 1194, No. 67903, slip op. at 14-15, 1990 Ill. LEXIS 82 (Ill. July 9, 1990); Hazelton [sic] v. Powhatan Nursing Home, No. CH 98287 (Va. Cir. Ct. Fairfax County Aug. 29, 1986), order signed (Sept. 2, 1986) (Fortkort, J.), appeal denied, Record No. 860814 (Va. Sept. 2, 1986), 6 Va. Cir. Ct. Op. 414 (Aspen 1987); Society for the Right to Die, Brophy v. New England Sinai Hospital, Inc.: Brief Amicus Curiae, 35 J. Amer. Ger. Socy., 669, 676 n.12 (1987). See also President's Commission for the Study of Ethical Problems in Medicine and Biomedical and Behavioral Research, Deciding to Forego Life-Sustaining Treatment 82-90 (1983).

In order to satisfy the legal conditions under which a living will can be implemented, physicians must certify that the appropriate medical condition exists. Living will statutes usually require that the medical condition be certified in writing by at least one attending physician who has personally examined the patient.[14] Some statutes also specify the standard of diagnostic certainty required (e.g., doctors must hold the "opinion" or must have a "reasonable degree of medical certainty" that the physical condition contemplated by the document has occurred).[15] In some states without statutes, confirmation requirements are enunciated in case law.[16] If neither statute nor case law offers specific guidance on the point at which a living will can be activated, health professionals must determine when the conditions for implementing a living will are present (for example, whether the patient is now in a terminal state and incapable of expressing her preferences). They will probably be protected from liability, even in case of diagnostic error, if they undertake diagnostic procedures consistent with standards of acceptable medical practice.

---

[14]Wis. Stat. Ann. §154.01(6) (West 1989). Hawaii's and Utah's statutes actually provide sample certification forms. Haw. Rev. Stat. §327D-10 (Supp. 1989); Utah Code Ann. §75-2-1105 (Supp. 1989).

[15]Ind. Code Ann. §16-8-11-9 (Burns 1990) (reasonable degree of medical certainty); Iowa Code Ann. §144A.2(8) (West 1989) (physician must hold "opinion"). For waiting period, see Colo. Rev. Stat. §15-18-104, 15-18-107 (1987 & Supp. 1989).

[16]John F. Kennedy Memorial Hosp. v. Bludworth, 452 So. 2d 921, 926 (Fla. 1984) (primary physician and at least two other physicians with specialties relevant to the patient's condition must certify condition); In re Estate of Longeway, 133 Ill. 2d 33, 549 N.E.2d 292, 298-299 (Ill. 1989); In re Jobes, 108 N.J. 394, 407-409, 529 A.2d 434, 440-442 (1987). For an example of the difficulties involved in making prognoses, see In re Application of Gannon (Coons), No. 0189-017460 (N.Y. Sup. Ct. Albany County April 3), N.Y.L.J. April 7, 1989 at 29, col. 4, vacated (April 11, 1989), as discussed in Steinbock, Recovery from Persistent Vegetative State?: The Case of Carrie Coons, Hastings Center Report 14 (July/Aug. 1989); Levy et al., Differences in Cerebral Blood Flow and Glucose Utilization in Vegetative Versus Locked-in Patients, 22 Annals of Neurology 673 (Dec. 1987) (describing the accuracy of positron emission tomographic (PET) scans in diagnosing vegetative states); Alvarado v. New York City Health & Hosp. Corp., 547 N.Y.S.2d 190 (Sup. Ct. N.Y. County 1989), vacated, 550 N.Y.S.2d 353 (1st Dept. 1990).

It is important to note that living wills, by their own terms, usually are not effective before a prognosis can be determined. Thus, the fact that a person with a living will is resuscitated in an emergency does not necessarily violate the terms of the document. On the contrary, that is the proper response until the medical conditions under which the document becomes effective are known to have occurred. Some states have clarified the role of emergency personnel by statute.[17] Courts have made it clear, too, that health professionals cannot invoke the "emergency" exception to provide life support to someone who is now decisionally incapacitated (e.g., a person anesthetized during surgery) if that individual specified in advance an unwillingness to undergo treatment in that situation.[18]

Physical condition may decide whether the living will can be implemented as a statutory directive. Many statutes limit the applicability of living wills to certain specified physical circumstances. If the patient is not in such circumstances, the living will cannot be invoked under—that is, with the protection of— the statute, though honoring an advance directive may be permissible under the common law of the state. As a practical matter, however, in states with living will laws, nonstatutory issues are usually dealt with under the same decisionmaking procedures as statutory ones. For example, if a patient whose condition falls outside the statutory definition of a "qualified patient" wants to reject life support, courts and physicians (if they plan to honor the request) most likely will require the same certification of condition as exists in the living will statute.

Descriptive Categories of Physical Conditions. The following are some of the physical conditions in which difficult terminal care decisions may arise.

1. "Permanent unconsciousness" is an umbrella term en-

---

[17]Md. Health-Gen. Code Ann. §5-607(b) (1990); Mont. Code Ann. §§50-9-102, 50-9-104, 50-9-204 (1989).

[18]Fosmire v. Nicoleau, 75 N.Y.2d 218, 224-225, 551 N.E.2d 77, 79-80, 551 N.Y.S.2d 876, 878-879 (1990); Leach v. Shapiro, 13 Ohio App. 3d 393, 469 N.E.2d 1047 (Ct. App. 1984).

compassing both the "persistent vegetative state" and the "irreversible coma." Since there was (and continues to be) confusion about the term "irreversible coma," permanent unconsciousness is increasingly becoming the favored term. "Permanent unconsciousness" includes all conditions in which purposeful interaction with the environment, awareness of pain or pleasure, and cognitive ability are permanently absent. Patients in a true irreversible coma appear permanently asleep, while those in persistent vegetative states have sleep-wake cycles and may exhibit reflexes that can be mistakenly perceived as awareness of environment.[19] Several courts and some statutes have authorized termination of treatment for permanently unconscious patients.[20]

2. "Minimal awareness" describes a state in which a person may be able to track objects with her eyes, respond to her name, and experience pain, but cannot make decisions about treatment. The group includes sufferers from AIDS-related neurological infections, Alzheimer's disease, brain tumors, stroke, and other types of neurological illness and injury.[21] Such patients may

---

[19]American Academy of Neurology, Position of the American Academy of Neurology on Certain Aspects of the Care and Management of the Persistent Vegetative State Patient, 39 Neurology 123-126 (Jan. 1989); Hastings Center Report 26-47 (Feb./March 1988) (collection of articles on the persistent vegetative state); American Medical Association Council on Scientific Affairs and Council on Ethical and Judicial Affairs, Persistent Vegetative State and the Decision to Withdraw or Withhold Life Support, 263 J.A.M.A. 426 (Jan. 19, 1990).

[20]Rasmussen v. Fleming, 154 Ariz. 207, 218, 741 P.2d 674, 685 (1987); In re Jobes, 108 N.J. 394, 529 A.2d 434 (1987); Brophy v. New Eng. Sinai Hosp. 398 Mass. 417, 497 N.E.2d 626 (1986); In re Welfare of Steinhaus (Minn. Redwood County Ct. Sept. 11), modified (Oct. 13, 1986) (Harrelson, J.); In re Bayer, No. 4131 (N.D. Burleigh County Ct. Feb. 5, 11 and Dec. 11, 1987) (Riskedahl, J.); Ark. Stat. Ann. §§20-17-201 to 20-17-218 (Supp. 1990); Idaho Code §§39-4503, 39-4504 (Supp. 1989); N.Y. Pub. Health Law §2965(5)(c)(ii) (McKinney Supp. 1990). Cf. Cruzan v. Director, Mo. Dept. of Health, 110 S. Ct. 2841, 111 L. Ed. 2d 224 (1990) (Court upheld Missouri's right to prohibit termination of life-sustaining treatment of permanently unconscious patients unless there is clear and convincing evidence that the patient wanted treatment terminated).

[21]In re Guardianship of Browning, 543 So. 2d 258 (Fla. Dist. Ct. App.),

recover fully or may, with treatment, be able once again to express their wishes despite lack of improvement in their underlying physical condition. (The second group might include patients with toxoplasmosis, pneumonia, gangrene, and accidental head trauma.)

In theory, an advance directive to refuse treatment might be implemented when a person enters a state of decisional incapacity, even temporarily.[22] In fact, however, there have been obstacles to enforcement of expressions of preference. Courts may assume that declarants would not have made such a request had they foreseen the full range of possibilities, for example, that through painless and inexpensive treatment they might regain mental capacity.[23] In light of the legal uncertainty, treatment should be provided unless the patient's wish to refuse is very clearly expressed in advance. The facility might also wish to seek judicial immunity for honoring the preference. (See §10.8.)

3. Some illnesses leave mental faculties intact but cause severe physical deterioration, destroying much of the ability to communicate (e.g., locked-in syndrome, Lou Gehrig's disease,

---

clarified, No. 88-02887 (Dist. Ct. App. May 3, 1989); 73 Op. Atty. Gen.—, No. 88-046, slip op. at 7-9 (Md. Oct. 17, 1988); In re Conroy, 98 N.J. 321, 486 A.2d 1209 (1985); In re Westchester County Med. Center (O'Connor), 72 N.Y.2d 517, 531 N.E.2d 607, 534 N.Y.S.2d 886 (1988); In re Beth Israel Medical Center (Weinstein), 136 Misc. 2d 931, 519 N.Y.S.2d 511 (Sup. Ct. N.Y. County 1987); In re O'Brien, 135 Misc. 2d 1076, 517 N.Y.S.2d 346 (Sup. Ct. 1987). See also Wray et al., Withholding Medical Treatment From the Severely Demented Patient: Decisional Processes and Cost Implications, 148 Arch. Internal Med. 1980 (Sept. 1988).

[22]In re E.G., 133 Ill. 2d 98, 549 N.E.2d 322 (1989); In re Brown, 478 So. 2d 1033 (Miss. 1985); Ridley, Accommodating Jehovah's Witnesses' Choice of Nonblood Management, 10 Perspectives in Healthcare Risk Mgmt. 17 (Winter 1990). See also §10.6 n.32 (blood transfusions).

[23]Randolph v. City of New York, 117 A.D.2d 44, 48-50, 501 N.Y.S.2d 837, 840-841 (1st Dept. 1986), affd. as modified, 69 N.Y.2d 844, 507 N.E.2d 298, 514 N.Y.S.2d 705 (1987); Evans v. Bellevue Hosp. (Wirth), No. 16536/87 (N.Y. Sup. Ct. N.Y. County July 27, 1987) (Sandifer, J.), N.Y.L.J., July 28, 1987, at 11, col. 1.; University of Cincinnati Hosp. v. Edmond, 30 Ohio Misc. 2d 1, 506 N.E.2d 299 (Ct. Comm. Pl. 1986); In re Estate of Dorone, 517 Pa. 3, 534 A.2d 452 (1987).

quadriplegia, or advanced cancer).[24] Patients in such conditions may have expressed their wishes in advance, but still efforts must be made to communicate with them when a treatment decision is needed. The patient's current wishes supersede the advance directive; the document should be honored only if the patient cannot communicate.[25]

§10.6.3 Kinds of Treatment at Issue

Terminal care decisions involve not only the patient's mental and physical states, but also the spectrum of medical interventions available. In selecting among treatment alternatives, a typical patient might consider comfort, expense, the probability of cure or improvement in either the immediate symptoms or the underlying condition, and whether the treatment will prolong life. Some will have other considerations that affect their choice of treatment.

The law has addressed certain types of treatment, approving and disapproving modes of care depending on the circumstances. The first part of this section notes those holdings; the second describes forms of treatment that are frequently at issue.

---

[24]Cases involving these types of patients include Bartling v. Superior Court, 163 Cal. App. 3d 186, 209 Cal. Rptr. 220 (Ct. App. 1984); Bouvia v. Superior Court (Glenchur), 179 Cal. App. 3d 1127, 225 Cal. Rptr. 297 (Ct. App. 1986), review denied (Cal. June 5, 1986); In re Rodas, No. 86PR139 (Colo. Dist. Ct. Mesa County Jan. 22, 1987), as modified (April 3, 1987) (Buss, J.); In re Application of Deel, 729 F. Supp. 231 (N.D.N.Y. 1990); Tune v. Walter Reed Army Med. Hosp., 602 F. Supp. 1452 (D.D.C. 1985); Satz v. Perlmutter, 362 So. 2d 160 (Fla. Dist. Ct. App. 1978), affd., 379 So. 2d 359 (Fla. 1980); State v. McAfee, 259 Ga. 579, 385 S.E.2d 651 (1989); In re Rivlin, No. 89-369904-AZ (Mich. Cir. Ct. Oakland County July 18, 1989) (Gage, J.); In re Culham, No. 87-340537-AZ (Mich. Cir. Ct. Dec. 15, 1987) (Breck, J.); In re Farrell, 108 N.J. 335, 529 A.2d 404 (1987); In re Requena, 213 N.J. Super. 475, 517 A.2d 886 (Super. Ct. Ch. Div.), affd., 213 N.J. Super. 443, 517 A.2d 869 (Super. Ct. App. Div. 1986) (per curiam); In re Jane Doe, 16 Phila. 229 (Pa. Ct. Comm. Pl. 1987); Doe v. Wilson, No. 90-364-II (Tenn. Ch. Ct. Feb. 16, 1990) (High, J.).

[25]Mont. Code Ann. §50-9-202(1) (1989); Doe v. Wilson, No. 90-364-II, slip op. at 4 (Tenn. Ch. Ct. Feb. 16, 1990) (High, J.).

The Legal Status of Treatment Choices.   Before specific types of treatment are discussed, several general principles concerning all treatment should be articulated. First, as noted in §10.3, there is no legal distinction between *withholding* and *withdrawing* treatment. Though healthcare professionals undoubtedly find the latter more difficult psychologically, the law's refusal to recognize a difference is supported by public policy considerations and the standards of medical practice. To hold otherwise could discourage health professionals from beginning potentially beneficial and lifesaving treatment for fear that, once begun, it could not be stopped, even if futile.[26] If a facility's policy or an individual professional's ethical preference conflicts with this principle, the patient should be informed that she cannot in that setting accept treatment on a trial basis (see §10.5). Healthcare facilities may wish to offer psychological support and training for staff who face emotional problems because of participation in life support termination.

Second, in general, decisionally capable patients may reject any type of treatment. Though an earlier view held that patients could reject only physically invasive treatment,[27] it is now well accepted that even painless and noninvasive care can be refused; treatment may be considered "invasive" merely because it is unwanted.[28]

Third, treatment options for decisionally incapacitated patients may be more limited. That is, the legal immunity of health professionals with respect to withholding or withdrawing treat-

---

[26]President's Commission for the Study of Ethical Problems in Medicine and Biomedical and Behavioral Research, Deciding to Forego Life-Sustaining Treatment 61-77 (1983).

[27]In re Quinlan, 70 N.J. 10, 40-41, 355 A.2d 647, 663-664, cert. denied sub nom. Garger v. New Jersey, 429 U.S. 922 (1976), diverged from in part, In re Conroy, 98 N.J. 321, 486 A.2d 1209 (1985).

[28]Rasmussen v. Fleming, 154 Ariz. 207, 222 n.24, 741 P.2d 674, 689 n.24 (1987); Brophy v. New Eng. Sinai Hosp. 398 Mass. 417, 434-438, 497 N.E.2d 626, 636-638 (1986); In re Conroy, 98 N.J. 321, 369-374, 486 A.2d 1209, 1233-1237 (1985); In re Torres, 357 N.W.2d 332, 340 (Minn. 1984); President's Commission for the Study of Ethical Problems, supra n.26, at 82-90.

ment for such patients may vary according to the type of treatment. Some living will statutes list the kinds of care that may be forgone; in other instances, courts have addressed what treatment may be rejected.[29]

Understanding these principles should help professionals working with patients. In seeking to effectuate patients' wishes, the professional must try to elicit or discover preferences about a wide variety of possible treatments. The task is complicated by the fact that many patients do not understand the available options at the time they execute an advance directive or must make a decision. For example, contemplating the possibility of becoming permanently unconscious, some people might decline anything that would prolong their life; others might want antibiotics and artificial feeding but no respiratory support. If the opportunity arises while a patient is still decisionally capable, health professionals can play a significant role in educating her so she may choose.

Patients can be helped to understand the value of being specific.[30] For instance, a generic rejection of "life support" when a certain physical state is reached is subject to more than one interpretation. In expressing that preference, the patient may or may not mean to refuse treatment (such as antibiotics and artificial feeding) that may be necessary for comfort but also prolongs life. It is impossible to anticipate every option, of

---

[29]Ill. Ann. Stat. ch. 110½ ¶702(2)(d) (Smith-Hurd Supp. 1989). For judicial statements, see §10.6 nn.31-41.

[30]73 Op. Atty. Gen.—, No. 88-046, slip op. at 19-25 (Md. Oct. 17, 1988); In re Westchester County Med. Center (O'Connor), 72 N.Y.2d 517, 531 N.E.2d 607, 534 N.Y.S.2d 886 (1988); Evans v. Bellevue Hosp. (Wirth), No. 16536/87 (N.Y. Sup. Ct. N.Y. County July 27, 1987) (Sandifer, J.), N.Y.L.J. July 28, 1987, at 11, col. 1 (living will of AIDS patient rejecting life support when "no reasonable expectation of recovering or regaining a meaningful quality of life" was ambiguous, since it did not indicate whether recovery was from AIDS or cognitive but still AIDS-infected state); Hazelton [sic] v. Powhatan Nursing Home, No. CH 98287 (Va. Cir. Ct. Fairfax County Aug. 29, 1986), order signed (Sept. 2, 1986) (Fortkort, J.), appeal denied, Record No. 860814 (Va. Sept. 2, 1986), 6 Va. Cir. Ct. Op. 414 (Aspen 1987). For drafting suggestions for specificity, see Living Wills and Health-Care Proxies, Murphy's Wills Clauses (Dec. 1988 & Supp. 1989). See also §10.6 n.8.

course, and repeated or exhaustive discussions would be painful to most patients. One compromise is to encourage patients to indicate whether their specific list of preferences is inclusive or exclusive. That is, do they want to reject only the treatments listed under the circumstances listed (exclusive), or do they also wish to reject, in advance, similar treatments in similar situations (inclusive)?

Descriptive Categories of Treatment Choices. Many treatment decisions involve acceptance or refusal of the following:

- antibiotics[31]
- artificial feeding (discussed below)
- blood transfusions[32]
- cardioversion[33]
- chemotherapy[34]
- comfort care (discussed below)
- dialysis[35]
- "do-not-hospitalize" orders[36]

---

[31]In re Severns, 425 A.2d 156 (Del. Ch. 1980). See also Hastings Center, Guidelines on the Termination of Life-Sustaining Treatment and the Care of the Dying 63-68 (1987); U.S. Congress Office of Technology Assessment, Life-Sustaining Technologies and the Elderly 331-354 (July 1987).

[32]Public Health Trust v. Wons, 541 So. 2d 96 (Fla. 1989); In re Brown, 478 So. 2d 1033 (Miss. 1985); Fosmire v. Nicoleau, 75 N.Y.2d 218, 551 N.E.2d 77, 551 N.Y.S.2d 876 (1990); In re Storar, 52 N.Y.2d 363, 420 N.E.2d 64, 438 N.Y.S.2d 266, cert. denied, 454 U.S. 858 (1981); In re Estate of Dorone, 517 Pa. 3, 534 A.2d 452 (1987). See also §10.6 nn.22, 23.

[33]Galvin v. University Hosp. of Cleveland, No. 115873 (Ohio Ct. Com. Pleas Cuyahoga County filed Sept. 8, 1987), as discussed in Miller, Right-to-Die Damage Actions: Developments in the Law, 655 Denver Univ. L. Rev. 181, 197 (1988). See also Kowey, The Calamity of Cardioversion in Conscious Patients, 61 Am. J. of Cardiology 1102-1107 (May 1, 1988).

[34]Custody of a Minor, 378 Mass. 732, 393 N.E.2d 836 (1979); Custody of a Minor, 375 Mass. 733, 379 N.E.2d 1053 (1978); Superintendent of Belchertown State School v. Saikewicz, 373 Mass. 728, 370 N.E.2d 417 (1977).

[35]In re Spring, 380 Mass. 629, 405 N.E.2d 115 (1980); In re Lydia E. Hall Hosp., 116 Misc. 2d 477, 455 N.Y.S.2d 706 (Sup. Ct. Nassau County 1982).

[36]Rasmussen v. Fleming, 154 Ariz. 207, 741 P.2d 674 (1987).

- "do-not-resuscitate" orders[37]
- medication[38]
- radiation[39]
- respirators[40]
- suctioning
- tracheotomy
- surgery, including amputation of gangrenous limbs[41]

Two among the listed items, artificial feeding and comfort care, merit further discussion.

"Artificial feeding" may be defined as technologically supplied nutrition and hydration, including hyperalimentation, intravenous feeding, and use of nasogastric, jejunostomy, or gastrostomy tubes. Whether and in what circumstances artificial

---

[37]In re Dinnerstein, 6 Mass. App. 466, 380 N.E.2d 134 (Ct. App. 1978); Custody of a Minor, 385 Mass. 697, 434 N.E.2d 601 (1982); In re Severns, 425 A.2d 156 (Del. Ch. 1980); Payne v. Marion Gen. Hosp., 549 N.E.2d 1043 (Ind. App. 1990); N.Y. Pub. Health Law §§2960-2978 (McKinney Supp. 1990); N.Y. Admin. Code tit. 10, §405.43; N.Y. State Department of Health Memorandum, Series 89-56 (July 13, 1989) (CPR requirements for prehospital personnel (such as ambulance attendants), including applicability of DNR orders); 1990 Tenn. Laws ch. 1082, to be codified in tit. 68, Tenn. Code Ann.; Joint Commission on Accreditation of Healthcare Organizations, Accreditation Manual for Hospitals MA. 1.4.12 (1991); 260 J.A.M.A. (Oct. 14, 1988) (collection of articles).

[38]People v. Robbins, 83 A.D.2d 271, 443 N.Y.S.2d 1016 (4th Dept. 1981) (no criminal liability for spouse who refused to call ambulance for wife who later died after she knowingly refused to take insulin); Commonwealth v. Konz, 498 Pa. 639, 450 A.2d 638 (Pa. 1982) (wife had no duty to seek medical attention for diabetic husband who refused insulin).

[39]In re Milton, 29 Ohio St. 3d 20, 505 N.E.2d 255 (1987), cert. denied sub nom. Ohio Dept. Mental Health v. Milton, 484 U.S. 820 (1987).

[40]Bartling v. Superior Court, 163 Cal. App. 3d 186, 209 Cal. Rptr. 220 (Ct. App. 1984); State v. McAfee, 259 Ga. 579, 385 S.E.2d 651 (Ga. 1989); In re Torres, 357 N.W.2d 332 (Minn. 1984); In re Quinlan, 70 N.J. 10, 355 A.2d 647, cert. denied sub nom. Garger v. New Jersey, 429 U.S. 922 (1976), diverged from in part on other grounds, In re Conroy, 98 N.J. 321, 486 A.2d 1209 (1985); In re Guardianship of Grant, 109 Wash. 2d 545, 747 P.2d 445 (1987), modified, 757 P.2d 534 (1988).

[41]Lane v. Candura, 6 Mass. App. 377, 376 N.E.2d 1232 (1978); State Dept. of Human Serv. v. Northern, 563 S.W.2d 197 (Tenn. App. 1978).

feeding may be refused are among the most controversial subjects in terminal care decision-making. Legislatures, courts, and medical organizations have addressed the issues.

Most living will statutes mention artificial feeding.[42] Though subject to differing interpretations, statutory language seems to fall into three categories: that which allows refusal of artificial feeding under certain circumstances;[43] that which does not;[44] and that which ties feeding in some way to comfort care (discussed below).[45] The third type of provision can be particularly difficult to interpret. When, for instance, a statute allows a patient to reject all treatment except that necessary for comfort, some authorities insist this means that no form of artificial feeding can be rejected (and still comply with the statute).[46] Others see such a proviso as requiring only certain kinds of artificial feeding that contribute to comfort.[47] Although dying without nutrition and hydration can be painful, that is not always the case. For example, a patient in a vegetative state or an irreversible coma feels no pain, by definition (as discussed above). Not providing nutrition and hydration may actually make the alert but dying patient more comfortable than inserting food and water through tubes into a body that cannot assimilate them.[48]

---

[42]For an updated map of statutory artificial feeding provisions, write to The Society for the Right to Die, 250 W. 57th St., NY, NY 10107.

[43]Alaska §18.12.010(c) (Sept. 1986); Colo. Rev. Stat. §§15-18-103, 15-18-104 (Supp. 1989); Ill. Ann. Stat. ch. 110½ ¶702(d) (Smith-Hurd Supp. 1990); Idaho Code §39-4504(1) (Supp. 1990).

[44]Ga. Code Ann. §31-32-2(5)(A)(1985); Wis. Stat. Ann. §154.01(5) (West 1989). Cf. Okla. Stat. tit. 63, §§3080.1 to 3080.5 (West. Supp. 1989), as amended in 1990 Okla. Session Laws Serv. ch. 268 (West) (separate law requiring artificial administration for decisionally incapacitated patient except under limited circumstances).

[45]Ariz. Rev. Stat. Ann. §36-3201(4) (1986); N.H. Rev. Stat. Ann. §137-H:2(II) (Supp. 1989).

[46]73 Op. Atty. Gen.—, No. 88-046, slip op. at 19-22 (Md. Oct. 17, 1988).

[47]Society for the Right to Die, Checklist Chart of Living Will Laws (1987); Society for the Right to Die, Handbook of Living Will Laws 6 (1987); Society for the Right to Die, Map of Tube Feeding Law in the United States (Oct. 15, 1989).

[48]For a discussion of situations in which artificial feeding can be painful,

It should be noted that even when a living will statute expressly prohibits rejection of artificial feeding, most courts to consider the issue have concluded that such prohibitive language in a statute cannot restrict a patient's right to refuse artificial feeding.[49] It is generally agreed that there is no analytic difference between this and other medical treatments.[50] Medical and ethical

---

see Cruzan v. Director, Mo. Dept. of Health, 110 S. Ct. 2841, 111 L. Ed. 2d 224, 247-49 (1990) (O'Connor, J., concurring); In re Conroy, 98 N.J. 321, 373-374, 486 A.2d 1209, 1236 (1985); Schmitz and O'Brien, Observations on Nutrition and Hydration in Dying Cancer Patients, in J. Lynn, ed., By No Extraordinary Means 29-38 (1989); U.S. Congress Office of Technology, Life-Sustaining Technologies and the Elderly 273-329, 434-436 (July 1987); Campbell-Taylor and Fisher, The Clinical Case Against Tube Feeding in Palliative Care of the Elderly, 35 J. Am. Geriatrics Socy. 1100 (Dec. 1987); Printz, Is Withholding Hydration a Valid Comfort Measure in the Terminally Ill?, 43 Geriatrics 84 (Nov. 1988); Ciocon et al., Tube Feedings in Elderly Patients: Indications, Benefits, and Complications, 148 Arch. Internal Medicine 429 (Feb. 1988). For a rare account of the actual experience of stopping artificial feeding for a permanently unconscious patient, see Lebowitz, Brophy Revisited: His Physician's View of Pain and Suffering, 1987 Massachusetts Medicine (Jan./Feb. 1987).

[49]In re Rodas, No. 86PR139 (Colo. Dist. Ct. Mesa County Jan. 22, 1987), as modified (April 3, 1987) (Buss, J.) (before law was amended to expressly authorize artificial feeding rejection); In re Guardianship of Browning, No. 74,174, 1990 Fla. LEXIS (Sept. 13, 1990); Corbett v. D'Alessandro, 487 So. 2d 368 (Fla. Dist. Ct. App.), review denied, 492 So. 2d 1331 (Fla. 1986); In re Estate of Longeway, 133 Ill. 2d 33, 549 N.E.2d 292 (1989); In re Gardner, 534 A.2d 947 (Me. 1987) (before amendment authorizing artificial feeding rejection); 73 Op. Atty. Gen.—, No. 88-046, slip op. at 19-23 (Md. Oct. 17, 1988). See also 54 Fed. Reg. 5321 (Feb. 2, 1989); Fla. Adm. Code §10D-29.110 (April 1988). Contra Couture v. Couture, 48 Ohio App. 3d 208, 549 N.E.2d 571 (Ohio Ct. App. 1989); Okla. Stat. tit 63, §§3080.1 to 3080.5 (West Supp. 1989), as amended in 1990 Okla. Sess. Laws Serv. ch. 268 (West); In re Guardianship of Grant, 109 Wash. 2d 545, 747 P.2d 445 (1987), modified, 757 P.2d 534 (1988).

[50]In re Conservatorship of Drabick, 200 Cal. App. 3d 185, 195-196 n.9, 245 Cal. Rptr. 840, 846 n.9 (Ct. App.), cert. denied, 102 L. Ed. 2d 387, 109 S. Ct. 399 (1988), rehearing denied, 102 L. Ed. 2d 816, 109 S. Ct. 828 (1989) (and authorities cited therein); Brophy v. New Eng. Sinai Hosp. 398 Mass. 417, 436 n.31, 497 N.E.2d 626, 637 n.31 (1986); In re Peter, 108 N.J. 365, 380-382, 529 A.2d 419, 427-428 (1987); Delio v. Westchester County Med.

sources concur that people have the same right to reject feeding as other care.[51] There are, however, exceptions.[52]

"Comfort care" usually refers to pain medication and, depending on the patient's condition, may also refer to artificial feeding (as discussed above). It is well accepted in the medico-

---

Center, 129 A.D.2d 1, 16-21, 516 N.Y.S.2d 677, 687-690 (2d Dept. 1987); Gray v. Romeo, 697 F. Supp. 580, 586-588 (D.R.I. 1988). See also Cruzan v. Director, Mo. Dept. of Health, 110 S. Ct. 2841, 111 L. Ed. 2d 224, 242, 248-249 (1990) (majority and O'Connor, J., concurring). Regulatory agencies have also explained that nonprovision of artificial feeding does not constitute neglect if based on patient preferences. 42 C.F.R. §483.10(b)(4) (Oct. 1, 1989); 54 Fed. Reg. 5321, 5335 (Feb. 2, 1989) (right to refuse artificial feeding is included in right to refuse treatment); Fla. Admin. Code §10D-29.110 (April 1988); N.Y. State Department of Health, Memo Series 89-94 (Oct. 20, 1989). See also 73 Op. Atty. Gen.—, No. 88-046, slip op. at 17-19 (Md. Oct. 17, 1988). Contra In re Guardianship of Grant, 109 Wash. 2d 545, 747 P.2d 445 (1987), as modified, 757 P.2d 534 (1988). For a complete list of artificial feeding cases, write to The Society for the Right to Die, 250 W. 57th St., NY, NY 10107.

[51]American Medical Association Council on Ethical and Judicial Affairs, Withholding or Withdrawing Life-Prolonging Medical Treatment §§2.20, 2.21, in Current Opinions of the Council on Ethical and Judicial Affairs of the American Medical Association (1989); American Academy of Neurology, Position Paper of the American Academy of Neurology on Certain Aspects of the Care and Management of the Persistent Vegetative State Patient, 39 Neurology 123-126 (Jan. 1989); Hastings Center, Guidelines on the Termination of Life-Sustaining Treatment and the Care of the Dying 57-62 (1987); American Dietetic Association, Position of the American Dietetic Association: Issues in Feeding the Terminally Ill Adult, 87 Am. Dietetic Assn. 78 (Jan. 1987); Steinbrook and Lo, Artificial Feeding—Solid Ground, Not a Slippery Slope, 318 New Eng. J. of Med. 286 (Feb. 4, 1988); J. Lynn, ed., By No Extraordinary Means (1989) (collection of essays on artificial feeding); O'Rourke (former director of Catholic Health Association), The A.M.A. Statement on Tube Feeding: An Ethical Analysis, 1986 America, 321 (Nov. 22, 1986); Paris and McCormick, The Catholic Tradition on Use of Nutrition and Fluids, America 356-361 (May 2, 1987).

[52]May et al., Feeding and Hydrating the Permanently Unconscious and Other Vulnerable Persons, 3 Issues in L. and Med. 203 (1987); American Nurse's Association Committee on Ethics, Guidelines on Withdrawing or Withholding Food and Fluid (1987); Weisbard and Siegler, On Killing Patients with Kindness: An Appeal for Caution, in J. Lynn, ed., By No Extraordinary Means 108-116 (1989).

legal community that patients should receive any treatment needed for comfort, regardless of whether it will lengthen or shorten life.[53] Similarly, nearly all living will statutes require that comfort care be offered even if other life-sustaining treatment is forgone.

When comfort care is likely to affect life span, it can seem problematic. One New Jersey court held that a person may choose a perhaps more painful but shorter dying process instead of a longer, less painful one.[54] The patient in that case declined artificial feeding. The situation may also arise with respect to patients receiving morphine for pain, Alzheimer's patients who refuse feeding, or patients with brain tumors who refuse steroids. (Steroids reduce uncomfortable intercranial pressure but often prolong dying.) Despite incidental effects on life span, both law and ethics approve the provision of comfort care at the patient's request.

§10.6.4 The Legal Context of the Decision

The procedures a facility follows in treating the dying depend on what is known of the patient's wishes. If the patient is decisionally capable, the task is easier than if he is decisionally incapable. If the patient is incapable, the question becomes whether he has executed a statutory advance directive. The facility must refer to the law of the jurisdiction for decision-making in the absence of statutory proxies or advance directives.

---

[53]State v. McAfee, 259 Ga. 579, 385 S.E.2d 651 (Ga. 1989); In re Jane Doe, 16 Phila. 229 (Pa. Ct. Com. Pl. 1987); Doe v. Wilson, No. 90-364-II, slip op. at 6 (Tenn. Ch. Ct. Feb. 16, 1990) (High, J.); Wanzer et al., The Physician's Responsibility Toward Hopelessly Ill Patients: A Second Look, 320 New Eng. J. Med. 844 (March 30, 1989); Hastings Center, Guidelines on the Termination of Life-Sustaining Treatment and the Care of the Dying 69-75 (1987); 17 Law, Med. & Health Care No. 3 (Fall 1989) (collection of articles on the case of Betty Wright).

[54]In re Requena, 213 N.J. Super. 475, 482-483, 517 A.2d 886, 890 (Super. Ct. Ch. Div.), affd., 213 N.J. Super. 443, 517 A.2d 869 (Super. Ct. App. Div. 1986) (per curiam).

The legal status and requirements of living wills have already been extensively reviewed. Another option available to patients is to appoint a proxy to speak on their behalf. The naming of a specific person for this purpose is often authorized under the jurisdiction's living will statute, by case law, or under a "durable power of attorney for health care" statute (see Appendix 10-1; a sample statutory form appears in Appendix 10-4). Such proxies are variously called healthcare or medical "surrogates," "decisionmakers," "agents," or "attorneys-in-fact" with "medical powers of attorney." Some statutes permit the proxy to act only when the patient has been declared "incompetent" (in which case the proxy is said to have "springing powers"). In other states, the proxy can make decisions from the time of appointment. Although all states have general durable power of attorney statutes, which usually cover financial matters, many (either in their general durable power statute or in a separate statute) authorize appointments for certain types of healthcare decisions. Providers should familiarize themselves with these statutes, and especially with the scope of the powers they convey.[55] General principles of the law of agency may allow people to appoint

---

[55]For citations to proxy provisions in living wills and durable powers of attorney for healthcare, see Appendix 10-1 to this chapter. For a map and comprehensive authority list for surrogate terminal care decision-making, write to The Society for the Right to Die, 250 W. 57th St., NY, NY 10107. For other authorities discussing healthcare proxies, see Cruzan v. Director, Mo. Dept. of Health, 110 S. Ct. 2841, 111 L. Ed. 2d 224, 249-250 (1990) (O'Connor, J., concurring); In re Peter, 108 N.J. 365, 378-379, 529 A.2d 419, 426 (1987); In re Westchester County Med. Center (O'Connor), 72 N.Y.2d 517, 528 n.2, 531 N.E.2d 607, 612 n.2, 534 N.Y.S.2d 886, 891 n.2 (1988) (dicta); Living Wills and Health-Care Proxies, Murphy's Wills Clauses 20-40 to 20-46 (Dec. 1988) (and authorities cited therein); Swidler, The Health Care Agent: Protecting the Choices and Interests of Patients Who Lack Capacity, 6 N.Y.L.S.J. Human Rights 1 (Fall 1988); Uniform Rights of the Terminally Ill Act §2, 9B U.L.A. at 70-73 (Supp. 1990). Other types of statutes authorizing proxies include Cal. Health & Safety Code §§1599.73, 1599.74 (West Supp. 1990); Md. Health Gen. Code Ann. §19-344(b)(3)(i) (1990); 73 Op. Atty. Gen.—, slip op. at 23-24, No. 88-046 (Md. Oct. 17, 1988); Mich. Comp. Laws Ann. §333.20201(6) (West Supp. 1989). See also Cohen, Patient's Rights Laws and the Right to Refuse Life-Sustaining Treatment in Nursing Homes: A Hidden Weapon for Patient Advocacy, 2 BioLaw S:231, 234-236 (Aug. 1989).

healthcare agents even in the absence of explicit statutory authority, but statutes serve to clarify their powers.[56]

If patients cannot speak for themselves when a decision must be made, and they have not executed a living will clearly applicable to their situation or appointed a proxy in writing, someone must decide for them. Frequently, health professionals consult the next of kin. If family members are agreed on the patient's preferences and can communicate them, or if family and physician agree on appropriate treatment regardless of the patient's previously stated preferences, there usually is no problem. Difficulties arise when (1) family members disagree with the patient's known preferences (but here the solution is simple: the patient's wishes control as a legal matter); or (2) the patient's preferences cannot be firmly established and the correct course of treatment is not entirely obvious.

In the latter case, statutory and case law may permit surrogate decision-making by family members, court-appointed fiduciaries (e.g., guardians), or even physicians.[57] Some living

---

[56]See Note, Appointing an Agent to Make Medical Treatment Choices, 84 Colum. L. Rev. 985 (1984); Swidler, supra n.55.

[57]For a discussion of the role of the family, see In re Conservatorship of Drabick, 200 Cal. App. 3d 185, 245 Cal. Rptr. 840 (Cal. Ct. App.), cert. denied, 102 L. Ed. 2d 387, 109 S. Ct. 399 (1988), rehearing denied, 102 L. Ed. 2d 816, 109 S. Ct. 828 (1989); McConnell v. Beverly Enter., 209 Conn. 692, 553 A.2d 596 (1989); John F. Kennedy Memorial Hosp. v. Bludworth, 452 So. 2d 921 (Fla. 1984); 73 Op. Atty. Gen.—, slip op. at 25-41, No. 88-046 (Md. Oct. 17, 1988); In re Jobes, 108 N.J. 394, 413-424, 529 A.2d 434, 443-447 (1987), stay denied sub nom. Lincoln Park Nursing & Convalescent Home v. Kahn, 483 U.S. 1036 (1987); In re Westchester County Med. Center (O'Connor), 72 N.Y.2d 517, 534 N.Y.S.2d 886, 531 N.E.2d 607 (1988); Gray v. Romeo, 697 F. Supp. 580 (D.R.I. 1988); In re Guardianship of Grant, 109 Wash. 2d 545, 565-568, 747 P.2d 445, 455-457 (1987), modified on other grounds, 757 P.2d 534 (1988) (and authorities cited therein). Some states have separate consent statutes that authorize family members to consent, but are silent about family ability to refuse consent. Ga. Code Ann. §§31-9-1 to 31-9-7 (1985 & Supp. 1989). Many states have "devolution" sections in their patients' rights statutes authorizing others, usually family members, to exercise the patient's rights, although it is still not clear if these statutes apply to life-sustaining treatment refusal. See Cohen, Patient's Rights Laws and the Right to Refuse Life-Sustaining Treatment in Nursing Homes: A Hidden Weapon for Patient

will statutes establish procedures to be followed in the absence of advance directives, often allowing decisions to be made jointly by the physician and one of a list of potential surrogates.[58] Some states have surrogate healthcare consent statutes or guardianship statutes that permit these people to decide for the patient. The statutes may, however, limit the kinds of decisions a surrogate can make; the statute may say, for example, that she may consent to treatment but say nothing about refusal of treatment.[59]

Advocacy, 2 BioLaw S:231, 234-236 (Aug. 1989). See also Rhoden, Litigating Life and Death, 102 Harv. L. Rev. 375 (Dec. 1988); Uniform Rights of the Terminally Ill Act §7, 9B U.L.A. 78 (Supp. 1990); American Medical Association Council on Ethical and Judicial Affairs, Withholding or Withdrawing Life-Prolonging Medical Treatment §§2.20, 2.21, in Current Opinions of the Council on Ethical and Judicial Affairs of the American Medical Association (1989).

[58]See, e.g., Ark. Stat. Ann. §20-17-214 (Supp. 1989). For a comprehensive list of living will statute provisions authorizing surrogate decisionmakers, see Society for the Right to Die, Checklist Chart of Living Will Laws (1987) (a more up-to-date list is also available from The Society for the Right to Die, 250 W. 57th St., NY, NY 10107). For a comprehensive list of citations for guardianship provisions concerning medical treatment, see Cohen, supra n.57, at 243 n.29.

[59]Some guardianship statutes expressly address the ability to make terminal care decisions; others mention the ability to consent but are silent about the ability to withhold consent. Still others make no mention of treatment, but courts have interpreted the term. Courts interpreting any guardianship language concerning the guardians' ability to reject life support for their wards include: Rasmussen v. Fleming, 154 Ariz. 207, 741 P.2d 674 (1987); In re Conservatorship of Drabick, supra n.57; McConnell v. Beverly Enter., 209 Conn. 692, 553 A.2d 596 (1989); Severns v. Wilmington Medical Center, 421 A.2d 1334 (Del. 1980); In re Guardianship of Browning, No. 74,174, 1990 Fla. LEXIS 1154 (Sept. 13, 1990); In re Estate of Greenspan, No. 67903, 1990 Ill. LEXIS 82 (Ill. July 9, 1990); In re Gardner, 534 A.2d 947 (Me. 1987); 73 Op. Atty. Gen.—, No. 88-046, slip op. at 25-31, 40-41, (Md. Oct. 17, 1988); Superintendent of Belchertown State School v. Saikewicz, 373 Mass. 728, 370 N.E.2d 417 (1977); In re Torres, 357 N.W.2d 332 (Minn. 1984); Cruzan v. Harmon, 760 S.W.2d 408 (Mo. 1988), affd. sub nom. Cruzan v. Director, Mo. Dept. of Health, 110 S. Ct. 2841, 111 L. Ed. 2d 224 (1990); In re Jobes, 108 N.J. 394, 529 A.2d 434 (1987), stay denied sub nom. Lincoln Park Nursing & Convalescent Home v. Kahn, 483 U.S. 1036 (1987); Leach v. Akron Gen.

The criteria for surrogate decision-making vary from state to state. One approach, described as "substituted judgment," is thought to be a subjective standard. It instructs the surrogate to make the decision the patient would have made, taking into account the particular individual's preferences. Both the literature and court decisions on terminal care decision-making reveal confusion about the relationship between the "clear and convincing evidence" and "substituted judgment" standards.[60] Some courts see the two as different, that is, that the former requires that there be clear evidence that the patient, not someone else construing patient preferences, actually made the decision, while "substituted judgment" refers to a decision by someone else construing patient preference. Other courts describe the two as overlapping, that is, that "substituted judgment" allows people to construe patient preferences if there is "clear" evidence that the patient would decide in a certain way, even if she did not actually express herself.[61]

Med. Center, 68 Ohio Misc. 1, 426 N.E.2d 809 (Com. Pl. 1980); Couture v. Couture, 48 Ohio App. 3d 208, 549 N.E.2d 571 (Ohio Ct. App. 1989).

[60]Courts disagreeing on what constitutes clear and convincing evidence (i.e., courts in the same case disagree) include: *Cruzan*, supra n.59; In re Jobes, supra n.59; In re Westchester County Med. Center (O'Connor), 72 N.Y.2d 517, 531 N.E.2d 607, 534 N.Y.S.2d 886 (1988); Elbaum v. Grace Plaza of Great Neck, 148 A.D.2d 244, 544 N.Y.S.2d 840 (2d Dept. 1989).

[61]For a discussion of the different evidentiary standards, see Cruzan v. Director, Mo. Dept. of Health, 110 S. Ct. 2841, 111 L. Ed. 2d 224 (1990). Courts using the clear and convincing evidence standard include: In re Gardner, 534 A.2d 947, 952-54 (Me. 1987) (subsequently modified by statute); In re Westchester County Med. Center, supra n.60; In re Storar, 52 N.Y.2d 363, 378-380, 420 N.E.2d 64, 72, 438 N.Y.S.2d 266, 274, cert. denied, 454 U.S. 858 (1981). Courts using the substituted judgment include In re Guardianship of Browning, No. 74,174, 1990 Fla. LEXIS 1154 (Sept. 13, 1990); Brophy v. New Eng. Sinai Hosp., 398 Mass. 417, 427-429, 497 N.E.2d 626, 631-632 (1986); In re Jobes, 108 N.J. at 409-420, 529 A.2d at 442-447; Gray v. Romeo, 697 F. Supp. 580, 587-589 (D.R.I. 1988). For other discussions of the application merits of the clear and convincing, substituted judgment, and best interest standards, see In re Estate of Longeway, 133 Ill. 2d 33, 549 N.E.2d 292, 299-301 (1989); In re Swan, 569 A.2d 1202 (Me. 1990); Couture v. Couture, 48 Ohio App. 3d at 213-214, 549 N.E.2d at 576; Comment, Judicial Postponement of Death Recognition: The Tragic Case of Mary

A few states have provided for an alternative—the "objective standard" or "best interest analysis." The patient surrogate is to make the decision that would be made by a reasonable person in that medical condition, considering such facts as pain and the risks and benefits of proposed treatment.[62] Obviously, these criteria can be difficult to apply. Health professionals may want to seek judicial clarification of the requirements in a particular case. In some jurisdictions, in fact, courts, not healthcare providers, must make these determinations.[63]

A patient may deal with more in her advance directive or oral statements of preference than the core issue of seeking or rejecting healthcare. It is not uncommon for a patient to express desires about organ donation after death, place of death, disposal of remains, and even preferences about financial expenditures on care. The facility should bring these matters to the attention

---

O'Connor, 15 Am. J.L. & Med. 301 (1989); Note, The Incompetent Developmentally Disabled Person's Right to Self-Determination: Right-to-Die, Sterilization, and Institutionalization, 15 Am. J.L. & Med. 333 (1989); Annas, Precatory Prediction and Mindless Mimicry: The Case of Mary O'Connor, Hastings Center Report 31 (Dec. 1988); Rhoden, Litigating Life and Death, 102 Harv. L. Rev. 375 (Dec. 1988).

[62]Rasmussen v. Fleming, 154 Ariz. 207, 221-222, 741 P.2d 674, 688-689 (1987); In re Conservatorship of Drabick, 200 Cal. App. 3d 185, 210-212, 245 Cal. Rptr. 840, 856-857 (Cal. Ct. App.), cert. denied, 102 L. Ed. 2d 387, 109 S. Ct. 399 (1988), rehearing denied, 102 L. Ed. 2d 816, 109 S. Ct. 828 (1989); In re Guardianship of Grant, 109 Wash. 2d 545, 567-568, 747 P.2d 445, 457 (1987), modified on other grounds, 757 P.2d 534 (1988). In re Beth Israel Med. Center, 136 Misc. 2d 931, 519 N.Y.S.2d 511 (Sup. Ct. N.Y. County 1987); Cruzan, 110 S. Ct. 2841, 111 L. Ed. 2d at 275-291 (1990) (Stevens, J., dissenting). The best interest test to authorize life-sustaining treatment refusal was rejected in Cruzan, supra n.59; In re Westchester County Med. Center (O'Connor), 72 N.Y.2d 517, 530-531, 531 N.E.2d 607, 613-614, 534 N.Y.S.2d 886, 892 (1988); In re Storar, 52 N.Y.2d 363, 380-384, 420 N.E.2d 64, 72-74, 438 N.Y.S.2d 266, 274-276.

[63]In re Estate of Longeway, 133 Ill. 2d 33, 549 N.E.2d 292, 300-302 (1989); 73 Op. Atty. Gen.—, No. 88-046, slip op. at 7-9, 38-40 (Md. Oct. 17, 1988); Leach v. Akron Gen. Med. Center, 68 Ohio Misc. 1, 426 N.E.2d 809 (Ct. Com. Pl. 1980); Superintendent of Belchertown State School v. Saikewicz, 373 Mass. 728, 755-759, 370 N.E.2d 417, 432-435 (1977), as clarified in In re Dinnerstein, 6 Mass. App. 466, 380 N.E.2d 134 (Ct. App. 1978).

of the appropriate parties. The enforceability of such requests depends on the jurisdiction.[64]

One group of patients, pregnant women, may find their decisions or those made for them limited by the fact of their pregnancy. Some living will statutes attempt to restrict the preferences expressed in the living will if the declarant is pregnant at the time of implementation. A few court decisions have considered whether limiting a pregnant patient's treatment options burdens her constitutional rights to privacy and bodily integrity. No clear answer to the question is available at this time.[65]

---

[64]McConnell v. Beverly Enter., 209 Conn. 692, 709, 553 A.2d 596, 605 (1989); In re Jobes, 108 N.J. 394, 415 n.10, 529 A.2d 434, 444 n.10, stay denied sub nom. Lincoln Park Nursing & Convalescent Home v. Kahn, 483 U.S. 1036 (1987). For organ donations, see Chapter 12 and Tenn. Code §32-11-103(d) (Supp. 1989). For the role of economics, see Lorenzen v. Employees Retirement Plan of Sperry & Hutchinson Co., 896 F.2d 228 (7th Cir. 1990) (widow who authorized removal of husband's life support three days before retirement was not entitled to lump sum of retirement benefits); U.S. Congress Office of Technology, Life-Sustaining Technologies and the Elderly 3-88 (July 1987); Callahan, Setting Limits: Medical Goals in an Aging Society (1987); Kapp, Response to the Living Will Furor: Directives for Maximum Care, 72 Am. J. Med. 855 (June 1982); Hastings Center, Guidelines on the Termination of Life-Sustaining Treatment and the Care of the Dying 119-126 (1987); *An Angry Man Fights to Die, Then Tests Life*, N.Y. Times, Feb. 7, 1990, at A1, col. 2 (McAfee case); Wray, et al., Withholding Medical Treatment From the Severely Demented Patient: Decisional Processes and Cost Implications, 148 Arch. Internal Med. 1980 (Sept. 1988); Dresser, Life, Death, and Incompetent Patients: Conceptual Infirmities and Hidden Values in the Law, 28 Ariz. L. Rev. 373, 399-404 (1986).

[65]Del. Code Ann. tit. 16, §2503(d) (1983); Note, Pregnancy Clauses in Living Will Statutes, 87 Colum. L. Rev. 1280 (1987); In re A.C., 573 A.2d 1235 (D.C. Ct. App. 1990), discussed in Annas, She's Going to Die: The Case of Angela C., Hastings Center Report 23 (Feb./March 1988); Jefferson v. Griffin Spaulding County Hosp. Auth., 247 Ga. 86, 274 S.E.2d 457 (1981). See also Kolder et al., Court-Ordered Obstetrical Intervention, 316 New Eng. J. Med. 192 (May 7, 1987).

C. Resolving Disputes

§10.7 Nonjudicial Resolution

Inevitably, problems arise in terminal care decision-making. Referring them for judicial resolution is costly, time-consuming, and emotionally stressful for all concerned. Most parties, therefore, including judges, seem to agree that whenever possible these controversies should be settled without resort to the courts.[1] In most instances, they can be. (As noted in §10.4.2, patients, family members, and staff should be told about the facility's dispute resolution procedures.) Statutes governing living wills, healthcare proxies, and surrogate decision-making usually offer civil and criminal immunity to healthcare professionals who comply with the statutes. If not, professionals may still be immune under specific case law so long as they adhere to accepted medical standards.[2]

The best means of settling problems seem to be clarifying facts, assumptions, and legal principles; educating those involved and improving communication; meeting to discuss the situation; and perhaps asking the advice of a facility ethics committee.[3]

The possibility of a factual misunderstanding should be

---

§10.7 [1]Rasmussen v. Fleming, 154 Ariz. 207, 223-224, 741 P.2d 674, 690-691 (1987); John F. Kennedy Memorial Hosp. v. Bludworth, 452 So. 2d 921 (Fla. 1984); In re Guardianship of Browning, No. 74,174, 1990 Fla. LEXIS 1154 (Sept. 13, 1990); In re L.H.R., 253 Ga. 439, 321 S.E.2d 716 (1984); In re Estate of Longeway, 133 Ill. 2d 33, 549 N.E.2d 292, 301 (Ill. 1989); In re Farrell, 108 N.J. 335, 341-343, 529 A.2d 404, 407-408 (1987).

[2]Cf. Barber v. Superior Court, 147 Cal. App. 3d 1006, 196 Cal. Rptr. 484 (Ct. App. 1983).

[3]For information on ethics committees, see Haw. Rev. Stat. §663-1.7 (Supp. 1989); Md. Health-Gen. Code Ann. §§19-370 to 19-374 (Michie 1990), as amended, 1990 Md. Laws ch. 545; Mont. Code Ann. §37-2-201 (1990); In re Quinlan, 70 N.J. 10, 44-51, 355 A.2d 647, 665-669, cert. denied sub nom. Garger v. New Jersey, 429 U.S. 922 (1976), diverged from in part, In re Conroy, 98 N.J. 321, 486 A.2d 1209 (1985); N.Y. Pub. Health Law §2972 (McKinney Supp. 1990); N.Y. Admin. Code tit. 10, §405.21(h)(3) (infant review).

investigated first, since it is the most easily resolved. Areas to probe include the patient's medical condition, patient preferences, generally accepted standards of medical practice and ethics, and legal requirements. For example, the family of someone who has been unconscious for a month following an accident may seem to the staff to be inappropriately eager to have life support discontinued. This may be, however, because they know the patient did not want to be kept alive in a permanently unconscious state but do not know that his condition has not yet stabilized and there is still reasonable hope for full recovery.

Family members might simply say, "We don't want him maintained artificially," without explaining that their request is based on clear evidence of the patient's wishes. Some health professionals may not know that medical ethics approves honoring patient preference even if it results in death, and that it is ethically permissible to forgo artificial feeding for permanently unconscious patients. Or they might be misinformed about the law, believing, for example, that it is always illegal to remove a respirator from a person who is not brain dead, or that life support must always be continued once it is begun.

Perhaps the misunderstanding can be identified and corrected during a meeting of interested parties. Possible participants include the patient, the family, the patient surrogate, the patient's and facility's attorneys, the attending physician, consulting specialists, the social worker, the risk manager, the ombudsman, the patient advocate, and members of an ethics or prognosis committee. (See Appendices 10-5 and 10-6 for sample forms for collecting information.) Depending on the legal and institutional requirements concerning the ability to make entries in a medical record following a meeting, a dated entry in the medical record, naming the participants and summarizing what took place, is probably helpful. (Or, if the report is lengthy, the entry should indicate where the full report is available.) If the patient or his surrogate executes a release-of-liability form (see Appendices 10-7 and 10-8), that too should be made a part of the medical record.

Each healthcare facility should have a dispute resolution

procedure. Many now use interdisciplinary committees, and in a few states a committee is required.[4] The composition, authority, and other characteristics of such a committee vary depending on facility preference or statutory requirements. Matters to be considered include whether the committee's decisions are binding or advisory; whether it evaluates medical ethics, medical prognoses, or both; whether proceedings are confidential; who serves on the committee; and precisely what its duties are. How these committees should function and what their effect is on liability (including documentation issues) are emerging areas of law.[5] A facility might wish to contact the ethics committee network to locate a model that would suit its institution.[6]

---

[4]Id.; Merritt, The Tort Liability of Hospital Ethics Committees, 60 S. Cal. L. Rev. 1239 (1987); Hastings Center, Guidelines on the Termination of Life-Sustaining Treatment and the Care of the Dying 99-105 (1987). Cases discussing the role of ethics committees include *Bludworth,* supra n.1; In re L.H.R., 253 Ga. 439, 321 S.E.2d 716 (1984); Superintendent of Belchertown State School v. Saikewicz, 373 Mass. 728, 370 N.E.2d 417 (1977); In re Torres, 357 N.W.2d 332, 335 n.2 (Minn. 1984); In re Jobes, 108 N.J. 394, 420-424, 529 A.2d 434, 447-450, stay denied sub nom. Lincoln Park Nursing & Convalescent Home v. Kahn, 483 U.S. 1036 (1987); In re Conroy, 98 N.J. 321, 486 A.2d 1209 (1985); *Quinlan,* 70 N.J. at 44-51, 355 A.2d at 665-669. For a comprehensive listing of healthcare institutional ethics committees, contact Cynthia B. Cohen, The Hastings Center, 255 Elm Road, Briarcliff Manor, NY 10510. See also Meisel, Chapter 15, The Right to Die (1989 & Supp. 1990); Glasser et al., Ethics Committees in Nursing Homes: Results of a National Survey, 36 J. Am. Geriatrics Socy. 150 (Feb. 1988); J. Monagle and D. Thamasma, eds., Medical Ethics 397-416 (1988). Brennan, Ethics Committees and Decisions to Limit Care: The Experience at the Massachusetts General Hospital, 260 J.A.M.A. 803 (Aug. 12, 1988); LaPuma et al., An Ethics Consultation Service in a Teaching Hospital, 260 J.A.M.A. 808 (Aug. 12, 1988); Cranford et al., Institutional Ethics Committees: Issues of Confidentiality and Immunity, 13 Law, Medicine & Health Care 52 (April 1985); McCarrick and Adams, Ethics Committees in Hospitals (Kennedy Institute of Ethics, Georgetown University, Washington, DC 20057) (June 1989).

[5]Id.

[6]For a compilation of ethics committee addresses, write to Cynthia B. Cohen, The Hastings Center, 255 Elm Road, Briarcliff Manor, NY 10510.

§10.8 *Judicial Resolution*

Regrettably, judicial intervention in terminal care decision-making cannot always be avoided. Most often, the need arises in cases involving a request to force or prevent treatment or to award monetary relief (discussed in §§10.9 and 10.10). In the situations in which a court's guidance is sought on treatment, a number of legal issues remain unclear at present. Precedents are few and varied on such questions as (1) who should institute the proceeding, a representative of the patient or a representative of the facility; (2) who are proper parties to it—the family, the facility, the third-party payor, the district attorney, or the state attorney general; (3) what legal relief can be sought—declaratory judgment, temporary or permanent injunction, or order to show cause; (4) what the proper forum is—state or federal court, and of what level; (5) whether the court must appoint a fiduciary (conservator or guardian) and guardian ad litem; and (6) who is responsible for court costs, guardian ad litem fees, and attorneys' fees.[1]

Until recently, it was accepted practice among health professionals to provide life-sustaining care as long as medically appropriate, even without patient consent. Health professionals believed they were legally required to do so—that provision of life-sustaining treatment was governed by different legal principles than other types of treatment.[2] Thus, a patient (or patient representative) who wished to have care terminated was required to gain court approval.

The newer trend is to shift the burden, that is, to assume

---

§10.8 [1]For a discussion of different types of procedural issues, see In re Storar, 52 N.Y.2d 363, 382-383, 420 N.E.2d 64, 73-74, 438 N.Y.S.2d 266, 276, cert. denied, 454 U.S. 858 (1981); In re Jane Doe, 16 Phila. 229, 235-239 (Pa. Ct. Com. Pl. 1987); In re Culham, No. 87-340537-AZ (Mich. Cir. Ct. Dec. 15, 1987) (Breck, J.); In re Guardianship of Grant, 109 Wash. 2d 545, 747 P.2d 445 (1987), modified, 757 P.2d 534 (1988); In re Jobes, 210 N.J. Super. 543, 510 A.2d 133 (Ch. Div.), review denied (N.J. March 10, 1986) (it is not guardian ad litem's role to fight for life support in all cases, but rather to pursue patient's best interest); In re Swan, 569 A.2d 1202 (Me. 1990).

[2]In re Spring, 380 Mass. 629, 405 N.E.2d 115 (1980).

that all treatment requires patient consent and any treatment to which the patient (or her representative) does not consent, including insertion of a nasogastric tube, cannot be provided without judicial authorization.[3] As noted earlier, if the patient is decisionally capable, or was when the decision was made, courts usually do not order treatment. Consent for routine nursing procedures and comfort care is either covered by the general consent form or is thought to be implied unless specifically rejected.[4]

Unless state law requires judicial intervention, healthcare providers are probably legally protected if they thoroughly document the patient's medical condition and prognosis, her wish to forgo treatment, and the decisionmaking process that was used. For a higher level of protection, the facility could ask a court either to authorize explicitly the decision to forgo treatment or to appoint a fiduciary to make decisions (specifically including decisions to refuse treatment) for a decisionally incapacitated patient. This effort, even if successful, may result in significant legal fees for the facility. If court approval is to be sought, however, there are advantages to the facility's initiating the request rather than asking the patient or her representative to do so. The primary benefits are that stress for the patient and family are reduced and that the facility controls the litigation.

Occasionally, disputes arise over unwillingness to provide treatment that the patient or family wants. The physician may consider the treatment unwarranted, either because it will be futile or because the burdens will outweigh the benefits. Although the law on this subject is just emerging, it appears that in general physicians will not be obliged to provide futile

---

[3]Public Health Trust v. Wons, 541 So. 2d 96, 98 (Fla. 1989) (hospital wishing to contest patient's treatment refusal must go to court); Quill, Utilization of Nasogastric Feeding Tubes in a Group of Chronically Ill, Elderly Patients in a Community Hospital, 149 Arch. Internal Med. 1937, 1940 (Sept. 1989); Hastings Center, Guidelines on the Termination of Life-Sustaining Treatment and the Care of the Dying 61-62 (1987); Fosmire v. Nicoleau, 75 N.Y.2d 218, 551 N.E.2d 77, 551 N.Y.S.2d 896 (1990) (notice requirements).

[4]See Chapter 7 and §10.6 n.18 addressing the limits of implied consent.

treatment. Still, health professionals may prefer to provide it rather than to litigate the matter.

D. Liability for Terminal Care Decisions

§10.9 Liability When Treatment Is Provided

There are strong incentives—costs in time, money, and reputation—to avoid even litigation that a healthcare facility or professional wins. From that perspective, terminal care decision-making is a particularly difficult area of medical practice and facility operation: the stakes are high and the law is uncertain. To name just one aspect of the dilemma, providers must consider under what circumstances they might be guilty of patient *abuse* for providing unwanted treatment and when they might be guilty of *neglect* for withholding it (as discussed in §10.2.1). However, some legal principles in the field can be identified, and some issues noted, of which the facility should be aware. (See also §4.8.7.)

To begin with, it is important to recognize the possibility of liability for providing unwanted treatment. Liability might derive from two sources: general tort law principles or statutory protections for patient preference. American jurisprudence has long acknowledged that a decisionally capable person may not be treated without his consent. A health professional who does so may be liable for battery, breach of a statutory duty, malpractice, or other wrongs; and, after *Cruzan*, there may be damages for constitutional violations.[1]

---

§10.9   [1]Cruzan v. Director, Mo. Dept. of Health, 110 S. Ct. 2841, 111 L. Ed. 2d 224, 241-242 (1990). Health professionals may be concerned about which members of the healthcare team bear ultimate responsibility for entering and implementing terminal care orders. Although no cases have directly addressed this issue, it appears that much of the obligation rests with the attending physicians, not the nurse or the institution. Cf. Sparks v. St. Luke's Regional Medical Center, 115 Idaho 505, 768 P.2d 768 (1988) (evidence

Awards of money damages for failure to obtain consent are relatively common. Some doubt remains, though, about the extent to which the general principle applies to life-saving treatment. In particular, what is the legal consequence of denying the request of a patient or an appropriate surrogate not to have life-sustaining treatment or of violating the terms of an advance directive to the same effect?

Some courts have held that informed consent principles apply to life-saving treatment just as to other treatment. They conclude that a health professional who imposes life-saving treatment against a patient's wishes (either contemporaneously or previously expressed) owes damages.[2] Others have declined to recognize a cause of action for damages in the case before them because the rights at issue were not clearly established when the events occurred.[3] Those decisions leave open the

---

supported that attending physician has responsibility regarding ventilator extubation order and hospital personnels' responsibility is to follow physician's order).

[2]Leach v. Shapiro, 13 Ohio App. 3d 393, 395, 469 N.E.2d 1047, 1051-1052 (Ct. App. 1984); Marcotte, Wrongful Life: Ohio Man Sues Hospital for Saving Him Against His Wishes, 1990 ABA Journal 31 (March 1990) (Do-not-resuscitate order allegedly ignored for patient Edward Winter); Margolick, Patient's Lawsuit Says Saving Life Ruined It, N.Y. Times (New York late edition), Mar. 18, 1990, at A1 (Winter case); Malette v. Shulman, 72 O.R.2d 417 (Ont. C.A. 1990) ($20,000 damage award upheld against physician who transfused unconscious Jehovah's Witness who had a Jehovah's Witness card rejecting blood transfusions in all circumstances); Lunsford v. Regents, No. 837936 (Cal. Super. Ct. S.F. County April 13, 1990) ($500,000 verdict awarded against hospital and surgeon for transfusing a child against Jehovah's Witness parents' wishes when transfusion was undertaken after making fraudulent representation to the parents) (more information on the case may be obtained from: Legal Department, The Watchtower, 25 Columbia Heights, Brooklyn, NY 11201). For more on civil damages for unwanted life support, see generally Miller, Right-to-Die Damage Actions: Developments in the Law, 65 Denver U.L. Rev. 181 (1988); Comment, Damage Actions for Nonconsensual Life-Sustaining Medical Treatment, 30 St. Louis U.L.J. 895 (1986); Merritt, The Tort Liability of Hospital Ethics Committees, 60 S. Cal. L. Rev. 1239 (1987).

[3]Bartling v. Glendale Adventist Med. Center, 184 Cal. App. 3d 961, 229 Cal. Rptr. 360 (Ct. App. 1986).

possibility of future awards. Some decisions question whether damages are ever appropriate for saving a life, and a few imply that overly aggressive attorneys should be chastised for filing on behalf of patients.[4]

Under another legal theory, damages may be appropriate for denying statutory rights to refuse treatment. No living will or healthcare proxy statute, by its terms, provides for damages against healthcare professionals who do not follow the directives. There are, however, patients' rights statutes and regulations that might be used to award damages against facilities. Most such statutes apply to extended care facilities or any facility that receives Medicare or Medicaid reimbursement. They usually specify that the patient has a right to refuse treatment and provide for monetary relief if rights are abridged.[5] Some courts, regulatory agencies, and commentators have applied these statutes to permit patients to terminate treatment, but not (so far) to award damages for unwanted treatment.[6]

Damage awards are not the only negative consequence of providing unwanted treatment. Though damage awards have not yet been awarded against healthcare providers, providers have been forced to bear other financial burdens. These include

---

[4]In re Spring, 380 Mass. 629, 638, 405 N.E.2d 115, 121 (1980); Ross v. Hilltop Rehab. Hosp., 676 F. Supp. 1528 (D. Colo. 1987), later proceeding, 124 F.R.D. 660 (D. Colo. 1988).

[5]Gray v. Romeo, 697 F. Supp. 580, 590-591 (D.R.I. 1988); Elbaum v. Grace Plaza of Great Neck, 148 A.D.2d 244, 544 N.Y.S.2d 840, 847 (2d Dept. 1989); 73 Op. Atty. Gen.—, No. 88-046, slip op. at 40-41 (Md. Oct. 17, 1988); 54 Fed. Reg. 5321, 5335 (Feb. 2, 1989) (federal Health Care Financing Administration, in comments to the new Medicare-Medicaid requirements for long-term care facilities, wrote that the residents' right to refuse to eat, drink, or be fed is included in the federal regulations recognizing the right to refuse treatment). See generally Cohen, Patient's Rights Laws and the Right to Refuse Life-Sustaining Treatment in Nursing Homes: A Hidden Weapon for Patient Advocacy, 2 BioLaw S:231 (Aug. 1989).

[6]Id.

attorneys' fees,[7] court costs,[8] guardian ad litem fees,[9] and uncollectible charges for the unauthorized care.[10]

There is no settled law on whether facilities must have procedures in place for making terminal care decisions in a timely manner. The possibility is at least suggested, however, by a decision of the New Jersey Supreme Court.[11] It held that while no absolute duty existed to establish procedures for removing life support after brain death, there was a duty to act reasonably, which the providers breached.

---

[7]Bartling v. Glendale Adventist Medical Center, 184 Cal. App. 3d 97, 228 Cal. Rptr. 847 (Ct. App. 1986), on remand, No. 500735 (Cal. Super. Ct. Los Angeles County Oct. 14, 1987) (Riley, J.) (awarded $160,000 in attorneys' fees); Wilmington Med. Center v. Severns, 433 A.2d 1047 (Del. 1981); Hoffmeister v. Coler, 544 So. 2d 1067 (Fla. Dist. Ct. App. 1989); Gray v. Romeo, 709 F. Supp. 325 (D.R.I. 1989); In re Clark, 212 N.J. Super. 408, 515 A.2d 276 (Ch. Div. 1986), affd., 216 N.J. Super. 497, 524 A.2d 448 (App. Div. 1987). But see In re Rosebush, No. 88-349180 AZ (Mich. Cir. Ct. Oakland County Nov. 30, 1988) (Kuhn, J.) (attorneys' fees denied).

[8]Fosmire v. Nicoleau, 75 N.Y.2d 218, 551 N.E.2d 77, 551 N.Y.S.2d 876 (1990); Northern v. State Dept. of Human Serv., 575 S.W.2d 946, 948 (Tenn. 1978).

[9]Rasmussen v. Fleming, 154 Ariz. 207, 222-223, 741 P.2d 674, 689-690 (1987); In re Conservatorship of Drabick, 200 Cal. App. 3d 185, 245 Cal. Rptr. 840, 857-858 (Cal. Ct. App.), cert. denied, 102 L. Ed. 2d 387, 109 S. Ct. 399 (1988), rehearing denied, 102 L. Ed. 2d 816, 109 S. Ct. 828 (1989). See also In re Jobes, 210 N.J. Super. 543, 510 A.2d 133 (Ch. Div.), review denied (N.J. March 10, 1986) (discussing role of guardian ad litem); In re Lydia E. Hall Hosp., 117 Misc. 2d 1024, 459 N.Y.S.2d 682 (Sup. Ct. Nassau County 1982).

[10]Alaska Stat. §18.12.070 (Sept. 1986); Cavagnaro v. Hanover, 236 N.J. Super. 287, 565 A.2d 728 (Super. Ct. Law Div. 1989) (hospital expenses incurred after confirmations of brain death are not compensable under New Jersey's "no-fault" act since they are not "reasonable" or "necessary"); Grace Plaza of Great Neck v. Elbaum, No. 19068/88 (N.Y. Sup. Ct. Nassau County January 9, 1990) (McCabe, J.), N.Y.L.J. Jan. 19, 1990, at 26, col. 4; 40 Tex. Ad. Code §16.1503(d)(10) (participation in Texas Medical Assistance program involving federal reimbursement is prohibited if treatment is ordered in contravention of living will). See also Kapp, Enforcing Patient Preferences: Linking Payment for Medical Care to Informed Consent, 261 J.A.M.A. 1935 (April 7, 1989).

[11]Strachan v. John F. Kennedy Memorial Hosp., 109 N.J. 523, 538 A.2d 346 (1988).

§10.10 Liability When Treatment Is Not Provided

Most healthcare professionals and administrators are more concerned about liability for not providing treatment than for providing it. It is essential to distinguish, however, between deliberate or negligent failure to supply wanted and needed treatment[1] on the one hand and nontreatment based on patient preference or futility on the other. The latter has far less potential for liability. Indeed, no provider has been found either civilly or criminally liable for stopping or failing to begin life-saving measures when this was consistent with patient (or surrogate) preference or was clearly futile.

Providers may fear suits from family members if they honor a patient's preference to forgo treatment and the patient dies. Although such suits have (rarely) occurred, their results are reassuring. The decisions indicate that lawsuits will not succeed if the patient's wishes are well-documented and medical negligence is not the cause of death, especially since all living will statutes have provisions immunizing providers who adhere to them.[2] Furthermore, family members have no independent right to participate in treatment decisions. If the patient is decisionally capable, it is neither customary nor legally appropriate to involve

---

§10.10 [1]Chambers v. Rush-Presbyterian St. Luke's Medical Center, 155 Ill. App. 3d 458, 508 N.E.2d 426, app. denied, 515 N.E.2d 102 (1987); Shorter v. Drury, 103 Wash. 2d 645, 695 P.2d 116, cert. denied, 474 U.S. 827 (1985) (release of civil liability for harm caused by patient's refusal of blood transfusion did not waive liability from negligent performance of surgery, which resulted in death); Payne v. Marion Gen. Hosp., 549 N.E.2d 1043 (Ind. App. 1990).

[2]See Appendix 10-1 for statutory citations. See also §10.7.3 supra for immunity provisions relating to ethics committees; Randolph v. City of New York, 117 A.D.2d 44, 48-49, 501 N.Y.S.2d 837, 839-841 (1st Dept. 1986), modified on other grounds and affd., 69 N.Y.2d 844, 507 N.E.2d 298, 514 N.Y.S.2d 705 (1987); Camp v. White, 510 So. 2d 166 (Ala. 1987) (jury verdict affirmed that physician not negligent for not reconnecting patient to a respirator when she orally refused to be reconnected); Miller, Right-to-Die Damage Actions: Developments in the Law, 65 Denver L. Rev. 181 (1988); Living Wills and Health-Care Proxies, Murphy's Wills Clauses 20-88 to 20-93 (Dec. 1988).

the family.[3] Thus, although facilities may feel more comfortable with a release from liability from family members, procuring such a release when the patient has refused treatment is unnecessary and has no legal effect. (On the contrary, a release from the patient or appropriate representative when the representative speaks for the patient is helpful and usually enforceable.)[4] Family members, however, do have certain rights concerning care of the patient's body once he is dead (see Chapter 12). Careful communication among health professionals and patients, and careful documentation of it, will allow professionals to meet their dual obligations to provide appropriate care and honor patient preferences.

Appendix 10-1
Advance Directive (Living Will and Healthcare Proxy) Statutes

(Updated citations may be obtained from: The Society for the Right to Die, 250 W. 57th St., New York, NY 10107.)

---

[3]Camp v. White, 510 So. 2d 166 (Ala. 1987); Kirby v. Spivey, 167 Ga. App. 751, 307 S.E.2d 538 (Ct. App. 1983); Morgan v. Olds, 417 N.W.2d 232 (Iowa Ct. App. 1987); Beck v. Lovell, 361 So. 2d 245, 250 (La. Ct. App. 1978), cert. denied, 362 So. 2d 802 (La. 1978); State v. McAfee, 259 Ga. 579, 385 S.E.2d 651 (Ga. 1989); In re Quinlan, 70 N.J. 10, 355 A.2d 647, cert. denied sub nom. Garger v. New Jersey, 429 U.S. 922 (1976), diverged from in part, In re Conroy, 98 N.J. 321, 486 A.2d 1209 (1985); Gravis v. Physicians & Surgeons Hosp., 427 S.W.2d 310 (Tex. 1968); Strickland v. Deaconess Hospital, 47 Wash. App. 262, 735 P.2d 74 (Ct. App.), review denied, 108 Wash. App. 2d 1028 (Wash. 1987). But see 1990 Fla. Laws 223, to be codified at Fla. Stat. Ann. §765.075.

[4]Shorter v. Drury, 103 Wash. 2d 645, 649-653, 695 P.2d 116, 119-121, cert. denied., 474 U.S. 827 (1985). For a discussion of releases with enforceable language for negligence, see chapter 5.

Alabama	Ala. Code §§22-8A-1 to 22-8A-10 (1984 & Supp. 1989) (living will).
Alaska	Alaska Stat. §§18.12.010 to 18.12.100 (1986) (living will).
	Alaska Stat. §§13.26.332 to 13.26.353 (Supp. 1989) (healthcare proxy).
Arizona	Ariz. Rev. Stat. Ann. §§36-3201 to 36-3210 (1986) (living will).
Arkansas	Ark. Stat. Ann. §§20-17-201 to 20-17-218 (1987 & Supp. 1989) (living will and healthcare proxy).
California	Cal. Health & Safety Code §§7185 to 7195 (West Supp. 1990) (living will).
	Cal. Civil Code §§2430-44, 2500-15 (West Supp. 1990) (healthcare proxy).
Colorado	Colo. Rev. Stat. §§15-18-101 to 15-18-113 (1987 & Supp. 1989) (living will).
	Colo. Rev. Stat. §§15-14-501 to 15-14-502 (1987) (healthcare proxy), as interpreted by In re Rodas, No. 86PR139, slip op. at 34-35, 38 (Colo. Dist. Ct. Mesa County Jan. 22, 1987, as modified April 3, 1987) (Buss, J.).
Connecticut	Conn. Gen. Stat. Ann. §§19a-570 to 19a-575 (West Supp. 1990) (living will).
	1990 Conn. Acts 90-71 (Reg. Sess.), to be codified at Conn. Gen. Stat. §1-43 (healthcare proxy).
Delaware	Del. Code Ann. tit. 16, §§2501 to 2509 (1983) (living will and healthcare proxy).
District of Columbia	D.C. Code Ann. §§6-2421 to 6-2430 (1989) (living will).
	D.C. Code Ann. §§21-2201 to 21-2213 (1989) (healthcare proxy).

Florida	Fla. Stat. Ann. §§765.01 to 765.15 (West 1986), as amended, 1990 Fla. Laws 223 (living will and healthcare proxy).
	1990 Fla. Laws 232, to be codified at Fla. Stat. Ann. §709.08 (healthcare proxy).
Georgia	Ga. Code Ann. §§31-32-1 to 31-32-12 (Michie 1985 & Supp. 1990) (living will).
	Ga. Code Ann. §§31-36-1 to 31-36-13 (Michie Supp. 1990) (healthcare proxy).
Hawaii	Hawaii Rev. Stat. §§327D-1 to 327D-27 (Supp. 1989) (living will).
	Hawaii Rev. Stat. §§551D-1 to 551D-7 (Supp. 1989), as authorized by §327D-26 (Supp. 1989) (healthcare proxy).
Idaho	Idaho Code §§39-4501 to 39-4509 (1985 & Supp. 1990) (living will and healthcare proxy).
Illinois	Ill. Ann. Stat. ch. 110½, ¶¶701 to 710 (Smith-Hurd Supp. 1990) (living will).
	Ill. Ann. Stat. ch. 110½ ¶¶804-1 to 804-12 (Smith-Hurd Supp. 1990) (healthcare proxy).
Indiana	Ind. Code Ann. §§16-8-11-1 to 16-8-11-22 (Burns 1990) (living will).
Iowa	Iowa Code Ann. §§144A.1 to 144A.11 (West 1989) (living will).
	Iowa Code Ann. §§633.705 to 633.706 (West Supp. 1990), as authorized by Iowa Code Ann. §144A.7(a) (West 1989) (healthcare proxy).
Kansas	Kan. Stat. Ann. §§65-28,101 to 65-28,109 (1985) (living will).
	Kan. Stat. Ann. §§58-625 to 58-632 (Supp. 1989) (healthcare proxy).

Kentucky	1990 Ky. Acts ch. 122, to be codified at Ky. Rev. Stat. Ann. §§311.622 to 311.644 (living will).
	1990 Ky. Acts ch. 123, to be codified at Ken. Rev. Stat. Ann. §§311.970 to 311.986 (healthcare proxy).
Louisiana	La. Rev. Stat. Ann. §§40:1299.58.1 to 40:1299.58.10 (West Supp. 1990) (living will and healthcare proxy).
Maine	1990 Me. Laws ch. 830, to be codified at tit. 18-A, §§5-701 to 5-714 (living will).
	Me. Rev. Stat. Ann. tit. 18-A, §5-501 (Supp. 1989) (healthcare proxy).
Maryland	Md. Health-Gen. Code Ann. §§5-601 to 5-614 (Repl. 1990) (living will).
	Md. Est. & Trusts Code Ann. §§13-601 to 13-603 (1974 & Supp. 1989), as interpreted by 73 Op. Atty. Gen.—, No. 88-046, slip op. at 23-24 (Md. Oct. 17, 1988) (healthcare proxy).
Minnesota	Minn. Stat. Ann. §§145B.01 to 145B.17 (West Supp. 1990) (living will and healthcare proxy).
Mississippi	Miss. Code Ann. §§41-41-101 to 41-41-121 (Supp. 1990) (living will).
	Miss. Code Ann. §§41-41-151 to 41-41-183 (Supp. 1990) (healthcare proxy).
Missouri	Mo. Ann. Stat. §§459.010 to 459.055 (Vernon Supp. 1990) (living will).
Montana	Mont. Code Ann. §§50-9-101 to 50-9-206 (1989) (living will).
Nevada	Nev. Rev. Stat. §§449.540 to 449.690 (Michie 1986 & Supp. 1989) (living will).
	Nev. Rev. Stat. Ann. §§449.800 to 449.860 (Supp. 1989) (healthcare proxy).

New Hampshire	N.H. Rev. Stat. Ann. §§137-H:1 to 137-H:16 (Supp. 1989) (living will).
New Jersey	N.J. Stat. Ann. §46:2B-8 (West Supp. 1989), as authorized in In re Peter, 108 N.J. 365, 378-379, 529 A.2d 419, 426 (1987) (healthcare proxy).
New Mexico	N.M. Stat. Ann. §§24-7-1 to 24-7-11 (1986) (living will).
	N.M. Stat. Ann. §§45-5-501, 45-5-502 (1989) (healthcare proxy).
New York	1990 N.Y. Laws, ch. 752, to be codified at N.Y. Pub. Health Law §§2980-2894 (healthcare proxy).
	N.Y. Pub. Health Law §§2960-2978 (McKinney Supp. 1990) (living will for DNR).
North Carolina	N.C. Gen. Stat. §§90-320 to 90-322 (1985) (living will).
	N.C. Gen. Stat. §§32A-1 to 32A-14 (Dec. 1984) (healthcare proxy).
North Dakota	N.D. Cent. Code §§23-06.4-01 to 23-06.4-14 (Michie Supp. 1989) (living will).
Ohio	Ohio Rev. Code Ann. §§1337.11 to 1337.17 (Supp. 1989) (healthcare proxy).
Oklahoma	Okla. Stat. Ann. tit. 63, §§3101-3111 (West Supp. 1990), as amended, 1990 Okla. Sess. Laws Serv. ch. 268 (West) (living will).
Oregon	Or. Rev. Stat. §§127.605 to 127.650 (1989) (living will).
	Or. Rev. Stat. §§127.505 to 127.585 (1989) (healthcare proxy).
Pennsylvania	Pa. Stat. Ann. tit. 20, §§5601 to 5607 (Purdon Supp. 1990) (healthcare proxy).
Rhode Island	R.I. Gen. Laws §§23-4.10-1 to 23-4.10-2 (1989) (healthcare proxy).

720

South Carolina	S.C. Code Ann. §§44-77-10 to 44-77-160 (Law. Co-op. Supp. 1989) (living will).
	H.B. 4444, to be codified at S.C. Code Ann. §§62-5-501, 62-5-502 (healthcare proxy).
South Dakota	1990 S.D. Laws ch. 412, to be codified at S.D. Codified Laws Ann. §§59-7-2.1, 59-7 (healthcare proxy).
Tennessee	Tenn. Code Ann. §§32-11-101 to 32-11-110 Supp. 1989) (living will).
	Tenn. Code Ann. §§34-6-101 to 34-6-107 as amended, 1990 Tenn. Pub. Acts ch. 831 (healthcare proxy).
Texas	Tex. Health & Safety Code §§672.001 to 672.021 (Vernon Supp. 1990) (living will and healthcare proxy).
	Tex. Rev. Civ. Stat. Ann. art. 4590h-1 (Vernon Supp. 1990) (healthcare proxy).
Utah	Utah Code Ann. §§75-2-1101 to 75-2-1118 (Supp. 1990) (living will and healthcare proxy).
Vermont	Vt. Stat. Ann. tit. 18, §§5251-5262 and tit. 13, §1801 (1987 & Supp. 1989) (living will).
	Vt. Stat. Ann. tit. 14 §§3451-3467 (Supp. 1988) (healthcare proxy).
Virginia	Va. Code §§54.1-2981 to 54.1-2992 (1988 & Supp. 1990) (living will and healthcare proxy).
	Va. Code §§11-9.1 to 11-9.4 (1989), as authorized by Va. Code §37.1-134.4 (Michie Supp. 1990) (healthcare proxy).
Washington	Wash. Rev. Code Ann. §§70:122.010 to 70:122.905 (Supp. 1990) (living will).
	Wash. Rev. Code Ann. §11.94.010 (1987 & West Supp. 1990) (healthcare proxy).

West Virginia	W. Va. Code §§16-30-1 to 16-30-10 (Repl. 1985) (living will).
	W. Va. Code §§16-30A-1 to 16-30A-20 (Supp. 1990) (healthcare proxy).
Wisconsin	Wis. Stat. Ann. §§154.01 to 154.15 (West 1989) (living will).
	1989 Wis. Laws 200, to be codified at Wis. Stat. Ann. §§155.01 to 155.80 (healthcare proxy).
Wyoming	Wyo. Stat. §§35-22-101 to 35-22-109 (1988) (living will and healthcare proxy).

See also Uniform Rights of the Terminally Ill Act, 9B U.L.A. 68-81 (Supp. 1990) (living will and healthcare proxy); Patient Self Determination Act, Pub. L. No. 101-508, §§4206, 4751 (effective December 1, 1991).

Appendix 10-2
Sample Statutory Living Will Rejecting
Life-Sustaining Treatment[1]

DECLARATION

Declaration made this _____ day of _____ (month, year). I, _____, being of sound mind, willfully and voluntarily make known my desire that my dying not be artificially prolonged under the circumstances set forth below and declare that:

If at any time I should have an incurable injury, disease or illness certified to be a terminal condition by two physicians who have personally examined me, one of whom is my attending physician, and the physicians have determined that my death will occur unless life-sustaining procedures are used and if the application of life-sustaining procedures would serve only to artificially prolong the dying process, I direct that life-sustaining procedures be withheld or withdrawn and that I be permitted to die naturally with only the administration of medication, food or

---

[1]This form, as suggested in Ariz. Rev. Stat. Ann. §36-3202(C) (1986), is typical of many other statutory forms. For citations to other statutes, see Appendix 1. Certain terms used in the document are defined as follows in the statute:

"Attending physician": "the physician selected by or assigned to the patient who has primary responsibility for the treatment and care of the patient." §36-3201(1).

"Life-sustaining procedure": "any medical procedure or intervention which in the judgment of the attending physician would serve only to prolong the dying process. Life-sustaining procedure does not include the administration of medication, food or fluids or the performance of a medical procedure deemed necessary to provide comfort care." §36-3201(4).

"Qualified patient": "a patient, eighteen years or more of age, who executes a declaration as provided in [§36-3202(C)] and who is diagnosed and certified in writing to be afflicted with a terminal condition by two physicians who personally examined the patient, one of whom is the attending physician." §36-3201(4).

"Terminal condition": "an incurable or irreversible condition from which, in the opinion of the attending physician, death will occur without the use of life-sustaining procedures." §36-3201(6).

fluids or the performance of medical procedures deemed necessary to provide me with comfort care.

In the absence of my ability to give directions regarding the use of life-sustaining procedures, it is my intention that this declaration be honored by my family and attending physician as the final expression of my legal right to refuse medical or surgical treatment and accept the consequences from such refusal.

I understand the full import of this declaration and I have emotional and mental capacity to make this declaration.

signed _____

city, county and state of residence _____

_____

The declarant is personally known to me and I believe him to be of sound mind.

witness _____

witness _____

Appendix 10-3
Sample Statutory Living Will Requesting Life-Sustaining Treatment[1]

LIFE-PROLONGING PROCEDURES DECLARATION

Declaration made this _____ day of _____ (month, year). I, _____, being at least eighteen (18) years old and of sound mind, willfully and voluntarily make known my desire that if at any time I have an incurable injury, disease, or illness determined to be a terminal condition I request the use of life-prolonging procedures that would extend my life. This includes appropriate nutrition and hydration, the administration of medication, and the performance of all other medical procedures necessary to extend my life, to provide comfort care, or to alleviate pain.

---

[1] This form requesting life-prolonging procedures is set forth in Ind. Code Ann. §16-8-11-12(c) (1990). Certain terms used in the document are defined as follows in the statute:

"Attending physician": "the physician who has the primary responsibility for the treatment and care of the patient." §16-8-11-2.

"Life-prolonging procedure": "any medical procedure, treatment or intervention that: (1) uses mechanical or other artificial means to sustain, restore, or supplant a vital function; and (2) serves to prolong the dying process." "Life-prolonging procedure does not include the provision of appropriate nutrition and hydration, the administration of medication, or the performance of any medical procedure necessary to provide comfort care or to alleviate pain." §16-8-11-4.

"Qualified patient": a patient who has been certified as qualified under [§16-8-11-14, which considers a patient qualified when (1) the attending physician has diagnosed the patient as having a terminal condition; and determined that the patient's death will occur from the terminal condition whether or not life-prolonging procedures are used; and (2) the patient has executed one of the documents authorized by §16-8-11-12 and was of sound mind when he or she executed the document]. §16-8-11-8.

"Terminal condition": "a condition caused by injury, disease or illness from which, to a reasonable degree of medical certainty; (1) there can be no recovery; and (2) death will occur from the terminal condition within a short period of time without the provision of life-prolonging procedures." §16-8-11-9.

725

In the absence of my ability to give directions regarding the use of life-prolonging procedures, it is my intention that this declaration be honored by my family and physician as the final expression of my legal right to request medical or surgical treatment and accept the consequences of the request.

I understand the full import of this declaration.

Signed _____

City, County, and State of Residence _____

_____

The declarant has been personally known to me, and I believe (him/her) to be of sound mind. I am competent and at least eighteen (18) years old.

Witness _____   Date _____
Witness _____   Date _____

Appendix 10-4
Sample Statutory Durable Power of Attorney (Proxy) for Health Care[1]

INFORMATION CONCERNING THE DURABLE
POWER OF ATTORNEY FOR HEALTH CARE

THIS IS AN IMPORTANT LEGAL DOCUMENT. BEFORE SIGN-
ING THIS DOCUMENT, YOU SHOULD KNOW THESE IMPOR-
TANT FACTS:

---

[1]This document is authorized by Vt. Rev. Stat. Ann tit. 14 §§3465, 3466 (Supp. 1988). For citations to other healthcare proxy statutes, see Appendix 10-1.

Except to the extent you state otherwise, this document gives the person you name as your agent the authority to make any and all health care decisions for you when you are no longer capable of making them yourself. "Health care" means any treatment, service or procedure to maintain, diagnose or treat your physical or mental condition. Your agent therefore can have the power to make a broad range of health care decisions for you. Your agent may consent, refuse to consent, or withdraw consent to medical treatment and may make decisions about withdrawing or withholding life-sustaining treatment.

You may state in this document any treatment you do not desire or treatment you want to be sure you receive. Your agent's authority will begin when your doctor certifies that you lack the capacity to make health care decisions. You may attach additional pages if you need more space to complete your statement.

Your agent will be obligated to follow your instructions when making decisions on your behalf. Unless you state otherwise, your agent will have the same authority to make decisions about your health care as you have had.

It is important that you discuss this document with your physician or other health care providers before you sign it to make sure that you understand the nature and range of decisions which may be made on your behalf. If you do not have a physician, you should talk with someone else who is knowledgeable about these issues and can answer your questions. You do not need a lawyer's assistance to complete this document, but if there is anything in this document that you do not understand, you should ask a lawyer to explain it to you.

The person you appoint as agent should be someone you know and trust and must be at least 18 years old. If you appoint your health or residential care provider (e.g. your physician, or an employee of a home health agency, hospital, nursing home, or residential care home, other than a relative), that person will have to choose between acting as your agent or as your health or residential care provider; the law does not permit a person to do both at the same time.

You should inform the person you appoint that you want him or her to be your health care agent. You should discuss this document with your agent and your physician and give each a signed copy. You should indicate on the document itself the people and institutions who will have signed copies. Your agent will not be liable for health care decisions made in good faith on your behalf.

Even after you have signed this document, you have the right to make health care decisions for yourself as long as you are able to do so, and treatment cannot be given to you or stopped over your objection. You have the right to revoke the authority granted to your agent by informing him or her or your health care provider orally or in writing.

This document may not be changed or modified. If you want to make changes in the document you must make an entirely new one.

You may wish to designate an alternate agent in the event that your agent is unwilling, unable or ineligible to act as your agent. Any alternate agent you designate will have the same authority to make health care decisions for you.

THIS POWER OF ATTORNEY WILL NOT BE VALID UNLESS IT IS SIGNED IN THE PRESENCE OF TWO (2) OR MORE QUAL-IFIED WITNESSES WHO MUST BOTH BE PRESENT WHEN YOU SIGN OR ACKNOWLEDGE YOUR SIGNATURE. THE FOL-LOWING PERSONS MAY *NOT* ACT AS WITNESSES:

    —the person you have designated as your agent;
    —your health or residential care provider or one of their employees;
    —your spouse;
    —your lawful heirs or beneficiaries named in your will or a deed;
    —creditors or persons who have a claim against you.

DURABLE POWER OF ATTORNEY FOR HEALTH CARE

I, _____, hereby appoint _____ _____ of _____ as my agent to make any and all health care decisions for me, except to the extent I state otherwise in this document. This durable power of attorney for health care shall take effect in the event I become unable to make my own health care decisions.

(a) STATEMENT OF DESIRES, SPECIAL PROVISIONS, AND LIMITATIONS REGARDING HEALTH CARE DECISIONS.

Here you may include any specific desires or limitations you deem appropriate, such as when or what life-sustaining measures should be withheld; directions whether to continue or discontinue artificial nutrition and hydration; or instructions to refuse any specific types of treatment that are inconsistent with your religious beliefs or unacceptable to you for any other reason.

_____

_____

_____

_____

(attach additional pages as necessary)

(b) THE SUBJECT OF LIFE-SUSTAINING TREATMENT IS OF PARTICULAR IMPORTANCE. For your convenience in dealing with that subject, some general statements concerning the withholding or removal of life-sustaining treatment are set forth below. IF YOU AGREE WITH ONE OF THESE STATEMENTS, YOU MAY INCLUDE THE STATEMENT IN THE BLANK SPACE ABOVE:

If I suffer a condition from which there is no reasonable prospect of regaining my ability to think and act for myself, I want only care directed to my comfort and dignity, and authorize my agent to decline all treatment (including artificial nutrition and hydration) the primary purpose of which is to prolong my life.

If I suffer a condition from which there is no reasonable prospect of regaining the ability to think and act for myself, I want care directed to my comfort and dignity and also want artificial nutrition and hydration if needed, but authorize my agent to decline all other treatment the primary purpose of which is to prolong my life.

I want my life sustained by any reasonable medical measures, regardless of my condition.

In the event the person I appoint above is unable, unwilling or unavailable to act as my health care agent, I hereby appoint _____ of _____ as alternate agent.

I hereby acknowledge that I have been provided with a disclosure statement explaining the effect of this document. I have read and understand the information contained in the disclosure statement.

The original of this document will be kept at _____

_____ and the following persons and institutions will have signed copies:

_____

_____

_____

In witness whereof, I have hereunto signed my name this _____ day of _____, 19____.

_____

Signature

I declare that the principal appears to be of sound mind and free from duress at the time the durable power of attorney for health care is signed and that the principal has affirmed that he or she is aware of the nature of the document and is signing it freely and voluntarily.

Witness: _____   Address: _____

Witness: _____   Address: _____

Statement of ombudsman, hospital representative or other authorized person (to be signed only if the principal is in or is being admitted to a hospital, nursing home or residential care home):

I declare that I have personally explained the nature and effect of this durable power of attorney to the principal and that the principal understands the same.

Date: _____
Address: _____

Name: _____

Appendix 10-5
Patient's Life-Sustaining Treatment Preferences Worksheet

NOTE: THIS FORM MUST BE COMPLETED BY SOCIAL WORKER/ PATIENT ADVOCATE (OR DESIGNEE) AFTER INTERVIEW WITH THE PERSON DESCRIBING THE PATIENT'S PREFERENCES ("DECLARANT") AND SHOULD BE PLACED OR REFERRED TO IN PATIENT'S MEDICAL RECORD. ANY QUESTIONS SHOULD BE DIRECTED TO [insert administrative title]. THE FACILITY'S LIFE-SUSTAINING TREATMENT POLICY (TERMINAL CARE) POLICY [insert policy identifying number] SHOULD ALSO BE CONSULTED. ATTACH ADDITIONAL PAGES IF NECESSARY.

BACKGROUND OF DECLARANT

1. Name _____
2. Age _____
3. Address _____
4. Nature and duration of relationship to patient _____
_____

SUMMARY OF RELIEF REQUESTED

5. Below is a list of treatments that may be at issue. For each type of treatment at issue, specify nature of relief requested (e.g., withdrawn, withheld, commenced, limited), and basis for relief requested (e.g., based on expressed wishes of patient, what the patient "would have wanted" if able to express, patient's best interest, medical futility):

acid/base corrective measures _____
antiarrhythmias (specify) _____
antibiotics (specify type and if oral or intravenous) _____
_____
artificially administered nutrients or fluids (specify whether nasogastric, gastrostomy, intravenous, hyperalimentation)
_____
blood transfusions or other blood products (specify) _____
_____

731

cardioversion _____

chemotherapy _____

defibrillation _____

dialysis _____

electrolyte corrective measures _____

"do-not-ICU" order _____

"do-not-resuscitate" order _____

medication (specify) _____

oxygen _____

physical therapy _____

radiation _____

respiratory support (including intubation) (specify) _____

_____

suctioning _____

surgery (including amputation of gangrenous limbs) _____

_____

tracheostomy tube _____

vasopressor/inotropic agents _____

other _____

UNDERSTANDING OF PATIENT'S CONDITION AND EFFECT OF TREATMENT DECISION REQUESTED

6. Diagnosis:

7. Prognosis (based on reasonable medical certainty). For each of treatments listed in (5) above for which treatment rejection is requested, specify likely consequence of continuing, limiting, beginning or stopping treatment (if possible specifying range or percentage of likelihood), in terms of: (a) life expectancy; (b) experience of pain/discomfort (if pain/discomfort is possibility, specify plan if any, and potential success of ability to reduce pain); (c) improvement (specify) in terms of life expectancy, ability to feel pain, cognitive awareness, other:

EVIDENCE OF PATIENT'S WISHES

8. If written evidence, attach copy.

	Yes	No
(a) Patient-appointed proxy (healthcare proxy, power of attorney for healthcare)	___	___
(b) Living will	___	___
(c) Other (specify) _____	___	___

732

9. If conversation, for each, provide the following information to the best of recollection:
   (a) date (if over a period of time, specify beginning and ending)
   (b) people present
   (c) circumstances (e.g., concerning patient's own condition; a condition of another person—specify relationship to person, e.g., friend, relative, person read about in newspaper); specify other person's mental and physical condition—if "terminal illness," specify disease; life-sustaining treatment patient was receiving; other)
   (d) content of statement, being as specific as possible about medical condition patient was discussing and types of treatment
   (e) patient's affect during conversation (e.g., flippant, serious, emotional)
10. Declarant's perception about patient's general values as it affects decisions concerning life-sustaining treatment (e.g., what type of life did he/she consider "meaningful," level of independence, level of concern of decision's affect on family or others psychologically and financially):
11. Other individuals who believe patient's wishes would be similar or different than as requested here. If any, list name, address, telephone number, relationship to patient, and anticipated position (e.g., similar or different) to patient of each:
12. Financial effect on declarant if patient dies:
13. Other comments:

_____

Signature of Individual Completing Form

_____

Print Name of Individual Completing Form

_____

Title

_____

Date Form Completed

Appendix 10-6
Patient's Medical Condition/Prognosis Worksheet

NOTE: THIS FORM MUST BE COMPLETED BY PATIENT'S ATTENDING PHYSICIAN AND PLACED IN PATIENT'S MEDICAL RECORD. ANY QUESTIONS SHOULD BE DIRECTED TO [insert administrative title]. THE FACILITY'S LIFE-SUSTAINING TREAT-MENT POLICY (TERMINAL CARE) [insert policy identifying number] SHOULD ALSO BE CONSULTED. ATTACH ADDI-TIONAL PAGES IF NECESSARY.

1. Name, title, specialty of physician completing form:
   _____

2. *PATIENT BACKGROUND INFORMATION*
   Name: _____
   Age: _____
   Date of Admission: _____
   Reason for Admission: _____
   Name of individual bringing patient to hospital (if any) and
     relationship to patient: _____
   Is the patient pregnant?
     Yes _____ (if yes, specify approximate weeks _____)
     No _____
   Does the patient have minor children?   Yes _____
     No _____
     If yes, specify ages _____
   If yes, list names of people and relationships to patient who
     might be able to care for children if patient is incapable of
     doing so:

3. Put a check (✔) next to each of the medical treatments listed
   below which the patient is currently receiving and the date
   it was instituted:
   acid/base corrective measures _____
   antiarrhythmias (specify) _____
   antibiotics (specify type and if oral or intraveneous) _____
   _____
   artificially administered nutrients or fluids (specify whether

nasogastric, gastrostomy, intravenous, hyperalimentation)

_____

blood transfusions or other blood products (specify) _____

_____

cardioversion _____

chemotherapy _____

defibrillation _____

dialysis _____

electrolyte corrective measures _____

"do-not-ICU" order _____

"do-not-resuscitate" order _____

medication (specify) _____

oxygen _____

physical therapy _____

radiation _____

respiratory support (including intubation) (specify) _____

_____

suctioning _____

surgery (including amputation of gangrenous limbs) _____

_____

tracheostomy tube _____

vasopressor/inotropic agents _____

other _____

4. Do you think the patient may need in the immediate future (approximately next two weeks) any of the treatments described in (3) above which s/he is not currently receiving?
   Yes _____   No _____
   If yes, list such treatments here:

5. Diagnosis (indicate if based on reasonable medical certainty, including probability, and range of percentages if possible); specify cause of condition and duration (if applicable, check against Part I of American Academy of Neurology statement on persistent vegetative state):

6. Bases for diagnosis (for each, list date of test and outcome):

7. Prognosis (indicate if based on reasonable medical certainty, including probability and range of percentages if possible).

For each of the treatments listed in (3) above for which rejection is requested, specify likely consequence of continuing or stopping treatment (if possible, specifying range or percentage of likelihood), in terms of: (a) life expectancy; (b) experience of pain/discomfort (if pain/discomfort is possibility, specify plan, if any, and potential success of ability to reduce pain); (c) improvement (specify in terms of life expectancy, ability to feel pain, cognitive awareness, other):

8. Ability of patient to understand consequences of accepting or rejecting treatment at issue (specify in as much detail as possible: date, contents and nature of conversations). Such discussions should include a description of the risks and benefits of each treatment in (3) above with relevant information in (5)-(7) above; statement that risks and benefits were explained and patient understood is not sufficient. If patient is incapacitated, indicate date of beginning of incapacity (if patient is temporarily incapacitated, indicate potential date of return of capacity):

9. Has physician ever personally received evidence of patient wishes?
   Yes _____   No _____
   (If yes, complete relevant sections of Patient's Life-Sustaining Treatment Preferences, Appendix 5)

10. Is physician willing to write and implement all orders to forgo treatment?
    Yes _____   No _____
    If no, indicate activities to which unwillingness applies, reason for unwillingness and extent to which such objections have been communicated to patient/surrogate:

11. Other comments/notes:

_____

Signature of Physician

_____

Date Form Completed

736

Appendix 10-7
Patient Consent, Release, Covenant Not to Sue and Waiver of Liability Concerning Rejection of Life-Sustaining Treatment

NOTE: THIS DOCUMENT MUST BE PLACED IN THE PATIENT'S MEDICAL RECORD. A COPY MUST BE PROVIDED TO THE PATIENT UPON REQUEST.

1. I, the undersigned, request that _____ (Facility) and any person associated with it honor my wishes to reject life-sustaining treatment expressed in this document and as otherwise known to them.

2. I specifically consent to *stopping* the following treatments:

3. I specifically consent to *not starting* the following treatments: .

4. I specifically consent to *limiting* the following treatments:

5. My attending physician _____ (print physician's name) has informed me that my diagnosis, based on reasonable medical certainty, is:

6. He/she has also informed me that my prognosis, based on reasonable medical certainty is:

7. He/she has also informed me of the consequences of stopping, not starting, and limiting the treatments listed above, all of which I understand.

8. (Optional—if not completed, draw a line through the paragraph and initial). If I become incapable of expressing my preferences, I appoint _____ (insert name and relationship) who resides at _____ (in-

sert address and telephone number) to make all medical decisions on my behalf, including decisions concerning the limiting, withholding, or withdrawal of life-sustaining treatment. I authorize him/her to make any decision concerning my care based on my wishes expressed while I was capable of so communicating, or if not expressed, based on what s/he thinks my wishes would have been if I had been able to express myself, or if unknown, based on what s/he thinks would be in my best interest. I intend this delegation to be honored to the full extent permitted by law, although it is possible that certain portions of the paragraphs may be unenforceable.

9. I and my next of kin hereby release and indemnify Facility, my physicians and any person associated with them from any liability in connection with compliance with this request. I and my next of kin agree to hold harmless and agree not to sue Facility, my physicians and any person associated with them with respect to any claim or liability arising therefrom.

I intend this document to be clear and convincing evidence of my wishes concerning life-sustaining treatment. I make these requests knowingly and voluntarily. I understand the consequences of making this request. I have been given the opportunity to ask questions and all my questions have been answered to my satisfaction.

Dated _____, 19 ____

_____   _____
[Signature of Next of Kin]   [Patient's Signature]

_____   _____
[Print Name]   [Print Name]

_____   _____
[Address]   [Address]

_____   _____
[Relationship to Patient]   [Telephone No.]

[Physician certifications, notarizations and/or witnessing requirements should be inserted to be consistent with other Facility's releases and consent forms.]

Appendix 10-8
Surrogate Consent, Release, Covenant Not to Sue and Waiver of Liability Concerning Rejection of Life-Sustaining Treatment

NOTE: THIS DOCUMENT MUST BE PLACED IN THE PATIENT'S MEDICAL RECORD. A COPY MUST BE PROVIDED TO THE SURROGATE UPON REQUEST.

1. I, the undersigned, request on behalf of _____ _____ (print patient's name), who is incapable of making the request himself/herself, that _____ (Facility) reject life-sustaining treatments for the patient as authorized by law.

2. I specifically consent to *stopping* the following treatments:

3. I specifically consent to *not starting* the following treatments:

4. I specifically consent to *limiting* the following treatments:

5. The patient's attending physician _____ (print physician's name) has informed me that the patient's diagnosis, based on reasonable medical certainty, is:

6. He/she has also informed me that the patient's prognosis, based on reasonable medical certainty, is:

7. He/she has also informed me of the consequences of stopping, not starting and limiting the treatments listed above, all of which I understand.

8. I hereby release and indemnify Facility, the patient's physicians and any person associated with them from any liability in connection with compliance with this request. I agree to hold harmless and agree not to sue Facility, the patient's physicians

and any person associated with them with respect to any claim or liability arising therefrom.

I make these requests knowingly and voluntarily. I understand the consequences of making this request. I have been given the opportunity to ask questions and all my questions have been answered to my satisfaction.

Dated: _____, 19 _____

_____

[Signature]

_____

[Print Name]

_____

[Address]

_____

[Telephone No.]

_____

[Relationship to Patient]

[Physician certifications, notarizations and/or witness requirements should be inserted to be consistent with other Facility's releases and consent forms.]

11 Reproductive Technologies

William A. Campbell

§11.0 Introduction

This chapter discusses the legal aspects of technologies used to achieve conception by means other than sexual intercourse and a resulting in vivo conception. The technologies to be discussed are in vitro fertilization (IVF), artificial insemination by donor (AID), and surrogate motherhood. The chapter emphasizes those issues of legal concern to the managers of healthcare facilities where the technologies are practiced and to the physicians who use them.

In one sense, there is little law to discuss regarding the use of reproductive technologies. Significant judicial decisions in the field can be counted on the fingers of one hand. Legislation regarding artificial insemination by donor deals mostly with the child's legal status, not with the procedure itself, and there is almost no legislation regarding in vitro fertilization. States have recently begun to enact laws dealing with surrogate motherhood, but few of these laws are likely to affect healthcare facilities and physicians participating in the transaction. "Law," however, has a broader meaning. As Robert M. Cover persuasively showed,[1]

---

§11.0   [1]The Supreme Court, 1982 Term—Foreword: *Nomos* and Narrative, 97 Harv. L. Rev. 4 (1983).

741

it also includes a society's traditions, moral beliefs, and narratives, and these traditions and beliefs will shape the legislation that regulates reproductive technologies. For this reason, the introductory materials include a discussion of some of the ethical concerns about use of the technologies.

Both participants in this field of medical practice and research and commentators have called for legislation to clarify liability questions and impose quality standards and recordkeeping requirements. Legislation has been especially needed in the fields of in vitro fertilization and surrogate motherhood. To aid the reader in understanding what sort of legislation is needed— and what may be expected—each section dealing with a particular reproductive technology includes recommendations for legislation from two studies that are especially thoughtful and well-reasoned. They are a student project at the University of Iowa College of Law[2] and the report of the Ontario Law Reform Commission.[3]

§11.1 Terminology

For the most part, the chapter follows generally accepted scientific and legal terminology. In two instances, however, it uses terminology that may be unfamiliar and needs to be defined. The first is that, following John A. Robertson[1] and the University

---

[2]Model Human Reproductive Technologies and Surrogacy Act, 72 Iowa L. Rev. 943 (1987) (hereinafter University of Iowa Model Act).

[3]Ontario Law Reform Commission, Report on Human Artificial Reproduction and Related Matters (1985) (hereinafter Ontario Report).

§11.1 [1]Robertson, Embryos, Families, and Procreative Liberty: The Legal Structure of the New Reproduction, 59 S. Cal. L. Rev. 939, 968-969. This is an excellent comprehensive analysis of the legal aspects of reproductive technologies. In a more recent article, Robertson favored the term "early embryo." See In the Beginning: The Legal Status of Early Embryos, 76 Va. L. Rev. 437 (1990), in which Professor Robertson carefully examines such questions as the enforceability of agreements regarding the disposition of pre-embryos, how to resolve disputes about the disposition of pre-embryos in the absence of agreements, and the implications for IVF procedures of a possible reversal of Roe v. Wade (410 U.S. 113 (1973)).

of Iowa model act,[2] the early blastocyst stage of the fertilized ovum is referred to as a "pre-embryo." At this stage of development, approximately the first six days[3] after fertilization, the fertilized ovum is not yet able to achieve implantation, and it does not have the characteristics it will later develop as an embryo. Thus, it is important in legislation to give this cluster of cells a legal status different from that of the implanted embryo. The second is that, although one of the sections in this chapter is headed "Surrogate Motherhood," following the terminology commonly used by both popular and legal writers on the subject, the term "surrogate mother" is not used to refer to a woman who agrees to be artificially inseminated, carry the baby to term, and then release it to the genetic father and his wife. As more than one writer has pointed out,[4] this is an incorrect use of the term; a true surrogate mother is one who rears a child that was born to another woman. The popular press has made widespread use of the incorrect term—as it has of the similarly incorrect "test-tube baby"—but that seems no reason to perpetuate the error. The University of Iowa model act uses the term "birth mother,"[5] which is the term used in the usual adoption context. The preferred usage, however, is "volunteer mother," which is the term used in the Florida statute[6] and which is useful for differentiating a mother in the situations to be discussed in this chapter from a birth mother in a usual adoption proceeding.

§11.2 Ethical and Policy Issues

The beginning point for most ethical and policy discussions of reproductive technologies is the understanding that infertility is

---

[2]University of Iowa Model Act, at 947, 952.

[3]Some scientists would extend the period of the pre-embryo to 14 days: from the time the process of fertilization begins until a single primitive streak appears. See Jones and Schrader, And Just What is a Pre-embryo? 52 Fertility and Sterility 189 (1989).

[4]See, e.g., Capron, Alternative Birth Technologies: Legal Challenges, 20 U.C.D. L. Rev. 679 n.1 (1987).

[5]University of Iowa Model Act, at 951.

[6]Fla. Stat. Ann. §63.212(1)(i)6.i (West 1989 Supp.).

a medical condition affecting a substantial portion of the population, and that, if medical science can develop and use safe and effective techniques to cure infertility or alleviate its consequences, social policy should encourage it to do so.[1] The technologies should clearly be employed within ethical limits; the difficulty is in finding agreement on what those limits are. For most people the ethical concerns differ depending on the reproductive technology. Artificial insemination by donor raises the fewest concerns; in vitro fertilization more concerns; and surrogacy arrangements the greatest number of ethical concerns.

The official position of the Roman Catholic Church is that all of the artificial reproductive technologies are to be condemned, because the resulting child is not the product of a conjugal act by a married couple, the only officially sanctioned form of sexual activity.[2] This, however, is an extreme position. For most persons, if the husband consents to his wife's being artificially inseminated by a donor, no ethical or policy issues are raised (although there are some medical issues to be dealt with) and the transaction is viewed simply as a private matter to remedy infertility. Artificial insemination by donor of an unmarried woman, however, may raise concerns about the welfare of the child, who will be reared by a single parent or in a nontraditional living arrangement. These concerns appear, however, to be the same as those about a child conceived through sexual intercourse and born to an unmarried woman. The feminist position appears to be that single women should have access to AID,[3] and one writer contends that a good argument can be constructed that single women have a constitutional right to AID.[4]

---

§11.2   [1] 2 Ontario Law Reform Commission, Report on Human Artificial Reproduction and Related Matters 141-142 (1985) (hereinafter Ontario Report).

[2] Congregation for the Doctrine of the Faith, Instruction on Respect for Human Life in Its Origin and on the Dignity of Procreation (1987).

[3] Andrews, "Alternative Modes of Reproduction," in N. Taub and S. Cohen, eds., Reproductive Laws for the 1990s: A Briefing Handbook 257, 284 (1988).

[4] Robertson, Embryos, Families, and Procreative Liberty: The Legal Structure of the New Reproduction, 59 S. Cal. L. Rev. 939, 962-963 (1986). This

The ethical concerns about in vitro fertilization divide into two categories. The first is about limits and where this technology may take us, concerns accurately described as anxiety about heading down a slippery slope.[5] Once we have allowed, and even encouraged, the use of IVF—out of compassion—to permit an infertile couple to conceive and bear a child of which they are the genetic parents, and we continue to refine and improve the IVF technology, we will—as we have done with other technologies—continue until we arrive at Huxley's brave new world: ectogenesis, gestation outside the body, and selection and grading of embryos. The way to deal with this concern is through the imposition of limits, without which there can be no morality.[6] The concern, then, is that our society's record in controlling the uses of technology is poor and that we are dealing here with a technology that enables its users to manipulate one of the most fundamental of all natural human functions, procreation. That no state or federal statute has been enacted that comprehensively regulates IVF indicates there is some basis for the concern about society's willingness or ability to place limits on the technology.

The second concern is about the welfare of the women for whom the technology is used in an effort to achieve pregnancy; that is, are they fully informed about the possible physical risks and discomforts, the psychological stresses, and the success rates for the procedure? This group of concerns is dealt with in the section on IVF.

Surrogate motherhood arrangements generate many conflicting views,[7] and proposals to prohibit or at least discourage surrogate contracts find several advocates.[8] On the other hand,

---

argument is fashioned from the contraceptive right of privacy cases and the abortion cases.

[5]Cowen, In the Rear and Limping a Little: Some Reflections on Medicine, Biotechnology, and the Law: The Roscoe Pound Lectures, 64 Neb. L. Rev. 548, 569 (1985).

[6]Id. at 564.

[7]See Colloquy: In re Baby M, 76 Geo. L.J. 1717 (1988), for essays by seven law professors on the subject.

[8]See Areen, Baby M Reconsidered, 76 Geo. L.J. 1741 (1988), and Ontario Report, at 233-272 (vol. 2).

it has been contended that if proper weight is given to the interests of the infertile wife, some surrogate arrangements should be allowed.[9] A special ethical concern is that payment for the volunteer mother's services is a form of baby-selling and will lead to economic exploitation of poor women, and this has prompted several states to prohibit such payments.[10] But payment to volunteer mothers is not universally condemned, and Lori Andrews's comments reflect the general ethical tensions in society over surrogate arrangements when she discusses the conflicting feminist views on this issue,[11] payment or no. For example, the argument that surrogacy arrangements should be regulated to protect women from exploitation can be countered by the argument that laws telling women what they can do with their bodies have frequently had the effect of placing women at a social and economic disadvantage. Professor Anita Allen sums it up well: "The lack of accord is radical. The issues are seemingly intractable."[12]

§11.3 In Vitro Fertilization and Pre-Embryo Transfer

§11.3.1 The Standard Procedure and Its Variations

In the standard in vitro fertilization procedure, a woman is given fertility drugs to regulate the timing of ovulation and to cause the development of several ova.[1] Shortly before the ova are mature they are aspirated from the ovary by either laparoscopy or the ultrasound procedure. The retrieved ova are then incu-

---

[9]Note, Redefining Mother: A Legal Matrix for New Reproductive Technologies, 96 Yale L.J. 187 (1986).

[10]See, e.g., Mich. Stat. Ann. §25.248(159) (Callaghan 1989-90 Supp.).

[11]Andrews, supra n.3, at 270-271.

[12]Allen, Privacy, Surrogacy, and the Baby M Case, 76 Geo. L.J. 1759 (1988).

§11.3 [1]The description in this section is taken from Seibel, a New Era in Reproductive Technology, 318 New Eng. J. Med. 828 (1988).

bated; the length of the incubation period depends on their stage of maturation. The ova are then placed in a petri dish with a specimen of the husband's sperm that has been washed and specially prepared to enhance the chances of fertilization. If fertilization occurs, three to five of the pre-embryos are transferred to woman's uterus by means of a special catheter. If implantation results, a pregnancy is achieved. The overall pregnancy rate for IVF centers in the United States is about 15 percent for each procedure in which ova are retrieved.[2] This compares with about a 31-percent pregnancy rate in nature.

Several variations exist on the standard IVF procedure. One is intrafallopian transfer of ova and sperm (gamete intrafallopian transfer, or GIFT). In this procedure, the retrieved ova and prepared sperm are transferred by means of laparoscopy to the fimbriated end of a fallopian tube, and fertilization takes place in the tube. Pregnancy rates for this procedure appear to be higher than for the standard IVF procedure.[3]

Some variations make use of donated gametes. One technique is to synchronize the menstrual cycles of the donor and recipient, artificially inseminate the donor with sperm of the husband or a donor, and then flush the fertilized ovum from the donor by lavage and transfer it to the recipient. One of the risks of this technique is that the lavage will fail to remove the pre-embryo and the pregnancy will continue in the donor. Another technique is to remove ova from the donor by means of laparoscopy, fertilize them in a petri dish with sperm of the husband or donor, and then transfer the pre-embryos to the uterus of the recipient. This technique can be enhanced by cryopreservation of the pre-embryos for later transfer and makes synchronization of menstrual cycles unnecessary.

---

[2] For 1987 the National IVF-ET Registry, of which there are 96 member clinics, reported an overall pregnancy rate of 16 percent, with four clinics accounting for 33 percent of the total. In Vitro Fertilization/Embryo Transfer in the United States: 1987 Results from the National IVF-ET Registry, 51 Fertility and Sterility 13 (1989).

[3] For 1987 the National IVF-ET Registry reported an overall pregnancy rate of 25 percent for GIFT procedures. Id.

§11.3.2 Statutes Affecting the Use of IVF Procedures

A serious legal problem with IVF procedures is that no statute comprehensively regulates the procedures.[4] As a result, many questions remain unanswered, and, worse, it is possible that statutes intended to regulate abortion or experimentation on fetuses may affect IVF procedures. The few statutes that do attempt to deal with IVF do so in a manner incompatible with the medical procedures that have been and are being developed. A particularly egregious example is an Illinois statute that provided that "[a]ny person who intentionally causes the fertilization of a human ovum by a human sperm outside the body of a living human female shall, with regard to the human being thereby produced, be deemed to have the care and custody of a child for the purposes of Sec. 4 of the Act to Prevent and Punish Wrongs to Children."[5] Thus, the statute appeared to make the physician performing the IVF procedure the legal custodian of any child conceived thereby. A federal suit, Smith v. Hartigan,[6] was required to be brought to determine that the statute did not mean exactly what it said. The plaintiffs, an infertile couple and their physician, challenged the constitutionality of the statute. The court dismissed the suit after finding that an opinion by the Cook County State's Attorney, supported by the Illinois Attorney General, stated that the statute did not prevent IVF procedures and was intended to give custody of the child to the supervising physician only if the embryo was not implanted, but at the same time the statute allowed the physician not to implant the embryo and thereby not cause a preg-

---

[4]This is in contrast with Australia where, in the state of Victoria, the minister of health, acting pursuant to the Infertility (Medical Procedures) Act of 1986, regulates clinics where the procedures are performed, consent procedures, and recordkeeping regarding births and the disposition of pre-embryos not transferred. See 1989 Rptr. Human Reprod. Law (Mar.-Apr.) 231-232.

[5]The statute was repealed in 1984. See Ill. Ann. Stat. ch. 38, §§8-27 through 8-29 (Smith-Hurd 1988 Supp.).

[6]556 F. Supp. 157 (N.D. Ill. 1983).

nancy. In short, the court found that the lawyers charged with enforcing this bizarre statute had rendered it meaningless through interpretation.

Another example of a statute that attempts to influence IVF procedures without comprehensively regulating them is New Mexico's Maternal, Fetal, and Infant Experimentation Act. In defining "clinical research," a section of the statute provides that the term does not embrace IVF if the procedure includes provisions "to insure" that every fertilized ovum is "implanted" in a female recipient.[7] This statute disregards any rights a couple may have to control the disposition of pre-embryos created from their ova and sperm, and it apparently confuses transfer of pre-embryos to a recipient with implantation (pregnancy). IVF procedures not meeting the statutory definition are regulated as clinical research.

By far the most troubling statutes that may affect IVF and lavage with pre-embryo transfer are those that broadly prohibit or regulate fetal research.[8] What, for example, is one to make of a Minnesota statute[9] that prohibits the use of a living human conceptus for any kind of research or experimentation except to protect the life or health of the conceptus? Or of a Louisiana statute[10] that prohibits any study of or experimentation on a human embryo except to preserve the life or to improve the health of the embryo? It has been recommended that before IVF procedures or lavage and embryo transfers are performed in states with statutes such as these an opinion from the attorney general or other responsible legal officer be requested concerning

---

[7]N.M. Stat. Ann. §24-9A-1D (Supp. 1986).

[8]Andrews, The Stork Market: The Law of the New Reproduction Technologies, A.B.A.J. 50 (Aug. 1984). See also L. Andrews, New Conceptions: A Consumer's Guide to the Newest Infertility Treatments Including In Vitro Fertilization, Artificial Insemination, and Surrogate Motherhood (1985). New Conceptions is an excellent work on the new reproductive technologies, covering their medical, emotional, and psychological as well as their legal aspects. Fetal research statutes that may affect IVF and embryo transfer are listed in Appendix D of New Conceptions.

[9]Minn. Stat. Ann. §145.422 (West 1988 Supp.).

[10]La. Rev. Stat. Ann. §87.2 (West 1986).

their effect on the procedures.[11] This was done in Massachusetts in 1983, and the District Attorney of Boston gave the opinion that the Massachusetts statute would not be violated if all fertilized ova were transferred.[12] On the other hand, a persuasive argument can be made that the fetal research statutes do not affect lavage and embryo transfer at all.[13] The argument runs as follows: Lavage of the pre-embryo from the donor is protected by Roe v. Wade[14] principles; once the pre-embryo is recovered, all efforts are directed toward its preservation and implantation; and in any event failure to transfer it is constitutionally protected because the intended recipient may decline pregnancy.

Three states, Pennsylvania, New Hampshire, and Louisiana, have enacted statutes to regulate some aspects of in vitro fertilization, though none has enacted a comprehensive regulatory statute. Pennsylvania requires facilities performing IVF to report on their work to the Commonwealth Health Director.[15] The report must be made quarterly and give the names of the persons conducting the procedure, the number of ova fertilized, the number of fertilized ova discarded, and the number of women to whom fertilized ova were transferred. New Hampshire requires the parties to IVF to receive medical evaluations and psychological counseling and prohibits maintenance of pre-embryos beyond 14 days of development unless cryopreserved

---

[11]Quigley and Andrews, Human In Vitro Fertilization and the Law, 42 Fertility and Sterility 348, 349 (1984).

[12]Id.

[13]Blumberg, Legal Issues in Nonsurgical Human Ovum Transfer, 251 J.A.M.A. 1178 (1984).

[14]410 U.S. 113 (1973). For discussions of constitutional rights to use the new reproductive technologies, see Ikemoto, Providing Protection for Collaborative, Noncoital Reproduction: Surrogate Motherhood and Other New Procreative Technologies, and the Right of Intimate Association, 40 Rutgers L. Rev. 1273 (1988); Robertson, Embryos, Families, and Procreative Liberty: The Legal Structure of the New Reproduction, 59 S. Cal. L. Rev. 939 (1986); and Robertson, Procreative Liberty and Control of Conception, Pregnancy, and Childbirth, 69 Va. L. Rev. 405 (1983).

[15]Pa. Cons. Stat. Ann. tit. 18, §3213(e) (Purdon 1983).

or transferred to a woman.[16] Louisiana imposes substantial restrictions on IVF. The pre-embryo is given legal status as a "biological human being" and is not to be considered the property of the facility where fertilization occurred or of the donors of the sperm and ovum.[17] A "viable in vitro fertilized ovum" is treated as a "juridical person," and its intentional destruction is prohibited.[18] Finally, IVF is to be performed only at a facility meeting the standards of the American Fertility Society and the American College of Obstetrics and Gynecology and under the direction of a medical doctor who possesses specialized training and skill in in vitro fertilization.[19]

What should be obvious from the discussion thus far is that legislation is sorely needed to deal with IVF and its variations.[20] Both the Ontario Law Reform Commission and the University of Iowa model act make numerous recommendations for regulating the procedure, and these recommendations are discussed subsequently in this chapter. Most of these recommendations are founded on the understanding that a pre-embryo does not share the same physical characteristics as a fetus or child and is not to be accorded the same legal status.[21] Any legislation that

---

[16] 1990 N.H. House Bill 1426-FN §§168-B:13 to 168-B:15 (effective Jan. 1, 1991).

[17] La. Rev. Stat. Ann. §9:126 (West Supp. 1990).

[18] Id. §9:129.

[19] Id. §9:128.

[20] See Lorio, Alternative Means of Reproduction: Virgin Territory for Legislation, 44 La. L. Rev. 1641 (1984).

[21] The Ontario Report expressly recognizes this different status by quoting from the United Kingdom, Royal College of Obstetricians and Gynaecologists, Report on In Vitro Fertilization and Embryo Replacement or Transfer (1983), para. 13.5 at 13: "Knowing as we do that in the natural process large numbers of fertilized ova are lost before implantation, it is morally unconvincing to claim absolute inviolability for an organism with which nature itself is so prodigal." Ontario Report, at 87 (vol. 1). The University of Iowa model act addresses the matter by defining "preembryo" as "the cell mass that results from fertilization of an ovum prior to implantation," University of Iowa Model Act, at 952, and then assigns rights to various parties to control and dispose of pre-embryos.

does not recognize this will very likely continue to present legal puzzles for those advising IVF practitioners and researchers, just as some of the fetal research statutes do now.

§11.3.3 Pretreatment Counseling and Consent

There are several levels to the recommended pretreatment counseling and consent procedures for IVF. At the most fundamental level, the couple should be fully informed about what is to take place, the risks to the woman from any surgical procedures, the risks and side effects from fertility drugs, and any other risks involved. They should have an opportunity to ask questions about the procedure, and their consent should be obtained on a written consent form.[22] Included in the disclosure should be information about the success rates of IVF procedures generally and at that particular facility.[23] This should be part of informed consent and may forestall any later claims by the couple that the facility misled them by inflated claims of success.

At the second level of pretreatment counseling, the University of Iowa model act recommends that the procedure be performed only in accordance with regulations adopted by the state health department and that both the man and woman successfully complete a medical evaluation,[24] which must include a physical examination and genetic screening, to minimize the risk of transmitting health or genetic problems to mothers or children.[25] In addition, while the model act makes them eligible, unmarried candidates for the procedure would be required to undergo a psychological evaluation,[26] which is designed to determine their suitability to become parents.[27]

---

[22]See generally, F. Rozovsky, Consent to Treatment: A Practical Guide, 24-58 (2d ed. 1990).

[23]Andrews, "Alternative Modes of Reproduction," in N. Taub and S. Cohen, eds., Reproductive Laws for the 1990s: A Briefing Handbook 257, 267 (1988).

[24]University of Iowa Model Act, at 970.

[25]Id. at 991-993.

[26]Id. at 970.

[27]Id. at 990-991.

Finally, it has been strongly recommended that patients undergoing IVF be given psychological counseling both before and after the procedure.[28] The University of Iowa model act requires that IVF participants receive counseling by a qualified mental health professional.[29] There are several reasons for this emphasis on psychological counseling. First, most couples who apply for IVF have already undergone extensive fertility tests and are trying to deal with the pain of their childlessness. Second, the applicants must be psychologically prepared for the failure of the procedure and must be assisted in dealing with that failure if it occurs. Finally, the desire to achieve pregnancy through a technology such as IVF arises from "a complex set of motivations and expectations surrounding a person's desire to have children,"[30] and these motivations and expectations should be understood before the person enters into an expensive and chancy procedure.

§11.3.4 Ovum Donors: Screening and Other Issues

As discussed in §11.3.1, one variation of the standard IVF procedure is to use donated ova, donated sperm, or both. A second variation is to artificially inseminate an ovum donor with the husband's sperm, remove the pre-embryo by lavage, and then transfer it to the wife. Both of these techniques involve donated gametes and raise their own separate legal concerns. The discussion here deals with the ovum or pre-embryo donor; the issues involving sperm donors are the same as in artificial insemination by donor and are discussed in §11.4.

The informed consent of donors must, of course, be obtained. To ovum donors, who will be given fertility drugs and who must undergo a surgical procedure for retrieval of the ova, all the risks and discomforts of the procedure must be fully

---

[28]Seibel, A New Era in Reproductive Technology, 318 New Eng. J. Med. 828, 833 (1988).

[29]University of Iowa Model Act, at 990, 993-996.

[30]Id. at 994.

explained.[31] With regard to pre-embryo donors, the risk that the pre-embryo may not be removed by lavage must be addressed and understood. Ovum donors should be counseled regarding the disposition of any fertilized ova that are not transferred to a recipient, and the donor's permission should be obtained—if possible—to transfer rights of control to the IVF facility or to the provider of the sperm or the couple seeking to achieve pregnancy. If this is not possible, consent should be obtained for cryopreservation or destruction.

Donors should be given a general health examination[32] and genetic screening,[33] and an age limit for donating should be set.[34] The University of Iowa model act requires all gamete donors to undergo a health and genetic examination pursuant to regulations promulgated by the state health agency.[35] Accurate and permanent records should be kept of the donor's medical examinations.[36]

It has long been the practice to pay sperm donors a nominal fee; ovum donors may also be paid for their services, and because of the possible risks and discomforts the pay may be significantly more than the amounts paid sperm donors.[37] The Ontario Law Reform Commission recommends that donors be paid reasonable expenses, but that payment should not become an inducement to make the donation.[38] Some fetal research statutes may, however, prohibit or restrict payment in the case of transfers of pre-embryos, and these statutes should be checked. For example, Minnesota prohibits the "sale" of a living "human conceptus."[39]

---

[31]Robertson, Ethical and Legal Issues in Human Egg Donations, 52 Fertility and Sterility 353, 358 (1989).

[32]Wadlington, Artificial Conception: The Challenge for Family Law, 69 Va. L. Rev. 465, 504-505 (1983).

[33]Lorio, Alternative Means of Reproduction: Virgin Territory for Legislation, 44 La. L. Rev. 1641, 1674 (1984).

[34]Id.

[35]University of Iowa Model Act, at 991-993.

[36]Recordkeeping is discussed in §11.4.4.

[37]Annas and Elias, In Vitro Fertilization and Embryo Transfer: Medicolegal Aspects of a New Technique to Create a Family, 17 Family L.Q. 199, 215 (1983).

[38]Ontario Report, at 169 (vol. 2).

[39]Minn. Stat. Ann. §145.422 (West 1988 Supp.).

§11.3.5 Control and Disposition of Pre-Embryos Not Transferred

As stated in §11.3.1, it is standard practice in IVF procedures to administer fertility drugs so that the woman produces multiple ova. In some IVF centers, only the number of ova intended to be transferred are fertilized.[40] In other instances, however, all of the ova are fertilized but not all are transferred to the woman in an attempt to achieve pregnancy. Thus, questions may be raised concerning what disposition is to be made of the pre-embryos not transferred and who has legal authority to decide what that disposition will be. The need for legislation on these issues is especially urgent to avoid repetitions of the *Davis* case in Tennessee.[41] In that case, an estranged husband and wife disputed custody of frozen pre-embryos created from their gametes. Mrs. Davis contended that she had authority over their disposition and could have them transferred to her in an attempt to achieve pregnancy or could allow them to be transferred to another woman. Mr. Davis contended that he had a veto power over their transfer to Mrs. Davis or anyone else. No contract existed to govern disposition of the frozen pre-embryos. The trial judge awarded custody to Mrs. Davis, and in doing so unnecessarily relied on the theoretical underpinning that the frozen pre-embryos were human beings and should be handled in a custody dispute as children of the couple. The Tennessee Court of Appeals reversed.[42] The court of appeals stated that awarding custody to Mrs. Davis, which might well have the consequence of causing Mr. Davis to become a parent against his will, was impermissible state action in violation of Mr. Davis's constitutionally protected right not to beget a child. In support of this position the court relied on U.S. Supreme Court decisions holding that the use of contraceptives is encompassed

---

[40]Robertson, Embryos, Families, and Procreative Liberty: The Legal Structure of the New Reproduction, 59 S. Cal. L. Rev. 939, 977 n.125 (1986).

[41]15 Fam. L. Rep. (BNA 1097) (Tenn. Ch. App. 1989). The calls for legislation have been more forceful in Great Britain than in the United States. See The Times (London) (Home News), Aug. 9, 1989, at 3.

[42]Davis v. Davis, 1990 WL 130807 (Tenn. App. Sept. 13, 1990).

in a constitutional right of privacy.[43] The court awarded joint control over disposition of the pre-embryos to Mr. and Mrs. Davis, and as a result Mr. Davis can prevent their being transferred in attempts to achieve pregnancy.

This subsection discusses the matter of control and disposition generally; the next section discusses the special case of cryopreservation.

In the absence of any statutes dealing with control and disposition, it would appear that the providers of the gametes, that is, the providers of the sperm and ova, have presumptive control over disposition of any pre-embryos that are not transferred.[44] Therefore, if pre-embryos are to be destroyed, donated for transfer to another woman, or frozen, written consent for the disposition should be obtained from both persons providing the gametes.

The Ontario Law Reform Commission recommends the following rules for control and disposition of pre-embryos that are not transferred:[45] When no donated gametes are used, the couple shall have joint legal control over fertilized ova not transferred. The couple may decide to donate them to another woman or couple, allow cryopreservation, or have them destroyed. When one member of the couple has contributed gametes and the other has not, legal control of fertilized ova shall rest with the person who contributed gametes. When either sperm or ova, or both, have been donated without restrictions, the donor should have no control over the use or disposition of fertilized ova. Where both sperm and ova have been donated without restriction, legal control of unused fertilized ova should rest with the physician, clinic, or other facility having possession of the ova.

The University of Iowa model act contains extensive provisions regarding control and disposition of gametes and pre-

---

[43]Carey v. Population Serv. Intl., 431 U.S. (1977); Eisenstadt v. Baird, 405 U.S. 438 (1972); Griswold v. Connecticut, 381 U.S. 479 (1965).

[44]Robertson, supra n.40, at 976. An analogy is drawn to "ownership" of body parts.

[45]Ontario Report, at 203-207 (vol. 2).

embryos.[46] It generally allows the parties to control disposition by written agreement and provides that the parties who contributed gametes to form the pre-embryo shall continue to exercise rights of control over the pre-embryo.[47] If the parties disagree, then the model act establishes a default scheme to give priority to certain rights.[48] For example, first priority is given to the sperm donor and second priority to the ovum donor.[49] The act also provides that a donor cannot transfer rights by will or intestate succession.[50]

§11.3.6 Cryopreservation and Banking

Cryopreservation of untransferred pre-embryos is likely to become a standard practice. Cryopreservation—freezing and storage[51]—enables IVF practitioners to make subsequent transfers in an attempt to achieve pregnancy if the first transfer is unsuccessful, and to do so without the expense and risks involved in another administration of fertility drugs and retrieval of ova.[52] Also, freezing and thawing a pre-embryo before transfer appears to increase its chances of survival.[53] Cryopreservation should be regarded as an experimental procedure involving human subjects and should be reviewed by a facility's institutional review board or similar agency.[54] In the absence of clear statutory directions,

---

[46]Model Human Reproductive Technologies and Surrogacy Act, 72 Iowa L. Rev. 943, 1002-1008 (1987).

[47]Id. at 1003-1004.

[48]Id.

[49]Id.

[50]Id. at 1006.

[51]In the procedure described by Drs. Sele, Racinet, Quenard, and Bergues, in Pregnancy After Oocyte Collection and Total Ovariectomy, 320 New Eng. J. Med. 1756 (1989), two pre-embryos were "deep-frozen at the two-cell and four-cell stages by using 1,2-propanediol with sucrose as a cryoprotectant."

[52]Grobstein, Flower, and Mendeloff, Frozen Embryos: Policy Issues, 312 New Eng. J. Med. 1584, 1584-1585 (1985).

[53]Robertson, Ethical and Legal Issues in Cryopreservation of Human Embryos, 47 Fertility and Sterility 371, 372 (1987).

[54]Id. at 379.

cryopreservation raises a number of legal questions to be dealt with by facilities performing this service. First is the matter of disposition of the pre-embryo. As discussed above, the gamete providers retain control over untransferred pre-embryos. Here, however, there are additional matters to be dealt with: what happens if the gamete providers die, divorce, or become unavailable during the period of cryopreservation.[55] The choices and possibilities should be carefully explained to the couple before cryopreservation, and the facility should obtain written directions and consent. The possibilities are donation to another woman or couple, destruction, or transfer of rights to the custodial facility for disposition as it wishes.

A second question is how long to allow the pre-embryo to develop before it is frozen. The Ontario Law Reform Commission summarizes the views of various study groups on this issue and recommends that pre-embryos not be allowed to develop more than 14 days after fertilization;[56] the University of Iowa model act also imposes a 14-day limit.[57] After 14 days, development of a true embryo usually begins.[58]

A third question, one also involving time, is whether limits should be set on how long a pre-embryo is kept in cryopreservation. Professor Robertson recommends setting no definite limits.[59] The Ontario Law Reform Commission recommends a 10-year limit, and at the end of that time the storage facility would be under a duty to destroy it.[60] The University of Iowa model act places no time limit on storage in the statute, but rather leaves the imposition of such a limit to the state health agency that regulates storage facilities.[61]

Any facility that is storing pre-embryos by cryopreservation is de facto a pre-embryo bank, and should be able to charge

---

[55]Id. at 373.
[56]Ontario Report, at 216 (vol. 2).
[57]University of Iowa Model Act, at 1001.
[58]Id.
[59]Robertson, supra n.53, at 375.
[60]Ontario Report, at 217 (vol. 2).
[61]University of Iowa Model Act, at 999-1000.

758

reasonable fees for this service.[62] The Ontario Law Reform Commission recommends that banking be allowed, but that it be conducted under a strict licensing and regulatory regime.[63] As discussed above, the University of Iowa model act would also allow banking, subject to regulation by the state health agency.

A recent case demonstrates that a written agreement regarding the disposition of frozen pre-embryos—though highly desirable—may not foreclose disputes on important issues. In York v. Jones,[64] a couple living in New Jersey was accepted in the Jones Institute's IVF program in Norfolk, Virginia. After several unsuccessful attempts at achieving pregnancy, six pre-embryos were frozen for later transfer to the wife. The couple executed a cryopreservation agreement drafted by the Jones Institute, which, among other things, provided that the couple could withdraw from the program at any time, that the pre-embryos would be stored only as long as they were active patients at the Jones Institute, that they would have "principal responsibility" to decide the disposition of the pre-embryos, and that should they no longer wish to attempt to achieve a pregnancy they could choose to have the pre-embryos donated to another infertile couple, donated for approved research, or discarded. The couple moved to California. They returned to Norfolk for another attempt, in which five of the cryopreserved pre-embryos were transferred. The attempt failed to achieve a pregnancy. The couple then requested the Jones Institute to release the remaining frozen pre-embryo for transport to the Institute for Reproductive Research at the Hospital of the Good Samaritan in Los Angeles. The Jones Institute refused, and the Yorks brought suit.

The court denied the defendants' motion to dismiss the suit, and in doing so relied on a bailment analysis. The court held that the cryopreservation agreement had created a bailor-bailee relationship regarding the Yorks' property, the pre-embryo.

---

[62]See Robertson, supra n.53, at 374.
[63]Ontario Report, at 172 (vol. 2).
[64]717 F. Supp. 421 (E.D. Va. 1989).

Under the law of bailments, a bailor has an absolute right to the return of the property when the purpose of the bailment has terminated. Thus the court found that the defendants could not insist that the couples' only options were the three choices specified in the agreement. The case was then settled, and the Yorks transported the frozen pre-embryo to Los Angeles.[65] Whether or not the court was correct in using a bailment analysis, the result reached seems correct: the terms of the cryopreservation agreement gave primary control over disposition to the couple who furnished the gametes.

§11.4 Artificial Insemination by Donor

§11.4.1 The Procedure

It has been observed by several writers that artificial insemination hardly rises to the level of a "technology," and that in fact it can be performed with something as inexpensive and unsophisticated as a turkey baster.[1] Nevertheless, it is a method of aiding reproduction by artificial means and is usually conducted in a hospital or clinic. The procedure is typically used to enable a wife to bear a child when her husband is infertile.[2] It is also used when the husband is fertile but risks passing on a genetic defect or disease.[3] The sperm "donor" is usually a medical student, resident, or graduate student who is paid a nominal amount.[4] At the time of the wife's ovulation, the donor's semen is placed in the wife's vagina near the cervix or in the cervical

---

[65]Robertson, In the Beginning: The Legal Status of Early Embryos, 76 Va. L. Rev. 437, 463 (1990).

§11.4 [1]See, e.g., Wikler, Society's Response to the New Reproductive Technologies: The Feminist Perspectives, 59 S. Cal. L. Rev. 1043, 1056 (1986).

[2]Currie-Cohen, Lutrell, and Shapiro, Current Practice of Artificial Insemination by Donor in the United States, 300 New Eng. J. Med. 585 (1979).

[3]Id.

[4]Id. at 587.

canal, and several attempts may be made before pregnancy is achieved.[5]

Although, as noted above, artificial insemination may be performed in the home with a rather ordinary kitchen implement and semen from a friendly donor, in practice it is usually treated as a medical procedure.[6] In at least five states, Arkansas, Connecticut, Georgia, Oklahoma, and Oregon,[7] a physician is required to perform the procedure; in Georgia, a physician who performs artificial insemination on a wife with her written consent and that of her husband is relieved of civil liability to them or to any children conceived by the procedure, except that for negligence.[8] In addition to this relief from liability and the usual reasons for obtaining informed consent, it is especially important to obtain informed consent from both husband and wife for an AID procedure because most state statutes legitimate the child born as a result of the procedure only if the husband consents.[9] Both the Ontario Law Reform Commission[10] and the University of Iowa model act[11] treat artificial insemination as a medical procedure, and the model act requires that it be performed in accordance with regulations issued by the state health agency.[12]

------

[5]Id.

[6]There are certain risks in using a friendly donor. Three cases have held that if the donor and an unmarried mother knew each other, the donor may be entitled to certain parental rights. See In re R.C., 755 P.2d 27 (Colo. 1989); Jhordan C. v. Mary K., 179 Cal. App. 3d 386, 224 Cal. Rptr. 530 (1986); and C.M. v. C.C., 152 N.J. Super. 160, 377 A.2d 821 (1977).

[7]Ark. Code Ann. §9-10-201 (1987); Conn. Gen. Stat. Ann. §45-69g(a) (West 1981); Ga. Code Ann. §74-101.1, §74-9904 (Harrison 1986); Okla. Stat. Ann. tit. 10, §553 (West 1987); and Or. Rev. Stat. §677.360 (1983).

[8]Ga. Code Ann. §19-7-21 (Harrison 1986).

[9]See Wadlington, Artificial Conception: The Challenge for Family Law, 69 Va. L. Rev. 465, 483-484 (1983).

[10]Ontario Law Reform Commission, Report on Human Artificial Reproduction and Related Matters 152 (1985) (hereinafter Ontario Report).

[11]Model Human Reproductive Technologies and Surrogacy Act, 72 Iowa L. Rev. 943, 967-969 (1987) (hereinafter University of Iowa Model Act).

[12]Id.

§11.4.2 Unmarried Women and Eligibility Issues

A troublesome issue in the absence of statutory guidance is whether unmarried women are eligible for artificial insemination. Two aspects of this question cause particular concern: whether a healthcare facility may be liable to the mother or child if it inseminates her and whether, if it refuses her request for insemination, a court will order it to honor the request. No cases have been found that impose liability for performing artificial insemination on unmarried women, but healthcare facilities that make the procedure available to single women should always require that the woman be over the age of 18 and that she sign a consent form acknowledging that she understands the consequences of the procedure and accepts legal responsibility for any child born as a result of the insemination. In addition, the facility may wish to require that single women undergo both a physical examination and a psychological evaluation as a condition of being artificially inseminated. The Ontario Law Reform Commission recommends that unmarried couples and single women be eligible for AID in certain circumstances.[13] The University of Iowa model act makes single women eligible if they successfully complete a physical examination and counseling.[14]

On the question whether a facility can be compelled to perform AID on a single woman, a persuasive argument can be made on the basis of the privacy, abortion, and family-rights cases that a single person has a constitutional right to the procedure enforceable against public and publicly funded facilities.[15] In a case involving Wayne State University, a single woman who was denied AID by the university challenged its "married only" rule in a federal suit. The suit was dismissed when the university dropped its marriage requirement.[16]

---

[13]The circumstances would be that the unmarried couple be in a stable relationship or that the unmarried woman demonstrate sufficient maturity and responsibility to warrant use of the procedure. Ontario Report, at 158 (vol. 2).

[14]University of Iowa Model Act, at 967-969.

[15]Robertson, Embryos, Families, and Procreative Liberty: The Legal Structure of the New Reproduction, 59 S. Cal. L. Rev. 939, 962-964 (1986).

[16]L. Andrews, New Conceptions: A Consumer's Guide to the Newest

The last piece of the puzzle that needs to be legislatively addressed if AID is to be administered to single women is the status of the sperm donor in such cases. The statutes that legitimate a child born from AID when the husband and wife consent to the procedure[17] have no applicability when a married couple is not involved; thus the donor's status as the legal father is uncertain, and the possibility exists that a donor—should the anonymity barrier be broken—could be held liable for support in a paternity action. The University of Iowa model act deals with this question by providing that no father-child relationship exists between the sperm donor and the child born to an unmarried woman by AID unless the donor signs a written statement in which he acknowledges the rights and responsibilities of parenthood.[18]

§11.4.3 Screening of Sperm Donors

The current system of screening of sperm donors for infectious and genetically transmitted diseases and defects is generally inadequate and is a potential source of liability. A 1979 study showed little effective genetic screening.[19] In 1985, four women in New South Wales, Australia, were reported to have AIDS antibodies after exposure to donor semen.[20] In 1987, the Journal of the American Medical Association reported a case in which hepatitis B was transmitted to a woman by donor semen used

---

Infertility Treatments Including In Vitro Fertilization, Artificial Insemination, and Surrogate Motherhood 176 (1985).

[17]See the statutes collected in Wadlington, Artificial Conception: The Challenge for Family Law, 69 Va. L. Rev. 465, 483 n.84 (1983).

[18]University of Iowa Model Act, at 955-956, 967-968.

[19]Currie-Cohen, Luttrell, and Shapiro, Current Practice of Artificial Insemination by Donor in the United States, 300 New Eng. J. Med. 585, 588 (1979): "Family histories were usually superficial, and biochemical tests were rarely performed. Most screening was performed by physicians who were not trained for this task."

[20]Correspondence from Jacqueline Morgan and Jim Nolan, Sydney, Australia, 314 New Eng. J. Med. 386 (1986).

in artificial insemination,[21] and an editorial in the same issue called for the screening of donors for sexually transmitted diseases as a standard practice.[22] A 1988 survey by the Congressional Office of Technology Assessment of 367 physicians conducting artificial insemination found that 44 percent screened semen for HIV, 28 percent screened for syphilis, 27 percent for gonorrhea, and 26 percent for hepatitis.[23] These deficiencies persist despite guidelines of the American Fertility Society that recommend screening for syphilis, hepatitis B, gonorrhea, chlamydia, CMV, and HTLV-III and call for genetic screening to exclude donors with, for example, cleft palate, spina bifida, and congenital heart malformation and those carrying sickle cell anemia and Tay-Sachs disease.[24]

Although lack of screening for either infectious diseases or genetic diseases or defects may expose a physician or healthcare facility to tort liability for negligence, the risk of liability may not be the same for each. In light of what is known about sexually transmitted diseases and the existence of standard tests for detecting the presence of those diseases, it seems clear that a facility that performs no testing on donor semen is an easy target for a negligence action.[25] On the other hand, lack of genetic screening presents a less clear case. It has been contended that in facilities where no trained geneticists are available, the

---

[21]Berry, Gottesfeld, Alter, and Vierling, Transmission of Hepatitis B Virus by Artificial Insemination, 257 J.A.M.A. 1079 (1987).

[22]Mascola and Guinan, Semen Donors as the Source of Sexually Transmitted Diseases in Artificially Inseminated Women: The Saga Unfolds (editorial), 257 J.A.M.A. 1093 (1987).

[23]N.Y. Times, Aug. 11, 1988, at 15, col. 1.

[24]New Guidelines for the Use of Semen Donor Insemination: 1986, 46 Fertility and Sterility 955 (Oct. 1986 Supp.).

[25]See Andrews, The Stork Market: The Law of the New Reproduction Technologies, A.B.A.J. 50, 56 (Aug. 1984). A possible analogy is to liability for the sale of tainted blood. See, e.g., Belle Bonfils Blood Bank v. Hangen, 195 Colo. 259, 579 P.2d 1158 (1978). In that case, the holding of liability was based on the court's finding that the blood bank was engaged in the sale of blood rather than in providing a medical service and therefore product liability rules applied. It is at least arguable that AID involves, in part, the sale of semen, especially where a sperm bank is part of the operation.

lack of screening would not be a lack of due care; but that in major medical facilities, where they *are* available, it would be.[26] The University of Iowa model act requires a medical evaluation of each gamete donor that must include a genetic and health history and a certification by the evaluator that the gametes are acceptable for use in an artificial insemination procedure.[27]

§11.4.4 Recordkeeping and Access Issues

Recordkeeping practices for AID procedures have been described as "woefully deficient"[28] and "minimal."[29] The lack of adequate records may be motivated by a desire to protect the anonymity of sperm donors, but it is contrary to the public interest. Records of the donor's identity, the results of his physical examination and genetic screening, and the identities of women impregnated with his sperm are important for several reasons. First, it is important that the child and his parents have access to this information should health or genetic problems develop in the donor that were undetected at the time of the donation.[30] Second, the number of inseminations with the sperm of a particular donor should be limited, to reduce the possibility of consanguineous marriages and to provide information about them before they occur.[31] Third, it should be possible for a child

---

[26]A. Holder, Legal Issues in Pediatrics and Adolescent Medicine 17-18 (2d ed. 1985). See also Wadlington, Artificial Conception: The Challenge for Family Law, 69 Va. L. Rev. 465, 505 (1983), speculating that it may be difficult to establish a standard of care because of the poor recordkeeping practices in AID procedures. In Moores v. Lucas, 405 So. 2d 1022 (Fla. Dist. Ct. App. 1981), physicians were held liable to the parents of a handicapped child for failure to diagnose and warn the couple that the wife was likely to pass on an inheritable disease. Accord Gallagher v. Duke Univ., 852 F.2d 733 (4th Cir. 1988).

[27]University of Iowa Model Act, at 991-992.

[28]Currie-Cohen, Luttrell, and Shapiro, Current Practice of Artificial Insemination by Donor in the United States, 300 New Eng. J. Med. 585, 589 (1979).

[29]Wadlington, supra n.26, at 472.

[30]University of Iowa Model Act, at 1011.

[31]Id. and Wadlington, supra n.26, at 497-498.

conceived through AID to obtain information about his biological father in certain instances.[32] And, fourth, the information is necessary to provide accurate public health and statistical information about AID procedures.[33]

The Ontario Law Reform Commission recommended that records of artificial conceptions be treated generally as medical records under applicable statutes and ethical rules.[34] The anonymity of gamete donors should be preserved, but a link between donor and recipient should be preserved in the records so that physicians can obtain medical information if it is necessary to diagnose and treat children conceived through the technology.[35] The commission recommended no legislation generally authorizing parents and children aged 18 or over to be given access to records of the donor's ethnic origin and genetic health, but instead recommended that the question of access to this information be left to the discretion of the physician who performed the procedure.[36] The University of Iowa model act creates a central registry in the state health agency where complete records are to be kept on gamete donors, recipients, and children conceived by the procedure.[37] The identity of gamete donors will be made available "only upon a showing of strict necessity supported by court order,"[38] and the central registry is required to notify any donor or parents of a child born as a result of the procedure of any information it acquires concerning a health risk posed to the donor or child.[39]

---

[32] Wadlington, supra n.26, at 499-500.
[33] University of Iowa Model Act, at 1011.
[34] Ontario Report, at 183-190.
[35] Id.
[36] Id.
[37] University of Iowa Model Act, at 1009-1010.
[38] Id. at 1010.
[39] Id.

§11.5 Surrogate Motherhood

§11.5.1 Arrangements

As a result of the publicity surrounding the Baby M[1] case in New Jersey, surrogate motherhood is the best-known and most controversial of the new reproductive technologies. Extremely difficult legal and ethical issues surround the procedure.[2] In the usual surrogate arrangement, when the wife is infertile or is the carrier of a genetic disease or defect, the married couple enters into a contract with a woman who is to be artificially inseminated with the husband's sperm, carry the baby to term, and then release the child to the father and his wife.[3] In commercial surrogacy arrangements, the husband and wife pay a substantial fee to the volunteer mother in addition to her medical expenses.[4]

For healthcare facilities and physicians, the legal issues presented by surrogacy arrangements are very similar to those in artificial-insemination-by-donor procedures. The one difference is that in surrogacy arrangements there are in a sense two gamete donors: the husband and the volunteer mother. Informed consent for the insemination procedure should be obtained from both, and both should be examined for infectious diseases and given a genetic screening. Questions about the validity of any surrogacy contract and custody of the child are not the facility's concern.

---

§11.5 [1]In re Baby M, 109 N.J. 396, 537 A.2d 1227 (1988). The court held that the commercial surrogacy contract in this case was in conflict with the prohibition of payments in regard of adoption and was a contract contrary to public policy and therefore void. The court held that the best interests of the child should govern the custody decision, and those interests were best served by awarding custody to the father and his wife, but giving the volunteer mother substantial visitation rights.

[2]See, e.g., symposia on volunteer motherhood in 16 Law, Med. and Health Care, Nos. 1 and 2 (1988) and Colloquy: In Re Baby M, 76 Geo. L.J. 1717 (1988).

[3]Wadlington, Artificial Conception: The Challenge for Family Law, 69 Va. L. Rev. 465, 474-476 (1983).

[4]Id.

§11.5.2 Legislation

Largely as a consequence of publicity from the Baby M case, many states have either recently enacted or are considering legislation to regulate surrogate motherhood arrangements.[5] (One might have hoped that the state legislatures would have addressed other forms of reproductive technology—IVF and AID—as well, but they have not.)[6] The recently enacted Florida and Michigan statutes illustrate the two major approaches taken in the legislation: regulation of surrogacy arrangements under an adoption model and voiding surrogacy contracts.

The Florida statute[7] prohibits "preplanned" adoption contracts in exchange for a valuable consideration, but provides that a "volunteer mother" may be paid for her medical, legal, and reasonable living expenses. The volunteer mother must be allowed seven days after the birth of her child to consent to adoption by the intended parents. Adoption of the child may only be accomplished with the approval of the state Department of Health and Rehabilitative Services and the court.

The Michigan statute[8] makes surrogate parentage contracts void and unenforceable as contrary to public policy. It prohibits the arranging of surrogate parentage contracts for compensation and makes the act punishable as a misdemeanor if engaged in by a "participating party" and as a felony if engaged in by a "nonparticipating party." Physicians and healthcare facilities do not appear to be included within the definitions of either participating or nonparticipating parties, but statutes that take the Michigan approach of imposing criminal sanctions on certain participants in surrogacy arrangements must be carefully read by counsel whose

---

[5]1988 Reptr. on Human Reprod. Law 199 lists 6 states that have enacted legislation recently and adds that approximately 100 bills are pending in state legislatures and the Congress.

[6]The National Conference of Commissioners on Uniform State Laws has also fallen short. Its Uniform Status of Children of Assisted Conception Act (approved 1988) deals only with surrogacy.

[7]Fla. Stat. Ann. §63.212(1)(i) (West 1989 Supp.).

[8]Mich. Stat. Ann. §§25.248(151) through 25.248(163) (Callaghan 1989-90 Supp.).

clients may be involved in the artificial insemination procedures that are part of a surrogacy arrangement.

The Ontario Law Reform Commission recommends that surrogacy arrangements be allowed but be closely regulated.[9] The arrangement must be approved in every case by a family court judge before artificial insemination is performed or a fertilized ovum is transferred. The volunteer mother would be represented by independent counsel. Surrogacy for nonmedical reasons would not be allowed. The court would review and approve all surrogacy contracts. Contracts could provide for immediate surrender of the child, compellable by court order, and the volunteer mother may be paid all costs and expenses, as approved by the court. If a handicapped child is born, the social parents (the husband-sperm donor and his wife) are treated as the parents for all purposes.

The University of Iowa model act[10] also authorizes surrogacy arrangements, but generally follows the adoption model. The entire arrangement, including the parties' eligibility and the terms of the contract, must be reviewed and approved by a court before the volunteer mother is artificially inseminated with the husband's sperm. The intended mother must be determined to be physiologically unable to bear a child without serious risk to her health or to the child's health before she is eligible to participate in a surrogacy arrangement. The volunteer mother must have a documented history of at least one uncomplicated pregnancy and vaginal delivery before she is eligible to participate. The volunteer mother has 72 hours following the birth of the child to decide whether she will keep the child.

§11.6 Conclusion

Law concerning the new reproductive technologies is largely undeveloped. Although the secondary literature, both legal and

---

[9]Ontario Law Reform Commission, Report on Human Artificial Reproduction and Related Matters 233-272 (1985).

[10]Model Human Reproduction Technologies and Surrogacy Act, 72 Iowa L. Rev. 943, 973-989 (1987).

ethical, is voluminous, statutory and case law that directly addresses the numerous issues created by these technologies is sparse. The state legislatures are, however, beginning to bestir themselves, largely as a result of the well-publicized Baby M case. Important developments to watch for in the next few years are statutory requirements for medical and genetic screening of gamete donors and court decisions imposing tort liability for failure to screen, licensing requirements for IVF facilities, statutory requirements regarding the disposition and cryopreservation of pre-embryos, and statutes that impose criminal or civil liability on physicians and healthcare facilities that participate in illegal surrogacy arrangements.

12

Organ Procurement and Transplantation

Lois L. Shepherd

§12.0 Introduction

Healthcare facilities throughout the nation have become increasingly involved in procedures for donating, removing, and transplanting organs. This involvement will only intensify as organ transplant operations become more common and the demand for suitable organs increases. Organ procurement and transplantation involve a number of legal issues. While litigation arising out of transplantation has been uncommon in the past, it is unlikely to remain so.[1] Increased legal controversy is predicted as a result of the increased numbers of healthcare facilities and professionals engaging in transplantation practice and from the fact that, as more transplantation procedures are performed, a "standard of care" is emerging to provide a legal measure by which to evaluate the conduct of transplant care providers.[2] The frequency of liability claims should also rise as a result of patients' developing higher expectations about the success of transplant operations.[3]

This chapter will first briefly describe the sources of the laws that bear on transplant issues. It will then describe the developing network of institutions that participate in organ procurement and transplantation. Next the chapter will explore the legal requirements and considerations that arise at each stage in the procurement and transplantation process. Most of the discussion focuses on cadaver organs. Issues relating specifically to the procurement of organs from living donors are considered separately and treated briefly. Artificial organs are not addressed. Furthermore, the emphasis is placed on solid organs rather than tissues such as skin because solid organ donation and transplantation raise the more difficult questions and are currently the subject of much legislative action and policy discussion.

The terms "donor" and "donee" are often used in the law and literature dealing with transplants in such a way that their

---

§12.0   [1] The infrequency of legal controversies in transplantation thus far is probably traceable to the caution that transplant teams and personnel have exercised in accepting donor organs, informing recipients about the dangers and prognosis of the procedures, and nurturing patient relationships. Rose, Medicolegal Problems Associated with Organ and Tissue Transplantations, 31 Med. Tr. Tech. Q. 100 (1984).

[2] Id. at 115; Overcast, Merriken, and Evans, Malpractice Issues in Heart Transplantation, 10 Am. J.L. & Med. 363, 366 (1985).

[3] Id.

meanings are ambiguous. "Donor" is sometimes used to refer to the decedent whose organs are donated (because there is usually no better term to use), but is more often and more properly used to identify the individual who has given permission for the donation, whether she is the decedent or a relative of the decedent. Similarly, a transplant recipient is sometimes called the "donee," when that term is more appropriately used to describe the institution or organization to which a donor has made the gift. In this chapter, the term "donee" will be used with this latter meaning.

A. The Legal and Institutional Framework

§12.1 Sources of Law

Organ procurement and transplantation are governed and affected by the following sources of law.

§12.1.1 State Statutes

Anatomical gift statutes prescribe the means by which individuals or their survivors may donate organs. They also extend immunity from legal liability to individuals and institutions involved in giving or receiving organs who, in good faith, are acting within the terms of the statutes or attempting to do so. The Uniform Anatomical Gift Act (UAGA) was adopted by the National Conference of Commissioners on Uniform State Laws in 1968[1] and has now been adopted with some variation in all 50 states and the District of Columbia. In 1987, the UAGA was revised in a number of significant ways. The Uniform Act is discussed in detail in Part B, Organ Procurement.

State law defines the standards for determining when death

---

§12.1   [1]Unif. Anatomical Gift Act, 8A U.L.A. 15 (1968).

occurs, whether that definition is embodied in the common law or in a determination-of-death statute. Persons removing organs for donation must pay strict attention to the law governing determinations of death in their jurisdiction. In 1989, 24 jurisdictions had adopted the Uniform Determination of Death Act. This Act is intended to provide comprehensive bases for determining death in all situations.[2] The Act and its predecessor, the Uniform Brain Death Act, which is still followed in some jurisdictions, promotes the availability of organs by removing legal liability for declaring patients dead who have been diagnosed as having total and irreversible cessation of brain functions although their respiration and circulation can be artificially supported.

State "required routine protocol" laws either require hospitals to ask relatives of patients who die if they would be willing to donate the decedent's organs or require hospitals to notify the family of the opportunity to donate. A measure designed to increase the supply of organs, the laws are aimed at overcoming physicians' and hospitals' traditional reluctance to intrude on grieving families to ask them for organ donations.

§12.1.2 State Case Law

There have only been a few reported cases bearing directly on organ procurement or transplantation issues. Those that have been reported, however, have been treated by commentators as having strong value as precedent.

§12.1.3 National Organ Transplant Act of 1984 (Pub. L. No. 98-507)

This Act provided for a national organ-sharing system and for the establishment of grants to organ procurement agencies

---

[2]Unif. Determination of Death Act, Prefatory Note, 12 U.L.A. 310 (Supp. 1989).

(OPAs) and prohibited the purchase of organs. The Act also established a 25-member Task Force on Organ Transplantation, with members representing medicine, law, theology, ethics, allied health, the health insurance industry, and the general public. In April 1986, the federal Task Force issued a final report that derived from members' discussions of medical, legal, social, ethical, and economic issues. It contains numerous specific recommendations targeted toward legislative bodies, government agencies, professional organizations, and the general public.[3]

§12.1.4 The Social Security Act

In late 1987 the Social Security Act was amended to add, in §1138 of the Act, new requirements relating to organ procurement and transplantation that hospital and organ procurement agencies must meet in order to participate in Medicare and Medicaid programs.[4] The Health Care Financing Administration has promulgated rules to implement §1138.[5] The requirements of the Act and the corresponding rules are discussed throughout this chapter where applicable.

§12.2 Institutional Roles in Transplantation

The advent of successful organ transplantation has witnessed the evolution of an institutional network for the solicitation, distribution, and transplantation of organs. In response to the new transplant technology, traditional institutions, such as hospitals, have taken on new roles, while some new institutions, such as organ procurement agencies, have sprung up. At first, the roles of these institutions were defined, quite naturally, in

---

[3]U.S. Department of Health and Human Services Report of the Task Force on Organ Transplantation, April 1986 [hereinafter Task Force Report].

[4]Section 1138 (42 U.S.C. §1320b-8(b)) was added to the Social Security Act by §9318(a) of the Omnibus Budget Reconciliation Act of 1986.

[5]See 53 Fed. Reg. 6526 (Mar. 1 1988).

response to transplant needs and without much involvement from government. Now, however, with recent federal legislation, there is a coordinated network of institutions with exclusive, sharply defined roles developing, whose practices are becoming subject to quite extensive governmental regulation. The institutions and their roles follow.

§12.2.1 Hospitals and Transplant Centers

All health care professionals involved in caring for potential organ and tissue donors are part of the organ procurement and transplantation system because of the opportunity they possess for soliciting the donation of organs. This includes nursing homes, since certain organs of the aged body (for example, the cornea) are suitable for donation. Medicare and Medicaid participation is now conditioned on a certain level of participation in the organ procurement process.[1]

A transplant center is a hospital designated by Medicare to furnish directly, for a specific organ or organs, transplantation and other medical and surgical specialty services required for the care of transplant patients.[2] Section 1138(a) of the Social Security Act requires a transplant center to be a member of, and abide by the rules of, the Organ Procurement and Transplantation Network (OPTN) in order to participate in the Medicare and Medicaid programs.[3] The effect of this statutory provision is to withhold Medicare or Medicaid payment from a hospital for *all* services, not just those relating to transplant services, if that hospital performs organ transplants but is not accepted for membership by the OPTN.[4]

---

§12.2 [1]See the discussion at §12.5.1 infra.

[2]53 Fed. Reg. 6526 (Mar. 1, 1988).

[3]In order to be a rule of the OPTN, the Secretary of Health and Human Services must have given formal approval to the rule. Furthermore, no action of the OPTN to deny an applicant membership status in the OPTN is effective unless ratified by the Secretary. 54 Fed. Reg. 51802 (Dec. 16, 1989).

[4]53 Fed. Reg. 6526, 6528 (Mar. 1, 1988). Even before §1138 was enacted, a number of private insurance companies restricted benefit coverage for transplants to institutions they had approved for such procedures.

776

§12.2.2 Organ Procurement Agencies

Organ Procurement Agencies (OPAs) coordinate activities relating to the recovery of donated organs, including providing for surgical retrieval and tissue typing, maintaining lists and tissue characteristics of potential recipients, and distributing organs to cooperating transplant centers. Often, at a hospital's request, the organ procurement agency will also be involved in securing consent for organ donations. In 1987 there were approximately 120 organ procurement agencies that Medicare paid for kidney acquisition services. About one-half of these OPAs are independently incorporated nonprofit entities whose sole function is the procurement of human organs. The remaining OPAs are hospital-based organ procurement agencies located within the administrative structure of a hospital approved to perform transplants.[5]

As with transplant centers, an organ procurement organization must meet certain qualification standards and be a member of the OPTN in order to be eligible to receive Medicare and Medicaid reimbursements.[6] Only one organ procurement organization will be designated by the Department of Health and Human Services per service area (a geographical area that includes a population of at least 2.5 million or yields at least 50 potential organ donors each year).[7]

§12.2.3 Tissue Banks

Tissue procurement programs obtain and process tissues for a variety of surgical needs. The programs are usually small, process only one type of tissue, and are largely self-supporting through fee-for-service arrangements. In 1986 there were 33 skin banks, 109 eye banks, and 164 bone banks.[8] Many tissue banks are currently either expanding from single-tissue to multiple-tissue

---

[5]53 Fed. Reg. 6526 (Mar. 1, 1988).
[6]§1138(b) of Social Security Act, 42 U.S.C. §1320b-8(b). See supra n.4.
[7]53 Fed. Reg. 6526 (Mar. 1, 1988).
[8]Task Force Report at 63, citing Eye Bank Association of America.

procurement or are developing cooperative agreements with other types of tissue banks and OPAs within their geographic area to coordinate donor identification and discussions with next of kin, with the aim of securing tissue and organ donation from the same cadaver.

§12.2.4 The Organ Procurement and Transplantation Network

In 1984 Congress provided for the establishment of an Organ Procurement and Transplantation Network (OPTN), which would be a private, nonprofit entity under contract with the Secretary of Health and Human Services to be the center for national organ distribution.[9] The United Network for Organ Sharing of Richmond, Virginia is currently under contract with the Secretary to function as the OPTN. Under the contract, the United Network for Organ Sharing is required to collect data on all organs donated in the country and maintain a list of all those awaiting transplants.

B. Organ Procurement

§12.3 Physical Suitability of Donors— A Determination of Death

The procurement of an organ typically begins in a hospital with the recognition that a patient is a potential donor. A person must meet two basic criteria to be considered an appropriate candidate for organ donation: she must be physically suitable for donation and she, or her family, must consent to the gift of organs.

The most medically desirable donor is the "brain dead"

---

[9]42 U.S.C. §274.

patient who has suffered total and irreversible loss of brain function but whose other body processes have been maintained by artificial means, thus preserving the viability of transplantable organs.[1] Traditionally, death was determined by the irreversible cessation of cardiac and respiratory functions. This method of determining death, however, came under attack several decades ago as failing to reflect advances in medical technology that permitted cardiac and respiratory activity to be mechanically maintained for some time even though the brain was no longer functioning. For organs to be preserved for transplant, the potential donor's cardiopulmonary system must continue functioning until the removal of the organs. A break from the traditional means of determining death was necessary if transplant programs were to exist; otherwise, the process of removing organs might be deemed to have "killed" the donor.[2]

Legislatures in more than half of the states have adopted laws that permit reliance on brain-related criteria for determining death.[3] Courts in other states have judicially recognized brain

---

§12.3 [1]The brain dead donor can supply items typically thought of as "organs," such as kidneys and hearts. By contrast, potential donors of tissue can be persons who have died from any cause except cancer, infection, or a rare disease. U.S. Department of Health & Human Services, Organ Transplantation Q. & A. (DHHS Publication No. HRS-A-OC 86-1) (Dec. 1985), at 10.

[2]See Schwartz, Bioethical and Legal Considerations in Increasing the Supply of Transplantable Organs: From UAGA to "Baby Fae," 10 Am. J.L. & Med. 397, 416 (1985). See also Comment, "The Bell Tolls for Thee": But When? Legal Acceptance of "Brain Death" as a Criterion for Death, 9 Am. J. Trial. Advoc. 331 (1985).

[3]Overcast, Merriken, and Evans, Malpractice Issues in Heart Transplantation, 10 Am. J.L. & Med. 363, 369 (1985); Comment, supra n.2, at 342 (1985). For states that have adopted laws that permit reliance on brain-related criteria for determining death, see: Ala. Code §22-31-1 (Supp. 1984); Alaska Stat. §9.65.120 (Supp. 1989); Ark. Stat. Ann. §20-17-101 (1987); Cal. Health & Safety Code §§7180-7182 (West Supp. 1985); Colo. Rev. Stat. §12-36-136 (1984); Conn. Gen. Stat. Ann. §19a-279h(b) (West Supp. 1989); Del. Code Ann. tit. 24, §1760 (1987); D.C. Code Ann. §6-2401 (1981); Fla. Stat. §382.009 (West Supp. 1989); Ga. Code Ann. §31-10-16 (1981); Haw. Rev. Stat. §327C-1 (1985); Idaho Code §54-1819 (1988); Ill. Ann. Stat. ch. 110½, §302 (Smith-Hurd 1934); Ind. Code Ann. §1-1-4-3 (Burns 1988); Iowa Code Ann. §702.8 (West 1979); Kan. Stat. Ann. §§77-204 to 77-206 (Supp. 1984);

death standards where statutory recognition has been lacking.[4] Whether statutory or judicial, the standards that have been adopted in the various states are not uniform, requiring that practicing physicians be familiar with the law of their jurisdiction.

Despite this general absence of uniformity, one definition of death has garnered recent support from a substantial number of jurisdictions. By 1989, 24 jurisdictions had adopted the Uniform Determination of Death Act (UDDA), approved by the National Conference of Commissioners on Uniform State Laws in August 1980.[5] The UDDA states that "[a]n individual who

---

La. Rev. Stat. Ann. §9.111 (West Supp. 1989); Me. Rev. Stat. Ann. tit. 22, §§2811 to 2813 (West Supp. 1986); Md. Pub. Health Code Ann. §5-202 (1984); Mich. Stat. Ann. §14.15 (1021) (Callaghan 1936); Miss. Code Ann. §§41-36-1, 41-36-3 (1972); Mo. Ann. Stat. §194.005 (Vernon 1983); Mont. Code Ann. §50-12-101 (1983); Nev. Rev. Stat. §451.007 (1985); N.H. Rev. Stat. Ann. §§141-D:1 to 141-D:2 (Supp. 1989); N.M. Stat. Ann. §12-2-4 (1978); N.C. Gen. Stat. §90-323 (1979); Ohio Rev. Code Ann. §2108.30 (Page Supp. 1985); Okla. Stat. Ann. tit. 63, §§3121 to 3123 (West Supp. 1990); Or. Rev. Stat. §432.300 (1953); Pa. Stat. Ann. tit. 35, §§10201 to 10203 (Purden Supp. 1989); R.I. Gen. Laws 1956, §23-4-16 (1982); S.C. Code Ann. §§44-43-450 to 44-43-460 (1984); Tenn. Code Ann. §68-3-501 (1987); Tex. Rev. Civ. Stat. Ann. art. 4447(t), §1 (Vernon Supp. 1984); Vt. Stat. Ann. tit. 18, §5218 (1981); Va. Code §54-325.7 (Supp. 1981); W. Va. Code §§16-10-1 to 16-10-3 (Supp. 1980); Wis. Stat. Ann. §146.71 (1957); Wyo. Stat. §§35-19-101 to 35-19-103 (Supp. 1985).

[4]Overcast, supra n.3, at 370 (1985) (partial citations). See, e.g., New York City Health & Hosp. Corp. v. Silsona, 81 Misc. 2d 1002, 367 N.Y.S. 2d 686 (Sup. Ct. 1975) (declaratory judgment on brain death standards under New York's Anatomical Gift Act). Some courts have recognized brain death standards in criminal homicide cases. See, e.g., State v. Fierro, 124 Ariz. 182, 603 P.2d 74 (1979) (removal of respiratory life-support system not proximate cause of gunshot victim's death); Commonwealth v. Golston, 373 Mass. 249, 366 N.E.2d 744 (1977), cert. denied., 434 U.S. 1039 (1978) (adopting a brain death standard to prove death in homicide case).

[5]Unif. Determination of Death Act, 12 U.L.A. 310 (Supp. 1989). The jurisdictions are Arkansas, California, Colorado, Delaware, the District of Columbia, Georgia, Idaho, Indiana, Kansas, Maine, Maryland, Mississippi, Missouri, Montana, Nevada, New Hampshire, Ohio, Oklahoma, Oregon, Pennsylvania, Rhode Island, South Carolina, Vermont, and Wyoming. For citations to code, see n.3, supra. Again, jurisdictions have adopted the Act in slightly varying forms. For example, Idaho's statute adds to the UDDA text

has sustained either (1) irreversible cessation of circulatory and respiratory functions, or (2) irreversible cessation of all functions of the entire brain, including the brain stem, is dead. A determination of death must be in accordance with accepted medical standards."[6] The UDDA thus recognizes that when artificial means of support preclude a determination under the common-law standard, death can be determined by the alternative procedures.[7] The Act is silent on acceptable diagnostic tests and medical procedures for determining death, leaving to the medical profession the formulation of acceptable medical practices.

There has been discussion in some state legislatures of amending determination-of-death statutes to include individuals born with anencephaly, a condition in which the brain has completely failed to develop. In general, states have been very cautious in enacting legislation in this area because of the complex issues involved.[8] Infants born with anencephaly do not meet the requirements for brain death under the UDDA and other brain death statutes since they are born with functioning

---

that the phrase "accepted medical standards" means "the usual and customary procedures of the community in which the determination of death is made," Idaho Code §54-1819 (1988), making the propriety of such determinations of even a more localized character.

[6]Unif. Determination of Death Act, 12 U.L.A. 310 (Supp. 1989). The Act is the result of an agreement between the ABA, the AMA, and the NCCUSL. Prefatory Note, 12 U.L.A. 310 (Supp. 1989). The UDDA supersedes the Uniform Brain Death Act, still the law in Alabama and West Virginia. The Uniform Brain Death Act stated that "[f]or legal and medical purposes, an individual who has sustained irreversible cessation of all functioning of the brain, including the brain stem, is dead. . . ." Unif. Brain Death Act §1, 12 U.L.A. 16 (Supp. 1989). Unlike this former Act, the UDDA applies in all situations because it includes the common-law definition of death as well.

[7]Unif. Determination of Death Act, Prefatory Note, 12 U.L.A. 310 (Supp. 1989).

[8]States Work to Increase Availability of Anatomical Gifts, 83 State Health Notes 4 (June 1988). See Note, Death Unto Life: Anencephalic Infants as Organ Donors, 74 Va. L. Rev. 1527 (1988) (arguing for legislation that provides a narrow exception to current whole brain death standard to allow anencephalic infants to serve as organ donors).

brain stems.[9] As an alternative to modifying statutory definitions of death, some legislatures have considered permitting parents of an anencephalic child to donate its organs even though this donation would not meet the current requirement set forth in the UAGA that organs may be removed only after a physician determines that the organ donor has died.[10]

§12.3.1 Limitations on Physicians Making Determinations of Death

The Uniform Anatomical Gift Act provides that the time of death of an organ donor is to be determined by the attending physician at death or, if there was none, by the physician who certifies death.[11] The physician who determines the time of death may not participate in any procedures for removing or transplanting a part unless the document of gift designates the particular physician for such procedures.[12] This prohibition is designed to avoid the possible conflict of interest that may exist between the attending physician and the transplant team in a time when speed is of the utmost importance.[13] The Commentary to the

---

[9]Between 2,000 and 3,000 anencephalics are born in the United States each year, constituting a large potential supply of newborn organs, whereas the supply is now virtually nil. Capron, Anencephalic Donors: Separate the Dead from the Dying, Hastings Ctr. Rep. 5 (Feb. 1987).

[10]See Capron, supra n.9 (criticizing such proposals). Although the issue of using anencephalic infants as organ donors has been treated by the press and some physicians as new, anencephalic infants were the major heart source for infant transplants in the United States more than two decades ago. The first human-to-human heart transplant in the country was performed using an anencephalic newborn donor. See Annas, From Canada with Love: Anencephalic Newborns as Organ Donors? Hastings Ctr. Rep. 36 (Dec. 1987).

[11]Unif. Anatomical Gift Act §8(b).

[12]Id. Pennsylvania has extended the prohibition against participation in the procedures by the physician certifying death to include "any of his professional partners or associates." 20 Pa. Cons. Stat. Ann. §8607(b) (Purdon 1975). Cotton and Sandler, The Regulation of Organ Procurement and Transplantation in the United States, 7 J. Legal Med. 55, 63 (1986).

[13]Comment, Unif. Anatomical Gift Act §8(b).

original Act indicates that the attending physician may communicate with the transplant team or potential donees, but it is unclear whether the attending physician can be a member of the transplant team, whether or not she participates in the "procedures."[14] The uncertainty in this provision may become less significant as more organ procurement agencies send in their own transplant teams once an attending physician in a hospital has determined a potential donor's death.

§12.3.2 Liability Relating to Determinations of Death

Neither the Uniform Anatomical Gift Act nor the Uniform Determination of Death Act specifically addresses the liability of persons who make determinations of death. Questions concerning liability could arise, for instance, if a physician used brain death criteria that were more liberal than those contained in the statute applicable in his jurisdiction. A physician could also make an error in assessing whether legal death in fact had occurred.[15]

While the UAGA clearly provides immunity to the surgeon who removes an organ in reliance on another physician's determination of death, it is unclear whether the Act's protection extends to the physician who makes the actual determination of death. No cases have yet decided this issue, although the Wisconsin Supreme Court has suggested exemption from liability for physicians acting in good faith in determining death.[16] That court, in Williams v. Hoffman, defined the scope of the immunity provision by noting that its application must be limited to matters relating to the mechanics of giving and receiving

---

[14]Schwartz, Bioethical and Legal Considerations in Increasing the Supply of Transplantation Organs: From UAGA to "Baby Fae," 10 Am. J.L. & Med. 397, 419 (1985).

[15]See Overcast, Merriken, and Evans, Malpractice Issues in Heart Transplantation, 10 Am. J.L. & Med. 363, 370 (1985).

[16]Williams v. Hoffman, 66 Wis. 2d 145, 223 N.W.2d 844, 76 A.L.R.3d 880 (1974).

anatomical gifts, the determination of time of death, and the removal of organs.[17] Valid arguments exist both for and against this application of the immunity provision.

Briefly, some arguments against the extension of immunity to death determinations are: (1) because the UAGA does not incorporate a specific death standard, it does not shield physicians making determinations of death; (2) the statute was intended to immunize physicians from liability only for actions taken *after* the donor is dead; and (3) a physician who negligently makes a declaration of death does not act in "good faith."[18] On the other hand, extension of UAGA immunity is supported by the fact that the physician's decision as to time of death is critical in the transplant procedure. Because §8(b) of the Act directs that the time of death is to be determined by the treating physician, this determination may be considered an action taken pursuant to the Act.[19]

The UDDA and other brain-death statutes are unhelpful here as well. While providing insulation from legal liability for declaring patients dead who do not meet the common-law definition of death but are considered "brain dead," these statutes do not address the question of liability for incorrect determinations of brain death. They simply provide that the determination of brain death must be made in accordance with acceptable medical standards. A "good-faith" effort to comply with medical standards is no protection, since there is no grant of good-faith immunity in most brain death statutes.[20]

---

[17]223 N.W.2d at 846.

[18]See Overcast, supra n.15, at 370-371 (1985).

[19]Id., citing Jeddeloh and Chatterjee, Legal Problems in Organ Donation, 58 The Surgical Clinics of N. Am. 245 (1978).

[20]Georgia is one state that has added a good-faith immunity provision to its version of the UDDA. See Ga. Code. Ann. §31-10-16 (1981). The Commentary to the UDDA states that it is unnecessary for the Act to address specifically the liability of persons who make determinations of death because "no person authorized by law to determine death, who makes such a determination in accordance with the Act, should, or will be, liable for damages in any civil action or subject to prosecution in any criminal proceeding for his acts or the acts of others based on that determination." This approach begs the question, What if a physician makes a good-faith attempt to act in accordance with the Act but fails to correctly diagnose death?

To summarize, healthcare facilities and their physicians cannot depend on any legal immunity in making determinations of death. Special care should thus be taken to make certain that determinations of brain death are accurate and well-documented. Hospitals may want to require that a second physician always confirm a determination of death made by another physician. Insurance coverage of this issue should also be scrutinized. Finally, careful explanation to the next of kin about when and why death will be declared can lessen the potential for litigation.[21]

§12.4 Acquiring Consent for an Organ Donation*

Once a patient has been identified as a candidate for donation, a hospital or organ procurement agency must have a legal basis for removing the organs. Under the Uniform Anatomical Gift Act, organs cannot be removed unless consent is obtained for the removal. Although the human body and its parts are not considered "property" that may be owned, bought, or sold, the body has traditionally been treated as "quasi-property" for some purposes, most notably to describe the right of a deceased person's next of kin to custody of the body in order to provide final rites and appropriate disposition or the survivor's right to bring a lawsuit for mutilation or other improper treatment of a corpse.[1] Anatomical gift statutes build on this conception by

---

[21]See infra §12.4.2; see also the discussion of Williams v. Hoffman, infra §12.8.

§12.4 *Some of the text of §12.4 is taken from Jane E. Baluss, Legal Issues in Organ Transplantation: Hospital Law in North Carolina (Institute of Government, 1985), pp. 11-14. Reprinted with permission.

[1]One commentator has observed: "It seems obvious that such 'property' is something evolved out of thin air to meet the occasion, and that in reality the personal feelings of the survivors are being protected, under a fiction likely to deceive no one but a lawyer." Prosser and Keeton on Torts §53, at 357 (5th ed. 1984), quoted in Strachan v. John F. Kennedy Memorial Hosp., 109 N.J. 523, 538 A.2d 346 (1988) (parent of suicide victim alleged hospital had committed tort of outrage and was responsible for inappropriate handling of

treating the transfer of body parts as a gift and prescribing procedures that must be observed in order for the gift and acceptance to be legally valid.[2]

Although the UAGA does not allow organs to be removed without express consent, another approach known as "presumed consent" or "required notification" has gained some support in this country and is widely used in others.[3] Under this approach, a reasonable effort must be undertaken by those seeking the donation to contact the decedent's next of kin in order to give them an opportunity to rebut the presumption that the decedent's organs will be donated. Although not widely practiced in the United States, this rule has been adopted in limited form by some states in order to increase donations. Medical ethicists continue to debate its propriety.[4] Maryland uses this approach

---

the body). For a discussion of the now universally accepted view that next of kin do not have an actual property right, but merely a limited right to possess the body for burial purposes, see Lawyer v. Kernodle, 721 F.2d 632 (8th Cir. 1983); Dougherty v. Mercantile-Safe Deposit & Trust Co., 282 Md. 617, 387 A.2d 244 (1978); Sinai Temple v. Kaplan, 54 Cal. App. 3d 1103, 127 Cal. Rptr. 80 (1976).

[2]For additional commentary on the Uniform Anatomical Gift Act, see D. W. Meyers, Medicolegal Implications of Death and Dying §§17:10-11 (1981); Best, Transfers of Bodies and Body Parts Under the Uniform Anatomical Gift Act, 15 Real Property, Probate and Trust J. 806 (1980); Dukeminier, Supplying Organs for Transplantation, 68 Mich. L. Rev. 811 (1972); Note, Human Organ Transplantation: Some Medico-Legal Pitfalls for Transplant Surgeons, 23 U. Fla. L. Rev. 134 (1970).

[3]Denmark, France, Israel, Norway, Spain, Sweden, and Switzerland have various forms of presumed consent laws. Childress, Artificial and Transplanted Organs, I Biolaw 303, 309 (1986). See also Cotton and Sandler, The Regulation of Organ Procurement and Transplantation in the United States, 7 J. Legal Med. 55, 66-67 (1986). One commentator has observed, however, that although the legal framework may be different, the actual practices appear to be much the same. France, for example, has a policy of presumed consent that does not require approval or ratification by the family, but health professionals in that country still seek familial consent. Childress, Some Moral Connections Between Organ Procurement and Organ Distribution, 3 J. Contemp. Health L. & Poly. 85, 93-94 (1987).

[4]In California in 1988 the heart of a man found unconscious on a sidewalk was transplanted six hours after the man died, still unidentified. California Man's Heart Is Transplanted Without Permission, N.Y. Times, April 24, 1988,

in certain emergency situations,[5] and California allows organs to be harvested after an unsuccessful "diligent search," including police investigation, for the next of kin.[6] A number of states permit medical examiners to remove corneal tissue when there is no known objection by the next of kin.[7]

Although all 50 states and the District of Columbia have adopted the mainframe of the Uniform Anatomical Gift Act, they have modified it to address their particular concerns. The following discussion applies to the official revised text of the UAGA as approved in 1987 by the National Conference of Commissioners on Uniform State Laws. Because the Act has been revised so recently, many state statutes still resemble the earlier version of the UAGA. It is especially important, then, for practitioners to refer to the statutes of their own states.

§12.4.1 The Individual Donor[8]

Sufficiency of the Individual's Consent. The philosophical orientation of the UAGA is toward recognition of an individual's

---

at 14, cols. 3-6. The case caused substantial debate among medical ethicists. One law and ethics professor was quoted as saying, "To take vital organs out of someone who is not identified is really incredible. If other people have done it, they haven't talked about it in the newspaper, that's for sure." Apparently, the doctors had followed California's statute, which requires a 24-hour police search for identification of relatives and questioning of visitors to the donor.

[5] Md. Est. & Trusts Code Ann. §4.509 (Supp. 1989).

[6] Cal. Health & Safety Code §7151.5 (West Supp. 1990). See supra n.4.

[7] See the discussion at §12.4.5 infra. The constitutionality of the corneal tissue removal statutes has been unsuccessfully challenged. See Georgia Lions Eye Bank v. Lavant, 255 Ga. 60, 335 S.E.2d 127 (1985) cert. denied sub nom. Lavant v. St. Joseph's Hosp., 475 U.S. 1084 (1986); State v. Powell, 11 Fla. L. Wk. 557, 497 So. 2d 1188 (1986), cert. denied sub nom. Powell v. Florida, 481 U.S. 1059 (1987); Tillman v. Detroit Receiving Hospital, 136 Mich. App. 683, 360 N.W.2d 275 (Mich. App. 1984).

[8] The following description of acceptable donors is derived from UAGA §2. Note that Georgia has separate provisions for adult and minor decedents. Ga. Code Ann. §§44-5-143, 44-5-143.1 (Supp. 1989).

right to determine the use of his organs, regardless of his family's wishes.[9] This orientation differs from past common-law developments in the United States, which either held there were no property rights in the corpse or recognized quasi-property rights belonging to the next of kin.[10] The UAGA explicitly recognizes both the decedent's and the family's limited rights in the corpse and assigns priority to the decedent's express wishes about donation.[11] The Act makes clear that consent of next of kin after death is not required if the donor has made an anatomical gift.[12] Nevertheless, physicians and transplant centers rarely proceed on the basis of the decedent's document of gift alone. Fear of negative publicity and concern for the well-being of the decedent's family have been cited as reasons for this unwillingness to proceed without the additional consent of the decedent's next of kin.[13] While it is understandable that no amount of legal protection will give a healthcare facility much comfort in the face of negative publicity, a shift in the approach made to families should be considered. Rather than seeking the consent

---

[9]Childress, Artificial and Transplanted Organs, I Biolaw 303, 305 (1986).

[10]See, e.g., Holland v. Metalious, 105 N.H. 290, 198 A.2d 654, 7 A.L.R.3d 742 (1964), in which the court upheld the objection made by the family of Grace Metalious (author of *Peyton Place*) to her will's direction that her body be given to a medical school for research.

[11]Childress, supra n.9.

[12]Unif. Anatomical Gift Act §2(h).

[13]See Prottas, The Rules for Asking and Answering: The Role of Law in Organ Donation, 63 U. Det. L. Rev. 183 (1985); R. W. Simmons, S. D. Klein, and R. L. Simmons, The Gift of Life: The Social and Psychological Impact of Organ Transplantations 31-34 (1977). One congressional report goes so far as to comment:

> Unfortunately, there is little concrete evidence in any country that donor cards have substantially increased the availability of organs or tissues for transplantation. Although the cards do provide important community awareness of the desirability of donation, the actual system used for organ retrieval . . . in the United States is dependent on receiving permission from the next of kin. . . . Many health and scientific experts place the blame [for the organ shortage] . . . on the medical profession itself. There is a reluctance by many doctors to assist in the transplantation process.

H. Rep. 769, 98th Cong., 2d Sess., reprinted in 1984 CIS H363-7. See also Childress, supra n.9.

of the next of kin when the decedent has executed a proper gift document, the facility could simply inform the family of the gift; it could then reconsider acting on the gift if the family expresses some disagreement with this course of action.

Section 2 of the revised UAGA provides that any individual who is at least 18 years of age may donate all or part of his own body, effective at his death.[14]

Required Procedure for Donating. An individual may make an anatomical gift only by means of a document of gift signed by the donor. Formerly, the UAGA required that two witnesses sign the gift document; this requirement has been deleted to simplify the making of anatomical gifts.[15] If the donor cannot sign, the document must be signed by another individual and by two witnesses, all of whom have signed at the direction and in the presence of the donor and of each other, and state that it has been so signed. If the document of gift is imprinted on a driver's license, revocation, suspension, expiration, or cancellation of the license does not invalidate the gift. An anatomical gift by will takes effect on the death of the testator, whether or not the will is probated, and the gift is unaffected by a declaration that the will is invalid for testamentary purposes.[16] (See Appendix 12-1 for a sample document-of-gift form.)

Amending or Revoking the Donation. An individual donor may amend or revoke an anatomical gift by means of (1) a signed statement; (2) an oral statement made in the presence of two individuals; (3) any form of communication during a terminal illness or injury addressed to a physician or surgeon;

---

[14]Unif. Anatomical Gift Act §2. Some states have adopted different age requirements. For example, Alaska sets the minimum age at 19 years. Alaska Stat. §13.50.010 (1985). Louisiana substitutes for the age requirement "who is competent to execute a will." La. Rev. Stat. Ann. §17.2352(A) (West) 1951.

[15]Comment, Unif. Anatomical Gift Act §2, 12 U.L.A. 8 (Supp. 1989).

[16]Because most organs must be harvested within several hours after death, the making of anatomical gifts by will is not practical. A donor card carried at all times on one's person is the best way to assure that one's desire to make a gift is carried out.

or (4) the delivery of a signed statement to a specified donee to whom a document of gift has been delivered. A donor can revoke or amend a gift by will by any of these means or in the manner provided for amending or revoking a will. A family member may not amend or revoke the donation of an individual.

Refusing to Donate. The superior right of the individual donor to do what she wishes with her body is also recognized in a new UAGA provision that allows a person to refuse to make an anatomical gift.[17] This amendment provides the option of refusal to individuals who are definitely opposed to the donation for any purpose or of any part of their body as an anatomical gift. An individual may refuse to make an anatomical gift by means of (1) a writing signed in the same manner as a document of gift; (2) a statement attached to or imprinted on an individual's driver's license; or (3) any other writing used to identify the individual as refusing to make an anatomical gift. During a terminal illness or injury, the refusal may be an oral statement or other form of communication. (See Appendix 12-2 for a sample refusal form.)

In the absence of contrary indications by an individual, an anatomical gift of a part is not a refusal to give other parts should adequate consent from the next of kin be obtained.[18] Similarly, in the absence of contrary indications by the donor, a revocation of an anatomical gift is not a refusal to make another anatomical gift; if an individual intends to refuse to make an anatomical gift, she should make the refusal in the manner specified in the Act.

§12.4.2 Gifts by Others[19]

Donation of all or part of a decedent's body may also be made by the following classes of persons, in order of priority: spouse,

---

[17]Unif. Anatomical Gift Act §2(i).

[18]Id. §2(j).

[19]Gifts by individuals other than the donor are treated in §3 of the revised UAGA.

adult child, either parent, adult sibling, grandparent, or decedent's guardian at death. However, donation by any such person is not proper when (1) the decedent has made an unrevoked refusal to make the anatomical gift; (2) a higher-priority person is available at the time of death; (3) the person who authorizes the donation knows of a refusal or contrary indications by the decedent; or (4) the person who authorizes the donation knows of opposition by another survivor who has equal or higher priority.[20] Similarly, a *donee* who knows of refusal or contrary indications by the decedent or objections by a survivor whose priority is equal to or higher than the offeror's priority may not accept the gift. Authorized donors other than the decedent may make a gift simply by signing a gift document (no witness required) or by transmitting a telegraphic, recorded telephonic, or otherwise recorded message or other form of communication from the person that is contemporaneously reduced to writing and signed by the recipient of the communication.[21] (See Appendix 12-3 for a sample document-of-gift form appropriate for donations by someone other than the individual donor.)

An anatomical gift by an authorized person may be revoked by any member of the same or a prior class if, before procedures have begun for the removal of a part from the body, the physician, surgeon, technician, or enucleator removing the part becomes aware of the revocation.[22] If a person of higher priority

---

[20]New York recently amended its gift act to further make consent invalid if either the donor or the donee has "reasons to believe that an anatomical gift is contrary to the decedent's religious or moral beliefs." N.Y. Pub. Health Law §§4301(2), 4301(3) (McKinney 1977 & West Supp. 1990).

[21]Unif. Anatomical Gift Act §3(c). The revised Act added "other form[s] of communication . . . contemporaneously reduced to writing and signed by the recipient." From this author's conversations with healthcare professionals involved in organ procurement, it appears that it has been the practice for many anatomical gifts to be given over the telephone and witnessed in writing, although the applicable anatomical gift statute requires telephonic gifts to be recorded. This revision to the UAGA may have been made in recognition of this common practice.

[22]Id. §3(d). "If there is no prior knowledge of the revocation by the individual removing the organ or tissue, the revocation is ineffective for any purpose and the anatomical gift may be procured and utilized as though no

is available, but does not make a gift, such failure is not an objection to the making of a gift, and a person of a lower priority may make the gift.

While the UAGA does not address the priority of rights among multiple donees when a donor has executed conflicting gift documents, this issue is not unknown. A New Hampshire court dealt with conflicting whole-body gifts, both of which were refused by the donees, by declaring execution of the gift impossible and awarding full custody of the body to the next of kin for burial.[23]

When soliciting organ donations from next of kin, it is good practice for the physician or hospital involved to explain to the patient's family the nature of the patient's condition, the time the organs will be removed, the extent to which the body will be cut or altered, and the procedure and timing of the legal determination of death. Such matters are likely to be unfamiliar and even confusing to prospective donors, especially when the decedent's life support will not be disconnected until the time for organ removal.[24] The physician or facility should ensure that the donor fully understands and agrees—before organs are removed. Such an approach would be consistent with the general principles of informed consent to medical procedures. Donor families also usually wish to know what happened as a result of the donation, although in satisfying a request for such information the hospital should preserve the confidentiality of the organ recipient.

The hospital must exercise care to ask the proper person for a deceased patient's organs and to be sure that no one with higher priority under the anatomical gift statute either is available to give consent or is known to object to organ donation. In a recent New York case, Nicoletta v. Rochester Eye and Human Parts Bank,[25] a father brought action against an eye bank and

---

attempted revocation had occurred." Id. §3, Comment, 12 U.L.A. 11 (Supp. 1989).

[23]Holland v. Metalious, 105 N.H. 290, 198 A. 2d 654, 7 A.L.R.3d 742 (1964).

[24]See the discussion of Williams v. Hoffman, infra §12.8.

[25]136 Misc. 2d 1065, 519 N.Y.S. 2d 928 (1987).

hospital to recover for physical, emotional, and psychological injuries he allegedly suffered as a result of the removal of his son's eyes for donation following a motorcycle accident. On the night of decedent's accident, a woman claiming to be the patient's wife signed a hospital form authorizing emergency treatment. After decedent's death, she signed another form permitting the removal of his eyes. The woman authorizing the donation was not the decedent's wife, although she had resided with him for ten years and was the mother of their two children. The court granted defendants' motion for summary judgment because testimony established as a matter of law that defendants acted in good faith. New York's anatomical gift act, like most states' anatomical gift acts,[26] provides that a person acting in good faith in accord with the terms of the Act is immune from civil and criminal liability.[27] Although a determination as to whether a person acted in good faith is usually a factual issue inappropriate on a motion for summary judgment, the court decided that the state legislature had created an objective standard by which the good faith of a donee could be measured.[28]

The court determined that the eye bank had acted in good faith by justifiably relying on the written permission form provided to it by the hospital. The hospital also acted in good faith in relying on the representations of the woman purporting to be the decedent's wife; nurses had questioned her identity when she signed the permission form and the woman's companions had not contradicted her answers. Furthermore, on the night of the accident the decedent's father had not challenged the woman's authority to sign the emergency treatment form.[29]

---

[26]See infra §12.8.

[27]*Nicoletta* is the only reported case dealing with the question of good faith in connection with anatomical gifts.

[28]"The Uniform Anatomical Gift Act establishes a statutory scheme which outlines the means of effecting an anatomical gift, the classes of individuals entitled to effect such a gift, and the circumstances under which such a gift must be deemed null and void. None of the previous good-faith cases have involved such a definitive standard by which to judge a defendant's conduct." 519 N.Y.S. 2d at 931.

[29]The court stated that "[t]o require further action on the part of the

In Tucker's Administrator v. Lower,[30] the hospital failed to
obtain permission for the gift at all. Tucker was brought to the
hospital with a severe head injury. Although he carried no
personal identification, his wallet contained a business card with
his brother's name. The hospital staff either did not find the card
or, finding it, did not act on it. A concerned friend of Tucker's
spent several hours at the hospital the day after his accident
trying to learn if Tucker had been admitted, but learned nothing.
The hospital staff made several calls to the police, who were
unable to locate Tucker's relatives. Approximately 24 hours after
he was admitted, Tucker was declared dead on the basis of
irreversible brain failure, life-support measures were discontinued, and his heart removed and transplanted into another
patient. Tucker's brother brought a $1 million wrongful death
action against the physicians involved in Tucker's treatment and
the subsequent transplant. The jury ultimately found for the
defendants. Its decision turned on the legal and medical acceptability of the brain death criterion used in declaring Tucker
dead.[31] The role played by the hospital's failure to notify and
obtain consent from the plaintiff cannot be determined because
no written opinion was produced. However, several accounts of
the case agree that this failure probably supplied the critical
motivation behind the brother's lawsuit,[32] which resulted in

---

defendant would not only impose an unreasonable duty on the Hospital, but
would also run afoul of public policy considerations, as such a decision would
tend to jeopardize the whole process of organ donation by causing unnecessary
delays, thereby frustrating the entire intent of the Uniform Anatomical Gift
Act." 519 N.Y.S. 2d at 932.

[30]No. 2381, Ct. Law & Eq., Richmond, Va. (May 25, 1972). In the absence
of a published opinion in this case, the information presented here has been
taken from discussions in R. Scott, The Body as Property 151-152 (1981); R.
W. Simmons, S. D. Klein, and R. L. Simmons, The Gift of Life: The Social and
Psychological Impact of Organ Transplantations 31-34 (1977); and Frederick,
Medical Jurisprudence: Determining the Time of Death of the Heart Transplant
Donor, 51 N.C.L. Rev. 174-176 (1972).

[31]This aspect of the Tucker case is discussed at length in 51 N.C.L. Rev.
181-184; however, the issues raised have been effectively resolved by enactment of the brain-death statutes.

[32]R. Scott, supra n.30; Simmons, supra n.30.

considerable notoriety[33] as well as legal expense for the defendant, though the plaintiff did not recover damages on the technical
issue of wrongful death.

While not the subject of a lawsuit, a recent incident in
California in which the heart of an unidentified man was
harvested after a diligent but unsuccessful attempt to identify
him and his next of kin caused considerable debate among
medical ethicists.[34]

§12.4.3 Donees

Valid donees include a hospital, physician, surgeon, or procurement organization who will use the donation for transplantation,
therapy, medical or dental education, research, or scientific
advancement; an accredited medical or dental school, college,
or university for use in education, research, or scientific advancement; and a specified individual for therapy or transplantation
needed by him.[35] A donee need not accept an anatomical gift.

Because it is possible to designate specified individuals,
professionals, or institutions, it has been suggested that donors
may likewise specify a group or groups that should receive or
should be denied the gift; a donor might, for example, specify
that a gift not be used for members of certain racial, religious,
or other groups.[36] The legal implications of a physician or
hospital donee's accepting a gift with restrictions contrary to

---

[33]The case received considerable adverse publicity, partly because the
transplant was one of the earliest performed in this country and partly because
of its racial overtones (Tucker is described as a black laborer).

[34]N.Y. Times, April 24, 1988, p. 14, cols. 3-6; see discussion supra §12.4,
n.4.

[35]Unif. Anatomical Gift Act §6. The 1986 federal Task Force recommended
that donated organs be considered "national resources." What impact such a
view might have on the right of donors to specify donees remains to be seen.
Most donors do not specify an individual recipient. The unlikelihood that a
tissue match would be successful makes such gifts quite rare. Under the UAGA,
however, donors do possess the right to make such choices.

[36]Childress, Some Moral Connections Between Organ Procurement and
Organ Distribution, 3 J. Contemp. Health L. & Poly. 85, 96 (1987).

public policy are unclear. The consequences of refusing such a gift are equally unknown, since there is no precedent for this issue. The question involves opposing moral and ethical concerns: if an organ procurement team refuses to accept a gift because it is subject to morally offensive restrictions, is it improperly ignoring another patient whose life could have been extended by the rejected organ? The courts have not yet faced these issues.

If a donee is not designated or if the donee is not available or rejects the anatomical gift, the anatomical gift may be accepted by any hospital.[37] If the donee knows of the decedent's refusal or contrary indications to make a gift, or that a gift by a member of a class having priority to act is opposed by a member of the same or a prior class, the donee may not accept the gift.[38]

§12.4.4 Execution and Delivery of the Gift

It is not necessary that a document of gift be physically delivered to a donee before the donor's death in order for the gift to be valid, but the donor may choose to deliver the gift document to a designated donee or to deposit it with any hospital, procurement organization, or registry office that accepts such documents for safekeeping and facilitation of the procedures after death. Such documents must be made available to interested parties for inspection after the donor's death.[39]

§12.4.5 Corneal Enucleations

At least 12 states have chosen to avoid the elaborate consent procedures for the removal of corneas and instead have adopted variants of a "presumed consent" law in this area.[40] These laws

---

[37]Unif. Anatomical Gift Act §6(b).
[38]Id. §6(c).
[39]Id. §7.
[40]Task Force Report at 30. See, e.g., Fla. Stat. §732.9185 (West Supp.

allow corneas to be taken "unless there is known objection" when the body of the deceased is under the jurisdiction of the coroner or medical examiner.[41] State laws allowing the removal of corneal tissue for transplant without giving notice to the next of kin have withstood constitutional attack. The Supreme Court, in Lavant v. St. Joseph's Hospital,[42] let stand a Georgia Supreme Court decision that the family of a deceased person has only a common-law right, not a constitutional right, to control the decedent's body. Because the common law may be modified or abrogated by the legislature, the General Assembly of Georgia had the power to authorize the "presumed consent" procedure. No notification or opportunity to object had to be provided under the due process clause of the Constitution. The same result has been reached with respect to Florida's and Michigan's cornea removal statutes.[43]

§12.4.6 Medical Examiner and Coroner Cases[44]

A coroner or medical examiner may release and permit the removal of a part from a body within that official's custody for transplantation or therapy if the official has received a request for the part from a hospital, physician, surgeon, or procurement

---

1989); Ky. Rev. Stat. Ann. §311.187 (Michie/Bobbs-Merrill Supp. 1988); and Md. Est. and Trusts Code Ann. §4.509.1 (Supp. 1989).

[41]The Task Force on Organ Transplantation concluded that these laws have been effective in increasing the supply of corneal tissue.

[42]See Georgia Lions Eye Bank v. Lavant, 255 Ga. 60, 335 S.E.2d 127 (1985), cert. denied sub nom. Lavant v. St. Joseph's Hosp., 475 U.S. 1084 (1986).

[43]State v. Powell, 497 So. 2d 1188 (Fla. 1980), cert. denied sub nom. Powell v. Florida, 481 U.S. 1059 (1987); Tillman v. Detroit Receiving Hosp., 360 N.W.2d 275 (Mich. App. 1984).

[44]Much of the following discussion is based on the treatment of this issue in Rose, Medicolegal Problems Associated with Organ and Tissue Transplantations, 31 Med. Tr. Tech. Q. 99, 108-109 (1984), and Overcast, Evans, and Merriken, Malpractice Issues in Heart Transplantation, 10 Am. J.L. & Med. 363, 372-374 (omitting citations).

organization.[45] Such authorization is permitted only if the official has made a reasonable effort, "taking into account the useful life of the part," to locate and examine the decedent's medical records and inform persons authorized to make a gift of their option to make (or object to making) an anatomical gift. The official must also not know of a refusal or contrary indication by the decedent or an objection by a person having authority to make the anatomical gift. The removal of the part must (1) be by a physician, surgeon, or technician, or by an enucleator in the case of eyes; (2) not interfere with any autopsy or investigation; and (3) be in accordance with accepted medical standards. Cosmetic restoration must be done, if appropriate.

An official releasing and permitting the removal of a part must maintain a permanent record of the name of the decedent, the person making the request, the date and purposes of the request, the part requested, and the person to whom it was released.[46]

Section 11(b) of the UAGA provides that the Act is subject to the laws of the state governing autopsies. In practice there is little conflict between organ retrieval and police investigation or autopsies. Cooperation between a procurement organization and the medical examiner usually permits the procurement of organs before an examination of the body without compromising subsequent civil or criminal litigation.[47] In a model program of such cooperation,[48] the attending physician, hospital, or transplant team notifies the medical examiner of potential deaths that may fall within the jurisdiction of the medical examiner's office as soon as the prognosis of death is determined. Such persons provide the history, the circumstances of death, and other pertinent data to the medical examiner's office. The medical

---

[45]Unif. Anatomical Gift Act §4.

[46]Id. §4(c).

[47]It is extremely rare for the necessity of a medical examination to preclude organ donation. Telephone conversation with Dr. Butts, North Carolina Examiner's Office (Oct. 24, 1986).

[48]This discussion describes the protocol followed by the medical examiner in Dade County, Florida, and nearby transplant programs. See Rose, supra n. 44.

examiner then decides on the basis of accepted forensic procedures and with attention toward any ongoing police investigation if it will permit organ retrieval. It can only release the part, of course, if it has authority under the anatomical gift act to do so, that is, if consent of the appropriate individuals has been obtained or is not required.

In medical examiner cases, particular care must be taken with documentation. As stated above, the UAGA sets forth the documentation required with respect to the release of the organ. Other documentation should be kept relating to the ongoing police investigation. In order to do this, the medical examiner should be present at the time of organ retrieval, or the transplant surgeon removing the organs should describe in detail the surgical dissection and the absence of injury to this area of the body. The attending physician, transplant team, and medical examiner should cooperate to produce detailed documentation of the following information: (1) the circumstances surrounding the injury; (2) the status of the victim when first viewed at the scene or examined at the hospital; (3) the status of the victim during hospitalization; (4) the evidence that led to the pronouncement of death; (5) the absence of injuries or other medical causes of death related to the donated organs; and (6) the medical examiner's or coroner's autopsy findings.[49] Records clearly indicating the fact of brain death, the irreversibility of the injury, and the actions of the transplant team are essential to the legal inquiry into cause of death. These records will show conclusively at any subsequent trial that organ donation was not an independent, intervening cause of death. Persons accused of murder or manslaughter have on various occasions attempted to claim that death was caused not by their actions but by the actions of physicians in organ retrieval, although courts have consistently refused this defense.[50] In addition to keeping ade-

---

[49]Id. at 109.

[50]This result follows logically from brain death statutes, which provide a legal basis for physicians to terminate life support systems where no brain function exists. See, e.g., State v. Holsclaw, 42 N.C. App. 696, 257 S.E.2d 650 (1979); California v. Saldana, 47 Cal. App. 3d 954, 121 Cal. Rptr. 243 (Cal. App. 1975); State v. Brown, 8 Or. App. 72, 491 P.2d 1193 (1971).

quate records, in cases of potential criminal prosecution it is also a wise practice for the transplant center to obtain the additional permission of the prosecuting attorney with jurisdiction over the case. Though not legally mandated in most states, obtaining the prosecuting attorney's permission is advisable to avoid charges of interference with criminal law enforcement.[51]

Although the cooperative efforts between transplant centers and medical examiner's offices will often be locally derived, some states have laws relating to procedures between the two institutions, and these should be consulted.[52]

§12.5 Obligations of Hospitals in Organ Procurement

To a great extent, the number of organs donated each year in any hospital depends on the hospital's involvement in securing consent from families of suitable donors. Although in some cases organ donation may be suggested by patients or their families, the possibility of donation more commonly is initiated by an attending physician, a hospital staff member, or a transplant coordinator who becomes aware of a potential donor through hospital records, making hospital rounds, or through information from someone who knows about the patient's case. New state and federal laws require hospitals to solicit organ donations from families of dead or dying patients who are suitable candidates for organ donation. These laws ensure a wider canvassing of the hospital population for potential donors and counter the traditional reluctance hospital staff have in approaching next of kin about organ gifts.[1]

---

[51]Overcast, supra n.44, at 374.

[52]See, e.g., Texas Stat. Ann. §49.25(6a) (Vernon 1979).

§12.5 [1]Despite their general acceptance, "required request" policies have not been without criticism. See Martyn, Wright, and Clark, Required Request for Organ Donation: Moral, Clinical, and Legal Problems, Hastings Ctr. Rep. 27 (April/May 1988) (maintaining that required request policies create conflicts of interest of substantial moral disvalue for practitioners, families, and society). For a response, see Caplan, Professional Arrogance and Public Misunderstanding, Hastings Ctr. Rep. 34 (April/May 1988).

§12.5.1 Federal Law

Section 1138(a) of the Social Security Act allows a hospital that otherwise meets the conditions of participation for the Medicare or Medicaid program to participate in either program only if it establishes written protocols to identify potential organ donors. The protocols must assure that families of potential donors are made aware that they have an option to donate (or to decline to donate) organs or tissue, while at the same time encouraging discretion and sensitivity with respect to the circumstances, views, and beliefs of the families of potential donors. Furthermore, the protocols must require that an organ procurement agency designated by the Secretary of Health and Human Services be notified of potential organ donors.[2]

§12.5.2 State Law

Before 1985, no state had a mandatory solicitation law of any variety. Since that year, however, state legislatures have adopted such laws with great speed. In 1988, 42 states and the District of Columbia had passed mandatory solicitation laws.[3] The 1987 revisions of the UAGA also included the addition of such a provision. Hospitals are required under the provision to routinely inquire of all patients admitted to a hospital whether they are an organ donor and, at or near the time of death of a patient, to request an anatomical gift from the next of kin.[4]

Typical "required request" laws passed by state legislatures require a hospital administrator, or her designated representative, to request donation of a suitable patient's organs at the time of death from persons who may legally consent to the anatomical gift. Exceptions to this duty of solicitation exist when the

---

[2] 42 U.S.C.A. §1320b-8. For purposes of §1138(a), the term "organ" means a human kidney, liver, heart, lung, or pancreas.

[3] 83 State Health Notes, June 1988, at 1.

[4] Unif. Anatomical Gift Act §5. The request is not required if an anatomical gift from the decedent would not be suitable.

administrator has actual notice of contrary intentions by the decedent, encounters opposition by any person qualified to donate the patient's organs, or has any reason to believe that the gift is contrary to the decedent's religious beliefs.[5] Many laws of this type, more appropriately called "required routine contact" laws, do not require actual solicitation but mandate only that hospitals create protocols through which next of kin will be notified about the possibility of donating organs or tissues.[6] Statutes also differ with respect to the following provisions: recording organ donation inquiries and decisions on death certificates; requiring the administrator to notify the regional organ procurement agency; and the extent to which state regulatory agencies are involved in monitoring compliance and establishing requirements for training of the health professionals who will make the requests.[7] Failure to comply with a state's required request law results in varying penalties. Some statutes appear to contain no enforcement mechanism,[8] while others provide for administrative or professional sanctions.[9] State licensing of hospitals may also be implicated,[10] as well as participation in a state's Medicaid program.[11]

Hospital officials who make solicitations should bear in mind that no one has an affirmative duty to be an organ or tissue donor,[12] and they should not press for donations after receiving a clear refusal.

---

[5]See, e.g., N.Y. Pub. Health Law §4351 (West Supp. 1987); Cal. Health & Safety Code §7184(a) (West Supp. 1987); Me. Rev. Stat. Ann. tit. 22, §2910 (West Supp. 1986); Wash. Rev. Code Ann. §68.08.650 (West Supp. 1987).

[6]See, e.g., Tenn. Code Ann. §68-30-110 (1987).

[7]Task Force Report, at 34. See statutes cited in nn.5 and 6 supra.

[8]See, e.g., N.Y. Pub. Health Law §4351 (West Supp. 1987).

[9]See, e.g., Unif. Anatomical Gift Act §5.

[10]See, e.g., Ky. Rev. Stat. §311.241 (Supp. 1986).

[11]83 State Health Notes, June 1988, at 2 (citing pending California bill).

[12]Conversely, is there a legal *right* to be a donor? This question has arisen in the context of condemned prisoners seeking state assistance to enable them to donate their organs after execution. North Carolina has allowed donation of organs by an executed prisoner. See *Barfield Will Donate Organs for Transplantation*, News and Observer (Raleigh, N.C.), Nov. 2, 1984; Campbell v. Wainwright, 416 F.2d 949 (5th Cir. 1969), cert. denied, 397 U.S. 953

§12.6 Other Programs to Encourage Donation

Driver's License Applications.   To encourage organ donation, most states routinely offer the opportunity to become a donor as part of a driver's license application.[1] Interested persons receive copies of the uniform donor card and explanatory materials, and the driver's license itself designates them as donors. Although signed donor cards constitute legally effective consent, they have played only a minor role in the current system of organ procurement.[2] Only a small percentage of the general public carries the donor cards,[3] and the cards are seldom found at the scene of fatal accidents or otherwise brought to the attention of physicians and families.[4] The impenetrable barrier to the effectiveness of donor cards, however, is physicians and hospitals themselves. Despite the Act's clear statement of the validity of gifts made by the properly executed gift document of an individual, hospitals and physicians have been opposed to proceeding on the basis of even a fully witnessed and legally adequate uniform donor card without also receiving permission from the patient's family.[5]

Tax and Organ Credits.   Tax incentives or rewards for donors have been seriously considered as well. Amendments to the Internal Revenue Code have been proposed that would provide

---

(1970) (refusal to transport prisoner under death sentence to another state for testing as kidney donor); see also Commentary, A Condemned Man's Last Wish: Organ Donation and a "Meaningful Death," 9 Hastings Ctr. Rep. 16 (1979).

§12.6   [1]Cotton and Sandler, The Regulation of Organ Procurement and Transplantation in the United States, 7 J. Legal Med. 55, 63 (1986). The revised UAGA recommends a driver's license form that allows an individual to designate her refusal to allow an anatomical gift. See Appendix 12-2.

[2]Task Force Report, at 29.

[3]A 1985 Gallup survey indicated that while 93 percent of Americans were aware of organ transplants, only 17 percent of them carried donor cards. U.S. Department of Health and Human Services, Organ Transplantation Q. & A. (DHHS Publication No. HRS-A-OC 86-1) (Dec. 1985), at 10.

[4]Task Force Report, at 29.

[5]Id.; see discussion supra §12.4.1.

income and estate tax deductions to decedents whose organs are donated.[6] Under one such proposal, a decedent's last taxable year would be allowed a $25,000 deduction for each qualified transplant donation.[7] State legislation for tax credits has been proposed as well.[8] Tax relief proposals for donors have been objected to on the ground that such indirect incentives are no different than direct payments, which are prohibited by federal law. There is also concern that such tax policies would benefit the middle and upper classes (who could benefit from a deduction) more than the poor.[9]

Several analysts in the field have also suggested a system of family credits for organ donations. Under a program of this kind, a family that participated in donations would acquire a position of priority for the receipt of an organ should one of its family members later require transplantation. The idea of family credits has not received very favorable response because it is considered threatening to the voluntary, cooperative system of donation currently in place.[10]

C. Removal and Distribution of Organs

§12.7 Statutory Procedures for Removal

A person who donates his own tissues may designate a specific surgeon or physician to carry out the procedures to remove the organ.[1] In the absence of a designation or if the designee is not available when the donor dies, the donee or other person authorized to accept the anatomical gift may employ or authorize

---

[6]See H.R. 540, 98th Cong., 1st Sess. (1983), which was not enacted.
[7]Id.
[8]83 State Health Notes, June 1988, at 3.
[9]Childress, supra n.7, at 312.
[10]Id.
§12.7 [1]Unif. Anatomical Gift Act §2(d).

any qualified person to perform the appropriate procedures.[2] All tissue-removal procedures must be performed by a physician or surgeon, except that in some states corneal enucleations may be performed by a licensed enucleator or technician, physician's assistant, registered or licensed practical nurse, or advanced medical student who has been trained and certified to carry out the procedure.[3] As noted earlier,[4] physicians who pronounce death are not allowed to participate in the procedures for removing or transplanting a part.

The donee of an entire body may authorize embalming and the use of the body in funeral services.[5] Some state laws require donees to do so when it will not destroy the gift, in order to take into account the interest of survivors in memorial ceremonies.[6] The donee of only part of the body must have the donated parts removed without unnecessary mutilation;[7] after removal of the organs, custody of the remainder of the body vests in the person who would normally be responsible for its final disposition.[8] Subject to these requirements, the rights created by an anatomical gift supersede all other rights in the body, except with respect to autopsies.[9] A valid gift also authorizes the donee to make any reasonable medical examinations necessary to determine the suitability of the gift for its intended use.[10]

---

[2]Id.

[3]Id.; see, e.g., N.C. Gen. Stat. §130A-406(e) (1943) ("qualified individual"); La. Rev. Stat. Ann. §17:2354.1 (West 1951) ("physician, technician, or other authorized person"); Del. Code Ann. tit. 24, §1783(d) (1981) ("qualified undertaker").

[4]See §12.3.1.

[5]Unif. Anatomical Gift Act §8(a).

[6]See, e.g., N.C. Gen. Stat. §130A-409.

[7]Unif. Anatomical Gift Act §8(a). This provision of the UAGA would suggest that the donee, even if an individual, might be subject to some liability for mutilation of the corpse. No reported cases suggest this view, however, and the provision is generally understood to place liability for mutilation on the physician removing the parts. The good-faith immunity provision of the UAGA should also apply to the donee, however.

[8]Unif. Anatomical Gift Act §8(a).

[9]Id. See discussion in §12.4.6.

[10]Id. §11(a).

§12.8 Liability for Treatment of Donors

Nothing in the law of anatomical gifts relieves physicians or hospitals of liability for negligence or malpractice in treating organ donors before their death. Section 11(c) of the revised UAGA provides that a person who acts in good faith in accord with the terms of the Act or with the anatomical gift laws of another state (or foreign country), or who attempts in good faith to do so,[1] is not liable for that act in any civil or criminal proceeding.[2] However, the treatment of the donor prior to death is considered outside the terms of the Act, and the immunity provision does not apply. This issue was squarely tested in the Wisconsin case of Williams v. Hoffman.[3]

In that case an accident victim with extensive brain damage was brought to the hospital on a Friday evening. During the night she suffered respiratory arrest and was placed on a respirator. The next morning her husband was informed that she had died, and he subsequently agreed to donate her kidneys. The woman was maintained on the respirator until 8:20 A.M. on Monday, when the attending physician pronounced her dead. The respirator was turned off and the kidney removal was begun. On the same morning, after having announced his wife's death at their church on Sunday and making funeral arrangements, the husband learned that his wife's body was not in the hospital morgue as he had thought, that she had not been pronounced dead until that morning, and that her kidneys were at that time being removed. He rushed to the hospital to determine her true condition and stop the operation, but he arrived too late.

---

§12.8 [1]Some state anatomical gift acts omit reference to the anatomical gift laws of another state or foreign country. See, e.g., Ga. Code Ann. §44-5-148(c) (1981).

[2]The state gift statutes sometimes vary the protection afforded by this immunity provision. For example, North Carolina has adopted a more stringent due care standard. N.C. Gen. Stat. §130A-409 (1943). Oregon's statute substitutes "with probable cause" for "in good faith." Or. Rev. Stat. §97.290(3) (1953). Missouri inserts "without negligence and" preceding "in good faith." Mo. Ann. Stat. §194-270(3) (1983).

[3]66 Wis. 2d 145, 223 N.W.2d 844, 76 A.L.R.3d 880 (1974).

Contending that his wife had not actually died until her kidneys were removed, the husband brought suit as her personal representative for assault, battery, and negligence; he also sued in his own right for willful and intentional mutilation of a corpse (or, alternatively, negligent mutilation of a corpse) and negligent communication of a premature and erroneous death message. Both the attending physician and the county that operated the hospital were named as defendants.

The defendants raised the immunity provision of the state's anatomical gift act as a defense to all of the complaints. The trial court upheld the assertion of total immunity against the plaintiff's challenge, and the plaintiff appealed to the state supreme court. That court rejected the defendants' assertion of total immunity, holding instead that the complaints on behalf of the deceased donor for negligence, assault, and battery while she was still alive did not fall within the immunity provision and that damages could be recovered if plaintiff could support his factual contentions. Complaints arising from the treatment of the donor before death were unprotected by the immunity provision's application to actions taken "in accord with the terms" of the statute; rather, that provision was limited to matters relating to the mechanics of giving and receiving anatomical gifts, the determination of time of death,[4] and the removal of organs without unnecessary mutilation.

The court in *Hoffman* held that the defendants could successfully raise the immunity provision as a defense to the complaint for mutilation of the corpse. The anatomical gift statute specifies that removal of organs from deceased donors must be performed without "unnecessary mutilation."[5] A phy-

---

[4]See the discussion at §12.3.2. The court also upheld the constitutionality of the good-faith immunity provision under the Wisconsin constitution. In dicta the court noted that the provision extending immunity to actions taken in compliance with other states' anatomical gift statutes did not unconstitutionally delegate Wisconsin's legislative powers to other legislatures, but merely reflected a policy decision to regard as lawful in Wisconsin actions that would be lawful elsewhere.

[5]Unif. Anatomical Gift Act §8.

sician's liability for unnecessary mutilation will thus depend on the factual determination of her "good faith" compliance.

It is instructive to note that the real impetus behind the *Hoffman* case was apparently the physician's or hospital's failure, when soliciting the organ donation, to tell the patient's husband the complete nature of her condition, the time the organs would be removed, and the procedure and timing of the legal declaration of death. Whether this failure by itself constituted a viable cause of action could not be addressed in *Hoffman*, since the appeal before the court was limited to the procedural issue of whether the lower court was correct in allowing the defendants to raise the immunity provision as an affirmative defense to the initial complaint before the factual merits of the case had been addressed.

Liability for incorrect determinations of death is discussed elsewhere.[6]

§12.9 Distribution of Organs

The National Organ Transplant Act makes it a federal crime to buy, sell, or otherwise benefit from commerce in organs in this country.[1] Violators of this provision are subject to a maximum fine of $50,000 and/or imprisonment for up to five years.[2] At least ten states have passed similar laws.[3]

---

[6]See the discussion at §12.3.2 supra.

§12.9   [1]National Organ Transplant Act, Pub. L. No. 98-507, 98 Stat. 2339 (1984). Despite this prohibition, a ten-month investigation conducted in 23 countries and published in the Pittsburg Press (The Challenge of a Miracle: Selling the Gift, by A. Schneider and M. Flaherty, Pittsburgh Press, Nov. 3-10, 1985) discovered a flourishing international market in buying, selling, and distributing kidneys. The investigation cited among practices in the United States the exportation and sale of 300 cadaver kidneys in 1984 and line-jumping by wealthy foreigners in American transplant centers. In other countries, live kidney donors are openly paid. Organs for Sale: From Marketplace to Jungle, Hastings Ctr. Rep. 3 (Feb. 1986). See Note, The Sale of Human Organs: Implicating a Privacy Right, 21 Val. U. L. Rev. 741 (1987) (arguing prohibition on sale of human organs infringes on fundamental right).

[2]National Organ Transplant Act.

[3]83 State Health Notes, at 4. See, e.g., statutes in California (1984), New

Aside from this prohibition against sale, there was very little governmental oversight of the distribution of donor organs until recently. In the absence of regulation, the early years of transplantation were characterized by a diversity of practices and protocols for histocompatibility testing, organ procurement, criteria for donor and organ acceptability, and patient selection.[4] The system was seen as "basically fair and, to a large extent, [it] has succeeded in distributing organs equitably."[5] Now the OPTN may prescribe rules for member organizations concerning the distribution of organs obtained within a transplant center.[6] Absent such rules, a transplant center may do whatever it wishes with organs obtained in-house, though as a practical matter the organ procurement organization with which it is affiliated will have policies on the distribution of organs.[7]

Currently, the two major criteria used to determine who will receive scarce organs are the probability of successful transplantation and the urgency of need. These criteria, reflecting "medical utility"—the maximization of welfare among patients suffering from end-stage organ disease—are widely accepted as just.[8] There is still much debate, however, over their application. For instance, is success measured by the length of a patient's life or its quality? There is also sometimes considerable tension between the urgency-of-need and the probability-of-success criteria.[9] The Task Force recommended in 1986 that a highly sensitized patient should be given priority over equivalently

---

York and Texas (1985), Georgia, Louisiana, Tennessee and West Virginia (1986), Florida, Illinois and Nevada (1987).

[4]Task Force Report, at 68.

[5]Id. at 85.

[6]53 Fed. Reg. 6544 (Mar. 1, 1988).

[7]Id.

[8]Childress, Artificial and Transplanted Organs, I Biolaw 303, 316 (1986). Medical utility is distinguished from social utility, which also has its proponents. Social utility would require consideration of a particular patient's, or type of patient's, value to society. See Childress, Some Moral Connections Between Organ Procurement and Distribution, 3 J. Contemp. Health L. & Poly. 85, 98-99 (1987).

[9]Id.

matched nonsensitized patients,[10] favoring in this regard the urgency-of-need criterion, since the success rates are lower for the sensitized patients than for the nonsensitized.[11] If two or more patients are equally suitable candidates for a particular organ according to medical criteria, the length of time a patient has waited for the organ has been seen as the fairest way to make the final selection.[12]

Other criteria have been applied in organ recipient selection. Age, lifestyle, the patient's support network, and whether the patient has already received one or more transplants have been variously considered and applied as additional factors to bear on the selection process. Arguments exist both for and against their importance.[13] More objectionable criteria, such a patient's ability to pay, have also been applied, drawing wide criticism. Reports that some nonresident, nonimmigrant aliens have received priority over American citizens for scarce organs donated

---

[10]Id.; Task Force Report, at 71-73, 83. A state of "sensitization" is indicated by the presence of antibodies to HLA antigens. Patients are exposed to foreign HLA antigens through blood transfusions, prior pregnancies, or by having had and rejected a previous organ transplant. Id. at 71. Over half of all patients waiting for a cadaveric kidney transplant in the U.S. are sensitized. Id.

[11]Childress, Artificial and Transplanted Organs, I Biolaw 303, 317 (1986).

[12]Task Force Report, at 86-89.

[13]See Task Force Report, at 89-91; Childress, supra n.11, at 317-319; Childress, supra n.8, at 85.

The Massachusetts Task Force on Organ Transplantation (1983) "flatly rejected arbitrary nonmedical criteria in the initial patient screening process." Annas, Regulating Heart and Liver Transplantation, 25 Jurimetrics 249, 252 (1985). Annas, a member of a statewide public task force, explained that "[F]or example, any specific age limit is an arbitrary excluder, although age can appropriately be taken into account as one possible factor that might influence ability to survive and prospects for rehabilitation." Likewise, alcoholics cannot be excluded from liver transplantation as a class, although active alcoholism is a factor to consider because it could affect the patient's ability to adhere to a rehabilitation regimen. Id. at 253. While the federal Task Force concluded in 1986 that patients with alcoholic cirrhosis do not do sufficiently well to be considered primary candidates for liver transplantation, this view has been challenged on both moral and medical grounds. See Liver Transplants for Alcoholics, The Wash. Post, Nov. 29, 1988, Health Section, at 14.

in the United States have led to a number of proposals to limit the number of transplants in any transplant center to be performed on nonimmigrant aliens.[14]

§12.10 Preservation of Donor Confidentiality

Hospitals should routinely safeguard the identity and privacy of all organ donors to the extent desired by the donor or, in the case of cadaver organs, by the surviving family. In current practice, even the recipient of an organ is not usually told the donor's identity. While this protocol of confidentiality has been established by hospitals out of respect for the privacy of donors and their families, the *legal* protection afforded this information is more dubious. American law is ambiguous about the confidentiality of medical records generally, and the mere identity of a patient, by itself, is rarely considered confidential.[1] There are only a few decisions that recognize a cause of action against healthcare providers for improper disclosure, and very few reported cases in which a provider paid damages.[2]

Can a hospital be required to disclose the names of donors? In Head v. Colloton,[3] the Iowa Supreme Court ruled that the state's public records statute did not require a state hospital to disclose to a potential transplant recipient the name of a potential

---

[14]Task Force Report, at 93-95.

§12.10   [1]A. Dellinger, Medical Records, in Hospital Law in North Carolina 29 (1986). Several recent cases and legislative enactments have protected the identities of patients with certain stigmatizing conditions. Id. at 37. In South Fla. Blood Serv. v. Rasmussen, 467 So. 2d 798 (Fla. Dist. Ct. App. 1985), a Florida court disapproved of disclosure when a person who contracted AIDS from a blood transfusion sought the names of the blood donors. Id. at 37, n.179.

[2]Id. at 29, 35.

[3]331 N.W.2d 870 (Iowa 1983). The case is discussed in detail in Kemna, Confidentiality of Organ Donor Registry Records Versus the Interest in Preserving Human Life, 5 J. Legal Med. 117 (1984) (urging that the *Head* decision should be read as relevant only to relief under the public records statute, leaving open possibility of equitable remedy under duty-to-rescue doctrine).

donor. The hospital was allowed to protect the potential donor's name because she was a "patient" of the hospital. The plaintiff in *Colloton* was a cancer patient seeking a bone marrow transplant who learned that the hospital where he was being treated had a registry of transplant donors[4] that included the name of a potentially compatible donor. He sought a court order directing the hospital either to request a marrow donation on his behalf or to release the potential donor's name so that he could approach her directly. The potential donor had submitted to tissue typing at the hospital to determine her suitability as a blood platelet donor for a member of her family. The hospital, when it subsequently established an experimental program involving bone marrow transplants between unrelated persons, placed this woman's name, without her knowledge or consent, in the bone marrow transplant registry. In fact, she had expressly refused to be listed as a general donor. The court refused to order the hospital to release the potential donor's name, holding that although the transplant registry was a "public record" within the meaning of the state's freedom-of-information statute,[5] the particular information sought was privileged as a patient record, since it was obtained as a result of the tissue-typing performed by the hospital's outpatient clinic.[6]

If a hospital possessed a registry of potential donors who did not undergo the tissue-typing at its own facilities, these names would not appear to be protected by *Colloton* as "patient records." This result suggests that hospitals should be careful to

---

[4]The hospital's donor registry was maintained in connection with an experimental program involving bone marrow transplants from unrelated donors, and the hospital's refusal to assist the plaintiff was consistent with its research protocol and institutional review committee procedures. Kemna notes that the plaintiff in *Colloton* first became aware of the potential donor's existence through a "leak by a hospital staff member that was contrary to established institutional procedures" and cautions that similar leaks "may be rare but should be anticipated in view of the human element of compassion" for terminally ill patients who are seeking donors. Kemna, supra n.3, at 132.

[5]Iowa's public records statute, Iowa Code §68 A.2 (1982), similar to the federal Freedom of Information Act, provided for liberal access by the general public to all public records. Id. at 121.

[6]331 N.W.2d at 876.

obtain and document consent from all persons included in any registry and to confine its registry to donors who could be considered patients. The identity of deceased donors is also unprotected, because the privilege associated with patient records does not extend past the life of a patient.[7]

Several cases have been reported involving the attempt by individuals who alleged they contracted AIDS from blood transfusions to obtain the names or patient records of blood donors. The analysis of the cases has been mixed, but the results are quite similar. In Gulf Coast Regional Blood Center v. Houston,[8] the blood center sought a writ of mandamus to compel the lower court to rescind its order requiring it to produce and make available to the plaintiff in a wrongful death action certain documents identifying blood donors. The court of appeals upheld the order, holding that the identification of blood donors is not an impermissible violation of their right to privacy, nor would disclosure violate any due process rights of the donors. However, the trial court imposed strict restrictions on the use of the discoverable information and prohibited plaintiffs from disclosing donor names or locations to third parties.

By contrast, the Supreme Court of Florida, in Rasmussen v. South Fla. Blood Service,[9] held that the privacy interests of blood donors and society's interest in maintaining a strong volunteer blood donation system outweighed the AIDS victim's interest in discovering the names and addresses of the donors. The court indicated that a method could be formulated to verify

---

[7]Dellinger, supra n.1, at 82. The failure of the law to provide broader protection to donor identity could deter organ donation if people perceive they will be the object of publicity should problems arise with the organs they donate. Consider a situation in Greensboro, North Carolina, in August 1986 in which physicians did not discover that a donor body was diseased with AIDS until two of its organs had already been transplanted into patients. The name of the decedent, an accident victim whose organs had been donated by his family, and his photograph were featured in local broadcasts and newspaper articles.

[8]745 S.W.2d 557 (Tex. App. 1988). *Gulf Coast* follows Tarrant County Hosp. Dist. v. Hughes, 734 S.W.2d 675 (Tex. App. 1987), an earlier case with similar facts.

[9]500 So. 2d 533 (Fla. 1987), 56 A.L.R.4th 739.

the blood donation organization's report that none of the donors was a known AIDS victim without disclosing the donors' identities.

A similar result was reached by the Supreme Court of Colorado in Belle Bonfils Memorial Blood Center v. District Court.[10] There the court, recognizing both the privacy interest of donors and the public's interest in maintaining a supply of volunteer blood, balanced these interests against those of the plaintiffs and determined that the AIDS patient was not entitled to obtain the name and address of the donor but could compel discovery of other information on donor record cards.

§12.11 Funding for Transplants

Third-party reimbursement for transplant procedures is becoming more readily available as transplant technology becomes less experimental. Medicare benefits are available to persons with end-stage renal disease undergoing kidney transplantation through the End Stage Renal Disease program (ESRD). Although coverage by the program was quite limited when first enacted by Congress in 1972, several reorganizations accomplished through amendments[1] have made the program's coverage policy fairly comprehensive. Post-transplantation Medicare coverage extends to 36 months, and reimbursement is provided to expenses incurred by live donors.[2] The Internal Revenue Code now precludes employer tax deductions for group health plans that do not cover end-stage renal disease, shifting some of the burden of ESRD coverage to private insurers.[3]

---

[10]763 P.2d 1003 (Colo. 1988). See also Krygier v. Airweld, Inc., 137 Misc. 2d 306, 520 N.Y.S.2d 475 (1987) (employing balancing test without reaching constitutional issues).

§12.11 [1]See Social Security Amendments of 1972, Pub. L. No. 603, 86 Stat. 1329 (1972); Social Security Act—End Stage Renal Disease Programs, Pub. L. 292, 92 Stat. 307 (1978); Omnibus Budget Reconciliation Act of 1981, Pub. L. No. 35, 95 Stat. 357 (1981).

[2]Cotton and Sandler, The Regulation of Organ Procurement and Transplantation in the United States, 7 J. Legal Med. 55, 76-77 (1986).

[3]Id. at 78.

The Health Care Financing Administration also permits Medicare coverage of cornea transplants, some bone marrow transplants, and some liver transplants for children.[4] In some cases, Medicare payment may also be made for heart transplantation.[5] Medicare's policy is to cover procedures deemed nonexperimental by the National Institute of Health, whose continued labeling as "experimental" of other transplantation therapies such as heart-lung, adult liver, lung, and pancreas transplants precludes Medicare coverage for these procedures. It has been suggested that, given the success of some of these procedures in recent years, the decision to classify them as experimental may be more political than scientific.[6] The costs of covering transplant procedures are tremendous.[7] Congressional and public pressure for extending coverage, however, is mounting, and Medicare funding may continue to expand in response. Beginning in 1987, Medicare began to pay for one year of cyclosporine treatment for all transplant recipients.[8]

The scope of benefits and eligibility requirements for Medicaid are determined by the states and vary considerably from state to state. Some states follow the Medicare guidelines, others fund procedures not covered by Medicare if prior authorization is obtained, and still others offer blanket coverage for all heart, liver, and pancreas transplants.[9] The tremendous cost of trans-

---

[4]Childress, Artificial and Transplanted Organs, I Biolaw 303, 321 (1986).

[5]53 Fed. Reg. 6526, Mar. 1, 1988; see Besharov and Silver, Rationing Access to Advanced Medical Techniques, 8 J. Legal Med. 515 (Nov. 1987) (citing U.S. Department of Health and Human Services, Health Care Financing Administration, HCFA Ruling No. HCFAR 87-1, Medicare Program: Criteria for Medical Coverage of Heart Transplants (April 6, 1987)). This ruling extended coverage retroactively to Oct. 17, 1986. The ruling sets forth certain selective criteria potential recipients must meet, causing Besharov and Silver to comment that by adopting these limitations on eligibility Medicare officials have opted for rationing in order to limit costs. Id. at 517.

[6]Cotton and Sandler, supra n.2, at 78-79.

[7]For the ESRD program alone the costs exceed $3 billion annually for approximately 75,000 patients. Childress, supra n.4, at 320-321.

[8]42 U.S.C. §§1320b-8, 1395rr (1986).

[9]Cotton and Sandler, supra n.80-81. States have the power to decide whether or not Medicaid will finance transplants and which procedures they

plant procedures, combined with the fact that for some patients a transplant is their only hope for survival, may produce significant litigation over Medicaid benefits in the future. Several important cases have already been decided.

In *Ellis v. Patterson*,[10] plaintiff brought suit for a determination that the Arkansas Medicaid plan must pay for her liver transplant. At the time of suit, the Arkansas plan only covered kidney and cornea transplants. The district court denied her relief, holding that Congress left to the states the choice of whether to include organ transplants in their Medicaid plans, and the court of appeals affirmed.

Medicaid requires participating states to provide "medically necessary" services, including inpatient and outpatient care, laboratory tests, and treatment by medical and nursing personnel. In addition, state Medicaid agencies may not arbitrarily deny coverage to eligible recipients solely because of their diagnosis.[11] The plaintiff argued that these two requirements compelled the state to fund the liver transplant she desperately needed.[12]

---

will finance. Once a state decides to finance transplants, it must provide reasonable funding and comparable care to similarly situated patients. Ellis v. Patterson, 859 F.2d 52 (8th Cir. 1988). A state cannot, then, out of budgetary concerns, limit its funding to a prescribed number of transplant patients. This requirement, along with the exorbitant cost of transplants, placed the Oregon legislature in a difficult situation in the spring of 1987 when it was found that a projected 34 patients would require transplants during the period from 1987 to 1989 at an estimated cost of $2.2 million. The legislature chose to discontinue Medicaid funding of all transplants but those of kidneys and corneas, choosing instead to extend its funding for basic healthcare to include about 1,500 persons not previously covered. This new policy suffered adverse publicity, sparked two lawsuits, and resulted in a boycott of organ donations organized by some low-income persons. In 1988, the state reinstated a somewhat modified transplantation program. Other states have also limited Medicaid financing of organ transplantation, recognizing their limited resources and the need to make a choice among competing healthcare needs. Welch and Larson, Sounding Board: Dealing with Limited Resources, 319 New Eng. J. Med. 171-173 (July 1988).

[10]859 F.2d 52 (8th Cir. 1988).
[11]42 U.S.C. §1396d(a)(1)-(5).
[12]Ellis was a ten-month-old baby girl suffering from a fatal liver condition, bilary atresia. The court reported the undisputed fact that if she received a

The court responded that such a line of analysis was appropriate in the usual case of a denial of necessary medical services. However, organ transplants are a special situation for which Congress has passed a separate section governing payment.[13] According to the court, the legislative history reveals Congress' intention that the states have discretion whether to include organ transplants in their Medicaid plans.

A similar case in Florida, Lee v. Page,[14] was decided differently. The court there ruled that the state must fund liver transplants where medically necessary. The court looked to Medicaid precedents and concluded that while a state may limit certain services for fiscal reasons, the state "cannot totally refuse to cover one service while covering others, or discriminate against one procedure because of the eligible person's condition or type of illness."[15] The *Ellis* court's statement that the argument that §1396b(i) gives states the option to exclude organ transplants was apparently not presented to the Florida District Court in *Lee.* Advocates of potential organ recipients have been successful in other states as well.[16]

In Todd v. Sorrell,[17] plaintiff also sought state Medicaid funding for a liver transplant. This time the basis for the denial

---

liver transplant she would have a 90 percent chance to live an active and normal life for at least the next five years; otherwise, she would die in less than two months.

[13]42 U.S.C. §1396(b)(i).

[14]No. 86-1081 CIV-J-14 (M.D. Fla. Dec. 19, 1986).

[15]Id., slip op. at 14.

[16]See, e.g., Allen v. Mansour, 395 N.W.2d 12, 153 Mich. App. 71 (1986) (ordering Michigan Department of Social Services to approve a prior authorization of a Medicaid-funded liver transplant for patient suffering from cirrhosis of liver due to alcoholism); Shannon v. Taylor, No. 87 C 1159 (N.D. Ill. Feb. 12, 1987) (bone marrow transplant was medically necessary, not experimental, and denial would violate Medicaid Act and regulations); Montoya v. Johnston, C.A. No. A-87-CA-97 (W.D. Tex. Feb. 18, 1987) (partial judgment issuing TRO and injunctive relief); (Feb. 20, 1987) (opinion and order) (court rejected Texas's self-imposed cap of $50,000 annually on inpatient Medicaid expenses in ordering Medicaid funding for liver transplants for plaintiff children); see generally Medicaid Transplant Litigation Proliferates, 21 Clearinghouse Rev. 20 (May 1987).

[17]841 F.2d 87 (4th Cir. 1988).

of funds was not that liver transplants were not covered but that the plaintiff, a 4-year-old girl, did not meet the first of eight criteria for selecting patients eligible for funded liver transplants. The sole reason for the state's refusal to fund the transplant was the fact that her condition was secondary bilary cirrhosis of the liver and not extrahepatic bilary atresia. The appellate court, in determining whether a preliminary injunction should have been granted, found sufficient merit in plaintiff's claim to support the injunction. In dicta, the court noted that an overly literal reading of the requirement of extrahepatic bilary atresia would clearly conflict with the provisions of 42 U.S.C. §1396(i)(1)(A) (1986), which requires states to adopt a plan providing written standards respecting coverage of transplants that treat similarly situated individuals alike in matters related to receipt of federal funds. In addition to meeting seven of the eight criteria, the effect of plaintiff's cirrhosis was virtually indistinguishable from the effect of bilary atresia. Because plaintiff was in substantial compliance with the transplant criteria, the court held she qualified for funding.[18]

Private insurers have also begun to cover transplants of extrarenal organs. In some plans coverage is incorporated into the regular policy, while in others it is included as an additional-cost rider.[19] Some states are requiring insurers to include coverage for certain transplants.[20]

Many people, however, still do not have policies that pay for organ transplantation procedures. In its April 1986 report, the federal Task Force recommended that "a public program should be set up to cover the costs of people who are medically eligible for organ transplants but who are not covered by private insurance, Medicare, or Medicaid and who are unable to obtain

---

[18]Case notes, Court Orders Preauthorization of Funds for Liver Transplant Patient, 21 J. Health & Hosp. Law 245-246 (Sept. 1988).

[19]Cotton and Sandler, The Regulation of Organ Procurement and Transplantation in the United States, 7 J. Legal Med. 55, 82-83 (1986).

[20]Georgia, for example, has enacted a bill mandating that certain insurance policies offer coverage for human heart transplants. Ga. Code Ann. §33-30-4.1 (1988).

an organ transplant due to lack of funds."[21] This recommendation indicates a strong interest in ending wealth discrimination in extrarenal organ transplantation.

D. Liability to Organ Recipients

§12.12 Physicians' Duty to Inform Patients of the Transplant Alternative

Can a physician be held negligent for failing to inform a patient of the possibility of transplantation?[1] Physicians have a general duty to advise their patients of standard alternative ways in which their condition may be treated before embarking on one method. Even if the physician is unable to offer the alternative treatment, she is required to explain it to her patient, and her failure to do so may be negligent. She must supply the patient with general information about the alternative form of treatment and, when appropriate, refer the patient to other physicians who are competent to perform the treatment.

The physician is not required to suggest an alternative treatment if she has a reasonable belief that it would not work in the particular patient's case. Whether or not the physician's decision to keep silent is negligent depends on the reasonableness of this assessment.

The range of alternative treatments a physician must explain to a patient is not without limits. A physician's duty to inform has been limited by some courts to matters that a reasonably knowledgeable practitioner in that physician's field would know.[2]

---

[21]Task Force Report, at 105.

§12.12 [1]Much of this discussion relies on Overcast, Merriken, and Evans, Malpractice Issues in Heart Transplantation, 10 Am. J.L. & Med. 363, 374-377 (1985). Because the healthcare principles discussed are general, citations to case law have been omitted.

[2]Holder, Physician's Failure to Obtain Informed Consent to Innovative Practice of Medical Research, 15 P.O.F.2d 711, 725.

Thus, with respect to some alternative methods of treatment, a general practitioner may be held to a less stringent duty to inform than certain specialists. The more widely accepted and acknowledged transplantation becomes, however, the more willing courts will be to recognize the duty of a nonspecialist to inform certain patients of the option of seeking a transplant.

The physician's duty to inform is further limited to explanations of alternatives that are "standard." How "standard" or "accepted" transplant procedures have become is a factual question for courts to decide. The specific transplantation procedure at issue would have to be addressed; those that have been proved more successful and less risky than others would require a duty to inform before the less proven procedures would require such a duty.

The scarcity of donor organs may be an additional factor in determining whether the duty to inform exists in transplant cases. If a physician perceives that a patient's chance of acceptance into a transplant program is small, she may wish to mention, but not to encourage her patient about, transplant possibilities. The legal outcome of such a decision by a physician is untested.[3] It is becoming increasingly clear, however, that public policy strongly disfavors not informing patients of the transplant alternative because of their apparent inability to pay.[4]

---

[3]Some commentators have noted that proximity to a transplant center should presumably not be a decisive factor in determining whether a physician has a duty to inform, because a patient most likely should make the decision whether to undergo travel in order to seek treatment. Overcast, supra n.1, at 376 n.50.

[4]The cost in 1986 of a heart transplant ranged from $51,000 to $110,000; the cost of a liver transplant, $68,000 to $238,000. Task Force Report, at 99 (omitting citations). But see Roberts, The Economics of Organ Transplants, 25 Jurimetrics 256, 261-267 (1985) (concluding that the fully allocated average one-year cost per patient is from $170,000 to $200,000 for heart transplants and from $230,000 to $340,000 for liver transplants).

Congress specifically requested the Task Force to address the issue of equitable access to donor organs, and the committee's report recommended funding initiatives for the purpose of ensuring that transplant procedures be made available to patients regardless of their ability to pay for them. Once a patient is selected for a transplant, funds can be collected from a number of

§12.13 Informed Consent

It is an axiom in healthcare law that a physician must obtain a patient's informed consent to treatment. Failure to do so constitutes negligence.[1] Among the general subjects courts have held that a physician must disclose to the patient are: (1) the patient's condition or problem; (2) the nature and purpose of the proposed treatment; (3) the risks and consequences of the treatment; (4) any feasible alternatives to the treatment; and (5) the patient's prognosis if the preferred treatment is not given.[2]

In transplantation, the two most critical issues about which potential transplant recipients should be informed are the material risks and possible complications associated with transplantation and the chances of the transplantation's success. In

---

sources to see that the procedure is carried through. The problem of inequitable access to organs may have more basic beginnings in that poorer patients are not referred for transplant consideration in the first place. This concern was expressed with respect to heart transplants in "Managing Our Miracles," Columbia University Seminars, PBS presentation broadcast on Oct. 14, 1986. The Task Force recommended that "health professionals provide unbiased, timely, and accurate information to all patients who could possibly benefit from organ transplantation so that they can make informed choices about whether they want to be evaluated and placed on a waiting list." Task Force Report, at 87.

§12.13 [1]See generally Chapter 7. Some jurisdictions continue to treat informed consent cases as arising out of the law of assault and battery. Overcast, Merriken, and Evans, Malpractice Issues in Heart Transplantation, 10 Am. J.L. & Med. 363, 377 n.57 (1985).

Two standards exist for determining when a breach occurs: one requires a physician to disclose that which a reasonable *medical practitioner* would disclose in similar circumstances; the other requires the physician to disclose what the average reasonable *patient* would want to know. Id. See also A. Rosoff, Informed Consent: A Guide For Health Care Providers (1981). For discussions related to this section, see Capron, Informed Consent in Catastrophic Disease Research and Treatment, 123 U. Pa. 1. Rev. 340, 367-368 (1974); Annas, Consent to the Anticipated Heart: The Lion and The Crocodiles, 13 Hastings Ctr. Rep. 20 (1983) (account of Dr. Christian Barnard's alleged overstatement to the first human transplant recipient of probability of operation's success).

[2]A. Rosoff, supra n.1. For a fuller discussion of each of these requirements as they relate to transplant procedures, see Overcast, supra n.1, at 378-381.

general, whether disclosure is necessary is determined by weighing both the probability that the risk will occur and its potential severity.[3] While the general body of case law on informed consent should be consulted to determine more exactly which risks might be considered "material" enough to necessitate disclosure, the general subjects that should be discussed with potential transplant recipients are: (1) the increased chance of infection due to the effects of immunosuppressive drugs; (2) the possibility of graft rejection; (3) the risk of transplant-related cancer;[4] and (4) the possibility of surgical and technical complications.[5] If failure to obtain informed consent results in litigation, a plaintiff must prove that the breach of duty caused injury. A patient must generally prove that a reasonable person under the same circumstances would have chosen a different course of treatment and thereby avoided the injury if the information in question had been disclosed. This will be difficult to prove in transplant cases, since transplantation is usually a last resort in which an unsuccessful operation could produce no worse result

---

[3] Id. at 380.

[4] The reported incidence of cancer in transplant patients surviving more than four years after transplant approaches 25 percent. Sheil, Transplantation and Cancer, cited in P. J. Morris, ed., Kidney Transplantation: Principles and Practice 335-350 (1979); Rose, Medicolegal Problems Associated with Organ and Tissue Transplantations, 31 Med. Tr. Tech. Q. 99, 114 (1984); Overcast, supra n.1, at 382. Cancer can be caused by the immunosuppressive agents or may be transplanted from the donor to the recipient. Id.

[5] Id. at 382-383; Rose, supra n.4, at 112-114. Overcast et al. suggest that courts could conceivably expand the scope of legally "material" information that must be disclosed to the heart transplantation patient to include such nonmedical aspects as: (1) the impact of the proposed procedure on the patient's family or job situation; (2) the likely cost of the proposed treatment and long-term care; (3) the necessity and cost of establishing residence near a treatment center for an extended period of time; or (4) the probability (or lack of same) that the procedure and follow-up treatment would be covered by the patient's insurance. While discussion of such issues is not traditionally considered to be the responsibility of the physician, in heart transplantation decisions these nonmedical considerations are "of utmost concern to the patient and may tip the balance in deciding whether or not to undergo treatment." Overcast, supra n.1, at 384-385.

than the current circumstances.[6] But although in many cases the alternative to transplant surgery is death, the issue of choice is not a closed one. It is possible that a jury would find that a reasonable person would prefer the death that would ensue absent a transplant over a prolonged life with painful complications and uncertain success.[7]

Although the probability of civil liability is low, obtaining informed consent from transplant recipients is a legal duty that must be satisfied by all healthcare professionals.

§12.14 Liability for Diseased or Defective Organs

The Uniform Anatomical Gift Act does not provide physicians with immunity for injuries sustained by transplant recipients. Instead, the liability of transplant care providers is determined by the same principles of tort law applicable in other medical contexts.[1] Because litigation in this area has been infrequent, the case law addressing questions of transplantation liability is slight. An analogy can be drawn, however, to a number of blood transfusion cases in which plaintiffs have advanced, with varying degrees of success, three different theories of recovery: negligence, implied warranty, and strict liability. The focus of most of the cases, and thus the discussion that follows, is the suitability of the donor tissue.

---

[6]This general view was expressed in McDermott v. Manhattan Eye, Ear & Throat Hosp., 26 App. Div. 2d 519, 270 N.Y.S.2d 955 (1966), affd. without opinion, 18 N.Y.2d 970, 278 N.Y.S.2d 209, 224 N.E.2d 717. One of plaintiff patient's contentions in this action was that her cornea transplant operation was contraindicated. The court observed that since the situation was "one of desperation" in which an unsuccessful operation could produce no worse result than the blindness that would ensue if nothing were done, going ahead was warranted.

[7]Overcast, supra n.1, at 385.

§12.14 [1]See, e.g., Carylon v. Weeks, 387 So. 2d 465 (Fla. Dist. Ct. App. 1980); Ravenis v. Detroit Gen. Hosp., 63 Mich. App. 79, 234 N.W.2d 411 (1975) cert. denied, 395 Mich. 824 (1975); Owen v. United States, 251 F. Supp. 38 (S.D. Cal. 1966).

§12.14.1 Negligence

A plaintiff asserting that a hospital's negligence resulted in an improper and harmful donor selection usually calls into question the care the defendant took to investigate the suitability of the organ. Under a negligence theory, liability should not attach unless the defect or disease in the organ could have been discovered with the exercise of due care. In Ravenis v. Detroit General Hospital,[2] the only reported case concerning defective solid organs, a Michigan jury found a hospital had been negligent in failing to set up a procedure that would ensure that its staff properly investigated the suitability of donated corneas. Portions of a potential organ donor's medical file that would have revealed that the donor had been afflicted with diseases that rendered the organs unsuitable for transplantation were not made available by the hospital to the physician who removed the donor's organs. The hospital was held liable to the transplant recipients who received the defective corneas because of this omission.

While the court in *Ravenis* focused on the failure to make available the donor's complete medical record, the hospital had also failed to establish procedures whereby standard tests would be performed on the organs themselves in order to detect the presence of certain diseases. A physician testified at trial that expert examination of the corneas under a slit lamp bimicroscope was required to determine the acceptability of the organs, and this procedure had not been performed. Liability could have been based on this omission as well.[3]

How exhaustively a physician must investigate the possibility of diseases or defects—by inquiry into the donor's medical history or by laboratory tests on the organ itself—in order to meet the relevant standard of "due care" remains at issue. In the blood transfusion cases, liability in negligence has been established in a number of cases for transfusion of incompatible

---

[2] 63 Mich. App. 79, 234 N.W.2d 411 (1975).

[3] Overcast, Merriken, and Evans, Malpractice Issues in Heart Transplantation, 10 Am. J.L. & Med. 363, 391 (1985).

blood because blood typing is a simple and routine procedure.[4] Providers have also been held liable for injuries resulting from the transfusion of blood contaminated with syphilis, since its presence is also easily detected by testing.[5] On the other hand, because reliable tests to detect serum hepatitis have not yet been developed, liability under a negligence theory for blood contaminated with hepatitis has never been proven.[6] Like hepatitis in blood transfusion cases, the presence of cancer cells in solid organs may not always be discoverable.[7]

While liability through negligence has not yet been established in any reported cases for blood contaminated with the Acquired Immune Deficiency Syndrome virus (AIDS), liability in the future should be anticipated as physicians and hospitals develop and implement standard procedures for testing blood and solid organs for the virus. In Kozup v. Georgetown University[8] the district court reviewed the medical chronology of the AIDS virus to determine what was known about AIDS by the medical community and when. The court concluded that it was not until 1984 that the medical community reached a consensus that AIDS was transmittable by blood, and it was not until 1985 that tests for antibodies sensitive to the virus were available to and recommended by the scientific and medical communities. Accordingly, the 1983 transmission of AIDS by infected blood was not the result of the defendant hospital's or blood bank's negligence.[9] A hospital's or blood bank's failure now to conduct

---

[4]See, e.g., Kyte v. McMillion, 256 Md. 85, 259 A.2d 532 (1969); Parker v. Port Huron Hosp., 361 Mich. 1, 105 N.W.2d 1 (1960); Redding v. United States, 196 F. Supp. 871 (D.C. Ark. 1961). Most cases in which incompatible blood has been transfused appear to result from clerical mistakes such as an attendant's picking up the wrong bottle, not from incorrect typing. See generally cases cited at Annot., 45 A.L.R.3d 1364.

[5]Overcast, supra n.3, at 390, citing Giambozi v. Peters, 127 Conn. 380, 16 A.2d 833 (1940).

[6]Id. at 390 (omitting citations).

[7]Id.

[8]663 F. Supp. 1048 (D.D.C. 1987), affd. in part, vacated in part by 851 F.2d 437 (D.C. Cir. 1988).

[9]See also McKee v. Miles Laboratories, 675 F. Supp. 1060 (E.D. Ky. 1987), affd. by McKee v. Cutter Laboratories, 866 F.2d 219 (6th Cir. 1989)

the tests that have since become standard in the industry would constitute actionable negligence. Some states have recently passed legislation requiring such tests to be performed.[10]

Accurate testing for defective conditions may be impeded by a number of factors. For example, in organ transplantation the cadaver donor's body may have been subjected to a number of blood transfusions before death, making it impossible to rely on the more simple blood tests to ensure the health of the organ.[11] The severe limitations on the viability of the organ outside the donor's body may also determine the kind and number of tests that should be performed.[12]

Courts have yet to develop specific criteria by which to determine if a physician or hospital has exercised due care in

---

(relying on *Kozup's* medical chronology to reach same result in negligence action against supplier of blood coagulant); Hermann, AIDS: Malpractice and Transmission Liability, 58 U. Colo. L. Rev. 63 (Winter 1986-1987).

[10]See, e.g., Ga. Code Ann. §44-5-151 (1988).

[11]In Greensboro, N.C. in August 1986, initial blood tests did not detect signs of the AIDS virus in a donor because his blood had been diluted by massive blood transfusions at the hospital where he died. Two Receive Organs from Man Exposed to AIDS, News & Observer (Raleigh, N.C.), Aug. 30, 1986, at 1A, col. 1. Two organ recipients were infected with the AIDS virus. N.C. Man's Organs Infect Recipients with AIDS Virus, Raleigh News & Observer, May 29, 1987, at 4A, col. 1. The "lesson learned" from this incident, according to a local immunopathologist, is that you must try to obtain a blood sample that is free from possible influence of drug therapy, transfusion, intravenous fluids, or other factors that affect the donor's normal blood state. Durham Morning Herald, Aug. 31, 1986, at 1C, col. 1. The case is the first reported in the United States in which AIDS was transmitted via donated organs erroneously believed to be safe. N.C. Man's Organs Infect Recipients with AIDS Virus, Raleigh News & Observer, May 29, 1987, at 4A, col. 1.

[12]Although there remains some debate on the matter, the prevailing view is that hearts can only be preserved for 4-6 hours, livers for 8-12 hours, and kidneys for 72 hours. Lungs cannot be preserved at all outside the body. Department of Health and Human Services, Organ Transplantation Q. & A. (DHHS Publication No. HRS-A-OC 86-1) (Dec. 1985), at 4. Some test results on hearts and livers are not always available before the time of transplant. According to the coordinator for the Carolina Organ Procurement Agency in Chapel Hill, N.C., these organs have a maximum 3-hour storage time, and it takes about 4½ hours to get some test results. Raleigh News & Observer, Aug. 30, 1986, at 1A, col. 1.

the selection of donor organs. The standard of care that courts will eventually develop will most likely consider the difficulties discussed here and also focus on the tests, medical history investigations, and other procedures that are generally practiced by transplant providers.[13]

§12.14.2 Strict Liability and Warranty

The blood transfusion cases suggest the possibility that plaintiffs in transplantation cases will assert implied warranty or strict liability theories of recovery. These theories have been advanced in a number of cases in which diseased or incompatible blood was transfused, on the basis that the transfusion constituted a "sale" of blood. Under implied warranty, the theory asserted is that since the blood was impure and unfit for its intended uses, the hospital or physician breached an implied warranty under a sales act or the Uniform Commercial Code.[14] Strict liability is asserted on the basis that blood that is diseased or defective is an unreasonably dangerous product for which the seller is strictly liable for consumer injuries.[15]

The attempt to characterize a blood transfusion as a "sale" in order to impose liability without fault has been generally unsuccessful. Most courts have chosen to characterize a hospital or physician's activities in blood transfusions as providing a service rather than engaging in the business of making a sale of blood.[16] Where courts have reached the opposite conclusion,

---

[13]Overcast, supra n.3, at 390.

[14]The relevant provisions of the Uniform Commercial Code are §2-314 (1976) (implied warranty of merchantibility covering fitness for ordinary uses); and §2-315 (implied warranty of fitness for particular purposes).

[15]See Restatement (Second) of Torts §402A (1965).

[16]See, e.g., Fisher v. Sibley Memorial Hosp., 403 A.2d 1130, 20 A.L.R.4th 129 (Dist. Colo. App. 1979). The court there reasoned that a blood transfusion could not be characterized as a product sold to the patient since it was merely a part of the overall treatment that the patient received from the hospital. The court also discussed society's interest in encouraging blood transfusion technology and practice, an interest that would not be furthered by the imposition

their decisions have often effectively been overturned by statute.[17] Most states have in fact adopted statutes that preclude the
imposition of legal liability without fault in blood transfusion
cases.[18] Such statutes may simply provide that the procurement

---

of strict liability. See also Roberts v. Suburban Hosp. Assn., Ct. Spec. App.
Md., No. 201 (Nov. 9, 1987) (AIDS transmission); Dibblee v. Dr. W. H. Groves
Latter-Day Saints Hosp., 12 Utah 2d 241, 364 P.2d 1085 (1961); Gile v.
Kennewich Public Hosp. Dist., 48 Wash. 2d 774, 296 P.2d 662, 59 A.L.R.2d
761 (1956); Glass v. Ingalls Memorial Hosp., 32 Ill. App. 3d 237, 336 N.E.2d
495 (1975); White v. Sarasota County Pub. Hosp. Bd., 206 So. 2d 19 (Fla.
App. 1968), cert. denied, 211 So. 2d 215; Perlmutter v. Beth David Hosp.,
308 N.Y. 100, 123 N.E.2d 792 (1954), rehg. denied, 308 N.Y. 812, 125 N.E.2d
869 (1955).

Some courts have treated blood banks differently, holding them strictly
liable for contaminated blood because their activities more closely resemble a
sale. See, e.g., Belle Bonfils Memorial Blood Bank v. Hansen, 195 Colo. 529,
579 P.2d 1158 (1978); De Battista v. Argonaut-Southwest Ins. Co., 403 So.
2d 26 (La. 1981) (since overturned by statute). Some state statutes that reject
strict liability for contaminated blood do not apply to blood banks. See, e.g.,
Wash. Rev. Code Ann. §70.54.120 (1985).

The strict liability claim has been rejected by courts on another basis as
well. Rather than defining blood as an unreasonably dangerous product, some
courts have reasoned that since hepatitis contamination cannot be detected,
blood is an "unavoidably unsafe product." A product of this kind is one that
cannot be made safe under present knowledge but the utility of which
outweighs the high risks involved in using it. Unavoidably unsafe products
cannot be the basis for a claim of strict tort liability. Restatement (Second) of
Torts §402A (k). See Fisher v. Sibley Memorial Hosp., 403 A.2d 1130, 20
A.L.R.4th 129 (D.C. App. 1979); Brody v. Overlook Hosp., 66 N.J. 448, 332
A.2d 596 (1975); Hines v. St. Joseph's Hosp., 86 N.M. 763, 527 P.2d 1075
(N.M. App. 1974), cert. denied, 87 N.M. 111, 529 P.2d 1232; cf. Cunningham
v. MacNeal Memorial Hosp., 47 Ill. 2d 443, 266 N.E.2d 897, 45 A.L.R.3d
1353 (1970) (superseded by statute on other grounds as stated in Glass v.
Ingalls Memorial Hosp., 32 Ill. App. 3d 237, 336 N.E.2d 495 (1975)).

[17]See Cunningham, supra n.16 (strict liability), effectively overturned by
Ill. Ann. Stat. ch. 111½, ¶5102-03 (Smith-Hurd 1971); Hoffman v. Misericordia
Hosp., 439 Pa. 501, 267 A.2d 867 (1970) (implied warranty), overturned by
Pa. Stat. Ann. tit. 42, §8333 (Purdon 1982).

[18]Greif, Hospital and Blood Bank Liability to Patients Who Contract AIDS
Through Blood Transfusions, 23 San Diego L. Rev. 875 (July-Aug. 1986)
(stating that only four jurisdictions in the United States have not legislatively

of blood and blood products for transfusion is for all purposes the rendition of a service and not a sale.[19]

The blood transfusion cases, closely analogous to disputes in solid organ transplantation, indicate that courts would be reluctant to impose liability without fault in this area as well. Solid organ transplantation is a valued medical procedure that courts should be hesitant to discourage by the imposition of strict liability on providers. Furthermore, the National Organ Transplant Act of 1984[20] prohibits the sale of organs, supporting the view that organ procurement and distribution involves a service to patients rather than the sale of a product. Finally, a number of states have passed statutes, similar to those relating to blood transfusions, that protect from strict liability persons involved in tissue and organ procurement and transplantation.[21]

---

barred application of products liability theories to blood and blood products); for discussion, see St. Luke's Hosp. v. Schmultz, 188 Colo. 353, 534 P.2d 781, 783 (1975); Overcast, Merriken, and Evans, Malpractice Issues in Heart Transplantation, 10 Am. J.L. & Med. 363, 394 (1985); cf. Shortess v. Touro Infirmary, 520 So. 2d 389 (La. 1988) (holding that hospital and blood bank could be held strictly liable for transfusion of blood contaminated with hepatitis); Casey v. Southern Baptist Hosp., 526 So. 2d 1332 (La. App. 1988) (statute removing strict liability in connection with blood transfusion unconstitutional because bill not given three readings after amended).

[19]In Cramer v. Queen of Angels Hosp., 62 Cal. App. 3d 812, 133 Cal. Rptr. 339 (1976), a hepatitis case, the court rejected an equal protection challenge to such a statute. Plaintiff's assertion that the distinction drawn by the statute between victims of contaminated blood transfusions and other tort victims was unconstitutional was rejected on the ground that the distinction drawn bore some rational relationship to a legitimate state purpose. The court reasoned that because the production and use of human blood for therapeutic purposes should be encouraged, those who provide these products should not bear the economic loss that might be imposed under the rule of strict liability because of their inability to detect hepatitis.

[20]See the discussion in §12.2.

[21]See, e.g., Conn. Gen. Stat. Ann. §19a-280 (West 1986); Ga. Code Ann. §§11-2-316(5), 51-1-28 (1981); Mo. Ann. Stat. §431.069 (West Supp. 1987); Or. Rev. Stat. §97.300 (1953). See McAllister v. American Natl. Red Cross, 240 Ga. 246, 240 S.E.2d 247 (1977) (statute not contrary to privileges and immunities clause of U.S. Constitution).

§12.15 Procedural Issues in Transplant Liability

In Brown v. Delaware Valley Transplant Program,[1] the Superior Court of Pennsylvania dealt with questions of change of venue in a suit brought against a transplant program for wrongful removal of the organs of a deceased relative. Venue was changed from the county in which plaintiffs brought suit to the neighboring county, in which decedent's body was discovered, the hospital where he was treated was located, and the vast majority of witnesses were located.

In a recent malpractice action involving the transplantation of a heart with an unmatching blood type, a Missouri appellate court, in State of Missouri ex rel. Wichita Falls General Hospital v. Adolph,[2] reached an unprecedented decision in refusing to allow a Missouri trial court to assert jurisdiction over a Texas hospital in a malpractice action; suit would have to be brought in Texas. The heart was harvested in Texas and transplanted in Missouri. The Missouri court's jurisdictional analysis followed the "minimum contacts" constitutional analysis, which requires "certain minimum contacts with [the forum] such that maintenance of the suit does not offend traditional notions of fair play and substantial justice."[3] The *Adolph* court found that the Texas hospital lacked "minimum contacts"; the contact was "random" and "fortuitous" since the heart might have gone to any state. The court also concluded that public policy prevented a finding that the assertion of jurisdiction over the Texas hospital would satisfy "fair play and substantial justice." The state's policy concern was that the imposition of jurisdiction over an out-of-state hospital might cause hospitals in the future to refuse to provide organs to Missouri residents.

---

§12.15   [1]371 Pa. Super. 583, 538 A.2d 889 (1988).

[2]728 S.W.2d 604 (Mo. Ct. App. 1987), cert. denied sub nom. Adolf v. Wichita Falls Gen. Hosp., 484 U.S. 927, 108 S. Ct. 292, 98 L. Ed. 2d 252 (1987). See discussion in Baron, Asserting Jurisdiction Over the Providers of Human Donor Organs: State of Missouri ex rel. Wichita Falls General Hospital v. Adolph, 92 Dickinson L. Rev. 393 (1988).

[3]International Shoe Co. v. State of Wash., 326 U.S. 310, 66 (1945).

E. Special Concerns with Living Donors

§12.16 Living Unrelated Donors

The use of living unrelated donors is very rare in this country. Before 1967, such donors provided 14.5 percent of transplanted kidneys, but since 1970 the number of kidneys obtained from living unrelated donors has been low.[1] The reluctance to allow donations to strangers arises from a concern that such donations are motivated by either money or coercion. In view of reports of a black market in kidneys, the federal Task Force in 1986 recommended that transplant centers demand objective proof of consanguinity and assign an advocate for the potential donor.[2] While this proposal may improve the condition of coerced or exploited donors, it does not address the problem of unrelated donors, such as spouses and friends, whose motives may be as altruistic as the motives of related donors. The responsibility of healthcare facilities is unclear, because they owe a duty of care both to the donor and to the transplant recipient. There is no current law specifying who may be a living donor. Until there is, the best rule for physicians and healthcare facilities to follow is not to turn away unrelated donors when related donors are unavailable. At the same time, facilities should be careful to ensure that the donor participates freely, out of altruistic motivation and not for financial remuneration, and that he understands all the risks and consequences of donation.

§12.17 Consent

Obtaining valid consent from living donors involves issues distinct from acquiring consent for cadaver gifts. Generally, a physician undertaking the removal of organs from a living donor

---

§12.16   [1]Childress, Artificial and Transplanted Organs, I Biolaw, 303, 305 (1986) (omitting citations).
[2]Id; Task Force Report, at 98.

should obtain a written consent that stipulates that the physician has explained and the donor understood the nature and purpose of the operation, the risks involved, and the possible consequences and complications.[1] Care should be taken not to allow any coercion of the potential donor. A physician's statement, for example, that a close relative will die without an individual's kidney would likely place considerable pressure on the potential donor and may invalidate the consent.[2] While questions about the relative's condition should be answered truthfully, physicians must be careful not to single out one individual as the only possible donor who could save the relative's life.

Physicians approaching individuals about live organ donation should remember that no one has an affirmative duty to be an organ or tissue donor. This principle was upheld when a Pennsylvania court refused to order a nonconsenting competent adult to donate bone marrow for a critically ill relative.[3] The proposed donor had consented to tissue-matching tests that indicated that he was the only suitable donor among the plaintiff's family, but he later refused to donate. A lower court had held that such an individual might be subjected to a legally imposed duty to provide tissues necessary to save the life of another when his own life and health would not be significantly threatened as a result and there was no other source of the needed material. However, the appeals court rejected this conclusion on ground that although there might be a moral obligation to donate tissues in such circumstances, to impose a

---

§12.17 [1]See Adams, Live Organ Donors and Informed Consent: A Difficult Minuet, 8 J. Legal Med. 555, 564 (1987). For an example of a consent form for use in obtaining the consent of a present donation by a living donor, see 15 Am. Jur. Legal Forms 2d, Physicians and Surgeons §202.108. For a consent form for a transplant donee, see id. at §202.107.

[2]Adams, supra n.1, at 568.

[3]Allegheny County Court, Pennsylvania (July 28, 1978). No published opinion is available; the information presented here is based on R. Scott, The Body as Property 151-152 (1981). See also Rose, Medicolegal Problems Associated with Organ and Tissue Transplantations, 31 Med. Tr. Tech. Q. 99, 102 (1984), citing Meisel and Roth, Must a Man Be His Cousin's Keeper? Hastings Ctr. Rep. (Oct. 1978).

legal duty to do so would violate the sanctity of individual moral choice and exceed the powers of the state to interfere with individual autonomy.

A recent case brought by a living donor, Lawse v. University of Iowa Hospitals,[4] illustrates the importance of approaching potential living donors with caution. Plaintiff contended that defendant hospital and doctor were negligent in not responding to his unwillingness to donate and that their "psychological manipulation" caused plaintiff to suffer when his remaining kidney failed. Although the court determined that plaintiff's claims were barred by the applicable statute of limitations, its opinion discusses in some depth the problem of obtaining truly voluntary and uncoerced consent from a living donor. Plaintiff contended and alleged that at age 23 he gave his kidney for his brother because he was assured by the doctor and the hospital that: (1) his brother would die without his kidney, when in fact he was doing well on dialysis; (2) there was basically no risk to him, it was like having an appendix removed, and (3) he was the best match. He also contended that: (1) he was not told his older brother had refused to donate his kidney; (2) other family members were told he was a match before he was; (3) he was given limited information; and (4) he was under duress.

The most difficult questions of consent arise when a minor or mentally incompetent individual[5] is the only or the most suitable match for organ transplantation.[6] These individuals are

---

[4]434 N.W.2d 895 (Iowa App. 1988).

[5]One note writer has identified three subgroups of legally incompetent individuals used as organ donors. They are "(1) an individual whose incompetence stems from a transient psychosis but who has a reasonable prospect of resuming his former social role upon recovery; (2) an individual whose incompetence arises from a mental condition, the prognosis of recovery from which is nil or virtually nil; (3) an individual with a long history of mental incompetency who will attain competence in the future including, for example, a child whose incompetence is present solely because of age." Note, Constitutional Law: Substantive Due Process and the Incompetent Organ Donor, 33 Okla. L. Rev. 128, 129-130 (1980).

[6]Despite widespread acceptance in the United States, few other countries allow routine use of organ donations from minors or mentally incompetent persons. Some countries prohibit organ donation by these persons. Adams,

incapable of giving legally valid consent.[7] Transplant care providers should therefore obtain the permission of both the incompetent donor and her guardian (usually the parents). Although there is little statutory authority, as a general rule a court order will also be required to remove an incompetent's organ. This precaution is taken because it is the state who is ultimately responsible for the donation under the doctrine of *parens patriae*.[8] Particular caution is advised when the parent or guardian has loyalties or duties to the potential recipient as well as to the donor—a proposed donation from a child to a sibling, for instance.

In determining whether it will grant authorization for the transplant, a court will usually analyze the facts before it using one of three methods: (1) the benefits test; (2) the doctrine of substituted judgment; or (3) a legislative alternative that falls somewhere between the two.[9]

In relying on the "benefits test," a court determines whether the transplant will emotionally or psychologically benefit the incompetent donor.[10] Courts using this test often inquire into

---

supra n.1, at 573. Some U.S. commentators have called for similar prohibitions in this country. Id. at 575.

[7]States may provide by statute whether and under what circumstances certain categories of persons can be live donors. For example, Michigan allows persons age 14 or older to donate a kidney without parental consent as long as a probate court approves. Mich. Comp. Laws §700.407 (1979); Adams, supra n.1, at 577.

[8]Rose, supra n.3, at 193; Adams, supra n.1, at 577 (citing Little v. Little, 576 S.W.2d 493 (Tex. Civ. App. 1979); Hart v. Brown, 29 Conn. Supp. 368, 289 A. 2d 386 (1972)).

[9]Note, supra n.5, at 130. This article is helpful in explaining the differences between the three types of analysis, as well as how they fare under constitutional scrutiny. See also Adams, supra n.1, at 577 and Murphy, Minor Donor Consent to Transplant Surgery: A Review of the Law, 62 Marq. L. Rev. 149 (1978) for similar models of court analyses.

[10]Note, supra n.5, at 130; Adams, supra n.1, at 578-579. In Little v. Little, 576 S.W.2d 493 (Tex. Civ. App. 1979), the court granted authorization for kidney donation where it found the existence of a close relationship between the sibling children, a genuine concern by each for the other's welfare, and that a successful transplant would increase happiness. Cf. In re Pescinski, 67 Wis. 2d 4, 226 N.W.2d 180, 182 (1975) (donation denied because sibling's

the closeness of the relationship between the donor and the donee to determine whether the donor's welfare would be impaired should the transplantation go unperformed and the donee suffer adverse health consequences.

Under the doctrine of substituted judgment, a court attempts to act for the incompetent donor as the donor himself would choose to act, were he of sound mind.[11] The court considers the former expressions of the ward made while competent (if there are any) as probative of how he would choose to act if presently competent, inquires into the ward's relationship with the proposed donee, and considers all other relevant factors that would bear on a competent individual's decision whether or not to donate.[12] The test is a subjective one, focusing on the individual's own circumstances, rather than an objective "reasonable person" standard.

Legislative alternatives may require similar inquiries into the general effects of the donation or may set out a specific set of prerequisites before the donation will be authorized.[13] One

---

death would cause donor no anguish); In re Richardson, 284 So. 2d 185 (La. App.), cert. denied 284 So. 2d 338 (La. 1973) (donation denied because benefited only potential recipient).

[11]Note, supra n.5, at 130. See Strunk v. Strunk, 445 S.W.2d 145 (Ky. 1969), where the donation of a kidney by a mentally incompetent adult to his brother was authorized on the basis of psychiatric testimony that the bond between the brothers was so strong that the death of the prospective recipient would impair the welfare of the incompetent donor. See also City Bank Farmers Trust Co. v. McGowan, 323 U.S. 594 (1945). See generally Robertson, Organ Donation by Incompetent and the Substituted Judgment Doctrine, 76 Colum. L. Rev. 48 (1976).

[12]Note, supra n.5, at 135-136. In re Pescinski, 67 Wis. 2d 4, 226 N.W.2d 180, 183 (1975) (Day, J., dissenting) (factors to consider in substituted judgment doctrine). For criticism of the substituted judgment doctrine, see Stone, Judges as Medical Decisionmakers: Is the Cure Worse than the Disease? 33 Clev. St. L. Rev. 579 (1986).

[13]See, e.g., Tex. Rev. Civ. Stat. Ann. art. 4590-2a, §2b (Vernon Supp. 1979), which requires the petitioning guardian to establish six prerequisites: the consent of the guardian; assent of the prospective donor; substantial need by donee and probability of benefit to donee; absence of a medically preferable alternative; a minimum of present and future risks to donor; and that the transplant be in donor's best interests. Note, supra n.5, at 131 n.38.

factor that inevitably weighs into the court's decision-making, whether or not it receives explicit recognition, is the ratio of the risk to the donor against the benefit to the recipient.[14]

§12.18 Physicians' Liability to Living Donors

Physicians and hospitals may be held liable for injuries caused by their negligence in physically removing donated tissues from living donors. The Uniform Anatomical Gift Act does not apply to donations by living donors; the good faith defense established in it is thus unavailable here. The legal redress of the donor in such instances is also not easily waived. Use of printed forms containing an exculpatory clause to shield hospitals from liability for negligent removal of anatomical materials has been rejected.[1]

While it is well-established that living donors can maintain causes of action under traditional negligence and intentional tort theories, the few cases reported have absolved the defendant physician or hospital on the facts. Of particular note is the reluctance of courts to find transplant care providers negligent

---

[14]See Rose, Medicolegal Problems Associated with Organ and Tissue Transplantations, 31 Med. Tr. Tech. 99, 104 (1984). For additional cases on incompetent organ donation see Masden v. Harrison, No. 68615 Eq. (Mass. Sup. Jud. Ct., June 12, 1957) and Foster v. Harrison, No. 68674 Eq. (Mass. Sup. Jud. Ct., Nov. 20, 1957), reported in Curran, A Problem of Consent: Kidney Transplantation in Minors, 34 N.Y.U.L. Rev. 891 (1959) (court considered psychiatric testimony of emotional impact upon donors; donations authorized); In re Richardson, 284 So. 2d 185 (La. App.) cert. denied, 284 So. 2d 338 (La. 1973) (retarded 17-year-old not permitted to donate kidney to sister because donation would not promote minor's best interest); Bonner v. Moran, 126 F.2d 121 (D.C. Cir. 1941); Annot., 139 A.L.R. 1366 (1941) (14-year-old not permitted to voluntarily consent to donate skin for aunt).

§12.18 [1]Smith v. Hospital Auth., Dade and Catossa Counties, 160 Ga. App. 387, 287 S.E.2d 99 (1981), holding such a release invalid as against public policy when (a) the hospital held a substantial "bargaining advantage" (the hospital credited patients' hospital fees for blood donations made by their relatives), (b) the donor relied on the hospital's skill and subjected himself fully to the risk of its carelessness, and (c) the release was buried in fine print on the back of a standard form presented for the donor's signature as a matter of routine.

on the ground that the need for such an operation could have been avoided. Thus, the Fifth Circuit has rejected a contention that physicians who performed a skin transplant on a child were negligent in deciding to perform the operation on a living donor instead of using skin from a cadaver and thereby subjecting the mother to a needless operation.[2] It also appears that hospitals and physicians will not be held liable to living donors for subjecting them to the medical risks of tissue removal because the prospective recipient's need for the donated tissues was created by the physician's or hospital's malpractice. Such a claim was strongly rejected in the New York case of Moore v. Shah,[3] in which a father who had donated a kidney for his son then sued the son's doctor for the negligent diagnosis and treatment that necessitated the transplantation. The court held that the physician owed no duty to the donor, who had never been his patient, and that to impose such a duty extending to all potential donors of organs for a given patient would create a group beyond the manageable limits of medical foresight.[4]

---

[2]Fleming v. Michigan Mut. Liability Co., 363 F.2d 186 (5th Cir. 1966). Abundant evidence was offered to support a finding that postmortem homographs were rarely used in the locale where the case occurred, were often dangerous from a medical point of view, and required strict compliance with various rules and regulations, which usually consumed a great deal of time.

[3]90 A.D.2d 389, 458 N.Y.S.2d 33 (1982).

[4]See also Sirianni v. Anna, 55 Misc. 2d 553, 285 N.Y.S.2d 709 (N.Y. Sup. Ct. 1967) where the court denied the claim that a physician's negligence in removing a donee's kidney gave rise to a cause of action in tort on the part of the donee's mother, who had donated one of her kidneys in order to save her son's life. The negligence of the surgeon, the court held, came to rest on the body of the son, and the act of donation by the mother was an independent, intervening act undertaken with full knowledge of the consequences. The later case of Petersen v. Farberman, 736 S.W.2d 441 (Mo. App. 1987), agreed with *Moore* and *Sirianni* ("Mother's decision to donate a kidney to her son was certainly laudable, but it does not fall within the purpose of the rescue doctrine.").

Appendix 12-1
Anatomical Gift by a Living Donor*

Pursuant to the Anatomical Gift Act, upon my death, I hereby give (check boxes applicable)
1. [ ] Any needed organs, tissues, or parts;
2. [ ] The following organs, tissues, or parts only _____
_____;

3. [ ] For the following purposes only _____
_____

(transplant-therapy-research-education)

_____   _____
Date of Birth   *Signature of Donor*

_____   _____
Date Signed

_____
Address of Donor

INSTRUCTIONS

Check box 1 if the gift is unrestricted, i.e., of any organ, tissue, or part for any purpose specified in the Act; do not check box 2 or box 3. If the gift is restricted to specific organ(s), tissue(s), or part(s) only, e.g., heart, cornea, etc., check box 2 and write in the organ or tissue to be given. If the gift is restricted to one or more of the purposes listed, e.g., transplant, therapy, etc., check box 3 and write in the purpose for which the gift is made.

Appendix 12-2
Refusal to Make Anatomical Gift**

Pursuant to the Anatomical Gift Act, I hereby refuse to make any anatomical gift.

---

*From the Unif. Anatomical Gift Act, 12 U.L.A. 7 (Supp. 1989).
**From the Unif. Anatomical Gift Act, 12 U.L.A. 7 (Supp. 1989).

838

Signature of Declarant

Address of Declarant

Date of Birth

Date of Signing

Appendix 12-3
Anatomical Gift by Next of Kin
or Guardian of the Person*

Pursuant to the Uniform Anatomical Gift Act, I hereby make this anatomical gift from the body of _____

Name of Decedent
who died on _____ at _____ in

Date   *Place*
_____.

City and State

The marks in the appropriate squares and the words filled into the blanks below indicate my relationship to the decedent and my wishes respecting the gift.

I survive the decedent as [ ] spouse, [ ] adult son or daughter, [ ] parent, [ ] adult brother or sister, [ ] grandparent, [ ] guardian of the person.

I hereby give (check boxes applicable):

[ ] Any needed organs, tissues, or parts;

[ ] The following organs, tissues, or parts only _____
_____;

[ ] For the following purposes only _____
_____.

Date

Signature of Survivor

Address of Survivor

---

*From the Unif. Anatomical Gift Act, 12 U.L.A. 9 (Supp. 1989).

13

Acquired Immunodeficiency Syndrome

Glen A. Reed and S. Wade Malone

§13.0 Introduction

Acquired Immunodeficiency Syndrome, or AIDS, swept into the
national consciousness in the 1980s much as poliomyelitis did
in the 1930s and 1940s.[1] Healthcare facilities could not, however,
look to the polio precedent to find immediate answers to the
legal problems associated with AIDS because the legal environment for healthcare facilities in the 1980s was strikingly different

---

§13.0   [1]See generally J. Paul, A History of Poliomyelitis (1971).

than that of the 1940s. In the three intervening decades, new
legal doctrines with profound effects on healthcare facilities had
emerged. Simple consent concepts had become a full-blown
doctrine, that of informed consent. Simple confidentiality requirements had developed into detailed confidentiality statutes
and regulations. The legal status of healthcare facilities had
changed from mere "workshops" in which physicians provided
services to full-scale providers of care with some degree of
ultimate responsibility for the care provided by independent
physicians. By the 1980s, patients with injuries resulting from
medical negligence were asserting their claims in court with
much greater frequency and vigor, and the size of awards in
medical malpractice cases had grown significantly faster than
the rate of inflation. The civil rights movement of the 1960s had
left in its wake numerous federal, state, and local antidiscrimination laws affecting not only employment and housing, but
also the provision of medical care in institutional settings.

Thus, even before the discovery of the human immunodeficiency virus (HIV), healthcare facilities were grappling with
numerous legal requirements and limitations on their conduct.
The virus and the disease, of course, arose independently from
these laws and were not envisioned at the time these laws
developed. The result is that a new disease that would have
raised relatively few legal issues and required relatively little
legal analysis in the 1940s raises a large number of legal issues
and requires a relatively complex analysis now. Fortunately,
after a few years of practical experience with the disease, a few
reported precedents, and a large volume of scholarship, answers
to many of the legal problems initially identified have become
fairly clear.[2]

---

[2]Some of the information written by one of the authors of this chapter
and included herein has been previously published by the American Academy
of Hospital Attorneys. See §13.4.2, n.5 infra.

A. Medical and Public Health Aspects of the Acquired Immunodeficiency Syndrome Epidemic

To have a clear understanding of the legal problems that AIDS creates for healthcare facilities, and to have any hope of finding the most appropriate solutions to those problems, it is essential to have a basic understanding of the nature of this disease.

§13.1 The AIDS Epidemic

The commonly accepted definition of "epidemic" is "an outbreak of a contagious disease that spreads rapidly."[1] Although AIDS is not likely to be as devastating as some of the epidemic diseases of earlier centuries,[2] it did spread rapidly prior to its discovery and may still be spreading at a significant rate.

§13.1.1 Definition of the Disease

"AIDS" has become the common name for a number of illnesses occurring in persons whose immune system has been weakened by the presence of the human immunodeficiency virus, or HIV. Early in the study of the virus and its effects, researchers and epidemiologists adopted detailed definitions to divide sick patients into groups with "full-blown AIDS," "AIDS-Related Complex (ARC)," lesser illnesses, and so forth. Now that it has become clear that apparently healthy persons with HIV infections are capable of spreading the disease and that a large percentage

---

§13.1 [1]The American Heritage Dictionary (1985 ed.).

[2]For a chronology of epidemics in the United States, see Report of the Presidential Commission on the Human Immunodeficiency Virus Epidemic 161-170 (U.S. Government Printing Office: 1988 0-214-701 : QL 3) (June 1988) (hereinafter Presidential Commission Report).

of infected persons will eventually become seriously ill, the focus has shifted from "AIDS" to "HIV infections."[3]

The Centers for Disease Control has developed a classification system for persons with HIV infections.[4] The first category, CDC I, consists of persons who, usually within a short time after exposure to the virus, have developed the symptoms of an acute infection. The symptoms include swollen lymph glands, fatigue, fever, and sometimes aseptic meningitis or rash. The second category, CDC II, consists of persons who have passed the initial infection period and are asymptomatic. CDC III consists of infected persons with a generalized and persistent lymphadenopathy, or swollen lymph glands, who do not have any other symptoms.

CDC IV is the category of HIV-infected persons with other clinical symptoms. CDC IV-A consists of persons with persistent constitutional symptoms, including fever, diarrhea, and weight loss. CDC IV-B consists of patients with various neurological symptoms including cognitive, affective, and sensory changes resulting from dementia, spinal cord disease, or nerve disease. CDC IV-C consists of persons with a secondary infectious disease associated with a defect in cell-mediated immunity.[5] CDC IV-D

---

[3]The first of the Presidential Commission's 20 major findings was:

The term "AIDS" is obsolete. "HIV Infection" more correctly defines the problem. The medical, public health, political, and community leadership must focus on the full course of HIV infection rather than concentrating on later stages of the disease (ARC and AIDS). Continual focus on AIDS rather than the entire spectrum of HIV disease has left our nation unable to deal adequately with the epidemic. Federal and state data collection efforts must now be focused on early HIV reports, while still collecting data on symptomatic disease.

Presidential Commission Report, at XVII.

[4]Centers for Disease Control, Classification System for Human T-Lymphotropic Virus Type III/Lymphadenopathy-Associated Virus Infections, 35 Morb. & Mort. Weekly Report 334 (May 23, 1986). The classification system is discussed in the Presidential Commission Report, at 8.

[5]The 18 specified diseases are:

1.   pneumocystis carinii pneumonia
2.   chronic cryptosporidiosis
3.   toxoplasmosis

consists of persons with one or more kinds of cancer known to be associated with HIV infection.[6] CDC IV-E consists of persons with other conditions or illnesses that may be associated with or complicated by an HIV infection.

§13.1.2 History of the Epidemic

Although there is some evidence that HIV existed decades ago, the first serious outbreak of the disease is now believed to have occurred in Zaire in 1976.[7] This was followed in 1981 by the reporting of increasing numbers of opportunistic infections in homosexual men in the United States.[8] This syndrome of opportunistic infections was not given the name "AIDS" until July 1982, a point at which 471 cases and 184 deaths had been

---

4. extra-intestinal strongyloidiasis
5. isosporiasis
6. candidiasis (esophageal, bronchial, or pulmonary)
7. cryptococcosis
8. histoplasmosis
9. mycobacterial infection with mycobacterium avium complex or M. Kansasii
10. cytomegalovirus infection
11. chronic mucocutaneous or disseminated herpes simplex virus infection
12. progressive multifocal leukoencephalopathy
13. oral hairy leukoplakia
14. multidermatomal herpes zoster
15. recurrent salmonella bacteremia
16. nocardiosis
17. tuberculosis
18. oral candidiasis (thrush)

Centers for Disease Control, supra n.4 at 337.
   [6]The specified cancers are Kaposi's sarcoma, non-Hodgkin's lymphoma (small, noncleaved lymphona or immunoblastic sarcoma), and primary lymphoma of the brain. Id.
   [7]R. Shilts, And the Band Played On 118 (1987).
   [8]Id. at 61-67.

reported.[9] That AIDS was caused by the virus that came to be known as HIV was not clearly established until April 1984.[10]

The Centers for Disease Control began tracking the extent of the disease before it was well understood. Beginning with 290 reported cases in 1981, the number of reported AIDS cases grew at an increasing rate each subsequent year through 1988:[11]

Year	New Reported Cases
1982	1,076
1983	2,933
1984	5,926
1985	11,038
1986	17,777
1987	25,987
1988	29,761
1989	35,375

The U.S. Public Health Service has projected that in 1992 there will be approximately 80,000 newly reported cases.[12]

§13.1.3 Incidence and Prevalence of the Disease

As of November 1, 1990, 298,914 cases of AIDS in 156 countries had been reported.[13] Although there is no system of consistent

[9]Id. at 168-171.

[10]Id. at 450-451.

[11]Centers for Disease Control, HIV/AIDS Surveillance Year-End Edition 15, 17 (Jan. 1990); telephone conference with CDC, Nov. 28, 1990. According to a report by the National Center for Health Statistics, AIDS was the 15th leading cause of death in the United States during 1987. *AIDS Was 15th Leading Cause of Death in 1987, Report Says*, AIDS Poly. & L., Mar. 22, 1989, at 8-9.

[12]*AIDS Medical Cost by 1991 Projected to Near $13 Billion*, AIDS Poly. & L., Jan. 25, 1989, at 2. One report estimates that the cumulative lifetime medical costs for treating those patients diagnosed as having AIDS beginning in 1988 will be $24.3 billion. *Cost for New AIDS Patients Predicted to Exceed $24 Billion*, AIDS Poly. & L., Mar. 8, 1989, at 3.

[13]Telephone conference with the Pan American Health Organization of the World Health Organization, Nov. 28, 1990.

reporting of HIV infections in the absence of serious clinical symptoms and no way of even detecting all such infections, epidemiologists estimated in 1986 that between 1,000,000 and 1,500,000 persons in the United States had HIV infections[14] and that the number of persons infected was increasing.[15] The Centers for Disease Control, using updated statistics, reported in February 1990 that approximately 1,000,000 persons in the United States had HIV infections in 1989 and that up to 2,000 newborns and 40,000 adults and adolescents are acquiring new infections each year.[16] Estimates of the number of persons infected worldwide range as high as 5,000,000.[17] At least one study predicts that up to 99 percent of all HIV-positive homosexual men will develop AIDS within 15 years of exposure.[18]

As of October 1990, the cumulative total of reported AIDS cases in the United States was 154,917, and the cumulative total of AIDS-related deaths was 95,774. The reported cases among adults and adolescents were distributed among the following sub-populations:[19]

---

[14]*PHS Conference Estimates 365,000 Cases Through 1992*, AIDS Poly. & L., June 15, 1988, at 5.

[15]The director of the World Health Organization's AIDS programs estimated that approximately one million people worldwide will contract the HIV virus in the next five years. *Frightening AIDS Forecast Offered to 6,500 Delegates*, AIDS Poly. & L., June 15, 1988, at 3.

[16]Centers for Disease Control, Estimates of HIV Prevalence and Projected AIDS Cases: Summary of a Workshop, October 31-November 1, 1989, 39 Morb. & Mort. Weekly Rep. 110, 111 (Feb. 23, 1990).

[17]The director of the World Health Organization's AIDS programs estimated that approximately one million people worldwide will contract the HIV virus in the next five years. *Frightening AIDS Forecast Offered to 6,500 Delegates*, AIDS Poly. & L., June 15, 1988, at 3.

[18]*Study Predicts 99% of Infected Men to Get AIDS*, AIDS Poly. & L., June 15, 1988, at 4.

[19]Centers for Disease Control, HIV/AIDS Surveillance 5-13 (Nov. 1990).

Transmission Category	Percentage of Cases Reported from Nov. 1989 to Oct. 1990	Percentage of Cumulative Cases Since 1981
Homosexual/Bisexual Male	56	60
Intravenous Drug Abuser	24	22
Homosexual/Bisexual Male and IV Drug Abuser	6	7
Hemophilia/ Coagulation Disorder Sufferer	1	1
Heterosexual	6	5
Recipient of Transfusion of Blood or Blood Components	2	2
Undetermined	5	3

In addition, among children under the age of 13, there were 784 cases reported from November 1989 through October 1990 and 2,686 cumulative cases.

In 1989, the rate of new reported adult and adolescent AIDS cases per thousand adults and adolescents was 0.140, with a rate of 0.199 for metropolitan areas and a rate of 0.061 for non-metropolitan areas. The rate per thousand males was 0.320.[20]

In 1986, the Centers for Disease Control estimated that by 1991 the cumulative number of AIDS cases in the United States would reach 270,000. In 1988, an estimate through the year 1992 was set at 365,000,[21] and in 1990 an estimate through the year 1993 was set at between 390,000 and 480,000.[22]

---

[20]Centers for Disease Control, HIV/AIDS Surveillance Year-End Edition 6, 15 (Jan. 1990).

[21]*PHS Conference Estimates 365,000 Cases Through 1992*, AIDS Poly. & L., June 15, 1988, at 5.

[22]Estimates of HIV Prevalance, supra n.16, at 117.

Since 1985, the United States armed forces have had a program of universal testing of all of their enlistees. During the period from 1985 to 1988, the rate of HIV infection (whether symptomatic or not) among these persons was 1.48 per thousand.[23] The rate of infection for older recruits, age 26 and up, was approximately 4.13 per thousand.[24] In a study of college students seeking health services at U.S. colleges the infection rate was reported as 3 per thousand.[25] In a study of an inner-city hospital emergency room the infection rate was 52 per thousand, with rates per thousand of 80 for black men, 41 for black women, 33 for white men, and 17 for white women.[26]

§13.2 Transmission of the AIDS Virus

§13.2.1 Persons Capable of Transmitting the Virus

Before HIV was well understood, many people believed that the presence or absence of "full-blown AIDS" had some significance in terms of the risks of transmission of the disease.[1] Although there is some evidence that the degree of contagiousness varies

---

[23]*False Positive Rate Low, Military Recruit Study Finds*, AIDS Poly. & L., November 2, 1988, at 7.

[24]*Recruits' Exposure Rate Stable, Pentagon Says*, AIDS Poly. & L., Dec. 17, 1986, at 4.

[25]*College Student HIV Infections 0.3%, CDC Survey Says*, AIDS Poly. & L., Nov. 16, 1988, at 6.

[26]*Far Higher Risks Said Possible for Emergency Room Personnel*, AIDS Poly. & L., June 29, 1988, at 3.

§13.2 [1]This type of distinction was one of the (at minimum) implicit grounds for the June 20, 1986 United States Department of Justice opinion (discussed infra) that held that persons with full-blown AIDS were handicapped under §504 of the Rehabilitation Act of 1973 while mere "carriers" of the disease were not. The opinion was rescinded on September 27, 1988, in part based upon "medical clarification" received from the surgeon general. See §13.8.1, nn.33-36 and accompanying text.

during the course of the illness, it has now been accepted that any person with an HIV infection is capable of transmitting the disease. This includes persons who have no symptoms at all.

§13.2.2 High-Risk Behaviors

In infected persons, HIV has been found in blood, semen, saliva, vaginal secretions, other bodily fluids,[2] and mother's milk. Despite early speculation that the disease might be transmitted through minimal contact with any of these substances, it has become increasingly clear that the reasonably likely methods of transmission are much more limited. These consist of inoculation or contact of broken skin with infected blood; contact with semen or vaginal secretions through sexual intercourse; and transmission from infected mothers to their babies in the womb, at delivery, or through breastfeeding. These modes of transmission explain the relatively high prevalence of the disease among certain population subgroups.

In June 1988, the Centers for Disease Control issued a release clarifying its position that the risk of acquiring an HIV or hepatitis B infection was so low in the case of certain body fluids that they would no longer be subject to the precautions previously issued by CDC with regard to blood and body fluids generally. The items no longer subject to such precautions are feces, nasal secretions, sputum, sweat, tears, urine, and vomitus, unless they contain visible blood.[3]

Public health officials in the United States have widely publicized the fact that the spread of the disease can be prevented by avoiding certain high-risk behaviors. A notice from the Surgeon General of the United States mailed to 107,000,000 individual households in 1988 classified the behaviors as follows:

---

[2]These include cerebro-spinal fluid, synovial fluid, and amniotic fluid. Centers for Disease Control, Update: Universal Precautions for Prevention of Transmission of Human Immunodeficiency Virus, Hepatitis B Virus, and Other Bloodborne Pathogens in Health-Care Settings, 37 Morb. and Mort. Weekly Report 377, 378 (June 24, 1988).

[3]Id.

Risky Behavior

- Sharing drug needles and syringes.
- Anal sex, with or without a condom.
- Vaginal or oral sex with someone who shoots drugs or engages in anal sex.
- Sex with someone you don't know well (a pickup or prostitute or with someone you know has several sex partners).
- Unprotected sex (without a condom) with an infected person.

Safe Behavior

- Not having sex.
- Sex with one mutually faithful, uninfected partner.
- Not shooting drugs.[4]

§13.2.3 Risks of Transmission in the Workplace

Monitoring efforts by the Centers for Disease Control have shown that HIV infections are not transmitted by "casual contact," such as shaking hands, hugging, sharing tools, working in close proximity, and so forth. Among the best evidence that the disease is not transmitted in this way is the complete absence of infections among healthcare workers and family members involved extensively in the care of AIDS patients where there is no sexual intercourse or subcutaneous exposure to blood or bodily fluids.[5]

---

[4]Understanding AIDS: A Message from the Surgeon General (U.S. Dept. of Health & Human Services, HHS Publication No. (CDC) HHS-88-8404) (1988).

[5]See Centers for Disease Control, Recommendations for Prevention of HIV Transmission in Health-Care Settings, 36 Morb. and Mort. Weekly Report 3S (Aug. 21, 1987); Centers for Disease Control, Update: Acquired Immunodeficiency Syndrome and Human Immunodeficiency Virus Infection Among Health-Care Workers, 37 Morb. and Mort. Weekly Report 229 (April 22, 1988); *Risks Small or Non-Existent for Family, Researcher Says*, AIDS Poly. & L., Feb. 24, 1988, at 2.

Although HIV infections are not transmitted in the workplace through casual contact, workers often believe that they are until the workers receive specific counseling on the subject. Most of the difficulty in dealing with HIV-infected employees or patients arises from the conflict between the fact that the disease is not spread by casual contact and the belief by many people that it is.

§13.2.4 Special Risks of Transmission in Healthcare Facilities

Due to the nature of some types of medical treatment, the risks of transmission of HIV infections are greater in healthcare facilities than they are in other workplaces. The major risks of transmission from infected patients to healthcare workers are:

1. accidental sticks with contaminated needles, including needles improperly prepared for disposal;
2. exposure to large quantities of blood in treating trauma;
3. exposure to blood during surgery; and
4. exposure to large quantities of infected blood or other fluids in laboratory accidents.

In 1988, the Centers for Disease Control reported on four studies of exposures of these types and concluded that the risk of acquiring an HIV infection after a needlestick exposure was less than 1 percent and that the risk from exposure to nonintact skin or mucous membranes was likely to be far less than that.[6]

There are no reported AIDS cases believed to have resulted from transmissions of HIV infections from healthcare workers to patients.[7] The types of activities believed to pose some risk of transmission, however, involve accidental cuts of the skin of the healthcare worker during surgery, trauma care, or dentistry.

---

[6]Centers for Disease Control, Update, supra n.5, at 231-233.
[7]Centers for Disease Control, Recommendations, supra n.5, at 15S.

§13.3 Tests for HIV Infections

HIV testing can serve several functions. These tests are used not only to perform clinical diagnoses, but also to screen donated blood, organs, breast milk, and semen, to provide data for epidemiological studies, and to provide information intended to prevent unnecessary exposures to the infection.[1]

§13.3.1 Types of Tests

The most widely used test for the presence of an HIV infection is an enzyme-linked immunosorbent assay, commonly referred to as ELISA. This test was originally developed to screen blood donors and is extremely sensitive. Typically, when testing individuals, a positive result on an ELISA test is followed by a second and possibly a third ELISA test. If the test results remain positive, a more sophisticated test is used to confirm a diagnosis of HIV infection. The most commonly used test for this purpose is known as the Western Blot Test. A carefully performed Western Blot Test will confirm that an HIV infection exists[2] and, based on present knowledge, that the person will be infectious for the indefinite future. Such tests do not themselves indicate whether a person "has AIDS" or meets any of the other classifications of the disease described above. These determinations can be made only through physician examinations of the patient's clinical signs and symptoms and by further laboratory studies.

ELISA and Western Blot tests only detect the presence of

---

§13.3 [1]Report of the Presidential Commission on the Human Immunodeficiency Virus, 73 (U.S. Government Printing Office: 1988 0-214-701 : QL 3) (June 1988) (hereinafter Presidential Commission Report).

[2]In a population with a 2 percent prevalence of HIV infection, the predictive value of a series of positive ELISA tests is approximately 80 percent, while the predictive value of a series of positive ELISA tests followed by a positive Western Blot Test is 99.97 percent. Centers for Disease Control, Recommendations for Prevention of HIV Transmission in Health-Care Settings, 36 Morb. and Mort. Weekly Report 3S, 13S-14S (Aug. 21, 1987).

antibodies to HIV. More sophisticated tests are being developed to detect the presence of the virus in a cell.[3] Because one must assume that a person with antibodies to HIV is infectious, such additional tests, while useful for research purposes and possibly for treatment, do not add information that contributes to a resolution of the most commonly raised legal issues for health-care facilities.

§13.3.2 False-Negative Results

Even though the ELISA test is extremely sensitive, it is possible for the blood of a person with an HIV infection to yield a false-negative result. The reason is that there is a certain period of time between the development of an HIV infection and the generation of antibodies that can be detected by these tests. This period is generally believed to last from 6 to 12 weeks after initial exposure to the virus,[4] but some researchers believe that in certain individuals the period could extend for a year or more.[5] Although other tests might be able to detect the presence of the virus in some persons during this early stage of the disease, such tests are too difficult and expensive to be used as a practical matter to reduce the chance of false-negative results except in very unusual cases. Due to the problem of false negatives, public health authorities recommend that persons who have experienced a known exposure to the virus receive repeated testing at specified intervals even though initial tests are negative.[6]

---

[3]See, e.g., *AIDS Virus Found to Hide in Cells, Eluding Detection by Normal Tests*, N.Y. Times, June 5, 1988, §1, at 1, col. 2 (discussing macrophage test); *New Test That Finds Hidden AIDS Virus Is a Sleuth with Value in Many Fields*, N.Y. Times, June 21, 1988, §C, at 1, col. 1 (discussing polymerase chain reaction (PCR) test).

[4]Centers for Disease Control, Recommendations for Prevention of HIV Transmission in Health-Care Settings, 36 Morb. and Mort. Weekly Report, 13S-16S (Aug. 21, 1987).

[5]N.Y. Times, June 5, 1988, §1, at 1, col. 2.

[6]See text accompanying §13.11.1, nn.17-20 infra.

§13.3.3 False-Positive Results

As stated above, false-positive results from a single ELISA test are fairly common and suggest nothing more than a need for additional testing. In the early years of the epidemic there was a belief that a significant number of false-positive results could occur even after the Western Blot Test. Some of these false-positive problems may have stemmed from a lack of quality control on the part of some of the private laboratories performing the tests. More recent studies indicate that although a false positive after a properly performed Western Blot Test is possible, the rate of occurrence is extremely low.[7]

Some healthcare facilities may consider screening programs for certain patients that make use only of initial ELISA tests and then treat every patient with a positive result as if they are infected. While this may serve some narrow purposes, it is important to keep in mind that once a healthcare facility has knowledge of a positive initial ELISA test result on one of its patients, the facility will have an obligation to see to it that sufficient additional testing is performed to either confirm or deny the patient's diagnosis.[8]

§13.4 Sources of Information and Recommendations for Healthcare Facilities

Many of the major legal issues raised in dealing with HIV-infected patients or employees will be resolved by referring to specific statutes or regulations designed to address those issues. In a number of jurisdictions, however, there will be no such

---

[7]See §13.3.2, n.5 supra. The Department of Defense testing program, applied to a subpopulation of enlistees with a low prevalence of HIV infections, had a false-positive rate of only 1 out of 135,187, or 0.0007 percent. *False Positive Test Rate Low, Military Recruit Study Finds*, AIDS Poly. & L., Nov. 2, 1988, at 7.

[8]See text accompanying §13.9, nn.1-16 infra.

specific law on some specific issues. In these jurisdictions the legal issues will have to be answered by analogizing AIDS to other diseases or handicapping conditions and by weighing certain rights enjoyed by the infected person against competing considerations.

Courts attempting to reach a proper result in such cases, as well as agencies and legislatures attempting to design appropriate new laws, have been influenced a great deal by the views and recommendations of several of the major organizations involved in dealing with the problem of AIDS. While dozens of organizations have issued policy statements and published reports, several such organizations and documents are particularly important for healthcare facilities.

§13.4.1 The Centers for Disease Control

The two federal agencies most deeply involved in developing information about the disease have been the National Institutes of Health and, to a greater extent, the Centers for Disease Control (CDC). The CDC is the leading authority on the incidence and prevalence of the disease, the characteristics of the disease affecting its spread from person to person, the risks of disease transmission, and methods of preventing disease transmission.

After several earlier releases, the CDC in August 1987 published its report entitled Recommendations for Prevention of HIV Transmission in Health-Care Settings.[1] In this document the CDC introduces the concept of *"universal* precautions,"* which involves treating every patient and every blood specimen as having an HIV infection. The report recommends that healthcare workers take special precautions to avoid needle sticks, cuts from sharp instruments, and exposures to blood, other bodily fluids, nonintact skin, and mucous membranes. Whenever such exposures are expected, the CDC recommends the use of gloves,

---

§13.4   [1]See Centers for Disease Control, Recommendations for Prevention of HIV Transmission in Health-Care Settings, 36 Morb. and Mort. Weekly Report 2S (Aug. 21, 1987).

masks, gowns, and eye coverings as appropriate. Resuscitation equipment is recommended as an alternative to mouth-to-mouth resuscitation.

Healthcare facilities are encouraged to provide training for all healthcare workers on the nature of the disease and on precautions against infections. The recommendations do not advocate the routine testing of all patients, but they do acknowledge that testing might be desirable for patients who are likely to expose healthcare workers to large amounts of blood and for healthcare workers regularly performing invasive procedures. The recommendations also acknowledge that some physicians may wish to use modified surgical procedures when dealing with infected patients and may request that patients consent to testing for such reasons. All such testing is to be performed only with consent. Appropriate counseling and confidentiality are recommended whenever such tests are given.

In June 1988, the CDC issued a clarification and supplementation of its recommendations in a report entitled Update: Universal Precautions for Prevention of Transmission of Human Immunodeficiency Virus, Hepatitis B Virus, and Other Blood-borne Pathogens in Health-Care Settings.[2] As noted above, this update exempted certain bodily fluids, for which the risks of HIV or hepatitis infection are very low, from universal precautions. The release also clarified that judgment should be exercised in selecting the appropriate type of protective barriers, that hand washing and other routine infection control procedures are still important, that gloves do not necessarily have to be worn by persons drawing blood samples in every case, and that universal precautions were not intended to alter healthcare facility waste management programs that had previously been recommended by the CDC.

In a series of reports, the CDC has also reported on every known case of direct exposure by healthcare workers to HIV-

---

[2]See Centers for Disease Control, Update: Universal Precautions for Prevention of Transmission of Human Immunodeficiency Virus, Hepatitis B Virus, and Other Bloodborne Pathogens in Health-Care Settings, 37 Morb. and Mort. Weekly Report 377 (June 24, 1988).

infectious material in the workplace. In the most recent of these reports, issued on June 23, 1989, CDC reported that in 5 studies of healthcare workers with such exposures in the United States, the United Kingdom, and Canada, only 6 out of a total 2,616 healthcare workers subsequently converted from a negative to a positive HIV antibody test status.[3] This extremely low rate of infection has been consistent since such studies began.

§13.4.2 The American Hospital Association

The American Hospital Association (AHA) has issued several sets of recommendations to its member institutions, culminating in a report entitled AIDS/HIV Infection: Recommendations for Health Care Practices and Public Policy.[4] In the report, the AHA endorses the universal precautions outlined by the Centers for Disease Control. The report recommends against routine testing of patients or staff, but does allow patient testing, with consent, in certain cases in which modified surgical techniques or other unusual precautions might be appropriate. The report recommends that HIV testing be done only with the informed consent of patients and that appropriate counseling accompany both the initial discussion of the test and communication of test results. The AHA emphasizes the need for confidentiality of test results and recommends that results be made available only to staff directly involved in caring for the patient.

The American Academy of Hospital Attorneys of the American Hospital Association issued a report in 1988 entitled AIDS and the Law: Responding to the Special Concerns of Hospitals, which surveys relevant legal principles and discusses some of

---

[3]Centers for Disease Control, Guidelines for Prevention of Transmission of Human Immunodeficiency Virus and Hepatitis B Virus to Health-Care and Public-Safety Workers, 38 Morb. and Mort. Weekly Report 6-8 (June 23, 1989).

[4]American Hospital Association, AIDS/HIV Infection: Recommendations for Health Care Practices and Public Policy, Report and Recommendations of the Special Committee on AIDS/HIV Infection Policy (1987-1988).

the legal questions confronting hospitals.[5] The report is generally consistent with CDC and AHA recommendations. An update to this report, reporting on judicial, legislative, and medical developments, was published in 1989.[6] The Office of Legal and Regulatory Affairs of the American Hospital Association has also issued a series of memoranda on specific legal issues entitled AIDS Issues Updates. These documents were issued periodically during 1988 and provide further elaboration on the AHA's recommendations as well as on legal developments.[7]

§13.4.3 The President's Commission on the Human Immunodeficiency Virus Epidemic

In 1987, President Reagan, by executive order, created the Presidential Commission on the Human Immunodeficiency Virus Epidemic. The Commission issued its report on June 24, 1988. Among the Commission's numerous findings were recommendations for stronger protections of confidentiality, stronger legal protections against discrimination against HIV-infected persons, and the institution of confidential notification programs in which public health authorities would contact and warn sexual partners of infected persons.[8] With regard to healthcare facilities, the Commission endorsed employee education and universal precautions, all possible steps to substitute autologous blood trans-

---

[5]AIDS Task Group of the American Academy of Hospital Attorneys, AIDS and the Law: Responding to the Special Concerns of Hospitals (Spring 1988) (hereinafter AAHA AIDS Task Group) (available from the American Academy of Hospital Attorneys, Chicago, Illinois).

[6]AIDS Task Group of the American Academy of Hospital Attorneys, AIDS and the Law: Responding to the Special Concerns of Hospitals (Nov. 1989 Update).

[7]The subjects covered by the memoranda were Legal Aspects of AIDS (Mar. 21, 1988); HIV Testing Following Employee Needle Stick or Mucous Membrane Exposure (May 26, 1988); HIV Testing and Informed Consent (July 1988); and HIV Confidentiality Issues (Nov. 1988). These memoranda are available from the American Hospital Association.

[8]Presidential Commission Report, at XVII-XIX.

fusions for homologous transfusions,[9] and notification of all persons who have received blood transfusions since 1977 that they should consider HIV testing and counseling.

§13.4.4 The American Medical Association

The American Medical Association (AMA) has also issued policy statements and recommendations relating to the AIDS epidemic. The document that is most relevant to certain of the legal issues is the AMA's Report of the Council on Ethical and Judicial Affairs: Ethical Issues Involved in the Growing AIDS Crisis.[10] In this document, the AMA advises its members that as a matter of ethics they should treat any HIV-infected patient whose condition is within their "current realm of competence." The report also deals with the issue of HIV-infected physicians and concludes that such physicians should refrain from actions that would raise an even minimal risk of transmission of the infection to a patient. The report endorses informing patients of any such risks of infection. With regard to the protection of third parties who might be at risk of infection from a physician's patient, the report advises that physicians should attempt to get patients to disclose their HIV infections voluntarily and that if they refuse, physicians should report the matter to public authorities and then directly to third parties if absolutely necessary.

---

[9]The recommendations stated:

> In health care facilities, all reasonable strategies to avoid a transfusion of someone else's blood (homologous transfusion) should be implemented by substituting, whenever possible, transfusion with one's own blood (autologous transfusion). Currently available techniques of autologous transfusion include predonation of one's own blood, recirculation of one's own blood during surgery (intraoperative autologous transfusion), blood dilution techniques (hemo-dilution), and post-operative collection for retransfusion (post-operative salvage).

Id. at XIX.

[10]American Medical Association Council on Ethical and Judicial Affairs, Ethical Issues Involved in the Growing AIDS Crisis (1987).

§13.4.5 Other Organizations

Persons searching for additional authorities addressing these issues will be able to locate numerous other sources, including reports by groups associated with the American Bar Association,[11] the National Education Association,[12] the American College of Physicians,[13] the National Academy of Science,[14] the American Association of Occupational Health Nurses,[15] the U.S. Office of Technology Assessment,[16] the American Federation of State, County, and Municipal Employees,[17] and the American Red Cross.[18]

§13.5 Issues Surrounding the Testing of Patients for HIV

§13.5.1 General Law on Informed Consent

The doctrine of informed consent evolved in the 1950s and 1960s, when courts imposed on physicians the duty to provide sufficient information on the nature and risks of the proposed

---

[11]American Bar Association AIDS Coordinating Committee, AIDS: The Legal Issues Discussion Draft of the American Bar Association AIDS Coordinating Committee (1988) (hereinafter AIDS: The Legal Issues (1988)).

[12]*NEA Urges AIDS Curriculum, Opposes Testing and Bias*, AIDS Poly. & L., July 15, 1987, at 4-5.

[13]*Physicians Group Affirms Patients' Right to Care*, AIDS Poly. & L., Mar. 9, 1988, at 3-4; *ACP Says: MDs Obligated to Care for AIDS Patients*, 10 Am. Medical News (Mar. 18, 1988).

[14]*Task Force Update Finds Some Needs Still Unmet*, AIDS Poly. & L., Dec. 16, 1987, at 9-10.

[15]*Nurses Urge OSHA Standard, Issues Resource Guide on AIDS*, AIDS Poly. & L., May 4, 1988, at 7.

[16]*OTA Study Says Campaigns are Difficult to Evaluate*, AIDS Poly. & L., June 15, 1988, at 8-9.

[17]*Federal Employee Unions Ask for Quick Regulation by OSHA*, AIDS Poly. & L., Feb. 10, 1988, at 6.

[18]*Behavior Hard to Change, Red Cross Survey Reports*, AIDS Poly. & L., Nov. 16, 1988, at 4.

treatment to permit a patient to give an intelligent and informed consent to treatment.[1] Every jurisdiction, by case law, statute, or regulation, requires that a patient give an informed consent in deciding whether to receive medical treatment.[2]

The law of most jurisdictions provides that a patient be given the following information:

1. the diagnosis;
2. the general nature of the contemplated procedure;
3. the risks involved;
4. the prospects of success;
5. the prognosis if the procedure is not performed; and
6. alternative medical treatment, if any.[3]

§13.5.2 Test Requirements as a Restriction on Access

Numerous court decisions have determined, with certain exceptions, that a healthcare provider is not duty-bound to admit or treat an individual.[4] Thus, if such duty is not imposed by federal or state statute or regulation, a healthcare provider can condition a patient's admission on an HIV test.[5] There are, however, at least three limitations on a facility's ability to require patient tests: (1) a duty to provide emergency care, (2) a duty to provide

---

§13.5 [1]Natanson v. Kline, 186 Kan. 393, 350 P.2d 1093 (1960); Salgo v. Leland Stanford Jr. Univ. Bd. of Trustees, 154 Cal. App. 2d 560, 317 P.2d 170 (1957). See generally Brandt, Health Care Workers and AIDS, 48 Md. L. Rev. 1, 36-38 (1989); American Hospital Association, HIV Testing and Informed Consent, AIDS Issues Update (July 1988); F. Rozovsky, Consent to Treatment (2d ed. 1990) (hereinafter Rozovsky); AIDS: The Legal Issues 92-96 (1988).

[2]See 2 D. Louisell and H. Williams, Medical Malpractice §22.17-22.68 (1989).

[3]Canterbury v. Spence, 464 F.2d 772 (D.C. Cir. 1972).

[4]Fabian v. Matzko, 236 Pa. Super. 267, 344 A.2d 569 (1975); Guerrero v. Copper Queen Hosp., 22 Ariz. App. 611, 529 P.2d 1205 (1974), rehg. denied, 23 Ariz. App. 172, 531 P.2d 548 (1975).

[5]See Klein, A Health Care Dilemma: Testing Patients for HIV, 21 J. Health and Hosp. L. 249 (1988) (hereinafter Klein).

access to public accommodations, and (3) a duty to provide care to handicapped individuals.

The first such limitation, the duty to provide emergency care, emanated from court decisions.[6] Many states have codified this principle.[7]

The second limitation on standard pre-treatment testing of patients for the HIV antibody derives from state statutes guaranteeing access to "public accommodations."[8] These state statutes typically define what constitutes a "public place of accommodation" in broad terms and prohibit denial of access because of a physical condition.

The third limitation on standard pre-treatment testing is a duty to provide care to handicapped individuals.[9] A person with AIDS is considered to be an individual with a handicap under the Rehabilitation Act (see §13.8.1). The cumulative effect of the Rehabilitation Act, its implementing regulations, and the *Arline* decision is that a healthcare facility subject to the Rehabilitation Act[10] may not deny or restrict the right of admission of an HIV-infected individual solely on the basis of handicap.[11]

Mandatory testing of all hospitalized patients for HIV has been opposed by the AMA, the AHA, and the majority of public health officials, including the CDC and the Surgeon General.[12]

---

[6]See, e.g., Williams v. Hosp. Auth. of Hall County, 119 Ga. App. 626, 168 S.E.2d 336 (1969); Stanturf v. Sipes, 447 S.W.2d 558 (Mo. 1969); Mercy Medical Center of Oshkosh v. Winnebago County, 58 Wis. 2d 260, 206 N.W.2d 198 (1973); Klein, at 249.

[7]See, e.g., La. Rev. Stat. Ann. §40:2113.4 (West Supp. 1990) ("Any general hospital licensed under this Part . . . shall make its emergency services available to all persons residing in the territorial area of the hospital . . .").

[8]See, e.g., N.Y. Exec. Law §296(2)(a) (McKinney 1982 & Supp. 1990); Wis. Stat. Ann. §942.04(1)(a) (1988 & West Supp. 1989).

[9]See §13.8.1, nn.1-37 and accompanying text supra; Klein, at 249.

[10]See §13.8.1, nn.15-21 and accompanying text supra.

[11]Id. See also Klein, at 249-253.

[12]In Dotson v. St. Mary's Hosp., No. 900017 (Super. Ct., Judicial Dist. of Waterbury, Conn. Mar. 30, 1989), the plaintiff filed suit against the hospital and his physician alleging that he was tested for HIV without his consent and contrary to his expressed wishes. AIDS Law & Litigation Reporter Monthly

In addition, testing is expensive for the hospital, for the patient, or for the third-party payor, and it carries with it obligations for counseling, confidentiality, and reporting that may involve a significant commitment of resources. Since a significant number of tests yield false-positive results, every positive initial test would have to be followed by more elaborate subsequent tests to determine an accurate diagnosis to communicate to the patient.[13]

On June 23, 1988, the Nemours Foundation adopted a policy that its three facilities (two in Delaware and one in Florida) would require testing of all current and prospective patients and employees for AIDS-related diseases, refuse admission to HIV-infected patients, and subject infected employees to transfer to jobs that did not involve patient care.[14] After being threatened with a lawsuit by the attorney general of Delaware,[15]

Rev. 46 (June-July 1989); see also *Hospital Sued Over Testing, Release of Medical Records*, AIDS Poly. & L., April 19, 1989, at 3-4. Three separate lawsuits were filed by individuals in Pennsylvania charging that physicians tested their blood for HIV antibodies without their permission. Doe v. Wills Eye Hosp., No. 5248 (Phila. Ct. Com. Pl.); Doe v. Dyer-Goode, No. 5249 (Phila. Ct. Com. Pl.); Doe v. Conly, No. 88-0486 (M.D. Pa. filed Mar. 31, 1988) (digested in *Three Lawsuits Claim Doctors Did Unauthorized HIV Tests*, AIDS Poly. & L., April 20, 1988, at 3-4). In *Dyer-Goode*, the trial court dismissed the case with prejudice. The Superior Court of Pennsylvania affirmed, holding that the doctor's HIV testing was not battery based on an absence of informed consent since the appellant had given his consent to have his blood withdrawn for a testing purpose. *Doctor Not Liable to Couple Over Unauthorized HIV Test*, AIDS Poly. & L., Dec. 13, 1989, at 4. The court found that the fact that an additional test, HIV, was performed on the blood did not constitute grounds for battery. Id.

[13]See, e.g., Kraus v. Spielberg, 37 Misc. 2d 519, 236 N.Y.S.2d 143 (N.Y. Sup. Ct. 1962). A small percentage of patients will have false-positive results even after multiple tests. See also Nurse Sues HIV Testing Center for Negligence After False-Positive Results, 3 AIDS Alert 192 (1988). (The plaintiff alleged he suffered severe emotional distress when the testing center twice erroneously told him he was HIV-infected. He also alleged the "mistakes resulted from careless procedures, not just false-positive test results.")

[14]*Private Hospital to Bar Patients with AIDS Virus*, N.Y. Times, June 25, 1988, at 28, col. 1.

[15]Letter from Charles M. Oberly, attorney general of Delaware, to William Winder, administrator, Nemours Health Clinic, (July 7, 1988) (advising

the Nemours Foundation "postponed" implementation of its policy.[16]

§13.5.3 Specific Laws on AIDS Testing

Many states have enacted specific laws on AIDS testing.[17] Although the language varies, many of those statutes require that the individual being asked to take an AIDS test be provided with information and explanations medically appropriate for that person including: accurate information regarding AIDS and HIV; an explanation of behaviors that reduce the risk of transmitting AIDS and HIV; an explanation of the confidentiality of information relating to AIDS diagnoses and HIV tests; an explanation of information regarding both social and medical implications of HIV tests; and disclosure of commonly recognized treatment or treatments for AIDS and HIV.[18]

In September 1988, Illinois amended its AIDS Confidentiality Act to delete the requirements that physicians obtain written consent before testing a patient for the HIV virus, provide information about AIDS, and provide counseling. In signing the bill, Governor James Thompson stated:

> The main objection to this bill is the elimination of the written informed consent requirement. Opponents argue that potential AIDS victims will not seek medical attention for fear that their rights of privacy will be violated. I feel strongly that more high risk individuals will receive care if health professionals can be assured of a safe work environment. In addition, repealing the mandated written consent will not eliminate a doctor's very

---

Nemours a lawsuit would be filed if the policy was put into effect or was not rescinded).

[16]*Delaware to Revise Controversial Testing Policy*, AIDS Poly. & L., July 13, 1988, at 3.

[17]See, e.g., Cal. Health & Safety Code §199.20-199.27 (West Supp. 1990); Del. Code Ann. tit. 16, §§1201-1204 (Supp. 1988); Ga. Code Ann. §§31-22-9.1 to 31-22-9.2 (Supp. 1989).

[18]Ga. Code Ann. §31.22-9.1(a)(6) (Supp. 1989); 1988 N.Y. Laws ch. 584 (S.9265-A).

important responsibility to discuss treatment and testing with patients, nor will it remove the duty to discuss findings and provide counseling. This obligation will continue to exist, regardless of my action on a particular piece of legislation.[19]

§13.5.4 Healthcare Facility Responsibilities

A long line of decisions has held that the responsibility for obtaining the informed consent of patients rests with physicians and not with healthcare facilities.[20] In the absence of circumstances demonstrating that a healthcare facility knew or should have known that the procedure was to be performed without consent, a facility will not be liable for the failure of a treating physician to obtain consent.[21] When a physician or other person employed by the facility provides treatment without obtaining the patient's informed consent, the facility can be held liable under the doctrines of respondeat superior, corporate negligence, and ostensible agency and estoppel.[22]

---

[19]Letter from James R. Thompson, governor of Illinois, to the members of the Illinois House of Representatives (Sept. 2, 1988). The Georgia legislature recently passed a bill that allows HIV tests to be administered to patients without their consent when a healthcare provider has been exposed to the patient's blood or other body fluids. See 1990 Georgia Laws 1187 (H.B. 842). See also Roeder, Legal Concerns: Hospitals Should Adopt Rules for HIV Testing Without Patient Consent, XXXIV, no. 4 Georgia Hospitals Today 8 (1990).

[20]See, e.g., Flannery v. President and Directors of Georgetown College, 679 F.2d 960 (D.C. Cir. 1982); Cooper v. Curry, 92 N.M. 417, 589 P.2d 201 (1978); Fiorentino v. Wenger, 19 N.Y.2d 407, 280 N.Y.S.2d 373, 227 N.E.2d 296 (1967).

[21]See, e.g., Lincoln v. Gupta, 142 Mich. App. 615, 370 N.W.2d 312 (1985); but see Magana v. Elie, 108 Ill. App. 3d 1028, 439 N.E.2d 1319 (1982).

[22]Bing v. Thunig, 2 N.Y.2d 656, 143 N.E.2d 3 (1957) (respondeat superior); Darling v. Charleston Community Memorial Hosp., 33 Ill. 2d 326, 211 N.E.2d 253 (1965), cert. denied, 383 U.S. 946 (1966) (corporate negligence found where hospital negligently failed to review treatment given to patient by staff physician); Mehlman v. Powell, 281 Md. 269, 378 A.2d 1121 (1977) (ostensible agency doctrine); see generally Reed, Expanding Theories of Hospital Liability: A Review, 21 J. Health & Hospital L. 217 (1988); J. Smith, Hospital Liability §3 (1989).

Although it is unarguably the responsibility of the patient's physician to make sure the patient is counseled with respect to an AIDS test, a healthcare facility should make sure a patient is counseled both before and after taking an HIV test.[23]

Before the test, as a part of obtaining the patient's informed consent, the healthcare facility should verify that the patient has been counseled on what the test entails and how it will be administered and verified. Following the test, patients should be counseled by trained personnel regarding the meaning of the test result.[24] In the case of positive results, patients should be advised of the importance of notifying their sexual partners of the results and of the need for partners to be counseled and tested. Infected patients should be advised of the importance of observing "safe" sexual practices and of what that means specifically. They should also be advised of symptoms that could indicate a need for medical attention. When appropriate, infected patients should be advised not to share needles with others, to avoid other blood to blood exposures, and to warn persons who may have had such contacts with them. Failure to counsel patients properly may potentially result in liability to the patient or to third parties such as sexual partners or even needle-sharing partners.[25] Unless required by specific statute or regulation, legally sufficient consents to HIV testing need not be in writing. Nevertheless, given the potential consequences of the test, it is advisable to document the informed consent process.[26] While documentation of a patient's authorization to be treated may be significant for a number of reasons, the paramount reason is to provide reliable evidence to use in an action based on a lack of consent.[27]

---

[23]Nurse Sues HIV Testing Center for Negligence After False-Positive Result, 3 AIDS Alert 193 (1988) (lawsuit alleges plaintiff was provided little or no counseling before, during, or after blood samples were drawn and was provided no counseling or referrals either time he was advised that he tested positive.).

[24]Id.

[25]Id.

[26]See American Hospital Association, AIDS Issues Updates 6 (July 1988).

[27]Rozovsky, at §12.1.

§13.6 *Confidentiality of Medical Information Regarding AIDS*

§13.6.1 General Law on Confidentiality

The requirement of patient confidentiality stems from rights of personal privacy recognized under common law and by the Constitution.[1] A state's statutes defining the physician-patient privilege, professional and healthcare facility licensure laws, and specific medical information confidentiality acts can all be relevant.[2] There are, however, some exceptions to such requirements. Disclosures that are reasonably necessary for the treatment of patients, for the protection of medical personnel, or to meet a clear public need are usually recognized as exceptions to confidentiality requirements.[3]

Unlawful breaches of confidentiality can result in various state-imposed sanctions and, more significant, civil liability for any injury caused.[4] Improper disclosure of accurate but confi-

---

§13.6 [1]Restatement (Second) of Torts §652A (1989); Eisenstadt v. Baird, 405 U.S. 438 (1972); Katz v. United States, 389 U.S. 347 (1967); Stanley v. Georgia, 394 U.S. 557 (1969).

[2]See, e.g., N.Y. Civ. Prac. L.&R. §§4504, 4507 (McKinney 1963 & Supp. 1990) (physician-patient privilege); Me. Rev. Stat. Ann. tit. 22, §1030 (Supp. 1988) (medical information confidentiality law).

[3]See, e.g., Whalen v. Roe, 429 U.S. 589, 602 (1977) ("Disclosures of private medical information to doctors, to hospital personnel, to insurance companies, and to public health agencies are often an essential part of modern medical practice even when the disclosure may reflect unfavorably on the character of the patient"); Doe v. Borough of Barrington, 58 U.S.L.W. 1121 (D. N.J. Jan. 29, 1990) (No. 88-2642) (holding municipality liable under 42 U.S.C.A. §1983 (West 1981 & Supp. 1989) for failing to adequately train its police officers about how AIDS is spread and the need for confidentiality).

[4]A hospital in Connecticut was sued recently by a patient alleging that he was tested for HIV without his consent and the positive results were released to his employer. Dotson v. St. Mary's Hosp., No. 90017 (Conn. Super. Ct. Mar. 30, 1989) (digested in *Hospital Sued Over Testing, Release of Medical Records,* AIDS Poly. & L., April 19, 1989, at 3). An Oklahoma health center was sued by a former patient for allegedly publicly disclosing the results of a positive HIV test. The suit alleges violations of 42 U.S.C. §1983 and an Oklahoma law guaranteeing the confidentiality of medical records. Miller v. McAlester

dential information regarding an HIV diagnosis can result in a civil action for invasion of privacy. The damages that may be alleged can include loss of employment, loss of housing, loss of or inability to obtain insurance, school expulsion, social stigma and harassment, and mental anguish. A disclosure of inaccurate information intimating that a person is infected with the HIV virus could constitute defamation and would be actionable per se in most states without any specific proof of damages.[5]

§13.6.2 Specific Laws on Confidentiality of AIDS Information

An individual's constitutional right to confidentiality and privacy must be balanced against the public's need for information regarding testing and treatment.[6] Underpinning the need for confidentiality is the public policy of encouraging patients to provide necessary information to doctors and hospitals to allow treatment and diagnosis.[7]

More and more states and localities are enacting laws with varying degrees of protection of the confidentiality of AIDS information.[8] Some states have established the confidentiality of

---

Regional Health Center, No. 89-83-C (E.D. Okla. Feb. 28, 1989) (digested in *Hospital Sued Over Release of Patient's Test Results*, AIDS Poly. & L., April 5, 1989, at 9-10). See generally Annot. Physician's Tort Liability Apart from Defamation for Unauthorized Disclosure of Confidential Information About Patient, 20 A.L.R.3d 1109 (1968).

[5]Restatement (Second) of Torts §572 (1977) ("One who publishes a slander that imputes to another an existing venereal disease or other loathsome and communicable disease is subject to liability without proof of special harm."); see also Laura, AIDS in the Workplace, 10 Whittier L. Rev. 397, 417 (1988) (discussing defamation suit filed by a physician at Johns Hopkins alleging the hospital carelessly disclosed information to the physician's colleagues that he had contracted AIDS).

[6]See generally Dunne and Serio, Confidentiality: An Integral Component of AIDS Public Policy, 7 St. Louis U. Pub. L. Rev. 25 (1988).

[7]See infra §13.6.2, nn.12,13 and accompanying text.

[8]Gostin, Public Health Strategies for Confronting AIDS: Legislative and Regulatory Policy in the United States, 261 J.A.M.A. 1627 (Mar. 17, 1989).

medical information held or maintained by a state agency, healthcare provider or facility, physician, laboratory, blood bank, or third-party payor indicating that a person has AIDS or ARC or is a carrier of the AIDS antibody.[9] With certain limited exceptions, some states have prohibited disclosure of test results that relate to the presence of the AIDS virus.[10]

New York passed a law taking effect February 1, 1989 that prohibits disclosure of testing information unless it is relevant to a person's healthcare or warranted by other narrow need-to-know concerns.[11] Massachusetts's confidentiality law simply states: "No health care facility . . . and no physician or health care provider shall . . . disclose the results of such test to any person other than the subject thereof without first obtaining the subject's written informed consent."[12]

AIDS-related lawsuits alleging violations of confidentiality laws are presently winding their way through the courts.[13] In a recent decision, a Kansas state district court held that Kansas's confidentiality laws prohibited an HMO from advising the ex-spouse of an HIV-positive male of his condition.[14]

§13.6.3 Waiver of Confidentiality by Patients

A patient may choose to disclose medical information by signing a release. Because a patient with AIDS may be unaware that he

---

[9]Id.

[10]Id.

[11]1988 N.Y. Laws ch. 584 (S.9265-A).

[12]Mass. Gen. L. ch. 111, §70F (Supp. 1988).

[13]See, e.g., *Miller*, supra n.4 (alleging that certain certain agents and employees of the healthcare facility informed various other individuals not associated with the facility of patient's positive test results); Doe v. Wills Eye Hosp., No. 5248 (Phila. Ct. Com. Pl.); Doe v. Conly, No. 88-0486 (M.D. Pa.) (digested in *Three Lawsuits Claim Doctors Did Unauthorized HIV Tests*, AIDS Poly. & L., April 20, 1988, at 3-4); Doe v. Shasta Gen. Hosp., No. 923362 Shasta City Super Ct., (digested in *Hospital Sued for Dumping, Illegally Testing Patient*, AIDS Poly. & L., Jan. 27, 1988, at 9-10).

[14]Doe v. Prime Health/Kansas City, Inc., No. 88-5149 (Dist. Ct. of Johnson County, at 11-12 (Oct. 18, 1988); see also N.Y. Times, October 20, 1988, §1, at 9, col. 1.

is waiving confidentiality by signing a release, the American Bar Association's AIDS Coordinating Committee has recommended special release requirements to encourage afflicted individuals to seek counseling and treatment.[15]

§13.7 Disclosures to Third Parties in Danger of Exposure to Infection

§13.7.1 General Law of Duty to Warn

Under traditional common-law principles, there was no duty to attempt to control the conduct of another person or to warn those endangered by such conduct.[1] The landmark decision Tarasoff v. Regents of the University of California[2] and its progeny[3] have modified that rule in the case of medical personnel with specific knowledge that a psychiatric patient is likely to harm another person and have imposed a duty to warn the affected party of such danger. Some courts have limited this duty to cases of clear threats of harm to a reasonably identifiable potential victim,[4] while other courts have accepted a broader duty simply to act prudently to prevent reasonably foreseeable harm.[5] Healthcare providers such as hospitals have been held liable under the doctrines of vicarious liability and estoppel for

---

[15]AIDS: The Legal Issues 106 (1988); compare 42 C.F.R. §2.31 (1989).

§13.7 [1]Restatement (Second) of Torts §§314, 315 (1965).

[2]17 Cal. 3d 425, 551 P.2d 334, 131 Cal. Rptr. 14 (1976).

[3]E.g., Jablonski by Pahls v. United States, 712 F.2d 391 (9th Cir. 1983); Chrite v. United States, 564 F. Supp. 341 (E.D. Mich. 1983); Doyle v. United States, 530 F. Supp. 1278 (C.D. Cal. 1982); Thompson v. County of Alameda, 27 Cal. 3d 741, 614 P.2d 728, 167 Cal. Rptr. 70 (1980); Heltsley v. Votteler, 327 N.W.2d 759 (Iowa 1982).

[4]See, e.g., Brady v. Hopper, 570 F. Supp. 1333 (D. Colo. 1983); Thompson v. County of Alameda, 614 P.2d 728 (Cal. 1980); McIntosh v. Milano, 168 N.J. Super. 466, 403 A.2d 500 (1979).

[5]See, e.g., Jablonski by Pahls v. U.S., 712 F.2d 391 (9th Cir. 1983); Lipari v. Sears, Roebuck Co., 497 F. Supp. 185 (D. Neb. 1980); Davis v. Lhim, 124 Mich. App. 291, 335 N.W.2d 481 (Mich. App. 1983); Bradley Center v. Wessner, 161 Ga. App. 576, 287 S.E.2d 716 (1982).

the negligence of physicians in failing to warn third parties.[6] It is unclear whether a warning must be given if the potential victim is already aware of the danger.[7] Courts have held that the threat must be "real," not abstract.[8]

Cases have identified a duty on the part of physicians to warn a patient's family of the danger presented by the patient's contagious disease.[9] Courts have held that physicians have a duty to warn persons at risk of infection in cases involving a variety of communicable diseases including syphilis, tuberculosis, typhus, smallpox, diphtheria, scarlet fever, and meningitis.[10] These cases involved situations in which neither the patient nor the family was advised of the risk of transmission or situations in which family members caring for a patient were improperly instructed regarding the risk of contagion. The cases do not reach the issue of a physician's responsibility to warn third parties at risk, where a competent adult patient has been fully counseled by the physician regarding the need to take precautions to protect those third parties.

---

[6]Joy v. Eastern Maine Medical Center, 529 A.2d 1364 (Me. 1987); Shepard v. Redford Community Hosp., 151 Mich. App. 242, 390 N.W.2d 239 (1976). See generally Closen and Isaacman, The Duty to Notify Private Parties of the Risks of HIV Infection, 21 J. Health & Hospital L. 295 (Nov. 1988) (hereinafter Closen and Isaacman).

[7]See, e.g., Heltsley v. Votteler, 327 N.W.2d 759 (Iowa 1982); Cairl v. State, 323 N.W.2d 20 (Minn. 1982).

[8]White v. United States, 780 F.2d 97 (D.C. Cir. 1986).

[9]Hofmann v. Blackmon, 241 So. 2d 752 (Fla. Dist. Ct. App. 1970) (tuberculosis).

[10]See, e.g., Jones v. Stanko, 118 Ohio St. 147, 160 N.E. 456 (1928); Davis v. Rodman, 147 Ark. 385, 227 S.W. 612 (1921); Fostgate v. Coronia, 65 N.J. 283, 321 A.2d 244 (1974), remanded, 66 N.J. 268, 330 A.2d 355 (1974); Shepard v. Redford Community Hosp., 151 Mich. App. 242, 390 N.W.2d 239 (1986); Gammil v. United States, 727 F.2d 950 (10th Cir. 1984); Skillings v. Allen, 143 Minn. 323, 173 N.W. 663 (1919); State v. Wordin, 56 Conn. 216, 14 A. 801 (1887); Simonsen v. Swenson, 104 Neb. 224, 177 N.W. 831 (1920).

§13.7.2 Specific Laws on Warnings to Third Parties Regarding AIDS

Notifying third parties at risk is generally viewed as a legal responsibility of the relevant state or local health department. There is a general consensus that a healthcare provider should not have a legal duty to warn a third party of another person's AIDS diagnosis, as some cases have held in other third-party-warning situations.[11]

There has been a groundswell of support urging states to develop contact-tracing programs to locate partners of HIV-infected people. A limited number of states, such as Colorado and Idaho, have already implemented such programs with a degree of success.[12] Based in large part on the success of Colorado's program, the AMA has recently recommended name reporting of HIV-positive patients to state health departments for tracing and notification.[13]

The President's Commission stated in its report that once a healthcare provider has counseled a patient on all relevant issues and the patient refuses to notify a sexual partner at risk, the healthcare provider should have the *option* (but not the *obligation*) to inform the sexual partner.

Some states (for example, New York), have enacted legislation that permits a physician to disclose HIV test results to the spouse, sexual partner, or needle-sharing partner of a person who tests positive if the physician believes the contact is in danger of infection and will not be warned by the infected person.[14] Under New York's law, physicians are granted im-

---

[11]Report of the Presidential Commission on the Human Immunodeficiency Virus 128 (U.S. Government Printing Office: 1988 0-214-701 : QL 3) (June 1988) (hereinafter Presidential Commission Report).

[12]*AMA Urges State Policies Stressing Confidentiality*, AIDS Poly. & L., July 13, 1988, at 11; *State and Local Officials Urge Adoption of Contract Tracing Programs*, AIDS Poly. & L., Dec. 14, 1988, at 2.

[13]*AMA Changes Policy on HIV Infection; Says Treatment Advances Warrant Names*, AIDS Poly. & L., Feb. 7, 1990, at 1-2.

[14]1988 N.Y. Laws ch. 584 (S.9265-A). See also Cal. Health & Safety Code §199.25 (West 1988).

munity from liability for warning the contacts of infected persons, for failing to warn contacts, and for disclosing HIV information to authorized persons.[15]

Some commentators believe that when the infected individual cannot reasonably be trusted to refrain from risky behavior or to inform at-risk partners, the healthcare provider should directly inform the at-risk third parties about potential risks of HIV infection without identifying the patient.[16]

§13.7.3 Healthcare Facility Policies on Warnings

Facility Obligations Versus Practitioner Obligations. All 50 states, either by statute or regulation, require that healthcare facilities report confirmed cases of AIDS to the appropriate governmental health agency in their jurisdiction.[17] When patients are under the care of an independently practicing physician, any duty to warn potentially at-risk individuals is the specific responsibility of the physician.[18] The healthcare facility has the general responsibility to ensure that the practitioner knows and discharges any legal obligation imposed on him or her.[19] Healthcare facilities can be directly liable for the acts or omissions of employee practitioners and, in some jurisdictions, physicians who act as "apparent agents" of the hospital. Thus, when a healthcare facility has an indication that an infected patient has not or will not identify a reasonably identifiable sexual partner, the patient's physician and hospital personnel should consider making such a warning.[20]

---

[15]1988 N.Y. Laws ch. 584 (S.9265-A).

[16]Closen and Isaacman, at 300.

[17]See, e.g., Md. Health-Gen. Code Ann. §18-334(c)(3)(1990); Cal. Health & Safety Code §§1603.1(c), 1603.1(d) (West Supp. 1988). A California court allowed a cause of action against a healthcare facility that failed to report a communicable disease that purportedly caused a third party to become infected. See Derrick v. Ontario Community Hosp., 47 Cal. App. 3d 145, 120 Cal. Rptr. 566 (1975).

[18]AAHA AIDS Task Group (Spring 1988), at 39.

[19]Id.

[20]See AAHA AIDS Task Group (Spring 1988), at 38-39; Closen and Isaacman, at 300.

Consent to Warnings as a Condition of Treatment. Subject to the limitations set forth in §13.5.2, supra, a healthcare facility can arguably require consent to warnings as a condition of treatment.[21] Many physicians have found it useful to state to patients their policies regarding warnings before treatment begins and to give the patients an opportunity to obtain another physician if they cannot agree on the terms of the relationship.

Warnings to Other Medical Providers. Confidentiality requirements virtually never extend to reasonably restricted communications to persons rendering direct care to a patient with an infectious disease. A failure to warn hospital employees providing treatment to an AIDS patient may subject the attending physician or the hospital to liability. On December 13, 1989, a West Virginia jury awarded $2 million to a hospital security guard who was bitten by an AIDS patient even though the plaintiff has shown no sign of infection.[22] The jurors found that the hospital should have warned the plaintiff that the patient had AIDS.[23] Several lawsuits are presently pending in which nurses are suing facilities for failure to warn, alleging the nurses unknowingly treated AIDS patients or patients suspected of being infected with the virus.[24]

---

[21]See supra §13.5.2, nn.4-16 and accompanying text.

[22]*Jury Awards Man $2 Million After Biting by AIDS Patient*, AIDS Poly. & L., Jan. 10, 1990, at 8.

[23]Id.

[24]See, e.g., Halverson v. Brand, No. 121, E.D. Appeal Docket 1987 (Pa. Super. Ct. Apr. 1988) (digested in *Nurse Says Emotional Trauma Caused by Failure to Inform*, AIDS Poly. & L., April 20, 1988, at 6); O'Callaghan v. Stone, No. 678 (Dist. Ct. Douglas Cty. Neb. filed Aug. 17, 1987) (digested in *Nurse Sues Over Exposure, Incubation Period at Issue*, AIDS Poly. & L., Oct. 7, 1987, at 6).

Disclosure to enable hospital personnel who are at risk to protect themselves is recommended as part of the healthcare facility's general obligations regarding the safety of its staff. In addition, the patient's diagnosis may be recorded in the medical record, where authorized personnel will have access to it. Of course, procedures should be established to limit such access to hospital employees with a need for the information in order to care for the patient, to protect themselves.

B. The Effect of AIDS on Patient Care

§13.8 Refusals to Treat AIDS Patients

There are a variety of highly relevant laws related to the refusal of healthcare facilities to treat AIDS patients, including the Federal Rehabilitation Act, the Americans with Disabilities Act, general state antidiscrimination acts, and specific state laws prohibiting discrimination against patients with AIDS.

§13.8.1 Federal Law

The Federal Rehabilitation Act.[1]   The Rehabilitation Act of 1973 (Rehabilitation Act) and its regulations prohibit discrimination on the basis of a "handicap."[2] Section 503 of the Rehabilitation Act prohibits such discrimination in employment by any significant federal contractor (in excess of $2,500) and is enforced through an administrative procedure administered

---

§13.8 [1]29 U.S.C.A. §793 et seq. (West Supp. 1988). See generally Note, Kushen, Asymptomatic Infection with the AIDS Virus as a Handicap Under the Rehabilitation Act of 1973, 88 Colum. L. Rev. 563 (1988) (hereinafter Kushen).

[2]29 U.S.C.A. §706(8)(B) (West Supp. 1989) defines "individual with handicaps" as:

> Any person who (i) has a physical or mental impairment which substantially limits one or more of such person's major life activities, (ii) has a record of such an impairment, or (iii) is regarded as having such an impairment.

45 C.F.R. §84.3(j)(2)(i)(1989) defines "physical or mental impairment" as:

> (A) [A]ny physiological disorder or condition, cosmetic disfigurement, or anatomical loss affecting one or more of the following body systems: neurological; musculoskeletal; special sense organs; respiratory, including speech organs; cardiovascular; reproductive, digestive, genito-urinary; hemic and lymphatic; skin; and endocrine; or (B) any mental or psychological disorder, such as mental retardation, organic brain syndrome, emotional or mental illness, and specific learning disabilities.

by the Office of Federal Contract Compliance Programs (OFCCP).[3] Section 504 of the Rehabilitation Act provides that no "otherwise qualified" handicapped person shall, "solely by reason of her or his handicap, be excluded from the participation in, be denied the benefits of, or be subjected to discrimination under any program . . . receiving Federal financial assistance."[4] Regulations implementing the Rehabilitation Act prohibit discrimination against any employee or applicant "[b]ecause of physical or mental handicap in regard to any position for which the employee or applicant for employment is qualified."[5]

Hospitals receiving Medicare funds are subject to §504.[6] Section 504 is enforced through an administrative procedure prescribed by Title VI of the Civil Rights Act of 1964,[7] which can result in a cutoff of federal funds or a court action brought by the federal agency involved.[8] Section 504, unlike §503, can also be enforced by private causes of action brought in federal court by individuals alleged to have suffered such discrimina-

---

[3]29 U.S.C.A. §793 (West Supp. 1989). On December 23, 1988, the OFCCP issued a policy statement that under §503 of the Rehabilitation Act all HIV-related conditions are to be considered handicaps and it will review and investigate claims of AIDS-based discrimination. *Labor Department Sets Policy on Handling HIV Bias Charges*, AIDS Poly. & L., March 22, 1989, at 4.

[4]29 U.S.C.A. §794 (West Supp. 1989). The definition of "program or activity" is set forth in a new §504(b), which was added by §4 of the Civil Rights Restoration Act of 1987. "Program or activity" is now given an institution-wide scope rather than the program- or activity-specific scope called for by the Supreme Court's decision in Grove City College v. Bell, 465 U.S. 555 (1984) (holding that only the program or activity receiving federal funds had to comply with federal antidiscrimination laws.) In enacting the Civil Rights Restoration Act of 1987, Congress overruled *Grove City.*

[5]41 C.F.R. §60-741.4(a) (1989); see also Southeastern Community College v. Davis, 442 U.S. 397, 406 (1979) (a "qualified handicapped person" is one who can perform the essential functions of his or her job "in spite" of a handicap).

[6]See, e.g., United States v. University Hosp. of the State Univ. of N.Y., 575 F. Supp. 607 (E.D.N.Y. 1983), affd., 729 F.2d 144 (2d Cir. 1984); Frazier v. Board of Trustees of Northwest Miss. Regional Medical Center, 765 F.2d 1278 (5th Cir. 1985).

[7]42 U.S.C.A. §2000d et seq. (West 1981 & Supp. 1989).

[8]29 U.S.C.A. §794a (West 1989).

tion.[9] For a plaintiff to prevail on a §504 claim she must establish: (1) that she is handicapped; (2) that she is "otherwise qualified" for the benefit or program participation being sought; (3) that she was excluded from or discriminated against in a federal or federally funded program; (4) that the discrimination occurred solely by reason of her handicap; and (5) that she was otherwise qualified to participate in the covered program.[10]

Section 505 was added by 1978 amendments to clarify what remedies are available under the Rehabilitation Act.[11] This section permits a court to take into account "[i]n fashioning an equitable or affirmative action remedy . . . the reasonableness of the cost of any necessary work place accommodation, and the availability of alternatives . . . in order to achieve an equitable and appropriate remedy."[12]

The Department of Health and Human Services (DHHS) is the federal agency responsible for promulgating regulations for hospitals' compliance with the Rehabilitation Act.[13] The regulations developed by the DHHS define "handicap" broadly enough to cover physical impairments arising from a disease such as AIDS and include within the scope of the Act's protection not only persons having such impairments but also persons "regarded as having such an impairment."[14]

Any analysis of a HIV-related discrimination claim under the Rehabilitation Act must begin with the Supreme Court's 1987 decision in School Board of Nassau County v. Arline.[15] In Arline, the Supreme Court considered two related questions: whether a person afflicted with tuberculosis, a contagious disease, may be considered a "handicapped individual" within the meaning of §504 of the Rehabilitation Act and, if so, whether

---

[9]See, e.g., Andrews v. Consolidated Rail Corp., 831 F.2d 678 (7th Cir. 1987).

[10]29 U.S.C.A. §794 (West Supp. 1989).

[11]Id. §794a(a)(1) (West Supp. 1989).

[12]Id. In addition, §505 permits a prevailing party, other than the United States, reasonable attorneys' fees as part of costs.

[13]45 C.F.R. §84.1 et seq. (1989).

[14]Id. §84.3(j)(1)(iii) (1989).

[15]107 S. Ct. 1123 (1987).

such an individual is "otherwise qualified" to teach school.[16] The Supreme Court held in the first instance that an individual such as the plaintiff in *Arline*, who had a record of a physical impairment that was contagious, was "handicapped" and was thus covered under §504. Under the Rehabilitation Act, the plaintiff thus had a cause of action for discrimination premised on fear of contagion of the disease.

On the question of whether the plaintiff was "otherwise qualified," the Court held that the paucity of factual findings by the district court precluded it from resolving whether Arline was, in fact, "otherwise qualified."[17] The Court agreed with amicus American Medical Association that a district court's inquiry on this issue should include:

> [findings of] facts, based on reasonable medical judgments given the state of medical knowledge, about (a) the nature of the risk (how the disease is transmitted), (b) the duration of the risk (how long is the carrier infectious), (c) the severity of the risk (what is the potential harm to third parties) and (d) the probabilities the disease will be transmitted and will cause varying degrees of harm.[18]

The Supreme Court advised that district courts making these findings "normally" should first "defer to the reasonable medical judgments of public health officials,"[19] and that then they must evaluate whether the employer could reasonably accommodate the employee under the established standards for that industry.[20] Under this analysis, therefore, whether a specific action is illegal or permissible will depend largely on medical and scientific evidence regarding the probability of transmitting the disease in light of the facts of the specific case.

In *Arline*, the Supreme Court specifically avoided the question of whether an otherwise healthy and asymptomatic person

---

[16]Id. at 1126-1131.
[17]Id. at 1131.
[18]Id.
[19]Id. at 1124.
[20]Id.

infected with a contagious disease can be considered "handi-capped" within the meaning of the Rehabilitation Act.[21] The definition of "regarded as having an impairment" in the regu-lations includes persons treated by others as if they had an impairment that substantially limits their "major life activities."[22] If a person who is HIV-infected and asymptomatic is discrimi-nated against because of a fear of contagion, even if that fear is baseless, such a person will, in all likelihood, be protected by the Rehabilitation Act.

Court and administrative decisions both before and after *Arline* have held that individuals with AIDS or HIV are covered under §504 and state statutes as individuals with handicaps.[23] In Doe v. Centinela,[24] a federal district court in California held that an asymptomatic HIV carrier who is excluded from a federally-funded hospital chemical dependency program because of the fear of contagion is regarded as handicapped within the meaning of §504 of the Rehabilitation Act and is entitled to protection unless the provider can demonstrate a compelling

---

[21]Id. at 1128 n.7; but see Doe v. Centinela Hosp., 57 U.S.L.W. 2034 (C.D. Cal., June 30, 1988).

[22]45 C.F.R. §84.3(j)(2)(iv) (1989).

[23]See, e.g. Chalk v. United States Dist. Ct. of Cal., 840 F.2d 701 (9th Cir. 1988); Cronan v. New Eng. Tel. Co., 41 FEP Cas. 1273 (Mass. Sup. Ct. 1986); Local 1812, AFGE v. United States Dept. of State, 662 F. Supp. 50 (D.D.C. 1987); OCR Complaint No. 04-84-3096 (Aug. 6, 1986) (holding that a North Carolina hospital violated the Rehabilitation Act by forcing a registered nurse believed to have AIDS to take a medical leave of absence); See, e.g., Doe v. County of Cook, No. 87-C-6888 (N.D. Ill.) (digested in AIDS Poly. & L., March 9, 1988, at 7); Doe v. Howard Univ., No. 88-3412 (D.D.C. filed Nov. 23, 1988) (digested in AIDS Poly. & L., Dec. 14, 1988, at 6). Compare Kohl by Kohl v. Woodhaven Learning Center, 672 F. Supp. 1226 (W.D. Mo. 1987) (holding that carriers of hepatitis B are covered by the Rehabilitation Act). See generally Kushen, supra n.1; AIDS: The Legal Issues, 152-178 (1988).

[24]57 U.S.L.W. 2034 (C.D. Cal., June 30, 1988). Centinela Hospital Medical Center required that all patients admitted to its chemical dependency program be tested for HIV; anyone with a positive test result would be excluded. The plaintiff in *Centinela* claimed he received assurances that he would not be dropped from the program if he agreed to take the test; when he tested positive he was dropped from the program. He sued, claiming he was covered by the Rehabilitation Act.

need for a policy excluding all HIV-infected people.[25] A New York State trial court, emphasizing that the hepatitis B virus is considered "far more contagious" than HIV, would not enjoin a New York City school policy that allowed students with HIV infection to attend public school after a case-by-case review was undertaken of their individual conditions.[26]

Federal district courts in California, Florida, and Illinois have found school students with AIDS to be entitled to the protection of the Rehabilitation Act and have ordered that they be readmitted to public schools.[27] The United States Court of Appeals for the Ninth Circuit ordered that a teacher who had been assigned to a nonclassroom job based on his AIDS diagnosis be returned to his classroom duties.[28]

On March 22, 1988, both houses of Congress voted to override President Reagan's veto of the Civil Rights Restoration Act of 1987.[29] By amending the definition section of the

---

[25]On January 10, 1989, the parties settled the suit with Centinela, agreeing to drop the requirement that all patients admitted to its chemical dependency program be tested for HIV and that any patients testing positive be excluded. See California Hospital Drops Rule Requiring AIDS Testing, 1989 Modern Healthcare 40 (Jan. 27, 1989).

[26]District 27 Community School Bd. v. Board of Educ. of the City of N.Y., 502 N.Y.S.2d 325 (Sup. Ct. 1986).

[27]Robertson v. Granite City Community Unit School Dist. No. 9, 684 F. Supp. 1002 (S.D. Ill. 1988); Doe v. Dolton Elementary School Dist. No. 148, No. 87-C-8713 (N.D. Ill. June 23, 1988); Doe v. Belleville Pub. School Dist. No. 118, 672 F. Supp. 342 (S.D. Ill. 1987); Thomas v. Atascadero Unified School Dist., 662 F. Supp. 376 (C.D. Cal. 1987); Ray v. School Dist. of Desoto County, 666 F. Supp. 1524 (M.D. Fla. 1987); see also Martinez v. School Bd. of Hillsborough Co., No. 87-1308-CIV-T-17(A) (M.D. Fla. Apr. 26, 1989), digested in *In Brief*, AIDS Poly. & L., May 3, 1989, at 9-10 (7-year-old neurologically handicapped girl will not have to be isolated from other seven students in a glass-walled booth while at school.)

[28]Chalk v. United States Dist. Court, 840 F.2d 701 (9th Cir. 1988); see generally Note, Chalk v. United States District Court Central District of California: A Major Victory for AIDS Employees Under the Federal Rehabilitation Act of 1973, 22 Akron L. Rev. 241 (1988).

[29]*Congress Overrides Civil Rights Veto, Codifies Handicap Provision of Arline,* AIDS Poly. & L., Mar. 23, 1988, at 1. The Civil Rights Restoration Act of 1987 is codified at 29 U.S.C.A. §706 (West 1985 & Supp. 1989).

Rehabilitation Act, the bill codified the Supreme Court's *Arline* decision. The amendment provides, with respect to employment, a specific qualification of the definition of an "individual with handicaps" in the context of contagious diseases and infections:

> For the purpose of sections 503 and 504, as such sections relate to employment, [the term "individual with handicaps"] does not include an individual who has a currently contagious disease or infection and who, by reason of such disease or infection, would constitute a direct threat to the health or safety of other individuals or who, by reason of the currently contagious disease or infection, is unable to perform the duties of the job.[30]

On June 24, 1988, the Presidential Commission's final report recommended legislation to protect HIV-infected people under federal law and also recommended a retraction of the Justice Department's June 23, 1986 memorandum that concluded that while a person with "full-blown AIDS is handicapped" under §504, a mere "carrier" of the disease is not.[31] On August 2, 1988, President Reagan ordered all federal agencies to adopt a policy based on Office of Personnel Management guidelines issued in March that recommended that "people with AIDS be allowed to continue working as long as they are able to maintain acceptable performance and do not pose a safety or health threat to themselves or others in the workplace."[32]

On September 27, 1988, the Justice Department reversed the position it had espoused in June 1986 and announced that §504 of the Rehabilitation Act covers all people infected with HIV, including asymptomatic carriers, and that no justification exists to single out contagion as a legitimate basis for discrimination.[33] The opinion, authored by Douglas Kmiec, Acting Assistant Attorney General of the Department's Office of Legal

---

[30]Pub. L. No. 100-259, §9, 102 Stat. 28, 31-32 (1988). The Presidential Commission Report stated, "It appears that this amendment is in concert with the *Arline* decision and codifies the existing standards applicable to Section 504." Presidential Commission Report, at 122.

[31]See generally Presidential Commission Report.

[32]*Reagan Proposal Responding to Report Excludes Anti-Discrimination Support*, AIDS Poly. & L., Aug. 10, 1988, at 1.

[33]Department of Justice Opinion (Sept. 27, 1988).

Counsel, concluded that (1) persons with AIDS are protected under the Rehabilitation Act even though AIDS is a contagious disease, and (2) asymptomatic HIV-infected individuals are handicapped under the Act.[34] The October 6, 1988 opinion gave three justifications for reversing the position set forth in the prior memorandum: (1) the *Arline* decision, (2) the enactment of the Civil Rights Restoration Act of 1987, and (3) "medical clarification" from then-Surgeon General C. Everett Koop.[35] The opinion noted that if an individual posed a threat to the health and safety of others or was unable to perform the job or satisfy the requirements of the program, that individual could be excluded if there was no reasonable way to accommodate these health and safety and performance concerns.[36] The opinion is binding on all executive agencies and recipients of federal funds and covers job applicants as well as current employees.

The Americans with Disabilities Act.   The Americans with Disabilities Act (Pub. L. No. 101-336, 104 Stat. 327 (1990)) will extend antidiscrimination provisions similar to the Rehabilitation Act to employers and public accommodations that are not recipients of federal funds during a phase-in period beginning in January, 1992. (Public accommodations will be covered as of January 1992; employers with over 25 employees as of July 1992; and employers with over 15 employees as of July 1994.) The public accommodations provisions of the Act will extend these antidiscrimination provisions to individual physician offices for the first time.

§13.8.2 State Antidiscrimination Acts

All 50 states and the District of Columbia prohibit discrimination against the handicapped in a variety of circumstances.[37] Forty-nine states plus the District of Columbia have enacted statutes prohibiting employment discrimination against the

---

[34]Id. at 29.

[35]Id. at 2-3 n.4.

[36]Id. at 27-28.

[37]Brockhoeft, *AIDS in the Workplace: Legal Limitations on Employer Actions*, 26 Am. Bus. L. J. 295 (1988) (hereinafter Brockhoeft).

handicapped.[38] Some states' enactments track the language of the Rehabilitation Act,[39] while other states take different approaches that, although stated differently, cover physical impairments arising not only from injury or congenital condition but also from illness or disease.[40]

In one of the first AIDS employment decisions, the Florida Commission on Human Relations was asked to determine whether Florida's antidiscrimination statute could provide redress to an employee fired because he had AIDS. The Commission found the statute applicable and found reasonable cause to believe that it had been violated.[41] In reaching its decision, the Commission ruled that there was an "absence of evidence to show with any reasonable probability that AIDS can be transmitted by casual contact that commonly occurs in the workplace."[42] The Commission further ruled that the employer "failed to show that there was a substantial risk of future injury or reasonable basis for its assessment of risk of injury to the [employee], other employees or the public by retaining [the employee]. . . ."[43] The employee subsequently filed federal Rehabilitation Act and constitutional claims (due process and equal protection) in federal court.[44] The case ultimately was settled, with the employee receiving reinstatement, over $190,000 in cash and benefits, and $56,000 in attorneys' fees.[45]

---

[38]Brockhoeft, at 295. Delaware prohibits such discrimination by gubernatorial executive order.

[39]See, e.g., Mass. Gen. Laws Ann. ch. 151B, §1 (West Supp. 1988); R.I. Gen. Laws §28-5-6(7) (1986). Some jurisdictions look to federal court decisions under the Rehabilitation Act to interpret their state statutes. See, e.g., Clarke v. Shoreline School Dist. No. 412, 106 Wash. 2d 102, 720 P.2d 793 (1986).

[40]See, e.g., Mich. Comp. Laws Ann. §37.1103(b)(i) (West Supp. 1988); Ohio Rev. Code Ann. §4112.01(A)(13) (Anderson 1988).

[41]Shuttleworth v. Broward County Office of Budget & Mgmt. Poly., FCHR No. 85-0624 (slip op.) (Florida Commn. on Human Relations, Dec. 12, 1985) (reproduced in AIDS Law & Litigation Reporter, at 1).

[42]Id. at 6 (slip op.).

[43]Id. at 7.

[44]Shuttleworth v. Broward County, 639 F. Supp. 654 (S.D. Fla. 1986) (denying motions to dismiss constitutional claims).

[45]Settlement Reached in Landmark Bias Suit, AIDS Poly. & L., Dec. 17, 1986,

A state trial court in Massachusetts has held in ruling on a motion to dismiss that its state statute prohibits employment discrimination because an employee has AIDS.[46] A California appeals court unanimously held that AIDS comes within the physical handicap coverage of California's Fair Employment and Housing Act.[47] Various state agencies have also issued policy statements to the effect that state statutes will be interpreted to protect persons with HIV or AIDS.[48]

§13.8.3 Specific Laws and Enforcement Policies on AIDS

A number of states have enacted exacting statutes that prohibit AIDS discrimination.[49] The scope of each state's statute varies.

---

at 1. The county also agreed to treat any employee with AIDS as handicapped under federal law.

[46]Cronan v. New Eng. Tel. Co., 41 FEP 1273 (Mass. Sup. Ct. 1986); 1 Indiv. Empl. Rts. Cas. (BNA) 651 (Mass. Ct. 1986). See also Racine Educ. Assn. v. Racine United School Dist., 129 Wis. 2d 319, 385 N.W.2d 510 (Ct. App. 1986) (Wisconsin Equal Rights Division of the Department of Industry, Labor and Human Relations found probable cause to believe that the school district violated state antidiscrimination laws by adopting a policy barring teachers with AIDS from employment in school settings).

[47]Raytheon Co. v. California Fair Employment & Housing Commn., 212 Cal. App. 3d 1242, 261 Cal. Rptr. 197 (1989) (court held defendant violated California's discrimination law by refusing to permit employee to work after he was diagnosed with AIDS). See also Isbell v. Poor Richard's, No. EH-352-87 (W. Va. Human Rights Commn., Sept. 1, 1988) (digested in *West Virginia Rights Agency Upholds Award to Fired Waiter*, AIDS Poly. & L., Oct. 5, 1988, at 6) (hearing examiner of the West Virginia Human Rights Commission found that AIDS is a handicap under West Virginia law and loss of employment solely on a "perception" that an employee has AIDS is unlawful).

[48]E.g., *Maine Law Bars Discrimination, Panel Says*, AIDS Poly. & L., April 9, 1986, at 6 ("The Maine Human Rights Commission said . . . that state law banning handicap discrimination in employment, housing and public accommodations covers AIDS-based discrimination."). As of December 31, 1988, 34 jurisdictions, either by decisions of courts, human rights commissions, or attorneys general opinions, have determined that handicap laws apply to AIDS- or HIV-infected individuals. Gostin, Public Health Strategies for Confronting AIDS: Legislative and Regulatory Policy in the United States, 261 J.A.M.A. at 1622-1623 (1989).

[49]H.R. 136, 134th Leg., 1988 Del. Laws; 1988 Fla. Sess. Law Serv. 380

885

For example, the Florida statute prohibits HIV-related discrimination in housing, accommodations, and government services;[50] its employment discrimination provisions extend protection to any person with AIDS or ARC in addition to asymptomatic carriers of the HIV virus.[51] Rhode Island's statute prohibits discrimination against HIV-positive persons in housing, employment, public accommodations, and the granting of credit and delivery of services.[52] Vermont's statute prohibits discrimination on the basis of positive HIV test results in decisions involving employment, school admissions, and provision of healthcare.[53]

One commentator has noted that as of December 31, 1988 "[l]egislation related to AIDS [had] been enacted in every state and the District of Columbia, with over 170 statutes passed. The next decade will likely bring an unprecedented number of disease specific statutes, particularly as the epidemic moves to mainstream populations—heterosexuals and children."[54]

In addition to the above-listed states, virtually every other state has considered or is presently considering some form of AIDS antidiscrimination litigation. It is likely that in the early 1990s every state will have AIDS antidiscrimination legislation of some type in place.

§13.8.4 Healthcare Facility Responsibilities

Policies on Employee Refusals to Care for Patients. One commentator has noted the "[w]orsening apprehension, prejudice

---

(West); Ga. Code Ann. §31-22-9 et seq.; 1988 R.I. Pub. Laws 405; Vt. Stat. Ann. tit. 21, §495(a)(6) (1989).

[50]1988 Fla. Sess. Law Serv. 380 (West). The Florida Comprehensive AIDS Act amends several Florida statutes as well as creating §§381.607 to 381.614. For a discussion of the Florida Act, see McHugh, AIDS in the Workplace: Policy, Practice and Procedure, 18 Stetson L. Rev. 1, 60-64 (1988) (hereinafter McHugh).

[51]1988 Fla. Sess. Law Serv. 380 at §45(1). One commentator believes this section "[w]ould also cover individuals 'regarded as' falling into any of these categories." See McHugh, at 61.

[52]1988 R.I. Pub. Laws 405.

[53]Vt. Stat. Ann. tit. 21, §495(a)(6) (1989).

[54]Gostin, supra n.48, at 1621.

and fear which stretch like a mine field between [healthcare workers] and their AIDS patients."[55] Although there have been 22 reported cases of workplace transmission of AIDS to healthcare workers, present medical research indicates that the risk of exposure to the AIDS virus in the healthcare setting is slight.[56]

Healthcare workers such as physicians and nurses have an ethical obligation to provide treatment to AIDS patients. The American Nurses Association mandates that "the nurse provide[ ] services with respect for human dignity and the uniqueness of the client unrestricted by considerations of social or economic status, personal attributes, or the nature of health problems."[57] A failure to provide such treatment is considered unprofessional conduct.

With respect to physicians, the American College of Physicians has stated that "[t]he denial of care to patients for any reason is unethical. . . ."[58] The American College of Physicians has also pronounced a physician's refusal to treat an AIDS-infected patient "morally and ethically indefensible."[59] The Council on Ethical and Judicial Affairs of the American Medical Association has taken a similar stance.[60]

---

[55]Gagliano, When Health Care Workers Refuse to Treat AIDS Patients, 21 J. Health and Hosp. L. 10, 255 (1988) (hereinafter Gagliano).

[56]See *Seroconversion After Exposure Found by Study to Be Minimal*, AIDS Poly. & L., June 28, 1989, at 6-7 (An ongoing study by the CDC's Cooperative Needlestick Surveillance Group found that "[a] health care worker's risk of HIV seroconversion following an exposure to infected blood is less than 1 percent and may be as low as four-tenths of 1 percent."); T. Banks, The Right to Medical Treatment, AIDS and the Law 175 (1987); but see Gagliano, at 256.

[57]American Nurses' Association Code for Nurses, No. 1., reprinted in M. Benjamin and J. Curtis, Ethics in Nursing, Appendix B (2d ed. 1986).

[58]*ACP Says: MDs Obligated to Care for AIDS Patients*, 10 Am. Medical News (Mar. 18, 1988); *Physicians Group Affirms Patients' Right to Care*, AIDS Poly. & L., Mar. 9, 1988, at 3; Gagliano, at 257.

[59]*ACP Says: MDs Obligated to Care for AIDS Patients*, 10 Am. Medical News (Mar. 18, 1988); *Physicians Group Affirms Patients' Right to Care*, AIDS Poly. & L., Mar. 9, 1988, at 3; Gagliano, at 257.

[60]Ethical Issues Involved in the Growing AIDS Crisis, 259 J.A.M.A. 1360 (1988). ("AIDS patients are entitled to competent medical service with compassion and respect for human dignity and to the safeguard of their confidences within the constraints of the law. . . . A physician may not

Physicians who are employed by a hospital waive their right to refuse to treat patients[61] and are required, with certain exceptions, to provide treatment to any patient a hospital admits.[62] The same principle applies to other employees.[63]

Despite these considerations, the threat of AIDS causes some healthcare workers to refuse to treat AIDS patients or perform job-related duties involving AIDS.[64] When this occurs, a healthcare facility, with employee education and counseling, can allay the fears of its workers. When a worker refuses to care for an AIDS patient he or she should initially receive further counseling. If the universal precautions of the CDC are followed,[65] any risk of transmission is negligible and should be considered a reasonable condition of the employee's work and not actionable. If an employee still won't treat an HIV-infected patient, a facility may attempt to accommodate such employee by a job transfer or may discipline him or her for insubordination.[66]

Policies on Independent Practitioner Refusals.   Generally, an independent physician is under no obligation to treat any patient, except in cases of emergency,[67] if a physician-patient relationship

---

ethically refuse to treat a patient whose condition is within the physician's current realm of competence solely because the patient is seropositive.")

[61]Hiser v. Randolph, 617 P.2d 774 (Ariz. Ct. App. 1980).

[62]See, e.g., Buttersworth v. Swint, 53 Ga. App. 602, 186 S.E.2d 770 (Ga. App. 1936).

[63]Many states have enacted statutes that protect hospital employees from discharge for refusal to participate in procedures such as abortions.

[64]See, e.g., Stepp v. Review Bd. of the Indiana Employment Sec. Div., No. 93A02-8707-EX-278 (Ind. Ct. App. 4th Dist. Apr. 4, 1988) (LEXIS, Indiana library).

[65]See text accompanying §§13.4.1, nn.2-4 supra.

[66]See, e.g., Stepp, supra n.64 (refusal to perform assigned laboratory tests on fluids with AIDS warnings justifies dismissal); Free v. Holy Cross Hosp., 153 Ill. App. 3d 45, 505 N.E.2d 1188 (Ill. App. Ct. 1987). In making a reassignment or transfer, however, a healthcare facility must act within the applicable limitations imposed by any collective bargaining agreement or the National Labor Relations Act. See text accompanying §13.10.4, nn.20-25 infra.

[67]1989 Current Opinions, Council on Ethical and Judicial Affairs of the American Medical Association §§8.11, 9.06.

does not exist. However, even a preexisting relationship may not guarantee continued treatment when a patient is stricken with AIDS, because the AIDS could be construed as a new (and different) illness.[68] Once a physician-patient relationship for treating a specific illness is established, the relationship must be maintained until treatment is completed unless terminated by both the patient and the physician, by the patient, by the physician with appropriate notice, or until medical treatment is no longer required. If a patient is in a life-threatening situation, a physician who refuses to continue to provide treatment could be sued for abandonment.[69]

Refusal to establish a physician-patient relationship because the patient has AIDS or an HIV infection may become a violation of federal law, however, when the public accommodations provisions of the ADA become effective in January 1992.

A New York State supreme court dismissed a complaint by a man suffering from AIDS on the ground that a physician's private office is not a public accommodation within the meaning of the State's antidiscrimination law.[70] The plaintiff had been a regular patient of the physician when he sought treatment in 1986 for a variety of ailments. Shortly after disclosing that he was suffering from AIDS he was told that the physician did not have the expertise to treat AIDS patients, and he was advised to seek treatment at an AIDS clinic.[71] The court rejected the plaintiff's claim of discrimination.[72]

---

[68]For an analysis of the positions of state medical licensing boards on requiring physicians to treat HIV-infected persons, see W. Dornette, AIDS and the Law, Appendix S (1989 Supp.).

[69]See, e.g., Norton v. Hamilton, 92 Ga. App. 727, 89 S.E.2d 809 (Ga. App. 1955); see generally Brandt, Health Care Workers and AIDS, 48 Md. L. Rev. 1, 43 (1989); Laura, AIDS in the Workplace, 10 Whittier L. Rev. 393, 427 (1988).

[70]Elstein v. State Division of Human Rights, N.Y. Sup. Ct. Onondago County, Aug. 15, 1988 (digested in 200 N.Y.L.J. 1, col. 3 (1988)).

[71]Id.

[72]The controlling statute listed "dispensaries, clinics, [and] hospitals," among others, as places of public accommodation. N.Y. Exec. Law §296(2)(a) (McKinney 1982 & Supp. 1988); see also Turk, AIDS: The First Decade, 14 Employee Relations L.J. 531, 543-534 (Spring 1989).

§13.9 Medical Malpractice in the Treatment of Infected Patients

§13.9.1 Sources of Liability in General

There are a variety of causes of action that a plaintiff in a case involving AIDS could bring against physicians, healthcare workers, and healthcare facilities, including:

1. breach of confidentiality;
2. failure to diagnose or misdiagnosis;
3. refusal to treat;
4. abandonment;
5. failure to provide counseling before testing;
6. failure to counsel after a positive test;
7. failure to inform the patient or his guardian or obtain an informed consent;
8. failure to warn third parties;
9. failure to properly conduct laboratory testing;
10. failure to adequate protect and/or warn workers and attending physicians;
11. blood bank and/or healthcare facility liability for transmitting the virus through improper or defective testing and screening procedures;
12. failure to inform patients of blood transfusion options.[1]

§13.9.2 Failure to Diagnose

As with other serious diseases and illnesses, a failure to diagnose or a misdiagnosis of AIDS may result in a delay or a lack of

---

§13.9 [1]See D. Louisell and H. Williams, Medical Malpractice §19A (1989); Hermann, Torts: Private Lawsuits about AIDS, in W. Dornette, AIDS and the Law 153 (1987); see also Baker and Arthur, AIDS in the Hospital Workplace: Theories of Hospital Liability, 24 Tort & Ins. L.J. 1 (Fall 1988); AIDS Malpractice Seen as Growing Problem for Health Care, AIDS Alert 205 (Dec. 1988).

treatment that may lead to an aggravated or exacerbated condition, unnecessary surgery, or premature death.[2] Of course, a significant factor in the award of any damages for a failure to diagnose would be the fact that there is, as of the time of this writing, no known cure for AIDS.

Plaintiffs in AIDS cases whose conditions have gone undiagnosed or misdiagnosed may be able to recover for emotional distress.[3] A plaintiff could seek to recover when she suffers psychological distress on discovering that treatment has been delayed, as well as when an erroneous diagnosis is made.[4]

There is as yet little case law on the issue of failure to diagnose dealing specifically with AIDS. In one case, however, a plaintiff who actually had an AIDS-related disorder but was misdiagnosed as suffering from asthma and psychosomatic illness was awarded $750,000 by a Massachusetts jury.[5] The plaintiff successfully argued that the misdiagnosis of her condition led to the necessity of longer hospital stays, an aggravation of her condition, and a shorter life span.[6]

---

[2]See, e.g., Willard v. Hutson 234 Or. 148, 378 P.2d 966 (1963) (failure to diagnose hemophilia; wrong diagnosis must be negligent and must be followed by improper treatment to the injury in order to be actionable).

[3]Cf. VanVleet v. Pfeifle, 289 N.W.2d 781 (N.D. 1980) (if physicians "were negligent in failing to diagnose cancerous condition," the fact that the patient would have eventually died, even if the cancer had been discovered sooner, does not relieve physicians of liability); MacMahon v. Nelson, 568 P.2d 90 (Colo. App. 1977) (defendant doctor's failure to diagnose cancerous tumor and resulting eight-month delay of removal caused plaintiff compensable emotional distress.)

[4]Cf. MacMahon.

[5]Ramos v. Harvard Community Health Plan, No. 86-4114 (Mass. Super. Ct., Middlesex County, Jan. 20, 1988). For a discussion of the *Ramos* case, see AIDS Malpractice Seen as Growing Problem for Health Care, AIDS Alert 205-208 (Dec. 1988).

[6]See id.; see also Maynard v. New Jersey, No. 89-143 (D.N.J. July 28, 1989) (digested in *Failure to Diagnose, Treat at Issue in New Jersey Suit*, AIDS Poly. & L., Sept. 20, 1989, at 8. In *Maynard* the judge refused to dismiss a suit against a doctor and nurse at a New Jersey prison who allegedly violated the civil rights of a prisoner by failing to diagnose and treat the inmate's AIDS-related illness. The court stated: "A medical need rises to the level of seriousness envisioned by *Estelle* [v. Gamble, 429 U.S. 97 (1976)] if that need is 'one that

§13.9.3 Failure to Counsel Patient Properly

When an individual is tested for AIDS, it is universally agreed that both pre- and post-test counseling should be given.[7] Prior to testing, counseling should be integrated with obtaining the individual's informed consent.[8] Some jurisdictions permit health-care providers to order an HIV test only after counseling the patient regarding the test.[9]

The Presidential Commission recommended in its report that the type and intensity of counseling accompanying the testing be guided by two factors—the test result and the reason the individual gives for seeking a test.[10] The Commission advised that a brochure could suffice when the test result is negative;[11] if the result is positive, then intensive personal counseling is recommended.[12] The Commission strongly recommended that the initial counseling after a positive test result include the distribution in writing of the following information: (1) the implications of the test result and the opportunity for further testing and counseling; (2) the responsibility to avoid spreading

---

has been diagnosed by a physician as requiring treatment or one that is so obvious that a lay person would easily recognize the necessity for a doctor's attention.' "

[7]Report of the Presidential Commission on the Human Immunodeficiency Virus 73-75 (U.S. Govt. Printing Office: 1988 0-214-701 : QL 3) (June 1988) (hereinafter Presidential Commission Report); see also 36 Morb. and Mort. Weekly Report 509 (Aug. 14, 1987); Laura, AIDS in the Workplace, 10 Whittier L. Rev. 397, 421-422 (1988).

[8]See, e.g., AIDS: The Legal Issues 97-98 (1988).

[9]See, e.g., Ga. Code Ann. §31-22-9.2(c) (Supp. 1989). "Counseling" is defined as providing the person with information and explanations medically appropriate for that person, which may include all or part of the following: accurate information regarding AIDS and HIV; an explanation of behaviors that reduce the risk of transmitting AIDS and HIV; an explanation of the confidentiality of information relating to AIDS diagnoses and HIV tests; an explanation of information regarding both social and medical implications of HIV tests; and disclosure of commonly recognized treatment or treatments for AIDS and HIV. Ga. Code Ann. §31-22-9.1(a)(6) (Supp. 1989).

[10]Presidential Commission Report, at 73.

[11]Id.

[12]Id. at 74.

the virus to other individuals and the means to accomplish that; (3) the responsibility for notifying the infected individual's sexual and drug partners; and (4) the availability of public health services to advise those individuals should the infected person refuse or be unable to do so.[13]

The Commission recommended counseling both before and after the administration of the test when an individual indicates that the reason for taking the test is high-risk behavior.[14] A person who has been involved in behavior that places him at high risk to develop the virus but who has a negative test should receive counseling regarding the meaning of the result and how he can remain uninfected.[15] Although there are, at the time of this writing, no known reported cases imposing liability for a failure to provide counseling, it is well-documented that positive HIV tests have led to depression and suicide.[16]

C. The Effect of AIDS on Healthcare Facility Personnel Policy

§13.10 Employment Discrimination

§13.10.1 Federal Antidiscrimination Laws

As noted above, the Rehabilitation Act prohibits discrimination against "individuals with handicaps."[1] Section 503 of the Rehabilitation Act prohibits discrimination in employment by federal agencies, by contractors and subcontractors who do more than $2,500 in business with the United States government, and by recipients of federal funds.[2] Section 504 provides in relevant

---

[13]Id.
[14]Id.; see also AIDS: The Legal Issues, at 98 (1988).
[15]Presidential Commission Report, at 74.
[16]See W. Dornette, AIDS and the Law §2.7A (1987 & Supp. 1989).
§13.10 [1]See supra §13.8.1, nn.1-36 and accompanying text.
[2]Id.

part: "No otherwise qualified handicapped individual in the United States, as defined in §706(7) of this title, shall, solely by reason of his handicap, be excluded from participation in, be denied the benefits of, or be subjected to discrimination under any program or activity receiving federal financial assistance."[3]

The Supreme Court, in the *Arline* decision, held that an elementary school teacher with contagious tuberculosis was a "handicapped person" within the meaning of the Rehabilitation Act.[4] Under the *Arline* decision a symptomatic or an asymptomatic HIV-infected individual is protected against discrimination if he or she is able to perform the duties of the job and does not constitute a direct threat to the health or safety of others, subject to an employer's making reasonable accommodations within the terms of the existing personnel policies.[5] Cases decided before and after *Arline* have held that people stricken with AIDS, as well as those infected with HIV, are protected by §504 of the Act and by state statutes.[6]

The Civil Rights Restoration Act of 1987 includes a provision that codifies the "otherwise qualified" standard discussed by the Supreme Court in *Arline*. This amendment[7] modifies the definitions section of the Rehabilitation Act to provide, in regard to employment, that the term "individual with handicaps" in the context of contagious disease and infections does not include "an individual who has a currently contagious disease or infection and who, by reason of such disease or infection, would constitute a direct threat to the health or safety of other individuals or who, by reason of the currently contagious disease

---

[3]29 U.S.C.A. §794 (West 1985 & Supp. 1989).

[4]School Bd. of Nassau County, Fla. v. Arline, 107 S. Ct. 1123 (1987); see supra §13.8.1, nn.15-22 and accompanying text.

[5]107 S. Ct. at 1130-1131 (1987).

[6]Id. See also Chalk v. United States Dist. Ct. of Cal., 840 F.2d 701, 46 FEP 279 (9th Cir. 1988); Raytheon Co. v. Fair Employment & Housing Commn., 212 Cal. App. 3d 1242, 261 Cal. Rptr. 197 (1989) (state law) (digested in *California Appeals Court Upholds Ruling that AIDS Is a Handicap Under State Law*, AIDS Poly. & L., Sept. 6, 1989, at 1, 10); Cronan v. New Eng. Tel. Co., 41 FEP 1273 (Mass. Sup. Ct. 1986) (state law).

[7]Pub. L. No. 100-259, §9, 102 Stat. 28, 31-32 (1988).

or infection, is unable to perform the duties of the job.''[8] The Justice Department's most recent opinion on the subject stated that before determining that an HIV-infected employee is not an ''individual with handicaps,'' an employer must first consider whether, consistent with the employer's existing personnel policies for the job in question, reasonable accommodation would eliminate the health or safety threat or enable the employee to perform the duties of the job.[9]

On December 23, 1988, the Labor Department's Office of Federal Contract Compliance Programs issued a policy statement regarding investigations under §503 stating that all HIV-related conditions are to be considered ''handicaps'' and that it will review and investigate complaints of AIDS-based discrimination.[10]

In July 1990, the President signed the Americans with Disabilities Act, which will prohibit discrimination based on disability by employers with 25 or more employees beginning in 1992 and employers with 15 or more employees beginning in 1994.

§13.10.2 State Antidiscrimination Laws

As described above,[12] numerous states have enacted statutes that prohibit discrimination on the basis of disability or physical handicap and that parallel the language of the Rehabilitation Act.[13] Other states have enacted statutes that cover physical

---

[8]Id.

[9]Department of Justice Opinion (Oct. 6, 1988), at 21-28. Id. at 27-28. Relying in part on the Department of Justice's opinion, the Department of Housing and Urban Development issued final regulations effective March 12, 1989, which state that HIV-infected individuals are protected from discrimination in housing and real estate transactions. See 54 Fed. Reg. 3232 (1989); see also *HIV Infection a Handicap Under Fair Housing Act Rules*, AIDS Poly. & L., Mar. 8, 1989, at 4.

[10]See *Labor Department Sets Policy on Handling HIV Bias Charges*, AIDS Poly. & L., Mar. 22, 1989, at 4.

[12]See supra §13.8.2, nn.37-48 and accompanying text.

[13]See supra §13.8.2, n.39.

impairments arising not only from injury or congenital conditions but also from illness or disease.[14]

§13.10.3 Specific Laws on Discrimination Against AIDS-Infected Employees

Use of HIV Tests. An increasing number of states have enacted statutes prohibiting or restricting HIV testing.[15] California is one state that prohibits the use of serologic test results in employment and insurance decisions.[16] Some states restrict an employer's ability to require an HIV test as a condition of employment.[17]

Prohibitions on Discrimination. Once an employee is diagnosed as having HIV or AIDS, or is perceived as having either affliction, the protections of the Rehabilitation Act and any applicable state antidiscrimination laws or ordinances are triggered.[18] Numerous jurisdictions have enacted some form of statute prohibiting employment discrimination based on AIDS.[19]

§13.10.4 The National Labor Relations Act

In any AIDS employment case the National Labor Relations Act (NLRA) may be relevant.[20] A healthcare facility whose employees are organized into a labor union must bargain over all wages,

---

[14]See supra §13.8.2, n.40.

[15]Schurgin, The Impact of AIDS Upon Health Care Employees, 21 J. Health and Hosp. L. 285 (Nov. 1988) (hereinafter Schurgin).

[16]Cal. Health & Safety Code §199.2 (West 1988).

[17]See e.g., Wis. Stat. Ann. §103.15(2)(b) (West 1988 & Supp. 1989).

[18]See supra §§13.8, nn.1-48 and accompanying text.

[19]Gostin, Public Health Strategies for Confronting AIDS: Legislative and Regulatory Policy in the United States, 261 J.A.M.A. 1622-1623 (1989).

[20]29 U.S.C.A. §151 et seq. (West 1973 & Supp. 1989) See generally AAHA Task Group (Spring 1988), at 47-48.

hours, and other terms and conditions of employment.[21] The National Labor Relations Board and courts have consistently held that changes in workplace rules, particularly those carrying disciplinary penalties, affect terms and conditions of employment, and therefore bargaining is mandated.[22] Thus, in order for a healthcare facility that is unionized to implement an AIDS policy, such policy or policies are subject to bargaining, unless the union has waived its right to bargain. In the absence of a waiver, an employer will be required to give prior notice to the union of any proposed AIDS policy and to bargain about such a proposal if requested to do so. When prior notice and bargaining are required, the parties are not required to reach agreement but only to bargain in good faith. If the employer and union bargain to an impasse, the employer may be permitted to implement unilaterally the term of the final offer made to the union prior to impasse.

Section 7 of the NLRA protects both union and nonunion employees' rights "to engage in . . . concerted activities for the purpose of collective bargaining or other mutual aid or protection."[23] Section 7's protection includes refusals by employees to work if a job is believed to be unsafe. As a general matter, a concerted refusal to work must be based on a good-faith perception that the employee would be exposed to a hazardous working condition.[24] Given the current status of medical evidence regarding AIDS, an employee may find it difficult to prove a good-faith perception of harm.[25]

---

[21]29 U.S.C.A. §174 (West 1978 & Supp. 1989).

[22]See, e.g., Gallenkamp Stores Co. v. NLRB, 402 F.2d 525, 529 n.4 (9th Cir. 1968) ("company rules concerning . . . employee discipline are mandatory bargaining subjects").

[23]29 U.S.C.A. §157 (West 1973 & Supp. 1989). Employees engaged in protected concerted activity may lose that protection if they engage in activity in an abusive manner. See, e.g., NLRB v. City Disposal Systems, 465 U.S. 822 (1984); see also Good Samaritan Hosp., 265 N.L.R.B. 618 (1982).

[24]See, e.g., Daniel Const. Co., 267 N.L.R.B. 1213 (1983).

[25]See, e.g., Schurgin, at 291; but see AIDS: The Legal Issues, at 74-75 (1988).

§13.10.5 Other Employment-Related Laws

Confidentiality of Personnel Information.   An employer may be liable for the tort of defamation for publishing a false statement that an employee has a contagious disease.[26] Of course, if the information that is disclosed is accurate and thus not defamation, the employee would have a cause of action based on invasion of privacy.[27] The employer would be able to assert a qualified privilege where a public or private interest is served.[28]

Workers' Compensation Laws.   Workers' compensation statutes in every state establish a system that pays specified amounts to employees injured by job-related illnesses or injuries and that imposes a liability for these costs on employers.[29] As a general matter, such statutes provide the employee's only remedy if the employee is injured or contracts an occupational disease at the place of employment. Claims arising from infectious diseases such as tuberculosis have been recognized under state workers' compensation statutes.[30] As a general rule, for an employee to recover workers' compensation she would need to establish that her illness was an occupational disease that was contracted on the job.[31] Courts have shown an inclination to find that a disease is occupational in nature if the disease can in any way be shown to have been derived from the facilities of the workplace. In the vast majority of diseases that AIDS patients develop, however, the employee would likely find it difficult to prove that the infection was contracted in the workplace rather than elsewhere.

---

[26]AAHA AIDS Task Group (Spring 1988), at 50.

[27]W. Dornette, AIDS and the Law, at §8.16; see also Restatement (Second) of Torts §652D (1977).

[28]Cf. Simonsen v. Swensen, 104 Neb. 224, 177 N.W. 831 (1920).

[29]See, e.g., Ga. Code Ann. §§34-9-1 to 34-9-367 (1988 & Supp. 1989); Ill. Rev. Stat. ch. 48, ¶172.42 (1988 & Supp. 1989); see generally 1B Larson Workers' Comp. Laws §41 (1987).

[30]Hovancik v. General Aniline & Film Corp., 8 A.D.2d 171, 187 N.Y.2d 28 (1959) (holding employee who shared pipe with co-employee who had tuberculosis was entitled to workers' compensation.)

[31]See, e.g., Fulton-DeKalb Hosp. Auth. v. Bishop, 185 Ga. App. 771, 365 S.E.2d 549 (Ga. Ct. App. 1988); Schurgin, at 290.

Contract Law.   Before any action is taken against an employee with HIV or AIDS, any relevant employment contracts, handbooks, or bargaining agreements must be examined.[32] Employment contracts may have grievance procedures and notice provisions regarding terminations.

Wrongful Discharge Law.   In the absence of a limiting statute or agreement of the parties, employment law presumes that private employment is "at will."[33] The employment-at-will doctrine permits either the employee or employer to terminate the employment at any time, without notice and without cause.[34] The concept of employment at will has been limited by the judicially created doctrine of wrongful discharge.[35] Numerous decisions have permitted wrongful discharge lawsuits based on the theories of contract liability,[36] the implied duty of good faith and fair dealing,[37] and tort liability premised on public policy.[38]

The Employee Retirement Income Security Act.[39]   The Employee Retirement Income Security Act (ERISA) prohibits an employer from discharging an employee "for the purpose of

---

[32]AAHA AIDS Task Group (Spring 1988), at 47.

[33]See AAHA AIDS Task Group (Spring 1988), at 48.

[34]Restatement (Second) of Agency §442, comment A (1958). See generally Hawkins, *Employment At Will: A Survey*, 39 Labor L.J. 525 (Aug. 1988).

[35]See generally Brockhoeft, AIDS in the Workplace: Legal Limitations on Employer Actions, 26 Am. Bus. L.J. 255, 265-278 (Summer 1988) (hereinafter Legal Limitations).

[36]See, e.g., Pine River State Bank v. Mettille, 333 N.W.2d 622 (Minn. 1983). The courts of at least 17 states have recognized some form of this exception. Legal Limitations, at 272 n.55.

[37]See, e.g., Cleary v. American Airlines, 111 Cal. App. 3d 443, 168 Cal. Rptr. 722 (1980); Fortune v. National Cash Register Co., 373 Mass. 96, 364 N.E.2d 1251 (1977). At least five states have recognized the implied duty of good faith and fair dealing. Legal Limitations, at 271 n.48.

[38]See, e.g., Kelsay v. Motorola, 74 Ill. 2d 172, 384 N.E.2d 353 (1978). At least 27 states have recognized or would likely recognize the public policy exception in an appropriate case. Legal Limitations, at 267 n.38. See generally American Hospital Association, The Wrongful Discharge of Employees in the Health Care Industry, No. 10 (Aug. 1987), at 3-7.

[39]29 U.S.C.A. §1140 (West 1985 & Supp. 1988).

·interfering with the obtainment of right to which [an employee] may become entitled" under an employee benefit plan. Health insurance is an ERISA covered benefit.[40] In contrast to the handicap discrimination laws, ERISA applies to all employers who maintain employee benefit plans. Thus, an employer who might not be prohibited by employee discrimination laws from discharging an employee could be precluded from terminating an employee with an HIV- or AIDS-related illness for the purpose of avoiding medical care costs.[41]

The Consolidated Omnibus Budget Reconciliation Act of 1986 amended ERISA to create an additional obligation with respect to employee benefits by requiring an employer to allow an employee who is discharged for reasons other than "gross misconduct" to continue to participate in the employer's group health plan for up to 18 months.[42] An employer may condition an employee's participation on the payment of premiums by the employee; however, the premiums may not be more than 2 percent above the normal premium for inclusion in the plan by an active employee.

§13.10.6 Infected Job Applicants

Regulations promulgated to implement §504 of the Rehabilitation Act prohibit an employer from engaging in broad inquiries into an applicant's handicapped status. Under the regulations, an employer "may not conduct a preemployment medical examination or may not make preemployment inquiry of an applicant as to whether the applicant is a handicapped person or as to the nature or severity of a handicap."[43] The regulations do permit an employer to make preemployment inquiries into

---

[40]See, e.g., Zipf v. American Tel. and Tel., 799 F.2d 889 (3d Cir. 1986); Folz v. Marriott Corp., 594 F. Supp. 1007 (W.D. Mo. 1984).

[41]See, e.g., Kross v. Western Elec. Co., 701 F.2d 1238 (7th Cir. 1983); State Div. of Human Rights v. Xerox Corp., 65 N.Y.2d 213, 480 N.E.2d 695 (N.Y. 1985).

[42]29 U.S.C.A. §§1161-1168 (1989 Supp.).

[43]45 C.F.R. §84.14(a) (1989).

"an applicant's ability to perform job-related functions."[44] Regulations also permit an employer to condition the offer of employment on the results of a medical examination undertaken before the applicant starts work, if such a test is required of all new employees regardless of handicap and the results of such an examination are used only in accordance with the requirements of the Rehabilitation Act.[45]

If the employer is subject to the Rehabilitation Act, then the employer must comply with the Act's requirements. In addition, state and local statutes and ordinances must be reviewed for prohibitions on the refusal to hire applicants because of AIDS conditions. One commentator has noted: "If the applicant is presently impaired in a way that prevents him from fully and effectively satisfying the various duties connected to the job, the employer has a legitimate interest in not hiring him."[46] Further, if the applicant is in remission at the time of application, but has lengthy hospital stays in his recent past, with lengthy incapacity reasonably expected in the near future, then the employer should not be required to hire the applicant.[47] On the other hand, if the applicant tests positive for HIV but has no symptoms and has the ability to perform the duties in question, he should be hired under ordinary circumstances.[48] A future inability to perform a job has been consistently held to be no defense in instances such as this.[49]

§13.10.7 Requirements to Report HIV Infections

A healthcare provider can and should implement a policy requiring employees to report known HIV infections. Once a

---

[44]Id.

[45]45 C.F.R. §84.14(c) (1989).

[46]W. Banta, AIDS in the Workplace 120 (1988).

[47]Id.

[48]Id.

[49]Chrysler Outboard Corp. v. Department of Indus., Labor and Human Resources, 14 FEP 344, 345 (Wis. Cir. Ct. 1976) (risk of future absenteeism does not constitute a legal basis for discriminating against handicapped individuals).

healthcare provider is notified that an employee is infected, the provider should take steps to ensure infection control. Of course, the employee's right to confidentiality must not be breached or the provider will be subject to possible civil liability.

§13.10.8 Imposing Testing Requirements on Employees

As noted above, regulations promulgated to implement the Rehabilitation Act govern employment-related testing by facilities that are subject to the Rehabilitation Act. An employer cannot require an individual to be tested for HIV unless it can show that such testing is "job-related"—not an easy task. A difficult issue arises with respect to employees who perform invasive procedures or are likely to be in contact with patients where blood-to-blood exposure may occur.[50]

More and more states are enacting statutes that prohibit or restrict HIV testing.[51] Mandatory testing of public employees raises constitutional claims under the Fourth Amendment.[52] A recent decision by the United States District Court for the District of Nebraska[53] held that the policy of a state agency in Nebraska that required certain employees to undergo mandatory testing for HIV violated the Fourth Amendment. The district court concluded that the state agency could not mandate such testing because

> [a]lthough pursuit of a safe work environment for employees and a safe training and living environment for all clients is a

---

[50]Schurgin, at 289.

[51]Gostin, Public Health Strategies for Confronting AIDS: Legislative and Regulatory Policy in the United States, 261 J.A.M.A. 1622-1623 (Mar. 17, 1989).

[52]See generally Comment, The Constitutional Implications of Mandatory Testing for Acquired Immunodeficiency Syndrome, 37 Emory L.J. 217 (Winter 1988).

[53]Glover v. Eastern Neb. Community Office of Retardation, 686 F. Supp. 243 (D. Neb. 1988).

worthy one, the policy does not reasonably serve that purpose. There is simply no real basis to be concerned that clients are at risk of contracting AIDS virus at the work place. These clients are not in danger of contracting the AIDS virus from staff members and such an unreasonable fear cannot justify a policy which intrudes on staff members' constitutional rights.[54]

The Eighth Circuit affirmed, holding that "[b]ecause the risk of disease transmission has been shown to be negligible in the [Eastern Nebraska Community Office of Retardation] environment, [the Eastern Nebraska Human Services Agency's] articulated interest in requiring testing does not constitutionally justify requiring employees to submit to a test for the purpose of protecting the clients from an infected employee."[55] On October 30, 1989, the United States Supreme Court denied certiorari.[56]

§13.10.9 Infected Employees

Employee Education and Counseling. With the ever-increasing number of AIDS patients, the need for a highly structured and detailed employee education and counseling program is paramount. The Presidential Commission recommends that all healthcare professionals become certified in infection control knowledge and participate in an appropriate education program.[57]

Removal of Employees from Contact with Patients. Many healthcare facilities prohibit HIV-infected healthcare workers from participating in direct patient care and assign them to other

---

[54]686 F. Supp. at 251.

[55]867 F.2d 461, 464 (8th Cir. 1989). See also Mandatory Tests for Nebraska Employees Struck Down by Federal Appeals Court, AIDS Poly. & L., Feb. 8, 1989, at 1.

[56]Eastern Neb. Community Office of Retardation v. Glover, 110 S. Ct. 321 (1989).

[57]Presidential Commission Report, at 34.

duties instead.[58] The Rehabilitation Act and cases interpreting it (and state antidiscrimination acts) require an employer to attempt to accommodate an infected employee. Unless the employee refuses to follow infection control procedure, transfer out of direct patient care is probably not warranted until the employee has symptoms that impair job performance.[59] The CDC has recognized that there may be increased risk of transmitting AIDS in certain specific direct patient care areas such as surgery and trauma care because the procedures performed in those areas involve repeated contact with exposed tissues of patients.

Some facilities have established programs in which infected employees who are asymptomatic receive counseling and referrals but their duties remain unaltered. For example, under a San Francisco General Hospital policy,[60] if an employee who is diagnosed with AIDS is in a position that encompasses direct contact with patients, the hospital's employee health service monitors the employee's condition on a monthly basis, analyzing whether that condition poses a threat to patients.[61] The M.D. Anderson Cancer Center in Houston has stated that it attempts to let employees with AIDS work as long as they desire, permitting the employees to set their own hours and take frequent breaks, as well as any other reasonable accommodations.[62] Dismissals only occur after excessive absenteeism and when other solutions have proved to be unsuccessful.

The California Medical Association issued guidelines in late 1989 to protect patients from the blood-borne infections of

---

[58]The Commission recommended that healthcare facilities have in place a policy for their AIDS- or HIV-infected employees. The Commission emphasized that any such policy should balance the responsibility of the healthcare facility to provide safe care to its patients with protection of the employment status of the worker. If such a balancing is not attempted, affected workers will be reluctant to identify themselves. Presidential Commission Report, at 33.

[59]See, e.g., HIV-Infected Health Care Workers Pose Delicate Problem, AIDS Alert 190 (Nov. 1988).

[60]Id.

[61]Id.

[62]Id.

healthcare workers, recommending that HIV-positive healthcare workers not perform invasive procedures but that disclosure of HIV status is not necessary when the healthcare worker does only non-risky procedures.[63]

On March 15, 1989, in a case apparently of first impression, the United States District Court for the Eastern District of Louisiana upheld the right of a hospital to fire a nurse because he refused to be tested for exposure to HIV or to divulge the results of a prior test.[64] The nurse, whose friend and roommate of eight years had died of AIDS, refused to be tested for AIDS or submit results from a previous test, claiming he was concerned about his employment if he was shown to have HIV.[65] The nurse's duties at that time included giving injections, starting intravenous lines, performing catheterizations, giving enemas, and changing dressings.[66] When he continued to refuse to be tested or submit previous test results he was fired for insubordination.[67]

The nurse brought suit under §504 of the Rehabilitation Act and under Louisiana's handicap law, alleging that he was fired because the hospital perceived him as handicapped premised on his alleged seropositivity.[68] The district court held in a trial without a jury that the hospital's actions did not violate §504 because (1) no evidence existed that any hospital personnel involved in the discharge "[e]ver concluded that he was seropositive" and (2) the nurse was not "otherwise qualified."[69] The court stated:

> The [hospital] had a legitimate and nondiscriminatory reason for discharging the plaintiff. The CDC guidelines . . . demonstrate the

---

[63]*California Doctors Issue Policy on Infected Personnel*, AIDS Poly. & L., Jan. 10, 1990, at 7-8.

[64]Leckelt v. Board of Commrs. of Hosp. Dist. No. 1, 714 F. Supp. 1377 (E.D. La. 1989) (digested in *Nurse's Firing for Test Refusal Upheld; Court Says Hospital Can Enforce Disclosure*, AIDS Poly. & L., April 5, 1989, at 1, 11-12).

[65]714 F. Supp. at 1382-1385.

[66]Id. at 1382.

[67]Id. at 1385.

[68]Id. at 1378-1379.

[69]Id. at 1385-1389.

need of a health care institution to monitor the health status of employees who have been exposed to infectious diseases, particularly diseases such as AIDS which are fatal to 100% of their victims, in order to protect patients and co-workers and to accommodate any current or future handicap of the employee . . . [70]

On August 28, 1990, the Fifth Circuit affirmed.[71]

Removal of Employees from Work Involving Invasive Procedures. The CDC does not recommend that healthcare workers with HIV infections be *routinely* restricted from performing invasive procedures, stating instead that such restriction should be determined on a case-by-case basis in conjunction with the employee's personal physician.[72] An attempt to transfer an HIV-infected nurse out of the surgical intensive care unit to another position in emergency critical care with the same salary and benefits resulted in a complaint against the hospital before the New York Commission on Human Rights in 1987.[73] The AMA has stated that it would probably be inappropriate for a physician infected with HIV to perform surgery, because the physician should not increase the risk of exposure of his patients even minimally.[74] A settlement of a federal suit brought by an infected

---

[70]Id. at 1389. The court also found that the hospital did not violate the Louisiana Civil Rights for Handicapped Persons Act, La. Rev. Stat. Ann. §46.2251 et seq. (West 1982 & Supp. 1990), stating that "[d]efendant's request for plaintiff's HIV test results was directly related to the requirements of his job." Id. The court further found that the defendant did not violate the plaintiff's Fourth Amendment or Louisiana constitution rights to privacy or the plaintiff's right to equal protection under the Fourteenth Amendment. Id. at 1390-1392.

[71]Leckelt v. Board of Commrs. of Hosp. Dist. No. 1, 909 F.2d 820 (5th Cir. 1990) (digested in *Hospital Right to Know HIV Status Disputed in Court of Appeals Hearing*, AIDS Poly. & L., Jan. 24, 1990, at 11-12).

[72]Centers for Disease Control, Recommendations for Prevention of HIV Transmission in Health-Care Settings, 36 Morb. and Mort. Weekly Report 3S, 16S (Aug. 21, 1987).

[73]Zeldis, Nurse Claims Bias by Hospital in Job Shift After AIDS Test, N.Y.L.J., Apr. 12, 1988, at 1, col. 3.

[74]Pear, *A.M.A. Rules that Doctors Are Obligated to Treat AIDS*, N.Y. Times, Nov. 13, 1987, at A14, col. 1.

physician at Cook County Hospital in Chicago who was barred from invasive procedures in October 1987 provides one solution: the physician was permitted to perform certain specific procedures using double-gloving and other precautions.[75]

Dealing with Employee Absenteeism.   As noted above, courts have rejected a future inability to perform a job because of anticipated excessive absences as a justification for terminations and refusals to hire. A healthcare provider who prematurely discharges an employee with AIDS because of excessive absenteeism could be faced with a discrimination suit based on the relevant local, state, or federal law. One possible solution for consistent and extensive employee absenteeism is an unpaid medical leave of absence, which would permit the employee to maintain his insurance.[76]

A healthcare facility, for legal and ethical reasons, should make every reasonable attempt to accommodate an employee infected with HIV or AIDS. If an employee must be terminated, the employer should attempt to negotiate a severance agreement that allows the employee to maintain his insurance.

§13.11 Obligations to Provide a Safe Working Environment

Healthcare facilities, like all other employers, have an obligation to provide for their employees a reasonably safe environment in which to work.[1] In the case of HIV, this does not require that all risks be removed from the healthcare facility, but it does require that reasonably available precautions be taught to employees, supported with necessary supplies and equipment,

---

[75]*Doctor, Hospital Settle Suit Over Staff Privileges,* AIDS Poly. & L., Sept. 23, 1987, at 8.

[76]See generally W. Banta, AIDS in the Workplace (1988).

§13.11 [1]This was a requirement of common law. Restatement (Second) of Agency §492 (1958). See Thigpen v. Executive Comm. of the Baptist Convention, 114 Ga. App. 839, 152 S.E.2d 920 (1966) (failure to warn nurse's aide of how to avoid an infection).

and enforced. The details of these requirements have been prescribed as a matter of federal law by the Occupational Safety and Health Administration.

§13.11.1 Federal Law on Safe Working Conditions

The Occupational Safety and Health Act. In 1970, Congress made the matter of workplace safety a subject of federal regulation by passing the Occupational Safety and Health Act.[2] This statute requires that each affected employer furnish to each employee "employment and a place of employment which are free from recognized hazards that are causing or are likely to cause death or serious physical harm."[3] The Act established a federal agency, the Occupational Safety and Health Administration (OSHA), to enforce its provisions and elaborate on the Act's requirements by promulgating detailed regulations.

As the number of AIDS patients in hospitals grew in the mid-1980s, disputes between healthcare workers and their employers regarding issues of workplace safety began to arise.[4] In 1986, organizations representing healthcare workers began to pressure OSHA to develop an emergency standard and specific regulations governing risks of exposure to HIV and other blood-

---

[2] 29 U.S.C.A. §651 et seq. (West 1985).

[3] Id. §654(a)(1).

[4] In July 1987, four kidney dialysis nurses charged that they were unlawfully dismissed from their jobs for requesting training and education regarding the safe handling of AIDS patients. *Fired Nurses File Suits Over Dialysis Treatment*, AIDS Poly. & L., July 15, 1987, at 7. On February 18, 1987, a San Francisco General Hospital nurse received a settlement in a workers' compensation case claiming that her fear of AIDS had caused a stress-related ulcer. She previously had lost a complaint to the California Labor Commissioner claiming that she was not permitted to wear adequate protective clothing in the hospital. *Nurse Wins Comp Claim Over Fear of AIDS*, AIDS Poly. & L., Feb. 25, 1987, at 2. The same nurse later filed an action claiming $100,000,000 in damages because the work-related stress caused her child to be born with a birth defect. *Nurse Charges AIDS Stress Caused Son's Birth Defects*, AIDS Poly. & L., April 22, 1987, at 6.

borne infections in healthcare workplaces.[5] In 1987, OSHA refused to adopt an emergency standard but did begin work on regulations, and it announced that it would begin a program of enforcement of its existing general regulations and statutory requirements even before such specific regulations were published.[6] In October 1987, the Department of Health and Human Services and the Department of Labor jointly published a notice entitled Protection Against Occupational Exposure to Hepatitis B Virus (HBV) and Human Immunodeficiency Virus (HIV).[7] During 1988, OSHA undertook a program of inspections and enforcement focused on healthcare facilities in 17 states and the District of Columbia.[8] By July 1988, 60 facilities had been inspected and a number of facilities had received notices of violations.[9]

In May 1989, OSHA published its proposed regulations on occupational exposure to blood-borne pathogens.[10] The regula-

---

[5]The American Federation of State, County, and Municipal Employees (AFSCME) petitioned OSHA for an emergency temporary standard covering AIDS and other blood-borne diseases in September 1986. *OSHA Asked for Emergency AIDS Rule*, AIDS Poly. & L., Oct. 8, 1986, at 4. In September 1987, the Federation of Nurses and Health Professionals called on healthcare employers to do more to provide safe working conditions in light of OSHA's failure to issue emergency workplace standards. *Employers Urged by Union to Provide Safer Conditions*, AIDS Poly. & L., Sept. 23, 1987, at 5. AFSCME and the Service Employees International Union filed a petition with OSHA for an emergency standard and a permanent rule-making on September 19, 1986 and FNHP filed such a petition on February 3, 1987. *Exposure Reports Prompt Permanent Rule Demands*, AIDS Poly. & L., June 3, 1987, at 3.

[6]*OSHA Denies Emergency Rule; Permanent Standard Promised*, AIDS Poly. & L., July 29, 1987, at 1.

[7]52 Fed. Reg. 41818 (Oct. 30, 1987). The notice was also mailed directly to over 500,000 employees.

[8]The states were New York, Florida, New Jersey, Pennsylvania, Massachusetts, Maryland, Louisiana, Virginia, Ohio, California, Texas, Illinois, Georgia, the District of Columbia, Washington, Connecticut, Colorado, and Michigan. *OSHA Sets Inspection Schedule for Health Care Facilities*, AIDS Poly. & L., Jan. 27, 1988, at 8.

[9]*OSHA Amends Compliance Order, Will Issue Safety Standard*, AIDS Poly. & L., July 13, 1988, at 10.

[10]54 Fed. Reg. 23042 (May 30, 1989).

tions require each employer to identify anticipated tasks and procedures that involve actual or potential exposure to blood or other potentially infectious material. Employers must then identify all employees whose duties include these tasks and document the results of these determinations.[11]

Infection Control Plans and Workplace Precautions.   Employers who have any employees subject to such exposures are required to have a written infection control plan that details the determination of potential exposure described above, the methods to be used to minimize or eliminate employee exposure, and the contents or a summary of the training program to be provided to employees.[12]

Certain aspects of the methods to be used to minimize employee exposure are prescribed by the regulations. The regulations require that universal precautions be observed in all instances that have the potential of contact with blood and other potentially infectious materials. "Universal precautions" is defined as "a method of infection control in which all human blood and certain human body fluids are treated as if known to be infectious for HIV, HBV and other blood-born pathogens." Universal precautions are discussed further below.[13]

The regulations also require that employers, wherever feasible, adopt engineering and work practice controls to minimize exposure.[14] The work practice controls prescribed in the regulations require hand washing at specified times, prompt removal and disposition of contaminated personal protective equipment, and the performance of certain procedures in a manner that will minimize splashing, spraying, and aerosolization of blood and other potentially infectious materials. These rules also prohibit used needles and other sharps from being

---

[11]54 Fed. Reg. 23135 (1989) (to be codified at 29 C.F.R. §1910.1030(c)).
[12]54 Fed. Reg. 23135 (1989) (to be codified at 29 C.F.R. §1910.1030(c)(1)(iv)).
[13]54 Fed. Reg. 23134 (1989) (to be codified at 29 C.F.R. §1910.1030(b)).
[14]54 Fed. Reg. 23135 (1989) (to be codified at 29 C.F.R. §1910.1030(d)(2)). This approach is required to be used in preference to the provision of personal protective equipment to employees.

sheered, bent, broken, recapped, or reshelved by hand, prohibit used needles from being removed from disposal syringes, prohibit eating, drinking, smoking, and other actions in areas where blood or other potentially infectious materials are present, and prohibit the storage of food and drink in refrigerators or other areas where blood or other potentially infectious materials are stored.[15]

The proposed regulations on protective work clothing and equipment contain specific requirements relating to the use of gloves; gowns; fluid-proof aprons; laboratory coats and head and foot coverings; face shields or masks and eye protection; and mouth pieces, resuscitation bags, pocket masks, or other ventilation devices.[16]

The proposed regulations relating to housekeeping require cleaning and disinfecting of all equipment and environmental and working surfaces after contact with blood or other potentially infectious materials. Specimens of blood or other potentially infectious materials, and all infectious waste, are required to be placed in closable, leakproof containers that are color-coded or labeled as constituting a "bio-hazard" as specifically prescribed in the regulations. All laundry that is or may be soiled with blood or other potentially infectious materials or that may contain contaminated sharps is required to be treated as if it were contaminated and handled as little as possible. Such laundry is required to be cleaned or laundered in such a way that any infectious agents present are inactivated or destroyed.[17]

Employee Medical Evaluations and Training. The regulations require that all employers provide, at no charge, to employees who are subject to potential exposure to infectious materials a medical evaluation covering any medical problems that could

---

[15]Id.

[16]54 Fed. Reg. 23135 (1989) (to be codified at 29 C.F.R. §1910.1030(d)(3)).

[17]54 Fed. Reg. 23136 (1989) (to be codified at 29 C.F.R. §1910.1030(d)(4)). The regulations also contain certain additional specific requirements for HIV and HBV research laboratories and production facilities. Id. at 29 C.F.R. §1910.1030(e).

interfere with the employee's ability to use protective clothing or receive an HBV vaccination. All employees occupationally exposed on an average of one or more times per month are required to be offered an HBV vaccination at no charge.[18]

Employees subject to potential exposures must be given training at the time of their initial employment. The training programs must include: a copy of the OSHA regulations; a general explanation of the epidemiology and symptoms of blood-borne diseases; an explanation of modes of transmission; an explanation of the employer's infection control program; an explanation of appropriate engineering controls, work practices, and personal protective equipment; information on how to use personal protective clothing and equipment; information on appropriate actions to take in an emergency; information on procedures to follow if an occupational exposure occurs; and an explanation of signs, labeling, and color coding relating to bio-hazards.[19]

Recordkeeping Requirements. The regulations also establish significant recordkeeping requirements. All employees subject to medical surveillance must have a written medical record, including hepatitis B vaccination information. These records are required to be kept confidential, may not be disclosed to any person within or outside the workplace except as required by law, and must be maintained for the duration of employment plus 30 years. Records of all training sessions, including persons conducting and attending the sessions, must be prepared and maintained for five years. All such records must be made available to OSHA on request, and employee medical and training records must be made available for inspection and copying on the request of infected employees.[20]

Practice Problems with Universal Precautions. The concept of universal precautions, when applied in a strict and literal sense, eliminates the need for any concern by healthcare workers about

---

[18]54 Fed. Reg. 23137 (1989) (to be codified at 29 C.F.R. §1910.1030(f).
[19]54 Fed. Reg. 23138 (1989) (to be codified at 29 C.F.R. §1910.1030(g)(2)).
[20]54 Fed. Reg. 23139 (1989) (to be codified at 29 C.F.R. §1910.1030(h)).

whether a particular patient, piece of soiled linen, or piece of contaminated waste is infected with HIV. Applying universal precautions means that all such items are assumed to be HIV-infected. Despite the OSHA requirements, healthcare facilities in areas with low-risk populations have found several practical problems with complete compliance with universal precautions. The requirements relating to medical waste and soiled linen, for example, may require special handling for a large proportion of a facility's total waste material and linen. The expense involved in such special handling can be substantial. As for surgery, several modifications of surgical procedure are identified by the Centers for Disease Control that, while appropriate for known or suspected HIV-infected patients, would compromise the quality of care and somewhat increase risks if consistently applied to all patients.[21]

During the promulgation process for the OSHA regulations, the Office of Management and Budget questioned whether employees should be required to delay or suspend life-saving procedures in emergency cases in order to comply fully with universal precautions.[22] Such actions would cause particular concern in areas where only a small percentage of persons receiving emergency care are actually HIV-infected. During the rule-making process, OSHA representatives claimed that they would take a "common sense" approach to enforcement of the standards.[23] The best advice for healthcare facilities who wish to avoid fines and other sanctions, however, is to comply with the standards as written.

§13.11.2 State Laws on Occupational Health and Safety

In addition to the federal Occupational Safety and Health Act, a number of individual states have strong programs of enforcement

---

[21]Centers for Disease Control, Recommendations for Prevention of HIV Transmission in Health-Care Settings, 36 Morb. and Mort. Weekly Report 3S, 14S-15S (Aug. 21, 1987).

[22]*Revised Proposal Seen in March on Blood-Borne Transmission*, AIDS Poly. & L., Feb. 8, 1989, at 6.

[23]Id.

of occupational safety requirements. In such states, enforcement is usually left to state officials. It seems likely that a number of these states will adopt regulations relating to AIDS and other blood-borne diseases that will be quite similar to the federal regulations.[24]

In March 1990, Kings County Hospital in Brooklyn, New York settled for an undisclosed amount a highly publicized case brought by a physician who alleged that the hospital's negligence in failing to adopt proper procedures for needle disposal resulted in her becoming HIV-infected from a needle prick in 1983.[25]

§13.11.3 Unsafe Conditions as Grounds for Concerted Refusals to Work

In addition to the protections of OSHA, employees also enjoy some protection against unsafe working conditions under §7 of the National Labor Relations Act. This provision protects the rights of employees "to engage in . . . concerted activities for the purpose of collective bargaining or other mutual aid or protection."[26] The protected activities include refusing to work if a job is believed to be unsafe. Under rulings of the National Labor Relations Board, the employee is protected if he has "a reasonably held belief that the conditions are unsafe."[27] As yet, there is no reported case dealing with the provisions of §7 in the case of a refusal to work based on a fear of HIV infection.

§13.11.4 Screening of Patients with HIV Tests

Screening Low-Risk Populations.   Before the concept of universal precautions emerged, many healthcare facilities at least

---

[24]Cf. §13.8.2, n.40 and accompanying text.

[25]Lubasch, *Out-of-Court Accord Ends Prego's Suit in AIDS Case*, N.Y. Times, March 9, 1990, at A14, col. 1.

[26]29 U.S.C.A. §157 (West 1973).

[27]Daniel Construction Co., 267 N.L.R.B. 1213 (1983).

considered whether the HIV status of all hospitalized patients should be determined so that special precautions could be used with the infected patients. Some people felt that these tests should be administered routinely and without the knowledge or consent of the patients.

Now that more is known about the low risk of transmission of these infections and the concept of universal precautions has become firmly established, such broad testing programs are generally regarded as inappropriate. In some jurisdictions HIV testing without consent would clearly be illegal. In jurisdictions without specific laws on the subject, those few hospitals that have attempted such programs have encountered such extensive opposition from members of the public and state agencies that they have abandoned the programs.[28]

Screening Limited Groups of Patients. The CDC, in its 1987 recommendations to healthcare workers, acknowledges that certain modified procedures or extraordinary precautions might be appropriate in the case of patients with known HIV infections. With regard to surgical procedures, for example, the CDC refers to eliminating hand-to-hand passing of sharp instruments; substituting stapling for hand suturing; use of electrocautery devices rather than scalpels; and the use of more extensive gowns.[29] The CDC recommendations leave open the possibility of requesting tests from certain patients whose history indicates they might be in high-risk groups so that such modified procedures could be used. The American Hospital Association's recommendations also acknowledge that testing might be appropriate for this purpose, but these recommendations do not advocate limiting requests for tests for these purposes only to subgroups of patients.[30]

---

[28]*Delaware Hospital to Revise Controversial Testing Policy*, AIDS Poly. & L., July 13, 1988, at 3 (Alfred I. DuPont Institute for Sick Children and Nemours Health Clinic); *Los Angeles Hospital Agrees to Drop Test Requirement for Rehab Program*, AIDS Poly. & L., Jan. 25, 1989, at 1 (Centinela Hospital Medical Center).

[29]Centers for Disease Control, supra n.21.

[30]American Hospital Association, AIDS/HIV Infection Policy: Ensuring a

Both the CDC and the AHA state that such tests should be performed only when a consent is given. As a practical matter, if such a program is adopted, the number of cases in which patients will withhold consent will be relatively few, and it may be possible, based on the patient's medical history, to simply assume that such a patient has an infection.

§13.11.5 Managing Known Exposures of Employees to HIV Infections

The OSHA regulations contain a specific procedure to be followed after any occupational exposure to blood or other potentially infectious materials. Employers are required to provide each employee who has had such an exposure with a confidential medical evaluation and follow-up at no cost to the employee. This procedure must include documentation of the route of exposure, the source patient, and the circumstances under which the exposure occurred. If the source patient is known and consents to an HIV test, such a test must be performed. A blood specimen from the exposed employee must be collected as soon as possible after the exposure and may be tested at that time or at a later date if the employee so requests.[31]

The employee must also be provided "safe and effective post-exposure prophylaxis for HIV and HBV." In accordance with CDC recommendations, if the source patient's HIV status is positive or unknown, this will include, in the case of HIV, periodic retesting of the employee to determine whether the employee has developed antibodies to HIV.[32] Under the CDC recommendations, if the source patient does not test positive for

---

Safe Hospital Environment: Report and Recommendations of the Special Committee on AIDS/HIV Infection Policy 1987/1988 12 (1988).

[31] *Delaware Hospital to Revise Controversial Testing Policy*, AIDS Poly. & L., July 13, 1988, at 3 (Alfred I. DuPont Institute for Sick Children and Nemours Health Clinic); *Los Angeles Hospital Agrees to Drop Test Requirement for Rehab Program*, AIDS Poly. & L., Jan. 25, 1989, at 1 (Centinela Hospital Medical Center).

[32] Centers for Disease Control, supra n.21, 16S-17S.

HIV, further testing of the employee is not mandated but should be made available. The OSHA regulations on this subject merely state that the exposed employee should be "managed according to standard recommendations for medical practice,"[33] which could be interpreted to incorporate the recommendations of the CDC.

---

[33]54 Fed. Reg. 23138 (1989) (to be codified at 29 C.F.R. §1910.1030(f)(3)(iv)).

IV

THE LEGAL
STRUCTURE OF
HEALTHCARE
FACILITIES

14 Corporate Organization, Reorganization, and Joint Venturing

Jean Gordon Carter

§14.0 Introduction*

Hospitals, nursing homes, and health maintenance organizations (HMOs) are legal entities. These healthcare facilities share the

---

§14.0*The author would like to thank Dean M. Harris of Moore & Van

921

legal requirements for existence and governance with other businesses such as General Motors Corporation. While some healthcare providers have special legal forms that result from the original formation of the facility, all providers must be legally organized and operated, often as a corporation. Still, healthcare facilities are special corporations subject to various requirements. Healthcare facilities are regulated by federal and state laws including those respecting licensure, accreditation, and third-party reimbursement requirements.

Many hospitals and some extended care facilities and HMOs are tax-exempt and must comply with requirements necessary to preserve this preferred tax status. These legal requirements affect the corporate form of healthcare providers. These same requirements can affect the ability of today's healthcare provider to compete for diminishing patient revenues and medical resources.[1] Private philanthropy, government assistance, third-party reimbursements, and patient dollars for healthcare facilities have declined while costs and sources of aggressive competition have risen. For example, physicians with staff privileges at a local hospital who once encouraged patients to use that hospital may now operate emergency services clinics and other clinics in direct competition with the hospital. Profit-makers have also entered the healthcare market. Healthcare providers facing pressures from such competitors must look for innovative ways to compete.[2]

Allen and Noah H. Huffstetler, III of Petrie, Stockton and Robinson for their assistance with this chapter.

[1]Many factors are lowering revenues, and owing to the rise in overall hospital costs third-party reimbursers have begun to stress cost control. For example, many insurance policies require preadmission screening to ensure that medical treatment and patient days are not excessive. Businesses, realizing that the cost of their employee insurance is rising, are also demanding efficient, cost-effective healthcare services. See Cunningham, What's Good for General Motors, 52 Hosps., J. Am. Hosp. Assn. 75 (1978). The result for hospitals is less patient revenues.

[2]Historically, hospitals have had various sources of capital. Early hospitals depended on philanthropy. Later, government directly subsidized them. More recently, hospitals have borrowed funds, often using tax-exempt bonds. Today,

Healthcare providers found new competitive methods increasingly necessary and popular during the 1970s. Corporate structures were reorganized, giving such facilities more flexibility to enter ventures unavailable to traditional providers. These new ventures may involve one or more other parties and thus are joint ventures.

This chapter considers corporate organization, reorganization, and joint venturing for hospitals, extended care facilities, and HMOs. Part A reviews basic corporate forms and governance, including the special issues for tax-exempt entities. Part B considers healthcare facility reorganization, the restructuring of the entity's corporate form to increase its legal flexibility. The chapter concludes with a discussion of joint venturing. Today's healthcare provider is trying to escape the restraints of traditional corporate form. Reorganization and joint ventures position healthcare providers to compete in today's healthcare environment.

A. Corporate Organization

§14.1 The Healthcare Provider as a Legal Entity

All healthcare facilities are formed as legal entities. Most are corporations, but some are trusts or subdivisions of political entities. The basic legal form of the entity will determine its governance and dictate some of its legal attributes and limitations. These attributes are in addition to those requirements common to all healthcare providers as healthcare providers.

Most hospitals, extended care facilities, and HMOs are legally formed as corporations and must be properly organized under the laws of their state with appropriate governing docu-

---

these past sources of capital have diminished, and hospitals must look to new sources of revenue: hospitals must be entrepreneurs. Goldsmith, Strategies for Surviving the Capital Shortage, 1982 Trustees 21 (Mar. 1982).

ments, including articles of incorporation, which are filed with the secretary of state or other offices in the state to create the corporation. After incorporation, the corporate governing board completes the organization of the corporation, including adopting bylaws for the corporation's governance.[1]

Once it is properly formed, the corporation achieves status as a separate legal entity, a corporation. This legal form will be respected by the law so long as the corporation respects its own corporate form by observing corporate formalities and maintaining its separate existence. For example, the corporation must have periodic board meetings and maintain separate books and records. By preserving its corporate form, a corporation maintains limited liability (so creditors may reach only its assets for its debts). If the corporation fails to maintain itself as a separate corporation, third parties may ignore the corporate form and reach the individuals behind the corporation. Such "piercing the corporate veil,"[2] while it's not lightly done, is a risk the healthcare corporation must avoid.

Some healthcare facilities exist as legal entities other than corporations. A special legal form often results from the initial creation of an entity. For example, a hospital may be founded as a trust, perhaps later achieving special status under state laws as a public trust. Other facilities are subdivisions of government entities. Some hospitals are owned by counties or involve hospital authorities. Other hospitals are corporations, leasing the hospital facility from the county that owns it. Each of these special legal forms may involve special requirements that are reflected in the entity's organizational documents and in state laws. Each healthcare provider must comply with the special requirements of its legal form.

---

§14.1 [1]See, e.g., H. Henn and J. Alexander, Laws of Corporations §§116-117, 133, at 266-272, 306-310 (3d ed. 1983).

[2]See id. §§146, 148, at 344-352, 354-356; Beautyman and Thallner, Does Hospital Restructuring Make Sense Today?, 20 Hosp. L. 121, 124 (1987). For a discussion of when courts will pierce the veil, see H. Henn supra n.1, at §148, at 354-356.

§14.2 Types of Corporations

Two basic types of corporations exist under the laws of many states: for-profit and nonprofit. For-profit corporations are businesses organized to earn a profit for their shareholders. Increasingly, hospitals are being organized as for-profit corporations. Most extended care facilities are also for-profit entities, as are many HMOs, particularly those that have been recently formed. In contrast, nonprofit corporations do not have shareholders who profit from the corporation's activities. Depending on state law, a corporation may have members[1] or even shareholders while retaining its earnings to further its corporate purpose. Nonprofit corporations may achieve tax-exempt status, as discussed below.

§14.3 Organizational Documents

All healthcare facilities, no matter what form they take, will have governing documents. A government hospital or a public trust may have state statutes as its primary governing documents. Corporations have articles of incorporation controlling their corporate existence, and often have bylaws providing the details of their governance.

The form for corporate articles of incorporation is determined by the law of the state of incorporation. For example, state law may require that the articles of incorporation provide the corporation's name, establish its purpose, describe its governing structure (including any members), name a registered agent and office, and establish the duration of the corporation.

---

§14.2 [1]Under the laws of some states, a nonprofit corporation may be either a membership or nonmembership corporation. Nonmembership corporations are governed by their boards of directors; membership corporations are governed by their members, who generally elect the board of directors. See, e.g., N.C. Gen. Stat. ch. 55A (1982); N.Y. Not-for-Profit Corp. Law art. 6 (McKinney 1970); Cal. Corp. code ch. 4 (West 1977). (The reader should consult the law of his or her own state.)

The articles may also provide for the disposition of assets on dissolution and for limitations on corporate activities.[1] Finally, the articles of incorporation may provide procedures for fundamental corporate changes such as amending the articles of incorporation.

Corporations also need corporate bylaws to direct their corporate governance and management.[2] The bylaws of the corporation provide for the directors or trustees, for the officers, and for members or shareholders, if any. Bylaws also delineate the powers of these trustees, officers, and members. The bylaws include procedural matters such as meeting schedules, notice requirements, quorum provisions, and election of officers and directors. Finally, bylaws may provide for committees, a fiscal year, a corporate seal, indemnity of board members and officers, and other needed structural provisions.

The articles of incorporation and bylaws or other governing instruments of accredited hospitals should comply with the requirements of the Joint Commission on Accreditation of Healthcare Organizations (JCAHO).[3] The JCAHO requires that the hospital governing instruments provide certain items including the responsibilities and selection process of the governing body and officers, provisions for and privileges of the medical staff, requirements for hospital auxiliaries, provisions for the hospital budget, requirements for the hospital chief executive, and policies on conflicts of interest. Hospital governing instruments should be initially prepared in compliance with JCAHO requirements, and they should be reviewed periodically for continuing compliance.

In addition to corporate bylaws, a hospital needs medical staff bylaws. These staff bylaws must be coordinated with the corporate bylaws of the hospital and should define the relationship between the board, administration, and medical staff. The specifics of such medical staff bylaws are beyond the scope of this chapter.

---

§14.3 [1] See H. Henn and J. Alexander, Laws of Corporations §§118-132, at 272-306 (3d ed. 1983).

[2] See id. §133 at 306-310.

[3] See Joint Commission on Accreditation of Healthcare Organizations, Accreditation Manual for Hospitals (1991).

§14.4 Corporate Governance

The authority for governing a corporation generally lies with its board of trustees or directors.[1] This body is charged with determining overall policy for the corporation. Depending on governance provisions, members of this board may be elected by the corporation's shareholders or members, appointed by government officials, or chosen by the other board members.[2] The board members must fulfill their duties with due care and good faith or be subject to liability for breach of duty.[3]

The board chooses the officers of the corporation, who carry out corporate policy.[4] These positions vary between corporations, as do the duties of the officers. All corporations have a chief executive officer, often referred to in healthcare facilities as the administrator, though such administrators are increasingly being given the title of president.

In addition, the hospital medical staff generally has its own governing structure, including a board and officers. This medical staff is responsible to the board of the hospital, but for decisions on certain medical functions the hospital board must depend on the medical staff and its board.

§14.5 Tax Status

While an increasing number of hospitals today are taxable, many nonprofit hospitals can qualify as tax-exempt. These tax-

---

§14.4 [1]Traditionally, many hospitals have had boards of trustees. Reorganized hospitals often have boards of directors. Perhaps use of the term "directors" rather than "trustees" stresses to board members the need for business decisions in addition to the traditional charitable activities. For discussions of the role of the hospital board, see R. Umbdenstock, So You're on the Hospital Board! (3d ed. 1987) and C. Bley and C. Shimko, A Guide to the Board's Role in Hospital Finance (1987).

[2]See, e.g., H. Henn and J. Alexander, Laws of Corporations §§192, 205, at 511-512, 555-558 (3d ed. 1983).

[3]See id. §234, at 621-625.

[4]See, e.g., id. §210, at 571.

exempt hospitals must fulfill special requirements to achieve and maintain this preferred tax status.[1] Also, many extended care facilities and HMOs are for-profit entities, though some can qualify as tax-exempt.

§14.5.1 Tax Exemption as a Hospital

Nonprofit entities can qualify as exempt from federal and often state taxes if the entity is organized and operated exclusively for tax-exempt purposes, with no part of its earnings inuring to the benefit of private parties. Exempt entities also cannot engage in prohibited lobbying.[2]

First, a tax-exempt entity must be "organized" for charitable purposes, which means that its governing documents must limit its purposes to charitable ones such as the promotion of health.[3] Generally, the articles of incorporation should state that the corporation will not do any actions inconsistent with its status as tax-exempt under I.R.C. §501(c)(3) and should also provide that, on dissolution, the corporate assets will continue to be used for exempt purposes.

In addition, a tax-exempt entity must be operated exclusively for its charitable purpose. Although the statute uses the term "exclusively," a tax-exempt entity can have some unrelated activities. However, if the unrelated activities become excessive the entity will lose its tax-exempt status. Unfortunately, the

---

§14.5 [1]A hospital that is part of a government entity may be tax-exempt but may not necessarily be subject to the restrictions on an I.R.C. §501(c)(3) tax-exempt entity. It could be subject to other restrictions, though.

[2]See I.R.C. §501(c)(3). (I.R.C. refers to the Internal Revenue Code of 1986, as amended.)

[3]Operating a hospital for the care of the sick has long been recognized as a charitable purpose so hospitals and related healthcare entities can be tax-exempt. See Rev. Rul. 56-185, 1956-1 C.B. 202; Rev. Rul. 69-545, 1969-2 C.B. 117. For an excellent source of information on tax-exempt entities, see B. Hopkins, The Law of Tax-Exempt Organizations (5th ed. 1987 & Supp. 1989). See also Hopkins and Beckwith, The Federal Tax Law of Hospitals: Basic Principles and Current Developments, 24 Duq. L. Rev. 691 (1985).

Internal Revenue Code and its regulations do not specify what percentage of unrelated activities will jeopardize tax-exempt status. Given the risk involved, the tax-exempt entity should minimize its unrelated activities.

Finally, a tax-exempt entity cannot provide private inurement to private parties instead of benefiting the public in general. Private parties may be incidentally benefitted because they are a part of the general public, but not because they are insiders. As an example, the IRS has recently scrutinized physician recruitment contracts because they provide special benefits to private physicians.[4] If the IRS finds one dollar of private inurement, the involved entity will lose its tax-exempt status.

§14.5.2 Unrelated Business Taxable Income

The income from a tax-exempt entity's activities other than charitable ones is subject to tax as Unrelated Business Taxable Income (UBTI). With certain modifications, UBTI is the gross income derived by an organization from any unrelated trade or business regularly carried on, less its related deductions.[5] An

---

[4]See Gen. Couns. Mem. 39,498 (Apr. 24, 1986), which questioned a guarantee of income to a physician. But see Gen. Couns. Mem. 39,674 (Oct. 23, 1987), in which the IRS seems to say such arrangements do not necessarily create private inurement, but they must be reviewed individually; Unpublished Private Letter Ruling on Physician Recruitment, The Exempt Organization Tax Rev. 330 (May 1990).

[5]I.R.C. §511 imposes a tax on the unrelated business taxable income of organizations described in §501(c). UBTI is the gross income derived by an organization from any unrelated trade or business regularly conducted by it, less the allowable deductions that are directly connected with it, with certain modifications. I.R.C. §512. An "unrelated trade or business" is any trade or business the conduct of which is not substantially related (aside from the need of the organization for income or funds or the use it makes of the profits derived) to the exercise of the organization's exempt purposes or functions. I.R.C. §513. A trade or business is "related" to the exempt purposes if the conduct of the business has a causal relationship to the achievement of the exempt purposes, and it is "substantially related" only if the causal relationship is a substantial one. To be substantially related to exempt purposes, the

unrelated business for a hospital is one not related to patient care, including inpatients and outpatients of the hospital facility.[6] For example, if a patient has a prescription filled in the hospital pharmacy, the income is tax-exempt; however, if a nonpatient has a prescription filled, then that income is unrelated and taxable. The rationale of taxing UBTI is to prevent tax-exempt entities from competing unfairly with taxable businesses. Unrelated business taxable income is taxed at rates similar to the corporate income tax rates.

§14.5.3 Taxable Entities

Some healthcare providers are for-profit entities. All income of these corporations is taxable, and such providers are not subject to the prohibitions discussed above for tax-exempt entities. These entities pay dividends to shareholders, who are then taxed on their dividend income. To avoid this double taxation, some corporations elect to be S corporations, with income taxed directly to shareholders.[7]

§14.6 Corporate Affiliations

Healthcare corporations can have corporate affiliations, including related corporations, and can merge with another entity.

---

business must contribute significantly to the advancement of the exempt purpose. See Treas. Reg. §1.513-1(d)(2) (as amended in 1983); B. Hopkins, The Law of Tax-Exempt Organizations, supra n.3, at 702-806; Janich and Sor, When Is an Activity "Substantially Related" to a Health Care Institution's Tax-exempt Purpose?, 20 Hosp. L. 193 (1987); Comment, The Effect of the Unrelated Business Income Tax on Today's Hospital, 13 Creighton L. Rev. 573 (1979).

[6]See Rev. Rul. 68-376, 1968-2 C.B. 246. See also Rev. Rul. 85-109, 1985-2 C.B. 165 and Rev. Rul. 85-110, 1985-2 C.B. 166.

[7]See I.R.C. §1361 et. seq. S corporations are subject to various limitations including ones on permissible shareholders and classes of stock.

§14.6.1 Affiliated Entities

Hospitals often have affiliated entities. These affiliates include hospital auxiliaries, which are often unincorporated associations providing volunteers for the hospital. Other affiliates may be corporations such as foundations, that support the hospital. Such corporations can be vital sources of community support for the hospital. These foundations can have their own governing boards, often independent of the hospital and its board.

§14.6.2 Mergers

A hospital may determine that merging with another hospital or entity such as a nursing home will benefit the hospital. Such mergers must comply with state law requirements for mergers, as well as other restrictions on corporations and hospitals. Also, federal and often state law prohibit mergers that restrain competition. A careful analysis of the effect of any merger on competition in the relevant markets should be made before merging. In limited circumstances, mergers that reduce competition may be permissible.[1]

---

§14.6 [1]Mergers may violate §7 of the Clayton Act (15 U.S.C. §18), §5 of the FTC Act (15 U.S.C. §45), and §§1 and 2 of the Sherman Act (15 U.S.C. §§1 and 2 (1982)). To determine violations, the Justice Department has issued certain merger guidelines in United States Department of Justice Merger Guidelines, Trade Reg. Rep. (CCH) No. 655 (Part II) (June 18, 1984). For discussions of antitrust laws and considerations in hospital mergers and joint ventures, see Cruz, Product and Geographical Market Measurements in the Merger of Hospitals, 91 Dick. L. Rev. 497 (1986); Groner, Hospital Mergers, Health Planning, and the Antitrust Laws: A Principled Approach to Implied Repeal, 7 J. Legal Med. 471 (1986); Comment, Defining the Relevant Market in Health Care Antitrust Litigation: Hospital Mergers, 75 Ky. L.J. 175 (1986-1987); Ponsoldt, Immunity Doctrine, Efficiency Promotion, and the Applicability of Federal Antitrust Law to State-Approved Hospital Acquisitions, 12 J. Corp. L. 37 (1986); Thompson and Scott, Antitrust Considerations and Defenses in Reorganizing for Multi-Institutional Activities, 26 St. Louis U.L.J. 465 (1982).

§14.7 Summary

Healthcare providers are legal entities, like other business entities. Often they are corporations and must act as corporations to preserve their special corporate status. Still, healthcare providers are subject to restrictions not imposed on other legal entities. Because these restrictions often prove to be a burden, many hospitals are reorganizing their legal forms.

B. Hospital Corporate Reorganizations

§14.8 Introduction to Corporate Reorganizations

A hospital corporate reorganization is a reshaping of the corporate structure[1] to allow more flexibility. In the past, hospitals have been sole corporations, subject to various regulatory and tax limitations. In contrast, a reorganized hospital system will have several affiliated entities. These new entities can provide services other than those offered by a traditional hospital, often free of some of the usual legal constraints. Although this section generally considers hospital reorganizations, similar reorganizations of HMOs or extended care facilities are possible.

§14.9 Reasons for Reorganizing

A corporate reorganization can offer many advantages to a hospital, but the hospital must first decide if it's worth it. The hospital should consider its current competitive position and

---

§14.8   [1]Although legally an extended care corporation or health maintenance organization could reorganize, the trend toward reorganization has generally been seen with hospitals and so this section focuses on hospital reorganization.

realistically assess its future, including any changes needed to fulfill its healthcare mission. Restructuring is a time-consuming process that requires a serious commitment by the hospital's board of trustees and administration. Without this commitment and without tangible goals expected from the reorganization, the hospital will find the process frustrating and the new corporate structure an administrative burden. Still, for the hospital committed to making reorganization work, the rewards can be many.

A reorganized hospital structure permits more flexibility for tax planning for a tax-exempt hospital than does a traditional, hospital-only structure. One of a charitable hospital's most valuable assets, its tax-exempt status, restricts the activities the hospital can perform while maintaining that status. Although a tax-exempt hospital must be operated for charitable purposes, it nevertheless is permitted to have limited amounts of UBTI, that is, income from activities other than its charitable purpose activities. If this UBTI becomes too large a percentage of hospital revenues, the IRS can revoke the hospital's exempt status, arguing that the hospital is not sufficiently charitable. One solution is to segregate UBTI activities into a taxable subsidiary, an entity common to reorganizations.

In addition, a tax-exempt hospital cannot provide private benefit or inurement to others. For example, the IRS may find that such benefit exists if a tax-exempt hospital serves as sole general partner in a limited partnership,[1] because all assets of a general partner are at risk for liabilities of the partnership. By creating a taxable subsidiary to serve as general partner, the hospital may be able to insulate itself from providing private

---

§14.9 [1]Recent IRS policy will permit a hospital to serve as sole general partner in certain limited partnerships. Such partnerships must further the charitable purpose of the hospital. See Gen. Couns. Mem. 39,546 (August 15, 1986). See also Note, The Participation of Charities in Limited Partnerships, 93 Yale L.J. 1355 (1984). Determining whether a venture furthers the hospital's charitable purpose requires a factual analysis. A hospital entering into such a limited partnership must be confident that it can succeed on this factual determination, because the risk from failing this test is loss of tax-exempt status.

benefit as well as from excessive UBTI. For many hospitals, such joint ventures not only may produce revenues for the hospital but also may strengthen ties with needed staff physicians who are partners in the joint ventures.

Careful planning can minimize taxes for a taxable subsidiary. For example, a taxable entity can offset any revenues against any expenses. In contrast, a tax-exempt entity can offset unrelated income against only certain expenses. By segregating profitable and unprofitable activities into a taxable subsidiary, the hospital system may better offset losses against revenues and therefore pay less taxes.[2]

Apart from the tax advantages, a corporate reorganization may have regulatory advantages. The original impetus for many hospital reorganizations was the wish to gain certain advantages from Medicare participation. With recent changes converting Medicare from a cost-reimbursement to a prospective-payment system, these advantages have been reduced for many hospitals.[3] Still, in some limited cases a hospital may be able to increase Medicare reimbursements by moving assets to other corporations; such a move may result in more favorable calculations for reimbursements where certain income-producing assets or activities are segregated from the hospital. Also in some circumstances, reorganizing might limit other restrictive Medicare provisions, such as provisions that require reimbursement for related entity services at that entity's cost.[4] Of course, Medicare

_____

[2]Of course, there are limitations on assignment of income or segregation of costs for the sole purpose of minimizing taxes. See, e.g., I.R.C. §482.

[3]Changes to Medicare provisions allow reimbursements on a fixed-amount, per-case payment system rather than a cost-reimbursement one. The older cost-reimbursement system required that certain nonoperating revenues offset costs. To avoid offset, hospitals tried to move their other revenue sources away from the hospital. See Squires, Corporate Restructuring of Tax-Exempt Hospitals: The Bastardization of the Tax-Exempt Concept, 14 L. Med. & Health Care 66. Many of the advantages of moving assets are now gone. See Beautyman and Thallner, Does Hospital Restructuring Make Sense Today?, 20 Hosp. L. 121, 124 (1987).

[4]See, e.g., 42 C.F.R. §413.17(a) (1987).

provisions can and will change, and the advantages of a reorganization strictly for Medicare reasons may be short-lived.[5] Furthermore, achieving Medicare advantages may require that the hospital have little control over its corporate affiliates, a price that many hospital boards are unwilling to pay.

Segregating hospital activities and assets may avoid certain interest income offsets in other third-party reimbursement contracts. Some reimbursement contracts require that investment income must offset certain costs, such as interest expenses in payment calculations. The income offsets may be avoided by moving to an affiliate the investment assets that generate this income. Contracts can change, though, and reorganizing strictly for contractual reimbursement reasons may give only a short-term advantage. Of course, this advantage may generate enough revenues to pay the transactional costs for a reorganization that will have other benefits.

Segregating activities into other entities may have certificate-of-need (CON) advantages under the laws of some states or may avoid application of the CON laws altogether.[6] Even if CON laws apply, the hospital system may strengthen its competitive position for winning a CON by having a separate corporation house the new activity. For example, the cost calculations for operating a nursing home outside of a hospital tend to be more favorable than those for a hospital-based nursing home. These lower projected costs increase the likelihood of obtaining a CON.

Another reason for segregating assets into an affiliated corporation is to insulate them from liabilities of the hospital. Conversely, the hospital may be protected from liability for high-risk activities carried out by an affiliated corporation. These advantages require strict attention to corporate formalities so that third parties are not able to ignore the separation between

---

[5]For a general discussion of the reimbursement aspects of reorganization, see L. Gerber, Hospital Restructuring: Why, Where & How (1983).

[6]But see, e.g., N.C. Gen. Stat. §131E-178 (1988). It may be difficult to show that an expenditure by a hospital affiliate is not on behalf of the hospital and thereby avoid the CON provisions.

the entities by "piercing the corporate veil." Still, the statutes of some states directly permit the "corporate veil" of a nursing home corporation to be pierced to reach its parent entity.[7]

Placing an activity in a separate corporation can also concentrate efforts on that activity. One example of such a special, segregated-function entity is a fundraising foundation. A traditional hospital foundation often was organized and operated by friends of the hospital; the hospital had no legal control over the foundation. In a reorganized system, however, the hospital legally can control a foundation through corporate provisions. Such a foundation can have directors who are fundraising friends of the hospital and who do not have the additional burden of serving on the hospital board. Furthermore, the foundation board can have more members than could serve effectively on the hospital board. The result is a stronger fundraising team.

Fundraising and hospital public relations may be helped by careful attention to accounting disclosure requirements and to the effect of such disclosures on the public's view of the hospital. For a sole corporation hospital, all financial information about the hospital is combined. However, in a group hospital arrangement, disclosure may be somewhat limited in some cases, subject to applicable accounting requirements. For example, the financial statements pertaining only to the hospital may be disclosed to the public, while financial information about the affiliates remains confidential.

Similarly, the presentation of financial information may improve the hospital's ability to obtain favorable financing. For example, the hospital could segregate an unprofitable venture into an affiliate, thus protecting the hospital's own financial standing from the effect of the losses. Still, lenders are becoming sophisticated about hospital reorganizations and should review the financial status of the hospital system as a whole in assessing financing. Lenders also may require all of the hospital affiliates to guarantee any hospital debt.

Another advantage of a reorganized hospital system is an

---

[7]See, e.g., Ill. Rev. Stat. ch. 111½, §§4151-119, 4153-601.

expansion of employee opportunities, which can help attract and retain valuable hospital personnel. The new system can provide a career path for the administrative personnel who are responsible for the various entities. Also, a hospital system, particularly a taxable subsidiary, may attract an employee or board member who traditionally has not been involved with nonprofit corporations; these entrepreneurs can bring innovative ideas.

A reorganized system may have other employee-related advantages.[8] Various attractive executive compensation packages may be offered by the different entities, though it is likely that the hospital group would be considered one control group for qualified benefit plans. It is also likely that the hospitals would be considered joint employers, particularly soon after reorganization;[9] however, it is possible that the separate corporations would be viewed as different employers for Fair Labor Standards Act purposes if the entities are truly separate. If the entities are separate, their employee hours would not be combined to determine minimum wage and overtime liability.

A reorganized hospital system can gain economies of scale throughout its operations. A more effective utilization of resources can provide more profits. Similar functions can be grouped together and managed by an expert. For example, the fundraising entity could have a trained staff to assist potential donors. Perhaps more important, necessary functions can be expanded to the optimum point and the excess capacity sold. For example, a hospital that buys a paging system for its staff will make a large investment in equipment. Once the hospital has the basic equipment, it can do paging for other parties at little additional cost. Such sales of services to outsiders can create UBTI, however, and may best be handled by a taxable affiliate. Thus, achieving economies of scale and tapping excess capacity can generate needed revenues.

Finally, any particular hospital may discover special advan-

---

[8]See S. Erf and J. Badel, Hospital Restructuring: Employment Law Pitfalls (1985) for a discussion of employment issues in hospital reorganizations.

[9]See 29 C.F.R. §791.2 (1988) for the factors indicating joint employers.

tages from reorganization. For example, two hospitals may reorganize together, creating a merger. The placement of a common holding company over both hospitals allows each to gain many of the benefits of a merger while retaining its own corporate identity and perhaps limited liability. A hospital also may affiliate with another type of nonprofit healthcare provider. Such affiliation can complement hospital services and may increase the revenue and fundraising potential of the other entity.[10] Under another structure, two hospitals may share services or undertake a joint venture through a common affiliate.[11] A creatively managed hospital can benefit from other advantages of reorganization.

§14.10 Steps in Reorganizing

The necessary steps for a corporate reorganization vary depending on each hospital's unique legal environment and reorganization goals. Certain steps common to most reorganizations are discussed below.

§14.10.1 Beginning the Reorganization

The first step in the reorganization process is for the board and the administration to ascertain whether reorganizing is appropriate. A hospital that is a sole corporation has a corporate structure that is simple and understandable. The lines of authority and governance are clear, and the cost of observing corporate formalities for the one corporation is low. If the hospital cannot identify clear advantages from reorganization, it should remain a sole corporation.

After the board and administration determine that a cor-

---

[10]For example, some grants require affiliation with a hospital.

[11]Shared services by hospitals may create taxable income unless all entities qualify as exempt. See, e.g., I.R.C. §501(e).

porate reorganization is appropriate, they can begin the reorganization process. The first step is selecting a reorganization team. This team should include the reorganization committee of the hospital board and a representative of the hospital administration, often the chief administrator. The hospital will need corporate and tax attorneys, preferably with healthcare and tax-exemption experience, to assist in properly structuring the new corporate entities, filing requests with the IRS, and complying with federal, state, and other regulations and requirements. In addition, the hospital's certified public accountants can assist with certain tax requests and provide guidance in developing a financially sound plan. The hospital must be aggressive in choosing attorneys and accountants whose experience in hospital reorganizations will help the hospital avoid pitfalls and develop a successful reorganized structure.

In addition to this important team, such a change requires the support of the board of trustees, the hospital administration and medical personnel, and often the community the hospital serves. Education of hospital trustees and staff about the reorganization is critical. Also, community public relations concerning the reorganization should not be ignored.[1] The team, while planning and implementing the new structure, must be aware of the many people who will be affected by the changes. Often these people can provide important input into the planning process.

Once formed, the team needs to review the hospital's goals and the reasons for the reorganization in order to develop an appropriate plan. Part of this analysis involves a review of the hospital's regulatory and legal environment to determine any special advantages possible from the reorganization and any restraints on it. After such a review, the team can create an appropriate structure.

---

§14.10 [1]Public misconceptions about the change can adversely affect the structure and ultimately thwart the reorganization. To avoid problems, some hospitals have employed public relations personnel to explain the reorganization to the media and public.

§14.10.2 Reviewing the Regulatory Requirements

Hospitals and other healthcare facilities are pervasively regulated by a variety of state and federal agencies. Therefore, regulatory matters are an important part of planning and implementing a corporate restructuring. The hospital's legal counsel must ensure that all required approvals are obtained and that the reorganization will not adversely affect the facility's regulatory status. Some specific areas of concern are discussed below.

Licensure.   State law provides for hospital licensure.[2] Generally, a hospital's license cannot be transferred or assigned except with consent of the state regulatory authority. If the reorganization will involve a transfer of the hospital to a different corporation, then it may be necessary to obtain approval for transfer of the license. However, most hospital reorganizations are accomplished by transferring ownership or control of the hospital corporation. For example, the hospital corporation may be acquired by a holding company that becomes the hospital's sole member. In such a case, the hospital corporation continues to exist and to operate as the licensed healthcare facility, and its license is not transferred. Even if the license will not be transferred, it is still advisable to obtain confirmation from the licensure agency that the reorganization will not affect the licensure status of the hospital.

Medicare and Medicaid Certification.   It is important to ensure that the reorganization will not adversely affect the hospital's status as a certified provider under the Medicare and Medicaid programs. As a precaution, the reorganization team should contact the applicable state agency to confirm that the reorganized hospital will retain its certified status.

Accreditation by the JCAHO.   In most cases it is unnecessary to obtain advance approval by the JCAHO for a corporate

---

[2]See, e.g., N.C. Gen. Stat. ch. 131E, art. 5 (1988); Ill. Ann. Stat. ch. 111½, ¶142-157 (Smith-Hurd 1988); Fla. Stat. Ann. ch. 395 (West 1986). (The reader should consult the law of his or her own state.)

reorganization, but when applicable the JCAHO should be notified within 30 days after completing the reorganization. Also, some reorganizations involve substantial changes that could affect a hospital's accreditation. For example, creation of a multihospital system may involve the establishment of a combined medical staff for two separate hospitals. Similarly, the JCAHO requires that certain functions be carried out by the governing board of a hospital, but a multihospital system may wish to perform some of those functions at the holding-company level. If such changes are contemplated, it is advisable to contact the JCAHO before the reorganization to ensure that there will be no adverse effect on the hospital's accreditation.

Certificate of Need Laws. Certificate-of-need laws regulate major expenditures and changes involving healthcare facilities.[3] State law will determine whether it is necessary to obtain a CON for a hospital reorganization. Before reorganizing, it is also important to ensure that the changes will not result in withdrawal of any CON for pending projects.[4]

The Hill-Burton Law. The federal Hill-Burton program was designed to assist public and other nonprofit hospitals in the construction and expansion of needed hospital facilities. If a hospital received grants, loans, or loan guarantees under the Hill-Burton program or other governmental programs, it may be necessary to obtain approval from the United States Department of Health and Human Services (HHS) for the corporate reorganization.

Under the Hill-Burton regulations, the transferor of a facility must notify HHS in writing within ten days after a transfer

---

[3]See, e.g., N.C. Gen. Stat. ch 131E, art. 9 (1988); Cal. Health & Safety Code pt. 1.5 (West 1979); Fla. Stat. Ann. §§381.701 to 381.715 (West Supp. 1989). (The reader should consult the law of his or her own state.)

[4]See, e.g., N.C. Gen. Stat. §131-189(c), which states that the Department of Facility Services may withdraw a certificate of need if the holder of the certificate, before completion of the project or operation of the facility, transfers ownership or control of the facility.

occurs.[5] The regulations define a "transfer" to include the conveyance of a facility to another entity. Even if the corporate reorganization does not involve an actual transfer of hospital assets, HHS may consider the creation of a holding company to govern the hospital as a transfer subject to HHS regulations.

If a facility assisted under the Hill-Burton program is transferred within 20 years to an entity that would not have been eligible for such assistance, the federal government can recapture an amount determined by a formula set forth by law.[6] Therefore, if there is any question as to the applicability of the Hill-Burton regulations, it may be preferable to notify HHS in advance of the reorganization to ensure compliance with all regulatory requirements.

The hospital also may need HHS approval for a corporate reorganization as a result of a prior agreement. For example, a Hill-Burton loan guaranty agreement may require HHS approval for any subsequent changes in the hospital's corporate structure. Therefore, any documents related to the agreement should be carefully reviewed to determine whether this type of contractual requirement exists.

§14.10.3 Performing the Due Diligence Review

In addition to the regulatory requirements, each hospital will have special reorganization concerns that the planning team can identify during a "due diligence" review.[7] This is an analysis of the hospital's current legal situation to determine any special situations or obstacles that will affect the reorganization. Some

---

[5] 42 U.S.C. §291i(a)(b) (Supp. 1983-1987). See 42 C.F.R. §124.703(a) (1988).

[6] See 42 U.S.C. §291i(a)(b). See also 42 C.F.R. §124.703(a).

[7] Due diligence is the care the law ordinarily requires a person to use in order to avoid liability. Black's Law Dictionary 411 (5th ed. 1979) calls common diligence "that degree of diligence which men in general exercise in respect to their own concerns." Here the term is applied to the need for carefully reviewing important legal documents before reorganizing a corporation.

obstacles may limit structural possibilities. Other items noted in the due diligence review will require special planning, consents, or waivers but will not ultimately restrict the reorganization. The review, while not a legal necessity, is prudent in order to protect the hospital from adverse consequences. Items that should be examined vary greatly from hospital to hospital, but include corporate documents, debt instruments, contractual agreements, and grants. The following sections discuss some of the items often examined during a due diligence review.

Corporate Governing Instruments. The hospital's current articles of incorporation and bylaws must be reviewed even though they probably will be amended as part of the reorganization process. The existing corporate documents govern the formalities necessary to amend the articles and bylaws. Also, the corporate documents may indicate special historic relationships that must be preserved or altered, such as an affiliation with a county. Bylaws often have management structure provisions, such as those governing the hospital committee structure, that may affect the new hospital system structure. Overall, the current hospital corporate documents are a good starting point to learn about the hospital.

Agreements with Government Entities. Agreements with government entities can indicate special circumstances, such as the fact that a hospital is public or that the hospital leases or has leased its facility from a government entity. State laws governing any such relationships must be reviewed prior to the reorganization. Relationships with government entities may need to be changed before a reorganization is possible.

Deeds. Deeds for hospital properties may have provisions—perhaps from the original gift of the hospital lands—that will limit the uses of the land; such provisions could limit reorganization transfers and the activities of the hospital system after the reorganization.

Debt Instruments and Bonds.   Debt instruments or bonds may have provisions limiting amendments of the hospital's governing instruments or limiting changes in the control structure of the hospital. Such agreements also may restrict transfers of assets to affiliated corporations. Failure to comply with these provisions could cause a default of the debt. In many cases lenders will consent to the desired reorganization changes, though such consents may require that the new hospital affiliates guarantee the debt. In addition, transferring assets during the reorganization could affect the hospital's credit or bond rating. For example, transferring investment assets to an affiliate will lower the hospital's net worth. The effect of transfers on the hospital's debt must be carefully considered, particularly if the hospital anticipates any future financing.

Other Governmental Funding.   Other types of governmental funding besides Hill-Burton funds may affect the reorganization. For example, public funding can subject a hospital to state open meetings laws that must be complied with for any valid corporate actions.[8]

Major Contracts.   Major contracts, including third-party reimbursement contracts, employment contracts, and physician agreements, may affect reorganization plans. For example, a contract may need to be assigned to the affiliate performing the contractual function. Such assignments generally require consent of the contracting parties. Other contracts require notice of corporate control changes (such as changes that might occur in a reorganization).

Tax Exemption Letter and IRS Forms 990 and 990-T.   The tax exemption determination letter from the IRS will generally show that a tax-exempt hospital is an Internal Revenue Code §501(c)(3)

---

[8]See, e.g., N.C. Gen. Stat. ch. 143, art. 33C (1987); N.Y. Pub. Off. Law art. 7 (McKinney 1988); Cal. Govt. Code §§54951.1, 54952.5, 54953 (West 1983). (The reader should consult the law of his or her own state.)

entity[9] and not a private foundation under I.R.C. §§509(a)(1) and 170(b)(1)(A)(iii). A review of the hospital's tax return (Form 990), including the UBTI tax return (Form 990-T), may provide tax-planning ideas for structuring the reorganization.

Financial Statements. The hospital's financial statements can reveal issues that must be addressed in the reorganization planning.

Medical Staff Bylaws. These bylaws must be coordinated with the new governing structure of the reorganized system. After the reorganization, for example, medical staff appointments may need to be made by the board of a parent company for the entire hospital system rather than by the hospital's board for the hospital alone.

Grants and Endowments. Certain major grants or endowments may restrict hospital activities or changes. For example, many grants require that the hospital retain its tax-exempt status.

Other Items. Additional issues that the reorganization team must address may be revealed by a review of board of trustees' minutes, consultants' reports, litigation pleadings, and other documents.

The due diligence review is different for every hospital. There is no substitute for a knowledgeable reorganization team working together to spot the issues, resolve them, and formulate a plan that works. Admittedly the review, while critical to a successful reorganization, is time-consuming. A knowledgeable team can identify the major issues during the early planning stages; therefore, a review should not unduly delay the restructuring process. Any necessary consents or waivers often can be obtained while the IRS is reviewing the reorganization plan.

---

[9]The Internal Revenue Code section prior to 1954 for tax-exempt hospitals was §101(6).

§14.10.4 Determining the Structure

After the due diligence review, the planning team can develop an appropriate structure for the reorganized hospital system. This structure depends on the hospital's current activities, but it also must have sufficient flexibility to provide for future needs. Therefore, creating the new structure involves considering the hospital's long-range plans. Though each hospital's plans and needs will differ from those of other hospitals, certain basic reorganized structures are commonly used.

The Basic Structure.   The three basic structures for reorganized hospital systems are the parent holding company, the hospital-as-parent, and the brother-sister arrangements. As discussed below, each structure has certain advantages and pitfalls.

The major concern in choosing any structure is determining the center of power for the reorganized system. In each model one corporation "controls" the others. The controlling entity is the "parent" corporation, regardless of its technical legal status.

The legal status of the parent corporation is directed by state law. Under the law of some states this parent entity can be the sole member of its nonprofit affiliates, a status equivalent to that of the sole shareholder of a for-profit corporation. Other state laws may necessitate different legal relationships.

The parent corporation will control its subordinate affiliates, or "subsidiaries."[10] It can, for example, elect directors, amend corporate documents, approve major corporate changes, and authorize budgets and large expenditures. The type and degree of control will depend on the hospital reorganization goals as well as state law. In any case, the parent entity must have sufficient control so that the hospital system has effective internal coordination. The parent's elements of control will be specified

---

[10]"Subsidiaries" is not technically the correct term for the subordinate affiliates with the parent as sole member, because "subsidiary" generally refers to a stock corporation that is owned by another corporation. "Subsidiaries" is used here, however, because conceptually it best describes the relationship between the sole member and its subordinate affiliates.

in the corporate documents of the parent entity and its subsidiaries. These control elements give the parent corporation control of its affiliates even if it is not the sole member of the subsidiaries. Thus, if being a sole member or shareholder is not permitted under state law or is not legally advisable,[11] the parent corporation can still control its affiliates.

The parent corporation (or another affiliate) can also be the sole shareholder of a for-profit corporation, the taxable subsidiary. As sole shareholder, the parent will have the usual rights of a shareholder under state law, which generally include the right to make fundamental changes and to elect directors. The parent corporation can have additional powers. However, the more these powers differ from ordinary shareholder powers, the greater the likelihood that the IRS will ignore the corporate form of the taxable subsidiary and consider it to be part of the parent entity, with attendant risk to the parent's tax-exempt status. The parent corporation may also be a shareholder of a taxable entity in a joint venture arrangement, as discussed in Part C.

The Parent Holding Company. A common reorganized hospital structure involves a parent holding company that controls both the hospital and the other nonprofit "subsidiary" corporations and that is the sole shareholder of a for-profit corporation. This model has one corporation whose fundamental purpose is to control the hospital system through its board of directors. Housing this board in a separate, governing parent entity emphasizes the board members' role as system managers rather than mere hospital board members. Therefore, the directors are more likely to focus on all of the subsidiaries rather than just on the hospital.

Another advantage of the parent holding company model is that it resembles for-profit holding companies, with which most board members are familiar. The primary disadvantage of the model is that it necessitates an additional corporation, the

---

[11]For example, making a parent entity the sole member is not advisable if state law has restrictive provisions affecting members of nonprofit entities.

parent entity, which must comply with all corporate formalities and tax requirements.

The Hospital-as-Parent.   An alternative is to make the hospital corporation a parent corporation with subsidiaries. This model eliminates one corporation, the parent holding company. The disadvantage of having the hospital as the parent entity is that the hospital board will tend to focus on the hospital rather than on the whole system. In addition, the intimate involvement of the hospital with the subsidiaries will make it more difficult to separate these subsidiaries from the hospital for reimbursement, liability, or tax purposes.

Brother-Sister Corporations.   The final basic reorganization arrangement is the brother-sister model, in which the hospital is not legally affiliated with the other corporations, but exerts control through common purposes or common directors. Having the affiliates share directors without an additional legal affiliation may have some regulatory, liability, or other advantages over the other models. However, in the brother-sister model, corporate coordination is difficult because control is indirect (through common board members) rather than direct (through a legal affiliation).

To achieve significant advantages using the brother-sister structure, it is necessary to minimize board overlap.[12] If the boards do not overlap, there is a stronger argument that the corporations are entirely separate and thus it is inappropriate to hold one corporation responsible for the others for reimbursement, tort liability, or other purposes. However, such an arrangement may not be workable. The separate boards may pursue their own goals without coordinating with their affiliates. The result, as some hospitals have learned, can be disastrous. Also, few hospital boards will give up control of functions or assets to entities they do not legally control. Arguably, giving up control is a breach of their fiduciary duties and creates improper private

---

[12]In the case of separate, nonoverlapping boards, the dominant corporation would seek to influence the others, though it might not legally control them.

benefit. Thus, while the brother-sister arrangement with no board overlap may have advantages, it has significant risks. Board overlap is discussed further at §14.10.5 infra.

One useful variation of the brother-sister arrangement is to create an independent fundraising foundation whose assets will be kept separate from those of the hospital. Historically, such foundations have developed at some hospitals and have been vital sources of community support. Of course, an independent foundation may not always use funds in the way the hospital board would prefer.

The Nonhospital "Subsidiaries." Each basic reorganization model can have many variations, based on the desired subsidiaries. The hospital should only create those entities that it realistically will need for its current and long-range goals. Extra subsidiaries can become an administrative burden.

Subsidiaries commonly used in hospital reorganizations include a fundraising foundation, an investment management company, one or more nonacute healthcare providers, and a taxable subsidiary. Of course, in the parent holding company model the hospital itself is a subsidiary. The many possibilities for and functions of subsidiaries are limited only by the imagination of the reorganization team.

A reorganized fundraising foundation, as discussed above, can be either controlled by the hospital system or be legally unrelated, a brother-sister entity to the hospital. Its board can include community leaders who can help with fundraising and provide community support for the hospital. Often these community leaders are too busy to serve effectively on the hospital's board but may enjoy and perform useful service on the foundation's board. Thus, a fundraising foundation can supply economic as well as public relations benefits for the hospital system.

A second common affiliate is an investment management corporation that houses the investment assets of the hospital system. Segregated into a separate entity, assets may be protected from hospital liabilities, so long as the hospital system observes all corporate formalities and avoids the "piercing of the corporate veil" by creditors. Segregating assets may also have third-party reimbursement advantages; one such advantage would be to avoid having interest income offset interest expense, which lowers reimbursements. Of course, the more closely the investment corporation is tied to the hospital through legal status or overlapping boards the less likely that any reimbursement calculations will exclude affiliate funds.

Hospital systems can include subsidiaries for nonacute healthcare functions, such as a nursing home. Separate corporations may avoid certificate-of-need provisions or enhance the hospital system's competitive position to receive a certificate of need. For example, a free-standing nursing home may appear more cost-efficient and thus more competitive for a contested certificate of need because overhead costs for a hospital tend to be higher than those for a nursing home. Certain free-standing services also may have reimbursement advantages. To determine the advantages, the reorganization team needs to review carefully the regulatory and other effects of moving functions to a separate entity.

Various other nonprofit subsidiaries are possible. For example, two already existing nonprofit entities may want to affiliate by becoming subsidiaries of a common parent. This arrangement can be used to "merge" two hospitals. Similarly, a hospital and an allied health entity can be affiliated under a common parent without eliminating their separate identities and corporate statuses. Other healthcare providers will find themselves better able to gain funding when affiliated with a hospital. Also, the hospital's real property could be moved to a separate entity to protect the property from hospital liabilities. If properly structured, such a property-holding entity may be tax-exempt.[13]

The Taxable Subsidiary.   Hospital systems often reorganize to create a taxable subsidiary, legally a for-profit entity owned by the hospital system. This entity allows the tax-exempt hospital system to perform functions that are not advisable for tax-exempt entities. Such functions could create too much unrelated income or arguably could have an element of private inurement

---

[13]See I.R.C. §501(c)(2).

that would jeopardize the hospital's tax-exempt status. Also, such a taxable entity could house functions that from a public relations standpoint do not seem appropriate for a tax-exempt hospital. Such activities may appear less threatening to community businesses if conducted by a taxable entity.

Recently the IRS has stepped up its scrutiny of taxable subsidiaries, arguing that a subsidiary that is a mere agent or instrument of a parent corporation should be combined with that entity for tax purposes, despite their separate legal forms.[14] Combining the two could taint the tax-exempt entity with taxable activities, thus jeopardizing its tax-exempt status. Various proposed changes to the law could impute a taxable subsidiary's activities to its parent.

The IRS currently reviews certain factors to determine if the taxable subsidiary is a mere agent for its parent and if, therefore, the tax-exempt parent and its taxable subsidiary should be considered as one entity. A general counsel memorandum[15] states that the subsidiary is not a mere agent of the parent if:

---

[14]For example, the conclusion of Gen. Couns. Mem. 39,508 (May 28, 1986), states that the IRS has not decided the question of the effect of the taxable subsidiary on the parent holding company in a hospital reorganization. See Priv. Ltr. Rul. 86-06-056 (Nov. 14, 1985). See also Lee and McCandlish, Trouble Ahead for Tax-Exempt Hospital Systems, 1986 Va. Hosp. Persp. 1 (Aug. 14, 1986). But see Priv. Ltr. Rul. 86-25-078 (Mar. 27, 1986); Priv. Ltr. Rul. 86-21-060 (Feb. 25, 1986); Purcell, Using For-Profit Subsidiaries to Preserve Exempt Status, 67 J. Taxn. 180 (1987).

The courts are less stringent than the IRS, providing that a corporation and its subsidiary are separate entities as long as the purposes for which the subsidiary is incorporated are the equivalent of business activities or as long as the subsidiary subsequently carries on business activities. Moline Properties v. Commissioner, 319 U.S. 436, 438-439 (1943); Britt v. United States, 431 F.2d 227, 234 (5th Cir. 1970). See B. Hopkins, The Law of Tax-Exempt Organizations 820-828 (5th ed. 1987 & Supp. 1989). When a corporation is organized with the bona fide intention of having some real and substantial business functions, its existence may not generally be disregarded for tax purposes. Britt, 431 F.2d at 234. Of course, if the parent corporation so controls the affairs of the subsidiary that the subsidiary is merely an instrumentality of the parent, the corporate entity of the subsidiary may be disregarded. Krivo Indus. Supply Co. v. Natl. Distillers and Chem. Corp., 438 F.2d 1098, 1106 (5th Cir. 1973), rehg. denied, 490 F.2d 916 (5th Cir. 1974).

[15]Gen. Couns. Mem. 39,326 (Jan. 17, 1985). This memorandum is

1. the subsidiary was organized for a bona fide business purpose;
2. any transactions between the tax-exempt and taxable entities are on an arm's-length basis;
3. the tax-exempt entity is not involved in the day-to-day management of the taxable subsidiary; and
4. a majority of the taxable subsidiary's directors are not directors, officers, or employees of the tax-exempt entity.

Private letter rulings address other factors, including sharing employees and facilities and having the taxable entity conduct businesses previously engaged in by the tax-exempt entity.[16] Unfortunately, these rulings do not define a clear test for determining when the subsidiary activities will be imputed to the parent. Instead, the IRS uses a facts-and-circumstances test. For protection, a hospital may want to apply for an IRS private letter ruling approving its taxable subsidiary. Such rulings are discussed at §14.10.7 infra.

§14.10.5 Creating the Corporations

After determining the appropriate reorganized structure, the planning team must create the new corporations and determine what changes are needed in the hospital's structure. The team's attorney can prepare the corporate governing documents for each hospital system entity. Preparing these documents requires many decisions, such as the structure of the boards, the desired officers, the appropriate committees, and the corporate names; each decision involves many considerations.[17]

---

modified somewhat by Gen. Couns. Mem. 39,598 (Jan. 23, 1987) and Gen. Couns. Mem. 39,646 (June 30, 1987).

[16]See, e.g., Priv. Ltr. Rul. 85-04-058 (Oct. 30, 1984); Priv. Ltr. Rul. 83-37-040 (June 14, 1983); Priv. Ltr. Rul. 82-44-114 (Aug. 6, 1982). See generally Purcell, supra n.14.

[17]For an excellent discussion on corporate aspects of hospital reorganizations, see L. Gerber, Hospital Restructuring: Why, Where, & How (1983).

First, each corporation must have a board of directors. Manageability is the key to structuring these boards. A reorganized hospital system will have several boards of directors, perhaps five or more. Unless these boards actually function as separate corporation boards—by meeting and preparing minutes, for example—courts may later be willing to deny the corporations' legal existence. Complying with the formal legal requirements, however, may easily become a burden for board members. One solution is to have a parent board with many members but smaller subsidiary boards. Another suggestion is to limit the number of board members serving on multiple boards.

It is also important to determine the optimum overlap between members of the affiliates' boards. For reimbursement and liability purposes, it may be advantageous to limit board overlap (to reduce the possibility that the courts or others will see the corporations as one). It should be noted that officers or employees of a corporation may be viewed as agents of their boards, thus creating overlap if these officers or employees serve on the board of an affiliate.

Board overlap can also have various tax consequences. Too much overlap may provide the IRS with the argument that the subsidiary is effectively the parent corporation. Such an argument could be made if a majority of the members of the parent board are members of a subsidiary board. For example, if the parent board has eleven members and six of those members serve on any subsidiary board, including the hospital board, then the subsidiary "controls" the parent. Also, the IRS is increasingly taking the position that less than a majority of the board of any taxable subsidiary should be members of the other boards. Such limited board overlap is one factor used to determine whether the taxable entity is merely an agent of its tax-exempt affiliates. In other cases, board overlap may be necessary. To avoid private foundation status with its attendant excise taxes and restrictions, a parent holding company may need majority overlap with the hospital board. Qualifying the parent holding company as a nonprivate foundation is discussed below in §14.10.7.

There are no absolute answers as to the appropriate board structures for a reorganized hospital system. The competing requirements for reimbursement, tax, and management purposes often dictate different board structures. The planning team must determine the structure that maximizes the most important reorganization goals. Equally important, the team must be sensitive to the concerns of the hospital's current board.

The planning team must address additional corporate governance issues. Each corporation will need officers. Determining the desired positions as well as the appropriate people to fill them generally involves reviewing previous executive positions in the hospital and current management personnel. At a minimum, each corporation should have a president and a secretary, but having additional officers is preferable. Also, the planning team must determine what board committees are needed and which corporations will have these committees.[18] For example, the medical staff committees may need to be in the parent company rather than the hospital if other subsidiaries will also have medical staffs. Of course, the current hospital committee structure will affect the new committee structures.

The new corporations also will need names. Often the names will reflect the public relations and marketing goals for the entities. For example, each affiliates' name may include the hospital's name to capitalize on the hospital's goodwill. In contrast, another hospital may prefer to give its affiliate names that are unrelated to the hospital, such as regional names, to attract new patients. The choice of new corporate names can be very important.

After determining the corporate structures, the attorney can prepare articles of incorporation and bylaws for the new corporations and proposed revised articles and bylaws for the hospital. The hospital's governing documents may need to be amended to give the parent company, if any, control of the hospital as sole member or otherwise. This parent company may

---

[18]Committees commonly located in the parent entity include executive, audit, finance, long-range planning, and public relations. Subject to accreditation and other requirements, the medical affairs committee and joint conference committee may be in the parent entity, particularly if entities other than the hospital will have medical staffs. Of course, each hospital has different committees.

have the power to elect the hospital board, amend the hospital's articles and bylaws, and review its budget; all of these powers will need to be reflected in the new corporate documents. In addition, all of the articles and bylaws for the tax-exempt affiliates must have certain provisions ensuring that the corporations will be tax-exempt and nonprivate foundations. The taxable subsidiary should have for-profit articles and bylaws, including shareholder provisions.

At this point, the board of trustees of the hospital could approve the new articles and bylaws in principle. Though this approval is not a legal necessity, it is an advisable step to ensure that the hospital board will agree to the ultimate reorganization plan. Also, it is critical that the hospital board understand and appreciate the proposed plan.

The new entities may now be incorporated and the new boards of directors may adopt the corporate bylaws, elect officers, and perform other necessary corporate actions. The taxable subsidiary's incorporation should be delayed until any desired IRS approval for this entity is obtained. Also, the hospital's revised articles and bylaws should not be formally adopted until after receipt of any desired IRS approvals, as discussed in §14.10.7 below.

§14.10.6 Determining Functional Transfers

As part of developing the reorganized hospital structure, the planning team considers the functions of each new corporation; these functions may require the transfer of assets or employees. For example, nonacute care assets can be moved to the nonacute healthcare subsidiary, and the investment assets can be transferred to the investment management corporation. The contractual, regulatory, and reimbursement requirements examined during the regulatory and due diligence reviews should guide the hospital in determining the propriety of asset transfers. Current employee benefits and taxes may affect the decision to transfer employees. By moving employees to new entities it may be possible to create advantages such as different employee benefits.[19] Employee and asset transfers should be addressed in sufficient detail during the planning stage to permit the request of any needed approvals.

An alternative to transfers of assets and employees is for the corporations to enter into leases or management agreements that transfer functions without actual transfers of assets or employees. The tax-exempt affiliates may be able to share, to some extent, assets and employees, though the better practice is to have agreements for such shared services. Any "sharing" arrangements with a taxable entity must have arm's-length, fair market value terms comparable to those for ordinary businesses, and there should be written documentation of these agreements.

In addition, each new corporation will need adequate capitalization and working capital. Otherwise, creditors may use undercapitalization as an argument for treating the corporations as a single entity. The amount of capital needed depends on the anticipated functions of a corporation. For example, a nonacute healthcare affiliate may need several months of working capital. The parent holding company may need capital to invest in its taxable subsidiary, but otherwise may need little capital. Depending on its nonprivate foundation status, the parent holding company may be able to have only limited capital.[20] The initial capitalization is important, though later asset transfers or loans to the new entities are possible.

§14.10.7 Preserving the Desired Tax Status

A tax-exempt hospital's most valuable asset is its tax-exempt status. The reorganization must preserve this status, and the

---

[19]For examples, labor negotiations and Fair Labor Standards Act provisions may be different between the entities as long as the entities are truly separate. The problem is that the affiliates may be considered joint employers such that they are treated as a sole employer for various labor and employee provisions. See S. Erf and J. Badel, Hospital Restructuring: Employment Law Pitfalls (1985).

[20]If the parent entity qualifies under I.R.C. §§509(a)(1) and 170(b)(1)(A)(vi), then one-third of its support must be from public sources, so the investment income produced by its capital will probably need to be limited. Therefore, its capital must be limited.

affiliates providing services that were previously part of the hospital should also be tax-exempt. Thus, the planning team needs to structure the reorganization carefully to ensure the desired tax status for all entities. A decision on tax status for the new entities requires approval from the IRS. Additional IRS approvals may be advisable to ensure the desired tax effects. Finally, the planning team needs to avoid other tax pitfalls in the reorganization process.

Tax-Exempt Status and Avoiding Private Foundation Status. As discussed above, nonprofit hospitals can be tax-exempt. Also, the IRS generally allows exempt status to hospital affiliates that provide hospital-related services.[21] The articles of incorporation and the bylaws, as well as the structure and activities, of the tax-exempt corporations must comply with the requirements of I.R.C. §501(c)(3) and its related regulations, as discussed above at §14.5.

The new tax-exempt corporations will wish to avoid private foundation status.[22] Private foundations, though "tax-exempt,"

---

[21]Such affiliates should be exempt as an integral part of the hospital. The IRS has provided other examples of entities eligible for tax-exempt status under I.R.C. §501(c)(3). See, e.g., Rev. Rul. 67-149, 1967-1 C.B. 133 (a trust to hold funds to satisfy malpractice claims against a hospital was exempt because the trust was an integral part of the hospital; such a trust performs a function that the hospital could otherwise perform). See Rev. Rul. 78-41, 1978-1 C.B. 148. But see Gen. Couns. Mem. 39,508 (May 28, 1986), which seems to provide that each nonprofit entity must have its own basis for exemption. The IRS appears to be questioning giving derivative exemption to groups of entities.

[22]Section 509(a) of the I.R.C. defines a "private foundation" as any organization described in I.R.C. §501(c)(3) except:

1) Certain organizations described in §170(b)(1)(A);

2) Other publicly supported organizations, meeting financial support tests; or

3) An organization that

a) Is organized, and at all times operated, exclusively for the benefit of, to perform the functions of, or to carry out the purposes of one or more organizations described in (1) or (2),

b) Is operated, supervised, or controlled by or in connection with one or more organizations described in (1) or (2); and

c) Is not controlled directly or indirectly by one or more disqualified

are subject to additional excise taxes, including a tax on net investment income, additional reporting requirements, and required annual distributions. For private foundations, there are prohibitions on activities such as self-dealing and investing in certain businesses, and there is increased risk to the tax-exempt status of a private foundation.[23] Violation of the private foundation limitations will subject the corporation to high penalty taxes. In addition, the tax treatment is less favorable for contributions to private foundations than for contributions to public charities.[24] Unintentionally creating a private foundation could adversely affect the reorganization structure and activities as well as subject the private foundation to taxes. For example, a private foundation cannot be a sole shareholder of another corporation, which means that it could not own a taxable subsidiary. Finally, it is not clear how the private foundation limitations would apply to transactions with affiliates in a hospital system.

There are several ways in which a tax-exempt corporation can avoid private foundation status. First, the corporation can be a "public charity," which for tax purposes means an entity that, because of its funding or its basic nature, is responsive to the public. By definition a hospital is a public charity.[25] The other forms of public charities relevant for hospital reorganizations are ones that receive a significant portion of their support from the general public or charitable activities. Such organizations are described in I.R.C. §§509(a)(1) by way of §§170(b)(1)(A)(vi) and

---

persons (as defined in I.R.C. §4946) other than foundation managers and other than one or more organizations described in (1) or (2).
See generally D. Gray, Nonprivate Foundations: A Tax Guide for Charitable Organizations (1978).

[23]See I.R.C. §4940 et seq. See also I.R.C. §§507-508. In general, the concept of and restrictions on private foundations are designed to prevent perceived abuses by certain charitable entities that are not considered sufficiently subject to public control. The private foundation rules make little sense for reorganized hospital affiliates, which are highly accountable to the public because of their hospital affiliation.

[24]See, e.g., I.R.C. §170(b)(1)(B).

[25]Hospitals are described in I.R.C. §170(b)(1)(A)(iii) and thus are nonprivate foundations under I.R.C. §509(a)(1).

509(a)(2). To oversimplify, a §170(b)(1)(A)(vi) entity must receive one-third (or one-tenth, with additional facts and circumstances) of its support from the government or general public, with no more than 2 percent of calculated support from any one source. A §509(a)(2) entity must receive more than one-third of its support from the public or charitable activities (with less than $5,000 or 1 percent coming from any particular source) and no more than one-third from unrelated or investment income. These support tests can be difficult to meet and can limit the activities of the corporation. Thus, meeting the tests will require careful planning and monitoring. Nevertheless, in some situations it is necessary for at least one of the reorganized system corporations to be such a publicly supported corporation, and until recently the parent holding company generally had to so qualify as publicly supported.[26]

As an alternative, an entity can qualify as a nonprivate foundation if by virtue of its corporate purpose and structure it supports a public charity.[27] The corporate governing instruments should provide appropriate support language. The hospital affiliates can generally qualify as supporting organizations because they support the hospital. Under current IRS policy, the

---

[26]IRS policy concerning qualifying the parent as a supporting organization has changed several times. The IRS has also changed its position on a parent corporation's being a supporting organization while having supporting organization subsidiaries. See, e.g., Gen. Couns. Mem. 39,508 (May 28, 1986). See generally McGovern, Restructured Nonprofit Hospitals, 1987 Tax Notes 405 (April 27, 1987).

[27]The Internal Revenue Code provides several requirements for an organization to be a supporting organization under §509(a)(3). First, under §509(a)(3)(C), a §509(a)(3) organization cannot be directly or indirectly controlled by disqualified persons, as defined. Second, under §509(a)(3)(A), it can be organized and operated for the exclusive benefit of, to perform the functions of, and to carry out the purposes of a specified §170(b)(1)(A) or §509(a)(2) organization. Finally, under §509(a)(3)(B), it can be operated, supervised, or controlled by or in connection with one or more organizations described in §509(a)(1) or (2). The regulations under §509(a)(3) discuss these requirements in painful detail. See Treas. Reg. §1.509(a)-4 (as amended in 1981).

parent holding company also may qualify as a supporting organization, but it may need majority overlap of its board with the hospital board.[28] If such board overlap is not desirable for regulatory or other purposes, then the alternative is to qualify the parent holding company as a public charity that meets the tests discussed above.

Determination of Exempt Status. To be recognized as a tax-exempt organization, an entity usually must file within 15 months of incorporation a Request for Determination of Tax-Exempt Status (Form 1023 or 1024). Such filings also establish that the corporation is a nonprivate foundation by its nature or that it requires an advance ruling period to permit it to gain the needed public support.[29] Form 1023 for I.R.C. §501(c)(3) entities requests detailed descriptions of the purpose, organization, and activities of the new tax-exempt corporation and requires proposed budgets for at least two years. These forms must be carefully completed (to avoid denial of exempt status) and then submitted to the IRS regional office for exempt organizations. However, if a reorganization private letter ruling is requested

---

[28]Gen. Couns. Mem. 39,508 concludes that the parent corporation in a reorganized hospital system can qualify as a supporting organization under I.R.C. §509(a)(3) so long as the parent and the publicly supported organization have management or control vested in the same persons. The rule of thumb for some entities discussed in this memorandum is that "no less than a majority of the persons who control or manage the supporting organization have the requisite commonality with the persons performing the same functions for each publicly supported organization supported or benefited." Gen. Couns. Mem. 39,508 (May 28, 1986). See Bromberg, Public Charity Status: Can the Organization Pass the Test?, 1986 Healthcare Fin. Mgmt. 70 (Nov. 1986). In addition, Gen. Couns. Mem. 39,508 provides somewhat reluctantly that an organization subordinate to a §509(a)(3) parent may also qualify under that section as a supporting organization if the subordinate organization and the publicly supported organization have management or control vested in the same persons.

[29]The advance ruling period for I.R.C. §509(a)(2) or 509(a)(1) (through §170(b)(1)(A)(vi)) organizations is five years. See Treas. Reg. §1.170A (as amended in 1980); Treas. Reg. §1.509(a)-3 (as amended in 1981). At the end of the advance ruling period the corporation should complete a form for the IRS to prove that it has qualified as a nonprivate foundation.

from the IRS national office, it is advisable to submit the tax exemption request forms as part of the letter ruling request so that one reviewer analyzes the entire reorganization. After approving these applications, the IRS will issue determination letters confirming the tax-exempt status of the new entities. The new corporations must request employer identification numbers using Form SS-4, Application for Employer Identification Number. In addition, the new nonprofit corporations need to be exempt from various state taxes, which will require compliance with state law.

Private Letter Ruling. As noted earlier, a critical part of the reorganization process is determining the effect of the reorganization on the hospital's tax-exempt status. Unfortunately, the effect of reorganization on a hospital's tax status is not specifically addressed by the I.R.C., Treasury Regulations, or IRS rulings.[30] The IRS has issued several general counsel memoranda on certain reorganization issues that reveal IRS policy but are not law. Also, the IRS has given several hundred private letter rulings to individual hospitals for their reorganizations. Unfortunately, private letter rulings are not legal precedents;[31] therefore, no hospital may rely on the letter rulings of another hospital. Until Congress or the IRS establishes formal law or regulations for hospital reorganizations, it is prudent to request a ruling[32] approving the hospital's reorganization.

Because the goal in obtaining the private letter ruling is to preserve the tax-exempt status of the hospital and its affiliates, this is the critical issue on which the IRS should be asked to rule. The IRS should also be asked for assurances that the proposed entities and the hospital will have nonprivate foundation status and that the reorganization transactions will not

---

[30]The reorganization provisions of I.R.C. §368 do not necessarily apply to I.R.C. §501(c)(3) entities.

[31]See I.R.C. §6110(j)(3).

[32]See Rev. Proc. 83-36, 1983-1 C.B. 763 for procedural requirements for private letter ruling requests. The IRS now charges a fee to issue a private letter ruling.

create any unanticipated unrelated business taxable income. The request can address transactions that will take place after the reorganization, such as sharing assets and creating affiliate loans and leases. Finally, the hospital can ask for a ruling on the tax effects of the taxable subsidiary.

A private letter ruling can require several months for approval. The time involved is more often a function of IRS review procedures than the specifics of the proposed reorganization. The hospital should use this delay to complete the regulatory and due diligence reviews and to establish the favorable public relations necessary to ensure a successful reorganization.

Additional Tax Considerations. The planning team must consider other federal tax issues. Many of these issues are not raised in the private letter ruling request because their tax effect is clearly provided or because the IRS is unlikely to rule on them. Also, the team needs to address state tax issues.

A critical issue is whether the reorganization will generate unrelated business taxable income. Efforts to avoid taxes on such income are likely to determine the placement of hospital activities.

Employee-related tax issues also must be considered. For example, transfers of employees may affect payroll taxes. Also, employee benefit plans may need to be amended to provide for transferred employees. In addition, the laws for benefit plans must be reviewed to ensure that no rules are violated by excluding affiliated employees.[33] Finally, the employees of taxable entities may not be eligible for all of the tax-exempt entities' deferred compensation plans.[34]

State tax laws cannot be ignored by a planning team

---

[33]The affiliated nonprofit entities may be considered as being under common control for I.R.C. §414(b) and 414(c), and thus the entities will be combined for applying the various rules for retirement plans. See Gen. Couns. Mem. 39,616 (June 27, 1986). See also I.R.C. §414(m).

[34]See, e.g., I.R.C. §403(b), which permits tax-deferred annuity plans only for employees of certain tax-exempt entities.

zealously working to achieve desirable federal tax results. In addition to receiving exemption from state income and franchise taxes, the new corporations may want exemptions from intangibles taxes, sales taxes, property taxes, or other state taxes. The hospital's exemptions from these taxes do not automatically extend to its affiliates; additional compliance with exemption requirements is needed.

§14.10.8 Implementing the Reorganization

After receiving the IRS private letter ruling and determination letters confirming continued tax-exempt status, and after completing the due diligence and regulatory reviews, the hospital can reorganize. The reorganization itself is very simple, even anticlimatic. The hospital must amend its articles of incorporation and bylaws to the new reorganized articles and bylaws. These new corporate documents affiliate the hospital with the other reorganization entities. For example, they may make the parent holding company the sole member of the hospital and make the hospital the affiliate of the other entities. These hospital amendments should be approved with full corporate formalities by the hospital board of trustees at a meeting. At this time the taxable subsidiary can be incorporated, and any reorganization asset or function transfers can be made. Some corporate housekeeping will probably be needed, too, such as the election of new directors and officers. The new corporations may need to establish banking relations and acquire insurance. They will need to set up books and records and execute any interaffiliate agreements. When these matters are attended to, the hospital reorganization is complete.

§14.11 After the Reorganization

The reorganization process continues long after the actual establishment of the new hospital structure. The board members and administrative staff need to concentrate on making the reorganization work and must look for ways to benefit from it. All board members and key employees need to understand the new system so they can maximize its advantages. New board members must learn about the system, and the hospital should develop a director's manual to assist them. In addition, the boards of the new subsidiaries must concentrate on their special functions to benefit the system as a whole.

§14.11.1 Maintaining the Separate Corporations

From a legal standpoint, the corporations are separate entities, not separate functions within one corporation, the hospital. Each entity must function as a corporation, observing all corporate formalities. For example, the corporate boards must have periodic meetings and must record minutes. Again, if the corporations fail to act as separate entities, then the law may treat all of the corporations as one entity, defeating the purposes of the reorganization.

The new corporations must work with each other to further the hospital system's goals. The tax-exempt entities have some flexibility in their affiliate dealings, but any transactions with the taxable subsidiary must be on an arm's-length basis, preferably with formal legal documentation. Failure to observe this requirement could jeopardize the tax status of the tax-exempt corporations. In addition, transactions between and among the tax-exempt affiliates should be reviewed and documented. For example, if an affiliate uses hospital properties, it is probably advisable for the hospital and the affiliate to sign a lease documenting the relationship.[1] Such documentation clarifies the corporations' finances for accounting purposes and minimizes the risk of third parties' considering the entities as one corporation for reimbursement and liability purposes. Furthermore, such an agreement can channel affiliate funds back to the hospital. It is important to remember that such payments to the

---

§14.11   [1]Such leases, signed by the hospital and its affiliate (and often by the same person) may look silly but could ultimately prove important.

hospital can create unrelated business taxable income under Code §512(b)(13) if the affiliate has any unrelated income or is taxable.[2]

§14.11.2 Using the Taxable Affiliates

One of the main reasons many tax-exempt hospitals are reorganizing is to create a taxable affiliate. The possibilities for this new taxable entity are many. The taxable entity can tap hospital resources and turn excess capacity into revenues. For example, hospital affiliates can use hospital resources to provide laboratory or paging services to doctors, as well as cleaning, computer, catering, and many other services to their community. In addition, the taxable entity can enter into new businesses unrelated to the hospital's healthcare purpose or activities, perhaps taking advantage of good business opportunities. The taxable affiliate can also enter into joint ventures in place of the hospital, because certain joint ventures could jeopardize the hospital's tax-exempt status.

The taxable entity can transfer its excess revenues to the hospital or hospital affiliates as appropriate. These revenue transfers can be through contracts under which the taxable entity pays the hospital for management personnel or use of facilities. Such payments, if they are deductible by the taxable entity, will probably create unrelated business taxable income for the tax-exempt recipient under Code §512(b)(13). As an alternative, the taxable entity can pay dividends to its parent entity, using after-tax dollars. Perhaps the taxable entity could make charitable contributions to the tax-exempt affiliates that would be deductible by the taxable entity and that would not

---

[2]See I.R.C. §512(b)(13). Perhaps this mechanical rule could be avoided by having an entity other than the subsidiary's parent receive the income. The IRS disagrees, though. See Gen. Couns. Mem. 38,878 (July 16, 1982). Also, the parent may avoid this rule if it owns less than 80 percent of the subsidiary. See generally Miller, Cut Income Taxes with Reorganization Planning, 1985 Healthcare Fin. Mgmt. 60 (April 1985).

be income to the recipients. It is likely, though, that the IRS would classify such contributions as dividends, and thus the taxable entity could not deduct them.[3]

§14.11.3 Certain Problems to Avoid

Having spent months planning and implementing the hospital reorganization, the hospital board and administration may experience one of two attitudes on completing the process: complacency or overzealousness. Either attitude can lead to frustration with the reorganized system.

A hospital that reorganized for a single, limited purpose— perhaps reimbursement maximization—may ignore the flexibility its new system gives it. It may neglect to direct attention to special functions in hospital affiliates. Such a hospital may find its reorganized structure a burden with too many corporations and boards and too much red tape. Ultimately, such a hospital may collapse its structure back into one corporation, particularly if the original reason for restructuring disappears.

The other extreme for a reorganized hospital is overzealousness. The hospital may be so intent on taking advantage of its new structure that it rushes into activities without fully considering their business advantages. Such a hospital may use its taxable affiliate to enter into joint ventures that are not economically sound. A variation of this overzealousness is the proliferation of new entities. After seeing the advantages of having separate functions in separate corporations, the hospital may create a separate corporation for each new function. Eventually this approach will create an unworkable corporate structure as well as an administrative nightmare.

Luckily, most reorganized hospital boards and administrative personnel will have carefully reviewed the reorganization goals during the planning stage and will have a realistic understanding of the uses and limitations of the reorganized system. Such hospitals will look for opportunities and will enter into new

---

[3]See Gen. Couns. Mem. 38,878 (July 16, 1982).

ventures that further the system's goals. They will also realize that the reorganization is not the cure for all of the hospital's problems. For these hospitals, the reorganization will be a success.

§14.12 Summary

Hospital reorganization is a long, detailed process demanding cooperation among and effort by the hospital board, administrative personnel, and outside advisors. The process can take at least a year and will require a thorough consideration of the hospital's current position and its long-range goals. Even after the reorganization is completed, the hospital must work to take advantage of and preserve its structure. Still, for the hospital committed to making the reorganization work, the rewards can be many. Most important, the properly reorganized hospital will find itself better able to compete for scarce revenues and resources in the current healthcare environment. This competition for revenues and resources may involve joint ventures.

C. Joint Ventures

§14.13 Introduction to Joint Venturing

A joint venture is a combination of some of the assets or abilities of two or more parties to accomplish a common goal.[1] The joint venturers agree on the contributions of each party and on the sharing of profits. Unlike a merger, a joint venture involves

---

§14.13 [1]For general discussions of joint ventures, see I. Snook and E. Kaye, A Guide to Health Care Joint Ventures (1987); L. Burns and D. Mancino, Joint Ventures Between Hospitals & Physicians (1987); and Elwood, Shields, and Bergman, Merging Health Care Institutions (1987).

participants who remain separate but whose resources are combined to benefit each venturer.[2]

More and more hospitals are entering into joint ventures, often involving their physicians, though other affiliations are possible.[3] For example, a joint venture could involve two hospitals or a hospital and outside investors. While this section generally focuses on hospital joint ventures, HMOs and extended care facilities face similar issues in their joint venturing.

§14.14 Reasons to Joint Venture

The best reason for joint venturing is to accomplish something together that the parties cannot accomplish as successfully alone. No joint venture should be undertaken unless it presents a good business opportunity and unless it is more advantageous for the parties to carry out the project together than to go it alone. The hospital must realistically assess any venture to assure that the venture furthers the hospital's goals.

A hospital's primary goal in joint venturing should be to further its provision of healthcare; for example, a hospital may want to provide a needed medical service for its community. Furthering the healthcare purpose often means increasing hospital revenues. Decreases in patient revenues and aggressive competition have forced hospitals to search for new sources of income. This goal may be accomplished directly (if the joint venture creates revenues) or indirectly (by strengthening relationships with staff physicians, who ultimately refer more patients to the hospital). Revenue-generating joint ventures may involve healthcare related services, such as providing expensive

---

[2] A "joint venture" refers not to a legal entity but to a relationship designed to accomplish limited goals, receive contributions from each venturer, give each venturer a joint venture interest in the venture, provide a sharing of profits and losses, and provide sharing of control. Roble and Mason, The Legal Aspects of Health Care Joint Ventures, 24 Duq. L. Rev. 455, 456 (1985).

[3] This section focuses on hospitals since hospitals have been active in joint venturing. Extended care facilities or health maintenance organizations could also consider similar joint ventures.

medical equipment, or may move outside the healthcare field, for instance to develop real estate.

"Market-oriented" reasons for joint venturing include increasing market share, increasing patient utilization, improving the hospital's competitive position, and diversifying its services. Financial reasons for joint venturing include raising capital from staff physicians or others to finance new activities. Conversely, physicians may view the hospital as a source of capital and hence a joint venture partner. Also, joint ventures may reduce the costs of services, particularly where one partner has special expertise or excess capacity that can benefit the joint venture. Similarly, joint ventures can produce economies of scale. For example, two hospitals can share essential support services such as billing to reduce each party's costs. Each participant can find its own rewards in joint venturing.[1]

§14.15 Legal Issues in Joint Venturing

Many legal issues affect joint venturing in the healthcare field and should be considered in forming a joint venture. These issues involve tax, antitrust, securities, employment, and other concerns.

§14.15.1 Tax Concerns

Healthcare joint ventures raise various tax concerns, particularly for tax-exempt hospitals.[1] These issues include protecting an exempt hospital's tax-exempt status, minimizing any UBTI, avoiding the detriment of the tax-exempt entity leasing rules, and complying with other relevant tax requirements.

---

§14.14 [1]Ernst and Whinney, Health Care Joint Ventures: Survey Results (1985). See also I. Snook and E. Kaye, A Guide to Health Care Joint Ventures 29-48 (1987); L. Burns and D. Mancino, Joint Ventures Between Hospitals & Physicians 7-20 (1987).

§14.15 [1]See L. Burns and D. Mancino, Joint Ventures Between Hospitals & Physicians 102-128 (1987).

Tax-Exempt Status. Any joint venture involving a tax-exempt hospital must be carefully structured to minimize the risk to the hospital's tax-exempt status. The greatest tax-exemption risk is an IRS challenge stating that the hospital's earnings are inuring to private parties;[2] if the IRS finds *any* private inurement, the hospital will lose its tax-exempt status. Private inurement may exist in any joint venture involving a tax-exempt entity, because a joint venture is a cooperative effort with both parties anticipating profits. The problem is that the hospital's "profit" is often not monetary, because the reason for many joint ventures is to attract medical personnel and patients. Thus, a joint venture may appear economically favorable to an outside party when its real advantage to the hospital is securing a needed physician. However, the IRS may challenge arrangements that appear to favor the noncharitable parties.

Joint ventures should be carefully structured to withstand a private benefit or inurement challenge. The hospital must fairly benefit from the venture and the other party must not profit excessively at the hospital's expense. The joint venture should be negotiated in an arm's-length manner with a fair return for each party. The hospital should consider documenting the financial feasibility and the commercial reasonableness of its ventures. Also, the hospital could request a private letter ruling from the Internal Revenue Service holding that the joint venture will not affect the hospital's tax-exempt status. Unfortunately, a private letter ruling can take several months, and often the IRS will not give a desired ruling because the questions asked are factual, not legal. Finally, as discussed above, a reorganized hospital could permit its taxable affiliate to enter into its joint ventures.

Unrelated Business Taxable Income. Another tax concern in joint venturing is generating UBTI for a tax-exempt hospital. A hospital's tax-exempt status can be jeopardized if it receives too

---

[2]See Myre, Significant Tax Issues in Hospital Related Joint Ventures, 75 Ky. L.J. 559, 560-564 (1986-1987) for a discussion of private benefit and inurement.

much unrelated business taxable income. Patient-related income from a joint venture is generally not UBTI. For example, the IRS found no UBTI in joint ventures formed to operate a magnetic resonance imaging machine,[3] a medical office building,[4] a nursing home,[5] and an ambulatory surgery center.[6] Also, passive income from joint ventures such as interest or rents from real property (and incidental personal property) is not UBTI[7] unless it involves debt-financed property or controlled subsidiary income.

Tax-Exempt Entity Leasing Rules. The tax-exempt entity leasing rules were designed to limit perceived abuses involving property leased to a tax-exempt entity or owned by a partnership with a tax-exempt partner. The fear was that special tax advantages such as accelerated depreciation and investment tax credits would be disproportionately allocated to taxable entities because the tax-exempt entities did not need those tax advantages. The result was the tax-exempt entity leasing rules, which reduce those tax advantages for any "tax-exempt use" property.[8] Because these tax-exempt entity leasing provisions can affect the tax attributes for all participants of a joint venture involving a tax-exempt entity, these rules should be considered in structuring a hospital joint venture. Still, after the Tax Reform Act of 1986, the tax-exempt entity leasing rules have less impact on hospital

---

[3]Priv. Ltr. Rul. 88-33-038 (May 20, 1988).

[4]Priv. Ltr. Rul. 85-28-080 (Apr. 19, 1985).

[5]Priv. Ltr. Rul. 87-17-057 (Jan. 28, 1987).

[6]Priv. Ltr. Rul. 87-15-039 (Jan. 13, 1987).

[7]See I.R.C. §512(b)(5).

[8]I.R.C. §168(g). See Myre, supra, n.2, at 570-572, and B. Hopkins, The Law of Tax-Exempt Organizations 770 (5th ed. 1987 & Supp. 1989). "Tax exempt use property" includes any tangible property that is leased to a tax-exempt entity. It also includes a share of property owned by a partnership with a tax-exempt partner if any partnership allocation to the tax-exempt entity is not a "qualified allocation." A "qualified allocation" is an allocation to the tax-exempt entity that has substantial economic effect, is consistent with the tax-exempt entity's other distributive share of partnership items, and remains the same throughout the term of the partnership.

joint venturing, since this Act limited many of the earlier tax advantages.[9]

Employee Benefits.   Joint ventures may effect the participants' employee benefit plans. The risk is that the plans will be combined so that in the aggregate they must meet the various requirements for qualified plans such as the nondiscrimination tests. The result could be loss of tax qualification for some of the joint venturers' benefit plans.[10]

Tax Shelters and Registration.   Joint ventures today are seldom "tax shelters,"[11] as they have been in the past. Still, the tax shelters as defined by the Internal Revenue Code must be negotiated.[12] Failure to register a tax shelter will result in various penalties. Thus, it is important to review any joint venture to see if tax shelter registration is required.

---

[9]For example, the tax-exempt entity rules require depreciation over 40 years using the straight-line method. This period is longer than the 31 years over which commercial real estate is now depreciated. Still, this difference is not as great as when depreciation was allowed over 19 (or 15) years prior to the Tax Reform Act of 1986. Thus, the impact of the tax-exempt entity rules on hospital joint ventures, while still present, is lessened.

[10]See I.R.C. §§414(b), (c), and (m). See also Roble and Mason, The Legal Aspects of Health Care Joint Ventures, 24 Duq. L. Rev. 455, 456 (1985); Gen. Couns. Mem. 39,616 (Mar. 12, 1987) (concerning the affiliations of non-stock entities under I.R.C. §414(c)).

[11]Prior to the Tax Reform Act of 1986, investors often used partnerships as tax shelters. For example, investors could use investment tax credits and accelerated depreciation to generate large tax losses in the early years of a partnership. These losses could then offset their other income, creating a tax shelter. Such tax shelters were useful to physicians and thus were attractive as joint venture forms created by hospitals for their medical staffs. The Tax Reform Act of 1986 eliminated many of the tax shelter benefits of partnerships. First, investment tax credits are no longer generally available. In addition, depreciation periods have been increased from useful life periods of 19 years to 31 years for commercial properties. Finally, limited partners generally can use passive losses only against passive income, and so passive losses cannot shelter other income. Thus, today's joint venture needs to be an economically sound business venture independent of its tax effects.

[12]See I.R.C. §6111.

§14.15.2 Antitrust Issues

All joint ventures involve two or more parties combining their resources to offer a new service or product. These two parties in different circumstances could be competitors; therefore, a joint venture between them arguably decreases competition and restrains trade. Federal and state antitrust laws prohibit contracts, combinations, and conspiracies in restraint of trade and also prohibit monopolization, attempts to monopolize, and conspiracies to monopolize.[13] Thus, joint ventures are subject to antitrust scrutiny.[14]

The antitrust laws do recognize some joint ventures as legitimate business enterprises despite the fact that they may limit competition. If former competitors pool their resources and share the risk of profit and loss, the joint venture may be viewed as a single entity competing in the marketplace rather than an unlawful combination of competitors.[15] Also, it may be permissible under certain circumstances to agree on the price for services as part of a joint venture that is treated as a new entity offering a different product or service from that which any of the individual venturers could have offered themselves.[16]

§14.15.3 Securities Law Concerns

Because a joint venture may involve an investment opportunity, federal and state securities laws may apply.[17] All offerings of securities are subject to the requirements of the federal Securities Act of 1933 (the Securities Act) and the securities laws ("Blue

---

[13]See, e.g., Sherman Act, 15 U.S.C. §§1-7 (1982); Robinson-Patman Act, 15 U.S.C. §§13-13b, 21a (1982).

[14]See Roble and Mason, The Legal Aspects of Health Care Joint Ventures, 24 Duq. L. Rev. 473-480 (1985); L. Burns and D. Mancino, Joint Ventures Between Hospitals & Physicians 143-157 (1987).

[15]Arizona v. Maricopa County Medical Socy., 457 U.S. 332 (1982).

[16]Broadcast Music, Inc. v. Columbia Broadcasting Systems, 441 U.S. 1 (1979).

[17]See L. Burns, supra n.14, at 71-79.

Sky" laws) of the states in which the offerings are made. Together, the federal and state securities laws require that any offering or sale of securities be registered with the applicable securities commission or be exempt from such registration, be accompanied by disclosure of all relevant material information, and be conducted in a nonfraudulent and nonmanipulative manner. Failure to comply with these laws could subject the issuer of the securities—often the hospital in hospital joint ventures—and its principals and officers to significant civil and criminal liabilities.

Federal Regulation of Securities Offerings. The Securities Act requires that any public offering of securities be registered with the Securities and Exchange Commission, unless the offering is exempt.[18] Federal registration is an expensive and time-consuming process. Fortunately, many offerings can qualify for exemptions from regulation or registration. First, federal regulation of offerings applies only to "securities."[19] A security may be involved if any investor expects his or her return to be the result of the efforts of others, regardless of the investment form. It may be possible to avoid classification of a joint venture as a security by having no passive joint venture participants. In addition, federal regulation does not apply to wholly intrastate offerings.[20]

Other joint ventures, while subject to federal regulation, may avoid federal registration. The most commonly used exemptions are those under Rules 504, 505, and 506 of Regulation D of the Securities Act. Rule 504 exempts certain offerings of less than $500,000. Offerings of less than $5,000,000 made to fewer than 35 nonaccredited investors can be exempt under Rule 505. Rule 506 permits offerings of an unlimited dollar amount made to fewer than 35 nonaccredited investors so long as certain disclosures are made. The 35 investors under Rules 505 and 506 do not include institutional investors or accredited investors.[21] To minimize the costs of securities law compliance,

---

[18]See 15 U.S.C. §§77-78 (1982).

[19]Securities Act §2(1), 15 U.S.C. §77(b)(1) (1982).

[20]15 U.S.C. §77(c)(a)(11) (1982).

[21]See Regulation D at 17 C.F.R. §§230.501 to 230.506 (1988).

a joint venture may be structured to fit within the preceding exemptions by limiting the number of investors or amount of capital raised. It is important to remember that even if a security is exempt from federal registration, the federal rules prohibit fraud, improper disclosures, and the manipulation of the securities market.[22] Therefore, all material information concerning the joint venture should be disclosed to the investors.

State Regulation of Securities Offerings. The states may also regulate the offering of securities, regardless of whether the securities are federally registered or regulated. Therefore, the laws of any state involved with a joint venture should be reviewed to determine their requirements.[23]

§14.15.4 The Hospital's Own Contracts or Governance

A hospital's own contracts or governance structure may limit its ability to joint venture. For example, its contracts, for instance its bonds, may limit its joint venturing. Prior to entering a joint venture, the hospital's governing instruments, financing documents, major agreements, and deeds should be carefully examined for limitations affecting any joint ventures. Such agreements may influence the structure of the joint venture.

§14.15.5 Public Hospitals

Public hospitals may be subject to statutes and constitutional provisions that govern their operation, structure, and activities. These provisions can limit a hospital's ability to joint venture. For example, the allowable uses of public funds and financing may affect joint ventures involving a public hospital.[24]

---

[22]See Rule 10b-5 derived from 15 U.S.C. §77(k) (1982).
[23]See, e.g., N.C. Gen. Stat. ch. 78A.
[24]See, e.g., N.C. Gen. Stat. §159-40 (1987); N.C. Const. art. V, §4.

§14.15.6 Corporate Practice of Medicine

State law may prohibit the corporate practice of medicine and limit the ability of corporations to practice medicine by employing physicians. Joint ventures should be structured to avoid application of these rules.[25] For example, the physicians providing medical services may need to be independent contractors to the joint venture so that the joint venture does not control their medical practices and thus is not engaged in the practice of medicine.

§14.15.7 Employment Issues

Joint ventures can raise employment issues. For example, the Fair Labor Standards Act regulates wages paid to and hours worked by employees. In some instances, the hours of an employee working for two or more employers will be combined to determine if this liability exists. Such aggregation can occur if the two employers are related in their control in such a way that they do not independently employ the employee.[26] This may arise in a healthcare joint venture in which hospital employees work full-time for the hospital and then additional time for the joint venture. In such a case the joint venture or the hospital may need to pay overtime to the employee. This overtime will be an additional expense for the joint venture or hospital.

§14.15.8 Ethical Considerations for Physicians

Joint ventures involving physicians may raise ethical concerns for the physician, since the physician joint venturer may profit

---

[25]See Roble and Mason, supra n.14, at 460-463; L. Burns, supra n.14, at 85-88.

[26]See U.S.C. §§201-219 (1982); 29 C.F.R. §791.2. See also Roble and Mason, supra n.14, at 483-487.

by referring a patient to the joint venture. To minimize abuses, various provisions limit such ownership or require physicians referring patients to their own facilities to give full disclosure to their patients.[27] New legislation could further restrict physician involvement in joint ventures, particularly those involving clinical laboratories.[28]

§14.15.9 Licensure and Accreditation

Some joint ventures need licenses to perform their anticipated services. Also, some joint ventures may desire accreditation, because such accreditation may increase patient and physician willingness to use the joint venture's services. In addition, some third-party payors may require accreditation and licensure before they will reimburse the joint venture for its services. Thus, applicable licensure and accreditation provisions should be reviewed in structuring a joint venture.[29]

§14.15.10 Certificate of Need

A healthcare joint venture may be subject to certificate-of-need laws in some states.[30] In that case, the joint venture must either obtain a certificate of need through what is often an expensive, competitive process or avoid the necessity of obtaining one. For example, depending on state law, a hospital affiliate participating in a joint venture might avoid certificate of need requirements that would apply if the hospital itself were the participant.

---

[27]See L. Burns, supra n.14, at 90-92.

[28]See, e.g., H.R. 939, 101st Cong., 1st Sess. (1989) and 42 U.S.C. §1395 nn.

[29]See L. Burns, supra n.14, at 82-89.

[30]For an analysis of the application of CON laws to joint ventures, see Roble and Mason, supra n.14, at 458-460.

§14.15.11 Medicare and Medicaid Issues

All healthcare joint ventures should be structured to maximize Medicare and Medicaid reimbursement, if possible. In addition, the joint venture must avoid certain Medicare and Medicaid prohibitions.

Using various methods, Medicare and Medicaid reimburse providers for services; these methods include cost reimbursement and prospective payments. Other services are not reimbursable. The specific reimbursement rules are detailed and subject to change, and an in-depth discussion of these rules is beyond the scope of this chapter. In general, the structure of any joint venture should be selected in light of the reimbursement methods allowed for its services.

Federal law prohibits any payments for referrals of patients whose care will be paid for by the Medicare or Medicaid programs.[31] Because an underlying purpose of many joint ventures is to increase patient referrals by strengthening ties with medical staff physicians, these antifraud and abuse (anti-kickback) provisions must be considered in structuring a joint venture.[32] In addition to obviously illegal activities such as kickbacks, the statute prohibits other financial arrangements between hospitals and physicians that are designed to increase referrals of reimbursement patients. At least one court has found it unlawful to pay a physician to induce him or her to use the payor's services, even if the payments were also intended to compensate the physician for professional services.[33] To minimize the risk of violating the antifraud and abuse provisions, joint ventures should not compensate anyone based on patient referrals. Regulations providing some safe harbors from these antifraud and abuse provisions may eventually be issued.[34] Also,

---

[31]See 42 U.S.C. §§1395n, 1396h.

[32]See Roble and Mason, supra n.14, at 463-470; L. Burns, supra n.14, at 129-142.

[33]See, e.g., United States v. Greber, 760 F.2d 68 (3d. Cir.), cert. denied, 474 U.S. 988 (1985); L. Burns, supra n.14, at 129-142.

[34]See, e.g., 54 Fed. Reg. 3088 (Jan. 23, 1989).

referrals involving clinical laboratories are subject to special prohibitions.[35]

§14.16 Basic Forms for Joint Ventures

All joint ventures involve certain basic forms or combinations of these forms: contracts, co-ownerships, partnerships, or corporations. Each of these forms has special legal characteristics that must be considered in structuring a joint venture.

§14.16.1 Contracts

The simplest form of joint venture is a contract. For example, the hospital could contract to perform management, billing, or paging services for physicians, utilizing its excess capacity. Also, the hospital could build a medical facility on the hospital campus and lease the medical facility by contract to physicians. Such an arrangement will strengthen ties with the physicians by physically locating them near the hospital. Thus, contractual joint ventures can provide revenues both directly and indirectly for the hospital.

The primary advantage of a contractual joint venture is its simplicity. A contract is a familiar type of arrangement. It can be prepared with relative ease and can be easily terminated when it expires (or earlier, according to its terms). Thus, a contractual joint venture is an easy first joint venture for a hospital.

The disadvantage of a contract is that it is more of an arm's-length agreement between separate parties than a true joint venture. While the parties have some interest in the results of each other's operations, they do not have a joint stake in the venture's profits. Thus, the parties do not realize all of the advantages of joint venturing.

The economic consequences of a contract are also simple.

---

[35]See 42 U.S.C. §1395 nn.

The hospital earns revenues from the contract. To the extent these revenues exceed the costs of providing the service, the hospital will realize a profit on the venture. If it is UBTI, the net income from a contractual joint venture will be subject to tax for a tax-exempt hospital.

§14.16.2 Co-ownerships

A second form of joint venture involves the co-ownership of property. For example, the hospital and the physicians could own real property as tenants-in-common, leasing this property to third parties. The shares of tenants-in-common can vary. For example, the hospital could be a 75 percent owner while the physicians own 25 percent of the property, with each party sharing profits in proportion to ownership interest. Like a contractual arrangement, co-ownership is simple and under-standable.

Co-ownerships have disadvantages as joint venture forms. For example, state law may have certain established legal principles governing the co-tenancy of property, particularly real property, that could ultimately adversely affect the joint venture relations of the parties. For example, under the law of some states one co-tenant can force the sale of the property and creditors of either co-tenant can reach the property.[1] In addition, co-tenancies are somewhat inflexible, not permitting practical business solutions to common problems such as the dissolution of the arrangement. The tax effects of co-tenancy arrangements by tax-exempt entities also are not clear. Thus, it is often preferable to establish a new entity, a partnership or corporation, to own the joint venture property. In certain situations co-tenancies may be useful, particularly where the joint venturers are related. For example, after a hospital reorganization, the separate tax-exempt corporations may find co-tenant ownership of property to be useful.

---

§14.16 [1]See, e.g., J. Webster, P. Hetrick, and J. McLaughlin, Webster's Real Estate in North Carolina §§114, 121, at 130, 136-138 (3d ed. 1988).

§14.16.3 Partnerships

A partnership between the hospital and others, such as physicians, is a true joint venture. Each party contributes capital to the partnership and shares in its profits. The parties have a joint stake in the success of the joint venture.

A partnership is a simple, flexible entity. The parties execute a written partnership agreement that defines their rights and responsibilities. The partners have wide latitude in structuring their agreement to fit their particular needs. The partnership agreement will define the capital contributions of each partner as well as their shares of profits. The agreement can define the responsibilities of the parties, for instance by designating a managing general partner, and can provide for the termination of the partnership. To the extent that a term is not specified in the agreement, state partnership law often provides guidance for the parties.

The major disadvantage of partnerships is that they lack limited liability: at least one partner must be liable personally for all debts of the partnership. Often the other participants will want the hospital to assume the role of sole general partner with full liability, a role that presents special risks for tax-exempt hospitals, as discussed below.

There are several issues unique to partnerships that the parties need to consider in structuring their partnership joint ventures.

General v. Limited Partnerships. There are two types of partnerships, general and limited. Every participant in a general partnership is liable for all debts of the partnership. Thus, a creditor of a general partnership can reach the personal assets of every partner. Although adequate insurance can provide protection, many individuals do not want to become general partners, particularly if they are not involved in the day-to-day operations of the entity. The alternative is to be a limited partner.

Limited partners have limited liability. They are generally liable for partnership debts only to the extent of the capital they invest in the partnership. Thus, they are protected from losses from the partnership other than (in most cases) the loss of their investment. This status is often desirable for investors in a partnership who will not be involved with the daily operations of the partnership. If a limited partner exercises too much control over or active involvement in the limited partnership, he or she will be considered a general partner despite technical legal status as a limited partner. Thus, a critical point in deciding between using a limited and a general partnership is the degree of actual involvement of the parties in the partnership. This involvement will also affect the necessary compliance with the securities laws, as discussed above.

All limited partnerships must have at least one general partner. This general partner will be fully subject to liability for the joint venture, so choosing an entity to bear this risk is often of critical concern.

Tax Issues of Partnerships.   For tax purposes, a partnership is considered a conduit.[2] It must file a tax return, but it is not subject to federal income taxation. Instead, all partners report on their personal tax returns their distributive share of the income, gains, losses, deductions, or credits of the partnership for the taxable year, whether or not actual distributions are made. Such income will be taxable to the tax-exempt hospital if the income is unrelated to the hospital's tax-exempt purpose. Related income is tax-exempt for a tax-exempt hospital.[3]

A partnership can be easily formed and later dissolved, without taxation in many cases. Thus, partnerships provide tax flexibility for the partners. Partnerships have a major tax disadvantage: they can be accidentally terminated. For tax purposes, a 50 percent change of ownership will terminate a partnership.[4] Inadvertent termination can create tax problems such as depreciation recapture, which means past depreciation deductions must be included in income.

Many partnerships, particularly those formed as tax shelters,

---

[2]See I.R.C. §§701 to 761 for the taxation of partnerships.
[3]See I.R.C. §512(c).
[4]See I.R.C. §708.

have disproportionate sharing of partnership profits and losses. For example, 99 percent of the losses may be allocated to the limited partners. The Internal Revenue Code provides that such allocations of income or loss as set forth in a partnership agreement will be respected provided they have "substantial economic effect." The essential test for substantial economic effect is whether the allocation may actually affect the dollar amount of the partners' shares of the total partnership income or loss independent of tax consequences.[5] One special problem for tax-exempt partners is that disproportionate allocations of profit and loss could lead to a challenge by the IRS arguing that the hospital is providing prohibited private inurement to the nonexempt partners.[6] Thus, a tax-exempt hospital entering into a partnership should consider having partnership profits allocated in accordance with capital interests.

Another special problem with partnerships is that the IRS classifies some state law partnerships as corporations for tax purposes. Classification as a corporation will significantly change the tax effects for the participants in the venture, because corporations are separate taxable entities while partnerships are conduits passing their tax attributes to their partners. The IRS has established tests for determining whether an entity will be taxed as a corporation or a partnership. This determination depends on whether the entity has more corporate or partnership characteristics. Corporate characteristics include continuity of life, centralized management, free transferability of interests, and limited liability.[7]

The IRS holds that a partnership has limited liability if the sole general partner has no substantial assets that creditors could reach or if it is merely a "dummy" acting as the agent of the limited partners. The necessity of having a general partner with

---

[5]See I.R.C. §704(b); Treas. Reg. §1.704-1 (as amended in 1988); Temp. Treas. Reg. §1.704-1T (1988); Temp. Treas. Reg. §7.704-1 (1976).

[6]See Rev. Rul. 69-633, 1969-2 C.B. 121, which holds that an exempt organization must receive income in proportion to its capital interest. But see Priv. Ltr. Rul. 84-32-014 (Apr. 9, 1984); Priv. Ltr. Rul. 83-01-003 (date not given).

[7]See Treas. Reg. §301.7701-2.

assets that is not a dummy entity can be a problem in a hospital joint venture in which the hospital's taxable subsidiary is the sole general partner of a limited partnership. The taxable subsidiary may need to be substantially capitalized[8] to avoid this problem.

The joint venture participants often want the hospital to serve as sole general partner in a limited partnership joint venture so that the hospital alone is fully liable for partnership debts. The IRS has imposed limitations on tax-exempt hospitals serving as general partners, particularly as sole general partners, in limited partnerships. At first the IRS said serving as sole general partner meant loss of tax-exempt status, because so serving created prohibited private inurement. The IRS has relaxed its position and will permit a tax-exempt hospital to serve as sole general partner if the partnership furthers the hospital's exempt purpose.[9] Still, the hospital needs to insulate itself from liability to the extent possible. The IRS recommends having an independent committee monitor the partnership. Also, the hospital should consider getting insurance to protect itself from the activities of the partnership. Of course, limiting the hospital's liability may increase the corporate characteristic of limited liability so much that the partnership will have too many corporate characteristics and be taxed as a corporation, as discussed above. Again, to protect its tax-exempt status, the hospital may prefer that its taxable subsidiary be the sole general partner.

---

[8] See Gen. Couns. Mem. 39,546 (Aug. 15, 1986).

[9] General Counsel Memorandum 39,005 holds that serving as a sole general partner does not per se create private inurement. Still, the IRS will closely review the particular situation to see that it furthers the exempt purpose of the tax-exempt entity. See Gen. Couns. Mem. 39,444 (Nov. 13, 1985); Gen. Couns. Mem. 39,546 (Aug. 15, 1986); Gen. Couns. Mem. 39,732 (May 19, 1988). See generally Bromberg, Can Joint Venture Threaten the Hospital's Tax-Exempt Status?, 1986 Healthcare Fin. Mgmt. 76 (Dec. 1986). Hopkins and Beckwith, The Federal Tax Law of Hospitals: Basic Principles and Current Developments, 24 Duq. L. Rev. 691, 718-721, 732-734 (1985). B. Hopkins, The Law of Tax-Exempt Organizations 829-843 (5th ed. 1987 & Supp. 1989).

§14.16.4 Corporations

The final joint venture form is a corporation. A corporation can be either for-profit or nonprofit. If the corporation's purpose is to make profits for parties who are not tax-exempt, the corporation will need to be a for-profit entity. Each participant in a corporate joint venture is a shareholder.

A joint venture corporation has the same legal requirements for its corporate existence as does a hospital corporation, as discussed above. Articles of incorporation and bylaws must be drawn up for a joint venture corporation. Its board of directors represents the interests of the shareholders. The number of directors and their relative voting power may, depending on the goals of the parties, reflect the control of the participating shareholders. The different parties can have different classes of stock or can use cumulative voting to give the desired proportionate control. For example, a hospital that has an 80 percent interest in the joint venture can own all of the Class A stock that is entitled to elect four directors of a five-member board; the other shareholder can own the Class B stock entitled to elect one director. The directors of the corporation then appoint or elect officers to operate the corporation.

The IRS in several private letter rulings has approved joint venture corporations formed by hospitals and others.[10] Still, the presence of shareholders other than the hospital increases the risk of private inurement flowing from the hospital to the other shareholders and, consequently, threatens the hospital's tax-exempt status. Joint venture corporations should comply with IRS guidelines for taxable subsidiaries of tax-exempt entities, discussed above, because the joint venture corporation is a taxable subsidiary even though the hospital is not the sole shareholder. With careful planning and attention, corporate joint ventures are possibilities for many hospitals.

The primary advantage of the corporate form is its limited

---

[10]Priv. Ltr. Rul. 86-35-045 (June 3, 1986). See generally Purcell, Using For-Profit Subsidiaries to Preserve Exempt Status, 67 J. Taxn. 180, 183 (1987).

liability. To preserve this advantage, the parties need to observe corporate formalities such as having meetings and keeping records of them; creditors and other third parties will then recognize the corporate form and should not be able to "pierce the corporate veil." Similarly, the corporation should be adequately capitalized.

Joint venture corporations, other than tax-exempt corporations, are taxable entities. While a corporation can be formed in a tax-free manner,[11] it is difficult to remove assets from a corporation without paying taxes.[12] If dividends are paid to the shareholders, they also will pay tax on these dividends, unless the shareholder is tax-exempt.[13] Generally, corporation profits are subject to a double tax. Certain deductible items flowing to the tax-exempt entity may be taxable if the rules of §512(b)(13), discussed above, apply.

§14.16.5 Summary

All joint ventures involve one or more of the preceding basic joint venture forms: contracts, co-ownerships, partnerships, or corporations. Even the most complex joint venture arrangement is ultimately made of those simple pieces.

§14.17 Common Examples of Joint Ventures

The possible types of joint ventures are varied and depend on the particular circumstances of the hospital and the other joint venturers. A few common joint venture types are discussed below.

---

[11]See I.R.C. §351.
[12]See I.R.C. §337.
[13]See I.R.C. §512(b).

§14.17.1 The Limited Partnership for Medical Activity

One common joint venture is the formation of a limited partnership with physicians to construct and operate a medical office building near the hospital. The hospital may serve as general partner, with staff physicians as limited partners. Each partner could share in the joint venture profits in accordance with its percentage of interest in the capital of the partnership. The hospital could own the real property and lease it to the partnership, thus producing extra revenues for the hospital. The partnership would then build the medical office building on the property and lease it to staff physicians. The partnership would receive rents from tenants of the facility. The taxable partners may be able to limit some taxes from the rents by taking depreciation and other operating expense deductions. Perhaps most important, the hospital will have medical staff physicians located near the hospital who presumably will refer their patients to the hospital. Many of those physicians will have an investment interest in the medical office building and will prefer to remain in the building.

A similar partnership arrangement could provide expensive medical equipment such as magnetic resonance imaging (MRI) equipment. For example, the hospital and physician investors working as partners could purchase an MRI. They could contract with physicians to operate the MRI. In addition to providing a new service to the community and generating revenues, this joint venture will provide the hospital with referring physicians who have a special interest in the joint venture's medical service.

§14.17.2 The Corporation for Medical Services

Another joint venture possibility is for the hospital and physicians to form a corporation to offer a new medical service. As an example, the hospital could provide 60 percent of the needed capital for an emergency services clinic and purchase all of the Class A stock that is entitled to elect three directors. Physician investors could purchase Class B stock that can elect two directors. Through its control of the three directors, the hospital will be able to legally control the corporation, though, depending on the governing instruments and state laws, the consent of one of the Class B directors may be needed for certain major changes. The corporation would contract with physicians as independent contractors to provide the medical services for the facility.

§14.17.3 The Physician Hospital Organization

Another possible joint venture is to form a Physician Hospital Organization (PHO), also known as a MeSH system (Medical Staff Hospital system). A PHO is a separate entity formed by a hospital and its staff physicians to represent their interests in a united way in negotiating contracts with third parties or entering into desirable investments. The PHO can be formed as a corporation, with the hospital and individual physicians owning the shares of stock in agreed proportions. As an alternative, the physicians can form a separate entity that owns the physician interest in the PHO, thus giving the physicians a more united interest in the PHO.

§14.17.4 The Shared Service Organization

Another special form of joint venture is a shared service organization, which is a cooperative venture between two hospitals. If properly structured, a cooperative venture can be tax-exempt under I.R.C. §501(e) and also be a nonprivate foundation. Such an entity must pay its net earnings to its participant hospitals. These ventures can provide services such as data processing, purchasing, billing, food services, laboratory services, communications services, and other specified activities.[1]

---

§14.17   [1]See Goodrich, Recent Developments in the Hospital Shared-Service Organization Controversy, 60 Neb. L. Rev. 35 (1981); Danely, Scutt, and Stonehill, Shared Service Alternatives Offer Flexible Tax Benefits, 1985 Healthcare Fin. Mgmt. 66 (May 1985).

The Supreme Court has held, however, that such hospital cooperatives cannot provide laundry services since §501(e) does not specifically list laundry services.[2]

§14.18 Summary

Many hospitals have formed successful joint ventures. The most successful joint ventures are ones in which the hospital and the other participants recognize a need for a facility or service in their community and form the joint venture to fulfill this need. This can result in profits for the parties as well as closer relations between them. Thus, hospitals competing in the current health-care environment may find joint ventures one key to survival.

D. Extended Care Facilities

§14.19 Extended Care Facilities Compared to Hospitals

Though the reorganization and joint venture portions of this chapter focus on hospitals, much of the information pertains to Extended Care Facilities (ECFs) also. Most ECFs are organized as corporations under the same laws as hospitals, and ECFs, like hospitals, engage in joint ventures and can in some cases undergo corporate reorganizations. In particular, hospitals have recently begun to affiliate with nursing homes to assure the availability of extended care beds for hospital patients who need continuing nursing care but no longer need acute medical care. Continuing care (life care) communities also enter into various affiliations to assure a range of services for their residents.

Significant differences exist between an average ECF and an average hospital, however, and these differences will ulti-

---

[2]H.C.S.C. Laundry v. United States, 450 U.S. 1 (1981) (per curiam).

mately have special legal ramifications. First, ECFs are much more likely to be for-profit entities than are hospitals. Second, ECFs are, on average, much smaller than hospitals. Because they are smaller, ECFs are more likely to be family-run businesses, which could qualify them for S corporation tax status,[1] freeing the corporation from corporate income tax. The small size of nursing homes has also made the economies of scale available through chain organizations more readily apparent. Therefore, organization of nursing homes into chains, with centralized management functions, is common for ECFs, though not for hospitals. Small nursing homes are unlikely to obtain advantages from the kinds of corporate reorganizations discussed in this chapter.

Specific federal and state laws, generally growing out of concern about financial or resident abuse in ECFs, may also subject ECFs to requirements that do not pertain to hospitals. First, a few states make a corporation that owns an ECF (but does not operate it) jointly liable for torts committed by the corporation that operates the facility if the two are affiliated and the owning corporation has significant control over the day-to-day operations of the facility. These provisions effectively provide for piercing of the corporate veil by statute.[2] Second, federal law imposes specific requirements on nursing homes for disclosure of changes in ownership or management of such facilities or of their officers, directors, agents, or managing employees.[3] Finally, some states also impose ownership or financial disclosure requirements on ECFs that are not imposed on hospitals.[4]

E. Conclusion

Healthcare providers as corporations must comply with the formalities of being a corporation. As these formalities begin to

---

§14.19   [1]I.R.C. §1361 et seq.

[2]See Ill. Rev. Stat. ch. 111½, §§4151-119, 4153-601.

[3]42 U.S.C. §§1395i-3(d)(1)(B), 1396r-(d)(1)(B).

[4]See, e.g., Ill. Rev. Stat. ch. lll½, §§4153-207, 4153-208.

burden the healthcare corporation, it can reorganize its corporate structure to position itself to compete for scarce revenues and resources. In addition, the healthcare provider can joint venture to further its healthcare goals. Thus can innovative providers increase their chances of survival in today's competitive healthcare environment.

15 Legal Characteristics of the Extended Care Facility

Timothy S. Jost

§15.0 Introduction

Extended care facilities (ECFs) are institutions in which persons with chronic healthcare needs receive health services over an extended period of time. The nursing facility is the most visible of these and is the institution with which this chapter is primarily concerned.[1] Also touched on are the legal characteristics of continuing care or life care communities, including facilities for independent living and for nursing care. This chapter does not address long-term psychiatric institutions.

About 1.5 million men and women live in 19,100 nursing facilities in the United States.[2] These people are characteristically among the oldest and most debilitated and dependent of our nation's citizens. Eighty-eight percent are over 65 years of age. Of these, 45 percent are aged 85 years or older. Over 90 percent of nursing facility residents aged 65 and older require assistance with bathing, three-quarters need help with dressing, and more than half have difficulty with bowel or bladder control.[3] Over half are commonly diagnosed as having chronic mental conditions.[4] As of 1986 there were about 700 continuing care retirement communities in the United States, each having an average of 200 independent-living apartments and 2 or 3 levels of on-site healthcare (personal care, intermediate care, or skilled care).[5]

In many respects extended care facilities resemble hospitals. Physically, they usually look like hospitals, with pastel-colored walls, tile floors, and metal or laminated furniture designed to endure rather than to please. Rooms in nursing facilities have hospital beds and call buttons; the corridors have hand rails and usually lead to a nurses' station. Legally, ECFs also resemble hospitals in many important respects. They are licensed by the state; they are subject to vicarious liability for injuries caused by

---

§15.0 [1]"Nursing facility" is defined in federal law as an institution "primarily engaged in providing to residents . . . on a regular basis, health-related care and services to individuals who because of their mental or physical condition require care and services (above the level of room and board) which can be made available to them only through institutional facilities." 42 U.S.C. §1396r(a)(1)(C) (Supp. V 1987).

[2]Hing, Use of Nursing Homes by the Elderly: Preliminary Data from the 1985 National Nursing Home Survey, 135 Advancedata 2 (May 14, 1987).

[3]Id. at 5.

[4]N. Eustis, J. Greenberg, and S. Patten, Long Term Care for Older Persons: A Policy Perspective 40 (1984).

[5]Tell, Wallack, and Cohen, New Directions in Life Care: An Industry in Transition, 65 Milbank Q. 551, 551 (1987).

employees to residents and to corporate liability for injuries caused by the facility's negligence; they are faced with many of the same corporate, tax, or employment law problems that hospitals encounter. Like hospitals, they must deal with legal and ethical problems in caring for the terminally ill or for patients who refuse treatment.

On the other hand, ECFs also possess peculiar characteristics that distinguish them from hospitals. ECFs tend to be smaller than hospitals—two-thirds of nursing facilities have fewer than 100 beds.[6] ECFs are much more likely to be proprietary, much less likely to be nonprofit or government-owned.[7] Physicians are much less present in ECFs than in hospitals. Nurse's aides are pervasive and bear much greater responsibility for care delivery than nurse's aides do in hospitals.[8]

ECFs also face legal problems somewhat different from those encountered by hospitals. ECFs are much more closely regulated by the state governments than are hospitals. In particular, ECFs are subject to more specific staffing requirements and more rigorous laws protecting residents' rights than are hospitals. Moreover, because the Medicaid program plays a pervasive role in financing long-term care in ECFs, ECFs are much more heavily regulated by the federal government than are hospitals. This chapter focuses on these unique legal concerns of ECFs.

A. Regulation of Extended Care Facilities

§15.1 State Regulation of Extended Care Facilities

§15.1.1 Licensure

All states require nursing facilities to be licensed. In addition, most states license one or more categories of facilities that offer

---

[6]Strahan, Nursing Home Characteristics: Preliminary Data from the National Nursing Home Survey, 131 Advancedata 3 (Mar. 27, 1987).

[7]Id. at 3.

[8]B. Vladeck, Unloving Care 17-22 (1980).

personal care and oversight, which go under different names including board and care, domiciliary care, residential care, or sheltered care facilities.[1] State licensure laws range from the very simple, requiring licensure and providing for criminal penalties or injunctive relief against unlicensed facilities,[2] to the extraordinarily complex, some of which are longer than the federal nursing facility statute. Most state laws also enumerate the standards that licensed facilities must meet (e.g., staffing requirements), establish rights for nursing facility residents, and provide for a range of sanctions to deal with substandard facilities.

Most states delegate to a licensing agency (usually the state health department) authority to adopt rules specifying the conditions that extended care facilities must meet to be licensed.[3] State nursing facility statutes often specify the general subjects that such regulations must address. For example, the Illinois statute mandates that the Health Department prescribe minimum standards regulating:

1. the physical plant of the facility (considering resident health, safety, comfort, and protection from fire hazard);
2. the number and qualifications of personnel (including specifications as to the number of staff hours per resident required for professional nursing care);
3. sanitary conditions in the facility;
4. diet and nutrition;
5. essential equipment;
6. habilitation and rehabilitation programs;
7. control of temperature and humidity;
8. development of evacuation and safety plans; and
9. maintenance of minimum financial resources.[4]

---

§15.1 [1]See American Bar Association, Board and Care Report: An Analysis of State Laws and Programs Serving Elderly Persons and Disabled Adults (1983).

[2]See Miss. Code Ann. §§43-11-5, 43-11-25, 43-11-27 (1981); N.D. Cent. Code §§23-16-04, 23-16-11, 23-16-12 (1978).

[3]See, e.g., Tex. Rev. Civ. Stat. Ann. art. 4442c, §7 (Vernon Supp. 1989); Minn. Stat. Ann. §144A.04(3) (West Supp. 1989); Ill. Stat. Ann. ch. 111½, ¶4153-202 (Smith-Hurd 1988).

[4]Ill. Stat. Ann. ch. 111½, ¶4153-202 (Smith-Hurd 1988).

Not surprisingly, these lists often mirror the concerns of the federal Medicaid and Medicare regulations (discussed below), though state statutes often have their peculiar twists, reflecting, for example, particularly bad experiences with nursing facility fires[5] or hazardous weather.[6]

The licensing agency is delegated power to enforce these standards through license denial or revocation. Because of the high stakes involved, nursing facility delicensure actions are frequently challenged on a variety of constitutional or administrative law grounds. Nursing facility delicensure has generally been upheld as a valid exercise of the state's police powers.[7] The courts have also generally rejected challenges brought by nursing facilities that claim that licensure statutes are excessively vague or leave too much discretion to the licensing agency and thus violate due process or the nondelegation doctrine.[8] Moreover, specific standards adopted by licensure agencies are usually upheld when questioned.[9]

Warrantless inspections of nursing facilities have uniformly been upheld as constitutional because the nursing facility industry is heavily regulated and because unannounced inspections are key to the regulatory process.[10] Unless there is a statute to

---

[5]See Ohio Rev. Code Ann. §3721.071 (Page Supp. 1988).

[6]See Ill. Stat. Ann. ch. 111½, ¶4153-202.1 (Smith-Hurd 1988).

[7]State ex. rel Eagleton v. Patrick, 370 S.W.2d 254 (Mo. 1963); Hoffman v. Moore, 70 A.D.2d 220, 420 N.Y.S.2d 771 (Ct. App. 1979).

[8]See Lackner v. St. Joseph Convalescent Hosp., 106 Cal. App. 3d 542, 165 Cal. Rptr. 198 (1980); People v. Gurell, 98 Ill. 2d 194, 456 N.E.2d 18 (1983). But see High Ridge Mgmt. Corp. v. State, 354 So. 2d 377 (Fla. 1977).

[9]See People v. Casa Blanca Convalescent Homes, 159 Cal. App. 3d 509, 206 Cal. Rptr. 164 (1984) (facility must be clean and sanitary); Kupferman v. New York State Bd. of Social Welfare, 60 App. Div. 2d 674, 399 N.Y.S.2d 949, affd., 47 N.Y.2d 738, 417 N.Y.S.2d 254, 390 N.E.2d 1178 (1977) (bedrooms must have minimum of 80 square feet per resident); In re Milcrest Nursing Home, 59 Ohio App. 2d 116, 392 N.E.2d 1097 (1978) (sprinkler system required). Cf. Koeble v. Whalen, 63 App. Div. 2d 408, 406 N.Y.S.2d 621 (1978) (regulations requiring facilities or services to meet "approval" or "satisfaction" of Commissioner too subjective).

[10]People v. Firstenberg, 92 Cal. App. 3d 570, 155 Cal. Rptr. 80 (1979), cert. denied, 444 U.S. 1012 (1980); Uzzilla v. Commr. of Health, 47 A.D.2d

the contrary, licensing and investigative agencies have also been able to gain access to records concerning residents kept by facilities.[11]

Much of the litigation concerning state enforcement actions involves administrative law issues. When a facility is subject to the threat of a sanction, state law usually requires the regulatory agency to give the facility adequate notice of the deficiencies with which it is charged and an opportunity for a hearing.[12] Ordinarily, the facility must exhaust its administrative remedies before challenging the regulatory action, and it may not in most instances introduce new evidence after the hearing has concluded.[13] Judicial review of an agency's decision will normally be on a substantial evidence basis,[14] though courts will reverse arbitrary or capricious agency action.[15]

Lack of state enforcement efforts in the past neither excuses a facility from compliance nor estops an agency from insisting on compliance.[16] Many state statutes require that a nursing facility be given an opportunity to correct violations before it

---

492, 367 N.Y.S.2d 795, appeal dismissed, 37 N.Y.2d 777, 375 N.Y.S.2d 97, 337 N.E.2d 604 (1975).

[11]See S. Johnson, N. Terry, and M. Wolfe, Nursing Homes and the Law: State Regulation and Private Litigation §§2-6, 2-7 (1985).

[12]Aurelia Osborn Fox Memorial Hosp. Socy. v. Whalen, 55 App. Div. 2d 495, 391 N.Y.S.2d 20 (1977); Fair Rest Home v. Commonwealth, Dept. of Health, 43 Pa. Commw. 106, 401 A.2d 872 (1979).

[13]Zieverink v. Ackerman, 1 Ohio App. 3d 10, 437 N.E.2d 319 (1981); Valley View Convalescent Home v. Dept. of Social & Health Servs., 24 Wash. App. 192, 599 P.2d 1313, review den., 93 Wash. 2d 1004 (1979).

[14]Geriatrics v. Colo. State Dept. of Health, 650 P.2d 1288 (Colo. App. 1982); Moon Lake Convalescent Center v. Margolis, 180 Ill. App. 3d 245, 535 N.E.2d 956 (1989); Boswell, Inc. v. Harkins, 230 Kan. 738, 640 P.2d 1202 (1982); In re Milcrest Nursing Home, 59 Ohio App. 2d 116, 392 N.E.2d 1097 (1978); Miller Home v. Dept. Pub. Welfare, 556 A.2d 1 (Pa. Commw. 1989).

[15]Villines v. Division of Aging and Mo. Dept. of Soc. Servs., 722 S.W.2d 939 (Mo. 1987).

[16]People v. Casa Blanca Convalescent Homes, 159 Cal. App. 3d 509, 206 Cal. Rptr. 165 (1984); Yanke v. State Dept. of Public Health, 162 Cal. App. 2d 600, 328 P.2d 556 (1958); Friedman v. Division of Health of Mo., 537 S.W.2d 547 (Mo. 1976).

can be sanctioned.[17] Where this is the case, the requirement will be enforced.[18] Where there is no such statutory requirement, however, due process does not stand in the way of expeditious action without opportunity for correction.[19] Indeed, the licensing agency can limit its consideration at a hearing to conditions existing in the facility at the time of an inspection, ignoring the facility's subsequent attempts at correction of the problems.[20] It can also consider the past compliance history of the facility in determining the appropriateness of the sanction.[21] In fact, however, many licensing agencies are willing to allow a facility with a history of deficiencies to remain licensed over a considerable period of time if the facility attains marginal compliance at some point in the correction process.[22]

For a comprehensive discussion of nursing facility licensure issues, see Annot., Licensing and Regulation of Nursing or Rest Homes[23] and S. Johnson, N. Terry, and M. Wolfe, Nursing Facilities and the Law: State Regulation and Private Litigation.[24]

§15.1.2 Intermediate or Alternative Sanctions

Delicensure has devastating consequences, not only for the owner and operator of the delicensed facility, but also for its

---

[17]Ill. Rev. Stat. ch. 111½, ¶4153-303 (Smith-Hurd 1988); Mo. Ann. Stat. §198.026 (Vernon Supp. 1989).

[18]Valley View Convalescent Home v. Dept. of Social and Health Servs., 24 Wash. App. 192, 599 P.2d 1313, review den., 93 Wash. 2d 1004 (1979).

[19]Boswell, Inc. v. Harkins, 230 Kan. 610, 640 P.2d 1202 (1988), app. dismissed, 459 U.S. 802 (1982); Commonwealth v. Brownsville Golden Age Home, 103 Pa. Commw. 449, 520 A.2d 926 (Pa. 1987), alloc. den., 529 A.2d 1083 (1988).

[20]*Casa Blanca*, supra n.16.

[21]Friedman v. Division of Health, 537 S.W.2d 547 (Mo. 1976); Ringwald v. Division of Health, 537 S.W.2d 552 (Mo. 1976); Colonial Gardens Nursing Home v. Commonwealth, Dept. of Health, 34 Pa. Commw. 131, 382 A.2d 1273 (1978).

[22]Jost, Enforcement of Quality Nursing Home Care in the Legal System, 13 L. Med. & Health Care 160, 169 (1985).

[23]53 A.L.R.4th 689 (1987).

[24](1985).

residents and staff. Delicensure most commonly leads to a forced sale but can also result in closure, with subsequent dislocation of the facility's residents and shrinkage of available bed supply.[25] For these reasons and others, state licensure agencies have traditionally been very reluctant to take action against facilities. This reluctance has undermined the credibility of state enforcement programs. In recent years, therefore, statutes have been adopted authorizing state agencies to use a variety of intermediate or alternative sanctions short of delicensure. The most common alternatives, now available in many states, are receivership, civil fines, admission holds, and rating systems. Two useful recent discussions of alternative sanctions are: Model Recommendations: Intermediate Sanctions for Enforcement of Quality of Care in Nursing Facilities, issued in 1981 by the ABA Commission on Legal Problems of the Elderly;[26] and State Regulation of Long-Term Care: A Decade of Experience with Intermediate Sanctions, by Sandra Johnson.[27]

Receivership statutes permit the state agency or agencies responsible for nursing facility regulation (usually including the licensing agency) to petition a court to place a manager in a seriously deficient facility, either to bring the facility back into compliance or to facilitate an orderly closure. Receivership is appropriate for a facility plagued with serious problems that the owners and administrator seem either unable or unwilling to remedy. All nursing facility receivership statutes allow the state agency to petition for receivership.[28] Some also permit facility

---

[25]There is considerable, though disputed, evidence that precipitous relocation of nursing home residents can cause deterioration or death, see Bourestom and Pastalan, The Effects of Relocation on the Elderly, 21 Gerontologist 4 (1981); Borup, Relocation Mortality Research: Assessment, Reply, and the Need to Refocus on the Issues, 23 Gerontologist 235 (1983); Cohen, Legislative and Educational Alternatives to a Judicial Remedy for the Transfer Trauma Dilemma, 11 Am. J.L. & Med. 405 (1986).

[26]This monograph includes a now somewhat dated 50-state survey.

[27]13 Law, Med. & Health Care 173 (Sept. 1985).

[28]See Colo. Rev. Stat. §25-3-108 (1982); Fla. Stat. Ann. §400.126(1) (West 1986); Iowa Code Ann. §135C.30 (West 1989); Kan. Stat. Ann. §39-954 (1986); N.Y. Pub. Health Law §2810(2)(a) (McKinney 1985); Wis. Stat. Ann. §50.05(4) (West 1987).

residents or their families or guardians to so petition.[29] Several states also allow for voluntary receivership when the facility ceases to be able to operate itself.[30] Grounds for receivership vary: some statutes only permit receivership when a facility is delicensed,[31] others authorize receivership in other emergencies[32] or when a facility has demonstrated an inability to comply with licensure standards.[33] Several statutes designate the enforcement agency as the receiver,[34] others allow the appointment of private receivers.[35] Most statutes provide an extensive list of powers and duties for the receiver,[36] though others allow the court to establish the receiver's powers.[37] Most statutes also afford the receiver some protection from liability.[38] Many statutes put time limits on the receiverships,[39] though others allow receiverships to continue until the problems are resolved that the receivership was imposed to address.[40]

---

[29]Ill. Rev. Stat. ch. 111½, ¶4153-503 (Smith-Hurd 1988); Mich. Comp. Laws Ann. §333.21751(1) (West 1980).

[30]Minn. Stat. Ann. §144A.14 (West 1989); N.Y. Pub. Health Law §2810(1) (McKinney 1985).

[31]N.Y. Pub. Health Law §2810(2)(a) (McKinney 1985); Mich. Comp. Laws Ann. §333.21751(1) (West 1980).

[32]Iowa Code Ann. §135C.30(2) (West 1989); Minn. Stat. Ann. §144A.15(2) (West 1989); Mo. Ann. Stat. §198.099(5) (Vernon 1983); Wis. Stat. Ann. §50.05(4) (West 1987).

[33]Pa. Stat. Ann. tit. 35, §448.814 (Purdon Supp. 1988).

[34]Kan. Stat. Ann. §§39-954, 39-963 (1986); Mich. Comp. Laws Ann. §333.21751(2) (West 1980).

[35]Ill. Ann. Stat. ch. 111½, ¶4153-506 (Smith-Hurd 1988); Md. Health-Gen. Code Ann. §19-336 (Supp. 1989); N.J. Stat. Ann. §26:2H-37 (West 1987).

[36]Conn. Gen. Stat. Ann. §9a-545 (West 1986); Fla. Stat. Ann. §400.126(3) (West 1986); Ill. Ann. Stat. ch. 111½, ¶4153-508 (Smith-Hurd 1988).

[37]Ariz. Rev. Stat. Ann. §36-429 (1986).

[38]Conn. Gen. Stat. Ann. §19a-547(a) (West 1986); Md. Health-Gen. Code Ann. §19-336 (Supp. 1989); N.Y. Pub. Health Law §2810(2)(d) (McKinney 1985).

[39]Ill. Rev. Stat. ch. 111½, ¶4153-504 (Smith-Hurd 1988); Kan. Stat. Ann. §§39-954, 39-963 (1986); Md. Health-Gen. Code Ann. §19-339 (1989 Supp.).

[40]Iowa Code Ann. §135C.30(3) (West. Supp. 1989); Mo. Ann. Stat. §198-128 (Vernon 1983).

Civil fines or forfeitures are appropriate when problems in a facility warrant a regulatory response but are not serious enough to justify delicensure or receivership. Fines or forfeitures are particularly appropriate when the problems are the result of decisions that are economically motivated and that might be made differently if the threat of monetary sanctions made the problematic course of conduct less profitable. Monetary sanctions can also assist in raising funds to finance other remedial efforts, such as receiverships. Civil fine statutes vary in the extent of the flexibility they allow enforcement agencies in assessing fines. Most statutes require classification of deficiencies and set maximums for each classification.[41] Some statutes additionally specify formulas for determining the appropriate fine.[42] Most statutes provide for daily accrual while the violation persists[43] or for an initial lump sum followed by additional increments that accrue daily.[44] Fines that accrue daily may offer greater incentives for correcting problems; however, such fines are more difficult to administer and may pose constitutional problems if the continuing accumulation makes it impossible for the sanctioned facility to seek judicial review.[45] Some statutes also permit amplified fines for repeat offenders, permitting the agency to address the problem of the facility that constantly cycles in and out of compliance.[46]

Civil fine statutes also take different approaches to the problem of collection. Statutes that require judicial action for collection of fines have proved problematic because of the

---

[41]Conn. Gen. Stat. Ann. §19a-527 (West Supp. 1989); Fla. Stat. Ann. §400-23 (West 1986); Or. Rev. Stat. §441.715 (1987).

[42]Ill. Rev. Stat. ch. 111½, ¶4153-305 (Smith-Hurd 1988); Mich. Comp. Laws Ann. §333.21799c (West 1980).

[43]Ariz. Rev. Stat. Ann. §36-431.01 (1988).

[44]Ill. Rev. Stat. ch. 111½, ¶4153-305 (Smith-Hurd 1988); Or. Rev. Stat. §441.715 (1987).

[45]Compare Oklahoma Operating Co. v. Love, 252 U.S. 331 (1920) and Oklahoma Gin Co. v. Oklahoma, 252 U.S. 339 (1920) with United States v. Ford Motors Corp., 402 F. Supp. 475 (D.D.C. 1975), affd., 425 U.S. 927 (1976).

[46]See Ill. Ann. Stat. ch. 111½, ¶4153-305(5), 4153-306 (Smith-Hurd 1988); Iowa Code Ann. §135C.40 (West 1989).

expense and delay inherent in litigation.[47] Statutes may be more workable that allow collection of fines from Medicaid payments[48] or permit the facility to pay a lesser fine immediately rather than resist collection and end up paying a greater fine if resistance proves unsuccessful.[49]

Admission suspensions achieve indirectly what civil fines achieve directly.[50] Because resident turnover in nursing facilities is high, a suspension of admissions immediately affects the facility's cash flow. A suspension of admissions also spares residents in the facility from relocation trauma.

Public rating of facilities by agencies attempts to direct the market so as to reward good facilities and penalize bad.[51] Overly subjective rating systems, however, have been successfully attacked as delegating too much discretionary authority to the agency.[52] Much the same purpose can be achieved through public posting or availability of inspection reports and complaint investigation results.[53] Other intermediate sanctions include injunctions[54] and placement of monitors within the facility on a full-time basis.[55]

---

[47]See Cal. Health & Safety Code §1428 (West Supp. 1989).

[48]Ill. Ann. Stat. ch. 111½, ¶4153-310 (Smith-Hurd 1988); Mich. Comp. Laws Ann. §333.21799d (West 1980).

[49]California formerly had such a scheme, but it was repealed in 1984. Its constitutionality was litigated and upheld, Lackner v. Perkins, 91 Cal. App. 3d 422, 154 Cal. Rptr. 138 (1979).

[50]See Cal. Health & Safety Code §1434 (West 1979); Fla. Stat. Ann. §400.121(4) (West 1986); Mich. Comp. Laws Ann. §333.21799b (West 1980); N.Y. Pub. Health Law §2806(2) (McKinney 1985).

[51]Fla. Stat. Ann. §400.023(3) (West 1986 and Supp. 1988); N.Y. Pub. Health Law §2803(1)(c) (McKinney 1985); Tex. Rev. Civ. Stat. Ann. art. 4442c, §7(a)(9) (Vernon Supp. 1989).

[52]High Ridge Mgmt. Corp. v. State, 354 So. 2d 377 (Fla. 1977). But see Greenwald v. Whalen, 609 F.2d 665 (2d Cir. 1979) (refusing to enjoin an application of the New York rating system).

[53]See Ill. Stat. Ann. ch. 111½, ¶4153-209, 4153-210, 4153-304 (Smith-Hurd Supp. 1988).

[54]Ill. Ann. Stat. ch. 111½, ¶4153-501 (Smith-Hurd 1988); Mo. Ann. Stat. §198.103 (Vernon 1983); Okla. Stat. Ann. tit. 63, §1-1931 (West 1984).

[55]Cal. Health & Safety Code §1430 (West Supp. 1989); Fla. Stat. Ann. §400.125 (West 1986); Minn. Stat. Ann. §144A.12 (West 1989).

§15.1.3 Criminal Prosecutions

While civil remedies are the normal means states adopt to address nursing facility problems, criminal prosecutions are becoming increasingly common. Since the late 1970s, nursing facilities and their personnel have been prosecuted under the Medicare and Medicaid fraud and abuse laws for defrauding these federal programs.[56] More recently, states have begun to prosecute those who physically abuse residents, seriously infringe on resident rights,[57] or mishandle patient funds.[58] Some states have gone further and prosecuted owners or administrators of nursing facilities for resident injuries resulting from neglect.[59]

Criminal prosecutions for neglect have been met with constitutional challenges claiming that general statutory definitions of neglect are too vague to support criminal prosecutions. State v. Brenner held that a statute proscribing "neglect" resulting in "unjustifiable pain and suffering" was sufficiently definite to withstand constitutional challenge.[60] People v. Gurell held that prosecution for violation of arguably vague state nursing facility standards was constitutionally permissible since the statute did not authorize prosecution for violation of the vague standards generally, but only for failing to correct specific violations identified by the Department of Public Health.[61]

Criminal prosecutions have raised difficult questions of causation and of evidence. In State v. Serebin,[62] the Wisconsin Supreme Court upheld the reversal of a trial court verdict that

---

[56]42 U.S.C. §1320a-7b (Supp. V 1987).

[57]See People v. Coe, 131 Misc. 2d 807, 501 N.Y.S.2d 997, affd., 126 App. Div. 2d 436, 510 N.Y.S.2d 470 (1986) (nurse convicted of having violated state health laws for having forcibly searched an elderly resident, who became agitated, collapsed, and died).

[58]State v. Pleasant Hill Health Facility, 496 A.2d 306 (Me. 1985).

[59]See State v. Serebin, 119 Wis. 2d 837, 350 N.W.2d 65 (1984); Mitchell v. State, 491 So. 2d 596 (Fla. App. 1986); State v. Brenner, 486 So. 2d 101, 60 A.L.R.4th 1143 (1986).

[60]Id. See also State v. Mckee, 392 N.W.2d 493 (Iowa 1988) (criminal neglect statute not unconstitutionally vague).

[61]98 Ill. 2d 194, 456 N.E.2d 18 (1983).

[62]119 Wis. 2d 837, 350 N.W.2d 65 (1984).

convicted a nursing facility administrator of reckless homicide in the death of a resident who had wandered from a facility, allegedly because the facility was inadequately staffed. The court held that the state had not proved beyond a reasonable doubt that adequate staffing would have prevented the death. The court affirmed, however, a conviction of the administrator for criminal neglect of residents resulting in malnourishment and bedsores, finding the proof of causation on these counts to be adequate.[63] In Mitchell v. State,[64] another criminal prosecution, the court affirmed admission of evidence that the defendant administrator had mistreated other residents, overcharged the victim's relatives, failed to pay the facility's debts, and mishandled another facility in another state. The court held that all of this evidence was relevant to the administrator's knowledge and motive.

An individual or entity convicted of patient abuse must be excluded from receiving payments under the Medicare and Medicaid programs for five years.[65] For a nursing facility, the effect of such an exclusion is devastating.

§15.1.4 Consumer Protection Laws

All states have unfair and deceptive trade practices acts (UDTPAs) that permit the state attorney general to bring lawsuits to protect consumers from abuses. Many of these acts also authorize private rights of action for injured consumers to protect themselves. In several states—Massachusetts, Texas, California, Arkansas, North Carolina, New York, and Ohio—state attorneys general have brought suits challenging nursing facility practices alleged to violate these laws.[66] In People v. Casa Blanca Convalescent

---

[63]See Note, State v. Serebin, Causation and the Criminal Liability of Nursing Home Administrators, 1986 Wis. L. Rev. 339 (1986).

[64]491 So. 2d 596 (Fla. App. 1986).

[65]42 U.S.C. §1320a-7(c)(3)(b) (Supp. V 1987).

[66]See Horvath and Nemore, Nursing Home Abuses as Unfair Trade Practices, 20 Clearinghouse Rev. 801 (1986).

Home,[67] for example, the state was awarded $167,500 in penalties and an injunction against a nursing facility in a UDTPA case. The court found that the conditions in the facility—including maggots and cockroaches on patients' bodies, burning of patients in baths, moldy food, and falsification of medical records—in addition to being violations of California's nursing facility regulations were also unfair trade practices. In other states UDTPAs have been used to open up nursing facilities that barred advocates from visiting residents and to penalize facilities that failed to provide adequate nutrition to residents.[68]

The UDPTAs of some states exclude from coverage industries like the nursing facility industry that are otherwise regulated by the state.[69] In states without such provisions, however, the UDPTA may provide the state with alternative remedies not available under its nursing facility statute. For example, UDPTAs often provide minimum damages, ranging from $25 to $2,000, for consumers who can establish unfair or oppressive trade practices but cannot establish actual damages; such a provision is especially useful in the nursing facility context, where actual damages are often hard to prove.[70]

§15.2 Federal Certification

§15.2.1 The Federal Role in Nursing Facility Regulation

For the last quarter century, the federal government has played a central role in defining the character of nursing facilities in the United States. The Medicare and Medicaid programs, established in 1965, provided coverage, respectively, for "extended care facilities" and "skilled nursing facilities." In 1971 Congress

---

[67]159 Cal. App. 3d 509, 206 Cal. Rptr. 164, 53 A.L.R.4th 661 (1984).

[68]Horvath and Nemore, supra n.66, at 804-807.

[69]See Okla. Stat. Ann. tit. 15, §754(2) (West 1990); Neb. Rev. Stat. §59-1601 (1988).

[70]Horvath and Nemore, supra n.66, at 809-810.

permitted optional coverage for a lower level of care, "intermediate care facilities" under the Medicaid program; a year later Congress established a single uniform definition of "skilled nursing facility" for both the Medicare and Medicaid programs.

Together the federal Medicare and Medicaid programs pay for about 45 percent of the nursing facility care consumed in this country.[1] In 1987, Medicaid spent $18.5 billion on nursing facility care, 48 percent of total Medicaid expenditures. Medicare paid for an additional $.6 billion in nursing facility care. Because the federal government pays for such a significant proportion of nursing facility care, more than 75 percent of the nation's nursing facilities, containing almost 90 percent of the nation's nursing facility beds, are certified for participation in the federal Medicare or Medicaid programs.[2] To be certified for Medicare or Medicaid participation, a facility must be surveyed periodically by a state survey agency, which must find the facility to be in substantial compliance with federal certification requirements. The original intent of Congress was probably that these requirements would merely supplement state licensing requirements; however, the federal government has taken the lead in nursing facility regulation in many states, with state licensing requirements and inspection procedures merely replicating their federal counterparts.

From 1974 until the late 1980s, the federal certification requirements[3] placed heavy emphasis on structural features of the nursing facility: the characteristics of its physical plant, the composition of its staff, and the contents of its by-laws and procedures. Little attention was paid to the actual process or outcome of resident care.[4]

The late 1980s have seen dramatic changes in federal nursing

---

§15.2 [1]Letsch, Levit, and Waldo, National Health Expenditures, 1987, 10 Health Care Financing Rev. 109, 122 (Winter 1988).

[2]Strahan, Nursing Home Characteristics: Preliminary Data from the National Nursing Home Survey, 131 Advancedata 2 (Mar. 27, 1987).

[3]Found at 42 C.F.R. pt. 405, subpt. K for Medicare, and at 42 C.F.R. pt. 442, subpts. D, E, and F for Medicaid.

[4]See, describing the history of federal policy regarding nursing homes, B. Vladeck, Unloving Care 30-70 (1980).

facility law.[5] Attempts in the early 1980s by the Reagan administration to deregulate nursing facilities unleashed a dramatic backlash. This backlash resulted in turn in a comprehensive, congressionally mandated review of federal nursing facility regulation by the prestigious Institute of Medicine[6] and in a consensus-for-change document endorsed by consumer, provider, and professional groups.[7] Simultaneous with these developments, the federal courts, in Smith v. Heckler,[8] determined that the Department of Health and Human Services (HHS) had breached its statutory obligations by failing to use a certification survey process that actually examined patient care in, not just the structural features of, nursing facilities.

§15.2.2 Substantive Requirements of the Omnibus Budget Reconciliation Act of 1987

These developments culminated with the adoption of the nursing facility reform provisions of the Omnibus Budget Reconciliation Act of 1987 (OBRA '87)[9] and in a new Medicare and Medicaid survey procedure.[10] The new law and survey procedure put much greater emphasis on the process and outcome of resident care, focusing on the services that the facility provides to residents and the effects of these services on the residents. The new statute also upgrades some staffing requirements (for example, requiring

---

[5]See, further describing these changes, Trocchio, New Nursing Home Quality of Care Standards, 5 Health Span 12 (Feb. 1988).

[6]Institute of Medicine, Improving the Quality of Care in Nursing Homes (1986).

[7]National Citizens' Coalition for Nursing Home Reform, Campaign for Quality Care in Nursing Homes (1987).

[8]Estate of Smith v. Heckler, 747 F.2d 583 (10th Cir. 1984); Smith v. Bowen, 675 F. Supp. 586 (D. Colo. 1987); Smith v. Bowen, 656 F. Supp. 1093 (D. Colo. 1987); Smith v. Heckler, 622 F. Supp. 403 (D. Colo. 1985).

[9]Pub. L. No. 100-203, §§4201-4218.

[10]42 C.F.R. §§488.100 et seq. (proposed 53 Fed. Reg. 22850 (June 17, 1988)). See also survey forms, procedures, and interpretive guidelines published in the Medicaid State Operations Manual, Transmittal No. 232 (September 1989).

training of nurse's aides and more extensive nursing coverage in some facilities); outlaws certain strategies that have been used to exclude Medicaid recipients from facilities; enumerates and emphasizes residents' rights; and requires states to develop a broader, and presumably more effective, armamentarium of enforcement devices. The law further prescribed a timetable for HHS and states to follow to assure full implementation of the law by 1990. The staffing, Medicaid discrimination, and residents' rights requirements of the 1987 nursing facility law will be discussed below in Parts B, C, D, respectively. The remaining substantive requirements, as well as the federal survey and enforcement process, are discussed here.

The new statute has separate, though similar, provisions governing skilled nursing facilities under Medicare[11] and nursing facilities under Medicaid.[12] The old distinction between skilled nursing facilities (SNFs) and intermediate care facilities (ICFs) is abolished, with ICFs generally being upgraded to SNF standards. Both the Medicare and Medicaid requirements generally mandate that facilities promote, maintain, and enhance the quality of each resident's life.[13] Each facility must have a quality assessment and assurance committee, composed of its director of nursing, a physician, and three members of the facility staff. This committee must meet quarterly to identify quality issues and to develop and implement plans to address quality deficiencies.[14] Facilities are to examine each resident at least once every three months and to comprehensively assess each resident's functional capacity, impairments, and medical problems at the time of admission and at least annually thereafter.[15] A written

[11]Pub. L. No. 100-203, §§4201-4206.
[12]Id. at §§4211-4218.
[13]42 U.S.C. §1395i-3(b)(1)(A) (Supp. V 1987); 42 U.S.C. §1396r(b)(1)(A) (Supp. V 1987).
[14]42 U.S.C. §1395i-3(b)(1)(B) (Supp. V 1987); 42 U.S.C. §1396r(b)(1)(B) (Supp. V 1987).
[15]42 U.S.C. §1395i-3(b)(3)(A) (Supp. V 1987); 42 U.S.C. §1396r(b)(3)(A) (Supp. V 1987); or upon any significant change in condition, see 42 U.S.C. §1395i-3(b)(3)(C)(i) (Supp. V 1987); 42 U.S.C. §1396r(b)(3)(C)(i) (Supp. V 1987). In addition, mentally ill or retarded Medicaid recipients are to be pre-

plan of care must be developed for each resident by a team including the resident's physician and the nurse responsible for the resident, with the participation of the resident or the resident's family. This plan must be based on the annual assessment and must address the medical, nursing, and psychosocial needs of the resident.[16] The facility must also provide services and activities to help each resident reach or maintain his or her "highest practicable physical, mental, and psychosocial well-being."[17] These services must be provided by qualified persons, and must include nursing services, specialized rehabilitative services, medically related social services, pharmaceutical services, dietary services, activities, and dental services.[18] Clinical records must be kept on each resident, including the resident's assessment and plan of care.[19]

To be certified for Medicare or Medicaid reimbursement, facilities must be licensed under applicable state and local law and must comply with Life Safety Code (fire) requirements and all other federal, state, and local laws and professional standards.[20] Facilities must also maintain infection control programs to ensure a safe environment.[21]

---

screened before admission to assure that a nursing home placement, instead of hospitalization in a mental hospital or placement in the community, is appropriate. 42 U.S.C. §1396r(b)(3)(F) (Supp. V 1987).

[16]42 U.S.C. §1395i-3(b)(2) (Supp. V 1987); 42 U.S.C. §1396r(b)(2) (Supp. V 1987).

[17]42 U.S.C. §1395i-3(b)(2) (Supp. V 1987); 42 U.S.C. §1396r(b)(2) (Supp. V 1987).

[18]42 U.S.C. §1395i-3(b)(4)(A) (Supp. V 1987); 42 U.S.C. 1396r(b)(4)(A) (Supp. V 1987). Nursing, nurse's aide training, and social work requirements are further described in Part C below.

[19]42 U.S.C. §1395i-3(b)(6)(C) (Supp. V 1987); 42 U.S.C. §1396r(b)(6)(C) (Supp. V 1987).

[20]42 U.S.C. §§1395i-3(d)(2), (4) (Supp. V 1987); 42 U.S.C. §§1396r(d)(2), (4) (Supp. V 1987). The Secretary may waive specific requirements of the Life Safety Code if rigid application would result in unreasonable hardship for a facility and waiver would not be unsafe for residents or personnel. Also, the Secretary may apply equivalent state fire safety law in place of the Life Safety Code.

[21]42 U.S.C. §1395i-3(d)(3) (Supp. V 1987); 42 U.S.C. §1396r(d)(3) (Supp. V 1987).

§15.2.3 Federal Survey and Certification Requirements

The survey and certification process mandated by OBRA '87 continues to rely on state survey agencies (usually the state health department) to verify compliance with the federal standards,[22] but in many other respects departs from the survey process in place prior to the Act. The state survey agency must inspect each certified nursing facility on average once every 12 months. To ensure continued compliance a standard survey, or an abbreviated version of it, may also be conducted within two months of a change of ownership, management, administration, or director of nursing.[23] The surveys must be unannounced; indeed, any person who notifies a nursing facility that a survey is imminent can be fined $2,000.[24] Each standard survey must examine—using a case-mix stratified sample of residents—the quality of care provided residents, "as measured by indicators of medical, nursing, and rehabilitative care, dietary and nutrition services, activities and social participation, and sanitation, infection control, and physical environment," and review resident care plans, assessments, and compliance with residents' rights rules.[25] If a facility is found to provide substandard care, it must be reinspected within two weeks using an extended survey.[26] The extended survey must include a larger sample of residents and be problem-oriented, in an attempt to discern what flaw of structure or process has resulted in the substandard care.[27] All

---

[22]Except for state-owned facilities, which must be surveyed directly by HHS, 42 U.S.C. §1396r(g)(1)(A) (Supp. V 1987).

[23]42 U.S.C. §1395i-3(g)(2)(A)(iii)(II) (Supp. V 1987); 42 U.S.C. §1396r(g)(2)(A)(iii)(II) (Supp. V 1987).

[24]42 U.S.C. §1395i-3(g)(2)(A) (Supp. V 1987); 42 U.S.C. §1396r(g)(2)(A) (Supp. V 1987).

[25]42 U.S.C. §1395i-3(g)(2)(A)(ii) (Supp. V 1987); 42 U.S.C. §1396r(g)(2)(A)(ii) (Supp. V 1987).

[26]42 U.S.C. §1395i-3(g)(2)(B) (Supp. V 1987); 42 U.S.C. §1396r(g)(2)(B) (Supp. V 1987).

[27]42 U.S.C. §1395i-3(g)(B)(iii) (Supp. V 1987); 42 U.S.C. §1396r(g)(B)(iii) (Supp. V 1987). An extended survey is not a prerequisite to enforcement

survey results must be made available to the public and posted at the facility. Information about substandard care must be shared with the nursing facility ombudsman (see §15.3, infra), attending physicians of patients receiving substandard care, the state board that licenses nursing facility administrators, and the state Medicaid fraud and abuse control units.[28]

All surveys are to be conducted by a multidisciplinary team, following a protocol to be established by HHS. The current survey procedure, formulated in response to the *Smith* litigation, will probably be continued in modified form under the new legislation. This multistep survey is designed to review the process and outcome of care delivered in the nursing facility.[29] The surveyors begin the survey by identifying both a randomly selected group of residents and a focused selection of residents with specified special care needs. The inspection team then tours the facility, examining all areas of the facility and conversing with residents, family members, and staff. The team concentrates on whether residents' needs—physical, emotional, psychosocial, and spiritual—are being met. The surveyors also are to review the physical environment and meet with resident council representatives, if a resident council exists. Next, the surveyors interview and observe the residents selected for the sample and compare the situation of the observed residents with what is reflected in the medical records of those residents. The surveyors then observe a drug pass (the distribution of medications to residents) and observe the dining area while a meal is served. Finally, a deficiency statement is formulated and is discussed with the facility at the exit conference. A separate survey reviews the administrative and structural features of the facility that were the focus of the old survey process, but is only used for initial certification surveys.

OBRA '87 also addresses concerns that facilities have

---

action. 42 U.S.C. §1395i-3(g)(2)(B)(iv) (Supp. V 1987); 42 U.S.C. §1396r (g)(2)(B)(iv) (Supp. V 1987).

[28]42 U.S.C. §1395i-3(g)(5) (Supp. V 1987); 42 U.S.C. §1396r(g)(5) (Supp. V 1987).

[29]See supra n.10.

expressed about the arbitrariness of a survey procedure that focuses on evaluations of process and outcome. States must implement programs to measure and reduce inconsistency in the survey process, must comprehensively train surveyors, and must assure that surveyors do not have conflicts of interest.[30] States must also educate nursing facility staff and residents as to state regulations, procedures, and policies.[31] HHS must review at least 5 percent of a state's facilities each year to validate the state survey results and must penalize the state if its surveys are substandard.[32] HHS may also conduct its own survey whenever it has reason to question the compliance of a facility with Medicare and Medicaid standards.

In addition to the survey process, each state must investigate complaints of violations of Medicare and Medicaid requirements and, where necessary, monitor problem facilities on-site.[33] States are specifically required to investigate allegations of resident neglect and abuse and of misappropriation of resident property. States must also maintain records concerning nurse's aides found guilty of these offenses as part of the nurse's aide registry that is also required by the legislation.[34]

§15.2.4 The Federal Enforcement Process

Historically, if a state survey agency found a facility to be out of compliance with Medicare or Medicaid certification standards, the only sanction was termination from participation in the program. If a state determined that conditions in a facility

---

[30]42 U.S.C. §§1395i-3(g)(2)(D), (E) (Supp. V 1987); 42 U.S.C. §§1396r(g)(2)(D), (E) (Supp. V 1987).

[31]42 U.S.C. §1395i-3(g)(1)(B) (Supp. V 1987); 42 U.S.C. §1396r(g)(1)(B) (Supp. V 1987).

[32]42 U.S.C. §1395i-3(g)(3) (Supp. V 1987); 42 U.S.C. §1396r(g)(3) (Supp. V 1987).

[33]42 U.S.C. §1395i-3(g)(4) (Supp. V 1987); 42 U.S.C. §1396r(g)(4) (Supp. V 1987).

[34]42 U.S.C. §1395i-3(g)(1)(C) (Supp. V 1987); 42 U.S.C. 1396r(g)(1)(C) (Supp. V 1987). See also infra §§15.7, 15.15.

justified decertification, the state could decertify it from the Medicaid program, and the Health Care Financing Administration could decertify it from the Medicare program.[35] Alternatively, if the deficiencies did not threaten resident health or safety, the state could recertify the facility subject to a correction plan.[36] Because decertification often put the nursing facility out of business, necessitating a traumatic relocation of residents and worsening an already tight nursing facility bed supply, facilities were often allowed to continue in the Medicare and Medicaid programs year after year with recurrent deficiencies.[37]

OBRA '87 addresses this basic lack of enforcement by requiring the state and federal governments to put in place a more extensive armamentarium of remedies to permit more flexible and appropriate responses to deficiencies.[38] In addition, OBRA '87 more clearly requires an appropriate regulatory response to identified problems. It also establishes redundancy of authority and responsibility for enforcement, in the hope that if a state fails to take action against a problem facility, HHS might (or vice versa).[39]

Under the new law, if a state's survey reveals that a facility is out of compliance with Medicaid certification requirements

---

[35]42 C.F.R. §§442.117, 489.53(b) (1988).

[36]42 C.F.R. §442.105 (1988).

[37]United States General Accounting Office, Medicare and Medicaid, Stronger Enforcement of Nursing Home Requirements Needed 14-19 (1987). A statute adopted in 1982, 42 U.S.C. 1396(a)(i) (repealed by the Nursing Home Reform Act of 1987), permitted states to suspend Medicaid payments for new admissions to substandard homes without decertifying them. This provision was cumbersome and could only be used after the facility was afforded a correction period and informal hearing, 42 C.F.R. 489.62 (1988). It was not widely used.

[38]See, discussing such remedies, National Senior Citizens Law Center, State Intermediate Sanctions for Nursing Homes (1988). See also, surveying implementation of OBRA '87 enforcement provisions, Gardiner and Malec, Enforcement of Nursing Home Regulations: OBRA Plus Two (Report to Senate Special Committee on Aging, Oct. 23, 1989).

[39]HHS has in fact had authority to "look behind" state determinations and terminate facilities certified by the state since 1980. 42 U.S.C. §1396a(a)(33)(B) (Supp. V 1987).

and that the deficiencies immediately threaten the safety of the facility's residents, the state may decertify the facility. Alternatively, the state may appoint temporary management to oversee the operation of the facility while it is either closed in an orderly fashion or brought into compliance.[40] If the facility is Medicare-certified, the Secretary of HHS may take similar steps.[41] If a state (or the Secretary of HHS if Medicare-certified facilities are involved) finds that a facility is out of compliance, but that the deficiencies do not immediately threaten the health or safety of residents, the same steps may be taken. Alternatively, the state may put an admission hold on the facility (refuse to pay for Medicaid residents admitted to the facility thereafter) or assess civil penalties against the facility for each day the facility is out of compliance.[42] When a survey determines that the facility is currently in compliance, but was not for some earlier period, the state (or the Secretary of HHS if Medicare facilities are involved) may assess civil fines for the period the facility was out of compliance.[43] Civil fines collected by the states must be used for specified enforcement-related expenses such as paying for relocation of residents or for temporary management expenses.[44]

HHS and the states are to develop criteria for applying sanctions. Such criteria must assure that remedies are applied expeditiously and that incrementally more serious remedies are imposed for repeated or uncorrected deficiencies.[45] In particular, the admission hold remedy must be imposed on any facility that

---

[40] 42 U.S.C. §§1396r(h)(1)(A), (2)(A)(iii) (Supp. V 1987). It may also impose any of the other sanctions permitted by the statute, including civil fines and admission holds.

[41] 42 U.S.C. §§1395i-3(h)(1)(A), (2)(A)(i), (2)(B)(iii) (Supp. V 1987).

[42] 42 U.S.C. §§1395i-3(h)(2)(A)(ii), (B) (Supp. V 1987); 42 U.S.C. §1396r(h)(1)(B), (2) (Supp. V 1987).

[43] 42 U.S.C. §1395i-3(h)(1)(B) (Supp. V 1987); 42 U.S.C. §1396r(h)(1)(B) (Supp. V 1987). Civil fines assessed by HHS may not exceed $10,000 a day. 42 U.S.C. §1395i-3(h)(2)(B)(ii) (Supp. V 1987).

[44] 42 U.S.C. §1396r(h)(2)(A) (Supp. V 1987).

[45] 42 U.S.C. §1395i-3(h)(2)(B) (Supp. V 1987); 42 U.S.C. §1396r(h)(2)(A) (Supp. V 1987).

is in violation of Medicare and Medicaid requirements for more than three consecutive months.[46] If a facility is found to have provided substandard care in three consecutive surveys, that facility must be subjected to an admission hold and be monitored until it establishes that it is and *will remain* in compliance.[47] States may also provide, and claim federal support for, incentive payments and public recognition for facilities that provide high-quality care.[48] Finally, states may use other alternative sanctions in place of those listed in the statute if they demonstrate to the Secretary that those sanctions are effective in deterring noncompliance and correcting deficiencies.[49]

If the state fails to take action against a deficient Medicaid facility, HHS may take any of the actions it could take against a deficient Medicare facility.[50] If a state finds a facility to be out of compliance with Medicaid requirements but decides not to terminate its certification, HHS may continue federal contributions for Medicaid funding for up to six months; but only if the state submits a plan and timetable for corrective action and guarantees to repay federal contributions if correction is not achieved.[51] Similarly, Medicare funding for substandard facilities may only continue for up to six months if there is a state plan and timetable for corrective action and if the facility agrees to repay payments made in the event that correction is not achieved.[52] If the state and HHS disagree as to whether a facility is out of compliance, whichever one finds the facility out of compliance prevails, and may proceed with applying the enforcement remedies enumerated in OBRA '87.[53]

---

[46]42 U.S.C. §1395i-3(h)(2)(D) (Supp. V 1987); 42 U.S.C. §1396r(h)(2)(C) (Supp. V 1987).
[47]42 U.S.C. §1395i-3(h)(2)(E) (Supp. V 1987); 42 U.S.C. §1396r(h)(2)(D) (Supp. V 1987).
[48]42 U.S.C. §1396r(2)(F) (Supp. V 1987).
[49]42 U.S.C. §1396r(h)(2)(B)(ii) (Supp. V 1987).
[50]42 U.S.C. §1396r(h)(3) (Supp. V 1987). It has the same authority with respect to state-owned nursing facilities that are Medicaid-certified.
[51]42 U.S.C. §1396r(h)(3)(D) (Supp. V 1987).
[52]42 U.S.C. §1395i-3(h)(2)(C) (Supp. V 1987).
[53]42 U.S.C. §1396r(h)(6) (Supp. V 1987).

OBRA '87 does not specify what procedural protections will be available to providers terminated or otherwise sanctioned. Under current regulations, states must permit a facility threatened with termination either a formal evidentiary hearing or an informal reconsideration on written evidence.[54] Medicare facilities are entitled to 15 days' notice of termination from HHS,[55] and are entitled to a hearing only after termination. Decertification without a pretermination hearing has generally been upheld as not in violation of the due process clause because of the strong governmental interest in protecting nursing facility residents and because of the questionable interest of the provider in continued participation in a benefits program.[56] Indeed, the attorneys and administrator of an ECF were recently ordered to pay $4,500 in attorneys' fees to the federal government when the ECF's attorneys obtained a temporary restraining order against termination of its Medicaid provider agreement without disclosing to the court this persuasive line of authority.[57] Given the strong emphasis in OBRA '87 on prompt and decisive enforcement action, it is unlikely that regulations implementing it will offer substantially more protection for providers than do the current regulations.

§15.3 The Ombudsman Program

A final quasi-regulatory program affecting extended care facilities is the federal-state long-term care ombudsman program. The

---

[54]42 C.F.R. §§431.153, 431.154 (1988). Under the "fast track" termination process established in 1986, nursing homes with serious deficiencies can be terminated in as little as 23 days with a highly abbreviated notice and response procedure. See Collier, Legal Issues in Long Term Care, in A. Gosfield, ed., 1989 Health Law Handbook 57, 76-77 (1989).

[55]Unless deficiencies pose an immediate threat to health and safety, in which case only two days' notice is given. 42 C.F.R. §489.53(c)(2) (1988).

[56]See Americana Healthcare Corp. v. Schweiker, 688 F.2d 1072 (1982), cert. denied, 459 U.S. 1202 (1983); Geriatrics Inc. v. Harris, 640 F.2d 262 (10th Cir. 1981), cert. denied, 454 U.S. 832 (1981); Green v. Cashman, 605 F.2d 945 (6th Cir. 1979); Case v. Weinberger, 523 F.2d 602 (2d Cir. 1975).

[57]Cedar Crest Health Center v. Bowen, 4 Medicare & Medicaid Guide (CCH) 38,205 (1989).

federal Older Americans Act requires[1] that states requesting funding under that Act establish an Office of the State Long-Term Care Ombudsman. This office must investigate and resolve the complaints of long-term care facility residents regarding the conduct of the facility in which they reside or of public agencies. The ombudsman office is also to collect and analyze data relating to complaints and conditions in long-term care facilities and to disseminate information about the problems and concerns of long-term care residents to policymakers.[2] The state must ensure that representatives of the ombudsman have access to long-term care facilities and their residents, as well as to the records of residents who consent to such review.[3] Ombudsmen must keep the identity of complainants confidential unless disclosure is consented to by the resident or ordered by a court.[4]

Most ombudsman programs have not been well-funded and operate largely on a volunteer basis. Ombudsmen vary in approach to their task, some functioning as resident advocates, others as mediators, still others largely as friendly visitors.[5] While they have no direct enforcement authority, ombudsmen have played a valuable role in identifying problems, resolving mis-understandings and conflicts, and maintaining a public presence in long-term care facilities.

B. Staffing Requirements

§15.4 The Administrator

Direct monitoring of the process and outcome of care delivery is the most visible use of the law to assure quality in nursing

---

§15.3   [1]At 42 U.S.C. §3027(a)(12) (Supp. V 1987).

[2]Regulations protecting the confidentiality of Ombudsman files are found at 45 C.F.R. §§1321.11(b), 1321.51 (1988).

[3]42 U.S.C. §3027(a)(12)(J)(iv) (Supp. V 1987). If a resident is incompetent and has no guardian, the ombudsman can review the records without consent.

[4]42 U.S.C. §3027(a)(12)(D) (Supp. V 1987).

[5]See A. Monk, L. Kaye, and H. Litwin, Resolving Grievances in the Nursing Home: A Study of the Ombudsman Program 77-138 (1984).

facilities. The law, however, also encourages maintenance of professional involvement in nursing facilities and enhancement of the skills of nonprofessional nursing facility employees as another means of improving quality. The administrator is certainly one of the key professionals in a nursing facility. A competent, caring, hard-working administrator can dramatically improve the environment of a nursing facility.

Since 1968, federal law has required that nursing facilities participating in the Medicaid program be directed by licensed administrators.[1] Federal law requires states to determine whether nursing facility administrators are of good character and otherwise suitable.[2] However, state requirements for licensure vary considerably. Twenty-three states, for example, require administrators to have earned a baccalaureate degree, while 10 require only a high school diploma.[3] Forty-three states require continuing education, with the number of hours required annually ranging from 10 to 315.[4] OBRA '87 requires HHS to promulgate standards for assuring the qualifications of nursing facility administrators and requires the states to implement these standards.[5] Once such standards are issued, OBRA '90 repeats the federal requirements for administrator licensing (H.R. 5835 §4801(e)(11), 101st Cong. 2d Sess., 136 Cong. Rec. H 12486).

§15.5 The Medical Director

OBRA '87 also requires that HHS promulgate regulations assuring that medical care in Medicare- and Medicaid-certified

----

§15.4 [1]42 U.S.C. §§1396a(a)(29), 1396g (1982). See Warzinski and Tourigny, State Licensure Requirements for Nursing Home Administrators: A History, 1987 J. Long-Term Care Admin. 6 (Spring 1987).

[2]42 U.S.C. §1396g(c) (Supp. V 1987).

[3]Warzinski and Tourigny, State Licensure Requirements for Nursing Home Administrators: A Comparison, 1987 J. Long-Term Care Administration 22, 23 (Fall, 1987).

[4]Id. at 24-25.

[5]42 U.S.C. §§1395i-3(e)(3), (f)(4) (Supp. V 1987); 42 U.S.C. §§1396r(e)(4), (f)(4) (Supp. V 1987). The administrator of a facility will need to meet these requirements for the facility to participate in the Medicare or Medicaid program. 42 U.S.C. §1395i-3(d)(1)(c) (Supp. V 1987); 42 U.S.C. §1396 r(d)(1)(C) (Supp. V 1987).

facilities is directed by a physician.[1] The medical director is responsible under current federal regulations for coordination within the facility to ensure the adequacy and appropriateness of the medical care. The director must assure that written by-laws and procedures adequately delineate the responsibilities of attending physicians and must serve as liaison to ensure that attending physicians fulfill their responsibilities.[2] The medical director is also responsible for monitoring the health status of facility employees, reviewing incidents and accidents on the premises, and assuring the adequacy of resident care policies.[3] In most facilities the medical director fills an important role in training, advising, and supervising the staff.[4] As a practical matter, the director, as the physician most readily accessible in the facility, also delivers much of the direct patient care and attends to matters such as certifying the deaths of residents who die in the facility.[5] To be certain that these important responsibilities are properly carried out, facilities should assure that their medical director is competent, has clear responsibilities, and is present in the facility with sufficient frequency to fulfill these obligations.[6]

§15.6 The Nursing Staff

One would expect that the nurse would be the most visible professional in a nursing facility. By definition nursing facilities provide nursing services, and research demonstrates that greater numbers of nurses in nursing facilities are associated with better

---

§15.5 [1]42 U.S.C. §1395i-3(f)(5) (Supp. V 1987); 42 U.S.C. §1396r(f)(5) (Supp. V 1987).

[2]42 C.F.R. §1122(a) (1988).

[3]42 C.F.R. §1122(b) (1988).

[4]Gerdes and Pratt, The Role of a Medical Director in a Nursing Home, 6 J. Gerontological Nursing 271 (1980); Ouslander, Medical Care in the Nursing Home, 262 J.A.M.A. 2582, 2588-2589 (1989).

[5]Id. at 273; M. Kapp, Preventing Malpractice in Long-Term Care 181 (1987).

[6]M. Kapp, supra n.5, at 71.

patient outcomes.[1] In fact, the nurse staffing level in many long-term care facilities is distressingly low and varies significantly from state to state.[2] Nursing facilities must compete with hospitals in a tight market for nurses, and they usually offer lower wages and poorer working conditions. Thus, turnover is high and staffing shortages are common.

The federal and state governments have taken varying approaches to the problem of nurse staffing shortages. The primary requirement of federal law is that there actually be a licensed practical or registered nurse in the facility at all times. To be Medicare-certified, a skilled nursing facility must provide 24-hour nursing coverage sufficient to meet the nursing needs of the residents and must employ a registered nurse on a daily basis to cover at least the day shift.[3] The facility may obtain a waiver from HHS permitting it to go without registered nurse coverage on weekends if it is located in a rural area where nursing facility services are otherwise not sufficiently available and if the facility's residents can get by without the attention of a registered nurse for 48 hours or other arrangements can be made for their care.[4] Requirements for Medicaid-certified facilities are identical, except that the states have broader waiver authority than HHS has under Medicare. A state can waive any of the coverage requirements if the facility can demonstrate that it has been unable to attract appropriate personnel despite diligent efforts (including offering prevailing wage rates); that the waiver will not threaten resident health and safety; and that a registered nurse or physician is immediately available by phone for the times when no nurse is present.[5]

State statutes commonly delegate to the state licensing

---

§15.6   [1]Institute of Medicine, Improving the Qualify of Care in Nursing Homes 101 (1986).

[2]Id. at 101-102.

[3]42 U.S.C. §1395i-3(b)(4)(C)(i) (Supp. V 1987).

[4]42 U.S.C. §1395i-3(b)(4)(C)(ii) (Supp. V 1987).

[5]42 U.S.C. §1396r(a)(4)(C)(ii) (Supp. V 1987). HHS must monitor the states' use of this waiver authority and intervene if it is used inappropriately. Id.

agency the authority to set nurse staffing requirements.[6] State regulations commonly impose minimum staffing ratios, which usually vary by number of residents and facility classification, and often also vary by shift and professional classification (RN or LPN) as well.[7] For example, Illinois requires that a skilled nursing facility provide 2.5 hours of nursing personnel per patient per day; that at least 40 percent of that time be on the day shift, 25 percent on the evening shift, and 15 percent on the night shift; and that 20 percent of the required hours be provided by licensed nurses.[8] In other states required minimum hours per resident per day range from as little as .4 hours per resident per day to as many as 4.[9] Where minimum required levels are low, however, many facilities exceed those requirements.[10] A comprehensive survey of state nursing care requirements for nursing facilities is compiled from time to time by the National Geriatrics Society.[11]

§15.7 Nurse's Aides

Most care in nursing facilities—as much as 90 percent—is delivered by nurse's aides.[1] Their work is physically demanding and emotionally challenging, their responsibilities heavy, and their environment often depressing. Yet nurse's aides characteristically have little training or education, are paid close to the minimum wage, have no prospects for advancement, and hence frequently move on to other jobs as quickly as possible. Turnover

---

[6]Ill. Ann. Stat. ch. 111½, ¶4153-202(2) (Smith-Hurd 1988); Minn. Stat. Ann. §144A.01(6) (West 1988); West Va. Code §16-5C-5(2) (1989).

[7]See Institute of Medicine, supra n.1, at 365.

[8]77 Ill. Admin. Code, §300.1230.

[9]Institute of Medicine, supra n.1, at 102.

[10]Id.

[11]National Geriatrics Society, Update to February 1986, Survey of Nursing Care Requirements in Nursing Homes in the States of the Union (1986).

§15.7 [1]Institute of Medicine, Improving the Quality of Care in Nursing Homes 90 (1986).

rates of 75 percent annually and absentee rates of up to 33 percent per shift are reported.[2]

The most common statutory response to this situation is to require nurse's aide training. As of 1985, 17 states mandated that nurse's aides receive from 15 to 60 hours of classroom training and from 20 to 100 hours of clinical training.[3] Most states provided a grace period of three to nine months to complete training, recognizing the fact that few aides can afford to obtain training before they seek employment. This potentially exacerbates the revolving door problem, however, since aides often leave the facility before the grace period ends and they are trained.

Under OBRA '87, all states were to have nurse's aide training and competency evaluation programs in place by October 1, 1990. HHS must specify requirements for the approval of nurse's aide training and competency evaluation programs including areas that must be covered in training programs, the required length (not less than 75 hours) and instructor qualifications for such programs, and procedures for determining competency both at the end of training programs and for aides currently employed.[4] These guidelines may permit facilities to operate their own training programs, but only if these programs comply with state requirements and only if the state is fully responsible for determining competency.[5] 1989 amendments to the 1987 Act also permit grandfathering of aides who have completed certain state training programs or worked for 24 months for the same employer as an aide (Pub. L. No. 101-239 §6901(b) (4)).

States must implement the HHS guidelines, approving and monitoring training programs and conducting competence eval-

---

[2]Id.; Stannard, Old Folks and Dirty Work: The Social Conditions for Patient Abuse in a Nursing Home, 20 Social Problems 329, 329-231 (1973).

[3]Institute of Medicine, supra n.1, at 366.

[4]42 U.S.C. §1395i-3(f)(2)(A) (Supp. V 1987); 42 U.S.C. §1396r(f)(2)(A) (Supp. V 1987). HHS proposed rules for nurse's aide training were published on March 23, 1990 at 55 Fed. Reg. 10938.

[5]42 U.S.C. §1395i-3(f)(2)(B) (Supp. V 1987); 42 U.S.C. §1396r(f)(2)(B) (Supp. V 1987).

uation.[6] States must also establish a nurse's aide registry listing all individuals who have completed a training course and passed a competency evaluation.[7]

Facilities must consult the state registry and relevant out-of-state registries before hiring an aide and may not employ an aide for more than four months unless he or she has passed a state training or competency evaluation program.[8] A facility may only use a nurse's aide to provide services for which the aide has demonstrated competency.[9] To ensure continuing competency, a facility must conduct regular in-service education and performance reviews for its aides.[10]

Some state laws impose additional requirements, for instance, that an aide be able to speak English or a language understood by a substantial number of the facility's residents[11] or have completed eight years of school.[12] Texas requires that nursing facilities report any new employees within 72 hours of

------

[6]42 U.S.C. §1395i-3(e)(1) (Supp. V 1987); 42 U.S.C. §1396r(e)(1) (Supp. V 1987).

[7]42 U.S.C. §1395i-3(e)(2), 42 U.S.C. §1396r-3(e)(2). The nurse's aide registry must also identify all aides found by the state to have abused or neglected a resident or misappropriated resident property, 42 U.S.C. §§1395i-3(e)(2)(B), (g)(1)(C) (Supp. V 1987); 42 U.S.C. §§1396r(e)(2)(B), (g)(1)(C) (Supp. V 1987). If the aide disputes the charges, he or she may include a statement in the registry, which must be disclosed along with the finding to any inquirer.

[8]42 U.S.C. §§1395i-3(b)(5)(A), (C) (Supp. V 1987); 42 U.S.C. §§1396r(b)(5)(A), (C) (Supp. V 1987). Discharge of an aide solely because of a finding of resident abuse by the state may, however, violate collective bargaining agreements, see Maggio v. Local 1199, Drug, Hosp. & Health Care Employee's Union, No. CV 88-1352 (E.D.N.Y., Dec. 4, 1988).

[9]42 U.S.C. §1395i-3(b)(5)(C) (Supp. V 1987); 42 U.S.C. §1396r(b)(5)(C) (Supp. V 1987). If an aide who formerly passed a state training or competency evaluation program has not done nursing-related work for 24 months before returning to work in a nursing home, he or she must take it over again. 42 U.S.C. §1395i-3(b)(5)(D) (Supp. V 1987); 42 U.S.C. §1396r(b)(5)(D) (Supp. V 1987).

[10]42 U.S.C. §1395i-3(b)(5)(E) (Supp. V 1987); 42 U.S.C. §1396r(b)(5)(E) (Supp. V 1987).

[11]Ill. Stat. Ann. ch. 111½, ¶4153-206(2) (Smith-Hurd 1988).

[12]Ill. Ann. Stat. ch. 111½, ¶4153-206(4) (Smith-Hurd 1988).

employment to the state Department of Human Services, which must then run a criminal conviction check on the employee.[13] If the check reveals a serious offense, the employee must be terminated.[14]

C. Admission and Medicaid Discrimination Issues

§15.8 Admission Agreements

The nursing facility admission process is, if handled properly, far more complex and comprehensive than the process through which patients are admitted to hospitals. The purpose of the hospital admission process is to identify the patient, responsible relatives, and sources of payment and to secure general consent to routine medical procedures. The nursing facility admission process addresses these considerations, but also initiates a long-term relationship between resident and facility. Pursuant to this relationship the nursing facility will provide room, board and medical and personal care to the resident over a potentially long period of time in exchange for the resident's meeting certain responsibilities, financial and otherwise. The nursing facility admission process is further complicated by the fact that the nursing facility resident is far more likely than the hospital patient to be mentally incompetent at the time of admission. The party who negotiates the admission contract with the facility, therefore, is often not the resident, but rather a surrogate, who may or may not have legal authority to contract for the resident. Finally, if the resident is a potential Medicaid recipient, the facility may desire to limit its responsibility to continue to serve the resident who no longer can finance his or her own care,

---

[13]Tex. Rev. Civ. Stat. Ann. art. 4442c, §18 (Vernon Supp. 1989).
[14]Id.

though the facility's attempt to impose such a limit may be illegal.[1]

The admission contract should address a variety of subjects. First, it should disclose the basic daily (or weekly or monthly) rate charged by the facility, services covered (or not covered) by that rate, the length of the advance notice to which the resident is entitled before the rate can be raised, the due date for payments, and any charges for late payments. If the facility requires a deposit, the agreement should state the amount of the deposit, what it covers, and under which circumstances it will be refunded. If the resident authorizes the facility to manage the resident's personal funds, a separate authorization should set out the terms of such an agreement, including the extent of the facility's management, any fees to be charged, whether the funds will be held in an interest-bearing account, and the form of accounting to which the resident is entitled.[2] If the resident's income or assets are being managed by someone else, that person should assume responsibility for charges owed the facility by the resident to the extent of the resident's income or assets.

The admission agreement, or an appended document, should enumerate the rights to which the resident is entitled under federal and state law.[3] In particular, the agreement ought to describe the notice and procedures to which the resident is entitled before being involuntarily transferred and the grounds on which such a transfer can take place. If the resident needs assistance with reading her mail, the facility should assure that the resident identifies a friend or family member to assist with this, or should obtain separate authorization from the resident for facility staff to give assistance. The facility should also disclose to the resident at the time of admission reasonable rules or regulations which the resident must observe (such as, for example, controls on smoking or on use of electric appliances or nonprescription medications).

---

§15.8 [1]See infra §15.9.

[2]See infra §15.14, addressing the facility's legal obligations for such an account.

[3]See infra §§15.12 to 15.17.

During the admission process the facility should secure a separate document containing a general consent signed by the resident (or a legally appropriate surrogate) to authorize provision of nursing care by the facility, administration of routine medications already used by the resident, and any anticipated routine and noninvasive treatments. The resident or surrogate should be given sufficient information to give informed consent to these services. The facility may ask the resident to authorize release of medical and other information to specified persons or agencies, such as the state Medicaid agency if Medicaid benefits must be sought. The facility should secure a copy of the resident's living will or durable power of attorney, if such exist. If the resident has not yet executed such documents, the facility may suggest that the resident consider taking this step.

Admission documents should be readable and understandable, using large type, clear print, opaque paper, and simple language. Facilities should adopting consider a multistage admission process, ideally lasting from two to four weeks. During this time, the resident should be familiarized with the facility, its services, and the admission contract through a tour and several discussions or interviews. Because many admissions occur directly from the hospital and are subject to the pressures of the discharge process, however, such familiarization often will not be possible. In any event, if the resident is being admitted by someone else, the facility should make sure that that person has legal authority to represent the resident.

§15.9 Medicaid Census Control Devices

Medicaid currently pays for about 40 percent of nursing facility care. Because Medicaid is the payor of last resort, taking over when other sources of payment are exhausted, all but the most wealthy residents are at risk of becoming dependent on Medicaid if their stay at a nursing facility is sufficiently prolonged. Medicaid is a voluntary program; nursing facilities need not participate if they do not wish to. Medicaid commonly pays substantially less for nursing facility care than facilities charge private (i.e., non-

Medicaid) residents.[1] Many nursing facilities accept Medicaid residents, however, despite the low payment rates, because they cannot attract enough private residents to fill their beds or because Medicaid payments may help to cover fixed costs or permit economies of scale. Moreover, many residents enter facilities as private patients and are kept on after their resources are consumed and they become dependent on Medicaid.

Because of the low levels of Medicaid payments in most states, however, many facilities accept Medicaid residents reluctantly and seek to discharge them whenever they can be replaced by private patients. As states have become increasingly parsimonious with Medicaid payments and nursing facility care has become increasingly expensive, facilities have tried to control their Medicaid census. Federal law probably does not forbid a nursing facility to favor private residents over residents dependent on Medicaid,[2] though some states do.[3] Recent federal and state legislative and regulatory initiatives have, however, outlawed many of the most common forms of Medicaid discrimination in an attempt to ensure that Medicaid applicants and recipients have access to nursing facility care.[4]

---

§15.9 [1]In Minnesota and North Dakota, Medicaid-certified nursing homes may not charge private residents more for basic services than the Medicaid rate. Minn. Stat. Ann. §256B.48 (West Supp. 1990); N.D. Cent. Code §50-24.4-19 (1987). See Minnesota Ann. of Health Care Facilities v. Minnesota Dept. of Public Welfare, 742 F.2d 442, cert. denied, 469 U.S. 1215 (1984) (holding the Minnesota statute to be constitutional).

[2]See United States General Accounting Office Memorandum, March 13, 1989, published in 1989-2 Medicare & Medicaid Guide (CCH), at 37,835. 42 U.S.C. §§1395i-3(c)(5)(B)(i) and 1396r(c)(5)(B)(ii) (Supp. V 1987) permit states to go further than the federal law in prohibiting admissions practices that discriminate against Medicaid recipients.

[3]See Conn. Stat. Ann. §19a-533(1986); N.J. Stat. Ann. §10:5-12.2 & 5-13 (West Supp. 1989); Wash. Rev. Code Ann. §74.42:055 (West Supp. 1989). See also N.Y.S. Health Facilities Assn. v. Axelrod, 143 Misc. 2d 870, 542 N.Y.S.2d 501 (Supp. 1989) (declaring regulation requiring admission quotas for Medicaid recipients invalid as exceeding legislative authority).

[4]See Nemore, Discrimination by Nursing Homes Against Medicaid Recipients: Improving Access to Institutional Long-Term Care for Poor People, 20 Clearinghouse Rev. 339 (1986).

§15.9.1 Duration-of-Stay Agreements

Until recently, the most common form of Medicaid discrimination was the duration-of-stay agreement, under which a private resident entering a Medicaid participating facility agreed not to convert to Medicaid for a specified period of time, usually ranging from one to five years.[5] The effect was to keep residents from converting to Medicaid even after they had become eligible, forcing them instead to leave the facility or seek help from friends or relatives.

Such agreements are now prohibited by federal law in facilities that participate in the Medicare and Medicaid programs. OBRA '87 provides that:

> A facility must—(i)(I) not require individuals applying to reside in the facility to waive their rights to benefits under [Medicare or Medicaid], (II) not require oral or written assurance that such individuals are not eligible for, or will not apply for, benefits under [Medicare or Medicaid] and (III) prominently display in the facility written information, and provide to such individuals oral and written information, about how to apply for and use such benefits and how to receive refunds for previous payments covered by such benefits.[6]

This statute supplements state statutes and attorney general opinions that in several states have held duration-of-stay agreements to be illegal.[7] Moreover, at least one court has refused to enforce a duration-of-stay contract, deeming it to be in violation of federal law and contrary to public policy.[8]

---

[5]National Senior Citizens Law Center, Nursing Home Private-Pay Admissions Requirements, 55 Nursing Home L. Letter 1 (1982).

[6]42 U.S.C. §1395i-3(c)(5)(A) (Supp. V 1987); 42 U.S.C. §1396r(c)(5)(A) (Supp. V 1987).

[7]See Me. Rev. Stat. §1826.2.H; Rev. Code Wash. ch. 74.42.055 §3(2)(a); Ohio Atty. Gen. Op. 85-063 (Sept. 24, 1985); Wis. Atty. Gen. Op. OAG-4-86 (March 7, 1986).

[8]Glengariff v. Snook, 122 Misc. 2d 784, 471 N.Y.S.2d 973 (1984).

§15.9.2 Responsible Party Agreements or Required Contributions

Some nursing facilities have refused to admit residents dependent on Medicaid unless a responsible party, sponsor, or guarantor signed the admission contract. Facilities have also required prospective residents or their families to make substantial payments to the facility as a condition of admission. Both practices are now prohibited in Medicare- or Medicaid-certified facilities. OBRA '87 forbids facilities to require third-party guarantees of payment as a condition for a resident's admission, expedited admission, or continued stay. OBRA '87 does, however, permit a contract with a resident's legal representative to assure payment from the resident's income or assets, as long as the representative incurs no personal financial liability.[9] OBRA '87 also prohibits facilities from requiring or accepting any consideration as a condition of admitting, expediting the admission, or permitting the continued stay of a Medicaid resident.[10] Even prior to the enactment of the federal prohibition, New York had prosecuted a facility criminally under state law for requiring a contribution.[11]

§15.9.3 Limited Bed Certification

Another common device used for Medicaid census control is to limit the number of beds available for Medicaid recipients in the facility. A nursing facility can accomplish this by seeking state Medicaid certification for only some of its beds, and then

---

[9]42 U.S.C. §§1395i-3(c)(5)(A)(ii), (B)(ii) (Supp. V 1987); 42 U.S.C. §§1396r(c)(5)(A)(ii), (B)(ii) (Supp. V 1987).

[10]Though this does not prohibit a home from accepting contributions from organizations or persons unrelated to Medicaid residents or potential residents, if they are not related to the admission of a Medicaid resident. 42 U.S.C. §§1396r(c)(5)(A)(iii), (B)(iv) (Supp. V 1987).

[11]See National Senior Citizens Law Center, Medicaid Discrimination: Litigation and Other Activities by State Attorneys General, 103 Nursing Home L. Letter 1, 2-4 (October 23, 1986) (describing prosecutions under N.Y. Pub. Health L. §2805-f(4)(b)(i) (McKinney 1985).

informing private residents in its non-Medicaid beds that they cannot convert to Medicaid because Medicaid beds are not available. About half the states permit this, though the Health Care Financing Administration has on several occasions ruled that it is impermissible.[12] While nothing in OBRA '87 explicitly forbids this practice, prohibitions in the statute against transferring residents who become eligible for Medicaid may make it impossible for facilities to discharge such residents, even if all certified beds are filled.[13] Moreover, if facility policies effectively require residents to waive their right to apply for Medicaid if they were initially admitted to a bed that was not Medicaid-certified, such policies would violate provisions of OBRA '87 prohibiting such waivers.[14] State acquiescence in limited bed certification has also been upheld in a federal court in Tennessee under pre-OBRA '87 Medicaid requirements and federal civil rights laws (because limited bed certification had the effect of limiting the access of blacks to nursing facilities).[15]

§15.9.4 Financial Disclosure Requirements

Still another device for limiting access by Medicaid recipients to nursing facilities is to require financial disclosure as a condition for admission. Some nursing facilities require potential applicants to disclose comprehensively their financial situation. If it appears that the applicant is currently or soon will be dependent on Medicaid, the facility denies admission. Otherwise, the applicant is admitted. This strategy has been advocated as an effective means of barring from the facility persons who are already Medicaid eligible, except in the few states that explicitly require

---

[12]See National Senior Citizens Law Center, Limited Bed Certification, 110 Nursing Home L. Letter 5 (Jan. 22, 1988).

[13]42 U.S.C. §§1395i-3(c)(2)(A), (5)(A) (Supp. V 1987); 42 U.S.C. §§1396r(c)(2)(A), (5)(A) (Supp. V 1987).

[14]42 U.S.C. §1395i-3(c)(5)(A) (Supp. V 1987); 42 U.S.C. §1396r(c)(5)(A) (Supp. V 1987).

[15]1990 Medicare & Medicaid (CCH) ¶38,519 (April 20, 1990).

Medicaid-certified facilities to accept a certain number of Medicaid recipients.[16]

Provisions of OBRA '87 that prohibit a facility from requiring promises that residents will not become Medicaid eligible may make financial disclosure requirements illegal if their purpose is to ensure that residents will remain in private-pay status.[17] Moreover, the prohibitions in OBRA '87 against transferring a resident who becomes Medicaid eligible bar facilities from discharging residents who become Medicaid eligible sooner than anticipated, or even residents who misrepresent their financial status in the disclosure form.[18]

§15.10 Differential Services and Medicaid Supplementation

Rather than barring Medicaid recipients outright, some facilities accept them but provide them with fewer services or amenities than are provided private-pay residents, unless relatives or others pay for these supplemental services.[1] It is a criminal offense to charge a resident extra for services covered by Medicaid.[2] OBRA '87, however, permits facilities to charge for services not covered by the state Medicaid plan. OBRA '87 first establishes a broad policy of nondiscrimination. Facilities "must establish and main-

---

[16]See statutes cited supra n.3.

[17]42 U.S.C. §1395i-3(c)(5)(A) (Supp. V 1987); 42 U.S.C. §1396r(c)(5)(A) (Supp. V 1987).

[18]42 U.S.C. §§1395i-3(c)(2)(A), (5)(A) (Supp. V 1987); 42 U.S.C. §1396r(c)(2)(A), (5)(A) (Supp. V 1987). A California statute permits facilities to request specific information about financial status and authorizes facilities to evict residents whose financial status is either "materially different than represented" or "fraudulently misrepresented," Cal. Health & Safety Code §§1439.7(a), (c), (d) (West Supp. 1989). This statute is, however, invalid to the extent that it conflicts with federal law. By contrast, an Illinois statute expressly prohibits discharging residents who become Medicaid eligible. Ill. Ann. Stat. ch. 111½, ¶4153-401.1(a) (Smith-Hurd 1988).

§15.10 [1]See Edelman, Family Supplementation in Nursing Homes, 18 Clearinghouse Rev. 504 (1984).

[2]42 U.S.C. §1320a-7b(d)(1) (Supp. V 1987).

tain identical policies and practices regarding . . . the provision of services required under the State plan for all individuals regardless of source of payment."[3] It proceeds, however, to permit facilities to charge residents for services not covered by the state plan to the extent that the resident is told at the time of admission or of conversion to Medicaid which services are not covered.[4] Presumably, facilities must provide without charge to the resident all care and services required by federal and state requirements. OBRA '87 delegates to HHS the responsibility to specify which additional items and services must be provided by the nursing facility without charge to patient funds.[5] At a minimum, the facility cannot charge for personal hygiene items and services.[6]

The position of OBRA '87 seems consistent with cases in some states permitting payments by relatives for services not covered by Medicaid.[7] Other states have, however, rejected supplementation. In Dunlap Care Center v. Iowa Department of Social Services, for example, the Iowa Supreme Court upheld the state's position forbidding private supplementation.[8] Similarly, a New York court refused to dismiss a criminal prosecution against a facility that had required supplemental payment for a private room for a Medicaid resident.[9] Presumably, OBRA '87 now preempts such state law, although a state can still block supplementation by including an item or service within the state plan.

---

[3]42 U.S.C. §1395i-3(c)(4)(A) (Supp. V 1987); 42 U.S.C. §1396r(c)(4)(A) (Supp. V 1987).

[4]42 U.S.C. §1396r-3(c)(4)(B) (Supp. V 1987); 42 U.S.C. §1396r(c)(5)(B)(iii) (Supp. V 1987).

[5]42 U.S.C. §1395i-3(f)(7) (Supp. V 1987); 42 U.S.C. §1396r(f)(7) (Supp. V 1987).

[6]Id.

[7]Resident v. Noot, 306 N.W.2d 311 (Minn. 1981) (resident's daughter can pay for private room without violating Medicaid law).

[8]353 N.W.2d 389 (Iowa 1984).

[9]New York v. Oppenheim, Ind. No. 1209/86 (N.Y. Sup. Ct., Queens Co. March 18, 1987), reported in National Senior Citizens Law Center, 107 Nursing Home L. Letter 7-8 (1987).

§15.11 Life Care Contracts

There are currently over 700 life care or continuing care communities in the United States that contract with their elderly residents to guarantee shelter, healthcare, and various social services for the remainder of the resident's life.[1] These arrangements usually involve a substantial payment up front (which could involve an assignment of all of the resident's currently owned and after-acquired property) and frequently involve periodic payments thereafter. Continuing care communities assure their residents access to nursing facility care, but may provide such care without cost beyond the initial payment, for a reduced charge, or on a fee-for-service basis.[2]

Life care contracts most frequently end up in litigation when a resident dies or leaves (for example, to be hospitalized) soon after he or she enters the facility.[3] Life care contracts frequently provide for probationary periods of from one to six months, during which the resident may terminate the contract and receive back the initial payment less the cost of the care received from the facility. Occasionally, they also include termination clauses allowing termination and a partial refund if adequate notice is given. Courts will usually allow recovery of all or part of initial payments by residents who die or leave the facility during such probationary periods or on invocation of termination clauses.[4] Where life care contracts do not include such clauses, however, or where the clauses do not apply, courts almost universally refuse refunds under life care contracts, rejecting

---

§15.11 [1]Tell, Wallack, and Cohen, New Directions in Life Care: An Industry in Transition, 65 Milbank Q. 551, 551, 552 (1987).

[2]Id. at 556.

[3]See Note, The Ties that Bind: Life Care Contracts and Nursing Homes, 8 Am. J.L. & Med. 153, 155-165 (1982); Annot., Validity and Construction of Contract Under Which Applicant for Admission to Home for Aged or Infirm Turns Over His Property to Institutions in Return for Lifetime Care, 44 A.L.R.3d 1174 (1970).

[4]Farrand v. Redington Memorial Home, 270 A.2d 871, 44 A.L.R.3d 1166 (Me. 1970); Lyon v. Willamette Lutheran Home, 240 Or. 56, 399 P.2d 895 (1965).

claims of unconscionability, lack of mutuality of obligations, absence or failure of consideration, or illegality of the contract as a wagering agreement.[5]

Several states have adopted statutes to address the problems that have been experienced by life care communities and their residents.[6] These statutes attempt to ensure that life care communities are financially viable by requiring preopening examination and certification,[7] escrowing of entrance fees,[8] maintenance of reserve funds,[9] or surety bonds.[10] Several of them attempt to control advertising[11] and most require disclosure of financial information[12] to ensure that life care residents can themselves evaluate the viability of a life care community they are considering.

State laws also address the content of the life care contract, providing for cooling-off periods of 7 to 90 days,[13] requiring a refund of remaining funds if the resident is dismissed from the facility,[14] or requiring that the facility clearly state its refund policy.[15] Several state laws attempt to give residents a lien or

---

[5]See Wilson v. Dexter, 135 Ind. App. 247, 192 N.E.2d 469 (1963); Steigelmeier v. West Side Deutscher Frauen Verein, 20 Ohio Ops. 2d 368, 88 Ohio L. Abs. 97, 178 N.E.2d 516 (1961); Pickard v. Oregon Senior Citizens Inc., 238 Or. 359, 395 P.2d 168 (1964).

[6]See H. Winklevoss and A. Powell, Continuing Care Retirement Communities: An Empirical, Financial and Legal Analysis, 225-258 (1984) (which includes a comprehensive analysis of these laws).

[7]See, e.g., Ariz. Rev. Stat. Ann. §20-1802(B) (Supp. 1988); Colo. Rev. Stat. §12-13-102(1) (1985); Mich. Comp. Laws Ann. §544.807 (1988).

[8]See, e.g., Minn. Stat. Ann. §80D.05 (West 1986); Cal. Health & Safety Code §1773.5 (West Supp. 1989); Ill. Ann. Stat. ch. 111½, 4160-7 (Smith-Hurd 1988).

[9]See, e.g., Fla. Stat. Ann. §651.035 (West Supp. 1989).

[10]Cal. Health & Safety Code §1773.5 (West Supp. 1989).

[11]Cal. Health & Safety Code §1789 (West Supp. 1989); Mich. Comp. L. Ann. §554.826(a) (1988).

[12]Fla. Stat. Ann. §651.091 (West Supp. 1989); Minn. Stat. Ann. §80D.04 (West 1986).

[13]Cal. Health & Safety Code §§1779(d) to 1779(f) (West Supp. 1989); Ariz. Rev. Stat. Ann. §20-1802(E) (Supp. 1988).

[14]Colo. Rev. Stat. §12-13-105 (1985).

[15]Fla. Stat. Ann. §651.055(1)(g) (West Supp. 1989).

preferred claim if the facility goes into liquidation.[16] Finally, statutes in Connecticut and Illinois permit life care community residents Medicaid eligibility only after the facility has fully consumed the resident's resources.[17]

D. Protection of Residents' Rights

§15.12 Protection of Residents' Rights Generally

Nursing facility residents are almost totally dependent on the facilities in which they live, not only for physical care and medical services, but also for dignity and human worth. Preservation of the rights of persons who are so abjectly dependent on institutions is always difficult—consider the experience of inmates of mental hospitals and prisons. Efficient operation of facilities often seems to require that residents be tractable and that resident resistance to institutional programs be deflected or overridden. Residents lack power and are often isolated from those outside the facility who could empower them. Nursing facility residents are normally severely debilitated—unable to assert, much less protect, their own rights. Staff are subject to norms within the facility that may not be supportive of respect for residents' rights, regardless of the official position of the facility and its administration. The law has, therefore, increasingly intervened to protect residents' rights.

Since the mid-1970s federal Medicaid and Medicare regulations have required facilities participating in those programs to

---

[16]Minn. Stat. Ann. §80D.08 (West 1986); Ariz. Rev. Stat. Ann. §20-1805 (Supp. 1988).

[17]Conn. Gen. Stat. Ann. §§17-116, 17-316 (West 1988); Ill. Ann. Stat. ch. 23, ¶3-1.5 (Smith-Hurd 1988). See Rowland v. Maker, 176 Conn. 57, 404 A.2d 894 (1978) (Medicaid cannot be denied unless assets are actually available); Cornue v. Department of Public Aid, 64 Ill. 2d 78, 354 N.E.2d 359 (1976) (upholding the Illinois statute).

respect enumerated residents' rights. Here again, OBRA '87 has made major changes, for the first time specifying residents' rights in a federal statute and elevating the importance of residents' rights in the process of assessing facility certification status. Many states have also independently adopted residents' rights statutes, as well as private right of action statutes permitting residents to sue to enforce those rights. Such laws are often vague, loosely worded, and subject to broad exceptions. Federal and state residents' rights laws do, however, establish a firm policy for protecting the rights of residents. Residents' rights statutes expose a facility to potential private liability and public sanction for violation of the rights they protect. Such laws also support owners and administrators who want to impress on their staff the need for respect of residents' rights.

§15.13 The Right to be Free from Physical and Chemical Restraints

One of the most frequently noted abuses in nursing facilities is the excessive use of restraints, especially chemical restraints.[1] Restraints occasionally may be necessary to deal temporarily with disturbed residents. Indeed, a facility may risk tort liability if it fails to control a disturbed or confused resident for that resident's own safety or for the safety of others.[2] It is not permissible, however, for a facility to restrain a resident merely for the convenience of its staff or so that the facility may operate with fewer employees.

---

§15.13 [1] Anon., Law, Research Can End Restraint Use in Nursing Homes, Say Panelists, 4 Quality of Care Newsletter (4) 6 (1989); Covert, Rodrigues, and Solomon, The Use of Mechanical and Chemical Restraints in Nursing Homes, 25 J. Am. Geriatric Socy. 85 (1977); Ray, Federspiel, and Schaffner, A Study of Antipsychotic Drug Use in Nursing Homes: Epidemiologic Evidence Suggesting Misuse, 70 Am. J. Pub. Health 485 (1980).

[2] Associated Health Systems, Inc. v. Jones, 185 Ga. App. 798, 366 S.E.2d 147 (1988); Juhnke v. Evangelical Lutheran Good Samaritan Home, 6 Kan. App. 2d 744, 634 P.2d 1132 (1981); Golden Villa Nursing Home v. Smith, 674 S.W.2d 343 (Texas Ct. App. 1984); Kujawski v. Arbor View Health Care Center, 139 Wis. 2d 455, 407 N.W.2d 249 (1987).

OBRA '87 specifies that nursing facility residents have: "[t]he right to be free from physical or mental abuse, corporal punishment, involuntary seclusion, and any physical or chemical restraints imposed for purposes of discipline or convenience and not required to treat the resident's medical symptoms."[3] It further provides that residents may be restrained only to protect their own physical safety or that of others, and then only under a physician's written order specifying the duration and circumstances of the restraint.[4] Finally, it specifies that psychopharmacologic drugs may be administered only if ordered by a physician as part of a written plan to eliminate or modify the symptoms for which the drugs are prescribed, and if the plan is annually reviewed by an external consultant for appropriateness.[5] The laws of many states are quite similar,[6] though some are even more specific. Ohio, for example, forbids the use of restraints for more than 12 hours in an emergency without a physician's order, requires the resident's physician to personally examine the resident before authorizing a restraint, and forbids authorization of restraints for more than 30 days unless the physician examines the patient again and renews the authorization.[7] Georgia requires that restrained residents be monitored every hour and released and exercised every two hours while awake.[8] Finally, a resident injured by restraints may sue for tort damages. A Texas jury, for example, recently awarded $39.4 million against a home in which an 84-year-old woman strangled

---

[3]42 U.S.C. §1395i-3(c)(1)(A)(ii) (Supp. V 1987), 42 U.S.C. §1396r(c)(1)(A)(ii) (Supp. V 1987).

[4]42 U.S.C. §1395i-3(c)(1)(A)(ii) (Supp. V 1987); 42 U.S.C. §1396r(c)(1)(A)(ii) (Supp. V 1987). HHS is to promulgate regulations specifying emergency situations in which restraints may be used until a doctor's order can reasonably be obtained.

[5]42 U.S.C. §1395i-3(c)(1)(D) (Supp. V 1987); 42 U.S.C. §1396r(c)(1)(D) (Supp. V 1987).

[6]Minn. Stat. Ann. §144.651(14) (West 1989); Fla. Stat. Ann. §400.022(j) (West 1986); Ky. Rev. Stat. §216.515(6) (1988); N.J. Stat. Ann. tit. 30, §13-3(f) (West 1981).

[7]Ohio Rev. Code §3721.13(13) (Page 1988).

[8]Off. Code Ga. Ann. §31-8-109 (1985).

while strapped in her bed (Texas Juries Get Tough on Restraints, 5 Quality of Care Advocate 5 (Mar./April 1990)).

There are often alternatives to drugs and physical restraints for dealing with confused or disturbed residents. For example, a variety of electronic devices have recently become available that notify facility staff if a resident wanders off, obviating the need for restraints. Training can also help to develop the attitudes and understanding that allow staff to cope with problem residents without using restraints.[9] Increased regulatory oversight of abuses of restraints may encourage facilities to adopt such approaches.

§15.14 Protection of Patient Property and Funds

Even publicly supported nursing facility residents receive a small monthly allowance with which they can purchase personal items and services such as clothing, cigarettes, candy, and transportation. These allowances are often held in "trust funds" for safekeeping until the resident needs them. There is considerable evidence that in the past the accounting for these funds was haphazard and embezzlement was common.[1] The Medicare and Medicaid Antifraud and Abuse Amendments of 1977 require an accounting for and prohibited commingling of these funds.[2]

---

[9]Soskis, Teaching Nursing Home Staff About Residents' Rights, 21 The Gerontologist 424, 427-428 (1981). See Associated Health Systems, Inc. v. Jones, 185 Ga. App. 798, 366 S.E.2d 147 (Ga. 1988) (holding facility liable for injury to a resident caused by another disturbed resident, observing that while residents' rights act prohibited facility from restraining the disturbed resident, it did not keep facility from restricting disturbed residents from public areas where conflict was likely or from subjecting them to additional observation and supervision, counselling, or behavioral controls.)

§15.14   [1]Kimsey, Tarbox, and Bragg, Abuse of the Elderly—The Hidden Agenda, I. The Caretakers and the Categories of Abuse, 29 J. Am. Geriatrics Socy. 465, 470-471 (1981); United States General Accounting Office, Improvements Needed in Managing and Monitoring Patients' Funds Maintained by Skilled Nursing Facilities and Intermediate Care Facilities (1976).

[2]Pub. L. No. 95-142, §21(a), 91 Stat. 1175, 1207.

OBRA '87 establishes more extensive and specific requirements for protecting patient funds. First, it forbids facilities from
requiring residents to deposit their personal funds with the
facility.[3] If a resident chooses to authorize a facility to maintain
personal funds, the resident must do so in writing.[4] The facility
must then deposit any resident's funds in excess of $50 in an
interest-bearing account separate from the facility's account
(crediting the interest to such account); maintain amounts under
$50 in a non-interest-bearing account; maintain a written record
of all transactions involving personal funds; afford the resident
or a legal representative reasonable access to the account; and
convey a resident's funds promptly to the estate upon his or her
death.[5] The facility must also notify Medicaid residents when
the amount in the resident's account comes within $200 of the
Medicaid asset limit, and thereby allow the resident to spend
the funds and avoid losing Medicaid eligibility.[6] Facilities must
purchase surety bonds or otherwise provide assurance of the
security of resident accounts.[7] Finally, the statute prohibits
facilities from charging personal funds for services covered by
Medicare or Medicaid.[8] State laws governing resident funds are
generally less specific,[9] but often require in addition a periodic
accounting to the resident.[10]

---

[3]42 U.S.C. §1395i-3(c)(6)(A)(i) (Supp. V 1987); 42 U.S.C. §1396r(c)(6)(A)(i)
(Supp. V 1987).

[4]42 U.S.C. §1395i-3(c)(6)(A)(ii) (Supp. V 1987); 42 U.S.C. §1396r(c)(6)(A)(ii)
(Supp. V 1987).

[5]42 U.S.C. §1395i-3(c)(6)(B) (Supp. V 1987); 42 U.S.C. §1396r(c)(6)(B)
(Supp. V 1987).

[6]42 U.S.C. §1396r(c)(6)(B)(iii) (Supp. V 1987).

[7]42 U.S.C. §1395i-3(c)(6)(C) (Supp. V 1987); 42 U.S.C. §1396r(c)(6)(C)
(Supp. V 1987).

[8]42 U.S.C. §1395i-3(c)(6)(D) (Supp. V 1987); 42 U.S.C. §1396r(c)(6)(C)
(Supp. V 1987).

[9]But see Ill. Rev. Stat. ch. 111½, ¶4152-201 (Smith-Hurd 1988); Md.
Health-Gen. Code Ann. §19-346 (1987 & Supp. 1989); Mo. Ann. Stat.
§198.090 (Vernon 1983) (all of which are at least as complex as the new
federal requirements).

[10]Wis. Stat. Ann. §50.09(1)(c) (West 1987) (monthly); Fla. Stat. Ann.
§400.022(d) (West 1986) (quarterly).

Protection of resident property within the institution presents an even more difficult problem than does protection of resident funds. Nursing facility residents—at least those who are alert—need ready access to their clothing and other personal items such as cosmetics and nonprescription drugs. Residents also often want to have at hand items that connect them with their past—jewelry, photographs, and mementos. Theft of personal property is one of the most common complaints concerning nursing facilities.[11] Property may be taken by employees or merely "borrowed" by other confused, wandering residents. State statutes often require facilities to allow residents to retain personal possessions as space permits unless the retention of such possessions would interfere with the rights of other residents.[12] Other states also require the facility to provide for the safekeeping of personal effects.[13] Protection of resident property is a task not readily subject to control through regulation or litigation and must be dealt with by a facility administration firmly committed to not tolerating pilfering in its facility.[14]

§15.15 The Right to be Free from Abuse

The most serious violation of residents' rights is intentional abuse. A recent study indicates that the prevalence of abuse, or of blatant neglect of elemental needs tantamount to abuse, in nursing facilities is very high.[1] Certainly the conditions in some

---

[11]Kimsey, Tarbox, and Bragg, supra n.1, at 470.

[12]N.H. Rev. Stat. Ann. §151:21.XIV (Supp. 1989); Ohio Rev. Code §3721.13(23) (1988).

[13]Minn. Stat. Ann. §144.651(22) (West 1989); Mich. Comp. Laws Ann. §333.20201(3)(c) (West Supp. 1988); Ann. Code Ga. §31-8-113(b) (1985) (also requires facility to keep a record of property deposited in secure part of facility).

[14]M. Kapp, Preventing Malpractice in Long-Term Care 108-112 (1987); Harris, Protecting Residents' Rights, 8 Am. Health Care Assn. J. 3 (Jan. 1982).

§15.15 [1]Pillemer and Moore, Abuse of Patients in Nursing Homes: Findings from a Random Sample of Staff (University of New Hampshire, Durham, New Hampshire) (1989). In this study of 577 licensed nurses and nurse's aides in 31 New Hampshire nursing homes, 81 percent admitted to

facilities are conducive to staff abuse of residents. These conditions include poor pay, undesirable working conditions, lack of training, and high absenteeism and turnover.[2] Furthermore, abuse is easily concealed. In many facilities, aides receive little direct supervision, particularly at night, and are often isolated with residents. Therefore, abuse by aides can go undetected by administrators and nurses.[3] Abused residents often do not complain, either because they are incapable of doing so or because they fear retaliation.[4] Even when residents do register complaints, they may not be believed.

Physical abuse of residents constitutes battery and is both a crime and actionable at the common law. Abuse also violates the residents' rights statutes of many states, which prohibit mental and physical abuse[5] or abuse and neglect.[6] The federal Medicaid law provides funding for Medicaid fraud control units in the offices of state attorneys general and specifies that the functions of these units must include reviewing complaints of resident abuse or neglect in facilities that receive Medicaid payments and must also include criminal prosecution of verified complaints.[7] A facility or individual convicted of patient abuse or neglect must be excluded from participation in Medicare or Medicaid.[8] As stated earlier, OBRA '87 requires states to investigate charges of resident neglect or abuse and of misappropria-

---

having observed at least one act of psychological abuse in the preceding year, and 40 percent to having committed a psychologically abusive act themselves. Thirty-six percent said they witnessed at least one act of physical abuse, and 10 percent admitted to having physically abused a resident themselves.

[2]Kimsey, Tarbox, and Bragg, Abuse of the Elderly—The Hidden Agenda, I. The Caretakers and Categories of Abuse, 29 J. Am. Geriatrics Socy. 465, 468 (1981); Stannard, Old Folks and Dirty Work: The Social Conditions for Patient Abuse in a Nursing Home, 329, 329-331 (1973).

[3]Stannard, supra n.2, at 333-335.

[4]Id. at 335-336.

[5]Conn. Gen. Stat. Ann. §19a-550 (West Supp. 1989); Ky. Rev. Stat. §216.515(6) (Michie/Bobbs-Merrill Supp. 1988); N.C. Gen. Stat. §131E-117(6) (1988).

[6]Ill. Ann. Stat. ch. 111½, ¶4152-107 (Smith-Hurd 1988).

[7]42 U.S.C. §1396b(q)(4) (1982).

[8]42 U.S.C. §1320a-7(a)(2) (Supp. V 1987).

tion of resident property.[9] If allegations involving a nurse's aide are substantiated after the aide is given an opportunity for a hearing to rebut such allegations, the state must retain this information in its nurse's aide registry and pass it on (accompanied by a brief response by the aide) to any who inquire of the registry.[10]

To encourage disclosure of abuse, several states have adopted abuse reporting statutes, some of which apply generally to abuse of the elderly and others of which are specifically applicable to nursing facility resident abuse.[11] These statutes vary in several respects, including who is required to report abuse, to whom the report should be made, and the consequences for failure to report. The statutes typically provide for confidentiality and immunity from civil or criminal liability for those who in good faith report abuse.[12] Several statutes also attempt to protect reporters against retaliation.[13] Since seriously abused residents often come into the care of physicians, who are becoming more and more accustomed to child abuse reporting, these statutes may prove helpful in ferreting out abuse.

§15.16 Dignitary, Privacy, Expressive, Associational, and Informational Rights

Federal and state residents' rights laws also protect a variety of dignitary, privacy, expressive, associational, and informational

---

[9]42 U.S.C. §1395i-3(g)(1)(C) (Supp. V 1987); 42 U.S.C. §1396r(g)(1)(C) (Supp. V 1987). See supra §15.7.

[10]42 U.S.C. §§1395i-3(e)(2)(B), (g)(1)(C) (Supp. V 1987); 42 U.S.C. §§1396r(e)(3)(B), (g)(1)(C) (Supp. V 1987).

[11]American Bar Association, Model Recommendations: Intermediate Sanctions for Enforcement of Quality of Care in Nursing Homes 32-34 (1981); Comment, Nursing Home Patient Abuse Reporting: An Analysis of the Washington Statutory Response, 16 Gonzaga L. Rev. 609 (1981).

[12]See, e.g., Ill. Ann. Stat. ch. 111½, ¶4153-609 (Smith-Hurd 1988); Mo. Ann. Stat. §198.070(7) (Vernon Supp. 1989); Tex. Health & Safety Code §444c.16(c)(d).

[13]Mich. Comp. Laws Ann. §333.21771 (West 1980); Ill. Ann. Stat. ch. 111½, ¶4153-609 (Smith-Hurd 1988).

rights. Some of these laws are very specific in their requirements. Under OBRA '87, for example, residents are entitled to choose their personal attending physician; to be informed participants in planning their care and treatment; to have privacy in communications and meetings with others; to have access to and be assured of confidential treatment of their personal and clinical records; to receive notice before their room or roommate is changed; to participate in resident and family groups; to examine federal or state survey results and correction plans; and to be informed of their rights at the time of admission and on reasonable request thereafter.[1] Specific and detailed provisions also assure that persons from outside the facility, such as family members, advocates, and service providers, will have access to the residents. Such provisions also protect the resident's right to refuse visitors and the facility's ability to enforce reasonable visitation policies with respect to social visitors.[2]

Other rights provisions, however, while equally important, may be more difficult to interpret and enforce. It may not be clear, for example, what is meant by provisions that assure a resident privacy in accommodations, or receipt of services with "reasonable accommodations of individual needs or services," or participation "in social, religious, and community activities."[3] Rights to accommodation of needs and to participation in activities are mandated only to the extent that they do not interfere with the rights of other residents, recognizing the fact that rights may sometimes come in conflict.[4] Facility management must be willing to train staff in the importance and meaning of such rights in order to ensure their implementation.

---

§15.16 [1]42 U.S.C. §§1395i-3(c)(1)(A)(i), (iii), (iv), (v), (vii), (ix), (B) (Supp. V 1987); 42 U.S.C. §§1396r(c)(1)(A)(i), (iii), (iv), (v), (vii), (ix), (B) (Supp. V 1987).

[2]42 U.S.C. §1395i-3(c)(3) (Supp. V 1987); 42 U.S.C. §1396r(c)(3) (Supp. V 1987).

[3]42 U.S.C. §1395i-3(c)(1)(A)(iii), (v), (vii), (Supp. V 1987); 42 U.S.C. §§1396r(c)(1)(A)(iii), (v), (vii), (Supp. V 1987).

[4]42 U.S.C. §§1395i-3(c)(1)(A)(v), (viii) (Supp. V 1987); 42 U.S.C. §§1396r(c)(1)(A)(v), (viii) (Supp. V 1987). Such conflicts may arise, for example, if one resident in a room chooses to smoke or watch television and the other objects.

State residents' rights statutes are quite similar to the federal statute, though some states provide additional rights. Georgia, for example, explicitly permits residents to use tobacco or consume alcohol.[5] Florida requires facility personnel to respect resident privacy by knocking before entering a resident's room.[6] Kentucky guarantees residents "the right to be suitably dressed at all times and given assistance when needed in maintaining body hygiene and good grooming."[7] New York assures a right to kosher food.[8]

§15.17 Transfer and Discharge Issues

A resident may be involuntarily discharged from a nursing facility or transferred between nursing facilities for a variety of reasons. For example, a discharge or transfer may be initiated by a decision of a state Medicaid agency that a resident no longer needs nursing care, or a decision of a facility that the resident is in default on financial obligations to the facility or is a troublemaker. There is considerable, though disputed, evidence that precipitous, unplanned relocation of elderly and debilitated nursing facility residents can seriously injure their health or even kill them.[1] Both the federal and state governments, therefore, have adopted provisions to protect residents against such transfers.[2]

If the transfer is initiated by the state Medicaid agency based on a utilization review determination, the resident (as well as the nursing facility administrator, attending physician, Medicaid agency, and, if possible, the next of kin or sponsor) is entitled

---

[5]Ga. Code Ann. §31-8-112(c) (1985) (unless a contrary policy of the facility is disclosed at admission and subject to facility safety rules and the rights of other residents).

[6]Fla. Stat. Ann. §400.022(1)(h) (1986) (except in emergencies).

[7]Ky. Rev. Stat. §216.515(20) (Michie/Bobbs-Merrill Supp. 1988).

[8]N.Y. Pub. Health Law §2803-c(3)(k) (McKinney 1985).

§15.17 [1]See supra §15.1 n.25.

[2]See Cohen, supra §15.1 n.25.

to notice of the decision.[3] If the decision results in reduction of Medicaid benefits, the recipient is entitled to a hearing to review the decision and to various procedural rights.[4] However, if a discharge decision is based on a determination by a facility or physician that nursing facility care is no longer necessary, the resident is not entitled to a hearing, even though the effect is to reduce Medicaid benefits.[5] If the discharge is based on a state decision to terminate Medicaid participation of the facility, the resident also has no constitutional right to a hearing.[6]

Facility-initiated transfers are controlled by federal and state law. Under OBRA '87, a facility may not transfer or discharge a resident unless:

   (i)   the transfer or discharge is necessary to meet the resident's welfare and the resident's welfare cannot be met in the facility;
   (ii) the transfer or discharge is appropriate because the resident's health has improved sufficiently so the resident no longer needs the services provided by the facility;
   (iii) the safety of individuals in the facility is endangered;
   (iv) the health of individuals in the facility would otherwise be endangered;
   (v)   the resident has failed, after reasonable and appropriate notice, to pay [or have Medicare or Medicaid pay] an allowable charge . . .
   (vi) the facility ceases to operate.[7]

The cause of the transfer or discharge must be documented in the resident's record, in most instances by a physician. Except in emergencies, the resident is also entitled to 30 days' notice

---

[3] 42 C.F.R. §§456.337, 456.437 (1988).
[4] 42 C.F.R. §§431.200, 431.220, 431.242 (1988).
[5] Blum v. Yaretsky, 457 U.S. 991 (1982).
[6] O'Bannon v. Town Court Nursing Center, 447 U.S. 773 (1980).
[7] 42 U.S.C. §1395i-3(c)(2)(A) (Supp. V 1987); 42 U.S.C. §1396r(c)(2)(A) (Supp. V 1987).

for transfer or discharges not initiated under clauses (ii) and (iii). The resident is also entitled to information about the right to appeal and how to contact the long-term care ombudsman or other relevant state advocacy agencies.[8] The state must also provide a fair process for hearing appeals from residents transferred or discharged by facilities, which must comply with guidelines established by HHS.[9] Several states have also addressed transfer and discharge issues,[10] though their statutes are generally less detailed than the federal law and will probably be preempted by it.[11]

§15.18 Private Enforcement of Residents' Rights

The rights provided by OBRA '87 and by most state laws are primarily enforced by the state licensing and certification authorities. Often, however, private litigation may be a more effective strategy for enforcement. Some courts have in the past

---

[8]42 U.S.C. §1395i-3(c)(2)(B) (Supp. V 1987); 42 U.S.C. §1396r(c)(2)(B) (Supp. V 1987).

[9]42 U.S.C. §§1395i-3(e)(3), (f)(3) (Supp. V 1987); 42 U.S.C. §§1396r(e)(3), (f)(3) (Supp. V 1987). The facility is also responsible for providing sufficient preparation and orientation to assure a safe transfer. 42 U.S.C. §1395i-3(c)(2)(C) (Supp. V 1987); 42 U.S.C. §1396r(c)(2)(C) (Supp. V 1987).

[10]See Conn. Gen. Stat. Ann. §19a-550(a)(4) (West Supp. 1989); Wis. Stat. Ann. §§50.03(5m), 50.09(1)(j) (West 1987 and Supp. 1988); Ill. Ann. Stat. ch. 111½, ¶¶4153-401 to 4153-423 (Smith-Hurd 1988). For an account of the operation of one such statute, see Hyman, The Nursing Home and Community Residence Facility Resident's Protection Act of 1985: Boon or Bane? 32 Howard L.J. 39 (1989).

[11]One of the issues latent in legislation prohibiting transfers without notice is whether a state can force a nursing facility that is losing money and wishes to close its doors to stay in operation until residents can be safely transferred. In Birnbaum et al. v. State of N.Y., 73 N.Y.2d 638, 543 N.Y.S.2d 23, 541 N.E.2d 23 (1989), a facility sued the state, claiming that the imposition of a receivership to permit orderly transfer or residents resulted in a loss to the facility that constituted a "taking" for which it should be compensated. The court rejected this contention, noting that the facility was aware of the notice requirement and should have given notice earlier of its intention to close.

permitted private lawsuits to enforce federal Medicaid regulations mandating respect for residents' rights.[1] Other courts have rejected private enforcement of the Medicaid requirements, holding that Congress intended that Medicaid regulations be enforced only through administrative action, thereby precluding private enforcement.[2] OBRA '87, along with its legislative history, specifies that its administrative remedies do not preclude common-law remedies, including private enforcement of requirements.[3]

State residents' rights statutes are not necessarily enforceable by private suits. Makas v. Hillhaven,[4] for example, rejected an argument that violation of the North Carolina residents' rights statute constituted negligence per se, noting that the statute was enforceable by the state administrative agency or through injunctive relief, not through a damage suit. To avoid such restrictive interpretations, a number of states have adopted statutes specifically permitting private lawsuits to recover for the violation of residents' rights.[5]

In Stiffelman v. Abrams,[6] a lawsuit was permitted under such a statute seeking substantial actual and punitive damages against a nursing facility by the estate of a resident who allegedly died from physical abuse suffered while in the facility. In another

---

§15.18 [1]Roberson v. Wood, 464 F. Supp. 983 (E.D. Ill. 1979); Butler, A Long-Term Care Strategy for Legal Services, 14 Clearinghouse Rev. 618 (1980); Wilson, Nursing Home Residents' Rights: Are They Enforceable? 18 The Gerontologist 255, 260-261 (1978).

[2]Stewart v. Bernstein, 769 F.2d 1088 (5th Cir. 1985); Fuzie v. Manor Care, 461 F. Supp. 689 (N.D. Ohio 1977).

[3]42 U.S.C. §1396r(h)(8) (Supp. V 1987); House Report No. 100-391(I), Omnibus Budget Reconciliation Act of 1987, at 472 (1987).

[4]589 F. Supp. 736 (M.D.N.C. 1984).

[5]See Cal. Health & Safety Code §1430 (West Supp. 1989); Mass. Gen. Laws. ch. 111 §70E (1985); N.J. Stat. Ann. §30:13-8 (West 1981); N.Y. Pub. Health Laws §2801(d) (McKinney 1985); American Bar Association, Model Recommendations: Intermediate Sanctions for Enforcement of Quality of Care in Nursing Home Facilities 30-32 (1981); S. Johnson, N. Terry, and M. Wolfe, Nursing Homes and the Law: State Regulation and Private Litigation §§2-6, 2-7 (1985).

[6]655 S.W.2d 522 (Mo. 1983).

case, a Georgia jury awarded $50,000 for emotional distress resulting from an involuntary transfer in violation of the state residents' rights statute.[7] In a third case, a New Jersey jury held a nursing facility and physician liable for $100,000 because they improperly transferred a resident.[8] Bregandy v. Richardson,[9] on the other hand, refused to permit the use of the state residents' rights statute as a ground for recovery in an ordinary negligence case.

Several state private-right-of-action statutes encourage private enforcement by providing for attorneys' fees awards, minimum damages, punitive damages, or multiple damages to encourage private enforcement.[10] Harris v. Manor Healthcare Corp.[11] upheld the grant of multiple damages under the Illinois statute, even though the plaintiff had not shown aggravated circumstances, recognizing that the statute was intended to encourage enforcement by private attorneys general. Wills v. De Kalb Area Retirement center[12] held that an action under the Illinois statute survives the death of the resident.

Even in the absence of a state private right of action, residents may sue to protect their rights under common-law tort or contract theories.[13]Free v. Franklin Guest Home,[14] for example, permitted a lawsuit based on provisions in an admission contract guaranteeing protection from abuse. Fuzie v. Manor

---

[7]Jackson v. Beverly Enter., C-85258 (Fulton Co. Ga., filed March 14, 1982), cited in Nemore, Protecting Nursing Home Residents: Tort Actions Are One Way, 21 Trial 54, 61 n.22 (Dec. 1985).

[8]Brehm v. Pine Acres Nursing Home, 190 N.J. Super. 103, 462 A.2d 178 (1983).

[9]134 Misc. 2d 327, 510 N.Y.S.2d 984 (Sup. Ct. 1987).

[10]Ill. Rev. Stat. ch. 111½, ¶4153-605 (Smith-Hurd 1988); Mo. Ann. Stat. §198.093 (Vernon 1983); N.Y. Pub. Health Law §2801-d (McKinney 1985).

[11]111 Ill. 2d 350, 489 N.E.2d 1374 (1986).

[12]175 Ill. App. 3d 833, 530 N.E.2d 1066 (1988).

[13]See, discussing such actions, Boggs and Connor, Nursing Home Tort Victims: Rights and Remedies, 53 Fla. Bar J. 11-14 (Feb. 1989); Note, Nursing Homes: Standards of Care, Sources of Potential Liability, Defenses to Suit and Reform, 37 Drake L. Rev. 699 (1988).

[14]397 So. 2d 47 (La. App. 1981).

Care[15] recognized a resident's right to sue as the intended beneficiary of the Medicaid provider contract between the state and the facility.

E. Conclusion

This chapter has emphasized the distinctive characteristics of law as it affects extended care facilities. Long-term care facilities are different from other healthcare facilities, and it is not surprising that in many respects the law pertaining to them is unique. The vast majority of legal issues that arise in long-term care facilities, however, are much the same as those that arise in any other institutional healthcare context. It is important, therefore, to consider not only the issues raised by this chapter, but also those raised in each of the other chapters, to competently address the legal problems of extended care facilities.

---

[15]461 F. Supp. 689 (N.D. Ohio 1977).

16 Legal Characteristics of the Health Maintenance Organization

Barbara Allan Shickich

§16.0 Introduction

Health maintenance organizations (HMOs) are similar in function to hospitals. Many of the same issues facing hospitals as providers of medical care also face HMOs. In addition, HMOs themselves pose issues for hospitals and healthcare providers. As the healthcare marketplace becomes increasingly competitive, hospitals are confronted by many options that frequently involve HMOs and other alternative delivery systems such as preferred provider organizations (PPOs) and competitive medical plans (CMPs). This chapter will define HMOs, PPOs, and CMPs and describe their unique legal features, emphasizing state and federal regulation of HMOs.

To place the current growth of HMOs and alternative delivery systems in historical context, this chapter also will trace the origins of HMOs and their early struggle for survival. The phrase "health maintenance organization" is only approximately 20 years old and was coined with the effort to obtain federal legislation to support the development of HMOs.[1] Since the early 1970s, the structure and operations of HMOs have been defined largely by state and federal legislation. Thus this chapter will provide an overview of the key provisions of the Model Health Maintenance Organization Act, adopted by the National Association of Insurance Commissioners, and the federal Health Maintenance Organization Act. It also describes the corporate structure of HMOs, state and federal limitations on HMO operations, and the role of HMOs in federal reimbursement programs such as Medicare and Medicaid.

A. The Origins of HMOs

§16.1 Outpatient Family Practice Plans

Health maintenance organizations existed in form long before the term was used to describe them. HMO-like entities originated in response to a need to provide healthcare at a reasonable cost to a defined population. A cornerstone in the delivery of care through an HMO was, and still is, outpatient care: reducing inpatient care, through a change in quantity and type of

---

§16.0   [1]J. Falkson, HMOs and the Politics of Health System Reform 32 (1980).

outpatient care, reduces the cost to the patient. Thus, HMOs began as outpatient family practice plans and were premised on prepayment of a fixed fee for a specific range of health services.

The first form of HMO might well have been the Boston Dispensary as it was operated before World War I.[1] The objective of the dispensary's administrator, Michael Davis, was similar to that of many early HMOs—the provision of quality healthcare, including preventive care, at a reasonable cost. He envisioned an outpatient clinic that not only would treat acute illnesses, but also would impart important principles of illness prevention such as cleanliness and proper diet. The vision was not shared by his contemporaries or colleagues.[2] At that time, outpatient hospital care was relegated to the status of a poor stepchild, with hospital clinic outreach programs "suffer[ing] from the stigma of welfare medicine and the antagonism of many ordinary physicians who saw them as a portent of 'medical socialism.'"[3]

§16.2 *Prepaid Group Practice Plans*

The taint of "medical socialism" associated with outpatient family practice plans did not fade with the development of prepaid group practice plans. If anything, its hue intensified. Further, the prepaid group practice plans ran afoul of the ten principles for medical service enunciated by the American Medical Association in June 1934.[1] The second and third principles stated that "no third party must be permitted to come between the patient and his physician in any medical relation" and that "the patient shall have absolute freedom to choose a duly qualified doctor of medicine . . . from among all those qualified to practice and who are willing to give service."[2] And the eighth principle stated that "any form of medical service

---

§16.1   [1]C. Rosenberg, The Care of Strangers 320 (1987).
[2]See id. for a discussion of this vision in a historical context.
[3]Id. at 322.
§16.2   [1]102 J.A.M.A. 2200-2201 (1934).
[2]Id.

should include within its scope all qualified physicians of the locality covered by its operation who wish to give service under the conditions established."[3] Prepaid group practice plans defined the relationship between the patient and the physician, determining the circumstances in which the plan would provide reimbursement for physician services. The patient could seek care only from those physicians who were part of the group practice. The cost of care provided by other physicians would not be paid for by the plan.

Notwithstanding these obstacles, prepaid group practice plans developed during the 1930s and 1940s. Some of the plans withered and died before the 1950s. Others survived, and some even thrived, despite strenuous challenges from organized medicine. In fact, some HMOs founded in the 1930s and 1940s have grown to be the leaders in the industry.

Many of the plans originated as contracts with employers. Plans that were generated and controlled by physicians, while inconsistent with the edicts of the medical establishment, suffered less from the taint of medical socialism and more from the charge of "unethical medical practice." In contrast, the plans that arose out of the cooperative movement were a genuine attempt to reorganize medical care by including not only principles of group practice, prepayment, and preventive medicine, but also consumer participation.[4]

In 1929 the Ross-Loos Medical Group, formed by physicians Donald Ross and H. Clifford Loos, contracted with the Los Angeles Water and Power Department to provide prepaid, comprehensive services for about 2,000 workers and their

---

[3]Id. at 2201.

[4]For a complete discussion of the political dynamics of the early development of prepaid group practice plans and health insurance in general, see Starr, The Triumph of Accommodation: The Rise of Private Health Plans in America 1929-1959, 7 J. Health Pol. Poly. & L. 580-628 (1982). Much of the discussion in §16.2 is based on the historical information found in that article and the references contained therein. Starr's analysis is centered on the role the AMA played in limiting the development of alternative healthcare financing options. For an excellent history of HMO development, see W. MacColl, Group Practice and Prepayment of Medical Care (1966).

families. The Ross-Loos Clinic grew with the addition of other employee groups to more than 12,000 workers and 25,000 dependents by 1935.

The Kaiser Foundation Health Plans had their origins with a surgeon named Sidney Garfield and several associates who provided medical care on a prepaid basis for men working at the Grand Coulee Dam for Henry J. Kaiser in 1938. During World War II, the Kaiser prepaid, comprehensive healthcare plan was expanded to include workers in shipyards and steel mills on the West Coast. In 1942 two Permanente Foundations were established, one to run a medical program in the Vancouver, Washington-Portland, Oregon region and one to run a medical program in the Oakland and Fontana, California, regions. Originally only serving Kaiser employees and their families, the plans were opened to the public in 1945. The Kaiser Foundation Health Plans have continued to grow, building a nationwide network of hospitals, clinics, and enrollees.

The first healthcare cooperative in the United States was established in 1929 at Elk City, Oklahoma. A "healthcare cooperative" may be defined as an organization established for the delivery of healthcare in a manner consistent with principles of equality and collective action and that emphasizes group practice, prepayment, preventive medicine, and consumer participation. The Elk City cooperative was created by a physician, Michael Shadid, who believed that medical care could be provided in a manner consistent with the democratic principles of the farm cooperatives surrounding Elk City. The federal government also supported the development of rural health cooperatives through prepayment plans set up by the Farm Security Administration in the 1930s and early 1940s.

Group Health Association of Washingtion, D.C. was established as a nonprofit cooperative in 1937 by the employees of the Federal Home Loan Bank. The Association was governed by a board elected by the members (enrollees), who initially were all federal employees. The plan hired physicians and provided medical and hospital care on a prepaid basis.

Group Health Cooperative of Puget Sound was established as a healthcare cooperative in Seattle, Washington in 1947. It was founded by members of the Grange, by the Aero-Mechanics Union, and by local consumer cooperatives. Capital for the project came from 400 families who contributed $100 apiece. The cooperative hired its own physicians and purchased a clinic and an adjoining 60-bed hospital. It offered comprehensive medical and hospital care on a prepaid basis. Today, Group Health Cooperative is the largest and most successful of the country's cooperative-style HMOs.

On the other side of the country, in New York City, a prepaid group practice plan was developed to alleviate the major source of financial distress among city employees, indebtedness caused by illness. Under the guidance and at the insistence of Mayor Fiorello La Guardia, 22 group practices including over 400 doctors were established in 1947 to provide medical services through the Health Insurance Plan of New York. The plan did not include hospital care because of limitations imposed at that time by New York state law. Thus, enrollees were required to enter into a separate contract with Blue Cross of New York for hospital care.

All of these fledgling prepaid group practices suffered from the slings and arrows of organized medicine. In many cases the antagonism took the form of disciplinary action by the local medical societies against the physicians participating in the plans. Frequently the action consisted of expulsion from the medical society, if the doctor was a member, or denial of admission if he was not. Lack of membership was a serious matter because physicians' hospital admitting privileges were often contingent on it.

Drs. Donald Ross and H. Clifford Loos were expelled by their local medical societies. In the case of the Elk City cooperative health plan, Dr. Shadid's state medical license was challenged repeatedly by the physician-controlled licensing authority and was retained only through intercession of the Oklahoma Farmers' Union with the governor and state legislature. Rather than expel Dr. Shadid and risk litigation, the county medical society dissolved and then reorganized 18 months later without him.

The American Medical Association (AMA) itself undertook

a campaign to quash Group Health Association. Cooperating with the local medical society, the AMA "threatened reprisals against any doctors who worked for the plan, prevented them from obtaining consultations and referrals and succeeded in persuading every hospital in the District of Columbia to deny them admitting privileges."[5] As a result of these actions, in 1938 the Justice Department indicted the AMA, the local medical organizations, and their officers for conspiracy in restraint of trade to destroy Group Health Association in violation of the Sherman Antitrust Act. In its defense, the AMA argued that medicine was a profession, not a trade, and that the antitrust laws did not apply to it. While the lower federal court accepted this view, the court of appeals and Supreme Court upheld the antitrust conviction.[6]

Group Health Cooperative of Puget Sound (GHC) suffered from similar efforts by the local medical society in King County, Washington to restrain trade in the furnishing of prepaid medical and hospital care. In 1949 GHC fought back and brought a civil suit against the King County Medical Society,[7] the King County Medical Service Bureau,[8] the King County Medical Service

---

[5]Starr, supra n.4, at 595.

[6]United States v. AMA, 110 F.2d 703 (D.C. Cir. 1940), affd., 317 U.S. 519 (1943). The court of appeals commented that the disciplinary action by the medical association "is just as much in restraint of trade as if it were directed against any other occupation or employment or business. And, of course, the fact that the defendants are physicians and medical organizations is of no significance. . . ." 110 F.2d at 711. The Supreme Court concurred with this conclusion: "As the Court of Appeals properly remarked, the calling or occupation of the individual physicians charged as defendants is immaterial if the purpose and effect of their conspiracy was such obstruction and restraint of the business of [GHA]." 317 U.S. at 528.

[7]The King County Medical Society was a nonprofit corporation composed of all but a very small number of licensed physicians (approximately 950) residing and practicing medicine in the county.

[8]The King County Medical Service Bureau was an unincorporated association composed of approximately 600 physicians who were members of the society.

Corporation,[9] a public hospital district, a private hospital, and several individual physicians.[10]

The dispute arose over GHC's industrial contracts, which competed with the Medical Service Corporation and, according to the Washington Supreme Court, offered more complete medical service.[11] The Medical Society had undertaken certain specific actions to limit contract medicine solely to that provided by the Medical Service Corporation. It provided in Article III, §8 of its bylaws that physicians "who shall engage in contract practice unless the same shall previously have been authorized by the Board of Trustees of this Society, or who as physician or surgeon shall serve on the staff of or perform work for the patients of, or shall perform work in, any institution or group or organization unless such services or work shall previously have been authorized by the Board of Trustees of this Society, shall be liable to censure, suspension or expulsion." It further adopted a resolution stating that the board of trustees considered it unethical for any member of the society to consult with any physician who was not a member of the society and who was doing contract practice on any contract patient. Finally, the society caused major hospitals in King County to adopt and enforce a bylaw or regulation restricting the right to become staff members or to practice therein to members of the King County Medical Society.

Although the defendants at the time of trial and on appeal argued that GHC services and facilities were inferior and that the GHC plan violated the AMA canon of ethics, the Washington Supreme Court found that the focus of the society's objection was not legitimately directed at the quality of care provided, but rather at the economic impact of GHC's industrial contracts. The Medical Society conceded that the GHC physicians would be admitted into the society even if they continued their individual membership contracts so long as they discontinued their indus-

---

[9]The King County Medical Service Corporation was a nonprofit corporation organized by members of the society to furnish medical care and hospitalization to the employees of businesses and industries in the county.

[10]Group Health Coop. of Puget Sound v. King County Medical Socy., 39 Wash. 2d 586 (1951).

[11]Id. at 602.

trial practice. Consequently, the court concluded that "this fact alone is sufficient to indicate that the Society's primary motive in opposing the Cooperative and its staff members is to restrain the competition which the Cooperative provides through its industrial contracts."[12]

In analyzing the prohibition against restraints of trade or competition found in Article XII, §22 of the Washington State constitution, the court found that "monopolies affecting price or production in essential service trades and professions can be as harmful to the public interest as monopolies in the sale or production of tangible goods."[13] The court concluded that the actions by the defendants were in violation of the constitution and enjoined the Medical Society from following any course of conduct that would have the effect of excluding applicants from membership in the society, discouraging consultations, and excluding physicians from practicing in hospitals on the sole ground that they were practicing contract medicine.

Through the courts, the prepaid group practice plans won the right to be free from attacks by organized medicine. By 1958 at least one writer had concluded that "all in all, group health plans now have sufficient legal approval to encourage their

---

[12]Id. at 638. The court went on to support a finding of restraint of trade:

> There can be no question but that the purpose of the combination in the instant case is to preempt and control all contract medicine practice in King County. If respondents are successful in this effort, there will be no competition in the contract medicine field. Members of the public will have no opportunity to choose between two or more plans offering this type or service. The result will be complete monopoly of this product throughout the county.

Id. at 640.

[13]In analyzing the application of Article XII, §22, the court found all elements of a monopoly present:

> It therefore appears that, in the relationship established and course of conduct pursued by respondents, there are present all three elements essential to the establishment of a monopoly or trust, within the meaning of the constitution. There is a combination or other arrangement between two or more corporations and associations; it is concerned with the production and sale of a product— prepaid medical and hospital service; and the purpose of the combination is to limit the production and fix the prices of that service with the object in view of restraining competition and creating a monopoly.

Id. at 645.

widespread growth."[14] The widespread growth did not come, however, until almost two decades later, and then only with the support of the federal government.

Between 1970 and 1973 both houses of Congress analyzed national health insurance and federal support for the development of HMOs. In 1973 Title XIII of the Public Health Service Act[15] was adopted and become known as the Federal Health Maintenance Organization Act of 1973. Among other things, the act provided federal financial assistance for the development of HMOs. As a result, hundreds of prepaid health care organizations have been developed since its implementation.

B. Defining the Alphabet Soup of Managed Care Systems

§16.3 Alternative Delivery Systems

Changes in methods for reimbursing healthcare and the increasing emphasis on cost containment and operational efficiency have led to the development of a variety of systems that combine healthcare insurance with healthcare delivery. These systems emphasize comprehensive healthcare and are called alternative delivery systems (ADSs) because they offer an alternative to traditional fee-for-service healthcare. Sometimes ADSs are referred to as managed care systems, because they provide a holistic approach to the delivery of healthcare through monitoring the use of healthcare services (utilization management) and giving physicians incentives to provide only healthcare services that are medically necessary and to do so in the least costly manner. ADSs include health maintenance organizations, pre-

---

[14]Hansen, Group Health Plans: A Twenty-Year Legal Review, 42 Minn. L. Rev. 548 (1958).
[15]42 U.S.C. §300e.

ferred provider organizations (PPOs), and competitive medical plans (CMPs).[1]

§16.4 Health Maintenance Organizations

An HMO may be described as "an organization which brings together a comprehensive range of medical services in a single organization to assure a patient of convenient access to health care services."[1] Three principles characterize an HMO:

(1) It is an organized system for the delivery of health care which brings together health care providers.

(2) Such an arrangement makes available basic health care which the enrolled group might reasonably require, including emphasis on the prevention of illness or disability.

(3) The payments will be made on a prepayment basis, whether by the individual enrollees, medicare, medicaid, or through employer-employee arrangements.[2]

An HMO may be a single entity or a group of entities bound together by contracts. The components of the HMO include:

- an organized health care delivery system capable of providing or arranging for ambulatory, inpatient, emergency and preventive medical services;
- voluntarily enrolled families and individuals who have

---

§16.3 [1]For an overview of ADSs, including HMOs, PPOs, and CMPs, see National Health Lawyers Association, Introduction to Alternative Delivery Mechanisms: HMOs, PPOs & CMPs (1986). See also Cowan, Alternative Health Care Delivery Systems: Health Maintenance Organizations and Preferred Provider Organizations, 1986 Legal Med. Ann. 235-250.

§16.4 [1]National Association of Insurance Commissioners (NAIC), Model Health Maintenance Organization Act, II Model Regulation Service at 430-432 (May 1982) (hereinafter Model HMO Act).

[2]Id.

chosen to contract individually or as members of a group with the HMO for health services;
- a financial plan that guarantees delivery of services on a prenegotiated and prepaid basis;
- an identifiable administrative organization that ensures legal, fiscal, public and professional accountability;
- arrangements by which the organization significantly bears the risk of providing health services and in some instances requires providers to share the risk.[3]

By both definition and structure, an HMO is vertically integrated, combining the functions of healthcare insurer and provider of healthcare services.

The National Association of Insurance Commissioners Model HMO Act includes these components in its suggested definition of an HMO:

Health maintenance organization means any person that undertakes to provide or arrange for basic health care services to enrollees on a prepaid basis. The organization may provide physician services directly through physician employees or under arrangements with individual physicians or a group or groups of physicians. The organization may also provide or arrange for other health care services on a prepayment or other financial basis.[4]

---

[3]J. Kress and J. Singer, HMO Handbook: A Guide for the Development of Prepaid Group Practice HMOs (1975).

[4]Model HMO Act, §2(6). The act also contains the following definitions of terms included in the definition of HMO:

"Basic health care services" means emergency care, inpatient hospital and physician care, and outpatient medical services. It does not include mental health services or services for alcohol or drug abuse.

"Health care services" means any services included in the furnishing of such care or hospitalization, as well as the furnishing to any person of any and all other services for the purpose of preventing, alleviating, curing, or healing human illness, injury or physical disability.

"Person" means any natural or artificial person including but not limited to individuals, partnerships, associations, trusts, or corporations.

Id. at §§2(2), 2(5), 2(7).

These various ways of describing an HMO allow wide latitude in the structure of the HMO, particularly in its arrangement for the provision of healthcare services. All HMOs, however, may be categorized as "open panel" or "closed panel" HMOs. The type of panel refers to the contractual relationship between the HMO and the physicians who provide care to the HMO members. In an open panel HMO, the HMO contracts with a number of individual physicians to provide healthcare services in their own offices. The physicians may provide care to fee-for-service patients as well as HMO members. In a closed panel HMO, the HMO employs or contracts with one or more single- or multi-specialty physician groups to provide primary healthcare services in central medical facilities owned or leased by the HMO. Physicians in a closed panel HMO provide care exclusively to HMO members.

Another way of identifying HMOs has been set forth by Interstudy, a healthcare research organization devoted to the study of HMOs that publishes an annual census of HMOs. Interstudy identifies four basic practice models: staff model plans, group model plans, individual practice associations, and primary care networks. The federal HMO act also recognizes these four models.[5] Each is distinguished from the others by the relationship between the HMO and its physician providers.

§16.4.1 Staff Model Plans

A staff model HMO is one in which the physicians and other healthcare providers are employed by the HMO. A staff model HMO also is a closed panel HMO in that it employs the physician groups who provide primary healthcare services to its enrollees in facilities provided by the HMO. Pursuant to the federal HMO Act, the health professionals in a staff model HMO are employees of the HMO who

---

[5]42 U.S.C. §300e(b)(3)(A).

(1) Provide services to HMO members at an HMO facility subject to the staff policies and operational procedures of the HMO;

(2) Engage in the coordinated practice of their profession and provide to members of the HMO the health services which the HMO has contracted to provide.

(3) Share medical and other records, equipment, and professional, technical, and administrative staff of the HMO; [and]

(4) Provide their professional services in accordance with a compensation arrangement, other than fee-for-service, established by the HMO. This arrangement may include, but is not limited to, fee-for-time, retainer or salary.[6]

Group Health Cooperative of Puget Sound and Group Health Association in Washington, D.C. were both established as staff model HMOs. Both continue to offer the majority of their services through that model.

§16.4.2 Group Model Plans

A group model HMO is one that is based on contractual relationship with its physicians. The physicians are organized in single or multi-specialty groups independent of the HMO. All of the physicians work together for the common good in all of their revenue-producing arrangements. The HMO contracts with the group as a whole to provide care to its enrollees. A group model HMO may be either an open or a closed panel HMO in that the services may be provided by the physicians in their own offices or in medical facilities owned or leased by the HMO.

The federal HMO Act defines a medical group that provides services in a group model HMO as a partnership, association, corporation, or other group composed primarily of members licensed to practice medicine or osteopathy, although the group

---

[6]42 C.F.R. §417.100 (1987).

may include other licensed health professionals; as their professional activity these members engage in the coordinated practice of their profession with a substantial portion (over 35 percent) being devoted to delivery of healthcare to members of an HMO.[7] Under federal regulations, the group is allowed to provide the balance of their services to fee-for-service patients, with the understanding that over time their practice will be composed exclusively of HMO patients. The coordination of the practice includes, among other things, pooling their income, distributing it in a manner unrelated to the provision of specific health services, and sharing health records, major equipment, and staff.[8]

The Kaiser Permanente Health Plans that operate in California, Oregon, and Washington are all examples of group model HMOs. The physicians are organized as a separate legal entity and contract with the administrative portion of the HMO to provide healthcare to its enrollees.

§16.4.3 Individual Practice Associations

A third variant of HMO practice models is the individual practice association (IPA). The HMO administrative organization contracts with individual physicians or small medical groups for the provision of healthcare services to its enrollees. Often the physicians will organize and form a legal entity solely for the purpose of contracting with the HMO. The physicians also provide healthcare services to private patients (or even in some instances to enrollees of more than a single HMO). The fee-for-service business constitutes the majority of the physicians' practice, and this regular business remains separate and apart from the financial arrangement with an HMO. The IPA once was considered to be the classic open panel HMO.

Under federal law, an IPA is defined thus as "a partnership, association, corporation, or other legal entity which delivers or arranges for the delivery of health services and which has

---

[7] 42 C.F.R. §417.100 (1987).
[8] 42 U.S.C. §300e-1(4); 42 C.F.R. §417.100 (1987).

entered into written services arrangement or arrangements with health professionals, a majority of whom are licensed to practice medicine or osteopathy."[9]

Many would argue that IPAs represent the future for the development of HMOs. IPAs are growing three times faster than staff panel or closed panel group model HMOs.[10] One researcher has projected estimates that during the 1990s two-thirds of all HMOs will be structured as IPAs.[11] The IPA model frequently is the most attractive for hospitals seeking to enter the HMO marketplace, because it allows broad physician participation through a physician-controlled organization linked to the hospital, with minimal disruption of existing practice arrangements.[12]

§16.4.4 Primary Care Networks

In the primary care network (PCN) model, practice clinics are brought together contractually by another entity to render healthcare. Primary care physicians contract with the HMO to provide care to its patients for capitation payments (payments per HMO patient for all services provided). The United States Code places these networks in the catch-all category of "health professionals who have contracted with the health maintenance organization for the provision of such services."[13]

The PCN is an open model HMO. The focal point is the primary care physician, whose principal function is the appro-

---

[9]42 C.F.R. §417.100 (1987). See 42 U.S.C. §300e-1(5). The statute requires that the individuals providing professional services do so in accordance with a compensation arrangement established by the entity and, to the extent feasible, that they share medical and other records, equipment, and professional, technical, and administrative staff.

[10]Welch, The New Structure of IPAs, 12 J. Health Pol. Poly. & L. 723, 724 (1987).

[11]Id.

[12]See Rosenfeld, Tully, and Rothenberg, Individual Practice Associations: The Future of Private Practice? 8 Whittier L. Rev. 441 (1986).

[13]42 U.S.C. §300e(b)(3).

priate delivery of healthcare. This physician serves as the "gatekeeper," with responsibility for all healthcare services delivered to the HMO enrollee.[14] Reimbursement mechanisms for a PCN vary. Frequently, capitation payments are used for the primary care services, with modified fee-for-service payments for specialty care, per diem payments for institutional services, and fee-for-service payments for the remainder.

§16.5 Preferred Provider Organizations and Exclusive Provider Organizations

A hybrid of an HMO and traditional insurance, a preferred provider organization (PPO) is a system of healthcare delivery characterized by a set of contractual arrangements among providers, payors, and consumers. It is defined as "arrangements between providers and at least one group purchaser whereby health care services are purchased for a specific population under negotiated terms."[1] PPOs generally are developed to serve a distinct geographical location. Many are sponsored by Blue Cross or Blue Shield organizations. Few, if any, are nationally recognized.

Providers associated with a PPO generally are paid on a

---

[14]See D. Avene and D. Hulet, The Primary Care Network—A Flexible Approach to Configure a Managed Healthcare System, in New Health Care Systems: HMOs & Beyond 128 (Group Health Institute 1986). Avene and Hulet argue that the primary care physician can:

1. assure quality, cost-effective care;
2. establish a contact point for accountability;
3. be provided an incentive to maintain appropriate practice patterns;
4. advise enrollees on appropriate types of care; and
5. be penalized for inappropriate referral care and enforce appropriate enrollee action.

§16.5 [1]AHA Office of General Counsel, Regulation of Preferred Provider Organizations: A Legal Guide for Hospital Executives, Legal Memorandum Number Eight (1986).

predetermined fee-for-service basis at or below their usual rates.[2]
The consumers are free to use non-PPO providers, but there are
strong financial incentives (in the form of reduced or eliminated
copayments and deductibles) to use preferred physicians and
hospitals.

The structure and form of PPOs vary widely. The PPO may
be a distinct corporate entity, a line of business of an existing
corporate entity, or an entity based solely on contracts. Its
common characteristics include:

1. a selected provider panel of physicians, hospitals or
   other types of professional and institutional providers;
2. contractual arrangements between providers and purchasers regarding services provided to patients;
3. negotiated payment terms (generally fee-for-service but
   often with a discount);
4. utilization control mechanisms;
5. a defined set of patients with an economic incentive to
   use the PPO providers; and
6. an administration that includes management information systems, claims processing, and quality assurance
   functions.[3]

PPOs are organized and controlled by one of three groups: (1)
brokers such as third-party administrators, insurance brokers,
and other entrepreneurs, with the PPO acting as an intermediary
between the providers and the buyers; (2) payors such as self-
insured employers, union trusts, and insurance carriers; or (3)
providers such as physicians and hospitals.

Unlike an HMO, whose structure and operation are determined by specific state and federal statutes, a PPO may be
structured so that it is largely unregulated by state or federal

---

[2]One description of a PPO states that it is "any arrangement in which (1)
some select group of patients (2) receives care from some select group of
providers at (3) less than retail rates." Blacker, Preferred Provider Organizations—A Panel Discussion, 6 Whittier L. Rev. 661, 691 (1984).

[3]AHA Office of General Counsel, supra n.1, at 2-3.

law. First, there is no federal statute dealing specifically with PPOs. The major federal legal issues concerning PPOs are antitrust provisions.[4] Second, state regulation of PPOs is a relatively recent development. In 1981 there were no PPO statutes, and as of 1986 only 20 states had enacted PPO legislation, primarily for the purpose of encouraging PPO development.[5] Even in the absence of state legislation, PPOs exist in 39 states as well as the District of Columbia and Puerto Rico.[6]

An exclusive provider organization (EPO) is a PPO that requires its enrolled consumers to use only preferred providers. If nonpreferred providers are used, the services are not paid for by the PPO. Thus, the distinction between an EPO and an HMO tends to disappear. One can argue that an EPO is susceptible to regulation either as an HMO or as an insurance company. For this reason, each EPO requires analysis under state laws and regulations governing HMOs, healthcare contractors, and insurance companies to determine the applicable requirements.

§16.6 Competitive Medical Plans

The phrase "competitive medical plans" (CMPs) was created by the Medicare amendments of the Tax Equity and Fiscal Respon-

---

[4]Provider-based PPOs are most susceptible to antitrust challenges because they potentially involve horizontal arrangements among providers. See Department of Justice, Press Release (Oct. 12, 1984), regarding the preparation of a civil antitrust law suit against Stanislaus PPO, Inc. Some relevant federal communications on PPO antitrust issues may be found in ALI-ABA, Health Care Industry: New Trends and New Problems 59-73 (1985). See also Roble, Knowlton, and Rosenberg, Hospital Sponsored Preferred Provider Organizations, 3 Law, Medicine & Health Care 208 (1984) and citations contained therein.

[5]States with PPO statutes as of August 1986 include California, Florida, Indiana, Illinois, Iowa, Kansas, Lousiana, Maine, Maryland, Michigan, Minnesota, Nebraska, New Hampshire, North Carolina, Oregon, Pennsylvania, Utah, Virginia, Wisconsin, and Wyoming.

[6]See Institute for International Health Initiatives, Clearinghouse on PPOs: Directory of PPOs and the Industry Report on PPO Development ix (June 1986).

sibility Act of 1982.[1] After amendment, §1876 of the Social Security Act authorized Medicare payments to CMPs (and federally qualified HMOs) through contracts under which the CMPs (and federally qualified HMOs) are reimbursed for furnishing covered services to Medicare beneficiaries.[2] A CMP must be operated by a legal entity operating according to state law. The sole function of the legal entity need not be to operate as a CMP, but the CMP must provide a minimum range of services (1) as defined by statute, (2) on a prepaid, capitation basis, and (3) primarily through physicians under either an employment or a contractual arrangement. The CMP must also assume financial risk for the provision of healthcare services and provide protection in the event of insolvency.[3]

---

§16.6   [1]Section 1876 of the Social Security Act, as amended by Pub. L. No. 97-248, §114 (codified in 42 U.S.C. 1395mm, note).

[2]See §16.12.1 infra for a discussion of the risk contracts that may be obtained by eligible HMOs and CMPs in providing healthcare to Medicare beneficiaries.

[3]42 C.F.R. §417.407(c) defines a CMP as follows:

A CMP is a legal entity that meets the following requirements:

(1) Except as specified in paragraph(s) of this section, the entity provides to its enrolled members at least the following services:

(i) Physicians' services performed by physicians.

(ii) Laboratory, X-ray, emergency, and preventive services.

(iii) Out of area coverage.

(iv) Inpatient hospital services.

(2) The entity receives compensation (except for deductibles, coinsurance, and copayments) for the health care services it provides to enrolled members on a periodic, prepaid capitation basis regardless of the frequency, extent, or kind of services provided to any member.

(3) The entity provides physicians' services primarily through

(i) Physicians who are employees or partners of the entity, or

(ii) Physicians or groups of physicians (organized on a group or individual practice basis) under contract with the entity to provide physicians' services.

(4) The entity assumes full financial risk under the procedures described in §110.108(b) of this title, on a prospective basis for the provision of health services listed in paragraph (c)(1) of this section, except that the entity may [obtain insurance in a manner consistent with this section or arrange for the physicians to assume the financial risk].

(5) The entity provides adequately against the risk of insolvency by

A CMP may be a state-licensed HMO, a PPO that allows prepayment of fees, a Blue Cross or Blue Shield medical service plan, an insurance company, or a self-funded hospital plan. A CMP affords much greater flexibility than the preceding forms for an entity to serve Medicare beneficiaries. Although a federally qualified HMO must be a separate legal entity to be eligible to enter into a contract with the Health Care Financing Administration to serve Medicare beneficiaries, a CMP need not be a separate legal entity. Many of the constraints on a federally qualified HMO in serving nonMedicare enrollees do not exist for a CMP.[4] It may have a more limited benefit package with unlimited copayments and deductibles. It also is not required to set a uniform rate for all individuals and all families of similar composition (community rating).[5]

To date, the majority of CMPs that have qualified to contract with the Health Care Financing Administration have been state-licensed HMOs. They are primarily entities that wish to provide services to Medicare beneficiaries on a contract basis without meeting the requirements of becoming a federally qualified HMO.

C. Selecting a Corporate Structure for an HMO

§16.7 Nonprofit HMOs

Staff and group model HMOs historically have been structured as nonprofit corporations. The nonprofit structure of HMOs was

---

meeting the fiscal and administrative management requirements of §110.108(a)(1)(i) through (iv) and (a)(3) of this title.

[4] See infra §16.11 for a discussion of the requirements to be a federally qualified HMO. See Krasner, HMOs and CMPs: Qualifying for the New Medicare Market, 2 Am. Med. Care and Rev. Assn. Newsl. 1 (1985) for a discussion of the advantages of CMP status.

[5] See infra §16.11.3 for a discussion of community rating.

reenforced, at least initially, by the federal HMO Act, which made federal grants and loans to HMOs available only to nonprofit entities.[1] Further, some state HMO laws encourage or require nonprofit structures for HMOs.[2]

As nonprofit corporations, tax-exempt status under the Internal Revenue Code (I.R.C.) has been available to these organizations. The HMOs may qualify as tax-exempt organizations under either §501(c)(3) or §501(c)(4) of the I.R.C. The greatest tax benefits are available to an organization that can qualify as a §501(c)(3) organization:

> Exemption from taxation under §501(c)(3) of the Code is available to: corporations, and any community chest, fund, or foundation, organized and operated exclusively for religious, charitable, scientific, testing for public safety, literary or educational purposes . . . no part of the net earnings of which inures to the benefit of any private shareholder or individual, no substantial part of the activities of which is carrying on propaganda, or otherwise attempting, to influence legislation (except as otherwise provided in subsection (h)), and which does not participate in, or intervene in (including the publishing or distributing of statements), any political campaign on behalf of (or in opposition to) any candidate for public office.

The advantages of nonprofit status under §501(c)(3) include exemption from federal (and usually state) income tax, state real estate and tangible personal property taxes, and some sales taxes. It also may enable the HMO to take advantage of certain tax-deferred annuity retirement and pension plans. Also, contri-

---

§16.7 [1]Under the initial federal HMO Act loan provisions, only loan guarantees were available to for-profit HMOs. In 1981 the HMO Act was amended to make loans funds available to for-profit HMOs as well as to nonprofit HMOs. See 42 U.S.C. §300e-4.

[2]In Minnesota, nonprofit operation is required under the state statute governing HMOs. In Mississippi and Montana, if an HMO is not a nonprofit corporation, it may be subject to all the regulatory requirements of an insurance company, including reserve requirements. In Alaska, which has no specific HMO statute, HMOs frequently qualify as hospital medical service corporations, which must be nonprofit corporations.

butions and gifts to the HMO are deductible for the donor, and foundations may make unrestricted gifts to the HMO.

Obtaining §501(c)(3) status used to be difficult for HMOs, but now HMOs that operate in a manner similar to a nonprofit hospital in providing charitable and emergency care are readily granted §501(c)(3) status. To qualify as an exempt organization under §501(c)(3), in general an HMO must be organized and operated as a charitable organization. It also must meet the same organizational and operational tests as a hospital.[3] The IRS initially took the position that an HMO could qualify as an organization described in §501(c)(4) but would not qualify as a §501(c)(3) organization.[4] This position was overruled by the tax court in South Health Association v. Commissioner.[5]

In that case, a staff model HMO organized as a nonprofit organization under the laws of Washington State sought §501(c)(3) status. Sound Health Association was a membership organization whose primary, but not sole, purpose was to provide a wide range of healthcare services to its members. Its goal was to provide comprehensive healthcare services to all members and the community. In analyzing whether the organization was entitled to §501(c)(3) status, the court noted that "neither the furnishing of medical care in general nor the operation of a hospital or HMO in particular, is specifically listed as a qualifying exempt activity within the meaning of section 501(c)(3). Thus the providing of medical services must fall, generally speaking, within the 'charitable purpose' to be exempt."[6] The court determined that the rendering of medical care is a charitable activity but that the nature and means of providing medical care must also be considered. Elaborating on this point, the court said, "[T]he tests applied to determine the [tax] status of a hospital are relevant to a determination of the status of an

---

[3]See Treas. Reg. §1.501(c)(3)-1. See also [1989] Stand. Fed. Tax Rep. (CCH) ¶¶ 3033.02-.0224 for a discussion of the organizational and operational tests.

[4]See Gen. Couns. Mem. 37,043 (Mar. 14, 1977).

[5]71 T.C. 158 (1978).

[6]Id. at 177.

HMO,"[7] and there are two standards by which a hospital may qualify for exempt status: (1) The community benefit standard of Rev. Rul. 69-545, which bases exemption on whether the organization benefits the community by making available emergency room services to all and furnishing other hospital services to patients able to pay, either directly or through third party reimbursement, and (2) the financial ability standard of Rev. Rul. 56-185, which bases exemption on whether the organization operates to the extent of its financial ability for those unable to pay.[8]

In comparing Sound Health Association with the hospital that was granted §501(c)(3) status in Revenue Ruling 69-545, the court concluded that Sound Health Association's policy of providing emergency care to any individual requiring such care, regardless of that individual's membership status or ability to pay, and its development of a plan to help subsidize individuals who wanted to subscribe but could not afford the monthly payments qualified the association as providing a community benefit.[9] Finally, the court concluded that the fact that the HMO was spreading the risk of paying for healthcare through its prepayment feature and was thus somehow in competition with commercial businesses was irrelevant.

The IRS has acquiesced in the *Sound Health Association*

---

[7]Id. at 178-179.

[8]Id. at 181.

[9]The IRS objected to the membership structure of Sound Health Association, arguing that it would result in "preferential treatment" to members. The court rejected this argument, noting that every charitable organization benefits only a certain segment of the community. The court added that preferential treatment is relevant only if the preferential treatment results in some private benefit, and it concluded that there was no insider benefit of the sort that would disqualify the Sound Health Association under §501(c)(3):

> The extension of the "insider test" for private benefit to a community-owned-and-operated HMO is not warranted under these facts. To equate an "insider" with potentially the whole community would so gut the insider test as to transmogrify it from a test of some precision in distinguishing private benefit to a test of such general application as to be useless.

Id. at 186-187.

decision, concluding that "staff model HMOs [may] be recognized as exempt under section 501(c)(3) because they promote health, and because they are instruments of the federal public policy underlying the HMO Act to encourage more efficient and economical delivery of health care."[10] Therefore a staff or group model HMO has a good possibility of obtaining §501(c)(3) tax-exempt status if it is organized and operated in a manner similar to the hospital in Revenue Ruling 69-545. However, it must meet both the organizational and operational tests.[11] Further, it would seem that an HMO must provide emergency care to individuals regardless of their enrollee status and regardless of their ability to pay for the care.

If an HMO cannot or chooses not to qualify as a §501(c)(3) organization, it can seek to be qualified as a social welfare organization under §501(c)(4). Section 501(c)(4) organizations are described as "civic leagues or organizations not organized for profit but operated exclusively for the promotion of social welfare . . . and the net earnings of which are devoted exclusively to charitable, educational, or recreational purposes." A social welfare organization is an organization that exclusively seeks to promote in some way the common good and general welfare of the people of the community.[12] Qualifying under §501(c)(4) exempts an HMO from paying federal income tax, but it does not provide the other tax advantages available to a §501(c)(3) organization.

An IPA or a PCN model HMO typically has difficulty obtaining tax-exempt status under either §501(c)(3) or §501(c)(4). The IRS has taken the position that nonprofit organizations composed of health professionals who have con-

---

[10]Gen. Couns. Mem. 38,735 (May 21, 1981).

[11]The IRS has stated that "under this approach the totality of the HMO's operations, e.g., its membership prepayment plan, whether membership is restricted or truly open to a sufficiently broad segment of the community served, the presence of a subsidized dues program, and whether health care services and health related activities directly benefit members and nonmembers, must be examined in determining whether private or public interests are served." Id. at 9.

[12]I.R.S. Reg. §1.501(c)(4)-1(2).

tracted to provide health services to the members or subscribers of various prepaid health service plans on a fee-for-service basis do not qualify for exemption from federal income tax as social welfare organizations under §501(c)(4), because they are not operated exclusively for the promotion of social welfare.[13] In evaluating an IPA model HMO (that intended to meet the federal HMO Act requirements) and an organization that resembled a PCN model HMO (that was not described in sufficient detail to determine whether it truly was a PCN), an IRS general counsel memorandum emphasized that because the physicians were compensated on a fee-for-service basis and the organizations performed primarily claims and billing functions, there was little to distinguish the organizations from insurance companies.[14] Distinguishing those characteristics that led the tax court to grant Sound Health Association §501(c)(3) status, the memorandum pointed out that neither of the organizations in question had any element of consumer control or input and neither made arrangements for providing medical care to indigent patients unable to pay for services not covered by the HMO contract.[15]

---

[13]In re Whether Nonprofit Organizations Composed of Physicians and Pharmacists That Are under Contract to Provide Health Services for a Fee to Prepaid Medical Plan Subscribers Qualify for a Tax Exemption as a Social Welfare Organization under Section 501(c)(4), Gen. Couns. Mem. 38,894 (Sept. 27, 1982).

[14]Id. Specifically, the memorandum read:

> One of the activities of . . . IPA is to provide an available pool of physicians that will abide by its fee schedule when rendering medical services to the member-patients of an HMO. . . . IPA then administers the claims received from its member-physicians and pays them according to its reimbursement agreement. The goal of . . . IPA is to reimburse 100% of the fees for services rendered. Thus, . . . IPA is similar to a commercial health insurance reimbursement program because it merely serves as an alternate method to the direct billing and collection of fees from patients. There is nothing inherently charitable or educational in the performance of administrative functions for physicians whose medical care delivery is not dependent on such services. [Footnote omitted.] Therefore, in our view, . . . IPA exclusively represents physicians who are seeking to maximize their income.

[15]The memorandum also notes that the physicians do not have a proprietary interest in the IPA or the PCN, but it concludes that that fact is not determinative. It finds that the intent of the organization is to help the

§16.8 For-Profit HMOs

As the growth of HMOs has shifted from staff and group model HMOs to IPA and PCN model HMOs, so has the trend shifted from nonprofit HMOs to for-profit HMOs.[1] This trend is particularly evident in California. When the Knox-Keene Act (the California HMO act) was first enacted in 1975, HMOs were exclusively nonprofit organizations. Beginning in the early 1980s, however, many of the HMOs licensed originally as nonprofit plans converted to for-profit status. As of 1986, most new HMOs seeking licensure were for-profit corporations. Most of these new HMOs are sponsored by publicly traded parent corporations and major insurance companies.[2]

The trend toward for-profit status was spurred by overall changes in the healthcare industry. The elimination of federal HMO funding ended any federal financial incentive to be non-

---

interests of the organizations' members. It states further:

> We therefore do not believe its activities alleviate a bona fide community problem: There is no difference between the amount of medical services available in the community before and after the creation of the organization, and there is no evidence in the administrative file that physicians' fees have been reduced as a result of the formation of the organization. The mere recitation by an organization that its activities promote health will not by itself justify an exemption from federal income tax under section 501(c)(4).

These conclusions indicate that the IRS would not be likely to grant tax-exempt status to a PPO. See Roble, Knowlton, and Rosenberg, Hospital-Sponsored Preferred Provider Organizations, 3 Law, Medicine & Health Care 208 (1984). See also Oddleifson, Tax Considerations Relating to Preferred Provider Organizations, in J. Waxman, ed., Attorneys & Physicians Examine Preferred Provider Organizations 77 (1984).

§16.8 [1]In 1981, 18 percent of all HMOs were for-profit entities. By 1985 that percentage had increased to 36 percent. Boochever, Health Maintenance Organizations, in J. Johnson, ed., Introduction to Alternative Delivery Mechanisms: HMOs, PPOs & CMPs 8 (1986). During 1987, for-profit HMOs grew by 23.6 percent, although nonprofit HMOs continued to have the majority of the HMO enrollees with 15.6 million members, or 54.1 percent of all HMO enrollees. Vignola, Health Maintenance Organization Higher Rates Brighten Prospects but Competition Dims Outlook, Salomon Bros. Newsl., May 1988.

[2]See generally Ostroff, Health Maintenance Organizations, 8 Whittier L. Rev. 377 (1986).

profit. At the same time, investors became interested in alternatives for reducing the costs of health insurance and delivery systems. Further, the increasingly competitive healthcare markets pressured HMOs to obtain capital to compete effectively.[3]

With the majority of new HMOs adopting a for-profit structure, many of the existing nonprofit HMOs sought to convert from nonprofit to for-profit status. Although such a conversion is simple from the standpoint of federal law, it can be a complex process under state corporate law.[4] The impediment under state law comes from the concept that nonprofit corporations hold their assets in a "charitable trust" for the benefit of the public. In order for a corporation not to violate this trust in becoming a for-profit entity, it must contribute the current value of its assets to a charitable use. The amount of this contribution, commonly known as a charitable trust settlement, is usually determined through arduous negotiations between the HMO and the state attorney general. This contribution may be made to an existing charitable organization or to a charitable foundation created by the converting HMO.

In an early and successful conversion—that of United States Health Care Systems, Inc.—the not-for-profit IPA model HMO was appraised as having a deficit and thus no charitable trust payment was required. Although a number of successful conversions followed, any of several risks may now make conversion less financially attractive. These include the possibility that (1) the charitable trust settlement is so high that it is not feasible to convert; (2) competitors seeking to purchase the HMO for an

---

[3]Few nonprofit, §501(c)(3) HMOs have been able to take advantage of financing through the issuance of tax-exempt revenue bonds by state healthcare facility authorities. The rigors of the financial and state and federal regulatory requirements are beyond the scope of all but the most well-established and stable HMOs.

[4]Boochever, supra n.1, describes the conversion process thus:

> Conversion procedures can generally be found in a state's corporations code in one of two basic forms. In the first procedure, the HMO simply adopts and files with the appropriate state department an amendment to its articles of incorporation deleting its not-for-profit provisions and adding provisions common for for-profit companies. In the second procedure, the HMO transfers substantially all of its assets to a for-profit corporation through a sale, merger or exchange.

amount greater than its appraised value may create controversy about the charitable trust settlement process; (3) falling HMO stock prices may reduce financial incentives to convert;[5] or (4) federal tax law may treat less favorably in future the deduction of accrued liabilities for for-profit IPA or PCN HMOs.[6]

§16.9 The Model HMO Act

HMOs are governed by state or federal law, or both. Prior to 1972, few states had a statutory framework to deal specifically with HMOs. The establishment, licensing, and oversight of HMOs was handled under general insurance laws, hospital and medical services corporation laws, other special statutes, or not at all. Most of these laws were unable to deal with the unique features of HMOs and unduly restricted their functioning. In the absence of well-developed state law, the National Association of Insurance Commissioners adopted the Model Health Maintenance Organization Act in 1972. It was designed specifically to address the unique features of HMOs.

In less than 20 years, virtually all of the states have adopted legislation to deal with HMOs. Only Alaska, the District of Columbia, and Hawaii do not have HMO statutes.[1] Many states

---

[5]See id. at 9 for a discussion of the conversion of HMO of Pennsylvania to U.S. Health Care Systems, Inc. and the attempted conversion of FHP, Inc.

[6]See Brooke, Dirig, and Yuhas, Taxation of HMOs After Section 461(h) and *General Dynamics*, 68 J. Tax. 358 (1988).

§16.9   [1]The following is a listing of the state HMO laws:

Alabama	Ala. Code §§27-21A-1 through 27-21A-32 (1986).
Alaska	No HMO statute. HMOs are regulated under the hospital or medical service plan statute: Alaska Stat. §21.87.330 (1984).
Arizona	Ariz. Rev. Stat. Ann. §§20-1051 through 20-1069 (1975) (Health Care Service Organizations).
Arkansas	Ark. Stat. Ann. §§66-5201 through 66-5228 (1975/ 1987).

California	Cal. Health & Safety Code §§1340 through 1399.64 (West 1979/1986) (Knox-Keene Health Care Services Plan).
Colorado	Colo. Rev. Stat. §§10-17-101 through 10-17-115 (1963/1986).
Connecticut	Conn. Gen. Stat. §§33-179a through 33-179t (1971/1987) (Health Care Centers).
Delaware	Del. Code Ann. tit. 16, §§9101 through 9115 (1982/1987). See also Del. Code Ann. tit. 18, §§6401 through 6406 (1987).
District of Columbia	None.
Florida	Fla. Stat. Ann. §§641.17 through 641.33 (West 1985/1987).
Georgia	Ga. Code Ann. §§33-21-1 through 33-22-28 (Michie 1979/1986).
Hawaii	No HMO statute. HMOs are regulated as prepaid healthcare plan contractors: Haw. Rev. Stat. §393-3 (1976/1985).
Idaho	Idaho Code §§41-3901 to 41-3934 (1974/1985).
Illinois	Ill. Rev. Stat. ch. 111½, ¶¶1401 to 1417 (1974/1987).
Indiana	Ind. Code Ann. §§27-8-7-1 through 27-8-7-18 (Burns 1979/1987) (Prepaid Health Care Delivery Plans).
Iowa	Iowa Code Ann. §§514B.1 through 514B.32 (West 1973).
Kansas	Kan. Stat. Ann. §§40-3201 through 40-3227 (1974/1987).
Kentucky	Ky. Rev. Stat. Ann. §§304.38-010 through 304.38-210 (Baldwin 1982/1986).
Louisiana	La. Rev. Stat. Ann. §§22:2001 through 22:2025 (West 1986).
Maine	Me. Rev. Stat. Ann. tit. 24-A, §§4201 through 4226 (1975/1986).
Maryland	Md. Ann. Code art. 19, §§701 through 734 (1982/1987).
Massachusetts	Mass. Gen. Laws ch. 176G, §§1 through 17 (1976/1986).
Michigan	Mich. Comp. Laws Ann. §§333.21001 through 333.21-098 (West 1982/1986).
Minnesota	Minn. Stat. §§62D.01 through 62D.30 (1973/1986).
Mississippi	Miss. Code Ann. §41-7-401 (1986).
Missouri	Mo. Ann. Stat. §§354.400 through 354.550 (Vernon 1983).
Montana	Mont. Code Ann. §§33-31-101 through 33-31-405 (1987).
Nebraska	Neb. Rev. Stat. §§44-3201 through 44-3291 (1978/1985).

1080

have used the Model HMO Act as the basis for their statutes.[2] Thus there are common statutory provisions regulating the

Nevada	Nev. Rev. Stat. §§695C.010 through 695C.350 (1973/ 1987).
New Hampshire	N.H. Rev. Stat. Ann. §§420-B:1 through 420-B:22 (1977/1985).
New Jersey	N.J. Rev. Stat. §§26:2J-1 through 26:2J-30 (1973).
New Mexico	N.M. Stat. Ann. §§59A-46-1 through 59A-46-31 (1985/1986).
New York	N.Y. Pub. Health Law §§4400 through 4413 (Consol. 1976).
North Carolina	N.C. Gen. Stat. §§57B-1 through 57B-25 (1979).
North Dakota	N.D. Cent. Code §§26.1-18-01 through 26.1-18-35 (1983).
Ohio	Ohio Rev. Code Ann. §§1742.01 through 1742.36 (Anderson 1976).
Oklahoma	Okla. Stat. tit. 63, §§2501 through 2510 (1975).
Oregon	Or. Rev. Stat. §§750.003 through 750.075 (1985).
Pennsylvania	Pa. Stat. Ann. tit. 40, §§83-101 through 83-119 (Purdon 1981).
Rhode Island	R.I. Gen. Laws §§27-41-1 through 27-41-29 (1983/ 1987).
South Carolina	S.C. Code Ann. §§38-33-10 through 38-33-300 (Law. Co-op. 1976/1987).
South Dakota	S.D. Codified Laws Ann. §§58-41-1 through 58-41- 97 (1974).
Tennessee	Tenn. Code Ann. §§56-32-201 through 56-32-335 (1986/1987).
Texas	Tex. Ins. Code Ann. arts. 20A.01 through 20A.35 (Vernon 1975/1987).
Utah	Utah Code Ann. 31A-8-101 through 312A-8-406 (1986/1987).
Vermont	Vt. Stat. Ann. tit. 8, §§5101 through 5113 (1979).
Virginia	Va. Code Ann. §§38.2-4300 through 38.2-4321 (1986).
Washington	Wash. Rev. Code Ann. §§48.46.010 through 48.46.920 (1975/1986).
West Virginia	W. Va. Code §§33-25A-1 through 33-25A-28 (1977).
Wisconsin	Wis. Stat. §§609.001 through 609.98 (1985/1987). See also Wis. Stat. §628-36(2m) (1983), which provides that the commissioner may make rules for HMOs.
Wyoming	Wyo. Stat. §§26-34-101 through 26-34-128 (1986).

[2]Alabama, Arkansas, Colorado, Delaware, Georgia, Illinois, Iowa, Kansas,

operation of HMOs. This section will discuss the provisions of the Model HMO Act. The reader must consult the law of his or her own state, whose provisions may differ from the model act described below.

§16.9.1 Licensing Procedures

In order to operate in a state, an HMO must apply for and obtain a license or certificate of authority from the applicable state government body (often the commissioner of insurance), as specified in §3(1) of the Model HMO Act:

> Notwithstanding any law of this state to the contrary, any person may apply to the commissioner (director, superintendent) for and obtain a certificate of authority to establish and operate a health maintenance organization in compliance with this act. No person shall establish or operate a health maintenance organization in this state, without obtaining a certificate of authority under this act.

The Model Act assumes that if the "person" making application for a certificate of authority is other than a natural person, the relevant state laws regarding corporations, partnerships, and trusts have been met.

The purpose of this subsection is not only to require the licensing of an HMO but also to establish a general override to existing state laws that restrict or prevent the formation or operation of health maintenance organizations.[3] In addition, §25

Louisiana, Maine, Minnesota, Mississippi, Missouri, Montana, Nebraska, New Jersey, New Mexico, North Carolina, North Dakota, Ohio, Rhode Island, South Carolina, Tennessee, Texas, Vermont, Virginia, West Virginia, and Wyoming all have HMO statutes based on or similar to the Model HMO Act.

[3]Some of the restrictions that the subsection is intended to override include prohibitions against the corporate practice of medicine and against advertising by professional groups and requirements that would designate the nature of physician participation in the HMO. See Model HMO Act, §3, comment, in I Model Regulation Service 430-7 (1986).

of the Model HMO Act specifically provides that the insurance law, the hospital and medical service corporation law, and certain other state law provisions do not apply to HMOs.

The HMO must supply an extensive list of information to the regulatory body. It must provide information concerning the nature of the organization and the persons responsible for conducting the affairs of the HMO. It must designate the geographic area it will serve and supply copies of contracts with providers, enrollees, and groups; a description of its quality assurance mechanisms; and the manner in which it proposes to involve consumers in matters of policy, operation, and complaint resolution. Financial statements showing assets, liabilities, and sources of financial support are also required.

When the appropriate governmental authority has reviewed the application, the authority must be satisfied that several conditions have been met. It must be assured that the healthcare services will be provided "in a manner enhancing availability, accessibility and continuity of service" and that there are procedures in place for ongoing quality assurance and analysis of operational and utilization statistics.[4] It must be convinced that the HMO "will effectively provide or arrange for the provision of basic health care services on a prepaid basis, through insurance or otherwise except to the extent of reasonable requirements for co-payments."[5] The HMO must be "financially responsible and may reasonably be expected to meet its obligations to enrollees and prospective enrollees."[6] Finally, enrollees

---

[4]NAIC, Model HMO Act §4(1)(b), in I Model Regulation Service 430-8 (1986). Comment to the Model HMO Act indicates some debate about the inclusion of certain standards regarding the quality of healthcare provided. The NAIC concluded that if states are to encourage HMOs through legislation, there must be some assurance that the healthcare services provided are of reasonable quality. The NAIC suggests that an evaluation of the HMO should consider whether the HMO has sufficient physicians to provide the promised services and whether the services are available at convenient locations and hours. Peer group and utilization review might be required. See Model HMO Act, in I Model Regulation Service 430-9 through 430-10 (1986).

[5]Id. §4(2)(c), at 430-9. HMOs are required to provide a minimum package of services on a prepaid basis. Copayments, however, are allowed.

[6]Id. §4(2)(d), at 430-9. Determining whether the HMO will have the

will be allowed to participate in matters of policy and operation.[7] Once licensed, an HMO must notify the governing authority of any material modification to the information on which the license was based.

§16.9.2 Powers

The Model HMO Act grants a broad range of powers to an HMO but requires prior approval by the state governing body for activities that might affect the financial condition of the HMO or its ability to meet its obligations.[8] The HMO is empowered to furnish healthcare services through either employed providers or those under contract. These services may include both basic and other healthcare services.[9] An HMO may enter into real property transactions relating to hospitals, medical facilities, and administrative facilities. It may make loans to medical groups under contract with it or to corporations under its control if the loans are related to the provision of healthcare services to enrollees. An HMO also is authorized to contract with insurance companies licensed in the state for the provision of insurance, indemnity, and reimbursement against the cost of healthcare services provided by the HMO. In addition, the HMO enjoys those powers available under the statute according to which it is organized, such as a nonprofit corporation statute or general corporation statute.

Insurers and hospital and medical service corporations also are granted certain powers under the Model HMO Act.[10] They

---

financial resources to fulfill its obligations to enrollees is one of the major challenges to state regulators. See §16.9.5 herein for a discussion of the specific financial requirements of the Model HMO Act.

[7]See §16.9.7 for a discussion of consumer participation.

[8]NAIC, Model HMO Act §5, in I Model Regulation Service 430-10 through 430-11 (1986).

[9]"Basic health care services" are defined as "emergency care, inpatient hospital and physician care, and outpatient medical services. [They do] not include mental health services or services for alcohol or drug abuse."

[10]NAIC, Model HMO Act §16, in I Model Regulation Service 430-19 (1986).

are authorized either directly or through a subsidiary or affiliate to organize and operate an HMO. Under this section, "[t]he business of insurance is deemed to include the providing of health care by a health maintenance organization owned or operated by an insurer or a subsidiary thereof." Further, insurers or hospital or medical service corporations are authorized to contract with HMOs to provide a variety of types of coverage, including coverage in excess of services for enrollees, coverage to deal with catastrophic situations, and coverage to provide protection to the enrollees in the event that the HMO becomes insolvent.

§16.9.3 Governance

The Model HMO Act states simply that "[t]he governing body of any health maintenance organization may include providers, or other individuals, or both."[11] Consumers are to be given an opportunity to participate in matters of policy and operation through advisory panels, referenda, or other mechanisms.

In this matter the intent of the Model HMO Act was to override restrictive laws related to membership of a governing body. But many states have rejected this portion of the Model HMO Act and have included specific requirements concerning the composition of the governing body. The most common requirement is the inclusion of a specific percentage of consumers or enrollees, generally ranging from 30 to 40 percent of the governing body.[12] In one state, physicians may not serve on the governing body.[13] In another state, no class of healthcare providers may be excluded from the governing body.[14] In other

---

[11]Id. §6, at 430-11.

[12]See, e.g., statutes of Colorado, Georgia, Iowa, Michigan, Minnesota, Oregon, Pennsylvania, South Carolina, South Dakota, and Washington.

[13]North Carolina provides that no professional association or individual may establish or operate an HMO.

[14]In Virginia the HMO may not exclude from its governing body any class of healthcare provider.

states, at least one physician must be on the governing body.[15] Each state's statute must be consulted before defining the structure of the governing body.

§16.9.4 Policy Requirements

An HMO is required under the Model HMO Act to offer "basic health services." These services are defined very generally in the Act as "emergency care, inpatient hospital and physician care, and outpatient services."[16] The Model HMO Regulations adopted by the NAIC elaborate on this definition.[17] The coverage is much less extensive than that required by the federal HMO Act. Many states, however, have extended the required coverage through the use of "mandated benefits." Mandated benefits may be divided into four different categories: specific services (for example, drug- and alcohol-abuse treatment), services for particular population groups (for example, adopted children), services related to professional specialty groups (for example, podiatrists), and services for specific diseases (for example, diabetes or kidney dialysis). Mandated benefits generally apply to healthcare insurers as well as to HMOs and Blue Cross and Blue Shield-type plans.

---

[15]In Arkansas the governing body must include at least one physician, one dentist, one pharmacist, one nurse, one consumer, and one enrollee. In Connecticut, one-fourth of the board of directors of a nonprofit HMO must be from the healing arts—at least two members must be a physician and a dentist—and another fourth must be composed of consumers, enrollees, or representatives of the public.

[16]NAIC, Model HMO Act §2(2), in I Model Regulation Service 430-4 (1986).

[17]See NAIC, Model Regulation to Implement Rules Regarding Contracts and Services of Health Maintenance Organizations, §8 in I Model Regulation Service 432-13 through 432-14 (1987). In general, the HMO is required to provide or arrange for the provision of emergency care services and medically necessary hospital services; medically necessary healthcare services performed, prescribed, or supervised by physicians or other health professionals in the hospital; and outpatient medical services, meaning "preventive and medically necessary health care medical services provided in a physician's office, a nonhospital based health care facility, or at a hospital."

The services offered must be defined in the "evidence of coverage" provided to each enrollee. The evidence of coverage must be a clear and concise statement of the healthcare services and benefits provided, with an explanation of any limitations, including copayments and deductibles, and "a clear and understandable description of the health maintenance organization's method for resolving enrollee complaints."[18] It must be filed with and approved by the appropriate governmental authority.

Charges for healthcare services also must be filed with the appropriate governmental authority. Under the Model HMO Act, HMOs are neither required to use nor prohibited from using community rating.[19] Charges may not be determined individually on the basis of a specific enrollee's health status but are to be based on actuarial principles for various categories of enrollees. Charges also may not be "excessive, inadequate, or unfairly discriminatory."[20]

§16.9.5 Financial Requirements

The Model HMO Act establishes financial requirements for HMOs in two areas: permitted investments and protection against insolvency. Investments are to be subject to statutory investment

---

[18]NAIC, Model HMO Act §8(1)(c)(E) in I Model Regulation Service 430-12 (1986).

[19]As the commentary to the Model Act states:

Reasonable underwriting classifications are permitted for the purpose of establishing the charges. Different charges may be imposed on different groups of enrollees. Such a rigid requirement as community rating would appear to be inappropriate when the competing financing mechanisms are not subject to such a constraint. The competitive disadvantage which such requirement might impose could impede the development of HMOs.

[20]The Model HMO Act commentary explains this standard as follows:

In applying the standard of excessive. inadequate, or unfairly discriminatory, it is contemplated that the commissioner may consider the amount necessary to assure a reasonable return on the initial and subsequent capital invested and an amount needed to accumulate adequate funds to stabilize the level of charges against fluctuation due to inflation, changes in medical technology and related causes.

requirements in the same manner as life and health insurers, except that HMOs are permitted to invest capital funds in facilities and services that will enable the HMO to meet its obligations with respect to the delivery of healthcare.[21]

The protection-against-insolvency provision requires the maintenance of a minimum capital account, a deposit of cash or securities in a minimum amount, and the organization's generation of additional amounts annually as a source of funds to meet its contractual obligations to enrollees. These requirements may be waived if the organization has sufficient net worth or an adequate history of generating net income to ensure its viability. They also may be waived if the HMO's performance is guaranteed by another financially strong organization.[22]

---

[21]In 1986 the NAIC adopted the detailed HMO Investment Guidelines (see I Model Regulation Service 435-1 through 435-14 (1986)).

[22]Pursuant to §13 of the Model HMO Act, all HMOs are required to have and maintain a capital account of at least $100,000. In addition, HMOs must make deposits, in part, as follows:

> (2) The amount for an organization that is beginning operation shall be the greater of: (a) five percent (5%) of its estimated expenditures for health care services for its first year of operation, (b) twice its estimated average monthly uncovered expenditures for its first year of operation or (c) $100,000. . . .
>
> (3) Unless not applicable, an organization that is in operation on the effective date of this section shall make a deposit equal to the larger of: (a) one percent (1%) of the preceding 12 months' uncovered expenditures, or (b) $100,000 on the first day of the fiscal year beginning six (6) months or more after the effective date of this section. . . .
>
> (5) When an organization has achieved a net worth not including land, buildings, and equipment of at least $1 million or has achieved a net worth including organization-related land, buildings, and equipment of at least $5 million, the annual deposit requirement shall not apply.
>
> The annual deposit requirement shall not apply to an organization if the total amount of the accumulated deposit is equal to 25% of its estimated annual uncovered expenditures for the next calendar year, or the capital and surplus requirements for the formation for admittance of an accident and health insurer in this state, whichever is less.

A new HMO is required to deposit an amount equal to 4 percent of its estimated annual uncovered expenditures in each succeeding year of operation subject to the limitation described in (5) above. An existing HMO must deposit amounts that increase from 2 percent the year after the deposit requirement becomes effective to 4 percent the fourth fiscal year after passage of the

Solvency protection is becoming an area of increasing concern for state HMO regulators as rapid growth and increased competition in the marketplace generate losses for some HMOs. Regulators' primary concern is to avoid potential harm to enrollees. To do so, states seek to ensure the financial viability of an HMO, which generally means that the HMO has "a fiscally sound operation, adequate provision against the risk of insolvency and that it has assumed full financial risk on a prospective basis for the provision of health care services."[23] The regulatory emphasis has been on (1) increasing initial and ongoing minimum net worth requirements, reserve requirements, and special deposits and (2) requiring that all contracts with providers include provisions holding the enrollees harmless in the event the HMO does not pay for the care provided.[24]

During 1986 and 1987, the NAIC adopted guidelines intended to address the regulatory needs arising from the rapid increase in the development of new health maintenance organizations. To help determine whether certain borrowed funds would be considered a liability for the purpose of regulatory review, the NAIC adopted "Guidelines for Long Term Debt to be 'Covered' Through Special Subordinated Surplus Notes."[25] To help determine the required deposit amount pursuant to §13 of the Model HMO Act, "Guidelines for Expenditures of Health

---

requirement. New York, New Mexico, Oregon, and Wyoming require deposits, capital accounts, or both similar to the pattern of the Model HMO Act.

[23]Meadows, Financial Viability of HMOs: How to Evaluate It, 6 Whittier L. Rev. 669 (1984). Meadows lists common financial problems for HMOs as lack of effective utilization controls, referral costs that are out of control, no incentive for physicians to control costs or utilization, underpriced premiums, underestimated costs, lack of favorable provider contracts or lack of provider network, fixed costs that are too high, and overestimation of marketing in terms of both too many and too few enrollees.

[24]See, e.g., California, which has identified services provided without a contractual agreement (and thus without a hold-harmless provision) to be an area of concern. The state now requires fee-for-service reimbursement to noncontracting providers in excess of 10 percent of total costs for healthcare services for the preceding 6 months, to be calculated each month, and an established reserve that is 120 percent of the calculated amount.

[25]NAIC, I Model Regulation Service 436-1 (1987).

Care Contracts to be 'Covered' Through Agreements with Providers" also were adopted.[26] Most recently, "Cash Management System Guidelines" were adopted.[27]

Although not included in the Model HMO Act, some states have considered establishing for HMOs guaranty funds similar to those required for insurers.[28] There is some risk associated with required participation in a guaranty fund. The additional cost to existing HMOs may jeopardize their solvency.

§16.9.6 Complaint Resolution

In addition to requiring that consumers or enrollees in HMOs have some opportunity for participation in policymaking and operation of the HMO, the Model Act requires that "every health maintenance organization shall establish and maintain a complaint system . . . to provide reasonable procedures for the resolution of written complaints initiated by enrollees."[29] HMOs also are required to maintain records and file reports with the appropriate governmental authority regarding the complaints made by enrollees.

Comments to the Model HMO Act identify two types of complaints, one related to the services provided by the HMO and the other related to coverage of services provided by insurance, by hospital or medical service corporations, or by some means other than by the HMO. For complaints related to services provided by the HMO, the Model Act suggests that the administrative procedure to handle complaints should "provide the mechanism through which enrollees receive a fair and proper

---

[26]Id. at 437-1.

[27]Id. at 438-1.

[28]Only Alabama and Illinois have established HMO guaranty funds. In North Dakota, Utah, and Wisconsin, HMOs are required to participate in life and health guaranty associations. Florida adopted a Rehabilitation Administration Expense Fund in October 1985 and required each HMO to contribute $10,000.

[29]NAIC, Model HMO Act §11(1)(a), in I Model Regulation Service 430-14 (1986).

opportunity to have their cases heard, including the use of binding arbitration as a means of resolving claims concerning coverage."[30] Many states have adopted the complaint-resolution requirements in their HMO statute. Many also have included specific time periods for resolution of the complaints, as recommended in the Model HMO Regulations Regarding Contracts and Services.[31]

§16.9.7 Consumer Protection Provisions

The Model HMO Act lists a set of prohibited practices. This list functions as a consumer protection provision for enrollees.[32] The use of untrue or misleading advertising or solicitations and any form of evidence of coverage that is deceptive are prohibited.[33] In addition, the general state provisions concerning unfair trade practices are made applicable to the HMO to the extent that they are not inconsistent with the nature of an HMO and thus clearly inappropriate. No entity may call itself an HMO unless licensed under the Act. Neither may an HMO, unless licensed as an insurer, call itself an insurer or use any similar name.

To ensure continuance of coverage available to enrollees to the extent possible, the Model HMO Act requires that an HMO "may not cancel or refuse to review an enrollee, except for reasons stated in the organization's rules applicable to all enrollees, or for the failure to pay the charge for such coverage,

---

[30]Id. §11, comment, at 430-15.

[31]NAIC, Model HMO Regulations Regarding Contracts and Services §9(D), in I Model Regulation Service 432-15 through 432-16 (1986). The Model Regulations require complaints to reach a final determination in not more than 90 days unless time is extended "(i) in the event of a delay in obtaining the documents or records necessary for the resolution of the complaint, or (ii) by the mutual written agreement of the health maintenance organization and the enrollee." Id. at §9(D)(3).

[32]NAIC, Model HMO Act §14, in I Model Regulation Service 430-17 through 430-18 (1986).

[33]The Model HMO Act specifically defines "misleading" and "deceptive." Id. at §§14(1)(b) and (c).

or for such other reasons as may be promulgated by the [appropriate state authority]."[34] Most HMOs develop policies or rules specifying actions that will result in cancellation of coverage. These provisions are usually incorporated in the evidence of coverage.

A recent area of consumer-protection concern has been discriminatory practices by HMOs. Several states prohibit discrimination between married and unmarried women in coverage and provision on maternity benefits.[35] Florida forbids discrimination on the basis of age and health status, and California prohibits discrimination due to blindness or partial blindness. Some states also prohibit HMOs from discrimination in enrollment policy against any person solely because of his or her status as a recipient of medical assistance or Medicare.[36]

§16.9.8 Dual Choice

A key provision in the Model HMO Act to assist in the development and growth of HMOs is the dual choice provision.[37] Dual choice requires that employers make available to employees the option to enroll in at least one HMO that offers services in the geographic areas in which a substantial number of employees reside. The requirement applies to both public and private employers having 25 or more employees and offering a health benefits plan. The same requirement also applies to employee benefit funds that offer their members any form of health benefit.

---

[34]Id at §14(3). The comment to this section suggests acceptable reasons for discontinuing coverage that are among the reasons often established by HMOs. These include terminating employment, terminating a group plan, moving out of the area served, moving out of an eligible class, failing to make reasonable copayment, refusing to accept services, misrepresenting information on the application, allowing a nonenrollee to use an HMO identification card to receive services, and failing to maintain a satisfactory physician-patient relationship.

[35]Most recently Colorado enacted such a provision.

[36]Minnesota, New York, and Ohio have such a provision.

[37]NAIC, Model HMO Act §29, in I Model Regulation Service 230-25 (1986).

Employers are not required to pay more for health benefits as a result of being required to offer an HMO option. An employer or benefit fund is required to pay to HMOs chosen by employees or members "an amount equal to the lesser of (a) the amount paid on behalf of its other employees or members for health benefits or (b) the health maintenance organization's charge for coverage approved by [the appropriate governmental authority pursuant to the HMO Act]."[38] In the event that there is a collective bargaining agreement, the selection of HMOs to be made available to employees must be made under that agreement. The dual choice provision in the Model HMO Act is very similar to §1310 of the federal HMO Act but would be applicable to state-licensed HMOs, which otherwise might not be able to take advantage of the federal dual choice provisions. Although rarely, if ever, enforced through litigation, the existence of a dual choice requirement under state law often helps an HMO gain consideration by employers who otherwise might not consider offering an HMO to their employees.

§16.10 Regulation of the Healthcare Industry

HMOs are subject to general statutory provisions that apply to healthcare delivery in general. Two common provisions that affect HMOs most particularly are restrictions on the corporate practice of medicine and legislation mandating that consumers be allowed to choose any physician to receive healthcare. Antitrust laws, both state and federal, also may have an impact on the organizational structure and operation of HMOs.

Some of the issues concerning regulation have been resolved in light of both state and federal HMO legislation. Perhaps more pertinent are the issues that these general provisions pose for the development and structure of other types of managed care systems such as PPOs and CMPs. Many of these issues are as yet unresolved.[1]

---

[38] Id.

§16.10 [1] See generally Kopit, An Overview of Regulatory Issues in PPO Contracting, in Waxman, ed., Attorneys & Physicians Examine Preferred Provider Organizations 19-22 (1984).

§16.10.1 Corporate Practice of Medicine

Restrictions on the corporate practice of medicine are based on the common-law rule that a corporation cannot engage in the practice of a learned profession through licensed employees unless it is legislatively authorized to do so. More specifically, the "corporate practice rule" prohibits a corporation from furnishing medical services for fees through doctors engaged and paid by it.[2] The rule exists in a majority of states and is based on "consideration of public policy, medical licensing laws, or professional standards."[3] Many states have narrow statutory exceptions to the general rule, allowing specifically identified corporations to engage in "the practice of medicine." These exceptions frequently limit participants in corporations that are to deliver healthcare to physicians.

The application and interpretation of the doctrine restricting the corporate practice of medicine vary widely. The legislative basis for codification of the general rule affects its scope. Judicial interpretations and professional licensure requirements also affect the impact of the doctrine.

During the 1930s, 1940s, and 1950s, restrictions on the corporate practice of medicine were invoked as a challenge to the creation and operation of group health plans (early HMOs).[4] For example, in one of the early Group Health Association cases, one of the challenges to the organization was that, as a nonprofit corporation employing a group of physicians to provide medical services to members, it was practicing medicine in violation of the medical licensing statute.[5] The challenge was rejected by the federal district court, which concluded that the nonprofit entity was not engaged in the practice of medicine. Some writers analyzing the cases have suggested that a distinction is made between nonprofit and for-profit entities in interpreting the rule.[6]

---

[2]W. Fletcher, Cyclopedia of the Law of Private Corporation §2525 (perm. ed. 1979).

[3]Hansen, Group Health Plan: A Twenty-Year Legal Review, 42 Minn. L. Rev. 527, 534 (1958).

[4]See id. at 534-536.

[5]Group Health Assn. v. Morr, 24 F. Supp. 445 (District Court for the District of Columbia 1938).

[6]Hansen, supra n.3, at 535-536.

Subsequently, with the enactment of state and federal HMO statutes, corporate-practice-of-medicine restrictions have become a moot issue. State HMO acts invariably include provisions that override inconsistent state law.[7] Similarly, the federal HMO Act specifies that restrictive state laws and practices do not apply to prevent federally qualified HMOs from operating.[8]

Without such statutory authorization, restrictions on the corporate practice of medicine do become an issue for PPOs.[9] If a PPO is taking a percentage of compensation or a specific fee from physicians, it may be in violation of the corporate-practice-of-medicine prohibitions.[10] If a PPO employs physicians or fails to disclose adequately to all parties that it is merely arranging for the provision of services, the doctrine could become problematic as well.[11] Depending on their structure, CMPs also may face challenges of illegal corporate practice of medicine. State-qualified HMOs that become CMPs, of course, would not face this obstacle. Furthermore, the nonprofit structure of some PPOs and CMPs may save them from a challenge.[12]

§16.10.2 Freedom of Choice Legislation

Another potential area of restriction in the operation of HMOs is state adoption of "freedom of choice" legislation. Freedom of

---

[7]See NAIC, Model HMO Act §3(1) and comments thereto, in I Model Regulation Service 430-6 through 430-7 (1986).

[8]42 U.S.C. §300e-10.

[9]Another related issue for PPOs is state restrictions and prohibitions on fee splitting. Many states prohibit physicians from sharing fees with individuals or with corporations for any professional service not professionally rendered by the recipient. One means of avoiding a charge of fee splitting is to characterize accurately the fees paid to the PPO as the cost of administrative services rather than the splitting of a professional fee. Also, the payment to the PPO could be fixed rather than based on the physician charges incurred.

[10]Kopit, supra n.1, at 20-21.

[11]Anthony, Preferred Provider Organizations, in J. Johnson, ed., Introduction to Alternative Delivery Mechanisms: HMOs, PPOs & CMPs 16 (1986).

[12]See, e.g., California Assn. of Dispensing Opticians v. Pearle Vision Centers, 143 Cal. App. 3d. See also Hansen, supra n.3, at 536 and cases cited therein.

choice is a philosophy that originated in the 1930s. It is based on the belief that patients should have the absolute freedom to choose any duly qualified physician to provide their healthcare and that any form of healthcare coverage or payments should support this freedom of choice. The philosophy, championed by organized medicine, clearly is antithetical to the closed panel HMO. Between 1939 and 1949, 17 states enacted laws requiring all medical service plans to allow free choice of physician, effectively ruling out prepaid group practice healthcare plans. Many of these laws were repealed or modified during the 1950s, being replaced with legislation that required employers or others providing healthcare plans to offer one traditional insurance plan that would allow freedom of choice and one plan that would limit choice through a prepaid group practice.

In the same manner that they dealt with corporate-practice-of-medicine restrictions, state HMO statutes and the federal HMO Act contain provisions that limit the applicability of freedom-of-choice restrictions.[13] These provisions should resolve the issue of the applicability of freedom of choice to HMOs. Unlike the corporate-practice-of-medicine restrictions, however, the issue has not become moot for HMOs. Between September 1986, and September 1987, legislators in many states proposed freedom of choice legislation that would apply specifically to HMOs as well as to other providers of healthcare coverage. The objective of the legislation was to require HMOs to reimburse any provider of healthcare services whether or not the provider was affiliated with the HMO plan. None of these proposals passed, but the resurgence of this issue clearly poses a threat to the cost savings and efficiencies of HMOs.

§16.10.3 Antitrust Considerations

Antitrust laws and principles are discussed in detail in another chapter of this book.[14] Therefore, this section will give only a

---

[13]See, e.g., NAIC, Model HMO Act §3(1), in I Model Regulation Service 430-6 through 430-7 (1986).
[14]See Chapter 3.

brief overview of the antitrust issues relevant to HMOs. The basis for this discussion is a policy statement issued by the Federal Trade Commission (FTC) in 1981.[15] The FTC has taken the position that HMOs have a potential dual role with respect to antitrust considerations: they have the potential both to promote competition in the healthcare marketplace and to restrain competition, because they usually involve a combination of physicians and institutions. The procompetitive potential for HMOs has led the FTC to conclude that their activities should be governed by the rule of reason and should not be declared illegal per se.

In evaluating HMOs, the FTC is concerned primarily with the basis for control of the plan. It distinguishes between provider-controlled HMOs and nonprovider-controlled plans. Control is determined on a case-by-case basis. However, if fewer than one-fourth of the governing body members are providers and there is no indication that those providers dominate the decisionmaking process, control will be found to rest with nonproviders. Nonprovider-controlled HMOs are treated as a single entity. They raise antitrust concerns only when they attempt to monopolize, exercise monopoly power, or take action with third parties to control or monopolize a segment of the market (concealed action). Provider-controlled HMOs, on the other hand, are subject to scrutiny as concerted activity.

The FTC also distinguishes between group- and staff-model HMOs and IPA-model HMOs, the former being considered merged plans and the latter, integrated plans. Merged plans are treated as nonprovider-controlled plans and subject to antitrust concerns only in attempts to monopolize, exercise monopoly power, or take concerted action with third parties. In the formation stage, merged plans may create antitrust concerns if 30 percent or more of the physicians in a geographic area are involved in the plan. Integrated plans are subject to scrutiny under the rule of reason. The market power of an HMO may determine the level of this scrutiny, although if the FTC believes

---

[15]46 Fed. Reg. 48, 982 (1981).

that the plan's policies or practices are developed for anticompetitive purposes, it may take action.[16]

PPOs raise significantly greater antitrust concerns than HMOs: "[T]he basic tension between PPOs and the antitrust laws is that by providing a means for competing providers to join in marketing their services, PPOs also provide a potential source of concerted activity and artificial interference with the competitive process."[17] The organizational structure and operational policies of the PPO determine the level of antitrust scrutiny and potential problems. Provider-sponsored PPOs are subject to market share analysis and integration just as provider-controlled, IPA-model HMOs are.

D. Federal Regulation of HMOs

§16.11 The Health Maintenance Organization Act of 1973

The House of Representatives has described the federal Health Maintenance Organization Act of 1973 as "one of our most important public health statutes."[1] The initial Act, adopted in 1973 as Public Law 93-222, was a response to a crisis in healthcare costs due to rampant inflation in the healthcare sector. It was adopted as an effort to control those costs by encouraging the development of HMOs through small grants and loans. The product of numerous philosophical and political disputes, the program was subject to much criticism[2] and has

---

[16]Id. at 48, 991.

[17]Proger, Practical Antitrust Concerns and Preferred Provider Organizations, in Waxman, ed., Attorneys & Physicians Examine Preferred Provider Organizations 63 (1984).

§16.11 [1]H.R. Rep. No. 100-417, 100th Cong., 1st Sess. 3 (1987).

[2]For a thorough discussion of the development of the federal HMO Act and an optimistic analysis of federal HMO policy, see J. Falkson, HMOs and the Politics of Health System Reform (1980). For a much more critical analysis,

been amended repeatedly to make the law more workable.[3] In 1981 the HMO Act was amended to phase out the federal financial aid portion of the program. Although not adopted, substantial amendments were proposed in 1987 to provide greater flexibility in the way HMOs were organized and operated, and thus to allow federally qualified HMOs to respond to the increasingly competitive healthcare marketplace. Throughout these amendments the HMO Act has continued to provide a structural framework for the development and operation of many HMOs that choose to be federally qualified. It also has provided the legal and financial impetus necessary to develop HMOs on a national scale.

§16.11.1 Operating and Fiscal Standards

One of the objectives of the federal HMO Act was to set a benchmark for the operation of HMOs. It was to establish standards and a qualification process that would ensure that federally qualified HMOs were fiscally sound and well-managed and that they provided good, economical healthcare.

The HMO Act sets very broad standards, leaving implementation to the secretary of the Department of Health and Human Services through regulations. To be federally qualified, an HMO must "have a fiscally sound operation and adequate provision against the risk of insolvency which is satisfactory to the Secretary, and have administrative and managerial arrangements satisfactory to the Secretary."[4] A fiscally sound operation is

---

which focuses on the implementation of federal HMO policy, see L. Brown, Politics & Health Care Organization: HMO as Federal Policy (1983).

[3]The HMO Act was amended in 1976 in Public Law 94-460 to make the law more workable and attempt to encourage further HMO development when the initial expectations of the program were not met. The act was amended again in 1978 by the HMO Amendments of 1978 (Pub. L. No. 95-559), which extended the program for an additional three years, increased the federal funds available for grants and loans, and sought to increase Medicare and Medicaid recipients' participation in HMOs.

[4]42 U.S.C. §300e(c)(1)(A).

demonstrated, among other things, by the HMO's total assets' being greater than its total unsubordinated liabilities, by sufficient cash flow and adequate liquidity to meet obligations as they become due, and by a net operating surplus.[5] The HMO must have a plan for handling insolvency that will ensure continued coverage for enrollees during the period for which they have prepaid.[6] Further, each HMO is required to purchase fidelity bonds for its officers and employees who handle funds and to purchase insurance coverage for professional liability and general casualty related risks.[7]

In order to meet the administrative and managerial requirements, an HMO need only have a policymaking body "which exercises oversight and control over the HMO's policies and personnel to assure that management actions are in the best interest of the HMO and its membership."[8] The policymaking body must be responsible for hiring and firing the chief executive.[9] The HMO must have personnel and systems to enable the HMO to "organize, plan, control and evaluate the financial, marketing, health services, quality assurance program, administrative and management aspects of the HMO."[10]

As with the Model HMO Act, a key concern in the operation of a federally qualified HMO is the protection of the enrollees. The HMO must assume full financial risk on a prospective basis for the provision of basic health services.[11] An HMO also must

---

[5] 42 C.F.R. §§417.107(a)(i)-(iii) (1987).
[6] 42 C.F.R. §417.107(a)(iv) (1987).
[7] 42 C.F.R. §§417.107(a)(v)-(vi) (1987).
[8] 42 C.F.R. §417.107(a)(2)(i) (1987).
[9] 42 C.F.R. §417.107(a)(2)(ii) (1987).
[10] Id.
[11] 42 U.S.C. §300e(c)(2). The HMO is allowed several alternatives, such as obtaining insurance to cover (1) the amount by which healthcare costs to any member for basic services exceed $5,000; (2) the cost of services provided to enrollees other than through the HMO due to medical necessity (such as out-of-area emergencies); or (3) 90 percent of the amount by which costs for any fiscal year exceed 115 percent of its income for the year. It may also make arrangements with providers to have them assume the financial risk on a prospective basis. See 42 C.F.R. §417.107(b) (1987).

ensure that no enrollee will be required to incur any liability for payments that are the legal obligation of the HMO.[12] Enrollees are to be provided with "full and fair disclosure" of the benefits, coverage, rates, procedures for obtaining benefits, grievance procedures, service area, participating providers, and financial condition of the HMO.[13] A federally qualified HMO may not discriminate in its enrollment. It is required to offer enrollment to "persons who are broadly representative of the various age, social, and income groups within the area it serves."[14] Neither may an HMO refuse to enroll an individual member of a group on the basis of health status, healthcare needs, or age.[15] A federally qualified HMO must have a meaningful grievance procedure to resolve disputes with enrollees,[16] and it must have an ongoing quality assurance program.[17] Further, a federally qualified HMO must make extensive and comprehensive reports to the Office of Health Maintenance Organizations, Department of Health and Human Services, concerning virtually every aspect of its finances and operations.[18]

HMOs seeking to be federally qualified must meet all of these fiscal and operating standards (as well as others described herein). An HMO must apply to be qualified and must pay a fee. Extensive information is required of the HMO, and usually a site visit is conducted by a variety of professionals to determine whether the HMO meets all requirements.

----

[12]42 U.S.C. §300e(c)(8); 42 C.F.R. §417.107(a)(3) (1987). The HMO may meet this requirement through the use of hold-harmless provisions in its agreements with providers, insurance companies, or financial reserves.

[13]42 C.F.R. §417.107(c)(1) (1987).

[14]42 U.S.C. §300e(c)(3)(A). Special exceptions are made for medically underserved populations and Medicare enrollees. See 42 C.F.R. §417.107(c)(2) (1987).

[15]42 C.F.R. §417.107(d) (1987).

[16]42 U.S.C. §300e(c)(6); 42 C.F.R. §417.107(g) (1987).

[17]42 U.S.C. §300e(c)(7); 42 C.F.R. §417.107(h) (1987).

[18]42 U.S.C. §300e(c)(9); 42 C.F.R. §417.107(j) (1987). Reports include the cost of operations; patterns of utilization of services; the availability, accessibility, and acceptability of services; and developments in health status of enrollees.

§16.11.2 Basic Services

To be federally qualified, an HMO must offer certain basic health services including:

(A) physician services (including consultant and referral services by a physician);

(B) inpatient and outpatient hospital services;

(C) medically necessary emergency health services;

(D) short-term (not to exceed twenty visits), outpatient evaluative and crisis intervention mental health services;

(E) medical treatment and referral services (including referral services to appropriate ancillary services) for the abuse of or addiction to alcohol and drugs;

(F) diagnostic laboratory and diagnostic and therapeutic radiologic services;

(G) home health services; and

(H) preventive health services (including (i) immunizations, (ii) well-child care from birth, (iii) periodic health evaluations for adults, (iv) voluntary family planning services, (v) infertility service, and (vi) children's eye and ear examinations conducted to determine the need for vision and health correction).[19]

In addition to this relatively comprehensive list of benefits, HMOs also are allowed to offer supplemental health services. These include such benefits as intermediate and long-term care, vision care, dental services, mental health services not included as a basic health service, long-term physical medicine and rehabilitative services, and prescriptive drugs.[20]

The comprehensive nature of the benefit package required of federally qualified HMOs often has been seen as an impediment to their development. A comprehensive benefit package obligates HMOs to offer a full panoply of services from the

---

[19]42 U.S.C. §300e-1(1).
[20]42 U.S.C. §300e-1(2).

outset, a generally costly undertaking. Further, it places HMOs at a competitive disadvantage with respect to indemnity plans and Blue Cross plans that are not required to offer and charge for services that enrollees may not desire. Establishing the definition of "basic services" was one of the controversial issues in the passage of federal HMO legislation.[21] Existing HMOs were reluctant to support legislation that would require the offering of benefits that could not be provided at a price competitive with those offered by existing indemnity plans. Others saw the comprehensive benefits as a first step toward national health insurance. With the expanding mandate of benefits at the state level, the benefit package offered by federally qualified HMOs has begun to be mirrored by state-licensed HMOs. Because the mandate of benefits applies to HMO competitors, the impediment as a comprehensive benefit package is reduced.

§16.11.3 Consumer Representation

The HMO Act originally specified the composition of the HMO policymaking body, requiring that one-third of the membership of that body be members of the HMO.[22] In 1978 that requirement was modified to make a distinction between private and public HMOs.[23] The Health Maintenance Organization Amendments of 1987, which were not enacted, suggested repealing this require-

---

[21]See J. Falkson, HMOs and the Politics of Health System Reform 133-164 (1980).

[22]Pub. L. No. 93-222, §2, 87 Stat. 914 (1973).

[23]42 U.S.C. §300e(c)(5). The distinction between private and public HMOs provides that an HMO shall:

(A) in the case of a private health maintenance organization, be organized in such a manner that assures that (i) at least one-third of the membership of the policymaking body of the health maintenance organization will be members of the organization, and (ii) there will be equitable representation on such body of members from medically underserved population served by the organization, and (B) in the case of a public health maintenance organization, have an advisory board to the policymaking body of the public entity operating the organization which board meets the requirements of clause (A) of this paragraph and to which may be delegated policymaking authority for the organization.

ment entirely.[24] It is likely that if amendments are passed, changes in requirements for the HMO policymaking body will be made.

Key components of the original HMO Act included the basic health services, which were to be offered on a prepaid basis without regard to the dates the health services were provided and with the prepaid periodic rates being fixed under a community-rating system. As that system was originally defined, the rates were to be determined on a per-person or per-family basis (taking into consideration the number of individuals in a family), with the rates being equivalent for all individuals and for all families of similar composition. Nominal differentials in rates were allowed only for differences in costs as a result of different patterns of healthcare use by individuals, small groups, and large groups; differences arising from group purchasing practices; and differences established for members enrolled under government contracts.

In 1981 the definition of community rating was modified to include all increased differentials in rates among members, thus introducing community rating by class. Federally qualified HMOs were granted the option of establishing rates based on the traditional community rating or establishing community rating by class for groups.[25] Community rating by class requires the HMO to classify all of the members of the organization into classes "based on factors which the health maintenance organization determines predict the differences in the use of health services by the individuals and families in each class."[26] Adjustments may be made for factors such as age and sex distribution of members. The HMO then must determine its revenue requirements for providing services to the members in each class and fix its rates accordingly.

The unadopted HMO Amendments of 1987 proposed an

---

[24]H.R. Rep. No. 100-417, 100th Cong., 1st Sess. 8 (1987).

[25]42 U.S.C. §3003-1(8); 42 C.F.R. §417.104(b) (1987). An HMO that offered health services prior to becoming federally qualified was not required to begin community rating until 48 months after becoming federally qualified. 42 C.F.R. §417.104(c)(1) (1987).

[26]42 U.S.C. §300e-1(8)(c)(i).

additional rating option, adjusted community rating.[27] Under such a rating system, HMOs would be able to set rates for specific groups, in particular for specific employer groups. The rates still would have to be set at the beginning of a policy year and based on the anticipated revenues required to provide services to that particular group.[28] There would be no year-end adjustment based on actual experience. Thus, an HMO still would be prohibited from setting a rate based on the actual experience of a particular group (experience rating), as practiced by indemnity carriers.

§16.11.4 The Federal Mandate

A benefit of federally qualified status for an HMO is the marketing advantage obtained by the federal mandate.

Under the federal mandate, commonly known as the dual-choice provision, all employers subject to the minimum-wage provisions of the Fair Labor Standards Act and employing 25 or more employees must offer their employees the opportunity to enroll in a federally qualified HMO as an alternative to the employer's existing health insurance program if requested or "mandated" to do so by a federally qualified HMO.[29] If employees are represented by a collective bargaining agent, the offer of membership in an HMO must be made first to the agent and then, if the offer is accepted, to the employees.[30] If an employer is mandated by more than one HMO, the employer must offer its employees a choice between one federally qualified HMO

---

[27]H.R. Rep. No. 100-417, 100th Cong., 1st Sess. 8-9 (1987).

[28]For groups of fewer than 100 persons, the HMO-adjusted community rate may not exceed the community rate by more than 20 percent.

[29]42 U.S.C. §300e-9; 42 C.F.R. §§417.150-417.159 (1987).

[30]42 U.S.C. §300e-9(a)(2). There was a good deal of controversy surrounding the initial interpretations of the mandate as they applied to organized labor. Therefore the law was amended in 1976 to require consultation with a collective bargaining agent if applicable. See 42 C.F.R. §417.159 (1987). See also J. Falkson, HMOs and the Politics of Health System Reform 168-169 (1980).

that is a staff or group model HMO and one federally qualified HMO that is an IPA or a PCN model HMO.[31]

Under the mandate, employers are not required to pay more than they would otherwise be required to pay for employee health benefits.[32] But the employer's contribution per employee for the HMO option must be equal, in terms of dollars and cents, to the largest contribution paid for an employee to another health benefits plan not exceeding the amount of the HMO premium.[33] It is possible that the provisions of the mandate will be modified to respond to concern that some HMO members use fewer services than employees in indemnity and self-insurance plans and therefore are not entitled to equal contributions. Any other modification will likely take the form proposed in the unadopted HMO Amendments of 1987 that employer contributions for employees who enroll in an HMO not "financially discriminate" against those employees.[34] Such a provision would enable employers to select options other than dollar-for-dollar equivalence to ensure equity among their employees.

§16.11.5 Preemption

One of the objectives of the HMO Act was to eliminate state barriers to HMOs. This was accomplished through the enactment of the preemption provision. Restrictive state laws and practices that prevent an entity from operating as an HMO are made inapplicable to federally qualified HMOs.[35]

The provision specifically preempts state laws and regulations that require medical society approval in order for an entity to furnish services, require that physicians constitute all or a percentage of an entity's governing body, require that the entity

---

[31]42 U.S.C. §300e-9(b); 42 C.F.R. §417.154 (1987).
[32]42 U.S.C. §300-9(c).
[33]42 C.F.R. §417.157(a)(2) (1987).
[34]H.R. Rep. No. 100-417, 100th Cong., 1st Sess. 9-11 (1987).
[35]42 U.S.C. §300e-10.

meet the requirements of an insurance carrier with respect to initial capitalization or financial reserves, or impose requirements that would prevent the HMO from complying with the federal HMO Act. In addition, states may not prevent a federally qualified HMO from soliciting members by advertising its "services, charges, or other nonprofessional aspects of its operation."[36]

§16.12 Medicare and Medicaid Regulations

A complete discussion of the application of Medicare and Medicaid regulations to HMOs and of the various nuances in the contracts between the federal government and HMOs is beyond the scope of this chapter.[1] Therefore, this section will provide only an overview of the fundamental principles applied to HMO contracts for providing services to Medicare and Medicaid beneficiaries.

HMO-specific Medicare and Medicaid regulations have been developed primarily during the last decade. Prior to the 1980s, a relatively small number of HMOs provided care to Medicare and Medicaid beneficiaries on a prepaid basis.[2] Most HMOs served the Medicare and Medicaid population on a fee-for-service basis. Over time, both the federal government and HMOs concluded that it would be mutually beneficial if HMOs were to provide care to Medicare and Medicaid beneficiaries on a prepaid, capitated basis. The federal government sought to take advantage of the cost efficiencies in the HMO system. HMOs sought to broaden the populations to whom their services were offered and to be reimbursed on a prepayment basis with appropriate incentives for their cost-efficient care.

The changes in Medicare enrollment became possible in

---

[36]42 U.S.C. §300e-10(b).

§16.12 [1]See 42 C.F.R. §417, subparts B & C (1987) for the complete Medicare and Medicaid regulations.

[2]The HMOs that were providing care to these populations were doing so on the basis of either uniquely negotiated agreements or demonstration projects. Group Health Cooperative of Puget Sound has one of the oldest Medicare prepaid, capitation agreements in the country.

1982 through the enactment of §114(a) of the Tax Equity and Fiscal Responsibility Act (TEFRA).[3] TEFRA adopted a fixed capitation payment system for Medicare beneficiaries enrolled in federally qualified HMOs and CMPs contracting with the Health Care Financing Administration (HCFA). Implementation of this new program, however, was delayed until 1985.

Similar changes affecting Medicaid beneficiaries also were made in federal and state law. Enrollment was made easier, and states made even more aggressive enrollment efforts to ensure participation in HMO cost savings.[4]

§16.12.1 Special Contracts

Through TEFRA, federally qualified HMOs and CMPs are able to enter into cost contracts and risk-basis contracts with HCFA. Reimbursement under either agreement is calculated using the average area per capita cost (AAPCC). Under a cost contract, an entity receives a capitation payment on an interim basis, with an annual adjustment to equal reasonable costs of Medicare services provided by the entity, subject to the AAPCC as an overall payment limit. Under a risk contract, an entity is paid a premium per member, per month, based on 95 percent of the AAPCC. The entity also calculates its adjusted community rate for Medicare beneficiaries, and the difference between 95 percent of the AAPCC and the adjusted community rate is to be returned to the Medicare beneficiaries in savings through lower payments from the HCFA, lower copayments, or greater benefits. The HCFA has the discretion to decide whether to contract with an entity, and the entity must be able to meet specific contract terms.[5] The entity also must fulfill both minimum and maximum

---

[3]Pub. L. No. 97-248 §114 (1982) (codified in 42 U.S.C. 1395mm, note).

[4]Between 1981 and 1985, Medicaid enrollment in HMOs tripled and the number of participating HMOs doubled. See R. Abrams, HMOs and Medicaid: Issues & Prospects, in New Health Care Systems: HMOs & Beyond 37 (Group Health Institute 1986).

[5]These contract terms require that the entity have providers who are Medicare certified; provide all Medicare services; provide additional services if

enrollment limits, including having at least 5,000 members if it is an urban plan and having at least 75 Medicare enrollees, but having no more than 50 percent of its enrollees be Medicare or Medicaid beneficiaries (with some exceptions). Regulations also define the basic benefit package to be offered, the marketing techniques that may and may not be used, the mechanism for enrollment, the mechanism for health screening where permissible, and virtually every other aspect of the services provided.

The entity benefits from these contracts through its increased ability to expand its market. Medicare and, to a lesser extent, Medicaid contracts make an HMO more attractive to investors, which increases the ability to raise capital. Increased patient volume along with specialized patient services such as home health care may allow these entities to increase their competitive posture through economies of scale.

§16.12.2 The Role of Professional Review Organizations

HMOs and CMPs are subject to review by professional review organizations (PROs) if they provide any care to Medicare beneficiaries. PROs are defined as "entities composed of licensed medical and osteopathic doctors who review services provided by the various medical specialties and subspecialties in hospitals and other facilities."[6] Under the Omnibus Reconciliation Act of 1986,[7] inpatient and outpatient services furnished to Medicare enrollees by HMOs and CMPs are to be reviewed for quality of care. An entity with Medicare risk contracts is required to

---

approved by the HCFA; conduct an annual, 30-day open enrollment; enroll all beneficiaries except those with end-stage renal disease; not disenroll on account of health status; provide 24-hour, 7-day emergency services; establish grievance procedures; agree to Medicare hearing requirements; maintain a quality assurance program; coordinate benefits; provide assurance of ability to assume financial risk and comply with financial disclosure requirements; and allow the HCFA to inspect and audit.

[6] 42 U.S.C. §1320c.
[7] Pub. L. No. 99-509, 99 Stat. 1874 (1986).

maintain written agreements with a PRO operating in the area in which the entity is located. The contents of these written agreements are defined by regulation.[8]

The scope of review by the PRO is very broad. The PRO must determine whether the quality of services (including both inpatient and outpatient services) provided by an entity meets professionally recognized standards of healthcare, including whether appropriate healthcare services have been provided and have been provided in an appropriate setting.[9]

The extent and nature of the review by PROs (or by nonPRO entities under contract with the HCFA to review HMOs) can be problematic for HMOs and CMPs. The reviewing entities and individuals sometimes are competitors of the entity being reviewed. Some have philosophical objections to the form of healthcare delivery offered by HMOs that may affect the objectivity of their review. For these reasons, the written agreements between the PRO and the HMO must be negotiated carefully. The HCFA may be required to intervene to resolve problems between HMOs and PROs.

§16.13 ERISA

As providers of healthcare benefit plans, HMOs are subject to the disclosure and reporting requirements of the Employee Retirement Income Security Act of 1974 (ERISA).[1] In addition, federally qualified HMOs are required by HMO regulation to provide to each employer, designee, or plan administrator "the information which is necessary to satisfy its reporting and disclosure obligations under ERISA insofar as that HMO is involved."[2] Because there are overlapping reporting requirements between ERISA and the HMO regulations, may HMOs

---

[8] 42 C.F.R. §466.71(a) (1987).
[9] 42 C.F.R. §466.72 (1987).
§16.13 [1] 29 U.S.C. §§1001-1461.
[2] 42 C.F.R. §417.107(m) (1987).

were concerned about duplication of reporting efforts. As a result of negotiations between the respective federal agencies that enforce the reporting requirements, uniform requirements were developed. Thus, information prepaid for one report may be used for other reports.

One emerging area of the law that may have an impact on HMOs is the interpretation and application of ERISA preemption provisions. ERISA contains a basic clause stating that the provisions of ERISA preempt state laws that relate to any employee benefit plan. It also contains a savings clause, which states that ERISA does not preempt state law that regulates insurance. Employee benefit plans are not deemed to be insurance in this context. However, in Metropolitan Life Insurance Company v. Massachusetts,[3] the Supreme Court held that where an ERISA plan purchases an insurance policy, the state's mandated benefit laws control the terms of the policy because those laws regulate insurance. As such, the mandated benefit laws are exempted from ERISA preemption by the savings clause.

In a more recent case, the Supreme Court concluded that the savings clause did not apply.[4] In that case an employee brought a bad-faith action against an insurance company, asserting that his disability claims under a group policy purchased as a part of an employee benefit plan had been mishandled. The Court concluded that the law of bad-faith actions "related to" employee benefit plans and therefore was preempted by ERISA. The savings clause did not apply, because bad-faith laws do not regulate insurance. The decision broadens the ERISA preemption provision to cover another entity (in that case the insurance company) that does business with an ERISA plan. The issue then arises as to whether a health plan doing business solely with an ERISA plan would be exempt from state HMO licensure under the same theory.

---

[3]471 U.S. 724 (1985).
[4]Pilot Life Ins. Co. v. Dedeaux, 481 U.S. 41 (1987).

E. Conclusion

HMOs are unique healthcare delivery systems. The state and federal laws governing the operation and structure of HMOs differentiate them from other healthcare facilities. Although HMOs share many common characteristics of hospitals as providers of medical care, their statutorily defined functions require separate consideration.

Table of Cases

References are to sections.

Table of Cases

Table of Cases

Table of Cases

Table of Cases

Table of Cases

Index

Artificial insemination, 11.4, 11.4.1,
11.4.2, 11.4.3, 11.4.4. *See
also* Reproductive technologies

"Baby Doe" regulations, 7.11,
7.11.1, 7.11.2
Baby M case, 11.5.1, 11.5.2
Bargaining units, 2.5.1
Battery, 4.8.1, 7.17.3
Benefits test, 12.17
"Best interest" analysis, 10.6.4
Board of directors, 14.10.5
Bona fide occupational qualification
(bfoq) defense, 2.6.3, 2.8.2
Bona fide seniority system and job
discrimination, 2.6.3, 2.8.2
"Borrowed servant" doctrine and
liability, 4.12.1
Brain death, determination of, 12.3
Breach of reasonable care duty,
4.0.2
proof of, 4.2
doctrine of res ipsa loquitur,
4.2.2
expert testimony requirement,
4.2.1
Brother-sister corporations, 14.10.4
Business judgment rule, 4.13.5
Business necessity defense, 2.6.3
Bylaws
corporate, 14.3, 14.10.5
staff, 14.3

Capacity to consent
assessment of capacity, 7.7
standards of decisional capacity,
7.7.1
tests of decisional capacity,
7.7.2
deciding for incompetent adults,
7.8
standards of decision, 7.8.2
who has authority, 7.8.1
presumption of capacity, 7.6
terminal care decisions, 10.3,
10.6.1

"Captain of the ship" doctrine,
4.12.1
Causation in torts, 4.0.3, 4.3
contributory negligence and, 4.3.3
intervening acts and, 4.3.1
standard of proof of, 4.3.2
Causes of action, AIDS liability,
13.9.1
Centers for Disease Control, 13.1.1,
13.1.2, 13.1.3, 13.2.2,
13.2.4, 13.4.1, 13.11.4,
13.11.5
Certificate of need. *See* CONs
Certification
extended care facilities, 15.2.1,
15.2.3
Charitable immunity doctrine,
4.11.1, 9.2.3
Child abuse and neglect
records, reporting, 8.14.6
Children's Justice Act, 8.14.6
Chiropractors, and staff privileges,
1.7.2
Civil fines, 15.1.2
Civil Rights Act (1866), 2.7
§1981, 2.7.1
Civil Rights Act (1871), 2.7
§1983, 2.7.2
Civil Rights Restoration Act (1988),
2.9.1, 6.6, 13.10.1
Clinical privileges, 1.2
allocation of, 1.6, 1.7, 1.7.1, 1.7.2
antitrust issues in denial of, 3.4.2
denial or revocation of, 1.8, 1.8.2,
1.8.3, 1.9, 1.10, 1.10.1,
1.10.2
regulation of, 1.4, 1.4.1, 1.5
COBRA, 4.10.2, 6.2.3, 13.10.5
Codes of ethics, 9.9
Comfort care, defined, 10.6.2
Commission on Biomedical
Research, 4.13.4
Commission on Medical Malpractice,
9.2.1
Community service obligation, 6.1.1
Comparable worth, 2.4.4
Comparative negligence, 4.3.3
Compensatory damages, 4.4.1
Conditions of participation in Medi-

Index

Index

Index

Index